Lecture Notes in Computer Science   12051

More information about this series at http://www.springer.com/series/7409

Anneli Sundqvist · Gerd Berget ·
Jan Nolin · Kjell Ivar Skjerdingstad (Eds.)

Sustainable Digital Communities

15th International Conference, iConference 2020
Boras, Sweden, March 23–26, 2020
Proceedings

Editors
Anneli Sundqvist ⓘ
OsloMet – Oslo Metropolitan University
Oslo, Norway

Jan Nolin ⓘ
University of Boras
Boras, Sweden

Gerd Berget ⓘ
OsloMet – Oslo Metropolitan University
Oslo, Norway

Kjell Ivar Skjerdingstad
OsloMet – Oslo Metropolitan University
Oslo, Norway

ISSN 0302-9743   ISSN 1611-3349 (electronic)
Lecture Notes in Computer Science
ISBN 978-3-030-43686-5   ISBN 978-3-030-43687-2 (eBook)
https://doi.org/10.1007/978-3-030-43687-2

LNCS Sublibrary: SL3 – Information Systems and Applications, incl. Internet/Web, and HCI

This Springer imprint is published by the registered company Springer Nature Switzerland AG
The registered company address is: Gewerbestrasse 11, 6330 Cham, Switzerland

Preface

As we pass into the third decade of the 20th century, in the age of big data, fake news, disinformation, information overload, and information divides, it is obvious that information scholars face broader challenges than ever before. At the same time, the iField has never been more relevant. During the 2020s we can expect an escalation of existing information technologies such as the Internet of Things (IoT), blockchains, 3D printing, and artificial intelligence (AI). Simultaneously, in this very decade mankind must attend to the 17 Sustainable Development Goals of United Nations Agenda 2030.

When the iSchool Community gathered for its 15th annual conference in Borås, Sweden, it was against this backdrop that we found it pertinent to pinpoint the theme of this year's iConference in terms of Digital Sustainable Communities. Here, in Scandinavia, we are part of the cold rush (server farms at the northern extremes of the globe) experiencing new ways in which the management of information generates a steadily increasing ecological footprint. With this theme we welcomed a broad range of contributions that help in understanding the seemingly limitless expansion of production, processing, and storage of information that we already have, and which can be expected to escalate immensely during the 2020s.

The 2020 conference was jointly organized by the iSchools at the University of Borås, Sweden, and Oslo Metropolitan University, Norway. Both of these schools have collaborated in various ways for several decades. Hosting the 2020 conference further strengthened the long-standing interplay between Scandinavian iSchools. This year the conference attracted a total of 402 contributions; including 88 full research papers, 93 short research papers, and 119 posters. Each paper was reviewed by two or three reviewers and each poster by two, both through a double-blind review process. Finally, 27 full research papers, 48 short research papers, and 76 posters were selected for the conference. The quality of the accepted papers was ensured by the high level of competition and rigorous review process resulting in acceptance rates of 30% for full research papers and 50% for short research papers. In addition, there was a total of 102 further submissions for the other, refereed conference tracks: the Visions papers, the Doctoral Colloquium, the Sessions for Interaction and Engagement, the Workshops, and the Student Symposium. A total of 469 recognized experts from around the world took part in the review process.

For the third time, the papers are published by Springer in their *Lecture Notes in Computer Science* (LNCS) series. These proceedings comprise complete versions of the full and short papers presented at the conference. This year the papers are organized into 14 thematic categories that represent the broad range of scholarship shared at the conference: sustainable communities, social media, information behavior, information literacy, user experience, inclusion, education, public libraries, archives and records, future of work, open data, scientometrics, AI and machine learning, and methodological innovation. Additionally, keynotes/keynote abstracts, posters, and visions papers are available in IDEALS – the Illinois Digital Environment for Access to Learning and Scholarship.

We want to sincerely thank all the reviewers who generously shared their knowledge as well as the 26 track chairs without whose expertise and hard work the conference never would have come to light. In this context we especially wish to make known our gratitude to the full and short papers chairs: Toine Bogers from Aalborg University, Jannica Heinström from Oslo Metropolitan University, and Geoff Walton and Frances Johnson both from Manchester Metropolitan University.

The iConference 2020 pushes the boundaries of information studies, explores core concepts and ideas, and creates new technological and conceptual configurations. The goal of the iConference series and these proceedings is to inspire conversation, encourage further research, and inform diverse audiences about today's critical information needs.

February 2020

Gerd Berget
Jan Nolin
Kjell Ivar Skjerdingstad
Anneli Sundqvist

Organization

Organizers

University of Borås, Sweden
OsloMet - Oslo Metropolitan University, Norway

Conference Chairs

Tor Arne Dahl	OsloMet - Oslo Metropolitan University, Norway
Helena Francke	University of Borås, Sweden

Program Chairs

Jan Nolin	University of Borås, Sweden
Kjell Ivar Skjerdingstad	OsloMet - Oslo Metropolitan University, Norway

Local Organizing Committee Chair

Alen Doracic	University of Borås, Sweden

Full Research Papers Chairs

Toine Bogers	Aalborg University, Denmark
Jannica Heinström	OsloMet - Oslo Metropolitan University, Norway

Short Research Papers Chairs

Frances Johnson	Manchester Metropolitan University, UK
Geoff Walton	Manchester Metropolitan University, UK

Posters Chairs

Masanori Koizumi	University of Tsukuba, Japan
Pamela McKenzie	Western University, Canada

Visions Chairs

Olof Sundin	Lund University, Sweden
Kim Tallerås	OsloMet - Oslo Metropolitan University, Norway

Workshops Chairs

Melanie Feinberg	University of North Carolina at Chapel Hill, USA
Henrik Jochumsen	University of Copenhagen, Denmark

Sessions for Interaction and Engagement Chairs

Martha Garcia Murillo	Syracuse University, USA
Radhika Garg	Syracuse University, USA
António Lucas Soares	McMaster University, Canada, and University of Porto, Portugal

Doctoral Colloquium Chairs

Simon Burnett	Robert Gordon University, UK
Anita Komlodi	University of Maryland, Baltimore County, USA

Doctoral Dissertation Award Chairs

Koraljka Golub	Linnaeus University, Sweden
Stasa Milojevic	Indiana University, USA
Lihong Zhou	Wuhan University, China

Early Career Colloquium Chairs

Ann-Sofie Axelsson	Chalmers University of Technology, Sweden
Isa Jahnke	University of Missouri, USA

Student Symposium Chairs

Terje Colbjørnsen	OsloMet - Oslo Metropolitan University, Norway
Carina Hallqvist	University of Borås, Sweden

Proceedings Chairs

Gerd Berget	OsloMet - Oslo Metropolitan University, Norway
Anneli Sundqvist	OsloMet - Oslo Metropolitan University, Norway

Volunteer Chairs

Camilla Holm	OsloMet - Oslo Metropolitan University, Norway
Jennifer Lea Thøgersen	OsloMet - Oslo Metropolitan University, Norway
Kalle Karlsson	University of Borås, Sweden
Hana Marčetić	University of Borås, Sweden

Sponsorship Chair

Nasrine Olson   University of Borås, Sweden

Conference Administration

Daniel Kristiansson   University of Borås, Sweden
Anette Trennedal   University of Borås, Sweden
Thea Devulder   OsloMet - Oslo Metropolitan University, Norway

Conference Coordinator

Clark Heideger   iSchools, USA

Reviewers Full and Short Papers iConference 2020

Konstantin Aal
Trond Aalberg
June Abbas
Jacob Edward Abbott
Pamela Abbott
Waseem Afzal
Noa Aharony
Michael Ahmadi
Shameem Ahmed
Isola Ajiferuke
Bader Albahlal
Dan Albertson
Daniel Gelaw Alemneh
Hamed Alhoori
Robert Allen
Wafaa Ahmed Almotawah
Sharon Amir
Lu An
Herbjørn Andresen
Muhammad Naveed Anwar
Clément Arsenault
Cristina Bahm
Alex Ball
Gitte Balling
Sarah Barriage
Syeda Batool
Edith Beckett
Gerd Berget
Andrew Berry

Dania Bilal
Wade Bishop
Toine Bogers
Maria Bonn
Erik Borglund
Christine L. Borgman
Jenny Bossaller
Ceilyn Boyd
Sarah Bratt
Jenny Bronstein
Jo Ann M. Brooks
Caroline Brown
Sarah Buchanan
Jhon Bueno
Iyra Buenrostro-Cabbab
Julia Bullard
Susan Burke
Christopher Sean Burns
Katriina Byström
Yao Cai
Francisco-Javier Calzada-Prado
Shujin Cao
Yu Cao
Hanna Carlsson
Daniel Carter
Vittore Casarosa
Biddy Casselden
Niel Chah
Tiffany Chao

Deborah Charbonneau
Hsin-liang Chen
Yi-Yun Cheng
Chola Chhetri
Yunseon Choi
Hans Dam Christensen
Heting Chu
Rachel Clarke
Johanna Cohoon
Monica Colon-Aguirre
Jordi Conesa
Anthony Joseph Corso
Andrew Martin Cox
Hong Cui
Mats Dahlström
Dharma Dailey
Rickard Danell
Peter Darch
Gabriel David
Rebecca Davis
Edward Claudell Dillon
Ying Ding
Bridget Disney
Brian Dobreski
Guleda Dogan
Kedma Duarte
Patrick Dudas
Catherine Dumas
Johanna Rivano Eckerdal
Emory James Edwards
Elizabeth Victoria Eikey
Johan Albert Eklund
Volkmar Engerer
Lisa Engström
Heidi Enwald
Ingrid Erickson
Kristin Eschenfelder
Yuanyuan Feng
Katrina Fenlon
Bruce Ferwerda
Guo Freeman
Henry A. Gabb
Maria Gäde
Chunmei Gan
Daniel L. Gardner
Jane Garner

Emmanouel Garoufallou
John Gathegi
Tali Gazit
Yegi Genc
Twyla Gibson
Prebor Gila
Tim Gorichanaz
Michael Gowanlock
Ann M. Graf
Elke Greifeneder
Jill Griffiths
Melissa Gross
Michael Robert Gryk
Mikael Gunnarsson
David Gunnarsson Lorentzen
Ayse Gursoy
Stephanie W. Haas
Jutta Haider
Oliver Haimson
Lala Hajibayova
Björn Hammarfelt
Xi Han
Fredrik Hanell
Susannah Hanlon
Preben Hansen
Joacim Hansson
Jenna Hartel
Morgan Harvey
Helmut Hauptmeier
Caroline Haythornthwaite
Daqing He
Jiangen He
Åse Hedemark
Jannica Heinström
Alison Hicks
Deborah Hicks
Niels-Peder Osmundsen Hjøllund
Shuyuan Mary Ho
Kelly M. Hoffman
Chris Holstrom
Liang Hong
Jiming Hu
Kun Huang
Ruhua Huang
Yun Huang
Gregory Hunter

Isto Huvila
Jette Hyldegård
Aylin Ilhan
Sharon Ince
Charles Inskip
Joshua Introne
Hamid R. Jamali
David Andrew Jank
Wei Jeng
Tingting Jiang
Erik Joelsson
Jenny Johannisson
Veronica Johansson
Frances Johnson
Jamie Johnston
Michael Jones
Soohyung Joo
Boryung Ju
Heidi Julien
Beth Juncker
Jaap Kamps
Amir Karami
Michelle M. Kazmer
Halil Kilicoglu
Jeonghyun Kim
Kyung Sun Kim
Vanessa Kitzie
Emily Knox
Kolina Sun Koltai
Yubo Kou
Yong Ming Kow
P. M. Krafft
Maximilian Krüger
Ravi Kuber
Sanna Kumpulainen
Serap Kurbanoglu
Birger Larsen
Elina Late
Jin Ha Lee
Keeheon Lee
Kijung Lee
Lo Lee
Noah Lenstra
Dirk Lewandowksi
Aihua Li
Daifeng Li

Kai Li
Meng-Hao Li
Louise Limberg
Chi-Shiou Lin
Jenny Lindberg
Maria Lindh
Zack Lischer-Katz
Chang Liu
Jiqun Liu
Annemaree Lloyd
Elizabeth Lomas
Kun Lu
Quan Lu
Christopher Lueg
Haakon Lund
Anna Lundh
Marc Lundstrom
Marianne Lykke
Clifford Lynch
Lai Ma
Long Ma
Monica Grace Maceli
Elena Maceviciute
Sirkku Maennikkoe Barbutiu
Yazdan Mansourian
Kate Marek
Jasmina Maric
Betsy Van der Veer Martens
Kathryn Masten
Matthew S. Mayernik
Samantha McDonald
Claire McGuinness
Pamela Ann McKinney
Florian Meier
Amanda Menking
Katarina Michnik
Shawne D. Miksa
Chao Min
Alex Mitchell
Matthew Mitsui
Ehsan Mohammadi
Lorri Mon
Camilla Moring
Atsuyuki Morishima
Heather Moulaison Sandy
Adrienne Muir

Gustaf Nelhans
Valerie Nesset
Chaoqun Ni
David M. Nichols
Hui Nie
Michael Nitsche
Rebecca Noone
Karen Nowé Hedvall
Kathleen Lourdes B. Obille
Bergman Ofer
Kyong Eun Oh
Benedict Salazar Olgado
Peter Organisciak
Virginia Ortiz-Repiso
Knut Oterholm
Yohanan Ouaknine
Ana R. Pacios
Kathleen Padova
Hyoungjoo Park
Min Sook Park
Laura Pasquini
Ei Pa Pa Pe-Than
Diane Pennington
Julia Pennlert
Olivia Pestana
Vivien Petras
Nils Pharo
Bobby Phuritsabam
Rachel Pierce
Ola Pilerot
Anthony Pinter
Alex Poole
Chen Sabag Porat
Devendra Potnis
Michael Preminger
Nathan Prestopnik
Jennifer Proctor
Jian Qin
Arcot Rajasekar
Sarah Rajtmajer
Angela U. Ramnarine-Rieks
Edie Rasmussen
Susan Rathbun-Grubb
Ming Ren
Laura E. Ridenour
Corinne Rogers

Abebe Rorissa
Vassilis Routsis
Melanie Rügenhagen
Kerstin Rydbeck
Ehsan Sabaghian
Athena Salaba
Ashley E. Sands
Madelyn Rose Sanfilippo
Sally Sanger
Vitor Santos
Maria Janina Sarol
Laura Saunders
Laura Sbaffi
Ingrid Schild
Kirsten Schlebbe
Sarita Schoenebeck
Kristen Schuster
Rainforest Scully-Blaker
Michael Seadle
John S. Seberger
Kalpana Shankar
Ryan Shaw
Kimberly Sheen
Elizabeth Jane Shepherd
Patrick Shih
Roswitha Skare
Olle Sköld
Mette Skov
Richard Slaughter
Catherine L. Smith
Hanna Maurin Söderholm
Jonas Söderholm
Il-Yeol Song
Daniel Southwick
Thomas Sødring
Clay Spinuzzi
Beth St. Jean
Gretchen Stahlman
Hrvoje Stancic
Caroline Stratton
Amber Stubbs
Besiki Stvilia
Shigeo Sugimoto
Chris Alen Sula
Yalin Sun
Ying Sun

Abstracts of Keynotes

Co-creating Digital Cultural Heritage: Unlocking Historic Archives and Records Through New Approaches to Digitisation

Lorna M. Hughes

School of Humanities, University of Glasgow, UK

Abstract. Mass digitisation of historic collections in archives, museums, libraries and universities has created a considerable volume of data for research across the disciplines, and opened up new lines of enquiry. Increasingly, community generated digital content can amplify and augment the 'official' digital collections, and open up previously hidden histories and encourage greater public engagement with the past. These collections have been developed through processes of co-creation, and they demonstrate how digitisation can enable our archives to expand beyond the physical boundaries of the repository, dissolving the physical boundaries which previously marked official from non-official, and creator from user. This approach highlights a fundamental shift in the material nature and location of the archive that is facilitated by the digital environment. This presentation will discuss examples of co-creation, and the digital affordances that enable it.

Civic Participation in the Datafied Society

Lina Dencik

Data Justice Lab, School of Journalism, Media and Culture,
Cardiff University, UK

Abstract. The use of data and algorithmic processes for decision-making is now a growing part of social life and helps determine decisions that are central to our ability to participate in society, such as welfare, education, crime, work, and if we can cross borders. Citizens are increasingly assessed, profiled, categorized and 'scored' according to data assemblages, their future behavior is predicted through data processing, and services are allocated accordingly. In a datafied society, state-citizen relations become quasi-automated and dependent on digital infrastructures. This raises significant challenges for democratic processes, active citizenship and public engagement. In this talk I will engage with the question of advancing civic participation in a context of rapid technological and social transformation, considering also experiments in new democratic practices to ensure legitimacy, transparency, accountability and intervention in relation to data-driven governance. In so doing, I will outline emerging terrains for developing civic agency in a datafied society.

Information Access for Evolving Media Usage

Jussi Karlgren

Spotify

Abstract. The media usage habits of the population at large change, which has effects for the educational system, for memory institutions, for the media industry, and therefore for those of us who develop technology for information access. Many of the current changes are easy to observe through introspection or through observing how people in our vicinity consume media and information: people read text on screens; watch lectures and educational material in video clips; listen to literary material and to short written texts superimposed on brief video clips to their near and dear; and stream music and movies instead of purchasing physical objects to place in shelves in their homes. There are very obvious challenges for technology having to do with how we make documents and their content accessible for search and exploration across media types, and we do not quite know what effects today's changes have on tomorrow's media usage. This talk will give some examples, and discuss one of the less obvious challenges: how to evaluate and validate new technology solutions. We know how to measure quality for systems designed to fulfil expressly formulated known information needs, but how can we measure quality of a system designed to entertain and delight? How can we assess the usefulness of systems for digital scholars? And what are the underlying assumptions that have governed the make-up of the experimental benchmarking of today's information systems?

Information Access For Evolving Media Usage

Contents

Social Media

Information Behavior

Information Literacy

Education

Public Libraries

Scientometrics

AI and Machine Learning

Methodological Innovation

Sustainable Communities

Empowering Women Through Access to Information: The Sustainability of a Community Informatics Project in Bangladesh

Misita Anwar and Viviane Frings-Hessami$^{(\boxtimes)}$

Monash University, Caulfield, VIC, Australia
{Misita.Anwar,Viviane.Hessami}@monash.edu

Abstract. Community informatics projects are designed to provide access to information and communication technologies (ICT) that will enable communities to meet their goals. Although their aim is to foster the development of skills that will contribute to the wellbeing of the communities, the sustainability of the formats in which the information is provided to the community groups is rarely taken into consideration during project development. This paper reports on how the challenge of ensuring the continuity of access to information is being addressed in the context of a community informatics project in rural Bangladesh. The PROTIC project has been working since 2015 in three remote villages of Bangladesh at empowering women working in agriculture by providing them with mobile phones and access to agricultural information through SMS, mobile applications and a dedicated call centre. In the last stage of the project, the Bangladeshi telecommunication partner is developing an application to store all the SMS that were sent to the participants during the course of the project and is making plans to keep the information up-to-date after the end of the project and to charge a subscription fee for access to it. However, the participants themselves, conscious of the fragility of digital formats, have taken steps to preserve the information that they found useful in more durable analogue formats. This paper discusses these two initiatives and argues that the continuity of access to information should be planned for from the beginning in community informatics projects in developing countries.

Keywords: Sustainable information · Community informatics · Analogue Back-ups

1 Introduction

This paper uses the example of a community informatics project implemented in Bangladesh to discuss how access to information can be maintained in a developing country after the end of a project. ICT for development (ICT4D) projects are designed to provide access to information and communication technologies that will enable communities to meet their goals (Heeks 2008; Thapa and Sæbø 2014; Unwin 2009). Although their aim is to foster the development of skills that will contribute to the

© Springer Nature Switzerland AG 2020
A. Sundqvist et al. (Eds.): iConference 2020, LNCS 12051, pp. 3–14, 2020.
https://doi.org/10.1007/978-3-030-43687-2_1

wellbeing of the communities involved, the sustainability of the formats in which the information is provided to the community groups is rarely taken into consideration during the development and the implementation of the projects. This paper discusses how the challenge of ensuring the continuity of access to information is being addressed by an ICT4D project that has been operating in rural Bangladesh since 2015. The Participatory Research and Ownership with Technology, Information and Change (PROTIC) project is a partnership between Monash University, Australia, Oxfam Australia and Oxfam Bangladesh, which has been working in three remote villages of Bangladesh at empowering women working in agriculture by providing them with access to agricultural information that could help them to improve their agricultural practices. Women in Bangladesh are actively engaging in agriculture and constitute more than 50% of the agricultural labour force (FAO 2011, p. 9; Rahman 2010; Lewis 2011). However, their contributions tend to be unacknowledged and unappreciated, and their mobility is restricted by social and cultural expectations that place a high importance on female honour and seclusion (Kabeer 1991; Rahman 2000, Rahman 2010; Lewis 2011; Guhathakurta and Banu 2017), as well as by the climate of Bangladesh, which is prone to frequent flooding and cyclones, especially in the South. It is in this context that three hundred women, 100 in each of three villages in three different parts of the country were provided with smartphones and phones credit, and that technical and support services were set up to develop agricultural content and provide it to the participants on a regular basis. Throughout the course of the project, three SMS were sent to the participants every week, two relating to agricultural production and one to the weather. A system of outbound dialling was put in place so that the women could listen to the texts of the SMS (or an extended version of them) if they preferred and a call centre was available to answer their questions. In addition, two mobile applications were developed specifically for the project, one on maize cultivation and one on agricultural subsidies. The goal of the project was that the women would learn the skills to access information by themselves. Therefore, little consideration was paid to the sustainability of the formats in which the information was provided. It is only in the fourth and last year of the project that some attention is being paid to the preservation of the information that was developed during the course of the project. The Bangladeshi telecommunication partner, Win Miaki, is developing an application to store all the SMS that their agronomists developed during the course of the project and is making plans to keep the information up-to-date after the end of the project. However, the village women themselves did not wait for their application to be developed. Two years into the project, they started taking steps to preserve the information that they found useful in more durable analogue formats. They started writing down the information they received from the call centre and the texts of the SMS in their notebooks and on sheets on brown paper that could be hung in their meeting rooms. They were motivated by their realisation of the fragility of the digital formats and their wish to preserve information that could be useful to them in the future.

This paper starts with a review of the literature on the sustainability of ICT4D projects and a section on the methodology used. The data for this paper was collected in three separate occasions: an in-depth semi-structured interview with Win Miaki staff on 28 March 2019, a workshop with PROTIC participants from two of the villages held in Dhaka on 27 March 2019, and follow-up focus group discussions in one of the villages in April 2019. The paper discusses the measures that have already been taken and may be taken in the future by the project partners, and those that were taken by the participants themselves to ensure that the information will still be accessible to them after the end of the project. The efforts made by the village women to preserve the information in formats that suited them show that the information was useful to them, and that they appropriated some practices that were introduced into their villages by development projects and adapted them to suit their needs. The authors argue that the continuity of access to information should be planned for from the beginning in community informatics projects in developing countries.

2 The Sustainability of ICT4D Initiatives

Sustainability is often defined as "[e]nsuring that the institutions are supported through projects and the benefits realised are maintained and continue after the end of the project" (IFAD and Rome 2006, p. 2). Based on this definition, a sustainability assessment would want to see whether the project outcomes would organically be sustained in the medium or longer term without assistance from external forces or organisations. It is also important to understand the context and the level of the sustainability. Since a development project is often a temporary event, sustainability will need to take into account the temporal nature of the project, which is not easy since short term priorities need to be reconciled with longer term sustainability (IFAD and Rome 2006). As most ICT-based interventions take place in local community contexts with minimal resources, ensuring the viability of the projects beyond the funding period is a pressing issue. Studies show that sustainability is a critical problem especially in low income environments where commercial services are often not viable (Unwin 2009; Sey and Fellows 2009).

The long-term sustainability is a challenge in many ICT4D projects. This problem is widely recognised in the literature on ICT4D (Marais 2015; De Zoysa and Letch 2013; Badsar et al. 2011; Heeks 2008). It is important to find viable solutions to this problem because the governments of developing nations and donor agencies have limited resources (Heeks 2008) and ICT4D failures will further discourage international agencies to invest in ICT in developing countries. However, while the sustainability of ICT initiatives in developing countries is among the major problems faced by the ICT4D community (Best 2010), little attention has been paid on how initiatives can be self-supporting. There are relatively few empirical case studies that examine long term sustainability (Best and Kumar 2008).

Many ICT4D initiatives are rolled out as pilot projects with the intention to scale up once they have proven effective. There is often an issue of lack of planning for scaling up the projects because the focus is on the implementation of the pilot. Also, the sheer cost of scaling up seems to be so high that many projects do not progress past the pilot phase. An increasing number of initiatives are now focusing on delivering services for poor people who can afford to pay a very small amount to get the benefits. Kleine and Unwin (2009) suggested that the most cost-effective way to implement such initiatives revolves around mobile telephony. They argued that if initiatives are developed with the intention that poor people will derive benefit, then their implementation should be at the cost of what these people can afford. This requires planning directed at providing appropriate and cost-effective services that meet people's needs. Development strategies in these cases call for multi-stakeholder involvement while accounting for the socio-economic characteristics and available resources of the target community (Sagar Kisan et al. 2013). Sustainable ICT4D strategy can also benefit from enhancing the skills and capacity of the communities to utilise the technological solutions made available by projects in order to develop resilience thinking (Marais 2011).

Researchers have suggested theoretical frameworks to help understand the reasons for the failure of ICT4D projects (e.g. Pade-Khene et al. 2011; Unwin 2009) and sustainability has been identified as a critical factor that influence success in ICT4D projects. To focus on the fundamentals underlying sustainability challenges, it is useful to examine the sustainability of ICT4D projects in terms of the many dimensions associated with project sustainability. The ICT4D literature distinguishes between five main types of sustainability: financial, social, institutional, technological, and environmental (Ali and Bailur 2007 p. 4–5): (1) Economic or financial sustainability is "the long-term ability of ICT projects to generate enough income to meet their operational and maintenance costs". (2) Technological sustainability is "the ability for a technology to exist for a long period of time without major shifts in hardware or software affecting its availability or durability". (3) Social sustainability "requires user buy-in and participation, taking account local traditions, considering differences within communities, empowering marginalized groups, sharing and aligning goals with local people and adapting to evolving community needs". (4) Institutional sustainability relates to "the buy-in of key institutional actors". (5) Finally, environmental sustainability is concerned with the plans for the eventual disposal or reuse of the technology when it reaches the end of its life. Such an evaluation system can assess sustainability in terms of how likely the project results will persist. The analysis of the sustainability of the PROTIC project that will be presented in this paper will be framed around these five types of sustainability.

3   Methodology

Data for this paper was collected on three separate occasions. Firstly, the authors organised on 27 March 2019 a one-day workshop with women participants of the PROTIC project from two areas, Borokupot in Satkhira district in the South of the country and Dakshin Kharibari in Nilphamari district in the North of the country. The workshop was originally planned to be held in one of the villages, but due to a security alert, the foreign researchers were not allowed to travel to the rural area and the workshop had to be held in the capital. This offered the researchers the opportunity to bring together women from two different areas. Six women from each village, selected by the local NGO partners, attended the workshop, which was facilitated by three PhD students and one Oxfam Bangladesh employee, who were all Bengali speakers. The workshop included several hands-on activities that were designed to evaluate the women digital literacy skills and to discuss their information preferences. Following this workshop, two focus groups were organised the next month in Borokupot to follow up on some issues that were raised during the workshop. The questions were prepared by the authors and the focus groups were facilitated by one of the PhD students, who had previously done fieldwork in the village. The workshop and the focus groups were recorded with permission from the participants and complied with Monash University's ethics procedures. The discussions were translated by two of the PhD students and analysed by the authors of this paper.

In addition to these activities with the PROTIC participants, the authors conducted an in-depth 2-h interview on 28 March 2019 with four senior staff members of Win Miaki at the Win Miaki offices in Dhaka. An Oxfam Bangladesh representative was also present during the interview. The interview was conducted in English and recorded with the participants' permission. The data was analysed by the authors and constitutes the main source for this paper.

4 Sustainability of PROTIC

4.1 Economic/Financial Sustainability

According to Ali and Bailur (2007), achieving the financial sustainability of a project is often the greatest challenge for ICT4D projects because they are usually funded by external donors for a limited period of time. They asserted that financial sustainability is especially problematic for projects that aim at ensuring equal access to the technology for those who cannot afford to pay for access (Ali and Bailur 2007). This is the case of PROTIC. Support for the participants will end with the end of the PROTIC project. Therefore, the issue that confronts the project is how to ensure that the participants will continue to have access to the information and that the content will be maintained and updated. In this case, financial sustainability includes the cost of maintaining the phones, the cost of providing internet access and access to the information, and the cost of updating the information.

Having been used for 3–4 years, many of the phones have started to deteriorate due to general wear and tear, loss of battery life, and functional hardware problems, such as broken screens and software malfunctions. Repairs and parts replacements are often required and this costs money. The cost of phone repairs is covered for the duration of the project, but, after the end of the project, participants will need to shoulder this cost, as well as that of replacing the phones when they reach the end of their lives. Internet access will be another cost for them to bear to keep accessing information. While data allowance is provided for the duration of the project, it is often not sufficient and participants purchase additional data themselves. After the project ends, they will need to think of ways to fund these expenses.

To ensure the continuing availability of the information, Win Miaki is planning to develop a mobile application that will house all the agricultural information sent to the women through various outlets for the past 4 years. The plan is for the application with the content to be downloadable to be used as an offline application. This would not cost much and this can be done before the project ends. However, since the information needs to be updated, there will be recurring costs. To cover these costs, Win Miaki proposes to charge the users a small monthly subscription fee. According to the latest evaluation survey they did among the participants, they believe that the women would be prepared to pay up to 100 Taka (about 1 Euro) for the subscription. According to a Win Miaki senior staff, "once people realise the benefit of this information, they will be willing to pay". He estimated that even if only 50% of the participants ended up subscribing to the application it should be sufficient to make it viable. Another Win Miaki senior staff suggested that the cost could be shared by a group of women since they have been sharing information among them. She argued that many of the women are feeling empowered by having access to the information and are actively sharing this information directly in their community or through social media. This sense of empowerment and ownership of the service will further its adoption within the wider community, not just among the PROTIC participants. Wider adoption means that the cost of maintaining the application could be covered and would benefit more people in the community. According to an Oxfam Bangladesh PROTIC staff, participants, particularly in the Northern area have reported that since their family income has increased as a result of the project, they managed to buy additional data allowance. This means that they can also be able to pay for phone maintenance or replacement as well as for the information service. However, in order to be able to do this, the women need to have some control over their family finances, which is often not the case in rural Bangladesh. Therefore, at this stage, we cannot say for certain whether or not the women would be willing and able to pay a subscription fee for the service.

An important achievement of the PROTIC project is that it helped the village women to acquire new skills, which enabled them to improve their economic position (Jannat et al. 2018). With their new digital literacy skills and access to the internet, women can for example find the market price for their crops and produce and therefore get a better price for them, or they can increase their production thanks to the information they have found. Women have also shown capacity to develop new small business opportunities. For example, two women are making pastry boxes, which they sell to shopkeepers in the district market through Facebook (Jannat et al. 2018). These examples of economic improvement are also contributing to the project's economic sustainability.

4.2   Technological Sustainability

PROTIC's initiative to focus on delivering services to relatively poor people through smartphones is a cost-effective solution. Innovative projects that provide SMS-based communication and turn mobile phones into a messaging hub can offer very real opportunities (Kleine and Unwin 2009). Technological sustainability is an important issue for projects relying on mobile phones because the technology changes quickly and is not designed for the long term. It is entwined with financial sustainability because financial resources are needed to replace broken or out-of date equipment. In the case of PROTIC, broken phones are becoming an important issue. It is expected that the participants will pay for new phones themselves when they wear out after the end of the project because they have understood how useful phones can be to them. The smartphones distributed to the participants, although at the low end of the price range, are of a relatively good quality. Considering more durable options with comparable price might prolong life expectancy, but without appropriate care the technology may deteriorate faster than expected. Instruction on proper care should accompany an ICT-based solution. Many accidents like broken screens, liquid damage and cracks from pressure have been reported among the PROTIC participants. Moreover, shared use of the phones among the families leads to overuse, which can reduce the performance of the phones.

The durability of the smartphones is only part of the problem of technological sustainability in PROTIC since the focus of the project is to provide women with relevant information and skills to access this information. The sustainability of the infrastructure and of the technology, i.e. the mobile application used to provide access to the information, are key issues. The planned mobile application development should pay attention to the design and accessibility of the system. Although the cellular network has been growing rapidly in many areas of the country, the limited 3G spectrum availability impacts on the quality of mobile services, particularly in rural areas (GSMA 2018). Culturally appropriate and user-friendly interfaces are important to sustain the application's use and software updates will be needed to safeguard the content and the application from security flaws. The mobile application will have some limitation since Bangladesh has many different agricultural areas with specific condition that will require a lot of customisation efforts from the application provider. There are existing mobile applications developed by government but these are not tailored to specific locations and climate conditions.

4.3 Social Sustainability

Social sustainability is concerned with the usefulness and relevance of the content provided by an ICT4D project to the needs of the recipients. This is a challenge that was addressed from the beginning by the PROTIC project, which aimed to be a participatory action project (Sarrica et al. 2019). The content of the information provided to the PROTIC participants was adapted to local needs of each of the three villages and to the changing needs of fragile ecosystems affected by climate change. Content was developed specifically for the villages in the project by Win Miaki, which sent every week two agriculture-related SMS and one weather-related SMS appropriate to each village (which means that a total of nine SMS might need to be prepared every week). Feedback was sought from the participants to inform the next phases of the project and steps were taken to adapt the content provided and the modes of delivery to the evolving needs of the participants and their increased ability at accessing and processing information. Two applications (one specifically for maize cultivation, one for agricultural subsidies) were developed and introduced in May 2017 (Jannat et al. 2018). In 2017, PROTIC started delivering messages about chickens and ducks to provide information about the prevention and treatment of common diseases, while at the same time some of the PROTIC women were trained in vaccinating poultry and livestock (Jannat et al. 2018). Moreover, since 2018, the feedback given by the PROTIC participants during monthly meetings was fed back into developing information that met the most pressing needs of the women in each of the three villages (Jannat et al. 2018). There is widespread evidence that the content provided by the project is shared with villagers who are not participants in PROTIC, which attests to its usefulness and relevance to the villagers' needs. For example, a woman from a neighbouring village has established a successful poultry business thanks to the PROTIC advice shared with her by one of the PROTIC women (Jannat et al. 2018).

During the course of the project, the PROTIC women developed documentation practices to capture themselves the content that they found useful in more durable formats, thereby working to ensure the sustainability of the information provided to them (Frings-Hessami et al. 2020). From early 2017, they started writing down the information they received from the call centre on loose pieces of paper, then they used notebooks, which had been provided to them during training sessions, to capture the information they found useful so that they could later have it handy if the same problem happened again to them or to their relatives or neighbours. It was quicker to refer to their notebooks than to phone again the call centre, which had limited working hours and which might be busy or not be able to give them the information straight-away. From the beginning of 2019, the women also started transcribing in their notebooks the text of the SMS after several incidents of lost data when phones went for repairs or when messages were deleted by mistake made them realise the fragility of the digital technologies and of the digital records. They thought that the messages contained information that was useful for them and they wanted to keep them for longer. In addition to using their notebooks, they also transcribed the SMS on sheets of brown paper, sorted out by topics, that they could hang in their community meeting places so that others, PROTIC members and non-members, could read them. This again shows that the content was useful not only for the project participants, but for their whole community, and that its impact was larger than the confines of the project, which contribute to its social sustainability. Both the practices of writing in notebooks and of using sheets of brown papers were new to the village women. They were not traditional practices in Bangladeshi villages (Frings-Hessami et al. 2020). The village women discovered them through development projects, such as PROTIC and REE-CALL, a larger development project also administered by Oxfam Bangladesh, in which they had participated, and they appropriated them to meet their own needs and the needs of their communities and to preserve the information that they wanted to keep for longer than what was made possible by the technology used in the project. They adapted a system that was not convenient and not sufficient so that it better met their needs. This again demonstrates the usefulness and the social acceptance of the project, which both will help to ensure its sustainability.

4.4 Institutional Sustainability

Working in a developing country is a highly political process. The project must be accepted by the key institutional actors at the national and at the local government levels. In Bangladesh, NGOs also play a key role and projects cannot proceed without their buy-in. There are over 23,000 registered NGOs (Karim 2011, p. 2). The NGO sector is quite diverse, ranging from many small local volunteer groups to powerful large-scale organisations with multimillion-dollar budgets (Lewis 2011). The NGOs provide essential services, such as microfinance, primary education, potable water, new skills training, and employment in the rural economy (Karim 2011). To implement the PROTIC project, the Bangladeshi NGO partner, Oxfam Bangladesh has been working with local NGOs in each of the three PROTIC villages. These local partners were responsible for conducting a variety of activities in the villages, including selecting the beneficiaries, organising orientation, training and capacity-building workshop, facilitating research activities, and implementing monitoring and reporting activities (Sarrica et al. 2019). Other partners were brought in for their technical expertise, such as Win Miaki and Research Initiatives Bangladesh (RIB), a research institute specialising in community development through participatory action research, as well as researchers and students from Bangladeshi universities (Sarrica et al. 2019). With so many partners involved, it is important to make sure that they all understand and concur with the project objectives and methodology and are committed to the success of the project (Sarrica et al. 2019). There is a risk that some of the local partners will interfere with the project, for example with the selection of the beneficiaries, or with the information flows in and out of the villages because they misunderstand the project's objectives or because they are following their own objectives. The institutional sustainability of the projects is dependent on the continuing support of the local partners. In the case of PROTIC, "the project design, governance, implementation, and evaluation, have had to take into account the divergent needs and capacities of all the stakeholders" and to make some compromises (Sarrica et al. 2019, p. 507).

A project implemented in Bangladesh must follow Bangladeshi laws, rules and customs. This is illustrated for example by the way Win Miaki operated as the provider of agricultural information for PROTIC. During the course of the project, Win Miaki developed information based on each village agricultural situation and climate conditions. Bound by regulations, they cannot send out the content they have developed before it has gone through a complex verification process, which involves consultation with technical experts, organisation of expert validation workshops and government approval. This requires close coordination and a good workflow process for the information to be available in a timely manner. The content of the information provided each week is related to the specific situation of each village at that time of the year. Some messages may be developed in answer to specific questions asked by farmers during the monthly meetings. Win Miaki have established a large database of agricultural information from their involvements with PROTIC and with various other projects, including government ones. They employ agricultural graduates to answer the call centre's queries. Through a content management system, these employees use the database as their first point of reference. If the information requested is not in the database, they can use other sources, but they must warn the callers that the information that they are providing has not been validated by the government.

4.5 Environmental Sustainability

The disposal of the phones has not been taken into account in the planning for PROTIC. In that sense, environmental sustainability may not be achieved. However, one of the key aims of PROTIC is to enable the village women to deal with climate change by providing them with up-to-date agricultural and meteorological information that takes into account the latest changes in the climate and the environment. This contributes to ensuring the sustainability of the project in a rapidly changing environment and it is one of the reasons for its popularity with the local populations.

However, maintaining the relevance of the information will necessitate continuous updates and will depend on measures being taken to ensure that this will happen.

5   Conclusions

Our study shows that some measures to ensure the social sustainability of the PROTIC project had been taken from the beginning of the project but that some aspect of sustainability had not been taken into consideration. PROTIC aimed to be a participatory action research project and for that reason, the local actors and the participants were consulted during the design of the project and regularly throughout its implementation, and their feedback fed into the provision of content and the methods of delivery of that content. However, the project focused on empowering village women through providing information to them and teaching them skills to access information by themselves, but it did not pay much attention to the sustainability of the formats in which the information was provided. In this context, the participants themselves took measures to preserve the information that was provided to them in more durable analogue formats. This is evidence to the usefulness of the content provided and to its social acceptance as well as to the new skills that the women acquired during the project. Future ICT4D projects should make plans to ensure the sustainability of the information from the beginning of the project, they should consider the durability of the formats in which they provide information, and they should support documentation practices that emerge spontaneously.

Working with multiple partners in a developing country is a complex process. It is essential to understand the local context, including the power structures, the infrastructure and the capabilities, and it is important for all the partners to understand and agree with the objectives of the project. PROTIC worked with local technical partners in developing and providing content that was adapted to the local needs and they responded to the participants' feedback and suggestions. The information provided by PROTIC was shared widely by the participants, multiplying its impact and, thereby, attesting to its relevance and usefulness. The mobile application being developed by Win Miaki to store all the content developed during the course of the project and the plans to continue updating the information are important steps to ensure the sustainability of the project and to broaden its impact by making the information available to the wider community at a low cost.

An important achievement of the PROTIC project is that it enabled village women to develop their confidence, acquire new skills and improve their economic situation. The setting up of successful business ventures thanks to the information provided by the project is an important flow-on effect that illustrates the social impact of the project. The phones may break and the provision of information may stop, but the women will retain the digital literacy skills that they have acquired and be able to use them to access information by themselves to meet their daily needs and to embark on new economic ventures that will improve their wellbeing and that of their communities.

References

Ali, M., Bailur, S.: The challenge of "sustainability" in ICT4D – Is bricolage the answer? In: Proceedings of the 9th International Conference on Social Implications of Computers in Developing Countries, Sao Paulo, Brazil, pp. 1–19 (2007)

Badsar, M., Samah, B.A., Hassan, M.A., Osman, N.B., Shaffri, H.A.: Predictor factors of telecentres outcome from the users perspectives in rural communities. Am. J. Appl. Sci. **8**(6), 617–627 (2011)

Best, M.L.: Understanding our knowledge gaps: or, do we have an ICT4D field? and do we want one? Inf. Technol. Int. Dev. **6**, 49–52 (2010)

Best, M.L., Kumar, R.: Sustainability failures of rural telecenters: challenges from the sustainable access in rural India (SARI) project. Inf. Technol. Int. Dev. **4**(4), 31–45 (2008)

De Zoysa, M.R., Letch, N.: ICT4D project sustainability: an ANT-based analysis. In: Proceedings of the Nineteenth Americas Conference on Information Systems, Chicago, Illinois, 15–17 August 2013, pp. 1–10 (2013)

Food and Agriculture Organisation (FAO): The state of food and agriculture 2010–2011. Women in agriculture: Closing the gender gap for development. FAO, Rome (2011). https://reliefweb. int/sites/reliefweb.int/files/resources/12C5112E3B7A2EDFC125784C0038AE91-Full_ Report.pdf. Accessed 23 Aug 2011

Frings-Hessami, V., Sarker, A., Oliver, G., Anwar, M.: Documentation in a community informatics project: the creation and sharing of information by women in Bangladesh. J. Doc. **76**(2), 552–570 (2020)

Guhathakurta, M., Banu, A. (eds.): Gendered Lives, Livelihood and Transformation: The Bangladesh Context. UPL, Dhaka (2017)

GSMA: Country overview: Bangladesh. Mobile industry driving growth and enabling digital inclusion (2018). https://www.gsmaintelligence.com/research/?file=a163eddca009553979bcd fb8fd5f2ef0&download. Accessed 27 Aug 2019

Heeks, R.: ICT4D 2.0: the next phase of applying ICT for international development. Computer **41**(6), 26–33 (2008)

IFAD: ARRI issues note: Sustainability. Internal document. IFAD, Rome (2006). https://www. ifad.org/documents/38714182/39710099/sustainability.pdf. Accessed 2 Sept 2019

Jannat, F., Chakraborty, T.R., Aktar, P., Stillman, L.: Evaluating a smartphone phone project in Bangladesh through community monthly meeting reports. In: Stillman, L., Anwar, M., (eds.) Proceedings of the 16th CIRN Conference, Prato, Italy, pp. 110–124 (2018)

Kabeer, N.: Cultural dopes or rational fools? Women and labour supply in the Bangladesh garment industry. Eur. J. Dev. Res. **3**(1), 133–160 (1991)

Karim, L.: Microfinance and its Discontents: Women in Debt in Bangladesh. University of Minnesota press, Minneapolis (2011)

Kleine, D., Unwin, T.: Technological revolution, evolution and new dependencies: what's new about ICT4D? Third World Q. **30**(5), 1045–1067 (2009)

Lewis, D.: Bangladesh: Politics, Economy and Civil Society. Cambridge University Press, Cambridge (2011)

Marais, M.: Analysis of the factors affecting the sustainability of ICT4D initiatives. In: Proceedings of the 5th International Development Informatics, Cape Town, pp. 100–120 (2011)

Marais, M.: ICT4D and Sustainability, pp. 1–9. Wiley Blackwell, Hoboken (2015). The International Encyclopedia of Digital Communication and Society

Pade-Khene, C., Mallinson, B., Sewry, D.: Sustainable rural ICT project management practice for developing countries: investigating the Dwesa and RUMEP projects. Inf. Technol. Dev. **17**(3), 187–212 (2011)

Rahman, S.: Women's employment in Bangladesh agriculture: composition, determinants and scope. J. Rural Stud. **16**(4), 497–507 (2000)

Rahman, S.: Women's labour contribution to productivity and efficiency in agriculture: empirical evidence from Bangladesh. J. Agric. Econ. **61**(2), 318–342 (2010)

Sagar Kisan, W., Shivaji Dadabhau, A., Singh, K.: Factors affecting the sustainability of ICT intervention for agricultural development – a review. Agric. Rev. **34**(3), 198–206 (2013)

Sarrica, M., Denison, T., Stillman, L., Chakraborty, T., Auvi, P.: "What do others think?" An emic approach to participatory action research in Bangladesh. AI Soc. **24**(3), 495–508 (2019)

Sey, A., Fellows, M.: Literature review on the impact of public access to information and communication technologies. CIS working paper/Center for Information and Society, University of Washington, no. 6 (2009)

Thapa, D., Sæbø, Ø.: Exploring the link between ICT and development in the context of developing countries: a literature review. Electron. J. Inf. Syst. Dev. Ctries. **64**(1), 1–15 (2014)

Unwin, T.: ICT4D: Information and Communication Technology for Development. Cambridge University Press, Cambridge (2009)

"In the Beginning, It Was Little Whispers… Now, We're Almost a Roar": Conceptualizing a Model for Community and Self in LGBTQ+ Health Information Practices

Vanessa L. Kitzie$^{(\boxtimes)}$, Travis L. Wagner , and A. Nick Vera

University of South Carolina, Columbia, SC, USA
kitzie@mailbox.sc.edu

Abstract. Although LGBTQ+ populations experience significant health challenges, little research exists that investigates their health from an informational perspective. Our study addresses this gap by exploring the health information practices of LGBTQ+ communities in South Carolina, focusing on how socio-cultural context shapes these practices. Thirty semi-structured interviews with South Carolina LGBTQ+ community leaders analyzed using open qualitative coding informed the development of a conceptual framework describing their information practices. Findings show that participants engaged in two broad types of practices – protective and defensive – as responses to risks and barriers experienced, which are in turn produced by social and structural factors. Findings advance information practices and marginalization approaches and offer ways for medical professionals to improve service to LGBTQ+ populations.

Keywords: Information practices · LGBTQ+ communities · Health information

1 Introduction

Lesbian, gay, bisexual, transgender, and queer (LGBTQ+) people face significant health challenges compared to their cisgender and heterosexual peers. These challenges are produced by social and structural factors, e.g., discrimination, resulting in mental and physical health disparities among this population [1–3]. Disparities can be specific to sub-groups under the broader LGBTQ+ umbrella and vary based on other intersecting, contextual, and identity-related aspects [1, 2, 4, 5]. A key factor contributing to these health challenges is informational, as LGBTQ+ people may experience difficulty learning about their healthcare needs, navigating the healthcare system, and addressing barriers to care [6, 7]. Despite the significance of information in shaping LGBTQ+ health outcomes, few studies investigate LGBTQ+ health from an informational perspective. Further, existing work frames this phenomenon using deficit-based models, which disempower LGBTQ+ populations [8].

LGBTQ+ residents in the Southern U.S. states may experience enhanced health challenges, since these regions have more conservative views of sexuality and gender identity on average [9]. South Carolina (SC) is a predominantly rural Southern state

© Springer Nature Switzerland AG 2020
A. Sundqvist et al. (Eds.): iConference 2020, LNCS 12051, pp. 15–31, 2020.
https://doi.org/10.1007/978-3-030-43687-2_2

with 2.9% of the population identifying as LGBTQ+ [10]. LGBTQ+ residents experience more severe health challenges as compared to the national averages, including heightened economic instability, unemployment, and lack of health insurance [11]. While some quantitative work documents the health challenges of SC LGBTQ+ residents [e.g., 10, 12] there exists an absence of qualitative research providing in-depth perspectives of how individuals navigate these challenges in their everyday lives.

This research addresses the above gaps by examining the health information practices of SC LGBTQ+ communities with a focus on how sociocultural context shapes these practices. By employing a social constructionist approach, the research envisions communities as engaging in information practices for personal and community empowerment in response to health challenges faced.

1.1 Theoretical Orientations

Information Practices Approach. Information behavior and practice are two umbrella concepts describing how people deal with information [13]. While their boundaries are blurry in practice, these concepts exhibit distinct epistemological and ontological understandings of information's social aspects [13, 14]. The cognitivist information behavior approach frames information needs as drivers of seeking and use. This framing has positivist and behaviorist metatheoretical underpinnings [15], which can be wielded against specific populations to suggest that any behaviors not adhering to this limited view are indicative of a personal failing requiring correction from experts [16–18].

Information practices represent constructivist and constructionist perspectives, where social and structural factors shape people's relationships with information. Information practices research focuses on the everyday life contexts in which people interact with information [19] and has uncovered relevant practices beyond seeking, including sharing and use [14]. We adopt an information practices approach for this study as it addresses how broader social and structural factors differentiate the health issues experienced by LGBTQ+ people from their heterosexual and cisgender peers. This perspective aligns with population health [20] and resilience approaches [21] addressing social and structural determinants of health.

Information Marginalization Theory. Information marginalization theory adopts a sociocultural lens to examine information inequality, wherein specific populations experience enhanced challenges in dealing with information [22]. Information poverty theory [23] and a constructivist grounded theory analysis [22] inform information marginalization theory. It has three components: (1) information marginalization factors, (2) individual-level behaviors, and (3) community-level practices. Per the theory, individual-level behaviors and community-level practices respond to information marginalization factors, often to defend/protect (used synonymously) against them [22]. This theory informs our information practices approach by identifying defensive/protective information practices as a typical response to social and structural inequalities and addressing how these practices operate at both individual and community levels of analysis.

2 Literature Review

Library and Information Science (LIS) scholars have applied an information practices approach to marginalized groups based on its strengths in attending to sociocultural context. Research highlights nuances and differences to traditional information seeking models and theories in ways that can potentially disrupt or re-situate them [14, 19, 23]. Several LIS studies offer insight into the unique relationship between information practices and information marginalization.

Studies examining information marginalization across a variety of populations demonstrate that despite engaging in certain practices that appear less "mainstream" [24] participants are knowledgeable and agentic in their information interactions. Specifically, they are aware of social and structural barriers to information and engage in information practices as measured responses. Examples include immigrants using tactical information like sharing between community elders and wandering to learn about a city's layout [25]; young parents sharing information via mobile technologies in lieu of "traditional" sources for health information [26]; and parents of individuals with disabilities designating a point person to gather information for the community based on limited access to health and wellbeing resources [22].

Few LIS studies focus on the information practices of LGBTQ+ populations. Existing work highlights the importance of community contexts, the need to manage the visibility of information practices, and community mistrust of outside information sources. Communities work together to maintain the trustworthiness of health information by establishing social capital and engaging in networked bonding and bridging to share information [27]. In other cases, the anonymity of online spaces provides a way for communities to safely seek information [28]. Other work considers the consumption of established LGBTQ+ information resources (i.e., media) within the community as purposeful "satisficing" based on the collective perception that limited representation is better than none [29]. Some research studies outside of LIS apply an informational focus to LGBTQ+ health; for instance, prior research identified how negative past experiences with health practitioners shaped LGBTQ+ patients' sharing and seeking practices, specifically disclosure management and avoidance [30, 31]. While these studies and related work begin a necessary dialogue around LGBTQ + information practices, there remain considerable gaps in the literature.

Those able to participate in institutional dialog about their identities and needs tend to come from privileged groups. As a result, studies examining LGBTQ+ identity and popular discourses at large center the needs and desires of cisgender, gay, white men and lesbians of relative wealth. This identity normalizes and dictates an LGBTQ + agenda exclusionary of non-white gay cisgender men [32]; transgender and gender nonconforming persons of color [33]; and non-Western LGBTQ+ individuals [34]. This lack of representation is evident in the studies overviewed [27–29], noting the overt presence of white, well-educated participants as a limitation. Similarly, much of the research focusing on LGBTQ+ individuals predominantly looked at millennial populations [28, 29]. Further, [27, 28]'s research recruited participants in mostly urban areas, reifying metronormativity narratives, which singularize the experiences of LGBTQ+ individuals inhabiting metropolitan spaces as universalized narratives [35].

Research reviewed describes how social and structural factors shape people's information practices. Additionally, those who are socially and structurally marginalized face unique challenges when dealing with information. How they address these challenges results in a series of nuanced practices that differ from those who do not experience such alterity. This study responds to a critical lack of information behavior and practices literature on LGBTQ+ individuals and focuses on their health information challenges, an unexplored area among this population. Further, it attends to some of the above sampling gaps by recruiting participants with diverse sexualities, gender identities, ages, races/ethnicities, and education levels from SC. The study addresses the following research question: How does sociocultural context shape the health information practices of SC LGBTQ+ communities?

3   Methods

This qualitative study was approved by the University of South Carolina Institutional Review Board (IRB) for expedited review (Pro0008587). We recruited 30 SC LGBTQ+ community leaders to participate in individual, semi-structured interviews between January – August 2019. This sample size is appropriate to study's goal of advancing theory rather than generating a priori codes [36, 37]. Leaders serve as vital stakeholders within their communities and have a valuable, macro-level vantage point from which to examine them. Our definition of "community" employs three criteria: (1) geography, participants reside or perform a majority of community work in SC, (2) social interaction, members engage in shared activities, and (3) ties, members are connected via shared LGBTQ+ identities [38]. Additional criteria specified that participants were 13 years or older. We included youth in our sample, given the many examples of dynamic youth LGBTQ+ leaders [39, 40]. Since some youth wished to participate without outing themselves to a parent or guardian, we obtained an IRB waiver of informed consent and instead collected youth assent [see also 30].

We used purposive sampling to collect names and contact information for over 100 visible LGBTQ+ and affinity organizations (e.g., social justice organizations, Unitarian Universalist Churches) in SC. We then contacted these organizations via email, asking them to nominate a leader to participate. Additional snowball sampling occurred at the end of each interview when we asked leaders to recommend other participants. Since data collection and analysis were iterative, we used theoretical sampling to identify perspectives that could flesh out or potentially contradict emergent findings, which led us to engage in additional recruitment via social media.

The semi-structured interview protocol addressed the following topics: (a) participant's involvement with the community, (b) participant and members identities, (c) community health questions and concerns, and (d) how the community addresses health questions and concerns. We structured questions from topic (d) based on [14] 's model of information practices, which divides them into seeking, sharing, and use. We also added creating as another relevant practice uncovered in research on teens and LGBTQ+ individuals [28, 29, 41]. Following interviews, we asked participants to elicit topics (c) and (d) further using information worlds mapping, a visual arts elicitation method [42]. We pre-tested the protocol and mapping exercise with three SC nonLGBTQ+ community leaders before participant interviews.

The mean and median interview duration was 78 min, and participants received a $50 cash incentive. Interviews were face-to-face at a public location of the participant's choosing except two interviews conducted over the phone. One participant was disabled and could not meet in-person, while another youth wanted to participate, but feared rejection from her family if they discovered her participation. In these two cases, participants did not engage in the mapping exercise. One or two paper authors attended each interview and took detailed field notes post-interview. All interviews were audiorecorded and transcribed verbatim.

Data sources were interview transcripts, field notes, and information worlds maps. Per [42]'s earlier work, we viewed the maps as supplemental to transcripts when performing analysis. We analyzed data using an open qualitative coding process borrowed from, but not identical to, grounded theory [43]. First, we individually hand-coded three transcripts using initial, process, and in vivo coding [37]. We then met to compare and discuss codes, generating a preliminary codebook. We applied this codebook to four additional transcripts, meeting six times to discuss emergent codes and compare them to existing ones [44]. After discussing and resolving coding discrepancies, we divided and independently coded the remaining transcripts. Then, we deployed focused and axial coding to describe conceptual categories and the relationships between them. We engaged in member-checking, sending participants their transcripts and fieldnotes to request removal of potentially identifying contextual information and comment on how well they reflected lived experiences [45].

4 Findings

4.1 Participant Demographics

The following Figs. 1 and 2 and Table 1 display participant demographic data. The majority of participants were young adults (18–35) and middle-aged (35–54), while their races/ethnicities reflected the broader state-level demographics for LGBTQ+ people [10]. Participant education levels varied but trended toward those with some degree of higher education. While the geographic distribution of participants spread across the state, more leaders resided in the Upstate and Midlands regions where LGBTQ+ and affinity organizations are prevalent and active. Fewer participants in the Coastal Lowcountry and Pee Dee regions likely reflects their smaller populations and less visible organizations. One exception was Charleston, which our sample under-represented. While the majority of participants identified as lesbian and gay, they employed many other labels to describe their sexualities and gender identities. These labels denote the inability of umbrella labels like LGBTQ+ to capture the multiplicity and fluidity of participant identities.

Fig. 1. Word cloud displaying participant gender and sexuality labels.

Fig. 2. Map of participant locations.

4.2   Conceptual Model of Participants' Health Information Practices

Data analysis and the study's theoretical orientation [14, 22, 23] informed the development of a conceptual model describing participants' health information practices (Fig. 3). The model's first component, contextual conditions, represent the underlying circumstances shaping how participants interact with health information. These conditions are broad, encompassing structural dimensions such as identity, geography, and politics. Gender identity and sexuality are overarching contextual conditions for this study and intersect with other conditions to produce qualitatively distinct health information practices.

Table 1. Participant age ranges, race & ethnicity, and education.

Age	N	Race & Ethnicity	N	Education	N
18–25	11	White	18	Some college credit	7
35–54	7	Black	7	Master's degree	6
55–64	4	Black, White	2	Associate degree	5
13–17	4	Black, Afro-Caribbean	1	Bachelor's degree	5
26–34	3	Aboriginal, Arab/West Asian, Black, White	1	In high school	2
65+	1	Black, White, Egyptian	1	In middle school	2
				High school diploma	1
				Doctoral degree	1
				GED or alt. credential	1

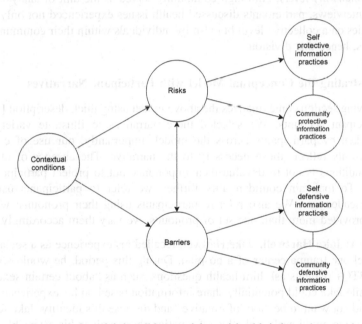

Fig. 3. Conceptual model describing participants' health information practices.

Contextual conditions produce two broad types of social and structural inequities: barriers and risks. Barriers are significant obstacles experienced in a specific spacetime arrangement that constrain individuals and communities from achieving desired informational outcomes. Examples of barriers identified by data analysis included family, law, and religion. Unlike barriers, which are actualized, risks represent perceived exposure to danger, harm, or loss that might result from engaging in specific information practices. Risks are often more specific than barriers, since barriers operate at the sociocultural level, whereas risks are more immediate and individualized. Examples of risks uncovered by data analysis were physical violence, being kicked out, and fear of the unknown. Barriers and risks are co-constitutive, with barriers commonly experienced by some rendered as potential risks to others and vice versa. Participants are not disempowered or lack agency because they face barriers and risks; instead, they respond to them to achieve particular informational outcomes.

Barriers and risks produce two distinct types of information practices: *defensive* and *protective*. *Defensive information practices* are instances where individuals or communities create, seek, share, and use information to defend against a barrier or barriers. These practices are reactive; individuals and communities deal with information as a direct response to the barrier(s). Individuals and communities engage in *protective information practices* to guard against a perceived risk or risks. These practices are proactive; while the risk did not yet occur, it has the potential to become actualized. Because barriers and risks are co-constitutive, defensive and protective information practices can co-occur. Both types of information practices can be divided further at the *self* and *community levels*. Although community served as the unit of analysis for this work, in interviews, participants discussed health issues experienced not only by their communities on a collective level but also by individuals within their communities and themselves, hence this division.

4.3   Illustrating the Conceptual Model with Participant Narratives

The following section contextualizes the above model using thick description [46] from four participant accounts. We selected these narratives to illustrate variety in the "paths" taken by participants across the model. Importantly, our use of contextual conditions only reflects those necessary to the narrative. The absence of other contextual conditions is not to devalue their importance but to protect participant confidentiality. To maintain confidentiality further, we refer to participants using self-selected pseudonyms. We also refer to participants using their pronouns; when participants provided more than one set of pronouns, we vary them accordingly.

Narrative 1: Jake Hartwell. Jake Hartwell recalled his experience as a social worker in the level one trauma center of a hospital. During this period, he would sometimes have LGBTQ+ patients ask him health questions, such as "about certain sexual practices." While Jake could potentially share information based on his experience as a gay man, he did not want to be "too informative" and disclose this identity. Jake felt it was inappropriate to out himself to do this information sharing given his ostensible role as a neutral and unbiased party in the field of social work: "I don't want to necessarily be like, 'Well, this is what I do, and this is how I do it,' just because that's not really appropriate." Instead, Jake provided his patients with information he thought they would need as LGBTQ+ individuals without disclosing his identity: "I want my patients to be able to see me as a blank canvas because if I tell them I identify this way, or I have this value, that might be something for them that might be harmful."

Several contextual conditions shape Jake's information practices. While likely true of multiple participants, Jake made it clear during member-checking that all of his intersecting identities (not solely the ones we initially highlighted) inform his practitioner role. Salient areas of Jake's identity include being bisexual, a person of color, young adult, first generation graduate student, and person of faith. While these identities shape Jake's social work practice by motivating and encouraging his work, they are not viewed by Jake to be appropriate to share with patients because they are not neutral. Key barriers that may shape Jake's decision to not share his personal experiences are homophobia and transphobia. These barriers can lead to the additional job-related risks of appearing unprofessional and doing harm by being "off-putting" to patients. To respond to these conditions, barriers, and risks, Jake engages in several information practices. First, he assesses his areas of expertise as a social worker, bisexual, a person of color, young adult, first generation graduate student, and person of faith to inform how and what information he conveys to his LGBTQ+ patients. We argue that such assessment constitutes a form of community protective information use, in which Jake protects against appearing unprofessional and doing harm by determining which parts of his experience and expertise rooted in these experiences are relevant to share and how to share them. In turn, Jake chooses to avoid sharing these experiences and expertise based on his intersecting identities with the understanding that this avoidance facilitates access to the very people whom he sees as his community. These people have LGBTQ+ identities, but also other marginalized identities, such as people from broken families or minority racial groups. Jake refers to this community as "the island of misfit toys," a descriptor illustrating the homophobia and transphobia barriers (among other, intersecting ones including racism) this community faces. Jake operates within these barriers to provide non-discriminatory care, even if he is doing so from a performed vantage point of neutrality. We regard this choice as self-defensive information sharing since Jake works to defend himself against barriers that could call into question his professionalism and the role of social work more broadly. We further categorize this practice as disclosure management and envision Jake as intentionally choosing not to disclose his identity to maintain his professional aspirations, which are to help his patients, including his community, with their health questions and concerns.

Narrative 2: Ben. Ben is a high school student who defined his community as comprised of other LGBTQ+ students: "So we only have four gay people at school and so- actually, no, we have [NAME]. [...] Okay, we have him. And yeah, it's only us." At school, Ben described meeting with community members outside on school grounds "near where we put our garden" against "a brick wall." Sometimes during these meetings, they will "get all our questions like, 'Who's going to the doctor's appointment?' [...] and so we go to the doctor's appointment and ask five questions." Ben also provided an example of a current health question her community has: "we're trying to– we've heard of PrEP. A lot of people have PrEP, but we don't even know how old you have to be to be on PrEP [...] it literally doesn't say on the website."

Contextual conditions relevant to this narrative are identity, education, and age. These conditions shape how Ben's community is treated, what information they can or cannot access, and how often they can access medical professionals based on when their parents, guardians, or other family members make appointments for them. Socioeconomic status and transportation serve as other contextual conditions since Ben's narrative suggests that at least some community members can afford a doctor's visit and get to the doctor's office.

Education constitutes a significant barrier to Ben and her community, who face homophobia and transphobia in school. Ben recalled a specific negative experience where these barriers intersected:

I have been called a [homophobic slur] in front of my teacher, and the teacher didn't do anything. She just was looking and was literally just texting on her phone. I sit two seats away from her. It's a row. She's in the corner. I was in the row that was three seats. I sit in the back one near the wall, and the boy was next to her desk. And he went right up to my desk and said it to me. And she was just on her phone texting still.

In this account, Ben signifies that school is a violent place for her and the community. Said violence can lead to the invisibility of LGBTQ+ identities illustrated by Ben's teacher ignoring his identity by allowing a peer to demean it. This invisibility is reinforced by the administration, namely the school principal who remains "really silent" on LGBTQ+ issues. While unstated by Ben, the contextual conditions of geography and law, and their related environmental and legal barriers can also produce this invisibility; SC has "no promo homo" laws, which render it illegal for health and sexuality education teachers to discuss homosexuality in a positive light.

A final barrier shaping Ben's community relates to family, as Ben characterized some of her members' families as "broken." This descriptor relates to their lack of acceptance for their LGBTQ+ children, as Ben recounted one community member who "when he first came out to his parents, he had an argument with his family, and they almost told him to get out." The concordant risk of being kicked out of one's home likely shapes how much health information Ben's community can create, seek, share, and use without family becoming aware of their LGBTQ+ identities.

These contextual conditions and barriers contribute to an information vacuum that produces an immediate lack of information about LGBTQ+ health issues, such as information to address the community's PrEP-related question. To defend against these barriers, the community relies on its members to engage in a specific form of community defensive information seeking and sharing in which one member serves as an information intermediary between a medical professional and the community's collective health questions and concerns. Community members employ these community defensive practices to maintain insularity of health questions and concerns based on a keen awareness that adults in their everyday lives do not have the information they need and are either indifferent or antagonistic to their LGBTQ+ identities.

Narrative 3: Shannon. College student Shannon recalled a traumatic experience consequential to her physical and mental health:

I have been gay-bashed. [My partner and I] foolishly thought it was a good idea to go to this– she loved country music, and we'd go to this country honky-tonk here in [CITY]. It's closed down now. It's a bar called [CLUB]. And we got cornered there in the parking lot afterwards. And it's a pretty scary situation like that. But after surviving that, I really became a staunch advocate of seeking out communities of people like myself because there are safety in numbers.

Shannon's experience of being gay-bashed illustrates the prevalence of physical violence, a significant health issue, experienced by participants and their communities. An essential set of contextual conditions and barriers producing this issue are temporal, as the violence occurred in 2004, which notes a marked difference in public visibility and legal acceptance for almost any LGBTQ+ person in the U.S. Shannon's experience occurred just over a decade before the Obergefell vs. Hodges ruling, which legalized same-sex marriage, and the Equal Rights Employment Commission ruled to include sexual orientation discrimination as a form of illegal discrimination.

Simply because this event happened in the past does not displace its import or likelihood of happening again. This observation is due to other, intersecting contextual conditions including gender identity and sexuality as they pertain to Shannon's understanding of living in a Southern rural town with a lack of legal protections for and political actors supportive of LGBTQ+ communities. Shannon envisions these intersecting conditions as producing legal and ideological barriers, which are unique and still relevant to the state in 2019: "[SC] is notoriously very right-wing. There's not a shred of protection for LGBTQ people at the state level, and there won't be as long as somebody like Henry McMaster is governor of South Carolina." This combination of barriers produced an environment in which not only were Shannon and her partner attacked for being in a same-sex relationship but also had no legal recourse to address the attack or prevent others from being targeted. Further, these barriers created a specter of potential physical violence, a notable risk that Shannon continues to face.

Shannon's resulting information practices are community protective, self-defensive, and self-protective. Specifically, Shannon engages in community protective sharing when advocating her community to "seek" out LGBTQ+ people to ensure "safety in numbers." Further, by taking her advice, Shannon engages in both self-protective and self-defensive information seeking. Her seeking out LGBTQ+ communities is self-protective because it responds to the risk of physical violence. This practice is also selfdefensive in addressing the unique environmental, ideological, and legal barriers she continues to face. The interrelationship between self-protective and self-defensive is illustrated further by Shannon: "If you live in a state like South Carolina that has no nondiscrimination laws, you have to insulate yourself and find places that protect you from the fact that you have no protection."

Narrative 4: Kim and Mocha. Our final narrative focuses on one interview taking place with two co-leaders of the same LGBTQ+ support group, Kim and Mocha. They reflected on the backlash they were receiving at the time of the interview due to Mocha's participation in an upcoming LGBTQ+ themed event at their local library. Upon the event's announcement, their organization's social media sites received threats of physical violence and detractors planned a day-of protest. As Mocha stated: "I didn't think 7,000 people in [CITY] had library cards until they heard [we] were coming to the library." Based on these threats and negative feedback, Kim stated that the upcoming event "has got me just freaked out." She expressed particular concern of physical violence during the event: "I mean, every time I think about it, I think about Mocha getting hurt. And the [other members] getting hurt." As a result of both preexisting threats and the imagined possibilities of what could occur, Kim detailed several strategies for assuring the safety of Mocha and other community members on the day of the event. One such concern for the event was parking that would allow Kim to escort participants to the library. She needed to have a defined location "to put [her] people's cars," ensuring it was the "safest location" in the area. Further, Kim wanted to ensure that any individuals counter-protesting (i.e., supporting the event) "were family" (i.e., belonged to the LGBTQ+ community) and would not be violent toward Mocha or others. Kim laid out potential strategies for action if someone were to try and attack Mocha: "If anybody goes near her, I'll knock [Mocha's partner] to get to her."

Aside from consistent, contextual conditions of gender identity and sexuality, other relevant ones are geography and ideology. These conditions produced related environmental, ideological, homophobia, and transphobia barriers wherein Kim and Mocha's relationship with Southern culture and its ideologies led them to feel unwelcome in multiple institutional spaces, including the library system hosting the event. Spirituality and religion each respectively served as a contextual condition and barrier, as Kim and Mocha both noted that the threats and antagonism came from extremist Christian organizations espousing homophobia and transphobia. Like Shannon, Kim and Mocha also experienced a temporal barrier, noting a resurgence of anti-LGBTQ+ sentiment in the wake of Donald Trump becoming president. Also similar to Shannon, a significant risk identified by Kim and Mocha was physical violence. Moreover, a litany of concerns about the event expressed by Kim and Mocha highlight another risk, fear of the unknown, wherein so many exterior factors could go wrong during the event that they could not possibly anticipate every threat. As Mocha explained: "You just don't know how they're going to come at you."

In response to these conditions, barriers, and risks, Kim and Mocha engaged in community protective information practices. Specifically, they used seeking to inventory the logistical steps they would need to protect themselves from a litany of risks (e.g., looking for safe places to park) and then created a series of responses to anticipated events (e.g., what to do if someone were to attack). Finally, they engaged in use through the proposed assessment of counter-protestors to determine whether they "were family." While Kim and Mocha did not specify the details of how to make this assessment, they are likely rooted in LGBTQ+ culture and community dynamics, particularly the importance of chosen family among those who may not be accepted for their identities by blood relatives.

5 Discussion

Findings continue to advance an information practices approach and information marginalization theory as viable frames from which to identify new dimensions of people's information interactions. Several findings aligned with those of prior theory and literature including the importance of mediation between the community, individual members, and outside information sources; the use of tactical and agentic information practices in response to social and structural barriers, including lack of representation within institutional contexts; and the viability of community as a context from which to assess information practices [22, 25–27, 29]. A significant contribution is the distinction between protective and defensive, extending the work of information marginalization research [22, 23]. This distinction highlights the fact that even if a participant does not face immediate constraints to their health information practices (barriers), they can still respond to perceived adverse outcomes produced by these barriers (risks). This finding aligns with a central claim of minority stress theory, positing that absent of immediate barriers, LGBTQ+ people still may experience stressors due to expectations that they will face these barriers in the future [47]. Findings also advance population health [20] and resilience [21] approaches within an informational context by reframing health information practices from resultant of personal failings to empowered and intentional acts. While some of the information practices of participants and communities appear to be uninformed or unsafe, when contextualized within the conceptual model, these practices become well-assessed and vetted within the community.

Findings have implications for service to LGBTQ+ populations within medical institutions. Specifically, we found that communities engage in defensive and protective practices to integrate outside health information into their communities in ways that are socially and informationally relevant. Leaders play a significant role in facilitating these practices by encouraging collective information sharing and exchange and acting as an intermediary between experts and their community. In this way, participants' information practices parallel those adopted by community health workers (CHW) who are trusted members or have specialized knowledge of their community and serve as an intermediary between them and health practitioners. Findings from this research can inform LGBTQ+ CHW training by incorporating the informational elements of health identified by the study's conceptual model. This implication is particularly salient given that provisions of the Affordable Care Act coupled with grant funding have increased the number and use of CHWs, however, they continue to lack standardized training [48].

Another practice-oriented implication is for medical professionals to center the nonprofessional knowledge and information practices of communities as central to informing practice. Another participant, Second, illustrates this strategy when explaining why she likes her physician: "She'll ask me for resources, and I'll share what I have, and she'll be like, 'Hey, I read this... Is this true?' Because sometimes they're given stuff that's not necessarily popular [within the community]." In this interaction, Second's doctor returns some of the power inherent to a patient-expert interaction to Second by seeking information that reflects the values of Second's community. This practice can be facilitated by LIS researchers and practitioners, who through sociocultural, empirical observation of LGBTQ+ communities can contribute to continuing education training specifically rooted in cultural competency for medical professionals. These trainings are necessary not only to inform a patient-expert interaction but also to assist medical professionals in sharing information sought and disseminated by a community. Given the consistent practices of mediating and exchanging information between an LGBTQ+ member to and for their broader community, we argue that the interoperability of self and community has significant impact in terms of resource and information distribution. While one practitioner may see providing additional information to one LGBTQ+ person as time-consuming or ineffective, the findings suggest that the extended distribution of this information has a ripple effect and can aid countless community members in unseen and unknown ways.

While this study has attended to clear gaps in representation across age, race/ethnicity, class, and regional lines, many groups remain overlooked. Particular absences existed among Latinx communities, a notable presence in SC. Moreover, while participants represented diverse identities within the broad LGBTQ+ umbrella, we were unable to represent specific identities, e.g., two-spirit, genderfluid, demisexual.

Further, we were limited by which SC LGBTQ+ communities wanted to be visible, as some remain purposefully hidden. We had a particular lack of participant representation from Charleston, which was somewhat surprising to us given the visibility and reach of prominent LGBTQ+ organizations in this area. Finally, we did not represent particular professions whose LGBTQ+ members face unique health needs, such as sex workers. The collectively missed populations noted here mean that our study overlooked multiple health issues and concerns.

We also acknowledge the inherent epistemic violence [49] latent to the categorical work done in our coding, naming, and mapping of LGBTQ+ information practices. Our choice to deploy ambit terms such as community/self and defensive/protective information practices reinforce the very binaries that LGBTQ+ individuals unsettle; in fact, one could describe many of our participants as existing within and doing these practices simultaneously. Further, as LGBTQ+ individuals, our participants' orientation toward concepts like community and self assume a universalized notion of these concepts rather than something experienced as a point of disorientation or even multiplicity [50]. Therefore, while we did not aim to essentialize our participants' experiences, the very act of naming these categories occurred and subsequent essentialisms emerged.

6 Conclusion

This research examined the health information practices of SC LGBTQ+ communities, addressing how sociocultural context shapes these practices. Informed by thirty semistructured interviews with community leaders, we developed a conceptual framework, which uncovered two distinct types of information practices, protective and defensive. This framework advances sociocultural theories of information practices, providing a preliminary step to theory-building and contributes to research extending our conceptual model to other groups experiencing information marginalization. Findings also offer ways for medical professionals to improve service to LGBTQ+ populations.

This work has several future directions: focus groups with community members to validate and expand findings from leader interviews; employment of more nuanced and embedded strategies to recruit participants underrepresented in the current sample; enhanced analysis of information worlds maps based on recent analytical recommendations from Greyson, Stoeveller, & Shankar (2019); and interviews with health and medical librarians, as well as medical practitioners to understand their information practices in relation to the LGBTQ+ communities they serve. Ultimately, this study and the future work discussed seeks to alter current perceptions of SC LGBTQ+ communities' health information practices as being inherently lacking to being purposeful and agentic. In doing so, our findings can inform both theory and praxis in generative directions by illuminating alternative ways of imagining not only how LGBTQ+ communities tactically deal with health information, but also how medical and information institutions can value LGBTQ+ communities as an already information-rich resource.

References

1. Institute of Medicine: The Health of Lesbian, Gay, Bisexual, and Transgender People: Building a Foundation for Better Understanding. National Academic Press, Washington, D. C. (2011)
2. Center for Disease Control and Prevention, LGBT Youth Homepage. https://www.cdc.gov/lgbthealth/youth.htm. Accessed 19 Nov 2019
3. HealthyPeople.gov Lesbian, Gay, Bisexual, and Transgender Health U.S. Department of Health Evidence-based Resources Homepage. https://www.healthypeople.gov/2020/topics-objectives/topic/lesbian-gay-bisexual-and-transgender-health/ebrs. Accessed 19 Nov 2019
4. James, S.E., Herman, J.L., Rankin, S., Keisling, M., Mottet, L., Anaf, M.: The report of the 2015 U.S.C transgender survey. National Center for Transgender Equality, Washington, D.C. (2016).   https://www.transequality.org/sites/de-fault/files/docs/usts/USTS%20Full%20Report%20-%20FINAL%201.6.17.pdf. Accessed 19 Nov 2019
5. Transgender Law Center at Southerners on New Ground. The Grapevine: A Southern Trans Report: Prioritizing Issues Impacting Transgender, Gender Nonbinary, and Gender Nonconforming Southerners. (2019). http://transgenderlawcenter.org/wp-content/uploads/2019/05/grapevine_report_eng-FINAL.pdf. Accessed 19 Nov 2019
6. Morris, M., Hawkins, B.: Towards a new specialization in health librarianship: LGBTQ health. J. Can. Health Librar. Assoc. 37(1), 20–23 (2016). https://doi.org/10.5596/c16-007
7. Romanelli, M., Hudson, K.D.: Individual and systemic barriers to health care: Perspectives of lesbian, gay, bisexual, and transgender adults. Am. J. Orthopsychiatr. 87(6), 714–728 (2017). https://doi.org/10.1037/ort0000306
8. Perrin, P.B., Sutter, M.E., Trujillo, M.A., Henry, R.S., Pugh Jr., M.: The minority strengths model: development and initial path analytic validation in racially/ethnically diverse LGBTQ individuals. J. Clin. Psychol. 76(1), 1–19 (2019). https://doi.org/10.1002/jclp.22850
9. Matthews, D.D., Lee, J.G.: A profile of North Carolina lesbian, gay, and bisexual health disparities, 2011. Am. J. Public Health 104(6), 98–105 (2014). https://doi.org/10.2105/AJPH.2013.301751
10. Williams Institute: LGBT people in South Carolina (2018). https://williamsinstitute.law.ucla.edu/wp-content/uploads/South-Carolina-fact-sheet.pdf. Accessed 19 Nov 2019
11. Mallory, C., Sears, B.: Discrimination against LGBT people in South Carolina. UCLA School of Law Williams Institute, Los Angeles, CA (2019). https://williamsinstitute.law.ucla.edu/wp-content/uploads/South-Carolina-ND-July-2019.pdf. Accessed 19 Nov 2019
12. Coleman, J.D., Irwin, J.A., Wilson, R.C., Miller, H.C.: The South Carolina LGBT needs assessment: a descriptive overview. J. Homosex. 61(8), 1152–1171 (2014). https://doi.org/10.1080/00918369.2014.872515
13. Savolainen, R.: Information behavior and information practice: reviewing the "umbrella concepts" of information-seeking studies. Libr. Q. 77(2), 109–132 (2007). https://www.jstor.org/stable/10.1086/517840
14. Savolainen, R.: Everyday Information Practices: A Social Phenomenological Perspective. Scarecrow Press, Lanham (2008)
15. McKenzie, P.J.: A model of information practices in accounts of everyday-life information seeking. J. Doc. 59(1), 19–40 (2003). https://doi.org/10.1108/00220410310457993
16. Frohmann, B.: The power of images: a discourse analysis of the cognitive viewpoint. J. Doc. 48(4), 365–386 (1992). https://doi.org/10.1108/eb026904

17. Talja, S.: Constituting "information" and "user" as research objects: a theory of knowledge formations as an alternative to the information-man theory. In: Vakkari, P., Savolainen, R., Dervin, B., (eds.). Information Seeking in Context: Proceedings of an International Conference on Research in Information Needs, Seeking and Use in Different Contexts, pp. 67–80. Taylor Graham, London (1997)

18. Julien, H.: Where to from here? Results of an empirical study and user-centered implications for information design. In: Wilson, T.D., Allen, D.K., (eds.) Exploring the Contexts of Information Behaviour, pp. 586–596. Taylor Graham, London (1999)

19. Savolainen, R.: Everyday life information seeking: approaching information seeking in the context of "way of life". Libr. Inf. Sci. Res. **17**(3), 259–294 (1995). https://doi.org/10.1016/0740-8188(95)90048-9

20. Marmot, M., Wilkinson, R.: Social Determinants of Health. Oxford University Press, New York (2005)

21. Colpitts, E., Gahagan, J.: The utility of resilience as a conceptual framework for understanding and measuring LGBTQ health. Int. J. Equity Health **15**(1), 60 (2016). https://doi.org/10.1186/s12939-016-0349-1

22. Gibson, A.N., Martin III, J.D.: Re-situating information poverty: information marginalization and parents of individuals with disabilities. J. Assoc. Inf. Sci. Technol. **70**(5), 476–487 (2019). https://doi.org/10.1002/asi.24128

23. Chatman, E.A.: The impoverished life-world of outsiders. J. Am. Soc. Inf. Sci. **47**(3), 193–206 (1996). https://doi.org/10.1002/(SICI)10974571(199603)47:3%3C193:AID-ASI3%3E3.0.CO;2-T

24. Thompson, K.M.: Furthering understanding of information literacy through the social study of information poverty. Can. J. Inf. Libr. Sci. **31**(1), 87115 (2007)

25. Lingel, J.: Information tactics of immigrants in urban environments. Inf. Res. **16**(4) (2011). http://www.informationr.net/ir/16-4/paper500.html. Accessed 16 Nov 2019

26. Greyson, D.: Health information practices of young parents. J. Doc. **73**(5), 778–802 (2017). https://doi.org/10.1108/JD-07-2016-0089

27. Veinot, T.C.: A multilevel model of HIV/AIDS information/help network development. J. Doc. **66**(6), 875–905 (2010). https://doi.org/10.1108/00220411011087850

28. Kitzie, V.: "That looks like me or something I can do": Affordances and constraints in the online identity work of US LGBTQ+ millennials. J. Assoc. Inf. Sci. Technol. **70**(12), 1340–1351 (2019). https://doi.org/10.1002/asi.24217

29. Floegel, D., Costello, K.L.: Entertainment media and the information practices of queer individuals. Libr. Inf. Sci. Res. **41**(1), 31–38 (2019). https://doi.org/10.1016/j.lisr.2019.01.001

30. Steinke, J., Root-Bowman, M., Estabrook, S., Levine, D.S., Kantor, L.M.: Meeting the needs of sexual and gender minority youth: formative research on potential digital health interventions. J. Adolesc. Health **60**(5), 541–548 (2017). https://doi.org/10.1016/j.jadohealth.2016.11.023

31. Schmitz, R.M., Sanchez, J., Lopez, B.: LGBTQ+ Latinx young adults' health autonomy in resisting cultural stigma. Cult. Health Sex. **21**(1), 16–30 (2019). https://doi.org/10.1080/13691058.2018.1441443

32. Duggan, L.: The Twilight of Equality?: Neoliberalism, Cultural Politics, and the Attack on Democracy. Beacon Press, Boston (2012)

33. Spade, D.: Normal Life: Administrative Violence, Critical Trans Politics, and the Limits of Law. Southend Press, New York (2015)

34. Puar, J.K., Rai, A.: Monster, terrorist, fag: the war on terrorism and the production of docile patriots. Soc. Text **20**(3), 117–148 (2002). https://www.muse.jhu.edu/article/31948. Accessed 19 Nov 2019

35. Halberstam, J.: In a Queer Time and Place: Transgender Bodies Subcultural Lives. New York University Press, New York (2005)
36. Strauss, A., Corbin, J.: Basics of Qualitative Research Techniques. Sage, Thousand Oaks (1998)
37. Saldaña, J.: The Coding Manual for Qualitative Researchers. Sage, Thousand Oaks (2015)
38. Hillary, G.A.: Definitions of community: areas of agreement. Rural Sociol. **20**, 111–123 (1995)
39. Worthen, M.G.: The interactive impacts of high school gay-straight alliances (GSAs) on college student attitudes toward LGBT individuals: an investigation of high school characteristics. J. Homosex. **61**(2), 217–250 (2014). https://doi.org/10.1080/00918369.2013. 839906
40. Weiser, S.M.: The art of resistance: an arts based understanding of activism. Unpublished doctoral dissertation, Columbia, SC (2018). https://scholarcommons.sc.edu/etd/4777. Accessed 19 Nov 2019
41. Koh, K.: Adolescents' information-creating behavior embedded in digital Media practice using scratch. J. Am. Soc. Inf. Sci. Technol. **64**(9), 1826–1841 (2013). https://doi.org/10. 1002/asi.22878
42. Greyson, D.: Information world mapping: a participatory, visual, elicitation activity for information practice interviews. In: Grove, A., (ed.) Proceedings of the American Society for Information Science and Technology, vol. 50, no. 1, pp. 1–4 (2013)
43. Strauss, A., Corbin. J.: Grounded theory methodology: an overview. In: Denzin, N., Lincoln, Y. (eds.) Handbook of Qualitative Research, pp. 273–285. Sage, Thousand Oaks (1994)
44. Charmaz, K.: Constructing Grounded Theory. Sage, Thousand Oaks (2014)
45. Creswell, J.W.: Qualitative Inquiry & Research Design: Choosing Among Five Approaches. Sage, Los Angeles (2013)
46. Geertz, C.: The Interpretation of Cultures. Basic Books, New York (1973)
47. Dentato, M.P., Halkitis, P.N., Orwat, J.: Minority stress theory: an examination of factors surrounding sexual risk behavior among gay and bisexual men who use club drugs. J. Gay Lesbian Soc. Serv. **25**(4), 509–525 (2013). https://doi.org/10.1080/10538720.2013.829395
48. Kangovi, S., Grande, D., Trinh-Shevrin, C.: From rhetoric to reality—community health workers in post-reform US health care. New Engl. J. Med. **372**(24), 2277 (2015). https://doi. org/10.1056/NEJMp1502569
49. Spivak, G.G.: "Can the subaltern speak?" In: Nelson, C., Grossberg, L., (eds.) Marxism and Interpretation of Culture, pp. 66–111. University of Illinois Press, Urbana (1988)
50. Ahmed, S.: Queer Phenomenology: Orientations, Objects, Others. Duke University Press, Durham (2006)

Cultural Activity Diversity and Community Characteristics: An Exploratory Study

Myeong Lee[1]([✉]) [iD] and Brian S. Butler[2] [iD]

[1] Department of Information Sciences and Technology,
George Mason University, Fairfax, VA 22030, USA
mlee89@gmu.edu
[2] College of Information Studies, University of Maryland,
College Park, MD 20740, USA
bsbutler@umd.edu

Abstract. Cultural diversity has been conceptualized and studied in different ways. On the one hand, cultural diversity can be conceptualized based on people's ethnic and national backgrounds. On the other hand, cultural dimensions are defined depending on people's behaviors and traits. Sociologists further categorized the latter depending on the degree of typicality in cultural artifacts/activities and individual's omnivorousness for cultural tastes. Although both aspects of culture-related concepts provide meaningful implications for urban characteristics, it is still unclear how these cultural dimensions are related to other characteristics of urban areas. This paper suggests a concept of *cultural activity diversity*, the diversity of cultural activities as a whole in a city. We provide an exploratory analysis of the relationships between cultural characteristics and socio-economic features across 14 and 28 urban areas in the U.S, respectively, using local event datasets.

Keywords: Local events · Cultural activity diversity · Urban characteristics

1 Introduction

When referring to *cultural diversity*, many studies focus on individuals' national and ethnic backgrounds because of one's high dependency on behavioral patterns and value systems that are embedded in nations and ethnic groups [4, 27]. Representative work of country- and ethnicity-based approaches to understanding an individual's cultural background is Hopfstede's cultural index that quantifies each country's cultural dimensions based on how social norms and collective values manifest in people's perceptions and their daily lives [20]. This kind of measure has been extensively used in studies that examined cross-national differences in behavioral and social dynamics [24, 28, 30].

The term, "cultural diversity," has been frequently used as an alternative to or in relation to national and ethnic backgrounds. Because of this, when scholars referred to social/physical manifestations of culture such as activities and

A. Sundqvist et al. (Eds.): iConference 2020, LNCS 12051, pp. 32–49, 2020.
https://doi.org/10.1007/978-3-030-43687-2_3

artifacts, they often used other terms such as *cultural tastes, cultural omnivorousness,* or *cultural specialization/capital* [5,6,21,31]. In other words, these terms are used for describing the cultural characteristics of individuals, communities, and/or their enactments in a conceptual space where the producers and audience of cultural artifacts co-exist. Research that focuses on the manifestation of culture has often studied in particular contexts such as the music consumption market, online search patterns, and place-driven characteristics in urban scenes [21,28]. Sociologists further classified the activity/trait-oriented dimension of culture. Some studies are based on individuals' cultural tastes and behaviors. This type of research often operationalized individuals' boundary-spanning behaviors across different genres (i.e., how many kinds of cultural products are consumed by individuals and how various their tastes are across different types), which scholars call *variety* from an *audience* perspective [5,15]. Conversely, as Goldberg and others suggest [15], organizational theory scholars have focused on *atypicality* from a *producer* perspective, which conceptualizes the extent to which a cultural product/artifact is different from existing genre systems (e.g., [10,28,33,42]).

Overall, cultural diversity can be defined and characterized in different ways. Each dimension of culture could be related to each other and might have something to do with other community performance indicators such as socio-economic status and safety [21]. However, it is not clear how the different dimensions of cultural diversity that range from ethnic heterogeneity to cultural omnivorousness are related to each other and to other community characteristics.[1] Although many studies have examined the relationships between one of the cultural dimensions and other community characteristics (e.g., ethnic heterogeneity vs. community engagement), the dynamics of diversity in local communities can be understood thoroughly only when all the cultural dimensions are taken into account. These theoretical gaps in the dimensions of cultural diversity imply that one dimension of cultural diversity could be an important intermediary process that shapes the effects of another.

This paper aims to explore the dynamics of cultural diversity and their substructures at the Census urban area level, which is a basis for understanding the sustainability of local communities and the digital communities that support it. To provide an initial exploration of the relationships between cultural diversity and other community characteristics, we use local event datasets such as data from Meetup.com, Yelp.com, and Eventful.com. By operationalizing city-level cultural diversity and examining their relationships with ethnic heterogeneity and socio-economic features, this paper provides a basis for further theorizing the cultural dynamics of local communities in the context of local activities.

---

[1] In this paper, the term "community" is used to denote any size of geographical boundaries in a general sense. A local community could range from a neighborhood to metropolitan areas. However, the data analysis in this paper precisely focuses on the Census Urban Area as the geographical unit of analysis.

2   Cultural Activity Diversity

Local events in the dataset include many different kinds of planned activities that range from farmers' market and music concerts to social movements and neighborhood gatherings, either organized by local residents or large organizations (but do not include accidental or un-planned events). The proportion of online events (e.g., webinars) in the data was less than 5%, and they were omitted from the analysis because it was conceptually unclear whether online events target particular cities. Viewing from the atypicality-omnivorousness lens, local events are a collection of localized markets (from a producer perspective) and social groups' activities (from an audience perspective). Even a single event could be created considering both of these dimensions when he or she plans a local event. For instance, a Yoga class organizer would want their events to be categorized as "Yoga" or "physical health" for increasing their visibility to the audience, abiding by existing categories on the websites. On the other hand, they might also want to differentiate themselves from the existing categories as part of marketing strategies (e.g., Yoga with a glass of wine).

Although the amalgamation of local activities and meetups provides senses of both the variety of consumers' contextualized, personal tastes (i.e., cultural omnivorousness) *and* producers' strategies for organizational success in the ecology of cultural/social markets (i.e., cultural atypicality), it is not quite accurate to conceptualize the entirety of activities using one of these notions. Therefore, this study suggests a new term, *cultural activity diversity*, as a means to understand the diversity of local events at the city level, which includes both of the cultural dimensions: the tendency of local activities to abide by established genre systems and a force to differentiate oneself from existing categories that is often shaped by event organizers' strategies.

Because cultural activity diversity consists of both forces to conform to and deviate from existing categories, other diversity dimensions and socio-economic features might be closely related to this construct. Particularly, ethnic heterogeneity and socio-economic deprivation are one of the important factors that have been studied extensively with regard to community characteristics [21,28,29,41]. Accordingly, this study builds upon the theoretical frameworks of community heterogeneity and socio-economic deprivation.

3   Ethnic Heterogeneity and Socio-Economic Deprivation

A motivation to study ethnic heterogeneity in local communities often stems from the high international mobility and inter-racial/ethnic dynamics within and across U.S. cities. Scholars have been particularly interested in the effects of community diversity in people's civic engagement. For example, Putnam argued that, in the short run, ethnic heterogeneity negatively affects social solidarity and trust between local residents [34]. This finding has been supported by many studies in sociology, political science, and economics. Costa confirmed, using datasets from the United States, international, and historical contexts, that homogeneous communities in terms of ethnicity and socio-economic status foster greater levels of social-capital production [9]. These findings are relatively consistent in different temporal and spatial contexts, with varying dimensions of community heterogeneity between cultural, racial, ethnic, and income diversity/inequality [2,3]: when ethnicity or nationality are homogeneous within a community, trust tends to be high [14].

Although many studies found that ethnic/national heterogeneity negatively affects community engagement and trust, there are also contradictory findings, even with similar datasets [12,25,37]. Abascal reexamined Putnam's work using the same survey dataset that the previous study used after reconceptualizing heterogeneity and combining census data [1]. They showed that ethnic heterogeneity has minimal or negligible effects on civic engagement when considering different perceptions of ethnic groups toward others. According to their study, it is the particular ethnic group size or dominance that shapes social trust, not the ethnic heterogeneity *per se*. This study concludes that some of the previous work on the effects of community heterogeneity mis-conceptualized "social capital" without integrating the *inter-group contact/conflict* literature [32] and overlooked the inconsistent nature of inter-ethnic dynamics (e.g., "community heterogeneity" has different meanings for white and non-white communities, respectively). Using a survey dataset from Canada, Stolle provides similar implications where social ties, that is, inter-ethnic contacts and their strengths, mediate the relationship between community heterogeneity and social trust within the community [39].

In addition to inter-ethnic contacts, socio-economic deprivation was found to be an important process that shapes community engagement. For example, with the fact that immigrants and people of color tend to be in a lower economic status compared to long-standing residents, Sturgis found that socio-economic deprivation is confounded with ethnic diversity in London, U.K. [40]. In the U.S. context, this confounding effect between socio-economic deprivation and ethnic heterogeneity still holds: through the national survey data collected for decades and redlining maps data, research showed that the racial zoning of the 1920's and 30's still predicts the poverty level in modern neighborhoods [26].

As a result, ethnic heterogeneity is positively correlated (or confounded) with the socio-economic deprivation of a community in the United States. However, it is still not clear whether and how cultural activity diversity, another dimension of cultural characteristics, is related to these two community characteristics at the city level. On the one hand, it is possible that, if ethnic heterogeneity is high, cultural activities might be created separately by different groups. If so, high ethnic heterogeneity will ultimately increase cultural activity diversity. On the other hand, it is possible that a high rate of socio-economic deprivation in a city might hamper the creation of diverse activities, especially among those who do not have enough resources, which might decrease cultural activity diversity. These potentially-conflicting inferences suggest the following research questions.

- RQ1: How is ethnic heterogeneity related to socio-economic deprivation?
- RQ2: How is ethnic heterogeneity related to cultural activity diversity?
- RQ3: How is socio-economic deprivation related to cultural activity diversity?

This paper explores these questions quantitatively using data from a sample of major U.S. cities. To generate variables, this study uses local event data that is collected from the three information sources, American Community Survey (ACS) from U.S. census, and geospatial data in Shapefile from U.S. census for defining the geospatial unit of analysis.

4   Hypotheses

Based on findings from previous studies on the relationship between ethnic heterogeneity and socio-economic deprivation and the inferences in the previous section, it is possible to hypothesize as follows for the research questions:

- H1: Ethnic heterogeneity would be positively correlated with socio-economic deprivation at the city level.
- H2: Ethnic heterogeneity would be positively correlated with cultural activity diversity at the city level.
- H3: Socio-economic deprivation would be negatively correlated with cultural activity diversity.

Although H2 and H3 are conflicting with each other if H1 is true, an underlying assumption behind these hypotheses is that the characteristics of cultural activities in a city are closely related to ethnic groups and their socio-economic resources.

5   Data

Local event data was collected (1) from January 2017 to August 2018 (20 months) targeting 14 U.S. cities and (2) from June 2018 to August 2018 (3 months) targeting 28 U.S. cities. The 14 cities for the twenty months were selected based on the propensity of tech start-up activities because the vibrant start-up culture of a city might be related to diverse meetups and the use of event-organizing technologies in the region [36]. The 28 cities for the three months were selected based on the largest populations. The underlying assumption was that cities with large populations would have more events organized both by organizations and citizens.

The target information sources are (1) Meetup[2], a website that allows anybody to create and attend diverse kinds of local events through joining "local groups", (2) Eventful[3], a website that allows users to create events and provides information about other local events, and (3) Yelp[4], a website that is intended for providing local business information but also provides affordances to create local events that are organized in local venues. Table 1 shows the descriptive statistics of total events in the datasets.

---

[2] https://meetup.com.
[3] https://eventful.com.
[4] https://yelp.com.

Table 1. Descriptive statistics of local events.

Data source		# of events	Mean # per city (SD)
Meetup	14 cities (20 months)	998,461	70,604 (42,953)
	28 cities (3 months)	196,554	6,778 (5,712)
Eventful	14 cities (20 months)	888,955	63,498 (61,225)
	28 cities (3 months)	420,709	14,507 (16,620)
Yelp	14 cities (20 months)	32,234	2,302 (1,951)
	28 cities (3 months)	7,260	250 (231)

Other data required for this study is collected from the U.S. Census Bureau website.[5] Particularly, urban area-level geographical boundaries in Shapefile, socio-economic status, socio-demographic information, and ethnic group population estimation in 2017 are collected from the American Community Survey (ACS) dataset.[6]

This study uses urban area-level Census regions (code 400) as the unit of geographical analysis. Because local information is disseminated and used in a metropolitan area following their mobility range, using Census Tracts or municipal city boundaries as the unit of analysis would be too small to reflect information users' dynamics; conversely, using the state or Census' statistical metro/micropolitan boundaries are too broad. Urban area boundaries do not follow municipal boundaries but cover urban regions based on high population density and are consistent with local event locations.

6   Approach

6.1   Event Data Disambiguation

Because a core part of this study is to measure cultural activity diversity, it is necessary to identify duplicate events across different information sources. However, there is no straightforward way to capture duplicate events because there is no shared key or ID between two or more websites. Furthermore, event titles and descriptions from different sources are often inconsistent with each other, even if they are physically the same event (maybe due to an ad-hoc provision of local information by different actors). This inconsistency suggests that event data needs to be disambiguated through multi-step, computational treatments rather than using a naïve text matching.

---

[5] U.S. Census: https://factfinder.census.gov.

[6] As of August 2018, the demographic/economic data for 2018 is not available from the U.S. Census. Because the ACS data is created annually and does not change dramatically in a short period of time, 2017 data is reasonable to use for the purpose of this study.

For that reason, machine learning techniques are used to disambiguate the data. We first generated pair-wise features for all the pairs of events from different websites. Pair-wise features between two events include the physical distance between two event locations, start time difference, Jaccard similarity between two titles and descriptions, and time overlap. After sorting the event pairs based on the similarity measures, about 500 pairs were manually compared and coded to specify whether each pair is actually the same event or not. These manually-coded data became the ground-truth data. Then, the Random Forests algorithm was used to train this ground-truth data ($F_1 = 0.99$ after tuning the model) [8]. Using this trained model, all the other pairs were disambiguated. Based on the machine learning result, duplicate events were removed from the combined datasets. Overall, 150,786 duplicate events out of 1,871,173 events were found across two or more websites for the 14-city data over 20 months ($M_{dup} = 10,770, SD_{dup} = 11,605, Rate_{dup} = 0.08$). For the 28-city data over 3 months, 55,159 duplicate events out of 611,047 events were found across two or more websites ($M_{dup} = 1,902, SD_{dup} = 2,734, Rate_{dup} = 0.09$). The titles and descriptions of the unique events are used to calculate cultural activity diversity.

6.2   Topic Modeling

Operationalizing cultural activity diversity needs to take both aspects of the cultural concepts into account. For example, local businesses, a large portion of local event organizers, often need to establish their brands to attract participants (who are potential customers). To do so, they would organize events that not only span existing genres, but also mix and incorporate diverse cultural elements as part of their strategies to be distinctive. Other small businesses and interest-based event organizers such as photography and concert-goers' groups might abide by the established genre systems of the website to benefit from the legitimatized market structure in attracting newcomers [17,18].

It is challenging to capture the dynamically-changing topics/genres of cultural activities using the pre-defined classifications of events on the websites. In other words, using an established genre system would be useful when focusing only on audience-based diversity. Instead, dynamically-changing genre systems can be better captured through unsupervised approach because this bottom-up approach makes it possible to consider both the audience-side enactments within the established genre systems *and* producer-side strategies to create novel/unique activities that comply less with existing classifications.

Topic modeling algorithms provide such capability for identifying the types of events, the volumes of activities across the generated topics, and their diversity in a city in an unsupervised way based on the corpus of event titles and descriptions. Particularly, Latent Dirichlet Allocation (LDA) is used to identify the spectrum of topics available in the event descriptions and titles [7]. After event topics are generated, each event is represented by a list of all the topics that have weights. Also, each topic is represented by a list of topical words with weights.

Based on these structures of topics, cultural scores are calculated for each topic. Two topics that have the largest and second-largest weights are selected for each event. Then, the topic with the largest weight adds two points and that with the second-largest weight adds one point. By extracting scores from all the events available in an urban area, this area can be represented with a list of topics where its elements are the scores that are calculated from the topic distribution of events. For example, the topics of cultural activities in Washington D.C., $C_{Washingon}$ can be represented as a list such as:

$$C_{Washingon} = [t_1 : n_1, t_2 : n_2, ..., t_i : n_i, ..., t_k : n_k]$$

where t_i is the index of the ith topic, k is the number of topics that is used in LDA, and n_i is the aggregate score of topic t_i. The number of topics n is determined using a benchmark algorithm that finds the best number of topics for LDA [16]. The priors for the LDA model were determined through plotting perplexity measures ($\alpha = 0.2, \beta = 0.7$).

After the number of topics and priors are determined based on the 180,647 random samples of events, a topic model is trained using the descriptions and titles of these samples (after pre-processing, 179,858 records in total are used for training the model). The title and description of each event are concatenated after pre-processing them (e.g., removing stop words and special characters, stemming words, etc.). Then, these tokens are used to run LDA. The trained LDA model is used to predict other events' topics, that is, how each event's description and title are represented as a list of topics and their distribution. The topic modeling results and the predictions based on the trained model are used as the basis for calculating cultural activity diversity for each city in each month.

6.3 The Measurement of Cultural Activity Diversity

Although a list-based approach, such as the Herfindahl-Hirschman Index (HHI) or Shannon entropy, makes it possible to operationalize the cultural activity diversity of a city in a computational way, the similarity and difference between topics could bias the computational model. For example, let us assume three different topics: jazz concerts, live guitars in the bar, and political movements. In a conceptual space of cultural activities, jazz concerts are more similar to live guitars in the bar than to political movements. In this case, using well-known diversity measures such as Shannon entropy or HHI for measuring cultural activity diversity could present a measurement bias. Using these measures treats jazz concerts and live guitars as being orthogonal to each other, just like the relationship between jazz concerts and political movements. Because of this potential measurement bias, scholars considered the distances between categories in the measurement in addition to balance and variety of entities across topics [15, 29, 33].

In a similar way, this study also takes the distances between topics into account. The distance between two topics is measured using cosine similarity. Because each topic is represented as a list of topical words and their distribution, it is possible to calculate the distance between two topics, $d_{i,j}$ (where i and j are the indices of two topics, T_i and T_j, respectively), with the angular form of cosine similarity, which is formulated as follows.

$$d_{i,j} = 2 \cdot \frac{cos^{-1}\left(\frac{T_i \cdot T_j}{|T_i||T_j|}\right)}{\pi} \tag{1}$$

Based on the topic modeling results that include the volumes of events across different topics and distances between topics based on cosine similarity, Rao-Stirling diversity index, D, is used as the cultural activity diversity measure, because it not only takes variety and balance into account (which is similar to Shannon entropy or HHI) but also considers disparity between topics in the measure [29, 35, 38].

$$D = \sum_{i,j(i \neq j)} d_{i,j} \cdot p_i \cdot p_j \tag{2}$$

where p_i and p_j are proportional representations of topic T_i and T_j, respectively, of an urban area (i.e., balance of cultural activity volumes between two topics), and $d_{i,j}$ is the degree of difference attributed to these two topics (i.e., disparity between two topics). The mean of the cultural activity diversity for each city in the 28-city dataset is presented in Table 2.

6.4   Variables

Key variables generated or collected for operationalizing the key constructs are presented in Table 3. The ethnic heterogeneity of an urban area is measured using HHI following the measure used in previous work [34, 40]. HHI quantifies the degree of entity concentrations across a set of categories [19].

$$H = 1 - \sum_{i=1}^{N} p_i^2 \tag{3}$$

where N is the number of ethnic groups and p_i is the share of ethnic group i.

Socio-economic deprivation is measured using five indicators of deprivation. "Poverty level," one of the five deprivation indicators, in Table 3 is the thresholds that are determined by U.S. Census Bureau based on family characteristics and is subject to change every year. To generate the poverty index, Principal Component Analysis (PCA) is used against these five indicators. The first component of the results (PC1) is used as the poverty index, which represents 60.45% of the five indicators.

Socio-economic inequality is also added as a variable to triangulate and elicit the pure effect of the poverty index. Socio-economic inequality is measured using the Gini index, one of the most popular measures used in many fields, including Economics.

Table 2. Average cultural activity diversity scores for the 28-city data over 3 months.

City	Mean Diversity	SD
San Antonio, TX	0.4519	0.00056
Houston, TX	0.4513	0.00037
Memphis, TN	0.4509	0.00043
Dallas, TX	0.4507	0.00040
San Diego, CA	0.4506	0.00062
Pittsburgh, PA	0.4504	0.00028
Fort Worth, TX	0.4504	0.00060
Chicago, IL	0.4500	0.00035
Charlotte, NC	0.4499	0.00027
Los Angeles, CA	0.4499	0.00049
Raleigh, NC	0.4497	0.00036
Durham, NC	0.4496	0.00052
San Francisco, CA	0.4495	0.00012
Nashville, TN	0.4494	0.00073
New York, NY	0.4494	0.00045
Columbus, OH	0.4493	0.00138
Philadelphia, PA	0.4492	0.00049
Austin, TX	0.4492	0.00035
Indianapolis, IN	0.4490	0.00051
Washington, DC	0.4490	0.00020
Baltimore, MD	0.4488	0.00087
Phoenix, AZ	0.4487	0.00021
Boston, MA	0.4485	0.00053
Detroit, MI	0.4481	0.00081
Jacksonville, FL	0.4480	0.00077
Seattle, WA	0.4476	0.00073
Denver, CO	0.4469	0.00019
San Jose, CA	0.4462	0.00050
El Paso, TX	0.4394	0.00459

Control variables (CV) follow the variables used in previous work on community heterogeneity and engagement. Because many of the previous work used individual-level survey data, control variables that are tailored to individuals such as whether one owns a house are not used. All other city-level control variables are used. In addition, some city-level variables that could give rise to the dependent variables are included. For example, the total number of the population might matter for cultural activity diversity, because local events tend to be more diverse in a city with a large number of people than that with a small number of population. In this case, the population needs to be controlled to correctly examine the effects of independent variables on cultural activity diversity. CVs include city population, ethnic group rate, foreign-born population, and time dummy variable with random effects.

Table 3. Key variables that represent constructs in the study and their measurements.

Construct/variable	Measurement
Ethnoracial heterogeneity	HHI of Six ethnoracial groups
Socio-economic segregation	Gini index
Population below poverty level	$\frac{N_{below\_poverty}}{N_{population}}$
Rented households (compared to owned)	$\frac{N_{rented\_households}}{N_{households}}$
Unemployment rate below poverty level	$\frac{N_{unemploy\_below\_poverty}}{N_{population}}$
Unemployment rate above poverty level	$\frac{N_{unemploy\_above\_poverty}}{N_{population}}$
People who holds less than bachelor's degree	$\frac{N_{less\_than\_bachelor}}{N_{population}}$
Poverty index	PCA of the five variables above
Cultural activity diversity	Rao-Stirling index

6.5   Analytical Models

H1 is tested only based on the ACS data. Because the ACS data does not have a temporal resolution within 2017 (i.e., only one value exists for each city for the entire year), multi-level regression models with a nested effect of the state on the dependent variable are used. Meanwhile, cultural activity diversity is based on the local event datasets, so the temporal granularity of this variable for H2 and H3 is higher than ACS-based variables (i.e., monthly-basis). To reflect this, the temporal factors are used as an indirect measure for ecological, platform-wide changes over time. Accordingly, the analytical models are the linear multi-level models (LMMs) where cultural activity diversity is nested within the time dummy variable.

A challenge in the data analysis comes from the number of data points. Because the unit of analysis is an urban area, the number of data points in regressions are too small to include many control variables. Increasing the number of control variables often leads to the overfitting issue. To deal with this challenge, this study uses two different approaches. The first one is the use of Bayesian-based regressions to run the linear multi-level models (LMM). Unlike regular LMMs, this approach minimizes the overfitting or multicollinearity issues by setting priors in estimating the distributions of parameters. Bayesian-based multi-level models estimate fixed- and random-effect parameters, γ's, through Markov Chain Monte Carlo (MCMC) rather than using maximum likelihood as regular LMM does [11].

The second strategy is to remove low-effect control variables from the model selectively. Although Bayesian-based LMM is strong in dealing with overfitting, it is not without limit in the number of independent variables. To select the variable(s) that can be removed from the model when necessary, baseline regressions are conducted against all the control variables. Based on these baseline tables, one or two control variables that have minimal effects on the DV are removed only if the number of variables goes beyond the capacity of the Bayesian-based LMM.

7 Results

Based on these analytical models and strategies, the summary of regression results is presented in Table 4. This table shows the estimates and confidence intervals. The original datasets for the regressions are the 14-area dataset over 20 months and 28-area dataset over 3 months. Because some differences are found between these two sets of regressions, the same models are tested against the 14-area dataset over 3 months for the same period that the 28-area data covers, so to infer the reasons for the differences.

H1 is for testing the baseline pattern to see if the theoretical framework from previous studies is consistent in the target cities. M8 and M9 in Table 4 test whether ethnic heterogeneity (HHI) is correlated with socio-economic deprivation (poverty index) or inequality (Gini index). The results show that ethnic heterogeneity is positively correlated with socio-economic deprivation for the 28-city dataset, while statistically not significant for the 14-city datasets. Meanwhile, socio-economic inequality is positively correlated with ethnic heterogeneity in the 14 cities over 20 months. This analysis partially supports the original findings from previous work.

M4 through M7 are for exploring the relationship between ethnic heterogeneity and cultural activity diversity (H2). The results show consistent patterns where ethnic heterogeneity is positively correlated with cultural activity diversity for the 14-city datasets (both 20- and 3-month datasets), even after controlling for socio-economic features, rejecting the null hypothesis of H2. However, this pattern is not statistically significant for the 28-city dataset. This inconsistency between the two sets of cities might be due to the effect of technology penetration. The 14 cities are sampled based on the high activity of technology start-ups. It is possible that a high rate of using event-based websites in the 14 cities reflects diverse populations' creation of local events; conversely, only part of the ethnic groups might have created events on the event-organizing websites in big cities due to varying technology penetration rates. In the case of the latter, ethnic heterogeneity would not have been reflected in the diversity of events that are visible online, even if their events are diverse in the real world.

M1 through M3 are for examining the relationship between socio-economic deprivation/inequality and cultural activity diversity (H3). Socio-economic deprivation is positively correlated with cultural activity diversity for the 14-city dataset over 20 months, which rejects the null hypothesis of H3 but counter-intuitive. Socio-economic inequality is also positively correlated with cultural

Table 4. Estimates based on the Bayesian-based multi-level regressions. The confidence intervals are at the 90% level (5% and 95%, respectively). Control variables are included in all the models but are not presented in this table.

	M1: Poverty			M2: Gini			M3: Poverty+Gini			M4: HHI			M5: HHI+Poverty		
	Est.	CI 5%	CI 95%	Est.	CI 5%	CI 95%	Est.	CI 5%	CI 95%	Est.	CI 5%	CI 95%	Est.	CI 5%	CI 95%
14 cities, 20 months ($N = 280$)															
Poverty index	1.45	1.14	1.75				0.34	−0.01	0.71				1.43	1.14	1.70
Gini index				2.31	2.00	2.63	2.04	1.65	2.45						
HHI										1.25	0.94	1.56	1.11	0.86	1.35
14 cities, 3 months ($N = 42$)															
Poverty index	−0.69	−1.54	0.20				−1.00	−1.83	−0.18				−0.41	−1.09	0.26
Gini index				0.93	0.19	1.64	1.74	0.43	1.88						
HHI										3.45	2.59	4.30	3.43	2.53	4.31
28 cities, 3 months ($N = 84$)															
Poverty index	−0.22	−0.55	0.11				−0.36	−0.72	0.02				−0.23	−0.57	0.11
Gini index				0.15	−0.11	0.42	0.26	−0.01	0.52						
HHI										−0.05	−0.72	0.61	0.05	−0.65	−0.74

	M6: HHI+Gini			M7: HHI+Gini+Pov			M8: HHI→Gini			M9: HHI→Poverty		
	Est.	CI 5%	CI 95%	Est.	CI 5%	CI 95%	Est.	CI 5%	CI 95%	Est.	CI 5%	CI 95%
14 cities, 20 months ($N = 280$)												
Poverty index				1.21	0.76	1.63				0.10	−0.01	0.20
Gini index	−0.45	−0.65	−0.24	−1.05	−1.34	−0.77	0.30	0.14	0.46			
HHI	1.45	1.09	1.79	1.57	1.23	1.86						
14 cities, 3 months ($N = 42$)												
Poverty index				−0.68	−1.45	0.10				0.07	−0.25	0.39
Gini index	−0.26	−0.78	0.26	−0.13	−0.66	0.43	0.37	−0.12	0.87			
HHI	3.37	2.24	4.50	3.30	2.12	4.41						
28 cities, 3 months ($N = 84$)												
Poverty index				−0.34	−0.74	0.05				0.46	0.10	0.83
Gini index	0.17	−0.08	0.42	0.29	0.01	0.57	−0.23	−0.75	0.29			
HHI	−0.07	−0.73	0.59	0.12	−0.57	0.84						

activity diversity for both the 14-city datasets over 3 and 20 months. This pattern is consistent with the explanation in the H2 test results. Although poverty and inequality could be a source of hampering local events, it might not be true in the cities where diverse populations are capable of using technology; rather, socio-economic variations might play a role as a source of diversity in such cities. This interpretation is partially supported by the results from the 28-city dataset. The positive effects of socio-economic variations and the negative effect of a lack of resources might conflict with each other in the 28-city dataset, resulting in a non-significant relationship in these cities.

8 Discussion and Limitations

8.1 Relationships Between Cultural Dimensions

One of the takeaways is that cultural dimensions are playing different roles in the dynamics of local communities. Ethnic heterogeneity is a source of cultural activity diversity. However, the diversity of cultural activities in a city might be affected or moderated by market forces, people's technology use, and their interplay. Because the data used in this paper does not provide information about intermediary processes between ethnic heterogeneity and cultural activity diversity about what factors are moderating or mediating their relationships, future studies need to further examine this gap by combining other datasets that indicate cities' technology penetration, key players in local activities, and businesses. Nevertheless, this exploratory analysis provides useful implications for cultural dynamics because it was possible to examine the relationship between different cultural dimensions (i.e., ethnic heterogeneity and activity-based diversity) that were often studied separately in different contexts of local communities.

8.2 Relationship Between Socio-Economic Features and Cultural Activity Diversity

Although there are some meaningful implications found from the regressions between socio-economic deprivation/inequality and cultural activity diversity, it is still unclear about their causal relationship. Local actors, such as local businesses and residents, often organize events with structures (e.g., payment process, group norms, and membership structure). Social agents surrounding such events, such as event attendants and local vendors, draw upon these structures and enact within the social boundaries [13]. If these boundaries reinforce their socio-economic classes, cultural activity diversity might negatively affect socio-economic deprivation and inequality in the long-run. Conversely, if people from diverse socio-economic classes are intermingled through local events, their interactions may foster people's exposures to various opportunities, which could ultimately relieve social segregation.

Also, while the analysis results suggest part of such dynamics through the positive correlation between socio-economic deprivation/inequality and cultural activity diversity, it is not clear whether the provision of local event information is less in the 28 cities or the social segregation in these cities is more polarized compared to the 14 cities. Technology penetration is one of the potential factors that should be taken into account, but a further examination of the provision of information is necessary to understand the dynamics surrounding socio-economic features and cultural diversity.

Finally, it is not only socio-economic features that could give rise to cultural activity diversity. There are many other community characteristics that could play as intermediary processes between ethnic heterogeneity and cultural activity diversity, such as safety level, technological infrastructures, and types of amenities. This study explored socio-economic features first because the theoretical frameworks about cultural diversity have been developed extensively in relation to deprivation as a confounding factor of ethnic heterogeneity, a widely-used dimension of cultural diversity. We expect that future studies develop a broader spectrum of theoretical frameworks by taking other community characteristics into account.

8.3   Limitations

As with other empirical studies, this study has limitations in the study design. Potential bias in the sampling of information sources could be critical. Adding other event data sources would have been greatly beneficial to this study. Still, sampling and scaling information sources are one of the most difficult challenges because there are only a few information sources that are commonly available across many U.S. cities. Facebook Events was one of the strongest candidates because of the platform's popularity; however, Facebook stopped providing city-level event data in early 2018, which led us to omit this option. Further efforts to find consistent information sources, such as newspapers and blogs, would improve the quality of this type of study.

Sampling a small number of cities is also a limitation. If testing M8 and M9 using the full ACS data in 2017, it is possible to see a clear pattern of the positive relationship between ethnic heterogeneity and socio-economic deprivation/inequality. However, due to the small number of data points, statistical power decreased significantly and provided only partial implications for the confounding effects. Although the data collection was limited because of the API limitations from the target information sources, sampling more cities in a randomized manner would help enhance this type of study in the future.

Finally, collecting local event data through informal sources would be significantly useful for future studies. Universal information sources that are available across different cities reflect only part of the available information [22,23]. A significant amount of local information is disseminated through word-of-mouth, local bulletin boards, and local mailing lists. Without considering these information sources, understanding the information provided in a city, a core part of identifying the causality between socio-economic features and cultural activity diversity, remains challenging.

9   Conclusion

Despite the limitations, this study is meaningful from several aspects. Theoretically and conceptually, this study sheds light on the relationships between different dimensions of cultural diversity as well as other community characteristics. Because the ways to operationalize cultural dimensions and the data sources that support them are becoming increasingly diverse these days, appropriate conceptualizations are essential, especially for data-driven studies. Through the exploratory analyses of different cultural dimensions at the city level, this paper provides a skeleton that can be used in different contexts and data.

Methodologically, this paper provides a framework to process and leverage local event descriptions to operationalize the cultural dimensions of urban areas. Because local events are already tagged with existing categories, choosing between topic modeling and existing genre systems for quantifying cultural diversity is often perceived as a data-driven, technical decision rather than a conceptual/theoretical one. This paper descriptively showcases a way to process data to measure a conceptual construct, not only through computational modeling but also by choosing reasonable techniques. Although there are many other parameters to consider to thoroughly measure cultural dimensions, leveraging unsupervised approaches in a conceptual space could benefit information scientists and cultural informatics researchers.

Practically, the cultural activity diversity measures can be used by policy-makers and cultural institutions in monitoring the change of local activities and related performance indicators. If policies and strategies can be designed based on the observations of multi-dimensional, cultural variables, rather than simple numbers of physical happenings, they will be able to better contribute to the sustainability of digital and physical communities synergizing each other.

Acknowledgment. This study is part of a larger study in the first author's dissertation work and has been extended from it. The first author's research was partially supported by the National Science Foundation's CHS program (#1816763) and through the Ann G. Wylie Dissertation Fellowship from the University of Maryland at College Park. We appreciate their generous support and reviewers' constructive feedback.

References

1. Abascal, M., Baldassarri, D.: Love thy neighbor? Ethnoracial diversity and trust reexamined. Am. J. Sociol. **121**(3), 722–782 (2015)
2. Alesina, A., Baqir, R., Hoxby, C.: Political jurisdictions in heterogeneous communities. J. Polit. Econ. **112**(2), 348–396 (2004)
3. Alesina, A., Ferrara, E.L.: The determinants of trust. Working Paper 7621, National Bureau of Economic Research, March 2000. https://doi.org/10.3386/w7621, http://www.nber.org/papers/w7621
4. Babacan, H.: Challenges of inclusion: cultural diversity, citizenship and engagement. In: Proceedings of International Conference on Engaging Communities, pp. 1–18. Queensland Department of Main Roads, August 2005

5. Bail, C.A.: The cultural environment: measuring culture with big data. Theory Soc. **43**(3–4), 465–482 (2014)
6. Bail, C.A., Brown, T.W., Wimmer, A.: Prestige, proximity, and prejudice: how Google search terms diffuse across the world. Am. J. Sociol. **124**(5), 1496–1548 (2019)
7. Blei, D.M., Ng, A.Y., Jordan, M.I.: Latent Dirichlet allocation. J. Mach. Learn. Res. **3**(Jan), 993–1022 (2003)
8. Breiman, L.: Random forests. Mach. Learn. **45**(1), 5–32 (2001)
9. Costa, D.L., Kahn, M.E.: Civic engagement and community heterogeneity: an economist's perspective. Perspect. Polit. **1**(1), 103–111 (2003)
10. Dubois, S.: Recognition and renown, the structure of cultural markets: evidence from French poetry. J. Cult. Econ. **36**(1), 27–48 (2012)
11. Gabry, J., Goodrich, B.: rstanarm: Bayesian applied regression modeling via Stan. R package version 2.18.2 (2018). https://CRAN.R-project.org/package=rstanarm
12. Gereke, J., Schaub, M., Baldassarri, D.: Ethnic diversity, poverty and social trust in Germany: evidence from a behavioral measure of trust. PLoS ONE **13**(7), e0199834 (2018). https://doi.org/10.1371/journal.pone.0199834
13. Giddens, A.: The Constitution of Society: Outline of the Theory of Structuration, vol. 349. University of California Press (1986)
14. Glaeser, E.L., Laibson, D.I., Scheinkman, J.A., Soutter, C.L.: Measuring trust. Q. J. Econ. **115**(3), 811–846 (2000)
15. Goldberg, A., Hannan, M.T., Kovács, B.: What does it mean to span cultural boundaries? Variety and atypicality in cultural consumption. Am. Sociol. Rev. **81**(2), 215–241 (2016)
16. Griffiths, T.L., Steyvers, M.: Finding scientific topics. Proc. Nat. Acad. Sci. **101**(Suppl. 1), 5228–5235 (2004)
17. Hannan, M.T., Carroll, G.R.: Dynamics of Organizational Populations: Density, Legitimation, and Competition. Oxford University Press, Oxford (1992)
18. Hannan, M.T., Freeman, J.: Organizational Ecology. Harvard University Press (1993)
19. Hirschman, A.O.: The paternity of an index. Am. Econ. Rev. **54**(5), 761–762 (1964)
20. Hofstede, G.: Culture's Consequences. Sage Publications, Beverly Hills (1980)
21. Hristova, D., Aiello, L.M., Quercia, D.: The new urban success: how culture pays. Front. Phys. **6** (2018). https://doi.org/10.3389/fphy.2018.00027
22. Lee, M., Butler, B.S.: How are information deserts created? A theory of local information landscapes. J. Assoc. Inf. Sci. Technol. **70**(2), 101–116 (2019)
23. López, C., Butler, B., Brusilovsky, P.: Does anything ever happen around here? Assessing the online information landscape for local events. J. Urban Technol. **21**(4), 95–123 (2014)
24. Mazanec, J.A., Crotts, J.C., Gursoy, D., Lu, L.: Homogeneity versus heterogeneity of cultural values: an item-response theoretical approach applying Hofstede's cultural dimensions in a single nation. Tour. Manag. **48**, 299–304 (2015)
25. Van der Meer, T., Tolsma, J.: Ethnic diversity and its effects on social cohesion. Annu. Rev. Sociol. **40**(1), 459–478 (2014). https://doi.org/10.1146/annurev-soc-071913-043309
26. Mitchell, B., Franco, J.: HOLC "redlining" maps: the persistent structure of segregation and economic inequality. NCRC Research (2018). https://ncrc.org/holc/
27. Ottaviano, G., Peri, G.: The economic value of cultural diversity: evidence from US cities. J. Econ. Geogr. **6**(1), 9–44 (2006)
28. Park, M., Park, J., Baek, Y.M., Macy, M.: Cultural values and cross-cultural video consumption on Youtube. PLoS ONE **12**(5), e0177865 (2017)

29. Park, M., Weber, I., Naaman, M., Vieweg, S.: Understanding musical diversity via online social media. In: Ninth International AAAI Conference on Web and Social Media (2015)
30. Pedrini, M., Bramanti, V., Cannatelli, B.: The impact of national culture and social capital on corporate social responsibility attitude among immigrants entrepreneurs. J. Manag. Gov. **20**(4), 759–787 (2016)
31. Peterson, R.A., Kern, R.M.: Changing highbrow taste: from snob to omnivore. Am. Sociol. Rev. **61**(5), 900–907 (1996)
32. Pettigrew, T.F.: Intergroup contact theory. Annu. Rev. Psychol. **49**(1), 65–85 (1998)
33. Pontikes, E.G., Hannan, M.T.: An ecology of social categories. Sociol. Sci. **1**, 311–343 (2014)
34. Putnam, R.D.: E Pluribus Unum: diversity and community in the twenty-first century the 2006 Johan Skytte prize lecture. Scand. Polit. Stud. **30**(2), 137–174 (2007)
35. Rao, C.R.: Diversity: its measurement, decomposition apportionment and analysis. Sankhy: Indian J. Stat. Ser. A **44**(1), 1–22 (1982)
36. Risen, T.: Where should you start your tech company?: A new study shows that the best city for tech isn't necessarily Silicon Valley. U.S. News (2016). https://www.usnews.com/news/articles/2016-05-11/where-should-you-start-your-tech-company. Accessed 3 May 2019
37. Schaeffer, M.: Can competing diversity indices inform us about why ethnic diversity erodes social cohesion? A test of five diversity indices in Germany. Soc. Sci. Res. **42**(3), 755–774 (2013). https://doi.org/10.1016/j.ssresearch.2012.12.018
38. Stirling, A.: A general framework for analysing diversity in science, technology and society. J. R. Soc. Interface **4**(15), 707–719 (2007)
39. Stolle, D., Soroka, S., Johnston, R.: When does diversity erode trust? Neighborhood diversity, interpersonal trust and the mediating effect of social interactions. Polit. Stud. **56**(1), 57–75 (2008)
40. Sturgis, P., Brunton-Smith, I., Kuha, J., Jackson, J.: Ethnic diversity, segregation and the social cohesion of neighbourhoods in London. Ethn. Racial Stud. **37**(8), 1286–1309 (2014). https://doi.org/10.1080/01419870.2013.831932
41. Uslaner, E.M.: The Oxford Handbook of Social and Political Trust. Oxford University Press, Oxford (2018)
42. Wang, P., Lee, M., Meng, X., Butler, B.: Toward an ecology theory of creativity in it products: a study of mobile device industry. In: Proceedings of the International Conference on Information Systems (ICIS), pp. 1–20 (2016)

Collecting and Organizing Citizen Opinions: A Dynamic Microtask Approach and Its Evaluation

Masaki Matsubara[1]([✉]), Yuhei Matsuda[2], Ryohei Kuzumi[3],
Masanori Koizumi[1], and Atsuyuki Morishima[1]

[1] Faculty of Library, Information and Media Science, University of Tsukuba,
1-2 Kasuga, Tsukuba-shi, Ibaraki 305-8550, Japan
{masaki,koizumi,mori}@slis.tsukuba.ac.jp
[2] Graduate school of Library and Media Studies, University of Tsukuba,
1-2 Kasuga, Tsukuba, Ibaraki 305-8550, Japan
yuhei.matsuda.2017b@mlab.info
[3] Public Relations Policy Division, Tsukuba city hall 1-1-1 Kenkyu-Gakuen,
Tsukuba, Ibaraki 305-8555, Japan
pln032@city.tsukuba.lg.jp

Abstract. Citizens' opinions are important information resources for democratic local governments. Since a mere collection of opinions is not easy to analyze, the collected opinions should be organized, so that the governments can effectively analyze it. Recently, web-based public opinion collection systems have been widely used, but many of them merely implement traditional methods. For example, collecting opinions in web-based questionnaire still use free-text fields, and organizing the collected opinions remains a cumbersome task for the government staff. This paper explores a new design space and proposes a scheme where citizens take part in organizing and classifying opinions while answering the questionnaire. In the scheme, we collect citizen opinions in a structured form, with a microtask interface that changes the list of choices dynamically. Our system has been used by Tsukuba city for several real-world opinion-collection projects. Our experience so far shows that the scheme is effective in organizing the collected opinions for analysis.

Keywords: Information integration · System development · Civic-tech · Public opinion data

1 Introduction

In the long history of democratic society, governments have developed several methodologies and rules to reflect citizens' opinions in their national and local policies, such as nationwide and local elections, several types of polls, online surveys, interviews, etc. [3,4,9]. Recently, political environments have rapidly changed in accordance with the emergence of information technologies and political instabilities. Due to this, evidence-based policymaking has been becoming a

© Springer Nature Switzerland AG 2020
A. Sundqvist et al. (Eds.): iConference 2020, LNCS 12051, pp. 50–65, 2020.
https://doi.org/10.1007/978-3-030-43687-2_4

fundamental basis for democratic countries in the 21st century. Opinion collection has become more critical for local governments than ever before [9, 27].

In order for local governments to capture citizens' opinions, they have started to utilize information technologies e.g., websites, smartphones, large LCD screens, SNS and QR codes have been used as interfaces to allow people to state their opinions [2, 5, 8, 13, 22, 27, 29, 34]. Unfortunately, a common feature of these attempts is simply using information technology as a tool to implement traditional methods, such as polls and surveys [26]. Implementing such traditional ways to collect public opinions does not allow for the full exploration of the potential new design capabilities made possible by information technologies. For instance, organizing collected opinions is still a cumbersome task for government staff, but this is an issue that could be improved with clever uses of information technology.

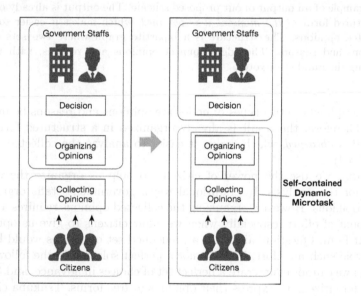

Fig. 1. The concept of our proposed scheme for collecting and organizing opinions. (left) In traditional opinion collection schemes, government staffs organize the collected opinions. (right) In contrast, citizens organize the opinions on the fly in our scheme.

This paper explores a new design space and proposes a scheme where citizens take part in organizing opinions while answering the questionnaire in self-contained dynamic microtask (Fig. 1). Here, opinions are individual answers to a posed question on their viewpoints, ideas, preferences, or judgements. We assume that there are reasons behind their opinions. In the scheme, we collect citizens' opinions in a structured way, with a microtask interface that changes dynamically the list of choices; if it receives a new opinion, it will be shown in the list of the choices in the task for future workers. The task also asks citizens what the reasons are for their opinions. The scheme outputs the collected opinions in a

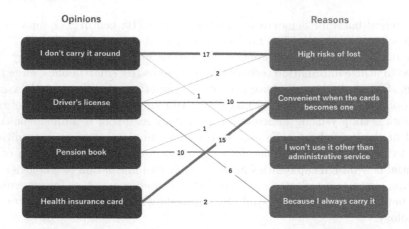

Fig. 2. Example of an output of our proposed scheme. The output is already organized in a structured form *at the moment it is obtained*, which makes it easier to analyze the collected opinions. The structure is a bipartite graph where two sets of nodes are opinions and reasons. The edges connect opinions and reasons, with the label representing the number of votes.

bipartite graph where two types of nodes are opinions and reasons behind them (Fig. 2). Therefore, the result is already organized in a structured form *at the moment it is obtained*, which makes it easier to analyze the collected opinions (See Sect. 4.4).

This way, we use the power of citizens to help us organize the collected opinions for the analysis. In traditional ways, government staffs organize the collected opinions. However, organizing the collected opinions requires a tremendous amount of effort, especially when we allow citizens to give us opinions in a free-text form. Questionnaire with a predefined set of choices would be desirable to avoid such an effort, but it is not a perfect solution in the following two points: (1) we cannot enumerate a perfect set of choices in advance, and (2) there is a need for citizens to express their opinions in free forms. Tsukuba city often receives complaints from citizens every time they conduct surveys only with a fixed set of choices - they want to express their opinions in a free-text form.

Contributions. Our contributions are as follows. (1) We propose a structured opinion collection method with self-contained dynamic microtasks, which is beyond just implementing traditional free text questions with information technologies. The method not only helps us collect their opinions, but allows us to *citizen-source* organizing the collected opinions. (2) We report our experience of several attempts with the proposed method conducted by Tsukuba city. (3) We show experimentally that the proposed method allows citizens to produce organized opinions in a structured form with few duplicate opinions. (4) We describe how the structured opinions make it easier to analyze them by applying existing analysis techniques to the collected opinions. In particular, we demonstrate a clustering result of opinions collected from the crowd was similar to the clustering result conducted by the city hall staff.

Limitations. Note that our scheme intends to give alternatives for free text questions for collecting opinions, and we do not assume that it replaces all types of questionnaires; it does not replace any statistical surveys where nobody must not be affected by others' opinions. Seeing other opinions when expressing their opinions has pros and cons. People may be led by the shown opinions, and can show their opinions more accurately [38]. How to deal with this issue in the system is an interesting future work but is out of the scope of the paper. One of the ways to avoid these effects is, for example, to show others' responses and ask for a vote after they enter their own opinions [14].

Another important limitation is that this paper focuses on a method for the structured collection opinion method and utilizes the simplest form of user interface. This worked well with the number of people in our experiment ($n = 415$), but as the number increases, the user interface will be a challenge because users have to browse a larger number of opinions. We need to devise sophisticated user interfaces to deal with it. For example, showing similar opinions when they enter their own opinions will be a possible solution.

The remainder of the paper is structured as follows. Section 2 gives related work. Section 3 explains the proposed scheme and our experience on several projects. Section 4 reports the results of the attempts conducted by Tsukuba city, and evaluates the effectiveness of the scheme.

2   Related Work

Many studies have addressed information technologies for collecting opinions from citizens. The most popular approach is to make it easier for citizens to report problems or answer survey questions without distributing paper-based surveys [26]. One of the common ways is to use the Web or smartphones so that citizens can report problems in cities as soon as they find them [16,19,22,25] or can answer survey questions connected to the locations [10,28].

One of the challenges in this approach is how to recruit people to perform the task [23]. Textizen [11] write questions on walls at bus stops to motivate citizens to answer questions. ThoughtCloud [7] uses tablets deployed at event places. Some studies develop dedicated equipment for motivating people to answer questions [18,35]. Some proposals use crowdsourcing to collect opinions from citizens [31]. Our contribution is independent of how to recruit people, and in fact, we used our methods in the real-world with different settings in terms of how to recruit people (Sect. 3.2).

The approaches above do not ask citizens to organize their opinions at all. The other extreme approach is to make places where citizens can discuss on given topics, so that citizens can generate new ideas or make decisions [15,17,24,33,36]. Like our approach, they introduce some *structures* into their schemes, such as clusters of topics [33], augmentations [17], and discussion trees [15]. The common

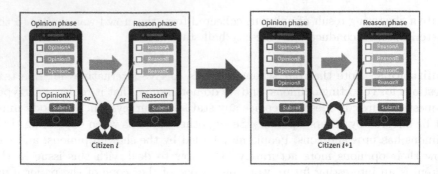

Fig. 3. Interface of the proposed framework. In the opinion phase, citizens can select the listed opinions or input new one into the free-text form. In the reason phase, citizens can select or input their reason in the same manner. When Citizen i submits new item with the free-text form, the inputted item will be listed when Citizen $i+1$ performs.

feature of these studies is asking citizens to do more than just answering survey questions, such organizing opinions and discussing them.

Compared to the two extreme approaches, our approach focuses on designing moderate solutions in two meanings. First, we do not ask citizens to do much more than answering the ordinary survey question. Therefore, they help us organize the questions with less effort. Second, we do not ask citizens to do things that judge (e.g., classify, give tags to) others' opinions. This is often a desirable property if the method is adopted by local governments, because the method is compatible with the Today's workflow to collect citizen opinions; it does not other than eliminating the burden for organizing opinions.

Applying NLP technologies is another approach to collect and analyze the citizen opinions. The most lightweight way is to extract citizen opinions from SNS such as Twitters [32]. This way is not appropriate for collecting opinions on the topics that are not popular among citizens, such as "what are desirable functions of citizen ID cards", and cannot replace paper-based surveys. Text mining is a typical way to analyze the opinions [20,21,37]. However, the outputs generally show the trends in opinions only and the methods do not replace the work being done by government employees today.

There are studies related to the IT-based surveys. Groves et al. [12] suggest that a low survey response rate may indicate that the risk of non-response error is high. Schober et al. [30] discuss the relationship between survey results and social media content. Some studies discuss the effect of different "modes" (e.g., Web-based, face-to-face, telephone-based, mobile) of surveys [1,6]. Considering these results is an interesting future work.

3   Proposed Method

3.1   Design

Figure 3 shows our proposed framework of the citizen opinion collection. It has two features. First, the set of choices grows; each task not only shows a set of choices to vote for, but also has a free-text form to which he or she can input his or her opinion, which appears in the list of choices in future tasks. Therefore, other citizens can choose it in performing the task. A key in this step is to keep the number of letters in the free text form small. We set the length 20 in our experiment. This restriction not only makes it easier to adopt it as a newly added choice, but also makes each opinion clear. If a citizen vote for an opinion from the listed choices, we count up the number of votes for it.

Second, the opinions are given in a structured form where the opinions and reasons for them are separated; After choosing his or her opinion, the citizen then moves to another step where he can enter the reason for it. What he does in the step is the same as that in the first step - he can choose one from a given set of reasons or he can write his own reason. Again, we limit the length of the free text opinion small (25 in our experiments).

As a result, the scheme outputs the collected opinions in a bipartite graph where two types of nodes are opinions and reasons behind them (Fig. 2).

3.2   Real-World Deployments

We have deployed the proposed system for three topics. First, the system collected the opinions on the re-development of the city's central area. The second topic was how to improve the counter service at the city hall. The third one was desirable services available to Citizen ID cardholders.

We tried several incentive structure, including (1) having a special workshop event, (2) putting posters with QR code to the system at the chairs in the waiting space for counter services of Tsukuba City Hall (Fig. 4), and (3) using crowdsourcing platforms. In our experience, we found that attracting people by the poster is not easy and using crowdsourcing services or special events attract more people. Note that crowdsourcing services are not appropriate for some topics for which opinions by local citizens is especially important. How to attract people is beyond the scope of the paper, and we omit further discussions.

Some of the statistics on (3) will be given in Sect. 4.

4   Evaluation

We evaluate two things on the output quality using the results obtained in our experience. First, we evaluate the quality of summarization, i.e., whether the citizens successfully summarize their opinions with our proposed scheme. For the purpose, we calculate the number of overlaps of the same of similar opinions that appear in the output of the scheme, and found that the scheme outputs a small portion of duplicate opinions, but the portion depends on how the scheme is deployed.

Fig. 4. Posters put at the back of chairs in the lobby of the City Hall. Each poster shows a QR code to access our system.

Second, in order to see the potential of structured outputs of collected opinions, we applied known techniques to analyze bipartite graphs. In particular, we compared the result of automatic clustering of collected opinions based on the reasons, and that made manually by the city hall staffs in the Citizen Card Initiative of Tsukuba city. In other words, we evaluated the differences between the on-the-fly labeling of opinions by citizens and the traditional two-phase classifications where opinions are classified by citizen-hall staffs after the opinions are collected. For the purpose, we asked the staff of the city hall to organize the collected opinions without showing the obtained reasons. The results showed that the proposed scheme can output a result that is compatible with those obtained manually by the city hall staffs.

4.1   Settings

Topic. The topic was "Desirable services available to Citizen ID cardholders" The citizen ID is the number similar to SSN in the US and assigned by the Japanese government to each citizen. Local governments provides a variety of services to the cardholder.

Tsukuba city has been collecting opinions on the topic since before. We made the initial set of eleven opinions compatible with the choices in the paper-based survey question. An example of such an opinion was "The card can be used as a bank or credit card" (opinions in the gray ground in Fig. 5).

As shown in Fig. 3, each citizen can choose one or more opinions from the given set or enter their own one. For the chosen or entered opinion, he or she can choose one or more reasons in the given list or enter their own one.

Citizen Recruitment. We used Yahoo! Crowdsourcing to recruit people who perform the opinion collection and organization tasks. We paid three yen (about 3 US cents) for each task. We used the crowdsourcing services because the topic was common to citizens in any local government and it is easy to recruit a large number of citizens in a short period of time with a low cost. In particular, we used two recruitment way: "Local recruitment" and "Nation-wide recruitment", i.e., we asked workers who live in the prefecture where the Tsukuba city situates and workers who live in Japan. As we will explain, we will see what happen if we recruit nation-wide workers on the crowdsourcing platform.

Note that the contribution of the paper is independent of how to recruit citizens. The discussions can be applied to any recruitment schemes including ones that we did in our real-world deployments (Sect. 3), such as the special event, and posters located at City Hall, although we found an interesting result that using crowdsourcing services are not necessarily good for our framework.

4.2   Statistics

Figure 5 shows the number of votes for each of the obtained opinions and reasons in "Local recruitment". Table 1 shows the statistics of the collected opinion and reasons. In "Local recruitment" experiment, the number of responses was 161, the final number of opinions (including "Nothing special") was 16, and that of reasons was 14. Therefore, the citizens added 6 opinions and 13 reasons, respectively, to the initial sets. The average number of opinions per person was 1.39, and the average number of reasons per opinion was 1.16. Most of people input 1 or 2 opinions with 1 reason in both conditions. It is worth noting that no one voted for one of the default opinions ("Library cards or care insurance cards").

Figure 6 (left) shows the relationship between the number of votes for each opinion and that of connected reasons in "Local recruitment". The right one shows the relationship between the number of votes for each reason and that of the connected opinions. As the figure shows, there is a clear positive correlation between the number of votes for each opinion (or reason) and that of the associated reasons (or opinions). This relationships were also observed in "Nation-wide recruitment".

4.3   Evaluation 1: Summarization Quality

One of the motivations of the proposed scheme is to crowdsource organizing the collected opinions to reduce the need for the city hall staffs to summarize the opinions. Thus, it is very important to evaluate whether the method can output the summarized results without duplicate opinions. As shown below, it showed fairly good result in terms of the quality of summarization, but we found that the quality heavily depends on how the scheme is deployed.

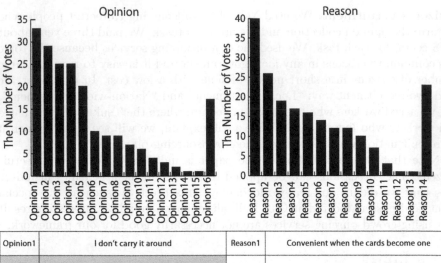

Opinion1	I don't carry it around	Reason1	Convenient when the cards become one
Opinion2	Driver's license	Reason2	I don't need bring many other cards
Opinion3	Identity proof function	Reason3	As an identification card
Opinion4	Health insurance card	Reason4	High risks of lost
Opinion5	Pension book	Reason5	I won't use it other than administrative service
Opinion6	Combine the back and forth on one side	Reason6	Because I always carry it
Opinion7	Seal registration certificate	Reason7	I don't think it is convenient
Opinion8	Useful cards in case of emergency	Reason8	Double-sided copy costs twice as much
Opinion9	Receiving administrative service	Reason9	I do not want to go to various places such as city hall and police for procedure
Opinion10	Name and address change according to moving or marriage	Reason10	Lacking essential functions other than accompanying function
Opinion11	Normally used card	Reason11	Troublesome
Opinion12	Credit card, point card	Reason12	I always carry it
Opinion13	Access to vital information	Reason13	Convenient to put the identification card together
Opinion14	IC card without number	Reason14	Nothing special
Opinion15	Cash card, credit card		
Opinion16	Nothing special		

Fig. 5. (bottom) Obtained opinions and reasons and (top) the number of votes for them. Colored cells represent initial set of items.

Table 1. Statistics of the collected opinions through web-based crowdsourcing

	Local recruitment	Nation-wide recruitment
#Participants	161	415
Average of #Opinions per person	1.39	2.06
#Added Opinions	6	18
#Obtained Opinions (O)	16	28
#Distinct Opinions (O')	14	20
#Duplicate Opinions Rate	12.5%	28.57%
Average of #Reasons per opinion	1.16	1.41
#Added Reasons	13	42
#Obtained Reasons (R)	14	43
#Distinct Reasons (R')	11	21
#Duplicate Reason Rate	21.43%	51.16%
Time	11 days	Four hours

We use duplicate rates in Table 1 for the quantitative evaluation of the proposed scheme on how it works well to summarize opinions. We determined whether each opinion is distinct by majority vote of 7 people. The duplicate rate for opinions is computed with the following equation:

$$D_{opinions} = \frac{|O| - |O'|}{|O|}$$

where O is the number of obtained opinions and O' is the number of distinct opinions. The duplicate rate for the obtained reasons is computed similarly with R and R'.

As Table 1 shows, the duplicate rates of the obtained opinions and reasons in "Local recruitment" are 12.5% and 21.43%, respectively. Figure 7 compares

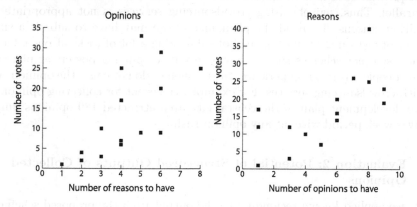

Fig. 6. (left) The number of votes and that of connected reasons for each opinion. (right) The number of votes and the number of connected opinions for each reason. A positive correlation can be observed between the number of votes for each opinion (or reason) and that of the associated reasons (or opinion).

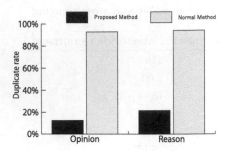

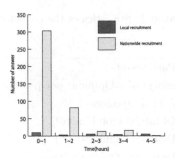

Fig. 7. Quantitative Evaluation of the Summarization

Fig. 8. Frequency distribution for the number of answers over time.

these duplicate rates with the theoretical rates $D0_{opinions}$ and $D0_{reasons}$ for the case where we do not use the proposed method. Here, $D0_{opinions}$ is computed with O being 161 (the number of answers). As the figure shows, our framework is effective in organizing collected opinions.

However, the duplicate rates are not zero even with our proposed method. We examined the task log and found that duplicated opinions were generated in the tasks performed in the early stage. We assumed that this happened because many workers answer the tasks *in parallel*, so that they can not see opinions by others and enter duplicate opinions.

This duplicate happens more in "Nation-wide recruitment". The duplicate rates of the obtained opinions and reasons are 28.57% and 51.16%, respectively. The number of overlaps is significantly higher than that in the "Local recruitment" experiment. Figure 8 shows the distribution of opinions in the time order. Obviously, the nation-wide attracted many workers as soon as the tasks were open.

This result suggests that it is important to avoid the rush of opinions, because the sequential data flow to update the list of choices does not work if tasks are in parallel. Thus, naively using crowdsourcing services is not appropriate for recruiting citizens. To avoid the phenomenon, we may have to submit a small number of tasks many times instead of submitting a lot of tasks at once. Or we should use other schemes such as having events or putting posters at places to recruit people. From our experience, those schemes do not cause the opinion rush as with crowdsourcing services. For example, the event for collecting opinion on the re-development plan of the central city area attracted 189 opinions during the two week period without any opinion rush.

4.4   Evaluation 2: Potential of Structured Outputs of Collected Opinions

Next, we applied known techniques to the output from the proposed scheme to see the potential of the structured outputs of collected opinions. The relationship between opinions and reasons in "Local recruitment" can be represented by a

Table 2. Set covers of opinions: These opinions cover any obtained reasons.

ID	Opinion
1	I don't carry it around
2	Driver's license
3	Identity proof function
8	Useful cards in case of emergency

bipartite graph as shown in Fig. 9. Nodes on both sides represent opinions and reasons, while each edge represents that an opinion is connected to a reason, associated with the number of votes.

The graph allows us to immediately know the backgrounds of their opinions, without neither analyzing the free-form opinions, nor preparing for choices for possible reasons. In the example, there are two different reasons for not carrying the Citizen ID cards - some citizens are concerned about the risk of lost, and some think the cards are just not convenient at all.

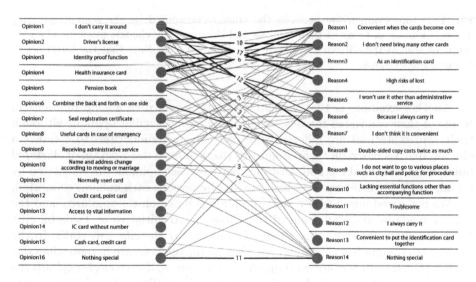

Fig. 9. Bipartite graph: the graph allows us to immediately know the reasons of their opinions, without neither analyzing.

An advantage of having such an structured output is that we can apply a variety of analysis techniques directly to the output. For example, we can compute *set covers* of opinions that cover any obtained reasons. Table 2 is a set cover for our output; if the administration adopts the opinions, it will cover hidden requirements (reasons) from citizens. This is practically important because we can find the minimum set of opinions to satisfy a lot of people.

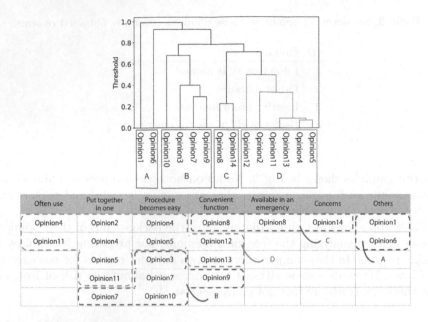

Fig. 10. (top) Comparison between the clusters computed by the cosine similarity among opinions in terms of their reasons and (bottom) the clusters made by the government staff in the Citizen ID initiative of Tsukuba City. Note that the latter set of clusters has overlaps.

Another example is that we can compute *similarities among opinions* in terms of their connected reasons, so that we can find similar opinions although their representations are different. We can use such similarities to conduct a cluster analysis based on them. Figure 10 (top) shows a dendrogram of clustered opinions by the Ward method. Distance between each opinions are calculated by cosine similarity using vector which created by reasons each opinion connected.

We compared our cluster results of opinions based on the similarity and the cluster made by the staff team of the Citizen card initiative of Tsukuba city. Figure 10 (bottom) shows the result of grouping by the city hall staffs. In the table, each column is a cluster, where some of the opinions are in more than one cluster (i.e., the clusters are overlapped). Each rounded dotted circle explains the clusters in Fig. 10 (top). As shown in the figure, the similarity-based clustering in terms of the obtained reasons was quite compatible with the manual clustering by experts.

5   Conclusion

This paper proposed a scheme that collects citizens' opinions in a structured way, with a self-contained microtask interface that changes dynamically the list of choices. Our scheme "citizen-source" organizing opinions being collected on the fly while they answer the questionnaire. The output is a structured bipartite graph that shows not only the opinions and reasons, but also the number of votes for them. Our evaluation result shows that the scheme outputs a summarized result with a good quality. In addition, we show that such a structured output allows us to directly apply well-known techniques for analyzing the output.

Our system has been being used by Tsukuba City in real-world opinion-collection projects. The future work includes incorporating effective recruitment strategies into our scheme and development of methods to analyze the output graph tailored to the needs of citizens' opinion analysis.

Acknowledgments. This work was partially supported by JST CREST Grant Number JPMJCR16E3 including AIP challenge program and JST Mirai Program Grant Number JPMJMI19G8, Japan.

References

1. Antoun, C., Couper, M.P., Conrad, F.G.: Effects of mobile versus pc web on survey response quality: a crossover experiment in a probability web panel. Public Opin. Q. **81**(S1), 280–306 (2017). https://doi.org/10.1093/poq/nfw088
2. Baldauf, M., Suette, S., Fröhlich, P., Lehner, U.: Interactive opinion polls on public displays: studying privacy requirements in the wild. In: Proceedings of the 16th International Conference on Human-computer Interaction with Mobile Devices & Services, MobileHCI 2014, pp. 495–500. ACM, New York (2014). https://doi.org/10.1145/2628363.2634222
3. Barnes, W., Mann, B.C.: Making local democracy work: municipal officials' views about public engagement. Nat. Civic Rev. **100**(3), 58–62 (2011)
4. Butt, M.: Result-oriented e-government evaluation: citizen's perspective. Webology **11**(1), 1–33 (2014)
5. Chua, A.Y., Goh, D.H., Ang, R.P.: Web 2.0 applications in government web sites: prevalence, use and correlations with perceived web site quality. Online Inf. Rev. **36**(2), 175–195 (2012)
6. Couper, M.P.: The future of modes of data collection. Public Opin. Q. **75**(5), 889–908 (2011). https://doi.org/10.1093/poq/nfr046
7. Dow, A., Vines, J., Comber, R., Wilson, R.: Thoughtcloud: exploring the role of feedback technologies in care organisations. In: Proceedings of the 2016 CHI Conference on Human Factors in Computing Systems, CHI 2016, pp. 3625–3636. ACM, New York (2016). https://doi.org/10.1145/2858036.2858105
8. Evans, L., Franks, P., Chen, H.M.: Voices in the cloud: social media and trust in canadian and us local governments. Rec. Manage. J. **28**(1), 18–46 (2018)
9. Fishkin, J.: When the People Speak: Deliberative Democracy and Public Consultation. Oxford Univerity Press, Oxford (2011). https://books.google.co.jp/books?id=iNsUDAAAQBAJ
10. Graeff, E.: Crowdsourcing as reflective political practice: Building a location-based tool for civic learning and engagement, September 2014
11. Granicus: textizen. https://www.textizen.com/
12. Groves, R.M., Presser, S., Dipko, S.: The role of topic interest in survey participation decisions. Public Opin. Q. **68**(1), 2–31 (2004). https://doi.org/10.1093/poq/nfh002
13. Isaksson, M., Jørgensen, P.E.F.: Connecting with citizens: the emotional rhetoric of norwegian and danish municipal websites. Nordicom Rev. **39**(1), 111–128 (2018)

14. Kawamoto, T., Aoki, T.: Democratic classification of free-format survey responses with a network-based framework. Nat. Mach. Intell. **1**(7), 322 (2019)
15. Kawase, S., et al.: Cyber-physical hybrid environment using a largescale discussion system enhances audiences' participation and satisfaction in the panel discussion. IEICE Trans. Inf. Syst. **101**(4), 847–855 (2018)
16. King, S.F., Brown, P.: Fix my street or else: using the internet to voice local public service concerns. In: Proceedings of the 1st International Conference on Theory and Practice of Electronic Governance, ICEGOV 2007, pp. 72–80. ACM, New York (2007). https://doi.org/10.1145/1328057.1328076
17. Klein, M.: Enabling large-scale deliberation using attention-mediation metrics. Comput. Support. Coop. Work (CSCW) **21**(4), 449–473 (2012). https://doi.org/10.1007/s10606-012-9156-4
18. Koeman, L., Kalnikaité, V., Rogers, Y.: "Everyone is talking about it!": a distributed approach to urban voting technology and visualisations. In: Proceedings of the 33rd Annual ACM Conference on Human Factors in Computing Systems, CHI 2015, pp. 3127–3136. ACM, New York (2015). https://doi.org/10.1145/2702123.2702263
19. Lee, C.S., Anand, V., Han, F., Kong, X., Goh, D.H.-L.: Investigating the use of a mobile crowdsourcing application for public engagement in a smart city. In: Morishima, A., Rauber, A., Liew, C.L. (eds.) ICADL 2016. LNCS, vol. 10075, pp. 98–103. Springer, Cham (2016). https://doi.org/10.1007/978-3-319-49304-6_13
20. Loures, T.C., Vaz de Melo, P.O., Veloso, A.A.: Generating entity representation from online discussions: challenges and an evaluation framework. In: Proceedings of the 23rd Brazillian Symposium on Multimedia and the Web, WebMedia 2017, pp. 197–204. ACM, New York (2017). https://doi.org/10.1145/3126858.3126882
21. Matsumoto, T., Sunayama, W., Hatanaka, Y., Ogohara, K.: Data analysis support by combining data mining and text mining. In: 2017 6th IIAI International Congress on Advanced Applied Informatics (IIAI-AAI), pp. 313–318, July 2017. https://doi.org/10.1109/IIAI-AAI.2017.165
22. Mergel, I.: Distributed democracy: Seeclickfix.com for crowdsourced issue reporting, January 2012
23. Miller, P.V.: Is there a future for surveys? Public Opin. Q. **81**(S1), 205–212 (2017). https://doi.org/10.1093/poq/nfx008
24. Network, G.O.I.: Online Consultation in GOL Countries: Initiatives to Foster E-democracy: Project Report (2001). https://books.google.co.jp/books?id=lAkbSQAACAAJ
25. Offenhuber, D.: Infrastructure legibility-a comparative analysis of open311-based citizen feedback systems. Camb. J. Reg. Econ. Soc. **8**(1), 93–112 (2015). https://doi.org/10.1093/cjres/rsu001
26. Price, V.: Public opinion research in the new century reflections of a former POQ editor. Public Opin. Q. **75**(5), 846–853 (2011). https://doi.org/10.1093/poq/nfr055
27. Reddel, T., Woolcock, G.: From consultation to participatory governance? a critical review of citizen engagement strategies in Queensland. Aust. J. Public Adm. **63**(3), 75–87 (2004). https://doi.org/10.1111/j.1467-8500.2004.00392.x
28. Sakamura, M., Ito, T., Tokuda, H., Yonezawa, T., Nakazawa, J.: Minaqn: web-based participatory sensing platform for citizen-centric urban development. In: Adjunct Proceedings of the 2015 ACM International Joint Conference on Pervasive and Ubiquitous Computing and Proceedings of the 2015 ACM International Symposium on Wearable Computers, UbiComp/ISWC 2015 Adjunct, pp. 1607–1614. ACM, New York (2015). https://doi.org/10.1145/2800835.2801632

29. Sandoval-Almazan, R., Gil-Garcia, J.R.: Assessing local e-government: an initial exploration of the case of Mexico. In: Proceedings of the 4th International Conference on Theory and Practice of Electronic Governance, ICEGOV 2010, pp. 61–65, ACM, New York (2010). https://doi.org/10.1145/1930321.1930335
30. Schober, M.F., Pasek, J., Guggenheim, L., Lampe, C., Conrad, F.G.: Social media analyses for social measurement. Public Opin. Q. **80**(1), 180–211 (2016). https://doi.org/10.1093/poq/nfv048
31. Schuurman, D., Baccarne, B., De Marez, L., Mechant, P.: Smart ideas for smartcities: investigating crowdsourcing for generating and selecting ideas forict innovation in a city context. J. Theor. Appl. Electron. Commer. Res. **7**(3), 49–62 (2012). https://doi.org/10.4067/S0718-18762012000300006
32. Seki, Y.: Use of twitter for analysis of public sentiment for improvement of local government service. In: 2016 IEEE International Conference on Smart Computing (SMARTCOMP), pp. 1–3, May 2016. https://doi.org/10.1109/SMARTCOMP.2016.7501726
33. Siangliulue, P., Chan, J., Dow, S.P., Gajos, K.Z.: Ideahound: improving large-scale collaborative ideation with crowd-powered real-time semantic modeling. In: Proceedings of the 29th Annual Symposium on User Interface Software and Technology, UIST 2016, pp. 609–624. ACM, New York (2016). https://doi.org/10.1145/2984511.2984578
34. Vargas, A.M.P.: A proposal of digital government for Colombia. In: Proceedings of the 11th International Conference on Theory and Practice of Electronic Governance, pp. 693–695. ACM (2018)
35. Vlachokyriakos, V., et al.: Postervote: expanding the action repertoire for local political activism. In: Proceedings of the 2014 Conference on Designing Interactive Systems, DIS 2014, pp. 795–804. ACM, New York (2014). https://doi.org/10.1145/2598510.2598523
36. Wright, S.: Government-run online discussion fora: moderation, censorship and the shadow of control1. The Br. J. Polit. Int. Relat. **8**(4), 550–568 (2006). https://doi.org/10.1111/j.1467-856X.2006.00247.x
37. Yamanishi, K., Li, H.: Mining open answers in questionnaire data. IEEE Intell. Syst. **17**(5), 58–63 (2002). https://doi.org/10.1109/MIS.2002.1039833
38. Yaniv, I.: Receiving other people's advice: influence and benefit. Organ. Behav. Hum. Decis. Process. **93**(1), 1–13 (2004). https://doi.org/10.1016/j.obhdp.2003.08.002. http://www.sciencedirect.com/science/article/pii/S0749597803001018

Indigenous Cultural Sustainability in a Digital World: Two Case Studies from Aotearoa New Zealand

Anne Goulding[✉] , Jennifer Campbell-Meier ,
and Allan Sylvester

Victoria University of Wellington, Wellington 6140, New Zealand
anne.goulding@vuw.ac.nz

Abstract. This paper explores issues relating to the impact of digital technologies on indigenous cultural sustainability. Adoption of digital technologies is represented as a double-edged sword for indigenous communities seeking to maintain and revitalize their cultures; while the affordances of digital technology can disseminate cultural information knowledge quickly, easily and globally, digitalization also raises questions about ownership, control and consultation. These issues are discussed in relation to two case studies from Aotearoa New Zealand from which key points for future research are identified.

Keywords: Cultural sustainability · Indigenous culture · Digital technologies

1 Introduction

The United Nations' Sustainable Development Goals (SDGs) [1] raise concerns about the sustainability of cultures into the future, highlighting the importance of safeguarding tangible and intangible cultural heritage, and the protection and promotion of diverse cultural expressions. None of the SDGs focus on culture specifically, despite pressure for its explicit integration within the post-2015 UN development agenda [2] but a number of the goals include culture and reference it their targets. SDGs 4 (Education), 8 (Work and Economic Growth), 11 (Cities and Communities) and 12 (Consumption and Production) all make some mention of culture with a focus on how culture can enable the SDGs. There is a growing recognition of the need for the protection of cultural heritage, vitality, and sustainability. Generations of inequitable and racialized policies mean that indigenous communities worldwide are in danger of losing touch with elements of their culture. Some have noted a tension between maintenance of indigenous culture and development [3]. The role of digital technologies in accelerating the trend towards cultural homogenization [4] has been highlighted although others perceive ways in which technology can empower indigenous peoples to reconnect with each other and their culture [5]. This paper surfaces issues related to indigenous cultural sustainability and digital engagement and suggests areas of importance for a future research agenda. To that end, a discussion of key concepts related to indigenous cultural sustainability in a digital context is followed by

A. Sundqvist et al. (Eds.): iConference 2020, LNCS 12051, pp. 66–75, 2020.
https://doi.org/10.1007/978-3-030-43687-2_5

analysis of two case studies from Aotearoa New Zealand that highlights key issues for further exploration and research.

2   Key Concepts

This section explores discussions of indigenous cultural sustainability in the literature, discussing concepts and ideas explored in the case studies.

2.1   Indigenous Culture

To begin, it is helpful to develop a clear understanding of culture. Eriksen defines culture as "the meaning content of human communities, the symbolic patterns, norms, and rules of human communities" [6] and this wide conceptualization of culture covers both material/tangible and immaterial/intangible culture. Material or tangible culture (art, weaving, dance, carvings, buildings, landscapes) is an expression of immaterial or intangible culture (beliefs, values, social organization and practices) [7]. Indigenous culture belongs to the original peoples of a land or region, in contrast to those who settled subsequently. The United Nations (UN) acknowledges indigenous peoples as those who keep and look after knowledge inextricably linked to their identity but also warn that indigenous culture is being undermined and threatened by development, domination and discrimination [8]. As a result, and reflecting a more general concern with sustainability, discussions of indigenous cultural sustainability have been growing since the turn of the century.

2.2   Cultural Sustainability

This paper refers to cultural sustainability as the preservation and continuation of tangible and intangible cultural capital, focusing predominantly on the representations of cultural heritage that can be passed on to future generations [9]. The main challenge to cultural sustainability is from increasing globalization, particularly human mobility (immigration and emigration) and the consequent impact on language, ethnic heritage, identity, and the distinctiveness of communities and societies. The most extreme outcome is cultural homogenization, "the process by which local cultures are transformed or absorbed by a dominant outside culture" [10]. Advances in technology have facilitated globalization processes and are often positioned as agents of cultural imperialism [11]. Alongside those raising concern about the negative consequences of Information and Communication Technologies (ICTs) for indigenous communities and the maintenance of their culture, however, are other voices suggesting that they can be harnessed to promote cultural sustainability. Digital technologies are thus conceptualized in the literature as a paradoxical "double-edged sword", with the potential to both erode and preserve indigenous culture and identity [12].

2.3 Digital Technologies and Cultural Sustainability

ICT development has been identified as a possible factor for a decline in indigenous cultural identity because of its power to reinforce and accelerate the dominance of colonizing modes of thought, culture, and values [13]. Exposure of indigenous communities to non-indigenous cultural values and information through digital technologies, with fewer opportunities for reinforcement of indigenous cultural heritage and languages, can lead to the loss of indigenous culture and identity [12]. There are also accounts of the misuse of indigenous cultural heritage and artefacts accessed via technology, raising questions of access and control [14]. The use of historic Māori portraits and mokomōkai[1] on goods for sale on an American arts website caused offence in Aotearoa New Zealand [15], for example, and illustrates the ease with which digital images and artefacts can be accessed and used in culturally unsafe ways.

There are, however, many instances of ICTs being used by indigenous people and communities to preserve and disseminate their cultural heritage. As long ago as 2006, Srinivasan highlighted the empowering potential of internet-based technologies for ethnic and indigenous peoples and researchers have continued to focus on how these communities can appropriate digital technologies to serve their cultural, political and social ambitions [16]. Dyson explores how ICTs enable indigenous Australians to document and access cultural materials, learn indigenous languages and protect indigenous cultural property [17], while Botangen et al. conclude that the use of Facebook among migrant Igorot people of the Philippines plays a significant role in the exchange, revitalization, practice, and learning of their indigenous culture [18]. Similarly, in Aotearoa New Zealand, O'Carroll found that the Internet and SNS (social networking sites) provide alternative ways for Māori to engage with aspects of their indigenous cultural identity [19], including accessing whakapapa (contextually rich geneology), learning te reo Māori (Māori language), and finding out more about cultural performing arts such as kapa haka (a Māori cultural or performing group).

The impact of digital technologies on indigenous cultural sustainability is complex, therefore, raising questions around homogenization, misappropriation and inappropriate use while simultaneously presenting opportunities for preservation and dissemination of important cultural information, knowledge and artefacts. These issues are explored through two case studies from Aotearoa New Zealand.

3   Case Studies

Māori, the tangata whenua (indigenous people of Aotearoa), today make up around 15% of the population [20]. Although colonization and successive historic government agendas of cultural assimilation and language domination during the nineteenth and twentieth centuries resulted in language, culture and identity loss [21], interest in both te reo Māori and Māori culture revived in the second half of the twentieth century [22]. This has prompted increasing demand for courses and resources from those keen to learn about the indigenous culture and language [23]. Digital technologies provide

---

[1] Preserved Māori tattooed heads: https://teara.govt.nz/en/ta-moko-maori-tattooing/page-5.

opportunities for more people to access mātauranga Māori (the ongoing empowerment and development of knowledge and ways of knowing, originating from ancestors and continuing into the future) and engage with the culture supporting its sustainability, but, as noted above, the use of technology for disseminating cultural artefacts and knowledge also requires safeguards to prevent misuse and misappropriation. The two case studies presented below illustrate the potential and precautions necessary for digital cultural sustainability.

3.1 The Digitisation of Robley's Moko; or Maori Tattooing[2]

The New Zealand Electronic Text Centre (NZETC) is an open access online repository of digitized and born-digital texts focused on New Zealand and Pacific Islands texts and heritage materials held by Victoria University of Wellington [24]. In 2007, a decision was made to digitize *Moko; or Maori Tattooing* written and illustrated by Horatio Gordon Robley and published in 1896 by Chapman & Hall in London [25]. Considered by some to be the seminal work on moko, the NZETC wanted to make this important piece of Aotearoa New Zealand's documentary heritage accessible while recognizing it contained images of ancestors, mokomōkai, and ancestral remains; mātauranga that should not be freely available to all. There were also concerns that the mokos illustrated in the text could be copied and used in a culturally unsafe manner. Following extensive consultation with potential user and source communities (librarians, academics, Māori and Ta Moko artists), the text was eventually presented with all images except those of mokomōkai and ancestral remains; place holders providing descriptions of images replace the illustrations along with an explanation of why they have been removed.

3.2 Arataki Cultural Tales

The Arataki app is a smartphone app launched in the Taranaki region of Aotearoa New Zealand in 2018. Using Bluetooth connectivity, the app provides cultural information and stories related to a range of sites around the country. Arataki provides visitors with a guided tour accompanied by Māori tales, legends and stories. New content is available at each site through which visitors can learn about the origin of Māori place names, and hear stories, proverbs, history and songs associated with each landmark presented in multiple formats including audio, video, images and text [26]. Stories and legends play an important role in the transmission of Māori cultural knowledge and in the pre-European oral culture survived through inter-generational transmission [27]. These oral traditions are an important part of Māori culture and identity, with stories handed down from generation to generation helping to explain the past, develop cultural understanding and experiences, and pass on learning. For the developer of Arataki, Lee Timutimu, the app combines his interest in technology with his passion for

---

[2] Although this is the title of Robley's work, we are aware that, among Māori, "tattoo" is not an adequate representation of the practices and traditions (Tikanga) of "moko" and is not considered a direct translation. See: https://www.tepapa.govt.nz/discover-collections/read-watch-play/maori/ta-moko-maori-tattoos-history.

Māori storytelling and is a way of ensuring important aspects of Māori cultural heritage and identity are passed on [26].

4 Analysis

While both these case studies demonstrate positive outcomes from the cultural sustainability perspective, as valuable indigenous cultural knowledge is being made more accessible for current and future generations, they also raise issues related to ownership, control and access, and consultation which Callaghan and Stevenson argue increase the complexity of decisions around the digitization of indigenous cultural heritage [28]. These form the basis of the discussion below.

4.1 Ownership

Copyright often protects the rights of the photographer, but not the rights of the creators of these artefacts, limiting use or reuse by the community. This important separation of the digital representation and 'ownership' of the medium can create a challenging tension. Indigenous cultures generally have a collective rather than individual notion of ownership. For indigenous people, the Western perspective of ownership focusing on individual property rights, such as those exerted in the 'ownership' of a photograph, overlooks the symbolic role that cultural heritage and artefacts play in cultural cohesiveness and vitality. This means that the artifacts and any representations of them belong to all the people [29] (dead, living, and not yet living). These different attitudes towards ownership are brought into stark relief when considering the history of colonization and the collection of indigenous cultural artefacts and representations of knowledge. The collecting practices of Western individuals and institutions means that those items once collectively owned are now legally the property of somebody else. Digitization of indigenous material culture can lead to a further loss. Although digitization can be a cost effective and acceptable method of virtually repatriating items or artefacts belonging to an indigenous community [30], a third of respondents in a study of the digitization of te reo Māori resources thought the decision of whether to digitize a resource should rest with the whānau (extended family) to which the information relates, and not the institutional "owners" [31].

For the NZETC, issues of ownership revolved around the appropriation of Māori cultural heritage in the form of moko designs. As Ngata et al. discuss, Māori are well aware of the potential commercial value of their unique art forms and are taking steps to protect them from exploitation [30]. The interactive and collaborative features of digital technologies have significantly expanded the potential for the re-use, re-shaping, and onward dissemination of digital cultural heritage, further complicating the issues of ownership [32].

In the case of Arataki, ownership in the strictest sense is probably not as relevant as Māori people believe that nobody owns history (but do have a strong sense of duty toward the preservation of history), which in the Māori worldview includes stories and legends [26] and ownership of folklore in indigenous culture is conceived as a collective, as opposed to individual, phenomenon. Indeed, the app could be said to be preserving the integrity of Māori stories as the tales are told by an experienced Māori storyteller who is committed to ensuring they are passed on accurately and with mana (authority, control, power, influence) [26]. The app is thus making space in a digital environment for the indigenous worldview and ways of knowing [33]. Nevertheless, Wyeld et al. recommend the development of protocols to respect and recognize the traditional owners of indigenous folklore and stories and their status as a body of knowledge that may be thousands of years old, as well as to protect them from misuse and abuse [34].

4.2 Control and Access

When considering control and access, the key issue is the clash of indigenous values which often place restrictions on certain cultural information, with Western principles of open access. While digitization of indigenous cultural heritage can contribute to cultural sustainability by making it widely accessible for those seeking to connect or reconnect with their cultural identity, without careful curation it can violate notions of the sacredness of information or images. In many indigenous cultures, access to certain cultural knowledge and artefacts is restricted and indigenous peoples have their own systems for management and access to their culture. Traditional access rights authorize indigenous custodians to regulate and restrict access to certain cultural knowledge and practice [35]. In the NZETC case, the images of mokomōkai and ancestral remains were considered tapu (sacred, prohibited, restricted) and were suppressed. Digitization may therefore be more straightforward for some cultures to engage with and adopt than others. The original tenet of the Internet was based on a Western model of open access to information for all, but this has led to barriers to participation for some cultures.

Another issue related to access and control is that much indigenous cultural knowledge and practice is not written and the act of capturing it in a format to be shared digitally can be problematic. For example, technology may impact on the nature of some indigenous cultural practices and traditions. The Māori performing art of kapa haka (group performance dance) is a good example here. The origins and authenticity of kapa haka are a matter of debate but Papesch argues that kapa haka can support and strengthen Māori cultural identity [36]. She suggests, however, that performances are increasingly being composed for cameras so that they can be recorded and transmitted, often via social media such as YouTube. She acknowledges that those who cannot attend performances will benefit from this digital access, but she experiences a sense of distance from the wairua (spirit, soul) of the performers when watching recordings. This raises a second issue related to the digital capture of indigenous culture for preservation and sustainability purposes - the extent to which they can truly reproduce the essence of the cultural artefact or practice. 37% of respondents in the study of the digitization of te reo Māori resources mentioned above, felt that digitization has a negative impact on the wairua of the item digitized [31]. While digital technologies can undoubtably enable indigenous communities to produce and communicate their culture in new ways, they do not necessarily fit well with traditional indigenous practices [37]. Spatiality is a significant attribute in stories and cultural practices [37], providing context for interpretation that may be missing in a digital format. The Arataki app with its blending of audio, video, images and text within the landscape attempts to provide a more authentic transfer of indigenous culture, although the extent to which digital solutions and sharing can ever provide satisfactory support for the sustainability for cultures predicated on oral traditions remains problematic.

4.3   Consultation

The discussions of ownership and control lead naturally to a consideration of the importance of consultation, participation and partnership in any efforts to make indigenous culture digitally available for sustainability purposes. The importance of involving indigenous community members in the creation and curation of any digital representation, and thereby recontextualization, of their cultural heritage and knowledge is clear. The development of specific protocols to protect digitized indigenous culture and guide practice in cultural heritage institutions is now established practice but the representation of indigenous culture through digital technology more broadly is generally uncontrolled and perhaps uncontrollable.

While both NZETC and developers of the Arataki app consulted widely with appropriate indigenous communities' representatives and stakeholders, the open nature of content creation on the internet means that this consultation is not possible for all expressions of indigenous culture made available digitally. Social media, for example, are not regulated by cultural custom [38] and while they can help indigenous people connect or reconnect with their culture, questions remain about the extent to which these media reproduce and strengthen culture as opposed to just facilitating connections and conversations [19].

5   Conclusion

Digital technologies can promote indigenous cultural sustainability by increasing access to tangible and intangible culture and encouraging active engagement and collaboration, especially for those members of indigenous communities unable to experience them in person [17–19]. As the case studies and other examples presented above demonstrate, technology, when used appropriately and when controlled by indigenous peoples themselves, can strengthen and disseminate important aspects of material and immaterial indigenous culture thus supporting their sustainability. Digital capture, preservation and sharing means that important elements of indigenous cultures can be passed on to future generations and have a key educative role for those both within and outside the community. Issues relating to ownership, control and consultation remain, however, and there are also other points to consider that could not be considered in depth in this paper due to its short format. There is, for example, a question about the impact of digital cultural content and practices for those cultures that have traditionally emphasized the importance of in-person and face-to-face communication and transmission of cultural norms and values. The issue of how technology may change some cultural practices is briefly touched on above and we need to consider how the capture and sharing of some indigenous cultural knowledge and practice via technology impacts on cultures predicated on oral traditions. Similarly, the digital representation of individual examples of indigenous culture can divorce them from their holistic context and give the impression that indigenous culture is static rather than a dynamic, evolving concept. Allied to this is the idea that indigenous peoples are creators and innovators of digital culture, not just consumers. While the examples provided in this paper are primarily from an Aotearoa New Zealand perspective, we know that colleagues and researchers around the world have experience of similar developments in other cultural contexts. Strathman [39], for example, discusses the issues that have arisen with some notable indigenous digital cultural heritage collaborative projects in Australia, Mexico, USA and Canada. She noted challenges related to software, security and financial sustainability which were not the focus of this paper but are additional considerations. We are eager to explore the issues raised in this paper and others on a wider basis to gain an understanding of how indigenous communities incorporate and apply ICTs for cultural sustainability on their own terms.

References

1. United Nations: Sustainable development goals. https://www.un.org/sustainabledevelopment/sustainable-development-goals/. Accessed 28 Aug 2019
2. Vlassis, A.: Culture in the post-2015 development agenda: the anatomy of an international mobilisation. Third World Q. **36**(9), 1649–1662 (2015)
3. Dockery, A.M.: Culture and wellbeing: the case of Indigenous Australians. Soc. Indic. Res. **99**(2), 315–332 (2010)
4. O'Connor, D.E.: Encyclopedia of the Global Economy. A Guide for Students and Researchers, p. 391. Academic Foundation, Westport (2006)
5. Roy, L., Chen, H., Cherian, A., Tuiono, T.: The relationship of technology, culture, and demography. In: Voogt, J., Knezek, G., (eds.) International Handbook of Information Technology in Primary and Secondary Education. Springer International Handbook of Information Technology in Primary and Secondary Education, vol. 20. Springer, Boston (2008). https://doi.org/10.1007/978-0-387-73315-9_48
6. Eriksen, T.H.: Small Places, Large Issues: An Introduction to Social and Cultural Anthropology. Pluto Press, London (2001)
7. Hill, L.L.: Indigenous culture: both malleable and valuable. J. Cult. Herit. Manage. Sustain. Dev. **1**(2), 122–134 (2011)
8. United Nations: Department of Economic and Social Affairs. Indigenous Peoples: Culture. https://www.un.org/development/desa/indigenouspeoples/mandated-areas1/culture.html. Accessed 28 Aug 2019
9. Throsby, D.: Linking ecological and cultural sustainability. Int. J. Divers. Organ. Communities Nations **8**(1), 15–20 (2008)
10. O'Connor, D.E.: Encyclopedia of the Global Economy. A Guide for Students and Researchers. Academic Foundation, Westport (2006)
11. Varan, D.: The cultural erosion metaphor and the transcultural impact of media systems. J. Commun. **48**(2), 58–85 (1998)
12. Resta, P.: ICTs and indigenous people. https://iite.unesco.org/files/policy_briefs/pdf/en/indigenous_people.pdf. Accessed 28 Aug 2019
13. Gill, S.S., Talib, A.T., Khong, C.Y., Kunasekaran, P.: Exploring the role of resources in ethnic minorities' adoption of information and communication technology in preserving their cultural identity in Malaysia. Asian Cult. Hist. **8**(1), 69–75 (2016)

14. Hunter, J., Koopman, B., Sledge, J.: Software tools for Indigenous knowledge management. In: Museums and the web (2003). https://files.eric.ed.gov/fulltext/ED482117.pdf. Accessed 28 Aug 2019
15. Forbes, M.: US arts website removes Māori images. Radio New Zealand National website (2016). https://www.rnz.co.nz/news/te-manu-korihi/306968/us-arts-website-removes-maori-images. Accessed 28 Aug 2019
16. Srinivasan, R.: Indigenous, ethnic and cultural articulations of new media. Int. J. Cult. Stud. 9(4), 497–518 (2006)
17. Dyson, L.E.: Cultural issues in the adoption of information and communication technologies by Indigenous Australians. In: Proceedings Cultural Attitudes Towards Communication and Technology, Murdoch University, Perth, pp. 58–71 (2004)
18. Botangen, K.A., Vodanovich, S., Yu, J.: Preservation of Indigenous culture among Indigenous migrants through social media: the Igorot peoples. In: Proceedings of the 50th Hawaii International Conference on System Sciences (2017)
19. O'Carroll, A.D.: Māori identity construction in SNS. Int. J. Crit. Indigenous Stud. 6(2), 2–16 (2013)
20. Stats NZ: Major ethnic groups in New Zealand (2019). https://www.stats.govt.nz/infographics/major-ethnic-groups-in-new-zealand. Accessed 21 Nov 2019
21. Ka'ai-Mahuta, R.: The impact of colonisation on te reo Māori: A critical review of the State education system. Te Kaharoa 4(1), 195–225 (2011). https://doi.org/10.24135/tekaharoa.v4i1.117. Accessed 28 Feb 2020
22. Te Ara. https://teara.govt.nz/en/maori/page-4. Accessed 21 Nov 2019
23. Education Central. https://educationcentral.co.nz/unprecedented-demand-for-te-reo-maori-classes/. Accessed 21 Nov 2019
24. NZETC. http://nzetc.victoria.ac.nz/. Accessed 21 Nov 2019
25. Callaghan, S., Stevenson, A.: "Moko; or Maori tattooing" project: a report on consultation. http://nzetc.victoria.ac.nz/tm/scholarly/tei-MokoDiscussionPaper.html. Accessed 21 Nov 2019
26. Poutama. Arataki Cultural Trails. https://poutama.co.nz/arataki-cultural-trails/. Accessed 21 Nov 2019
27. Metge, J.: Time & the art of Maori storytelling. J. New Zealand Stud. 8(1), 2324–3740 (1999)
28. Stevenson, A., Callaghan, S:. Digitisation and Matauranga Maori (2008). http://researcharchive.vuw.ac.nz/handle/10063/608. Accessed 21 Nov 2019
29. Simpson, T.: Claims of indigenous peoples to cultural property in Canada, Australia, and New Zealand. Hastings Int'l Comp. L. Rev. 18, 195–221 (1994)
30. Ngata, W., Ngata-Gibson, H., Salmond, A.: Te Ataakura: Digital taonga and cultural innovation. J. Mater. Cult. 17(3), 229–244 (2012)
31. Crookston, M., Oliver, G., Tikao, A., Diamond, P., Liew, C.L., Douglas, S.L.: Kōrero Kitea: Ngā hua o te whakamamatitanga: the impact of digitised te reo archival collections (2016). https://interparestrust.org/assets/public/dissemination/Korerokiteareport_final.pdf. Accessed 21 Nov 2019
32. Ihimaera, W.: A Maori perspective. JNZL: J. New Zealand Lit. 9, 53–55 (1991)
33. Winter, J., Boudreau, J.: Supporting self-determined Indigenous innovations: Rethinking the digital divide in Canada. Technol. Innov. Manage. Rev. 8(2), 38–48 (2018)
34. Wyeld, T.G., Leavy, B., Carroll, J., Gibbons, C., Ledwich, B., Hills, J.: The ethics of indigenous storytelling: using the torque game engine to support Australian aboriginal cultural heritage. In: DiGRA Conference (2007)
35. Nakata, M., Byrne, A., Nakata, V., Gardiner, G.: Indigenous knowledge, the library and information service sector, and protocols. Aust. Acad. Res. Libr. 36(2), 7–21 (2005)

36. Papesch, T.R.B.: Creating a modern Maori identity through Kapa Haka (2015). https://ir. canterbury.ac.nz/handle/10092/11263
37. Rodil, K., Winschiers-Theophilus, H.: Indigenous storytelling in Namibia: sketching concepts for digitization. In: 2015 International Conference on Culture and Computing (Culture Computing), pp. 80–86. IEEE, October 2015
38. Brown, D., Nicholas, G.: Protecting indigenous cultural property in the age of digital democracy: institutional and communal responses to Canadian first nations and Māori heritage concerns. J. Mater. Cult. **17**(3), 307–324 (2012)
39. Strathman, N.: Digitizing the ancestors: issues in indigenous digital heritage projects. Int. J. Commun. **13**, 18 (2019)

Perceptions of AR4D Researchers on Documentation of Agricultural Indigenous Knowledge in Uganda

Christine Kiconco[(✉)] and Constant Okello-Obura

East African School of Library and Information Science, College of Computing
and Information Sciences, Makerere University, Kampala, Uganda
christinah.kiconco@gmail.com, obura2007@gmail.com

Abstract. This paper reports preliminary findings from a Doctoral study on Agricultural Indigenous Knowledge (AIK) in Agricultural Research for Development (AR4D) Organizations. AIK is increasingly recognized as an important resource that should be harnessed for agricultural development. However, lack of formal documentation of AIK poses a great risk of its possible extinction. There is also lack of interest in AIK by AR4D researchers [1–3] which could be due to negative perceptions. However, no study has explored AR4D researchers' perceptions of AIK and how they influence their attitude towards AIK documentation. The study therefore examined the relationship between perceptions and AIK documentation among AR4D researchers in AR4D organizations in Uganda. A mixed methods approach with a cross-sectional survey design was employed to collect data across all nine Zonal Agricultural Research and Development Institutes (ZARDIs). The population was 149 from which a sample of 103 was determined based on Krejcie and Morgan (see pg.4). Of the 103 respondents randomly selected to participate in the survey, so far, 78 had filled the online questionnaire giving a response rate of 76%. Of 9 Research Directors purposively selected to participate in face-to-face interviews, 4 had been obtained. Survey data was analyzed using SPSS while interview data content analysis was done. Preliminary results revealed a positive attitude towards AIK among Research Directors while majority AR4D researchers showed less interest in AIK. Correlations between perceptions and AIK documentation were significant implying that perceptions of AIK determine attitude towards AIK documentation.

Keywords: Perceptions · Documentation · Agricultural Indigenous Knowledge · AR4D researchers

1 Introduction

The term Agricultural indigenous knowledge is defined by [4] as a collection of theoretical, declarative, procedural and dynamic understandings of the natural and social aspects of agricultural production. AIK is variously labelled as local knowledge, traditional ecological knowledge, indigenous technical knowledge (ITK) or traditional environmental knowledge [5–7] to refer to the knowledge that is not acquired from

A. Sundqvist et al. (Eds.): iConference 2020, LNCS 12051, pp. 76–87, 2020.
https://doi.org/10.1007/978-3-030-43687-2_6

formal learning. Agricultural Indigenous Knowledge (AIK) in this study therefore is used interchangeably with Indigenous Technical Knowledge (ITK) to mean the same thing. Although AIK has for many generations survived through oral tradition with no written documents for recording and dissemination [8], the rapid changes in modern society pose serious threats to AIK survival. Documenting AIK presents numerous benefits to society including organization and preservation for future generations, collaboration and partnerships among a broad range of actors, educational uses as well as integration into development programs [9–12]. According to [9], documentation is primarily a process in which traditional knowledge is identified, recorded and organized as a means to dynamically maintain, manage, use, disseminate and/or protect the knowledge. However, negative perceptions of this knowledge within the scientific community today, seem to have resulted in a lack of interest in its documentation. According to Cambridge Dictionary, [13] perception is a belief, attitude or opinion held by many people based on appearances.

For decades, lack of interest in AIK has been associated with the 19th century negative attitudes towards western knowledge which contributes to the neglect of AIK in development programs [14]. Although in Africa, AIK remains one of the most valuable resources owned by rural people, it has also been the least mobilized for sustainable development [15]. Studies such as that of [16] reveals that development experts are generally dismissive of AIK in relation to conventional knowledge and technologies to which [17] identifies as negative perceptions. Similarly, [18] indicates that AIK is inhibited by perceptions, attitudes and belief systems. On the other hand, [19] argues that people who use indigenous knowledge are associated with poverty, backwardness and superstitions. Perhaps this is the reason why AIK is not given sufficient attention in development programs.

1.1   Uganda's Context

Uganda is endowed with 65 indigenous communities each with its unique cultural values, beliefs, practices and heritage [20]. This diversity contributes to a wealth of AIK [21]. AIK offers many problem solving strategies for rural farmers to cope with rapid changes in the environment including climate change, crop and animal pests and diseases [22–24], loss of soil fertility [22–24], weather prediction [3, 25, 26] preservation of food [22, 27] among others. Indeed, [28] recommends that such AIK practices should be promoted in development endeavors. Unfortunately, AIKs in Uganda are disappearing at an alarming rate without much effort to document them [25, 29–33]. The threats to AIK loss are more perturbing as the country has the youngest population in the world [34, 35]. This means that as an elder dies, AIK is lost. Similarly, majority of AIK holders are illiterate with limited use of modern ICTs [1, 36, 37]. Unless efforts are made to document AIK in formal settings, this valuable knowledge may be lost forever.

Although, Uganda recognizes the value of AIK through a policy framework [21, 38, 39], development experts have not paid much attention to AIK documentation. For instance, the Kampala Declaration7 on Indigenous Knowledge for Sustainable Development [39] urges the National Agricultural Research Organization (NARO) to spearhead the identification, documentation and sharing of AIK for benefits to the society [39, 40]. NARO is the apex body for guidance and coordination of all agricultural research activities in Uganda's National Agricultural Research System [40, 41]. NARO does this through its sixteen Public Agricultural Research Institutes (PARIs); seven National Research Institutes (NARIs) and nine Zonal Agricultural Research and Development Institutes (ZARDIs). ZARDIs carry out both applied and adaptive research for specific ecological zones to directly benefit farmers at the grassroots. Even though, ZARDIs' research programs often involve the use of farmers' AIK practices that generate new knowledge, their efforts to systematically document AIK remain obscure [41, 42]. Previous research reveals that, agricultural researchers were generally dismissive of AIK [2, 23] which [33] associates with negative perceptions. The study therefore sought to examine the relationship between perceptions and AIK documentation among AR4D researchers in NARO ZARDIs in Uganda.

1.2   Research Questions

1. How do AR4D researchers perceive AIK?
2. What is the relationship between AR4D researchers' perceptions of AIK and AIK documentation?
3. What challenges affect AIK documentation efforts in AR4D organizations in Uganda?

Research Hypothesis [H0]: There is no relationship between perceptions and AIK documentation. The null hypothesis is tested at 0.05 level of significance.

2   Methodology

2.1   Study Design

A cross-sectional study design was used to investigate the relationship between perceptions and AIK documentation in an AR4D organization in Uganda. The study utilized both qualitative and quantitative methods and tools.

2.2   Study Setting

The study was conducted in ZARDIs which are 9 of the 16 Public Research Institutes of National Agricultural Research Organization [40]. The choice of ZARDIs was based on their mandate and strategic positioning across the country mainly in rural settings where they are positioned to address agricultural problems at the grassroots. ZARDIs are indicated by red circles on the map below (Fig. 1).

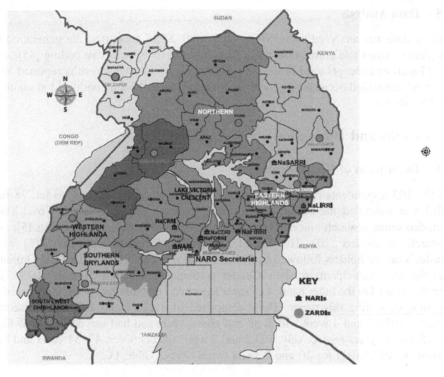

Fig. 1. Above shows the location of ZARDIs across Uganda. Retrieved from: https://www.naro. go.ug/

2.3 Population and Sampling

The study population was 149 AR4D researchers comprising of Senior Research Officers, Research Officers, Research Assistants and Research Technicians. A corresponding sample size of 103 was determined based on Krejcie and Morgan sample table. According to [43], the sample size equivalent to 149 is 103. To avoid bias, 103 was divided by 9 ZARDIs to include all in the sample. As such, 11 AR4D researchers were randomly selected from each ZARDI to participate in a survey totaling to 103. On the other hand, all 9 Research Directors of the 9 ZARDIs were purposively selected to participate in face-to-face interviews on the basis on their position as top managers.

2.4 Data Capture Procedure

Survey data were collected from AR4D researchers using an online self-administered questionnaire submitted through Google forms. The questionnaire was based on a four-point Likert scale anchored on: strongly disagree (0) to strongly agree (3). In addition, a face-to-face interview with the help of an interview guide was used to collect qualitative data from Research Directors.

2.5 Data Analysis

Survey data was analyzed using SPSS version 20. SPSS supported the generation of frequency counts and correlations [44]. Content analysis by selective coding [45], was used based on concepts used in the survey. Preliminary interview results reported here were not quantified because only 4 of the 9 interviews had been conducted at the time of this paper.

3 Results and Discussion

3.1 Description of Respondents

Of the 103 respondents randomly selected to participate in the survey, so far, 78 had filled and submitted the online questionnaire giving a response rate of 76%. They included senior research officers (16); research officers (37); research assistants (5); and research technicians (20). The largest percentage of respondents 42 (54%) were Master's degree holders followed by PhD 16 (21%), Bachelors 14 (18%) and Diploma had the least participants 6 (8%). Gender participation entailed 54 male (69%), 24 female (21%). On the other hand, 4 of the 9 Research Directors had been interviewed at the time of writing this paper. These comprised of 3 males and 1 female. Research Director (RD) 1 and 4 were within 55 and above years and had served in AR4D field for 15 and 18 years respectively. RD 2 and 3 were aged between 47–54 years and had served in AR4D field for 10 and 7 years respectively (Table 1).

Table 1. Below shows the categories of participants

Particulars of respondents		Frequency	Percent	Cumulative percent
Gender of respondents	Male	54	69.2	69.2
	Female	24	30.8	100.0
	Total	78	100.0	
Age of respondents	23–30	5	6.4	6.4
	31–38	27	34.6	41.0
	39–46	33	42.3	83.3
	47–54	11	14.1	97.4
	55 and above	2	2.6	100.0
	Total	78	100.0	
Level of education	PhD	16	20.5	20.5
	Masters	42	53.8	74.4
	Bachelors	14	17.9	92.3
	Diploma	6	7.7	100.0
	Total	78	100.0	
Job title	Senior research officer	16	20.5	20.5
	Research officer	37	47.4	67.9
	Research assistant	5	6.4	74.4
	Research technician	20	25.6	100.0
	Total	78	100.0	

(*continued*)

Table 1. (*continued*)

Particulars of respondents		Frequency	Percent	Cumulative percent
Number of years in AR4D field	0–3	9	11.5	11.5
	4–6	21	26.9	38.5
	7–10	29	37.2	75.6
	11–13	11	14.1	89.7
	14–16	3	3.8	93.6
	17–20	2	2.6	96.2
	24–26	3	3.8	100.0
	Total	78	100.0	

3.2   Perceptions of AIK Among AR4D Researchers

Question 1 sought to establish AR4D researchers' perceptions of AIK. Results from the survey revealed the following:

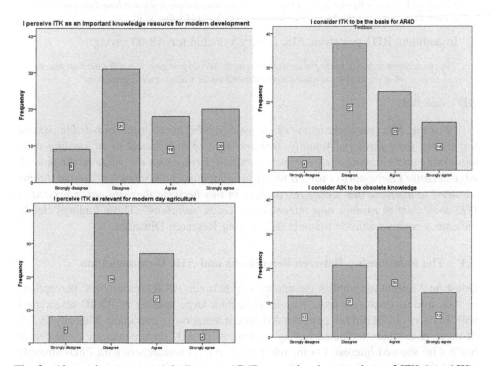

Fig. 2. Above shows grouped findings on AR4D researchers' perceptions of ITK (see AIK). Source: Field data

Results in Fig. 2 above, reveal negative attitudes towards AIK among AR4D researchers. Majority 31 (40%) did not perceive AIK as important while 20 (26%) strongly agreed. On relevance, 39 (50%) did not perceive AIK as relevant compared to 27 (35%) that agreed. In regards to AIK as basis for AR4D, 37 (47%) disagreed while 23 (30%) agreed. On the perception that AIK is obsolete knowledge, 32 (41%) agreed compared to 21 (27%) that disagreed. This finding agrees with that of [14] that indigenous knowledge is unproductive, irrelevant and backward perhaps why that development experts are generally dismissive of AIK in relation to conventional knowledge.

Results from interviews with four Research Directors on the hand revealed an appreciation of AIK as a very important knowledge resource for AR4D. For instance; RD1 said that:

"ITK (see AIK) is very important; it forms the basis for our research. It works for farmers and has been for a very long time. You see, new initiatives we scientists are getting come from local knowledge".

Similarly, RD2 said that:

"I consider ITK very useful for our research activities. We take advantage of what is already existing with farmers though it is not the focus. You know, we are a science based organization, so even though we get the knowledge from farmers, we add value to it".

In addition, RD3 perceived AIK as very valuable for AR4D saying:

"This local knowledge is basis for modern research. We do not give it much attention but we realize it is what rural communities largely depend on to sustain their agriculture".

RD4 said that:

"For me, ITK is a cornerstone of our research because all the knowledge that we test comes from farmers. Actually, farmers have often accused us of stealing their knowledge and claiming it as our own initiative. I recognize the value of this knowledge because I have always used it on my farm together with science of course. I think we need to motivate our young researchers in this because they are not interested in ITK, they want to explore new interesting scientific solutions". These findings clearly indicate a positive attitude towards AIK among Research Directors.

3.3   The Relationship Between Perceptions and AIK Documentation

Question 2 sought to establish the relationship between AR4D researchers' perceptions of AIK and its documentation. Results indicate a large number of AR4D researchers with Masters (75%) did not consider AIK documentation as important. Majority 59.0% of these researchers indicated having no interest in AIK documentation compared to 6.4% who showed interest. On the other hand, AR4D researchers with PhDs strongly agreed that AIK was important. This agrees with results from interviews in which all Research Directors (PhDs) also perceived AIK as important. For instance, RD3 explained that:

"Though we have come to realize that AIK is valuable to us, no deliberate efforts had been made to document AIK at my institute. We tend to consider AIK as means to an end".

Similarly, RD4 said that:

"I feel that ITK should be documented because knowledgeable people die with the knowledge". This shows a positive attitude towards AIK documentation.

A null hypothesis was tested using Pearson correlation coefficient. Pearson correlation test is a relevant test for continuous variables. As such, it was deemed relevant because initially categorical data based on Lickert scale (interval) was used to generate composite mean indexes that became continuous variables (Table 2).

Table 2. Pearson correlation showing relationship between perception and AIK documentation.

	Perceptions	Documentation
Perceptions		.504**
		.000
Documentation	.504**	
	.000	
No of respondents	78	78

**. Correlation is significant at the 0.01 level (2-tailed).

The result in the table above reveals a significant relationship between perception and AIK documentation ($r = 0.504$; $p < 0.01$). The null hypothesis is rejected. This implies that an AR4D researcher's perception of AIK influences his/her attitude towards its documentation. A researcher with a positive perception of AIK will have a positive attitude towards AIK documentation.

3.4 Challenges to AIK Documentation in AR4D Organizations in Uganda

Question 3 sought to establish the challenges to AIK documentation. Results show lack of proper coordination of AIK documentation efforts as the greatest challenge (97%). Lack of ITK unit to coordinate documentation came second (96%). Inadequate modern ICT tools for ITK documentation (94%), Negative attitudes towards traditional knowledge (91%), Lack of training on how to document ITK (90%), Lack of guidelines on standard formats for ITK capture and Lack of awareness of Intellectual property rights relating to ITK documentation both scored (85%), Lack of financial capacity to sustain long term ITK documentation projects (81%), Institutional policy does not provide clear guidelines on ITK documentation (71%), Lack of motivation for indigenous knowledge (69%), Poor recognition of ITK (64%), Language barrier (56%), Lack of knowledge management expert to provide guidance on ITK documentation and Inadequate staff capacity for long term ITK projects scored (53%). On the other hand, Lack of trust limiting AIK acquisition was not considered a challenge as (50%) disagreed compared to (46%) that agreed. Although literature search could not find any study on AIK in AR4D organizations, the above findings relate to those of [37].

4 Discussion

Findings from interviews revealed an appreciation of AIK as an important resource for AR4D. Similarly, results from the survey show that AR4D researchers with PhD perceived AIK as important. Contrary, majority of AR4D researchers with Masters perceived AIK as less important. These researchers' age fall between 20–38 years. This implies that older AR4D researchers appreciate AIK unlike the young researchers. This finding agrees with previous studies such as [33, 46]. On feelings regarding AIK documentation, all interviewed admitted that, though they understood the importance of AIK, no deliberate efforts had been made to systematically document it. Similarly, majority 50% strongly agreed that no deliberate efforts had been made to document AIK in their ZARDIs. Generally, majority 50% strongly agreed that deliberate efforts should be made to document AIK in ZARDIs compared to 8% that disagreed. It was further revealed that AIK was not a priority in ZARDIs' research agenda perhaps the reason why they had not implemented projects for documenting AIK. This perhaps could be due to the policy environment that does not clearly provide for AIK documentation. However, it was acknowledged that ZARDIs are strategically positioned to document AIK. Majority 60% strongly agreed that their ZARDIs are strategically positioned to document AIK. Findings from interviews were in agreement empathizing that ZARDIs should take on the responsibility for AIK documentation. Findings revealed a strong relationship between perceptions and AIK documentation. Correlations between perceptions and AIK documentation were significant. The null hypothesis was rejected which implies that AR4D researchers' perceptions of AIK determine their attitude towards AIK documentation.

5 Conclusion and Recommendations

AIK is an important knowledge resource that urgently needs to be systematically documented before extinction. Findings from the study clearly show a strong relationship between perception and AIK documentation. AIK was perceived as important among Research Directors. However, majority young researchers showed less interest in AIK. ZARDIs have a lot of potential to document AIK due to their strategic positioning across the country majorly in rural settings where they are in direct physical contact with rural farmers at the grassroots. The challenge remains that AIK is not a priority in ZARDIs' research agenda. This calls for realignment of government policies and where necessary support the documentation, management and integration of AIK into AR4D. This is likely to increase appreciation of AIK especially among young researchers. It is therefore important that NARO works closely with its ZARDIs to establish AIK units that can identify and document AIK in a systematic manner. It is incumbent upon NARO and its ZARDIs to work together and adopt best AIK documentation practices that make it possible for AIK to be accessible for today's development and the future.

References

1. Aluma, J.R.: Integration of indigenous knowledge (IK) in agriculture and health development processes in Uganda. Uganda J. Agric. Sci. **42**(3), 11–14 (2010)
2. Lusembo, P., Kabanyoro, R., Akello, B., Fernandez, M., Sebaganzi, R.: Testing alternative approaches for research and development in Uganda: the experience of Mukono Agricultural Research and Development Centre (ARDC). Afr. Crop Sci. Conf. Proc. **7**, 1315–1319 (2005)
3. Aluma, J.R.W., Akwang, A.A., Mwesigwa, V.T.: Report on Integrating Indigenous Knowledge (IK) in Agricultural Research Workshop. NARO, Kampala (2001)
4. Wall, C.R.L.: Knowledge management in rural Uzbekistan: peasant, project and post-socialist perspectives in Khorezm (2006)
5. Masinde, M., Bagula, A.: ITIKI: bridge between African indigenous knowledge and modern science of drought prediction. Knowl. Manag. Dev. J. **7**(3), 274–290 (2011)
6. Soh, M.B.C., Omar, S.K.: Small is big: the charms of indigenous knowledge for sustainable livelihood. Procedia-Soc. Behav. Sci. **36**, 602–610 (2012)
7. WIPO. Traditional knowledge – operational terms and definitions: Intergovernmental Committee on Intellectual Property and Genetic Resources, Traditional Knowledge and Folklore. Geneva (2010)
8. Lodhi, S., Mikulecky, P.: Management of indigenous knowledge for developing countries. Commun. Manag. Technol. Innov. Acad. Glob. **5**, 94–98 (2010)
9. WIPO, "Documenting traditional knowledge: A toolkit." WIPO (2017)
10. Kaniki, A.M., Mphahlele, M.K.: Indigenous knowledge for the benefit of all: can knowledge management principles be used effectively? South Afr. J. Libr. Inf. Sci. **68**(1), 1–15 (2013)
11. Egeru, A.: Role of indigenous knowledge in climate change adaptation: a case study of the Teso Sub-Region, Eastern Uganda. Indian J. Trad. Knowl. **11**(2), 217–224 (2012)
12. Koohafkan, P., Altieri, M.A.: Globally important agricultural heritage systems: a legacy for the future. Food and Agriculture Organization of the United Nations, Rome (2011)
13. Cambridge Dictionary, "Perception defined" (2019)
14. Agrawal, A.: Indigenous and scientific knowledge: some critical comments. Antropologi Indonesia (2014)
15. Maunganidze, L.: A moral compass that slipped: Indigenous knowledge systems and rural development in Zimbabwe. Cogent Soc. Sci. **2**(1), 1266749 (2016)
16. Moyo, B.H.Z.: The use and role of indigenous knowledge in small-scale agricultural systems in Africa: the case of farmers in Northern Malawi. University of Glasgow, Glasgow (2010)
17. Sinha, B.: An appraisal of the traditional post-harvest pest management methods in Northeast Indian uplands. Indian J. Trad. Knowl. **9**(3), 536–543 (2010)
18. Meyer, H.W.: The influence of information behavior on information sharing across cultural boundaries in development contexts. Inf. Res. Int. Electron. J. **14**(1), 1–13 (2009)
19. Ponge, A.: Integrating indigenous knowledge for food security: perspectives from the millennium village project at Bar-Sauri in Nyanza Province in Kenya. In: International Conference on Enhancing Food Security in the Eastern and Horn of Africa regions, 2011, Kampala, Uganda, pp. 16–17 (2011)
20. Uganda Government: National Development Plan (NDPII). Uganda Government, Kampala (2015)
21. MGLSD, "Uganda National Culture Policy." Ministry of Gender, Labour and Social Development (MGLSD) (2006)
22. Haumba, E.N., Kaddu, S.: Documenting and disseminating agricultural indigenous knowledge for sustainable food security in Uganda. Univ. Dare-s-Salaam Libr. J. **12**(1), 66–86 (2017)

23. Unger, J.: Evaluation of local knowledge applied by farmers towards management of crop pests and diseases in the Masaka region, Uganda (2014)
24. Akullo, D., Kanzikwera, R., Birungi, P., Alum, W., Aliguma, L., Barwogeza, M.: Indigenous knowledge in agriculture: a case study of the challenges in sharing knowledge of past generations in a globalized context in Uganda. In: World Library and Information Congress: 73rd IFLA General Conference, Durban, South Africa, pp. 19–23 (2007)
25. Haumba, E.: Challenges of Documenting and Disseminating Agricultural Indigenous Knowledge for Sustainable Food Security in Soroti District. Makerere University, Kampala (2015)
26. Mutasa, M.: Knowledge apartheid in disaster risk management discourse: Is marrying indigenous and scientific knowledge the missing link?" Jamba: Journal of Disaster Risk Studies 7(1), 1–10 (2015)
27. Tweheyo, R.: Indigenous knowledge and food security: enhancing decisions of rural farmers. University of Groningen, Groningen (2018)
28. Asogwa, I.S., Okoye, J.I., Oni, K.: Promotion of indigenous food preservation and processing knowledge and the challenge of food security in Africa. J. Food Secur. 5(1), 75–87 (2017)
29. Okello-Obura, C.: Documenting agricultural indigenous knowledge and provision of access through Online Database platform. Library Philosophy & Practice (2018)
30. Openjuru, G.L.: Indigenous Knowledge, pp. 17–35. Sense Publishers, Rotterdam (2017)
31. Green, D., Raygorodetsky, G.: Indigenous knowledge of a changing climate. Clim. Change 100(2), 239–242 (2010)
32. Orlove, B., Roncoli, C., Kabugo, M., Majugu, A.: Indigenous climate knowledge in southern Uganda: the multiple components of a dynamic regional system. Clim. Change 100(2), 243–265 (2010)
33. Agea, J.G., Lugangwa, E., Obua, J., Kambugu, R.K.: Role of indigenous knowledge in enhancing household food security: a case study of Mukungwe, Masaka District, Central Uganda. Indilinga Afr. J. Indig. Knowl. Syst. 7(1), 64–71 (2008)
34. NPA, Uganda Vision 2040. National Planning Authority (NPA), Kampala, Uganda (2013)
35. UBOS, "Statistical abstract" (2012)
36. Naanyu, M.: Integration of indigenous knowledge with information and communication technologies in coping with effects of climate change and variability on agriculture in Kajiado County, Kenya. University of Nairobi, Kenya (2013)
37. Lwoga, E.T., Ngulube, P., Stilwell, C.: Challenges of managing indigenous knowledge with other knowledge systems for agricultural growth in sub-Saharan Africa. Libri 61(3), 226–238 (2011)
38. Ajayi, O.C., Mafongoya, P.L. (eds.): Indigenous Knowledge Systems and Climate Change Management in Africa. Technical Center for Agricultural and Rural Cooperation (CTA), Wageningen (2017)
39. Gorjestani, N.: Indigenous knowledge for development. Protecting AND Promoting Traditional Knowledge: Systems, National Experiences AND International Dimensions, p. 265 (2004)
40. NARO, "NARO annual report 2016/17," NARO, Enteebe, Uganda (2017)
41. NARO, "NARO training policy," Poilcy (2011)
42. Mbigidde, V.A., Kashaija, I.N., Mugwanya, B.Z.: Strengthening communication and knowledge management for increased agricultural productivity: a Ugandan case study. In: Fifth African Higher Education Week and RUFORUM Biennial Conference 2016, Linking Agricultural Universities with Civil Society, the Private Sector, Governments and Other Stakeholders in Support of Agricultural Development in Africa, pp. 385–393. RUFORUM (2016)

43. Krejcie, R.V., Morgan, D.W.: Determining sample size for research activities. Educ. Psychol. Measur. **30**(3), 607–610 (1970)
44. Pickard, A.J.: Research Methods in Information. Facet publishing, London (2013)
45. Flick, U.: Introducing Research Methodology: A Beginner's Guide to Doing a Research Project. Sage, Thousand Oaks (2015)
46. Mosissa, R., Jimma, W., Bekele, R.: Knowledge management strategy for indigenous knowledge on land use and agricultural development in Western Ethiopia. Univ. J. Agric. Res. **5**(1), 18–26 (2017)

Reimagining Small World: A Preliminary Model

Priya Kizhakkethil[(✉)] [iD]

University of North Texas, Denton, Texas, USA
priyakizhakkethil@my.unt.edu

Abstract. The concept of a small world was developed out of studies that looked at socio-economically and informationally poor communities, characterized by social types and social norms which constrain access to information. This paper presents a preliminary model of a reconceptualized small world, and associated concepts, designed to study a world whose members are not purposively seeking information nor is it informationally poor. The ongoing qualitative study covered by this paper, looks at a gendered online community, a diaspora small world, formed around a shared interest in reading and writing fan fiction and the spaces they occupy. Viewing small world and information ground as complementary constructs, early observations lend credence to the value in reconceptualizing small world from the perspective of information ground and vice versa.

Keywords: Diaspora · Small world · Fandom

1 Introduction

Globalization has resulted in the transnational movement of people creating diaspora communities, and in today's networked world, technology is used by these communities to stay in touch with not only friends and family but also, in many ways, as a tool to keep in touch with their cultural roots. Information and communication technologies enable the synchronous transnational participation in everyday life thereby altering the diasporic experience (Hegde 2016). Srinivasan and Pyati (2007) argued that diaspora information behavior should be studied within the dynamic contexts of globalization and diaspora. Most research on immigrant communities tend to focus on place-based scenarios, but Srinivasan and Pyati (2007) stated that online diasporic environments are equally important as their information environments tend to be more global and emphasized the need to study virtual diasporically mediated grounds such as diaspora web sites, including news sites, social networking sites, and chat room among others, as information grounds. Media plays an important role in the acculturation process of immigrants, and the host country's role in the same has been noted and studied (Raman and Harwood 2016; Dalisay 2012). Contemporary literature also notes the role played by home country or ethnic media in the process, especially for the provision of scripts which enable those in a diaspora to enact and embody their "ethnicity in a transnational, transmedia global culture" (Ramasubramaniam and Doshi 2017, p. 183). Migration can also be viewed as gendered journeys, and even though the migratory

A. Sundqvist et al. (Eds.): iConference 2020, LNCS 12051, pp. 88–95, 2020.
https://doi.org/10.1007/978-3-030-43687-2_7

flows of women are not new in human mobility history, women's perspectives and experiences and their increasing role and significance have been largely underestimated and underexplored, due to the problematic assumption that migration is overwhelmingly male (Kim 2013; Suman 2018). From an information science perspective, Kim (2016) noted the absence of interest in the personal lives of women, with most information studies concentrating on information behavior in work-related contexts. Pollak (2015) notes that in comparison to the overwhelming quantity of studies which look at information behavior in professional and formal contexts, very little is known about experience based and non-documentary information which can be found in informal or non-formal contexts including leisure.

Fan communities are not just consumers but produce cultural products which Busse (2017) describes as artistic works as well as cultural documents. The gendered nature of fan communities have been noted by multiple authors including Jenkins (2007) who views fandom as an imagined and an imaginative community. Long (2003) writing on women's book clubs, notes the need to look at reading as a social practice and how adopting a reader-centered model leads to the viewing of reading as a form of cultural practice and behavior that carries out "complex personal and social functions for those who engage in it" (p. 22). These sort of spaces may be needed by women as a place where their concerns can be vocalized, to chronicle the peculiarities of their lives, while expanding their cultural repertoires through "dialogue with narrative in books or from other women's lives, to name what delights or troubles them, to explore dissociations between what matters to them and the social strictures or ideological frameworks that fail in important ways to address them" (p. 219). This paper covers an ongoing (data collection stage) research study which looks at women belonging to the Indian diaspora and their participation in the leisure activity of fan fiction reading and writing, forming part of an online community. Long (2003) holds that reading groups may embody the concept of a deliberative space, a "counterhegemonic publics" (Fraser 1989, p. 167), riding the boundary between public and private sphere. These gendered diasporic environments which are "privately public and publicly private" (Papacharissi 2010, p. 142) can also be seen as online book clubs and as small worlds and have been termed as "virtual zenanas". A social or cultural practice seen across South Asia and across religions too, "zenana" refers to the part of a house or dwelling which belongs to girls and women. Viewing these virtual zenanas as a small world, it was felt reconceptualization of a small world is required for the purpose of the study. This paper is a continuation from the early stage of the study presented as a poster at the ASIS&T 2019 annual meeting (Kizhakkethil and Burnett 2019), and showcases a preliminary model along with some early observations.

2 Small World

The concept of small world is associated with the work of Elfreda Chatman in the Library and Information Science (LIS) world. The concept was used to study the everyday world of socio-economically and informationally poor communities and Chatman drew on the work of Alfred Schutz and Manfred Kochen among others in the use and development of the concept. These worlds were described by her as having a certain degree of predictability as far as everyday happenings are concerned and people are seen to share "physical and/or conceptual space within a common landscape of cultural meaning" (Chatman 2000, p. 3). Small world is defined as a "community of like-minded individuals who share coownership of social reality" (Chatman 1999, p. 213). The smallness of the world comes from the structuring and defining of daily activities by means of a set of social norms and behaviors specific to its localized context (Burnett and Jaeger 2011). The theory of normative behavior explicated the concept of small world in a full sense comprising the concepts of social type, social norms, world view and information behavior (Chatman 2000; Burnett et al. 2000). Observing that Chatman's work focuses on tightly bound small worlds where information from beyond its boundaries are rarely looked at, along with a failure to adequately account for the interactions that can take place between various small worlds and the broader society in which they exist, Burnett and Jaeger (2011) drew on the work of Juergen Habermas, especially the concepts of public sphere and life-world as explicated by him, and combined the same with the theory of normative behavior to build the theory of information worlds.

Chatman's functional sociology approach to her work has been noted by Savolainen (2008) and her small world concept along with its social norms and values also fits in with the model of 'homo soiologicus' which "explains action by pointing to collective norms and values, i.e., to rules which express a social 'ought'; social order is then guaranteed by a normative consensus" (Reckwitz 2002, p. 245). In a functional sociology approach the emphasis is placed on group specific norms and roles which can have the effect of constraining information seeking. Even though Chatman's studies show the importance of context, Savolainen (2008) avers that a broader view of information seeking should be adopted in today's times characterized by extensive and easily accessible networked resources and "increasing individualization characteristic of reflexive modernization" (p. 6). As a result people may be less prone to pressures induced by norms that can direct information seeking. The structural functional approach in sociology is associated with the work of Robert Merton and has been drawn on by Chatman especially the concept of insider-outsider. While Alfred Schutz was critical of the models of 'homo sociologicus' and 'homo economics' (Reckwitz 2002), whose work Chatman drew on in developing the small world concept. The applicability of the theory of normative behavior in studying virtual worlds was noted by Burnett et al. (2000) with normativity perceived in frequently asked questions (FAQs) that are posted in virtual spaces, as well as social types perceived in the world of feminist book sellers. But Worrall (2014) who used the theory of information world (the theory of normative behavior is a part of the same) in studying communities fostered by LibraryThing and Goodreads found that social ties played a larger role, more than social type, where "getting to know one another is more of a process of establishing social ties than socially typing others" (p. 209). Another thing noted in this study was a sense of community forged around common and shared interests and values.

2.1 Small World Reimagined

To describe a world which coalesces around a common interest, along with a common cultural background and in some cases a common experience of being part of a diaspora, the concept of small world is useful. But it is felt that a re-imagination, a reconceptualization of small world, especially a virtual one is required for the present study. The reason for this is, (1) the world being looked at is not informationally poor, (2) the people who populate this world are not explicitly looking for or seeking information, and (3) there is no organizational or institutional structure to impose order which could lead to the establishment of norms. It is felt that setting aside information (and information behavior), an attempt should be made to picture this world, to understand it as a context in which information is experienced and then identifying associated practices that surround such an experience (Kizhakkethil and Burnett 2019). As expressed by Chatman (1996), "the process of understanding begins with research that looks at their social environment and that defines information from their perspective" (p.205). Based on the researcher's observation and understanding of the world under study, and drawing on a review of relevant literature, a preliminary model of a small world is presented below (Fig. 1).

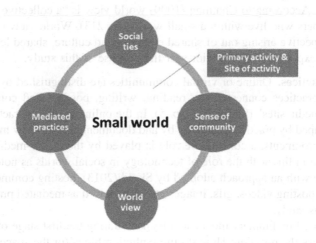

Fig. 1. Preliminary model of a small world with associated concepts.

The concepts listed below are seen as aspects or features of this reconceptualized preliminary model of a small world. These concepts would be used to guide the interpretation and analysis of qualitative data, while remaining open to themes that the data will present.

Primary Activity and Site of Activity. A small world is a social world and according to Strauss (1978), social worlds have one primary activity and a site(s) where these activities take place. This aspect of a social world is also in line with the concept of an information ground and is also characteristic of a third place as enunciated by Oldenburg (1999). Fisher and Naumer (2006) notes that people gather at an information ground for a primary instrumental purpose where social interaction can be seen as a primary activity, with information flow its by-product.

Social Ties. The establishment of connections through the process of interactions between people who share a common space is referred to as social ties. Engaging in common pursuits help people establish connections between each other and "feel part of a community-as-social-world" (Worrall 2014, p. 220).

Sense of Community. A sense of community is defined by McMillan and Chavis (1986) as having four elements. First is membership, defined as a "feeling of belonging or of sharing a sense of personal relatedness" (p. 9). Second is influence, defined as a "sense of mattering, of making a difference to a group and of the group mattering to its members" (p. 9). Third is reinforcement defined as "integration and fulfillment of needs" (p. 9). The fourth element is shared emotional connection which is "the commitment and belief that members have shared and will share history, common places, time together, and similar experiences" (p. 9). In a study using the concept of information grounds to look at Seattle's Polish community, it was found that social interactions led to the establishment of a sense of community and also in helping the maintaining of Polish ethnic identity (Fisher and Naumer 2006).

World View. According to Chatman (1999) world view is "a collective set of beliefs held by members who live within a small world" (p. 213). World view is defined as a common perspective arising out of shared ethnicity and culture, shared leisure interest, and even the experience of migration, for the purpose of this study.

Mediated Practices. Online or virtual communities are distinguished by the presence of mediated practices connected to "reading, writing, posting, and commenting via various new media sites" (Skold 2013, p. 5). In the online world, interactions between people are shaped by practices mediated by and documented in the new media ecology. In virtual environments, a constitutive role is played by these new-media documents, and this is also in line with the role of technology in social worlds as noted by Strauss (1978). In line with an approach adopted by Skold (2013), posting comments, replying to comments, posting videos, gifs, images etc., are viewed as mediated practices for the purpose of this study.

The proposed preliminary model will be used during the first stage of the research study to address the question: How do the fanfiction blogs (or the spaces afforded by them) form and function as a small world? The research population comprises of women belonging to the Indian diaspora and who are also fans of an Indian TV show titled "Iss Pyaar Ko Kya Naam Doon". Adopting a qualitative research approach, data in the form of comments posted on five fanfiction blogs (purposively sampled) and semi-structured interviews (at the time of writing this paper, fourteen (14) participants have been recruited and twelve (12) interviews have been completed) are been collected currently. Even though these works are in the public domain, following best ethical practices, no URLs to the fan work mentioned are provided, and any sort of identifiable information (like online ids) has been removed.

3   Early Observations

Initial observation of collected data, shows support for the concepts of the preliminary small world model, other than worldview. Reading and in some cases writing fan fiction is the primary activity of this small world and there are multiple sites in the form of blogs (based on popularity those hosted on Wordpress.com have been chosen for the study), where this activity takes place. Some authors/blog holders have separate tabs that act as places for general chats. In the blog hosting a story titled "Second chances", the author has posted this (Fig. 2):

Dear Friends

feel like chatting some more – more than the chapter posted? There is a

Chatter's corner now... find the link to it on top... ☺ Stories are like magpies –

they like forming sisterhood and sisterhood needs a corner for a good chat. ☺

Fig. 2. Example of the concept 'primary activity and site of activity'

This is very much in line with the concept of information ground where social interaction is seen as a primary activity. Social ties and a sense of community can be seen in comments like the one below (Fig. 3):

Anagha.. I too joined IF pretty late and missed journeys... But with this bunch... I have had

the pleasure to be of some real wonderful journeys.. Its like going on a pucnic with the

family.

The wait seems frustrating initially, but when you start interacting, you will love the wait

too.. Its like a train trip... Its most fun when we make friends with co-passengers ☻

Fig. 3. Example of the concepts 'social ties' and a 'sense of community'

A participant had this to say in her interview, indicative of social ties and a sense of community:

"In addition to reading mind-blowing work of the various authors, I have had the chance to interact with wonderful ladies whom I met in the virtual world. People from all walks of life seem to converge in this virtual world which I heard, is fondly called "Sapno Ki Duniya (SKD)" – the world of your dreams. True that. You are transported into a different world for some time. It is relaxing. And the interaction with fellow readers makes it all the more engaging."

Another participant who writes fan fiction and maintains blogs had this to say about the sense of comfort she feels in this small world, especially pointing to the gendered nature of the same:

"Kind of like being in a Co-ed school vs a girls school. I used to study in a Co-ed school where we were always on our guard. Talk a certain way, behave in a certain manner. When I joined

an all girls school later on, it was as though, suddenly there were no restrictions. It felt as though I had been let loose."

Mediated practices in the form of posting comments, liking comments, replying to comments, posting videos, images, gifs are in many ways what constitutes this small world. Strauss (1978) highlighted the role played by technology in a social world, which he described as "inherited or innovative modes of carrying out the social world's activities" (p. 122) and mediated practices as affordances of technology like the blogs themselves, could be seen in the same manner. Interactions that happen via these mediated practices result in the establishment of social ties and in engendering a sense of community. Practices like posting songs, images and gifs are also seen as a way of expressing one self. A participant who enjoys posting images and gifs had this to say:

"I am a strong believer of "A picture is worth a thousand words". Sometimes the point I am trying to make becomes more obvious when I use a pic/gif/song instead of writing it down."

From these early observations nothing has showed up to support the presence of a world view. Jenkins (2008) drawing on Cohen (1985) mentions that differences of opinion, world view and other fundamentals should be seen as normal and inevitable between members of a community. Membership in a community implies a sense of things which match and the "participation in a common symbolic domain" (p. 136) which does not mean either a "consensus of values or conformity in behavior" (p. 136). These ideas along with notions of social identity open up fascinating avenues to explore and world view as conceptualized by Chatman may not be a good fit in reconceptualizing small world.

4   Conclusion

The need for exploring how information grounds could form part of small worlds was noted by Fisher and Naumer (2006) and this point was reinforced by Savolainen (2009) who argued for the research potential in seeing information ground and small world as complementary constructs. New attributes of spatial and social factors may be found if we were to reconceptualize small world from the perspective of information ground and vice versa. This study is an attempt in this direction and with early observations giving credence to the idea, it is hoped the study can contribute towards conceptual and theoretical work in the field of LIS.

References

Burnett, G., Jaeger, P.T.: The theory of information worlds and information behavior. In: Amanda, S., Heinstrom, J. (eds.) New Directions in Information Behavior, pp. 161–177. UK, Emerald (2011)

Burnett, G., Besant, M., Chatman, E.A.: Small worlds: normative behavior in virtual communities and feminist bookselling. J. Am. Soc. Inf. Sci. Technol. **52**, 536–547 (2000)

Busse, K.: Framing fan fiction: literary and social practices in fan fiction communities. University of Iowa Press, Iowa (2017)

Chatman, E.A.: The impoverished life-world of outsiders. J. Am. Soc. Inf. Sci. **47**(3), 193–206 (1996)

Chatman, E.A.: A theory of life in the round. J. Am. Soc. Inf. Sci. **50**(3), 207–217 (1999)

Chatman, E.A.: Framing social life in theory and research. New Rev. Inf. Behav. Res. **1** (December), 3–17 (2000)

Cohen, A.P.: The Symbolic Construction of Community. Tavistock, London (1985)

Dalisay, F.: Media use and acculturation of new immigrants in the United States. Commun. Res. Rep. **29**(2), 148–160 (2012)

Fisher, K.E., Naumer, C.M.: Information grounds: theoretical basis and empirical findings on information flow in social settings. In: Spink, A., Cole, C. (eds.) New Directions in Human Information Behavior, pp. 93–111. Springer, Dordrecht (2006). https://doi.org/10.1007/1-4020-3670-1_6

Fraser, N.: Unruly Practices: Power, Discourse, and Gender in Contemporary Social Theory. University of Minnesota Press, Minneapolis (1989)

Hegde, R.S.: Mediating Migration. Polity, Malden (2016)

Jenkins, H.: Afterword: the future of fandom. In: Harrington, C., Gray, J., Sandvoss, C. (eds.) Fandom, Identities and Communities in a Mediated World, pp. 357–364. New York University Press, New York (2007)

Jenkins, R.: Social Identity, 3rd edn. Routledge, New York (2008)

Kim, J.: Information practices during life transition: Korean immigrant women's everyday life information seeking and acculturation (Doctoral dissertation) (2016)

Kim, Y.: Transnational Migration, Media and Identity of Asian Women: Diasporic Daughters. Routledge, New York (2013)

Kizhakkethil, P., Burnett, G.: Virtual zenana: reimagining small world. Proc. Assoc. Inf. Sci. Technol. **56**(1), 693–695 (2019)

Long, E.: Book Clubs: Women and the Uses of Reading in Everyday Life. University of Chicago Press, Chicago (2003)

McMillan, D.W., Chavis, D.M.: Sense of community: a definition and theory. J. Commun. Psychol. **14**(1), 6–23 (1986)

Oldenburg, R.: The Great Good Place: Cafes, Coffee Shops, Bookstores, Bars, Hair Salons, and Other Hangouts at the Heart of a Community. Da Capo Press, Cambridge, MA (1999)

Papacharissi, Z.A.: A Private Sphere: Democracy in a Digital Age. Polity, Cambridge (2010)

Pollak, A.: Words to live by: How experience shapes our information world at work, play and in everyday life (Doctoral dissertation, University of Western Ontario) (2015)

Raman, P., Harwood, J.: Media usage and acculturation: Asian Indian professionals in Silicon Valley. J. Intercult. Commun. Res. **45**(5), 355–373 (2016)

Ramasubramanian, S., Doshi, M.J.: Ethnic performance, language proficiency, and ethnic media use among Indian American immigrants. J. Int. Intercult. Commun. **10**(3), 183–200 (2017)

Reckwitz, A.: Toward a theory of social practices: a development in culturist theorizing. Eur. J. Soc. Theory **5**(2), 243–263 (2002)

Savolainen, R.: Small world and information grounds as contexts of information seeking and sharing. Libr. Inf. Sci. Res. **31**, 38–45 (2009)

Savolainen, R.: Everyday Information Practices. The Scarecrow Press Inc., Lanham (2008)

Suman.: Gendered migrations and literary narratives: writing communities in the South Asian diaspora. Millennial Asia **9**(1), 93–108 (2018)

Sköld, O.: Tracing Traces: a document-centered approach to the preservation of virtual world communities. Inf. Res. **18**(3) (2013). http://www.informationr.net/ir/18-3/colis/paperC09.html

Srinivasan, R., Pyati, A.: Diasporic information environments: Re-framing immigrant-focused information research. J. Am. Soc. Inf. Sci. Technol. **58**(12), 1734–1744 (2007)

Strauss, A.: A social world perspective. Stud. Symb. Interact. **1**(1), 119–128 (1978)

Worrall, A.: Roles of Digital Libraries as Boundary Objects within and Across Social and Information Worlds (Doctoral dissertation, Florida State University) (2014)

Informational Boundary Work in Everyday Life

Pamela J. McKenzie[✉] (iD)

The University of Western Ontario, London, ON N6A 5B9, Canada
pmckenzi@uwo.ca

Abstract. Everyday life often requires a great deal of work to manage the multiple domains that comprise it (e.g., paid work, family care, household maintenance, body and health management, leisure, education, social life, and community or religious involvement). This "boundary work" includes the ongoing categorization of life domains, the establishment and negotiation of boundary permeability, and the crossing of boundaries. The boundaries between the domains of everyday life are negotiated differently by different people and by the same person over time as life circumstances change. Information Science research tends to dichotomize "everyday life" and workplace information practices. Scholars seeking to understand the character of everyday life information practices must attend to the informational work required to (a) place, maintain, and challenge boundaries among life domains, and (b) orchestrate the bridging or crossing of those boundaries. This paper uses the example of keeping track of municipal waste collection to explore the informational work of managing, maintaining, and crossing boundaries in everyday life. Some participants recorded "garbage day" in centrally-located personal information management (PIM) tools shared with household members. By doing so, they integrated the task of waste disposal into an everyday life with other household members that included multiple domains, including paid work. Others' approaches categorized waste collection as separate from the inside life of the household. The study provides evidence that participants engaged in boundary work **within** their non-work lives, beyond simply establishing boundaries between work and home.

Keywords: Personal information management · Everyday life · Information practices · Categorization · Work-life balance · Boundary work

1 Introduction

For many people, everyday life requires a great deal of often unwaged work to manage their participation in multiple domains (e.g., paid work, family care, household maintenance, body and health management, leisure, education, social life, and community or religious involvement). This work includes the ongoing categorisation of life domains, the establishment and negotiation of boundary permeability, and the crossing of boundaries, which Nippert-Eng [1] calls "boundary work." The boundaries between the domains of everyday life, including "work" and "home," are negotiated differently by different people and by the same person over time as life circumstances change.

© Springer Nature Switzerland AG 2020
A. Sundqvist et al. (Eds.): iConference 2020, LNCS 12051, pp. 96–103, 2020.
https://doi.org/10.1007/978-3-030-43687-2_8

Information scholars seeking to understand the character of everyday life information practices must attend to the informational work required to (a) place, maintain, and challenge boundaries among life domains, and (b) orchestrate the bridging or crossing of those boundaries. This paper presents initial findings on the informational work of managing, maintaining, and crossing domain boundaries in everyday life, illustrated through the exemplar of keeping track of municipal waste collection. As Haider [2] shows, the concrete practices of environmental routines such a disposing of waste embed information practices.

2 Literature Review

Researchers in several disciplines have considered the interface between work and non-work domains. A major shortcoming of this literature has been its overall assumption that work and non-work are discrete, separate, and non-overlapping entities. The work-life literature therefore largely neglects the interaction among everyday life domains [3]. It also neglects the interfaces within domains (e.g., work-work conflict for those holding multiple jobs) and outside of paid employment (e.g., school-life conflict) [4]. With few exceptions (e.g., [5–7]), information scholars similarly dichotomize workplace and everyday life information practices, conceiving of "everyday life" as what takes place outside of the workplace, rather than considering the varieties within and interactions across these domains.

Boundary theory is one of the most prominent ways of conceptualizing "the ways that people create, maintain, or change perimeters between work and non-work domains" [3, p. 463; 8]. Boundary theory developed independently of the theory around boundary objects [9] and it focuses on the categorisation work of individuals rather than on the development and use of tools to span boundaries within communities of practice. It shares with boundary object scholarship an understanding of category boundaries, including those between "work," "home," and other domains of everyday life, as socially constructed; this means that boundaries, their features, and their meanings are ongoing accomplishments, negotiated and transformed through social practices, among social actors, and over time. Boundary theory understands the individual, not as a passive reactor to broader environmental conditions, but as an active agent who participates in the ongoing co-construction of domain boundaries in interaction with others [10]. It is therefore commensurate with a social practices approach to information phenomena [11].

Several scholars have used boundary theory to explore the ways that individuals set, manage, and cross boundaries in everyday life. Nippert-Eng [1] showed that individuals used informational tools like calendars to manage, by flexible tactics of integration and segmentation, the boundaries of work and non-work domains. Campbell Clark et al. [12] considered how individuals engage in daily micro-level role transitions across three everyday life boundaries: work-home, work-work, and work-third-space. Within Information Studies, Thomson [13] studied remote workers whose sole professional office was located in their homes. She showed that these workers actively made decisions about the permeability of their "information boundaries" through creating and maintaining physical, temporal, and psychological boundaries.

Information scholars have studied boundary spanning in workplace settings such as interdisciplinary research environments (e.g., [14]) and have considered the role of boundary objects (e.g., [15]), but there has been little research to date, within or outside of IS, on the informational aspects of maintaining and crossing boundaries among the domains of everyday life more broadly (e.g., [7]).

This paper builds on the work of Nippert-Eng and Thomson by showing how a single task, household waste disposal, is represented through informational tools such as calendars and document collections in ways that reveal the informational work of creating, maintaining, challenging, and crossing domain boundaries in everyday life. Taking this focus reveals strategies of information work that operate beyond single everyday life domains and, in so doing, allows us to begin to see "everyday life" beyond simply what takes place outside of paid work [5, 6].

3   Methods

My research team[1] and I collected data from 47 participants (31 presenting as women and 16 as men) in two Canadian provinces. I selected participants purposively to represent a wide variety of everyday life situations, sampling to maximize variation of household arrangements, work characteristics, and roles participants occupied in domains beyond work and household (e.g., manager of a chronic illness, hobbyist, student). The team and I interviewed participants about what they "keep track of" in their lives overall and how they do it, and we photographed spaces, objects, and physical and electronic documents participants discussed.

I analysed the resulting data set, which comprises over 56 h of interviews (2200 transcribed pages), and more than 1100 photographs. I used NVivo 12 to analyse thematically within a constructionist framework, which assumes that "meaning and experience are socially produced and reproduced" and seeks "to theorize the socio-cultural contexts, and structural conditions" that underlie and enable individual accounts [16]. First, I undertook two rounds of broad content coding to identify what participants mentioned keeping track of, and then to specify the domains (e.g., household, family, work, education, health) mentioned in those accounts. Next, I analyzed these transcript passages, and the photographs associated with them, for evidence of the setting, management, or crossing of boundaries between two or more domains in participants' lives. Analysis was recursive, using strategies of constant comparison [17]. Data collection and analysis conformed to Canadian guidelines on ethical research on human subjects [18]. To maintain confidentiality, I identify participants by a generic initial. Quotes are edited for brevity and clarity (e.g., removing false starts and irrelevant text).

As Nippert-Eng points out, even something as mundane as the placement of a calendar enacts boundaries. The tools participants used to keep track of household waste collection serve as a site for exploring the informational work of managing,

---

[1] Elisabeth Davies, Nicole Dalmer, Cameron Hoffman-McGaw, Lucia Cedeira Serantes, Sherilyn Williams, Lola Wong.

maintaining, and crossing boundaries in everyday life. In the two provinces where we collected data, household waste collection was managed municipally. In many cities and regions, garbage, recycling, and/or compost collection occurred predictably on the same day each week, and little informational work was required to keep track of this task. In other regions, collection schedules varied from week to week; for example an eight-or-more-day rotation that resulted in a different collection day from week to week, or multi-week schedule that maintained the same collection day but alternated what was collected each week (e.g., compost or recycling). For participants living in those cities, keeping track of what was being collected and when was a task that required a great deal of personal information management [19]. The tools they used to keep track of when and how to put household waste out for collection reveal the multiple ways in which participants categorised this everyday task, the domains to which they saw it belonging, and the ways they represented these domains in relation to one another. In short, these tools offer a window into the shape and character of participants' everyday lives.

4   Findings

Several participants recorded rotating "garbage days" on household calendars or in document collections that they shared with members of their households. Six of these were located in the kitchen, and the seventh on a telephone table in the front hall. As Eliot et al. [20] have found, the kitchen serves as an important contextual location for information in households, with refrigerator doors and bulletin boards as common sites for hosting domestic information including reminders and scheduling.

When asked how she kept track in her home, Participant 9 immediately mentioned the monthly municipal calendar with preprinted garbage collection dates. She and her partner kept it on the refrigerator as their "home calendar," on which they recorded tasks and events as well as using it to track garbage day:

> We use the calendar as a, "Okay, let's talk about what's going on for us. If [Partner]'s out of town for a couple of days, we have to coordinate about who can take the dog. But we have to coordinate all of that stuff. Or having a drink with friends, or... like a haircut, stuff like that, dentist appointments. It gets on the home calendar.

Participant 6 worked part-time and saw clients in her home workspace. She lived with her husband, who was taking parental leave, and their baby. She posted her monthly municipal waste collection calendar on her kitchen wall, alongside a set of small blackboard squares that she used to record her and her family's day-to-day activities over the course of each week:

> We keep our garbage schedule here, and I look there, and when I update whether it's a compost or recycling day. Just kind of, everything shows up. So right now, day off, anniversary, a market I do, all of my appointments, the fact that it's a holiday's up there, the fact that you guys are coming [to do this interview] ...and we had to go to a farm to get produce...like, kind of everything shows up there.

Participant 6 listed her client appointments so that her husband would know when he was sole carer for the baby. Although she did not write on the municipal garbage calendar, its placement alongside the blackboard calendar squares allowed her to integrate waste collection into work, family, and leisure aspects of her everyday life.

Three other participants kept waste collection information in a larger document collection on their refrigerator doors. Participant 40's recycling calendar shared the space with coupons and flyers for local events that he and his wife might attend, while Participant 41's garbage calendar sat near to a calendar that indicated the year's breaks and holidays for her daughter's school. P29 categorised waste removal with food, placing her compost bin instructions next to baking instructions from a pizza box. All three of these participants also used their refrigerator door to hold a flyer explaining how electricity pricing changed through the course of each day, categorising waste collection with energy use, suggesting a "sustainability" category.

Participant 34, the sole adult in a household with two teenagers and a medically fragile toddler, had just moved house and did not have a municipal waste calendar for her new neighbourhood. She recorded "garbage day" on the packed monthly kitchen calendar she shared with the two older children. Along with the one-time "moving day" and weekly "laundry day;" this calendar recorded reminders of the toddler's many medical appointments and logged her daily vital statistics and emergency trips to the hospital. It noted the dates when school fees were due and the deposit date for the baby's government disability allowance, the family's primary source of income; family birthdays and anniversaries; and social events including a community bonfire.

These participants integrated the task of waste disposal into an everyday life with other household members that included multiple domains: general household operations, child and pet care, social and family activities, important family milestones such as birthdays and anniversaries, leisure, physical health and well-being, food provisioning, financial management, and paid work when it affected participants' availability for family care. The final participant who integrated waste disposal into a broader household category was Participant 35, a member of a retired couple living on a farm, whom we interviewed together. She wrote "garbage day" on the agenda she kept in the front hall, where, like the previous participants, she had also recorded things like symphony concert dates, medical appointments, a reminder about the dog's flea medicine, and birthdays and anniversaries.

Her husband, Participant 36, took a different approach. For him, waste collection was not part of household life but rather part of outdoor work, maintenance, and farming.

> P36: I have a calendar in the garage. And I write on that calendar when the recycle day.
> Interviewer: So what kinds of things go on the calendar in the garage and how is that different from what goes on [the front-hall agenda]?
> P36: Well, garbage day was one. Recycle, because that's the area that the garbage is. So I keep it there, so all I have to do is look up to see if it's this week. Other things out there I keep my phone numbers for the gas guy on-, a couple lawn mower guys that I've used because I have a phone out there. Frequently used numbers for farm things are out there.

Two other participants took this approach: Participant 10 did not write on her municipal garbage calendar, and used a separate kitchen calendar for social and household items. She placed the garbage calendar by her back door, beside the jeans she only wore when mowing her lawn, thus categorising garbage and recycling with outdoor maintenance. The only calendar in Participant 5's kitchen was the recycling and garbage calendar, which covered an entire year with squares too small to be useful for recording any other information. By separating this stand-alone garbage calendar from all of the kinds of household and workplace information that other participants included, Participant 5 showed that he firmly segmented his personal information management by domain. As he explained, calendars were for work-related events, not for domestic life:

I've never in my all entire life used calendars. I will at work, but never in my personal life because I would just know when things were due, when I get the bill I would pay it or I knew what date.

P13 and P44, both of whom were interviewed in their workplaces, recorded information about household waste disposal on mobile tools. P44 listed "garbage" in a crowded paper agenda that integrated a large number of domains. It also recorded assignments for her night classes, the return of a colleague to work after an absence, an acquaintance's upcoming surgery, car logistics, and a busy day for her partner. P13's transcript demonstrates how boundary practices may change over time, in his case from more integrating to more segmenting, and from collaborative to individual strategies. He explained that he had formerly used multiple shared calendars, integrated across two separate groups of work colleagues and his home life: "There was my personal calendar and then two other work calendars that were shared with two other groups of people that I had all visible on one Google Calendar." Now, however, he recorded important events on workplace lists and then transferred them to a single Google calendar that he accessed on his phone and did not share, either with his domestic partner or with his work colleagues. Although he explained that he included some personal events, like a birthday party, on this calendar, the week of the interview it contained only four items: three work-related meetings and "Recycle." Despite their differences, these two participants documented waste disposal as an individual task not shared with partners or coworkers nor differentiated from their work lives, both because it was recorded along with work details and because they carried the phone and agenda with them across domains.

5   Discussion and Conclusion

Although it is a small and easily overlooked activity, keeping track of household waste collection required active information work for all of these participants. This work was not limited to the use of calendars and agendas; more than one participant mentioned using the presence of garbage or recycling bins outside neighbors' houses as a backup reminder when their other tools failed them. Waste removal is itself a physical and organizational boundary-spanning endeavour. Physically, waste is created within the household and then removed to a distant location. Organizationally, household members participate in waste disposal but it is initiated and controlled by the municipality they live in, so they have little control over it. This task therefore provides a helpful window into the ways that informational tools support the creation, maintenance, challenging, and crossing of boundaries among domains in everyday life.

Nippert-Eng describes boundary work as a mental and physical sculpting process that can result in a wide variety of different experiences as each individual carves out their own categories and relationships in relation to the broader system of cultural concepts within which they are embedded. She argues that we place the boundary between categories such as home and work "through extensive, detailed decisions at each possible meeting point between realms. Choices to place our calendars somewhere and to use each for certain things are countered by choices of where not to put calendars and what kinds of activities each will not include" [1, p. 579]. By showing how participants categorise waste collection as a task, this paper has shown that they place boundaries within the home and work realms as well as between them.

The informational boundary work associated with keeping track of waste collection is situated within the broader context of participants' everyday lives. As Nippert-Eng observes [1, p. 563],

> by focusing on individuals' boundary work – the constraints and negotiations that concretize classification systems and their categories – social scientists can gain a great deal of insight into how society, itself, might exist. We also can acquire unique understandings about how individual members of a society create and understand their everyday lives.

Attending to the ways that individual participants conceptualized and recorded information about this minor task reveals the varying characteristics of everyday life as "the totality of lived experience" [6, p. 399] for each participant. These characteristics provide insights that information studies scholars might use in order to explore the complexities of "everyday life" as a context for information practices.

References

1. Nippert-Eng, C.: Calendars and keys: the classification of 'home' and 'work'. Sociol. Forum **11**(3), 563–582 (1996)
2. Haider, J.: The environment on holidays or how a recycling bin informs us on the environment. J. Doc. **67**(5), 823–839 (2011)
3. Beigi, M., Shirmohammadi, M., Otaye-Ebede, L.: Half a century of work-nonwork interface research: a review and taxonomy of terminologies. Appl. Psychol. **68**(3), 449–478 (2019)
4. Kelliher, C., Richardson, J., Boiarintseva, G.: All of work? All of life? Reconceptualising work-life balance for the 21st century. Hum. Resour. Manag. J. **29**(2), 97–112 (2019)
5. Savolainen, R.: Everyday Information Practices: A Social Phenomenological Perspective. Scarecrow Press, Lanham (2008)
6. Ocepek, M.G.: Bringing out the everyday in everyday information behavior. J. Doc. **74**(2), 398–411 (2018)
7. McKenzie, P.J., Davies, E.: Genre systems and "keeping track" in everyday life. Arch. Sci. **12**(4), 437–460 (2012)
8. Ashforth, B.E., Kreiner, G.E., Fugate, M.: All in a day's work: boundaries and micro role transitions. Acad. Manag. Rev. **25**(3), 472–491 (2000)
9. Star, S.L., Griesemer, J.R.: Institutional ecology, 'translations' and boundary objects: amateurs and professionals in Berkeley's Museum of Vertebrate Zoology, 1907–39. Soc. Stud. Sci. **19**(3), 387–420 (1989)
10. Kreiner, G.E., Hollensbe, E.C., Sheep, M.L.: Balancing borders and bridges: negotiating the work-home interface via boundary work tactics. Acad. Manag. J. **52**(4), 704–730 (2009)
11. Savolainen, R.: Information behavior and information practice. Reviewing the "umbrella concepts" of information seeking studies. Libr. Q. **77**(2), 109–132 (2007)

12. Campbell Clark, S.: Work/family border theory: a new theory of work/family balance. Hum. Relat. **53**(6), 747–770 (2000)
13. Thomson, L.: When I've packed it in and they send me something: information boundaries in professional home offices. In: Proceedings of the ASIST Annual Meeting, vol. 50 (2013)
14. Palmer, C.L.: Information work at the boundaries of science: linking library services to research practice. Libr. Trends **45**(2), 165–191 (1996)
15. Huvila, I., Anderson, T.D., Jansen, E.H., McKenzie, P.J., Worrall, A.: Boundary objects in information science. J. Assoc. Inf. Sci. Technol. **68**(8), 1807–1822 (2017)
16. Braun, V., Clarke, V.: Using thematic analysis in psychology. Qual. Res. Psychol. **3**(2), 77–101 (2006)
17. Corbin, J.M., Strauss, A.: Basics of Qualitative Research: Techniques and Procedures for Developing Grounded Theory. Sage, Thousand Oaks (2007)
18. Canadian Institutes of Health Research, Natural Sciences and Engineering Research Council of Canada, Social Sciences and Humanities Research Council of Canada: Tri-council Policy Statement: Ethical Conduct for Research Involving Humans - TCPS2. Public Works and Government Services Canada, Ottawa, Ontario (2018)
19. Jones, W.: Keeping Found Things Found: The Study and Practice of Personal Information Management. Morgan Kaufman Publishers, Burlington (2008)
20. Elliot, K., Neustaedter, C., Greenberg, S.: Time, ownership and awareness: the value of contextual locations in the home. In: Beigl, M., Intille, S., Rekimoto, J., Tokuda, H. (eds.) UbiComp 2005. LNCS, vol. 3660, pp. 251–268. Springer, Heidelberg (2005). https://doi.org/10.1007/11551201_15

Ya Hasra: An Exploratory Study on Online Communities of Moroccan Jews, Christians and Muslims Dealing with Their Common Cultural Heritage

Yohanan Ouaknine[✉] [iD] and Noa Aharony [iD]

The Information Science Department, Bar Ilan University, Ramat Gan, Israel
Yohanan.ouaknine@ois.co.il

Abstract. The purpose of this paper is to present preliminary results for the study of online communities of Moroccan Jews, Christians, and Muslims, dealing with their shared cultural heritage in social networks. The phenomenon of non-conflictual inter-religious online communities appears to be limited to the Moroccan nostalgia groups and received marginal attention in social networks research.

Drawing on literature covering nostalgia and information behavior, a mixed-methods approach was followed using questionnaires with closed and open questions. Descriptive statistics and qualitative data were collected.

Although several studies were published on the shared cultural heritage of Moroccan Muslims, Christian, and Jews and on Information Behavior, there is a lack of research on the impact of nostalgia on information sharing in these online communities. Using multicultural Facebook groups, this research aims to shed light on the impact of nostalgia on cultural heritage preservation, in online communities initiated by Muslims, Christians, or Jews, by studying how nostalgia may increase information sharing.

Preliminary results revealed that the primary motivation for information sharing in these online communities is the preservation of the common cultural heritage and the need to renew ties between friends and communities of different religions. Some results suggest that nostalgia of the collective cultural past could be used to respond to the present needs of the community.

Keywords: Nostalgia · Online communities · Information behavior and sharing · Cultural heritage

1 Introduction

1.1 Jews, Muslims, and Christians from Morocco: A Common Cultural Heritage

The Moroccan Jewish community numbered approximately 250,000 persons in the early sixties. This community had solid roots in the expulsion of Jews from Spain

---

"Ya Hasra" is a term in Moroccan Arabic expressing nostalgia or "good old times".

© Springer Nature Switzerland AG 2020
A. Sundqvist et al. (Eds.): iConference 2020, LNCS 12051, pp. 104–113, 2020.
https://doi.org/10.1007/978-3-030-43687-2_9

during the Inquisition, in the population movements ruled by the Roman Empire, in the Berber communities and up to the exodus of Jews from Jerusalem, almost 2000 years ago. Nowadays, only 1% of this community still resides in Morocco, while the vast majority left for Israel, France, Canada, United States of America and many other destinations [1]. A second community in Morocco was mainly comprised of French colons who lived in Morocco under the French protectorate and after the Independence of Morocco. As of December 31, 2017, 54,000 French nationals were registered with the French consulates in Morocco [2]. A third group is comprised of 4.5 million Moroccans natives living abroad, representing approximately 15% of Morocco's population [3].

Other linguistic communities are the Moroccan speaking Tamazight (Berberic) or Spanish. All the communities used French and Moroccan Arabic, known as "Darija" as their primary language.

Two separate immigration processes occurred in the French and Jewish communities. The first was the separation of Jews from their Muslim and Christian neighbors and their integration in their countries of adoption. A second immigration process after the independence of Morocco was the return to France of a large part of the Christian community, mostly composed of French nationals.

Ritter [4] uses the concept of "Diaspora" to define the "social configuration of transnational connections of individuals who identify with the same roots, practices, or languages" and adapts it to Moroccan who choose to live out of Morocco [4]. Today's online Moroccan communities in Facebook express a need to fill the cultural gap and to renew cultural ties with lost traditions. Moroccan Jews, Christians and Muslims and their descendants seek information about their cultural heritage, and online communities are an accessible source of information. This heritage is expressed by cultural memorabilia of Morocco, discussions about traditions and folkloric artifacts but also by practical information [4].

Illman and Sjö [5] studied Facebook groups as a possible platform for inter-religious encounters. While in early days of Internet research, online communities were expected to support and inspire inter-religious dialogue, research shows that online groups actually develop conflictual discussions between religious groups, because of individual tend to prefer information sources that reinforce their beliefs [5].

Museums and libraries are the major players of the preservation of the communities heritage [6] but they are not alone. This exploratory study may contribute to the advancement of the Cultural Heritage Preservation on the web, by understanding the factors that impact online communities, motivates their members to preserve their cultural heritage in social networks like Facebook and promotes inter-religious dialogue.

2 Related Work

2.1 Nostalgia

Hepper, Ritchie, Sedikides, and Wildschut [7] conceptualized Nostalgia as multifaceted blended emotion "involving remembering, reminiscing, thinking, and reliving the past" with positive and negative emotions. They see in Nostalgia a focused past experience, usually related to childhood and youth [7], related to close relationships and associated with more positive feelings such as happiness than negative feelings [8]. The researchers compiled a list of 35 features expressing the diverse facets of nostalgia. Davalos et al. called these facets "Triggers" and considered that nostalgia is usually evoked by triggers involving pictures, smells, music, objects or information about homeland, remembering individuals, places or experiences [9].

The sociologist Fred Davis [10] stated that nostalgia that took place in the past *does not imply* that the past was its cause. Davis [10] argues that nostalgia uses the past to recreate a *newly* constructed past that answers the needs of a community or a person [10]. This reconstruction may take place in an online community [9] or among friends. Moderators in these two groups may publish elements triggering nostalgia among members, like music, pictures, or movies.

Recent research shows that these methods are already used in online brand communities to promote "Nostalgic products that may have a cognitive feature, referring to memories associated with key moments or someone's youth, and an affective component, which connects these memories with affective experiences existing in past times" [11]. These methods triggers positive reactions among users of online brand communities and encourage them to buy products linked to nostalgic moments.

2.2 Information Behavior in Nostalgia Groups

Savolainen [12] proposed in the ELIS model (Everyday Life Information Seeking) social and cultural factors that affect the way people search for information in their daily life. A central concept in the ELIS model is the "Mastery of Life" - the way people identify specific projects and issues in everyday life and solve problematic situations with a selection of information sources and channels and seeking of orienting and practical information [12]. The need to solve a problematic situation generally leads to a motivation to seek information. In a study examining the antecedents of user acceptance of an audio-visual heritage archive, Ongena, van de Wijngaert, & Huizer [13] found that Nostalgia proneness had a strong effect on the intention to **use** cultural heritage archive service and propose to research the effect of memorable images on information behavior [13]. In this study, we explore the possibility that Nostalgia proneness has an effect on the intention to **share** cultural heritage.

Routledge [8] considers that the motivational approach to the study of Nostalgia was not studied enough in psychology. He argues that people are motivated to avoid unpleasant states and approach pleasant ones, and that negative psychological states trigger nostalgia, which in turn promotes positive psychological states [8]. In this exploratory study, we propose that negative psychological states might trigger nostalgia which in turn, may promote information sharing.

The information behavior, which includes participation, seeking and sharing information in Nostalgia online communities may be related to these two approaches – The social and cultural factors proposed by Savolainen [12], and the motivational approach proposed by Routledge [8].

3 Methodology

3.1 Research Questions

The main objective of this exploratory study is to describe online communities dealing with cultural heritage in its digital form and explain how nostalgia can increase information sharing in these online communities.

As an exploratory research of a new topic, it will not be representative of all online nostalgia communities due to its small sample size. Nevertheless, this research offers a valuable insight and reliable methodology for future theory development in this domain.

3.2 Data Collection

The research was conducted in Facebook groups dealing with Morocco and multi-cultural communities in June 2019. The researchers posted an invitation in 41 groups to participate in the research and 32 persons answered the questionnaire within the first week. For this preliminary research, the questionnaire was published in French, which is one of the languages spoken by all the communities. Facebook groups were collected by using the Facebook search box for Moroccan heritage topics related to the three religious' groups. The groups were selected on the basis of six criteria: (1) Multicultural online community; (2) sharing pictures and stories about their cultural heritage; (3) one year or more of activity; (4) no political or commercial activities; (5) more than 200 members and (6) public groups. The themes were identified by reading and coding the description of the Facebook group with MaxQDA 2020 software [14]. Figure 1 presents the major themes of the Facebook groups where researchers posted the invitation to the survey.

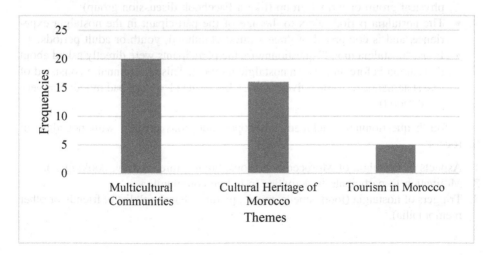

Fig. 1. Frequency of main themes in Facebook groups

Three major themes were expressed in announcement or information parts of the Facebook pages, as presented in Fig. 1. 49% of the pages focused on Multicultural relations between Muslim, Jewish and Christian communities ($N = 20$). 39% of the Facebook groups focused on Cultural heritage of Morocco, including pictures, old movies, architecture or cooking ($N = 16$). In the last theme, 5 Facebook groups (12%) featured Morocco as an attractive touristic destination. The list of Facebook groups and their links can be found here: https://bit.ly/2lPCOZV.

3.3   Data Analysis

Measures. Three closed questionnaires were used to gather data: Demographics, information behavior, and nostalgia. The full survey in French can be found here: https://forms.gle/F8yCZqBgQ3vS9x2d8

1. The demographics section included the following variables: Age, education level, family situation, religious community and place of birth.
2. The "information behavior" questionnaire was employed to measure different, underlying constructs and consisted of five statements, rated on a five-point Lickert scale (1 = strongly disagree; 5 = strongly agree). The scale had a high level of internal consistency, as determined by a Cronbach's alpha of 0.85 in this study. This questionnaire was adapted from the research of Ongena, van de Wijngaert, & Huizer [13] about Nostalgia proneness having an effect on the intention to share cultural heritage.
3. The nostalgia section was based on Routledge works [8] and his argument that negatives psychological states triggers nostalgia which might, in turn, trigger information sharing. This section includes the following questions:

   • The nostalgia moment refers to the situation when one is nostalgic: alone, in a physical group or virtual group (like a Facebook discussion group).
   • The nostalgia period refers to the age of the participant in the nostalgia experience, and is comprised of three values: childhood, youth or adult periods.
   • In the "nostalgia mood" questionnaire, the participants were directly asked about their mood before and after a nostalgic moment. This questionnaire consisted of five statements, rated on a five-point Lickert scale (1 = very bad mood; 5 = very good mood).

A fourth questionnaire included three open questions dealing with nostalgia of Morocco:

1. Aspects of nostalgia of Morocco (emotions, architecture, history, cooking…).
2. Motivation to participate in activities in online communities.
3. Triggers of nostalgia (food, smells, music, pictures, Facebook list of friends or other memorabilia).

4   Results

4.1   Participants

32 persons answered the questionnaire within one week of its publication. Half of the participants were women ($N = 16$). 62.5% of the participants were graduates ($N = 20$). 78.1% were born in Morocco ($N = 25$). Their average age was 52.7 years, SD = 14.2, range = 22–82. 59.4% of the participants were married ($N = 19$). 40.6% of the participants declared that their parents belong to the Muslim community ($N = 13$), 31.3% to the Christian community ($N = 10$) and 28.1% to the Jewish community ($N = 9$).

4.2   Information Behavior

A one-way ANOVA was conducted to determine if the information behavior score was different for groups of different religious background. Participants were classified into three groups: Muslim ($N = 13$), Christian ($N = 10$) and Jewish ($N = 9$). The information behavior score increased from the Christian group ($M = 2.78$, SD = .83), to the Jewish group ($M = 3.6$, $SD = 0.75$), to the Muslim group ($M = 3.82$, $SD = 1.14$). The differences between these religious groups were statistically significant, $F(2, 31) = 3.9$, $p < .05$, $\eta^2 = .21$.

4.3   Nostalgia

Nostalgia Period
Figure 2 shows that nostalgia experience is related mainly with childhood and youth period.

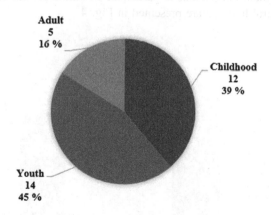

Adult
5
16 %

Childhood
12
39 %

Youth
14
45 %

Fig. 2.   Nostalgia by age period.

Nostalgia Moment
Figure 3 shows three situations where participants experienced a nostalgia moment: (1) alone; (2) with friends or family and 3; in an online discussion. Frequencies shows

that the largest nostalgia situation occurs when the participant is alone of with friends and family. Only three participants stated that the Nostalgia moment occurs in online discussions.

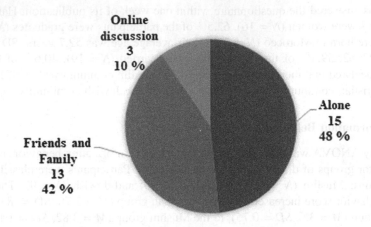

Fig. 3. Nostalgia moment by social groups.

4.4 Qualitative Analysis

Qualitative data was coded with MaxQDA, a software primarily intended for this purpose [14]. Three main themes were expressed in the open questions. (1) Motivations to participate in Moroccan culture and heritage groups in Facebook; (2) Aspects of nostalgia of Morocco and (3) Triggers that initiate nostalgia.

Motivations. The main motivations to participate in online communities dealing with the Moroccan cultural heritage are presented in Fig. 4.

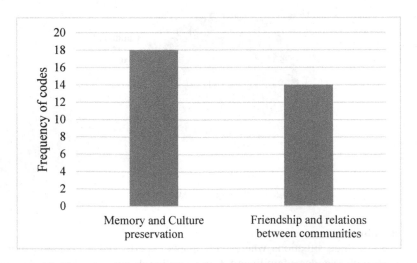

Fig. 4. Occurrences of the motivations to participate in online communities

Two themes expressing the motivation to participate in online communities were categorized in the text. These themes are presented in Fig. 4: (1) Memory and Culture preservation of a heritage common to the three religions (75.0%) and (2) the expression of friendship and relations between the different communities (58.3%).

Aspects of Nostalgia of Morocco. The aspects of nostalgia of Morocco are presented in Fig. 5.

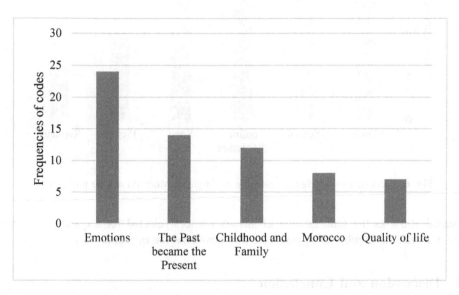

Fig. 5. Occurrences of aspects of nostalgia of Morocco in participants' answers

In this question, the researchers asked participants to define, in their own words and language, what Nostalgia of Morocco is. The major part of participants answered in French, and some in Arabic. Five themes were expressed in theses answers, as presented in Fig. 5: (1) Emotions linked to nostalgia like sadness, joy or pride (82.8%); (2) A reconstruction of the past in the present, mainly related to the good relations between communities that should be reestablished (48.3%); (3) Childhood and family (41.4%); (4) The country of Morocco, the sea, the architecture and the folklore (27.6%) and (5) the quality of life, expressed by sentences like "everything was simple then, a different approach of life, a feeling of freedom…" (24.1%).

Triggers of Nostalgia Triggers initiating nostalgia of Morocco are presented in Fig. 6.

The last open question asked about the triggers that initiate a Nostalgia moment. Six themes are expressed in theses answers, as presented in Fig. 6: (1) Food is linked to smell and taste of Moroccan cooking (66.7%); (2) School relates to pictures of class, discussions about teachers or school friends (53.3%); (3) Online discussion relates mainly to Facebook posts and comments (50.0%); (4) Songs and Music (46.7%); (5) Pictures and movies depicting Moroccan sites or persons (33.3%) and (6) Romantic moments, mainly in the youth period (20.0%); The total response percentages may

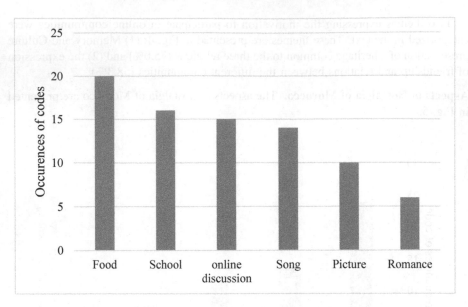

Fig. 6. Occurrences of triggers initiating nostalgia of Morocco among participants

exceed 100% as the total number of answer choices selected for a question can be greater than the number of respondents that answered the question.

5 Discussion and Conclusion

This paper presents an exploratory methodology and results for the mapping of the facets of Nostalgia in online communities dealing with Moroccan cultural heritage, and the role of nostalgia in the motivation to participate in these communities.

A major limitation of this study is the small sample size. Nevertheless, the findings of this study offer validation of previous findings, confirm the reliability of the information behavior questionnaire and may help to shed light on an emerging topic.

Preliminary findings of this study present a significant correlation between Information behavior in Cultural heritage communities and Religious groups. The findings about information behavior and religious groups may suggest that Ritter's definition of Diaspora about groups of individuals who share mutual roots, practices, or languages may be adapted to these online communities. Results from the qualitative analysis suggested that memory and culture preservation may be the factors of the motivation to participate in these religious groups.

The findings also show that members of these communities may use Nostalgia and an idealized past to answer present needs, following Davis argument [10]. A major topic expressed in participants' answers was related to the need to reestablish the good relations between the three communities. Surprisingly, Political matters, and especially the Israeli-Arab conflict, did not appear in the text. Findings about Nostalgia moment in social groups and Nostalgia period were consistent with previous studies [7, 8].

Nevertheless, the fact that a very small number of participants experienced nostalgia in Online discussion might imply that these discussions were genuine and not professionally moderated.

This exploratory research intended to shed light on a new and unknown topic: the preservation of cultural heritage shared by three different religious communities of Morocco, in Facebook. Future research will propose a model linking Nostalgia, Well-being, Information Behavior and Cultural heritage preservation in online communities. We also intend to extend the scope of the communities by proposing surveys in all the languages spoken by the Moroccan diaspora. In this spirit, we intend to translate the survey into Moroccan Arabic, Moroccan Amazigh, Spanish, English and Hebrew in future research.

References

1. Zafrani, H.: Two Thousand Years of Jewish Life in Morocco. KTAV Publishing House Inc., Jersey City (2005)
2. France Diplomatie: Dossier Pays: Maroc. https://www.diplomatie.gouv.fr/fr/services-aux-citoyens/preparer-son-expatriation/dossiers-pays-de-l-expatriation/maroc/
3. Boukharouaa, N., et al.: The Moroccan diaspora and its contribution to the development of innovation in Morocco. In: Global Innovation Index, pp. 123–131 (2014)
4. Ritter, C.S.: The Moroccan diaspora in Istanbul: experiencing togetherness through participatory media. Cult. Anal. 1, 49–66 (2017)
5. Illman, R., Sjö, S.: Facebook as a site for inter-religious encounters: a case study from Finland. J. Contemp. Relig. 30, 383–398 (2015). https://doi.org/10.1080/13537903.2015.1081341
6. Loach, K., Rowley, J., Griffiths, J.: Cultural sustainability as a strategy for the survival of museums and libraries. Int. J. Cult. Policy 23, 186–198 (2017). https://doi.org/10.1080/10286632.2016.1184657
7. Hepper, E.G., Ritchie, T.D., Sedikides, C., Wildschut, T.: Odyssey's end: lay conceptions of nostalgia reflect its original Homeric meaning. Emotion 12, 102–119 (2012). https://doi.org/10.1037/a0025167
8. Routledge, C.: Nostalgia: A Psychological Resource. Routledge, Abingdon. (2016). https://doi.org/10.4324/9781315669311
9. Davalos, S., Merchant, A., Rose, G.M., Lessley, B.J., Teredesai, A.M.: "The good old days": an examination of nostalgia in Facebook posts. Int. J. Hum. Comput. Stud. 83, 83–93 (2015). https://doi.org/10.1016/j.ijhcs.2015.05.009
10. Davis, F.: Nostalgia, identity and the current nostalgia wave. J. Pop. Cult. 11, 414–424 (1977). https://doi.org/10.1111/j.0022-3840.1977.00414.x
11. Koetz, C., Tankersley, J.D.: Nostalgia in online brand communities. J. Bus. Strategy 37, 22–29 (2016). https://doi.org/10.1108/JBS-03-2015-0025
12. Savolainen, R.: Everyday life information seeking: approaching information seeking in the context of "way of life". Libr. Inf. Sci. Res. 17, 259–294 (1995). https://doi.org/10.1016/0740-8188(95)90048-9
13. Ongena, G., van de Wijngaert, L., Huizer, E.: Acceptance of online audio-visual cultural heritage archive services: a study of the general public. Inf. Res. 18, 1–20 (2013)
14. Kuckartz, U., Rädiker, S.: Analyzing Qualitative Data with MAXQDA: Text, Audio, and Video. Springer, Cham (2019). https://doi.org/10.1007/978-3-030-15671-8

... with less that a very small number of purchases in experience. Consider the Online discussion might imply that these discussions were positive and non-positive simultaneously limited.

This exploratory research aimed to shed light on a new and relatively unexplored phenomenon of cultural heritage shared by three different religious communities in Morocco. Facebook. Future research will propose a model linking foreign/Jews being Jewish and Cultural heritage preservation in online communities. We also intended to broaden the scope of the communities by proposing surveys in all the languages spoken by the Moroccan diaspora. In this study, we tried to translate the survey into Moroccan Arabic, Moroccan Amazigh (in English and Hebrew) in future research.

References

1. Zafrani, TA: Two Thousand Years of Jewish Life in Morocco. KTAV Publishing House, Inc. Jersey City (2005)
2. France Diplomatie Dossier Pays Maroc. https://www.diplomatie.gouv.fr/fr/dossiers-pays/maroc/presentation-du-maroc/article/presentation-du-maroc/
3. Ben Barouch, N. et al.: The Moroccan diaspora and its contribution to the development of innovation in Morocco. Int. J. Innovation Stud. 1, 123–134 (2018)
4. Pillar, Ghis: The Moroccan diaspora in Ignored Agent uniting to interest, through emergency media. Oele Anat. J. 6(1)2012 ...
5. Benit, R. Site as Facebook: a site for international enclosure a conservation from Studland. J. Cultural Right 10, 382–394 (2015). https://doi.org/10.1080/1355203591.2015.1063544
6. Losch, E., Rowley, J.: Online cultural sustainability: a strategy for the survival of museums and culture. Int. J. Cult. Policy 23, 186–193 (2016). https://doi.org/10.1080/10286632.2016.1145657
7. Heppler, F., Ruodes, T. Danzfeldt, C., Wilkinson, C. who study's and an emergency distance support a design of heritage sentiment. Comm. 12(10)6 (2016). https://doi.org/10.1002/...
8. Prodanti, C. Sarangan, A Pecshang and Internet, Routledge. Abingdon (2016). https://books.routledge.com/...
9. David, A.S. Medium, Anrey, S. O. Millar, J.C.: Lay to share. Internet 324: The avenue of life education in emergency in Facebook users. Proc. Hum. Comput. Study 82, 86–93 (2013). https://doi.org/10.1016/...
10. Linetsk, I Experimented Identity and the communities in audit. J. Exp. Cult. 21, 411–424 (2017). https://doi.org/10.1177/...
11. Kerres, J. Linakov, V.D.: Facilitation in media. Communication processes. J. Data Manage. 37, 202–209 (2017). https://doi.org/10.1016/...
12. Sprecher, S.: Prosperity for information seeking processes and information seek of in the construction of the relationship. Comput. Hum. Behav. 33 (2015). https://doi.org/10.1016/...
13. Dacey, G., Kemal, Wilfred, H.V.: ... in the performance of online scale education in new knowledge-based reasons to the young use of the use of ... J. Comput. 18, 1–9 (2013)
14. Thomas, D.C. Ahrend, S.: Collective agency in community of practice. J. Org. Vol. Arbana and Comm. Online, J. Conn. 2015). http://www.Wustingroup.bic/10.1016/...

Social Media

Trolling Trump

Pnina Fichman(⊠)

Indiana University, Luddy Hall #2114, 700 N. Woodlawn St.,
Bloomington, IN 47405, USA
fichman@indiana.edu

Abstract. This study aims to gain a better understanding of a global collective process of trolling Donald Trump's inauguration speech. One hundred videos with satirical trolling content were posted over a three-weeks period in 2017. We performed thematic content analysis of sixty videos, each represents a different country to understand the role of national culture and crowd work in global trolling. Results show that all the videos involve satirical trolling behaviors, regardless of national boundaries, and that we found that similar to prior research on collective intelligence, processes of innovation, replication, and customization were evident.

Keywords: Global trolling · Donald Trump · National culture · Collective intelligence · Satire

1 Introduction

This paper focuses on global trolling, as it manifests itself on YouTube in the form of videos with overt satirical political content. While early research focused attention on deviant behaviors and malevolent trolling, more recently the focus shifted to satirical, ideological, collective, and political trolling from countries around the globe [e.g., 21]. Some scholars studied motivation behind trolling behavior [e.g., 1, 20], while others focused on the perceptions and reactions to trolling [e.g., 5]. Only some prior research on trolling can be generalized, because forms of trolling and types of perpetrators have diversified with time. One understudied aspect of trolling is its global reach.

There is research on specific cases of trolling from various countries around the globe, including USA [e.g., 6], UK [e.g., 23], China [21], Israel [20], Italy [2], New Zealand [15], and Russia [27]. Collectively, these studies raise a question about the extent and nature of trolling globally. Specifically, it is unclear to what extent motivations, perceptions, and reactions to trolling behavior differ from one country to another. One would expect both similarities and differences in global trolling, because research suggests that trolling behaviors differ from one socio-technical context to another; different communities and different platforms interact differently with online trolling. Furthermore, it is also unclear if global trolling can involve more than one country. It is possible, for example, that shared motivations or ideology can bridge over national, socio-cultural, and geographical boundaries on online platforms.

Studying global trolling seems to be timely and necessary because of the rise in media accounts of Chinese and Russian trolling, and the proliferation of the "state-sponsored

© Springer Nature Switzerland AG 2020
A. Sundqvist et al. (Eds.): iConference 2020, LNCS 12051, pp. 117–129, 2020.
https://doi.org/10.1007/978-3-030-43687-2_10

trolling" phenomenon [e.g., 17]. Specifically, there is a need to address questions about global trolling, such as: What are the signs of and motivations for global trolling? What tactics and behaviors characterize global trolling? How do these resemble other trolling manifestations? How does culture impact global trolling events?

Further, research on collective intelligence processes mostly ignored the impact of trolling or national culture on these processes. Collective intelligence, as an umbrella term, refers to the knowledge that emerges from people collaborating, and it is discerned as shared intelligence. Levy [12, p. 13] defines it as "a form of *universally distributed intelligence*, constantly enhanced, coordinated in real time, and resulting in the effective mobilization of skills. …[t]he basis and goal of collective intelligence is mutual recognition and enrichment of individuals rather than the cult of fetishized or hypostatized communities." He argued that technology enhanced the ability of collectives to pool together their knowledge through interactions. Collective intelligence fuels the most advanced inventions and is a powerful tool for innovation and growth. An applicable and known example of collective intelligence playing the role of a powerful tool is the telephone; it was ideas across generations that allowed for the evolution of the telephone. More recently, online platforms allowed for and capitalized on ideas such as wisdom of the crowds [e.g., 22, 24]. Scholars studied these processes and examined the outcomes of mass collaboration in knowledge creation, for example, by focusing on Wikipedia [e.g., 7, 25]. In the broadest of terms, research on collective intelligence needs to be done in order to seek understanding of human behavior in general, and in particular in trolling instances, or across cultures.

We designed a study that analyzes YouTube videos from sixty countries, as a case of global trolling, in order to address 2 research questions: (1) What are the features of this global trolling event? (2) What are the collective intelligence attributes of this global trolling event? This study is unique and timely in that it focuses on global and ideological trolling, analyzing internet videos as a medium of trolling, that together exhibit the outcome of collective intelligence process.

2   Background

There is no consensus on the definition of trolling or what even constitutes it; trolling behavior ranges in manifestations, meanings, contexts, and effects. Trolling is defined here as [5, p. 6]: "a repetitive, disruptive online deviant behavior by an individual toward other individuals or groups". However, because we are focusing on the "America First" event, countries rather than individuals are at the center of our trolling attention. While early research focused attention on deviant behaviors and malevolent trolling, the focus has now shifted to satirical, ideological, collective, and political trolling from countries around the globe [2, 21, 27]. With regards to this paper, studies of collective, ideological and satirical trolling cases of American, Chinese and Russian trolls are most applicable [2, 3, 21, 27]. Trolling behaviors include provocativeness, intentionality, repetitiveness, pseudo-sincerity, and satire [19, 20]. Trolls can employ specific tactics to be provocative in specific situations [3], for example, through various outrage tactics such as lying, name-calling, insulting, or simply through the use of vulgar language [4].

Satire and ideological trolling are of particular interest, given that they seem to be a ubiquitous part of online interactions [3]. Humor "is defined as an amusing social experience that "benignly" violates norms" [13, p. 3], and trolls are known to violate community norms malevolently [20] or use community norms satirically to promote their ideology [3]. While humor involves appropriate violations of communication norms, malevolent trolling involves aggressive and inappropriate violation of norms. What is appropriate is subjective and varies across cultures [13]. This context-dependent nature of humor becomes even more complex when considering also the sociotechnical context of this global trolling [18] in which the America First event took place. Unfortunately, there is no cross-cultural research on trolling [5] or satire trolling, and very little cross-cultural research on humor [13]. However, it was found that in collectivistic culture (China, Korea, and Thailand, for example) humor was used for group bonding and individuals used self-deprecating humor, while individuals in individualistic countries (such as Canada, Germany, and US) were more likely to use self-enhancing humor [13].

Research on collective intelligence attracted much scholarly attention. Nickerson and his colleagues focused, for example, on the effect of exposure to original ideas in crowdsourcing ideation [26], reuse for customization [11], and crowds designing an object collectively [16], applying theories of idea exposure and idea generation [11], knowledge and reuse for replication and innovation [16], and combinatorial conjecture of creativity and human conceptual combination [26]. They found that crowdsourced idea generation and the exposure to an original idea may affect participants' motivation and their cognitive process. People are more likely to generate original ideas and filter out unoriginal ideas; however, it is often difficult for people to build on an original idea [11]. In another study they found that metamodels are more likely to be reused than models; designs that are generated from metamodels are less likely to be reused than other designs; metamodels will exhibit amplified reuse when created by members with higher levels of community experience; finally, metamodels are more likely than models to lead to designs similar to themselves, and therefore are less likely to lead to dissimilar designs [11]. In a third study, they found that a third-generation design of a chair was deemed more creative than the first, and features of the chair had been added, inherited and modified across the generations; essentially, crowd-based design processes are effective and highly encourage more creativity [16]. It is still unclear how people that participate in collaborative actions online can be productive or destructive, and which tactics are more constructive. It is also unclear how features of the collective outcome (be it a product, a design, an article, a video, or an answer) move through the generations of the combination of ideas process. Further, it is unclear what type of ideas should be attended to when it comes to generating good ideas by others. Above all, there is still much that needs to be addressed in this context, such as how creativity evolves across different cultures on a global-scale after being exposed to an initial and original source.

3 Method

In order to address the research questions, we choose a global trolling event that was reported in *Vanity Fair* on February 5, 2017 by Laura Bradley, who wrote an article titled "Europe is Trolling Trump". What began as a European trolling phenomenon turned quickly into a global trolling events with dozens of countries involved from around the globe.

3.1 Data Collection

Data, in the form of brief videos, was publicly available online. Using a snowball method and following an initial sample from Bradley's article (February 5, 2017), data was collected between February 6–February 24, 2017 on four separate dates. Only publicly available videos were captured and saved as files on shared folders for future analysis. We collected 100 videos and analyzed a total of 60 videos from various countries. Included in our sample are those videos that were published in February 2017 with the repeated theme, "America First [county name] Second". Each video provides a parody version on Trump's inauguration comment "America First" and then typically included humorous reasons why that country should be considered second.

Sixty out of these 100 videos were then uploaded into Nvivo 12, a software for qualitative data analysis. The 40 videos that were not included in our sample are those that represent regions, such as Europe or the Muslim World, and unrecognized countries and other entities, such as Mars, Westeros, Commander Geek, or Teen responses. All the videos are in English and they all begin with a variation of the statement "this is a message from the government of [country name]". Typically, there was only one video per country, and in cases where there were 2 videos from a single country (India and Israel), we included only the first video that was published from this country. This resulted in 60 videos, each from a different country.

3.2 Data Analysis

Based on content analysis we addressed the first research questions, while comparative case analysis addressed the other question. At the time we completed our data analysis many of the videos had been removed and were no longer available online. A coding scheme was developed from the data, using an iterative process of coding and discussion among the three coders. Each code was described and an example was provided to ensure coding reliability; codes with frequency of less than 10 instances were removed, as they were not significant enough for further analysis. Codes were grouped into four broad categories: trolling behaviors, trolling tactics, structural codes, and content. The unit of analysis for categories (trolling behavior, trolling tactics, and structural codes) was the video as a whole. For the content category, the unit of analysis for coding was 15-s intervals; coding involved assigning codes to each 15-s segment of the video. Two coders coded the data and intercoder reliability test was conducted on 10% of the videos by a third coder. Intercoder reliability was high at 91.4% with a Cohen Kappa of K = 0.829.

While we noticed in the content analysis some trends with the appearance of new codes over time and disappearance of others, we could not easily parse out trends over time, and a more nuanced analysis was required. We then wrote a brief case synopsis for each video in each stage; these were about half a page long each. Through continued comparative analysis between cases we identified themes that are common across the cases in a given stage, based on which we conducted a comparative case analysis between stages [14]. The themes that emerged include, for example, opening statements (e.g., "This is a message from the government of [insert country's name].") and closing requests (e.g., "We totally understand that it will be America first, but can we say [country name] second"). Tracing these themes through the five stages reveal a few that remained constant, such as the use of vulgar language, and others that varied from one stage to another, such as the nature of references to other countries.

The sixty videos ranged in length from 1:46 min (Russia) to 12:19 min (Germany), with an average of 4:07 min. There was a significant correlation between the length of video and country rank on Hofstede's Individualism/Collectivism ($r = -.66$, $p < .05$) and length of video and country rank on Hofstede's Indulgence dimension ($r = -.29$, $p < .05$) [10]. Collectivist cultures are considered to be less direct (more indirect) and less succinct (more elaborate) compared with individualistic cultures, which might explain why collectivistic countries had longer videos than individualistic countries [e.g., 8, 9]. Furthermore, longer videos were correlated with countries that suppress individual gratifications and regulate it through strict social norms. A little over half of the videos (52%) included an English narrator, most of the videos (84%) included subtitles in English and/or their local language, a closing request in the majority of videos (93%) to have their own country second (or even tenth in one instance), and half of them (52%) included an introduction that puts that video in the context of a local satirical TV show, in their own local language.

To address the second research question, we grouped the videos into 5 stages, based on assumed video publication date, to examine global collective intelligence change over time. We grouped countries into one stage solely based on our data collection dates. The first stage included the six videos that appeared in the *Vanity Fair* article on February 5, 2017 (stage 1); the second stage included the eleven additional videos that the *Vanity Fair* article added by February 6 (stage 2). Then we collected video through Google and YouTube searches on three occasions: eight videos on February 9 (stage 3), twenty videos on February 12 (stage 4), and fifteen additional videos on February 24 (stage 5).

Table 1 provides the names of the countries in each stage, along with average video length by stage. As we can see in Table 1, average video length varied between stages; yet there was no noticeable pattern of evolution, except that the range in the first stage showed the largest variety in length.

Table 1. Countries, regions, and length of videos by stage.

Stage	Countries	Length (avg. and range)
1	Belgium, Denmark, Germany, Netherland, Portugal, Switzerland	5:22 (1:58–12:19)
2	Canada, Finland, France, Italy, India, Kazakhstan, Lithuania, Luxembourg, Mexico, Morocco, Romania	3:50 (1:42–6:41)
3	Austria, Bulgaria, Croatia, Czech Republic, Iran, Moldova, Namibia, Slovenia	4:03 (3:29–5:58)
4	Australia, Brazil, Burkina Faso, China, Hungary, Iceland, Israel, Japan, Kosovo, Macedonia, New Zealand, Nigeria, Pakistan, Philippines, Russia, Singapore, Spain, Turkey, Uganda, the UK	3:45 (1:46–5:28)
5	Algeria, Armenia, Columbia, Egypt, Greece, Hong Kong, Ireland, Malaysia, Malta, Poland, Sweden, Syria, Taiwan, Tunisia, Ukraine	4:19 (3:00–5:54)

4   Findings and Discussion

To gain a better understanding of the global trolling phenomenon, we present our findings and discuss them under two sections, each addressing one research question: (1) To what extent is the "America First" event a case of global trolling? (2) What are the collective intelligence attributes of this global trolling event across and within countries?

4.1   Trolling Trump as Global Trolling

To address the first research question, we identify the nature of this global trolling event by describing the trolling behaviors and tactics we found in our data and examining them in light of online trolling research.

Overall, we found that the most frequent codes are the main categories, with references to Trump (#198) and the use of Trump language (#193), as well as to trolling behaviors (#157); these appeared in all the videos and were coded more than once per video. Specific codes that appeared frequently include references to the culture of the (video) sponsor country (#190), and references to another country (#129), as well as the use of the hyperbole trolling tactic (#114), in which the video exaggerates one's strengths or another's weaknesses. Clearly the frequent references to Trump are unique to this case study and are expected as this is the subject of the videos. The frequent references to sponsor country and to other countries in all the videos is indicative of the global and international scope of this event. Finally, the common utilization of trolling behaviors, and specifically the hyperbole tactic in the videos, supports the argument that this event is an instance of (global) trolling.

Furthermore, typical trolling behaviors [19], such as repetitive, provocative, pseudo-sincere, and satirical trolling behaviors, characterize all sixty videos. Holistically, the videos exhibit a repetition of satirical provocation by mocking Trump's inauguration speech and his "America First" campaign. The repetition occurs not only across videos, but also within a single video. The most extreme manifestation of repetition is in the China video that involved nothing but clips of Trump's repeatedly saying "China" at various speeches and interviews. Similarly, a repetition of clips of Trump referring to "Denmark" appears as part of the Swedish video. This repetitive trolling behavior by all contributors continued for a three-week period, resembling the repetition pattern of other events, such as the case of Chinese collective trolling [21], or state-sponsored trolling activities [17]. The duration of the Chinese collective trolling repetitions was a few days, but state-sponsored trolling can last longer than a couple of weeks, with several peaks. The "America First" event continued for about three weeks. This might be because the production of video is significantly more time-consuming than simply posting a text message or image on Facebook, Twitter, or Weibo. Another possible explanation is that a global spread of an idea takes longer as it crosses geographical, national, language, and cultural boundaries.

Table 2. Frequency and percent of trolling tactics.

Tactic	Description	Frequency	Percent
Hyperbole	Exaggerating one's strengths or another's weaknesses	114	23
Insulting	Statement meant to insult an individual or group of people	44	9
Personal attacks	Statement meant to target an individual	17	4
Sarcasm (Other)	Using irony to mock other countries	24	5
Sarcasm (US)	Using irony to mock the US	29	6
Swearing	Using vulgar language, usually to elicit a reaction	16	4
Derailment tactic	Purposefully leading a conversation off course, including: latching onto an unimportant detail; going completely off topic; inserting oneself into a conversation uninvited	77	15
Insane troll logic	Refers to claims that cannot be argued against because they are so absurd and detached from reality that they are nonsensical. Entails arguments so blatantly illogical that people assume that it must be done on purpose or that the arguer must be "crazy"	33	7
Lying tactic	Making an untrue statement, from simply lying to pure fantasy	36	7
Misappropriation of jargon	Adopting and playing with normative speech patterns for the group	26	5
Politeness tactic	Use of polite language such as "thank you" and "please" in trolling	69	14
Straight man tactic	Responding to others in an overly serious manner; for ex. taking humorous or sarcastic comments literally	8	1

As can be seen in Table 2, the "America First" global trolling event involved typical trolling tactics [3]. The most common tactics include the hyperbole arguments (23% of all tactics), exaggerating the weaknesses of either Trump, US, or other countries, or the strengths of their own country.

A typical example appears in the Sweden video, as the narrator, using Trump's voice and intonations, argues: "Sweden is the best country of all of Europe. Better than the Netherlands, better than Switzerland, and especially better than Denmark." This was followed by the derailment tactic (15%), which involved leading the conversation off track by latching onto an unimportant detail. The narrator started with an articulation of Sweden's strengths, when mentioning Denmark, but switched into making insulting comments on the Danish people, saying that they are the "Mexicans of the Scandinavia", and then included random clips of Trump saying "Denmark" at his various speeches, jumped into the "nuke Denmark" comment, mentioned IKEA, and finally followed with comments on the Trump organization, meatballs, furniture, and the wall bordering Mexico. Another common tactic was the politeness tactic (14%), which involved the use of "thank you," "please," or honorific mention, such as "Dear Mr. President". The repetitive politeness mocks the president, but also addresses him with appropriate honorific; in this context, it adds a sarcastic tone in the opening of all the videos.

Other trolling tactics found in our analysis included insulting (9%), lying (7%), sarcasm (towards others (6%) or the US (6%)), misappropriation of jargon (5%), swearing (4%) and personal attacks (4%) (Table 1). These trolling tactics resemble those identified in individual satire trolls' posts [3]. While each tactic on its own may not constitute trolling, the amalgamation of tactics and trolling behaviors, repeated over and over again, does.

Thus, we conclude that the "America First" case of global trolling resembles individual trolling behaviors and tactics, with global manifestation. Global trolling is less personal, but more ideological and collective.

4.2   Collective Intelligence in Global Trolling

We describe here the global trolling collective intelligence process based on our comparative case analysis, through five stages, addressing the second research question. Trolling Trump as a global trolling event evolved over a three-week period following Trump's inauguration speech and involved videos from 60 countries. We identified five stages in which the videos were posted. Each stage featured patterns of references that evolved between one stage to another and an evolving format of the closing request. At first, videos followed a relatively simple format of "America First, 'X Country' Second," as shown in the Netherlands videos, which was the first one posted. Then, in later stages, many renditions of this request appeared, including, for example: "America first, Netherlands Second, but can we say Lithuania third" (Lithuania, stage 2), "Unlike other countries we are not aspiring to be second, but 51st" (Czech Republic, stage 3), or even "Israel First, America Second" (Israel, stage 4). The same pattern was observed also on the eleven videos that emerged within regions in Germany. The Germany region videos, all in the 4th and 5th stages, displayed the same format of the opening and closing requests as other videos in these stages.

Besides the evolution of the opening and closing request, three significant references were noticeable: (1) China; (2) the gay community; and (3) Muslims/Arabs. None of these references appeared in the first stage, but they start to appear in stage 2, for example, with reference to China in the Luxembourg video. An increasing number of videos began to incorporate these references, to the point that in the fifth stage, 10 of the 14 videos included at least one reference to China, the gay community, and Muslim/Arabs.

The opening statement and closing request are important components of this global trolling event. The closing request starts as a simple remark and becomes progressively more intricate across the stages. The videos in stage one simply stated "We totally understand that it will be America first, but can we say [country name] second"; only a couple of exceptions diverged from this format. One exception is Germany, which in addition to this statement introduced a joke that would be repeated numerous times later, suggesting "If you were wanting to push the red button on us, then this is where we are located on the map" and showing a map where they highlighted Italy instead. Another variation in closing request in stage one appears in the Belgium video, saying "We totally understand it is going to be America first, but can we say Belgium second, or tenth… we don't care." The rank order (and name) of countries included in the closing request attracted much attention in videos in later stages. Both these notions help show how collective intelligence is upheld within all of these videos across stages, perhaps because they build into the simple satirical statement a complex statement about international relations (which country is their enemy, which country has an important role in global affairs), and mock Trump's impulsive behavior.

In stage two, most of the countries continue the pattern set up by the first group of videos, ending their videos either with the simple request, or with one of the two variations that were introduced in the first stage. For example, Luxembourg, Morocco, and Italy all included the bombing joke after their closing request. Again, a couple of videos here diverted in a way that affected videos in later stages. Specifically, Lithuania requested, "We totally understand if it is America first, Netherlands second, but can we say Lithuania third." For the first time, the video directly referenced the Netherlands, the first country to post a trolling video, and by doing so, parodically gave them priority in global affairs.

In stage three, these specific variations on the closing request continued, while a few elaborated further. One video, from Iran, added to the intricacy of global affairs and referenced several countries that produced videos in prior stages, in their closing request, asking to be only ahead of their primary enemy, Iraq, stating, "We totally understand that it is going to be America first, and a lot of other countries already claimed to be second. We can't compete with Netherlands, Switzerland, Portugal, Denmark, or other European countries, but how about Iran before Iraq". The Czech Republic, in another video, took their closing request a step further by stating "not aspiring to be second, but 51st of the United States". This exact joke was then repeated in later videos from Greece and Ireland, setting up a new trend in which various countries claim to became part of the United States, instead of competing for their rank globally.

In stages 4 and 5, the videos followed the general format of the closing request as in the previous stages but incorporated new ideas such as Israel (stage 4) claiming to take precedence over all the countries and to be ahead of the United States, showing the seal with "Israel first, America Second." Egypt (stage 5) decided to outline the United States as a part of its bombing joke instead of a neighboring country. In the earlier stages the videos would conclude with the request "America First, X Country Second", but in stages 4 and 5 it became a point to add additional comments after it. For instance, the United Kingdom (stage 4), after the closing request, added comments such as "Your greatest friend... seriously we love you... I need to tweet this..." and continued along those lines for 15 s after the request.

Referring to another country and to other videos was not limited to the opening and closing statements. One common reference was to China, typically in an insulting tone. There were none in stage 1, but by stages 2 and 3, there were brief references to China by Luxembourg and India, and in stage five, 7 of the 12 videos incorporated a type of insulting or degrading trolling comment towards China. Mocking both Trump's and the other counties' fixation with China is the video from China in the fourth stage, which only included a repetition of one word "China". Another common reference to other countries in the videos involved direct reference to early videos and their respective countries, by either insulting the country or citing their video. In stage one, all the videos insulted the Netherlands, as did many of the later stage videos as well. Insulting the Netherlands developed into a relevant feature across all stages of the videos. In stage five, Armenia directly quoted Turkey's video from stage four with the comment of "the country not the bird" and also directly quoted Bulgaria's video (stage three) of them "wanting to be tenth." There were also many instances where countries from later stages would insult countries from previous stages in their videos such as Iran (stage three) insulting India (stage two). Iran's closing request is also another example of this; they stated "We can't compete with Netherlands, Switzerland, Portugal, Denmark, or other European countries..." which refers to all the videos in the first stage. With this occurring, ideas can be directly traced from source to source.

Unlike the closing request, which became more complex with each stage, until it reached stagnation by stage five, the general format of the opening request did not change much until the fifth stage. The format of the opening statement is as follows: "This is a message from the government of [insert country's name]." In stage five a variation was introduced by the Hong Kong video, saying instead "This is a message on behalf of Her Majesty's request because the government of Hong Kong is too busy right now." This introductory statement criticizes their own country, and as such it became a way to excuse late adopters, who joined the trolling game later. Syria's video followed that same presentation by stating, "This is a message on behalf of all people from Syria because the government is too busy." At this stage, Taiwan had also changed their opening request to say "This is a message from the government of China, but you can just call us Taiwan," turning its opening request into a satirical comment on a controversial international affair.

Collective intelligence in global trolling resembles and enhances prior research in other settings, media, or platforms, and other creative processes and outcomes. As others have shown, creativity in mass crowd production is a result of combination of ideas [16], as well as the influence of the original idea [26]. In this global trolling event, the evolution of videos over time picked ideas from the first videos, early videos, and from later videos, combining them into new creations of videos. The impact of the original idea, in the form of the video from the Netherlands, continued to influence the later videos in content, style, and ideas that were incorporated into all the videos. The impact of this first video was evident in subsequent videos not only through the replication of ideas, such as opening and closing requests, but also in making direct reference to the video. Furthermore, in global trolling we identified similar processes of replication, innovation, and customization as others have discussed in the context of Thingiverse 3D models, for example [11]. The use of Trump voiceover in the videos illustrates replication that was adopted by video creators across the globe throughout the various stages of the global trolling event. At the same time, the closing and opening remarks were customized for each country and each region with specific manifestations, as well as stage-related variations. Innovation occurred over time, not only through country-specific customizations, but also in the introduction and through the evolution of major references to gay people, China, and Muslims.

This global trolling event, using YouTube videos, while resembling collective intelligence processes, results in a different outcome – trolling on a global scale while using videos. The repetitive nature of ideas in this case is the backbone of trolling. Sharing ideas in videos, across the YouTube platforms, triggered both shared creativity and pooled skills of video creators, from 60 countries across the globe, enabling them to join the event, by posting their unique creations on YouTube. Together they troll and their trolling videos creation are more sophisticated over time. Cultural and geographical differences became instrumental in the construction and evolution of trolling globally; instead of barriers to knowledge sharing these differences became the building blocks of collective intelligence.

5 Conclusions

This study examined a global trolling event, "America First," with the intention to identify whether global trolling exists, and if so, what trolling behaviors and tactics characterize global trolling, and what are the specific cultural manifestations of global trolling. We found that this is indeed a case of global trolling, exhibiting repetitive, provocative, pseudo-sincere, and satirical trolling behaviors, across all videos, regardless of sponsored countries. The study also examined collective intelligence processes; we found that similar to prior research, processes of innovation, replication, and customization were evident, as well as clear impact of the original idea, from the first Netherland's video, and throughout the five stages. We found support for these processes in video creation, while prior research focused on text or designs; across geographical, political, and national boundaries, while prior research largely disregarded these boundaries; and in online settings with naturally evolving creative processes that spans three weeks.

References

1. Buckles, E.E., Trapnell, P.D., Paulhus, D.L.: Trolls just want to have fun. Pers. Individ. Differ. **67**, 97–102 (2014)
2. Ferrari, E.: Fake accounts, real activism: political faking and user-generated satire as activist intervention. New Media Soc. **20**(6), 2208–2223 (2018)
3. Fichman, P., Dainas, A.: Graphicons and tactics in satirical trolling on Tumblr.com. Int. J. Commun. **13**, 4261–4286 (2019)
4. Fichman, P., Peters, E.: The impacts of territorial communication norms and composition on online trolling. Int. J. Commun. **13**, 1016–1035 (2019)
5. Fichman, P., Sanfilippo, M.R.: Online Trolling and Its Perpetrators: Under the Cyberbridge. Rowman & Littlefield, Lanham (2016)
6. Flores-Saviaga, C., Keegan, B.C., Savage, S.: Mobilizing the Trump train: understanding collective action in a political trolling community (2018). https://arxiv.org/pdf/1806.00429. pdf
7. Giles, J.: Internet encyclopedias go head to head. Nature **438**, 900–901 (2005)
8. Gudykunst, W.B.: Bridging Differences: Effective Intergroup Communication, 3rd edn. Sage Publications, Thousand Oaks (1998)
9. Gudykunst, W.B., Ting-Toomey, S.: Verbal communication styles. In: Gudygunst, W.B., Ting-Toomey, S., Chua, E. (eds.) Culture and Intercultural Communication, pp. 99–117. Sage Publications, Newbury Park (1988)
10. Hofstede, G., Hofstede, G.J., Minkov, M.: Cultures and Organizations: Software of the Mind, 3rd edn. McGraw-Hill, New York (2010)
11. Kyriakou, H., Nickerson, J.V., Sabnis, G.: Knowledge reuse for customization: metamodels in an open design community for 3D printing. MIS Q. **41**(1), 315–332 (2017)
12. Lévy, P.: Collective Intelligence: Mankind's Emerging World in Cyberspace. Perseus Books Group, Cambridge (1997). Transl. by R. Bononno
13. Lu, J.G., Martin, A.E., Usova, A., Galinsky, A.D.: Creativity and humor across cultures: where Aha meet Haha (2019). https://doi.org/10.1016/B978-0-12-813802-1.00009-0
14. Miles, M.B., Huberman, A.M.: Qualitative Data Analysis: An Expanded Sourcebook, 2nd edn. Sage Publications, Thousand Oaks (1994)
15. McCosker, A.: Trolling as provocation: YouTube's agonistic publics. Converg. Int. J. Res. New Media Technol. **20**(2), 201–217 (2014)
16. Nickerson, J.V., Yu, L.: Cooks or cobblers? Crowd creativity through combination. In: Proceeding of CHI, pp. 1393–1402 (2011)
17. Nyst, C., Monaco, H.: State-sponsored trolling. Institute for the Future (2018). https://docs. google.com/viewer?url=http%3A%2F%2Fwww.iftf.org%2Ffileadmin%2Fuser_upload% 2Fimages%2FDigIntel%2FIFTF_State_sponsored_trolling_report.pdf
18. Sanfilippo, M.R., Yang, S., Fichman, P.: Trolling here, there, and everywhere: perceptions of trolling behaviors in context. J. Assoc. Inf. Sci. Technol. **68**(10), 2313–2327 (2017)
19. Sanfilippo, M.R., Fichman, P., Yang, S.: Multidimensionality of online trolling behaviors. Inf. Soc. **34**(1), 1–13 (2018)
20. Shachaf, P., Hara, N.: Beyond vandalism: Wikipedia trolls. J. Inf. Sci. **36**(3), 357–370 (2010)
21. Sun, H., Fichman, P.: Chinese collective trolling. In: Proceedings of 81st Annual Meeting of the Association for Information Science and Technology, pp. 478–485 (2018)
22. Surowiecki, J.: The Wisdom of the Crowds. Anchor Books, New York (2004)
23. Synnott, J., Coulias, A., Ioannou, M.: Online trolling: the case of Madeleine McCann. Comput. Hum. Behav. **71**, 70–78 (2017)

24. Tapscott, D., Williams, A.D.: Wikinomics: How Mass Collaboration Changes Everything. Penguin Group Inc., New York (2007)

25. Viegas, F.B., Wattenberg, M., Kriss, J., van Ham, F.: Talk before you type: coordination in Wikipedia. In: Proceedings of the 40th Annual Hawaii International Conference on System Sciences, pp. 575–582 (2007)

26. Wang, K., Nickerson, J.V., Sakamoto, Y.: Crowdsourced idea generation: the effect of exposure to an original idea. Creat. Innov. Manag. **27**(2), 196–208 (2018)

27. Zelenkauskaite, A., Niezgoda, B.: "Stop Kremlin trolls:" ideological trolling as calling out, rebuttal, and reactions on online news portal commenting. First Monday (2017). https://doi.org/10.5210/fm.v22i5.7795

Perceived Use and Effects of Social Media for 1 to 2.5 Generation Immigrant College Students with Depression: Results from a Mixed Methods Survey

Christopher C. Frye[1]([⊠]), Linh G. Ly[2], Julissa Murrieta[3], Linda Sun[1], Courtney S. Cochancela[4], and Elizabeth V. Eikey[5]

[1] The iSchool Inclusion Institute (i3), University of Pittsburgh, Pittsburgh, PA 15260, USA
{ccf15,lis69}@pitt.edu

[2] The iSchool Inclusion Institute (i3), University of Washington, Seattle, WA 98195, USA
linh.lgly@gmail.com

[3] The iSchool Inclusion Institute (i3), University of Maryland, College Park, College Park, MD 20742, USA
jmurriet@umd.edu

[4] The iSchool Inclusion Institute (i3), College of Westchester, White Plains, NY 10606, USA
ccochancela@cruiser.cw.edu

[5] The iSchool Inclusion Institute (i3), University of California, San Diego, La Jolla, CA 92697, USA
elizabethveikey@gmail.com

Abstract. As social media becomes more prevalent, understanding its use and its relationship with mental health is crucial, especially among marginalized populations. Immigrant college students in the United States face unique challenges that put them at an increased risk of experiencing depression. Due to barriers surrounding mental health disclosure and treatment, immigrant students may turn to social media for support. In this paper, we present the results of a mixed methods survey conducted on the perceived use and effects of social media among 83 immigrant undergraduates (from generation 1 to 2.5) with depression. Most participants perceived social media as having no effect on depression. However, others perceived social media as improving depression more than worsening it. Overall, participants feel belonging and supported but report some feelings of isolation, loneliness, and comparison when engaging with social media. Many report using social media as a distraction technique by engaging with uplifting content, which is viewed as having a positive impact on depression symptoms. For immigrant college students, it is important to feel connected and supported on social media when experiencing mental health issues while avoiding comparison and navigating the disclosure of sensitive information. While social media has an opportunity to be a promising space for immigrant college students with depression and provide access to culturally relevant resources, there are a number of challenges that need addressed.

© Springer Nature Switzerland AG 2020
A. Sundqvist et al. (Eds.): iConference 2020, LNCS 12051, pp. 130–150, 2020.
https://doi.org/10.1007/978-3-030-43687-2_11

Keywords: Social media · Immigrant · College student · Mental health · Depression · Marginalized populations

1 Introduction

Social media may be an important space for people who face increased barriers to mental health treatment and disclosure, such as students of different immigrant generations. The population of immigrant college students has been increasing in universities across the United States (US) [9]. In fact, immigrant students comprised 24% of universities' populations from 2011 to 2012 [9]. While depression is a major challenge among college students generally [55], immigrant college students experience several additional stressors that increase their risk of depression. For instance, they often face unique struggles, such as discrimination from others and pressure to improve family's socioeconomical status, that negatively affect their mental health [9, 19].

The exact cause of depression is unknown [63], but it can impact one's life dramatically. Depression increases one's suicide risk, causes loss of interest in activities, and negatively affects academics, work, and personal life [63]. The Centers for Disease Control and Prevention (CDC) reported that untreated depression often becomes a chronic disease, and many people with depression go untreated [22, 63]. Research has shown that only about 36% of students with depression receive treatment [22], and this may be worse for immigrant students. For example, a study on Asian-American and Caucasian undergraduate students revealed that only 8.6% of Asian-American students received mental health treatment versus 17.9% of the general population [1]. People may be reluctant to seek treatment because of stigma [21, 42, 57], which may be exacerbated for marginalized and minority groups [29, 42], views about mental health issues [61], and representation of healthcare providers and access issues [16].

Individuals unable or reluctant to seek professional mental health services or disclose their mental health concerns face-to-face may turn to social media to find support, seek information about depression, and even manage their symptoms. This is unsurprising; according to Pew Research Center [7], 88% of 18 to 29 year-olds use some form of social media. Research has shown that individuals with mental health concerns between 18 to 24 are heavy social media users and are more likely to engage in social media to connect with others [27]. This may be even more likely for immigrant college students, who face additional stigma around mental health and lack of representation. Social media may play a crucial role in finding and feeling supported for this specific population.

Although some studies highlight the negative effects of social media in the context of mental health [37, 47, 52], there is evidence that social media has benefits for those with depression symptoms by facilitating social support and connectivity [6, 15, 23, 56]. While research has investigated other marginalized groups' experiences [5, 16, 30, 36], few studies have examined the use and perceptions of social media among immigrant college students [41]. This is an issue given the high rates of depression in college populations and the unique challenges immigrant students face.

In order to begin to fill this gap, we focus on students who were born in a country outside of the US and moved to the US (sometimes referred to as generation 1 to 1.75[1]) as well as those born in the US but whose parent(s) were born in a country other than the US (sometimes referred to as generation 2 and 2.5) [50, 51, 54]. Our study investigates perceptions and uses of social media among immigrant college students with depression. We discuss how this research has implications for our understanding of social media's role in mental health among immigrant students, as well as for the design of social media platforms. We identified the following research questions:

RQ1: What social media platforms do immigrant undergraduates use?

RQ2: In general, how do immigrant undergraduates perceive social media's effect on their depression?

RQ3: When using social media, to what extent do they:

> *(a) ...feel belonging?*
> *(b) ...feel supported?*
> *(c) ...feel isolated?*
> *(d) ...feel alone?*
> *(e) ...engage in comparison?*
> *(f) ...engage in distraction?*

RQ4: How does social media affect immigrant undergraduates' depression in positive and negative ways?

RQ5: What type of improvements to social media do immigrant undergraduates request?

2   Methodology

2.1   Measures

We developed a survey in Qualtrics to better understand social media's potential role in the lives of immigrant college students with depression. Data was collected in April 2018. Data quality was determined by both check questions embedded in the survey, as well as eligibility questions.

Culture and Immigrant Status. Participants were asked to identify their heritage culture other than American/US and their native language. They were also asked multiple choice questions about their birth country and their parents' birth countries to determine their immigrant generation, according to the Moffett definition [40], as shown in Table 1.

---

[1] For a description, see Table 1.

Table 1. Immigrant generation descriptions

Immigrant generation	Description
1	Moved to the US after age 17
1.25	Moved to the US between ages 13–17
1.5	Moved to the US between ages 6–12
1.75	Moved to the US before age 6
2	Born in the US and both parents born outside of the US
2.5	Born in the US and one parent born outside the US

Depression. We included the 21-item Beck's Depression Inventory II (BDI-II) [2]. These questions cover the psychomotor range of depressive symptoms, which include feelings of worthlessness, loss of focus, difficulty sleeping, appetite levels, and loss of energy. Each item is scored on a 0 to 3 range, and the accumulated score from the 21 items is calculated. The three ranges of scores convey the severity of depression symptoms experienced: minimum = 0 to 13, mild = 14 to 19, moderate = 20 to 28, and severe = 29 to 63. The BDI-II is reliable, and studies suggest it more accurately differentiates between depressed and non-depressed individuals [2]. Through multiple choice questions, we asked participants whether they had ever received a clinical diagnosis of and treatment for depression.

Social Media Platforms. We developed a list of 70 popular social media platforms from around the world to ensure we included a diverse set. This multiple answer question allowed participants to select all platforms they use as well as write in additional platforms not listed.

Social Media Perceptions and Improvements. In order to assess general perceptions of social media's effect on depression, participants were asked to select all that apply: "Social media makes my depression better," "Social media makes my depression worse," "I don't think social media affects my depression at all." Based on their selection, participants received open-ended follow-up questions to understand how social media impacts them in positive and negative ways. All participants received an open-ended question to elicit suggestions for improvements and feature changes. Using a Likert scale from 1-Strongly Disagree to 7-Strongly Agree, we also asked to what extent does social media relate to the following constructs:

Belonging & Support: We included these constructs because research has shown that lower sense of belonging [24, 31] and lower perceived social support [24, 59] are associated with greater severity of depression. Questions included: "In general, using social media... (1) makes me feel supported, (2) gives me a sense of belonging."

Loneliness & Isolation: We assessed perceptions of reduced connection because perceived isolation and loneliness are associated with depression [16]. Therefore, we asked two questions: "In general, using social media makes me feel... (1) isolated, (2) alone."

Comparison: Comparison was included because social comparison is related to depression symptoms both on social media [5] and in general [10]. We investigated this by asking: "In general, using social media makes me compare myself to others."

Distraction: Distraction was assessed because it has been shown to reduce depressive episodes [24, 26]. Participants answered the following question: "I use social media to distract me from my thoughts."

2.2   Ethical Considerations

We received Institutional Review Board (IRB) approval from the University of California, Irvine to conduct this study. The survey was reviewed by a certified mental health counselor to ensure that our questions were appropriate. Further, we included some individuals with lived experience during the creation of instruments. In the survey, we provided free mental health resources and included information and ways to access the National Suicide Prevention Lifeline for individuals who scored above a 0 on the suicidal thoughts section of the BDI-II. Additionally, we provided a space at the end of the survey for participants to share any additional information they wished.

2.3   Recruitment and Eligibility

We recruited participants through Amazon Mechanical Turk (mTurk) and through our personal social media accounts (Facebook, Twitter, and Instagram). Our participants were compensated $2 for approximately 20 min of their time. Eligibility criteria included: currently reside in the US; identify as an immigrant (either they were born in another country and moved to the US or one or both of their parents were born in another country but they were born in the US); 18 to 24 years old; currently an undergraduate; use at least one social media platform; speak English; and have experienced depression symptoms within the last 12 months. Participants were excluded if they have a history of a manic episode, schizophrenia, or bipolar disorder because the needs of these disorders may be distinctly different than the needs of those with depression.

2.4   Participants

In our final analysis, we had 83 participants (139 responses: 28 removed for being incomplete, and 28 excluded based on quality checks). Eighty of those participants were recruited directly via mTurk and 3 were recruited through personal social media accounts. When asked about gender in an open-ended question, participants responses included male ($n = 50$) and female ($n = 33$). Their age ranged from 18 to 24 (mean = 21.5; SD = 12.54). Forty-two participants were immigrant generations 1–1.75, and 41 were 2–2.5. The most commonly reported heritage culture was Mexican ($n = 15$), followed by Chinese ($n = 10$). More demographic information can be found in Table 2.

Regarding diagnosis and treatment, the majority ($n = 64$) had not received a clinical diagnosis or sought professional treatment. Based on the BDI-II, the mean depression score among participants was 21.25 (SD = 12.54) (moderate), which is significantly higher than norms of undergraduates in the US (norms: mean = 9.14, SD = 8.45; our participants: mean = 21.25, SD = 12.54) [13]. Although there are no clinical cut-off points, research suggests 13 or higher may be considered depressed [20], and 74.7% ($n = 62$) of our participants reached this threshold. However, scores less than 13 may not necessarily mean "not depressed" but rather lower symptom severity. This is important as all participants identified as experiencing depression, and there may be cultural differences in perceptions of depression symptoms.

Table 2. Participants' demographic information

Category	Participant breakdown
Immigrant generation	1 ($n = 6$, 7.2%) 1.25 ($n = 8$, 9.6%) 1.5 ($n = 13$, 15.7%) 1.75 ($n = 15$, 18.1%) 2 ($n = 26$, 31.3%) 2.5 ($n = 15$, 18.1%)
Heritage culture	Mexican ($n = 15$) Chinese ($n = 10$) African ($n = 7$) German ($n = 6$) Filipino ($n = 5$) French, Japanese ($n = 3$) Kenyan, Indian, Thai, Irish, Pakistani, Latino, African American ($n = 2$) Lithuanian, Vietnamese, English, Cuban, Nigerian (Igbo), Ukrainian, Cape Verde, Mien, Italian, Peruvian, Haitian, Hispanic, Moroccan, Puerto Rican, Latin, Jamaican ($n = 1$)
Native language	English ($n = 43$) Spanish ($n = 13$) French ($n = 4$) Chinese, Cantonese, German ($n = 3$) Filipino, Mandarin ($n = 2$), Filipino ($n = 2$) Japanese, Lithuanian, Hindi, Vietnamese, Urdu, Ukrainian, Portuguese, Gonja, Swahili, Danish ($n = 1$)
Race	Asian ($n = 23$) White ($n = 23$) Hispanic, Latino, or Spanish ($n = 17$) Black or African American ($n = 15$) Middle Eastern or North African ($n = 3$) American Indian or Alaska Native ($n = 1$)
Year in school	1st year ($n = 10$) 2nd year ($n = 20$) 3rd year ($n = 30$) 4th year ($n = 21$) 5th year ($n = 2$)
Degree pursuing	Bachelor's degrees ($n = 70$) Associate's ($n = 11$) Multiple ($n = 1$) Other ($n = 1$)
Student status	Full-time ($n = 68$) Part-time ($n = 15$)

2.5   Data Analysis

We used Excel, R, and JASP to compute counts, means, and standard deviations. We inductively coded participant responses from open-ended questions in an iterative manner and then generated broader themes. Our process was as follows: we first had six researchers individually go through the data to become familiar with it. Then as a group, we met to discuss themes we noticed. We created a document based on this discussion that we used to develop a preliminary codebook. The codebook was iteratively revised based on practice coding and discussions in the group. For the final coding process, four researchers individually coded the responses from the participants in a separate Excel document. We coded 17 responses for making depression better, 27 for making depression worse, and 81 responses for improvements. Each response was coded with up to 3 codes; however, this was rare, as most only had 1 code. Then researchers met to compare and discuss these codes. Any responses we did not have full agreement on were thoroughly discussed among the group until we reached consensus.

3   Results

3.1   Social Media Use (RQ1)

Respondents were asked to name all social media platforms that they used in their everyday lives. As illustrated in Table 3, Facebook (86.75%, $n = 72$) was the most commonly used social media platform among participants, followed by 43 who use YouTube, 41 who use Instagram, 36 who use Snapchat, and 32 who use Reddit. On average, participants reported using 4.40 (SD = 2.63) different social media platforms, but the number of platforms used ranged from 1 to 14.

Table 3.   Social media platforms

Type of social media platforms	# of participants
Facebook	72
YouTube	43
Instagram	41
Snapchat	36
Reddit	32
Twitter	25
LinkedIn, Tumblr	12
Google+	10
WeChat	5
Flickr, QQ	4
DeviantArt, Gaia Online, Funny or Die, Telegram, MeetUp, Kik	3
Myspace, Ask.fm, Vine	2
Vkontakte, LiveJournal, StumbleUpon, MyHeritage, Baidu Tieba, We Heart It, Sina Weibo, Delicious, Taringa, Skyrock, Last.fm, Tagged, MeetMe, Doubon, Xanga	1

3.2   Quantitative Data on Perceptions (RQ2, RQ3)

While we allowed participants to choose multiple answers to reflect the dynamic nature of social media and take a nuanced approach to thinking about perceived impact, participants tended to have one perception (rather than multiple perceptions) of social media's effects. As Fig. 1 shows, in terms of participants' perceptions of social media's effects on their depression, 46.99% (*n* = 39) of participants reported that social media does not influence their depression.

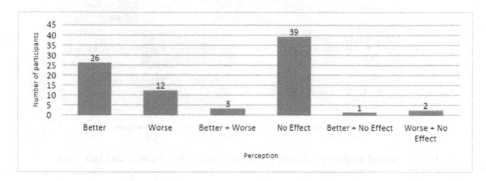

Fig. 1. Participants' perceptions of social media's impact on depression

While only 14.46% *(n* = 12) felt social media worsened depression, 31.33% (*n* = 26) reported that it makes it better. A small portion of participants reported that social media both makes their depression better and worse (*n* = 3), followed by worse and no effect (*n* = 2) (meaning social media can at times have negative implications and sometimes none), and better and no effect (*n* = 1) (meaning social media can at times have positive implications and sometimes none).

Out of all participants, 55.42% (*n* = 46) at least somewhat agreed that social media gives them a sense of belonging, and 61.45% (*n* = 51) at least somewhat agreed that social media makes them feel supported (Fig. 2). Of all participants, 54.22% (*n* = 45) at least somewhat agreed that they use social media as to distract them from their thoughts.

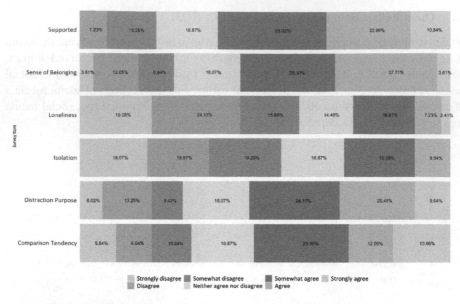

Fig. 2. Social media's perceived effect on participants' feelings and behaviors

Most participants (51.81%, $n = 43$) at least somewhat agreed that social media makes them compare themselves to others. Although the extent to which participants reported reduced connection from social media use was less than comparison, we found some participants indicated social media leads to perceptions of reduced connection. Specifically, 28.92% ($n = 24$) at least somewhat agreed that social media makes them feel isolated, and 26.51% ($n = 22$) at least somewhat agreed that social media makes them feel alone.

3.3   Qualitative Data on How Social Media Is Positive and Negative (RQ4)

Perceived Positive Effects. In terms of how social media improves depression, two themes emerged (Table 4).

Table 4. Themes regarding how social media has a positive impact on depression

Theme	# of codes[a]
Connecting with similar others	13
Uplifting content and distraction	13
Other	1

[a]Represents 27 of the 30 participants who reported social media improves depression

Thirteen discussed how social media allowed them to find and connect with others, often focusing on connecting with others who have similar experiences and sharing information with each other in a safe space. Feelings of connectedness improved participants' perceptions of their own experiences and provided them with ideas on how to cope. For instance, P10 said: *"It [social media] makes my depression better because I learn I'm not the only one. There's other people going through the same problems, and I'm also with them. We're struggling together and finding ways to help each other."* Similarly, understanding that other people are going through similar struggles helps users, as illustrated by this P11's words: *"It [social media] helps me to connect with others who are experiencing depression in their daily lives and see how they cope with it."* Not only is social media useful to garner support from online friends, but it also helps participants stay in contact with trusted friends or family. For example, P60 explained, *"It [social media] helps me keep in touch with people that talk me through and give me advice about my depression."* Engaging with similar others on social media helped to create safe spaces, where it is easier to discuss depression and its impact on individuals' lives. One participant described: *"I can connect with people experiencing the same problems with school. The forum is easier to talk about this issue" [P16].* Through social media, immigrant college students can connect with other individuals. This foster feeling of support and belonging as well as potential avenues for seeking advice and help, which are perceived to improve depression symptoms.

About half of the participants who reported that social media positively impacts their depression made comments related to distraction and engaging with positive or uplifting content (*n* = 13). These responses focused on how social media distracts the participant with happy content, such as images and videos, in order to avoid thinking about depressing thoughts. Participants often reported using social media to escape from their thoughts by engaging with content from others. For instance, P24 said: *"I am able to take my mind off things for a while and focus on other stuff. It helps me recharge."* Another participant expressed that seeing joyous content distracted them and improved their depressed mood: *"It's [social media's] full of funny clips that make me laugh and distract me from depressing thoughts or thinking a lot" [P21].*

Perceived Negative Effects. In terms of how social media worsens depression, two themes emerged (Table 5).

Table 5. Themes regarding how social media has a negative impact on depression

Theme	# of codes[a]
Comparison	13
Reduced connection	4
Other	1

[a]Represents 17 participants who reported social media worsens depression

Thirteen discussed how social media facilitates feelings of comparison because participants often perceive other users' lives as happier or better than theirs, which exacerbates their depression symptoms. For example, one participant described negative feelings when viewing friends' posts on social media: *"I see a lot of my friends post about how they are doing in their life and most of them seem to be doing a lot better than me. Seeing their posts makes me feel like I am doing poorly in comparison. I like my friends, but it makes me sad when I see them achieving their goals and flaunting it"* *[P49]*. The constant feed of social media does not help either, as users are bombarded with posts and updates from others that can lead to comparison. For example, this participant said: *"Facebook makes my depression worse because I am forced to see how good everyone else's life is. Like all of the pictures and all of the details of their vacations. The photo section is the worst. Also, the relationship status"* *[P54]*.

Our qualitative findings also help shed some light as to how social media reduces connection. Of individuals who reported social media worsens their depression, some ($n = 4$) explained how social media made them feel isolated or alone. One participant expressed the isolating environment social media creates: *"Seeing all those people doing things without me makes me feel more lonely and sad, especially when it's the people you believe to be your friends"* *[P61]*. When looking through others' photos and posts, users may feel excluded from offline activities hosted by their friends. For instance, P58 stated: *"It [social media] makes me lonely because I know no one really cares, everyone is so wrapped up in themselves."* This feeling may be further exacerbated by the physical form lack of interaction takes on social media platforms. For example, one participant said: *"People don't respond to my messages. People don't like my posts or pictures that much"* *[P67]*. Some participants also discussed spending too much time online than interacting offline, which resulted in feelings of isolation and loneliness. For example, P77 said, *"I waste time online instead of interacting with people [which makes me depression worse]."*

3.4 Qualitative Data on Improvements (RQ5)

We asked all participants to explain how they would change social media to better suit their needs (Table 6). We describe the four themes that emerged for those who did have suggestions below.

Table 6. Recommendation for improvements

Theme	# of codes[a]
Improved connection	16
Increased protections and more positive content	15
Better access to resources and outreach	11
More culturally inclusive	6
Other	9
Not sure/no changes	24

[a]Represents 80 participants who provided a response for this question

Improved Connection. Immigrant college students want social media platforms to provide easier ways to connect and more specific spaces to locate individuals with similar lived experiences. For example, P40 said they want *"to have people join like-minded groups together to be there for each other."* Some participants described a need for more support groups, as illustrated in the following quote: *"A support group. It's easy to message people and put a hang out. Being in a group with positive people who understand people with depression can help" [P10].* Immigrant college students also want specific cultural groups to reduce stigma, as illustrated by P30: *"Develop a group that encourages immigrants especially in the Hispanic community to talk about depression so it's not as much of a taboo topic."*

Increased Protections and More Positive Content. Participants requested that social media provide options to promote more positive, happy content while reducing more dismal content that may unintentionally lead to more negative emotions, thoughts, and comparison. For instance, P49 explained how it would be useful for social media to get more user feedback to personalize the experience and tailor content to users' needs: *"I think that I would want to see features that pop up and ask if a post is making you feel sad, maybe give you options to look at happier things, if the post detects that it is about depression."* With machine learning techniques, social media platforms can help identify negative and depression-triggering posts, so that more happy content is promoted on users' online feeds. Participants also suggested positive content include ways to minimize comparison, as illustrated by P75: *"[I] would not have the ability to give like... I would change these features because it makes them feel less included if they do not get as many likes from their peers and makes them feel less adequate about themselves."* Although less common, participants expressed wanting to feel safer on social media in order to communicate with others. P54 expressed: *"I wish there was a feature to screen out ugly messages on Facebook, or to block the comments on You-Tube so you don't have to see them. The world is so hateful sometimes."* Other participants spoke similarly about having a filtering feature to improve their experience *"by having less racial stereotypes and removing trolls" [P37].*

Better Access to Resources and Outreach. There is an opportunity for these platforms to connect students to mental health resources, engage in outreach efforts, and reduce stigma around depression. For example, P51 stated: *"Improve access to free or affordable help for immigrant college students with depression."* Participants also recommended that social media platforms create more easily accessible safe spaces that have options to find support from others but also offer depression-related content without requiring users disclose their identity: *"Have a dedicated area available on all social media platforms to deal with depression for college students. Also, anonymity would really help. Some social media has that, but most platforms don't" [P32].* Others recommended resources to help immigrant students understand the impact of social media: *"Some aspects of social media that I would change would be to have greater access to information about how social media affects a young individual's cognition and how it may affect their personality" [P61].* Some participants felt these strategies could be useful in encouraging openness about depression and reducing stigma.

More Culturally Inclusive. Some participants requested that social media promote more cultural inclusivity through encouraging different viewpoints, as illustrated by P24: *"More inclusiveness and views outside the US."* Similarly, more language options would show a commitment to supporting people from diverse backgrounds. For example, one participant requested *"material available in different languages or in setting more familiar to them [immigrant students] because it might make them more comfortable viewing the material"* [P25].

4 Discussion

4.1 The Need for Culturally Relevant Information and Resources

Nearly half of participants did not feel as though social media has any effect on their depression and a portion reported that no changes to social media should be made despite studies showing social media's negative effects on mental health [7, 37, 55]. This could be partially due to cultural differences in perceptions of mental health and the role of more general-purpose technologies, like social media. Research has shown that cultural values influence perceptions of mental health [3, 14, 38, 60]. For example, Carpenter-Song et al. [14] found that Euro-Americans recognize mental illnesses and seek out mental health services while Latinos and African Americans tend to downplay mental illnesses and thus are less likely to seek treatment.

Cultural differences can also influence whether individuals recognize their experiences as related to mental health. This means that in order to reach these populations, information must resonate with them. This notion is supported by prior literature that highlights the need for resources to provide respectful information in a holistic fashion for individuals by relating to their culture and mental health [34]. Having more culturally relevant information about the potential downsides to social media may help immigrants understand when to engage with and disengage from social media; further, knowing how to best engage with these platforms can help students have a better relationship with them. Further, social media could be one way to disseminate culturally competent mental health resources. This was echoed by some participants, who felt social media platforms could be a free and easy way to share this type of information.

Extant literature showcases existing frameworks that can be used to accomplish this (e.g., Bernal et al. [12]). Social media platforms can choose appropriate articles to promote and Facebook and other platforms could spend more time and effort delivering videos on how to deal with depression, memes and informative pictures regarding treatment options, or inspiring quotes in immigrants' native language, which was mentioned by some of our participants.[2]

---

[2] It is important to note that although increasing access to more culturally competent resources and information about social media will benefit immigrant college students, social media platforms are not a replacement for clinical treatment.

4.2   Tradeoffs in Fostering Connection

We found immigrant college students want to connect with others to get support for depression. This is unsurprising, as prior research suggests that students suffering from at least moderate depression prefer to talk about it on social media rather than in person [50]. Over half of participants in our study agreed that social media makes them feel a sense of support and belonging, and that connection with others on social media improved their depression. This is important, given that higher sense of belonging [35, 46], higher perceived social support [13, 59], and lower perceived isolation and loneliness [59] are associated with lower depression severity. Our findings are congruent with prior literature by Zhang [62], who found college users who receive support on Facebook in response to disclosing stressful life events have reduced depression symptoms. While these studies highlight how connecting with others on social media is important for those with depression [32], social media's role in fostering belonging and support may be even more critical for immigrant students. Immigrant undergraduates may face additional challenges that may not fit with the picture of a "traditional" college student. Challenges such as discrimination [55], bullying [45], and financial barriers [33] can negatively impact their mental health. Because they may be geographically separated from friends and family who share their cultural identity, social media may act as a bridge to keep them in contact with loved ones [49]. Although friends and family connections are important, it may be difficult for some immigrant students to reach out to family or friends about their mental health concerns because of cultural differences in perceptions of depression and mental health generally [17]. Social media can help fill this gap by connecting immigrant students with others who share both their cultural identity and lived experiences with depression.

Comparison Compromises Connection. Despite many positive aspects of social media, many participants reported that social media does increase feelings of loneliness, isolation, and comparison. For some immigrant students with depression, social media exacerbates feelings of loneliness either because they are not getting physical signs of support (e.g., messages, likes, etc.) or they "feel alone together" (i.e., so many people are there but none to support them). It is possible that perceived isolation offline translates to similar feelings online. Further, while loneliness and isolation may be motivating factors for turning to social media, attempting to connect with others may inadvertently result in students comparing themselves to other users. We found that many participants felt social media makes them compare themselves to others, which is congruent with prior literature on the relationship between comparison and poor mental health [18, 44, 58]. The very nature of social media makes it more likely that users will engage in comparison. Social media tends to be one-sided; users often present their best self, an idealized representation of their actual lives, which does not encompass negative parts. This makes it easier to feel as though others are doing better, as highlighted by participants in our study, which is in line with prior research [7, 8, 44]. To counteract this tendency to compare, social media could allow users to decide if they want to view engagement metrics, such as likes, number of comments, etc. These often quantitative features may be problematic for some users who are inclined to compare their numbers to others'. Interestingly, this idea recently gained traction by Facebook and Instagram, who are experimenting with removing likes from the platforms to reduce the pressure of posting and worrying about the quantity of likes [34]. This type of change not only could reduce comparison but could also increase connection by encouraging users to post for support and quality interactions rather than altering post content solely to receive more likes.

Disclosure Compromises Connection. Traditionally, social media's purpose was to facilitate communication, which could be used for entertainment and marketing. Over time, however, social media users have appropriated these platforms to fulfill various needs from sharing political news to recruiting for employment to acquiring information about health conditions. Due to the number of different types of users, the role of the platform itself has been called into question. How can social media adequately support the needs of these different subgroups while balancing the goals of the platform itself? Moreover, it has become clear that users' needs are dynamic, and they use these platforms in more than one way. Immigrant college students' needs across the platform may change. For example, their needs and requirements when they use social media to connect with other immigrant students with depression to get support are different than when they use social media to connect with individuals from their academic institution to learn about new course offerings. In the former case, students may need to disclose their experiences as an immigrant as well as their mental health.

There is an inherent tradeoff that becomes apparent when acknowledging the larger context of this work. While it is clear that fostering spaces on social media for immigrant students with depression is important, connecting immigrant students not only with others who share similar mental health experiences, but also individuals who are immigrants could be counterintuitive to the individuals seeking support, as it is unclear how this information could be used in the future and by whom (e.g., [39, 43]). Thus, having one's identity in any way tied to this information could be problematic. This kind of information sharing could create an environment where the cultural stigma of mental health is exacerbated, causing immigrant students to avoid sharing their personal information and unintentionally reducing the likelihood of receiving the support and resources they want and need.

One potential protection is ensuring anonymity on spaces dedicated to mental health. This is different from current ways of connecting immigrant college students (i.e., closed Facebook groups) because a user's identity is still apparent. A user may not want to have their personal information available when discussing sensitive topics, especially because it is not clear who will see their interactions and how this information will be used. This notion is similar to Andalibi et al. [4], who described the process of adding an extra layer of security when talking about sensitive experiences. Anonymized spaces facilitate hybrid identities. For example, immigrant college students could keep the same appearance to friends and family but remain anonymous when connecting with others to fulfill their mental health needs. However, this comes with its own challenges. For instance, how can social media platforms intervene if bullying occurs or threats to the individual or others are made? This is a larger problem that will require cooperation among industry, policy, and research.

4.3   Distraction and Positive Content: Benefits and Challenges

Our study shows that immigrant students are using social media as a distraction mechanism and requesting more positive and happy content. Social media's role as a distractor may be critical for immigrant students and other marginalized groups who may be less likely to receive traditional mental health services – meaning they may turn to social media as an outlet more than others. However, what is unclear is whether using social media for distraction is a positive way to disrupt ruminative thought or an avoidance coping strategy that exacerbates depression and anxiety. On one hand, social media platforms may help immigrant students get out of negative thought and emotional cycles by providing them with content to distract them and other topics about which to think. This is congruent with Radovic et al. [50], who found that searching for entertaining content and using social media as a distraction were positive uses of social media among depressed individuals. This makes sense given that depression is associated with negative thoughts cycles, referred to as rumination [42, 53]. Individuals who engage in rumination often find it difficult to disengage from mood-congruent thoughts, and research has suggested that distraction may play a crucial role in alleviating negative mood [32, 36].

It is important to note that our qualitative findings reveal that the content of the distraction may be critical. Even the type of positive content may matter. While happy content, such as funny videos and memes may help reduce negative feelings and thoughts, the impact of positive content either related to themselves or others may vary from person to person. For instance, viewing birthday party photos posted by one's friends or seeing a post that makes one recall positive memories when depressed may negate the positive effects of distraction. Research supports this: Joorman et al. [32] found that depressed individuals' sad moods worsened when they recalled positive memories. Therefore, future research must carefully evaluate the type of social media content used as distraction and how it relates to depression symptoms.

Further, social media may function as a maladaptive coping strategy, as individuals may use social media sites to avoid real-world stressors via their distracting feature. For instance, Rideout and Fox [50] demonstrated how students with moderate to severe depression symptoms use social media to avoid their problems compared to students with no depression. Positive content being ever present on social media and being easily accessible via mobile devices can allow immigrant college students to stay distracted on social media longer. As prior work notes, "It is possible that people who are socially anxious or depressed use multitasking with media as a distraction technique to avoid experiencing negative emotional states" (p. 7) [11]. However, this could facilitate an avoidance coping strategy, worsening their psychopathology.

5   Limitations

Recruiting using mTurk likely limited the diversity of our sample. More participants identified as men than women, and most identified as White or Asian, meaning our sample is not representative of all immigrant undergraduates in the US. In some cases, using mTurk may compromise the quality of responses [25]. Also using the BDI-II comes with limitations due to the ordering of questions and norms and gender bias issues embedded in this measure [28]. The ordering of open-ended questions in the survey also could have influenced the type of responses from participants. Additionally, participants self-identified as immigrants and were grouped into generations based on answers regarding birth county. Some participants may be international students, who face unique challenges and may have different perspectives compared to immigrant students, though the distinction is blurry. Furthermore, we relied on participants' ability to recall experiences. Self-reporting of health statuses is subject to different interpretations and perceptions by each participant [48]. While future work is needed, we caution others to carefully consider ethics around this topic and population.

6 Conclusion

Immigrant college students represent an increasing portion of college students in the US. As depression becomes a concerning issue among them, it is important to explore their perceptions of social media's role in depression. From the data collected from 83 immigrant college students via a mixed methods survey, we found the majority of immigrant students perceive that social media has no effect on their depression, followed by positive effects. Immigrant students felt that social media provides them with a sense of belonging and support by allowing them to connect to similar others or be distracted by positive content. However, some reported feelings of comparison and isolation when using social media platforms. Our research advocates for social media to better suit immigrant undergraduates' needs by highlighting both perceived benefits and negative consequences. By increasing culturally relevant information and resources, fostering connection across hybrid identities, decreasing the quantifiable aspects associated with comparison, and adapting positive content to users' needs, social media may be one possible positive outlet for immigrant college students with depression. Our research study is one of the first that focuses on immigrant college students' perceptions of social media in relation to depression.

Acknowledgements. We would like to thank iSchool Inclusion Institute (i3) Director Dr. Kayla Booth, our research advisor and i3 Assistant Director Dr. Elizabeth Eikey. This work was supported by the National Center for Research Resources, the National Center for Advancing Translational Sciences, and the NIH (UL1 TR001414). It is solely the responsibility of the authors and does not necessarily represent the official views of the NIH.

References

1. Abe-Kim, J., et al.: Use of mental health-related services among immigrant and US-born Asian Americans: results from the National Latino and Asian American study. Am. J. Public Health **97**(1), 91–98 (2007)
2. Beck, A.T., Steer, R.A., Brown, G.K.: Beck Depression Inventory-II. San Antonio **78**(2), 490–498 (1996)
3. Abdullah, T., Brown, T.L.: Mental illness stigma and ethnocultural beliefs, values, and norms: an integrative review. Clin. Psychol. Rev. **31**(6), 934–948 (2011)

4. Andalibi, N., Morris, M.E., Forte, A.: Testing waters, sending clues: indirect disclosures of socially stigmatized experiences on social media. In: Proceedings of the ACM on Human-Computer Interaction, vol. 2, no. CSCW, p. 19 (2018)
5. Andalibi, N., Ozturk, P., Forte, A.: Depression-related imagery on instagram. In: Proceedings of the 18th ACM Conference Companion on Computer Supported Cooperative Work and Social Computing, pp. 231–234. ACM (2015)
6. Andalibi, N., Ozturk, P., Forte, A.: Sensitive self-disclosures, responses, and social support on instagram: the case of #depression. In: Proceedings of the 2017 ACM Conference on Computer Supported Cooperative Work and Social Computing, pp. 1485–1500. ACM (2017)
7. Anderson, M., Jiang, J.: Teens, social media & technology 2018. Pew Research Center, 31 May 2018
8. Appel, H., Gerlach, A.L., Crusius, J.: The interplay between Facebook use, social comparison, envy, and depression. Curr. Opin. Psychol. 9, 44–49 (2016)
9. Arbeit, C.A., Staklis, S., Horn, L.: New American Undergraduates: Enrollment Trends and Age at Arrival of Immigrant and Second-Generation Students. Statistics in Brief, NCES 2017-414. National Center for Education Statistics (2016)
10. Bagroy, S., Kumaraguru, P., De Choudhury, M.: A social media based index of mental well-being in college campuses. In: Proceedings of the 2017 CHI Conference on Human Factors in Computing Systems, pp. 1634–1646. ACM (2017)
11. Becker, M.W., Alzahabi, R., Hopwood, C.J.: Media multitasking is associated with symptoms of depression and social anxiety. Cyberpsychol. Behav. Soc. Netw. 16(2), 132–135 (2013)
12. Bernal, G., Bonilla, J., Bellido, C.: Ecological validity and cultural sensitivity for outcome research: issues for the cultural adaptation and development of psychosocial treatments with Hispanics. J. Abnorm. Child Psychol. 23(1), 67–82 (1995)
13. Brausch, A.M., Decker, K.M.: Self-esteem and social support as moderators of depression, body image, and disordered eating for suicidal ideation in adolescents. J. Abnorm. Child Psychol. 42(5), 779–789 (2014)
14. Carpenter-Song, E., Chu, E., Drake, R.E., Ritsema, M., Smith, B., Alverson, H.: Ethno-cultural variations in the experience and meaning of mental illness and treatment: implications for access and utilization. Transcult. Psychiatry 47(2), 224–251 (2010)
15. Cavazos-Rehg, P.A., et al.: An analysis of depression, self-harm, and suicidal ideation content on Tumblr. Crisis 38, 44–52 (2016)
16. Cruwys, T., et al.: Feeling connected again: interventions that increase social identification reduce depression symptoms in community and clinical settings. J. Affect. Disord. 159, 139–146 (2014)
17. De Choudhury, M., Sharma, S.S., Logar, T., Eekhout, W., Nielsen, R.C.: Gender and cross-cultural differences in social media disclosures of mental illness. In: Proceedings of the 2017 ACM Conference on Computer Supported Cooperative Work and Social Computing, pp. 353–369. ACM (2017)
18. De Vries, D.A., Kühne, R.: Facebook and self-perception: individual susceptibility to negative social comparison on Facebook. Pers. Individ. Differ. 86, 217–221 (2015)
19. Deenanath, V.: First-generation immigrant college students: an exploration of family support and career aspirations. Graduate School of University of Minnesota (2014)
20. Dozois, D.J., Dobson, K.S., Ahnberg, J.L.: A psychometric evaluation of the Beck Depression Inventory-II. Psychol. Assess. 10(2), 83 (1998)
21. Eisenberg, D., Downs, M.F., Golberstein, E., Zivin, K.: Stigma and help seeking for mental health among college students. Med. Care Res. Rev. 66(5), 522–541 (2009)

22. Eisenberg, D., Golberstein, E., Gollust, S.E.: Help-seeking and access to mental health care in a university student population. Med. Care **45**(7), 594–601 (2007)
23. Ellison, N.B., Steinfield, C., Lampe, C.: The benefits of Facebook "friends:" social capital and college students' use of online social network sites. J. Comput. Mediat. Commun. **12**(4), 1143–1168 (2007)
24. Fisher, L., Overholser, J., Ridley, J., Braden, A., Rosoff, C.: From the outside looking in: sense of belonging, depression, and suicide risk. Psychiatry (N. Y.) **78**(1), 29–41 (2015)
25. Fort, K., Adda, G., Cohen, K.B.: Amazon mechanical turk: gold mine or coal mine? Comput. Linguist. **37**(2), 413–420 (2011)
26. Gonzales, A.L., Hancock, J.T.: Mirror, mirror on my Facebook wall: effects of exposure to Facebook on self-esteem. Cyberpsychol. Behav. Soc. Netw. **14**(1–2), 79–83 (2011)
27. Gowen, K., Deschaine, M., Gruttadara, D., Markey, D.: Young adults with mental health conditions and social networking websites: seeking tools to build community. Psychiatr. Rehabil. J. **35**(3), 245 (2012)
28. Hagen, B.: Measuring melancholy: a critique of the Beck Depression Inventory and its use in mental health nursing. Int. J. Mental Health Nurs. **16**(2), 108–115 (2007)
29. Hautasaari, A., Yamashita, N., Kudo, T.: Role of CMC in emotional support for depressed foreign students in Japan. In: Proceedings of the 2017 CHI Conference Extended Abstracts on Human Factors in Computing Systems, pp. 2614–2621. ACM (2017)
30. Homan, C.M., Lu, N., Tu, X., Lytle, M.C., Silenzio, V.: Social structure and depression in TrevorSpace. In: Proceedings of the 17th ACM Conference on Computer Supported Cooperative Work and Social Computing, pp. 615–625. ACM (2014)
31. Joiner Jr., T.E., et al.: Main predictions of the interpersonal-psychological theory of suicidal behavior: empirical tests in two samples of young adults. J. Abnorm. Psychol. **118**(3), 634 (2009)
32. Joormann, J., Siemer, M., Gotlib, I.H.: Mood regulation in depression: differential effects of distraction and recall of happy memories on sad mood. J. Abnorm. Psychol. **116**(3), 484 (2007)
33. Kanno, Y., Varghese, M.M.: Immigrant and refugee ESL students' challenges to accessing four-year college education: from language policy to educational policy. J. Lang. Identity Educ. **9**(5), 310–328 (2010)
34. Kleinman, Z.: Facebook hints at hiding likes, 3 September 2019. http://bbc.com/news/technology-49562978. Accessed 5 Sept 2019
35. Kondrat, D.C., Sullivan, W.P., Wilkins, B., Barrett, B.J., Beerbower, E.: The mediating effect of social support on the relationship between the impact of experienced stigma and mental health. Stigma Health **3**(4), 305 (2018)
36. Li, G., Zhou, X., Lu, T., Yang, J., Gu, N.: SunForum: understanding depression in a Chinese online community. In: Proceedings of the 19th ACM Conference on Computer-Supported Cooperative Work and Social Computing, pp. 515–526. ACM (2016)
37. Lin, L.Y., et al.: Association between social media use and depression among US young adults. Depress. Anxiety **33**(4), 323–331 (2016)
38. Masuda, A., Boone, M.S.: Mental health stigma, self-concealment, and help-seeking attitudes among Asian American and European American college students with no help-seeking experience. Int. J. Adv. Couns. **33**(4), 266–279 (2011)
39. Maurer, R.: Social media information now required from all visa applicants, 5 June 2019. https://www.shrm.org/resourcesandtools/hr-topics/talent-acquisition/pages/social-media-information-required-all-visa-applicants.aspx. Accessed 5 Sept 2019
40. Moffett, D.: Is an immigrant considered first or second generation?, 11 March 2019. https://www.thoughtco.com/first-generation-immigrant-defined-1951570. Accessed 5 May 2019

41. Murrieta, J., Frye, C.C., Sun, L., Ly, L.G., Cochancela, C.S., Eikey, E.V.: #Depression: findings from a literature review of 10 years of social media and depression research. In: Chowdhury, G., McLeod, J., Gillet, V., Willett, P. (eds.) iConference 2018. LNCS, vol. 10766, pp. 47–56. Springer, Cham (2018). https://doi.org/10.1007/978-3-319-78105-1_6
42. Nolen-Hoeksema, S., Wisco, B.E., Lyubomirsky, S.: Rethinking rumination. Perspect. Psychol. Sci. 3(5), 400–424 (2008)
43. Office of the Federal Register: Implementing immediate heightened screening and vetting of applications for visas and other immigration benefits, ensuring enforcement of all laws for entry into the United States, and increasing transparency among departments and agencies of the Federal Government and for the American people (2017). https://www.federalregister.gov/documents/2017/04/03/2017-06702/implementing-immediate-heightened-screening-and-vetting-of-applications-for-visas-and-other. Accessed 5 Sept 2019
44. Panger, G.: Social comparison in social media: a look at Facebook and Twitter. In: CHI 2014 Extended Abstracts on Human Factors in Computing Systems, pp. 2095–2100. ACM (2014)
45. Pottie, K., Dahal, G., Georgiades, K., Premji, K., Hassan, G.: Do first generation immigrant adolescents face higher rates of bullying, violence and suicidal behaviours than do third generation and native born? J. Immigr. Minor. Health 17(5), 1557–1566 (2015)
46. Powell, J., Clarke, A.: Information in mental health: qualitative study of mental health service users. Health Expect. 9(4), 359–365 (2006)
47. Primack, B.A., et al.: Use of multiple social media platforms and symptoms of depression and anxiety: a nationally-representative study among US young adults. Comput. Hum. Behav. 69, 1–9 (2017)
48. Quan-Haase, A., Young, A.L.: Uses and gratifications of social media: a comparison of Facebook and instant messaging. Bull. Sci. Technol. Soc. 30(5), 350–361 (2010)
49. Radovic, A., Gmelin, T., Stein, B.D., Miller, E.: Depressed adolescents' positive and negative use of social media. J. Adolesc. 55, 5–15 (2017)
50. Rideout, V., Fox, S.: Digital health practices, social media use, and mental well-being among teens and young adults in the US (2018)
51. Rumbaut, R.G.: Ages, life stages, and generational cohorts: decomposing the immigrant first and second generations in the United States. Int. Migrat. Rev. 38(3), 1160–1205 (2004)
52. Shensa, A., Escobar-Viera, C.G., Sidani, J.E., Bowman, N.D., Marshal, M.P., Primack, B. A.: Problematic social media use and depressive symptoms among US young adults: a nationally-representative study. Soc. Sci. Med. 182, 150–157 (2017)
53. Takano, K., Tanno, Y.: Self-rumination, self-reflection, and depression: self-rumination counteracts the adaptive effect of self-reflection. Behav. Res. Ther. 47(3), 260–264 (2009)
54. Trevelyan, E.N., et al.: Characteristics of the US Population by Generational Status, 2013. US Department of Commerce, Economic and Statistics Administration, US Census Bureau (2016)
55. Tummala-Narra, P., Claudius, M.: Perceived discrimination and depressive symptoms among immigrant-origin adolescents. Cult. Divers. Ethnic Minor. Psychol. 19(3), 257 (2013)
56. Veretilo, P., Billick, S.B.: Psychiatric illness and Facebook: a case report. Psychiatr. Q. 83(3), 385–389 (2012)
57. Vidourek, R.A., King, K.A., Nabors, L.A., Lynch, A., Merianos, A.: College students' perceived confidence in mental health help-seeking. Int. J. Mental Health Promot. 16(2), 83–90 (2014)
58. Vogel, E.A., Rose, J.P., Roberts, L.R., Eckles, K.: Social comparison, social media, and self-esteem. Psychol. Pop. Media Cult. 3(4), 206 (2014)
59. Wang, J., Mann, F., Lloyd-Evans, B., Ma, R., Johnson, S.: Associations between loneliness and perceived social support and outcomes of mental health problems: a systematic review. BMC Psychiatry 18(1), 156 (2018)

60. Wong, E.C., Collins, R.L., Cerully, J., Seelam, R., Roth, B.: Racial and ethnic differences in mental illness stigma and discrimination among Californians experiencing mental health challenges. Rand Health Q. **6**(2), 6 (2017)
61. Young, C.B., Fang, D.Z., Zisook, S.: Depression in Asian-American and Caucasian undergraduate students. J. Affect. Disord. **125**(1–3), 379–382 (2010)
62. Zhang, R.: The stress-buffering effect of self-disclosure on Facebook: an examination of stressful life events, social support, and mental health among college students. Comput. Hum. Behav. **75**, 527–537 (2017)
63. Depression. Centers for Disease Control and Prevention (CDC) (2017). https://www.cdc.gov/mentalhealth/basics/mental-illness/depression.htm. Accessed 2 July 2017

Mobile Instant Messenger as a Hub for Mixed Work and Personal Conversation

Group Chat Switching Patterns and Usage Strategies of the Users

Youngchan Jeong⬛, Hyelan Jung⬛, and Joongseek Lee⁽⊠⁾⬛

Seoul National University, Seoul 08826, Republic of Korea
ycmailcase@gmail.com, joonlee8@snu.ac.kr

Abstract. Because mobile instant messengers (MIM) are actively used for work, the problem of personal chats and work chats being mixed in one medium arises. For an empirical study of this problem, we collected chat log data recorded on the actual site. Based on this, we analyzed the distribution of chats according to work situation and the switching pattern between personal and work chats. We also conducted interviews to examine the strategies that MIM users use to manage this situation. The pattern of switching between work and personal conversations more than three times occurred the most. In addition, users complained about the problem and wanted to manage it by turning off alarms or delaying notification check and scanning at once. Based on this, the study pointed out that the existing countermeasures for blocking the app itself are less effective when work and personal chats are used simultaneously in an MIM. The study also argued for the need for a new management approach to selectively manage in-app behavior. In particular, this study classified six patterns of switching between work and personal conversations based on log analysis; this result can be widely applied to related problem-response strategies in the future.

Keywords: Mobile instant messenger · MIM · KakaoTalk · Task switching · Log analysis · Cyberslacking · Work-life balance

1 Introduction

Because smartphones are actively used for work purposes [1, 2], personal and work use are mixed in a single medium. In particular, mobile instant messengers (MIM) are widely used for work conversations as well as personal conversations because of the ease of use and access, file transfer feature, lack of additional costs, and the ability to use group chats [3–5]. For this reason, work and personal conversations take place simultaneously in MIM. Because of this, at work sites, there are problems with employees having personal conversations with MIM during work hours. At the same time, at home, there is a problem of increasing stress and workload while exchanging work communications after work [6, 7]. As a result, the use of MIM is blurring the boundary between work and personal domains [8, 9]. Because of this, users are

© Springer Nature Switzerland AG 2020
A. Sundqvist et al. (Eds.): iConference 2020, LNCS 12051, pp. 151–168, 2020.
https://doi.org/10.1007/978-3-030-43687-2_12

exposed to pervasive multitasking and task-switching between simultaneous conversations, experience cognitive burdens, and find it difficult to distinguish work from leisure [1, 2, 10, 11].

To solve these problems, there have been attempts at technical, social, and academic aspects. First, technically, service providers such as Apple and Google provide block-centered management functions [12–14]. These functions prevent notifications from the specified app at the specified time and restricts use. They also provide the ability for users to manage themselves by showing how much each user has used each app for a day or a week. On the social side, people have argued for the need for self-regulation of users to prevent so-called cyberslacking behaviors [15] that involve using smartphones for non-business purposes at work. Particularly in Korea, where this study was conducted, there have been discussions and legislation to prevent post-work contact as a social issue [16, 17]. On the academic side, research has been conducted to find the optimal notification time point by reducing unnecessary notifications or delaying the time to solve interruption problems caused by notifications [18–21] (Fig. 1).

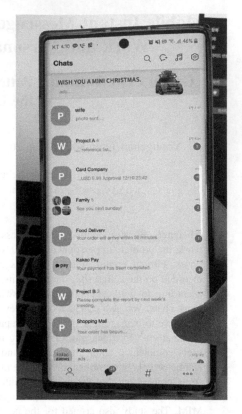

Fig. 1. Example of using MIM. New chat messages appear in the work chat room and the personal chat room, resulting in switching between different chat rooms. (P: personal, W: Work, Red dots: new) (Color figure online)

However, these approaches are mainly based on blocking the app itself or blocking notifications from the app; thus, there is a limit in solving the problem of mixing personal and work use in a single app such as an MIM. In addition, a study showed that even having a short refresh time using an MIM, even during work hours, contributes to increased productivity [22, 23]. This suggests that a more complex and microscopic strategy of human-computer interaction domain is needed beyond the blocking approach.

To create effective management methods, empirical analysis on how work and personal conversations are mixed in MIM during work and leisure time is required. However, previous studies have mainly analyzed app-level usage behaviors rather than micro interactions in one app and were also limited in capturing actual usage behaviors by collecting data through surveys [24–27]. Against this background, in this study, we collected an automatically recorded MIM conversation log from the field and conducted an empirical analysis. We also analyzed the switching pattern to observe the mix between work and personal conversations over time. In addition, user interviews were conducted to investigate how users manage conversations in this mixed situation, revealing motives and alternative use strategies that are difficult to observe in quantitative analysis. This study was conducted in accordance with the following research questions:

(1) How do patterns of switching between work and personal conversations in MIM appear compared to other apps?
(2) What is the distribution of MIM usage according to the work situation, and what are its characteristics?
(3) What is the pattern of switching between work and personal conversations within the MIM?
(4) How do MIM users manage the mixed situation between work and personal conversations?

2 Background

This study was conducted as a follow-up to the author's study of smartphone use behavior at work [8]. Accordingly, we would like to describe the parts of the existing research that are linked to this research. This chapter describes the results associated with RQ1.

In the previous study, a total of 45,398 smartphone app usage logs were collected from 18 participants over 72 h to analyze usage patterns and app usage rates according to work conditions. As a result, the highest usage in both work and non-work use was recorded in MIM. In particular, the proportion of MIM usage was 50% for work use at work and 41% for work at non-work hours. The app-switching analysis also showed the highest frequency of switching between MIM and productivity apps (Excel, Word, Notepad, etc.). In the case of switching to another app after using the productivity app, the conversion to MIM was 33.12%, which was the highest compared to other apps. Similarly, when using other apps and switching to productivity apps, the conversion rate in MIM was 36.2%, the highest. We concluded that MIM act as a bridge between work and personal use. Based on these findings, this study was conducted to analyze MIM usage behavior in a more specific and additional way in terms of in-app behavior.

3 Related Works

With the development of information and communication technology and the spread of smart personal devices such as smartphones and tablet PCs, the boundary between work and leisure is blurred [27–29]. Using smartphones for work can overcome space-time constraints, increase the efficiency of work and communication, and improve productivity [30–32]. Lee et al. [32] surveyed 185 people who had used smartphones for more than six months in their work, claiming that smartphones had a variety of positive effects on their work as computing devices. With smartphones, people said they could work anywhere, anytime, and that they were able to play an organizational role better. However, due to the nature of being connected anywhere, anytime, workers may be interrupted in their spare time or experience increased workload [27, 29]. Mark et al. said multitasking can increase stress, and interruption results in increased workload and pressure [33, 34]. In particular, MIM are some of the most used apps for work on smartphones [3, 8]. Cho et al. [35] studied KakaoTalk, the most widely used MIM in Korea, and examined the complex effects of dependence on MIM apps, work relevance, information ambiguity, and fatigue of use on work organizational life. Lee [36] also revealed that informal online communication using KakaoTalk has a positive impact on work performance. In other words, the position that MIM are helpful for work and the position that they are negative coexist.

However, micro and empirical studies on what types of work and personal conversations take place based on actual MIM conversation data have not been actively conducted. The survey method was widely used in the smartphone and MIM work utilization studies conducted so far [35, 37–39]. Therefore, in this study, we empirically analyzed the distribution of micro conversations and the type of switching between work and personal conversations using conversation log data.

4   Method

4.1   Log Data Collection

In this study, we collected MIM chat logs from smartphone users. We chose Kakao-Talk, the most commonly used MIM in Korea. KakaoTalk is a MIM app serving about 50 million users in Korea. Like other MIMs such as Whatsapp or Wechat, the main function is to open a chat room and send and receive messages. Users can also create group chat rooms between multiple users to send files, photos, videos, addresses, locations, and contacts. Users can turn alarms on and off for individual chat rooms. Participants in the study were limited to those who currently perform certain tasks at fixed working hours every day at work. We recruited using snowball sampling through KakaoTalk group chat. A total of 10 participants were enrolled. Initially, 16 participants were recruited, but during the relatively long-term log collection of 3 months, 6 people dropped and 10 were the final participants. Eight participants were in their 20 s and two were in their 30 s. To collect work and personal conversations separately, the chat log was collected by instructing the user to select three of the most frequently used work and personal chat rooms. To filter out inactive chat rooms, a preliminary interview was conducted to determine the number of chat rooms that participants were active in at least five days a week. Based on this, we established the number of chat rooms - three of each- to use for research. The data were collected online; participants were informed of the anonymity and post-investigational disposition of all data and provided informed consent. To ensure that we did not collect unnecessary personal information, the users extracted the logs directly from their smartphones and then processed the conversation data files using Microsoft Excel's VBA macro manufactured and distributed by the researcher and sent them to the researcher. This macro is designed to load the KakaoTalk conversation text file and automatically delete its contents, leaving only the send and receive information and time of the messages, as shown in Fig. 2 below.

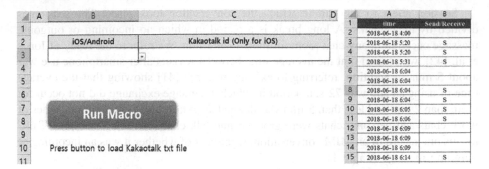

Fig. 2. Example of VBA macro (Right: dashboard, Left: Result)

4.2 Log Data Processing

A total of 60 chat room data were collected, 6 for each participant. (3 for work chat, 3 for personal) We analyzed 92 days of chat logs collected in 2018. The collected data were combined by participants, as shown in Fig. 3. To classify the talk log data into the used and unused areas, we classified them into sessions by referring to previous studies [40, 41].

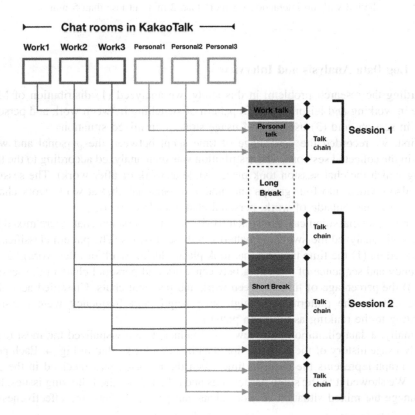

Fig. 3. Visualization of Classification method for Sessions and Talk chains

Session refers to the part in which the conversation took place. The session is divided by long breaks. A long break is a period in which no incoming or outgoing message occurred in any chat room for more than 5 min. We refer to the study of Jones et al. [42], who found that the average time between revisits after smartphone use was about 5 min. In addition, referring to existing research [41] showing that the average time of using an app was 72 s, a period in which a message exchange did not occur for more than 2 min and less than 5 min was defined as a short break. In addition, series of work chats and personal chats were grouped into talk chains within a session. "Talk" means one record of an MIM conversation, regardless of whether it was an incoming or outgoing message (Table 1).

Table 1. Description of terms and measures

	Description
Session	Independent conversation periods separated by long breaks
Talk	One KakaoTalk message in the log data
Talk chain	Period of continuous conversation with the same characteristics (work or personal)
Long break	Period with no interaction for more than 5 min
Short break	Period with no interaction for more than 2 min but less than 5 min

4.3   Log Data Analysis and Interview

Regarding the research problem, in this study, we analyzed (1) distribution of MIM usage in working and leisure time, (2) pattern of switching between work and personal chats in session, and (3) users' MIM usage strategy in mixed situations.

First, we recorded the percentage of time spent between the personal and work chats in the collected sessions. The distribution was then analyzed according to the time during which the chat session took place (while at work or after work). The sessions were also divided into four groups and analyzed: personal chat at work, work chat at work, work chat outside of work, personal chat outside of work.

Second, we classified cases in which work chats and personal chats were mixed in a session and analyzed the switching patterns in these sessions. The pattern classification was based on (1) the time that the chat took place (during work or after work), (2) the frequency and sequence of switching between work and personal chats in the session, and (3) the percentage of time between work and personal chats. Classified according to the criteria, the patterns with high time length and frequency were classified according to the ranking as the main pattern.

Finally, a data-elicitation interview was conducted. We visualized the most recent weekly usage history of the collected log data in a graph like that in Fig. 4. Each point in the graph represents the point in time when the message was received in the chat room. We showed it to the study participants and asked about the following issues: how to manage the mixed situation of work chats and personal chats, the effectiveness of existing methods to block the use of messengers, the use of personal conversations at work, and the method of handling work conversations during leisure. For each participant, 30 min of 1:1 and face-to-face interviews were conducted. After the interviews, based on the questions, three experts in the Human-computer interaction field classified the responses first. After discussion, we reviewed each other's classification and determined the final classification.

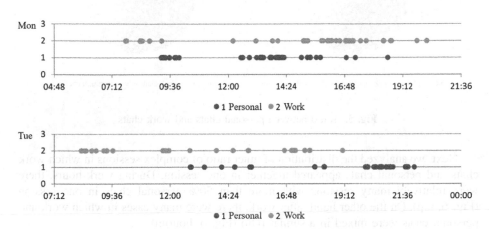

Fig. 4. Data visualization example for data elicitation interview

5   Results

5.1   Quantitative Observations

Through the survey, we collected a total of 198,505 talk logs over 92 days and categorized them into 17,248 sessions. Of these, 7,670 sessions took place during work hours and 9,578 sessions took place after work. Business hours in this analysis referred to the regular working hours for each participant collected through user interviews. The ratio of work chats to personal chats in each session according to work situation is shown in Fig. 5. First, there were 5,289 sessions consisting only of private chats during work hours, 69% of the total, and 24% of sessions consisting only of work chats. Similarly, after work, personal chat-only sessions made up 73% and work chat-only sessions constituted 22%. Complex sessions were less frequent than work chat only sessions or personal chat only sessions in terms of frequency. This analysis showed that work chats and personal chats were used for both work hour and after work. This shows a mix problem with chat.

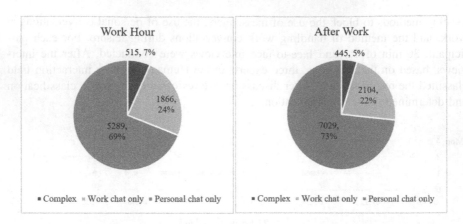

Fig. 5. Ratio between personal chats and work chats

Next, we analyzed the distribution of inner ratio of complex sessions in which work chats and personal chats appeared together in one session. During work hours, there were relatively many sessions with more than 50% personal chats in one session (Fig. 6, top). On the other hand, after work, there were many cases in which work and personal chats were mixed in a similar ratio (Fig. 6, bottom).

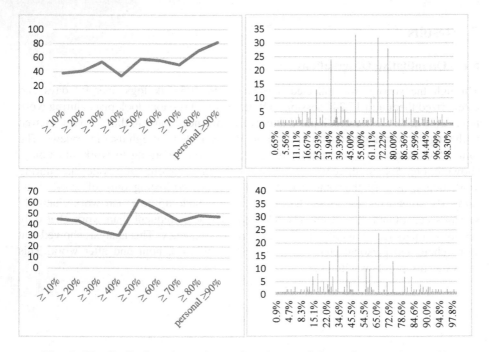

Fig. 6. The distribution of complex sessions (top: work hours, bottom: after work)

Based on this distribution, the sessions were classified into four groups (personal at work, work chat at work, work chat outside of, personal chat outside of work) to identify the characteristics of the sessions according to the usage context. In the case of complex sessions, based on the internal session rate, if the work chat rate was higher, it was classified as a work session, whereas when the personal chat rate was higher, it was classified as a personal session. For example, a personal chat at work session includes those with a personal chat only session occurring during work hour and a relatively higher proportion of personal chats in a complex session. 71 of the complex sessions with the same proportion of work chat and personal chat were not included in this analysis. To prove the significance of group distribution, a one-way analysis of variance (ANOVA) was performed on each group feature (Table 2). The names of the four sessions are abbreviated. To show the characteristics of each group, we analyzed the number of sessions in each group and the total usage time. We also see the average number of talks and the average time spent in a session. We analyzed the rate at which users initiated a session by sending a message directly. We also described participation rate which mean how many messages the user sent out of all the messages in a session.

Table 2. Description of session groups

	PatW	WatW	WatNW	PatNW	F/P (Dunnett)	Total
Number of sessions	5,572 (32.4%)	2,065 (12%)	2,296 (13.4%)	7,244 (42.2%)		17,177
Total usage time in minutes	27,431 (36.6%)	8,927 (12%)	9,827 (13.1%)	28,661 (38.3%)		74,846
Average talk within a session	13.09	9.49	12.46	10.62	7.084/0.000**	
Average usage time for each session (minutes)	4	4	4	3	18.358/0.000**	
Average rate of initiating a chat for each session (1 = Yes, 0 = No)	0.39	0.21	0.15	0.35	202.931/0.000**	
Average participation rate for each session	0.37	0.22	0.17	0.36	265.284/0.000**	

The number of sessions was highest in the order of PatNW, PatW, WatNW, and WatW. There were more personal chat sessions than work chat sessions. This was shown in the same order as use time. Average talk messages were highest in personal conversation (PatW). Compared to work chats, personal chat sessions were often started by sending a message first (PatW = 39%, PatNW = 35%). On the other hand, work chats outside of work were more likely to be started by others than by participants themselves. Participation rate was also high in the PatW and PatNW sessions. As a result, we observed that people participated more actively in personal chats regardless of work situation. Nevertheless, it has been shown that MIM is also used in work chats by 25%. In addition, the number of talks is relatively high during WatNW sessions, indicating that more messages are sent and received during work chat after work hour.

5.2 Switching Patterns in a Session

In relation to RQ3, we analyzed how switching between work and personal chats took place within a session. This analysis was based on switching between talk chains. The analysis included only sessions that showed at least one switch between the work talk chain and the personal talk chain. The total number of sessions included in the analysis was 960 (5.57%, out of a total of 17,248). The length of each session was 10,751 min (out of 74,846 min, 14.4%). The number of switches among the classification criteria was set to 1, 2, and 3 or more times considering that 66.3% (N = 636) of the sessions had 2 or fewer instances of switching. In Table 3, the number in parentheses indicates the time duration, in minutes.

Based on this analysis, we categorized 960 sessions into six main patterns, taking into account the session frequency and the mean and median time (Fig. 7). The classified pattern occupies 59.27% (N = 569) of the total by frequency and 81.23% (t = 8733 min) of the total based on the usage time and thus includes the majority of

Table 3. Session classification distribution by switching pattern and work situation.

Number of talk-chain switches	Order of switching	Talk time share within a session	Session count and time by work situation		Total	Average usage time within a session
			Work hours (time, minutes)	After work (time, minutes)		
1 time	A: Work → Personal	Work < Personal	30 (232)	23 (144)	174 (1049)	(6.03)
		Work > Personal	33 (326)	20 (195)		
		Work = Personal	32 (80)	36 (72)		
1 time	B: Personal → Work	W < P	37 (284)	27 (235)	238 (1162)	(4.88)
		W > P	30 (188)	30 (197)		
		W = P	58 (144)	56 (114)		
2 times	C: Work → Personal → Work	W < P	2 (48)	3 (30)	84 (791)	(9.42)
		W > P	38 (302)	40 (407)		
		W = P	1 (4)	0 (0)		
2 times	D: Personal → Work → Personal	W < P	86 (943)	48 (488)	140 (1482)	(10.59)
		W > P	1 (7)	2 (28)		
		W = P	1 (6)	2 (10)		
Over 3 times	E: Multiple switches	W < P	73 (1829)	71 (1529)	324 (6267)	(19.34)
		W > P	76 (1277)	50 (1392)		
		W = P	17 (118)	37 (122)		
Total					960 (10751)	(11.2)

the analyzed objects. Sessions not included in the main pattern are classified into other types. The 960 sessions included in the classification were included in each pattern independently without overlapping.

- Pattern 1. Wandering between work and personal chats (N = 324, 34.75%, t = 6267, 58.3%). This means that the user did not focus on either work or personal chats during a single period of usage which means a session. The sessions included in this pattern mean that the user has used to move back and forth between work and personal chats more than three times. This was the largest portion of the overall pattern.

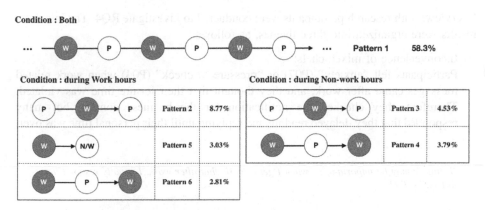

Fig. 7. Switching patterns between work and personal talk chain in a session.

- Pattern 2. Work between cyberslacking (N = 86, 8.96%, t = 943, 8.77%). This is a pattern of returning to a personal chat after a brief work chat in the middle of a personal chat during working hours. It includes 2 switches. The sessions included in this pattern indicated that a high percentage of personal chats were used during the work hour. This can be seen as cyberslacking. In spite of switching to a work chat in the middle, the user returned to his or her personal chat and continued cyberslacking.
- Pattern 3. Interruption by work chat (N = 48, 5%, t = 488, 4.53%). In this pattern, during after-work hours, a personal chat is interrupted by a work chat for a while, but the personal conversation is returned to. This includes two switches. This shows the user attempting to return to the personal chat in the original context.
- Pattern 4. Focus on work after work hours (N = 40, 4.17%, t = 407, 3.79%). This is a pattern in which a personal chat is briefly engaged in in the middle of a work chat during after-work hours, but then the work chat is returned to. The work chat rate is higher than the private chat in session. This shows a focus on work chat after work, even though it was disturbed by personal chat.
- Patter 5. Personal chat after work (N = 33, 3.43%, t = 326, 3.03%). This pattern occurs when one switch occurs. This is a pattern in which a long work chat is engaged in first during work hours, and then the user transfers to a personal chat. This shows that the user starts his or her personal chat after processing the work chat first.

- Pattern 6. Returning to work (N = 38, 3.96%, t = 302, 2.81%). This pattern includes two switches. During work hours, a work chat session is interrupted by a private conversation, but then the work conversation is returned to. The work conversation proportion is higher than that of the personal conversation. The work chat was interrupted by a personal chat during work but shows an effort to return to work.
- Pattern 7. Other (N = 391, 40.73%, t = 18.78%).

5.3   Qualitative Findings

Interviews with research participants were conducted to investigate RQ4. The interview results were organized into three themes, as follows.

- Inconvenience of mixed chats:
  Participants felt "anxiety" (P07) or "pressure to check" (P04) when work related messages came after work, and they thought that their leisure time was violated. Therefore, they checked the notification for the business contact, but many responded that they delayed reading and replying until their personal time was over.

"I think it may be important, so when I get a work chat after work, I usually respond immediately." – P02

"I'm annoyed with work chats after work, so I just check and ignore them and read them very late at night or go to work the next day." – P03

In a personal chat during work, almost all participants experienced moments of disturbance. Receiving personal contact during work "distracted" (P08) participants and made them "anxious because of the accumulation of notifications in personal chat rooms" (P07).

- Strategies of users:
  Participants used several strategies to manage the mix of work and personal chats. The most common way was to turn off alarms for disturbing chat rooms, mainly trying to focus on work by turning off alarms for private chat rooms during business hours.

"When I'm busy, I turn off all personal chat room notifications and try not to check. I practiced a rule that I only checked once an hour."-P04

In addition, a large number of respondents used the defer and scan strategy (P02–04, P06–10). In this strategy, participants first defer a reply to a personal chat that arrives during work and then later enter a chat room in their spare time. They scan the entire chat and dismiss the notification. In this process, users quickly identify and respond to what needs to be answered. There were also strategies for considering work colleagues and chat counterparts.

"When badge accumulates, I scroll down and see if there's anything I need to reply and turn off. I also check the preview pop-up when a message comes in to decide whether or not to enter the chat room."– P08

"I go to the bathroom and use KakaoTalk to avoid being discovered by my colleagues when I'm talking to a friend. And I always send the last message as an emoticon, so my friends won't be noticed by their coworkers because of the kakaoTalk notification."-P01

"In order to keep others from knowing I'm in a private chat, I intentionally send a personal chat while talking about work. I act as if I am at work."– P09

However, in some cases, this management strategy failed due to work chat notifications. Respondents said they turned on the MIM to check for work messages and naturally saw personal conversation notifications, or vice versa (P01–P04, P07–P09). In this case, users enter all chat rooms with notifications, so switching occurs.

- Effectiveness of blocking policy:
  There were many skeptical responses to blocking MIM and chat rooms during and after work to prevent mixing between work and personal chats. P01 replied, "Even after work, I have to respond to the request for necessary materials because there are still other colleagues in the office." P05 said, "Blocking itself is impossible. If your boss or team member wants to write it, you have no choice but to write it." In addition to these responses, P07 said, "Even if KakaTalk is eliminated, colleagues or supervisors will be contacted by other means such as phone calls, texts and e-mails in case of emergency. That's why it is necessary to respond anyway." P08 replied, "If policy prevents people from having private conversations with KakaoTalk, they will have a different way of doing things personally at work." For this reason, simply blocking KakaoTalk is not a strategy for solving problems.

6 Discussion

In this study, we used a quantitative approach to analyze the distribution of chats in MIM (KakaoTalk app) and the pattern of switching between work and personal conversations (RQ2, 3). In the interview, we also looked at how users assess and manage situations in which work and personal chats are mixed (RQ4). This chapter describes some of the issues that emerged from this process.

The analysis showed that KakaoTalk is used in a mix of work and leisure. Quantitative analysis showed that the MIM is actively used for both business and personal chats. In addition, the switching analysis results showed that the pattern in which the users switched between the work chat and personal chat more than three times consecutively is a session was the highest. In the qualitative approach, participants were found to be uncomfortable because their work and leisure were interrupted by the mix of personal and work chats. These results indicate that measures are needed to address this problem, but there is no effective management method now. Users didn't turn off the alarm even if they were disturbed considering the possibility of an important contact. Even if the user turns off the alarm of a certain chat room, when the user opens the app, all notifications are shown. This can induce a user to check a chat that is not related to work. These results provide the basis for arguing that the effectiveness of existing management policies and services, which focus on blocking the use of apps, is low. As smartphones are actively used for work, the boundary between work and life is blurred. It's practically impossible to go back to the past when smartphones weren't in the office. In this situation, rather than using a separation policy that prohibits personal use during work, a strategy is needed to accept the switching phenomenon between work and personal messages caused by smartphones and manage them effectively. Therefore, there is a need for a technical approach in terms of HCI to enable selective managing according to the situation at the in-app behavior level. For example, a sender or receiver can create a hierarchy of messages so that non-urgent messages don't sound an alarm when they're at work. Or, if the MIM adds the ability to set priority alarms for a particular chat room, the user must first check for new messages in this chat room so they can see other chats.

Six major patterns were derived from the switching analysis. Interestingly, the whole chat personality was influenced by whether the start of the chat was from a personal chat or from a work chat. For example, in the case of Pattern 2 (work between cyberslacking) or Pattern 3 (interruption by work), the session was started with a personal chat, and the personal chat weight was high throughout the session. Similarly, Pattern 4 (focus on work after work hours) or Pattern 6 (returning to work) began with work chats, and most sessions had high work chat levels. This allows us to infer the need for a feature to help start a chat with a message that matches the work situation as a strategy to reduce switching and mix. For example, if system provider adds a MIM feature that encourages user to start using MIM as a work chat during work hour, user will most likely return to work even if it is interrupted by a personal chat in between.

The interviews gathered strategies by which MIM users attempt to manage the mix of conversations. In particular, the 'defer and scan' strategy which means stacking chats without reading them one by one and looking roughly to select important chats later in spare time can be considered in developing alternative functions. Currently, most MIMs use the same notification method for all talks. If different notification methods can be set according to the importance of the talk, it could help the user reduce the time taken to scan the talk and selectively accept only the necessary information. In addition, during the interview process, there was a reaction that even if the MIM is blocked, work contact is expected to come by other means anyway. Also, reactions were gathered that users would expect cyberslacking with other tools anyway. From this, it can be concluded that simply blocking the app is not useful. In this situation, a strategy is needed to manage interruptions faster and easier.

7   Conclusion

In this study, we analyzed the 92-day log data recorded in the field, exploring how work and personal chats take place in MIM and what the patterns are. We conducted a qualitative investigation into the management strategies users used. As a result, a mixture of work and personal chats was observed in the MIM. The MIM was more commonly used for personal chats, but at the same time, about 25% of the chats were business chats. In addition, the switching analysis showed the most frequent pattern of switching between work and personal chats to be more than three times, which shows that users simultaneously switch between work and personal chats. During interviews, users reported feeling uncomfortable using mixed chats, and various users described various strategies to manage them. Based on these results, we concluded that the existing countermeasures against app blocking are not effective. Based on these conclusions, we argue that at the in-app behavior level, micro-selective management strategies that enable more detailed management of work and personal chats need to be discussed in the HCI field.

However, this study has a limitation in that the number of study participants was relatively small and the age group was biased. To compensate for this, we tried to extend the log collection period to analyze relatively large amounts of data. However, further research needs to be carried out with a larger number of participants to make the research results generalizable. In terms of content, this study is limited in that it does not observe the transition between different work chat rooms. Further observations of this area will be made in future studies, as switching between chats of the same kind can also interfere with each other. Also, this study was done log-based, so we didn't analyze the content of the conversation. For example, personal chat also can be done in the work chat room. In addition, the same message can be accepted by someone as personal and by others as work. Therefore, this part should be studied in depth in the future through content analysis. In addition, the study was conducted on only one MIM app. Given the high likelihood of a mix of work and personal behavior in a variety of apps, from e-mails to phone calls to text messages, there is a need for more analysis. Since the amount and pattern of switching for each medium may be different, it will be necessary to study the comparison.

Despite these limitations, it is expected that this study will be useful in the context of growing social discussions about the problems of deviation from work due to MIMs and the stress of engaging in work chats after work. In a situation where we can't go back to the past before using smartphones, we need to find ways to manage them to reduce the disadvantages rather than block the use of smartphones. This study has the advantage of analyzing the pattern of how users are using smartphones based on a large amount of usage logs in this changing environment. In addition, the results can provide contributions to deriving a strategy for coping with mixed use and switching problems in the future by identifying the pattern of switching between work and personal chats in detail and collecting users' problem-solving strategies.

References

1. David, P., Kim, J.H., Brickman, J.S., Ran, W., Curtis, C.M.: Mobile phone distraction while studying. New Media Soc. **17**, 1661–1679 (2015). https://doi.org/10.1177/1461444814531692
2. Ludwig, T., Dax, J., Pipek, V., Randall, D.: Work or leisure? Designing a user-centered approach for researching activity "in the wild". Pers. Ubiquit. Comput. **20**, 487–515 (2016). https://doi.org/10.1007/s00779-016-0935-7

3. National Information Society Agency: Ministry of Science and ICT, Republic of Korea. Survey on Smartphone Dependence, Ministry of Science and ICT, Sejong (2019)
4. Lee, U., et al.: Hooked on smartphones: an exploratory study on smartphone overuse among college students. In: Proceedings of the 32nd Annual ACM Conference on Human Factors in Computing Systems, pp. 2327–2336. ACM, Toronto (2014). https://doi.org/10.1145/2556288.2557366
5. Church, K., De Oliveira, R.: What's up with WhatsApp? Comparing mobileinstant messaging behaviors with traditional SMS. In: Proceedings of the 15th International Conference on Human-Computer Interaction with Mobile Devices and Services, pp. 352–361. ACM, Munich (2013). https://doi.org/10.1145/2493190.2493225
6. Shin, I.-G., Seok, J.-M., Lim, Y.-K.: Too close and crowded: understanding stress on mobile instant messengers based on proxemics. In: Proceedings of t the 2018 CHI Conference on Human Factors in Computing Systems, pp. 1–12. ACM, Montreal (2018)
7. O'Neill, T.A., Hambley, L.A., Bercovich, A.: Prediction of cyberslacking when employees are working away from the office. Comput. Hum. Behav. **34**, 291–298 (2014). https://doi.org/10.1016/j.chb.2014.02.015
8. Jeong, Y., Jung, H., Lee, J.: Cyberslacking or smart work: smartphone usage log-analysis focused on app-switching behavior in work and leisure conditions. Int. J. Hum.-Comput. Interact. **36**, 1–16 (2019). https://doi.org/10.1080/10447318.2019.1597574
9. Oh, S., Kim, Y.-Y., Lee, H.: Smart work: blurring work/nonwork boundaries and its consequences. J. Digit. Converge. **11**, 191–198 (2013)
10. Madden, K.: Phone Use and Attention: A Multitasking Study. Celebrating Scholarship & Creativity Day, 138. (2017). http://digitalcommons.csbsju.edu/elce_cscday/138
11. Lang, A.: Using the limited capacity model of motivated mediated message processing to design effective cancer communication messages. J. Commun. **56** (2006). https://doi.org/10.1111/j.1460-2466.2006.00283.x
12. Support.apple.com: Use Do Not Disturb on your iPhone, iPad, and iPod touch. https://support.apple.com/en-us/HT204321
13. Support.apple.com: Use Screen Time on your iPhone, iPad, or iPod touch. https://support.apple.com/en-us/HT208982
14. Google.com: Digital Wellbeing. https://wellbeing.google/
15. Vitak, J., Crouse, J., Larose, R.: Personal internet use at work: understanding cyberslacking. Comput. Hum. Behav. **27**, 1751–1759 (2011). https://doi.org/10.1016/j.chb.2011.03.002
16. Cho, J.: A study on the right to disconnect. Labor Law Rev. **46**, 103–138 (2019)
17. Lee, S.G., Lee, J.H.: The use of smart devices at work, issues and improvement plans on working hours - mainly on the KakaoTalk prohibition act after work. J. Labor Law **38**, 145–180 (2016)
18. Mehrotra, A., Musolesi, M., Hendley, R., Pejovic, V.: Designing contentdriven intelligent notification mechanisms for mobile applications. In: Proceedings of the 2015 ACM International Joint Conference on Pervasive and Ubiquitous Computing, pp. 813–824. ACM, Osaka (2016). https://doi.org/10.1145/2750858.2807544
19. Shin, I., Seok, J., Lim, Y.: Ten-minute silence: a new notification UX of mobile instant messenger. In: Proceedings of the 2019 CHI Conference on Human Factors in Computing Systems, pp. 442–454. ACM, Glasgow (2019). https://doi.org/10.1145/3290605.3300672
20. Okoshi, T., Ramos, J., Nozaki, H., Nakazawa, J., Dey, A.K., Tokuda, H.: Reducing users' perceived mental effort due to interruptive notifications in multi-device mobile environments. In: Proceedings of the 2015 ACM International Joint Conference on Pervasive and Ubiquitous Computing, pp. 475–486. ACM, Osaka (2015). https://doi.org/10.1145/2750858.2807517

21. Fischer, J.E., Greenhalgh, C., Benford, S.: Investigating episodes of mobile phone activity as indicators of opportune moments to deliver notifications. In: Proceedings of the 13th International Conference on Human Computer Interaction with Mobile Devices and Services, p. 181. ACM, Stockholm (2011). https://doi.org/10.1145/2037373.2037402
22. Kim, S., Park, Y.A., Headrick, L.: Daily micro-breaks and job performance: general work engagement as a cross-level moderator. J. Appl. Psychol. **103**, 772–786 (2018). https://doi.org/10.1037/apl0000308
23. Trougakos, J.P., Beal, D.J., Green, S.G., Weiss, H.M.: Making the break count: an episodic examination of recovery activities, emotional experiences, and positive affective displays. Acad. Manag. J. **51**, 131–146 (2008). https://doi.org/10.5465/AMJ.2008.30764063
24. Kim, I., Jung, G., Jung, H., Ko, M., Lee, U.: Let's FOCUS: mitigating mobile phone use in college classrooms. Proc. ACM Interact. Mob. Wearable Ubiquit. Technol. **1**, 1–29 (2017). https://doi.org/10.1145/3130928
25. Chou, M.C., Liu, C.H.: Mobile instant messengers and middle-aged and elderly adults in taiwan: uses and gratifications. Int. J. Hum.-Comput. Interact. **32**, 835–846 (2016). https://doi.org/10.1080/10447318.2016.1201892
26. Duxbury, L., Smart, R.: The myth of separate worlds: an exploration of how mobile technology has redefined work-life balance. In: Creating Balance?: International Perspectives on the Work-Life Integration of Professionals, pp. 269–284 (2011). https://doi.org/10.1007/978-3-642-16199-5_15
27. Lee, K., Kim, K.: The Impact of Using Smart Devices on Worker's Life. KoreaLabor Institute, Sejong (2015)
28. Thomas, K.J.: Workplace technology and the creation of boundaries: the role of VHRD in a 24/7 work environment. Adv. Dev. Hum. Resour. **16**, 281–295 (2014). https://doi.org/10.1177/1523422314532092
29. Duxbury, L., Smart, R.: The "Myth of Separate Worlds": an exploration of how mobile technology has redefined work-life balance. In: Kaiser, S., Ringlstetter, M., Eikhof, D., Pina e Cunha, M. (eds.) Creating Balance?, pp. 269–284. Springer, Heidelberg (2011). https://doi.org/10.1007/978-3-642-16199-5_15
30. Corno, F., De Russis, L., Roffarello, A.M.: AwareNotifications: multi-device semantic notification handling with user-defined preferences. J. Ambient Intell. Smart Environ. **10**(4), 327–343 (2018). https://doi.org/10.3233/AIS-180492
31. Dén-Nagy, I.: A double-edged sword?: A critical evaluation of the mobile phone in creating work-life balance. New Technol. Work Employ. **29**, 193–211 (2014). https://doi.org/10.1111/ntwe.12031
32. Lee, K.Y., Kim, K., Lee, M.: Are smartphones helpful? An empirical investigation of the role of smartphones in users' role performance. Int. J. Mob. Commun. **15**, 119 (2017). https://doi.org/10.1504/IJMC.2017.10001838
33. Mark, G., Wang, Y., Niiya, M.: Stress and multitasking in everyday college life: an empirical study of online activity. In: Proceedings of the 32nd Annual ACM Conference on Human Factors in Computing Systems, pp. 41–50. ACM, Toronto (2014). https://doi.org/10.1145/2556288.2557361
34. Mark, G., Gudith, D., Klocke, U.: The cost of interrupted work. In: Proceedings of the 26th Annual ACM Conference on Human Factors in Computing Systems, p. 107. ACM, Florence (2008). https://doi.org/10.1145/1357054.1357072
35. Cho, J., Kim, H.: Effects of KakaoTalk uses on organizational factors including organizational identification, organizational support, and job satisfaction. Media Econ. Cult. **16**, 42–77 (2018)

36. Lee, J.M.: Water-cooler effect in informal communication at work: focusing on Kakao talk of smart-phone user. J. Korea Contents Assoc. **13**, 362–369 (2013). https://doi.org/10.5392/jkca.2013.13.03.362

37. So, S.: Mobile instant messaging support for teaching and learning in higher education. Internet High. Educ. **31**, 32–42 (2016). https://doi.org/10.1016/j.iheduc.2016.06.001

38. Ariffin, Z., Omar, S.Z.: Usage of Whatsapp in relation to employee engagement in a telecommunication company. Int. J. Acad. Res. Bus. Soc. Sci. **8**, 434–452 (2018). https://doi.org/10.6007/ijarbss/v8-i1/3818

39. De Benedictis, A., et al.: WhatsApp in hospital? An empirical investigation of individual and organizational determinants to use. PLoS ONE **14**, e0209873 (2019). https://doi.org/10.1371/journal.pone.0209873

40. Meyer, J., Wasmann, M., Heuten, W., El Ali, A., Boll, S.C.J.: Identification and classification of usage patterns in long-term activity tracking. In: Proceedings of the 2017 CHI Conference on Human Factors in Computing Systems, pp. 667–678. ACM, Denver. (2017). https://doi.org/10.1145/3025453.3025690

41. Böhmer, M., Hecht, B., Schöning, J., Krüger, A., Bauer, G.: Falling asleep with Angry Birds, Facebook and Kindle – a large scale study on mobile application usage. In: Proceedings of the 13th International Conference on Human Computer Interaction with Mobile Devices and Services, vol. 11, pp. 47–56. ACM, Stockholm (2011). https://doi.org/10.1145/2037373.2037383

42. Jones, S.L.: Revisitation analysis of smartphone app use. In: Proceedings of the 2015 ACM International Joint Conference on Pervasive and Ubiquitous Computing, pp. 1197–1208. ACM, Osaka (2015). https://doi.org/10.1145/2750858.2807542

The Attitudes of Chinese Online Users Towards Movie Piracy: A Content Analysis

Yao Lyu[1] , Juan Xie[1,2(✉)] , and Bingbing Xie[3]

[1] School of Information, Florida State University, Tallahassee 32304, USA
xiejuan9503@163.com
[2] School of Information Management, Nanjing University,
Nanjing 210023, China
[3] School of Information Management, Wuhan University,
Wuhan 430072, China

Abstract. Movies piracy has raised growing concerns in digital time. However, most studies on movie piracy focused on university students, paying less attention to the exploration of the comprehensive factors among online users, especially in Chinese context. To narrow these gaps, the current study aimed at investigating the attitudes of Chinese online users towards movie piracy and examined the factors that influence the attitudes. Taking a piracy case of a Chinese movie *"The Wandering Earth"* as an example, we collected 735 comments from two *Sina Weibo* posts through web crawling. Through a content analysis based on social cognitive theory (SCT), we found that the attitudes of online users ranged from supporting, opposing pessimistically to opposing movie piracy. We also found out outcome expectancies, self-control, social learning, moral disengagement and environmental factors contributed to these attitudes. The factors of users' attitudes were consistent with the explanation on piracy behavior of SCT and contributed to enriching SCT in Chinese context. This research provided a better understanding of movie piracy among online users with qualitative insights and had some implications.

Keywords: Movie piracy · Content analysis · Social cognitive theory · Digital piracy · Chinese online users

1 Introduction

Digital piracy is defined as "the illegal copying or downloading of copyrighted software and media files" [1]. With the facilitation of internet technology, digital piracy has been rampant online. Books, software, music, and video files are the main targets of online digital piracy [2] and the piracy of different types of media is influenced by different factors [3]. Particularly, movie piracy has raised growing concerns due to its widespread and huge economic damages [4].

Previous studies investigating the determinants of users' movie piracy (e.g., [5–8]) were mostly under the guidance of less comprehensive theories, investigating limited movie piracy factors with quantitative approaches. Moreover, the previous research often used student samples, paying less attention to general online users. In addition,

A. Sundqvist et al. (Eds.): iConference 2020, LNCS 12051, pp. 169–185, 2020.
https://doi.org/10.1007/978-3-030-43687-2_13

most studies focused on western culture, leaving movie piracy in eastern culture under-represented. Therefore, focusing on general online users in Chinese context, this study intends to explore more comprehensive movie piracy factors qualitatively with the following research questions:

RQ1. What are the attitudes of Chinese online users towards movie piracy?
RQ2. What are the factors that influence their attitudes?

2 Literature Review

2.1 Movie Piracy

Compared to software and music, movie piracy received less attention, while piracy behaviors in different media types were driven by different factors [3, 9]. Movie piracy refers to any activity related to unauthorized use of movies, including illegally recording, stream-ripping, uploading, downloading or streaming movies [7]. Based on theory of planned behavior, a study in UK investigated how novelty-seeking related to illegal downloading [10]. Redondo and Charron [8] proved that the Spain download-ers' unwillingness to pay was highly associated with their pirating behaviors. Their results were consistent with the cognitive dissonance theory. In Netherlands, Jacobs et al. [6] applied social cognitive theory and indicated that curiosity and ambition, social environment and perceived attitudes, and habits drove online technological forum users and university students to download pirated movies. An Indian study identified illiteracy, high price, unemployment, insufficient law enforcement, as well as poor infrastructure to be responsible for the rampant online movie piracy [11]. In Phau et al.'s research, habitual conduct, affection, facilitating conditions and attitudes were found to significantly influence Australian university students' intention on illegally downloading movies [7]. Drawing upon self-control theory and social learning theory, the link between low self-control and movie piracy has been revealed among US college students [12]. Same result was also found among high school students in the US [13]. In a comparison of determinants of movie piracy between US students and Kuwait students, it was reported that subjective norm only influenced Kuwait students significantly, while moral obligation only influenced US students significantly [5].

Most previous movie piracy research was conducted on student samples and in western countries (e.g., US, UK, Australia, and Netherlands). The current research body paid less attention to a more general population and sociocultural differences (e.g., China) [3]. Lin, Qiu, Li, and Cheng examined why general online users in China viewed pirated movies [14]. Based on the theory of panned behavior, this research recognized personal factors (perceived benefits of pirated movies, personal require-ments of movie quality and attitudes towards movie piracy), internet factors (the permeating of pirate movies, the spread through social networks and the accessibility of pirate movies), as well as enforcement factors (potential risks and punishing force of the government) on movie piracy. However, it overlooked social learning factors and moral engagement, which were spotted in social learning theory [15] and social cog-nitive theory [16]. In addition, the research analyzed online questionnaire feedback rather than respondents' original thoughts, leaving a gap for qualitative insights. Therefore, it is necessary to conduct a study on general Chinese online users to investigate more movie piracy factors with a qualitative approach.

2.2 Social Cognitive Theory

Previous studies on digital piracy applied focused theories (e.g., neutralization theory, self-control theory and cognitive dissonance theory) and comprehensive theories (e.g., the theory of planned behavior, the theory of reasoned action and social cognitive theory). A comprehensive theory can contribute to more movie piracy factors. Among the comprehensive theories, the theory of planned behavior or the theory of reasoned action associated strong rationality with piracy behavior. However, piracy was not only committed through careful and rational planning [3]. On the other side, socialization models (e.g., social cognitive theory) were stronger in unifying multiple levels of movie piracy theories [3]. Therefore, we chose social cognitive theory (SCT) as our theoretical framework.

SCT assumed that behaviors were learnt in social context, which included moral, environmental, irrational and rational factors. This theory has been tested in various topics such as communication, health behavior and criminal behavior. In digital piracy, SCT factors were categorized as outcome expectancies, self-efficacy and self-regulation, social learning, moral disengagement, and environmental determinants [3, 16]. Outcome expectancies refer to piracy behaviors' psychological aspects, including perceived benefits, risks, costs and associated punishment. Social learning shows the ability and practice to learn new behaviors by watching others, reflected by peer association, prior experience or habit and social norms. Self-efficacy, or self-regulation, is the ability to control one's behavior through self-control and self-monitoring. Moral disengagement describes individuals' neutralization of wrongdoing by justifying illegal actions. Additionally, environmental determinants consist of external or physical factors that could further influence piracy behavior (e.g., age, education and gender).

3 Methodology

3.1 "The Wandering Earth" Case

The Wandering Earth is a Chinese movie released on the first day of the 2019 Chinese New Year (Feb. 4th). It became a blockbuster after release and suffered serious piracy at the mean time. Pirated versions of this movie were of high picture quality and could be either viewed on free streaming websites or shared through cloud storage platforms with little charge (as low as 1 CNY, about 0.15 USD). To date, the piracy of *The Wandering Earth* has totally caused 150 million USD loss on the movie's box office revenue [17].

3.2   Data Collection and Cleaning

Sina Weibo is the most popular Chinese social media platform. This platform, just like *Twitter*, provides rich information to study users' attitudes and behaviors, and all posts and comments on the platform are publicly available. Since the broke out of the piracy case, 1150 related posts has been posted with 22,657 comments gathered and 478 official accounts involved.

Among these official accounts, *ThePaper.cn* (澎湃新闻) is one of the most popular Chinese general news media, while *Sina Finance* (新浪财经) is one of the media channels of *Sina Weibo* specialized in finance and related law issues. The comments of their posts present a wide range of opinions of the Chinese online population. The current study took all 735 comments under two posts of *ThePaper.cn* and *Sina Finance* discussing the piracy case as dataset. The data was collected during April 4th–5th, 2019, by a Python web crawler developed by the third author. The study was approved by the Office of Human Subjects Research at Florida State University.

In the data cleaning process, relevant comments are those mentioning movie piracy directly or indirectly and providing their standpoints on movie piracy; irrelevant comments fail to meet these requirements, such as those only discussing movie plots, showing local ticket prices, and commenting purely with pictures and/or emojis. Four hundred and thirty comments were left after removing duplicated and irrelevant ones.

3.3   Content Analysis

Our content analysis started with a pilot study of ninety comments. In the pilot study, we found three attitudes on movie piracy (MP): supporting MP, opposing MP and pessimistically opposing MP (Table 1). Further, we labelled attitudes as intuitive or rational ones depending on whether they were backed up with reasons or not; comments without reason were labeled as intuitive one while those with reasons were rational. We did not differentiate pessimistic attitude, since all pessimistic comments provided reasons to argue why it was impossible to eliminate MP.

As for intuitive comments, we coded their tactics [18, 19]. For example, in the pilot study, we found that users applied insulting, trolling and sarcasm words to intuitively express their attitudes. Furthermore, we formed a more specified categorization for rational comments. Comments holding a strong view which remained unchangeable were categorized as absolute ones; while those that might shift when condition(s) changed were categorized as conditional ones.

To investigate factors behind these attitudes, we developed a coding book based on SCT. First, the attitudes toward consuming pirated digital sources could be driven by outcome expectancies, such as saving money, enjoyment of goods, quality of digital goods and perceived punishment/risk [6, 8, 20]. We thereby classified the price and audiovisual effect of both authorized and pirated movies, the quality of the movie as well as perceived sanction by law enforcements into this category. Additionally, in the pilot study, we found that the responsibility of the future of movie industry and the specific support of Chinese authorized movies contributed to opposing MP. The responsibility and the preference on nationality are consistent with the adoration of a specific artist/producer in SCT [21]. Moreover, watching free versions of digital goods

Table 1. The coding book of attitudes.

Category	Subcategory	Definition	Example
Supporting MP	Intuitively supporting	Supporting movie piracy without reasons	"Anyone who wants the free movie website, pls pm me"
	Absolutely rationally Supporting	Supporting movie piracy with reason(s) and without condition	"When you take all big apples, you need to leave some small ones to those in lower income levels"
	Conditionally rationally supporting	Supporting movie piracy with reason(s) in certain condition(s)	"You asked for piracy by setting the prices too high"
Opposing MP	Intuitively opposing	Opposing movie piracy without reasons	"Let's combat against MP!"
	Absolutely rationally opposing	Opposing movie piracy with reason(s) and without condition	"It's heart breaking for movie producers to see their effort get pirated"
	Conditionally rationally opposing	Opposing movie piracy with reason(s) in certain condition(s)	"No matter it is a good movie or not, I will anyway go to theater to support it, because it is made in China"
Pessimistically opposing MP	–	Opposing movie piracy, but without confidence that piracy can be eliminated	"Pirated movies are usually attached with Casino ads (to gain profit), it is hard to cut this industry chain in a short time"

and then deciding if they are worth paying (sampling effect) affects piracy consumption [22], which is also supported by some comments in the pilot study. Therefore, we included movie industry responsibility, movie nationality and sampling effect into outcome expectancies additionally.

Social learning also plays an important role in shaping these attitudes. In social learning processes, individuals either evaluate their behaviors based off subjective norms that are socially recognized as acceptable [3, 23], or comply with the force of habit, which was generated from previous MP experience [6]. To be noticed, the awareness of intellectual property was classified into subjective norms but not perceived sanctions by law enforcements, since MP consumers are barely punished by law enforcements in China. Therefore, judging MP behaviors as immoral is more effective than coitizing them based on law enforcements.

Additionally, self-control was found to be able to influence users' attitude on MP in pilot study. Knowing that MP is immoral or illegal, users might oppose MP because of self-control or support it due to low self-control.

For comments which supported MP, users applied moral disengagement as well to justify their MP behaviors. They denied the harm of their pirating behaviors [7]. For example, they considered that it is acceptable to watch a pirated movie once they have ever paid for it (one for all); besides, they argued that MP causes no avenue loss and hence should not be opposed (victimless crime) [24].

Table 2. The coding book of factors.

Category	Subcategory	Definition	Example
Outcome expectancies	Movie industry responsibility	Users are responsible for the future of movie industry	"If you hope the movie industry to produce more wonderful movies, you are not supposed to watch any pirated one"
	The audiovisual effects in theater	Users' feelings about audiovisual effects in theater	"You cannot experience the special effects of this movie from pirated versions, you need go to a theater"
	The audiovisual effects of pirated movie	Users' feelings about audiovisual effects of pirated movie	"Watching those versions recorded in theaters makes me dizzy, I' d rather waiting for cracked 1080p versions"
	The price of authorized movie	Users' perceived price of authorized movie	"You asked for piracy by setting the prices too high"
	The price of pirated movie	Users' perceived price of pirated movies	"I prefer watching pirated movies for free rather than paying for them"
	Movie quality	Users' perceived movie quality	"You need to pay for this wonderful movie and support the producers' efforts"
	Sampling	Watching free versions of digital goods and then deciding if they are worth paying.	"If I watched a free one first and think it's a nice movie, and then I go to a theater and watch it again, would I be judged?"
	Perceived sanction	The perceived sanctions from laws enforcements	"Selling pirated movies is asking for trouble at this time (the government is rigorously suppressing MP)"
	Movie nationality	Where the movie was produced domestically or not	"No matter it is a good movie or not, I will anyway go to theater to support it, because it is made in China"
Social learning	Subjective norm	A set of requirements that regulate behaviors to be socially recognized as acceptable	"Why are they so shameless? They even showoff for having watched pirated movies"
	MP habit	Habits of consuming pirated movies among wide range of users	"Most Chinese have downloaded and watched pirated movies and used pirated software"

(*continued*)

Table 2. (*continued*)

Category	Subcategory	Definition	Example
Self-efficacy	Self-control	The ability to keep oneself away from piracy behaviors	"I never go to any cinema and I always watch pirated movies. I support to combat with MP, but I cannot keep myself from watching them"
Moral disengagement	One for all	Watching pirated movies after paying for one time in theater	"Pls pm me the free website, p.s. I've already watched it in a theater"
	Victimless crime	Piracy doing no harm to movie industry	"People who watch pirated movies will never go to theater, so there's no harm (of the piracy) to box office revenue"
Environmental factors	Individual characteristics	Users' physical factors, such as disability and pregnancy	"There are only 3D versions in our local theaters, but 3D makes me feel dizzy"
	Geographical factors	The geographic characteristics of theaters	"There is no theater in my town"
	Accessibility of authorized alternatives	The accessibility of authorized movies in online platforms	"There is neither theater in our village and nor authorized movie available online"
	MP market	A balance between copyright holders, piracy merchants and consumers in movie market	"When you take all big apples, you need to leave some small ones to those in lower income levels"
	Pirated resources	The richness of available pirated resources	"Pirated versions have been uploaded on YouTube. YouTube has become a habitat for pirated resources"

The last category in SCT is environmental factor. The environmental factors consist of individual characteristics and external factors. In the context of viewing MP, individual characteristics could be their pregnancy, marital as well as health status, and external factors include geographic factors, accessibility of authorized alternatives, MP market and the rampant MP resources.

The coding schema of factors is shown in Table 2. For each comment, the most significant one or two factors were coded.

The two authors coded all 430 comments separately according to the coding schema. As for users' attitudes, the Cohen's Kappa intercoder reliability was 0.771 (>0.70), showing an acceptable degree of agreement [25]. For the factors, a Cohen's kappa consistency of 0.723 was reached, which is also satisfactory [25]. Finally, the two authors reached a consensus on the coding results after discussions.

4   Findings

In all 430 relevant comments, 112 of them supported MP, 268 comments opposed MP, and 50 opposed MP pessimistically.

4.1   Attitudes Supporting MP

Intuitively Supporting. Intuitive comments did not show reasons for their attitudes. We nonetheless identified several tactics that were applied in the intuitive expressions (Table 3).

Table 3. Tactics and examples in intuitively supporting MP comments.

Attitude	Tactic	Example
Intuitively supporting	Stating the support to MP	"As audience I do not care if it is pirated or not as long as I can watch"
	Indicating having engaged in MP or being willing to engage	"I watched a super high picture quality version in XX channel"
	Showing where to find the pirated movies	"Who wants the website address (of the pirated movies), I can give you"
	Trolling	"I'm so scared, come on, arrest me…"
	Sarcasm	"Those rich guys just envy us that we don't need to pay for watching"
	Hurling insults	"I watched pirated movies and so what? Your mom is dead!"

In comments intuitively supporting MP, we identified that people plainly stated their opinions or attacked other users who opposed MP with dirty words. The plain comments involved directly stating the support to MP, indicating having engaged in MP or being willing to engage, or showing where to find pirated movies; at the meantime, the "dirty" ones attacked users who opposed MP by trolling, sarcasm or hurling insults.

Absolutely Rationally Supporting. Absolute supports to MP were decided by unconditional factors, such as MP habits, victimless crime, sampling, MP market, one for all, individual characteristics and self-control (Table 4). By referring to MP habits, the supporters argued that piracy was a rooted and unchangeable habit for all users. For example, everyone had engaged in piracy and thus nobody could blame others for it.

"Most Chinese, including your parents, have downloaded and watched pirated movies and used pirated software, go to disdain your parents."

Table 4. Factors of supporting and opposing MP.

Attitude (#)	Absolute factors (#)	Conditional factors (#)
Absolutely rationally supporting MP (24)	MP habits (7), victimless crime (6), sampling (5), MP market (3), one for all (1), individual characteristics (1), self-control (1)	–
Conditionally rationally supporting MP (49)	–	The price of authorized movie (28), the price of pirated movie (6), geographical factors (6), The audiovisual effects of pirated movie (4), individual characteristics (3), movie quality (1), perceived sanction (1), the availability of authorized alternatives (1), self-control (1)
Absolutely rationally opposing MP (72)	Subjective norm (52), perceived sanction (8), movie industry responsibility (5), The audiovisual effects in theater (5), movie nationality (2), movie quality (1)	–
Conditionally rationally opposing MP (103)	–	The audiovisual effects in theater (54), movie nationality (14), movie quality (10), movie industry responsibility (7), The audiovisual effects of pirated movie (7), subjective norm (3), the price of pirated movie (3), perceived sanction (2), the price of authorized movie (2), victimless crime (2), individual characteristics (1)

Besides, the supporters tended to believe that piracy caused little loss on box office revenue. They also justified the existence of MP market, indicating the MP market was a complementary part to authorized movie market. For example, MP allowed people in lower income levels to consume or make profit from movies.

> *"When you take big apples, you need to leave some small ones to those in lower income levels, otherwise you are against the Natural Law (有人吃肉有人喝汤，你想吃干舔净,有伤天理)."*

Sampling was another significant motivation for piracy: people tried out the quality of movies to decide buying tickets or not. Additionally, some users considered watching pirate movies was acceptable as long as they had paid for the movie once (at least), which is called "one for all".

Conditionally Rationally Supporting. While absolute MP supporters were decided by unchangeable factors, conditional ones were driven by situational factors, such as the price of authorized movie, the price of pirated movie, geographical factors and the audiovisual effects of pirated movie (Table 4). These factors were conditional because they could only influence people under certain conditions, thus suggesting their attitudes might change if the conditions changed. For example, some MP supporters argued that the high price of authorized movies made them choose pirated movies, implying they might choose authorized ones if the price was low.

"You asked for piracy by setting the prices too high."

Some also applied geographical factors to support MP, saying that there was no movie theater in their village and they could only watch pirated versions online. The audiovisual effect of pirated movie was another conditional factor for supporting piracy: as for the *the Wandering Earth* case, some of the pirated sources were of great audiovisual effects and hence contributed to the supportive attitudes. Some individual characteristics were also referred to as reasons for supporting movie piracy. For example, some users had to watch pirated versions online, because the movies available in local theaters were not suitable for them:

"There are only 3D versions in our local theaters, but 3D makes me feel dizzy."

4.2 Opposing MP

Intuitively Opposing. Intuitive commenters applied three tactics to oppose MP (Table 5).

In most comments in this category, slogans combined with exclamation marks appeared repeatedly to exclaim their opposing attitudes. Other comments showed actual actions along with attitudes. For example, some users indicated having reported illegal retailers or resources or having gone to theaters with family members and friends. Similar to intuitive comments supporting MP, some comments in this type also hurled insults to people who had opposite opinions.

Absolutely Rationally Opposing. People who absolutely opposed MP provided two common reasons, as shown in Table 4. First, they argued that subjective norms required a protection of copyright, because the protection showed respect to movie producers' time and efforts. Therefore, any type of privacy was considered as disrespectful and hence should be prohibited. Second, some people were afraid of being punished by laws enforcements.

"It's heart breaking for movie producers to see their effort get pirated."

"Why are they so shameless? They even showoff for having watched pirated movies."

Besides, several comments showed that audience was responsible to the development of movie industry. MP itself and users' supporting attitude on MP could stop producers making good movies in the future and finally destroy the industry.

"Producers have invested much money on this movie, if we all watch pirated movies, no one is going to produce good movies in the future."

Table 5. Tactics and examples in intuitively opposing MP comments.

Attitude	Tactic	Example
Intuitively opposing	Repeating the slogan	"It's everyone's responsibility to combat MP!"
	Indicating actual actions	"I just reported seven (pirated movie retailers) on *Taobao* and *Xianyu* (two Chinese online shopping websites, similar to *eBay*)"
	Hurling insults	"You watch pirated movies, your mom dies"

Conditionally Rationally Opposing. In this category, most comments indicated they only opposed MP when the audiovisual effect in theater was much better than that of pirated versions (Table 4). Movie nationality was also mentioned frequently in comments opposing MP: some audience would go to pay for a movie as long as it was a Chinese movie. Additionally, in this case, they took the quality of the movie into consideration, and they opposed the piracy of good movies while felt neutral on the piracy of bad movies.

"I support to combat the piracy of (good) movies like this (the Wandering Earth), but the piracy of other movies (which are not so good) is OK to me."

Besides, if users thought the pirated movie was of low audiovisual effect, the price of tickets in the theater was reasonable, or the price pirated movies was too high, they chose to oppose MP.

However, some comments mentioned perceived sanction to oppose MP in another way: selling pirated movies was unwise when the government was restrictedly suppressing MP.

"Selling pirated movies is asking for trouble at this time (when the government is rigorously suppressing MP) (现在卖盗版不是往枪口上撞吗)."

Individual characteristics were applied as well. For instance, a user said, as a single man, going to theaters alone made him feel lonely, so he preferred to watch online movies at home.

4.3 Pessimistically Opposing MP

The factors influencing the attitude of pessimistically opposing MP is shown in Table 6. People who opposed MP pessimistically acknowledged that MP should be prevented, yet it was impossible to eliminate MP. The most common reason they provided was that a large number of pirated resources were easily accessed online, through platforms such as *WeChat, Weibo, YouTube*, as well as some piracy websites.

> *"Pirated versions have been uploaded on YouTube; YouTube has become a habitat for pirated resources."*

They furthermore referred to MP market, indicating the piracy industry driven by profit was tremendous. Therefore, eliminating MP was impossible.

> *"Pirated movies are usually attached with Casino ads (to gain profit), it's hard to cut this industry chain in a short time."*

By referring to MP habits, people argued that piracy mentality was rooted deeply in a certain group of audience. Additionally, some pirated movies were of high audio-visual effect. These factors together made opposing MP difficult.

Table 6. Factors of pessimistically opposing MP.

Attitude (#)	Factors (#)
Pessimistically opposing MP (50)	Pirated resources (16), MP market (11), MP habits (11), The audiovisual effects of pirated movie (8), the price of pirated movie (1), perceived sanction (1), subjective norm (1), self-control (1)

5 Discussions

5.1 The Attitudes of Chinese Online Users Towards MP

In this study, we found three types of attitudes on movie piracy of Chinese online users, ranging from supporting, pessimistically opposing to opposing MP. The intuitive ones, either supporting or opposing MP, show the ungrounded attitudes through repeating slogan, insulting, etc. The popularity of this type of attitudes can be partly explained by technological affordances and cultural practices of the entertainment-oriented social media platform, *Weibo*.

In rational attitudes, conditional ones are only applicable in certain situations. Besides the factors that are common in all piracy cases, e.g., the price of authorized/pirated versions and the sanctions of law enforcements, some factors that are particularly relevant to movie are identified. For instance, when audience thinks the audiovisual effects of the movie can only be enjoyed in theaters, they tend to oppose pirated versions; on the contrary, if the pirated versions have equivalent audiovisual effects with those in theaters, they might accept pirated movies. These specific factors extend the coverage of the comprehensive model of information seeking (CMIS) which indicates that information behaviors are particularly influenced by information carrier characteristics [26].

Pessimistic attitudes opposing MP mainly describe the rooted piracy foundation across the nation to show the difficulty in eliminating MP. Even though the users agree to eliminate MP, their attitudes are infirm. These attitudes can be attributed to the current status of information property protection in China: China has been suffered from piracy for decades and now is determined to eliminate it [27–29]; at this time, some consumers are aware of the necessity of eliminating MP but feel helpless due to the tremendous existence of it.

5.2 Factors Influencing Attitudes

We found 19 factors behind the attitudes. The results support the explanation power of SCT on MP attitudes. We found that outcome expectancies, including perceived rewards and costs, influenced MP related attitudes. In other words, audience needs to weigh benefits and risks when making decisions [3]. As for perceived rewards, it is found that the audiovisual effects in theaters or that of pirated movies and sampling effect motivate users to support or oppose MP. For example, some audience members tend to object MP when they consider that theaters provide better movie experience than that of pirated movies; moreover, some users think that watching a pirated movie helps them decide whether or not to pay for it, thus avoiding paying for a unworthy movie. Similar results have been found in a study that the perceived rewards such as utility and quality of digital goods exert a small-to-medium correlation with piracy [3].

In addition to these factors, we found movie quality, the responsibility to movie industry, and movie nationality were considered as benefits. When a movie is of high quality, audience is more apt to pay for it because of the respect to producers; at the meantime, audience wishes there will be more high-quality movies in the future, so they pay for good movies to financially support the producers so that they can keep producing. More interestingly, Chinese audience is more likely to pay for Chinese movies than those from other countries. These factors echo previous research findings that the adoration of a specific artist/producer helps opposing MP [21].

Perceived costs, including the price of authorized or pirated movies and perceived sanctions by law enforcements are identified as factors that drive users away from certain attitudes. It is found that people tend to watch a movie for free but not to pay for it when the price is too high; besides, although MP provides free movies, users nonetheless oppose MP because they are afraid of being punished by law enforcements [21].

Other than outcome expectancies, we identified social learning factors, including subjective norms as well as habits. Subjective norms refer to a set of standards of behaviors that are morally acceptable in a society. Specifically, in the MP context, it is argued that pirating movies is not normal or acceptable (just like stealing children from parents) and hence should be denounced and resisted [23]. In our study, many Chinese patrons are reported to shape their attitudes toward MP according to subjective norms. This finding is inconsistent with an American study which found that moral beliefs did not have a strong link with perceptions on MP [12]. On the other hand, the force of habits is found to have exerted influence on viewers' perceptions on MP [30]. Piracy has been rampant in China for several decades due to the lack of regulation. Under this condition, many users take watching pirated movies for granted.

The factors of moral disengagement include "one for all" and "victimless crime". Based off deterrence theory, cognitive dissonance theory and neutralization theory, moral disengagement presents how people justify their behaviors although they know the behaviors are immoral. Exactly, some pirated movie consumers show their rationales for committing piracy even though they understand the immorality of MP [31,

32]. For example, some patrons contended that watching pirated versions should not be judged if they already paid for the movie; moreover, some even argued that watching pirated movies did not harm the movie's box office avenue.

We additionally found that the low self-control of online users contributed to their MP perceptions as well. Some users were aware of the harm and risk of MP, but they nonetheless consumed pirated sources due to a lack of self-control and self-regulation, which is supported by previous studies (e.g., [12]).

Environmental factors were rarely introduced in previous studies [3], nonetheless we identified sufficient examples in this category, such as geographical factors, accessibility of authorized alternatives, MP market and pirated resources. The value of information good in an "ecosystem" is enabled by sociotechnical infrastructures [33]. Accordingly, we identified infrastructures such as the access to theaters and authorized alternatives in the MP context. For instance, there are no theaters in some villages in China, thereby forcing audience there to choose online versions; moreover, when there is no authorized version in the internet, audience tends to watch pirated ones [7]. There are also comments showing that the MP market is too tremendous to be destroyed, which echoes a study in US, indicating that pirated copies are cheaper and hence more welcome [34]. Individual characteristics were also found to be influential. For example, some new mothers cannot leave their babies alone and babies are not welcome in theaters, thereby forcing the mothers to watch online movies at home. Interestingly, we identified bachelor as an important factor: single people prefer watching movies at home rather than in theaters.

From the above discussion, we found that culture plays a significant role in influencing the attitudes of Chinese online users. Confucianism holds a dominant position in Chinese society. It is not a religion but an ethical system that holds the cultivation of virtue and enhancement of humanity in high regard rather than laws or religious principals [35]. Therefore, the sense of judgement by social norms contributes more to attitudes on MP than perceived sanctions by laws. Besides, virtue promotion is achieved by a continuous process from people themselves, their families to the whole society, showing the interpersonal closeness and ties. Thereby, on one hand, Chinese users attach great important to the companion from their spouses and children when watching movies. On the other hand, they also find themselves responsible for the maintenance of social order, as supported by the Patriotism and movie industry responsibility found in the study. In addition, Confucianism encourages moderation and being patient, which partly explains why some people being opposed to a radical elimination of MP. However, the traditional culture has been challenged in modern times. In the MP case, for example, rampant pirated resources and market, as well as the inequality of infrastructure between rural and urban areas have brought some problems to maintain the goal of virtuous living.

6 Implications

The current study has two theoretical implications. First, the results are aligned with the categories of social cognitive theory, and expands some detailed subcategories based on Chinese context. It is reported that online activities in different cultural backgrounds can be affected by culture differences [19]. In this study, we found personal physical factors, responsibility, movie nationality, geographical factors, MP market and pirated resources are related to Chinese sociocultural structure. Second, different attitudes on MP were found to be affected by different kinds of factors in the theory. For example, people often absolutely support or oppose MP for social learning factors, while their conditional attitudes are often affected by outcome expectancies such as prices, audiovisual effects and movie quality. The easy availability of pirated resources is the main reason for pessimistic attitude, which was seldom found in other types of attitude. Moreover, MP market and piracy habit are also significant in pessimistic attitude.

This study also has some practical implications. Since moral justification is a significant factor in the results, the government should inform users that piracy is not morally acceptable by specific reasons, e.g., the serious avenue loss caused by MP. Furthermore, the government can emphasize the dependence of movie industry on the support of audience to call on audience's sense of responsibility, thus raising the awareness of the long-term damage of MP. Social organizations and celebrities can also contribute by educational communication with the public. In addition, building more theaters or providing authorized alternatives help keeping people from online MP.

7 Conclusion

To investigate the attitudes of Chinese online users on MP and the factors behind the attitudes, we conducted a content analysis with a Chinese MP case. We found that attitudes among users ranged from supporting MP, opposing MP pessimistically to opposing MP. Factors influencing Chinese online users' attitudes included outcome expectancy, self-efficacy, social learning, moral disengagement and environmental factors. The findings echoed the explanation of MP behavior by SCT and enriched SCT by identifying some detailed cultural factors in Chinese context.

However, there are some limitations. First, self-control and self-regulation factors usually measured by scales in SCT cannot be fully investigated in this qualitative study. Additionally, we didn't differentiate the attitudes of consumers and retailers of MP products. Moreover, although users' attitudes can be examined through online comments, more empirical work should be done to figure out the relationship between their attitudes and actual actions.

Acknowledgments. We thank Dr. Besiki Stvilia for his suggestions on this paper. The second author would like to thank China Scholarship Council (CSC) for financially supporting her visit in Florida State University.

Declaration of Interest. None.

References

1. Al-Rafee, S., Cronan, T.P.: Digital piracy: factors that influence attitude toward behavior. J. Bus. Ethics **63**(3), 237–259 (2006). https://doi.org/10.1007/s10551-005-1902-9
2. Peitz, M., Waelbroeck, P.: Piracy of digital products: a critical review of the theoretical literature. Inf. Econ. Policy **18**(4), 449–476 (2006)
3. Lowry, P.B., Zhang, J., Wu, T.: Nature or nurture? A meta-analysis of the factors that maximize the prediction of digital piracy by using social cognitive theory as a framework. Comput. Hum. Behav. **68**, 104–120 (2017)
4. Rob, R., Waldfogel, J.: Piracy on the silver screen. J. Ind. Econ. **55**(3), 379–395 (2007)
5. Al-Rafee, S., Dashti, A.E.: A cross cultural comparison of the extended TPB: the case of digital piracy. J. Glob. Inf. Technol. Manag. **15**(1), 5–24 (2014)
6. Jacobs, R.S., Heuvelman, A., Tan, M., Peters, O.: Digital movie piracy: a perspective on downloading behavior through social cognitive theory. Comput. Hum. Behav. **28**(3), 958–967 (2012)
7. Phau, I., Teah, M., Liang, J.: Investigating the factors influencing digital movie piracy. J. Promot. Manag. **22**(5), 637–664 (2016)
8. Redondo, I., Charron, J.-P.: The payment dilemma in movie and music downloads: an explanation through cognitive dissonance theory. Comput. Hum. Behav. **29**(5), 2037–2046 (2013)
9. Fleming, P., Watson, S.J., Patouris, E., Bartholomew, K.J., Zizzo, D.J.: Why do people file share unlawfully? A systematic review, meta-analysis and panel study. Comput. Hum. Behav. **72**, 535–548 (2017)
10. Urbonavicius, S., Dikcius, V., Adomaviciute, K., Urbonavicius, I.: Movie piracy: how novelty-seeking relates to illegal downloading. EuroMed J. Bus. **14**(1), 21–30 (2019)
11. Gupta, P.K., Venkataramani, B.: Evaluation of movie piracy using an integrated approach of interpretive structural modelling and MICMAC analysis. Int. J. Indian Cult. Bus. Manag. **11**(1), 43–58 (2015)
12. Higgins, G.E., Fell, B.D., Wilson, A.L.: Low self-control and social learning in understanding students' intentions to pirate movies in the United States. Soc. Sci. Comput. Rev. **25**(3), 339–357 (2007)
13. Malin, J., Fowers, B.J.: Adolescent self-control and music and movie piracy. Comput. Hum. Behav. **25**(3), 718–722 (2009)
14. Lin, X., Qiu, Z., Li, J., Cheng, L.: The influencing factors of viewing network pirate film in China. In: 12th International Conference on Service Systems and Service Management (ICSSSM), pp. 1–4. IEEE (2015)
15. Akers, R.: Social Learning and Social Structure: A General Theory of Crime and Deviance. Routledge, New York (2017)
16. Bandura, A.: Social Foundations of Thought and Action. Prentice Hall, Englewood Cliffs (1986)
17. Batlle, E., Neuschmied, H., Uray, P., Ackermann, G.: Recognition and analysis of audio for copyright protection: the RAA project. J. Am. Soc. Inform. Sci. Technol. **55**(12), 1084–1091 (2004)
18. Xin Hua Daily Finance. http://www.xhfmedia.com/newsdetail.htm?id=1902140050. Accessed 14 Sept 2019
19. Sanfilippo, M., Yang, S., Fichman, P.: Trolling here, there, and everywhere: perceptions of trolling behaviors in context. J. Assoc. Inf. Sci. Technol. **68**(10), 2313–2327 (2017)
20. Sun, H., Fichman, P.: Chinese collective trolling. Proc. Assoc. Inf. Sci. Technol. **55**(1), 478–485 (2018)

21. Cockrill, A., Goode, M.M.: DVD pirating intentions: angels, devils, chancers and receivers. J. Consum. Behav. **11**(1), 1–10 (2012)
22. Chiou, J.S., Cheng, H.I., Huang, C.Y.: The effects of artist adoration and perceived risk of getting caught on attitude and intention to pirate music in the United States and Taiwan. Ethics Behav. **21**(3), 182–196 (2011)
23. Steinmetz, K.F., Tunnell, K.D.: Under the pixelated jolly roger: a study of on-line pirates. Deviant Behav. **34**(1), 53–67 (2013)
24. Cho, H., Chung, S., Filippova, A.: Perceptions of social norms surrounding digital piracy: the effect of social projection and communication exposure on injunctive and descriptive social norms. Comput. Hum. Behav. **48**, 506–515 (2015)
25. Siponen, M., Vance, A., Willison, R.: New insights into the problem of software piracy: the effects of neutralization, shame, and moral beliefs. Inf. Manag. **49**(7–8), 334–341 (2012)
26. Tong, Z., Yan, F., Hao, J.: Digital copyright protection in China. Publ. Res. Q. **24**(1), 48–53 (2018). https://doi.org/10.1007/s12109-008-9049-z
27. Lombard, M., Snyder-Duch, J., Bracken, C.C.: Content analysis in mass communication: assessment and reporting of intercoder reliability. Hum. Commun. Res. **28**(4), 587–604 (2002)
28. Gu, J.: From divergence to convergence: institutionalization of copyright and the decline of online video piracy in China. Int. Commun. Gaz. **80**(1), 60–86 (2018)
29. Liu, X., Zha, Y.: Copyright protection of digital movies using the coalition of technology and law in China. Chin. Stud. **07**(04), 259–276 (2018)
30. Johnson, J.D., Meischke, H.: A comprehensive model of cancer-related information seeking applied to magazines. Hum. Commun. Res. **19**(3), 343–367 (1993)
31. Akbulut, Y.: Exploration of the antecedents of digital piracy through a structural equation model. Comput. Educ. **78**(C), 294–305 (2014)
32. Brown, M.E., Trevino, L.K., Harrison, D.A.: Ethical leadership: a social learning perspective for construct development and testing. Organ. Behav. Hum. Decis. Process. **97**(2), 117–134 (2005)
33. Kos Koklic, M., Kukar-Kinney, M., Vida, I.: Three-level mechanism of consumer digital piracy: development and cross-cultural validation. J. Bus. Ethics **134**(1), 15–27 (2016). https://doi.org/10.1007/s10551-014-2075-1
34. Jetha, K., Berente, N., King, J.L.: Digital and analog logics: an analysis of the discourse on property rights and information goods. Inf. Soc. **33**(3), 119–132 (2017)
35. Hofstede, G.: Culture's Consequences: Comparing Values, Behaviors, Institutions, and Organizations Across Nations. Sage Publications, Thousand Oaks (2001)

Information Quality of Reddit Link Posts on Health News

Haichen Zhou[1,2] and Bei Yu[2(✉)]

[1] Nanjing Agricultural University, Nanjing 210095, Jiangsu, China
haizenchow@gmail.com
[2] Syracuse University, Syracuse, NY 13244, USA
byu@syr.edu

Abstract. Inaccuracy has been a common problem in news coverage of scientific research. This problem has been particularly prevalent in health research news. Health research news usually spreads from research publications and press releases to news and social media. In this study we examined the information quality of the Reddit link posts that introduce health news stories. We developed a coding schema to annotate the inaccurate information in a sample of 250 link posts on health research news within the Reddit community *r/Health* in 2018. The result shows that most link posts simply copied the original news headlines verbatim, while some paraphrased the news stories by adding, deleting, replacing, and combining content. We found that 12 paraphrased link posts contained inaccurate information that may mislead the readers. The most common type of inaccuracy is exaggeration resulted from changing the original speculative claims to direct causal statements by removing the modal verbs such as "may" and "might". The result shows that although the link posts of health news were generally faithful to the original news stories, exaggerated claims may lead to false hope for researchers and patients.

Keywords: Reddit · Health news · Paraphrasing · Information quality

1 Introduction

Inaccuracy has been a common problem in news coverage of scientific research [1, 2]. This problem has been particularly prevalent in health research news [3, 4]. Health research news usually diffuses from research publications and press releases to news and social media [3]. Inaccuracy has been attributed to journalists' lack of training or the appeal to sensationalism to arouse readers' interest [5], and has been found not only in non-credible sources like tabloids, but also in prestige newspapers and even academic press releases from the researchers' own institutions [3]. For example, exaggerated health advice, exaggerated causal claims from correlational findings and inference to humans from animal studies have been frequently found in press releases and news stories [3]. The exaggerations may result in wrong medical decisions and serious health consequences [6].

With the popularity of social media, health research news has also been spread to social media. Certain online discussion communities, such as Reddit, have become a

© Springer Nature Switzerland AG 2020
A. Sundqvist et al. (Eds.): iConference 2020, LNCS 12051, pp. 186–197, 2020.
https://doi.org/10.1007/978-3-030-43687-2_14

curated news source for the general public [7]. As a social news aggregation, web content rating, and discussion website[1], Reddit has a number of subreddit communities, such as *r/Health*, where participants can post links to health news stories. Different from Facebook and Twitter, Reddit implements the voting and comment functions to help the community filter out low-quality health information [8]. Reddit users are asked to provide an interesting title and text comment when post a link to a health news story[2]. They can also upvote and downvote a post. Through this collective effort, high quality content is expected to rise to the top [9]. Despite the wisdom of the crowd, many factors such as low health literacy[3] might affect Reddit voters' judgment; therefore, the accuracy of the top posts is still questionable [10–12]. Some studies have raised concern about this issue. For example, health information retrieved through social media was ranked as the least reliable source compared with information from physicians, family/friends and web search results [11]. In addition, health-related posts on social media were found to blend evidential and subjective experiential knowledge, which might result in inaccuracy [12]. A few studies examined the information quality of Reddit specifically. In [13] doctors were asked to evaluate a sample of posts related to diseases such as diabetes and AIDS on three websites, including Reddit, and found a small proportion (4 of 79) was considered as factually incorrect. Positive correlation between quality and popularity of Reddit posts has also been reported [14]. Despite the satisfactory findings, these prior studies examined the text posts only, and left out the link posts. Different from text posts, where the content is entirely in text, the link posts introduce external content by providing links and author comments. Since link posts are an important node in the path of information sharing [15], more research is needed to understand the misinformation introduced during link posting.

In this study we conducted a content analysis to examine the information quality of the Reddit link posts on health news. Since the subreddit *r/Health* does not allow text posts, and thus provides an ideal data source for studying misinformation in link posts. Glenski et al. [7] found that the majority of users in Reddit are headline browsers. They only view the summary headlines (the title in Reddit posts) and ignore the content or the comments. 73% of posts were rated without viewing the content at first. This means the quality of the summary headline written by authors in Reddit plays a key role in disseminating accurate health information on Reddit. The summary headlines are often paraphrased from the original news headlines. An examination of the types and quality of paraphrases can foster deeper understanding of the types and frequencies of inaccuracy, and thus shed light on potential strategies for curbing the misinformation dissemination in Reddit or other popular social media. Hence we focus on analyzing the quality of the paraphrases in the summary headlines. We aim to answer the following research questions:

RQ1. What are the common ways of paraphrasing when users link post health news?
RQ2. How often did inaccuracy occur in the paraphrases and what are the types of inaccuracy?

---

[1] https://www.redditinc.com/.

[2] https://i.imgur.com/y1Lix2T.png.

[3] https://nnlm.gov/initiatives/topics/health-literacy.

This paper is organized as follows. Section 2 offers a review of related work. In Sect. 3, the data preparation, sampling, and annotation are described, after which, in Sect. 4, the research results are discussed. In Sect. 5, the conclusions are drawn.

2 Related Work

2.1 Information Quality on Reddit Community

To date, prior research on Reddit posts has examined some aspects of the content and the community, such as the popularity of posts [16] and the structure and dynamics of the discussion forums [17]. In comparison, the information quality of the Reddit posts was less studied. Overall, a few studies have found satisfactory result regarding the information quality of Reddit posts in several topic areas. For example, Straub-Cook [18] examined the posts about public affairs in r/Seattle, and found that users were good at navigating and filtering the vast array of information sources. Aniche et al. [19] found that content reliability was not perceived as an issue by users in r/programming. A possible explanation is that since the main topics in this subreddit are about technical discussion and code sharing, the reliability of these topics may not be too difficult to assess for users with programming experience. Cole et al. [13] asked doctors to evaluate a sample of answers to health-related questions in three websites including Reddit, and found that the health information in the answers was generally accurate; only a small amount of information was assessed as poor quality. In addition, some authors explored the relationship between observed popularity and estimated quality (number of votes a post after minimizing the impact of social influence bias and inequality in visibility) in Reddit. The result shows that popularity is a relatively strong signal of quality [14]. Despite the satisfactory findings, these prior studies examined the text posts only, and left out the link posts, which is the focus of this study.

2.2 Paraphrase

Writing summary headlines after reading the articles can be regarded as a kind of paraphrase. In the area of computational linguistics, paraphrase has been well studied due to its application in information extraction [20], machine translation [21], plagiarism detection [22] and question answering [23]. Some studies have developed taxonomies for paraphrase. For example, Culicover [24] first proposes four types of paraphrase in 1968: transformational, attenuated, lexical, derivational, and real-world. Recently, Bhagat and Hovy [25] categorized the types of paraphrase into 26 categories focusing on the lexical level changes. Vila et al. [26] develop a two-tier taxonomy setting out 26 categories grouped into five classes: lexicon based changes, morphology based changes, syntax based changes, semantics based changes, and discourse based changes. Fujita [27] presents a lexical and structural paraphrase taxonomy containing six classes, namely paraphrases of single content words, function-expressional paraphrases, paraphrases of compound expressions, clause-structural paraphrases, multi-clausal paraphrases, as well as paraphrases of idiosyncratic expressions. These taxonomies were specifically designed for linguistic studies, and many defined categories do not apply to our study of the Reddit posts. Drawing on these prior studies, we developed a simplified taxonomy that is tailored to the purpose of identifying inaccurate information. This taxonomy will be described in the next section.

2.3 Types of Inaccuracy in Health Research News

To date, researchers and media watchdogs (such as Health News Review) have been conducting manual content analysis to estimate and monitor the quality of health research news [3, 28–30]. These efforts have resulted in rich knowledge on the types of inaccuracy, especially exaggeration. Several evaluation criteria have been manually developed, such as [3, 30, 31]. Sumners et al. [3] focused on three types of exaggerations: health advice not mentioned in journal articles, causal claims from correlational findings, and human inferences from research on non-humans. Woloshin and Schwartz [32] checked the mentions of study limitations and exaggerated data presentation. Several media watchdogs, including Media Doctor Australia [28], Media Doctor Canada [29], and Health News Reviews in the United States [30], have been using a detailed 10-criteria list for media monitoring [33]. The 10 criteria used by Health News Reviews are: cost, benefit, harm, evidence, disease-mongering, funding, existing approaches, availability, novelty, and sensational language. In this study we will compare the content of the Reddit link posts and the original health research news to examine whether inaccuracy occurred during this paraphrasing process and what are the common types of inaccuracy introduced by paraphrasing.

3 Method

Our research method included multiple steps. First, we chose the Reddit health community *r/Health* as the study case and downloaded all data in the year of 2018. We then cleaned the invalid data and formed the final dataset. A sample set of posts was then selected and annotated based on our paraphrase taxonomy. Finally, we investigated the relationship between the inaccuracy and paraphrase types.

3.1 Data Preparation

The posts and related metadata in 2018 were downloaded using Pushshift.io (A website that crawls social network data in real time and open data for researchers)[4]. In total, we collected 108,235 posts. Among them were a number of advertisements and other invalid posts with no more than one comments and scores (equal to upvote minus downvote). Therefore, we removed the posts with one or zero comments and scores, and those not written in English. Finally, we obtained 4,335 valid posts.

---

[4] https://pushshift.io/.

To focus on the posts that may contain inaccurate paraphrases, we removed the headlines that were copied verbatim from the original news source. First, we used the python package Newspaper[5] to collect the headlines from the original news sources (A). Second, we examined whether each text posted by authors in Reddit (B) is the same as the original headline (string(A) == string(B)). In this process, 1,389 posts were found to be the same, 2,611 different, and 335 not verifiable because the original news page cannot be accessed or parsed. Therefore, the 2,611 paraphrased posts were used for developing the sample data set through random sampling. Among the paraphrased posts, three authors contributed nearly half (1,079) of the posts.

3.2   Sampling and Annotation

A sample of 250 paraphrased posts were randomly selected and annotated by one annotator. Since the posts follow the zipf law that most posts were contributed by a few authors, we selected 50 posts from each of the top 3 authors and 100 posts from all other authors. As we mentioned in Sect. 2.2, current taxonomies were specifically designed for linguistic studies, and many defined categories do not apply to our study of the Reddit posts. Hence we induced our own taxonomy based on the most obvious changes the authors made. For example, if a paraphrased post only deleted one word from original news, that post will be annotated as "Delete". The inductive coding resulted in five types of paraphrase: Copy & Paste, Combine, Add, Delete, and Replace. Table 1 lists the category and description. Table 2 shows the examples of both original sentences and paraphrased sentences in each category. Some sentences used more than one type of paraphrase.

Table 1. A taxonomy of paraphrase types and descriptions.

Paraphrase type	Description
Copy & Paste	The author copied and pasted sentences from the original news or press release
Combine	The author combined multiple original sentences together
Add	The author added their own words or sentences to the original sentence
Delete	The author deleted some of the words or phrases in the original sentence
Replace	The author replaced the words or phrases in the original sentence with their own words or phrases (also including rephrasing the whole sentences)

---

[5] https://github.com/codelucas/newspaper.

Table 2. Examples of sentences and paraphrase types.

Paraphrase type	Original sentence	Posted sentence
Combine	"City hosp **uses alcohol to cure** heart disease The **doctors** made use of a process known as alcohol septal ablation, in which pure alcohol is used to burn the extra mass The man was suffering from **hypertrophic cardiomyopathy**, a common disorder in which heart muscles grow thick, sometimes causing sudden death"	"Doctors use alcohol to cure hypertrophic cardiomyopathy"
Add	"Scientists Discovered What Causes Dementia"	"Scientists **Have** Discovered What Causes Dementia"
Delete	"'Raw water' is now a health trend, **because of course it is**"	"'Raw water' is now a health trend"
Replace	"A large body of evidence stretching from bench to bedside suggests that environmental stressors associated with hospitalization are toxic. Markers of allostatic overload, including elevated levels of cortisol, catecholamines, and inflammatory markers, **have been associated with** adverse outcomes after hospital discharge"	"Researchers develop the theory that the toxicity of hospitalization - lack of sleep, nutrition, activity; abundance of stress, disruption, noise, confusion - **can** have physiologic adverse effects that last long after discharge"

4   Results and Discussion

Before answering RQ1 and RQ2, we report the descriptive statistics of the health subreddit. Compared with the famous community *r/science* (21,806,873 users), the size of *r/Health* (616,042 users) is not large. To make the current participation pattern of *r/Health* clear, we collected the data of the most recent year 2018 and observed the data in two dimensions: post number and author number. Figure 1 shows the plotted numbers of both post and author. The two numbers seem to follow the same pattern, and both declined near the end of the year.

RQ1. What are the common ways of paraphrasing when users link post health news?

Since one post may use multiple types of paraphrase, we annotated each occurrence of paraphrase, and then calculated the number and percentage of posts used in each type. Table 3 shows that "copy and paste" was the most common type of paraphrase; it was used in 121 posts (48.4%). "Replace" was also frequently used (32.4%). "Add" and "Delete" were less common (13.2% and 22.8% respectively). Table 4 shows examples of common types of paraphrase.

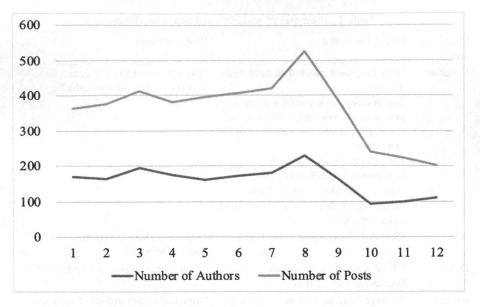

Fig. 1. Trend of the Reddit health community by month

Table 3. Paraphrase type distribution

Paraphrase type	Count	Percentage
Copy & Paste	121	48.4%
Combine	26	10.4%
Add	33	13.2%
Delete	57	22.8%
Replace	81	32.4%

Table 4. Examples of common types of paraphrase

Paraphrase type	Example
Add	**Time** (in the future), **Location** (in America), **Sources** (finds new research, Science, PubMed, in a new study, Interesting study), **Triggering discussion** (is there a downside), **Function words** (have), **Content words** (alone, deep, disease, neurocognitive scores)
Delete	**Time** (Tuesday), **Sources** (study says, Gallup found), **Function words** (but, and, a, its, their)
Replace	**Simplicity** (and = &, two = 2, percent = %, United States = US, administration officials = admin, The tattoo and the hospital's decision = It), **Personal habits** (said = told, predicted = suggests, favored = vote for, recently = just), **Certainty** (may = can, may = activated, would = could)

RQ2. How often did inaccuracy occur in the paraphrases and what are the types of inaccuracy?

Drawing on the categorization of inaccuracy in prior studies [3], we categorized the 12 posts with inaccurate information into four types: *exaggerated causal claims* (7 posts), *exaggerated inference to human or larger population* (1 post), *unconfirmed new claim* (1 post), and *other factual errors* (3 posts).

Exaggerated causal claim is a major type of misinformation in health research press releases and news stories [3]. In our sample data, we found seven posts containing exaggerated causal claims. In these paraphrases, the authors often removed the modal verbs (such as "may" and "might") that were used to mitigate the certainty in the original news, resulting in increased certainty and exaggerated claims. For example, in Ex. 1, the original news on a potential link between the *Tau* protein and Alzheimer's diseases was exaggerated as if it is a direct causal finding by removing the modal verbs and replacing the original phrase of "strong link" with a direct causal verb "activate". Since this claim and other relevant claims on the cause of Alzheimer's disease [34] are extremely important for finding treatments for Alzheimer's disease, which is affecting 44 millions of people in the world, the exaggerated claims may lead to false hope for researchers and patients.

Ex. 1 Original News: New evidence suggests a mechanism by which progressive accumulation of Tau protein in brain cells **may** lead to Alzheimer's disease. Scientists studied more than 600 human brains and fruit fly models of Alzheimer's disease and found the first evidence of a **strong link** between Tau protein within neurons and the activity of particular DNA sequences called transposable elements, which **might** trigger neurodegeneration.

Paraphrased Post: Tau **Activates** Transposable Elements in Alzheimer's Disease.
In the other cases of exaggerated causal claims, "may" was replaced by "can", "have been associated with" replaced by "can", "associated with" replaced by "as a result", "would" replaced by "could", "would prevent" replaced by "prevents", and "could reduce the number" replaced by "without", indicating exaggeration from correlational or conditional causal findings to direct causal claims.

Exaggerated inference from animal studies to humans, or from small samples to larger population has been found in previous studies [1]. In our data set we found only one post that removed important research details, resulting in exaggerated inference from a small group of patients to all patients. In Ex. 2, the paraphrased post removed the information that the new treatment will be tested on three patients only, and large-scale clinical trial is expected in the future. Since study design [35] is considered important information for understanding the strength of the research findings, removing the detail on the small sample size could result in a false belief that the treatment is available to all patients.

Ex. 2. Original News: Scientists in Japan now have permission to treat people who have heart disease with cells produced by a revolutionary reprogramming technique. On 16 May, Japan's health ministry gave doctors the green light to take wafer-thin sheets of tissue derived from iPS cells and graft them onto diseased human hearts. In their technique, Sawa and his colleagues use iPS cells to create a sheet of 100 million heart-muscle cells. Once Sawa's team has treated its **three patients**, it will apply to conduct a **clinical trial** involving a further seven to ten people.

Paraphrased Post: Scientists in Japan now have permission to treat people who have heart disease with tissue derived from human induced pluripotent stem cells. Sheets of up to 100 million heart muscle cells grown in a lab will be surgically applied to diseased hearts.

Another post (Ex. 3) combined two findings, one on children's yoghurts and the other on organic yoghurts into a new, unconfirmed claim on "children's organic yoghurts".

Ex. 3. Original News: In our survey of yogurts sold in the UK, we found that less than 10% were low sugar – almost none of which were **children's yogurts**. We also found that **organic** products, often viewed as healthier options, contained some of the highest levels of sugar.

Paraphrased Post: Organic children's yogurts found to have some of the highest sugar contents in the product line.

Other factual errors were also found. In Ex. 4, the author of the following paraphrase misunderstood the meaning of "genomes" and replaced the phrase "1 million or more volunteers" with "1 million genomes", indicating the author's lack of biomedical knowledge. In Ex. 5, one sentence not found in the original news was added, inserting unconfirmed information. In another post, "$60" was replaced by "$37", probably a typo.

Ex. 4. Original News: NIH launches All of Us research program this week. The National Institutes of Health (NIH) announced this week plans to open national enrollment for the All of Us Research Program on May 6. The goal of the program is to **enroll 1 million or more volunteers**. Through the program, the volunteers will agree to share information about themselves over many years. "All of Us is an ambitious project that has the potential to revolutionize how we study disease and medicine," Health and Human Services Secretary Alex Azar said.

Paraphrased Post: The US is launching a massive effort to **sequence 1 million genomes** and link them to personal health in order to better study disease and medicine.

Ex. 5. Original News: A new, eye-wateringly high estimate of the cost of obesity in the US. A report released this week puts a surprisingly high figure on the societal cost of obesity in the US: $1.72 trillion annually, or 9.3% of GDP. By far the biggest chunk of that $1.72 trillion is the $1.24 trillion chunk attributed to the "indirect" costs of obesity: the "work absences, lost wages, and reduced economic productivity for the individuals suffering from the conditions and their family caregivers," the report explains. That is, the bulk comes from costs other than healthcare spending.

Paraphrased Post: A new study estimates the obesity estimate costs $1.7 trillion a year in the US alone. Or more than $5,000 per person per year. Increased risk of **arthritis, back/knee pain, early disability, early retirement, diabetes, heart disease, cancer** all drive this cost.

The RQ2 result shows that although most link posts were faithful to the original news content, a small number of posts contained distorted information regarding the major research finding, study design, and other factual information. The most common type of misinformation is the exaggerated causal claims, which account for more than half of the problematic posts. The exaggerated causal claims, exaggerated inference to larger population, and new claim invented with no evidence may result in misunderstanding and false hope for researchers and patients.

5 Conclusions

In this study, we sampled 250 link posts from the Reddit health community *r/Health* in 2018, and examined the inaccurate information introduced when authors paraphrased the original health news stories. The result shows that most posts simply copied the original news content verbatim, while some paraphrased by adding, deleting, replacing, and combining content. We found a total of 12 paraphrased posts that contained inaccurate information. The most common type of inaccuracy is exaggeration resulted from changing the original speculative claims to direct causal statements by removing the modal verbs such as "may" and "might". Although the link posts were generally consistent with the original news stories, the small number of exaggerated claims may lead to false hope for researchers and patients. This study provides a first-step information quality scan of the link posts on Reddit. Due to the limited amount of data included in this study, a larger-scale study is needed to be able to generalize the finding to the broader community of volunteers for science communication on social media.

References

1. Tankard, J.W., Ryan, M.: News source perceptions of accuracy of science coverage. Journal. Q. **51**, 219–225 (1974). https://doi.org/10.1177/107769907405100204
2. Pellechia, M.G.: Trends in science coverage: a content analysis of three US newspapers. Public Underst. Sci. **6**, 49–68 (1997). https://doi.org/10.1088/0963-6625/6/1/004
3. Sumner, P., et al.: The association between exaggeration in health related science news and academic press releases: retrospective observational study. BMJ **349**, g7015 (2014). https://doi.org/10.1136/bmj.g7015
4. Chang, C.: Inaccuracy in health research news: a typology and predictions of scientists' perceptions of the accuracy of research news. J. Health Commun. **20**, 177–186 (2015). https://doi.org/10.1080/10810730.2014.917746
5. Fahnestock, J.: Accommodating science: the rhetorical life of scientific facts. Writ. Commun. **15**, 330–350 (1998). https://doi.org/10.1177/0741088398015003006
6. Buhse, S., Rahn, A.C., Bock, M., Mühlhauser, I.: Causal interpretation of correlational studies – analysis of medical news on the website of the official journal for German physicians. PLoS ONE **13**, e0196833 (2018). https://doi.org/10.1371/journal.pone.0196833
7. Glenski, M., Pennycuff, C., Weninger, T.: Consumers and curators: browsing and voting patterns on reddit. IEEE Trans. Comput. Soc. Syst. **4**, 196–206 (2017). https://doi.org/10.1109/TCSS.2017.2742242

8. Brossard, D., Scheufele, D.A.: Science, new media, and the public. Science **339**, 40–41 (2013). https://doi.org/10.1126/science.1232329
9. Ovadia, S.: More than just cat pictures: Reddit as a curated news source. Behav. Soc. Sci. Libr. **34**, 37–40 (2015). https://doi.org/10.1080/01639269.2015.996491
10. Zhao, Y., Zhang, J.: Consumer health information seeking in social media: a literature review. Health Inf. Libr. J. **34**, 268–283 (2017). https://doi.org/10.1111/hir.12192
11. de Belt, T.H.V., Engelen, L.J., Berben, S.A., Teerenstra, S., Samsom, M., Schoonhoven, L.: Internet and social media for health-related information and communication in health care: preferences of the Dutch general population. J. Med. Internet Res. **15**, e220 (2013). https://doi.org/10.2196/jmir.2607
12. Sharma, R., Wigginton, B., Meurk, C., Ford, P., Gartner, C.: Motivations and limitations associated with vaping among people with mental illness: a qualitative analysis of Reddit discussions. IJERPH **14**, 7 (2016). https://doi.org/10.3390/ijerph14010007
13. Cole, J., Watkins, C., Kleine, D.: Health advice from internet discussion forums: how bad is dangerous? J. Med. Internet Res. **18**, e4 (2016). https://doi.org/10.2196/jmir.5051
14. Stoddard, G.: Popularity dynamics and intrinsic quality in Reddit and hacker news. In: ICWSM (2015)
15. Record, R.A., Silberman, W.R., Santiago, J.E., Ham, T.: I sought it, i Reddit: examining health information engagement behaviors among Reddit users. J. Health Commun. **23**, 470–476 (2018)
16. Horne, B.D., Adali, S., Sikdar, S.: Identifying the social signals that drive online discussions: a case study of Reddit communities. In: 2017 26th International Conference on Computer Communication and Networks (ICCCN), pp. 1–9 (2017)
17. Medvedev, A.N., Delvenne, J.-C., Lambiotte, R.: Modelling structure and predicting dynamics of discussion threads in online boards. J. Complex Netw. **7**, 67–82 (2019). https://doi.org/10.1093/comnet/cny010
18. Straub-Cook, P.: Source, please? Digit. Journal. **6**, 1314–1332 (2018). https://doi.org/10.1080/21670811.2017.1412801
19. Aniche, M., et al.: How modern news aggregators help development communities shape and share knowledge. In: 2018 IEEE/ACM 40th International Conference on Software Engineering (ICSE), pp. 499–510 (2018)
20. Shinyama, Y., Sekine, S.: Paraphrase acquisition for information extraction. In: Proceedings of the Second International Workshop on Paraphrasing, vol. 16, pp. 65–71. Association for Computational Linguistics, Stroudsburg (2003)
21. Callison-Burch, C., Koehn, P., Osborne, M.: Improved statistical machine translation using paraphrases. In: Proceedings of the Main Conference on Human Language Technology Conference of the North American Chapter of the Association of Computational Linguistics, pp. 17–24. Association for Computational Linguistics, Stroudsburg (2006)
22. Barrón-Cedeño, A., Vila, M., Martí, M., Rosso, P.: Plagiarism meets paraphrasing: insights for the next generation in automatic plagiarism detection. Comput. Linguist. **39**, 917–947 (2013). https://doi.org/10.1162/COLI_a_00153
23. Fader, A., Zettlemoyer, L., Etzioni, O.: Paraphrase-driven learning for open question answering. In: Proceedings of the 51st Annual Meeting of the Association for Computational Linguistics, Long Papers, vol. 1, pp. 1608–1618. Association for Computational Linguistics, Sofia (2013)
24. Culicover, P.W.: Paraphrase generation and information retrieval from stored text. Mech. Transl. Comput. Linguist. **11**, 78–88 (1968)
25. Bhagat, R., Hovy, E.: What is a paraphrase? Comput. Linguist. **39**, 463–472 (2013). https://doi.org/10.1162/COLI_a_00166

26. Vila, M., Martí, M.A., Rodríguez, H.: Paraphrase concept and typology. A linguistically based and computationally oriented approach. Procesamiento del Lenguaje Nat. **46**, 83–90 (2010)

27. Fujita, A.: Automatic generation of syntactically well-formed and semantically appropriate paraphrases (2005)

28. Smith, D.E., Wilson, A.J., Henry, D.A.: Monitoring the quality of medical news reporting: early experience with media doctor. Med. J. Aust. **183**, 190–193 (2005). https://doi.org/10.5694/j.1326-5377.2005.tb06992.x

29. How well do Canadian media outlets convey medical treatment information? https://www.ncbi.nlm.nih.gov/pmc/articles/PMC3090174/

30. Schwitzer, G.: How do US journalists cover treatments, tests, products, and procedures? An evaluation of 500 stories. PLOS Med. **5**, e95 (2008). https://doi.org/10.1371/journal.pmed.0050095

31. Chang, C.: Inaccuracy in health research news: a typology and predictions of scientists' perceptions of the accuracy of research news. J. Health Commun. **20**, 177–186 (2015)

32. Woloshin, S., Schwartz, L.M.: Press releases: translating research into news. JAMA **287**, 2856–2858 (2002)

33. Moynihan, R., et al.: Coverage by the news media of the benefits and risks of medications. N. Engl. J. Med. **342**, 1645–1650 (2000)

34. Greenberg, S.A.: How citation distortions create unfounded authority: analysis of a citation network. BMJ **339**, b2680 (2009)

35. Cyranoski, D.: 'Reprogrammed' stem cells approved to mend human hearts for the first time. Nature **557**, 619 (2018)

Saudi International Students' Perceptions of Their Transition to the UK and the Impact of Social Media

Anas Alsuhaibani[1,2]($\boxtimes$), Andrew Cox[1]($\boxtimes$), Frank Hopfgartner[1]($\boxtimes$), and Xin Zhao[1]($\boxtimes$)

[1] Information School, University of Sheffield, Sheffield, UK
{ahalsuhaibani1, a.m.cox, f.hopfgartner,
xin.zhao}@Sheffield.ac.uk
[2] Department of Information Systems, College of Computer Engineering
and Sciences, Prince Sattam Bin Abdulaziz University, Al-Kharj, Saudi Arabia
ah.alsuhaibani@psau.edu.sa

Abstract. In their transition to a new country, international students often feel lost, anxious or stressed. Saudi students in the UK in particular may face further challenges due to the cultural, social and religious differences that they experience. There is a lot of evidence that social media play a crucial role in this experience. By interviewing 12 Saudi students from different cities in the UK, the aim of this study is to investigate how they perceive their transition to the UK and how social media is involved. The analysis indicates that Saudi students' perceptions of transition tend to fall in to one of two markedly different camps. Some students see transition as an opportunity to detach themselves from their home country and to engage with the new society. Those students turn to social media as a tool allowing them to build bridges with the new society. Other students feel less enthusiastic to make a full engagement with the UK society. Those students find social media as a good tool to maintain connections and links with family and friends in their home country.

Keywords: International students' transition · Study abroad · Social media · Saudi international students

1 Introduction

The UK is one of the top destinations for international students with approximately 460,000 foreign students studying in the UK in 2017/18 [1]. There is great diversity in nationality of international students in the UK and Saudi Arabia is one of the top seven sending countries, with more than 14,000 higher education students in 2017/18 [2]. Study abroad for an international student is usually considered a major life event that involves multiple changes to their cultural, social, and academic environments [3–5]. Comparing international students to domestic students shows that the former face more challenges in their studies and in adjusting to university life [6, 7]. The concept of transition 'indicates the progression from familiar to the unknown and involves the

© Springer Nature Switzerland AG 2020
A. Sundqvist et al. (Eds.): iConference 2020, LNCS 12051, pp. 198–208, 2020.
https://doi.org/10.1007/978-3-030-43687-2_15

adoption of new challenges culturally, socially, and cognitively' [19 p. 2]. International students at their transition are more likely to suffer from different psychological issues (e.g., anxiety, loneliness, depression or stress) [3, 6, 8, 9]. Saudi students may encounter further challenges compared to other international students, because of the differences in culture, religion, language and academic system [10].

International students tend to spend more time on social media than domestic students [11], this is due to their increased need of social support and communication [12]. A recent study of the use of social media by Korean and Chinese students in the US found that they spend on average about 6.5 h of their day online [13]. Sandel [14] found that international students spend on average approximately two hours per day communicating with friends and families. Social media can help in increasing students understanding of the potential host country's culture and it may facilitate their cultural transition [14–16]. Furthermore, it may be helpful in supporting the 'language adjustment' of international students [17]. On the other hand, social media may have negative social and academic impacts on international students. It can hinder the students' engagement with the new society [18] and distract them from their studies [19].

Thus, the transition is a very sensitive period for international students and social media can play a major role. However, much more needs to be understood about how international students perceive their transition and how they use social media at this point in their lives, including whether and how it affects different nationalities in different ways. Given the sensitivity of the transition period on the students' life, the increased number of Saudi students in the UK and their high use of social media, and the specific challenges and differences that Saudi students face, this research investigates the role of social media in Saudi students' transition when studying in the UK. This research builds on work published in 2019 [20]. The aim of this research will be achieved by answering the following questions:

1. How do Saudi students perceive their transition to the UK?
2. How do they perceive the impact of social media during their transition?

2 Literature Review

A simple model has been proposed by Menzies and Baron [21] to explain the experience of international students' transition to a host country (see Fig. 1). This model suggests that the sojourner passes through five phases during their transition. The authors assume that student at the "pre-departure" phase anticipates their experience of studying abroad and has a neutral mood [22, 23]. This is followed by the "arrival" and the "honeymoon" phases, in which students are positive, and are excited and eager to explore the new country [21, 23]. The student then reaches the "party's over" stage where they begin to realise the environmental, cultural, and academic differences, which lead them to feel depressed and anxious [21, 23–25]. Finally, the "healthy adjustment" phase occurs when the student feel that they adjusted to the life in the host country and they have got used to it [21]. While this model captures key aspects of experience, it does feel rather linear and simplistic. For example, Blue and Haynes [22] critiqued this model and argued that the healthy adjustment may not always happen. Following the after the party's over phase, students may have another phase called "crisis" which is very negative and may lead them to return home.

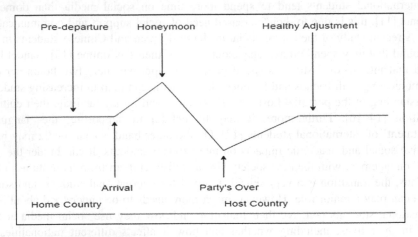

Fig. 1. International students' transition model. Adapted from [21]

Along with the increased use of social media, it has been reported by a number of studies [13–17] that social media is implicated in the students' sojourn and plays a role in their experience of transition. It has been argued that international students during their time abroad consider social media as a source of academic and daily life information [26]. Social media can also play a positive role in increasing the students' academic and social engagement [16]. Sandel [14] reported that social media can support the adjustment of international students through "relational bonds", "psychological well-being", "sociocultural skills" and meeting "informational needs" [14]. For Chinese and Indian students in Australia, Martin and Rizvi [27] claimed that students used social media as a tool to explore the new place and culture. This can increase the students' sense of belonging to a new city and positively affect their adjustment. However, despite the positive views of most authors in this area, it is important to acknowledge that social media may also negatively influence students' transition. Guo, Li and Ito [18] acknowledged that social media could have a dual impact: as well as its helpful roles, it can adversely affect international students by isolating them from the new society and making them more distracted. Other researchers [19] reported that for students as a whole, the uncontrolled use of social media negatively affects their academic performance and achievement.

There is a lot of debate about the impact of social media on students. Little of this seems to have been tied to the specific context of international students' transition. Furthermore, more studies are required to see how social media can affect different nationalities in different ways. In a recent systematic review conducted by Sleeman, Lang and Lemon [28], they reached the conclusion that future researchers are recommended to focus on students coming from "less researched" countries. To the best of the researchers' knowledge, this will be one of the first studies that observes Saudi students' transition and their use of social media in the UK. Accordingly, therefore, this research aims to make an important contribution to this under explored area by producing a strong base that can support further studies and investigations in the field of students' transition and social media.

3 Methods

This paper is a part of a larger study investigating the transition of Saudi students to the UK and their use of social media. A sequential mixed methods approach (qualitative then quantitative) will applied, using semi-structured interviews, followed by Twitter data analysis. This paper will only focus on and report the findings of an initial analysis of the results of the first qualitative method interviews. Twelve Saudi students who are using social media and pursuing or planning to pursue their higher education in the UK were recruited. The reason for including students who are planning to study in the UK is that this study focuses on all the stages of the transition. According to Menzies and Baron [21], the experience of transition starts before arriving in the host country. Other participants in the study were already in the UK. All had been there for less than a year, as McLachlan and Justice and Prescott and Hellsten [4, 29] have argued, the student's transition period usually lasts up to 12 months after their arrival in the host country. Participants were recruited from different locations in the UK and to represent different levels of study, different ages, genders and family status. The interviews were conducted face-to-face, via phone or Skype, depending on the participants' preference and lasted between 42 and 102 min. During the interviews, students were asked to draw their transition timeline, identify the stages which they gone through, the difficulties that they had and their emotions during these phases. They also discussed what they drew with the interviewer. For phone and Skype interviews, students were asked to scan their drawing and send it to the interviewer. Table 1 shows more details about the participants.

Data was analyzed thematically using Braun and Clarke's six steps approach [25]. In order to ensure that codes and themes were derived from the data, the coder (first author) sought to set aside, as far as possible, his own assumptions and beliefs while undertaking the analysis. Furthermore, meetings with other researchers were conducted regularly during the data collection and analysis to ensure the balance of the data interpretation. Recruitment for the interviews was based on the principle of voluntary, informed consent and approved by the University of Sheffield prior to data collection.

Table 1. The interview participants

Participant	Gender	Age	Marital status (children)	Since when in the UK	City in the UK	Degree
M1	Male	28	Married (1)	Not arrived yet	Sheffield	Ph.D.
F1	Female	28	Single	Not arrived yet	Sheffield	Ph.D.
M2	Male	26	Single	8 months	Manchester	English course then Master
F2	Female	24	Single	6 months	Newcastle	English course then Master
F3	Female	30	Single	10 months	Manchester	English course then Ph.D.
F4	Female	31	Single	11 months	Sheffield	English course then Master
F5	Female	40	Single	11 months	Sheffield	English course then Master
M3	Male	35	Married	10 months	Durham	Masters
F6	Female	27	Single	12 months	Birmingham	Masters
M4	Male	38	Married (6)	9 months	Southampton	Ph.D.
M5	Male	35	Married (1)	12 months	Brighton	Ph.D.
F7	Female	34	Married (2)	7 months	Leicester	Ph.D.

4　Results and Discussion

4.1　Transition Period

As previously mentioned, transition for international students is a major life change. Some researchers in the area have argued that students usually start to get into the mood of transition three months before their traveling day. They also argue that the transition usually lasts for six to 12 months [4, 29]. Participants' views in this study varied in when they felt they started to get into the mood of transition and in when they adjusted to the life in the UK (if they did at all).

Similar to the model of transition presented by Menzies and Baron [21], on a timeline of their transition, students were asked to draw their feeling and emotions and to identify factors that motivate their happiness or sadness. Figures 2 and 3[1] below represent samples of students' drawings. In explaining Fig. 2, the student claimed that she entered the mood of transition around 3 months before her traveling day when she received the offer of study. She was like most students in this research, nervous and stressed before traveling to the UK. For this student and most other students, this is usually triggered by fears about the new experience, place and environment. This is

---

[1] Annotations have been included near to the students' handwritings to make them easier to read.

clearer for students who have no experience in living in a different country and for those who are weak in English:

> 'My mood in the days around the travel day was really bad; I lost my appetite in the last three days in Saudi Arabia. This is because I was afraid of moving to a different and western society especially for me as a Muslim girl with weak English language.' [F4].

> 'A few days before my departure to the UK, I was extremely nervous. I was questioning myself about my decision to study abroad' [M2].

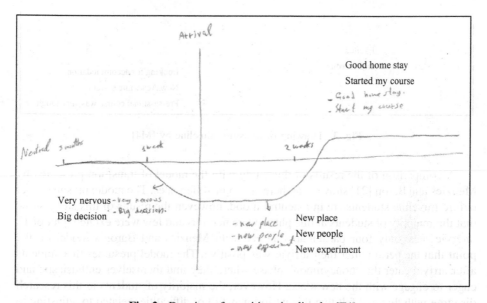

Fig. 2. Drawing of transition timeline by [F4]

For other students, their negative mood may last longer after arrival and this was reinforced by difficulties they faced in the UK. In Fig. 3, the student suggests that the stress period was after arriving and it was triggered by difficulties with searching for accommodation and adjusting to the new academic system:

> 'After arriving in the UK, I was very nervous due to the difficulties I faced with finding the accommodation. I started my pre-sessional course as soon as I arrived in the UK and I was very busy […]. Anyway, after about two months, I found suitable accommodation and my family joined me in the UK. I also started my Ph.D. study, so, by that time I felt that I settled in life in the UK' [M4].

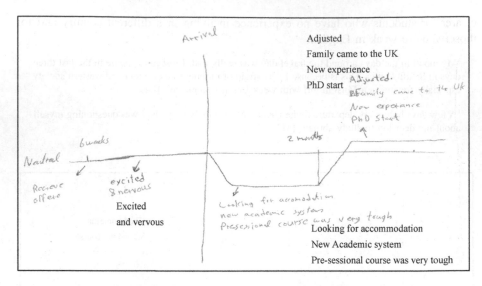

Fig. 3. Drawing of transition timeline by [M4]

A comparison of the results of this study with the model of transition presented by Menzies and Baron [21] shows that there are some differences. The model presumes that before traveling students are in a neutral mood, however, the results of this study show that the majority of students at this phase were nervous and few were excited. Out of 12 interviewees, only four participants agreed with Menzies and Baron's model on the point that the period after their arrival was positive. The model presumes that students after arrival enter the "honeymoon" phase where they find themselves enthusiastic and eager to engage with the new place. However, the majority of students in this research disagree with that and felt that this period was full of difficulties related to adjusting to the new place, adjusting to the new academic system and finding accommodation.

4.2 How Students Perceive Transition

Perceptions of transition tended to fall in one of two markedly different camps. Some students see transition as an opportunity to make a break from their home country and to engage with the new society:

'I see my life in the UK as a good opportunity for me to engage with the UK community. In addition to the academic goals that I have, I am also planning to achieve some personal goals learning about other cultures and engaging with new people' [F5].

This is usually clear for students who are eager to know about other cultures or those who want to develop their English language.

Other students believed that they came to the UK mainly for academic purposes and they are not enthusiastic to make a full engagement with the UK society:

'I do not see myself very excited to learn about the UK culture and to engage with the society […]. When I have free time, I would prefer to spend it with Saudi friends. I feel that we have more things in common and I enjoy chatting with them more than others.' [M5].

This can be attributed to the difference in culture, religious and social life, considering the conservative Muslim society that Saudi students came from [30]. Furthermore, it might be related to the fact that the majority of Saudi students are sponsored by employers in Saudi Arabia with an obligation to return immediately following the end of their studies. Therefore, these students usually see their time in the UK as a temporary period and do not see the point of mixing with other cultures as important [31]. Students with these views are usually more connected with their people in Saudi Arabia and the Saudi community in the UK.

It was also found that how the students perceive the transition is usually related to their push and pull factors. Push factors are those motivations related to why the student wants to study abroad. On the other hand, pull factors are those related to the selection of a destination, institution or specific program of study [32–34]. This study found that students who are personally motivated by the pull factor of the opportunity to study abroad perceive the transition as a life experience from which they can learn a lot. Those students are usually more willing to engage with the UK society and culture:

'I decided to study abroad because I think that people should develop themselves; and interacting with a new culture and people is a type of development' [F3].

On the other hand, students who are motivated to study abroad because of the lack of programs of studies in Saudi Arabia (which is a push factor for sending students abroad [35]) may see their experience of studying abroad as something they are obliged to do:

'To be honest, I would prefer to do my Masters in Saudi Arabia, but since my major was not provided in Saudi Arabia I had to go to the UK' [F4].

'My main motivation to study abroad is my work; if I have the choice I will not go abroad. I have commitments with my family and children in Saudi Arabia' [M4].

4.3   How Social Media Is Related to Students' Transition

There was a strong relationship between how the students perceive transition and their behavior on and their use of social media. Students who are more willing to detach themselves from the Saudi society usually make a shift in their content and communication on social media. For example, some students reported that they created new accounts on social media (i.e. new accounts on WhatsApp, Snapchat or Twitter) as soon as they arrive to the UK. The reason for doing this is that they want to restrict these accounts for the UK content and communications. Those students usually make limited access to the online Saudi content because they want to weaken their ties with their Saudi life. They believe that this can have positive impacts on their engagement with the new society:

'Once I arrived to the UK, I created a new WhatsApp account, but I gave this number only to a few people in Saudi Arabia. The reason behind that is I want to focus on my studies and life here in the UK. I still contact my family and Saudi friends on social media but very rarely' [F5].

This finding supports another result by Li and Chen [36], who argued that having host country friends on social media and exploring a host country content can make a positive impact on the cultural adjustment of international students. These students' views also concur with those of another previous study [37] that found that social media could positively affect the language adjustment of international students:

'In the UK, I also started to use a platform called Meetup and I have a positive experience with it. It allowed me to meet new people who have common interests; we meet and talk and that helped me to improve my English.' [M2].

In contrast, students who were not keen to engage with the new society made few changes to their social media use. The results show little attempts from these students to use social media as a tool to help with their social engagement with the new society. Many participants who have this view reported that they found social media to be a tool to keep them connected with their family and friends back home. Families in Saudi Arabia are very connected and children even if they are adults usually spend a lot of time with their parents [30, 38]. Therefore, some students thought that this is an advantage of social media because they do not want to be disconnected from their home country:

'We are a very connected family and especially for my parents I do not want them to feel that I am far away from them, so, I am always in contact with them on social media.'[M4]

'I feel that social media is making a link for me with my country and family. Social media is the only way that keeps me updated with them.' [M5]

5   Conclusion and Future Work

This paper has investigated how Saudi international students in the UK perceive transition and how they use social media during that period. It has shown that the perception of transition can follow two different patterns. Some students see transition as an opportunity to detach themselves from their home country and to engage with the new society. For them social media allows them to build bridges with the new society and engage with it. On the other hand, others believe they came to the UK mainly for academic purposes and they do not have to make a full engagement with the UK society. Social media is a way to maintain ties for those who want to be connected with their home family or friends.

In future work, a second quantitative method that includes retrieving Saudi students' content on Twitter will be implemented. This method includes applying content analysis and using text mining to further examine changes in behavior and to test and extend the results of the first method.

References

1. NUFFIC Homepage. https://www.nuffic.nl/en/internationalisation/facts-and-figures/higher-education/global-mobility/sending-and-receiving-countries. Accessed 23 Sept 2019
2. Ministry of Education. https://www.moe.gov.sa/en/Pages/default.aspx. Accessed 21 Sept 2019

3. Chen, C.P.: Common stressors among international college students: research and counseling implications. J. Coll. Couns. **2**(1), 49–62 (1999)
4. McLachlan, D.A., Justice, J.: A grounded theory of international student well-being. Int. J. Theory Constr. Test. **13**(1), 17–32 (2007)
5. Searle, W., Ward, C.: The prediction of psychological and sociocultural adjustment during cross-cultural transitions. Int. J. Intercult. Relat. **14**(4), 449–464 (1990)
6. Hechanova-Alampay, R., Beehr, T.A., Christiansen, N.D., Van Horn, R.K.: Adjustment and strain among domestic and international student sojourners: a longitudinal study. Sch. Psychol. Int. **23**(4), 458–474 (2002)
7. Burns, R.B.: Study and stress among first year overseas students in an Australian university. High Educ. Res. Dev. **10**(1), 61–77 (1991)
8. Wu, H., Garza, E., Guzman, N.: International student's challenge and adjustment to college. Educ. Res. Int. **2015**, 1–9 (2015)
9. Andrade, M.S.: International students in English-speaking universities: adjustment factors. J. Res. Int. Educ. **5**(2), 131–154 (2006)
10. Arafeh, A.K.: From the Middle East to the Midwest: The Transition Experiences of Saudi Female International Students at a Midwest University Campus (2017)
11. Gray, K., Chang, S., Kennedy, G.: Use of social web technologies by international and domestic undergraduate students: implications for internationalising learning and teaching in Australian universities. Technol. Pedag. Educ. **19**(1), 31–46 (2010)
12. Delwar Hossain, M., Veenstra, A.S.: Online maintenance of life domains: uses of social network sites during graduate education among the US and international students. Comput Hum. Behav. **29**(2), 697–702 (2013)
13. Park, N., Song, H., Lee, K.: Social networking sites and other media use, acculturation stress, and psychological well-being among East Asian college students in the United States. Comput. Hum. Behav. **36**(1), 38–46 (2014)
14. Sandel, T.L.: "Oh, I'm Here!": social media's impact on the cross-cultural adaptation of students studying abroad. J. Intercult. Commun. Res. **43**(1), 1–29 (2014)
15. Raymond, J., Wang, H.: Computers in human behavior social network sites and international students' cross-cultural adaptation. Comput. Hum. Behav. **49**(4), 00–11 (2015)
16. Forbush, E., Foucault-Welles, B.: Social media use and adaptation among Chinese students beginning to study in the United States. Int. J. Intercult. Relat. **50**(3), 1–12 (2016)
17. Alshehab, H.M.: Female Saudi international students daily practices on social media in Australia. Int. J. Innov. Educ. Res. **5**(12), 39–77 (2017)
18. Guo, Y., Li, Y., Ito, N.: Exploring the predicted effect of social networking site use on perceived social capital and psychological well-being of Chinese international students in Japan. Cyberpsychol. Behav. Soc. Netw. **17**(1), 52–58 (2014)
19. Al-Rahmi, W.M., Othman, M.S.: The impact of social media use on academic performance among university students: a pilot study. J. Inf. Syst. Res. Innov. **4**, 1–10 (2016)
20. Alsuhaibani, A., Cox, A., Hopfgartner, F.: Investigating the role of social media during the transition of international students to the UK. In: iConference 2019 Proceedings (2019)
21. Menzies, J.L., Baron, R.: International postgraduate student transition experiences: the importance of student societies and friends. Innov. Educ. Teach. Int. **51**(1), 84–94 (2014)
22. Blue, J.L., Haynes, U.: Preparation for the overseas assignment. Bus. Horiz. **20**(3), 61–77 (1977)
23. De Cieri, H., Dowling, P.J., Taylor, K.F.: The psychological impact of expatriate relocation on partners. Int. J. Hum. Resour. Manag. **2**(3), 377–414 (1991)
24. Zapf, M.K.: Cross-cultural transitions and wellness: dealing with culture shock. Int. J. Adv. Couns. **14**(2), 105–119 (1991). https://doi.org/10.1007/BF00117730

25. Brown, L.: The incidence of study-related stress in international students in the initial stage of the international sojourn. J. Stud. Int. Educ. **12**(1), 5–28 (2008)
26. Zhao, X.: Social media and the international student experience. Int. Educ. Res. Netw. (2016)
27. Martin, F., Rizvi, F.: Making Melbourne: digital connectivity and international students' experience of locality. Media Cult. Soc. **36**(7), 1016–1031 (2014)
28. Sleeman, J., Lang, C., Lemon, N.: Social media challenges and affordances for international students: bridges, boundaries, and hybrid spaces. J. Stud. Int. Educ. **20**(5), 391–415 (2016)
29. Prescott, A., Hellsten, M.: "Hanging together even with non-native speakers": double edged challenges in the transition experience. Int. High. Educ. 75–95 (2003)
30. Al-Saggaf, Y.: The effect of online community on offline community in Saudi Arabia. Electron. J. Inf. Syst. Dev. Ctries. **16**(1), 1–16 (2004)
31. Binsahl, H.M., Chang, S., Bosua, R.: Exploring the factors that impact on Saudi female international students' use of social technologies as an information source. In: PACIS, pp. 201–210 (2015)
32. Mazzarol, T., Soutar, G.N.: "Push-pull" factors influencing international student destination choice. Int. J. Educ. Manag. **16**(2), 82–90 (2002)
33. Ahmad, S.Z., Buchanan, F.R.: Choices of destination for transnational higher education: "pull" factors in an Asia Pacific market. Educ. Stud. **42**(2), 163–180 (2016)
34. Krzaklewska, E.: Why Study Abroad? – An Analysis of Erasmus Students' Motivations (2008)
35. Yakaboski, T., Perez-Velez, K., Almutairi, Y.: Collectivists' decision-making: Saudi Arabian graduate students' study abroad choices. J. Int. Stud. **7**(1), 94–112 (2017)
36. Li, X., Chen, W.: Facebook or Renren? A comparative study of social networking site use and social capital among Chinese international students in the United States. Comput. Hum. Behav. **35**(1), 16–23 (2014)
37. Qiu, W.: Language Adjustment of International Students in the US: A Social Network Analysis on the Effects of Language Resources, Language Norm and Technology (2011)
38. Binsahl, H., Chang, S.: International Saudi female students in Australia and social networking sites: what are the motivations and barriers to communication. In: ISANA International Academy Association Conference, vol. 112, pp. 1–12 (2012)

"On the left side, there's nothing right. On the right side, there's nothing left:" Polarization of Political Opinion by News Media

Shuyuan Mary Ho[1(✉)], Dayu Kao[2], Wenyi Li[1], Chung-Jui Lai[2], and Ming-Jung Chiu-Huang[2]

[1] Florida State University, Tallahassee, FL 32306, USA
smho@fsu.edu
[2] Central Police University, Guishan District, Taoyuan 333, Taiwan, ROC
camel@cpu.edu.tw

Abstract. Political opinions as expressed by the news media have created the phenomenon of polarization in the United States. Modern news agencies have always considered objectivity as being of primary importance. When opinions inadvertently color the facts, the resulting information manipulation can create confusion, and chaos. This study attempts to understand the language differences as expressed by the U.S. news media in the conveyance of political opinions, and to identify predictive language-action cues that can differentiate writing styles of right-wing news media from those of left-wing news media on Twitter. Original tweets from news media agencies were collected and analyzed using logistical regression analysis during September 2019. The study identifies a statistical significance with regards to cognitive loads, analytical thinking, and political sentiment profiles of tweets to allow for better ways of differentiating political opinions between the news media, from right-wing to left-wing. This suggests that news media of the left-wing and right-wing could employ more neutral writing styles to reduce political polarization. The study contributes to our understanding of the language strategies employed by the news media in terms of influencing the public opinions.

Keywords: Sentiment analysis · Polarization · Political opinion mining · Information manipulation · Language-action cues · Social media · Twitter

1 Introduction

As the public has rapidly adopted social media, government agencies also increasingly use social media to announce policy changes and to reach out directly to citizens. For example, Obama successfully established Twitter, Facebook, MySpace, and other social media as integral parts of his political campaign toolbox [1]. More recently, President Trump regularly tweets his opinions, and uses his twitter feed to direct government policy. The direct feed of news and policies from White House administration has allowed citizens' easy access to what was once privileged information,

A. Sundqvist et al. (Eds.): iConference 2020, LNCS 12051, pp. 209–219, 2020.
https://doi.org/10.1007/978-3-030-43687-2_16

but this has also created a wide range of space for interpretation by the news media. The phenomenon of political opinions being spread easily and quickly on social media by the news agencies is resulting in an increasingly polarized populace. Tripathi and Naganna [2] pointed out a challenge inherent in this process—opinion spamming; propaganda spread by different political parties to influence and perhaps mislead public opinion. It is becoming important to understand the evolution of subjective opinion as presented by formerly objective news media agencies.

Tripathi and Naganna [2] suggested three types of opinions: direct, indirect, and comparative (p. 1628). This research aims to conduct a comparative study regarding the difference of opinion as expressed among news media agencies, and especially with regards to social media. We thus ask the question: *Can we computationally identify a news media's political opinions based on language in their tweets*? This short paper is outlined as follows. In the second section, we review literature on political sentiment analysis, opinion mining and classification. Then, we specifically focus on studies about how Twitter reveals political sentiment around election campaigns. In the third section, we describe our study framework, data collection, data filtering strategies, and data selection criteria. In the fourth section, we present our data analysis, in particular the logistic regression analysis, the results and the implications. In the fifth section, we conclude the study with potential contributions, challenges and directions for future studies.

2   Political Opinion Mining and Sentiment Analysis

Yu and Kaufmann *et al.* [3] conducted a study on political opinion mining. Datasets from the 1989–2006 senatorial speeches and 2005 House speeches were collected to compare with the level of sentiment revealed in the business news domain and movie reviews. LIWC (Linguistic Inquiry and Word Count) was used to extract linguistic expressions and features, and SVM was adopted to classify texts for future research. They discovered that the average sentiment level of congressional debate is higher than that of neutral news articles, but lower than that of movie reviews.

Below we will review studies on sentiment analysis particularly focused on political opinion mining for Presidential Elections.

2.1   2009 German Presidential Election

Similar to Yu et al.'s [3] study using LIWC, Tumasjan and Sprenger *et al.* [1, 4] analyzed political tweets across 6 parties to predict the German federal election in 2009. Twitter provides the public with the ability to "microblog" their opinions, making it a good channel for predicting public opinions regarding election results. Both online sentiment and the offline political landscape were analyzed, concluding that Twitter can be a valid mirror of the political landscape, and provide evidence for predicting the election outcome in Germany. Stieglitz and Dang-Xuan [5] also studied the same German election, but their study focused on sentiment analysis expressed on Twitter; that is, the original tweet and retweet behaviors regarding political communication. Based on the relationships between original tweets and retweets, the study was able to identify a group of influential users on Twitter that had a significant impact on the populace. By analyzing linguistic features using LIWC, the study further discovered that the more the affective words were used on tweets, the more likely the original tweets would be retweeted. Dang-Xuan and Stieglitz [6] additionally conducted a blog study and found out that clearly articulated sentiment (i.e., with either positive or negative emotion) will affect their readers, and will likely receive feedback. More-over, their readers tended to participate more with the emotionally-charge discussions on their blogs. Stieglitz and Dang-Xuan [7] conducted a third study regarding political opinions and associated posts on Facebook, to identify that emotionally-charged (i.e., both positive and negative emotion) comments or posts on Facebook will trigger more feedback and recurring posts.

2.2   2012 U.S. and French Presidential Election

Wang and Can et al. [8] developed a system to collect real-time data on the 2012 US Presidential Election as reflected on Twitter. In their proposed baseline model, they used human annotators from Amazon Mechanical Turk (AMT) to get human feedback on the sentiment model, and then adopted naïve Bayes model to tokenize and classify tweets. Nooralahzadeh and Arunachalam et al. [9], on the other hand, conducted a Twitter study on both US and French Presidential elections occurring in 2012. They compared the sentiment—specifically the hashtag analysis—as a type of topic modeling that prevailed before and after the presidential election. The hashtag network results revealed strong ties and connections in the communities studied.

2.3   2016 U.S. Presidential Election

Alashri and Sandala et al. [10] conducted a topical modeling study to analyze Facebook posts in order to better understand the nature of modern online discourse. The study identified the characteristics of people who interacted with candidates during 2016 elections, and was able to identify linguistic features of the associated posts, along with the phenomenon that results in political polarization. Jordan and Pennebaker et al. [11] also conducted a study on the 2016 US Presidential election that compared online posts regarding candidates' Trump and Clinton's emotional tones and authenticity. The study identified that that Trump's debate language was low with regards to analytic/formal thinking, but high in negative emotional tone and authenticity. Clinton, by contrast, was high in analytic and positive emotions, but low in authenticity. The study further analyzed the associated tweets of the candidates, and identified that as Clinton-related tweets became more analytical, her poll numbers dropped—whereas Trump-related tweets became higher in positive emotion and in analytic thinking, and resulted in higher subsequent polling.

3   Study Framework

In order to understand political opinion as tweeted by news media agencies about the current Trump administration, our study collected data that was tweeted directly by the news media, and not the retweets.

3.1   Data Collection

We collected tweets using Twitter stream API, a Python program, using the keyword "Trump." A total of 831,013 tweets were collected on September 10–11, 2019. Retweet data varied from January 30, 2018 through September 11, 2019 (Table 1).

Table 1. Size of dataset

Timeline	Tweets	Retweets	Total
Total	211,249 (25.42%)	619,764 (74.58%)	831,013 (100%)

3.2   Data Filtering and Selection Criteria

As our research question focuses on the news media's original tweets, retweets were not considered unless they contained the original tweets from the news media. Thus, only original tweets remained in the final dataset; 1,344 tweets in total. Our tweets selection criteria are described below.

1. Unformatted data not sorted and classified by the Python was removed.
2. Original tweets were separated from retweets.
3. News media's account names were sorted to extract the tweets.
4. The dataset was divided into three categories[1] of news media agencies; left-wing, central, and right-wing. Table 2 gives an overview of the news media agencies that fall in the scope of the study. The data on 'central' category is used as a baseline dataset for the purpose of comparing with the analyses between the right-wing and the left-wing.
5. Remaining tweets and retweets of non-relevant accounts were removed.

Table 2. Data description

Category	Tweets	Example
Left-wing	850 (63.24%)	Alternet, CNN Opinion, Democracy Now, The Daily Beast, The Huffington Post, The Intercept, Jacobin, Mother Jones, MSNBC, The New Yorker, The New York Times Opinion, The Nation, Slate, Vox, Mashable, ABC, The Atlantic, BuzzFeed News, CBC, CNN Online News, The Economist, The Guardian, NBC, The New York Time Online News, NPR Opinion, Politico, TIME, The Washington Post, CBS, The Daily Show, Newsweek, VanityFair

(continued)

---

[1] Allsides.org media bias rating: https://www.allsides.com/media-bias/media-bias-ratings.

Table 2. (*continued*)

Category	Tweets	Example
Right-wing	158 (11.76%)	Fox News Online News, Reason, The Wall Street Journal Opinion, Examiner, The Washington times, The American Spectator, Breitbart, The Blaze, CBN, The Daily Caller, Daily Mail, The Daily Wire, Fox News Opinion, The Federalist, National Review, New York Post, Newsmax
Central	336 (25%)	AP, Reuters, Bloomberg, The Christian Science Monitor, The Hill, BBC, USA Today, The Wall Street Journal Online, NPR Online News
Total	1,344 (100%)	

4   Data Analysis

Our data is analyzed with sentiment, and then we performed a logistic regression analysis. We employed a comparative sentiment analysis study using LIWC2015 to extract linguistic features of tweets, microblogging messages, and to categorize the news media agency's opinions. The texts were extracted and counted as word frequencies into 90 different types of psychology items using the LIWC default dictionary Pennebaker and Boyd *et al.* [12].

Then, we employed the logistic regression analysis to analyze the statistical significance of these categories across left-wing and right-wing. The right-wing news media is set as 1 while the left-wing is set as 0.

4.1   Cognitive Loads

Table 3 refers to the variables concerning the percentage of total words on cognitive loads within the extracted tweets. Figure 1 also illustrates that both right-wing and left-wing news media employ more cognitive loads in their tweets than news media espousing neutral opinions. Comparatively speaking, the left-wing news media use higher words of cognitive load than those of right-wing. Table 3 shows that the absolute Z-values of cognitive process, cause, discrepancy, and differentiation are greater than 1.96 ($p < 0.05$). Therefore, cognitive process, cause, discrepancy, and differentiation are statistically significant in differentiating between opinions from the left-wing and opinions from the right-wing.

Table 3. The logistic regression and the t-test of cognitive loads.

Coefficients	Estimates	St. error	Z-value	Left-wing	Central	Right-wing
Intercept	−1.649	.124	−13.269***			
Cogproc	−.102	.028	−3.679**	5.54	3.32	4.77
Cause	.129	.048	2.710**	1.15	.88	1.29
Discrep	.169	.054	3.088**	.63	.30	.87
Tentat	−.048	.050	−.971	1.46	.80	.98
Certain	.068	.046	1.483	.83	.39	.98
Differ	.155	.047	3.313***	1.18	.93	1.47

Note: *** $p < .001$, ** $p < 0.01$, * $p < 0.05$

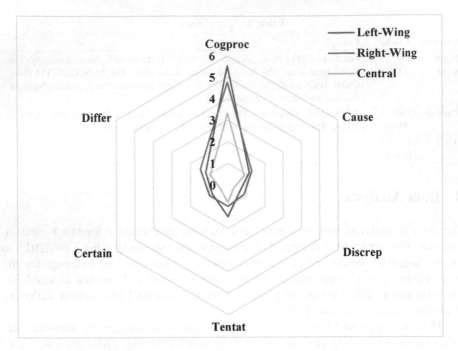

Fig. 1. The spider chart of cognitive loads.

4.2   Affective Processes

Table 4 refers to the variables concerning the percentage of total words on affective processes within the extracted tweets. Based on Fig. 2. news media from the right-wing employed less words of affective processes than those of the left-wing. It seems that the left-wing tends to use more words of the affective process than those news media taking a neutral stand. Table 4 shows that individual affective words are not statistically significant to differentiate new media from the right-wing to the left-wing since all the absolute Z-values are less than 1.96 ($p > 0.05$).

Table 4. The logistic regression and the t-test of affective processes.

Coefficients	Estimates	St. error	Z-value	Left-wing	Central	Right-wing
Intercept	−1.489	.123	−12.089***			
Affect	−.294	.226	−1.299	4.51	4.15	3.85
Posemo	.257	.228	1.129	2.21	2.17	1.98
Negemo	.290	.230	1.259	2.19	1.97	1.84
Anx	−.197	.111	−1.770	.33	.22	.16
Anger	.011	.061	.173	.84	.63	.84
Sad	−.244	.129	−1.890	.33	.34	.14

Note: *** $p < .001$, ** $p < 0.01$, * $p < 0.05$

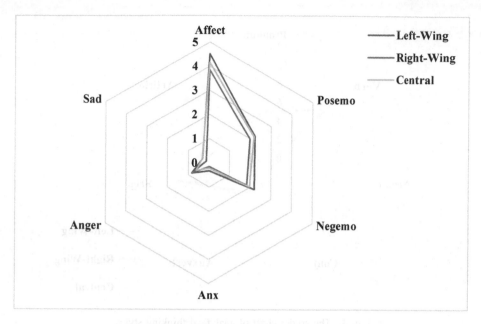

Fig. 2. The spider chart of affective processes.

4.3   Analytical Thinking Styles

Table 5 refers to the variables concerning the percentage of total words on analytical thinking styles within the extracted tweets. Figure 3 illustrates that news media from both right-wing and left-wing are similar to each other, and employ competitively more words of analytical thinking than those of the neutral stand. Table 5 reports that the absolute Z value of "article" and "verb" are great than 1.96 (p < 0.05), which informs statistical significance to differentiate between left-wing and right-wing.

Table 5. The logistic regression and the t-test of analytical thinking styles.

Coefficients	Estimates	St. error	Z-value	Left-wing	Central	Right-wing
Intercept	−1.442	.232	−6.212***			
Pronoun	−.025	.019	−1.303	4.98	4.35	5.13
Article	−.066	.024	−2.781**	4.76	3.26	3.80
Prep	−.030	.017	−1.708	10.42	10.08	9.48
Auxverb	−.006	.033	−.177	4.06	3.22	4.52
Conj	.018	.030	.602	2.27	1.67	2.41
Negate	.042	.052	.807	.77	.66	.99
Verb	.046	.022	2.067*	8.33	7.06	9.39

Note: *** p < .001, ** p < 0.01, * p < 0.05

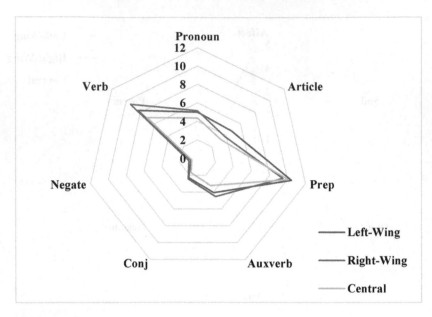

Fig. 3. The spider chart of analytical thinking styles.

4.4   Profiles of Political Sentiment

Table 6 refers to the variables concerning the percentage of total words on the profiles of political sentiment within the extracted tweets. Figure 4 illustrates that all three news media express equally about the present events and news. Table 6 that the absolute Z values of "sad," "focus past," "work" are statistically significant to differentiate between left-wing and right-wing sentiment due to the absolute Z-values are greater than 1.96 ($p < 0.05$).

Table 6. The logistic regression and the t-test of profiles of political sentiment.

Coefficients	Estimates	St. error	Z-value	Left-wing	Central	Right-ring
Intercept	−1.442	.176	−8.213***			
Posemo	−.024	.032	−.736	2.14	2.17	1.96
Negemo	−.012	.047	−.260	2.20	1.99	1.81
Anx	−.150	.112	−1.337	0.34	.23	0.16
Anger	.013	.062	.206	0.88	.63	0.83
Sad	−.281	.133	−2.116*	0.29	.36	0.14
Certain	.031	.045	.695	0.80	.39	0.96
Focuspast	.068	.028	2.442*	1.92	1.04	2.34
Focusfuture	−.033	.050	−.658	0.82	.76	0.78
Work	−.05	.022	−2.192*	5.14	4.66	4.01
Money	.002	.046	.050	0.83	.62	0.72

Note: *** $p < .001$, ** $p < 0.01$, * $p < 0.05$

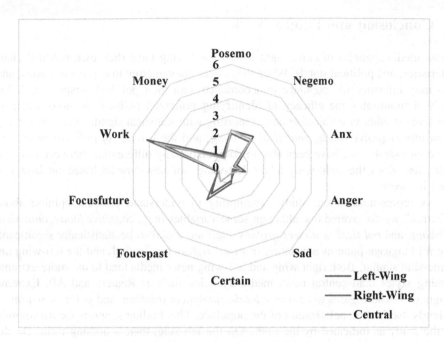

Fig. 4. The spider chart of profiles of political sentiment.

However, news media from the right-wing tends to focus more on the past than both media from the left-wing and neutral stand. It also appears that the news media from the right-wing tends to be more certain than the left-wing; but the media with the neutral stand does not often employ words with certainty (e.g., always, never) in their tweets.

4.5   Discussion and Implication

Based on the above analysis, we identified that the *affective process* does not lend statistical significance in differentiating the tweets of the left-wing from those of the right-wing news media. However, the following language-action cues including *cognitive loads* (such as cognitive processes, cause, discrepancy, and differentiation), *analytical thinking* (such as article, verb), and *profiles of political sentiment* (such as sad, focus past, and work) of tweets do lend statistical significance, and were a better way of differentiating between the political opinions of news media, from the right-wing to the left-wing. Nonetheless, the diagrams (Figs. 1, 2, 3 and 4) showed similar patterns among left-wing, right-wing and neutral, and subtle differences among the three news media categories are not observable.

5 Conclusion and Future Work

News media agencies of either right-wing or left-wing have their own political characteristics, and political stands. When they tweet, they attempt to express opinions, and this may influence the populace in accordance with their political perspectives. This study demonstrates the efficacy of identifying polarized political opinions and perspectives in otherwise objective news reporting with statistical significance—especially regarding *cognitive loads, analytical thinking*, and the *profiles of political sentiment*. We conclude that we have been able to computationally differentiate between political opinions—from the right-wing to the left-wing—of news media based on language used in tweets.

As represented in our study—attempting to understand political opinion about "Trump," we discovered that although some variables (e.g., *cognitive loads, analytical thinking*, and *political sentiment profiles*, etc.) are found to be statistically significant, overall language patterns emanating from the right-wing, central, and the left-wing are somewhat similar. Both right-wing and left-wing news media tend to use more extreme writing styles than central news media agencies such as Reuters and AP. Extreme language—with regards to *cognitive loads, analytical thinking*, and *political sentiment*—lends itself to the polarization of the populace. This finding supports the assumption of the study as indicated by the title: "On the left side, there's nothing right. On the right side, there's nothing left." To reduce polarization, research suggests that news media of the left-wing and right-wing should employ more neutral writing styles as manifested by the central news media agencies. Returning to the historical practice of presenting objective news without including opinion would reduce political polarization over time.

The current research results can be considered as an initial study for constructing a prediction model to process and analyze political opinions as reflected in the general populace. Our future work will include confirming predictor variables and consolidating potential prediction model from multiple Twitter feeds. We will further use the prediction model to analyze original tweets from individuals in order to understand and visualize how public political opinions are being polarized by the news media. We may further predict in terms of which side—left or right—is more popular as reflected in the results of the 2020 U.S. President Election.

Acknowledgements. The authors wish to thank Florida Center for Cybersecurity (FC2) Capability Building Program for the grant #FC2-3910-1007-00-B, 07/01/2018—06/30/2020. The authors also wish to thank Conrad Metcalfe for his editing assistance.

References

1. Tumasjan, A., Sprenger, T.O., Sandner, P.G., Welpe, I.M.: Predicting elections with Twitter: what 140 characters reveal about political sentiment. In: Proceedings of the Fourth International AAAI Conference on Weblogs and Social Media (ICWSM 2010), pp. 178–185. Association for the Advancement of Artificial Intelligence, Washington, DC (2010)

2. Tripathi, G., Naganna, S.: Opinion mining: a review. Int. J. Inf. Comput. Technol. **4**(16), 1625–1635 (2014)
3. Yu, B., Kaufmann, S., Diermeier, D.: Exploring the characteristics of opinion expressions for political opinion classification. In: Proceedings of the 9th Annual International Digital Government Research Conference, Montreal, Canada, pp. 82–91 (2008)
4. Tumasjan, A., Sprenger, T.O., Sandner, P.G., Welpe, I.M.: Election forecasts with Twitter: how 140 characters reflect the political landscape. Soc. Sci. Comput. Rev. **29**(4), 402–418 (2011). https://doi.org/10.1177/0894439310386557
5. Stieglitz, S., Dang-Xuan, L.: Political communication and influence through microblogging-an empirical analysis of sentiment in Twitter messages and retweet behavior. In: Proceedings of the 2012 45th Hawaii International Conference on System Sciences (HICSS'45), pp. 3500–3509. IEEE Computer Society, Hawaii (2012). https://doi.org/10.1109/hicss.2012.476
6. Dang-Xuan, L., Stieglitz, S.: Impact and diffusion of sentiment in political communication-an empirical analysis of political weblogs. In: Proceedings of the 2012 Sixth International AAAI Conference on Weblogs and Social Media (ICWSM 2012), pp. 427–430. Association for the Advancement of Artificial Intelligence, Dublin (2012)
7. Stieglitz, S., Dang-Xuan, L.: Impact and diffusion of sentiment in public communication on Facebook. In: Proceedings of the 2012 European Conference on Information Systems (ECIS 2012), pp. 1–13. Association for Information Systems (AIS) (2012). aisel.aisnet.org/ecis2012/98
8. Wang, H., Can, D., Kazemzadeh, A., Bar, F., Narayanan, S.: A system for real-time Twitter sentiment analysis of 2012 U.S. presidential election cycle. In: Proceedings of the 50th Annual Meeting of the Association for Computational Linguistics (ACL 2012), pp. 115–120. Association for Computational Linguistics, Jeju Island (2012)
9. Nooralahzadeh, F., Arunachalam, V., Chiru, C.: 2012 presidential elections on Twitter-an analysis of how the US and French election were reflected in tweets. In: Proceedings of the 2013 19th International Conference on Control Systems and Computer Science. IEEE, Bucharest (2013). https://doi.org/10.1109/cscs.2013.72
10. Alashri, S., Sandala, S.S., Bajaj, V., Parriott, E., Awazu, Y., Desouza, K.C.: The 2016 US presidential election on Facebook: an exploratory analysis of sentiments. In: Proceedings of the 2018 51st Hawaii International Conference on System Sciences (HICSS'51), pp. 1771–1780. University of Hawaii, Waikoloa Village, Hawaii Big Island (2018). https://doi.org/10.24251/hicss.2018.223
11. Jordan, K.N., Pennebaker, J.W., Ehrig, C.: The 2016 U.S. Presidential candidates and how people tweeted about them, 1–8 (2018). https://doi.org/10.1177/2158244018791218. Special collection: SMaPP global special issue
12. Pennebaker, J.W., Boyd, R.L., Jordan, K.N., Blackburn, K.: The development and psychometric properties of LIWC2015. University of Texas at Austin (2015)

How to Initiate a Discussion Thread?: Exploring Factors Influencing Engagement Level of Online Deliberation

Jieli Liu$^{(\boxtimes)}$ and Pengyi Zhang

Department of Information Management, Peking University, Beijing 100871,
China
{liujieli, pengyi}@pku.edu.cn

Abstract. Online platforms provide a public sphere for discussion, debate, and deliberation among citizens. The engagement of online deliberation enables participants to exchange viewpoints and form communities. This paper aims to explore the influencing factors on engagement level of online deliberation by examining the relationship between an initial post's content features and length and the engagement of the discussion thread it initiates. We sampled 254 discussion threads with 254 initial posts and 2934 following posts and conducted quantitative and qualitative analysis of the posts. Findings show that initial posts which are longer and allocentric (as opposed to egocentric) would evoke longer following posts in a discussion. Different content type (social interaction, claim, argument) of initial posts would lead to significant different engagement, arguments would trigger higher level engagement (average posts per participant and average length of posts in discussions). Whether an initial post holds a clear position has no significant impact on discussion engagement. These findings contribute to a deeper understanding of online deliberation and its engagement and can be useful in promoting engagements in online deliberation.

Keywords: Online communities · Online deliberation · Initial post ·
Engagement

1 Introduction

With the blooming of social media and online communities, people have been increasingly active in sharing information about and expressing points of views on public issues. Online platforms, such as Facebook, Quora, Weibo, and Zhihu, provide an open and inclusive platform for (often heated) discussions and deliberations. Users of these sites may gather around a topic such as "equal rights" and have long and heated discussions and deliberations by posting messages and sharing information and knowledge. These discussions may be not governed or without any political agenda, belonging to a notion of deliberation called "discursive participation", discussing public issues outside the governments' operation [1]. These discussions allow users to exchange knowledge by asking and answering questions, by initiating and responding to a thread, and so on [2]. It is important for users to engage online discussions which

© Springer Nature Switzerland AG 2020
A. Sundqvist et al. (Eds.): iConference 2020, LNCS 12051, pp. 220–226, 2020.
https://doi.org/10.1007/978-3-030-43687-2_17

can develop greater awareness of the reasons behind different views and increase political engagement and general community participation [3, 4].

Aiming to reveal reasons for intensive engagements, this short paper explores the following research question: what factors influence the engagement of online deliberation? Building on prior research, we used a set of indicators for discussion engagement, such as numbers of posts and participants in a thread, average posts per participant, average length of posts in a thread [5, 6]. We are interested in what content features (such as content type of posts, orientation of elaboration, and statement of a clear position) and length of an initial post in a discussion. We sampled 254 discussion threads of topic topics in the public sphere related to citizens' daily lives and may influence people's decision making. We hope to contribute to promoting the engagement of deliberation and establishing a prosperous online public sphere.

2 Related Research

Online deliberations are triggered by influential public problems and participants of the discussion have stake in these discussion and interchange rational and critical arguments to explore a potential answer [7]. Deliberation can be conceptualized as an idealized category within the broader notion of call "discursive participation". The form of activity is discourse with other citizens focusing expressing different views, learning positions of others, and understand of public concern. Occurring though online and off-linc mcdia, it involves private individuals in informal and unplanned exchanges outside the government operation [1]. Participants can benefit from online deliberations and discussions in many forms such as increased knowledge levels [8]. The quality of knowledge sharing is crucial to online deliberation.

Most prior research has focused on the quality of deliberations [5, 6, 9] Some research has studied the relationship with level of argumentation and deliberation. For example, Halpern and Gibbs compared the deliberations in Facebook and YouTube, and found that deliberation quality (measured as equality of participation, level of argumentation, conversational coherence, politeness, civility, and message length) differs between social media platforms. For example, user-to-user messages were longer in Facebook than in YouTube, associated with the higher level of identification [6]. Participation and massage length can be used as indicators for deliberation qualities and discussion engagement. Zhou et al. investigated the characteristics of deliberation on the Guangzhou Daily website through content analysis of posts and measured the quantity of the posts and participants, topicality, nature of the argument (i.e. justification, complexity and civility), and responsiveness and homogeneity of contributions. The findings indicate a public sphere in China online space is emerging but not yet mature enough to expose to disagreement [5]. Xiao and Askin examined people commonly concerned the notability of the topic in deletion deliberation, and non-unanimous debates had more participants than unanimous debates [9]. Researchers classify posts in online discussion into egocentric and allocentric expression now try to investigate whether orientation of elaboration will make a difference to discussion engagement [10]. The position held by people often influence the ongoing of opinion interaction [11]. Therefore, we try to explore the relationship between position of initial posts and discussions they lead to.

3 Methods

The data set was collected from Zhihu.com using a Web crawler in March 2019. Zhihu is one of the largest online Q&A communities in China, In addition to posting and answering questions, participants also use Zhihu as an online community for knowledge exchange and discussion by commenting on others' posts, generating discussion threads among several participants. We sampled two widely discussed topics, "feminism" and "same-sex marriage", due to their increasing publicity and attention from the public.

We sampled 254 threads of discussion under nine question pages about the topics ("feminism" and "same-sex marriage") with different numbers of replies. There are a total number of 3,964 posts on the nine pages. Among them, there are 1,030 posts that does not generate any replies. The rest of the 2,934 posts, belong to 254 threads with 254 initial posts and 2,680 replying posts.

The first author and a MLIS student coded content features (including content type, orientation of elaboration, and position of argument) independently, discussed and resolved the disagreements. Cohen's kappa values of position, orientation of elaboration, and content type are 0.89, 0.86, 0.84 respectively. We calculated external features automatically (including numbers of posts and participants, and length). Some examples are shown in Table 1.

We measured the level of engagement in a thread with the following aspects:

(a) *# of posts*, which was measured by total number of posts in a discussion;
(b) *# of participants*, which was measured by total number of participants in a discussion;
(c) *average posts per participant*, which was measured by average numbers of posts by per person;
(d) *average length of posts*, which was represented average string length of each post.

Statistic tests (correlation, Mann-Whitney U Tests, and K-Wallis Tests) are conducted to test the relationships between features of the initial post and the level of engagement as measured above.

Table 1. Features of initial post

Indicators	Categories	Definition with examples
Content type [6, 10]	Social interaction	Greeting, personal attacks, compliment, and other expression
	Claim	Sharing unsupported personal opinion or information without reasoning
	Argument	Putting forward one's own viewpoints and using argumentation to prove. Arguments based on external sources such as quotes, data, examples or websites

(continued)

Table 1. (*continued*)

Indicators	Categories	Definition with examples
Orientation of elaboration [6, 10]	Egocentric	Elaborating one's own arguments/advice/feeling, citing one's own experience, asking question from personal knowledge base, social interaction (e.g., "From my experiences…", "I remember when…" "I want to know…whether") or citing books, reading materials, and knowledge learned before (e.g., "I had read… before")
	Allocentric	Comparing and synthesizing others' multiple perspectives, citing others' opinion and give response. For examples: • Judgment: "I agree with you… because", "Your opinion is too …, because", "… you mention above is right, but…" • Summarization: "All of posts below is …, and I believe that…" • Extended understanding: "Your advice can apply to … these field, and I think…" • Cite other's opinion and reply: "… had referred …, but I think…"
Position	Clear support	Clearly support feminism or same-sex marriages
	Clear oppose	Clearly oppose feminism or same-sex marriages
	Unclear	Do not clearly express the position to the topic, discuss both position or hold neutral position
Length		String length of initial post

4 Results

4.1 Content Type

We classified the content of the initial posts into three categories: claims, argumentation, and social interaction. The percentage of claim is 59.84%, argumentation is about 26.77%, social interaction type initial posts is 13.39%. To determine whether content types of initial posts have an impact on discussion engagement, we conducted a Kruskal-Wallis Test (shown in Table 2). The result from Kruskal-Wallis Test shows content type has a significant on average posts per participant of discussion ($\chi^2(2) = 6.706$, $p < .05$). Participants post more comments per person in discussions initiated by arguments (mean rank = 145.22) than claims (mean rank = 125.49) and social interactions (mean rank = 104.10). This suggests that arguments can trigger more engaged or in-depth discussion, while social interactions remain at a shallow level of engagement.

Table 2. Impact of content type on discussion engagement

Type	N	Average posts per participant			Length		
		Mean rank	λ^2	P	Mean rank	λ^2	P
Social interaction	25 (9.84%)	104.10	6.706	.035	68.78	43.487	.000
Claim	176 (69.29%)	125.49			120.39		
Argument	53 (20.87%)	145.22			178.82		

The results show that there is a significant difference in average length of posts between different content type, $(\chi^2(2) = 43.487, p < .001)$. Arguments (mean rank = 178.82) trigger longer following posts in average, followed by claims (mean rank = 120.39) and social interactions (mean rank = 68.78).

4.2   Orientation of Elaboration

The percentage of egocentric initial posts is 66.54% (n = 254), while the percentage of allocentric initial posts is 33.46%. To test the influence of initial post's orientation of elaboration discussion engagement, we conducted Mann-Whitney U Test (results shown in Table 3).

Table 3. Impact of orientation of elaboration discussion engagement

Orientation of elaboration	Average length of post in discussion			
	N (%)	Mean rank	U	P
Egocentric	164 (64.57%)	117.78	5786.000	0.004
Allocentric	90 (35.43%)	145.21		

The results indicate that discussion average length is significant longer for allocentric expression (mean rank = 145.21) than egocentric expression (mean rank = 117.78), U = 5786.000, p < .01. Allocentric posts initiate longer following posts than egocentric posts in average. This suggests that by referring to and building on others' statements, one could elicit longer replies with perhaps more thoughtful response.

4.3   Position

Fewer people hold a clear position (14.57%), while most of participants (85.43%) do not clearly express their position or of supporting or against a particular issue. Mann-Whitney U Test shows that whether a participant hold a clear position has no significant impact on discussion engagement. A possible explanation might be that people respond to a post not because a particular position but because of how it expresses the position, such as content type, orientation of the expression, and so on.

4.4 Length of Initial Post

A correlation analysis reveals a significant correlation ($r = .534$, $p < .001$) between initial post length and the average length of posts in the discussion thread. This finding suggests that longer initial posts generate longer reply posts in discussion. This might be because longer initial posts contain more information and more complex ideas, which can evoke longer reply in replies.

5 Conclusion and Discussion

This study aims to contribute to a deeper understanding of online deliberation engagement by analyzing several factors related to the initial post of a discussion thread. Our results suggest that (1) arguments (other than claims and social interactions) initiate discussions with more average posts per person and longer posts; whether the initial post has a clear argument position does not have any significant influence on the engagement level of the discussion. (2) allocentric elaborations invite longer replies in a discussion thread; (3) longer initial posts tend to have longer replies in a thread.

The results suggested that how a discussion thread is started has significant influence on the engagement of the participants in that discussion. Intuitively, longer initial posts may be able to convey more complex ideas which tend to get more replies than shorter posts with simple facts or opinions. Halpern and Gibbs used massage length as an indicator of deliberation quality, and found that longer message provide more justification for the arguments [6]. Arguments would raise more involved discussion than claims and social interactions, with more participants and posts. Prior research found that there were more participants in a discussion in non-unanimous situations than unanimous situations [9]. Perhaps arguments are more likely to happen in non-unanimous situations where different ideas and viewpoints get shared and debated. Allocentric expressions that build on others' posts generate longer replies, perhaps others feel the need to address the reference first before expressing one's own statement [10]. These findings can be useful in stimulating more in-depth online deliberation.

There are several limitations in this study. We sampled discussion threads from about topics in the areas of civic rights, which could have unique discussion and deliberation patterns comparing to other topics. We only examined features of the initial posts, future work can explore other impact factors such as characteristics of the author. Other features such as the use of pronoun and sentiment of the initial post still need exploring. For example, research found that employees who used significantly more pronouns of "we" and "they" indicated a greater involvement with the organization [12]. Emotion plays an essential role in effective communication on social issues [13], which may also has an impact on online deliberation engagement. Future studies can analyze the discussion content to examine factors other than the initial post such as characteristics of the participants that influence the engagement of discussion and to explain how and why discussions develop over time.

Acknowledgement. This research is supported by NSFC Grant #71603012.

References

1. Carpini, M.X.D., Cook, F.L., Jacobs, L.R.: Public deliberation, discursive participation, and citizen engagement: a review of the empirical liter. Ann. Rev. Polit. Sci. **7**, 315–344 (2004)
2. Liu, J., Wang, Y.: Information worth spreading: an exploration of information sharing from social q&a to other social media platforms. Proc. Assoc. Inf. Sci. Technol. **53**, 1–5 (2016)
3. Cappella, J.N., Price, V., Nir, L.: Argument repertoire as a reliable and valid measure of opinion quality: electronic dialogue during campaign 2000. Polit. Commun. **19**, 73–93 (2002)
4. Price, V., Cappella, J.N.: Online deliberation and its influence: the electronic dialogue project in campaign 2000. IT Soc. **1**, 303–329 (2002)
5. Zhou, X., Chan, Y.-Y., Peng, Z.-M.: Deliberativeness of online political discussion: a content analysis of the Guangzhou daily website. J. Stud. **9**, 759–770 (2008)
6. Halpern, D., Gibbs, J.: Social media as a catalyst for online deliberation? Exploring the affordances of Facebook and YouTube for political expression. Comput. Hum. Behav. **29**, 1159–1168 (2013)
7. Habermas, J., Habermas, J.: The Structural Transformation of the Public Sphere: An Inquiry into a Category of Bourgeois Society. MIT press, Cambridge (1991)
8. Min, S.-J.: Online vs. face-to-face deliberation: effects on civic engagement. J. Comput.-Mediat. Commun. **12**, 1369–1387 (2007)
9. Xiao, L., Askin, N.: What influences online deliberation? A wikipedia study. J. Assoc. Inf. Sci. Technol. **65**, 898–910 (2014)
10. Ke, F., Xie, K.: Toward deep learning for adult students in online courses. Internet High. Educ. **12**, 136–145 (2009)
11. Medaglia, R., Yang, Y.: Online public deliberation in China: evolution of interaction patterns and network homophily in the Tianya discussion forum. Inf. Commun. Soc. **20**, 733–753 (2017)
12. Sherblom, J.C.: Organization involvement expressed through pronoun use in computer mediated communication. Commun. Res. Rep. **7**, 45–50 (1990)
13. Roeser, S.: Risk communication, public engagement, and climate change: a role for emotions. Risk Anal.: Int. J. **32**, 1033–1040 (2012)

Analysis of YouTube's Content ID System Through Two Different Perspectives

Liliana P. Salas$^{(\boxtimes)}$

University of Arizona, Tucson, AZ 85721, USA
lsalas@email.arizona.edu

Abstract. Computer engineering and law seem to be two distant disciplines that go in opposite directions. In fact, most lawyers and IT-engineers tend to consider that their fields do not have much in common, but today's reality requires much more collaboration between the two. This paper presents an analysis of YouTube's Content ID system from two different perspectives: Lex Informatica and Legal Risk Management, in order to determine the link between technology and law. Therefore, by highlighting the importance of this relationship, this paper aims to assess the weaknesses, benefits, and challenges that professionals in these scientific fields face today and invites them to collaborate in a more efficient manner to avoid the violation of users' rights.

Keywords: YouTube · Content ID · Lex Informatica · Legal Risk Management · Law · Technology

1 Introduction

The rise of the Internet as a new place of social relations has presented challenges in all fields and particularly to law-makers and IT-engineers. On one hand, law makers must create adequate regulations to face new social changes that are introduced by information technologies, while IT engineers must adjust their creations, so they can comply with the law. However, this interaction between these two sciences reflects a disconnection that merits an analysis where their deficiencies, virtues and challenges are exposed. Academics have had to introduce perspectives in order to explain and face this problem [1]. "Lex Informatica", and "legal risk management", are two key perspectives that allow to highlight the interaction between these two fields in a pragmatic way.

The purpose of this paper is to analyze the relationship between technology and law through a case study within the two perspectives mentioned above. The automated filtering system, Content ID, used by YouTube and largely criticized by users will be selected to address the task. This system, designed by IT-engineers with a clear purpose of providing a technological system to safeguard the rights of copyright holders and to reduce the risks of potential lawsuits, presents serious challenges to legal science since users' rights are threatened and the implementation of this system puts the burden of proof on users instead of rightholders without providing any legal support to said users. Therefore, by selecting the Content ID system as a case study, it turns out to be ideal

© Springer Nature Switzerland AG 2020
A. Sundqvist et al. (Eds.): iConference 2020, LNCS 12051, pp. 227–234, 2020.
https://doi.org/10.1007/978-3-030-43687-2_18

for the purposes of this short paper, as the frictions between technology and law are clearly manifested.

After providing important background information, the perspective of "Lex informatica" will be shown by the interaction between Content ID and law. How is technology enforcing legal rights? Can technology really serve the law? How is technology undermining legal rights? Can technology create new rules? These questions will be discussed in Sect. 3.

Next, the perspective of "legal risk management" will be addressed by presenting the way in which YouTube is managing legal risks. What kind of legal risks is a business such as YouTube facing? How are those risks evaluated? How might technology help to mitigate some legal risks and increase others? How is YouTube managing that new imbalance? These are the questions that will be addressed in Sect. 4.

After discussing the case study through all both perspectives, we will have more grounds to highlight the benefits, barriers, and challenges that technology is facing in the area of law.

2 Background

YouTube is an online service that was created in 2005 with the purpose to provide a platform in which users can share all kinds of videos in a friendly way under some contractual limitations. Due to its success in October 2006, "the popular online video service announced the news of its acquisition by Google for $1.65 billion in stock" [2]. However, surveys showed that between seventy-five and eighty percent of all videos hosted on YouTube infringed on copyright law [3]. The large amount of pirated content on YouTube put Google in a very compromising situation.

Although some companies started to sue YouTube before Google's acquisition [4], lawsuits notably increased afterwards. Viacom, a company owner of the rights of abundant copyright material, sued Google claiming contributory infringement and vicarious liability [5]. Therefore, according to case law judgments, the burden of proof of copyright infringement is placed on copyright owners, so they are required to establish that "the defendant has knowledge of the infringing activity and induces, causes, or materially contributes to the infringing conduct" [6]. On the other hand, in order for vicarious liability to exist it is necessary to demonstrate that the "defendant has the right and ability to supervise the infringing conduct and has an obvious and direct financial interest in the infringement" [3]. However, without completing the trial, Google launched an automated Content ID system that seeks to detect possible infringements of copyright law. YouTube explains the operation in a practical video which states:

"Copyright holders give us copies of their audio recordings and videos that they want us to look for on YouTube. We (...) put these files in a database. (...) Every time you upload a video to YouTube, we quickly compare (...) in our entire database, looking for a match. (...) Each time Content ID finds a match, we do what the copyright holder asks us to do with that video; either block it, leave it up, or even start making money from it" [7].

Nevertheless, this system has been largely criticized by YouTube users who claim that the system ignores the doctrine of "fair use" which protects creativity under legal limitation even if the content is derived from the work of another, and thus when the system blocks lawful videos, the technology is undermining their rights [3].

3 Content ID as an Example of Lex Informatica

3.1 What Is Lex Informatica?

Cyberpaternalist School authors were the pioneers in developing the concept of "Lex Informatica" [8]. While some use the term solely to denote a possible system for conflicts of law relating to the Internet, others establish that technology provides effective tools for regulation [8]. Either way, the term "Lex Informatica" can be summed up as "a set of technological rules for information that flows as imposed by technology or networks and might constitute an extra regulatory instrument to adopt decisions" [9].

3.2 Interaction Between Content ID and Law

The Content ID system is a "good example of what Lessig coined in his influential book, Code and Other Laws of Cyberspace, "upstream filtering": filtering imposed from above without the knowledge or often the consent of the users whose access it affects" [10].

Reidenberg says that: "policy choices are available either through technology itself, through laws that cause technology to exclude possible options, or through law that causes users to restrict certain actions" [11]. Google's automated filter system is a clear example of technology restricting certain actions (uploading videos) in which law has established a certain framework.

Although law is not obliging companies to develop such technologies, it is providing the legal framework of intellectual property and Content ID is a technological mean mostly designed to protect copyright holders' interests, as well as acting as a shield for companies like Google from numerous lawsuits. In this way, Content ID is enforcing legal rights by excluding the possibility of copyright infringement on website platforms, and as some authors have stated: "Electronic Copyright Management Systems are more capable than legislation of protecting an author's copyright" [12].

However, this kind of system could undermine users' rights under the legal doctrine of fair use. Ironically, well-known Professor Lawrence Lessig was a victim of the Content ID system which matched his academic lecture video with the recording of the Phoenix song "Lisztomania" [13]. Lessig launched legal proceedings against Liberation, the Melbourne-based company who owns the rights of the song, alleging that a takedown notice from them had undermined his right under the "fair use" doctrine. Although the parties already settled their dispute in which Liberation Music accepted to pay Lessig for "the harm it caused", clearly the Content ID system has flaws and not all users have the fortune of being a worldwide recognized lawyer with the means to bring the issue to trail and win.

One group of YouTube users commonly affected by Content ID are video game reviewers. In a notable case, American commentator Joe Vargas uploaded a video titled "Youtube Copyright Disaster! Angry Rant" in 2013 on his widely followed YouTube Channel in which he complained of how the system had flagged 62 of his video game review videos and was subsequently blocking him from receiving profit from his work [14]. Like many Youtubers, Joe relies on his review content as a source of income and he has continued to post more "rant" videos on the subject as the problem continues to affect users. Lessig and Vargas are just two examples of how this automated system largely overlooks many cases that ought to be protected by the fair use doctrine and ultimately can drive users away from YouTube causing the media platform to suffer losses.

It is important to note that, as demonstrated in Lenz v. Universal Music Corp, "(…) Rightholders must consider "fair use" before issuing a take-down notice" [15]. Therefore, Content ID should be a system built to serve the law by matching probable copyright infringement as Ian Walden mentioned, but by proceeding to block content without first analyzing the "fair use" doctrine it could be argued that this is an attempt by technology to change the law. The Content ID appeal procedure established by Google for users who believe their videos were unfaithfully blocked or removed has created a "guilty until proven innocent system," which clearly switches the burden of proof.

In Campbell v. Acuff-Rose Music, Inc., the Supreme Court explained that "fair use is not a bright-line test and that there is no presumption for or against the fair use of a work" [16]. It is a basic procedural legal principle that generally states that plaintiffs have the burden of proof. In this case, copyright holders must prove infringement (now replaced by Content ID technology), but they have a legal and jurisprudence duty to analyze possible "fair use" before creating a take-down notice. Clearly Content ID is violating legal rules and that is where the relationship between legal science and IT-engineers must be improved, so when designing systems or technological platforms, their creations are adjusted to existing regulations. In this case, Content ID, should have considered the burden of proof principle in copyright infringement and the fair use doctrine, so that its system would be consistent with those postulates.

Therefore, while technology is serving the law it could also be undermining users' rights, and simultaneously switching the burden of proof requirement from the copyright owner to the user. This kind of interaction must be revised, and alternatives provided, because when technology is serving the law, under no circumstances can that service undermine other rights.

4   How YouTube Might Be Managing Legal Risks

4.1   What Is Legal Risk Management (LRM)?

There is not a unified definition, however, almost all definitions reference expressing legal uncertainties and measuring them by their potential effects [17]. Professor Moorhead points to two main legal risks: "one which is specific to an individual organization or its objectives" and another one in which "the law itself gives rise to a result which is both unplanned and unwelcome" [18].

4.2 Legal Risks YouTube Faces

YouTube's business model mainly faces legal risks in relation to copyright infringement since their success relies on the content posted by their users. It is important to recall that during the trial Viacom v. YouTube it was determined that around 80% of YouTube content was infringing copyright. Therefore, all regulation and case law related to copyright infringement by online platforms are relevant to assess an LRM.

Although safe harbor provisions exist under the Digital Millennium Copyright Act-DMCA and the European regulatory framework, these do not protect online service providers from being sued, and in some cases, losing their legal immunity due to their actions or contractual clauses, and thus a significant economic harm to their businesses. For instance, in the Napster case the court found that "the right and ability to supervise the infringing activity and their direct financial interest in such activities" were determinants to prove contributory copyright infringement [19]. In Viacom's trial the plaintiff alleged that YouTube "reserves and exercises the unfettered right to block or remove any video", most likely to compare YouTube's action with the Napster case [20].

Therefore, the YouTube LRM assessment must focus on analyzing the sources in order to mitigate copyright infringement liability and provide solutions either through conventional means such as contracts or others such as technology, for example.

4.3 Assessing Legal Risk Management

The well-known Napster case proved that too much control over third party content, either by contract or facts, might allow online companies to lose their safe harbor. Hence, an LRM task can be demonstrated in their Terms of Service (TOS). The inclusion of sentences such as: "(...) YouTube has no control over, and assumes no responsibility, for the content (...)" "(...) YouTube reserves the right to decide whether Content violates these TOS for reasons other than copyright infringement" certainly mitigates a legal risk [21].

DMCA and European regulatory Frameworks do not oblige companies to adopt automated filtering systems. However, there might be a legal risk for companies that do not adopt such systems to be sued. For instance, in SABAM cases [22] the EUCJ had to rule on the possibility of allowing these systems. Although until now the EUCJ had ruled in favor of the online companies, and thus the legal risk was low, it does not mean that the window is closed to future lawsuits against them, for not having those kinds of systems. For instance, in a very strange decision a judge in Germany now wants YouTube to install additional keyword-based filters to its platform despite already having Content ID [23].

4.4   Technology as a Measure

The use of technology in order to mitigate legal risks can be proven by Google's decision to adopt Content ID. It mitigates the risk of litigation only by copyright holders that have provided their material to the Content ID database and eliminates the same risk for companies that are awaiting that service, such as SABAM in Belgium.

However, the adoption of Content ID also creates new risks. For example, users of Content ID may fall victim if the system fails at matching, also, YouTube users whose content has been removed mistakenly can suffer from profit loss. Although it is unlikely that Content ID will fail to operate correctly, the practice of controlling content through the act of matching might result in YouTube losing their safe harbor.

Users can allege a contractual breach according to the contract clause 7.B. You-Tube's right for removing content without prior notice relies only on events "other than copyright". It is important to remark that YouTube cannot change these kinds of clauses, otherwise it can lose its safe harbor by controlling content. According to clause 6.F. of the TOS, removing content which infringes copyright is only possible upon "proper notification" and under DMCA, so giving material to Content ID cannot be interpreted as a proper notification. Therefore, both the Content ID system and internal appeal process constitute a breach of the TOS and can be held liable in court. It is also important to highlight that YouTube's TOS are a "take it or leave it" basis contract, hence, case law in relation to standard contracts had established that any grey clause must be interpreted in users' favor.

Google could manage this new legal risk by cancelling the Content ID internal process and sending all matches to copyright holders who must initiate the DMCA take-down notice procedure after analyzing the "fair use" doctrine. In relation to the other new risk that arose, YouTube must be sure that copyright holders are releasing ISP from any liability in contractual clauses in an event of failure by using the Content ID database.

5   Conclusion

The perspectives of "Lex Informatica", and Legal Risk Management had been analyzed through a case study, Content ID, which involves the issues concerning the relation between computers and law. The intention was to highlight the benefits, weaknesses, and challenges of such interrelation.

As for the benefits it is noted that technology provides the law with new mechanisms so it may be enforced in a quicker way due to current social needs. Thereby, in Intellectual Property law, Content ID can impede the infringement of copyright resulting in a useful tool for rightholders as well as for businesses such as Google that can mitigate their legal risks through technology.

As for the weaknesses it is important to highlight that technology might undermine other rights and even create new standards opposed to the law. Thus, in copyright law, such systems might undermine the doctrine of "fair use" and switch the burden of proof principle to the weakest party. In this case, a "guilty until proven innocent system" has been imposed on lawful users. Hence the importance of IT-engineers receiving legal advice when creating these systems so as to avoid infringements on rights and comply with regulations.

Finally, regarding challenges it can be pointed out that the relationship between computers and law is inescapable. Hence, in order to achieve system to respect legal principles, lawyers and IT-engineers should work closely to detect and treat failure promptly. As Charles Clark once said "the answer to the machine is in the machine" [24].

References

1. Vraalsen, F., Lund, M.S., Mahler, T., Parent, X., Stølen, K.: Specifying legal risk scenarios using the CORAS threat modelling language. In: Herrmann, P., Issarny, V., Shiu, S. (eds.) iTrust 2005. LNCS, vol. 3477, pp. 45–60. Springer, Heidelberg (2005). https://doi.org/10.1007/11429760_4
2. Kim, E.C.: YouTube: testing the safe harbors of digital copyright law. S. Cal. Interdisc. LJ **17**, 139 (2007)
3. Bartholomew, T.B.: The death of fair use in cyberspace: YouTube and the problem with content ID. Duke L. Tech. Rev. **13**, 66 (2014)
4. Frey, A.: To sue or not to sue: video-sharing web sites, copyright infringement, and the inevitability of corporate control. Brook. J. Corp. Fin. Com. L. **2**, 167 (2007)
5. Text of Viacom Complaint. https://online.wsj.com/public/resources/documents/ViacomYouTubeComplaint3-12-07.pdf. Accessed 01 Dec 2019
6. Peguera, M.: Secondary liability for copyright infringement in the web 2.0 environment: some reflections on Viacom v. Youtube. J. Int. Commer. Law Technol. **6**(1) (2011). https://ssrn.com/abstract=1716773
7. Google Statement. support.google.com/youtube/answer/2797370?hl=en. Accessed 01 Feb 2019
8. Patrikios, A.: Resolution of cross-border e-business disputes by arbitration tribunals on the basis of transnational substantive rules of law and e-business usages: the emergence of the lex informatica. U. Tol. L. Rev. **38**, 271 (2006)
9. Reidenberg, J.: The rule of intellectual property law in the internet economy. Hous. L. Rev. **44**, 1073 (2007)
10. Lessig, L.: Code and Other Laws of Cyberspace (2009). ReadHowYouWant.com
11. Reidenberg, J.R.: Lex informatica: the formulation of information policy rules through technology. Tex. L. Rev. **76**, 553 (1997)
12. Walden, I., Hörnle, J. (eds.): E-Commerce Law and Practice in Europe. Elsevier, Amsterdam (2001)
13. Tan, C.: Lawrence Lessig v Liberation Music Pty Ltd: YouTube's hand (or bots) in the over-zealous enforcement of copyright. Eur. Intellect. Prop. Rev. **36**(6), 347–351 (2014)
14. YouTube Copyright Disaster! Angry Rant. https://www.youtube.com/watch?v=JQfHdasuWtI. Accessed 16 Dec 2019
15. O'Donnell, K.: Lenz v. Universal Music Corp. and the potential effect of fair use analysis under the takedown procedures of section 512 of the DMCA. Duke L. Tech. Rev. 1 (2009)
16. Timkovich, E.T.: The new significance of the four fair use factors as applied to parody: interpreting the court's analysis in Campbell v. Acuff-Rose Music, Inc. Tul. J. Tech. Intell. Prop. **5**, 61 (2003)
17. Leitch, M.: ISO 31000: 2009—the new international standard on risk management. Risk Anal. Int. J. **30**(6), 887–892 (2010)
18. Moorhead, R., Vaughan, S.: Legal risk: definition, management and ethics, 31 March 2015

19. Stern, R.: Napster: a walking copyright infringement? IEEE Micro **20**(6), 4–5 (2000)
20. Peguera, M.: Secondary liability for copyright infringement in the web 2.0 environment: some reflections on Viacom v. Youtube. J. Int. Com. L. Tech. **6**, 18 (2011)
21. YouTube Terms of Service
22. Kulk, S., Zuiderveen Borgesius, F.: Filtering for copyright enforcement in Europe after the Sabam cases. Eur. Intellect. Prop. Rev. **34**(11), 791–794 (2012)
23. Marino, G.: YouTube is not GEMA's main offender. J. Intellect. Prop. Law Pract. **7**(9), 644–646 (2012)
24. Clark, C.: The answer to the machine is in the machine. In: The Future of Copyright in a Digital Environment. Information Law Series, vol. 4, pp. 139–145. Kluwer Law International (1999)

Information Behavior

Depression Management as Lifestyle Management: Exploring Existing Practices and Perceptions Among College Students

Jordan Dodson[1,5]($\boxtimes$), Naika Saint Preux[2,5], Jenni Thang[3,5], and Elizabeth V. Eikey[4,5]

[1] The University of North Carolina at Chapel Hill, Chapel Hill, NC, USA
jordodson@gmail.com
[2] The College of Westchester, White Plains, NY, USA
naikasp4@gmail.com
[3] Indiana University Bloomington, Bloomington, IN, USA
jennysui22@gmail.com
[4] University of California, San Diego, CA, USA
elizabethveikey@gmail.com
[5] The iSchool Inclusion Institute (i3), Pittsburgh, USA

Abstract. Research is limited on college students' existing approaches to managing depression, which are important to understand before designing and recommending non-digital and digital tools. We conducted a mixed methods survey with 109 college students about their awareness of and interest in non-digital and digital tools, what tools they use, how they use them, and their perceived effectiveness. In general, students are aware of and interested in both non-digital and digital tools. Therefore, we cannot discount the utility of both non-digital and digital tools, even among high technology users. We found 78 participants use non-digital tools, such as paper, art, and checklists, and 80 participants reported using digital tools, such as social media, texts, and YouTube/vlogging. From students' perspectives, depression management is lifestyle management. Thus, they often use a combination of tools for connection and support, catharsis and outlet, keeping busy and distraction, organization and planning, and emotion and thought analysis and regulation, and they perceive these tools to be at least somewhat effective in managing their depression. This research emphasizes the need to understand current practices and perceptions and can be used as a foundation for other researchers, clinicians, and educators as they continue to find ways to support college students with depression.

Keywords: Depression · Self-monitoring · Non-digital and digital tools · College students · Mental health

1 Introduction

Many college students deal with depression symptoms [23]. In fact, one study found approximately 30% of college students reported being depressed [38]. A review article by Ibrahim et al. [23], found that anywhere from 10–85% of university students have

© Springer Nature Switzerland AG 2020
A. Sundqvist et al. (Eds.): iConference 2020, LNCS 12051, pp. 237–255, 2020.
https://doi.org/10.1007/978-3-030-43687-2_19

depression. Depression causes loss of interest in activities and can negatively affect academic, work, and personal life and can increases one's suicide risk [31]. According to Hunt and Eisenberg [22], one in ten reported considering committing suicide.

Given the need for in-the-moment support and supplemental care, there is great promise in digital mental health tools for college students, especially given the popularity of technology among this age group [19, 34]. There are numerous studies on the development, evaluation, and understanding of digital mental health tools [4, 10, 16, 17, 37]. Mobile apps, in particular, have garnered a lot of attention because they are one type of tool that may reduce barriers to help seeking and offer improved interaction modalities and even passive data collection. In recent years, a plethora of depression apps have appeared [33]. Literature in this space tends to focus on the design of depression management apps [27], whether or not they adhere to evidence-based practices and approaches to treatment (like Cognitive Behavior Therapy [CBT]) [21], and their effectiveness [4], including the impact of the overall user experience of the interfaces on users' symptoms [3].

While there is numerous research on mobile apps for depression [4, 21, 27], few studies focus on how these apps and other self-management practices for depression play out in college students' everyday lives. Further, some studies suggest these types of condition-specific apps may be underutilized [12, 13]. Even if we address the lack of scientific evidence in apps and test the efficacy of such tools, we will have no impact unless they are used. Thus, adoption and retention of appropriate tools remains a potential issue [25, 29]. Individuals may not adopt apps or other digital mental health tools because they do not adequately address or support their needs [29]. Part of the problem may lie in our conceptualization of depression management and lack of understanding of what individuals already do to manage depression.

Pushing apps may do a disservice to students and ignore their existing strategies. This is a critical point; self-management existed long before technologies were created to assist with the process. Therefore, rather than continuing to design new apps (and other digital tools) for depression management, we need a better understanding of what college students are already doing to manage depression. In order to investigate this, we conducted a mixed methods survey study with 109 college students, some have been professionally diagnosed with depression and some have depression symptoms but have not sought a clinical diagnosis[1]. We identified five research questions:

RQ1: To what extent are college students aware of non-digital and digital tools to manage depression?
RQ2: To what extent are college students interested in managing depression using non-digital and digital tools?
RQ3a: What non-digital tools do college students already use to manage their depression?
RQ3b: What is their perceived effectiveness of this combination of non-digital tools in managing their depression?

---

[1] For the purposes of this research, depression refers to both self- and professionally-diagnosed depression.

RQ4a: What digital tools do college students already use to manage their depression?
RQ4b: What is their perceived effectiveness of this combination of digital tools in managing their depression?
RQ5: How do they use non-digital (a) and digital tools (b) to manage depression?

By investigating what college students are already doing and their perceptions of how effective these tools are, we take a human-centered approach to uncover latent needs that can be explored to design both non-digital and digital tools that better align with users' goals and lives. We focus on "tools" as a response to the prevalence of research on mobile apps, which are one class of tools but not the only ones used in depression management. By tools, we mean any and all items (physical or otherwise) used to aid managing depression. Further, we believe that viewing students' depression management through the lens of digital vs. non-digital provides a way forward for designing products, services, or systems to support depression management. This research has implications for our understanding of what college students want in order to effectively manage their depression, which is important for technology designers, researchers, mental health professionals, and college educators. Further, this work touches on the various types of modalities used to create and share information and may serve as a foundation in understanding ways to disseminate information pertaining to depression, making this information valuable to scholars in the Information Science community.

2   Methodology

2.1   Eligibility

Our focus was undergraduate students because depression is one of the most common health problems for this population [28, 40]. In order to be eligible to participate, individuals had to (1) be currently enrolled in a college or university in the United States, (2) be between 18 and 25 years old, and (3) have experienced depression symptoms within the last 12 months. Participants could be either self-diagnosed or clinically-diagnosed. We included a self-diagnosed population due to the stigma of mental health and the difficulty surrounding seeking and receiving mental health treatment and diagnosis from a healthcare provider [15]. However, it is important to note that depression symptoms do not necessarily equal clinical depression. In order to narrow our findings to depression, participants were not eligible to participate is they had a history of mania, bipolar disorder, or schizophrenia. This is because individuals with mania, bipolar disorder, or schizophrenia may have unique needs [2, 7, 18, 20]. As compensation, we offered the chance to enter to win one of two $50 e-gift cards via a raffle. Participants were not obligated to take the survey to be entered. Participants' contact information was not linked to their data in order to ensure privacy and confidentiality, and winners were picked at random.

2.2 Recruitment

We recruited participants through Facebook advertisements, posting to our own social media accounts (Facebook, Snapchat, and Instagram), and posting to online communities (GroupMe private group chats, Discord servers) related to people of color, LGBTQ+ issues, mental health, and universities (e.g., university listservs and university-related Facebook groups) as well as posting to survey sharing Facebook groups and websites (i.e., surveytandem.com). We ran three separate Facebook ads over the course of 3 months (February 14-March 4, 2019; April 9–16, 2019; April 15–22, 2019).

2.3 Survey

The survey consisted of questions pertaining to demographics, depression, awareness of tools, and existing practices and perceptions of digital and non-digital tools.

Demographics. The demographics section of the survey consisted of questions about a participant's age, gender, sexual identity, student status, immigrant status, employment, household annual income, and race. The gender question was open-ended and the racial identity question allowed for multiple choices to be selected in order to remain as inclusive as possible. The remainder of the demographic questions were multiple choice.

Depression and Depression Symptoms. We included two yes or no questions to understand if participants had been clinically diagnosed and if they are currently receiving professional treatment. To assess symptoms, we used Beck's Depression Inventory (BDI-II), a 21-item self-report instrument intended to assess the existence and severity of symptoms of depression [6]. The questions are scored on a scale from 0–3. A score is calculated by adding the scores of each individual item. A total score of 0–13 is considered in the minimal range, 14–19 is mild, 20–28 is moderate, and lastly 29–63 is severe.

Awareness of and Interest in Tools. In order to gain a better understanding of participants' awareness of and interest in non-digital and digital tools, we asked them to rate their level of awareness on a scale from 1-Strongly Disagree to 5-Strongly Agree.

Tools for Depression Management and Perceived Effectiveness. We generated a list of non-digital and digital tools for our survey based on feedback provided by college students on different methods they use informed by literature surrounding this topic. We created a list to reduce participant burden and to spark participant memory, and we provided options for participants to input their own tools if not on the list. After participants selected each tool they use, we asked them how their selected tools are used to manage their depression through an open-ended question. We created separate questions to inquire about the usage of non-digital and digital tools in order to clearly identify the reasons as to why participants may use one category of tool as opposed to the other. We also asked participants to rate how effective the combination of non-digital tools and digital tools is in their depression management on a scale from 1-Strongly Disagree to 5-Strongly Agree. Scales were intentionally kept consistent across measures where possible in order to reduce participant burden and confusion.

2.4   Participants

In total, we gathered 221 responses to our survey. After removing unfinished surveys, ineligible participants, and responses from individuals who incorrectly answered our data quality check question, we were left with 109 responses. The Appendix provides a detailed chart of all participant demographics; however, we highlight some information. The mean age of our participants was 20.50 (SD = 1.81). Out of 109 participants, 51.38% (n = 56) were professionally diagnosed with depression, and 48.62% (n = 53) were not. Additionally, 34.58% (n = 37) were seeking professional treatment, 60.75% (n = 65) were not, and 6.42% (n = 7) preferred not to answer. Using the BDI-II, the mean depression score across participants was 28.16 (SD = 12.10) (moderate). Over half (55.04%, n = 60) of our participants reported having severe depression symptoms, 19.27% (n = 21) reported having moderate depression symptoms, 13.76% (n = 15) reported having minimal depression symptoms, and 11.93% (n = 13) reported having mild depressive symptoms. Although there are no clinical cut-off points, Dozois et al. [11] suggest 13 or higher may be considered depressed. Out of our 109 participants, the majority (57.80%, n = 63) identified as female, male (15.60%, n = 17), or non-binary (12.84%, n = 14). With regards to sexual identity, 44.95% (n = 49) of our participants identified as straight or heterosexual, followed by bisexual (18.35%, n = 20). The majority of participants identified as White (60.55%, n = 66) followed by Multiracial (14.68%, n = 16). In terms of education status, there was a fairly even split across grade levels, and 33.94% (n = 37) participants identified as a first-generation college student. Out of the 12 possible household income categories, under $10,000 was the most common response (24.77%, n = 27).

2.5   Data Analysis

For the open-ended questions, we used an inductive approach to analyze our data. The main purpose of the inductive approach is to create themes in a raw data set that allows for patterns and recurring themes to emerge [36]. Our approach first consisted of each of us becoming familiar with the data and then individually taking notes and creating initial codes. Then we came together as a group to discuss our notes and codes and develop a preliminary codebook. The preliminary codebook was tested by having each person individually code all responses. We again came together as a group to refine, collapse, and add codes to create our final codebook with ten possible codes, as shown in Table 1. Once the codebook was refined, we re-coded each response individually, and then compared codes as a group. Final codes were determined through group discussion and consensus. Although we set no limit on the number of codes each answer could have, responses ended with up to three codes, but most had two codes. For quantitative data, we used Excel to compute counts, means, standard deviations, etc. where appropriate.

Table 1. Final codes and their descriptions

Theme	Description
Organizing and planning	Using tools to track or record activities, tasks, responsibilities, etc., especially in the future; organizing aspects of the person's life; planning one's day or time
Tracking	Tracking, monitoring, or logging different aspects of lifestyle (e.g., mood, triggers) over time and things in the past to see changes or progress over time; looking back over a period of time to see changes, patterns, trends, etc.; recording aspects of one's life to see how they improve or change; using tool(s) as a record
Keeping busy and distraction	Focusing one's attention, energy, thoughts, etc. on something else (other than current thoughts, feelings); often directing attention away from mental health symptoms, such as negative thoughts our emotions; using tool(s) to avoid over-thinking; attempting to "get out of one's head" or engage in distraction
Catharsis and outlet	Expression of emotions, thoughts, or feelings; using tool(s) as an outlet to express oneself; using tool(s) to lift a burden or weight off their shoulders or to relieve pressure or vent; "getting out" or releasing emotions or feelings
Emotion and though analysis and regulation	Using tool(s) to help analyze emotions and cognition and how they affect their mental state, emotions, and thoughts; process of analyzing thoughts and emotions (not just releasing them or distractions them); identifying symptoms, distorted thoughts, and emotions; processing or understanding their emotions and thoughts (e.g., trying to "work it out" or "work through it"); identifying warning signs for symptoms
Connection and support	Finding and/or connecting with other people, robots, or entities; getting or giving support; being social; feeling less alone or more connected to people generally
Information seeking	Looking online for information regarding health
Entertainment	Using tool(s) to entertain oneself
Motivation	Motivating oneself; stimulating interest or enthusiasm to do something; sometimes seeing other people's content and feeling motivated; helping to keep productive
Other	Did not fall into one of the above categories or the participant did not provide enough information to interpret and code

3 Findings

3.1 Awareness of and Interest in Different Types of Tools (RQ1, RQ2)

When asked about their awareness of using non-digital and digital tools for depression management, 71.56% (n = 78) of participants at least somewhat agreed that they were aware of non-digital tools, and 71.56% (n = 78) at least somewhat agreed that they were aware of digital tools for depression management, as shown in Fig. 1. Also shown in Fig. 1, 63.30% (n = 69) at least somewhat agreed that they were interested in using non-digital tools to manage depression. The majority of participants (67.89%, n = 74) were at least somewhat interested in using digital tools.

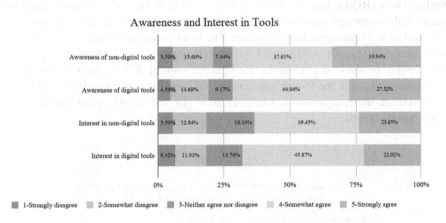

Fig. 1. Reported awareness of and interest in using digital and non-digital tools for depression management

3.2 Types of Tools Used

Non-digital Tools (RQ3a, b). Out of 109 total participants, 71.56% (n = 78) reported that they use at least one non-digital tool to manage their depression compared to 27.53% (n = 28) who reported not using any. As shown in Fig. 2, the most common tools that our participants used were paper (n = 50), art (such as drawing, painting, and doodling) (n = 29), and checklists (n = 22). When asked about their perceived effectiveness of the combination non-digital tools they use, 66.67% (56 out of 78) of

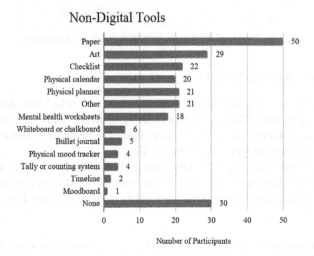

Fig. 2. Types of non-digital tools used to manage depression

participants at least somewhat agreed that the tool or combination of tools are effective in helping them manage their depression, while 16.67% (13 out of 78) at least somewhat disagreed.

Digital Tools (RQ4a, b). As shown in Fig. 3, 79.82% (n = 87) of participants used digital tools to manage depression, while 19.27% (n = 23) did not use any non-digital tools and (n = 4) preferred not to answer. The most commonly used tools were social media (n = 51), texts (n = 34), and YouTube/vlogging (n = 26). In terms of perceived effectiveness of these digital tools, 59.77% (52 out of 87) of participants at least somewhat agreed that the tool or combination of tools they use are effective in helping them manage their depression, while 17.24% (15 out of 87) participants at least somewhat disagreed.

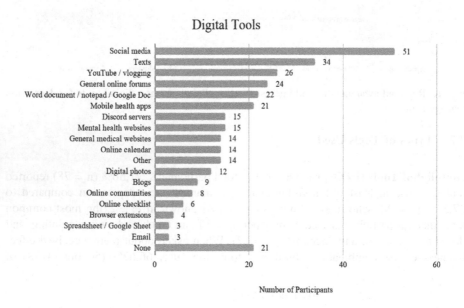

Fig. 3. Types of digital tools used to manage depression

3.3 How Tools Are Used (RQ5)

Participants[2] who used non-digital and/or digital tools were asked *how* they use them to manage their depression. Through our qualitative analysis, multiple themes emerged around non-digital and digital tool use, some of which overlap and some of which are unique across the tool category, as shown in Fig. 4.

There were clear differences in how non-digital and digital tools are used. For example, the most prominent ways non-digital tools are used were catharsis and outlet (n = 23) and organizing and planning (n = 18). Whereas, digital tools are more

---

[2] Not every participant answered how they use these tools: 75 participants answered "how" regarding non-digital tool usage and 80 for digital tool usage. Participants could provide multiple reasons.

commonly used for connection and support (n = 35) and keeping busy and distraction (n = 21). Emotion and thought analysis and regulation as well as tracking were reported about equally for both non-digital and digital tools. Entertainment, information seeking, and motivation were the least commonly reported and also unique to digital tools. We provide more details about the five most commonly reported themes across these tools.

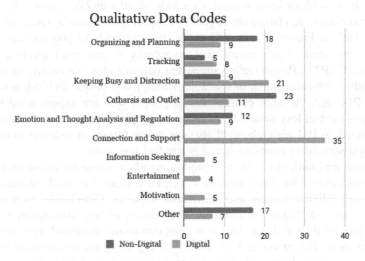

Fig. 4. Reasons participants used digital and non-digital tools

Connection and support (n = 35) was unique to digital tools. Participants talked about using social media, general online communities and forums, online health communities, Discord servers, texts, email, YouTube or vlogging, digital photos, blogs, mobile health apps, mental health websites, and general health or medical websites. Many participants discussed feeling isolated and using digital tools to either feel less alone by relating to others' experiences or actually connecting with other people. A lot discussions of social media focused on actual interactions. For instance, P22 said, *"I find that tools like Discord and social media really help because my depression can make me feel very lonely and isolated. And since I deal with issues body image issues and social anxiety, interacting with other people 'IRL' [in real life] can be nerve-racking and socializing online helps since I feel more in control. I can engage and disengage when I choose, and my physical body isn't an issue in discussions."* Another participant talked about using social media to connect with friends: *"Social media allows me to vent about my feelings and receive positive reinforcement from friends"* [P12]. Similarly, P42 also described interacting with friends via social media and texting: *"In general, social media [and] texting in photos keep me in touch with my friends so I feel less isolated."*

Although many people talked about getting support from people they know, some people also expressed concerns and preferred to connect with people they do not necessarily know very well: *"I specifically use social media places that aren't tied to my primary accounts where most people that I know irl [in real life] are. I want to be heard but I'm scared of people that I know hearing it. But even on some accounts where I know more people, I will try to find others with experiences of mental illness to hear about their experiences. That helps me [feel] less alone"* [P41]. Similarly, many participants noted the importance and value of anonymity when interacting with others as a form of depression management. For example, P76 talked about engaging with a *"large community where I can communicate with other people going through the same struggles as me without being judged. Can hide identity and be completely open."*

One participant even talked about getting support from a non-human entity: "There is a 'chat bot' on Facebook called 'Woebot' that responds to you and can schedule check ins and stuff. That's pretty cool, especially if you can't reach a personal friend/contact" [P23]. Part of feeling supported was this idea that online, an individual can find others who are similar or relatable, which made people feel less isolated. For example, P14 said, "It helps connect me to people who are experiencing the same thing, makes me feel less alone." In some cases, people do not even have to interact to feel connected, as P31 highlighted: "I also use online forums or websites to read about other people with other issues so it makes me feel less alone."

Catharsis and outlet (n = 34) was predominantly a reason for non-digital tool use (n = 23) but also seen for digital tools (n = 11). Participants frequently reported writing on paper or in digital formats and sometimes drawing. Participants often described writing as a way of "letting emotions out" or venting without consequences and as a means to process their feelings. This was most commonly discussed when referring to non-digital tools. For example, P12 said, *"Writing gives me an opportunity to vent without consequence. I can 'tell' anything to my journals and not risk being judged."* Similarly, P1 described how writing is a way to express feelings, especially in the absence of others: *"Since I don't really have anyone who I could talk to or would listen to me, I get everything down on paper about how I am feeling and how I feel. I just have to get it out somewhere because I can't keep it all inside."* Along those same lines P13 said, *"To me writing things out helps me express my emotions more rather than keeping it in. Sometimes there are too many things on my mind and so I prefer to write it out, and it sometimes releases a little bit of weight off my shoulder."* Similarly, one participant stated, *"I mostly journal to get my feelings out and understand them from a more distanced perspective, rather than just staying in my own head"* [P56].

One interesting aspect of non-digital tools was the ability to easily discard anything written. For example, P15 said that *"[it] helps to write things down to clear my mind, [and you] can easily erase [it] or throw [it] away after venting."* Drawing as a non-digital tool was also briefly mentioned as an outlet for expressing emotions. For instance, P14 explained how drawing has been therapeutic: *"Drawing has always helped with my depression as it is a way to get the feelings out without issues."*

Although not as common, participants also reported writing in digital or online spaces as a way to express their emotions: "I type up letters to friends/ex friends on a Google Doc explaining how I feel but I don't send them out, I don't have their names it in either only I know who they're for but they're just to help me express how I feel about our relationship" [P1]. P31 also talked about using digital journaling: "I use notepad to write down my feelings if I'm having a bad day because it helps me put my feelings into perspective." In addition to writing, one participant also mentioned using an audio journal: "The audio journal helps give me an outlet to express my feelings" [P35]. Another way of using digital tools to express feeling was to post online. For example, P3 said, "I also write and post anonymously to get my feelings out." Although less common, some participants report using apps. For instance, P103 said, "…I also use the app Vent as a way to self-harm without actually harming myself or others."

Keeping busy and distraction (n = 30) was reported for both non-digital (n = 9) and digital tools (n = 21) although more common for digital tools. Most frequently, digital tools, such as social media, YouTube channels and vlogs, were used to distract participants from their thoughts and emotions. For example, P6 said, "*Social media is solely a distraction. On worse mental health days, it serves as an alternate reality.*" Similarly, another participant described using social media as a distraction mechanism but also expressed concerns about the negative consequences: "*Social media is also a way for me to veg out of my bad thoughts. However, it can be equally as harmful and often causes me to not do what is important*" [P52]. Referring to YouTube and mobile health apps, P46 stated, "*They provided a distraction from all the surrounding stress and intrusive thoughts.*" Similarly, P71 said, "*Distractions from the thoughts depressing me are often very useful with suicidal thoughts. YouTube videos provide a semi-endless supply of distracting visual content. Same with social media.*"

Some also talked about non-digital methods like drawing on paper. In addition to an emotional outlet, drawing helped participants disengage from their thoughts, as highlighted by multiple participants: "*I also like to draw because it gets my mind off of things*" [P13], and "*I draw and write to help distract myself and not think or over-think*" [P3]. Similarly, P25 and P26 both discussed drawing as a way to distract them from their own thoughts: "*Drawing gets me out of my head*" [P25] and "*It is pretty mindless, but drawing mindlessly distracts me*" [P26].

For *organizing and planning* (n = 27), participants reported using mostly non-digital tools (n = 18), such as physical calendars, planners, checklists, paper, and whiteboards or chalkboards. However, some (n = 9) reporting using digital tools (n = 9), such as calendars and checklists. A number of participants described using these types of tools to stay organized and accomplish tasks: "*My [non-digital] calendar allows me to lay out all of my obligations and stay organized. It helps me to be able to look at my entire month and see what I need to do by when*" [P2]. P6 also explained this by saying, "*I use post it notes to create to-do lists so I can focus on tasks rather than my brain going crazy.*" Some participants also explained how digital tools were used to stay on task as well: "*An online calendar supplements my physical calendar*" [P50] and "*The [digital] calendar helps keep me organized and aware of appointments*" [P35]. Part of keeping track of plans also seemed to encourage participants to complete them. For example, P9 said, "*[These non-digital tools] keep me on a schedule. I can push through a day if I have a basic list of things I should accomplish.*"

Along those same lines, some participants felt that staying organized reduced procrastination, which is important because procrastination can reinforce negative feelings: "*[This non-digital tool] helps me keep track of things I need to do so I don't procrastinate as bad*" [P4]. Similarly, P93 stated, "*It is really helpful for me to have a visual of the things that are going on with me and the things that I am going to have to tackle that week. Knowing my schedule and having a checklist right in my face, makes it so I can't ignore it for that long and so I feel more motivation to do it."* Others also described how planning their days using tools helped to reduce feelings of being overwhelmed and increase positive affect. For instance, P1 discussed how staying organized improved mood: *"A [non-digital] checklist helps me manage my tasks and it makes me feel better thinking I am organized with a checklist. Feels good to check off things."* Similarly, P10, said, *"Managing my time in school [using non-digital tools] helps me to not get overworked with deadlines and keep an uplifted mood."* Others described how these non-digital tools made them feel less overwhelmed and more in control. For instance, one participant said, *"The rest of the [non-digital] tools, calendars, checklists, worksheets are to make sure I can keep up with school and feel less overwhelmed by having things to check off"* [P56]. P58 uses these non-digital tools *"because I feel like I have more control over my day and it is not outside of my hands. When I plan out my day I do not feel lost or confused."* Part of organization and time management was coping with stress, as highlighted by P3: *"Stress makes everything worse so by organizing my life [using non-digital tools], I manage to help lower stress."* Some participants also reported using digital checklists to manage their schedules: *"[Digital] checklists break down tasks into more manageable things so I don't feel overwhelmed"* [P42].

Participants reported using both non-digital (n = 12) and digital tools (n = 9) for **emotion and thought analysis and regulation** (n = 21). Some participants used these tools to better fundamentally understand their emotions and cognition. Participants use these tools to gain a deeper understanding of the emotions and thoughts that arise in their lives and take action to change their emotion and thought patterns. For instance, P7 relayed how writing helped them evaluate their emotions: *"Writing out my thoughts helps me process my emotions and evaluate them objectively. Often, it helps me to see that the thing I am upset about is not as bad as I make it out to be and I can take steps to remove myself from the mindset."* A key point here is how writing for this individual leads to change. Similarly, P2 also stated, *"Well I use notepad to write down my feelings if I'm having a bad day because it helps me put my feelings into perspective. I also use online forums or websites to read about other people with other issues so it makes me feel less alone."* In these cases, participants work through their own feelings from a different point of view. Additionally, participants also described engaging in activities that help them analyze their relationships with others. For example, one participant mentioned that writing unsent letters helped them evaluate their relationships with friends and even ex-friends: *"I type up letters to friends/ex friends on a google doc explaining how I feel, but I don't send them out. I don't have their names it in either; only I know who they're for, but they're just to help me express how I feel about our relationship"* [P36].

4 Discussion

4.1 Depression Management as Lifestyle Management

We found students with depression use a variety of non-digital and digital tools to assist with not only the students' depression and emotion management, but also overall lifestyle well-being. We identified primary reasons college students use various tools to manage depression, which can help us understand students' needs from their own perspectives and why multiple tools may be necessary. Participants reported managing symptoms through writing out and analyzing their feelings and emotions, reaching out to friends and family, and taking their mind off of their situation completely, as well as managing other aspects of their lives through organizing their daily schedules and working through their depression symptoms. For these students, depression management is more than traditional treatment approaches; it is lifestyle management. Thus, this work provides further evidence that illness management should be considered as lifestyle management but in the context of depression. As found in prior research, chronic illnesses (like diabetes and chronic pain) are often managed alongside the other demands of daily life [1, 5, 8, 26]. Many of these students' current practices for managing depression are inseparable from other practices common to all students, like managing a schedule of various tasks and appointments (which may include classes, extracurricular activities, and possibly part or full-time employment) and emotionally coping with career and developmental needs, life transitions, and stress [24]. Depression management is about addressing the effects depression has on college students' day-to-day lives, including their emotions, thoughts, and activities. It may be difficult to develop a singular tool that can adequately address all of these needs. However, we can devise ways to support a multitude of practices - i.e., their "tool box." It is important to note that depression-specific tools like dialectical behavior therapy (DBT) worksheets or depression-related mobile apps need to be actively sought out and are often used in conjunction with therapy – meaning clinicians and mental health professionals may be the gatekeepers to some of these specific tools. This can be problematic when students face barriers to seeking formal treatment.

4.2 The Value of Non-digital and Digital Tools

This study suggests that both non-digital and digital tools are a valuable part of a students' tool box. Thus, non-digital tools cannot be discounted in the hype around digital mental health. These results show that the affordances of different types of tools may make some better suited for different aspects of depression management. For example, non-digital tools allowed participants to put their emotions, thoughts, and other concepts outside of themselves and into something with which they can physically interact in a private way. Although the importance of designing tools for collective illness management is evident [30], these findings highlight the need for personal and private components. Digital tools, on the other hand, gave our participants the opportunity to interact with others online experiencing similar symptoms, access motivational and entertaining content, and seek out information pertaining to their symptoms. Interestingly, the percentage of students who agreed non-digital tools were effective was higher than the percentage of people who agreed digital tools were effective. Our research provides us with a foundation to ask the questions: How might digital depression management tools add to the non-digital tool experience, and how might non-digital depression management tools add to the digital tool experience?

4.3   Understanding Tool Appropriation

Many of the most commonly used tools are appropriations of tools intended for purposes other than depression management. For example, social media, Google and Word documents, physical calendars, and checklists were not designed specifically to support users with depression. However, college students re-purpose these and view them as tools in their depression management efforts. This is consistent with other research on the use of non-depression specific tools being used to manage depression [9, 32]. The appropriation of digital tools to explicitly support mental health has been seen among other mental health conditions [13, 14]. The re-purposing of these everyday lifestyle management tools for depression carries both positive and negative implications. On one hand, many of the tools that our participants said they use were tools that many of them have easy and free access to and may use for school or communication purposes anyway. When using lifestyle management tools, participants are able to complete a lifestyle-related task and lessen the intensity of their symptoms at the same time. For instance, when using physical calendars, participants can plan their day and alleviate stress but using just one tool. This removes the burden of having to use multiple tools to address both depression and lifestyle-related needs, which can be beneficial for a busy college student.

On the other hand, lifestyle management tools are not specifically designed for depression management. Thus, many of these general tools may not meet the specific needs of college students with depression, and at worst, they could lead to unintended negative consequences. In our study, for instance, the most common digital tool used was social media. Participants found social media to be useful in connecting with others who share similar lived experiences. However, social media can potentially be harmful; students may also engage in comparison or track what others are doing, which can worsen their symptoms [35, 39]. This can even be true of non-digital tools. For example, writing may be useful to release emotions and thoughts, but it may unintentionally facilitate rumination, exacerbating negative mood.

4.4   Implications

Understanding how college students currently utilize these tools to manage their depression is important for a number of different stakeholders. Information Science and Human Computer Interaction experts gain a better understanding of the mediums used to create, share, and disseminate information in this context, which aid in the design and deployment of content and information systems. In addition to the results reported and discussed thus far, cross-cutting themes that emerged across findings offer opportunities for design. For example, students' responses suggest *a desire for control, benefits of externalizing thoughts and emotions,* and *the need to balance private management with social support and interpersonal interactions.* These findings can influence future designs of digital tools (including mobile apps) and non-digital tools. Further, mental health professionals and university clinicians can utilize this research to consider how they may fill gaps in their assessment and treatment of students. They may suggest non-digital tools like physical calendars and planners to reduce stress, art to release emotions, and writing to work through them. Professionals can also advise students on their use of various digital tools, especially social media, YouTube channels, and Discord servers. Similarly, college educators will also benefit from knowing which tools college students use to cope with their depression, as they can develop better intervention strategies and programs based on what students are already doing. For example, because many students reported using social media for depression management, educators may consider developing programs that engage with students on these platforms.

5 Limitations and Future Work

One limitation we faced was the homogeneity of our population sample. The majority of the participants identified as White, female, and heterosexual. Because of this, our results are not those of a diverse group of college students and do not represent all college students. To keep participants anonymous, we did not ask for any information about the schools they attended or their field of study, which means this may not represent participants from different types of schools or majors. Thus, our future work will focus on getting more students with different backgrounds. Further, we plan to utilize interview methodology to get a richer understanding of how and when these tools are used, how they fit together, and how well they address students' needs. Ratings of effectiveness were self-reported, so future work should address whether perceived effectiveness translates to better well-being.

6 Conclusion

Depression can impact all aspects of an individual's life. Thus, it makes sense that college students describe using a variety of both non-digital and digital tools to manage their depression. Many participants use these tools for more than just reflecting on their depression symptoms, including navigating other parts of their lives (their social circles, future tasks, and creative endeavors) in order to alleviate the burden of their symptoms. Thus, depression management is a form of lifestyle management, and we must design tools accordingly. We are not necessarily suggesting that one tool should or can be designed to support all of these needs. Rather, we highlight the different roles these tools play in college students' own conceptualization of depression management. Students' approaches to managing depression may be supported by a combination of tools—digital, non-digital, and even hybrid—that they appropriate and combine based on personal preferences and needs. Thus, when designing tools, we cannot think just about translating traditional depression treatment approaches to digital formats; we have to consider latent needs such as those that emerged from this study. While there is much promise and excitement around digital tools, we cannot discount the role of non-digital tools and the interplay between non-digital and digital mediums.

Acknowledgements. We would like to thank iSchool Inclusion Institute (i3) Director Dr. Kayla Booth, i3 Assistant Director and our research advisor Dr. Elizabeth Eikey, and Michael Depew, as well as the 2017, 2018, and 2019 cohorts. This work was supported by the National Center for Research Resources, the National Center for Advancing Translational Sciences, and the NIH (UL1 TR001414). It is solely the responsibility of the authors and does not necessarily represent the official views of the NIH.

Appendix

See Table 2

Table 2. Participant demographics

Category	Details
Depression diagnosis	Yes (n = 56)
	No (n = 53)
Current professional treatment	Yes (n = 37)
	No (n = 65)
	Prefer not to answer (n = 7)
Gender	Female (n = 63)
	Male (n = 17)
	Non-binary (n = 14)
	Woman (n = 3)
	Transgender (n = 2)
	Gender-queer (n = 2)
	Trans male (n = 2)
	Gender-neutral (n = 1)
	Genderfluid (n = 1)
	Cis male (n = 1)
	Man (n = 1)
	Masculine (n = 1)
	Androgyne (n = 1)
Sexual identity	Straight or heterosexual (n = 49)
	Bisexual (n = 20)
	Pansexual (n = 12)
	Gay, lesbian, or homosexual (n = 8)
	Asexual (n = 7)
	Queer (n = 5)
	Questioning (n = 4)
	Prefer not to answer (n = 4)

(continued)

Table 2. (*continued*)

Category	Details
Racial identity	White (n = 66)
	Asian (n = 11)
	Black or African American (n = 8)
	Hispanic, Latinx, or of Spanish origin (n = 5)
	Middle Eastern or North African (n = 2)
	Black or African American, Asian (n = 2)
	Black or African American, White (n = 2)
	Hispanic, Latinx, or of Spanish origin, White (n = 2)
	Middle Eastern or North African, White (n = 2)
	Asian, White (n = 2)
	Prefer not to answer (n = 7)
Student status	1st year (n = 26)
	2nd year (n = 25)
	3rd year (n = 19)
	4th year (n = 28)
	5th year (n = 3)
	Other (n = 8)
Household income	Under $10,000 (n = 27)
	$10,000–$19,999 (n = 10)
	$20,000–$29,999 (n = 6)
	$30,000–$39,999 (n = 6)
	$40,000–$49,999 (n = 10)
	$50,000–$59,999 (n = 9)
	$60,000–$69,999 (n = 7)
	$70,000–$79,999 (n = 9)
	$80,000–$89,999 (n = 2)
	$90,000–$99,999 (n = 4)
	$100,000–$149,999 (n = 10)
	$150,000 or above (n = 8)
	Prefer not to answer (n = 1)

References

1. Aarhus, R., Ballegaard, S.A.: Negotiating boundaries: managing disease at home. In: Proceedings of the SIGCHI Conference on Human Factors in Computing Systems, pp. 1223–1232. ACM, New York (2010). https://doi.org/10.1145/1753326.1753509
2. Addington, D., et al.: Depression in people with first-episode schizophrenia. Br. J. Psychiatry **172**(S33), 90–92 (1998). https://doi.org/10.1192/s0007125000297729
3. Anderson, K., et al.: Mobile health apps to facilitate self-care: a qualitative study of user experiences. PLoS ONE **11**(5), e0156164 (2016). https://doi.org/10.1371/journal.pone.0156164
4. Arean, P.A., et al.: The use and effectiveness of mobile apps for depression: Results from a fully remote clinical trial. J. Med. Internet Res. **18**, 12 (2016). https://doi.org/10.2196/jmir.6482
5. Bayliss, E.A., et al.: Understanding the context of health for persons with multiple chronic conditions: moving from what is the matter to what matters. Ann. Fam. Med. **12**(3), 260–269 (2014)

6. Beck, A.T., et al.: Beck Depression Inventory-II
7. Beigel, A., Murphy, D.L.: Unipolar and bipolar affective illness: differences in clinical characteristics accompanying depression. Arch. Gen. Psychiatry **24**(3), 215–220 (1971). https://doi.org/10.1001/archpsyc.1971.01750090021003
8. Corbin, J., Strauss, A.: Managing chronic illness at home: three lines of work. Qual. Sociol. **8**(3), 224–247 (1985). https://doi.org/10.1007/BF00989485
9. Dodson, J., et al.: Investigating health self-management among different generation immigrant college students with depression. In: Taylor, N.G., Christian-Lamb, C., Martin, M.H., Nardi, B. (eds.) iConference 2019. LNCS, vol. 11420, pp. 213–221. Springer, Cham (2019). https://doi.org/10.1007/978-3-030-15742-5_20
10. Doherty, G., et al.: Engagement with online mental health interventions: an exploratory clinical study of a treatment for depression. In: Proceedings of the SIGCHI Conference on Human Factors in Computing Systems, pp. 1421–1430. ACM, New York (2012). https://doi.org/10.1145/2207676.2208602
11. Dozois, D.J.A., et al.: A psychometric evaluation of the Beck Depression Inventory–II. Psychol. Assess. **10**(2), 83–89 (1998). https://doi.org/10.1037/1040-3590.10.2.83
12. Eikey, E.V., Chen, Y., Zheng, K.: Do recovery apps even exist? Why college women with eating disorders use (but not recommend) diet and fitness apps over recovery apps. In: Taylor, N.G., Christian-Lamb, C., Martin, M.H., Nardi, B. (eds.) iConference 2019. LNCS, vol. 11420, pp. 727–740. Springer, Cham (2019). https://doi.org/10.1007/978-3-030-15742-5_69
13. Eikey, E.V., et al.: The use of general health apps among users with specific conditions: why college women with disordered eating adopt food diary apps. In: American Medical Informatics Association (AMIA) Symposium, San Francisco, CA (2018)
14. Eikey, E.V., Reddy, M.C.: "It's definitely been a journey": a qualitative study on how women with eating disorders use weight loss apps. In: ACM CHI Conference on Human Factors in Computing Systems (CHI), pp. 1–13. ACM, Denver (2017). https://doi.org/10.1145/3025453.3025591
15. Epstein, R.M., et al.: "I didn't know what was wrong:" how people with undiagnosed depression recognize, name and explain their distress. J. Gen. Intern. Med. **25**(9), 954–961 (2010). https://doi.org/10.1007/s11606-010-1367-0
16. Firth, J., et al.: The efficacy of smartphone-based mental health interventions for depressive symptoms: A meta-analysis of randomized controlled trials **16**(3), 287–298 (2017). https://doi.org/10.1002/wps.20472
17. Fleming, T., et al.: Beyond the trial: systematic review of real-world uptake and engagement with digital self-help interventions for depression, low mood, or anxiety. J. Med. Internet Res. **20**(6), e199 (2018). https://doi.org/10.2196/jmir.9275
18. Forty, L., et al.: Clinical differences between bipolar and unipolar depression. Br. J. Psychiatry **192**(5), 388–389 (2008). https://doi.org/10.1192/bjp.bp.107.045294
19. Fox, S.: Health topics. Pew Research Center
20. Häfner, H., et al.: Schizophrenia and depression: challenging the paradigm of two separate diseases - a controlled study of schizophrenia, depression and healthy controls. Schizophrenia Res. **77**(1), 11–24 (2005). https://doi.org/10.1016/j.schres.2005.01.004
21. Huguet, A., et al.: A systematic review of cognitive behavioral therapy and behavioral activation apps for depression. PLoS ONE **11**(5), e0154248 (2016). https://doi.org/10.1371/journal.pone.0154248
22. Hunt, J., Eisenberg, D.: Mental health problems and help-seeking behavior among college students. J. Adolesc. Health **46**(1), 3–10 (2010). https://doi.org/10.1016/j.jadohealth.2009.08.008

23. Ibrahim, A.K., et al.: A systematic review of studies of depression prevalence in university students. J. Psychiatr. Res. **47**(3), 391–400 (2013). https://doi.org/10.1016/j.jpsychires.2012. 11.015

24. Kitzrow, M.A.: The mental health needs of today's college students: challenges and recommendations (2003)

25. Krebs, P., Duncan, D.T.: Health app use among US mobile phone owners: a national survey. JMIR mHealth uHealth **3**(4), e101 (2015). https://doi.org/10.2196/mhealth.4924

26. Lim, C.Y., et al.: Facilitating self-reflection about values and self-care among individuals with chronic conditions. In: Proceedings of the 2019 CHI Conference on Human Factors in Computing Systems. Association for Computing Machinery (2019). https://doi.org/10.1145/ 3290605.3300885

27. Løventoft, P.K., et al.: Designing daybuilder: an experimental app to support people with depression. In: Proceedings of the 12th Participatory Design Conference: Exploratory Papers, Workshop Descriptions, Industry Cases, vol. 2, pp. 1–4. ACM, New York (2012). https://doi.org/10.1145/2348144.2348146

28. Lyubomirsky, S., et al.: Dysphoric rumination impairs concentration on academic tasks. Cogn. Ther. Res. **27**(3), 309–330 (2003). https://doi.org/10.1023/A:1023918517378

29. Mohr, D.C., et al.: Three problems with current digital mental health research… and three things we can do about them. Psychiatr. Serv. **68**(5), 427–429 (2017). https://doi.org/10. 1176/appi.ps.201600541

30. Murnane, E.L., et al.: Personal informatics in interpersonal contexts: towards the design of technology that supports the social ecologies of long-term mental health management. In: Computer Supported Cooperative Work and Social Computing (CSCW) (2018). https://doi. org/10.1145/3274396

31. National Institute of Mental Health: Depression. https://www.nimh.nih.gov/health/topics/ depression/index.shtml#part_145397. Accessed 12 Sept 2019

32. Rubanovich, C.K., et al.: Health app use among individuals with symptoms of depression and anxiety: a survey study with thematic coding. JMIR Ment. Health **4**(2), e22 (2017). https://doi.org/10.2196/mental.7603

33. Shen, N., et al.: Finding a depression app: a review and content analysis of the depression app marketplace. JMIR mHealth uHealth **3**(1), e16 (2015). https://doi.org/10.2196/mhealth.3713

34. Smith, A., Anderson, M.: Social media use 2018: demographics and statistics. Pew Research Center (2018)

35. Tandoc, E.C., et al.: Facebook use, envy, and depression among college students: Is facebooking depressing? Comput. Hum. Behav. **43**, 139–146 (2015). https://doi.org/10. 1016/J.CHB.2014.10.053

36. Thomas, D.R.: A general inductive approach for qualitative data analysis (2003)

37. Torous, J., Powell, A.C.: Current research and trends in the use of smartphone applications for mood disorders. Internet Interv. **2**(2), 169–173 (2015). https://doi.org/10.1016/J. INVENT.2015.03.002

38. Vidourek, R.A., et al.: Students' benefits and barriers to mental health help-seeking. Health Psychol. Behav. Med. **2**(1), 1009–1022 (2014). https://doi.org/10.1080/21642850.2014. 963586

39. Vogel, E.A., et al.: Social comparison, social media, and self-esteem. Psychol. Popul. Media Cult. **3**(4), 206–222 (2014). https://doi.org/10.1037/ppm0000047

40. Vredenburg, K., et al.: Depression in college students: personality and experiential factors. J. Couns. Psychol. **35**(4), 419–425 (1988). https://doi.org/10.1037/0022-0167.35.4.419

Influencing Factors of the Identity of Japanese Animation Fans Among Chinese Adolescents: A Grounded Theory Study

Yiqi Liang[1,2], Xiaoqun Yuan[2(✉)], Shuying Chen[2,3], and Jinchao Zhang[2]

[1] School of Journalism and Communication, The Chinese University
of Hong Kong, Shatin, Hong Kong SAR, China
[2] School of Information Management, Wuhan University, Wuhan, Hubei, China
yuan20030308@whu.edu.cn
[3] Department of Psychology, Sun Yat-sen University,
Guangzhou, Guangdong, China

Abstract. Individuals are increasingly exposed to vibrant cultures because of the development and popularity of new media, such as social networking and online video. Introduced to China 40 years ago, Japanese animation is prevalent among Chinese adolescents, which has been documented in much literature. However, few studies focus on the factors which make a Chinese adolescent become a Japanese animation fan, and the important factor explaining how people adopt the identity from different cultures. This study aims to deal with these questions by developing a model of influencing factors of the identity of Japanese animation fans among Chinese adolescents. The grounded theory was introduced and data used for analysis were collected from 39 Japanese animation fans among Chinese adolescents by in-depth interviews. The results suggest that audience environment, perceived quality of Japanese animation and supply and demand matching degree are three main factors impacting the identity of Japanese animation fans among Chinese adolescents.

Keywords: Identity · Japanese animation · Fandom · Chinese adolescents · Grounded theory

1 Introduction

Television, movies, music, the Internet and other media have made contributions to the rapid and wide spread of ideas of different cultures, which has a huge impact on the formation of cultural identity (Arnett Jensen 2003). Japanese animation is one of the dynamic popular cultures, which was introduced into China 40 years ago. In December 1980, China Central Television broadcasted the first Japanese animation – Astro Boy, marking the official entry of Japanese animation into China. China is the biggest comics market in the world with 5 million readers, most of them are teenagers. For these adolescents, Japanese animation is their major choice (Fung et al. 2019). This preference for Japanese animation not only has a considerable effect on the share of animation market, but may also on their individual fan identity. In fact, fandom is an

© Springer Nature Switzerland AG 2020
A. Sundqvist et al. (Eds.): iConference 2020, LNCS 12051, pp. 256–267, 2020.
https://doi.org/10.1007/978-3-030-43687-2_20

extremely affect-laden form of investment in the liking of or interest in a particular object or idea (Thorne and Bruner 2006; Chung et al. 2008). Individuals engage with fandom in different ways from the point of view of identity development and belonging, which results in a process of learning to overcome identity ambiguity (Seregina and Schouten 2017). Numerous studies have shown that fandom aids identity building and self-reflection (Spigel and Jenkins 1991; Sandvoss 2005; Jenkins 2006a, 2006b, 2007, 2014; Smith et al. 2007; Chung et al. 2008), extending the value of fandom outside its limited consumption context (Seregina and Schouten 2017).

Identity, as a philosophical and logical concept, was put forward by Erikson (1959), which was a central topic of consumption, as people turn to products and brands for meaning in their lives (Seregina and Schouten 2017). The beginning of this concept focused on the individual's self-identity. Tajfel first defined social identity as "the individual's knowledge that he belongs to certain social groups together with some emotional and value significance to him of this group membership" (Tajfel 1972). According to the work of Hogg et al. (2004), he proposed this concept when he studied social categorization, ethnocentrism, social comparison, and intergroup relations. This idea had been further developed to social identity theory (Tajfel and Turner 1979).

In fact, how to identify different groups and their influencing factors is an important topic. Melnick and Wann (2011) investigated the sport fandom in Australia with a convenience sample of 163 university students, the investigation results suggested that compared with similar data obtained from US, these Australian students were judged greater sport consumers and more heavily identified with the sport fan role and a favorite team. Taylor (2015) tried to explore the nature of fan behavior and factors associated with salience of fan identity with both online and offline questionnaires, the result showed that empathy and the tendency to experience transportation into fictional narratives contributed to stronger fan identity salience. These studies both used questionnaire survey research, which was appropriate for the given purposes. But the questions of the questionnaire were designed with several 'fixed' answers, which is not suitable for the study on the influencing factors of social identity. To quantify each influencing factor, researchers need more spaces to disclose new or revelatory responses. Although qualitative research has been suffering the criticism that it does not adequately justify its assertions, the grounded theory has continued to prove useful for researches and to help readers see the rigor of concept development and theory building (Gioia et al. 2013). Rottmann et al. (2016) probed factors influencing the acceptance of leadership identity by engineers through grounded theory. They interviewed engineers employed by four Canadian engineering-intensive firms and the findings suggested important implications for engineering leadership educators.

Identity is individuals' subjective perceptions of who and what they are. The concept in this study is grounded in the empirical operation of asking interviewees if they belong to Japanese animation fans. In this regard, this study applies the grounded theory to figure out influencing factors of identity of Japanese animation fans among Chinese adolescents. The research questions are: (1) What are the unique features of Japanese animation that attract Chinese adolescents? (2) What are the influencing factors of the identity formation?

2 Methodology

2.1 Grounded Theory

As this study aims to explore the influencing factors of the identity of Japanese animation fans and how these factors work, a qualitative grounded methodology is used. To the contrary of a deductive research approach that begins with theory and moves from the definition of concepts and their proposed relations out to the "real world", the grounded theory encourages researchers to develop their own theory grounded in data systematically collected and analyzed (Glaser and Strauss 1967; Strauss and Corbin 1998). The intent of the grounded theory is to generate or discover a theory or abstract analytical schema of a phenomenon that relates to a particular situation grounded in the experience and perceptions of the participants (Strauss and Corbin 1998). In order to develop a sustentative theory, this approach allows for a much wider range of data than other qualitative methodologies (Goulding 2002). The data that can be used for grounded theory include interview notes, observations, company reports, secondary data, even statistics, etc. (Goulding 2002). Thus, the grounded theory is suitable for this study of full understanding how Japanese animation fans among Chinese adolescents developed identity.

Though grounded theory has diversified since its initial development, especially the splits between Glaser and Strauss, the founders of grounded theory, luckily, it is methodological rather than ontological and epistemological aspects that have been cited as the main source of divergence (Helen and Cowley 2004). This study will follow Strauss and Corbin's (1998) systematic approach, which delineates distinct steps in data collection and analysis with open coding, axial coding and selective coding. Following these principles and procedures of grounded theory, open interviews are conducted in this study, primarily to maintain open-mindedness in the early phases of the field research.

2.2 Sample

The participants were recruited online and offline. Online recruitment was undertaken through posting recruitment information in online virtual communities of Japanese animation fans. Offline recruitment included introduction from acquaintances and random interview in Comic Con. Finally, 39 Japanese animation fans were selected as participants. There were 20 male and 19 female participants. All of them were students aged between 14 and 23. Nine of the participants were junior high school students, five were in senior high school and 24 were in college. To obtain representative samples, these participants were recruited from different provinces and regions in China. 17 of the participants were from Guangdong Province and 12 from Hubei Province. The remaining 10 participants came from Guangxi, Sichuan, Shanxi, Hebei, Henan, Jiangsu and Jiangxi Provinces.

2.3 Data Collection

Grounded theory starts with empirical details expressed in interview transcripts and field notes and attempts to build a theoretical structure "bottom up" from this base (Langley 1999). Similar to existing qualitative researches (Sinclair 2016), the core of grounded theory is the semi-structured interview, which is implemented to obtain both retrospective and real-time accounts for those people experiencing the phenomenon of theoretical interest. Therefore, the data of this study was collected from semi-structured individual interviews with 39 Japanese animation fans, each of them was carried out through either Internet or face to face and lasted from 15 min to 3 h. Before the interview, the main purpose of this study was briefly introduced to each participant. Then, the interview began with participants answering demographic information. After this, they were asked seven open-ended questions, which were designed to collect information on the identities of Japanese animation fans and their influencing factors. Following the work of Phinney (1992), the identity in this paper was investigated three aspects: cognition, emotion and behavior. The cognitive component was related to one's cognition of being a member in a specific social group; the emotional component was linked to the affective commitment to the group; and the last component was associated with their identity behavior. During the interview, the participants were encouraged to express the views on their own identities in these three aspects, and the questions were designed to elicit details of the participant's identity formation, as shown in Table 1. After the interview, the data was timely collated. Furthermore, follow-up interviews were scheduled for further verification in the case when there were inconsistencies or ambiguities in the statements of the interviewees. The average follow-up interviews of these participants were more than twice. The 76 669 words of interview materials were collected from February 20 to April 5, 2019. Data were kept confidential and protected. Participants were interviewed anonymously. No identifying information of the participants was collected. Based on these steps, it is clear that the interview materials presented the real and complete thoughts of the interviewees as far as possible.

Table 1. Semi-structured interview questions

Number	Questions
1	Do you regard yourself as a fan of Japanese animation?
2	Please comment on Japanese animation and tell me why
3	Could you please describe for me what you consider your identity of Japanese animation?
4	What factors influence your thoughts of your identity?
5	Please describe the identity behavior in your daily life
6	What factors influence occurrences of your identity behavior?
7	What else can you tell me about your identity of Japanese animation fans and its influencing factors that we may not have discussed?

3 Data Analysis

Conducting the research with grounded theory requires that data collection and data analysis occur simultaneously (Glaser and Strauss 1967) when data analysis occurs through an iterative process referred to as "constant comparison" (Corbin and Strauss 1990; Glaser 1965; Glaser and Strauss 1967) and sampling and data analysis proceeds until the theory reach the point of theoretical saturation. Following Strauss and Corbin's systematic approach, open, axial, and selective coding were also used to analyze the data.

Firstly, during open coding, which began soon after the start of data collection, each transcript was analyzed in sentences or groups of sentences reflecting a single idea. These units were labeled with codes to reflect that idea or concept (Strauss and Corbin 1990). Then similar codes were grouped into different categories. Implementing the method of "constant comparative" (Glaser 1965), code names were iteratively revised and categories were further broken down to reflect the experience of the participants. Finally, 22 concepts and 10 categories were achieved in open coding stage, such as the story of Japanese animation, the character of Japanese animation, the music of Japanese animation, etc. Based on the open coding, axial coding aims to classify these categories into their corresponding father-categories. In this study, three main categories were generated by axial coding, which were audience environment, perceived quality of Japanese animation and supply and demand matching degree. After that, selective coding tried to establish a core category and to construct a sustentative theory by linking these codes to a central phenomenon. In this study, the core category was the identity of Japanese animation fans. Finally, theoretical saturation was reached at a sample of 24. What's more, the other 15 samples were analyzed and the results showed that no new or different themes emerged, indicating that the theory generated from this research had reached the point of saturation.

4 Results

In axial coding stage, three main categories emerged including audience environment, perceived quality of Japanese animation and supply and demand matching degree and each main category had several subcategories with them (see Table 2). In selective coding stage, a core phenomenon was decided and the interactions between core phenomenon and other categories were identified. In this case the core phenomenon was the identity of Japanese animation fans among Chinese adolescents. Finally, the theory emerged as the concepts were combined into an integrated framework that explained the phenomenon of identity formation of Japanese animation fans (Strauss and Corbin 1998). This model indicates the factors that influence the formation of the identity of Japanese animation fans among Chinese adolescents (see Fig. 1).

4.1 Audience Environment

The first factor that influences the development of identity is audience environment, including audience availability, costs, recommendation and audience alternativeness.

Table 2. Categories and subcategories from axial coding

Categories	Subcategories
Audience environment	Audience availability
	Cost
	Recommendation
	Audience alternativeness
Perceived quality of Japanese animation	Story
	Painting style
	Character
	Music
Supply and demand matching degree	Growth promotion
	Spiritual balance

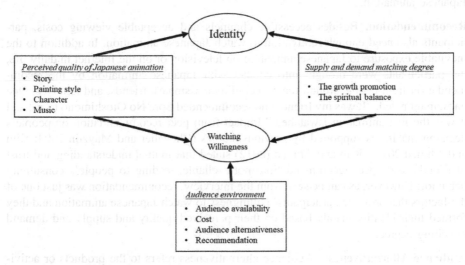

Fig. 1. Influencing factors of the identity formation of Japanese animation fans among Chinese adolescents

It is the external condition influencing Japanese animation fans' identity formation by affecting their willingness to watch. That is, when all these environmental factors drive audiences to watch Japanese animation, they are more likely to form the identity as Japanese animation fans.

Audience Availability. Audience availability is one of the environmental factors on identity formation. If the audiences can't access the Japanese animation, it will be impossible for them to form the identity as Japanese animation fans. For the participants, television and Internet are reliable channels to access Japanese animation. During their childhood, they watched various animations produced by the mature Japanese animation industry on TV, and gradually formed the habit of watching

Japanese animation. Although less and less Japanese animation could be broadcasted on TV due to the restrictions on foreign animations, Japanese animation didn't disappear in Chinese adolescents' life. The participants turned to the Internet, a border platform where they could watch what they want without constraints on time or space, for Japanese animation. Video websites such as bilibili, Acfun, iQIYI and Tencent animation were their major choices to watch Japanese animation.

Costs. The cost that participants should afford when watching Japanese animation is mainly their time and academic stress rather than economic cost because most Japanese animation can be watched for free on the Internet in China. When the heavy burden of homework left them little time for leisure, they would reduce the time spent on watching animation. One participant noted, "Recently, I am following an animation named Haikyu, which was recommended by my teacher. Generally, I spent one hour and a half on animations, but sometimes I was so busy that I would only watch them on weekend." It is clear that viewing costs will influence their willingness to watch Japanese animation.

Recommendation. Besides accessible channels and acceptable viewing costs, participants also need enough motivation to watch Japanese animation. In addition to the inevitable exposure to Japanese animation on television or on the Internet in daily life, the participants were brought into contact with Japanese animation by the recommendation from people around them, including classmates, friends, and relatives. One participant noted, "It was my friend who recommended Sora No Otoshimono to me and it was the first animation I watched." Impact from peer recommendation on people's decision making is supported by previous studies (Chevalier and Mayzlin 2004; Kim and Ahmad 2012). Kim and Ahmad (2012) stated that mutual understanding and trust of friends made peer recommendation more reliable, leading to people's consuming behavior. However, as can be seen from the interview, recommendation was just one of the factors that promote participants' willingness to watch Japanese animation and they formed their identity mainly based on their perceived quality and supply and demand matching degree.

Audience Alternativeness. Audience alternativeness refers to the products or activities that audience can select to replace Japanese animation. The culture environment where participants lived in was complicated. Since they got access to digital devices such as television, computer and mobile phone at a young age, participants were exposed to various culture products. In addition, entertainment didn't occupy their whole life. They naturally needed to study, exercise and cultivate other interests and hobbies. There is a place for Japanese animation in their hearts, as one participant said, "Japanese animation is quite appealing to me and I have no interest in the TV drama. The girls in TV series are not as cute as those in animation. In fact, there is also no way to compare the two", but these products and activities fought with Japanese animation for participants' time. When there are many alternative cultural products and activities which are more suitable for the needs of audiences, their willingness to watch animation will be reduced. One participant stated, "Now I think games are more important to me in my life and I don't feel like catching up on new anime works now because of the lack of time."

4.2   Perceived Quality of Japanese Animation

Perceived quality of Japanese animation precisely includes the evaluation on the quality of its four attributes, i.e. story, painting style, characters and music. The judgment is made according to their own criteria which derive from quality of alike products the participants watched before.

Story. The themes, plots and connotations of story have a crucial impact on identity formation. Those in wide range of subjects with novelty attracted the participants. One participant stated, Stories about monsters in traditional view were always horrible and terrible, while the "Natsume's Book of Friends" presented warm-hearted stories about short encounter and separation between the protagonist and monsters. Besides, because of its broad target audience, there were rich connotations in Japanese animation, which appealed to the participants as well. One participant stated, "Japanese animation had changed my idea that animation was only oriented to young children. Particularly, EVA was an in-depth work and it made me feel proud of watching animation."

It can be seen that if the quality of story in Japanese animation met their evaluation criteria, the participants would have stronger watching willingness and identity, and vice versa. One participant stated, "I prefer to the previous works, new released animations are more and more 'feimeng' (meaning unnecessary sexual descriptions in animations) which are meaningless."

Painting Style. The painting style of Japanese animation, including character and background design, also has an influence on identity formation. The participants were fascinated by the novel painting style, especially good-looking appearances of characters when the identity first began to form. One participant stated, "I was fond of Japanese animation because of its girlish painting style at the beginning. I remember the first animation I watched was Shugo Chara. The painting style of it was novel for me and there was no such painting style in domestic animation. I fell in love with it at the first sight."

If the quality of painting style was higher than the evaluation standard already formed by the participants, they would be more willing to watch Japanese animation and have a stronger identity, and it was the same in reverse. One participant stated, "I do not follow up most of the new released now because the quality is a little bit, you know…there are too many Isekai works (referring to the portal fantasy subgenre of Japanese animation) and the characters in these works almost look the same, the arrangements of storyboard are not as good as before."

Characters and Music. The participants paid much attention to character setting and music in Japanese animation. In terms of characters, Most of Japanese animation took teenager boys or girls as main characters, whose stories easily won identification of the participants. The setting of the protagonists' characters in animation impressed the participants particularly, such as bravery, persistence and other recognized good qualities. One participant stated, "I like Japanese animation because the personalities of the leading roles were very attractive. They are all brave teenagers and I can see the determination in their eyes."

As another important component of Japanese animation, animation music refers to the music in an animated work, including the title song (OP), the ending song (ED), background music and character songs. Appropriate choice of music made audience more integrated into the story. One participant stated, "At first I listened to background music of Jigoku Shojo by chance and thought it was great. After a search of its plot, I found it very interesting and wanted to watch a few episodes. Unexpectedly I couldn't stop myself from watching it."

The perceived quality of these attributes of Japanese animation effects their identity formation. And it should be noticed that the results reflect that high quality of characters and music has positive effects on the identity formation while characters and music in low quality doesn't have negative impact on it. Differently, story and painting style of low quality will impair their identity formation and good quality can enhance it.

4.3   Supply and Demand Matching Degree

Another key component of identity formation is their supply and demand matching degree. The participants described in details their harvest from Japanese animations that included growth promotion and spiritual balance. These gains further stimulated their demands of Japanese animation.

The Growth Promotion. The growth promotion refers to interest, inspiration and social satisfaction that Japanese animations brought to them. Firstly, the protagonist's love and persistence for a particular activity, which were displayed in animations of entertainment and sports themes, stimulated the participants' interest in the same entertainment and sports. One participant stated, "I had learned the piano for two years in primary school. But at that time, I didn't like the piano very much and even felt tired of practicing it over and over again. After that, I happened to watch 'Your Lie in April' recommended by my friend, and I was really moved by the animation. Kousei, the hero and his friends were good at playing the piano, and I would like to be like them. I began to love the piano inspired by them."

Secondly, when encountering confusing and perplexing situation in life, the participants often found answers and absorbed life philosophies from Japanese animation. One participant stated, "I used to worry about being unwelcome or excluded at school, and I was often misunderstood by others because I didn't communicate well with them. However, after reading a lot of stories in Japanese animations, I understood that it was unnecessary for me to live like others."

Thirdly, during puberty, due to hormone levels changes, adolescents' desire and curiosity about the opposite sex are evoked. However, when to and how to make friends with the heterosexual are determined by cultural expectations. Asian teens tend to have friends of the heterosexual later and have fewer friends than their western counterparts (Berk 2017). During this period, the participants had little contact with the heterosexual in reality. Their cognitive desire about the heterosexual was not realized, while they could have access to the heterosexual in Japanese animation, and even found the ideal type in the animation.

The Spiritual Balance. The participants also maintained spiritual balance and keep a good mental state through catharsis and cure by watching Japanese animation. Japanese animation was an outlet for them to escape from strain for a while because there are a large number of action and adventure themes in Japanese animation. These themes of animations, with exciting atmosphere and shocking scenes, were regarded as 'hot blood' style in the eyes of Japanese animation fans in China. The 'hot blood' refers specifically to the emotions of feeling radical, impulsive and full of strength and courage. Under the stimulation of such emotional infection, they could vent their frustration when they were under great pressure or encountered setbacks. One participant stated, "Watching Japanese animation is a good way for me to get rid of my stress. It makes me relax."

The participants were also "cured" by many heart-warming works in Japanese animation. There were several reasons reported by the participants why they loved these heart-warming works. Firstly, watching Japanese animation was a good way for participants to fill the void. Secondly, Japanese animation provided participants with a temporary escape from reality. On their way to adulthood, the participants shouldered greater responsibility and were under the increasing pressure which they couldn't cope with. At that time, they would choose to immerse themselves in fantasy, hope and comfort offered by Japanese animation. One participant stated, "I am increasingly fond of Japanese animations, because the reality becomes more and more realistic." Another participant also mentioned a similar view, "I think most of the Japanese animation represent a different world, where plots and interpersonal relationship are totally different from the reality, such as complete trust among people." Thirdly, the participants felt to be understood by characters in animations. Most of the main characters in animations are middle or high school students, whose experiences are alike that of the participants some degree. This kind of character setting, which enhances the audience's sense of substitution and immersion, caters to the mainstream audience's taste. The participants were touched by the struggle and persistence to achieve a certain goal, the courage to take the first step, and the friendship and growth with friends around. The characters in Japanese animations even shared their personal feelings, which might have never been mentioned to others or could not be understood in real life by the participants.

5   Conclusion

The identities of Japanese animation fans among Chinese adolescents are affected by three main components, namely audience environment, perceived quality of Japanese animation and supply and demand matching degree. This study examines the influencing factors of the identity of Japanese animation fans in the Chinese context. It helps not only to understand the situation that Japanese animation prevails among Chinese youth, but also to comprehend the reasons why people adopt identity from different cultures. There are several limitations in this study. First, this study was focused in two regions (Guangdong province and Hubei province). Testing the proposed model with various populations of Japanese animation fans among Chinese adolescents will further strengthen and refine the model. Second, this model only focused on the identity of Japanese animation fans among Chinese adolescents.

Conducting additional research on the model will further improve its generalization on other situations such as fans of other animations and cultural products.

References

Arnett Jensen, L.: Coming of age in a multicultural world: globalization and adolescent cultural identity formation. Appl. Dev. Sci. **7**(3), 189–196 (2003)

Berk, L.E.: Exploring Lifespan Development, 4th edn. Pearson, New York (2017)

Chevalier, J.A., Mayzlin, D.: The effect of word of mouth on sales: online book reviews. J. Mark. Res. **43**(3), 345–354 (2004). Social Science Electronic Publish

Chung, E., Beverland, M.B., Farrelly, F., Quester, P.: Exploring consumer fanaticism: extraordinary devotion in the consumption context. In: Advances in Consumer Research – North American Conference Proceedings, vol. 35, pp. 333–340 (2008)

Erikson, E.H.: Identity and the life cycle. Psychol. Issues **1**, 18–164 (1959)

Fung, A., Pun, B., Mori, Y.: Reading border-crossing Japanese comics/anime in China: cultural consumption, fandom, and imagination. Glob. Media China **4**(1), 125–137 (2019)

Gioia, D.A., Corley, K.G., Hamilton, A.L.: Seeking qualitative rigor in inductive research. Organ. Res. Methods **16**(1), 15–31 (2013)

Glaser, B.: The constant comparative method of qualitative analysis. Soc. Probl. **12**(4), 436–445 (1965)

Glaser, B., Strauss, A.: The Discovery of Grounded Theory: Strategies for Qualitative Research. Weidenfeld & Nicholson, London (1967)

Goulding, C.: Grounded Theory: A Practical Guide for Management, Business and Market Research. Sage, London (2002)

Heath, H., Cowley, S.: Developing a grounded theory approach: a comparison of Glaser and Strauss. Int. J. Nurs. Stud. **41**(2), 141–150 (2004)

Hogg, M.A., Abrams, D., Otten, S., Hinkle, S.: The social identity perspective: intergroup relations, self-conception, and small groups. Small Group Res. **35**(3), 246–276 (2004)

Jenkins, H.: Fans, Bloggers, and Gamers: Exploring Participatory Culture. New York University Press, New York (2006a)

Jenkins, H.: Convergence Culture: Where Old and New Media Collide. New York University Press, New York (2006b)

Jenkins, H.: The Wow Climax: Tracing the Emotional Impact of Popular Culture. New York University Press, New York (2007)

Jenkins, H.: Fandom studies as I see it. J. Fandom Stud. **2**(2), 89–109 (2014)

Kim, Y.A., Ahmad, M.A.: Trust, distrust and lack of confidence of users in online social media-sharing communities. Knowl. Based Syst. **37**(2), 438–450 (2012)

Langley, A.: Strategies for theorizing from process data. Acad. Manag. Rev. **24**(4), 691–710 (1999)

Taylor, L.D.: Investigating fans of fictional texts: fan identity salience, empathy, and transportation. Psychol. Popul. Media Cult. **4**(2), 172–187 (2015)

Melnick, M.J., Wann, D.L.: An examination of sport fandom in Australia: socialization, team identification, and fan behavior. J. Symb. Log. **50**(4), 502–509 (2011)

Phinney, J.S.: The multigroup ethnic identity measure: a new scale for use with diverse groups. J. Adolesc. Res. **7**(2), 156–176 (1992)

Rottmann, C., Sacks, R., Reeve, D.: Engineering leadership: grounding leadership theory in engineer's professional identities. IEEE Eng. Manag. Rev. **44**(2), 91–109 (2016)

Sandvoss, C.: Fans: The Mirror of Consumption. Polity, Cambridge (2005)

Seregina, A., Schouten, J.W.: Resolving identity ambiguity through transcending fandom. Consum. Mark. Cult. **20**(2), 107–130 (2017)

Sinclair, S., et al.: Sympathy, empathy, and compassion: a grounded theory study of palliative care patients' understandings, experiences, and preferences. Palliat. Med. **31**(5), 437–447 (2016)

Smith, S., Fisher, D., Cole, S.J.: The lived meaning of fanaticism: understanding the complex role of labels and categories in defining the self in consumer culture. Consum. Mark. Cult. **10**(2), 77–94 (2007)

Spigel, L., Jenkins, H.: Same bat channel, different bat times: mass culture and popular memory. In: Uricchio, W., Pearson, R. (eds.) The Many Lives of the Batman, pp. 117–148. British Film Institute, London (1991)

Strauss, A., Corbin, J.: Basics of Qualitative Research: Techniques and Procedures for Developing Grounded Theory, 2nd edn. Sage, Thousand Oaks (1998)

Strauss, A., Corbin, J.: Basics of Qualitative Research: Grounded Theory Procedures and Techniques. Sage, Thousand Oaks (1990)

Tajfel, H.: Social categorization. In: Moscovici, S. (ed.) Introduction à la Psychologie Sociale, vol. 1, p. 292. Larousse, Paris (1972)

Tajfel, H., Turner, J.C.: An integrative theory of intergroup conflict. In: Austin, W.G., Worchel, S. (eds.) The Social Psychology of Intergroup Relations, pp. 33–47. Brooks/Cole, Monterey (1979)

Thorne, S., Bruner, G.C.: An exploratory investigation of the characteristics of consumer fanaticism. Qual. Mark. Res. Int. J. **9**(1), 51–72 (2006)

Creating a Space for "Lowbrow" Information Behavior: From Dime Novels to Online Communities

Diana Floegel[1]([⊠]) [iD], Heather Moulaison-Sandy[2] [iD],
Ariel Hammond[1] [iD], and Sarah G. Wenzel[3]

[1] Rutgers University, New Brunswick, NJ 08901, USA
djfl85@scarletmail.rutgers.edu
[2] University of Missouri, Columbia, MO 65211, USA
[3] University of Chicago, Chicago, IL 60637, USA

Abstract. Both information behavior and social informatics research concern themselves with the formation and evolution of digital communities and online environments. However, literature to date focuses heavily on formal, professionalized, and normative resources and contexts at the expense of other materials and environments, including those centered around "entertaining" content such as fiction. In this paper, we present a historical narrative centered on paperback fiction and its creation, then relate that narrative to other fiction formats and current online fiction collectives, such as fanfiction archives. We adopt the perspective that fiction—often denigrated as "lowbrow" material, especially within an information science scholarly canon—can and should be considered an information resource in order to broaden social informatics and information behavior work so that they move away from normative conceptions of information and its interactors. We conclude with promising theoretical and practical directions to continue this work in the future.

Keywords: Information behavior · Social informatics · Cultural studies · Mass-market formats

1 Introduction

Digital communities in online environments inherit from the information practices that precede them. These systems are products of the epochs and of the creators and other actors who shape their progression over time. Oftentimes, scholarship bifurcates communities and the information they interact with into a highbrow and lowbrow binary. "Highbrow" describes resources and communities classified as intellectual and therefore elite, while "lowbrow" refers to more popular resources created and disseminated to general audiences [1]. Distinctions between highbrow and lowbrow materials are imperfect and problematic; differences between categories are constructed and therefore neither determined nor absolute [2], and the binary itself tends to reflect and reify systemic inequities [3].

© Springer Nature Switzerland AG 2020
A. Sundqvist et al. (Eds.): iConference 2020, LNCS 12051, pp. 268–277, 2020.
https://doi.org/10.1007/978-3-030-43687-2_21

The problematic nature of highbrow/lowbrow distinction becomes apparent when connections are drawn between highbrow materials and canon. Venues and materials considered to be highbrow often comprise canon, or texts that are cast as most essential to a particular discipline, time period, place, or genre [1]. Though "canon" is neither singular nor static, canonical spaces typically overrepresent privileged perspectives (e.g., western, white, wealthy, male, and educated) [3], meaning overlapping constructions of canons and a high/lowbrow binary perpetuate inequities in a variety of cultural spaces and narratives. This is especially troubling because canonical sources tend to shape dominant cultural and educational discourses that reinforce traditional knowledge structures and reify insider/outsider dynamics surrounding who can access and interact with certain types of content.

Meanwhile, content cast as lowbrow and, often, non-canonical tends to be denigrated and thus less influential in hegemonic discursive spaces. A great deal of content cast as lowbrow is created and consumed by marginalized people—e.g., those who may not have the power to infiltrate and influence mainstream canons. Sometimes, less formalized "lowbrow" resources might be considered a revolution in the information ecosystem; they have the potential to propose alternative, unvetted responses to information problems with more radical content in less traditional forms or genres. Thus, the "lowbrow" label is both artificial and a misnomer, and it may be used to discount material that troubles more dominant conceptions of culture [4, 5].

We observe that, as a discipline, information science focuses heavily on formal information resources that may be considered highbrow, thus missing opportunities to focus on resources more typically cast as lowbrow, including "entertaining" fictional works that are excluded from literary canons [6]. Because information science prioritizes the study of "elite" resources such as academically-oriented nonfiction [e.g., 7], its discursive practices reinforce highbrow/lowbrow distinctions and consequently shape and support research that neglects "lowbrow" materials. Additionally, scholarship in areas such as information behavior produces and promotes theories that reflect privileged populations [8], and subsequently can be argued to have an implicit interest in epistemically supporting a hegemonic canon.

For example, information behavior scholarship often focuses on the practices of formalized experts in traditional work settings [49]. It follows that many theories of information behavior reflect the privileged positionalities found within these contexts; they overrepresent white, wealthy, and educated people and consequently generalize their information interactions and cast marginalized or alternative practices as "other" [8]. Theories of everyday information behavior, for example, typically focus on professionals [49] or hobbyists [50] with little attention to the structural power dynamics that underscore all information interactions [51]. In general, the information behavior "canon" promotes an individualized perspective and overrepresents privileged people's practices.

How does this affect digital communities in online environments? In online communities, current information sources that are crowdsourced or collaboratively produced not by professionals, but rather by less formally recognized types of experts, enthusiasts or others wishing to participate, tend to be less recognized than more formalized resources and spaces [9]. Practices of online communities that focus on creating and sharing fiction, for example, are undertheorized in the information science literature, though some notable exceptions exist [e.g., 10]. Indeed, fiction can provide not only entertainment but also perspectives that serve as prominent information resources for individuals who are underrepresented within more formalized content. Thus, "entertaining" mediums typically neglected by information science scholarship can be considered informative [11]. This is extremely relevant to social informatics work, which aims to bring social science perspectives to computing with a focus on individual and collective interactors, as well as social dynamics and processes [12, 13].

Like information behavior, social informatics adopts an individualized perspective that overrepresents formal resources and neglects marginalized communities. Research in the domain of algorithmic inequities, for example, often does not meaningfully engage with structural articulations of constructs like gender [52] and race [53], instead focusing on individualized notions of bias and fairness as they are instantiated in technologies such as facial recognition software [54]. This limits theory development and has real-world consequences for marginalized communities who are targeted by these technologies. Further, social informatics work that does engage with less formalized online communities typically overlooks manifestations of power in such spaces [36].

As a result, in this paper we adopt the perspective that fiction can and should be considered an information source [6], a perspective that supports the study of a variety of online communities, and that will continue efforts to broaden information science work so that it moves away from normative conceptions of both information and its interactors. To support this argument and to begin to carve space for "lowbrow" materials, we present a historical narrative centered on paperback fiction and its creation, then relate paperbacks' trajectory to other fiction formats and related online fiction collectives, such as fanfiction communities.

2   Making Space for the "Lowbrow" in Information Science

2.1   The Rise of Mass-Market Paperbacks

To make a case for the place of mass-market information, including popular fiction and works by and for marginalized communities, we begin by tracing the trajectory of paper-bound materials in the US, starting with the paperback. In the mid-19th century, a number of popular and inexpensive newspapers and magazines featured stories and fiction designed to appeal to mass audiences. As publishers experimented with other low-cost text-based formats, the novel-length mass-market paperback was born [14]. Dime novels were an example – paperbacks produced at a furious pace while being entertaining (though often formulaic) and affordable. As much a format (i.e., small, paper-covered book) as a shorthand for the fiction contained within, they offered adventure and escape, intrigue and stories and types of characters that were not available through other information channels. Publishers marketed them as wholesome to avoid possible censorship, and were able to point to Horatio Alger's rags to riches stories or moral cowboys valiantly protecting American values in the West, for example, to demonstrate this virtue [15].

Such stories did not fit into hegemonic constructions of "cultured" highbrow fiction that "serious" sources were producing [14],[1] though they did often reflect dominant (e.g., white and male) perspectives.[2] The violence portrayed in Westerns [14] and detective fiction was criticized as having the potential to contaminate readers [15]. Dime novels have been and are still often framed as lowbrow content, and have only recently been recognized for their contribution to, and reflection of, American cultures they represented [16]. Though they maintained some moralizing normativity, they addressed less mainstream topics than other works at the time.

2.2 Paperbacks and Marginalization

Authors writing in certain paperback sub-genres[3] engaged in more subversive story-telling that at least partly challenged canonical trends. For example, though they fed into many pervasive stereotypes surrounding queerness, lesbian pulp novels featured queer women whose stories deviated from patriarchal conceptions of gender and sexuality [17]. Counter-cultural groups such as the Beats created and engaged with paperbacks to facilitate the spread of their non-conformist ideals [18], going so far as to create the first paperback-only bookstore in North America [19]. Additionally, African-American authors have consistently used developing technologies to publish works which counter mainstream notions about themselves, and to give voice to their own experiences [20], a tradition which spans from the early newspaper stories of the mid-1800s to online communities today.

The presence and availability of these stories indicates that as they evolved as a format, paperbacks provided their readers with information that was not available via more formalized channels. However, even content that appeared subversive in paper-backs was often curbed or co-opted by wider structural forces operating in opposition to non-dominant epistemologies and positionalities. For example, though lesbian pulp provided a slate of queer protagonists, it was written with the "male gaze" in mind and it often did not serve the communities it claimed to represent [21, 22]. Some lesbian pulp novels advanced anti-queer and anti-communist Cold War agendas that cast both queer and communist discourses as dangerous and in need of intervention [21].

---

[1] According to Reynolds, the educated classes (in his words, a "small minority") in the United States in the 1890s were reading highbrow fiction in such as Stephen Crane's *Red Badge of Courage* and Oscar Wilde's *The Picture of Dorian Gray* – these pieces appeared in highbrow serials such as *Harper's Magazine* and *Lippincott's Magazine*. Other "serious" magazines included *The Century, The Nation, The Arena,* and *The Atlantic.*

[2] Of the detective fiction analyzed by Bedore from the 19th century, 96% of the detectives were men, as well as 85% of the criminals. A very small number of non-white characters appeared, with only 4 in the role of the detective (out of 165), 18 as criminals (out of 447), 10 as victims (out of 255). An additional 5 had roles as informants and 8 were in secondary roles.

[3] The original genres/sub-genres associated with dime novels and early mass-market paperbacks included Westerns, detective fiction/crime drama, romance novels, and stories for boys.

2.3   Access and Infrastructure in Paperback Publishing

Much as current online community members have needs for infrastructure, including Internet access and a device upon which to access the Internet [23], access to paperbacks was heavily dependent upon available platforms, technologies, and fiscal resources.

As the market for cheaply produced niche publications proved itself, and technological advances were made,[4] smaller presses were quickly bought out by larger publication houses [24]. This provided wider distribution and readership, but ultimately undercut paperbacks' subcultural challenge, and removed additional avenues for marginalized voices [24]. Therefore, while some paperbacks perhaps made attempts at subversion, more powerful institutional forces intervened in their efforts, as can happen with marginalized forms of entertainment [25]. Paperbacks ultimately assimilated to or were appropriated by normative narratives and publishing structures; however, practices such as self-publishing and genres such as urban fiction continue to challenge these circumstances. Paperbacks both contest and adapt to normative information channels.

The rise of personal computers in the late 20th century, and the development of the internet in the early 21st, has amplified creative voices and communities in many fields of marginalized literature, including comics, zines, and fanfiction. Scholarship argues that online venues often facilitate creation of and access to ideas that might otherwise be excluded from literary discourse [26], though such venues may also reflect and amplify inequities. Thus, other genres of marginalized literature may be examined in light of their connections to, and perhaps evolution from, paperbacks.

2.4   Beyond Paperbacks: Comics, Zines, Fandom and Online Collectives

From as early as the 1930s and through today, marginalized voices found an outlet in comic books. Comics grew from the newspapers of the late 19th century, with the inaugural American comic said to be that of the Yellow Kid in the Hearst newspapers, beginning in 1895. While comic strips developed as early as 1904, the comic book per se was not created until 1933 [27]. Comics continued as a relatively subversive genre until the 1950s when it was decided that they were dangerous for children, at which point, fearing governmental regulation or censorship, in 1954 the comic code was put into place by comics publishers themselves. It forbade publishing comics that had sexual overtones, violence, etc. In its wake, the large mainstream comics companies of today, particularly Marvel and DC, emerged as the titans of the industry against which smaller companies struggle and in opposition to which subversive content found a voice. For example, there was still room for publications such as *MAD Magazine*—a satirical and occasionally scatalogical publication—and the *Village Voice*, which published a great deal of queer content from New York City. In the 1960s, comics started to shake themselves free of the code and in 1968, according to Hilary Chute, the first "underground"—or limited-run, small press, locally distributed—comic was sold [27]. Underground comics and even what today are called "graphic novels" continued

---

[4] For example, advances in lithographic printing and wire racks.

in the margins of the publishing world until Art Spiegelman's *Maus* won mainstream recognition.

Zines evolved from the science fiction "fanzine" in the 1930s and exploded with the development of photocopiers and other technologies in the late 1970s. Over the course of the next forty years, they evolved in response to societal and technological changes. Zine content, then and now, ranges from political diatribe to autobiographical "perzines." The heyday of the photocopied black-and-white zine was in the 1980s and 90s, when they were distributed largely by hand and traded at various places, including punk music venues. Zines helped give rise to third wave feminism, in both the countercultural Riot Grrrl Press with influential zine authors such as Kathleen Hanna, Pagan Kennedy, and Miranda July, as well as within academia [28]. As the internet developed, zines moved online, where posting and responses are immediate, and combinations of visual and textual material can be further explored. At the same time, the availability of color photocopying added a new dimension to zines, which expanded to include photozines and minicomics. However, while zines can be a subversive genre that allows marginalized individuals to voice their opinions and experiences, they are by no means fully democratized; zines by women of color such as Nguyen's *Evolution of a Race Riot*, for example, are often left out of both popular and academic conversations, and zine communities may be unwelcoming to people of color more generally [29]. Thus, technological progression does not negate systemic inequities.

Fanfiction represents another area where members of more general publics may rewrite or challenge canonical stories or events [30]. While fanfiction has been marginalized in many forms of mainstream discourse including academia [31], it highlights intersections between information practices, systems design, and community formation [9]. Like some paperbacks, fanfiction deviates from canon by literally rewriting it, and certain forms of fanfiction such as "slash" reorient normative stories to center alternative narratives [32, 33].

Though fan collectives existed long before internet infrastructure, online channels contributed to a boon of transnationally connected digital communities who work collaboratively to craft and disseminate various works. Many of these communities formed in resistance to monetization and common industrial publishing practices [9, 34]. Due to internet affordances, fanfiction communities enact digitally facilitated potentialities that twentieth-century paperback authors were perhaps unable to imagine. These burgeoning literary communities use a variety of media including text-based blog or story-hosting platforms, visual renditions of poetry, oral storytelling on podcasts, or a combination of the above.

The possibilities for authorial development are greater in online communities than ever before, as the theory of distributed mentorship argues, because the feedback and guidance afforded by these new technologies are not bound by time and space [40]. Additionally, in a similar fashion to creating small niche printing presses and gaining technical skill by doing so, those who engage in online communities develop computing skills which can be leveraged beyond their literary platforms; this is especially beneficial for women and people of color who are currently marginalized in computer science [41]. Indeed, one of the key characteristics of online communities is knowledge flow, both into and out of the community, and it is argued that knowledge collaboration is a crucial sustaining element for such communities [42].

This is not to say, however, that fanfiction represents a utopic vision of the internet or online community-building. On the contrary, though literature on fanfiction often focuses on its subversive practices, this scholarship and actual fan communities tend to be structured by the whiteness and cis/heteronormativity that exist within and outside of the internet: The "masses" who write and read fanfiction, as well as the marginalized communities represented by these practices, often exclude or are antagonistic toward fans of color and other marginalized fans [3, 26, 35]. The velocity of feedback, both positive and negative, can be overwhelming and detrimental to budding authors, which begs for author protection on these platforms. Online literary authors and readers are also widely lambasted in popular culture, and though the psychological complexities of online literary works are beginning to be addressed, they are not free from problematic representations [43].

Additionally, as with the takeover of niche paperback publishers by larger publishing houses, these online spaces are not immune to market forces, as illustrated by recent events surrounding the buying and selling of the social media site Tumblr [37]. Online communities are also not free from power structures, though the extent of their effect is uncertain, as some indicate that traditional hierarchies have less effect on online communities than assumed [44], while others indicate that these structures are quite prevalent [45], even within communities which expressly aim to subvert them. This variability may be due to the communities studied, range of platforms being used, influence of informal leaders [46], or a combination thereof.

3   Implications and Conclusion

This preliminary research project suggests that information science—especially information behavior and social informatics—may expand its own canon and challenge its epistemic assumptions by more carefully engaging with forms of entertainment and the online communities that they inspire. Examinations of such materials may demonstrate tensions between cultural subversion and wider systemic inequities that curb creative information practices within capitalist social structures. Fiction may help information science reckon with its own contributions to problematic highbrow and lowbrow binary constructions, and it may also further efforts to include marginalized perspectives and creation in information practice research [25, 38]. To that end, we demonstrate that these resources are not "lowbrow" at all. Overall, including these resources could move both information behavior and social informatics away from individualized canonical models and toward structural engagement with information interactions.

Today's online communities owe a debt to the undertheorized formats that emerged in the US and were often cast as lowbrow at the turn of the 20th century. This paper begins to address the gap in our knowledge of information behavior as it applies to the creation and consumption of resources that both entertain and inform. Future work intends to further examine the cultural and related theoretical implications of including fictional resources in information science scholarship, as well as the historical and social trajectories of mass-market paperbacks in and beyond the US. It also intends to explore avenues for sustainable library preservation of born-digital media [39, 47, 48]. This provides needed historical, cultural, and critical perspectives relevant to social informatics research. Our work demonstrates that "sustainable" online communities are not only present-day phenomena; they can be contextualized along wider trajectories that attend to marginalized formats, people, and collectives in order to bring more perspectives to bear on information science work.

References

1. Lauter, P.: Transforming a literary canon. Trans.: J. Incl. Scholarsh. Pedag. **26**(1), 31–33 (2016)
2. Jagose, A.: Queer Theory: An Introduction. NYU Press, New York (1997)
3. Thomas, E.: The Dark Fantastic: Race and the Imagination from Harry Potter to the Hunger Games. NYU Press, New York (2019)
4. Bourdieu, P.: Distinction: A Social Critique of the Judgement of Taste. Harvard University Press, Cambridge (1984)
5. Radway, J.A.: Reading the Romance: Women, Patriarchy, and Popular Literature. University of North Carolina Press, Chapel Hill (1991)
6. Floegel, D., Costello, K.L.: Entertainment media and the information practices of queer individuals. Libr. Inf. Sci. Res. **41**(1), 31–38 (2019)
7. Case, D.O., Given, L.M.: Looking for Information: A Survey of Research on Information Seeking, Needs, and Behavior, 4th edn. Emerald Group Publishing Limited, Bingley (2016)
8. Henrich, J., Heine, S.J., Norenzayan, A.: The weirdest people in the world? Behav. Brain Sci. **33**, 61–135 (2010)
9. Fiesler, C., Morrison, S., Bruckman, A.S.: An archive of their own: a case study of feminist HCI and values in design. In: CHI 2016 Proceedings. ACM, New York (2016). http://dx.doi.org/10.1145/2858036.2858409
10. Pecoskie, J., Hill, L.: Beyond traditional publishing models: an examination of the relationships between authors, readers, and publishers. J. Doc. **71**(3), 609–626 (2015)
11. Gray, J.: Television Entertainment. Routledge, New York (2008)
12. Kling, R.: What is social informatics and why does it matter? Inf. Soc. **23**(4), 205–220 (2007)
13. Sanfillipo, M., Finchman, P.: The evolution of social informatics research (1984–2013): challenges and opportunities. In: Finchman, P., Hosenbaum, H. (eds.) Social Informatics: Past, Present, and Future, pp. 29–55. Cambridge Scholars Publishing, Newcastle upon Tyne (2014)
14. Reynolds, Q.J.: The Fiction Factory: Or From Pulp Row to Quality Street: The Story of 100 Years of Publishing at Street & Smith. Random House, New York (1955)
15. Bedore, P.: Dime Novels and the Roots of American Detective Fiction. Palgrave Macmillan, New York (2013)
16. Sullivan, L.E., Schurman, L.C.: Pioneers, Passionate Ladies, and Private Eyes: Dime Novels, Series Books, and Paperbacks. The Hawthorne Press, Binghamton (2009)
17. Bauer, H., Cook, M. (eds.): Queer 1950s: Rethinking Sexuality in the Postwar Years. Palgrave Macmillan, New York (2012)
18. Hemmer, K.: Encyclopedia of Beat Literature. Infobase Publishing, New York (2010)
19. City Lights Bookstore. http://www.citylights.com/

20. Hill, M.: Toni Morrison and the post-civil rights African American novel. In: Cassuto, L., Eby, C.V., Reiss, B. (eds.) The Cambridge History of the American Novel, pp. 1064–1083. Cambridge University Press, Cambridge (2011)

21. Keller, Y.: "Was it right to love her brother's wife so passionately?" Lesbian pulp novels and US lesbian identity, 1950–1965. Am. Q. 57(2), 385–410 (2005)

22. Nealon, C.S.: Invert-history: the ambivalence of lesbian pulp fiction. New Lit. Hist. 31(4), 745–764 (2000)

23. Fidel, R.: Human Information Interaction: An Ecological Approach to Information Behavior. The MIT Press, Cambridge (2012)

24. Brouilette, S.: Corporate publishing and canonization: "Neuromancer" and science-fiction publishing in the 1970s and early 1980s. Book Hist. 5, 187–208 (2002)

25. Floegel, D., Costello, K.L.: "We just decided to do it ourselves": extending theories of information poverty and small worlds with institutional small worlds and queer world-building. J. Crit. Libr. Inf. Stud. (in press)

26. Hellekson, K., Busse, K. (eds.): The Fan Fiction Studies Reader. University of Iowa Press, Iowa City (2014)

27. Chute, H.: Why Comics? HarperCollins Publishers, New York (2017)

28. Gottlieb, I., Wald, G.: Smells like teen spirit: Riot Grrrls, revolution, and women in independent rock. Crit. Matrix 7(2), 11–68 (1993)

29. Arroyo-Ramirez, E., Chou, R.L., Freedman, J., Fujita, C., Orozco, M.: The reach of a long-arm stapler: calling in microaggressions in the LIS field through zine work. Libr. Trends 67 (1), 107–130 (2018)

30. Coppa, F.: A brief history of media fandom. In: Hellekson, K., Busse, K. (eds.) Fan Fiction and Fan Communities in the Age of the Internet, pp. 41–60. MacFarland & Company Inc, Jefferson (2006)

31. DeKosnik, A.: Rogue Archives: Digital Cultural Memory and Media Fandom. The MIT Press, Cambridge (2016)

32. Duggan, J.: Revising hegemonic masculinity: homosexuality, masculinity, and youth-authored Harry Potter fanfiction. Bookbird: J. Int. Child. Lit. 55(2), 38–45 (2017)

33. Hoad, C.: Slashing through the boundaries: heavy metal fandom, fan fiction and girl cultures. Media Music Stud. 3(1), 5–22 (2017)

34. Coppa, F.: An archive of our own. In: Jamison, A. (ed.) Fic: Why Fanfiction is Taking Over the World, pp. 302–308. Smart Pop, Dallas (2013)

35. Noble, S.: Algorithms of Oppression: How Search Engines Reinforce Racism. NYU Press, New York (2018)

36. Pande, R.: Squee from the Margins: Fandom and Race. Iowa University Press, Iowa City (2018)

37. Perano, U., Primack, D.: Verizon agrees to sell Tumblr to owner of Wordpress. AXIOS. https://www.axios.com/verizon-tumblr-wordpress-automattic-e6645edd-bc73-45c2-9380-9fe8ca34291f.html

38. Gorichanaz, T.: Information creation and models of information behavior: grounded synthesis and further research. J. Librariansh. Inf. Sci. 50, 998–1006 (2019)

39. Quirk, L.: Proliferating ephemera in print and digital media. Engl. Stud. Canada 42(3/4), 22–24 (2016)

40. Campbell, J., Aragon, C., Davis, K., Evans, S., Evans, A., Randall, D.: Thousands of positive reviews: distributed mentoring in online fan communities. In: Proceedings of the 19th ACM Conference on Computer-Supported Cooperative Work & Social Computing, pp. 691–704. ACM, New York (2016)

41. Fiesler, C., Morrison, S., Shapiro, R.B., Bruckman, A.S.: Growing their own: legitimate peripheral participation for computational learning in an online fandom community. In: Proceedings of the 2017 ACM Conference on Computer Supported Cooperative Work and Social Computing, pp. 1375–1386. ACM, New York (2017)
42. Faraj, S., Jarvenpaa, S.L., Majchrzak, A.: Knowledge collaboration in online communities. Organ. Sci. **22**, 1224–1239 (2011). https://doi.org/10.1287/orsc.1100.0614
43. Long, S.: 'Euphoria"'s controversial One Direction scene teaches a lesson on 'real person fan fiction'. https://www.dukechronicle.com/article/2019/09/euphorias-controversial-one-direction-scene-teaches-a-lesson-on-real-person-fan-fiction
44. Ardichvili, A., Maurer, M., Li, W., Wentling, T., Stuedemann, R.: Cultural influences on knowledge sharing through online communities of practice. J. Knowl. Manag. **10**, 94–107 (2006). https://doi.org/10.1108/13673270610650139
45. Bourdon, I., Kimble, C., Tessier, N.: Knowledge sharing in online communities: the power game. J. Bus. Strategy **36**, 11–17 (2015). https://doi.org/10.1108/JBS-04-2014-0044
46. Huffaker, D.: Dimensions of leadership and social influence in online communities. Hum. Commun. Res. **36**, 593–617 (2010). https://doi.org/10.1111/j.1468-2958.2010.01390.x
47. DIY Book Scanner. https://www.diybookscanner.org/en/index.html
48. Johnson, R.J., Fong, C.L.: The expanding universe of Sherlockian fandom and archival collections. Transform. Works Cult. **23** (2017). https://doi.org/10.3983/twc.2017.0792
49. Ocepek, M.: Bringing out the everyday in everyday information behavior. J. Doc. **74**, 398–411 (2018)
50. Hartel, J.: Managing documents at home for serious leisure: a case study of the hobby of gourmet cooking. J. Doc. **66**, 847–874 (2010)
51. Gibson, A.N., Martin, J.D.: Re-situating information poverty: information marginalization and parents of individuals with disabilities. J. Assoc. Inf. Sci. Technol. **70**, 476–487 (2019)
52. Keyes, O.: The misgendering machines: Trans/HCI implications of automatic gender recognition. In: Proceedings of the ACM on Human Computer Interaction, no. 88. ACM, New York (2018)
53. Huq, A.Z.: Racial equity in algorithmic criminal justice. Duke Law J. **88**(663) (2019). Paper no. 663
54. Bennet, C.L., Keyes, O.: What is the point of fairness? Disability, AI, and the complexity of justice. In: Workshop-AI Fairness for People with Disabilities, 21st International ACM SIGACCESS Conference on Computers and Accessibility. arXiv:1908.01024

Challenges and Opportunities of ACM Digital Library: A Preliminary Survey on Different Users

Shaobo Liang[1], Daqing He[2(⊠)], Dan Wu[1], and Haoge Hu[1]

[1] Wuhan University, Wuhan 430072, Hubei, China
[2] University of Pittsburgh, Pittsburgh, PA 15212, USA
dah44@pitt.edu

Abstract. As currently the ACM Digital Library (ACM DL) is developing its new version, this study aimed to understand the usages of ACM DL. Through focusing on the existing critical barriers for different DL users in their usages of the current ACM DL, this study aimed to identify important potential directions for the further developments of the new ACM DL. A survey was conducted among different countries, and 157 valid responses were collected. The results show information access barriers to the current ACM DL in the aspects of resource formats, browsing experience, and searching experience. We then proposed several design changes that can help developers of the ACM DL and other DLs to design more user-centered DL interfaces.

Keywords: Digital Library · Information access · Online survey

1 Introduction

Digital library (DL) refers to an online database of digital resources, including text, images, audios, videos, and other digital formats [1]. DL varies greatly in size and scope, and can be maintained by individuals or organizations [2]. In recent years, along with more powerful archiving and information accessing technologies being developed, various academic institutions and professional associations have developed different DLs for hosting diverse published or online digital contents. However, technologies evolve fast, thus it is important for the DL community to constantly identify existing barriers from users and develop further improvement to the DL system.

As one of the oldest and the most authoritative web archives for computing literature, the ACM Digital Library (ACM DL) is a "research, discovery and networking" platform, containing the full-text collection of all ACM publications[1]. It serves as a repository for high-quality literature on computing literature and provides rich inter-linking relationships among authors, works, institutions, and special interest groups within the ACM community [3]. With the development of more accessible

---

[1] dl.acm.org.

© Springer Nature Switzerland AG 2020
A. Sundqvist et al. (Eds.): iConference 2020, LNCS 12051, pp. 278–287, 2020.
https://doi.org/10.1007/978-3-030-43687-2_22

technologies and information technologies, the ACM DL has developed the new version of its interface [4] to provide a more user-centered interface and service.

Although this new version is still in trial stage, and there is not a large number of users accessing the information via this new version, the developers of the new ACM DL have been actively cooperating and discussing with the whole computing communities on how to enhance the new ACM DL system and its services. Therefore, we conducted a survey to investigate users' current usage inside the existing ACM DL, including the motivations, goals, search tasks, access methods, the challenges, as well as the attitudes and needs towards personalized function about the recommendation, search, interface, and notification. We aim to find out users' needs and obstacles through the survey results, and recommend improvements to the ACM DL via the new design.

2 Related Works

There have been many attentions to the DL users' information behaviors in the literature. Researchers studied the users' intents when using DLs, their information needs, behaviors, their desires which could influence the design of the DLs.

Marchionini, Plaisant and Komlodi [5] conducted a study of Library of Congress Digital Library's interfaces. They proposed that DLs in large scale should consider the users' different roles and tasks, and provide personalized user interface tailored for different users' roles and tasks.

In addition, different groups of users have various activity characteristics in DLs. For instance, users can have different search strategies (such as using different retrieval fields) [6]. Researchers examined DL users' clickstream data, and found out that users' search activities are less exploratory [7]. Islamaj et al. studied the PubMed users' needs and behavior, and found that the three main search fields used by the users are search by author, gene/protein, and disease. They also demonstrated that the analysis of users' search preference could contribute to improving biomedical information retrieval [8].

Users' DL needs on mobile devices became more personalized. Toms et al. argued that the research on DL should not only focus on users' information search tasks but also users' DL experience including the playfulness and pleasure, because the experience will affect the users' willingness of using DLs [9]. DLs can analyze the users' diverse preferences to establish user portrait through transaction log data, which can enhance their personalized services [10]. Franke et al. studied the recommendation algorithm based on the DL users' historical log, and improved the recommend services of DLs [11]. Willson and Given compared the differences between searches on DL and searches on WWW. They found that DL users needed more user-centered interface design [12]. Others also stated that the personalized interface could meet different user groups with different search skills and preferences [13].

The research on the information needs and behavior characteristics of the DL users can effectively help the DLs improve services. Especially under rapid development of information technology, DLs should reform their services better. However, the existing researches have not focused on needs and barriers of ACM DL users. Through this research, we can provide suggestions for the development of new ACM DL.

3 Study Design

3.1 Research Questions

In this study, we focused on the different groups of users' critical barriers in accessing the current ACM DL and the potential directions for improving in the new ACM DL. Consequently, the research questions in this study are:

RQ1: What are the obstacles in the aspects of information needs and information access methods inside the current ACM DL among different user groups?

RQ2: What are the users' attitudes and needs towards personalized function to improve the DL's services?

3.2 Questionnaire and Participants

As ACM DL's users come from all around the world, we want to collect the responses from a wide range of users. This motivated us to adopt web survey via an online questionnaire as the data collection method. Although other qualitative methods like interview can help investigate users' views in-depth, it is too difficult to recruit users from different regions around the world.

As shown in Table 1, the questionnaire is in English, and contains 25 questions that are divided into six different modules. These modules cover important aspects of information access and services in DLs. The online version of the questionnaire can be found at [14]. To align the research questions in this paper, the discussion here will mainly concentrate on the questions in module 1 and modules 3–6. We used the method of "snowball" to recruit the participants via social media and e-mail. The survey was published on a professional online survey service platform (http://wjx.cn).

In total of 157 valid questionnaires were returned. Among all valid responses, male accounts for 44.6% and female accounts for 55.4%.

Table 1. Question groups in the survey.

Module	Survey contents	Questions
1	General background of users (age, gender, occupation, environment, education, geographical location)	Q1–Q7
2	Users' motivations, goals, tasks when using ACM DL	Q8–10
3	Users' information needs and access methods	Q11–13 and Q16–18
4	Users' critical existing barriers in current ACM DL	Q14–15
5	User's attitudes towards to personalized recommendation, interface, and search service	Q19–23
6	User's attitudes towards to notification and engagement	Q24–25

More than half of the responses (54.1%) were between the age of 22–30. 80.2% of the responses were students, including undergraduate students (24.8%) and graduate students (55.4%). The responses from university faculty and staff accounted for 15.3%.

Most of the responses received a college degree or higher. In terms of geographical demographics, the responses from East Asia accounted the most at 63.7%, followed by North America (15.3%) and Europe (10.19%). In this study, we mainly compared the differences among different regions, different positions (student and non-student), and different environments (academia and non-academia).

4   Results

4.1   Challenges in Information Access Among Different User Groups

The Needs for the Diverse Collection. From the answers in the survey, 78.3% of responses indicated that users mainly looked for the PDF resources inside ACM DL. We conducted a further investigation on what formats do users want have beyond PDF in Q12. As shown in Fig. 1, different user groups have diverse format preference in the DL collection, but the majority want papers in HTML5 format. Users from East Asia and student group also showed high needs for papers in XML format.

The Barriers to Information Access Process. For many years, ACM DL has greatly benefited authors, readers, and researchers of the computing community. However, responses to Q14 still show barriers preventing users from accessing the information they want. Table 2 reveals that more than half users couldn't find the relevant results when using ACM DL, and users find difficult to obtain certain elements inside papers (such as tables, figures, and datasets) too. Besides, other mentioned obstacles include confusing labels of subject areas (46.91%), difficulties to locate papers via links to SIGs (Special Interest Groups) (43.21%), and old labels of Computing Classification Scheme (43.21%).

Furthermore, we investigated the information access methods used by different groups of users when they looked inside ACM DL (Q13). As shown in Fig. 2, users still would like to use different information access methods, although the use of simple keyword search accounts for the most.

Through analyzing answers to Q15, we find that users' views about the access methods for ACM DL should be enhanced. As shown in Fig. 3, the major access barriers for accessing ACM DL are searching, including the simple keyword search and advanced search. Especially for users from Europe and East Asia, and users from academia, they had more complaints about advanced search. Besides, there are many dissatisfactions with browsing using different subject areas, browsing through SIGs, and browsing using ACM subject CCS.

4.2   Opportunities for ACM DL's Improvement

In this section, we investigated different users' attitude and willingness to the redesign and new features of ACM DL. Through Q19–Q21, the results showed that most users (64.9%) hold a positive attitude to personalized recommendation and search service, and majority of users would be willing to create a personal profile inside the DL using their email.

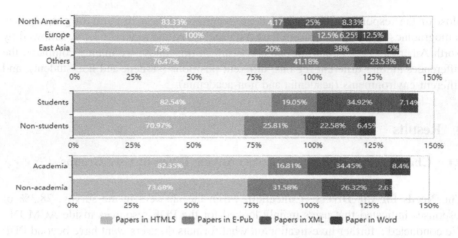

Fig. 1. Comparison of needs for diverse collection among different user groups.

Table 2. Barriers for information access inside ACM DL.

Barriers	Percentage
Search engine in the DL cannot find relevant papers	62.96%
Search engine in the DL cannot search on tables, figures and datasets inside paper	50.62%
Papers are not easily located via links to ACM publications	40.74%
Papers are not easily located via links to Special Interest Groups	43.21%
The labels of subject areas are confusing, need update	46.91%
The labels of CCS are confusing	43.21%
The categories of CCS are too old for my needs	39.51%
Collection missing the materials I look for, such as presentation videos	27.16%

The Needs for Customized Interface. When asked whether do users want to change the elements inside the webpage of ACM DL to customize the user interface, most users reported that they hope to change the position of navigational components. Specifically, the users from North America concerned about adding or deleting certain elements, while the users in East Asia and Europe focused on the font and navigation buttons in personalized user interface more. Results are shown in Fig. 4.

The Needs for Personalized Search Support. Further analysis showed that different groups of users all wished to get more personalized search support in the ACM DL. The questions about personalized search support are shown in Table 3.

Query terms suggestion is the most needed support (67.52%), followed by personalized ranking of the results based on the user's search history (54.14%), browsing history (50.96%), and research interests (49.68%). In addition, most users hold welcome attitudes toward personalized recommendation based on their privacies (such as searching, browsing, and clicking history) when they accessed the ACM DL.

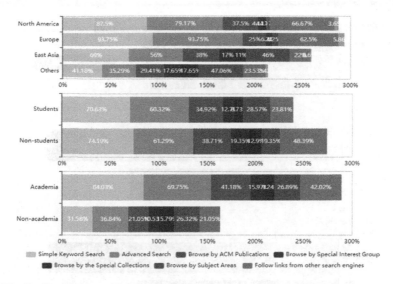

Fig. 2. Comparison of information access methods among different user groups.

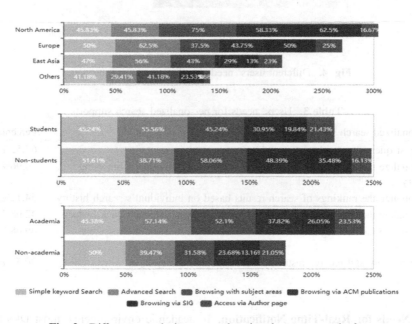

Fig. 3. Different users' views on enhancing the access methods.

There are no obvious differences in the needs for search support among different user groups, except for the needs for multilingual information retrieval. The users from Europe (50.44%) and users from East Asia (47.69%) had more need for searching in their native language.

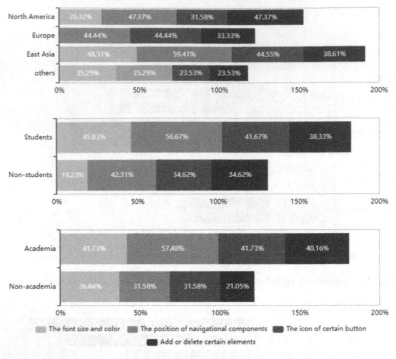

Fig. 4. Different users' needs for the customized interface.

Table 3. Users' needs for personalized search support.

Personalized search support	Percentage
Suggest query terms when typing the query	67.52%
Personalize the rankings of search results based on individual's browsing history	50.96%
Personalize the rankings of search results based on individual's search history	54.14%
Personalize the rankings of search results based on individual's click history	42.68%
Personalize the rankings of search results based on individual's research interests	49.68%
Enter a query and receive results in your own native language	30.57%

The Needs for Real-Time Notification. In academic environments, most DLs have improved the contents recommendation based on users' subscriptions. Through the Q21, most users preferred the recommendation about articles (85.99%), journals (70.06%), and conferences (60.51%). We compared the different groups of user's needs about real-time notification through Q24.

From Fig. 5, the North America users needed the notification about upcoming ACM conference mostly (78.95%), but the users from Europe had more requirements about call for special issue (88.89%). As for East Asia users, they wished get more support

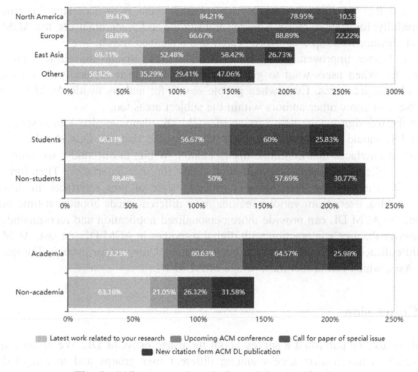

Fig. 5. Different users' needs for real-time notification.

about latest work related to their researches (69.31%). In total, the users from Europe and North America had more needs for real-time notification. Interestingly, the non-student users concentrated on latest work than the student users. This might be because most users from the non-student group are university faculty members.

5 Discussions

This study investigated the different users' information access barriers when using the current ACM DL, and studied their attitudes and willingness towards personalized features inside the new version of ACM DL. Our findings can help ACM DL understand the challenges they faced and the opportunities they can enhance the service level.

As for the challenges of ACM DL, users need more support about the collection format, not just the PDF files. ACM DL can enhance their access about various resources, such as the datasets, figures, and tables inside papers, and supplementary materials. For instance, they should provide more resources in HTML 5 format for users in Europe and users of the student group and academia group. It can help these users complete their information tasks better. In the aspect of information access methods, ACM DL should focus on functions of searching and browsing. Many users expressed that there were many barriers prevent them from accessing information successfully; for users in North America and Europe and academia users, the ACM DL should enhance its simple keyword search and advanced search.

The further improvement of the DL should be around the subject areas of ACM DL. When users want to get updated on some areas, naturally they look for particular subject areas. Even when people search for authors inside ACM DL, they may want to know other authors within the subject areas too.

In the redesign for the new version of ACM DL, there are also some aspects that ACM DL should focus. Previous work [5] proposed that the DLs should develop consistent interfaces that minimize disorientation. While, in our study, we found that users in different regions have different needs for user interfaces. Therefore, the ACM DL can consider developing a different style of user interfaces in different regions. Also, users from various regions have different needs about real-time notification; the ACM DL can provide more personalized notification and recommendation to improve the user's interaction with digital resources in ACM DL. At last, ACM DL should enhance the multilingual information retrieval support for users in Europe and East Asia, which can attract more usage of ACM DL.

6 Conclusion

In this study, we published a survey about the usage of ACM DL. We compared the difference in information access among different user groups and investigated the different users' attitudes and needs towards personalized function to improve the DL's services. Through the analysis of results, we proposal some insights on how to improve the new version of ACM DL. The ACM DL serves diverse user communities and thus needs to develop appropriate interfaces for varied users and needs. The limitation of this study is mainly at the analysis of survey. Due to the design of the survey, we could not use statistical methods to examine the results.

Acknowledgement. This work is an outcome of project "User Seeking Behavior Modeling and Search Technology Development Within Multi-Device Integrated Search Environment" (No. 71673204) supported by National Natural Science Foundation of China.

References

1. Arms, W.: Digital Libraries. MIT Press, Cambridge (2000)
2. Witten, I.H., Bainbridge, D., Nichols, D.M.: How to Build a Digital Library. Morgan Kaufmann, San Francisco (2009)
3. ACM Digital Library. https://dl.acm.org/. Accessed 10 Sept 2019
4. Next ACM Digital Library. https://dlnext.acm.org/. Accessed 19 Sept 2019
5. Marchionini, G., Plaisant, C., Komlodi, A.: Interfaces and tools for the Library of Congress national digital library program. Inf. Process. Manag. **34**(5), 535–555 (1998)
6. Dinet, J., Favart, M., Passerault, J.M.: Searching for information in an online public access catalogue (OPAC): the impacts of information search expertise on the use of Boolean operators. J. Comput. Assist. Learn. **20**(5), 338–346 (2004)

7. Jiang, T., Wang, M., Gao, H.: A search log analysis of OPAC users' searching behavior-a case study of Wuhan University library. Doc. Inf. Knowl. **167**, 46–56 (2015)
8. Islamaj Dogan, R., Murray, G.C., Névéol, A., Lu, Z.: Understanding PubMed® user search behavior through log analysis. Database (2009)
9. Toms, E.G., Dufour, C., Hesemeier, S.: Measuring the user's experience with digital libraries. In: Proceedings of the 4th ACM/IEEE-CS Joint Conference on Digital Libraries, pp. 51–52. ACM, New York (2004)
10. Dongzhi, B.: Current situation and influence of the three network convergence. China New Telecommun. **4**, 5–10 (2010)
11. Franke, M., Geyer-Schulz, A., Neumann, A.: Building recommendations from random walks on library OPAC usage data. In: Zani, S., Cerioli, A., Riani, M., Vichi, M. (eds.) Data Analysis, Classification and the Forward Search. Studies in Classification, Data Analysis, and Knowledge Organization, pp. 235–246. Springer, Heidelberg. (2006). https://doi.org/10.1007/3-540-35978-8_27
12. Willson, R., Given, L.M.: The effect of spelling and retrieval system familiarity on search behavior in online public access catalogs: a mixed methods study. J. Am. Soc. Inf. Sci. Technol. **61**(12), 2461–2476 (2010)
13. Hutchinson, H.B., Bederson, B.B., Druin, A.: The evolution of the international children's digital library searching and browsing interface. In: Proceedings of the Conference on Interaction Design and Children, pp. 105–112. ACM, New York (2006)
14. A Survey about ACM Digital Library Usage. https://www.wjx.cn/jq/39294761.aspx. Accessed 19 Sept 2019

Watching, Playing, Making, Learning: Young Children's Use of Mobile Devices

Kirsten Schlebbe[✉] [iD]

Humboldt-Universität zu Berlin, Unter den Linden 6, 10099 Berlin, Germany
schlebbe@ibi.hu-berlin.de

Abstract. Mobile devices provide additional opportunities for families with young children to seek, exchange, and use information. This paper presents an exploratory interview study with representatives from 19 families. The goal of the study was to examine how young children and their families use mobile devices and whether this usage includes information seeking activities or other activities that can be linked to the children's information behavior. Results indicate that the children show a great variety of information-related activities while using the mobile devices. Activities that may appear as pure entertainment at first glance also have to be considered in the context of the children's information behavior. The results contribute to a better understanding of young children's experiences in relation to mobile devices and raise new questions about the information behavior of young children in general.

Keywords: Children · Information behavior · Mobile devices

1 Introduction

Young children's use of mobile devices has steadily increased during the last decade [1]. Whether parents use a Wikipedia entry to show their children what a specific animal looks like or children engage in video chatting with their grandparents, mobile devices provide various opportunities for families to seek, exchange, and use information.

This paper presents an exploratory interview study with representatives from 19 families with children aged one to six years from Germany, Denmark, and Italy. The goal of the study was to explore the following questions from an information science perspective:

RQ1: How do children aged one to six years use mobile devices?
RQ2: Does this usage include information seeking activities or other activities that can be linked to the children's information behavior?

The preliminary results presented in this paper contribute to a better understanding of young children's experiences in relation to digital and especially mobile devices and raise new questions about the information behavior of young children in general.

The paper is organized as follows. Section 2 presents an overview of relevant research about young children's use of mobile devices and their information behavior. Section 3 describes the methodology of the study. Section 4 presents and discusses the

© Springer Nature Switzerland AG 2020
A. Sundqvist et al. (Eds.): iConference 2020, LNCS 12051, pp. 288–296, 2020.
https://doi.org/10.1007/978-3-030-43687-2_23

results of the interviews. In Sect. 5 the outcomes of the study are summarized and an outlook on further research is given.

2 Relevant Research

2.1 Young Children's Use of Mobile Devices

A *mobile device* can be defined as, "a portable, wireless computing device, possible to carry without additional equipment and small enough to be used while held in the hand" (p. 197) [2]. Typical examples of such devices are smartphones and tablets.

Between 2011 and 2017, the proportion of American households with children eight years of age and younger possessing at least one mobile device increased from 52% to 98%. 42% of the children in this age group owned a tablet and 4% a smartphone. The amount of time children spend with the devices each day has tripled since 2011. As of 2017, children were spending an average of 48 min per day on mobile devices. When children used these devices, they spent most of their time watching TV or videos followed by playing mobile games [1].

In Germany, these numbers are comparatively lower. In 2019, 2% of four to five year old children owned a tablet and only 1% had a smartphone. However, the shared use of mobile devices in families was significantly higher, with about 20% of children aged four to five being allowed to co-use a tablet and/or smartphone [3].

These studies show that a growing percentage of young children regularly use mobile devices for different activities. In light of these findings, we must now ask: how does the use of mobile devices impact the information behavior of children and their families?

2.2 Studying Young Children's Information Behavior and Practices

Various studies have examined the information behavior of children and young adults, but this research tends to focus on school-aged children and adolescents (*e.g.,* [4–11]). As a consequence, younger children are underrepresented in the field of information behavior research [12, 13].

In recent years there have been some important efforts to correct this gap in the research. Barriage and Searles [14] conducted a study examining the information seeking activities in family interactions of ten girls between the ages of three and six years. Their results indicate that "information seeking typically occurs in response to ongoing talk and action, with few instances of information seeking unrelated to the locally immediate context of the family interactions" (p. 1). Barriage [15] also conducted a survey with 31 parents whose children were between the ages of four and eight years to examine young children's everyday life information practices related to their hobbies and interests. She found that "young children exhibit a heavy reliance on interpersonal interactions for information seeking and information sharing, while information use is more likely to be an individual activity" (n.pag.).

While these studies are dealing with the information practices of young children in general, other researchers have focused specifically on children's behavior in the digital environment. Agarwal [16] examined the use of touch devices by toddlers and preschoolers through a single-case study. His results indicate, among other things, that the child experienced information overload and distraction while using the devices. Given *et al.* [12] studied the everyday life information seeking of 15 Australian children three to five years old in the home, using video recordings of the children's interaction with information technologies. Their results show that the "children engage in artistic and sociodramatic play, as well as early literacy and numeracy activities [...]" and, in this way, "gather information to shape future learning activities" (p. 349).

While previous studies have begun to investigate young children's information practices in general as well as their activities in the digital environment from an information science perspective, further studies are urgently needed to gain deeper insight.

3   Method

This research is part of a larger study looking at the information behavior of young children in relation to their use of mobile devices. This short paper reports of the preliminary results of 19 semi-structured exploratory interviews with 22 parents of 19 families with 22 children aged one to six years who had prior experience using mobile devices. A later stage of the research project will focus on the children's perspectives.

The interviews were conducted over a period of nine months. Participants were recruited through a combination of convenience and snowball sampling. Sixteen of the families lived in Germany, two families were in Denmark, and one was in Northern Italy. Because of the geographic distribution of the participants, six interviews were carried out face-to-face, three by video call, and ten by phone. Two interviews were conducted in English, and 17 interviews were conducted in German. The quotes included in this article were translated from the original language into English. The length of the interviews varied between 30 and 60 min. In three cases both parents took part in the interview. In nine cases only the mother and in seven cases only the father of the family was questioned. Table 1 describes the study sample in detail.

Ten of the children were female and twelve male. Regarding the examined ages, the sample had a strong focus on the age of three to five years, with 17 of 22 children in this range. Two children were six years old, three children were younger than three years. Seven of the families had additional younger and/or older children, which were not included in the study since they did not belong to the age group examined.

The questions during the interviews focused on two main areas. The first set of questions concerned the technological equipment available to the children, the general use of the devices (*e.g.*, frequency, duration, and context of use) and specific applications and functions used. The second set of questions focused on the information-related activities of the children linked to the equipment.

Table 1. Study sample.

Fam.	Children[a] (age in years)	Siblings (age in years)	Interviewee/s	Resid.	Lang.
A	Anna (5) ♀	–	Father	DK	en
B	Bo (5) ♂	Brother (16)	Mother	DK	en
C	Christian (4) ♂	–	Mother	DE	de
D	Diana (5) ♀, Daniel (4) ♂	–	Father & Mother	DE	de
E	Eric (1) ♂	–	Mother	DE	de
F	Finn (3) ♂	Brother (7)	Father & Mother	DE	de
G	Greta (4) ♀	Twins (<1)	Father	DE	de
H	Henry (3) ♂	Sister (<1)	Father	DE	de
I	Isabell (6) ♀	–	Father	DE	de
J	Jacob (5) ♂, Julia (3) ♀	–	Mother	DE	de
K	Karla (2) ♀	–	Mother	DE	de
L	Louis (2) ♂	–	Mother	DE	de
M	Max (3) ♂	Brothers (<1, 11), Sister (13)	Father	DE	de
N	Nina (6) ♀, Nora (4) ♀	–	Father	DE	de
O	Olivia (3) ♀	–	Mother	DE	de
P	Paul (3) ♂	Twins (<1)	Mother	DE	de
Q	Quentin (3) ♂	–	Father	DE	de
R	Robert (5) ♂	–	Father & Mother	DE	de
S	Sina (4) ♀	Brother (7)	Mother	IT	de

[a]For the purpose of anonymization, the children were given pseudonyms.

All interviews were recorded and transcribed verbatim. For the analysis of the data, different coding methods were combined with a focus on descriptive coding [17]. The software MAXQDA was used for transcribing and analyzing the data.

The limitations of the study should also be mentioned. A larger and more diverse sample would have been desirable. The exploratory approach and the relatively broad age range led to a strong heterogeneity of the results. For a subsequent study, it would be useful to limit the investigation to a more specific age group and selected usage contexts. Especially critical is the fact that the children's perspective was only indirectly taken into account. Therefore, a follow-up study is currently being prepared to address the points of criticism mentioned above.

In the following section, the preliminary results of the data analysis are presented and discussed.

4   Results and Discussion

4.1   Children's General Use of Mobile Devices

The definition of a *mobile device* was kept relatively open during the interviews. The interview questions focused on the use of tablets and smartphones, but many parents also talked about other portable devices such as laptop computers or digital cameras.

All 22 children have already used a tablet and 20 children have used a smartphone at least in some form. In general, the different mobile devices could be assigned to different functions and usage contexts. While the tablet was rather seen as a device for the whole family, the smartphones were regarded as the parents' devices and were used less often by the children. Only a few children (4) possessed their own mobile devices in the form of specific tablets designed for children.

The majority of the children used mobile devices regularly, ranging anywhere from daily to about once a week. Only two of the families had a more limited use of mobile devices. In these families, the children used mobile devices very rarely and at irregular times. One of these cases was the youngest child in the sample (Eric, 1.5 years). Some use cases were part of the families' daily routine, such as watching children's TV series at bedtime or playing with an app while the parents were cooking dinner. Other activities such as taking photos happened more spontaneously or only in particular situations.

While the older children were allowed to use the devices at least in part alone, the younger children were usually supervised by the parents. One reason for this may be that the younger children were often dependent on the help of their parents when using the devices, while the older children generally showed more independence.

Since most of the children were not able to read or write yet, they navigated through visual features like icons or thumbnails. Four families reported that their children had used voice control before.

4.2   Children's Activities and Preferences

The interviews with the parents indicated that their children engaged in a great variety of activities related to the mobile devices. Tablets and smartphones were seen as all-in-one solutions that work as a television, a computer, a communication device, and a camera at the same time. The children used the devices to watch online videos, play with various apps, listen to music, video chat with family and friends, and to look at photos or videos or to take pictures themselves. Figure 1 shows the activities of the children mentioned by the parents during the interviews. The size of the boxes depends on the number of children who have already performed these activities, according to their parents.

Communication via digital devices was mentioned by all interviewees, but this was in most cases strongly supervised and directed by the parents. Some families also preferred to use a laptop computer for this purpose. Overall, the children in this study engaged in passive activities such as watching videos or looking at photos and/or videos rather than in more interactive activities such as playing games, drawing, or making music. However, a majority of the children (16 of 22) had used mobile devices

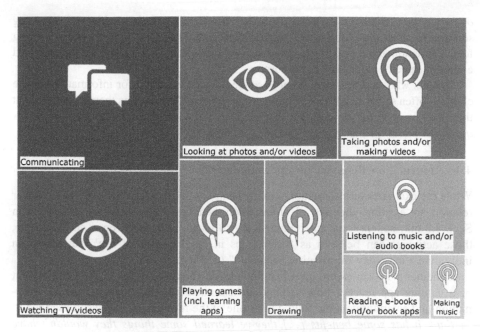

Fig. 1. Children's activities mentioned by the parents.

for taking photos and making of videos, two activities that are more interactive than passive.

It is important to mention that some activities were carried out rarely (*e.g.*, reading book apps) and others almost daily (*e.g.*, watching videos). According to the parents, watching TV/videos, playing games, looking at photos and/or videos, and communicating were the most common activities for the majority of the children. Regarding the total amount of time children spent with the devices, watching TV/videos took up the largest proportion of time in many families. These results are consistent with earlier studies [1]. However, it should be noted that these aspects were strongly dependent on the child's interests and age as well as on the parents' rules. As a consequence, the behavior of some children differed from this standard profile.

4.3 Parents as Search Assistants

Using the devices for typical information seeking activities, *e.g.*, using search engines or online encyclopedias, was named by half of the families interviewed. However, these activities were mentioned only after follow-up questions from the interviewer and took place irregularly and in situations where there was a specific information need.

In these situations, the parents acted as search assistants or lay information mediaries [18] for their children. Often pictures or videos of things unknown to the child were searched for: *"This is what I do together with the children and show them: This is what a whale looks like or, um, [...] something like an ibex [...] you can show a picture or a little video, how the ibex actually walks around in the mountains and not in a cage or something"* (Father D). Other examples mentioned included using web mapping services to show the children the geographic location of a specific place or searching for information about events the children would like to visit. Usually, the parents used common search engines for these purposes.

Parents who said that they do not use the devices to search for information for the children often stated that they can answer their children's questions themselves and that they do not need the devices for this purpose: *"I think I can easily answer all his questions myself at the moment [laughs]"* (Father Q).

4.4   Information Behavior or Entertainment

While the examples of information seeking behavior described in Sect. 4.3 have a clear relation to existing theories of information behavior, the activities described in Sect. 4.2 may appear to be entertainment at first glance. But as Given *et al.* [12] argue, those activities can be seen as "early steps in the 'mastery of life' that define an individual's everyday information behaviors" (p. 346).

Whether a TV series provides first knowledge about the work of a fire department or a gaming app teaches how to play an instrument, the boundaries between information and entertainment are fluid. Or, as one of the mothers interviewed described it: *"I think it has some benefits [...] they've learned some things they wouldn't have learned if they didn't consume it. [...] For example, there's Pixi, a TV series, and it's all about facts. [...] they've learned a lot from it...they've definitely expanded their knowledge."* (Mother J).

Case and Given [19] also refer to the confluence of information and entertainment and notice: "The conceptual overlap is not new, but rather something we used to gloss over in studying information behavior" (p. 133).

5   Conclusion and Future Work

The goal of the study presented in this paper was to examine how young children and their families use mobile devices and whether this usage includes information seeking activities or other activities that can be linked to the children's information behavior. Therefore, an exploratory interview study with parents of children aged one to six years who had prior experience with mobile devices was conducted.

Results indicate that the children show a great variety of information-related activities while using the mobile devices. Typical information seeking activities were named by half of the families interviewed. In these situations, the parents acted as search assistants for their children. Watching TV or videos, playing games, looking at photos and/or videos and communicating were the most common activities for the majority of the children. As already mentioned above, these activities that may appear as pure entertainment at first glance must also be considered in the context of young children's information behavior. In this area, further research is certainly needed.

Another interesting aspect that could not be discussed in this paper but will be examined in a more in-depth analysis in the future was the impact of parental influence. The interviews showed that parents greatly influenced the children's use of the devices by limiting the frequency and duration of use as well as the access to particular content. This raises questions about whether this parental influence also has an impact on the children's information behavior, not only in the digital context, but also with regard to the general information behavior of young children.

References

1. Rideout, V.: The Common Sense census: media use by kids age zero to eight. Common Sense Media, San Francisco (2017)
2. Stal, J., Paliwoda-Pękosz, G.: A SWOT analysis of using mobile technology in knowledge providing in organisations. In: International Conference on ICT Management for Global Competitiveness and Economic Growth in Emerging Economies (ICTM2018), Wrocław, Poland, 22–23 October 2018 (2018)
3. Kinder Medien Studie (2019). https://kinder-medien-studie.de/wp-content/uploads/2019/08/KMS2019_Berichtsband.pdf. Accessed 13 Sept 2019
4. Agosto, D.E., Hughes-Hassell, S.: People, places, and questions: an investigation of the everyday life information-seeking behaviors of urban young adults. Libr. Inf. Sci. Res. 27(2), 141–163 (2005)
5. Bilal, D., Kirby, J.: Differences and similarities in information seeking: children and adults as Web users. Inf. Process. Manag. 38(5), 649–670 (2002)
6. Cooper, L.Z.: A case study of information-seeking behavior in 7-year-old children in a semistructured situation. J. Am. Soc. Inf. Sci. Technol. 53(11), 904–922 (2002)
7. Foss, E., et al.: Children's search roles at home: implications for designers, researchers, educators, and parents. J. Am. Soc. Inf. Sci. Technol. 63, 558–573 (2012)
8. Meyers, E.M., Fisher, K.E., Marcoux, E.: Making sense of an information world: the everyday-life information behavior of preteens. Libr. Q. 79(3), 301–341 (2009)
9. Todd, R.J.: Adolescents of the information age: patterns of information seeking and use, and implications for information professionals. Sch. Libr. Worldwide 9(2), 27–46 (2003)
10. Vanderschantz, N., Hinze, A., Cunningham, S.J.: "Sometimes the internet reads the question wrong": children's search strategies & difficulties. Proc. Am. Soc. Inf. Sci. Technol. 51(1), 1–10 (2014)
11. Vanderschantz, N., Hinze, A.: A study of children's search query formulation habits. In: Proceedings of the 31st International BCS Human Computer Interaction Conference (2017). Article 7
12. Given, L., Winkler, D.C., Willson, R., Davidson, C., Danby, S., Thorpe, K.: Watching young children "play" with information technology: everyday life information seeking in the home. Libr. Inf. Sci. Res. 38, 344–352 (2016)
13. Spink, A., Heinström, J.: Information behaviour development in early childhood. In: Spink, A., Heinström, J. (eds.) New Directions in Information Behaviour, pp. 245–256. Emerald, Bingley (2011)
14. Barriage, S.C., Searles, D.K.: Astronauts and sugar beets: young girls' information seeking in family interactions. In: Grove, A. (ed.) Proceedings of the 78th ASIS&T Annual Meeting: Information Science with Impact: Research in and for the Community. Richard B. Hill, Silver Spring (2015). Article 27
15. Barriage, S.: 'Talk, talk and more talk': parental perceptions of young children's information practices related to their hobbies and interests. Inf. Res. 21(3) (2015). Paper 721. http://InformationR.net/ir/21-3/paper721.html

16. Agarwal, N.K.: Use of touch devices by toddlers or preschoolers: observations and findings from a single-case study. In: Bilal, D., Beheshti, J. (eds.) New Directions in Children's and Adolescent's Information Behavior Research, pp. 3–37. Emerald, Bingley (2014)
17. Saldaña, J.: The Coding Manual for Qualitative Researchers, 2nd edn. Sage, Thousand Oaks (2013)
18. Abrahamson, J.A., Fisher, K.E.: 'What's past is prologue': towards a general model of lay information mediary behaviour. Inf. Res. **12**(4), 1–21 (2007)
19. Case, D., Given, L.M.: Looking for Information. A Survey of Research on Information Seeking, Needs, and Behavior, 4th edn. Emerald, Bingley (2016)

How Likely Are College Students to Be Influenced by Others in Small-Group Projects: A Study on Group Compositions and Coursework-Related Collaborative Information Seeking Behavior

Tien-I Tsai[1](✉) and Chun-Hsien Chuang[2]

[1] National Taiwan University, Taipei 10617, Taiwan
titsai@ntu.edu.tw
[2] National Taiwan University Library, Taipei 10617, Taiwan

Abstract. Small-group teaching has been a preferred pedagogy in many college-level courses. It is crucial for college students to seek information with peers in their small groups to achieve their learning goals. While peer influence has been proven as one of the factors in students' information seeking behavior, the role of group compositions in collaborative information seeking remains unclear. In order to reveal how college students are influenced by their peers in their collaborative information seeking process in real-life situations, the current study used a multi-mode survey design to collect data. Five-hundred and thirty-five students participated in the survey. Results showed that while homogeneous and heterogeneous groups regarding gender and disciplinary compositions were evenly distributed, most groups were homogeneous regarding students' year of study. When collaboratively seeking information for a small-group project, students typically agreed that other peers in the group influenced their collaborative information behavior. While gathering information, students especially considered peers' opinions; they also tended to give up information if their peers do not need it, especially when in a homogeneous group. However, in heterogeneous groups, students tended to change the sources consulted when gathering information. Pedagogical implications and suggestions for future research were provided.

Keywords: Information behavior · Collaborative information behavior · Group compositions

1 Introduction

Small-group teaching has been a preferred pedagogy in many universities [1]. With this pedagogy, small-group projects are widely used in course planning, and thus most college students have experiences working in small-group projects. While working in small groups, it is essential for students to gather information needed with their peers to accomplish their tasks and to fulfill their course requirements.

© Springer Nature Switzerland AG 2020
A. Sundqvist et al. (Eds.): iConference 2020, LNCS 12051, pp. 297–304, 2020.
https://doi.org/10.1007/978-3-030-43687-2_24

When discussing effective small-group teaching or small-group project planning, higher education research emphasizes the dynamics of group compositions [2]. And the group composition can be discussed by group members' demographics such as gender, age, and ethnicity [3]. In college settings, group compositions are typically discussed by students' gender, ethnicity, study levels/year-of-study, disciplines, skills, or academic performance [4, 5]. However, in the current study setting, college students were less diverse in ethnicity, and it is more difficult to measure their skills or performance across different areas of study. The current study focuses on group compositions in terms of students' gender, study levels, and disciplines.

While many studies argued heterogeneous groups have their benefits on students' learning, other studies argued the other way around [4]. It remains unclear how group compositions are related to students' collaborative information behavior in small-group projects.

Collaborative information seeking can be broadly defined as seeking information towards the same goals with a group of people [6–9]. Drawing upon Shah's series of collaborative information seeking studies, the contexts of collaborative information seeking are typically complex and require group decision making [6–8]. Peer influence is one of the crucial factors in individuals' information behavior [10]. When discussing collaborative information seeking, peer influence could be even more important, and it is worthy of study. Nevertheless, relevant studies typically introduce students' own demographics rather than their group compositions [e.g., 8, 9].

Furthermore, previous studies typically investigating collaborative information seeking either used an experiment to evaluate how an information system perform to enhance collaborative information seeking [6–8], or interviewed a small number of participants regarding their collaborative information seeking processes [9]. Only very few studies examined how peers influence plays a role in college students' information seeking behavior [11]. The current study aims to investigate students' perceptions of their collaborative information seeking behavior in non-hypothetical situations. The critical incident technique was used in our survey design to help college students recall their collaborative information seeking in their real-life learning experiences.

The research questions of the current study are as follows:

(1) How likely are students influenced by other peers in the small group while collaboratively seeking information for coursework-related projects?

(2) Do students within different group compositions (in terms of gender, study level, and discipline) tend to be influenced by other peers in the small group to a different extent while collaboratively seeking information for their projects?

2 Methods

2.1 Data Collection

In order to enhance the response rate of the survey, the current study used a multi-mode survey design—web survey and print survey—to collect data. After one round of pilot testing and revisions, the web survey was distributed through many university Facebook groups and pages, as well as the university bulletin board system (BBS; a popular online forum). Flyers with a QRcode to the survey link were distributed across the dorms on campus. Researchers' own personal connections were also used to disseminate the web survey. The print questionnaire was distributed in various courses offered by different departments with the permission of the instructor.

The survey instrument consisted of three major parts: (1) background questions regarding students' small-group projects, (2) how students were influenced by other peers in their small groups while seeking information for the project, and (3) students' demographic information. And critical incident technique was used to help students recall their collaborative information seeking experience. Students were asked to answer the questions based on their successful small-group project experience during the past year. Prior to the formal questionnaire questions, a set of filtering questions were set to make sure that participants all had experience working in a small-group project during the past year. And the small-group project meets the following criteria: the small group were with a size of 3 to 6 students (including themselves); the project lasted between 3 to 6 months (half to whole semester) in length; the small-group project is for completing a for-credit formal course offered by the department of the university. Questions regarding students' small-group projects mainly included: information about the course, the type of the project, the number of students in the small group, group composition in terms of gender, study level (underclassmen and upperclassmen), and discipline. Questions regarding how students were influenced by other peers while seeking information were developed base on Pern (2010) [11] and included six items (see results and discussion). Demographic questions included: gender, study level, and discipline.

2.2 Participants

Participants of the current study were college students at a research university in Northern Taiwan. While underclassmen (50.8%) and upperclassmen (49.2%) were quite evenly distributed, more female students (65.2%) participated in the current study. And according to the Ministry of Education discipline categories, nearly half of the students were from soft disciplines—humanities and social sciences (44.9%). Nearly one-third were from hard-applied sciences (30.7%). About one-fifth were from soft-applied disciplines—law and business (17.8%), and only 6.7% from hard sciences. Although the distribution of the study participants did not reflect the university population, this may reflect the disciplines that require students to work on long-term small-group projects in courses.

2.3 Data Analysis

After cleaning the data, 535 valid responses were used for data analysis. An overview of students' demographics and group compositions were first analyzed with descriptive statistics. The extent to which students were influenced by other group members while selecting information sources was also examined by descriptive statistics.

The current study aims to investigate whether or not students within homogeneous and heterogeneous groups perform differently in their collaborative information seeking behavior. Each group composition variables (i.e., gender composition, study-level composition, and disciplinary composition) were first categorized into homogeneous and heterogeneous groups (i.e., all-male/all-female vs. mixed-gender groups; all-underclassmen/all-upperclassmen vs. mixed-level groups; same-discipline vs. cross-discipline groups). T-tests were then performed to analyze whether or not students within different group compositions were influenced by other group members to a different extent.

3   Results and Discussion

3.1   Group Compositions

Homogeneous and heterogeneous groups were identified based on students' gender, study-level (year-of-study), and disciplinary compositions. As shown in Table 1, homogeneous and heterogeneous groups regarding gender and disciplinary composition were more evenly distributed than the study-level composition. Most groups were homogeneous groups in terms of their study-level compositions. One possible explanation is that college courses typically targeting students in a certain year of study. However, most elective courses in the study setting take students from sophomores, juniors, and seniors. And due to students' own course planning (e.g., planning for a double major/minor, obtaining a specialty certificate, etc.), it is also very common for students to take their required courses in the year other than as planned by the department. Given that most groups were formed by students themselves, students supposed to have the opportunities to form mixed-level groups. However, they seemed not to do so. Although more detailed evidence was needed, this phenomenon may reveal that students tend to form their groups with peers in the same year of study.

Table 1. Overview of group compositions.

Group composition	Homogeneous groups	Heterogeneous groups
Gender composition	45.2%	**54.8%**
Study-level composition	**72.7%**	27.3%
Disciplinary composition	**50.8%**	49.2%

3.2   Influence of Peers on Collaborative Information Seeking

Students were asked to what extent they agree or disagree with the six statements regarding how they were influenced by other peers in the small group during their collaborative information seeking process for the coursework-related project. As shown in Fig. 1, every single item was rated with an average above 3 (neutral). This means when working collaboratively, students typically agreed that their collaborative information behavior was influenced by other peers in the small group.

Specifically, "giving up information when it is not needed by peers" was rated the highest among all six items ($M = 4.39$, $SD = 0.81$). When gathering information, students tended to "corroborate thoughts with peers" ($M = 4.17$, $SD = 0.61$) and

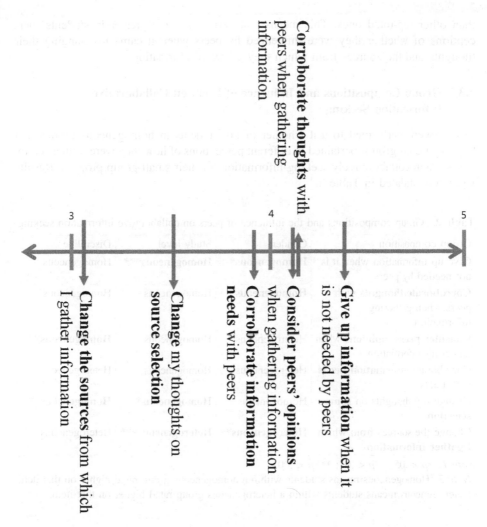

Fig. 1. Overview of the extent to which students were influenced by their peers in the small groups when collaboratively seeking information. *Note:* All items were rated by students on a 5-point Likert scale where 1 = strongly disagree and 5 = strongly agree. Vertical gray lines = 3, 4, and 5. The length of the vertical arrows indicates the standard deviation of each item.

"consider peers' opinions" ($M = 4.16$, $SD = 0.71$). Students also tended to corroborate their information needs with peers ($M = 3.97$, SD = 0.69). In spite of the above items, students were less likely to change their thoughts on source selection ($M = 3.53$, $SD = 1.04$) or change the sources from which they gather information ($M = 3.12$, $SD = 1.01$).

It is interesting that, in general, students seemed to take peers' thoughts and opinions into serious consideration but somewhat retained their own thoughts on source selection and their own ways of gathering information. Nevertheless, it is also worthy of notice that the standard deviations of the lower-rated two items were higher than other top-rated ones. This means that variations were greater in students' perceptions of whether they were influenced by peers when it came to changing their thoughts and the sources from which they gathered information.

3.3   Group Compositions and Influence of Peers on Collaborative Information Seeking

T-tests were performed to test whether or not students in homogeneous groups and heterogeneous groups pertained to different perceptions of how they were influenced by peers when collaboratively seeking information for their small-group projects. Results were consolidated in Table 2.

Table 2. Group compositions and the influence of peers on collaborative information seeking.

Group composition	Gender	Study level	Discipline
Give up information when it is not needed by peers	**Homogeneous***	**Homogeneous*****	Homogeneous
Corroborate thoughts with peers when gathering information	**Homogeneous***	Homogeneous	Homogeneous
Consider peers' opinions when gathering information	Heterogeneous	Homogeneous	**Homogeneous****
Corroborate **information needs** with peers	Heterogeneous	Homogeneous	Heterogeneous
Change my thoughts on **source selection**	Homogeneous	**Homogeneous***	**Homogeneous*****
Change the sources from which I **gather information**	**Heterogeneous****	**Heterogeneous*****	Heterogeneous

Note 1: $*p < .05$; $**p < .01$; $***p < .001$

Note 2: Homogeneous means students within a homogeneous group rated higher on that item; Heterogeneous means students within a heterogeneous group rated higher on that item.

No matter which types of homogeneous groups students were in, it seemed that students were more likely to be influenced by peers when it comes to giving up information, corroborating thoughts with peers, or changing their thoughts on source selection. When in a heterogeneous group, students were more likely to change the sources from which they gather information.

Specifically, comparing to their counterparts in the heterogeneous groups, students in same-gender groups were especially likely to give up information when not needed by peers ($p < .05$) and to corroborate thoughts with peers ($p < .05$); students in the same-study-level groups were also more likely to give up information when not needed by their peers ($p < .001$); students in same-discipline groups were more likely to consider peers' opinions ($p < .01$). It is interesting that students were more likely to change their thoughts on source selection in same-study-level groups ($p < .05$) and in same-discipline groups ($p < .001$). This phenomenon can be explained by studies arguing that same-gender students may have good rapports and interactions [3, 12], and same-age students are easily communicated [13]. Students could possibly trust their peers in homogeneous groups and may not want to generate potential conflicts. Thus, students may give up information not needed by other peers and consider other peers' thoughts. On the other hand, students in mixed-gender groups ($p < .01$) and mixed study-level groups ($p < .001$) were especially more likely to change the sources from which they gather information. Although changing the sources while gathering information may not always be good, it could be an important learning process for students to try different sources in their information seeking processes.

4 Conclusion

When forming small groups for a course project, students may form either homogeneous or heterogeneous groups regarding gender and discipline, but they tended to form a homogeneous group regarding study level/year of study. When seeking information collaboratively for a small-group project, students typically agreed that their collaborative information behavior was influenced by other peers in the group. Students especially took peers' thoughts and opinions into consideration while gathering information, and tended to give up information if it is not needed by their peers. The above situations happened especially when in a homogeneous group. When in a heterogeneous group, students tended to change the sources from which they gather information.

As suggested in the findings of the current study, within a mixed-study-level group, students seemed to be encouraged to try different sources in their collaborative information seeking processes. However, students tended not to form mixed-study-level groups while working on their small-group projects. It is important for instructors to facilitate heterogeneous group formation in class. Specifically, before group formation, it would be important for the instructor not only to encourage students to form heterogeneous groups but also to spend some course time helping students know one another.

Future studies can further expand the questionnaire and incorporate interviews into the study design so that these phenomena can be further explained. For instance, the current study was not able to judge whether more positive or negative influences were brought to the students based on the ratings of items in the questionnaire. It would also be intriguing for future studies to use an action study design to evaluate how group compositions are related to their project performance in classroom settings throughout the semester. Although some studies (e.g., Jensen & Lawson, 2011) argue that heterogeneous groups may not work as well as that has been proven in the Western culture [4], the current study reveals that heterogeneous groups may have its value inspiring students to try to take different actions on their information seeking behavior.

Even if the current study used critical incident technique and asked students to recall a successful small-group project, the current study only focused on exploring a general overview of how college students were influenced by other peers within different group compositions. It was not able to prove which group compositions are more effective than others and/or how group compositions may affect their performance on small-group projects. Future studies can further examine how students' group compositions and their collaborative information seeking behavior are related to their project outcomes in order to further discuss whether or not heterogeneous groups work better than homogeneous groups. Overall, the study findings still shed some light on small-group pedagogy and serve as a foundation of future research on college students' coursework-related collaborative information seeking behavior.

References

1. Mills, D., Alexander, P.: Small Group Teaching: a Toolkit for Learning. The Higher Education Academy, York (2013)
2. Jaques, D.: Learning in Groups: a Handbook for Improving Group Work, 3rd edn. RoutledgeFalmer, London (2004)
3. Williams, K.Y., O'Reilly, C.A.: Demography and diversity in organizations: a review of 40 years of research. Res. Organ. Behav. **20**, 77–140 (1998)
4. Jensen, J.L., Lawson, A.: Effects of collaborative group composition and Inquiry instruction on reasoning gains and achievement in undergraduate biology. CBE Life Sci. Educ. **10**(1), 64–73 (2011)
5. Moore, R.L.: The effect of group composition on individual student performance in an introductory economics course. J. Econ. Educ. **42**(2), 120–135 (2011)
6. Shah, C.: Collaborative Information Seeking: the Art and Science of Making the Whole Greater than the Sum of All. Springer, Berlin (2012). https://doi.org/10.1007/978-3-642-28813-5
7. Shah, C.: Collaborative information seeking. J. Assoc. Inf. Sci. Technol. **65**(2), 215–236 (2014)
8. Hansen, P., Shah, C., Klas, C.-P. (eds.): Collaborative Information Seeking: Best Practices, New Domains and New Thoughts. Springer, Heidelberg (2015). https://doi.org/10.1007/978-3-319-18988-8
9. Wu, M.-M., Foster, J.: Exploring factors for collaborative group investigation. J. Educ. Media Libr. Sci. **47**(2), 123–146 (2009)
10. Lancaster, F.W.: Needs, Demands, and Motivation in the Use of Sources of Information. University of Illinois at Urbana—Champaign (1995)
11. Pern, K.-J.: Factors Influencing Consideration of Information Behaviours of Undergraduate Students: Taken Tamkang University as Example. Master's thesis. Tamkang University, Taiwan (2010)
12. Alagna, S.W., Reddy, D.M., Collins, D.: Perceptions of functioning in mixed-sex and male medical training groups. Acad. Med. **57**(10), 801–803 (1982)
13. Schaffer, S.P., Chen, X., Zhu, X., Oakes, W.C.: Self-efficacy for cross-disciplinary learning in project-based teams. J. Eng. Educ. **101**(1), 92–94 (2012)

Information Literacy

Educating for Democracy? The Role of Media and Information Literacy Education for Pupils in Swedish Compulsory School

Hanna Carlsson[1]([ID]) and Olof Sundin[2]([ID])

[1] Department of Cultural Sciences, Linnaeus University, 351 95 Växjö, Sweden
hanna.carlsson@lnu.se
[2] Lund University, 221 00 Lund, Sweden

Abstract. This paper reports a study of pupils' experiences of media and information literacy education in five Swedish schools by answering the following overarching question, *what roles do the teaching of information seeking and critical assessment of information play for pupils in their school-work as well as in their everyday life?* Pupils in ninth grade were asked to fill in a questionnaire regarding their use of digital technology as well as their thoughts on media and information literacy education. The study shows that many pupils are knowledgeable about the terms of production pertaining to *content* in most online sources they mention. Still, infrastructural meaning-making that take into consideration issues of personalization, data integrity and surveillance, are largely lacking. The study also shows that the school's teaching is central to the pupils' development of a critical stance towards the information that they encounter online. These findings underline the importance of how schools choose to treat media and information literacy education. It is concerning then that infrastructural meaning-making is quite absent in the pupils' responses.

Keywords: Media and information literacy · Infrastructural Meaning-making · Information search

1 Introduction

Today's globalized information age is characterized by an ever-increasing wealth of information. Accompanying this information growth is an equally mounting proportion of misinformation, forming part of a changed information infrastructure that among other things blurs the boundaries between producer and consumer and where the influence of commercial platforms and algorithms is steadily increasing. The role played by propaganda and so-called fake news in the 2016 American president election, as well as the construction of the expression "alternative facts" could be seen as illustrative examples of this development, a development that brings the importance of critical assessment of information in a democratic society to the fore. This paper reports a study of pupils' experiences of media and information literacy education in five Swedish schools by answering the following overarching question, *what roles do the teaching of information seeking and critical assessment of information play for pupils in their school work as well as in their everyday life?* We argue that to possess

© Springer Nature Switzerland AG 2020
A. Sundqvist et al. (Eds.): iConference 2020, LNCS 12051, pp. 307–326, 2020.
https://doi.org/10.1007/978-3-030-43687-2_25

knowledge about the infrastructure from which information is gained and to be able to make use of this knowledge in everyday life should be recognized as corner stones of active citizenship in a democracy of our times.

Compulsory school plays an important role for making sure that everyone has an equal opportunity to critically assess information in order to make those well-informed choices that the liberal democracy depends upon. We argue that compulsory schooling also should provide pupils with intellectual tools for unpacking the information infrastructure that not only partakes in shaping how they learn and live but also co-shapes the basis of contemporary society. However, previous research points to the difficulties of making information seeking (IS) and critical assessment of information (CAI) a part of teaching and learning (e.g. Gross and Latham 2009; Rieh and Hilligoss 2008; Sundin 2015; Sundin and Carlsson 2016). Hence, more research is called for in order to gain more knowledge on this topic.

Sweden makes an interesting case for this study since adjusting compulsory school to, and preparing pupils for the digitized society is a high-profile area. At the same time Sweden is reported to be one of the countries where Russian propaganda is spread in both traditional media and social media (Kragh and Åsberg 2017). Sweden holds a long tradition of embracing inquiry-based learning, accompanied by new technologies for information seeking in the classroom (Alexandersson and Limberg 2012). This peda-gogical turn has arguably contributed to making information seeking and critical perspectives on and assessment of information important fields of knowledge in Swedish schools. In contemporary Swedish educational policy digital literacy is addressed not merely as a question of being able to use digital technology but also as a question of ensuring that pupils have the tools to take a critical stance in a democratic society (e.g. The Swedish Ministry of Education 2017).

Although information seeking and critical assessment of information are mentioned in relation to most subjects in the Swedish national curriculum, they are particularly pointed out as essential fields of knowledge for Swedish and Civics and are here explicitly related to the question of democracy. Hence, how information seeking and critical assessment of information are learned in relation to these subjects is the focus of this study. We chose to focus on pupils in ninth grade, which is the last compulsory grade in the Swedish school system. The pupils are then between fourteen and fifteen years old. In Sweden, most young people of that age can be expected to have their own smartphone and to use social media and search-engines frequently. Furthermore, most Swedish schools, including the schools in this study, provide pupils with personal laptops or tablets through so-called 1 to 1 initiatives. Swedish nine graders can thus be expected to encounter and handle vast amounts of information of various kinds both in and out of school. This, along with almost having fulfilled their compulsory schooling and as such should be "fully trained" by the Swedish school system in IS and CAI, made us choose pupils of this grade for participation in the study.

2   Research on Media and Information Literacy in School Settings

The student-centered pedagogy has co-developed with a growing awareness in information studies research of students' increased responsibility for IS CAI, as well as of the development of these into fields of knowledge being taught and assessed by educators (Alexandersson and Limberg 2012). How pupils seek and assess information are consequently widely studied phenomena within information studies. Several research projects have studied IS and CAI as objects of teaching and learning. For instance, Kuhlthau (2004) as well as Limberg and her colleagues (e.g. Lundh and Limberg 2008; Limberg and Alexandersson 2010; see also Rieh et al. 2016) have pointed to the connections between IS and learning. Several studies also point to challenges with student-centered pedagogy by showing pupils' troubles when seeking information (e.g. Gross and Latham 2012; Large et al. 2008; Pan et al. 2007). Francke et al. (2011) claim that pupils tend to identify IS as searching for facts, at the expense of a more overall understanding of a topic (c.f. Blikstad-Balas and Hvistendahl 2013; Todd 2006). Additionally, previous research has shown that pupils often have a simple understanding of facts and tend to construct a dichotomy between facts and opinions (Alexandersson and Limberg 2003). Furthermore, earlier research has consistently confirmed a relationship between low proficiency and overestimation of competence in relation to information literacy (Gross and Latham 2012; Mahmood 2016).

Another starting point for research on IS and CAI in school settings in recent years has been the increasing significance of digital technology and the use of social media and search engines that has changed the information infrastructure of schools considerably (c.f. Sundin and Carlsson 2016). Research on online searching and information literacy demonstrates the difficulties pupils have in critically assessing information (Francke and Sundin 2012; Julien and Barker 2009; Rieh and Hilligoss 2008). An interest in online searching in relation to literacy is not widely spread outside information studies, but there are exceptions. For example, the educational scholars Morrison and Barton (2018) argue for the need to develop search engine literacy training and communication studies scholars Hargittai et al. (2010) show how assessment of information already starts when choosing a search engine.

Moreover, several studies point to the struggles pupils have in understanding how search engines work (c.f. Sundin and Carlsson 2016; Julien and Barker 2009). Andersson (2017) shows in her ethnographic study of how teenagers search for information that Google is often invisible to young people and primarily associated with school assignments. As pointed out by Sundin and colleagues, search engines today constitute an infrastructure that has become so naturalized that it is often taken for granted (Sundin et al. 2017; Haider and Sundin 2019) and as such they represent new and different challenges for information literacy education. In conclusion, this points to the importance of updating the teaching of IS and CAI in compulsory school in order to adapt it to the changing ways in which knowledge is being used, produced and communicated in society today (Francke and Sundin 2016).

3 Infrastructural Meaning-Making

A concept guiding the analysis presented in this paper is that of information infrastructure, here understood as "networks constituting the conditions for knowing and hence constructing what is to be known, the importance of this knowledge and how it can be accessed and stored" (Sundin and Carlsson 2016, p. 990). Conceptualizing information – and the conditions for how it is disseminated, accessed and stored – as infrastructure, allows for an analysis of media and information literacy (MIL) education that recognizes information and knowledge production as co-constructed by material, and social structures both shaping and being shaped by society (Haider and Sundin 2019; c.f. Bowker 1994, 1996). In contemporary society those material and social structures are deeply ingrained in the capitalist ideology. Hence, the information infrastructure cannot be meaningfully approached, analytically nor empirically, without recognizing that a few commercial actors, such as Google, Amazon, Facebook, Apple and Microsoft, and their business models for commodifying information access, now control this central feature of society. Plantin et al. (2018, p. 295) describe this in terms of a dialectic development as "the platformization of infrastructure and the infrastructuralization of platforms". Building on the work of Plantin and colleagues, we here deploy the concept of platform in order to recognize the influence of the capitalist spirit (cf. Mager 2012) and its consequences for the current information infrastructure.

Established understandings of MIL have been criticized for failing to embrace the whole palette of critical dimensions that the platformized information infrastructure presents us with. Such critical dimensions concern for instance the opaqueness of search engines and the algorithmic governance of social media flows. In their book *Invisible search and Online Search Engines*, Haider and Sundin (2019) argue for what they refer to as infrastructural meaning-making as a way of addressing some of the limitations identified when MIL is applied to the platformized information infrastructure of today. With the analytical concept of infrastructural meaning-making Haider and Sundin (2019) claim that making sense of the platformized information infrastructure involves not only to posses the skills for finding and being able to critically assess information and information sources. It equally involves being able to problematize the perceived neutrality of algorithm driven search and to understand why specifically you encounter particular information. Talking about infrastructural meaning-making then is in every aspect a socio-technical approach to MIL that brings together meaning, materiality, trust, skills and understanding in an assemblage situated in the specific cultural and societal conditions of the capitalist information age.

Having said the latter, Haider and Sundin also argue for the need to accept the limitations of educating MIL. You do not convert someone who holds a strong belief in the anti-vax movement with MIL education. In fact, as Boyd (2017) argues, education for MIL could actually reinforce the problem it was supposed to solve. MIL is also about trust and trust takes time to emerge. An interest in trust makes clear that MIL is not (only) an individual ability. For the purpose of this study the concept of infrastructural meaning-making is used normatively, as a way of framing aspects that we believe that a MIL education with democratizing ambitions ought to consider. An important aspect of this meaning-making is the ability to take a critical stance, however, equally important is to be able to have a reasonable trust in those societal institutions, e.g. universities, schools and libraries, that produce knowledge at the same time as the critical perspective is not thrown overboard. To trust information and to critically assess information are to some extent two practices in conflict with each other.

4 Method

The findings reported in this paper form part of a larger study that was conducted during spring 2017. The larger study comprised data from interviews with teachers and librarians, textual analysis and a questionnaire directed at pupils, and was conducted at five schools situated in southern Sweden.[1] Including several schools allowed for comparisons that made explicit more general patterns as well as particularities in the individual schools. For the purpose of this paper, we focus on the perceptions of the participating pupils expressed in the questionnaire. When selecting schools for the study we looked for schools of different size and location as well as with different forms of management (both private and public). Although the five schools that finally agreed to participate do meet the initial criteria for selection, it should be noted that despite their differences the schools also share many characteristics. It should also be noted that common attitudes or a formal policy regarding how IS and CAI should be approached and taught is not always present at the participating schools. This means that our findings foremost reflect the attitudes and experiences of individual pupils, although the schools and their different settings provide a necessary and regulating framework for both teaching and learning, that probably affects the answers we received. Table 1 gives an overview of the participating schools.

In order to get a rich and broad picture of the pupils' perspectives on how IS and CAI are taught and learned at the different schools, pupils in ninth grade were asked to fill in a questionnaire with questions regarding their use of digital technology as well as their thoughts on MIL education. Only pupils of those teachers that chose to participate in the study were offered to fill in the questionnaire. Hence, the number of participating pupils varies between the schools (see Table 1). Both pupils and parents were informed about the study in advance and that participation was voluntary. Altogether 37 pupils chose not to participate, whereas 231 did participate. The questionnaires were answered during class with one of the researchers present to answer questions. The research complies with the ethical guidelines in Good Research Practice (Swedish Research Council 2017).

The questionnaire consisted of nineteen questions, out of which eight were altogether qualitative and text based. Eleven questions were multiple-choice, with the possibility to comment one's answer. The length and reflective quality of the text-based answers and comments varied greatly both between pupils and between schools. Pupils from school 4 rarely commented or answered the text-based questions whereas pupils

---

[1] Carlsson and Sundin (2017). Sök- och källkritik i grundskolan. En forskningsrapport [Search critique and critical assessment of information in compulsory school. A research report]. Lund: Lunds universitet.

Table 1. Participating schools

School	Private/public	Total no. of pupils	Pupils in 9th grade	No. of participating pupils
1	Private	≈400	≈60	17
2	Public	≈520	≈60	57
3	Private	≈540	≈50	47
4	Public	≈600	≈130	91
5	Public	≈850	≈90	27
Total		≈2910	≈430	231

from school 2 and 5 generally provided extensive and rich comments and answers. Due to these differences, school 2 and 5 are more visible when findings are presented and discussed. When the text-based answers are quoted, the authors have translated these parts of the material into English. Some grammatical adjustments have been made to facilitate readability.

In a first step of the analysis of the questionnaires the answers of the multiple-choice questions were compiled using SPSS, whereas the text-based answers and comments were analyzed through careful and repeated readings in order to establish common themes for each school as well as for the sample as a whole. At the second step of analysis the results from the questionnaires were analyzed with a closer attention paid to the theoretical perspective.

5   Pupils' Perspectives on Information Seeking and Critical Assessment of Information

5.1   Tools and Platforms for Information Seeking in School

In order to gain a deeper understanding of how Swedish nine graders interact with and make sense of the contemporary information infrastructure, the pupils where asked about what tools and platforms they use when looking for information to be used for school assignments. Regarding tools a majority of the participating pupils state that they use a laptop or tablet provided by school. It is also quite common to use one's own, or a parent's smartphone tablet or laptop. Only 2% state that they use a public desktop in the classroom or the school library (Appendix Table 2). It is interesting to note the high use of private mobile devices, which suggest that these pupils mainly interact with the information infrastructure through exceedingly customized and personalized interfaces, in line with the platformization of infrastructure, pointed out by Plantin et al. (2018).

Regarding platforms used in the given context, most respondents state that they turn to Wikipedia followed by search-engines such as Google and Bing and NE.se – the Swedish national encyclopedia online, YouTube and online forums. Social media are rarely used by the respondents in the given context (Appendix Table 3). In the following, we comment some of the platforms. The extensive use of Wikipedia is not surprising. Previous research show that people put considerable trust in ranking lists of search engines (Pan et al. 2007; cf. Kammerer and Gerjets 2012), and regularly choose from the first hits (Pan 2009). Wikipedia often turns up at the top of those lists (Höchstötter and Lewandowski 2009) and is as such a convenient choice. As stated by one of the respondents "I also use Wikipedia since the platform is quite big and usually when you search for some information, Wikipedia always turns up as the first alternative" (PS2).

Pupils that comment on their choice of YouTube refer to the advantages of being able to encounter information orally and as moving images. As expressed by one pupil: "[i]f I use YouTube to find facts /.../ you can find teachers that talk about the thing you're looking for" (PS3). Others remark that YouTube is not a platform where one starts one's search, rather one is directed to YouTube through links from other sites. The answers indicate an awareness of the diversity of the platform and how it can be used differently for different purposes.

In their written comments, the pupils in many cases have reflexive discussions about to their usage of most platforms. In this sense, those who commented, appear to be quite knowledgeable about some conditions of the current information infrastructure, and express strategies for handling its challenges. Still, the pupils' focus is mostly on evaluating the credibility of the content of the information they encounter on these platforms rather than demonstrating any infrastructural meaning-making. Comments that express awareness of a more contextualized critique, involving questions such as "Why do I encounter this information at all", (cf. Sundin and Haider 2016) are largely lacking.

Google does not seem to be neither promoted nor banned by teachers. Rather, Google appears more to be a naturalized tool, which echoes findings of previous studies that point to how Google has become an invisible part of everyday life (c.f. Sundin et al. 2017; Haider and Sundin 2019). When comparing to how the pupils discuss and reflect on their use of search engines with their use of the other platforms, search engines are not addressed with the same amount of critical awareness regarding credibility, function and terms of production. Even if some pupils recognize how the search engine works, the pupils appear to put a lot of trust in Google, which also corresponds well with findings in previous research (cf. Sundin and Carlsson 2016).

> Google is not in itself a source of information but a search engine. One can with the help from Google find sources easier. Usually Google automatically sorts and orders sites and links so that the most relevant ends up at the top and when it comes to a topic where information changes often or news come up, Google makes sure to show the most relevant, to make searching easier. If a company or a site has paid Google to end up higher on the site (which benefits both sides, Google & the company), this is made explicit. So the risk of getting irrelevant information without knowing it is low.
>
> *PS2*

Given the absence of contextualizing discussions of Google and social media, that take into consideration for instance issues of personalization, data integrity and surveillance, there is reason to believe that this type of critique has not been prevalent in the MIL education that the pupils have attended. Pupils' perceptions of this education are discussed in the next section.

5.2   The Pupils' Perceptions of MIL Education

Most of the pupils in the present study state that they have been taught about CAI and IS. Only 7 pupils stated that they had not received any such education (Appendix Table 4). Those pupils who gave a positive response were asked to elaborate on their education, how it was done, what it contained and important things they learned. Their answers vary greatly. Several indicate that they cannot remember how the teaching was organized or what it contained while others made extensive descriptions of more or less detail.

> At school we have had CAI every now and then. One time we had a test in Civics where we would review a source and write if we thought it was relevant or not. We have also learned about CAI in general and learned that it is very important to review the sources we use. In addition, sometimes when we do assignments in Civics and Science we have to critically assess the sources we used.
>
> *PS2*

The vast majority of pupils who answered the text-based question describe that they had been taught how to value the credibility of a source while only a few describe that they had been taught about IS. One pupil describes that in the teaching of IS they had to learn "[h]ow one seeks facts and information in the easiest way. The use of key words and how to filter the answers" (PS2). Another pupil writes that they had been taught, "how you search on Google to find what you are looking for, for example by removing certain words you do not want to include, etc." (PS1).

When students are more specific about what they have learned, certain things come up frequently, for example, to always compare different sources, to be critical of online forums and social media and instead use NE.se [a Swedish commercial encyclopaedia], as well as being aware of the author's intention for writing the text. Running through the answers are descriptions of checklists of various kind that correspond with the traditional criteria for source criticism: authenticity, time, dependence and tendency: "Who has written the text? Why was the text written? When is the text written? e.g. language, sincerity. Are there more sources that state the same thing?" (PS5) The text-based responses give the impression that the pupils have a more or less vague picture of the content of the education of IS and CAI that they received during seventh to ninth grade. Previous research has pointed to the difficulties of making these activities a part of teaching and learning (e.g. Limberg and Sundin 2006), which might partly explain why the pupils have such vague memories of this part of their education. However, those who answered have quite a clear picture of what they have learned, which is largely expressed in the form of checklists for the critical assessment of text-based information. Checklists, such as these, have been criticized in the information literacy literature, among other things, for not considering contextual aspects (Meola 2004; cf. Elmborg 2006; Tuominen et al. 2005).

A large majority of the pupils' state to have use for what they have learned about IS and CAI when working with school assignments (Appendix Table 5). However, there are various reasons why the pupils find what they have learned useful. Some find this knowledge important because school assignments require credible facts and information. One pupil expresses that "for every writing task that requires you to have relevant and correct facts I use the different methods I learned in school to find credible facts"

(PS5). Others point out that CAI forms part of the basis for their grade. For some however, the education seems superfluous. "Most of what I've learned from the teaching of CAI, I believe, falls under 'common sense'" (PS5).

5.3 Pupil's Perceptions of Their Own Abilities

A majority of the pupils' states that they perceive of themselves as good or very good at searching for information for school assignments online (Appendix Table 6). The pupils were also asked about their ability to critically assess online information. Here too, the majority of pupils estimates their ability to be good, but fewer perceive of themselves as "great", in comparison with the ability to search for information (Appendix Table 7). These results correspond well with results from investigations where similar questions have been posed to Swedish teenagers about their abilities regarding CAI. (e.g. The Swedish Ministry of Education 2016) as well as with earlier research (Gross and Latham 2012; Mahmood 2016).

A few pupils have chosen to comment their answers. In their comments some pupils express doubts in relation to their ability to critically assess information, as exemplified below.

> I consider myself to be critical of what I read, because I've seen so many facts that are wrong on the Internet. My weakness is people I look up to that I would easily believe no matter what they say, and when I simply want to look for small stuff, it could be that I just turn to the first ever site.
>
>   *PS3*

This type of self-critical approach is not expressed in relation to the ability of searching for information, which confirms the results of the multiple-choice questions. This may indicate that the pupils are not aware of the difficulties and critical dimensions of IS, to the same extent, as they are when it comes to CAI. For some, to be good at searching for information simply means finding what you are looking for. One pupil writes "I rarely have trouble finding facts for my assignments and therefore consider myself okay at online information searching" (PS2). A few also refers to a broader experience of Internet use: "Because we work digitally all the time in school, I'm very used to navigating information on the Internet" (PS2). There are also examples of including more query related aspects: "I find it easy to know what I should enter in the search box in order to find the information I'm looking for" (PS3). From the comments it appears that IS is primarily understood as a technical skill.

Furthermore, the ability of IS is often enmeshed or confused with the ability to critically assess information. One pupil gives the following comment to the question: "Do you think you are good at searching for news, facts and information for school information online?"

> I'm not world class. But it works well because I ask myself questions that show whether the source(s) have true theories or not. The questions are, for example, who is the owner of the source? Can you get in touch with him? Have many other sources written similar things? Are there any connections between the sources? Why was the source created? WHEN was the source created is almost always the most important. Is it an open source (who can change and type text) or is it perhaps that the source is a blog or the like where many can state their opinions?
>
>   *PS2*

From the pupils' answers, IS stands out as a mean to an end and not as an object of learning in its own right. It is compared to the critical assessment of sources, quite invisible (Sundin and Carlsson 2016; Haider and Sundin 2019).

5.4   The Role of MIL Education in Pupils' Everyday Life

The increased use of digital tools and platforms by young people means that they get access to information in new ways also outside school (cf. Andersson 2017). When the pupils in the present study were asked about what tools they used for information searching in their spare time, the majority indicated that they use their own phone. Many also state that they use their own computer and/or tablet (Appendix Table 8). When asked what platforms they use in their leisure time, social media and search engines are at the top of the list (Appendix Table 9). In a text-based question, students were asked to share what they do when using the platforms. The answers show that they are used for different purposes, which roughly can be divided into four categories: entertainment, socializing and staying in touch with family and friends, searching for information and facts and keeping up to date. One pupil writes:

> The social media I use are mostly to check updates about everyday things that my friends post. I use Snapchat to talk to my friends. I use Youtube for entertainment and sometimes information. In case I want to find out something in particular I use Google and Wikipedia.
>
> *PS2*

Another pupil expresses herself as follows:

> I almost only ticked the boxes for social media as they are the services I use a lot in my spare time to stay in touch with friends and family. Googling things is something you do every day, to find something or simply because you're bored. When I use Facebook it's for chatting with other people. There are many links to articles on Facebook but most are unreasonable "click-bait" to get readers. Youtube I use to watch videos for entertainment. I usually go to different forums, once again mostly for entertainment.
>
> *PS5*

The quotes above point to the difficulty of associating platforms with certain parts of life. Search engines, Wikipedia and Youtube are the services used extensively both at school and in pupils' everyday life (Appendix Table 9). Many pupils critically assess and discuss the information they encounter and use in their spare time. More than half (67%) of the pupils' state that they always or sometimes come across information that they question whether they can trust when they are online. Several pupils also express that they relate critically to the content of discussions with friends and acquaintances on, for example, Snapchat.

> On snapchat, you can't believe everything you hear, or what people want you to believe (e.g. that rape victims are lying and a convicted rapist being innocent). I'm always critical when it comes to information people post on snapchat, and I try to constantly get as much information as possible, from both parties, when there's, for example, some dispute or fight mentioned.
>
> *PS2*

In the quote above, the pupil talks about how she applies the methods the school teaches of CAI, to assess information and rumors in social media in her spare time. This indicates that the school's teaching may be influential outside the classroom. Another student expresses this even more clearly.

> I use social media daily like Instagram and twitter and there you get a lot of information, I usually trust blindly what it says but lately, because of the work we have done in school I've become more critical of everything I read there. I know that information rarely is checked and it's easy to lie on social media.
>
> *PS2*

In the questionnaire the pupils were explicitly asked if they felt that the school's teaching of IS and CAI was useful for them even in their spare time. More than half indicate that this is the case to some extent (Appendix Table 10). The vast majority also states that they have only been educated about IS and CAI in school.

> I've learned all the techniques I know from school. Before I learned about critical assessment of information, I believed everything online, even though it was completely absurd. I thought that if you wrote something, it had to be true.
>
> *PS2*

Those who specify alternatives highlight that they learned from the advice of parents, or other family members, as well as friends or through own experiences of encountering false information online. Otherwise, there are occasional examples of pupils stressing, for instance, events in the media as alternative sources of knowledge to the school's teaching.

The text-based responses indicate that the school's teaching is central to the pupils' development of a critical stance towards the information they encounter online. For those pupils who have parents that discuss the issue, this more informal education appears to play an important role. However, merely a few mentions that they get this support at home. These findings underline the importance of how schools choose to treat IS and CAI as objects of teaching and learning. It is concerning then that the infrastructural meaning-making we argue for is largely lacking.

6 Discussion and Conclusions

The results from this study give insight into how pupils, that are about to finish Swedish compulsory school, reason about information search and critical assessment of information, and the role played by school in these matters. Many pupils who provided comments demonstrate a quite impressive awareness about certain aspects of the information infrastructure they depend on for their education and in everyday life. Our analysis shows that the pupils are knowledgeable about the terms of production pertaining to *content* in most online sources they mention, such as social media and Wikipedia, and appear to be trained to compare different sources in order to establish the credibility and trustworthiness of the information they find and encounter. These aspects are of great importance and should be expected to be captured by MIL education in a digital age. Still, the infrastructural meaning-making that we argue to be equally important, is not present in the pupils' responses to any larger extent. One reason for this could be that although social media, Wikipedia and online forums are examples of peer-to-peer production enabled by digital technology, in relation to critical assessment of information, they are more easily translated and compared to the conditions of print media. In a sense Wikipedia and social media are remediations of newspapers and encyclopedias from a previous print-based information infrastructure, albeit of course with different material conditions for the production and dissemination of information. Critical assessment can then conveniently be turned into a question of authorship and establishing provenience in relation to content, by applying criteria that draw on traditional source criticism in the shape of checklists.

Search engines arguably order knowledge in ways that evade notions of a remediation of a print-based information infrastructure. How this ordering works, that this ordering even takes place, is largely black boxed and invisible and thus much more difficult to grasp and capture in MIL education. Google's ranking list comes off as a neutral given, and not as a result of culturally situated algorithmic governance (Haider and Sundin 2019). Hence, although questions of authorship and content of course are still relevant, they need to be supplemented by other forms of understanding assessment, which traditional criteria for source criticism fail to capture. This requires knowledge of the platformized information infrastructure that not all teachers are likely to possess, which in our findings are illustrated by the pupils' lack of discussions of these issues. Given the importance pupils state that the schools' instruction on critical assessment of information has, this is a problem that needs to be addressed.

Related to the invisibility of search engines is the invisibility of search as an object of critique and learning, which has been observed also in previous research (Sundin 2015; Sundin and Carlsson 2016). Most pupils in this study state that they perceive of themselves as good at both finding and assessing information, but there is a tendency to embed searching into critical assessment or to treat it as merely a set of practical skills. Although these activities cannot be meaningfully teased apart, when failing to treat them as separate phenomena, pupils run the risk of not capturing the critical aspects of search, which is an important aspect of infrastructural meaning-making.

As pointed out in the introduction of this paper, active citizenship requires the ability to understand the complexity of the current information infrastructure. It is important to note here that infrastructural meaning-making is not merely about critique – it is also about trust (Haider and Sundin 2019). The findings of this study do not give any clear picture of how the pupils navigate between these positions. What we can tell is that they have learned to be critical towards information they encounter online. Whether Swedish compulsory school has succeeded in also building that trust in society's knowledge institutions, that democracy depends on, is for another study to find out. The important job of building trust is however not simply a task for MIL education, not even for compulsory schooling. It is a political undertaking for society at large.

The pupils participating in this study express to have skills and competences to handle some challenges that the contemporary information infrastructure poses, still important pieces of the puzzle, that is infra-structural meaning-making, appear to be missing. The most important conclusion drawn from this study then is that we must turn talk about the importance of information search and critical assessment of information into action and discuss what it actually can be, how it should be taught and what it means to be media and information literate in contemporary society.

Appendix 1: Tables of Results

Table 2. Tools for formation seeking in school

Tool	Total no. of pupils	%
Private phone	118	49,4
Private tablet	45	18,3
Private computer/laptop	113	47,3
Tablet from school	32	13,4
Computer/laptop from school	177	74,1
Public desktop	6	2,5
Other	11	4,6

Table 3. Platforms for information seeking in school

Service	Total no. of pupils	%
Search engines	192	80
NE.se	157	66
Wikipedia	193	81
Instagram	5	2
Facebook	13	5
YouTube	91	38
Twitter	6	3
Snapchat	7	3
Online newspapers	114	48
Online forums	36	15
Other	17	7

Table 4. Have you, as you recall it, being taught about critical assessment of information and information seeking during your xxx school years?

	Total no. of pupils	%
Yes	124	52
Yes, but not a lot	80	34
Neither little nor a lot	18	8
No, not at all	7	3
Don't know	7	3
No reply	3	1
Total	239	100

Table 5. Have you had use for what they you've learned about information searching and critical assessment of information when working with school assignments?

	Total no. of pupils	%
Yes, always	94	39
Yes, sometimes	97	41
No, seldom	20	8
No, not at all	5	2
Don't know	19	8
No reply	4	2
Total	239	100

Table 6. Do you think of yourself as good at searching for facts, news and information for school assignments online?

	Total no. of pupils	%
Yes, very good	101	42
Yes, ok	115	48
Neither good nor bad	12	5
No, not so good	6	3
No, not good at all	3	1
No reply	2	1
Total	239	100

Table 7. Do you think you are good at deciding if you can trust news, facts and information you find online?

	Total no. of pupils	%
Yes, very good	62	26
Yes, ok	139	58
Neither good nor bad	32	13
No, not so good	3	1
No, not good at all	1	1
No reply	2	1
Total	239	100

Table 8. Which of the following tools do you usually use in your spare time? You can tick multiple options

Tool	Total no. of pupils	%
Private phone	214	90
Private tablet	62	26
Private computer/laptop	151	63
Borrowed tablet	13	5
Borrowed laptop	41	17
Borrowed desktop	6	3
Family computer	22	9
Other	18	8
No reply	3	1

Table 9. Which of the following platforms do you usually use in your spare time? You can tick multiple options.

Service	Total no. of pupils	%
Search engines	178	75
NE.se	43	18
Wikipedia	113	47
Instagram	155	65
Facebook	138	58
YouTube	194	81
Twitter	46	19
Snapchat	160	67
Online newspapers	80	34
Online forums	55	23
Other	15	6
No reply	3	1

Table 10. Do you feel that you have use for what you have learned in school about information searching and critical assessment of information school when you're online in your spare time, for example when Googling or using Social Media?

	Total no. of pupils	%
Yes, always	50	21
Yes, sometimes	103	43
No, seldom	47	20
No, not at all	14	6
Don't know	17	7
No reply	8	3

Appendix 2: Questionnaire for Pupils, Year 9, Spring Semester 2017, Translated from Swedish

By answering this questionnaire, I agree to participate in the study *Search critique and critical assessment of information in compulsory school* (see information letter).

First, we kindly ask you to answer some questions about searching for and critically assessing information in school.

1. Which of the following tools do you usually use to search for information and facts online in relation to school assignments? You can tick several options.

   ☐ Private phone
   ☐ Private tablet
   ☐ Private computer/laptop
   ☐ Tablet from school
   ☐ Computer/laptop from school
   ☐ Public desktop
   ☐ Other

2. Which of the following platforms do you usually use to search for information and facts on the Internet in relation to school assignments? You can tick several options.

   ☐ Google, bing or other search engine
   ☐ NE.se
   ☐ Wikipedia
   ☐ Instagram
   ☐ Facebook
   ☐ Youtube
   ☐ Twitter
   ☐ Snapchat
   ☐ Online newspapers (e.g. Dagens nyheter, Sydsvenskan, Svenska dagbladet [Swe. dish newspapers])
   ☐ Online forums (e.g. Flashback)
   ☐ Other

3. Tell us why you choose use the services you ticked in question 2 to search for facts and information on the internet in relation to school assignments.

4. Tell us why you do not choose to use certain services mentioned in question 2 to search for news, facts and information in relation to school assignments.

5. Do you think of yourself as good at searching for facts, news and information for school assignments online?

   ☐ Yes, very good
   ☐ Yes, ok
   ☐ Neither good, nor bad
   ☐ No, not so good
   ☐ No, not good at all

6. Do you think you are good at deciding if you can trust news, facts and information you find online?

   ☐ Yes, very good
   ☐ Yes, ok
   ☐ Neither good, nor bad
   ☐ No, not so good
   ☐ No, not good at all

7. Have you, as you recall it, being taught about critical assessment of information and information seeking during your xxx school years?

   ☐ Yes
   ☐ Yes, but not a lot
   ☐ Neither little nor a lot
   ☐ No, not at all
   ☐ Don't know

8. If you have been taught about critical assessment of information and information seeking, tell us about how it was done and what it contained

9. If you have been taught about critical assessment of information and information seeking, make a list of five important things you learned.

10. If you have been taught about critical assessment of information and information seeking, do you recall any school librarian being involved?

   ☐ Yes
   ☐ No
   ☐ Don't know
   ☐ My school do not have a school librarian

11. Have you had use for what they you've learned about information searching and critical assessment of information when working with school assignments?

   ☐ Yes, always
   ☐ Yes, sometimes
   ☐ No, seldom
   ☐ No, not at all
   ☐ Don't know

12. Which of the following tools do you usually use in your spare time? You can tick multiple options.

☐ Private phone
☐ Private tablet
☐ Private computer/laptop
☐ Tablet from school
☐ Computer/laptop from school
☐ Public desktop
☐ Other

13. Which of the following platforms do you usually use in your spare time? You can tick multiple options.

☐ Google, bing or other search engine
☐ NE.se
☐ Wikipedia
☐ Instagram
☐ Facebook
☐ Youtube
☐ Twitter
☐ Snapchat
☐ Online newspapers (e.g. Dagens nyheter, Sydsvenskan, Svenska dagbladet [Swedish newspapers])
☐ Online forums (e.g. Flashback)
☐ Other

14. Tell us about what you do when you use the platforms you ticked in question 13

15. Do you come across news, facts, or other information that you question whether you can trust when using the platforms, you ticked in question 13?

☐ Yes, always
☐ Yes, sometimes
☐ No, seldom
☐ No, not at all
☐ Don't know

16. If you answered yes to question 15, please give examples on one or several occasions when such a thing happened

17. Do you feel that you have use for what you have learned in school about information searching and critical assessment of information school when you're online in your spare time, for example when Googling or using Social Media?

☐ Yes, always
☐ Yes, sometimes
☐ No, seldom
☐ No, not at all
☐ Don't know

18. Apart from the school's teaching, tell us about other ways that you have learned to decide whether you can trust information you encounter online?

19. Do you have any tricks that you have learned outside school that you use to decide whether you can trust information you encounter online? Tell us about them here.

References

Alexandersson, M., Limberg, L.: Constructing meaning through information artefacts. New Rev. Inf. Behav. Res. **4**, 17–30 (2003)

Alexandersson, M., Limberg, L.: Changing conditions for information use and learning in swedish schools: a synthesis of research. HumanIT **11**(2), 131–154 (2012)

Andersson, C.: The front and backstage: pupils' information activities in secondary school. Inf. Res. **22**(1) (2017). CoLIS paper 1604 http://InformationR.net/ir/22-1/colis/colis1604.html. Accessed 12 Sept 2019

Blikstad-Balas, M., Hvistendahl, R.: Students' digital strategies and shortcuts. Nord. J. Digit. Lit. **8**(1), 32–48 (2013)

Bowker, G.C.: Science on the Run: Information Management and Industrial Geophysics at Schlumberger, 1920-1940. MIT Press, Cambridge (1994)

Bowker, G.C.: The history of information infrastructures: the case of the international classification of diseases. Inf. Process. Manag. **32**(1), 49–61 (1996)

Boyd, D.: Did media literacy backfire? J. Appl. Youth Stud. **1**(4), 83 (2017)

Elmborg, J.: Critical information literacy: implications for instructional practice. J. Acad. Librariansh. **32**(2), 192–199 (2006)

Francke, H., Sundin, O., Limberg, L.: Debating credibility: the shaping of information literacies in upper secondary schools. J. Doc. **67**(4), 675–694 (2011)

Francke, H., Sundin, O.: Negotiating the role of sources: educators' conceptions of credibility in participatory media. Libr. Inf. Sci. Res. **34**(3), 169–175 (2012)

Francke, H., Sundin, O.: Del 4: Källkritik och nya publiceringsformer. Modul: Kritisk användning av nätet [Part 4: Critical assessment and new forms of publication. Modul: Critical use of the net]. The Swedish Ministry of Education, Stockholm (2016)

Gross, M., Latham, D.: What's skill got to do with it?: information literacy skills and self-views of ability among first-year college students. J. Am. Soc. Inform. Sci. Technol. **63**(3), 574–583 (2012)

Gross, M., Latham, D.: Undergraduate perceptions of information literacy: defining, attaining, and self-assessing skills. Coll. Res. Libr. (2009)

Haider, J., Sundin, O.: Invisible Search and Online Search Engines. The Ubiquity of Search in Everyday Life. Routledge, New York (2019)

Hargittai, E., Fullerton, L., Menchen-Trevino, E., Thomas, K.Y.: Trust online: young adults' evaluation of web content. Int. J. Commun. **4**(27), 468–494 (2010)

Höchstötter, N., Levandowski, D.: What users see: structures in search engine results pages. Inf. Sci. **179**(12), 1796–1812 (2009)

Julien, H., Barker, S.: How high school students evaluate scientific information: a basis for information literacy skills development. Libr. Inf. Sci. Res. **31**(1), 12–17 (2009)

Kammerer, Y., Gerjets, P.: How search engine users evaluate and select web search results: the impact of the search engine interface on credibility assessments. In: Lewandowski, D. (ed.) Web Search Engine Research, pp. 251–279. Emerald, Bingley (2012)

Kuhlthau, C.: Seeking Meaning: A Process Approach to Library and Information Services, 2nd edn. Libraries Unlimited, Westport (2004)

Large, A., Nesset, V., Beheshti, J.: Children as information seekers: what researchers tell us. New Rev. Child. Lit. Librariansh. **14**(2), 121–140 (2008)

Limberg, L., Sundin, O.: Teaching information seeking: relating information literacy education to theories of information behaviour. Inf. Res. **12**(1) (2006). http://informationr.net/ir/12-1/paper280.html. Accessed 12 Sept 2019

Limberg, L., Alexandersson, M.: Learning and information seeking. In: Bates, M.J., Maack, M. N. (eds.) Encyclopedia of Library and Information Science, 3rd edn. Taylor & Francis, New York (2010)

Lundh, A., Limberg, L.: Information practices in elementary school. Libri: Int. J. Libr. Inf. Serv. **58**(2), 92–101 (2008)

Mager, A.: Algorithmic ideology. How capitalist society shapes search-engines. Inf. Commun. Soc. **15**(5), 769–787 (2012)

Mahmood, K.: Do people overestimate their information literacy skills? A systematic review of empirical evidence on the Dunning-Kruger effect. Commun. Inf. Lit. **10**(2), 199–213 (2016)

Meola, M.: Chucking the check-list: a contextual approach to teaching undergraduates web-site evaluation. Portal: Libr. Acad. **4**(3), 331–344 (2004)

Morrison, R., Barton, G.: Search engine use as a literacy in the middle years: the need for explicit instruction and active learners. Lit. Learn.: Middle Years **26**(3), 37 (2018)

Kragh, M., Åsberg, S.: Russia's strategy for influence through public diplomacy and active measures: the Swedish case. J. Strateg. Stud. **40**(6), 773–816 (2017)

Pan, B., Hembrooke, H., Joachims, T., Lorigo, L., Gay, G., Granka, L.: In Google we trust: users' decisions on rank, position, and relevance. J. Comput.-Mediat. Commun. **12**, 801–823 (2007)

Plantin, J.-C., Lagoze, C., Edwards, P.N., Sandvig, C.: Infrastructure studies meet platform studies in the age of Google and Facebook. New Media Soc. **20**(1), 293–310 (2018)

Rieh, S.Y., Hilligoss, B.: College students' credibility judgments in the information-seeking process. In: Metzger, M.J., Flanagin, A.J. (eds.) Digital Media, Youth, and Credibility. The John D. Catherine T. MacArthur Foundation Series on Digital Media and Learning, pp. 49–72. The MIT Press, Cambridge (2008)

Rieh, S.Y., Collins-Thompson, K., Hansen, P., Lee, H.J.: Towards searching as a learning process: a review of current perspectives and future directions. J. Inf. Sci. **42**(2), 19–34 (2016)

Sundin, O.: Invisible search: Information literacy in the Swedish curriculum for Compulsory schools. Nord. J. Digit. Lit. **10**(4), 193–209 (2015)

Sundin, O., Carlsson, H.: Outsourcing trust to the information infrastructure in schools: how search engines order knowledge in education practices. J. Doc. **72**(6), 990–1007 (2016)

Sundin, O., Haider, J., Andersson, C., Carlsson, H., Kjellberg, S.: The search-ification of everyday life and the mundane-ification of search. J. Doc. **73**(2), 224–243 (2017)

Swedish Research Council: Good Research Practice, Stockholm (2017)

The Swedish Ministry of Education: IT-användning och IT-kompetens i skolan. Skolverkets IT-uppföljning 2015 [IT-use and IT-competence in school. The Ministry of Education's evaluation 2015]. The Swedish Ministry of Education, Stockholm (2016)

The Swedish Ministry of Education: Curriculum for the compulsory school, preschool class and school-age educare (revised edition). The Swedish Ministry of Education, Stockholm (2017)

Todd, R.J.: From information to knowledge: charting and measuring changes in students' knowledge of a curriculum topic. Inf. Res. **11**(4), paper 264 (2006). http://InformationR.net/ir/11-4/paper264.html. Accessed 12 Sept 2019

Tuominen, K., Savolainen, R., Talja, S.: Information literacy as a sociotechnical practice. Libr. Q. **75**(3), 329–345 (2005)

Co-learning in a Digital Community: Information Literacy and Views on Learning in Pre-school Teacher Education

Fredrik Hanell[(✉)] [iD]

Linnaeus University, 35106 Växjö, Sweden
fredrik.hanell@lnu.se

Abstract. Through analysing how different views on learning enable pre-school teacher students to distinguish and use affordances offered by digital tools and the learning environment, this paper seeks to connect modes of appropriation, identity positions and information activities to types of information literacy. Identity, particularly views on learning, is analysed to find out how a Facebook group to some students remains a sustainable digital community throughout teacher education. The paper reports results from a netnographical study conducted between 2012 and 2015. The material used in the analysis consists primarily of 12 semi-structured student interviews and 6 teacher interviews. In the thematic analysis, a socio-cultural perspective on identity is applied. The concept affordance is used to analyse how identity is connected to use of digital tools and the learning environment. The findings show how the appropriation of the Facebook group is connected to identity positions and views on learning in two types of information literacy: a relational information literacy and a pragmatic information literacy. The normative function of co-learning is found to be an important aspect of the learning environment of pre-school teacher education that explains why the digital community can be experienced as either including or excluding.

Keywords: Information literacy · Pre-school teacher education · Identity · Learning · Social media

1 Introduction

Digitalisation is transforming society in a multitude of ways as communication and use of information increasingly is mediated by digital tools. In the education sector, commercial actors and policy makers are pushing digital tools into educational settings [1, 2] promoting substantial public investments in digital infrastructure. Simultaneously, individual students and teachers employ popular digital tools in creative ways to realise "new" ways of learning [e.g. 3, 4]. In a recently completed PhD-project[1], a netnographic study conducted between 2012–2015 sheds light on the meeting between Swedish teacher education and new forms of literacies connected to use of digital tools.

---

[1] This paper is based on a PhD-project partly reported in [5–7] and published in full in Swedish as [8].

© Springer Nature Switzerland AG 2020
A. Sundqvist et al. (Eds.): iConference 2020, LNCS 12051, pp. 327–342, 2020.
https://doi.org/10.1007/978-3-030-43687-2_26

In the netnographic tradition where ethnographic methods are applied to study online interactions [9, 10] digital communities are often a starting point. A digital community is a group of people that interacts socially and develops relations by means of a common (digital) place [9]. In this paper, I present key findings from the netnographic study that shows how affordances from the learning environment, digital tools and views on learning interact and can help to explain how a Facebook group to some students and teachers remains interesting and useful throughout the course of teacher education, making the group a sustainable digital community, while others left the group or chose not to participate actively.

A focal point in the reported study is the enactment of information literacies. In the context of this paper, information literacy is understood as an aspect of a practice, such as digital group-based learning, consisting of information activities performed to achieve specific goals in a specific context. The cultural dimension of information literacy in pre-school teacher education has been studied previously through analysing how students perform and describe information activities as digital tools are used and appropriated [5, 6]. Two modes of appropriating a Facebook group have been identified: as a relation-building tool and as a collaborative problem-solving tool [5]. When appropriated as a relation-building tool, central information activities include initiating open discussions and using humour and irony to build relations. Students appropriating the group as a collaborative problem-solving tool instead request and share information directly connected to teacher education. In this paper, the psychological dimension of information literacy is focused through the concept identity, particularly views on learning. This paper therefore elaborates on and deepens previous research on how different identity positions (discussion-oriented student, goal-oriented student and customer-oriented student) can be connected to different ways of sharing information in pre-school teacher education [7]. Through analysing how different views on learning enable students to distinguish and use affordances offered by digital tools and the learning environment, this paper seeks to connect modes of appropriation, identity positions and information activities to types of information literacy. Two research questions guide this investigation:

1. How can modes of appropriation, identity positions and information activities be connected to types of information literacy as students use a Facebook group during pre-school teacher education?
2. How can views on learning explain how the Facebook group for some students remained interesting and useful throughout teacher education while other students left the group or chose to be inactive participants?

2   Theoretical Framework

The socio-cultural perspective applied in this paper draws our attention to how human actions are mediated by tools and situated in social settings [11]. Applied to information literacy, a socio-cultural perspective makes clear that "people's use of information cannot be meaningfully separated from the tools that are an integral part of social practices" [12, p. 95]. Scribner and Cole [13] describes literacy as having both a cultural and a psychological dimension. Literacy, understood as "socially organized practices which make use of a symbol system and a technology for producing and disseminating it" [13, p. 236], therefore entails both the cultural aspects of how tools mediate, for example, written language and the psychological dimensions of how individuals conceptualise and learn written language. In this paper, Scribner and Cole's view on literacy is used as a point of departure to frame information literacy as an aspect of socially organized practices. Pre-school teacher education is considered an overarching practice, including several practices such as digital, group-based learning. Information literacy, as an aspect of the social practice of pre-school teacher education, can be studied by analysing information activities, connected to specific practices, and accounts of these activities.

A socio-cultural perspective on identity, as suggested by Penuel and Wertsch [14], conceptualises identity as commitment in three domains [15, 16]: fidelity (commitment to persons you trust), ideology (commitment to ideas making the world and your place in it comprehensible), and work (commitment to a career choice that may realise hopes for the future). Understood in this way, identity is an important aspect for understanding how – and why – tools are appropriated and information activities performed [cf. 7]. To facilitate the analysis of how identity is connected to use of digital tools and properties of the learning environment, the concept affordance is used.

Affordances describe properties in the environment related to the capabilities of an individual to use them [17]. Hence, affordances can be seen as identified social situations or material properties that may mediate actions in a certain situation. A crucial aspect of learning is consequently the ability to identify and use affordances. In this paper, the concept affordance is used as an analytical tool to integrate enabling and constraining properties of tools and settings, including identity and views on learning, in the analysis of accounts of information activities. Accounts of information literacy are always connected to norms, for example descriptions of how learning takes place [18]. Identity and values of the individual as well as norms within the social practices where the individual acts therefore affect the identification of affordances.

3   Previous Research

Swedish pre-school teacher education is rooted in a seminar tradition, educating teachers for younger pupils, and Fröbel-seminars educating kindergarten teachers [19]. Friedrich Fröbel – pedagogue and philosopher – viewed children as human plants in need of good care to realise their potential, and teachers as "gardeners" providing supervision and suitable conditions rather than formal instruction [19]. The importance of free play, creativity, social interaction and relations as a foundation for learning are still communicated in pre-school teacher education, something we will return to below when views on learning are discussed.

A common ground for practice-oriented research on information literacy, and much research on digital literacy, is how for example Scribner and Cole [13] frame literacy as socially constructed and consisting of both technical skills and meaning-making aspects. Researchers in this tradition, studying the Swedish context, describe a gap between the ideas behind information literacy conveyed in school and changes in pupils' information activities when digital tools are used [e.g. 20–22]. Several studies [e.g. 22–26] also point out that schools and higher education need to better support the development of a literacy with a deeper critical understanding of use of digital tools. These previous studies suggest a negotiation taking place in the meeting between formal education and digital tools where information activities, views on education and views on digital tools are reshaped. They also suggest we need a better understanding of the complexity of young people's education-related use of digital tools if the formal education system is to support the development of more critical forms of literacy. The present study seeks to contribute in addressing this issue.

Within information literacy research, identity can be used as an analytical tool to deepen our understanding of how information activities are performed. From different perspectives, LIS-researchers have made the relation between identity and information literacy visible: Lloyd [27] and Sundin [28] explore the development of professional identity, Meyers [29] investigates identity construction among children in virtual settings, Rivano Eckerdal [30] studies young women's conversations about contraceptives, and Hjøllund [23] explores social media use in upper-secondary school. However, further research is needed to better understand how identity is related to information literacy in educational settings. When it comes to teacher students, there seems to be no previous studies of the connection between information activities and identity.

LIS-research on Facebook use in educational settings has focused on issues connected to information literacy and information sharing. Schreiber [31] shows how a Facebook practice can overlap the written assignment practice among university students. Hjøllund [23] demonstrates how use of Facebook among pupils in upper-secondary school can provide new opportunities to express identity and use information, but at the same time, the urge to receive satisfaction from affirmation by others on Facebook can divert attention from formal learning. Similar to Boyd [32], Hjøllund also points out that digital tools can lead to an overlap of different contexts. Research on information sharing shows that the materiality of tools affect how information is shared [33], and Mansour and Francke [34] illustrate how information sharing is related to assessment of credibility. Among general Facebook users, Syn and Oh [35] find that social engagement is the most important motivation to share information on Facebook. The interest in materiality and credibility distinguishes LIS-studies from the high number of other studies of information sharing on Facebook.

Since most students are familiar with Facebook and use it more frequently than other digital platforms, it is attractive to use in higher education [36]. Facebook groups seem to be the most popular function since they are suitable for information sharing (as shared information is accessible for everyone in the group simultaneously regardless of time and place) and afford specialized content-driven communication [37]. Previous studies also suggest that students appreciate to be able to reach teachers swiftly in an informal setting [38] and Facebook may also provide a unique way to nurture relationships between teachers and students [39, cf. 4]. According to Aaen and Dalsgaard [37], there is a lack of studies that include the context around Facebook groups, such as physical settings and other digital tools. Similarly, Greenhow and Lewin [40] suggest that there is a need for ethnographic accounts of how digital tools are used for learning, in a wider sense than just formal learning, something that the present study contributes with.

Similar to other studies of Facebook use in education settings, studies focusing on teacher education [41, 42] find that Facebook groups can offer teacher students valuable opportunities for communication and facilitate learning. How identities of teacher students are expressed and shaped in digital settings is fairly unexplored [43], even though identity is considered to be a crucial component affecting perspectives and ways of acting among teachers [44]. In a study of a student-led Facebook group (without teachers) Lu and Curwood [43] investigate how teacher students identities develop. In line with previous studies, the authors find that most of the students remained passive partly because they believed a verbal minority used the group to express themselves. We will return to the reasons behind why some students are highly active, while others avoid using a Facebook group actively, when the results are presented and discussed below. Next, the design of the present study will be described.

4 Research Design

This paper reports results from a netnographical study at a Swedish pre-school teacher education[2] conducted between 2012 and 2015. Netnography is an ethnographic approach for doing research online [9, 10]. As mentioned above, a starting point for several netnographic studies is the concept digital[3] communities. A digital community is a group of people interacting socially, developing relations through a common (digital) place facilitating this interaction [9]. Digital communities represent a part of people's everyday experiences on internet and are used for both information sharing and emotional support. Recently, anthropological research has questioned concepts such as community, leading Kozinets [10] to reconsider digital communities as the starting point for netnographic research. Because of how the numerous contexts and opportunities for interaction offered by the internet interacts with – and intensify – the multifaceted and situational properties of identities, it may be problematic to describe persons interacting in a Facebook group as members of a community. For these reasons, Kozinets [10, p. 100] reframes netnography as an approach for studying social experiences online, or "online networks of social interaction and experience". While uncritical overuse of the community concept is questionable, I still consider digital community a useful term to describe the Facebook group discussed in this paper. In line with the theoretical underpinnings of the study, shifting identity positions and ways of using and understanding the group are considered even though I apply the community concept. The digital community studied is a Facebook group used by teachers and more than 200 pre-school teacher students enrolled in teacher education 2011.

Material generated by the study includes online material, mainly from the Facebook group used by students and teachers, but also field notes from participant observations, transcribed interviews and a field diary (Table 1).

---

[2] Swedish pre-school teacher education is a 3.5-year university education (210 credits in the European Credit and Accumulation System).

[3] Kozinets speaks of "online communities" but in this paper, I choose to use "digital communities" which also is in line with the notion of a "digital place".

Table 1. Material generated by the netnographic study.

Part of the study	Material
Part 1 (April–June 2012)	201 conversations from the Facebook group. Interviews with 3 students and 2 teachers. 11 pages of field notes
Part 2 (November 2013–February 2014)	147 conversations from the Facebook group, 104 conversations from the Facebook groups of two teams. Material from Google Drive, Prezi, and blogs. Interviews with 9 students and 4 teachers. 27 pages of field notes and 4 pages of field diary
Part 3 (September 2014–January 2015)	83 conversations from the Facebook group. 3 pages of field notes

Throughout the study, conversations from Facebook groups and material from other digital tools were collected in text documents and coded thematically. In the analysis, conversations were also studied naturalistically, as they were unfolding in the Facebook group, to better understand the experience of the interface and the graphic content.

To gain a deeper understanding of the participants use and understanding of digital tools in the learning environment of teacher education, I was active in the field *in corpore* [9] during the second part of the study, and detailed field notes and a field diary were produced. Interviews were conducted during the first two parts of the study, and they were analysed to contextualise and validate results from digital interactions [45] and to better understand the perspective of the participants [46] – something particularly important when analysing identity. Given the aim of this paper, the findings primarily report results from the analysed interviews. Applying a socio-cultural perspective on information literacy, I analysed the netnographical material using the concepts affordances and identity. The analytical concept affordance was used to investigate the interplay between enabling and constraining factors of the learning environment, appropriation of digital tools and identity. Inspired by theoretically informed ethnography [47], the inductive process of coding also contained a cross-fertilisation between theory and empirical material. Recurring themes of interviews, conversations and observations were identified and comparatively analysed to highlight similarities and significant differences.

5   Results and Analysis

The use of the Facebook group in the socio-cultural setting of pre-school teacher education is carried out in relation to, and partly as a response to, enabling and constraining properties of other tools, material and organizational aspects of university education, and norms of the learning environment.

5.1   Enabling and Constraining Properties of Digital Tools

One important tool is the virtual learning environment (VLE) that teachers and students are prescribed to use by the university. In several accounts, the VLE is described as a necessary, but inadequate, tool for the pedagogical needs at the teacher education. The VLE can be said to serve as a backdrop that illuminates the affordances of other digital tools by example of its own shortcomings. When it comes to the Facebook group, it is particularly the enabling of discussions that makes the tool interesting according to Kristian, a teacher:

> But this Facebook group is for discussion. About things related to our education, about pre-school and learning in general, and about children and young people. For us who share this interest – here we can meet, it is a meeting place. [The VLE] carries official course- or education information. That is there. That is where documents such as course guides and course plans are. And there is, like, official statements from course leaders. Then we can talk about it in the Facebook group. Interview with Kristian, 120608[4]

Thus, Kristian views the VLE as a vehicle for formal course information while the Facebook group offers a place for students and teachers to discuss course content and share information concerning issues related to pre-school teacher education. This view is often shared by students who appropriate the group as a relation-building tool while students who appropriate the group as a collaborative problem-solving tool tend to consider it a channel for sharing official course information [5]. The teacher Kenneth, similar to Kristian, describes the difference between the VLE and the group in terms of meeting the students in various types of conversations:

> I am often very happy to get this look behind the scenes. That's based on an idea that I am not comfortable in this simple teacher role. I mean where it is about course plans, transfer and assessment. If I hadn't had any other ambitions I would probably have remained on [the VLE] because it would have been easier for everyone involved. If I have the idea that I want the students to meet children as humans, and not hide behind a teacher role, I think that then I should try to live it on a university level – I want to meet students not only as students but also in other conversations. Interview with Kenneth, 140108

This quote illustrates the identification of two affordances – properties of the environment enabling actions [17] – connected to certain norms when it comes to how learning is understood: the group enables discussions and a more equal dialogue between students and teachers. While the VLE might be suitable for the "simple teacher role", the Facebook group better facilitates informal communication where students are approached not merely as students. Kenneth suggests another teacher role, connected to a certain view on learning, stipulating that in conversations beyond assessment and transfer of knowledge, students and teachers should be able to meet and discuss as people (we will return to norms and views of learning below). In this view, the overlap of different contexts made possible by social media is considered constructive, as opposed to findings from previous research on school pupils' information literacy [23].

---

[4] All quotes have been translated from Swedish by the author.

5.2   Material and Organizational Aspects of the University Education

The learning environment comes with constraining properties in terms of limited contact hours, and few chances of physical meetings, between students and teachers. This poses a challenge for Kenneth who seeks to teach and interact with the students through "nurturing relationships", something that is difficult when opportunities to meet with students are scarce: "the idea that relations are something that you nurture and develop is not working during this course. I basically only meet them for assessment" (Interview with Kenneth, 120530). Therefore, the group becomes an important arena for regular contact between students and teachers and for nurturing relationships, something that Kenneth and other teachers believes to be a necessary condition for learning. A post to the group made by Kristian exemplifies a type of information activity where affordances of the group are used to nurture relationships:

> Today and yesterday have been fun days at work. I have you to thank for that. Nice.
> Let's continue like this! Facebook conversation, 120417

Drawing on how Moll et al. [48] describe the nurturing of relationships as important for learning, Francis [4] suggests that nurturing practices are vital when students collaborate online. The nurturing of relationships can create a sense of familiarity and makes it easier to ask for, and to receive, assistance from others. Nurturing practices afforded by the group are a necessary component that allows the teacher students to appropriate the group as a tool for learning, either as a relation-building tool or as a collaborative problem-solving tool [5].

From a student perspective, Anna argues that the Facebook group is important since the entire class with more than 200 students lacks other functional ways to communicate and get together. The students only meet for "some lectures or so, but then you don't talk to each other, you only see each other. So we really only talk through [the Facebook group]" (Interview with Anna, 120530). This means that the group is appealing to both students and teachers who want to engage in discussions in addition to the few opportunities provided by lectures and seminars. The socio-cultural setting of pre-school teacher education seems to provide few alternatives to practice the ideals of learning emphasising open discussions and meetings with others. In practice, opportunities to nurture and build relations and to create a learning environment that teachers such as Kristian and Kenneth envision are severely constrained due to limitations connected to few contact hours with students and large groups of students during lectures. For these reasons, the affordances offered by the group are important to achieve the pedagogical ideals conveyed by Kristian and Kenneth – in particular to support open discussions and the nurturing of relationships – ideals shared by students positioning themselves as discussion-oriented students [7].

These affordances of the Facebook group are not identified or appreciated by everyone. Some teachers and students see problems with how the group is used for open discussions, in particular when anxious students use the group to request formal information: "it become that kind of hysteria as soon as some small, small thing happened. Instead of checking with your group's teacher you blurted out to [...] the Facebook group" (Interview with Linus, 140107). Another student critiques how the group is used to share information with low topical relevance to teacher education: "it was only actually, excuse the phrase, but pure shit written there. [...] So you felt, no, this is like completely unserious, I shan't be a part of this" (Interview with Kristoffer, 140130). Similarly, Erik is sceptical of the advantages of the group, even though he remains a member: "to me the [Facebook group] is just a road to anxiety. [Karl laughs] Because there are, there are too many with different ideas and in the end, you sit there and think: I have gone about it...completely...wrong" (Interview with Karl and Erik, 131218).

By critiquing a perceived lack of relevant and correct information useful for their studies, Linus, Kristoffer and Erik provide examples of the identity position goal-oriented student [7]. As opposed to students who position themselves as discussion-oriented students and appropriate the group as a tool for relation-building, goal-oriented students tend not to fully acknowledge the value of joking or informal conversation as components of the nurturing practices mentioned above. This is not to say that students who position themselves as goal-oriented students are not at all interested in the nurturing capacities of the group. However, the examples above from goal-oriented students suggest that when conversations create insecurity, anxiety or frustration, the effect can be the opposite of nurturing or relation-building. This observation echoes findings from previous research [43] suggesting that repeated sharing of information by a few individuals that seems irrelevant to others can discourage several students from participating in conversations. Both an uneven level of activity and different perceptions of the purpose of a Facebook group seem to be recurring issues when Facebook is used in educational settings. As suggested above, a key to understand how use of the group is understood and justified among the students and teachers is how learning is understood as co-learning. Next, we will explore co-learning and how different views on learning can explain how affordances of digital tools are identified and how information activities are undertaken.

5.3   Norms of the Learning Environment

A part of the learning environment that deeply affects how affordances of digital tools are identified, understood and used in pre-school teacher education is norms connected to views on learning. The view on learning as co-learning is identified in Hanell [7] as an ideological form of commitment [15, 16] that shapes the identity position discussion-oriented learner and consequently affects how information is shared. The notion of co-learning affects how roles of students and teachers are perceived, and both students and teachers repeatedly refer to co-learning when they discuss their views of digital tools. From a socio-cultural perspective, a central idea is that tools mediate and shape both actions and cognitive processes [e.g. 11, 49]. However, when Anna reflects on how discussions and learning are affected by digital tools to some extent, she also points out that her view on learning might be more important than the tools she use. In an interview, Anna describes her motivation as a pre-school teacher student:

> I like to discuss, things, I mean this co-learning – I like it. [...] Now if you think that you should work for co-learning, which is a bit like... Perhaps a concept in the world of pre-schooling, learning from each other... then perhaps you should do it yourself first. Interview with Anna, 131216

Similar to Anna, Irma describes how the notion of co-learning influences her actions as a student:

> Now if we think about the idea of co-learning, and that it is this we – I – start with in any case. Otherwise I wouldn't even have come to school to begin with, but kind of be sitting with my text books. Interview with Irma, 131216

In line with how Anna describes the importance of her view on learning, Kristian asserts that his view on teaching and the role of the teacher is the main issue rather than the use of various digital tools:

> It is not only that I use Facebook to communicate with my students, but that I choose to be another kind of teacher than the teacher traditionally has been. And that is really a much bigger step than to use Facebook. Interview with Kristian, 140120

In a sense, Facebook is used to implement the notion of co-learning that entails a student-active pedagogy where knowledge is created collaboratively in open discussions. This view on learning emphasises the importance of relations in the process of learning. The role of the teacher is less connected to traditional classroom-authority and the transfer of knowledge, but more to being a supervisor that facilitates students' learning. Interestingly, the notion of the "traditional" teacher-role associated with authority and the transfer of knowledge that both Kenneth and Kristian critique and aim to avoid has not historically been influential in pre-school teacher education. This traditional teacher-role is associated with schooling, not pre-schooling, and the teaching of older pupils. The critique of the "traditional" teacher-role can be related to the traditional image of the pre-school teacher, emanating from Fröbel's kindergartens and the pre-school teacher seminars, with strong beliefs that pre-schooling should not mimic schooling and that teachers should act as supervisors [19].

Apart from co-learning, two other views on learning are visible in the material. These views reflect different norms and understandings of the roles of students and teachers, and how university education is perceived. Students who position themselves as goal-oriented learners commit to a career choice (becoming a pre-school teacher) and consequently focus on finishing compulsory assignments and to acquire a diploma (preferably without unnecessary efforts) [7]. This view on learning can be framed as an instrumental view on learning. Kristoffer describes how other students would write posts about dead pets or how they had fell and injured themselves – conversations that Kristoffer thought irrelevant in relation to teacher education. In this way, Kristoffer illustrates how students who position themselves as goal-oriented learners might not identify the affordance open discussions offered by the Facebook group. Rather, they prefer the sharing of correct and relevant information.

Students who position themselves as customer-oriented learners commit to a neoliberal view on learning [7, cf. 50]. Education is perceived as a commodity, the student as a customer and the teacher as a salesman. A type of information activity connected to this identity position is voicing discontent, often in relation to practical issues where teachers are considered to be responsible for negative outcomes. One example of this is when a student realises that a lecture will be held in a building not commonly used: "But why? Feels completely unnecessary when we've had all the other three years here…" (Facebook conversation, 141007). After other students have explained where the building is located, a teacher writes that the change had to be made because the large lecture hall in the main building was already booked. Practical issues, beyond the control of individual teachers, explained the circumstances. However, students positioning themselves as customer-oriented students tend to direct their discontent towards the teachers because they are seen as representatives of the university and as such responsible for the "commodity" the students have paid for.

During the last part of the study, the normative function of co-learning in the social practice of pre-school teacher education is visible. Among the information activities in the Facebook group, the identity position discussion-oriented student is dominating [7]. At this point, during the last semester of teacher education, few active members of the group reflect the other two identity positions and the alternative views on learning.

6   Discussion

When descriptions of information activities form narratives that construct identities of teacher students, for themselves and for others [see 14], the psychological dimension of information literacy is made visible. The previous section shows how identity, particularly views on learning, interacts with affordances of digital tools and the learning environment when information activities are undertaken. In this way, the present study supplements previous research on information literacy and identity [e.g. 23, 27, 28, 30] with an analysis of the connection between views on learning (as an aspect of identity) and information literacy.

Through information activities, information literacy emerges as an aspect of the social practice of pre-school teacher education when this practice meets a Facebook practice [cf. 31]. In the table below, the first research question is addressed as the connection between information literacy, appropriation and identity is described (Table 2).

Table 2. The connection between appropriation, identity and information literacy.

	Relational information literacy	Pragmatic information literacy
Mode of appropriation	Relation-building tool	Collaborative problem-solving tool
Identity position	Discussion-oriented	Goal-oriented/Customer-oriented
View on learning	Co-learning	Instrumental/Neoliberal
Relation teacher-students	Non-traditional, informal	Traditional, formal
Typical information activities	Sharing and requesting information that constructs identity, builds relations and initiates open discussion; reflecting and questioning	Sharing and requesting relevant and correct information; voicing discontent, protesting

In Hanell [5], two different modes of appropriating the group are identified: as a relation-building tool and as a collaborative problem-solving tool. In the table above the two modes of appropriating the group are connected to three types of identity positions identified in Hanell [7], linked to different ways of sharing information: discussion-oriented student, goal-oriented student and customer-oriented student. When the group is appropriated as a relation-building tool, and when students position themselves as discussion-oriented students, information shared and requested often serves to build relations, construct identity and spark open discussions – often with humour and irony as key components of these information activities. This identity position and this mode of appropriation are connected to a relational information literacy, characterized by a commitment to co-learning in the ideological domain, and a non-traditional and informal approach to student-teacher relations. Grounded in the view on learning as co-learning, a relational information literacy is connected to the historical heritage of pre-schooling and the social practice of pre-school teacher education.

On the other hand, students who appropriate the group as a collaborative problem-solving tool, and position themselves as goal-oriented learners, tend to share and request information directly related to, and useful for, formal aspects of teacher education. This mode of appropriation and the identity positions goal-oriented student and customer-oriented student are connected to a pragmatic information literacy. This type of information literacy reflects both instrumental (goal-oriented student) and neoliberal (customer-oriented student) views on learning as well as a traditional and formal view on student and teacher roles. In terms of commitment, goal-oriented students commit to pre-schooling as a career choice while customer-oriented students commit to a neoliberal ideology, suggesting a certain *quid pro quo* mentality within a pragmatic information literacy.

Information literacy is connected to norms [18]. The normative view on learning as co-learning is historically rooted in the development of the pre-school teacher profession and pre-school teacher education. The way the teachers explicitly distance themselves from "traditional schooling" and the importance both students and teachers place on social interactions and relations echo ideals from Fröbel's kindergarten and the seminar-tradition of Swedish pre-school teacher education [19]. In connection to the second research question, the findings above show how the idea of co-learning provides explanations for how and why digital tools are used in pre-school teacher education. The critique of the traditional teacher-role, associated with authority and the transfer of knowledge, and a social-constructivist view on learning as co-learning provides an ideological rationale for the use of digital tools. Previous research suggests that Facebook groups can provide teacher students with valuable opportunities for communication [41, 42]. Depending on the motivations of the participants, Facebook can support learning communities [42]. The digital community in the Facebook group becomes an important arena for realising the credo of co-learning, emphasising the building of relations and open discussions between students and teachers. These ambitions are difficult to achieve outside of the digital community, given the material and organizational aspects of teacher education.

However, norms and information activities connected to co-learning can be both including and excluding. The interplay between pedagogical ideals and enabling and constraining properties of the learning environment makes affordances of the Facebook group identifiable and appealing for several teachers and students. The discourses surrounding digital tools, reflecting both technological determinism and overinflated optimism [51], likely interact with the ideals of co-learning and contributes in framing digital tools as natural and even necessary to use. At the same time, students who reflect instrumental or neoliberal views on learning, in a pragmatic information literacy, can be repelled by what they perceive to be irrelevant or misleading information. The preference for relevant and correct information is in line with how Facebook groups are considered suitable for information sharing partly because they enable specialised, content-driven communication [37]. Information activities connected to a relational information literacy with nurturing properties for students who embrace the ideal of co-learning can in fact be the opposite of nurturing for students with different views on learning.

These results can be related to findings from Lu and Curwood [43] who identify two categories of teacher students using a Facebook group. One category of students expresses identity through identification with other students and is helpful, supportive and sociable. The other category instead expresses resistance towards social norms related to group-activities. Among the pre-school teacher students, the normative view on learning as co-learning has including properties for students who consider learning to be a social and relational process. Students with more individualistic preferences, often positioning themselves as goal-oriented or customer-oriented learners, instead appear to be gradually alienated by the ideal of co-learning. The tendency to share information in the community is lower among these students, which is coherent with previous research describing social engagement as the most important motivation to share information on Facebook [35]. Co-learning is a dominating norm within the social practice of pre-school teacher education, but not fully accepted. The tendency to commit to co-learning explains why some students consider the digital community interesting and useful, while students who reject or resist the norms of co-learning instead leave the community or choose to be inactive participants. Future research should continue to investigate how views on learning interact with information activities in different digital settings.

7 Conclusions

This paper shows how the appropriation of Facebook [5] can be connected to the positioning of identity [7] and views on learning in two types of information literacy: a relational information literacy and a pragmatic information literacy. The psychological dimension of literacy [13] is explored through an analysis of how co-learning, and instrumental and neoliberal views on learning, are expressed in accounts of information activities in a digital community. The normative function of co-learning is found to be a significant aspect of the socio-cultural environment of pre-school teacher education that can explain how a digital community using a Facebook group can be experienced as either including or excluding.

References

1. Cuban, L.: Oversold and Underused: Computers in the classroom. Harvard University Press, Cambridge (2001)
2. Player-Koro, C.: 'Roll-out neoliberalism' through one-to-one laptop investments in Swedish schools. IRPPS Monografie, pp. 75–84 (2014)
3. Adalberon, E., Säljö, R.: Informal use of social media in higher education: a case study of Facebook groups. Nord. J. Digit. Lit. 12(4), 114–128 (2017). https://doi.org/10.18261/issn. 1891-943x-2017-04-02
4. Francis, R.J.: The Decentring of the Traditional University: The Future of (Self) Education in Virtually Figured Worlds. Routledge, London (2010)
5. Hanell, F.: Appropriating Facebook: enacting information literacies. Hum. IT 12(3), 5–35 (2014)
6. Hanell, F.: Information activities and appropriation in teacher trainees' digital, group-based learning. Inf. Res. 21(1) (2016)
7. Hanell, F.: Teacher trainees' information sharing activities and identity positioning on Facebook. J. Doc. 73(2), 244–262 (2017)
8. Hanell, F.: Lärarstudenters digitala studievardag: informationslitteracitet vid en förskollärarutbildning. Diss. Lund: Lunds universitet (2019)
9. Kozinets, R.V.: Netnography: Doing Ethnographic Research Online. Sage, Los Angeles (2010)
10. Kozinets, R.V.: Netnography: Redefined, 2nd edn. Sage Publications, Thousand Oaks (2015)
11. Wertsch, J.V.: Mind as Action. Oxford University Press, New York (1998)
12. Limberg, L., Sundin, O., Talja, S.: Three theoretical perspectives on information literacy. Hum. IT 11(2), 93–130 (2012)
13. Scribner, S., Cole, M.: The Psychology of Literacy. Harvard University Press, Cambridge (1981)
14. Penuel, W.R., Wertsch, J.V.: Vygotsky and identity formation: a sociocultural approach. Educ. Psychol. 30(2), 83–92 (1995). https://doi.org/10.1207/s15326985ep3002_5
15. Erikson, E.H.: Childhood and Society, 2nd edn. Penguin Books, Harmondsworth (1965)
16. Erikson, E.H.: Identity, Youth and Crisis. Norton, New York (1968)
17. Gibson, E.J., Pick, A.D.: An Ecological Approach to Perceptual Learning and Development. Oxford University Press, Oxford (2000)
18. Rivano Eckerdal, J.: Libraries, democracy, information literacy, and citizenship: an agonistic reading of central library and information studies' concepts. J. Doc. 73(5), 1010–1033 (2017). https://doi.org/10.1108/JD-12-2016-0152
19. Tellgren, B.: Från samhällsmoder till forskarbehörig lärare: kontinuitet och förändring i en lokal förskollärarutbildning. Diss. Örebro: Örebro universitet (2008)
20. Francke, H., Sundin, O.: Negotiating the role of sources: educators' conceptions of credibility in participatory media. Libr. Inf. Sci. Res. 34(3), 169–175 (2012). https://doi.org/ 10.1016/j.lisr.2011.12.004
21. Francke, H., Sundin, O., Limberg, L.: Debating credibility: the shaping of information literacies in upper secondary school. J. Doc. 67(4), 675–694 (2011). https://doi.org/10.1108/ 00220411111145043
22. Sundin, O., Francke, H.: In search of credibility: pupils' information practices in learning environments. Inf. Res. 14(4) (2009)
23. Hjøllund, N.-P.O.: Begærets subjekt og informationskompetence: en re-installering af subjektet. Diss. Copenhagen: Københavns Universitet (2017)

24. Julien, H., Barker, S.: How high-school students find and evaluate scientific information: a basis for information literacy skills development. Libr. Inf. Sci. Res. **31**(1), 12–17 (2009). https://doi.org/10.1016/j.lisr.2008.10.008

25. Selwyn, N.: The digital native - myth and reality. Aslib Proc. **61**(4), 364–379 (2009). https://doi.org/10.1108/00012530910973776

26. Sormunen, E., Tanni, M., Alamettälä, T., Heinström, J.: Students' group work strategies in source-based writing assignments. J. Assoc. Inf. Sci. Technol. **65**(6), 1217–1231 (2014). https://doi.org/10.1002/asi.23032

27. Lloyd, A.: Informing practice: information experiences of ambulance officers in training and on-road practice. J. Doc. **65**(3), 396–419 (2009). https://doi.org/10.1108/0022041091095 2401

28. Sundin, O.: Nurses' information seeking and use as participation in occupational communities. New Rev. Inf. Behav. Res.: Stud. Inf. Seeking Context **3**, 187–202 (2002)

29. Meyers, E.M.: Tip of the iceberg: meaning, identity, and literacy in preteen virtual worlds. J. Educ. Libr. Inf. Sci. **50**(4), 226–236 (2009)

30. Rivano Eckerdal, J.: Information, identitet, medborgarskap: unga kvinnor berättar om val av preventivmedel. Diss. Lund: Lunds universitet (2012)

31. Schreiber, T.: Conceptualizing students' written assignments in the context of information literacy and Schatzki's practice theory. J. Doc. **70**(3), 346–363 (2014). https://doi.org/10.1108/JD-01-2013-0002

32. Boyd, D.M.: It's Complicated: The Social Lives of Networked Teens. Yale University Press, New Haven (2014)

33. Pilerot, O.: Making design researchers' information sharing visible through material objects. J. Assoc. Inf. Sci. Technol. **65**(10), 2006–2016 (2014). https://doi.org/10.1002/asi.23108

34. Mansour, A., Francke, H.: Credibility assessments of everyday life information on Facebook: a sociocultural investigation of a group of mothers. Inf. Res. **22**(2), 1–17 (2017)

35. Syn, S.Y., Oh, S.: Why do social network site users share information on Facebook and Twitter? J. Inf. Sci. **41**(5), 553–569 (2015). https://doi.org/10.1177/0165551515585717

36. Manca, S., Ranieri, M.: Is it a tool suitable for learning? A critical review of the literature on Facebook as a technology-enhanced learning environment. J. Comput. Assist. Learn. **29**(6), 487–504 (2013). https://doi.org/10.1111/jcal.12007

37. Aaen, J., Dalsgaard, C.: Student "Facebook" groups as a third space: between social life and schoolwork. Learn. Media Technol. **41**(1), 160–186 (2016). https://doi.org/10.1080/17439884.2015.1111241

38. Bosch, T.E.: Using online social networking for teaching and learning: Facebook use at the University of Cape Town. Commun. South Afr. J. Commun. Theory Res. **35**(2), 185–200 (2009). https://doi.org/10.1080/02500160903250648

39. Mazer, J.P., Murphy, R.E., Simonds, C.J.: I'll see you on "Facebook": the effects of computer-mediated teacher self-disclosure on student motivation, affective learning, and classroom climate. Commun. Educ. **56**(1), 1–17 (2007). https://doi.org/10.1080/03634520601009710

40. Greenhow, C., Lewin, C.: Social media and education: reconceptualizing the boundaries of formal and informal learning. Learn. Media Technol. **41**(1), 6–30 (2016). https://doi.org/10.1080/17439884.2015.1064954

41. O'Bannon, B.W., Beard, J.L., Britt, V.G.: Using a Facebook group as an educational tool: effects on student achievement. Comput. Sch. **30**(3), 229–247 (2013). https://doi.org/10.1080/07380569.2013.805972

42. Charteris, J., Parkes, M., Gregory, S., Fletcher, P., Reyes, V.: Student-initiated Facebook sites: nurturing personal learning environments or a place for the disenfranchised? Technol. Pedagogy Educ. **27**(4), 459–472 (2018). https://doi.org/10.1080/1475939X.2018.1507924

43. Lu, Y., Curwood, J.S.: Update your status: exploring pre-service teacher identities in an online discussion group. Asia-Pac. J. Teach. Educ. **43**(5), 438–449 (2015). https://doi.org/10.1080/1359866X.2014.960802

44. Day, C., Kington, A., Stobart, G., Sammons, P.: The personal and professional selves of teachers: stable and unstable identities. Br. Edu. Res. J. **32**(4), 601–616 (2006). https://doi.org/10.1080/01411920600775316

45. Davies, C.A.: Reflexive Ethnography: A Guide to Researching Selves and Others. Routledge, London (2008)

46. Spradley, J.P.: The Ethnographic Interview. Holt, New York (1979)

47. Willis, P., Trondman, M.: Manifesto for ethnography. Cult. Stud./Crit. Methodol. **2**(3), 394–402 (2002). https://doi.org/10.1177/14661380022230679

48. Moll, L.C., Amanti, C., Neff, D., Gonzalez, N.: Funds of knowledge for teaching: using a qualitative approach to connect homes and classrooms. Theory Pract. **31**(2), 132–141 (1992). https://doi.org/10.1080/00405849209543534

49. Säljö, R.: Digital tools and challenges to institutional traditions of learning: technologies, social memory and the performative nature of learning. J. Comput. Assist. Learn. **26**(1), 53–64 (2010). https://doi.org/10.1111/j.1365-2729.2009.00341.x

50. Saunders, D.B.: Exploring a customer orientation: free-market logic and college students. Rev. High. Educ. **37**(2), 197–219 (2014). https://doi.org/10.1353/rhe.2014.0013

51. Selwyn, N.: Minding our language: why education and technology is full of bullshit … and what might be done about it. Learn. Media Technol. **41**(3), 437–443 (2016). https://doi.org/10.1080/17439884.2015.1012523

Digital Natives and Digital Immigrants in the Creative Economy

How These Groups Adopt and Continually Use Digital Technologies

Shahrokh Nikou$^{(\boxtimes)}$ (iD), Suellen Cavalheiro, and Gunilla Widén

Åbo Akademi University, Fänriksgatan 3B, 20500 Turku, Finland
{shahrokh.nikou, suellen.cavalheirirosilva,
gunilla.widen}@abo.fi

Abstract. As digitalisation disrupts businesses ever more profoundly, the concern is growing about how creative workers and designers use digital technologies in their day-to-day practices. This study investigates factors that influence the intention of creative workers to use digital technology. The relationships between digital literacy, perceived usefulness (PU), perceived ease of use (PEOU), social norms, attitude towards use, and intention to use digital technology were examined for a sample of 377 respondents. Structural Equation Modelling (SEM) results show that digital literacy significantly impacts the intention to use digital technology. Attitude towards use mediates the relationships between PU, PEOU, and social norms to intention to use digital technology. Based on the results, theoretical contributions and implications are discussed.

Keywords: Digitalisation · Information literacy · Digital literacy · Digital immigrants · Digital natives

1 Introduction

With each new generation, it is possible to identify nuances concerning the previous one in regard to, e.g., the adoption and usability of the emerging technologies. The rapid development of digital technologies and the rising of the digital age were taken differently from generations. The active population in the labour market during the last decades have witnessed tremendous changes that affected their ways of interacting professionally and socially. The generations that have reached adulthood in a society where personal devices and digital technologies are omnipresent will be entering the workplace where this social transformation already took place. In the previous generations, it was necessary to adapt most of their daily activities for information sharing and social interaction to a reality that is standard nowadays [1]. It is common sense to perceive that the younger generations tend to deal with new technologies, and its constant renewal, with higher capacities and literacy (e.g., information and digital) levels than previous generations [2]. Through the analysis of these individuals, Prensky [3, 4] adopted the denomination of digital natives and digital immigrants. Establishing,

© Springer Nature Switzerland AG 2020
A. Sundqvist et al. (Eds.): iConference 2020, LNCS 12051, pp. 343–362, 2020.
https://doi.org/10.1007/978-3-030-43687-2_27

in this way, a division of how these two audiences interact with and use digital technologies. According to Prensky [3, 4] the digital natives represent those who were born around the 1980s along with the emergence of the new digital technologies, and therefore more exposed to it. Those who were born before the 1980s are in the group known as digital immigrants, being exposed to digital technologies (e.g., Internet and personal computers) in adulthood, thus, requiring a more significant adaptation to digital technologies. Despite the use of digital technologies and tools by the two groups, they present contrasting characteristics that demarcate their generations [5]. As pointed out by Kesharwani [6], a large part of the academic studies that propose to analyse these two groups, treat their characteristics as mutually exclusive. One of the main factors used in the division of these groups has been the age [3, 4] of the target audience. Added to this age segmentation, there is a higher focus in academic research on studies that address digital natives, as they are the younger audience and present characteristics that tend to spread in the future generations.

However, this age division is questioned by some academics who propose more detailed studies of the interactions of these two groups with digital technologies [5, 7, 8]. It should be considered that the digitalisation, connectivity, and integration supported by digital tools [9] reaches contemporary society as a whole and that literacy, whether digital or not, is a competence that depends on practice, frequency of use and the ability to use digital technologies. In this regard, we argue that a classification of digital natives and digital immigrants, primarily based on the assessment of their competence as well as their behaviour towards digital technologies, would be the best possible scenario. Besides, it does not nullify the revolutionary rupture of connectivity and integration induced by the digitalisation that has been affecting the future generations. Such an analysis provides a more comprehensive perspective of how this technological wave has absorbed not only different ages but groups with a distinct personality, demographic, and social characteristics.

In order to put this indication under analysis and in the attempt to classify digital native and digital immigrant with other criteria than age, the core theoretical objective of this paper is to investigate if the engagement and the frequency of use of creative professionals with their software of graphic design, video editing, and web development applications can be used instead of age factor to classify digital native and digital immigrants. The primary purpose of using creative professionals for the investigation is twofold: (i) the workers in the creative industries and economic sectors are characterised by the use of individual creativity and exploitation of intellectual property [10] and (ii) previous studies point to the creative industries as the vanguard in the adoption of new technologies [11, 12]. The question that guides this research is *"what factors impact creative workers' intention to use digital technology in their day-to-day routines?"*. To answer this question, we devise an integrated theory-based model from conventional adoption theories, also adding digital literacy as a separate construct. Data will be collected through an online questionnaire and will be analysed through Structural Equation Modelling (SEM) technique.

2 Literature Review and Hypotheses Development

The use of digital tools, and therefore digitalisation to improve work process performance has been adopted by most, if not all, economic and industrial segments. For the creative industries, the effects of digitalisation are heterogeneous, since this set of industries has a diverse range of sectors, each one with its own processes and business models. However, due to the proximity in the relationship between creativity, innovation, and digital technologies, creative workers have demonstrated intense fluency in digital literacy and the use of digital technology to perform their work [13]. In the study performed by Van Laar et al. [12], where managers and senior executives from Dutch creative industries were asked about the skills needed for creative industry workers, it becomes clear that digital literacy is a factor of extreme relevance to the segment. The results show that creative workers usually have a high fluency in digital literacy, even when considering groups with a considerable age difference. This indication leads to the belief that professionals linked to the creative industries have a high level of digital literacy that is continually updated due to their work needs [12, 13]. Digital literacy is "the ability to understand information and—more important—to evaluate and integrate information in multiple formats that the computer can deliver" (Gilster as cited in Pool, p. 6) [28, 29].

We use items from the "Digital Native Assessment Scale" (DNAS) proposed by [14] as one of the available, statistically tested and validated instruments in the literature to measure the digital competency level of the creative workers. However, it should be noted that other frameworks, such as EU Digital Competence Framework [54] could be used as an alternative framework to DNAS. We used this framework, because it discards the age division, relying primarily on the subjects' self-report regarding their degree of digital literacy.

2.1 Digital Natives and Digital Immigrants

The term "digital natives" was first adopted by Prensky [3, 4] to describe a generation that grew up in a society where digital technologies were already standard in the daily lives of their individuals. In the academic literature, other terms were used to denominate the same generation, such as "Net-Generation" [15], "Millennials" [16] and "iGeneration" [17]. Among the characteristics that identify digital natives, the most prominent is their exposure to the Internet and new digital technologies from an early age. These individuals, when reaching adulthood, have already spent a considerable part of their lives using technological devices, digital applications, and connected to the world wide web. According to [3, 4], the heavy exposure to the digital environment since a young age supposedly affected their brain development differently from previous generations. Digital natives are used to transmitting and receiving information fast, preferably using instant message application, where they can use graphics and images to convey concepts and ideas. They tend to perform more than one task at the same time, often networking with other individuals. As a counterpart to this cohort, [3, 4] denominated individuals out of this range of characteristics as "digital immigrants". Although they may become proficient in the use of some digital technologies, digital immigrants are conditioned to use it differently from the digital natives [5]. For them, the information must be transmitted legibly and formalised textually (e.g., by email). Digital immigrants share data conditioned with an existing necessity and tend to discuss ideas and opinions in small groups of peers. They are more productive when focused on one task at a time, using digital technologies to increase the quality of their performance rather than to connect with others.

However, this characterisation based on the age has been criticised by many researchers such as [5] and for the premise of the digital technologies effect in the brain development of digital natives [18–20]. By including digital literacy, we aim to address this academic debate by exploring different classification factors that goes beyond the age.

In addition to digital literacy, other factors also impact creative workers' intentions to use digital technologies. By analysing the academic literature, it is possible to identify some efforts in precedent investigations of the use of the digital technologies applied within the initial adoption construction of the Technology Acceptance Model [21]. Some articles provide a correlation between the Technology Acceptance Model (TAM) and the Theory of Planned Behaviour (TPB) [22] for the elaboration of a longitudinal study [6, 23, 24]. Nevertheless, as this research is limited to only one wave questionnaire delivery, due to the importance of TPB, social norms and attitude towards use will be used together with constructs of TAM and digital literacy to devise a theory-based conceptual model, see Fig. 1.

2.2 Perceived Ease of Use

Perceived ease of use (PEOU) refers to the degree of easiness associated with the use of digital tools. In the theoretical model stipulated in this research, the concept of perceived ease of use is extracted from TAM [21]. Previous research suggests that perceived ease of use also affects perceived usefulness and has greater relevance in the early stages of adopting a new behaviour [21, 25]. Moreover, this paper assumes that due to rapid and constant technology upgrades, perceived ease of use has significant relevance to audience attitude towards use of digital technology (i.e., work tools); hence:

H1a. *Perceived ease of use has a significant effect on perceived usefulness*
H1b. *Perceived ease of use has a significant effect on attitude towards use*

2.3 Perceived Usefulness

Perceived usefulness (PU) refers to the degree of trustworthiness attributed by the individual regarding the gain in performance through the use of digital technologies. The employment of this construct in the research model is an aggregation of similar concepts from an examined model in the literature review: TAM [21]. In this paper, we argue that PU influences the creative workers' attitude towards use of digital technologies and we expect that the PU to be a strong predictor of attitude towards use of digital technologies; hence:

H2. *Perceived usefulness has a significant effect on attitude towards use*

2.4 Social Norms

Social norms (SN) refer to the degree of interference of other individuals in the decision making of an individual's intention to use digital technology [26]. This construct is similar to the "subjective norms" [21, 22] or "social influence" [25]. Directly or indirectly (through the attitude towards use), we assume that social norms influence creative workers' behaviour in relation to their interaction with technology [27], where the opinion of third parties, closely related to the individual, are significant in shaping their own evaluation. Social norms influence decision making in a complex way and are susceptible to a variety of contingent influences [22]. This paper assumes that the social pressure exerted by SN, not only directly affect the intention to use digital technology but also influences the attitude towards use of technology of creative workers; hence:

H3a. *Social norms have a significant effect on intention to use digital technology*

H3b. *Social norms have a significant effect on attitude towards use*

2.5 Attitude Towards Use

Attitude towards use refers to the affective reaction of the individual when using a technology [25]. It is associated with the individual's liking, joy, and pleasure when making use of a technology [25]. For some cases, this construct may represent the strongest predictor of behavioural intent [2, 25]. More detailed analyses indicate that attitudinal constructs regarding the use of technology are more significant when the theoretical model considers constructions related to the expectation of effort and performance [27]. In studies related to digital natives and digital immigrants, [2] state that the higher is the individual's confidence in its ICT skills, the more positive their attitude toward using digital technology. This paper assumes that attitude towards use influences the intention to use digital technology for creative workers; hence:

H4. *Attitude towards use has a significant direct effect on intention to use digital technology*

2.6 Digital Literacy

Digital literacy refers to the attitude and ability of individuals to appropriately use digital tools to identify, access, generate, integrate, and evaluate digital resources, building new knowledge, creating media expressions, and communicating with others [30, p. 135]. An individual is considered digitally literate when demonstrating technical and operational skills to use ICT and digital technology in daily activities [31]. By classifying digital natives and digital immigrants by age group, the study placed those of a certain age into a predefined group with insufficient comprehension of their cognitive and technical abilities [32]. On the other hand, by classifying digital natives and digital immigrants by their exposure, experience, proficiency and engagement with digital technology, the gap between different ages is bound to the improvement of their ICT skills [14]. The digitally literate individual should be a critical thinker, who can responsibly make use of the Internet, who can select appropriate software to their needs and used it with the capability to seek and evaluate digital information for learning and performing tasks [31, p. 1068], hence:

H5a. *Digital literacy has a significant effect on intention to use digital technology*
H5b. *Digital literacy has a significant effect on attitude towards use*

2.7 Intention to Use

The intention to use digital technology refers to the degree to which individuals would use the technology in their day-to-day routines [33]. Different studies propose that intention to use digital technology is related to perceived ease of use and perceived usefulness [34, 35]. This construct is related to motivational factors, which makes it the most crucial determinant in predicting the decision to take a specific action [22]. In this research, the intention to use digital technology is considered as the outcome variable to evaluate the intention to use digital technology of creative workers within their work activities. Figure 1 shows the proposed model.

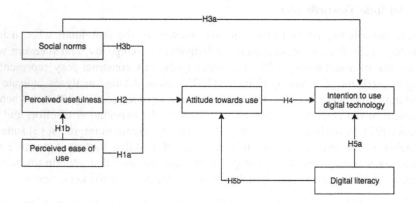

Fig. 1. Research model

3 Methodology

The methodology employed in this paper focuses on developing a better understanding of how creative workers use their ICT skills to deal with their digital work tools. Thereby, the quantitative approach through Partial Least Squares Structural Equation Modelling (PLS-SEM) using Smart-PLS software was employed. The PLS-SEM method was chosen primarily for its broad application in academic research [36, 37].

All the items used within each construct were selected from validated measures, undergoing minor adjustments to better fit to the context of this research. Items for measuring PU, PEOU and attitude towards use, each with five items, were derived from [21]. Items for SN and intention to use digital technology, each with five items, were derived from [21, 25]. Finally, digital literacy has been measured with items based on the digital native assessment scale [14]. The choice of a survey questionnaire was based on the accessibility and easiness in collecting quantitative data, enabling the researcher to perform data analysis efficiently. All survey items were measured on the 7-point Likert scale from "1 = strongly disagree" to "7 = strongly agree", see Appendix 1.

3.1   Data Collection

The sample of participants was limited to creative workers who perform their artistic activities through the use of digital tools. Within this group, only self-employed, individuals belonging to a creative collective, or individuals working in small businesses were included. In the case of small companies, a total of 50 employees was considered a delimiting factor for participation in this research. It was a strategic decision in order to select creative workers that are out of the reality imposed by large corporations within the creative economy. It is considered that in large corporations, the use of digital tools can be dictated by commercial agreements not related to the functionalities of these tools. As well as its accessibility may be limited or even prohibited depending on the position and function held by the employee. These bureaucracies are expected to be smaller or even non-existent in the case of small businesses and freelancers. The profile of these creative workers can be found by the exposure of their online portfolio or through online platforms and communities developed for the dissemination of creative work (e.g., Behánce, Dribbble, GitHub, among others). The choice of these professional profiles was random, given the need to include different genres, occupations, and locations.

During four-week of July 2019, the questionnaire was distributed to participants presenting the following characteristics: (i) currently working as a creative worker, positioning themselves as the creator of their own work, (ii) identify themselves as a freelancer, self-employed, start-up, studio, or group of independent artists, (iii) the work created by them must be unique, that is, represent an original perspective that embodies the vision of the creator and (iv) for SMEs cases, no signs should be found that the company belongs to or is part of a medium or large business.

A total of 380 questionnaires were returned, 3 participants did not answer the questionnaire properly and were excluded from further analysis. As suggested by [40], the non-response bias test was performed. The first 25% of respondents were compared with the final 25% of respondents for all survey items using the chi-square test. The result showed that the participants do not differ significantly, thus concluding that the answers collected from the sample are not biased. Of the respondents, 70% were males, and 30% were females. The median age of the respondents was 33 years old. Most of the participants were from Europe (43.2%), followed by participants from South America (26.3%). When we asked whether the respondents have migrated from their original country where they born, only 21% said yes. The majority of the respondents were full-time freelancer (40.3%), and 28% reported that they were full-time employed by SMEs. The majority of the respondents had at least six years or more experience working as an artist or as a creator, see Table 1.

Table 1. Descriptive statistics of the respondents

Descriptive statistics of the respondents	Pooled sample	Digital native (DNAS above Mean)	Digital immigrant (DNAS below Mean)
Sample size	377 (100%)	188 (49.9%)	189 (50.1%)
Median age	33 years	32 years	34 years
Gender			
Male	262 (69.5%)	124 (32.9%)	138 (36.6%)
Female	110 (29.2%)	61 (16.2%)	49 (13%)
Other	5 (1.3%)	3 (0.8%)	2 (0.5%)
Original continent			
Africa	34 (9.0%)	20 (5.3%)	14 (3.7%)
Asia	42 (11.1%)	25 (6.6%)	17 (4.5%)
Europe	163 (43.2%)	69 (18.3%)	94 (24.9%)
North America	31 (8.2%)	19 (5.0%)	12 (3.2%)
Oceania	8 (2.1%)	3 (0.8%)	5 (1.3%)
South America	99 (26.3%)	52 (13.8%)	47 (12.5%)
Migrated from the place of origin			
Yes - Reside in a different country	79 (21.0%)	40 (10.6%)	39 (10.3%)
No - Reside in the origin country	298 (79.0%)	148 (39.3%)	150 (39.8%)
Level of education			
High School Diploma	48 (12.7%)	28 (7.4%)	20 (5.3%)
Bachelor's degree	219 (58.1%)	108 (28.6%)	111 (29.4%)
Master's degree	77 (20.4%)	43 (11.4%)	34 (9.0%)
Ph.D.	2 (0.5%)	0 (0.0%)	2 (0.5%)
Other	31 (8.2%)	9 (2.4%)	22 (5.8%)
Employment type			
Full-time as a freelancer	152 (40.3%)	77 (20.4%)	75 (19.9%)
Full-time as a SME employee	106 (28.1%)	48 (12.7%)	58 (15.4%)
Part-time as a freelancer and as a SME employee	46 (12.2%)	25 (6.6%)	21 (5.6%)
Part-time as a freelancer	67 (17.8%)	35 (9.3%)	32 (8.5%)
Part-time as a SME employee	6 (1.6%)	3 (0.8%)	3 (0.8%)
How long have you been working as an artist/creator			
Less than 2 years	15 (4.0%)	9 (2.4%)	6 (1.6%)
From 2 to 5 years	116 (30.8%)	60 (15.9%)	56 (14.9%)
From 6 to 10 years	130 (34.5%)	64 (17%)	66 (17.5%)
From 11 to 15 years	63 (16.7%)	33 (8.8%)	30 (8%)
From 16 to 20 years	37 (9.8%)	15 (4%)	22 (5.8%)
More than 21 years	16 (4.2%)	7 (1.9%)	9 (2.4%)

4 Data Analysis and Results

The mean-split of the scores collected from Digital Native Assessment Scale (DNAS) [14] was employed as a classification factor between digital native (above mean; N = 188) and digital immigrants (below mean; N = 189). The maximum DNAS score possible was 84 (12-items on a 7-point Likert scale), and the mean among the participants was 68 (81% of the maximum score possible) indicating the majority of the participants with high the level of digital literacy skills.

The same similarities were found in the analysis of the respondents' self-perception regarding frequency of use and proficiency with the digital work tools, see Table 2.

4.1 Measurement Analysis

We analysed the research model in two stages (a) measurement model assessment and (b) structural model assessment [42]. The assessment of the reliability and validity was performed through the outer loadings, composite reliability, and average variance extracted (AVE) [43]. As indicated by [44] the values of outer loadings should be above .70, all indicators, except for few items, loaded significantly on their respective constructs with primary loadings more than .70. Moreover, the values of CR, which is the assessment of the internal consistency were all above the threshold of .70 or higher [41]. For convergent validity, we examined the value of AVE for each latent variable

Table 2. Respondent self-perception regarding frequency of use and proficiency

Respondent self-perception regarding frequency of use and proficiency	Pooled sample	Digital native (DNAS above Mean)	Digital immigrant (DNAS below Mean)
Sample size	377 (100%)	188 (49.9%)	189 (50.1%)
Digital Native Assessment Scale (DNAS) 12-Items: (7-point Likert scale from "1 = strongly disagree" to "7 = strongly agree".)			
Grow up with Technology	M = 6.50	M = 6.79	M = 6.21
Comfortable with Multitasking	M = 6.28	M = 6.81	M = 5.74
Reliant on Graphics for Communication	M = 4.67	M = 5.69	M = 3.66
Thrive on Instant Gratifications	M = 5.11	M = 5.91	M = 4.32
Please indicate how often do you use the following digital technologies (hardware): (5-point Likert scale from "1 = I do not use it" to "5 = several times a day")			
Smartphone	M = 3.95	M = 3.98	M = 3.93
Desktop Computer	M = 3.08	M = 3.04	M = 3.13
Laptop Computer	M = 3.23	M = 3.30	M = 3.16
Tablet Computer	M = 2.15	M = 2.27	M = 2.04
Graphics Tablet (e.g., Wacom Intuos)	M = 2.83	M = 2.83	M = 2.83
Professional Camera	M = 1.94	M = 2.01	M = 1.88

(*continued*)

Table 2. (*continued*)

Respondent self-perception regarding frequency of use and proficiency	Pooled sample	Digital native (DNAS above Mean)	Digital immigrant (DNAS below Mean)
Please indicate how often do you use the following digital technologies (software): (5-point Likert scale from "1 = I do not use it" to "5 = several times a day")			
Raster Graphics Editor (e.g., Photoshop)	M = 3.65	M = 3.72	M = 3.57
Vector Graphics Editor (e.g., Illustrator)	M = 3.03	M = 3.15	M = 2.91
Motion Graphics Editor (e.g., After Effects)	M = 1.81	M = 1.84	M = 1.79
Video Editor (e.g., Premiere)	M = 1.62	M = 1.68	M = 1.57
3D Modelling Editor (e.g., Cinema 4D)	M = 1.69	M = 1.77	M = 1.60
Team Collaboration App (e.g., Slack)	M = 2.07	M = 2.08	M = 2.07
Task Management App (e.g., Asana)	M = 1.71	M = 1.74	M = 1.68
Please indicate your expertise level using the following digital technologies (software): (5-point Likert scale from "1 = novice" to "5 = expert")			
Raster Graphics Editor (e.g., Photoshop)	M = 4.30	M = 4.36	M = 4.24
Vector Graphics Editor (e.g., Illustrator)	M = 3.71	M = 3.84	M = 3.58
Motion Graphics Editor (e.g., After Effects)	M = 2.23	M = 2.27	M = 2.20
Video Editor (e.g., Premiere)	M = 2.18	M = 2.15	M = 2.21
3D Modelling Editor (e.g., Cinema 4D)	M = 2.02	M = 2.05	M = 1.99
Team Collaboration App (e.g., Slack)	M = 2.25	M = 2.27	M = 2.23
Task Management App (e.g., Asana)	M = 1.82	M = 1.87	M = 1.76

and all values, expect of digital literacy (.494), were above the recommended value of .50 [45]. We also assessed the Cronbach's alpha (α) for the internal consistency of latent constructs, and all values except for social norms (.69) were above .70. Nevertheless, as Cronbach's alpha tended to provide a conservative measurement in PLS-SEM and it is used to measure internal consistency reliability, some researchers [45, 46] recommended using the CR as a replacement, which should be .70. In our analysis, the lowest CR value is .832 [41] see Table 3.

Table 3. Reliability and validity

Construct	Items	Factors loadings	t-Statistic	Cronbach's α	CR	AVE
Perceived ease of use	PEU1	.874	66.713	.777	.867	.685
	PEU2	.851	32.595			
	PEU3	.745	16.202			

(*continued*)

Table 3. (*continued*)

Construct	Items	Factors loadings	t-Statistic	Cronbach's α	CR	AVE
Perceived usefulness	PU1	.731	14.462	.853	.895	.631
	PU2	.835	30.402			
	PU3	.844	42.048			
	PU4	.751	19.833			
	PU5	.779	22.218			
Social norms	SN1	.817	17.505	.686	.857	.750
	SN2	.908	26.514			
Attitude towards use	ATU1	.782	21.819	.842	.894	.680
	ATU2	.865	44.195			
	ATU3	.860	40.882			
	ATU5	.773	13.930			
Intention to use digital technology	IU1	.615	13.148	.843	.889	.618
	IU2	.834	28.096			
	IU3	.759	21.186			
	IU4	.845	26.845			
	IU5	.822	33.256			
Digital literacy	DL1	.726	10.677	.761	.832	.494
	DL2	.785	16.746			
	DL3	.724	20.324			
	DL4	.689	30.784			
	DL5	.750	19.033			
	DL6	.682	26.239			

Note: CR = Composite Reliability; AVE = Average Variance Extracted.

For discriminant validity, we used the square root of AVE for each latent variable to establish discriminant validity [47, 48], and all the values were higher than other correlation values among the latent variables, see the values in bold on the diagonal in Table 4.

Table 4. Discriminant validity

Constructs	ATT	DL	INT	PU	PEOU	SN
Attitude towards use	**.824**					
Digital literacy	.417	**.673**				
Intention to use digital technology	.700	.535	**.786**			
Perceived usefulness	.699	.506	.673	**.794**		
Perceived ease of use	.553	.416	.565	.522	**.828**	
Social norms	.469	.387	.516	.498	.358	**.866**

4.2   Structural Analysis

To test the research hypotheses and to assess the significance of relationships between constructs in the model, we used SmartPLS. The SEM results showed that the intention to use digital technology was explained by variance of 58%. Moreover, attitude towards use and perceived usefulness were explained by variance of 55% and 27%, respectively. The PLS-SEM analysis showed that attitude towards use had the strongest effect on the intention to use digital technology ($\beta = .52$, $t = 9.85$, $p < .001$), therefore and H4 is supported by the model. The relationships between PU ($\beta = .49$, $t = 7.97$, $p < .001$), PEOU ($\beta = .20$, $t = 3.65$, $p < .001$) and SN ($\beta = .17$, $t = 3.60$, $p < .001$), were found to be significant to attitude towards use, thus H1a, H2 and H3b were supported by the model. The path between PEOU to PU was significant ($\beta = .52$, $t = 8.98$, $p < .001$), thus H1b is supported. Social norms also directly impact ($\beta = .21$, $t = 3.60$, $p < .001$) the intention to use digital technology, therefore H3a was also supported.

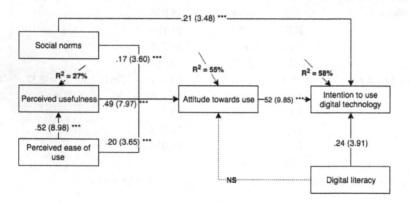

Fig. 2. Conceptual results

The SEM analysis revealed interesting results in relation to digital literacy. While, we found a direct relationship between digital literacy and the intention to use digital technology ($\beta = .24$, $t = 3.91$, $p < .001$), the result showed that digital literacy had no significant impact on the attitude towards use. Thus, only H5a was supported by the model (see Fig. 2). Moreover, the result showed that the total indirect effects between digital literacy and intention to use digital technology is not significant. In other words, no mediation effect of attitude towards use could be found between digital literacy and intention to use digital technology. Finally, we found that attitude towards use mediates the path relationships between PU ($\beta = .26$, $t = 6.55$, $p < .001$), PEOU ($\beta = .12$, $t = 4.14$, $p < .001$) and SN ($\beta = .07$, $t = 2.55$, $p < .01$) to intention to use digital technology.

4.3 Multigroup Analysis (MGA)

To classify the respondents as digital natives and digital immigrants and using other factors rather than the age [5, 7, 8], we used the scores on the Digital Native Assessment Scale (DNAS) [14] to examin the model. As mentioned, DNAS is a more consistent classification factor than the age as it allows to label individuals based on their proficiency and competency with the digital technologies. Thus, we performed the DNAS analysis in a mean-split of participants score, identifying the digital native (above mean; N = 188) and digital immigrants (below mean; N = 189). The MGA results showed that these groups differed from each other on several path relationships. For instance, while for digital natives, the path between digital literacy and intention to use digital technology was not significant, it was found to be significant for digital immigrants ($\beta = .27$, $t = 3.91$, $p < .001$).

More interestingly, the path between SN and attitude towards use was found to be significant only for the digital immigrants ($\beta = .19$, $t = 2.91$, $p < .005$). We also found a significant relation between SN and intention to use digital technology, applicable only for digital natives ($\beta = .23$, $t = 3.52$, $p < .001$). Given that [32] argued that it is possible for adults to become digital natives as much or more than the younger generations through, e.g., skills acquisition, increasing the frequency of use, and continuing interaction with digital technologies. Our results, using the DNAS framework for the classification, supported this idea by showing several differences between these two groups. The differences between the groups were observable only through creative workers' proficiency in using digital tools and not based on their age.

5 Discussion

In this paper, we devised a theory-based model to examine creative workers' intention to use digital technologies in their day-to-day routines. We developed an integrated conceptual model, comprising of six constructs (e.g., digital literacy, intention to use, social norms). Moreover, unlike common practice that tends to divide individuals based on their age, in this paper, we refrained from this approach and used the classification index based on the Digital Native Assessment Scale (DNAS) from [14] to classify creative workers as digital natives and digital immigrants. By classifying the respondents based on their scores on the DNAS items and irrespective of their age, the digital native group presented higher engagement with digital technologies than digital immigrants, considering their perspective in how often they use these tools. The digital natives also showed higher skills when considering their own proficiency using digital technologies. Moreover, the SEM results showed that social norms had a different impact on the attitude towards use and intention to use digital technology when respondents were classified into digital native and digital immigrants. From the results obtained, we can assume that the engagement of digital natives and digital immigrants can be leveraged by increasing their exposure to opportunities to interact with digital technologies. However, how these opportunities of interaction are perceived by these groups (e.g., peer collaboration, instructor guidance, professional demands) will depend on the distinct effect of social norms on their behaviour.

Our results also complemented prior studies such as [49, 50] who also indicated that in order to classify individuals, we need to emphasise on the impact of socio-demographic variables on engagement and ability to use digital technologies rather than the age criteria. Hsieh et al. [51, p. 3] focused on socio-economic criteria to demonstrate how geographic location can influence digital inequality, "the inequality in the access and use of information technology". Studies like these indicated that differences in location and social levels can influence the level of digital literacy of the older generations and the younger ones. In other words, it can impact their awareness, attitude and ability towards use, critical and evaluative sense, as well as cognitive and technical skills when handling digital technologies [30, 31].

6   Conclusion, Future Work and Limitations

In this paper, in response to the academic debate on the classification of the individuals as digital natives and digital immigrants, we contribute to the literature by exploring Digital Native Assessment Scale (DNAS) [6–8]. The SEM results show that DNAS is a more consistent classification factor than the age, as we found significant differences between the respondents. Our findings show that individuals with less exposure and access to new technologies can be positioned as digital immigrants, even if they are born after 1980. The same can occur with individuals born before 1980 when located in socio-demographic conditions where their exposure to digital technologies is enhanced. We used creative workers as the subjects of our research because prior studies argue that creative workers, due to the nature of their creative works, have a high fluency in digital literacy that is continually updated due to their work needs [12, 13]. Our results supported this assumption by showing how creative workers perceive and state their use of digital technologies in their daily work practices.

Furthermore, the results of multigroup analysis contribute to literature and support other scholars' assumption [32, 49] that not all individuals from the youngest generations are digital natives. With a consistent classification based on exposure and engagement with digital technologies, it is assumed here that digital immigrants can continuously improve their level of digital literacy. We argue that to identify digital natives and digital immigrants, in the first step, we need to assist them in the adoption and breadth of use technologies. For instance, by creating an environment where digital technology engagement can be built and strengthen, companies can provide to their audience anxiety reduction when encountering new tools and leading them to interact with new technologies more comfortably [5, 7].

Regarding some limitations of the research presented here, it should be noted that participants under analysis are presumed to have a high level of digital literacy, which was observed by their high DNAS score, in average 81% of the maximum. Individuals less digitally literate than creative workers could exhibit distinct path associations in the constructs proposed in the research model. Even so, possibilities of analysis within these group of creative workers were not fully explored. An analysis that investigates with more detail on how the socio-demographic system from different location influence the creative worker's technology engagement is essential. In addition, it should be made clear that the associations of individuals with the digital tools performed in this research were closely related to the execution of their work tasks. The engagement of this audience with digital tools in their leisure time has not been performed, which may result in different perspectives regarding the classification of individuals.

Overall, in future research, new studies must consider digital natives and digital immigrants as a dynamic classification that has by its nature the condition of being modified in relation to the individuals' exposure to new technologies versus time. Digital natives and digital immigrants have their importance in the social environment to which they interact, incorporating different perspectives and outlining different ways for the adoption and use of technologies [52, 53].

Acknowledgement. This work was supported by Academy of Finland, project The Impact of Information Literacy in the Digital Workplace [grant number 295743].

Appendix. Measurement Instrument

Construct	Code	Items	Source
Social norms	SN1	Most professionals from my field use digital tools	Taylor and Todd [38, 39]
	SN2	Professionals that I admire use digital tools	
	SN3	I have to use digital tools because my clients require it	
	SN4	Professionals that use digital tools have more prestige than those who do not	
	SN5	In my field, those who use digital tools have a high profile	
Perceived usefulness	PU1	Using digital tools enable me to accomplish my work tasks more quickly	Davis [21]; Thompson et al. [26]
	PU2	Using digital tools enhance my effectiveness in my work	
	PU3	Using digital tools can significantly increase the quality of output of my work	
	PU4	Using digital tools increase my chances of getting more jobs	
	PU5	Using digital tools increase my chances of getting jobs well-paid	

(*continued*)

(*continued*)

Construct	Code	Items	Source
Perceived ease of use	PEU1	It is easy for me to get the expected result with digital tools	Davis [21]
	PEU2	It is easy for me to become a skilled user of digital tools	
	PEU3	It takes too long to learn how to use digital tools to make it worth the effort	
	PEU4	Working with digital tools is complicated. It is difficult to understand what is going on	Thompson et al. [26]
	PEU5	Overall, I find digital tools easy to use	
Attitude toward use	ATU1	The actual process of using digital tools is pleasant	Davis [21]; Thompson et al. [26]
	ATU2	Digital tools make my work more interesting	
	ATU3	I work better using digital tools	
	ATU4	Digital tools enable me to be a self-directed and independent worker	
	ATU5	Once I started working with digital tools, I find it difficult to avoid	
Intention to use digital technology	IU1	I do not hesitate to use new digital tools in my work processes	Venkatesh et al. [25]
	IU2	I plan to continue using digital tools in my work processes for years to come	
	IU3	I intend to use the next versions of digital tools in my work processes	
	IU4	I am very likely to use digital tools to create my work digitally	
	IU5	I would recommend to other professionals in my field to use digital tools	

(*continued*)

(*continued*)

Construct	Code	Items	Source
Digital Literacy - *Digital Natives Assessment Scale (DNAS)*	*Grow up with technology*		Teo [14]
	DNAS1	I use the Internet for work and leisure every day	
	DNAS2	When I need to know something, I search first online	
	DNAS3	I keep in touch through devices with friends and online communities every day	
	Comfortable with multitasking		
	DNAS4	I can check email and chat online at the same time	
	DNAS5	When using the Internet for my work, I am able to listen to music as well	
	DNAS6	I am able to use more than one application on the computer at a time	
	Reliant on graphics for communication		
	DNAS7	I use pictures and figures more than words when I wish to explain something	
	DNAS8	I use a lot of graphics and icons when I send messages	
	DNAS9	I use pictures to express my feelings and ideas better	
	Thrive on instant gratifications and rewards		
	DNAS10	I wish to be rewarded for everything I do	
	DNAS11	I expect the websites that I regularly visit to be constantly updated	
	DNAS12	When learning something new, I prefer to learn those that I can use quickly first	

References

1. Purcell, K., Rainie, L., Mitchell, A., Rosenstiel, T., Olmstead, K.: Understanding the participatory news consumer. Pew Internet Am. Life Proj. **1**, 19–21 (2010)
2. Nikou, S., Brännback, M., Widén, G.: The impact of digitalization on literacy: digital immigrants vs. digital natives. In: 27th European Conference on Information Systems (ECIS), Stockholm, Sweden, 8–14 June (2019)

3. Prensky, M.: Digital natives, digital immigrants part 1. Horizon **9**(5), 1–6 (2001)
4. Prensky, M.: Digital natives, digital immigrants part 2: do they really think differently? Horizon **9**(6), 1–6 (2001)
5. Vodanovich, S., Sundaram, D., Myers, M.: Research commentary—digital natives and ubiquitous information systems. Inf. Syst. Research **21**(4), 711–723 (2010)
6. Kesharwani, A.: Do (how) digital natives adopt a new technology differently than digital immigrants? A longitudinal study. Inf. Manag. 103170 (2019)
7. Tufts, D.R.: Digital Adults: Beyond the Myth of the Digital Native Generation Gap. Fielding Graduate University, Santa Barbara, CA (2011)
8. Wang, Q.E., Myers, M.D., Sundaram, D.: Digital natives and digital immigrants. Bus. Inf. Syst. Eng. **5**(6), 409–419 (2013)
9. Parida, V.: Digitalization. In: Frishammar, J., Ericson, Å. (eds.) Addressing Societal Challenges, pp. 23–38. Luleå University of Technology (2018)
10. Higgs, P.L., Cunningham, S.D., Bakhshi, H.: Beyond the creative industries: Mapping the creative economy in the United Kingdom (2008)
11. Huws, U.: Labor in the Global Digital Economy: The Cybertariat Comes of Age. NYU Press, New York (2014)
12. Van Laar, E., Van Deursen, A.J., Van Dijk, J.A., de Haan, J.: Twenty-first-century digital skills for the creative industries workforce: perspectives from industry experts. First Monday **24**(1) (2019)
13. Cavalheiro, S.: The Impact of Digitalization on Creative Economy: How Digital Technologies Enable to Increase Creativity Value (2019)
14. Teo, T.: An initial development and validation of a Digital Natives Assessment Scale (DNAS). Comput. Educ. **67**(C), 51–57 (2013)
15. Tapscott, D.: Growing up digital: the rise of the net generation. Educ. Inf. Technol. **4**(2), 203–205 (1998)
16. Oblinger, D., Oblinger, J.L., Lippincott, J.K.: Educating the Net Generation. Boulder, Colo.: EDUCAUSE, c2005. 1 v.(various pagings): illustrations (2005)
17. Rosen, L.D.: Rewired: Understanding the iGeneration and the Way They Learn. St. Martin's Press (2010)
18. Helding, L.: Digital natives and digital immigrants: teaching and learning in the digital age. J. Singing **68**(2), 199 (2011)
19. Smith, G.: A critical look at the role of technology as a transformative agent. Technol. Hum. Educ. Narrat. (8) 65–77 (2011)
20. Thompson, P.: The digital natives as learners: technology use patterns and approaches to learning. Comput. Educ. **65**, 12–33 (2013)
21. Davis, F.D., Bagozzi, R.P., Warshaw, P.R.: User acceptance of computer technology: a comparison of two theoretical models. Manag. Sci. **35**(8), 982–1003 (1989)
22. Ajzen, I.: The theory of planned behavior. Organ. Behav. Hum. Decis. Process. **50**(2), 179–211 (1991)
23. Kim, S.S.: The integrative framework of technology use: an extension and test. MIS Q.: Manag. Inf. Syst. **33**(3), 513–537 (2009)
24. Po-An Hsieh, J.J., Wang, W.: Explaining employees' extended use of complex information systems. Eur. J. Inf. Syst. **16**(3), 216–227 (2007)
25. Venkatesh, V., Morris, M.G., Davis, G.B., Davis, F.D.: User acceptance of information technology: toward a unified view. MIS Q. **27**(3), 425–478 (2003)
26. Thompson, R.L., Higgins, C.A., Howell, J.M.: Personal computing: toward a conceptual model of utilization. MIS Q. **15**(1), 125–143 (1991)

27. Venkatesh, V., Morris, M.G., Ackerman, P.L.: A longitudinal field investigation of gender differences in individual technology adoption decision-making processes. Organ. Behav. Hum. Decis. Process. **83**(1), 33–60 (2000)
28. Gilster, P.: Digital Literacy. Wiley, New York (1997)
29. Pool, C.: A conversation with Paul Gilster. Educ. Leadersh. **55**(3), 6–11 (1997)
30. Martin, A.: DigEuLit–a European framework for digital literacy: a progress report. J. eLiteracy **2**(2), 130–136 (2005)
31. Ng, W.: Can we teach digital natives digital literacy? Comput. Educ. **59**(3), 1065–1078 (2012)
32. Helsper, E.J., Eynon, R.: Digital natives: where is the evidence? Br. Edu. Res. J. **36**(3), 503–520 (2010)
33. Joo, Y.J., Park, S., Lim, E.: Factors influencing preservice teachers' intention to use technology: TPACK, teacher self-efficacy, and technology acceptance model. J. Educ. Technol. Soc. **21**(3), 48–59 (2018)
34. Chow, M., Herold, D.K., Choo, T.M., Chan, K.: Extending the technology acceptance model to explore the intention to use Second Life for enhancing healthcare education. Comput. Educ. **59**(4), 1136–1144 (2012)
35. Lee, D.Y., Lehto, M.R.: User acceptance of YouTube for procedural learning: an extension of the Technology Acceptance Model. Comput. Educ. **61**, 193–208 (2013)
36. Hair, J.F., Risher, J.J., Sarstedt, M., Ringle, C.M.: When to use and how to report the results of PLS-SEM. Eur. Bus. Rev. **31**(1), 2–24 (2019)
37. Sarstedt, M., Ringle, C.M., Hair, J.F.: Partial least squares structural equation modeling. In: Handbook of Market Research, pp. 1–40 (2017)
38. Taylor, S., Todd, P.A.: Understanding information technology usage: a test of competing models. Inf. Syst. Res. **6**(2), 144–176 (1995)
39. Taylor, S., Todd, P.: Assessing IT usage: the role of prior experience. MIS Q. **19**(4), 561–570 (1995)
40. Armstrong, J.S., Overton, T.S.: Estimating nonresponse bias in mail surveys. J. Mark. Res. **14**(3), 396–402 (1977)
41. Hair, J.F., Ringle, C.M., Sarstedt, M.: PLS-SEM: indeed, a silver bullet. J. Mark. Theory Pract. **19**(2), 139–152 (2011)
42. Gefen, D., Straub, D.: A practical guide to factorial validity using PLS-Graph: tutorial and annotated example. Commun. Assoc. Inf. Syst. **16**(5), 91–109 (2005)
43. Hair, J.F., Hult, G.T., Ringle, C.M., Sarstedt, M.: A Primer on Partial Least Squares Structural Equation Modelling (PLS-SEM). Sage Publication, Thousand Oaks (2013)
44. Hulland, J.: Use of partial least squares (PLS) in strategic management research: a review of four recent studies. Strateg. Manag. J. **20**(2), 195–204 (1999)
45. Bagozzi, R.P., Yi, Y.: On the evaluation of structural equation models. J. Acad. Mark. Sci. **16**(1), 74–94 (1988)
46. Hair, J.F., Sarstedt, M., Ringle, C.M., Mena, J.A.: An assessment of the use of partial least squares structural equation modelling in marketing research. J. Acad. Mark. Sci. **40**(3), 414–433 (2012)
47. Henseler, J., Ringle, C.M., Sarstedt, M.: A new criterion for assessing discriminant validity in variance-based structural equation modelling. J. Acad. Mark. Sci. **43**(1), 115–135 (2015)
48. Fornell, C., Larcker, D.F.: Evaluating structural equation models with unobservable variables and measurement error. J. Mark. Res. **18**(1), 39–50 (1981)
49. Kennedy, G.E., Judd, T.S., Churchward, A., Gray, K., Krause, K.L.: First-year students' experiences with technology: are they really digital natives? Australas. J. Educ. Technol. **24**(1), 108–122 (2008)

50. Sharafi, P., Hedman, L., Montgomery, H.: Using information technology: engagement modes, flow experience, and personality orientations. Comput. Hum. Behav. **22**(5), 899–916 (2006)
51. Hsieh, J.P.A., Rai, A., Keil, M.: Addressing digital inequality for the socioeconomically disadvantaged through government initiatives: forms of capital that affect ICT utilization. Inf. Syst. Res. **22**(2), 233–253 (2011)
52. Fortunati, L., Taipale, S., de Luca, F.: Digital generations, but not as we know them. Convergence **25**(1), 95–112 (2019)
53. Lindell, J.: A methodological intervention in cosmopolitanism research: Cosmopolitan dispositions amongst digital natives. Sociol. Res. Online **19**(3), 1–14 (2014)
54. Carretero, S., Vuorikari, R., Punie, Y.: The Digital Competence Framework for Citizens. Publications Office of the European Union (2017). https://publications.jrc.ec.europa.eu/repository/bitstream/JRC106281/web-digcomp2.1pdf_(online).pdf

Peeling Back the Layers: Deconstructing Information Literacy Discourse in Higher Education

Alison Hicks[(✉)] and Annemaree Lloyd

University College, London (UCL), London, UK
a.hicks@ucl.ac.uk

Abstract. The discourses of information literacy practice create epistemological assumptions about how the practice should happen, who should be responsible and under what conditions instruction should be given. Analysis of a wide range of documents and texts emerging from the Higher Education (HE) sector suggest that information literacy (IL) is shaped by two competing and incongruent narratives. The outward facing narrative of information literacy (located in information literacy standards and guidelines) positions information literacy as an empowering practice that arms students with the knowledge and skills to battle the complexity of the modern information world. In contrast, the inward facing narrative (located in information literacy texts) positions students as lacking appropriate knowledge, skills and agency. This deficit perception, which has the capacity to influence pedagogical practice, is at odds with constructivist and action-oriented views that are espoused within information literacy instructional pedagogy. This presentation represents the first paper in a research programme that interrogates the epistemological premises and discourses of information literacy within HE.

Keywords: Information literacy · Positioning theory · Discourse analysis

1 Introduction

Drawing from an ongoing analysis of discourses and practices that shape information literacy in higher education (ILiHE), this paper presents an epistemological account of the discourse of information literacy. The intention of this research is to interrogate the institutional approach to the practice and delivery of information literacy by peeling back the layers of the broader information literacy narrative. The findings presented here are part of a larger programme of research that is exploring how librarians, students and the practice of IL are positioned within the higher education sector.

The questions that guide this section of the ILiHE project are:

- How does the discourse of ILiHE position information literacy in professional guidelines, models and texts?
- How does the discourse of ILiHE position students as learners?

An epistemological account of information literacy within the higher education (HE) sector leads us, as researchers, to question information literacy practice according

© Springer Nature Switzerland AG 2020
A. Sundqvist et al. (Eds.): iConference 2020, LNCS 12051, pp. 363–372, 2020.
https://doi.org/10.1007/978-3-030-43687-2_28

to the discourses (how reality can be known/what knowledges and ways of knowing are legitimised and accepted) that shape and situate it (the relationship between the knower and what is known/how information literacy happens in HE); its characteristics (the principles, assumptions that guide the process of knowing and action), and the possibility for the practice to be shared and repeated by others in the same HE setting.

The emerging analysis of ILiHE suggests that information literacy is characterised by outward-facing statements (located in information literacy standards and guidelines) that position IL as an empowering practice, with inward-facing articulations (located in information literacy texts) positioning students as deficient and unable to successfully engage with the practice to inform their learning. This leads us to assert that disparities between these outward and inward-facing narratives form one of the most fundamental and problematic failures of ILiHE, because the starting point of the narrative of ILiHE and the operationalisation of the practice becomes a deficit approach rather than an approach that focuses on the strengths and knowledges that diverse student cohorts bring to the construction of the ILiHE information landscapes. We also propose that this ongoing marginalisation may, in part, contribute to students' resistance to engage with these ideas.

We further suggest that while much research has been conducted into the operationalisation of ILiHE, the field cannot progress until the foundational tensions between these two faces of practice has been resolved. We argue that the inward IL narrative requires re-examination to focus on the strengths of IL practice and its capacity to accommodate diversity rather than to promote deficiency while the outward narrative of IL must be reframed to highlight more of the complex and messy dimensions of IL practice. Failing to acknowledge and address these tensions creates the risk of minimising the sustainable aspects of information literacy as a core practice of student learning.

2 Literature Review

The last decade has seen the emergence of a second wave of institutional information literacy models. Starting with the UK's ANCIL model, which was released in 2011 [1], and the Metaliteracy model, which was created in the US by Jacobson and Mackey in 2013 [2], the Association of College and Research Libraries (ACRL) released the Framework for Information Literacy in Higher Education in 2016 [3], its first major update of information literacy since 2000 [4]. These new guidelines, which built on long-standing critiques of traditional information literacy standards and documents [5–7], aimed to update information literacy for the challenges posed by dynamic and changing information environments. In further focusing attention on information literacy concepts rather than skills and competencies, they marked a significant turn for a field that has tended to emphasise positivist methods of instruction and assessment.

The release of this second wave of documents has not been without controversy [8]. Commentators questioned what was lost through the profession's explicit move away from standard practice [9], and there was a sudden resurgence of interest in the standards-based VALUE rubric for information literacy, which was published by the Association of American Universities and Colleges in 2013 [10]. Unease with the dramatic change in focus further catalysed the publication of a number of texts that were designed to help librarians translate these more flexible institutional models into practice (see Appendix A). However, by and large, institutional backing for these documents, coupled with practitioners' espousal of problem-based learning [11] and the flipped classroom [12], amongst other initiatives, marks a growing acceptance of constructivist theories of learning within information literacy teaching research and practice.

These developments have, nonetheless, failed to translate into a broad examination of the practice of information literacy in higher education as it is represented by institutional and other core guiding documents. While Martin [13] scoped four different UK models of information literacy, her work pre-dated the emergence of recent US models of practice. Furthermore, whilst a number of initial small-scale critiques of the ACRL Framework have been published [14, 15], there has been little critical exploration of other prominent models of practice or a sustained exploration of the ideas and principles that are presented through these modernising narratives. These oversights provide an important justification for our programme of study.

3   Methodology

The overall aim of the ILiHE project is to interrogate and unpack the discourses and practices of information literacy in Higher Education as they relate to students and librarians. For the first stage of the project, a discourse analytical approach was employed to identify the discourses which surround and bind institutional narratives of information literacy within higher education. Texts that were analysed included preambles to the five major English-language information literacy models that have been published since 2010 as well as introductions to books that specifically explore these models (see Appendix A). Book introductions and preambles to institutional models were selected for the framing work that they do to position and contextualise information literacy. This approach also enabled us to carry out an in-depth study of the institutional narratives of information literacy that, as professional documents, serve to both codify and sanction teaching librarian practices. Academic articles were excluded from this sample because of their typical focus on classroom practice and the tendency to avoid framing major information literacy concepts. While the exclusion of empirical and critical articles is a limitation of this study, the focus on institutional narratives provides a useful preliminary way to untangle and draw attention to competing perspectives and expectations within information literacy teaching practices.

3.1   Discursive Approach and Positioning Theory

Discourse is conceptualized in this paper as a complex network of relationships that wind between and entangle people, texts and ideas, leading them to enact practices within agreed boundaries. A discourse analytical approach emphasises social construction of reality and acknowledges the multiplicity of this construction. In the context of information literacy discourse, Lloyd [6] has argued that information literacy is composed of different contexts, different concepts and different truths and that the discourses of higher education that influence the practice and practising of information literacy do not accommodate informal learning, non-textual sources of information or the diversity of learning approaches that students bring to their information practices in the higher education sector. In effect, the discourse community that supports ILiHE creates tensions for students who are not privy to how or why the practice is operationalised in this context, in terms of what knowledges are accepted and which ways of knowing are validated [16–18].

Information literacy is a practice that is socially enacted [19], and in this study, positioning theory is used as a framework that will allow us to describe how discourses of ILiHE construct and position the performativity of students to create a specific type of interaction and way of *doing IL* within higher education. Positioning theory has been applied within LIS to studies of mature-aged students and academic information behaviours [20] and physician-patient interaction [21]. We also draw upon other fields where positioning theory has been applied [22–25].

Positioning theory is located within a constructivist framework and can be useful in understanding the interactional relationship between actors and the discursive texts related to their practices. Moghaddam and Harré [24, p. 2] describe positioning theory as "how people use words (and discourse of all types) to locate themselves and others." Positioning can consequently be seen as a productive process that involves the social construction of particular individuals and groups as "culturally imagined types" [22, p. 130]. In further asserting that "it is with words that we ascribe rights and claim them for ourselves and place duties on others," Moghaddam and Harré [24, p. 3] also signal the moral codes that govern these narratives as well as the ways in which positioning serves as an "intelligible map" [25, p. 232] for interaction. In the present research, we aim to illuminate how the discursive texts of ILiHE position both information literacy and learners. As Slocum-Bradley [26, p. 81] points out, it is only by understanding "how we construct social reality, we can construct more consciously to sustain norms that promote the ends we profess to desire."

4   Findings and Analysis

Preliminary analysis of book introductions and the preambles of institutional models of information literacy practice suggests the emergence of two distinct narratives. The overall outward-facing narrative positions ILiHE in terms of empowerment and authority over complex, messy, volatile and often fragile information environments. This narrative is in contrast to the inward-facing discourse, which positions students in terms of their deficiencies within the discursive framework of higher education. Both discourses act to enable and constrain information literacy practice.

4.1   How Is IL Positioned as a Practice in HE?

In the texts and the institutional preambles that were investigated in this study, the discourse of information literacy is described as both practised and agile. Practised information literacy references statements about the assumed generic and timeless aspects of information literacy, which supports the capacity for lifelong learning. This understanding situates information literacy as a set of "core" [27, p. 3], "foundational" [3, p. 2] or "basic" ideas [28, p. viii] that are mastered progressively [29, p. 6; 10, p. 1] and form the "foundation of autonomous learning" [1, p. 6]. The agile theme establishes the discourse in terms of transferability of skills, the transformative nature of the practice and the capacity to develop reflexivity, openness (to perspectives) and critical thinking. In this theme, information literacy is positioned as "flexible" [3, p. 2; 1, p. 4] and not "something learned once and for all" [30, p. xv] as well as "cyclical" [28, p. 3] and collaborative [3, p. 3; 1, p. 4; 31, p. xv].

While there is a certain tension between these themes, they feed into an overarching discourse of information literacy as "empowerment" or the idea that information literacy will 'empower' learners with the skills or understandings that they need to make informed choices in their current and future endeavours. The themes of practised and agile also act to authorise a specific epistemology (ways of knowing) and knowledge claim, which establishes the contextual foundations of the practice by which students' practising is evaluated.

4.2   How Are Learners in HE Positioned by the IL Discourse?

In contrast, book introductions reveal that the discourse surrounding student's engagement with information literacy instruction affords learners a social position that emphasises their lack of capacity to learn the information skills associated with the practice. Within this narrative, students are positioned as struggling under the weight of their deficit, which variously positions learners as overwhelmed, passive and uncritical and, in some instances, as plagiarisers.

Learners are positioned as overwhelmed when they are perceived to be unable to cope with an "oversaturated information ecosystem" [31, p. xix] that drowns us in information [32]:

> "students need to learn how to deal with the ocean of information that surrounds them" [29, p. 10].

Within this framing, information overload is viewed as constraining the ability of students to action their learning, creating the conditions which produce passive students who are unmotivated, lacking in persistence and dependent upon others. Learners are positioned as unmotivated when they are seen to devalue information literacy ideals:

> "someone might be aware that they should carefully evaluate the information they find… yet not care enough to actually do it" [32].

A perceived tendency to give up too easily means that students are similarly positioned as lacking in persistence and patience in their research endeavours:

> "they need to be persistent in the search for information" [29, p. 10].

Students' passivity subsequently positions them as uncritical of sources or actions of others. Within this theme, the students' lack of agility creates a narrative that suggests inflexibility:

> "this process requires the researcher to be flexible… and to keep an open mind" [29, p. 9].

Students' lack of criticality further positions them as ignorant of the skills and knowledge that they will need to be successful within today's information environments, which is often portrayed through metaphors that emphasise students' lack of voice:

"before an encounter with a threshold concept, the novice is in a blissful state of ignorance" [28, p. 3].

More commonly, students are positioned as being unable to understand variation or nuances within information environments:

"It means… not just reverting to long-standing habits only because they are familiar" [32].
"Students tend to see all information sources as equal unless instructed otherwise" [29, p. 7].

These issues are exacerbated by students' feelings of overconfidence [33, p. 10].

The discourse also characterises students as plagiarisers who lack the capacity to understand the ethical obligations of academic practice. Within this framing, students are positioned as disrespectful of others' intellectual property as well as liable to make irresponsible decisions:

"ethical use of information is a concept that students struggle to understand" [29, p. 7].
"[information literacy instruction] is… crucial for their development as informed and responsible citizens" [34, p. xv].

5   Discussion

The discourse of information literacy in the higher education sector is composed of both outward-facing and inward-facing narratives. The outward-facing discourse of information literacy positions the practice as empowering learners by facilitating a critically reflexive engagement with information. Against this discourse is the inward discourse, which positions higher education students as lacking the capacity to develop strategies to inform their learning and meet the rules of academic practices.

The difference between these narratives is striking but not unexpected. Deficiency could be interpreted as an important rationale for information literacy instruction, which empowers the learner to unlock their potential and make more informed and healthy decisions. Within this framing, empowerment is positioned as a "self-evident good" [35, p. 53] that enables individuals (or communities) to exercise power in the determination of their everyday life [36].

However, when we position students as deficient, we retreat from the idea that information literacy empowers learners to control their lives. Instead, a narrative that centres upon a lack of ability subtly reframes empowerment in terms of top-down behaviour modification by establishing and holding learners accountable to specific activities and indicators of expertise. Establishing a "fundamental contrast between those who know and those who are ignorant, between the morally superior and the morally inferior" [37], the emphasis on expert awareness further reinforces the illusion of empowerment by drawing learners into "participating in processes and decisions over which they have little meaningful control" [35, p. 58].

Within the context of this study, these ideas suggest that the narratives of empowerment and deficiency are politicised rather than neutral. This leads to further questions about whom or what is empowered, under what conditions or circumstances deficiency is evaluated, and which discourses prevail [19, 38]. Responding to these questions forms the basis of future work by the authors.

6 Conclusion

In previous research, Lloyd [6, p. 87] argued that:

> The current dominant paradigm of information literacy... produces a deficit model of information literacy which does not take into account the importance of informal learning or other sources of information which are accessed through communication or action. This reduces the power of information literacy and the way in which information education is undertaken by students and undergraduates.

Almost fifteen years on from this statement and despite the wider adoption of constructivist models of education, there is little evidence present in the texts reviewed as part of this analysis to suggest that the practising of ILiHE and the narrative that influences these practises has altered. However, for the practice of information literacy to be sustainable in the HE context, our analysis suggests that authors (of texts, preambles, standards and guidelines) and researchers working in this sector should focus more closely on the ways in which these statements and documents position both IL and students. Future research should continue to explore these ideas as well as to extend this study by examining, for example, how librarians as well as students and information literacy are positioned within institutional narratives.

Appendix A

Information literacy models

- A new curriculum for information literacy (ANCIL) (Secker & Coonan, 2011)
- Framework for information literacy for higher education (ACRL, 2016)
- Metaliteracy (Jacobson & Mackey, 2014)
- Seven pillars of information literacy (SCONUL, 2011)
- VALUE rubric (AACU, 2013)

Books

- Metaliteracy
  - Jacobson, T. E., Mackey, T. P.: Metaliterate learning for the post-truth world. Chicago: Neal-Schuman (2019).
  - Jacobson, T. E., Mackey, T. P.: Metaliteracy in practice. Chicago: Neal-Schuman (2016).
  - Mackey, T. P., Jacobson, T. E.: Metaliteracy: Reinventing information literacy to empower learners. London: Facet Publishing (2014).

- Framework
  - Bravender, P., McClure, H., Schaub, G.: Teaching information literacy threshold concepts: Lesson plans for librarians. Chicago: ACRL (2015).
  - Burkhardt, J. M.: Teaching information literacy reframed: 50+ framework-based exercises for creating information-literate learners. Chicago: Neal-Schuman (2017).
  - Godbey, S., Wainscott, S., Goodman, X.: Disciplinary applications of information literacy threshold concepts. Chicago: Neal-Schuman (2017).
  - Harmeyer, D., Baskin, J. J.: Implementing the information literacy framework: A practical guide for librarians. Lanham: Rowman & Littlefield (2018).
  - Jacobson, T.: Foreword. In Harmeyer, D., Baskin, J.J. (eds.), Implementing the information literacy framework: A practical guide for librarians, Lanham: Rowman & Littlefield (2018).
  - McClure, R.: Rewired: Research-writing partnerships in a frameworks state of mind. Chicago: Neal-Schuman (2016).
  - McClure, R., Purdy, J. P.: The future scholar: Researching and teaching the frameworks for writing and information literacy. Medford, NJ: ASIST (2016).
  - Oberlies, M. K., Mattson, J. L.: Framing information literacy: Teaching grounded in theory, pedagogy, and practice. Chicago: Neal-Schuman (2018).
- Seven Pillars/Metaliteracy
  - Hosier, A., Bullis, D., Bernnard, D., Vobish, G., Holden, I., Pitera, J., Loney, T., Jacobson, T.: The Information literacy user's guide: An open, online textbook. https://textbooks.opensuny.org/the-information-literacy-users-guide-an-open-online-textbook/, last accessed 2019/8/29.
- ANCIL
  - Coonan, E., Secker, J.: Rethinking information literacy: A practical framework for supporting learning. London: Facet (2013).

References

1. Secker, J., Coonan, E.: A New Curriculum for Information Literacy: Curriculum and Supporting Documents. https://newcurriculum.wordpress.com/project-reports-and-outputs/. Accessed 29 Aug 2019
2. Jacobson, T.E., Mackey, T.P.: Proposing a metaliteracy model to redefine information literacy. Commun. Inf. Lit. 7(2), 84–91 (2013)
3. ACRL (Association of College and Research Libraries). Framework for information literacy for higher education. http://www.ala.org/acrl/standards/ilframework. Accessed 29 Aug 2019
4. ACRL (Association of College and Research Libraries). Information literacy competency standards for higher education. www.ala.org/ala/acrl/acrlstandards/standards.pdf. Accessed 29 Aug 2019
5. Bruce, C.: The Seven Faces of Information Literacy. Auslib Press, Adelaide (1997)
6. Lloyd, A.: Information literacy: different contexts, different concepts, different truths? J. Librariansh. Inf. Sci. 37(2), 82–88 (2005)
7. Tuominen, K., Savolainen, R., Talja, S.: Information literacy as a sociotechnical practice. Libr. Q. 75(3), 329–345 (2005)

8. Bombaro, C.: The framework is elitist. Ref. Serv. Rev. **44**(4), 552–563 (2016)
9. Drabinski, E., Sitar, M.: What standards do and what they don't. In: McElroy, K., Pagowsky, N. (eds.) Critical Pedagogy Handbook. Neal-Schuman, Chicago (2016)
10. AACU (Association of American Colleges and Universities). Information literacy VALUE rubric. http://www.aacu.org/value/rubrics/information-literacy. Accessed 29 Aug 2019
11. Smith Macklin, A.: Integrating information literacy using problem-based learning. Ref. Serv. Rev. **29**(4), 306–314 (2001)
12. Arnold-Garza, S.: The flipped classroom teaching model and its use for information literacy instruction. Commun. Inf. Lit. **8**(1), 7–22 (2014)
13. Martin, J.: Refreshing information literacy: learning from recent British information literacy models. Commun. Inf. Lit. **7**(2), 115–127 (2013)
14. Morgan, P.K.: Pausing at the threshold. Portal: Libr. Acad. **15**(1), 183–195 (2015)
15. Wilkinson, L.: The problem with threshold concepts. Sense and Reference (2014). https://senseandreference.wordpress.com/2014/06/19/the-problem-with-threshold-concepts/. Accessed 29 Aug 2019
16. Burkholder, J.M.: Interpreting the conventions of scholarship: rhetorical implications of the ACRL Framework. Portal: Libr. Acad. **19**(2), 295–314 (2019)
17. Elmborg, J.: Critical information literacy: implications for instructional practice. J. Acad. Librariansh. **32**(2), 192–199 (2006)
18. Kapitzke, C.: (In)formation literacy: a positivist epistemology and a politics of (out)formation. Educ. Theory **53**(1), 37–53 (2003)
19. Lloyd, A.: Information literacy as a socially enacted practice: sensitising themes for an emerging perspective of people-in-practice. J. Doc. **68**(6), 772–783 (2012)
20. Given, L.: Discursive constructions in the university context: social positioning theory and mature undergraduates' information behaviours. New Rev. Inf. **3**, 127–142 (2002)
21. McKenzie, P.: Positioning theory and the negotiation of information needs in a clinical midwifery setting. J. Am. Soc. Inform. Sci. Technol. **55**(8), 685–694 (2004)
22. Holland, D., Leander, K.: Ethnographic studies of positioning and subjectivity: an introduction. Ethos **32**(2), 127–139 (2004)
23. McVee, M., Silvestri, K., Barrett, N., Haq, K.: Positioning theory. In: Alvermann, D., Unrau, N., Sailors, M., Ruddell, R. (eds.) Theoretical Models and Processes of Literacy. Routledge, New York (2019)
24. Moghaddam, F., Harré, R.: Words, conflicts and political processes. In: Moghaddam, F., Harré, R. (eds.) Words of Conflict, Words of War: How the Language We Use in Political Processes Sparks Fighting. Praeger, Santa Barbara (2010)
25. Tirado, F., Gálvez, A.: Positioning theory and discourse analysis: some tools for social interaction analysis. Hist. Soc. Res./Historische Sozialforschung **33**(1), 224–251 (2008)
26. Slocum-Bradley, N.: The positioning diamond: a trans-disciplinary framework for discourse analysis. J. Theory Soc. Behav. **40**(1), 79–107 (2010)
27. Bravender, P., McClure, H., Schaub, G.: Teaching Information Literacy Threshold Concepts: Lesson Plans for Librarians. Neal-Schuman, Chicago (2015)
28. Godbey, S., Wainscott, S., Goodman, X.: Disciplinary Applications of Information Literacy Threshold Concepts. Neal-Schuman, Chicago (2017)
29. Burkhardt, J.M.: Teaching Information Literacy Reframed: 50+ Framework-Based Exercises for Creating Information-Literate Learners. Neal-Schuman, Chicago (2017)
30. Jacobson, T.E., Mackey, T.P.: Metaliteracy in Practice. Neal-Schuman, Chicago (2016)
31. Harmeyer, D., Baskin, J.J.: Implementing the Information Literacy Framework: A Practical Guide for Librarians. Rowman & Littlefield, Lanham (2018)

32. Hosier, A., et al.: The Information literacy user's guide: an open, online text book. https://tex tbooks.opensuny.org/the-information-literacy-users-guide-an-open-online-textbook/. Accessed 29 Aug 2019

33. Mackey, T.P., Jacobson, T.E.: Metaliteracy: Reinventing Information Literacy to Empower Learners. Facet Publishing, London (2014)

34. Jacobson, T.: Foreword. In: Harmeyer, D., Baskin, J.J. (eds.) Implementing the Information Literacy Framework: A Practical Guide for Librarians. Rowman & Littlefield, Lanham (2018)

35. McLaughlin, K.: Empowerment: A Critique. Routledge, Abingdon (2016)

36. Adams, R.: Empowerment, Participation and Social Work. Palgrave Macmillan, New York (2008)

37. Furedi, F.: I don't want to have my awareness raised, thanks. http://www.frankfuredi.com/newsite/article/i_dont_want_to_have_my_awareness_raised_thanks. Accessed 29 Aug 2019

38. Walton, G., Cleland, J.: Information literacy: empowerment or reproduction in practice? A discourse analysis approach. J. Doc. **73**(4), 582–594 (2017)

Where is Search in Information Literacy?
A Theoretical Note on Infrastructure
and Community of Practice

Olof Sundin

Lund University, 221 00 Lund, Sweden
olof.sundin@kultur.lu.se

Abstract. In this conceptual paper theory of infrastructure is combined with one of situated learning, with a focus on search and search engines. The aim of the paper is to make a theoretical contribution to the information literacy research field by discussing theoretical contradictions as well as strengths when combining the two theoretical perspectives. Search engines and their use are part of the contemporary information infrastructure and are a such often not thought of when being used. It is argued that a critical perspective on information literacy in relation to search seems to demand that they are treated as situated and general at the same time. The paper concludes that sociomaterial perspectives on information literacy research offers both infrastructures and practices a place.

Keywords: Information literacy · Infrastructures · Situated learning · Search engines

1 Introduction

I have a ten-year-old son who sits a lot with his iPhone. He uses the internet mostly through visible applications on his phone. Sometimes when he searches for something he just writes a few words in the address field and then off he goes. This is not a rational use of a certain general-purpose web search engine based on specific criteria. For him, this is just finding what he wants. Mostly he asks me or my wife to find very specific things, such as the 10 most beautiful goals by Zlatan Ibrahimović, who is the best goalkeeper ever, or a photo of the biggest pike that you can fish. We have not yet discussed how search engines work because so far he is not interested and they have not yet broached this issue in school. He basically treats search engines as facts machines. Moreover, in school he and his class have searched for information, but they have not talked about what they have done or how and why they got the search result they did. At least not according to my son. In fact, the Curriculum for the compulsory school, preschool class and school-age educare [1] states that for his age one of the core contents of the school subject Swedish is: "Searching for information in books, periodicals and on websites for children using search engines on the internet". That is, they are supposed

© Springer Nature Switzerland AG 2020
A. Sundqvist et al. (Eds.): iConference 2020, LNCS 12051, pp. 373–379, 2020.
https://doi.org/10.1007/978-3-030-43687-2_29

to search for information, but they are not supposed to learn how searching the internet works. Search is treated as a neutral tool for learning something else.

In this conceptual paper I combine a theory of infrastructure with one of situated learning, with a focus on search and search engines. Thereby I do not aim to just bring search engines into information literacy research, but I also aim to make a theoretical contribution to the field by discussing theoretical contradictions as well as strengths when combining the two theoretical perspectives. A starting point is that searching for information has become such a self-evident part of everyday life that talking about a search-ification of everyday life as well as a mundane-ification of search is justified [2, 3]. That is, everyday-life practices of all kinds have been suffused by search to such an extent that it is actually difficult to identify the activity. At the same time, searching has become so easy, so mundane, that anyone without any particular skill or knowledge can do it and still get what most people would regard as a satisfying result.

The next section discusses infrastructure as a conceptual device and how that complies with situated learning and, more precisely, the theory of community of practice. Thereafter, a couple of interview transcripts are discussed followed by a short conclusion.

2   Learning to Use the Infrastructure of Search

Theoretical engagements with the notion of infrastructure often have a focus on information [4–6]. An infrastructure is tangible in the various sociomaterial relations that make it possible and which enable the carrying out of certain functions in society, such as the electricity grid is tangible in being able to read in the dark, to charge the car or to search for information online. Infrastructures are sociomaterial also in the sense that they include classifications, standards, regulations and so forth, which all shape its materiality in specific ways [7]. That is, they also include norms and values of how, when and where they should be used. One key idea from infrastructure studies is how infrastructures, when they work properly, tend to go unnoticed. Geoffrey Bowker and Susan Star [5, p. 33] formulate this as, "[t]he easier they are to use, the harder they are to see".

Often, you only notice infrastructures when you are new to an infrastructure or when they break down. An example of the first instance is when travelling from UK to Sweden. You immediately notice the electricity infrastructure because of the different standards for power plugs. As inhabitants in UK are used to having problems with electricity standards when travelling, they might remember to carry out a quick Google search for "standards", "charger" and "Sweden" before embarking on a journey. The first link tells you: "In Sweden the power plugs and sockets are of type F. The standard voltage is 230 V and the standard frequency is 50 Hz" (https://www.power-plugs-sockets.com/gb/sweden/). When living in Sweden, this is, in most situations, everyday-life knowledge that you do not need to know; however, when travelling it becomes important. As long as they do what they are supposed to do, you hardly think about the electricity system and its standards. For newer technology, this is not always the case. Recently, I bought a plug-in hybrid car that can be charged with electricity. I learned quickly that in Sweden there are at least 12 different standards – as you can see from

Fig. 1. Different charging standards for electric car batteries in Sweden 2019-07-30.

this picture (see Fig. 1) taken from a Swedish website on how to find your nearest charging station (https://www.uppladdning.nu/).

The standards are developed to accommodate car companies, national and supra-national regulations, battery factories, electrical companies and so forth. The standards compete and, to some extent, supplement each other. For me, as a new owner of a chargeable car, the infrastructure for plug-in hybrid cars has certainly not become invisible in the same way as the workings of petrol stations is invisible to me when filling the tank of the car. Furthermore, a number of competing companies supply the electricity and, in contrast to petrol stations, it is often necessary to have a separate account with each of the companies if you want to use them. I need to learn how to use the infrastructure.

For general-purpose search engines, as well as for social media and other con-temporary digital services, it is obvious, without going into the details, how they are made and remade every time they are used. All digital traces of individual use are aggregated at a collective level which then shapes further use through, for example, the autocorrect function and, of course, the search result as such. Besides user data, the infrastructure of search also consists of indexes and algorithms, as well as a number of standards, templates, and classifications and the devices used. For the ordinary user, if noticed at all, a search engine is just an empty white query box (or an address field) in which you write what you want to find or do. Another trait of this conceptual device of infrastructure is that it emerges in practice and that it, accordingly, must be investigated as parts of practices [6, p. 379]. The analytical starting point is not on the technology as such or its different parts – user data, index, algorithms – but how the infrastructure is used, for example in the practice of tourism and how search engine use emerges there, or the practice of schooling and how search engine activities today are embedded in that practice. A further trait of infrastructures – together with their standards and classifications – is that they are not neutral. For an ordinary citizen, it is enough that there is light when the lamp is switched. But a critical citizen could ask questions, for example about prices of electricity, how bulbs can be recycled and whether the elec-tricity is from renewable energy or fossil fuel. In order to read on a winter evening in Northern Europe, you just turn on the light, but if you want to become a critical citizen, you have to make the infrastructure visible and learn more about it.

How do you learn to use an information infrastructure such as search engines? Just as with electricity, which you can use by just switching on the lamp, many times you just have to type a word to get a result that is at least good enough. At the same time, the workings of search engines for a large number of sectors have dramatic consequences in society, such as for business, tourism, politics and schools. Again, you do not have to know very much in order to find out something about what you are looking for. But just as with electricity, if you want to be an informed and critical citizen this is not enough. For example, research has convincingly demonstrated that search engines are not neutral, but in fact can reinforce prejudice [e.g. 8], that they gather your data in a way that affects your privacy [9], that they are not just tools for finding information but also contribute to establishing what knowledge there is to know [10], and that they can be manipulated by groups with a particular agenda who identify so-called data voids and formulate and popularize phrases and keywords that people thereafter use in order to find extremist content [11]. That is, you have to learn the implications search engines have for different avenues in life. Again, search engines should not be seen as a constant variable effecting something else. Instead, they are more and more parts of social practices in life which they, together with other actors in the practice, shape and reshape.

In information literacy research, a number of scholars lean on situated learning [e.g. 12] and/or practice research [e.g. 13] when understanding how information literacy is learned and enacted in various practices [e.g. 14–17]. Information literacy research with a sociocultural and practice theoretical interest often underlines the need to talk about literacies, rather than literacy, in order to stress the situatedness of literacy. It is taken for granted that practices and their embedded information activities are tied to local communities to such an extent that references to generalised competences, abilities or knowledge are problematized and sometimes even criticized.

3   Learning the Infrastructure of Search

Web search engines are extremely complex technologies whose development is based on input from a number of academic fields – including computer science, information science and general linguistics – and they are situated within legal frameworks, cultural practices and economic systems. They have continuously changed since the first web search engine (Webcrawler) was launched in 1994, and their development has since moved outside academia and closer to the business sector [18]. Furthermore, search engines are increasingly inbuilt into the operating systems of computers, smartphones, tablets and in all kinds of connected gadgets and devices. They are moving in a direction where text input is supplemented with voice assistance for use, such as in my plug-in car. Search engines are everywhere, yet at the same time they are not thought of at all by most people.

During the spring of 2019, I conducted 32 couple interviews with 62 late teenagers (17–19 years). The interviews are part of the larger project "Algorithms and Literacies: Young people's understanding and society's expectations".[1] The interviews were a way for us to make people reflect on what they normally do not think about; to reflect about their epistemological practices of finding out something. In this paper I will only

---

[1] The research complies with the ethical guidelines in Good Research Practice (Swedish Research Council, 2017); the research project has been reviewed by Swedish Ethical Review Board for the South of Sweden and according to their decision it does not fall under the Swedish Research Act (203:460).

very briefly address two specific interview questions, namely variants of: "Do you remember when you started using social media" and "Do you remember when you used Google for the first time?". Almost all interviewed teenagers could identify the first social media applications they used. Two of the participants were Linda and Louise, both 18 years old. They went to upper secondary school taking a technology programme in the south of Sweden:

Researcher: Do you remember when you started using social media?
Linda: Yes, I was only allowed to start using Facebook when I was 13. It was one such age limit, but everyone around me started earlier. But I remember it. And then, the other social media, like Instagram, I think got a little bit earlier. And then Snapchat when it was released like in 2014.
Louise: I had ... I like didn't care about Facebook, but then it seemed like, "yes, everyone has Facebook. Maybe there is something good with Facebook? "[giggle] But like, let's see if I can remember how old I was, like 13–14 something. And since then, I've added social media in relation to what friends around me used and what I've seen worked. I think I got Snapchat in let's say nine grade and started using it like that there.

The interviewed youth often associated their first distinct social media experience with their first smartphone that gave access to a new world. Facebook – despite the fact that they do not use it so much anymore – was the most often-mentioned application through which the participants were introduced to social media. Directly after the participants answered the question about experiencing social media for the first time, I asked, "[d]o you remember when you used Google for the first time?". The answers to that question were in nearly all cases less clear than to the question about social media. Many participants hesitated when trying to remember when they started to use Google or similar search engines, but in general it was a much earlier experience which was far more difficult to remember. The interview quoted above continues:

Researcher: But do you remember when you started to use Google, searching on Google?
Louise: No. [giggle]
Researcher: Was it much earlier?
Linda: Yes.
Louise: It is a lot older. I remember in like second grade, on the school computers ... using Google, but no, I don't know.
Linda: No, I don't remember either. It just feels like you've always used Google.
Louise: and after a while you started to realize what it was, but you have used it before. Just so like "freely", I don't know.

If social media was connected to their first smartphone, it appears that Google was connected to their first computer use. While social media clearly relate to their everyday life and leisure, search engine use was often related to school practices. Google was so much inscribed into school practices and the introduction of computers that, when asked, they remembered starting to use it even before they knew what it was. While social media applications are easily identified and demarcated, also in relation to one's biography, search engines are difficult to discern as a program separate from the computer as such.

For Bowker and Star [5 p. 35, 293f], with reference to Lave and Wenger [12], the process of becoming a member of a community of practice (learning) implies that the infrastructures of the community become more and more invisible. In relation to information literacy this could be regarded as somewhat of a contradiction. Visualizing information infrastructures, such as the role and function of search engines in social practices, is a necessary part of promoting information literacy in educational contexts at the same time as learning in a community implies becoming more and more blind to its infrastructure. There appears to be a need to make a distinction between learning for use and learning for critical use. A critical use also entails being able to switch between pragmatic and critical use depending on the situation. Furthermore, the infrastructure of search is today the same in many communities [3 pp. 55–57]. In a situated sense there are always norms and expectations of when and how a search engine should be used or not. You are for example usually supposed to put the phone away during dinner and in schools. In a generic sense, enacting information literacy implies also certain skills, abilities and knowledges that have weight beyond specific practices and communities.

4   Short Conclusion

When my son, whose experience I used to introduce this short paper, searches for something, he thinks that he finds facts, that he gets straightforward answers to straightforward questions, not that he uses search engines to gauge a topical area. To search using general-purpose web search engines is an activity that is now tied to a large number of practices. Search engines constitute a crucial contemporary information infrastructure and, as such, in everyday life they are invisible to most people. As argued above, search engines (most often Google), despite their central role in contemporary society, are often not even thought of when starting to use them, as exemplified in the quotations above. In the interviews I have conducted, it became clear that the anecdotal observation of my ten-year old also applies more widely to older youths. This finding challenges how infrastructures have been dealt with in relation to communities of practice, as referred to above, in at least two ways: Firstly, according to infrastructure studies combined with situated learning theory, the infrastructure should be easier to recognize when you enter a community of practice as a new member. However, the interviews reveal that search engines almost never seem to have been a visible information infrastructure for the current generation of teenagers. This can be compared to social media, which in almost all interviews were easy to identify and talk about. Secondly, infrastructure studies note how infrastructures are tied to specific communities.

For sure, search engines are given meaning differently in for example schools compared to leisure practices, but they are also in some respects the same in different communities. If we want to emphasise critical perspectives, we also need to extricate literacy from its practice-based existence and discuss crucial affordances of technology such as search engines. A critical perspective on information literacy demands that we situate searching and search engines in specific communities of practice. Yet, we also need to explore how search and search engines tie different practices and different communities of practice together. We further need to acknowledge that critical information literacy is not an abstraction, but that it needs to encompass critical awareness of the interlinked commercial, social and political interests of the actually existing contemporary general-purpose search engines acting as multi-sided platforms.

That is, we need to bring in sociomaterial perspectives to information literacy research in which both infrastructures and practices and, above all, how practices are part of infrastructures, are given a place.

References

1. Swedish National Agency for Education: Curriculum for the compulsory school, preschool class and school-age educare (Lgr11), Stockholm (2018)
2. Sundin, O., Haider, J., Andersson, C., Carlsson, H., Kjellberg, S.: The search-ification of everyday life and the mundane-ification of search. J. Doc. **73**(2), 224–243 (2017)
3. Haider, J., Sundin, O.: Invisible Search and Online Search Engines: The Ubiquity of Search in Everyday Life. Routledge, Abingdon (2019)
4. Bowker, G.C.: The history of information infrastructures: the case of the international classification of diseases. Inf. Process. Manag. **32**(1), 49–61 (1996)
5. Bowker, G.C., Star, S.L.: Sorting Things Out: Classification and Its Consequences. MIT Press, Cambridge (2000)
6. Star, S.L., Ruhleder, K.: Steps toward an ecology of infrastructure: design and access for large information spaces. Inf. Syst. Res. **7**(1), 111–134 (2015[1996])
7. Orlikowski, W.J.: Sociomaterial practices: exploring technology at work. Organ. Stud. **28**(9), 1435–1448 (2007)
8. Noble, S.U.: Algorithms of Oppression: How Search Engines Reinforce Racism. NYU Press, New York (2018)
9. Hoofnagle, C.J.: Beyond Google and evil: how policy makers, journalists and consumers should talk differently about Google and privacy. First Monday **14**(4) (2018). https://firstmonday.org/ojs/index.php/fm/article/view/2326/2156
10. Rogers, R.: Digital Methods. MIT Press, Cambridge (2013)
11. Golebiewski, M., Boyd, D.: Data voids: where missing data can easily be exploited. Data and Society (2018). https://datasociety.net/output/data-voids-where-missing-data-can-easily-be-exploited/
12. Lave, J., Wenger, E.: Situated Learning: Legitimate Peripheral Participation. Cambridge University Press, Cambridge (1991)
13. Schatzki, T.R.: Practice theory: an introduction. In: Knorr-Cetina, K., von Savigny, E., Schatzki, T.R. (eds.) The Practice Turn in Contemporary Theory, pp. 1–14. Routledge, Abingdon (2001)
14. Hicks, A.: The theory of mitigating risk: information literacy and language-learning in transition. Högskolan i Borås, Borås (2018)
15. Limberg, L., Sundin, O., Talja, S.: Three theoretical perspectives on information literacy. Hum. IT: J. Inf. Technol. Stud. Hum. Sci. **11**(2) (2012). https://humanit.hb.se/article/view/69/51
16. Lloyd, A.: Recasting information literacy as sociocultural practice: implications for library and information science researchers. Inf. Res. **12**(4) (2007). http://InformationR.net/ir/12-4/colis34.html. Paper colis34
17. Tuominen, K., Savolainen, R., Talja, S.: Information literacy as a sociotechnical practice. Libr. Q. **75**(3), 329–345 (2005)
18. Van Couvering, E.: The history of the Internet search engine: navigational media and the traffic commodity. In: Spink, A., Zimmer, M. (eds.) Web Search. Information Science and Knowledge Management, vol. 14, pp. 177–206. Springer, Heidelberg (2008). https://doi.org/10.1007/978-3-540-75829-7_11

What They Talk About When They Talk About the Need for Critical Evaluation of Information Sources: An Analysis of Norwegian and Swedish News Articles Mentioning 'Source Criticism'

Kim Tallerås[1] and Olle Sköld[2]

[1] Department of Archivistics, Library and Information Science,
Oslo Metropolitan University, Oslo, Norway
[2] Department of ALM, Uppsala University, Uppsala, Sweden
olle.skold@abm.uu.se

Abstract. In the so-called 'post-truth' era the need for skills that allow (digital) information to be critically evaluated has garnered considerable attention and discussion. In the library and LIS domains, researchers, librarians, and libraries have recurrently and strongly argued to play important roles in the effort to solve the many challenges offered by increasingly mundane-ified, invisible, and powerful online information infrastructures. Little is known, however, about the proliferation of such arguments in broader societal debate and dialogue. The empirical basis if this paper is an analysis of 100 news articles published by major Swedish and Norwegian media outlets mentioning the term "source criticism". The analysis focused on (1) what is being talked about in conjunction with the notion of source criticism; and (2) who is talking with authority on the topic of source criticism. Of particular interest was the extent to which libraries, librarians, and LIS are ascribed important and authoritative positions in the discussions. The findings showed that although libraries are referenced in some of the articles, neither the library sector as such nor LIS research has any sort of meaningful presence in public discourse on misinformation, disinformation, and other negative information trends. The stark difference between how the positions and possible contributions of libraries, library professionals, and LIS research are rendered in public and professional and academic library discourses is a significant hindrance for the library research and practice domains to realize their manifold productive potential of in the larger context of present-day information machineries, politics, and culture.

Keywords: Source criticism · Public discourse · Misinformation

1 Introduction

LIS has a long-standing tradition of engaging with the multiplex scenario of how people search for, assess, and otherwise engage with information in areas of professional and non-professional life innately tied to post world-wide-web information

© Springer Nature Switzerland AG 2020
A. Sundqvist et al. (Eds.): iConference 2020, LNCS 12051, pp. 380–388, 2020.
https://doi.org/10.1007/978-3-030-43687-2_30

technology. From the mid-2000s and onward, a strand of digitally-oriented LIS scholarship has gained prominence in terms of its impact, wide-spectrum relevance, and prolificacy. Research in this strand sets out to examine the present-day information landscape and its hegemonic modes of information production and use from the interrelated perspectives of algorithmic influence, and the functionalities and results of search engines and data aggregators in the social-media space (e.g., Andersen 2018; Andersson 2017; Huvila 2016; Lewandowski 2008; Lewandowski 2012; Rieh 2004; Sundin 2017). This turn towards critical examinations and renderings of large-scale online information infrastructures in LIS is mirrored in the broader layers of library discourse. In our so-called 'post-truth era'—characterized by fake news, filter bubbles, spread of conspiracy theories in online media and a more general tendency towards information flows based on opaque and personalized algorithms (Lewandowsky et al. 2017)—libraries are often positioned as independent and trustworthy suppliers of information that to a certain degree can act outside of the capitalist logic of the social-media and search-engine industries and, further, offer resistance to hate-speech and other forces that facilitate the erosion of public dialogue (Chen, X. et al. 2015; Chen, Y. 2015; Lenker 2016). Similarly, librarians are recurrently cast as the mediators of the literacies (information, media, digital) required to safely, with precision and sufficient critical capacity navigate and use online information ecologies (Cooke 2017; Fichtelius et al. 2019). LIS researchers, librarians, and the library sector are thus argued to play pivotal parts in solving the political, social, and cultural challenges offered by increasingly mundane-ified, invisible, and powerful online information infrastructures (Haider and Sundin 2019). Little is known, however, about the proliferation of such arguments in broader societal debate and dialogue.

The purpose of this paper is to address this knowledge gap by investigating the extent to which libraries, librarians, and LIS are ascribed important and authoritative positions in the struggle to lessen the impact of negative information trends (misinformation, conspiracy theories, fake news, highly divisive speech) in online communication also outside the bounds of current library and (library and) information science discourses. This is an important step in the multi-stage process of gaining research-based insights into the actual and potential democratic roles of libraries, library professionals, and LIS research in the larger context of present-day information machineries, politics, and culture.

2   Research Design

The empirical basis of the paper consists of an analysis of 100 newspaper articles published in the Swedish and Norwegian media outlets between January and December 2018. The outlets were chosen as the specific empirical setting for this study because of their strong focus on current major debates and events, their different modes of expression (news articles, editorials, interviews, chronicles) and diverse subjects (tech, culture, politics). Content analysis (Krippendorff 2004) and intersubjective coding techniques inspired by Charmaz (1983) were employed in the processing of the articles. The concept of 'source criticism' (Nor. 'kildekritikk'; Swe. 'källkritik') was used as a sensitizing device and as an analytical point of focus.

2.1 Conceptual Framing

Source criticism is a North European concept that originates from the study of biblical and historical sources. Although it can be linked to specific theoretical assumptions, methodologies, disciplines or professions (e.g., history), the concept is popularly used in Scandinavian countries to denote critical evaluations of information sources in a more general sense. Swedish Wikipedia, for example, defines source criticism as the practice of conducting "critical assessment of source material and of the credibility of statements given in an information source" (authors' translation; Källkritik, n.d.). When the Norwegian Library Association translates IFLA's infographic guideline "How to spot fake news" (Norwegian Library Association 2017), they describe it as "eight steps of source criticism" (authors' translation), whereas IFLA on their English-language web page combine concepts like "critical thinking" and "media and information literacy" to describe their guideline (IFLA 2019). Source criticism further has been cast as an important, but on its own insufficient, tool in confronting pressing present-day information concerns (Sundin and Haider 2018). From an epistemological point of approach, source criticism can be tied to constructivist understandings to knowledge production (Steensen 2018) and it has been argued to provide valuable resources in an era where "knowledge and truth are increasingly understood as constructions" (Steensen 2018 p. 187).

Given the broad signification and recent increase in usage—especially in a Nordic context—of the concept of source criticism is a reasonable operationalization to employ in the data collection and data analysis processes underpinning this paper.

2.2 Methods and Materials

The articles that form the basis of this paper were gathered via Retriever (www.retriever.no), a news-archive and analysis platform with wide Nordic and international coverage. Truncated searches were performed for articles containing the keywords 'källkritik' and 'kildekritikk' in a series of established and influential Norwegian and Swedish online and print outlets. The Norwegian outlets included in the Retriever-search were Aftenposten, Dagsavisen, Klassekampen, Dagbladet, VG, NRK, and TV2 Nyheter. The Swedish counterparts were Aftonbladet, Svenska Dagbladet, Dagens Nyheter, SVT Nyheter, Expressen, and Metro. The search was limited to articles published in 2018. 50 items per country were selected for analysis, leaving the total at 100. If several articles contained very similar content, only the most recent one was included in the analysis. The article selection process proceeded in reverse-chronological order from late December 2018 and continued until the quota was reached.

Once the corpus was collated the processing of the articles was conducted with guidance from descriptive and investigative schemes of analysis inspired by content-analysis methodology (Krippendorff 2004). The categories of the descriptive scheme were the articles' country and date of publication, journal outlet, and genre (news story, editorial, et cetera). The investigative scheme directed analytic attention towards two points of focus meant to bring into view the roles of libraries, librarians, and LIS research as they emerge in discussions of negative information trends in public discourse. The points of focus were: (1) what is being talked about in conjunction with the notion of source criticism; and (2) who is talking with authority on the topic of source criticism. The coding of data proceeded hermeneutically and in reiteration between conducting trial analyses and (re)establishing codes and code definitions (see e.g., Charmaz 1983). The present paper's authors both participated in the article analyses, and the coding procedure and results were developed intersubjectively during this process.

3   Analysis and Findings

The selection strategy employed in this paper did not result in an equal distribution of articles between the outlets included in the study, but it produced a dataset that represents a multi-outlet snapshot of public discourse in connection to discussions about source criticism in Sweden and Norway during 2018. Svenska Dagbladet (18), Aftenposten (17), SVT News (16), and Dagbladet (16) were most well-represented, with the remaining outlets having between two and nine inclusions. The analysis showed few notable differences between Norwegian and Swedish articles in terms of content and interlocutors. For this reason, no comparisons between Norwegian and Swedish outlets will be conducted.

Over half of the articles (53%) were opinion pieces (chronicles, comments, editorials). The remaining ones were either portrait interviews (3%) or regular news stories (44%).

3.1   What Do They Talk About?

About fifty independent topics were identified in the analysis. These topics constitute an overview of what is being talked about when the articles talk about source criticism. Often, the articles include more than one topic, for example the prevalence of fake news and how this should be handled as an educational problem in schools. Table 1 lists the ten most common topics found in the article dataset.

Given the general media coverage following the 2016 US presidential election and the 2016 UK Brexit referendum, it is not surprising that the most common topic related to source criticism is fake news, dis- and misinformation. These topics were thematized either as independent phenomena, or as mentioned above, be related to other topics such as educational issues or political influence. The topic source criticism at school occurs almost as frequently as fake news, dis- and misinformation. An interesting feature of this topic is that there are only a few mentions of school libraries as relevant institutions in the mediation of source-criticism skills, and the articles that do, are usually chronicles written by librarians or other representatives of the library sector. These chronicles also contain the only mentions of libraries and librarians in the dataset. When source criticism at school is being talked about, it is usually about curriculum developments or general considerations about how source criticism needs to be better incorporated into the school system.

Specific source-critical methods are mentioned in some of the articles, but always a very abstracted way. For example, a commentator warns that insights into citation

Table 1. The ten most common topics in the dataset, the percentage of topic mentions in the total no. of articles, and topic inclusion criteria.

Topic	Percentage of mentions	Inclusion criteria
Fake news, dis- and misinformation	30%	Articles directly mentioning the concepts fake news, dis- or misinformation
Source criticism at school	26%	Articles thematizing educational issues in relation to source criticism
Source criticism in journalism	16%	Articles thematizing journalistic work in relation to source criticism
Methods of source criticism	14%	Articles where practical methods for source criticism are discussed or mentioned
Political influence	9%	Articles thematizing issues like the use of social media to influence voters or interference in elections by foreign powers
Conspiracy theories	8%	Articles thematizing the prevalence and spread of conspiracy theories
Fact checking	7%	Articles thematizing professional practices of fact checking
Metoo	6%	Articles thematizing the metoo movement and phenomenon
Study of historical sources	6%	Articles discussing methods for approaching and interpreting historical sources
Online hate speech	6%	Articles thematizing online hate speech

techniques, as they are currently taught in higher education, is not enough to fight misinformation. The overall impression is that source criticism is not dealt with in any substantial way. Source criticism is mostly mentioned as something that is important, but the concepts or the methods and approaches that it plausibly could entail are not detailed or discussed. As aforementioned 53% of the articles were different types of opinion pieces, and an objective of the opinion genre is to problematize. The genre-bound nature of opinion pieces may hence explain our observations that the discussion of source criticism in the studied dataset is largely about the lack of source criticism, either in terms of concrete abilities or in the form of a critical mindset. And as outlined above, source criticism is seen to be mostly lacking in schools and in journalistic practice. Of key importance for the purpose of this paper is the almost complete lack of mentions where libraries, librarians or LIS research are referenced as some kind of solution or resource in efforts to handle misinformation, disinformation, or other negative information trends.

3.2   Who Are Talking?

The analysis of the articles also focused on the backgrounds of the authors of opinion articles, or people who were interviewed or otherwise referenced as experts or authorities on the topic of source criticism. Additional background information like the academic disciplines of researchers and the field of proficiency of non-academic experts were registered when available. The findings show that people with a wide array of academic and professional backgrounds are cast as having authority on the topic of source criticism. As shown in Table 2, the most common group of people 'talking' in these articles are representatives from professional fields. Two of these fields stand out; journalists (22% of articles) and teachers (10% of articles). This is in line with the findings of what is being 'talked about', namely education and journalism (see Table 1). The journalists and teachers commonly are authors of opinion articles and brought in as experts on source criticism most often in the context of their own profession, but also as more general experts concerning digital developments or fake news. The data also shows a long tail of people with professional backgrounds who appear only a few times, ranging from school librarians to psychologists and lawyers to experts on cybercrime and civil defense.

Table 2. Backgrounds of interlocutors mentioned in more than 2% share of the articles.

Interlocutor background	Percentage of mentions
Expert or representative from a professional field	30%
Academic	22%
Representative of an institution/organization/firm	21%
Representative of a NGO/interest group	13%
Debater or intellectual	7%
Politician	6%

22 of the articles involve academics in some role. As shown in Table 3, six of these belong to the field of media, communication or journalism. Philosophers, historians and military researchers occur three times each. Among the list of different academic disciplines that occur only once there are representatives from pedagogy, literature and economics, but none from the LIS field.[1]

Table 3. The four academic disciplines with more than one mention.

Academic discipline	No. of mentions
Media, Communication, Journalism	6
Philosophy	3
History	3
Military and civil defense research	3

[1] As mentioned above there are a few librarians figuring as professional experts in the material, but these do not represent LIS or any neighboring academic fields.

4   Discussion and Concluding Remarks

Negative information trends like misinformation, disinformation, fake news, and hate speech has garnered considerable attention in the professional and research literature of the library and LIS fields. Early studies of online misinformation (e.g., Drobnicki and Asaro 2001; Fitzgerald 1997; Floridi 1996) describe the phenomena and outline possible counteractive strategies in ways that are largely similar to those of today. Drobnicki and Asaro (2001) trace the history of online misinformation back to pre-digital hoaxes and fabrications and point to that the efficacy of their online counterparts is facilitated by the speed of Internet communications, the lack of control instruments, and distributed authorship. Two principal suggested means of lessening the impact of negative information trends can be found among the early studies of misinformation in Internet environments: the establishment of information services that would promote quality information (characterized by factualness, plurality, integrity) (Floridi 1996) and the strengthening of source-critical skill sets among users (Fitzgerald 1997).

This paper shows that these suggested means resonate greatly with core arguments of present use. One of the main reasons put forward in professional and academic literature to support the position that libraries, librarians, and LIS research have important roles to play in the struggle to come to grips with online misinformation and related negative information trends is the significant usefulness of traditional library values, librarianship know-how—e.g., the capacities needed to "ensure that people have access to *quality information*" (Fallis 2015, p. 402, emphasis in original), and the theoretical tools of LIS ('search', 'relevance', see e.g.,. Haider and Sundin 2019) in this context (Fallis 2015; Sullivan 2018). The arguably most ubiquitously discussed contribution of the library research and practice sectors is the ability to envision and mediate the literacy required to raise users' 'resistance' to misinformation and to develop the skills needed to competently find, evaluate, and use online information sources (Cooke 2017; Lenker 2016; Walsh 2010). This literacy is largely framed to be a matter of procedure (e.g., source criticism), a critical mindset, and the proper application of resources ("When in doubt … Ask a librarian") (Harvard 2017). On the other hand, it has been claimed that librarians "can't fight fake news" (Sullivan 2018, p. 1146) because they don't have the full understanding of the problem, and because their traditional solutions are not sufficient to solve the it.

While this paper does not shed light on librarians' abilities to counteract negative information trends like misinformation and fake news per se, it clearly highlights that there is a stark difference between how the positions and possible contributions of libraries, library professionals, and LIS research are rendered in public discourse and in the professional and academic library discourses. The library and LIS literatures engage with fake news, misinformation, and similar phenomena with notable confidence and ambition. This engagement is not solely situated under the auspices of the library- and LIS-spheres, but is rather positioned on the wider playing field of current democratic society and the large-scale information-related issues facing them. The findings of the present study paint a picture that differ to a radical extent: although libraries are mentioned in some of the analyzed articles, neither the library sector as such nor LIS research has any sort of meaningful presence in Swedish and Norwegian public discourse on misinformation, disinformation, and other negative information trends.

The articles in the dataset that did stress the importance of library-related skills, knowledges, or perspectives did emerge from the sector itself and are thus not part of how the sector is viewed upon by those outside of the library and LIS domains.

Looking ahead, recent proposals for national library strategies in Norway (Ministry of Culture 2019) and Sweden (Fichtelius et al. 2019) indicate that the Scandinavian library sector may have a continuing—perhaps even increasing—interest to cast themselves as important actors in the efforts to develop societal, political, and cultural strategies robust to the pressures of misinformation, disinformation, conspiracy theories, and the like. Sullivan (2018) shows, drawing on examples from e.g., IFLA, ALA, and Harvard University libraries, that a similar dynamic exists also in the North American library sector. Greatly differing renderings of the positions and possible contributions of libraries, library professionals, and LIS research in public and professional and academic library discourses could be a significant hindrance for the library research and practice domains to realize their manifold productive potential of in the larger context of present-day information machineries, politics, and culture. If the sector is to succeed in this, both in the form of legitimizing genuine practices and institutions, and in the form of communicating the knowledge the sector has to contribute, systematic and research-based efforts must be initiated with the purpose to investigate paths of action that can let libraries, librarians, and LIS research to shift their positions in the relevant areas of public debate.

References

Andersen, J.: Archiving, ordering, and searching: search engines, algorithms, databases, and deep mediatization. Media Cult. Soc. **40**(8), 1135–1150 (2018)

Andersson, C.: "Google is not fun": an investigation of how Swedish teenagers frame online searching. J. Doc. **73**(6), 1244–1260 (2017)

Charmaz, K.: The grounded theory method: an explication and interpretation. In: Contemporary Field Research, pp. 109–126. Waveland Press, Prospect Heights (1983)

Chen, X., Sin, S.-C.J., Theng, Y.-L., Lee, C.S.: Why students share misinformation on social media: motivation, gender, and study-level differences. J. Acad. Librariansh. **41**(5), 583–592 (2015)

Chen, Y., Conroy, N.J., Rubin, V.L.: News in an online world: the need for an "automatic crap detector". Proc. Assoc. Inf. Sci. Technol. **52**(1), 1–4 (2015)

Cooke, N.A.: Posttruth, truthiness, and alternative facts: information behavior and critical Information consumption for a new age. Libr. Q. **87**(3), 211–221 (2017)

Drobnicki, J.A., Asaro, R.: Historical fabrications on the Internet. Ref. Libr. **35**(74), 121–164 (2001)

Fallis, D.: What is disinformation? Libr. Trends **63**(3), 401–426 (2015)

Fichtelius, E., Persson, C., Enarson, E.: Demokratins skattkammare: Förslag till en nationell biblioteksstrategi. Kungliga biblioteket, Stockholm (2019)

Fitzgerald, M.: Misinformation on the internet: applying evaluation skills to online information. Emerg. Libr. **24**, 9–14 (1997)

Floridi, L.: Brave.Net.World: the internet as a disinformation super-highway? Electron. Libr. **14**(6), 509–514 (1996)

Haider, J., Sundin, O.: Invisible Search and Online Search Engines: The Ubiquity of Search in Everyday Life. Routledge, Abingdon (2019)

Harvard: Fake news, misinformation, and propaganda (2017). https://guides.library.harvard.edu/fakeadu/fake. Accessed 16 Sept 2019

Huvila, I.: Affective capitalism of knowing and the society of search engine. Aslib J. Inf. Manag. **68**(5), 566–588 (2016)

Krippendorff, K.: Content Analysis: An Introduction to Its Methodology, 2nd edn. Sage, Thousand Oaks (2004)

Lenker, M.: Motivated reasoning, political information, and information literacy education. Portal: Libr. Acad. **16**(3), 511–528 (2016)

Lewandowski, D.: Search engine user behaviour: how can users be guided to quality content? Inf. Serv. Use **28**(3–4), 261–268 (2008)

Lewandowski, D.: Web Search Engine Research. Emerald, Bingley (2012)

Lewandowsky, S., Ecker, U.K.H., Cook, J.: Beyond misinformation: understanding and coping with the "post-truth" era. J. Appl. Res. Mem. Cogn. **6**(4), 353–369 (2017)

Rieh, S.Y.: On the web at home: information seeking and web searching in the home environment. J. Am. Soc. Inf. Sci. Technol. **55**(8), 743–753 (2004)

Sullivan, M.C.: Why librarians can't fight fake news. J. Librariansh. Inf. Sci. **51**(4), 1146–1156 (2018)

Sundin, O.: The search-ification of everyday life and the mundane-ification of search. J. Doc. **73** (2), 224–243 (2017)

Walsh, J.: Librarians and controlling disinformation: is multi-literacy instruction the answer? Libr. Rev. **59**(7), 498–511 (2010)

IFLA: How to spot fake news (2019). https://www.ifla.org/publications/node/11174. Accessed 16 Sept 2019

Ministry of culture: Rom for demokrati og dannelse Nasjonal bibliotekstrategi 2020–2023. Kulturdepartementet, Oslo (2019)

Norwegian Library Association: Oppdag falske nyheter: How to spot fake news (2017). https://norskbibliotekforening.no/2017/03/oppdag-falske-nyheter-how-to-spot-fake-news. Accessed 16 Sept 2019

Steensen, S.: Journalism's epistemic crisis and its solution: disinformation, datafication and source criticism. Journalism **20**(1), 185–189 (2018). https://journals.sagepub.com/doi/full/10.1177/1464884918809271

Sundin, O., Haider, J.: Källkritik, självkritik och källtillit. In: Carlsson, U. (ed.) Medie- och informationskunnighet i den digitala tidsåldern - en demokratifråga: Kartläggning, analyser, reflektioner, pp. 59–61. Nordicom, Göteborg (2018)

Wikipedia Contributors: Källkritik (2019). https://sv.wikipedia.org/wiki/K%C3%A4llkritik. Accessed 16 Sept 2019

User Experience

A Cross-cultural Study on Information Architecture: Culture Differences on Attention Allocation to Web Components

Gao-Ming Tang[1], Hsin-Yuan Hu[2], Shih-Yi Chen[3], and Wei Jeng[2(✉)]

[1] Carnegie Mellon University, Pittsburgh, PA 15213, USA
[2] National Taiwan University, Taipei 10617, Taiwan
wjeng@ntu.edu.tw
[3] National Chengchi University, Taipei 11605, Taiwan

Abstract. A well-designed web information architecture (IA) supports the findability and usability of web content to ensure efficient and effective user experience. This study aims to investigate how web visitors from different cultures allocate their attention to the four main systems (*labeling*, *organization*, *navigation*, and *searching*) in IA. We conducted a user study comprised of observation tasks, sketch sessions, and questions regarding participants' attention allocation, as well as background questionnaires regarding demographics, cultural dimensions, and personal traits. A total of 33 student participants from Taiwan (TW) and the US were recruited. Our preliminary results find that the less complicated content a website displays, the more participants are aware of IA and its components in general. We also found that US participants usually pay more attention to text labels on a webpage, whereas TW participants are more likely to evenly distribute their attention to both text and image objects. The ultimate goal of this study is to shed light on the topic of culture-specific IA in global web communities.

Keywords: Information Architecture · Web design · Cultural customization IA

1 Introduction

While English information content dominates today's World Wide Web, the total number of non-English Internet users, such as those in China and India, has grown dramatically in the past decade, topping one billion as of 2018 [14]. Assuming web visitors prefer content in their native languages, it is likely that more and more websites will support multiple languages in the future.

Information Architecture (IA) is the art and science of organizing and labeling information objects, which enables users' seamless search and navigation activities, on a website to create a better user experience [15]. However, since the majority of IA principles and practices are rooted in English web content, it is not surprising that there

---

G.-M. Tang—This work was done while Gao-Ming Tang was at National Taiwan University.

A. Sundqvist et al. (Eds.): iConference 2020, LNCS 12051, pp. 391–408, 2020.
https://doi.org/10.1007/978-3-030-43687-2_31

is a lack of empirical IA studies examining the characteristics or influences across English and non-English cultures.

Prior studies regarding cultural characteristics on web design either center on aesthetic judgments [5] or lack empirical data [13]. To deepen understanding of the topic and stimulate further discussion for the web society community, we conducted a user study to gather data about how web visitors in different cultures allocate their attention to four aspects in an IA, namely: labeling, organization, navigation, and searching. In addition to attention allocation, we also capture web visitors' perceptions and preferences regarding a website. Consequently, the ultimate goal of our study is to shed more light on cultural studies in website development and society. Specifically, we investigate the following research questions in this paper:

(1) How are web visitors' cultural backgrounds associated with their attention allocation to web components?
(2) How are culturally different web visitors' preferences and perceptions regarding web components associated with the four IA systems (labeling, organization, navigation, and searching), respectively? What are the characteristics of these web components?

Based on the results, we seek to contribute to the information science community and information professionals in two ways. Firstly, web developers or designers will be able to take our findings into consideration during the design process, e.g., customizing websites in accordance with the expectations and natural habits of local societies when accessing the digital world. Additionally, as web design trends are significantly updated every decade, we take the opportunity to discuss the applicability of Hofstede's cultural dimensions on website components and design in the late 2010s. After discovering patterns of today's cultural customization in IA, we are one step closer to form sustainable guidance that can be followed by future generations.

2   Literature Review

2.1   Theories of Cultural Differences

Related projects with regard to cultural characteristics, including Hall's high-context and low-context cultures [10] and Hofstede's cultural dimensions theory [11], are two commonly discussed conceptual frameworks in the cross-cultural realm. The former uses the terms high/low context to describe how explicitly people encode messages in their communication. Not only can a high-context message be communicated through language and rules, but it can also be encoded and decoded through personal status or other contextual elements, such as body gestures and facial expressions. Conversely, in a low-context culture, messages are mainly handled with wording or other protocol that is explicitly announced. Hofstede's cultural dimensions theory [11] is a cross-cultural conceptual framework identifying several facets of characteristics of different countries. Hofstede divides cultural characteristics into these dimensions: power distance, individualism, uncertainty avoidance, masculinity, and later added long-term orientation. They can be explained as follows: *Power Distance* (PDI): the extent to which the less powerful accept and expect that power is unequal; *Individualism* (IDV): the degree to which people in a society are integrated into a group; *Uncertainty Avoidance* (UAI): the extent to which a society is tolerant of ambiguity; *Masculinity* (MAS): a society's preference for achievement, heroism, assertiveness, and material rewards for success; *Long-term Orientation* (LTO): the connection of the past to current and future actions. In contrast to Hall's communication styles between cultures, Hofstede presents a more categorical structure for describing cultural differences.

There are several studies regarding the cultural characteristics of how people see and process information in the field of psychology. Chua, Boland, and Nisbett [4] state that there are different cognitive styles between East Asians and Westerners, which leads to different behaviors when viewing scenes [2]. In particular, Chua's study finds that East Asians tend to pay more attention to background context, whereas Westerners tend to chase focal objects in the scene. Thus, the implication can be derived: East Asians value the concept of harmony and view things in a more holistic way, while Westerners tend to be more analytic and goal-driven.

2.2   Culture and Web Design

Literature related to culture and web design commonly appeared in the 2000s. Most of the studies correspond with Hofstede's cultural dimensions theory, examining how web design strategies are adjusted in different cultures. Marcus and Gould [13] compare how website interfaces differ across the cultural dimension spectrum. For instance, in high Power Distance Index (hereafter: PDI) cultures, websites are usually very structured and focus on expert or authority representation. In high Uncertainty Avoidance Index (hereafter: UAI) cultures, website interfaces are usually simple, with limited choices and restricted amounts of data, in order to prevent users from feeling lost. Singh and Pereira [16] developed the Cultural Values Framework to identify the relations between features of websites and cultural factors. Their research sampled websites from four countries, and the results are consistent with the conclusions found by Hofstede [11] and Hall [10]. El mimouni and MacDonald [6] investigated American and Arabic websites based on Hofstede's PDI dimensions and Marcus and Gould's elements of design. The study observed 60 websites for their main page navigation hierarchical features, navigation diversity, number of hyperlinks, search options, etc. With the exception of navigation diversity, the other aspects are confirmed to be significant, suggesting that cultural differences are associated with developers' choice of web components. In another study, Cyr and Trevor-Smith [5] examined whether webpages in different cultures display web design differently in terms of eight facets: language usage, layout, symbols, content and structure, navigation, links, multimedia, and colors. Goyal, Miner, and Nawathe [8] later utilized Cyr and Trevor-Smith's coding scheme and analyzed whether cultural differences appeared between BRIC and the US on their government websites. Their findings confirm that differences exist, especially between China and the US in their web design, while the rest (Brazil, Russia, and India) do not completely fit their culture in web design.

The aforementioned studies provide a fine starting point and insight into the substantial measurements that can capture how cultural characteristics influence web design. However, some lack of empirical evidence (e.g., Marcus and Gould [13]), and most were not carried out in the past decade (e.g., Cyr and Trevor-Smith [5]). Our study centers on four IA systems and Hofstede's cultural dimension theories and conducts an empirical experiment to present the association between culture and web design.

3   Methodology

3.1   Research Design

We adopt a lab experimental method that allows us to collect web visitors' attention allocation and measure their perceptions and preferences regarding IA components. An experiment session is divided into two sequential parts: The Main Study and Background Studies. We report the research design and considerations in the following sections.

3.2   Main Study

In the Main Study, participants were asked to observe four websites and answer a series of IA-related questions for each website. Because a website's content may change at any time, we used a screenshot of each website to avoid biases caused by seeing different content or layouts. Although using a screenshot instead of a live link limits how participants can interact with the website (e.g., the participants receive no response from their clicks), they are still able to scroll up and down to browse the webpage.

Although attention is described as behavior of how people selectively concentrate on information with limited cognitive processing resources [1], we believe that viewing a static picture would not significantly affect our investigation on participants' attention allocation. Based on our pre-test study involving ten college students, each participant in the experiment is encouraged to spend up to two minutes observing a webpage. It is worth noting that previous studies on the topic of attention allocation suggest that no apparent difference is found between a 5-second limit and a longer timeout [7, 9].

We designed an instrument using Qualtrics, an online questionnaire software. The instrument consists of 7 open-ended and 5 close-ended questions. Questions were divided into four groups based on the concept that we would like to understand:

(1)   How do participants feel about the webpage? [*feelings about a webpage*]
(2)   What do participants like or dislike about the webpage? [*preferred objects or components of a webpage*]
(3)   The degree to which participants are aware of each of the IA systems (in the 5-point Likert scale: 1 = not at all aware; 5 = extremely aware) [*the awareness of a webpage's IA*]
(4)   If participants select 2 to 5 points in the previous question for any of the IA systems, they would be asked to further describe how they are aware of it.

The constructs in the aforementioned instrument follow an indirect questioning technique, to intentionally avoid offering participants explicit information about specific terms related to IA systems. Instead of asking "*Are you aware of the navigation features in this webpage*" to locate the concept of the navigation system, we say "*how can one find needed information other than using the search function: users do not input any search terms, but find information by clicking on it.*"

It is worth noting that a sketch session was added to this instrument after the pre-test, as the pre-testers seemed unable to remember some detail about the webpage in the given time. We also observed that pre-test participants were overwhelmed by the tasks: they may become stressed if they have forgotten what they just saw and this could influence the quality of data collection. As a result, each participant is allowed to sketch what they've seen about the webpage, which can assist them as they answer the questionnaire.

3.3 Task Selection

Just as related work often considers using political, charity, or educational types of websites as experimental materials (e.g., Cyr and Trevor-Smith [5], El mimouni and MacDonald [6], Goyal et al. [8], etc.), we consider top-ranked global university websites, because universities often have adequate funding to invest more in website construction. Because the complexity of a website structure may influence users' attention allocation, we would also like to sample websites with varying complexity levels. We randomly sampled 15 universities from the top 100 World University Rankings 2018 (timeshighereducation.com), and 20 people helped rate the complexity on a 9-point Likert scale basis. After calculating the score of each sample, we sorted these 15 webpage screenshots in ascending order and grouped them into low, medium, and high complexity groups. We then randomly drew one from each group. Based on this randomization procedure, the University of Toronto (hereafter: UToronto), the California Institute of Technology (hereafter: Caltech), and the Korea Advanced Institute of Science and Technology (hereafter: KAIST) were selected as the webpages used in our experiment, representing *low*, *medium*, and *high* complexity designs, respectively.

A training session was placed as the first set of tasks. We adopted U of Washington's main page as the training session, which was randomly selected from the ranking. The remaining three sets of tasks (low, medium, and high complexity) were applied to a Latin Square design. Considering first language differences among our participants, we used the default language version of the university websites and applied an online translation tool to control the experimental settings.

3.4 Background Studies

To investigate cultural and personal characteristics, we designed two sets of instruments for background studies, based on Chien et al. [3]. The first set is the Big Five Inventory [12]. It contains 44 questions about a person's personality, such as "*I see myself as someone who is talkative,*" "*tends to find fault with others,*" or "*does a thorough job,*" using a 5-point Likert scale (1 = disagree strongly; 5 = agree strongly). Participants selected a number for each statement that most closely reflects them. The other instrument set is the Cultural Value Scale (CVSCALE) [17], a 26-item instrument also using a 5-point Likert scale to assess Hofstede's cultural dimensions on the individual level.

3.5   Experiment Procedure

The experiment procedure is presented in Fig. 1. The experiment was conducted in a laboratory environment, in which at most 5 participants were present concurrently. Each participant was seated with a computer showing the instrument, as well as note-taking tools and the consent form.

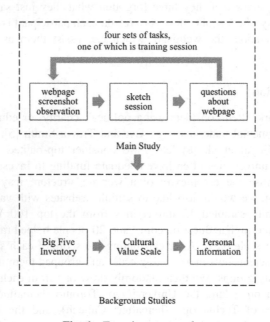

Fig. 1. Experiment procedure.

In the Main Study section, participants were asked to complete four sets of tasks, in which the first set is a training session that familiarizes participants with the experiment process. For each task, participants saw a screenshot of a webpage, which they could spend at most 2 min observing. After observation, the screenshot was shut down, and we gave the participant a piece of paper for notetaking in writing and/or drawing forms. After finishing their sketches, participants moved on to answer questions about the webpage. The length of the Main Study session ranges from approximately 40 to 90 min.

After completing the Main Study section, participants were asked to complete the background questionnaires, including the Cultural Value Scale and the Big Five Inventory questionnaires mentioned above, and also provided personal information including age, gender, degree status, etc.

3.6   Participants

We selected participants from Taiwan (hereafter: Group TW) and people from the United States (hereafter: Group US). Participants must be students who attended K-12 education in their home countries. To approach participants, recruiting information was disseminated through social media, such as local online forums, Facebook, Reddit, etc. We also contacted the Office of International Affairs, a similar unit to the International Students Office in the US, at National Taiwan University to help promote the recruitment. We eventually recruited 33 participants in total: 15 in Group US and 18 in Group TW.

Ethics. The study was reviewed by the Research Ethic Office (equivalent to Institutional Review Board approval) at National Taiwan University and meets all the necessary criteria for minimal risk review (no. 201711HS017) in May 2018.

3.7   Data Analysis

Based on the data collected from the experiment, we analyze both text and visual data, including scores of awareness and descriptions of IA, webpage sketches from the Main Study, along with cultural values and Big Five scores from the Background Study. According to our analysis progress, in this paper, we present and discuss only text documents along with cultural values.

Data Preparation. We framed out the web components used in three webpages respectively and qualified these components (see example in Fig. 2). The qualifiers were named in a neutral way and revised by our research team. Secondly, we referred to the descriptions of the four IA systems from our participants and matched them with our qualifiers. For example, in the descriptions of the organization system of UToronto from participant-US04: *"future students, current student, alumni, faculty, donors etc. [sic]. close the top of the website, but had a search function in the top right. There was[sic] social media at the bottom too."* We then coded "menu on the top," "search icon/bar," and "social media icon" respectively for the organization system (see Table 1 for more examples). After coding every response from both Groups TW and US in four IA systems, the graphics were produced by Gephi and are shown in the next section (see Figs. 4 and 5).

Data Analysis. In order to echo our research questions, we reported cultural values and compared the differences in awareness of IA systems between Groups TW and US by using both quantitative and qualitative analysis. We first arranged all the text documents in spreadsheet style formats and calculated both Groups TW and US participants' awareness regarding the three webpages. As for the background studies, we calculated the cultural value according to previous studies [3]. The SPSS software is applied for the above statistical analysis. Following Chien et al. [3], all questions and responses in both the Main and Background studies for Group TW were translated into Traditional Chinese characters. Also, due to our research design in task selection, we could further discuss the influence of different web complexity levels in participants' perceptions from different cultures.

external links

menu on the top

school badge
icon

hero image

heading

image-news

content-news

heading

content-articles

image-articles

heading

footer

search icon/bar

dropdown list

school name

image-events

content-events

social media
icons

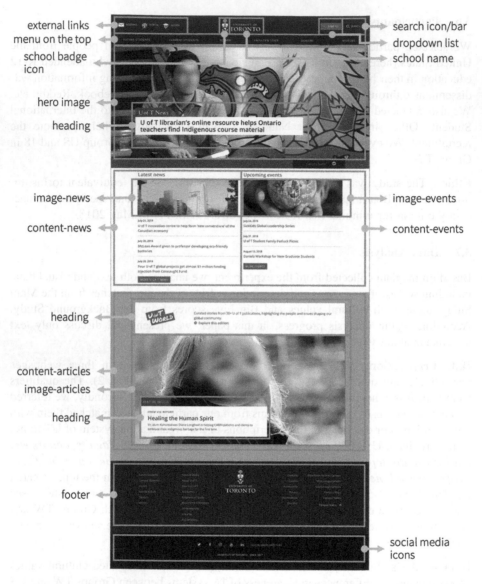

Fig. 2. Webpage coding example (UToronto).

Visual Analysis. In addition to the above analysis, we proposed another visual analysis in order to discover web components that participants pay more attention to a webpage. For a more in-depth discussion regarding which web components participants have used to describe IA, we demonstrate the relations between web components with IA systems by using Gephi. Since an effective visualization helps enhance readability and understanding of complex data, producing these graphics could help us delve into participants' responses about IA systems, complementing our previous analysis.

Table 1. Coding examples.

Participant	Task	IA	Responses	Qualifiers
TW01	UToronto	Org.	*The top layer has the identity of the website viewer Next is the **latest news**. Then there is **the message of the school publishing center**. The **footer** puts on other **social platforms** (but it seems that there is no last update time)*	Menu on the top; content-news; content-articles; footer; social media icon
US03	Caltech	Org.	*It does so through different sections of the webpage, each labeled by a **header text** at the top of the section, then **photos**, **videos**, **text**, and/or **graphics** that will give information about the school*	Heading; image-news; media-video; content-news; content-events
US12	KAIST	Lab.	***Student-related information seems to be at the top**, and **other info at the bottom** (although I can't recall the exact labels)*	Menu on the top; footer
TW12	Caltech	Sea.	*There is a little **magnifier** in the upper right corner, which is supposed to be the search function. But it is not easy to find out*	Search icon/bar
US14	UToronto	Nav.	*There are several site navigation links **at the webpage's bottom**, and there is a **"jump to"** navigation menu right next to the **search bar** in the upper right corner*	Footer; dropdown list; search icon/bar

4 Preliminary Findings

We report our early findings in three sections. Firstly, we report participants' demographics and cultural characteristics as an *overview*. Secondly, we report and discuss the relationship between participants' cultural backgrounds and their awareness. Finally, we present graphics showing connections between web components and IA systems.

4.1   Participants Overview

Demographics. As shown in Table 2, a total of 33 student participants were recruited for the experiments, including 18 participants in Group TW and 15 participants in Group US.

Table 2. Demographics of the participants.

		TW (N = 18)	US (N = 15)	Total
Gender	Female	10	8	18
	Male	8	7	15
Age	18–24	16	10	26
	25–34	2	4	6
	35–44	0	1	1

Cultural Value Scale (*CVSCALE*). The CVSCALE, a 26-item scale with five individual cultural values, suggests there is a significant difference in the Uncertainty Avoidance Index (UAI) and Masculinity (MAS) dimensions between the two groups, as Table 3 illustrates. Our result shows some similarities, compared to the prior work, e.g., Chien et al. [3]. Both UAI and Individualism (IDV) is higher in Group US, while PDI is higher in Group TW. However, in our result, only UAI shows a significant difference.

Table 3. CVSCALE rated scores. [a]One of the data points of Group US is two standard deviations below the mean of UAI and is therefore excluded in our analysis.

	TW (N = 18)	US (n = 14[a])	p-value
PDI	2.00	1.76	.247
UAI	3.44	3.90	.041
IDV	3.04	3.13	.691
MAS	2.18	1.64	.043
LTO	3.72	4.06	.139

4.2   Effects on Awareness: Culture and Complexity

We further use a mixed-model ANOVA to determine the differences in IA awareness. Country (US/TW) and complexity (low/medium/high) are the between-subject variables, and four types of IA-specific perceived awareness (organization, labeling, searching, and navigation) are the within-subject factors. No interaction effect is found between the culture and complexity variables across different types of awareness. However, statistical effects are found in the website complexity as well as cultural comparisons.

Cultural Effects. As shown in Table 4, the analyses reveal significant cultural effects on navigation awareness ($F_{1,93} = 5.95$, $p = .017$), in which the US participants rate higher in navigation awareness than TW; however, no statistical effect is suggested in the remaining IA awareness.

Table 4. IA awareness in different cultures.

	TW	US	F-value/p-value
Labeling (LAB)	3.70	3.78	$F_{1,93} = .12/p = .733$
Organization (ORG)	3.95	4.11	$F_{1,93} = .75/p = .390$
Navigation (NAV)	3.39	3.89	$F_{1,93} = 5.95/p = .017**$
Search (SEA)	3.74	3.78	$F_{1,93} = .03/p = .872$

Complexity Effects. The analysis of variance suggests that website complexity is negatively associated with awareness scores in organization, labeling, and searching systems (Table 5). The results can mean that increased website complexity leads to lower perceived IA awareness. However, the differences slightly decrease if the participant can appropriately use search functions, as marginal differences ($p = .055$) are found between low and high complexity in search awareness.

Table 5. IA awareness in the degree of complexity.

	High	Med	Low	F-value/p-value	Post-hoc (Bonferroni)
LAB	3.30	3.82	4.11	$F_{2,93} = 4.880$ $p = .010$	Low > High ($p = .008$)
ORG	3.43	4.22	4.43	$F_{2,93} = 10.084$ $p < .001$	Low > High ($p < .001$) Low > Med ($p = .003$)
NAV	3.17	3.69	4.06	$F_{2,93} = 6.406$ $p = .002$	Low > High ($p = .002$)
SEA	3.59	3.43	4.26	$F_{2,93} = 4.980$ $p = .009$	Low > High ($p = .055$) Low > Med ($p = .011$)

4.3   Analysis of Textual Descriptions

Figure 3 shows another measurement of participants' awareness: the description word count on four IA systems in different web complexity levels by both groups. Since participants are able to elaborate more about familiar topics, we consider that the word count of their responses could be one objective index to represent awareness. In both groups, participants tend to describe organization systems in more detail, while describing search systems with less detail, even within different web complexity levels.

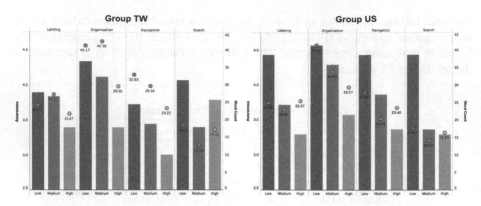

Fig. 3. Participants' awareness and word count of descriptions on four IA systems.

Besides the word count, we also examined participants' textual descriptions for IA-specific systems. Word frequency was calculated to verify participants' perceptions of the webpage. Even though participants in both groups viewed the same webpage, the groups mention different web components. For example, "heading" only appears in Group TW, whereas "navigate" is only mentioned by US participants.

4.4 Visualization on Textual Descriptions

Using a network visualization layout, Figs. 4 and 5 represent participants' descriptions of four IA systems with web components. The layout mainly presents in a dual circle form. The inner circle represents the four IA systems, and the outer circle is the web components appearing on each webpage. The connections between IA systems and web components are generated if participants mentioned the component in the IA systems. The bigger the size and the darker the color of an IA system at the inner circle, the more components were mentioned by the participants. For the outer circle, the bigger the size of the individual components, the more participants have mentioned individual components. The width of an edge represents the degree of participants' attention, e.g., the thicker the link, the more the participants mentioned this component in the Main Study.

There are also components that were not linked to IA systems, i.e., the black dots outside the circle, which illustrate that no participant mentioned these components at all. It is worth noting that these figures only record the relations between the web components and IA systems that we could clearly capture from participants' responses. It is possible that participants could describe these systems with other descriptions instead of using web components, and this does not mean that they were unaware of these systems. Note that the links between web components and IA systems may not be "precisely" connected. These connections can only represent which components were noticed and used by participants to describe the system when answering the questions. Since there were no bottom-up user studies at the time of the establishment of IA principles from Rosenfeld et al. [15], generating these figures could help us understand what web components really help the participants in these IA systems, which is one of

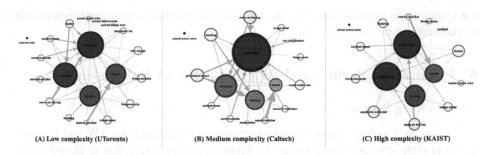

Fig. 4. Connections between web components and IA systems in different degrees of complexity.

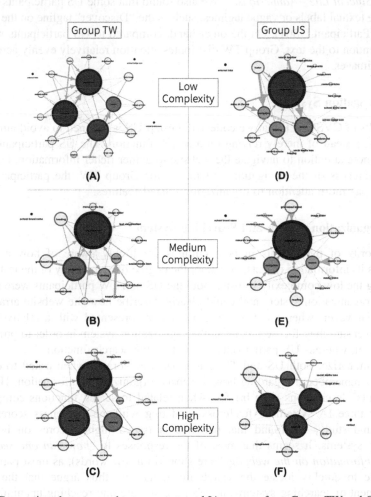

Fig. 5. Connections between web components and IA systems from Group TW and Group US.

the extra contributions of this research. Further discussion regarding these figures will be presented in the following section.

5 Cultural Similarities and Differences for IA Sub-systems

5.1 Labeling System

Regarding the labeling system of web components, we noticed that TW and US participants share several browsing patterns. Most participants were able to identify both textual and visual labels during the experiment. For example, participant-US09 stated, *"The webpage labels their content with brief, one to three word explanations: 'Did you know?' 'Student Life' 'Admissions.'"* We also found that some US participants disliked imprecise textual labels or vague taglines, such as the "Discover" tagline on the Caltech website (Participant US01). On the other hand, compared to US participants who pay more attention to the text, Group TW distributes attention relatively evenly across both text and images.

5.2 Navigation System

The results of CVSCALE that we collected, Group US is inclined to avoid ambiguous situations, instead of merely relying on a search function. The US participants might allocate more attention to navigate the website to gather richer information, leading to better awareness of the navigation system. As for Group TW, the participants were found to pay more attention to organization related features.

5.3 Organization System and Searching System

The majority of participants in both cultures are highly aware of how a website organizes its information objects, no matter the degree of complexity of the task. While observing the low complexity website, both the US and TW participants were satisfied with the organization system and could clearly describe how the website arranges its content. However, when the TW participants were presented with a relatively complicated website, they focused more on the organization system in order to process the rich content, whereas US participants focused on the search function.

To summarize, both US and TW participants elaborated when asked to describe what they remembered regarding how a website organized its information. However, participants' descriptions were briefest when related to search functions compared to the other three IA systems. After cross-validating with the awareness scores in the Background study, we found that participants issued higher scores on both IA's searching systems. It seems that most of the responses to *"how can one search for specific information on the webpage"* are short (in a few words), as most participants were able to quickly locate the search functions. We thus argue that the current development of searching systems in web IA is mature and reaching unanimity.

5.4   Website Complexity on Attention Allocation

To further investigate the influences of varying degrees of website complexity on participants' attention allocation, we used networking graphs to illustrate the relationship between web components and IA systems.

According to Fig. 4, there are significant differences among the three tasks. Based on the participants' reports, the more complex a website is, the less complicated a web-component network it forms. As shown in Fig. 4C, KAIST has fewer nodes in its web-component network, which means participants could only identify a few web components during the experiment. We found that the low complexity website has more nodes (Fig. 4A), and participants were able to distribute their attention to all four IA systems, judging by the similar size of four systems.

In the matter of cultural effect versus complexity, we also noticed that the concentration of graphics among Group TW is distinct from the counterpart of Group US, as in Fig. 5. In low and medium complexity tasks, US participants mentioned several components associated with the organization system (Fig. 5D and E). However, with regard to the complex website, US participants tend to pay more attention to other IA systems instead of the organization system (Fig. 5F). Compared with the US layouts, the size of the nodes in the network layouts in TW (Fig. 5A, B, and C) did not change dramatically when the complexity increased. We argue that the TW participants not only focused on the organization system, but also the navigation and labeling systems across three degrees of complexity. It is also noted that the size of the searching system in Fig. 5C is apparently small among IA systems. However, its link is the thickest, showing that participants merely used a small number of components such as "search icons/bar" to refer to the searching system.

There are some web components not mentioned by participants, and therefore have no connection with IA systems, e.g., "school brand name" in Fig. 5A. However, these components might be overlooked due to their obscurity. For instance, the purpose of "external links" on the low complexity website is confusing (Fig. 5A), using jargon and terms that only students or professors in the university would be familiar with.

6   Discussion

6.1   Awareness and Attention Allocation on IA Systems

We further discuss the differences in participants' attention allocation between two cultural groups, triangulated with our background questionnaire results. Our CVSCALE results suggest our US participants received higher scores on UAI, suggesting they may be sensitive to information ambiguity and would like to avoid it while interacting with a webpage. This can reflect the mean differences found in navigation systems between two cultural groups: Group US is found higher across four IA systems, as shown in Fig. 3. While navigation system represents an intuitive and natural way of finding information in a first-seen webpage, a significant high awareness to the navigation system and high UAI in Group US shows their concern of navigation system to reduce possible information anxiety derived.

We also found that US values textual labels over icons or images, whereas Group TW is more broadly distributed. We argue that TW participants are not eager to seek any information at first sight, but tend to sense the environment by browsing and observing the given page as a whole. This finding is aligned with previous studies such as Chua et al. [4] and Boduroglu et al. [2]: East Asians tend to consider parts of objects in relation to the whole. In spite of being inconsistent with Hofstede's study, we found a higher UAI score in Group US, meaning the participants are inclined toward processing the information as quickly as possible to avoid the ambiguity of the messages that a webpage carries.

6.2   The Similarities in Cultural Dimensions Between Groups

Our findings' inconsistency with Hofstede's study is especially apparent in UAI and Long-term Orientation (LTO), where the data results in the opposite of Hofstede's conclusion. One possible reason for this can be that our participants, as predominately college students, are experiencing a similar stage of life, sharing a similar college/living environment which may influence their preferences to some degree. Therefore, this lack of diversity of education status and individual living background, may explain the difference from Hofstede's study, which took place in multiple countries in working conditions.

7   Managerial Implications

In light of our findings, we offer several suggestions to web designers and developers. We expect that these implications may help professionals build a suitable and culture-friendly website.

7.1   Visitors Prefer Less Complicated Design

Firstly, web visitors prefer a low complexity website, no matter their cultural background. The simplicity of web components largely enhances usability due to a higher awareness of IA systems. If a website is inevitably constructed in a complicated way, rendering a noticeable search feature would be a compensation for information findability.

7.2   Visitors from Different Cultures May Behave Differently with a Complicated Design

Our US participants tend to seek searching functions on a complicated website, whereas Group TW maintains similar browsing behavior no matter the complexity of the website. Therefore, to optimize the user experience for US website visitors, we suggest that web developers/designers enhance the features in searching and navigation IA systems, such as enlarging search icons and navigation menus. This will allow US visitors to find needed information more effectively. Selection and organization of the content are of crucial importance for TW participants, due to the continuation of their browsing habits across a website's different levels of complexity. Because they prefer navigating rather than searching a website, web developers/designers should be careful when arranging content; otherwise, information is likely to be overlooked.

7.3 US Visitors Care About the Text Labels

Finally, Group US indicates concern regarding the clarity of labeling systems, while Group TW distributes their attention in a holistic way on both text and images. Therefore, it is inferable that websites built for US visitors should display precise wording as well as informative images.

8 Concluding Remarks

This study investigates how a web visitor's cultural background is associated with the attention of web components in different IA systems. We discovered that web visitors in the US and Taiwanese cultures are less aware of the IA systems of complicated websites, due to the overwhelming amount of information objects. We also discovered that participants from both cultures allocate their attention to different IA aspects of the websites. For instance, text labels received more attention than image-based labels by Group US, whereas Group TW distributed their attention to both relatively evenly.

8.1 Limitation

As mentioned in the Methodology section, website screenshots were used in the experiment to minizine webpage content changes over time and to allow participants to focus on general impressions of the webpage. However, participants were not able to interact with the web components by clicking while observing, which possibly hindered them from navigating the website in a natural way. This experimental setting may also diminish the navigation system, e.g., many present-day global navigation systems are hover-driven. In addition, the participants from Group US were recruited while they were in Taiwan, including students and short-term students such as exchange or visiting students, which may result in a bias in sampling: those who have already stayed in Taiwan for a time might be immersed in Asian culture to some degree, compared to lifelong US residents.

8.2 Future Directions

Our future work includes seeking other independent variables, such as personality traits of participants that we collected. We are also interested in analyzing participants' sketches of each website, which is expected to become rich supplemental data. We would also recommend that future researchers adopt other cultural theories in order to interpret the findings from a more comprehensive perspective.

Acknowledgments. This work was financially supported by the Ministry of Science and Technology (MOST) in Taiwan, under #MOST 108-2636-H-002-002- and MOST 107-3017-F-002-003-, and the Center for Research in Econometric Theory and Applications (Grant no. 107L900204) from The Featured Areas Research Center Program within the framework of the Higher Education Sprout Project by the Ministry of Education (MOE) in Taiwan.

References

1. Anderson, J.R.: Cognitive Psychology and Its Implications, 7th edn. Worth Publishers, New York (2010)
2. Boduroglu, A., Shah, P., Nisbett, R.E.: Cultural differences in allocation of attention in visual information processing. J. Cross Cult. Psychol. **40**(3), 349–360 (2009)
3. Chien, S.-Y., Lewis, M., Sycara, K., Liu, J.-S., Kumru, A.: Relation between trust attitudes toward automation, Hofstede's cultural dimensions and big five personality traits. Proc. Hum. Fact. Ergon. Soc. Annu. Meet. **60**(1), 841–845 (2016)
4. Chua, H.F., Boland, J.E., Nisbett, R.E.: Cultural variation in eye movements during scene perception. Proc. Natl. Acad. Sci. **102**(35), 12629–12633 (2005)
5. Cyr, D., Trevor-Smith, H.: Localization of web design: An empirical comparison of German, Japanese, and United States website characteristics. JASIST **55**(13), 1–10 (2004)
6. El mimouni, H., MacDonald, C.M.: Culture and information architecture: a study of American and Arab academic websites. Proc. Assoc. Inf. Sci. Technol. **52**(1), 1–4 (2015)
7. Five Second Test. https://fivesecondtest.com/. Accessed 2018
8. Goyal, N., Miner, W., Nawathe, N.: Cultural differences across governmental website design. In: Proceedings of the 4th International Conference on Intercultural Collaboration, pp. 149–152. ACM Press, New York (2012)
9. Gronier, G.: Measuring the first impression: testing the validity of the 5 second test. J. Usability Stud. **12**(1), 8–25 (2016)
10. Hall, E.T.: Beyond Culture. Doubleday, New York (1976)
11. Hofstede, G., Hofstede, G.J., Minkov, M.: Cultures and Organizations: Software of the Mind. McGraw-Hill, New York (2010)
12. John, O.P., Srivastava, S.: The big-five trait taxonomy: history, measurement, and theoretical perspectives. In: Pervin, L.A., John, O.P. (eds.) Handbook of Personality: Theory and Research, pp. 102–138. Guilford Press, New York (1999)
13. Marcus, A., Gould, E.W.: Crosscurrents: cultural dimensions and global web user-interface design. Interactions **7**(4), 32–46 (2000)
14. Number of Internet users in selected countries in 2018. https://www.statista.com/statistics/271411/number-of-internet-users-in-selected-countries/. Accessed 2019
15. Rosenfeld, L., Morville, P., Arango, J.: Information Architecture: For the Web and Beyond, 4th edn. O'Reilly Media, Sebastopol (2015)
16. Singh, N., Pereira, A.: The Culturally Customized Web Site: Customizing Web Sites for the Global Marketplace. Butterworth-Heinemann, Burlington (2005)
17. Yoo, B., Donthu, N., Lenartowicz, T.: Hofstede's five dimensions of cultural values at the individual level: development and validation of CVSCALE measuring. J. Int. Consum. Mark. **23**(2), 193–210 (2011)

"Defying Stereotypes Is a Plus": Classifying Gender, Sex, and Sexuality Content in Visual Materials

Hyerim Cho[1][✉] and Amanda Menking[2]

[1] University of Missouri, Columbia, MO 65211, USA
hyerimcho@missouri.edu
[2] University of Toronto, Toronto, ON M5S 1A1, Canada
amenking@gmail.com

Abstract. As engagement with various types of visual materials like graphic novels and video games has increased, users have become aware of how gender, sex, and sexuality are presented in these materials. To understand the information needs of these users, the first author adopted diary study and interview methods based on the uses and gratification theory. Through thematic analysis of this data, we learned participants wanted to search for visual materials based on gender and sexuality representation and depictions of sexual activities. To situate this finding in the context of existing ratings and recommendations systems, we then used domain analysis to evaluate a maximum variance sample of these systems. We learned currently available visual material ratings and recommendations systems fail to meet users' gender and sexuality related search needs. We discuss the relationship between classification systems and censorship to unpack the challenges of providing more descriptive and nuanced classifications of visual materials. Our findings identify gaps in current ratings and recommendations systems and suggest ways to move toward more equitable information access.

Keywords: Visual materials · Gender · Sexuality · Recommendation systems

1 Introduction

I am a parent at a progressive all-girls middle school [...]. Our family has "adopted" the library [...] and I would like to add 5–10 manga series to the collection. [...] I have started reading some titles I got from the public library, but the choices are many. So far, I've read the first volume of Bleach (which I liked in general, but disqualified itself when Orihime's brother suggested she "just shove those magnificent boobs in his face and let HIM attack YOU") and OnePiece (no major female characters, but at least not demeaning).

The excerpt above was taken from a post to AnimeNewsNetwork, an English-language forum for fans of anime and manga. As the poster asks, how does a parent find manga series featuring women in a positive light [28]? More broadly, how does a user new to narrative heavy visual materials—comic books, graphic novels, anime, manga, and video games—determine whether a particular item meets their needs?

© Springer Nature Switzerland AG 2020
A. Sundqvist et al. (Eds.): iConference 2020, LNCS 12051, pp. 409–418, 2020.
https://doi.org/10.1007/978-3-030-43687-2_32

Visual materials have become increasingly popular in recent years with more than 40% of all U.S. adults playing video games [36] and the North American comic book and graphic novel market growing to over $1 billion USD [37]. While teenage boys and young men remain the largest demographic groups playing video games [36], women over 50 are more likely to play video games than men their age [2]. Understandably, as more people have started to engage with these forms of media, concerns about how gender, sex, and sexuality content are portrayed in visual materials have also increased. In the last decade, researchers have studied games [21, 22, 32] comics [13] and anime [23] to ask questions about the representations of women [18, 31], particularly from the perspectives of communication and gender studies. Information science scholars, however, are in a unique position to participate in this conversation and attempt to satisfy information users' needs by organizing and providing access to the "right" materials. Here, the definition of "right" differs depending on audience; one user may seek visual materials that are inclusive, while another may seek the opposite.

Current retrieval and recommendation systems struggle with addressing these issues. Like the parent in the introduction, many users have become more aware of representation, and they want to search for materials presenting more realistic and diverse representations of gender, sex, and sexuality. However, current search options are limited and do not satisfy this need. In this paper, we share our findings from a comparison between a subset of interview and diary data (hereafter referred to as *study data*) collected by the first author and analyzed by both authors and a domain analysis of current ratings and recommendations systems for visual materials (hereafter referred to as *r/r systems*) conducted by both authors. As we compare these two datasets, we ask:

RQ1. What kinds of concerns about gender, sex, and sexuality content do visual materials users express? What do they say they want and need?

RQ2. How well do current visual material ratings and recommendations systems meet these needs?

Our contribution is twofold: first, we specifically identify gender, sex, and sexuality content related information needs of visual material users; second, we identify gaps between these needs and current *r/r systems*, suggesting how the latter may be improved.

2   Previous Studies

This study sits at the intersection of several bodies of work; we have chosen to focus on the most relevant [34]. First, we review research about depictions of gender, sex, and sexuality in visual materials from media, communications, and gender studies scholars. Then we discuss work from information scientists who have studied visual material users' needs. Finally, we briefly review literature about ratings systems in general.

In the past few decades, scholars in media and communications studies have investigated a range of topics related to the portrayal of gender, race, and sexuality in visual materials like video games [14, 21, 32, 42], graphic novels, comics and anime [13, 23], and in more traditional forms of visual media like television [4, 15, 26, 39] and movies [3, 29, 35, 43]. For example, Chess has critiqued the heteronormativity of video game narratives [5] and explored questions of diversity in terms of sex and ethnicity in video game commercials [6] while Shaw and colleagues have considered lesbian, gay, bisexual, transgender, and queer (LGBTQ) representation in digital games [41]. Information science scholars, however, have been slower to address questions about representation in visual materials, particularly with regard to users' search experiences. Important exceptions include Kitzie's [25] recent examination of how social networking sites and search engines shape identity-related information practices of LGBTQ millennials in the U.S.; however, Kitzie does not focus on visual materials.

When searching for visual materials, users need various subject accesses to satisfy their information needs. For example, Cho, Donovan, and Lee [8] created a taxonomy for video games' visual styles that enables users to search for games based on their different aesthetic styles. Similarly, Lee and colleagues [27] identified different appeal factors of playing video games, such as *Narrative, Challenge,* and *Sensation.* Similarly, Cho et al. [9, 10] found 19 different features that users need when they search for anime, including *Theme, Mood, Characters, Artwork/Visual Style,* and *Audio Style.* Having robust subject access in *r/r systems* enhances visual material users' search experiences, letting them conduct relevant and contextual searches.

The challenges of creating subject access to address gender, sex, and sexuality content in visual materials cannot be discussed without also touching on rating systems in general. Historically, ratings systems did the work of censorship. In fact, the British Board of Film Classification (BBFC), which we discuss in more detail below, began as the British Board of Film *Censors.* As Martin and Reagle [30] note, citing a version of the Recreational Software Advisory Council (RSAC) website accessed in 1997, a rating or content advisory system may classify content in ways that are *descriptive* (provides a description of the content and may provide indicators about content categories) or *evaluative* (makes a judgement about the content and appropriateness, usually based on age). Citing a former case study by the second author, Martin and Reagle [30] add the following terms: *deterministic* (a process based on methodology that assumes objectivity) and *non-deterministic* (a process based on the opinions of a group or organization).

We extend previous work by addressing gender, sex, and sexuality content in visual materials from an information science perspective with attention to the possibility of using *descriptive* and *deterministic* processes to better classify items to meet users' needs.

3   Methods

This short paper reports on an exploratory study that draws from a subset of data collected during a larger study. Because we noted certain emerging themes in the diary study and interview data collected by the first author, we then performed a domain analysis of current ratings and recommendations systems for visual materials. We detail methods for both the larger study and for this short paper below.

After receiving Institutional Review Board approval, the first author recruited visual material users, defined for this study as people who are interested in or enjoy more than one narrative-heavy visual material (i.e., someone who reads graphic novels and plays video games). Recruitment was conducted via social media, relevant fan communities, and library bulletin boards; snowball sampling was also used. All potential participants were 19 years or older. Once we observed data saturation [11, 38], the first author ceased recruitment and data collection, resulting in 26 participants. Participants received $50 USD as a token of appreciation for their time.

The first author used a self-reporting diary study and semi-structured follow-up interviews to collect data from February 2018 to April 2018. These methods were chosen based on the Uses and Gratification (U&G) perspectives; U&G posits that audiences are active in their media selection and use [33, 39] and are, thus, "sufficiently self-aware to be able to report their interests and motives in particular cases, or at least to recognize them when confronted with them in an intelligible and familiar verbal formulation" [24, p. 511]. As a theoretical foundation, U&G was also adopted to create the codebook for analyzing the qualitative data.

After recruitment, participants kept track of activities relevant to visual material seeking needs or consumption via two diary templates (Google Forms)—one for a typical day and one for an atypical day (e.g., weekends, off-days, vacations). Participants were asked to make entries for 10 days. When a participant completed the diary, a follow-up interview was scheduled. In the follow-up interviews, the first author asked questions about participants' specific visual material diary records in addition to their general visual material needs and search behaviors. On average, interviews lasted 30 min, were audio-recorded with permission, and then transcribed verbatim.

As noted above, this short paper reports on a subset of diary study and interview data [7]. After we identified gender, sex, and sexuality related themes in the study data via iterative open coding [11], we conducted a domain analysis focusing on currently available visual material ratings and recommendations systems (*r/r systems*), following the guidelines suggested by Hjørland [20]. Specifically, we analyzed ESRB[1] (video games), DC Comics[2] (comic books), BBFC[3] (films and videos including animated shows such as anime and cartoons), and Tokyopop[4] (graphic novels and manga), focusing on their content descriptors and rating definitions. To select these sources, we used maximum variation purposive sampling [17] based on popularity and prevalence in visual material fan communities. From these four sources, we collected: 19 rating categories (e.g., *E: Everyone, T: Teen,* and *M: Mature*); 10 different definitions of each rating categories; 27 content descriptors related to gender, sex, and sexuality (e.g., *Sexuality, Nudity,* and *Discrimination*); and 21 subheadings and/or descriptions (e.g., *Sexual Violence: Depictions of rape or other violent sexual acts*) for review.

4   Findings and Discussion

We begin by answering our first research questions (RQ1): *What kinds of concerns about gender, sex, and sexuality do visual materials users express? What do they say they want and need?* In our *study data,* our thematic analysis revealed two emerging

---

[1] https://www.esrb.org/ratings/.

[2] https://www.dccomics.com/ratings.

[3] https://bbfc.co.uk/what-classification/classification-guidelines.

[4] https://icv2.com/articles/comics/view/10114/tokyopop-details-ratings-criteria.

concerns as expressed by participants—representation of gender and sexuality and depictions of sexual activities. Additionally, participants said they wanted to know whether materials included representative characters and they needed to know whether they would be confronted by depictions of non-consensual sexual activities *before* they selected visual materials. Below, we discuss these issues and, in response to RQ2, we critique current *r/r systems* for visual materials accordingly.

4.1 Representation

In their study of characters in video games, Williams and colleagues [42] found "a systematic over-representation of males, white and adults and a systematic under-representation of females, Hispanics, Native Americans, children and the elderly." A decade later, in the *study data* participants voiced similar concerns:

I try and go through and find games and media that feature non-male protagonists. I feel like there are so much out there that follows a white male protagonist, and it's kind of boring. It's just nice to see someone like myself reflected in media. (P23)

I like comics and media written for/by LGBT folks, and this one in particular is a nice mix of artistic inspiration and feeling connection. (P4)

As P23 and P4 note, they try to look for visual materials featuring characters with whom they can relate. In fact, when we coded instances of *representation, identification* often co-occurred. But representation alone isn't enough. P26 reported:

I very strongly gravitate towards shows that have complex female characters and that happens with me over and over again. I have opted out of watching TV shows or anime that weren't very diverse or I felt like the female characters were flat or were not very accurate [...] they weren't very convincing. (P26)

Study participants expressed a strong desire to see themselves—women, gender non-binary users, "LGBT folks," and others—reflected in the media they consume in a way that is not demeaning or tokenizing ("flat," "not very accurate"). Yet, despite the fact that representation has been discussed in the visual media community for years [e.g., 21, 32, 42] current *r/r systems* do not fully support searches for different types of characters, subjects, or plots. For example, while major streaming services like Netflix offer combined tags (i.e., "Action & Adventure Featuring a Strong Female Lead," "LGBTQ Dramas") for TV shows and movie, for visual materials like animation and anime, only broad terms like "Anime Series," "Japanese Anime," or "Family Animation" are provided, treating the medium itself as a genre.

Although the definitions or detailed descriptions of content descriptors are not readily available in *r/r systems* (e.g., Netflix, Amazon Prime Video, and Google Play) that have implemented BBFC's rating information (see Figs. 1 and 2), BBFC's attempt to address gender and sexuality issues in their content descriptors is noteworthy. Specifically, BBFC's rating system contains content descriptors such as "Discrimination", showing the level of, and the types of, discriminations depicted in an item (e.g., *"The work as a whole must not endorse discriminatory language or behaviour, although there may be racist, homophobic or other discriminatory themes and language"*).

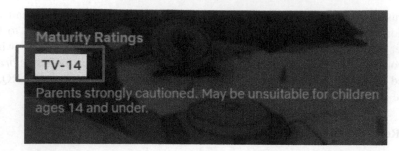

Fig. 1. A screenshot of Netflix anime series *The Seven Deadly Sins*' (2014) details information page.

Fig. 2. A screenshot of Amazon Prime Video anime series *Cardcaptor Sakura's* (2000) details information page.

4.2   Depictions of Sexual Activities

In our domain analysis of currently available *r/r systems*, we noted a lack of granularity when it comes to depictions or natures of sexual activities, such as sexual consent. This kind of information is particularly important when users may be triggered by scenes of non-consensual sex (such as P17) or simply want to avoid particular kinds of content (such as P26):

> *Part of the reason I tend to view less more comic books and TV is it can be very difficult to predict what's going to trigger me in advance. I have a history of sexual violence and so there's a lot of stuff around sexual consent in media that is really terrible. So, it can be very difficult to figure out how to reliably find something that's not going to trigger me more when I'm already doing really badly. (P17)*

> *Right, so, I did actually quit watching that, and it was the consensual element [that] was the hard pass. Like, it makes me uncomfortable to watch. I don't think the it doesn't seem genuine to me, and I don't think the responses to that level of lack of consent is realistic in my opinion. I don't think it is. I also was really put off by the very like slut shaming dialogue in it. (P26)*

Aside from BBFC, the *r/r systems* we reviewed fail to provide more intuitive and in-depth content descriptions for visual materials (see Fig. 3), merely describing the materials as containing "Sexual Content" or "Sexual Innuendo." Tokyopop (see footnote 4) attempts to provide more detailed information about scenes with nudity and sex, containing content descriptors such as "Non-sexual Nondescript Nudity" or "Sexual-Partial Nudity." However, for an *r/r system* to address different natures of sexual activities, descriptors with more contextualized information need (e.g., Non-consensual sexual act) to be created to satisfy users' needs.

Rating categories	Descriptions		Content descriptors	Subheadings/Descriptions
			Sexuality	Sexual Content: Non-explicit depictions of sexual behavior, possibly including partial nudity
E: Everyone	N/A			
E 10+: Everyone 10+	N/A			
T: Teen	N/A	Sexuality		Sexual Content: Non-explicit depictions of sexual behavior, possibly including partial nudity
M: Mature 17+	N/A			
Ao: Adults only 18+	N/A			Sexual Violence: Depictions of rape or other violent sexual acts
RP: Rating pending	N/A			Suggestive Themes: Mild provocative references or materials
				Sexual Themes: References to sex or sexuality
E: Everyone	Appropriate for readers of violence and/or some content			Strong Sexual Content: Explicit and/or frequent depictions of sexual behavior, possibly including nudity
T: Teen	Appropriate for readers ag violence, language and/or	Nudity		Nudity: Graphic or prolonged depictions of nudity
	Appropriate for readers ag moderate violence, mild pr suggestive themes.			Partial Nudity: Brief and/or mild depictions of nudity
T+: Teen plus				
	Appropriate for readers ag intense violence, extensive profanity, nudity, sexual themes and other content suitable only for older readers.			
M: Mature			N/A	N/A
	A U film should be suitable for audiences aged four years and over, although it is impossible to predict what might upset any particular child. U films should be set within a positive framework and should offer reassuring counterbalances to any violence, threat or horror. If a work is particularly suitable for pre-school children, this will be indicated in the ratings info.		Nudity	Occasional nudity with no sexual context
U Universal: Suitable for all			Sex	Only very mild sexual behaviour (for example, kissing) and references to such behaviour.
			Discrimination	Discriminatory language or behaviour is unlikely to be acceptable unless clearly disapproved of.

Fig. 3. Process of domain analysis in this study (partial dataset).

To be clear, participants did not express a puritanical desire to avoid all depictions of sexual activities or to censor sexual content in general; rather, they wanted to be more aware and have an option to actively choose a visual material instead of being a passive user. However, as the BBFC notes [44], it is a challenge not to give away major plot spoilers by providing more detailed warnings or content descriptors. How, then, might classification systems address these needs without censoring content or divulging too much information? We take up this question below.

4.3   Classification Systems and Censorship

Ratings and recommendations systems are socially and politically constructed and often lack reliability and validity [12, 19] (returning to [30], they can be *evaluative* and *non-deterministic*). Moreover, they can also be leveraged to perpetuate censorship. Take, for example, current library practices. Rubin [40] states that materials focusing on "diverse titles," such as "nonwhite main or secondary characters, LGBT main or secondary characters, disabled main or secondary characters" (p. 496) tend to be challenged. Citing the ALA's 2015 report on frequently challenged books [1], Rubin writes, "over the last ten years, 52% of the top 100 books challenged or banned included diverse content and 80% of the top ten banned in 2014 contained diverse content" (p, 496). According to Downey [16], one of the self-censorship rationales librarians often employ is *"it's hard to find LGBT-themed books"*; that is, even librarians excuse the exclusion of diverse materials by acknowledging the current limitations of classification and search. As information scientists, we can and should question ourselves: *What can we do to create more search-friendly environments for diverse visual materials that promote equity in gender and sexuality representations?*

5   Conclusion and Future Work

Visual material users today represent a far broader spectrum than straight, cisgender teenage boys and young men. This means users expect more from visual materials and are searching for items they consider "right" for them. As one participant noted in their diary response, visual materials "defying stereotypes is a plus." To meet users' needs, we must think carefully about how we classify gender, sex, and sexuality content in visual materials and explore design interventions that address tensions without resolving them. For example, one can imagine creating a system in which Quick Response (QR) codes are used to address some users' needs to know more details about content while respecting other users' desires to avoid spoilers. One can also imagine designing a system that aggregates existing *r/r systems* and allows users to build upon these, generating their own personalized *r/r systems* that then use machine learning to predict matches. We plan to pursue these ideas in future work and invite others to join us. As information scientists, we are in a unique position to spearhead efforts towards more inclusive information experiences. By addressing visual material users' needs with regards to gender, sex, and sexuality content and by enhancing the contexts of content descriptions in future *r/r systems*, we will be able to encourage more thoughtful and equitable information access and better serve a wider range of users.

References

1. American Library Association: Frequently Challenged Books of the 21st Century. http://www.ala.org/advocacy/bbooks/frequentlychallengedbooks/top10
2. Anderton, K.: Women over 50 are playing more video games than men. https://www.forbes.com/sites/kevinanderton/2019/01/29/women-over-50-are-playing-more-video-games-than-men-infographic/#6bf4ec761093
3. Benshoff, H., Griffin, S.: America on Film: Representing Race, Class, Gender, and Sexuality at the Movies. Wiley, West Sussex (2011)
4. Billings, A., Eastman, S.: Selective representation of gender, ethnicity, and nationality in American television coverage of the 2000 summer olympics. Int. Rev. Sociol. Sport **37**, 351–370 (2002). https://doi.org/10.1177/101269020203700302
5. Chess, S.: The queer case of video games: orgasms, heteronormativity, and video game narrative. Crit. Stud. Media Commun. **33**, 84–94 (2016). https://doi.org/10.1080/15295036.2015.1129066
6. Chess, S., Evans, N.J., Baines, J.J.: What does a gamer look like? Video games, advertising, and diversity. Telev. New Media **18**, 37–57 (2016). https://doi.org/10.1177/1527476416643765

7. Cho, H.: Understanding users of cross-media information: contexts, gratifications, and features focusing on visual narrative materials (2019)
8. Cho, H., Donovan, A., Lee, J.H.: Art in an algorithm: a taxonomy for describing video game visual styles. J. Assoc. Inf. Sci. Technol. **69**, 633–646 (2018). https://doi.org/10.1002/asi.23988
9. Cho, H., Schmalz, M.L., Keating, S.A., Lee, J.H.: Information needs for anime recommendation: analyzing anime users' online forum queries. In: 2017 ACM/IEEE Joint Conference on Digital Libraries (JCDL), pp. 1–3. IEEE, Toronto, ON, Canada (2017)
10. Cho, H., Schmalz, M.L., Keating, S.A., Lee, J.H.: Analyzing anime users' online forum queries for recommendation using content analysis. J. Doc. **74**, 918–935 (2018). https://doi.org/10.1108/jd-08-2017-0122
11. Corbin, J.M., Strauss, A.L.: Basics of Qualitative Research: Techniques and Procedures for Developing Grounded Theory. SAGE, Los Angeles (2015)
12. Coyne, S.M., Callister, M.A., Gentile, D.A.: Media violence and judgments of offensiveness: a quantitative and qualitative analysis. Psychol. Pop. Media Cult. **5**, 372–389 (2016)
13. Danziger-Russell, J.: Girls and Their Comics: Finding a Female Voice in Comic Book Narrative. Scarecrow Press, Lanham (2013)
14. Dill, K.E., Thill, K.P.: video game characters and the socialization of gender roles: young people's perceptions mirror sexist media depictions. Sex Roles **57**, 851–864 (2007)
15. Dow, B.: Ellen, television, and the politics of gay and lesbian visibility. Crit. Stud. Media Commun. **18**, 123–140 (2010). https://doi.org/10.1080/07393180128077
16. Downey, J.: Self-censorship in selection of LGBT-themed materials. Ref. User Serv. Q. **53**, 104–107 (2013). https://doi.org/10.5860/rusq.53n2.104
17. Etikan, I.: Comparison of convenience sampling and purposive sampling. AJTAS **5**, 1 (2016). https://doi.org/10.11648/j.ajtas.20160501.11
18. Ferguson, C.J.: Positive female role-models eliminate negative effects of sexually violent media. J. Commun. **62**, 888–899 (2012)
19. Gentile, D.A., Humphrey, J., Walsh, D.A.: Media ratings for movies, music, video games, and television: a review of the research and recommendations for improvements. Adolesc. Med. Clin. **16**, 427–446 (2005)
20. Hjørland, B.: Domain analysis in information science: eleven approaches – traditional as well as innovative. J. Doc. **58**, 422–462 (2002). https://doi.org/10.1108/00220410210431136
21. Ivory, J.D.: Still a man's game: gender representation in online reviews of video games. Mass Commun. Soc. **9**, 103–114 (2006). https://doi.org/10.1207/s15327825mcs0901_6
22. Jansz, J., Martis, R.G.: The Lara phenomenon: powerful female characters in video games. Sex Roles **56**, 141–148 (2007)
23. Jiang Bresnahan, M., Inoue, Y., Kagawa, N.: Players and whiners? Perceptions of sex stereotyping in Animé in Japan and the US. Asian J. Commun. **16**, 207–217 (2006). https://doi.org/10.1080/01292980600638728
24. Katz, E., Blumler, J.G., Gurevitch, M.: Uses and gratifications research. Pub. Opin. Q. **37**, 509–523 (1974)
25. Kitzie, V.: That looks like me or something i can do": affordances and constraints in the online identity work of US LGBTQ+ millennials. J. Assoc. Inf. Sci. Technol. **54**, 222–231 (2019). https://doi.org/10.1002/asi.24217
26. Lauzen, M., Dozier, D., Horan, N.: Constructing gender stereotypes through social roles in prime-time television. J. Broadcast. Electron. Media **52**, 200–214 (2008). https://doi.org/10.1080/08838150801991971

27. Lee, J.H., Clarke, R.I., Cho, H., Windleharth, T.: Understanding appeals of video games for readers' advisory and recommendation. RUSQ **57**, 127 (2017). https://doi.org/10.5860/rusq. 57.2.6529

28. LHanson11: Manga recs for girls middle school? (2014). https://www.animenewsnetwork. com/bbs/phpBB2/viewtopic.php?t=2907330

29. Madžarević, G., Soto-Sanfiel, M.: Positive representation of gay characters in movies for reducing homophobia. Sex. Cult. **22**, 909–930 (2018). https://doi.org/10.1007/s12119-018-9502-x

30. Martin, C.D., Reagle, J.: An alternative to government regulation and censorship: content advisory systems for the internet. Cardozo Arts Entertain. Law J. **15**, 409–427 (1997)

31. Martins, N., Williams, D.C., Harrison, K., Ratan, R.A.: A content analysis of female body imagery in video games. Sex Roles **61**, 824 (2009)

32. Near, C.E.: Selling gender: associations of box art representation of female characters with sales for teen- and mature-rated video games. Sex Roles **68**, 252–269 (2013). https://doi.org/10.1007/s11199-012-0231-6

33. Oliver, M.B.: Affect as a predictor of entertainment choice: the utility of looking beyond pleasure. In: Hartmann, T. (ed.) Media choice: a theoretical and empirical overview, pp. 181–198. Routledge, New York (2009)

34. Onwuegbuzie, A.J., Leech, N.L., Collins, K.M.T.: Qualitative analysis techniques for the review of the literature. Qual. Rep. **17**, 56 (2012)

35. Pennell, H., Behm-Morawitz, E.: The empowering (super) heroine? The effects of sexualized female characters in superhero films on women. Sex Roles **72**, 211–220 (2015)

36. Perrin, A.: Five facts about Americans and video games. https://www.pewresearch.org/fact-tank/2018/09/17/5-facts-about-americans-and-video-games/

37. Reid, C.: Selling Graphic Novels in a Changing American Marketplace 1. https://www. publishersweekly.com/pw/by-topic/industry-news/comics/article/78393-selling-graphic-novels-in-a-changing-american-marketplace.html

38. Robinson, O.C.: Sampling in interview-based qualitative research: a theoretical and practical guide. Qual. Res. Psychol. **11**, 25–41 (2014). https://doi.org/10.1080/14780887.2013. 801543

39. Rubin, A.M.: Television use by children and adolescents. Hum. Commun. Res. **5**, 109–120 (1979). https://doi.org/10.1111/j.1468-2958.1979.tb00626.x

40. Rubin, R.: Foundations of Library and Information Science. ALA Neal-Schuman, an imprint of the American Library Association, Chicago (2016)

41. Shaw, A., Lauteria, E.W., Yang, H., Persaud, C.J., Cole, A.M.: Counting queerness in games: trends in LGBTQ digital game representation, 1985–2005. Int. J. Commun. **13**, 1544–1569 (2019)

42. Williams, D., Martins, N., Consalvo, M., Ivory, J.D.: The virtual census: representations of gender, race and age in video games. New Media Soc. **11**, 815–834 (2009)

43. Young, L.: Fear of the Dark: "Race", Gender and Sexuality in Cinema. Routledge, New York (1996)

44. Ratings info. https://bbfc.co.uk/what-classification/what-bbfc-ratings-info

User Experience to Inform the Design of a Search Infrastructure for Open Educational Resources

Tamara Heck[1(✉)] iD, Valentyna Kovalenko[2], and Marc Rittberger[1] iD

[1] Information Center for Education,
DIPF | Leibniz Institute for Research and Information in Education,
Rostocker Straße 6, 60323 Frankfurt am Main, Germany
heck@dipf.de
[2] Darmstadt University of Applied Sciences, Darmstadt, Germany
valentyna.kovalenko@stud.h-da.de

Abstract. Open education includes the access and use of freely licensed material, which is known as open educational resources. Since the idea evolved about 20 years ago, the movement faces the challenge to motivate educators to actively use, create and distribute open learning resources. The reasons are that educators do not know where to find such resources for their discipline, and if they know common web sources, they find it hard to seek for the most relevant material. By now, there are several information seeking services for openly licensed educational material that differ in structure and functions in many respects. Some services as well offer functions to upload one's own material. A challenge for those services is to offer appropriate seeking and filtering functions to allow users an efficient and easy search. The following paper reports on a user-oriented study that evaluates six search services for open educational resources. A qualitative approach was chosen to better study the specific target group and new evolving search services. The study informs the designing of a decentralized infrastructure that offers seeking educational material from different higher educational institutions within Germany.

Keywords: Information seeking · User experience · Open educational resources

1 Introduction

A central goal of open education is the access to freely licensed and available educational material for learners and educators [1]. This material is referred to as open educational resources (OER). The nature of OER can be described by the five "r's", that is the licence of OER allows every user to retain, reuse, revise, remix and redistribute OER [2, 3]. Since the idea of OER, the movement faces the challenge to motivate educators to actively use, create and distribute open learning resources. One reason stated in surveys [4, 5] is that educators do not know where to find such resources for their discipline. They think that for their own discipline sharing educational material is uncommon and thus not available [4]. To make OER accessible and

A. Sundqvist et al. (Eds.): iConference 2020, LNCS 12051, pp. 419–427, 2020.
https://doi.org/10.1007/978-3-030-43687-2_33

findable, educational institutions like universities, but as well other providers and voluntary user communities established online repositories and search sites. Additionally, existing providers like libraries expanded their information services to make OER searchable. For example, libraries added an additional metadata field to their search mask to allow the filtering for OER, which means resources that are licensed with one of the three Creative Commons license CC-0, CC-BY or CC-BY-SA. By now, there are several information seeking services for openly licensed educational material that differ in structure and functions in many respects. In Germany, the web portal and service OERInfo[1] gives an overview of existing OER web sources, it lists 16 services and platforms that focus on OER search (Sep 2019) – despite other existing repositories that include closed and openly licensed material. Studies that give an overview of functions of open educational resource repositories (ROER) show some diversities [6, 7]. Some repositories do not only allow the search for OER, but the upload of new user resources as well. Other social functions are the creation of user profiles and own bookmark lists and the option to comment and add tag.

Regarding OER seeking, services show differences in the number filter options. Offering filters to refine search results allows for a finer search of relevant resources that users might need for their purpose. Hereby, a crucial aspect is the metadata and its quality. On the one hand, there is a lack of metadata as resource creators do not fill out metadata fields. On the other hand, metadata standards for learning material, like LOM or LRMI, differ in their fields and values and make filtering less efficient. The following study is part of a project that aims at designing a concept for a decentralized infrastructure that allows a user efficient search for OER from divers higher educational institutions within Germany [8, 9]. On a system basis, it deals with challenges regarding metadata aggregation and mapping. From a user-oriented point of view, it faces issues like users' attitudes towards using and sharing open educational material and users seeking behavior. User studies on OER deal with user attitudes towards openness as well as using and creating open learning material [10, 11]. Our study concentrates on the analysis of user experience with OER search services. Here, we see a need because we are dealing with a specific user group, i.e. educators who seek material for their specific teaching context, and we are dealing with new search services that show differences in their design, functions and scope. In order to design a useful and usable service for higher education lecturers, we would like to understand more about how lecturers interact with OER search services.

The following qualitative study applied experimental search scenarios to analyze information seeking on six OER search services. The study will inform the designing of a decentralized infrastructure that offers seeking educational material from different higher education institutions within Germany. We apply a user-oriented design for the overall project. The development of the infrastructure will go along with user studies that evaluate single service functions together with potential users. The study introduced here focused on lecturers at German universities. The research questions were:

---

[1] https://open-educational-resources.de/.

- How do educators experience OER search services?
- What are relevant functions for educators for finding learning material for their teaching?

Section 2 introduces the study design. Section 3 includes first results and recommendations.

2 Qualitative User Study Design

The study builds on the information service evaluation model [12] that gives a comprehensive overview of evaluation aspects aggregated from several other information service models. The focus was on the user perspective of experiencing an information service. As OER search services in Germany are quite new and not used by many higher education lecturers yet, we decided to run a qualitative approach instead of an online usability survey. Moreover, our qualitative data is able to reveal lecturers' personal attitudes in a better way.

We designed two search tasks that each participant had to do. Those tasks were adapted for each search service as the chosen services greatly differ in their design and functions. Prior to designing the search tasks, we asked participants to tell us about their teaching subjects and course types. A first task for each participants was: *"You are preparing your current seminar with the focus on (for example digital education) and seek educational licensed material that allows you to use, edit and share with others."* The second task was more specialized and ask for example to search for a picture that allows re-editing.

The user study for each participant included the following steps (Fig. 1):

- General questions on knowledge about OER and the search services
- 2 × tasks for two search services each
- Interview on experiences during the search and service use

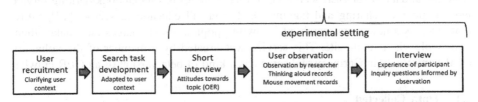

Fig. 1. Process of the experimental setting in the qualitative approach.

Our participant target group were lecturers with teaching responsibility at any German university, who know what open educational resources are (explicit use of OER or OER creation was not a criteria). Participants were recruited via mailing lists and personal contacts that disseminated study invitations. We recruited six participants, each of them did search tasks in two different services, so each service was tested by two participants. We did not collect any personal information about the participants. The teaching areas of the participants differ and cover educational research as well as information and computer science.

We chose our search services according to four criteria. Services shall allow the search for learning resources (not OER only, but with a strong focus on them), they are offered by German providers, they focus on the higher education sector or have many resources for higher education, and they are free to use. Our main sources to find German services were the OERInfo and the OER world map[2] pages (status Nov 2018). Those criteria led to six services shown in Table 1. Other services were either not free to use or had a very strong focus on school education.

Table 1. Search services and their features.

Feature	Service					
	OERHörnchen	DDB	Edutags	HOOU	ZOERR	OpenRub
Service type (according to OER world map)	Meta search engine	Online library	Social bookmarking service	Repository	Repository	Repository
URL	https://oerhoernchen.de/suche	https://www.deutsche-digitale-bibliothek.de	https://www.edutags.de/	https://www.hoou.de	https://www.oerbw.de/edu-sharing/components/search	https://open.ruhr-uni-bochum.de/

OER search services in Germany differ in their focus and functions as they have different providers. Thus, the websites have different looks and users cannot rely on similar designs to help them navigate through diverse services. The three repositories were explicitly established to foster the use and creation of OER, mainly within their own university. ZOEER is a service for all university educators in one federal state. The Deutsche Digitale Bibliothek (DDB) is an online library service that offers the search for Germany's cultural and scientific resources. It has a typical search service structure and allow for OER search via a filter. Edutags is a social bookmarking service with a focus on sharing and tagging OER from all educational sectors [13]. OER-Hörnchen is a new meta-search site crawling popular OER sources and makes them searchable via a single site. This service was created by a member of the voluntary OER community in Germany and serves as a kind of beta version of an OER crawler.

2.1 Data Collected

We collected user data for different purposes. In a short semi-structured interview, we ask about the users' attitude towards OER use and experience with searching OER (semi-structured short interview). During the search tasks we observed participants and made notes if we realized they had difficulties with their search. We as well recorded those search tasks and participants were prompted to think aloud. After participants

---

[2] https://oerworldmap.org/.

completed their search tasks, they were able to talk about their experience based on our observation and participants' thinking aloud monologues. Recorded interviews and thinking aloud phases were analyzed afterwards.

3 Results and Discussion

3.1 Awareness and Use of OER and Services

The interviews with the educators revealed that they know about resource licenses and their restrictions and as well about specific OER licenses. However, some feel insecure and are not sure if they have all knowledge that is needed. None of the lecturers did create and share OER, a fact that several quantitative studies found out as well [4]. Participants were not aware of the specific OER search services. They search for non-restricted learning material like OER within common sites like Google Scholar or Wikipedia, or they use textbooks and magazines. For example, Google image search offers a license filter. However, participants stated that a more structured search is needed. One participant complained that they find a lot of OER online, but the specific search for material that fits their context and topic is hard to find. Restricted sources like textbooks offer better material, but this material is often not openly licensed. This participant stated that this circumstance prevent them from sharing their created teaching resources as those resources is based on resources from textbooks that are not openly licensed.

3.2 Type of Resources and Granularity

Regarding OER types, it is striking that lecturers seek single pictures or exercises instead of learning units or courses. The granularity of OER is widely discussed, several levels of OER are suggested like textbooks or learning units [14]. An OER granularity model for higher education suggests six levels [15]: a single learning object, a unit of several objects that belong to a higher education seminar, that is part of a module, within a specific semester, for a specific study subject. The model shows the difficulty of assigning a one dimensional hierarchy to learning objects. For example, single seminar courses can be part of several modules and target groups. A multi-hierarchical system is possible, but would complicate an easy seeking design for users. If users need single learning resources for their teaching, a system provider has to consider whether a granularity model is efficient. If a granularity model is applied, an explicit metadata field that includes information on the resource's granularity is needed.

3.3 Interface and Additional Metadata

Regarding the usability of the search services, participants had minor complaints. They expected a well-arranged design and felt disrupted by additional features besides the search mask like links and videos. One participant that evaluated OERHörnchen, the metasearch service, claimed that they first though the service would offer a simple search mask like Google "*and that is why you forget to scroll down*" (p1 on OER-Hörnchen). That is the participant overlooked the diverse search masks of OER-Hörnchen that set a kind of pre-filter. The same participant preferred the DDB search mask that was easier to use for them.

Some participants were irritated by the license filter. Either they expected to find OER only and did not see any need to apply a filter, like with the service OER-Hörnchen, or participants were not able to find the filter easily. Those pitfalls need to be improved to increase seeking experience and OER use. Otherwise, users tend to use closed material. Moreover, participants stated that they wanted to see a resource's license directly as metadata shown in the result list.

Some OER were perceived as learning resource for students rather than a resource that lecturers could use to add to their teaching material. A filter for refine target groups might help lecturers to do a proper refinement. Metadata standards include fields that specify target groups. However, this is still a problem to be solved as resources can be interesting for diverse target groups. Here, additional metadata about a resource learning goal and scope is helpful to further refine results.

3.4 Learnings for Creating an OER Infrastructure

The overall findings show that participants are not aware of current search services that focus on OER, but they find them helpful when those services support the search for topical learning material with specific learning goals that fit their teaching. This finding goes along other studies stating that current OER repositories need to facilitate the retrieval of OER that are appropriate for users' context and learning goals [6]. As more learning resources will enter the services, searching and filtering functions need to be improved. Improving metadata quality through applied standards and additional information like user-generated data (tags, comments, rating) will become crucial.

Regarding our first question, our participants experienced the evaluated services positively, some participants had problems with finding functions within the service interface. Services could be facilitated further when providers explicitly state the main purpose of those search services. One participant recommended to *"display the purpose of the web offering through short texts and additional information what is to be found on the site"* (p1 on DDB service). That means the search masks need to be the most prominent feature on the site.

Moreover, a search service has to explicitly state which kind of resources it offers, that is openly licensed material only or open and closed resources. In the latter case and with regard to our second question, participants want to have a more prominently placed filter function search for license metadata to be able to directly choose resources with open licenses. One participant recommended to place the license filter *"directly besides the search mask"* (p1). Other relevant search functions include specific filters for learning resources like target group and learning goals. One participant recommend that a service shall not only display media types, but *"didactical methodological materials"* (p3 on DDB). This aspect goes along with the purpose of a service. Some participants preferred a more concrete guidance by the service and stated that *"[a service] does not quite focus on university material"* (p2 on Edutags and HOOU). That is either a service needs to focus on resource for a specific educational sector only, or it needs more filter functions to allow resource restriction. The participant further complaint that *"you cannot choose a topic, but a category. [Categories] like social and natural sciences or no topics, but disciplines*" (p2 on HOOU). Another participant recommended "*further filter options to limit results on topics*" (p3). As our participants rather searched for single learning objects, more research has to be done to find out of the establishment of a granularity model is useful ad efficient.

Besides the search functions that our participants evaluated, services like ZOERR provide a direct uploading function to give educators the option to share their own resource. Other services run a background service for sharing material. With regard to the idea of OER – which includes not only the access and use of OER, but the creation, remixing and sharing as crucial elements to foster open education and resource quality [16, 17] – providers might need to expand their services. Santos Hermosa et al. [6] analyzed OER repositories on indicators such as re-use and re-mix. For example, open formats of OER are relevant to enable users to easily re-mix resources. User communities could support bottom-up quality evaluation. Elements of user communities include:

- visibility of system users and their activities
- the opportunity to comment, rate and add additional information about the resource, like prescribed metadata fields or user-generated tags
- the opportunity to communicate with others

Edutags as a social bookmarking system applied some user function. Some activities like comments are visible for all system users. Thus, a social bookmarking function could be a sub-part of an OER search service. HOOU as well offers user community functions for registered users. As our participants did not use any services before their evaluation, they did not state on any user community functions and did not recognize those in Edutags. Future research has to be done to analyze the usefulness of those functions for higher education lecturers.

4   Conclusion

With our study we wanted to get deeper insights into user search behavior of OER and more specifically on seeking appropriate OER for their teaching. We applied a qualitative approach with search tasks, observation and open interviews to allow participants to talk about their experience. This gave us a first impression of our target group that will be able to use the decentralized OER search infrastructure and first hints on what we need to consider in designing this infrastructure. Our main findings suggest a search service where users understand its purpose immediately and are informed about the kind of resources they can find. The service should include specific metadata fields that allow users to search for resources that fit their purpose. More research has to be done on those field values and the appropriateness for users as well as on differences regarding higher education disciplines and their specific need.

References

1. UNESCO: Paris open declaration. Paper presented at the World Open Educational Resources (OER) Congress, Paris, France (2012). http://www.unesco.org/fileadmin/MULTIMEDIA/HQ/CI/CI/pdf/Events/Paris%20OER%20Declaration_01.pdf
2. van Damme, D.: Open educational resources: a catalyst for innovation in education (2017). https://www.open-science-conference.eu/wp-content/uploads/2016/02/vanDamme_Open-Educational-Resources-A-Catalyst-for-Innovation-in-Education-Berlin-Open-Science-Conference-22-March-2017.pdf
3. Wiley, D.: The Access Compromise and the 5th R (2014). https://opencontent.org/blog/archives/3221
4. Heck, T., et al.: Survey: open science in higher education (2017). https://zenodo.org/record/400561/files/TIB_OS_wiss_Poster_3_2017_RZ.PDF
5. Allen, E., Seaman, J.: Opening the textbook. Educational resources in U.S. higher education (2017). http://www.onlinelearningsurvey.com/reports/openingthetextbook2017.pdf
6. Santos-Hermosa, G., Ferran-Ferrer, N., Abadal, E.: Repositories of open educational resources. An assessment of reuse and educational aspects. IRRODL **18**, 84+ (2017). https://doi.org/10.19173/irrodl.v18i5.3063
7. Zervas, P., Alifragkis, C., Sampson, D.G.: A quantitative analysis of learning object repositories as knowledge management systems. Knowl. Manag. E-Learn. Int. J. **6**, 156–170 (2014). http://www.kmel-journal.org/ojs/index.php/online-publication/article/download/240/241
8. Kerres, M., Hölterhof, T., Scharnberg, G., Schröder, N.: EduArc. Eine Infrastruktur zur hochschulübergreifenden Nachnutzung digitaler Lernmaterialien. Synergie 07 (2019). https://uhh.de/en4om
9. Heinen, R., Kerres, M., Scharnberg, G., Blees, I., Rittberger, M.: A federated reference structure for open informational ecosystems. JIME **2016**, 33 (2016). https://doi.org/10.5334/jime.413
10. Bossu, C., Brown, M., Bull, D.: Adoption, use and management of open educational resources to enhance teaching and learning in Australia: final report to the office for learning & teaching (2013)
11. Boston Consulting Group: The Open Education Resources Ecosystem: an Evaluation of the OER Movement's Current State and its Progress Toward Mainstream Adoption. William and Flora Hewlett Foundation, California (2013). https://hewlett.org/wp-content/uploads/2016/08/The%20Open%20Educational%20Resources%20Ecosystem.pdf
12. Schumann, L., Stock, W.G.: The information service evaluation (ISE) model. Webology **11**, 1–20 (2014)
13. Rehm, M., Heinen, R., Schanberg, G.: Edutags - social bookmarking for teachers: a German case study (2014)
14. Kerres, M., Heinen, R.: Open informational ecosystems. The missing link for sharing resources for education. Int. Rev. Res. Open Distrib. Learn. **16** (2015). https://doi.org/10.19173/irrodl.v16i1.2008

15. Mandausch, M.: Annotationskonzept für Bildungsressourcen (2017). https://www.ice-karlsruhe.de/wp-content/uploads/2017/12/2017-12-01-Annotationskonzept.pdf
16. Stagg, A., Bossu, C.: Educational policy and open educational practice in Australian higher education. In: Blessinger, P., Bliss, T.J. (eds.) Open Education. International Perspectives in Higher Education, pp. 115–135. Open Book Publishers, Cambridge (2016). http://oro.open.ac.uk/id/eprint/57224
17. Blessinger, P., Bliss, T.J.: Introduction to open education: towards a human rights theory. In: Blessinger, P., Bliss, T.J. (eds.) Open Education. International Perspectives in Higher Education, pp. 11–29. Open Book Publishers, Cambridge (2016). https://doi.org/10.18278/ijoer.1.1.5

The Effects of Message Framing on Online Health Headline Selection: A Mediation of Message Credibility

Tingting Jiang[1,2](✉) (iD), Xi Wu[1] (iD), Ying Wang[1] (iD), and Ye Chen[3] (iD)

[1] School of Information Management, Wuhan University, Wuhan, Hubei, China
tij@whu.edu.cn
[2] Center for Studies of Information Resources, Wuhan University, Wuhan, Hubei, China
[3] School of Information Management, Central China Normal University, Wuhan, Hubei, China

Abstract. The acquisition of health information is conducive to promoting the public's health literacy and improving citizens' health. The display of online health information often features an entering page that lists headlines hyperlinked to health article pages. Among the various techniques that help increase headline effectiveness, this study was particularly interested in message framing (gain/loss framing) and investigated how it influenced headline selection in the form of fixation and clicking and considered message credibility as a possible mediator. Based on an eye-tracking experiment, this study found that gain-framed headlines received a larger fixation count, a longer fixation duration, and a larger clicking count. In addition, message credibility had partial mediating effects on the relationship between message framing and fixation count and that between message framing and clicking count. The findings provide useful implications for creating effective online headlines in the health domain and enrich our understanding of how information characteristics affect information selection.

Keywords: Message framing · Health information · Headline selection · Message credibility · Eye-tracking experiment

1 Introduction

An increasing number of people are acquiring health information on the Internet, which is a global trend. In China, the users of Internet medical care services have reached 253 million, accounting for 32.7% of all Internet users [1]. Women are more interested in health information than men. They seek for health information more frequently, not only for themselves, but for their family [2]. The incidence and mortality rates of cancers kept rising during the past decade. Cancers are becoming more and more common among young people [3, 4], with breast cancer, cervical cancer, and ovarian cancer among the leading causes of women's death [5].

Online health articles are written with an attempt to persuade people to adopt a healthy behavior [6]. Various techniques have been used to increase the persuasiveness

© Springer Nature Switzerland AG 2020
A. Sundqvist et al. (Eds.): iConference 2020, LNCS 12051, pp. 428–437, 2020.
https://doi.org/10.1007/978-3-030-43687-2_34

of health massages, and message framing is one of them. Prospect theory provides the theoretical basis for message framing [7]. An identical message can be framed in two ways, gain framing and loss framing. The former refers to emphasizing the benefits of engaging in a healthy behavior, while the latter the costs of engaging in an unhealthy behavior [8].

It is interesting to notice that more and more headlines of online health articles are created in the form of gain or loss framing. For examples, "moderate weight loss will make you feel pleasant" is a gain-framed headline, and "excessive weight loss will induce negative emotions" is a loss-framed one. The display of online information often features an entering page that lists headlines hyperlinked to article or content pages [9], which also applies to the health domain. The effectiveness of headlines determines what will be read and what will be ignored [10].

Given the abundance of existing research on the use of message framing in the content of health articles, this study instead focused on gain/loss-framed headlines of cancer-related information and investigated how they attracted female users' attention and clicks. In particular, message credibility was taken into account for being an important factor influencing the persuasiveness of framed messages [11]. An eye-tracking experiment was conducted to capture users' eye movements and selection behavior in response to cancer-related headlines for which message framing was manipulated. The goal of this study is to provide practical implications for public health organizations to create effective headlines and better serve female audience and creating effective headlines.

2 Literature Review

2.1 Message Framing and Persuasiveness

Message framing and the persuasiveness of framed messages have been widely investigated in the health domain. Researchers have measured the persuasiveness of gain/loss-framed health information in terms of intention, behavior, attitude, and resolve [8, 12–17]. It has been found that gain-framed messages significantly promoted disease prevention behavior, e.g. smoking cessation, physical activity, and healthy eating, as well as health knowledge acquisition. However, most studies obtained no evidence showing a direct effect of message framing on persuasiveness. A number of studies also took into account the moderating effects of individual characteristics, e.g. emotional state [17, 18], social comparison orientation [19], approachavoidance motivation [20], self-efficacy [12], and racial identity [21], as well as information characteristics, e.g. temporal consequences [14, 22], evidence type [23], and communication mode [24]. When these moderators were introduced into the studies, message framing was found to influence the persuasiveness of health information related to smoking, exercises, diet, and so on.

2.2 Information Headlines and Selection

Despite the lack of focused research on the headlines of health information, researchers have devoted great efforts to exploring news headline techniques. It was suggested that the major role of an online news headline is to attract users' attention to the news story, and sometimes it need to entice them to click and open the news articles [25].

When increasing the effectiveness of a headline, news providers may consider a variety of verbal techniques, including sensationalism, selectivity, negativity, using questions, quotes, numbers, and special words and word length, so on and so forth [10, 26–28]. Besides news headlines, researchers have also investigated widely how the presentation (e.g. position, format, title length, and popularity and recency indicators, etc.) of various types of online information, such as search results and product information, influences users' attention and behavior.

Attention and behavior are two basic levels of information selection. Attention is selective in nature, and it determines to which stimuli in the environment our perceptual system is addressed [29]. The observable behavior, such as clicking and commenting, might be inconsistent with attention [30]. It has been found that external links [31], pictures [32], larger font size [33] would increase users' fixation duration. The use of numbers, simplification, negativity could encourage people to click on the headline [10, 27, 28].

2.3 Message Credibility

Message credibility is one of the most important dimensions of information credibility, the others being source credibility and media credibility. It is an internal characteristic of the content itself that may make the information more or less believable [34]. The measurement of perception of message credibility often involves the evaluation of accuracy, authenticity, and overall believability [35].

It has been found that the credibility of political news or advertising could be increased by value framing (i.e. resonating with people's moral values) and positive tone (i.e. conveying the message with amiable, heartfelt language) [11, 36]. Loss-framed health information related to physical activity had lower message credibility [11]. In addition, message credibility was found to have a positive moderating effect on the association between the negative affect of tobacco warnings and the perceived effectiveness of warnings [37] as well as a mediating effect on the association between advertising characteristics (e.g. surprise) and the intention of word of mouth [38].

3 Methods

3.1 Participants

This study recruited 60 female participants who were undergraduate or postgraduate students aging between 19 and 26, with an incentive of 50RMB. It was required that they had used the Internet to acquire health information and they had an interest in learning about cancer-related information. It should be mentioned that 4 participants were excluded from the eye-tracking experiment because of calibration problems.

3.2 Apparatus and Stimuli

The experiment was conducted on a mockup mobile health website built with the prototyping tool Axure to simulate two types of pages. A navigation page displays a list of health headlines, and each headline is hyperlinked to a consumption page where the corresponding health article is displayed.

A total of 30 real headlines/articles related to three popular cancer topics for women, i.e. cervical cancer, ovarian cancer, and breast cancer, were collected widely from online health sources. Each topic contained 10 headlines, 5 gain-framed and 5 lossframed.

The original headlines were modified to different degrees to control other possible factors, such as length and use of punctuation or special characters. To minimize the influence of position, this study created two different designs of headline displaying sequence based on a 2 * 2 Latin square. That is, gain-framed and loss-framed headlines appear alternately on the navigation page; but the first design starts with a gain-framed headline while the second loss-framed.

3.3 Task and Procedures

In the experiment, the 56 participants were asked to surf the mockup site in a way they visited health websites or applications on mobile devices for their own sake. There was no time limitation set for the experiment. Their attention and clicking were captured with a Tobii Pro X3-120 eye tracker and the built-in screen recorder respectively.

At the beginning of the experiment, the researchers briefly described the surfing task and calibrated the eye tracker using 5 calibration points. Then the participants started to perform the task. They might click into the consumption pages to read the health articles, but this study was only interested in their interaction with the navigation page or the headlines. An Area of Interest (AOI) was created for each headline so that fixation data could be exported in terms of AOI rather than the entire page.

Upon completion, the participants needed to complete a post-questionnaire which was used to check whether gain/loss framing was successfully manipulated for the headlines and to collect the participants' perception of the message credibility of the headlines [35].

4 Results

4.1 Gain/Loss Framing Manipulation Check

The 30 cancer-related health headlines involved in the experiment were manipulated to reflect gain/loss framing. Manipulation checks were performed in the first place to make sure that the framing of the headlines was perceived as intended. Each headline was evaluated on a 7-point scale (1 to 7: "very negative" to "very positive"). A significant difference (t = 3.69, p < .001) was found between the perception of gain-framed headlines (Mean = 5.87, SD = 1.00) and loss-framed headlines (Mean = 2.18, SD = 1.23). In other words, the message framing manipulation for the experiment was successful.

4.2   Effects of Message Framing on Headline Selection

The participants' selection of gain/loss-framed health headlines was observed at two levels, i.e. attention (i.e. fixation count and total fixation duration) and behavior (i.e. clicking count). According to the descriptive statistics, the 56 participants paid attention to 1,337 headlines in total, including 675 gain-framed and 662 loss-framed, and further clicked on 290 of them, including 178 gain-framed and 112 loss-framed. The gain-framed headlines had a larger average fixation count (Mean: 7.19 > 6.27), a longer average total fixation duration (in second; Mean: 1.46 > 1.19), and a larger average clicking count (Mean: .26 > .17) than the loss-framed ones. There existed a strong correlation between fixation count and total fixation duration ($r = .91$, $p < .01$). Both fixation count ($r = .28$, $p < .01$) and total fixation duration ($r = .29$, $p < .01$) were correlated with clicking count.

The linear regression analysis was employed to examine the effects of message framing on fixation count and total fixation duration which are both numerical variables. As can be found in Table 1, significant results were obtained for both fixation count ($\beta = .09$, $p < .01$) and total fixation duration ($\beta = .12$, $p < .01$). Specifically, gain-framed headlines attracted a significantly larger fixation count and a significantly longer fixation duration. Whether message framing would influence clicking count was determined with the binary logistic regression analysis as clicking count is a categorical variable, either clicking or not clicking. The results in Table 2 indicate a significant effect of message framing on clicking count: the participants were more likely to click on gain-framed headlines ($\exp(B) = 1.76$, $p < .001$).

Table 1. Effects of message framing on fixation count and total fixation duration

Dependent variable	Module	Unstandardized coefficients		Standardized coefficients	t	Sig.
		B	Std. error	Beta		
Fixation count	(constant)	6.28	.20		32.04	.00
	Message framing	.92	.28	.09	3.34	.00
Total fixation duration	(constant)	1.19	.04		28.32	.00
	Message framing	.27	.06	.12	4.47	.00

4.3   Mediating Effects of Message Credibility

The message credibility of each headline was evaluated using a 7-point scale consisting of three dimensions, i.e. how accurate, authentic, and believable it is. Table 3 shows that loss-framed headlines were perceived significantly more credible than gain-framed ones ($\beta = -.16$, $p < 0.01$).

This study conducted a mediation test on message credibility. According to a popular approach for testing mediation [39], mediating effect exists when (1) message framing influences fixation count, total fixation duration, and clicking count; (2) message framing influences message credibility; and (3) the direct effects of message framing on fixation count, total fixation duration, and clicking count decline (partial

Table 2. Effect of massage framing on clicking count

Dependent variable		B	S.E.	Wald	df	Sig	Exp(B)
Clicking count	(constant)	−1.59	.10	235.66	1	.00	.20
	Message framing	.57	.14	17.35	1	.00	1.76

Table 3. Mediating effect of message credibility

Step	Predictor	Dependent variable	Beta/exp(B)	p-level
1	Message framing	Fixation count	.09**	.001
	Message framing	Total fixation duration	.12**	.00
	Message framing	Clicking count	1.759**	.00
2	Message framing	Message credibility	−.10**	.00
3	Message framing (a)	Fixation count	.10** (a)	0.00 (a)
	Message credibility (b)		.06* (b)	.03 (b)
	Message framing (a)	Total fixation duration	.13** (a)	.00 (a)
	Message credibility (b)		.04 (b)	.12 (b)
	Message framing (a)	Clicking count	1.86** (a)	.00 (a)
	Message credibility (b)		1.24** (b)	.00 (b)

*p < 0.05, **p < 0.01

mediation) or disappear (full mediation) when message credibility is added as a predictor. Also shown in Table 3, when message credibility was added as a predictor (β = .06, p = .03), the effect of message framing on fixation count was still significant (β = .10, p = .00); when message credibility was added as a predictor (β = 1.24, p = .00), the effect of message framing on clicking count is still significant (β = 1.86, p = .00). That is, message credibility partially mediated the relationship between message framing and fixation count and clicking count. However, there was no mediating effect of message credibility on the relationship between message framing and total fixation duration (β = .04, p = 0.12).

5   Discussion and Conclusions

This study was interested in the use of message framing in headlines of cancer-related online health information and observed female participants' attention and behavior when they interacted with gain/loss-framed headlines in an eye-tracking experiment. It contributes to the existing literature which was limited to the message framing of health information content and mainly examined its effects on people's behavioral intentions collected via questionnaire surveys.

5.1   Implications for Online Headline Creation

The eye-tracking experiment in this study involved two types of health headlines, i.e. gain-framed and loss-framed. As the results show, the former type attracted more fixations and clicks and held the participants' eyes for a longer duration. When headline effectiveness is measured in terms of attention and behavior, gain-framed headlines were superior to loss-framed ones in the context of cancer-related information. This echoes a few previous studies which found that gain-framed messages were more effective in promoting health knowledge level or encouraging disease prevention behavior. Also, this study detected positive correlations among fixation count, fixation duration, and clicking count, which provided additional evidence that implicit attention and explicit behavior are related [40].

This study presents important practical implications for creating online health headlines, especially those related to cancers. Cancer information avoidance is a common phenomenon detrimental to public health. It is used as a stress coping strategy, i.e. reducing emotional uncertainty by increasing cognitive uncertainty [41]. This may work for the current, but in the long run, people will probably lose the chance of surviving a fatal disease that can be prevented or treated if they have relevant knowledge [42]. In practice, online health information provider should think carefully about the way they create a headline since it determines to a great extent whether the hyperlinked article will be opened. Using gain-framed headlines is an effective technique to increase the chance of opening. Reducing people's resistance to cancer-related information is the important first step to enhance their health literacy and ultimately life quality.

5.2 The Message Credibility of Differently Framed Headlines

As mentioned above, previous studies of message framing were interested in the moderating effect of affective (e.g. mood) and cognitive factors (e.g. self-efficacy). Differently, this study introduced message credibility as a mediator in order to explore how message framing played its effect on people's interaction with health headlines. It was found that message credibility had a partial mediating effect on the relationship between message framing and fixation count and that between message framing and clicking count, suggesting that the influence of message framing on attention and behavior was engendered via its influence on message credibility in part. It is interesting to find that loss-framed headlines were more credible but received less fixations and clicks than gain-framed headlines.

Since loss-framed information emphasizes costs, it often uses negative vocabulary to state bad consequences. In this study, the loss-framed headlines were related to cancers, so the bad consequences involved could be very terrible, such as "endangering life". When encountering unwanted information that may reduce pleasure or arouse fear, people will avoid such information, refusing to reveal the content [43]. Moreover, women respond to negative emotional stimuli more strongly for having a higher level of neuroticism than men [44, 45]. The female participants in this study tended to avoid the loss-framed headlines even if they perceived them to be more credible. The fact might be that the more credible the loss-framed headlines, the more fear or discomfort they felt, and the more likely they reduced fixation and clicking.

5.3 Future Research

This study had several limitations that could be addressed in future work. First, a homogeneous convenient sample was involved in the experiment. Second, the current study only involved three health topics related to cancer. Different choices of topics might affect the results of the research. The researchers plan to conduct a further experiment to include more heterogeneous participants and more health topics, in order to increase the generalizability of the findings. Third, only message credibility, a cognitive factor, was considered as a mediator for present. There is evidence showing the impacts of affective factors on people's intention and behavior. It will be interesting to see whether affective factors also play their roles in mediating the relationship between message framing and headline selection.

Acknowledgement. This research has been made possible through the financial support of the National Natural Science Foundation of China under Grants No. 71774125 and No. 71874129.

References

1. Yuanshihui. http://www.yuanshihui.cn/detail/a667b93559b41cfe350e7deb. Accessed 16 Sept 2019
2. Chen, W., Zheng, R., Baade, et al.: Cancer statistics in China, 2015. CA: Cancer J. Clin. **66** (2), 115–132 (2016)
3. Fidler, M.M., Gupta, S., Soerjomataram, I., Ferlay, J., Steliarova-Foucher, E., Bray, F.: Cancer incidence and mortality among young adults aged 20–39 years worldwide in 2012: a population-based study. Lancet Oncol. **18**(12), 1579–1589 (2017)
4. Sohu: https://www.sohu.com/a/237497515_100100380. Accessed 22 Nov 2019
5. Sohu: http://www.sohu.com/a/259911832_782458. Accessed 16 Nov 2019
6. Zebregs, S., van den Putte, B., Neijens, P., et al.: The differential impact of statistical and narrative evidence on beliefs, attitude, and intention: a meta-analysis. Health Commun. **30** (3), 282–289 (2015)
7. Major, L.H.: Mental health news: how frames influence support for policy and civic engagement intentions. J. Health Commun. **23**(1), 52–60 (2018)
8. van't Riet, J., Werrij, M.Q., Nieuwkamp, R., et al.: Message frame and self-efficacy influence the persuasiveness of nutrition information in a fast-food restaurant. Food Qual. Prefer. **29**(1), 1–5 (2013)
9. Noguti, V.: Post language and user engagement in online content communities. Eur. J. Mark. **50**(5/6), 695–723 (2016)
10. Blom, J.N., Hansen, K.R.: Click bait: forward-reference as lure in online news headlines. J. Pragmat. **76**, 87–100 (2015)
11. Borah, P.: Interactions of news frames and incivility in the political blogosphere: examining perceptual outcomes. Polit. Commun. **30**(3), 456–473 (2013)
12. Jensen, J.D., Ratcliff, C.L., Yale, R.N., et al.: Persuasive impact of loss and gain frames on intentions to exercise: a test of six moderators. Commun. Monogr. **85**(2), 245–262 (2018)
13. Gallagher, K.M., Updegraff, J.A.: Health message framing effects on attitudes, intentions, and behavior: a meta-analytic review. Ann. Behav. Med. **43**, 101–116 (2012)
14. De Bruijn, G.J., Budding, J.: Temporal consequences, message framing, and consideration of future consequences: persuasion effects on adult fruit intake intention and resolve. J. Health Commun. **21**(8), 944–953 (2016)

15. Steward, W.T., Schneider, T.R., Pizarro, J., et al.: Need for cognition moderates responses to framed smoking-cessation messages 1. J. Appl. Soc. Psychol. **33**(12), 2439–2464 (2003)
16. Bernstein, M.H., Wood, M.D., Erickson, L.R.: The effectiveness of message framing and temporal context on college student alcohol use and problems: a selective e-mail intervention. Alcohol Alcohol. **51**(1), 106–116 (2015)
17. Persky, S., Ferrer, R.A., Klein, W.M., et al.: Effects of fruit and vegetable feeding messages on mothers and fathers: interactions between emotional state and health message framing. Ann. Behav. Med. **53**, 789–800 (2018)
18. Keller, P.A., Lipkus, I.M., Rimer, B.K.: Affect, framing, and persuasion. J. Mark. Res. **40**(1), 54–64 (2003)
19. Hoffner, C., Ye, J.: Young adults' responses to news about sunscreen and skin cancer: the role of framing and social comparison. J. Health Commun. **24**(3), 189–198 (2009)
20. Gerend, M.A., Shepherd, J.E.: Using message framing to promote acceptance of the human papillomavirus vaccine. Health Psychol. **26**(6), 745 (2007)
21. Lucas, T., Manning, M., Hayman, L.W., et al.: Targeting and tailoring message-framing: the moderating effect of racial identity on receptivity to colorectal cancer screening among African-Americans. J. Behav. Med. **41**(6), 747–756 (2018)
22. Gerend, M.A., Cullen, M.: Effects of message framing and temporal context on college student drinking behavior. J. Exp. Soc. Psychol. **44**(4), 1167–1173 (2008)
23. Robbins, R., Niederdeppe, J.: Testing the role of narrative and gain-loss framing in messages to promote sleep hygiene among high school students. J. Health Commun. **24**(1), 84–93 (2019)
24. Elbert, S.P., Ots, P.: Reading or listening to a gain-or loss-framed health message: effects of message framing and communication mode in the context of fruit and vegetable intake. J. Health Commun. **23**(6), 573–580 (2018)
25. Arapakis, I., Lalmas, M., Cambazoglu, B.B., et al.: User engagement in online news: under the scope of sentiment, interest, affect, and gaze. J. Assoc. Inf. Sci. Technol. **65**(10), 1988–2005 (2014)
26. Tenenboim, O., Cohen, A.A.: What prompts users to click and comment: a longitudinal study of online news. Journalism **16**(2), 198–217 (2013)
27. Lai, L., Farbrot, A.: What makes you click? The effect of question headlines on readership in computer-mediated communication. Soc. Influ. **9**(4), 289–299 (2014)
28. Kuiken, J., Schuth, A., Spitters, M., et al.: Effective headlines of newspaper articles in a digital environment. Digit. Journal. **5**(10), 1300–1314 (2017)
29. Donsbach, W.: Psychology of news decisions: factors behind journalists' professional behavior. Journalism **5**(2), 131–157 (2004)
30. Wendelin, M., Engelmann, I., Neubarth, J.: User rankings and journalistic news selection: comparing news values and topics. Journal. Stud. **18**(2), 135–153 (2015)
31. Vraga, E., Bode, L., Trollerrenfree, S.: Beyond self-reports: using eye tracking to measure topic and style differences in attention to social media content. J. Commun. Methods Meas. **10**(2–3), 149–164 (2016)
32. Ulloa, L.C., Mora, M.M., Pros, R.C., et al.: News photography for Facebook: effects of images on the visual behaviour of readers in three simulated newspaper formats. J. Inf. Res. (2015)
33. Rello, L., Baezayates, R.A.: Good fonts for dyslexia. In: Conference on Computers and Accessibility (2013)
34. Fogg, B.J., Marshall, J., Laraki, O., et al.: What makes web sites credible? A report on a large quantitative study. In: Proceedings of the SIGCHI Conference on Human Factors in Computing Systems, pp. 61–68. ACM, New York, NY, USA (2001)

35. Appelman, A., Sundar, S.S.: Measuring message credibility: construction and validation of an exclusive scale. Journal. Mass Commun. Q. **93**(1), 59–79 (2016)
36. Meirick, P.C., Nisbett, G.S.: I approve this message: effects of sponsorship, ad tone, and reactance in 2008 presidential advertising. Mass Commun. Soc. **14**(5), 666–689 (2011)
37. Mutti-Packer, S., Reid, J.L., Thrasher, J.F., et al.: The role of negative affect and message credibility in perceived effectiveness of smokeless tobacco health warning labels in Navi Mumbai, India and Dhaka, Bangladesh: a moderated-mediation analysis. Addict. Behav. **73**, 22–29 (2017)
38. Dinh, T.D., Mai, K.N.: Guerrilla marketing's effects on Gen Y's word-of-mouth intention–a mediation of credibility. Asia Pac. J. Mark. Logist. **28**, 4–22 (2015)
39. Baron, R.M., David, A.K.: The moderator-mediator variable distinction in social psychological research: conceptual, strategic, and statistical considerations. J. Pers. Soc. Psychol. **51**(6), 1173–1182 (1986)
40. Kim, E., Liang, T., Meusel, C., et al.: Optimization of menu-labeling formats to drive healthy dining: an eye tracking study. Int. J. Hosp. Manag. **70**, 37–48 (2018)
41. Chae, J.: Who avoids cancer information? Examining a psychological process leading to cancer information avoidance. J. Health Commun. **21**(7), 837–844 (2016)
42. Vrinten, C., Boniface, D., Lo, S.H.: Does psychosocial stress exacerbate avoidant responses to cancer information in those who are afraid of cancer? A population-based survey among older adults in England. J. Psychol. Health **33**(1), 117–129 (2018)
43. Sweeny, K., Melnyk, D., Miller, W., et al.: Information avoidance: who, what, when, and why. Rev. Gen. Psychol. **14**(4), 340–353 (2010)
44. Malouff, J.M., Thorsteinsson, E.B., Rooke, S.E.: Alcohol involvement and the five-factor model of personality: a meta-analysis. J. Drug Educ. **37**(3), 277–294 (2007)
45. Coen, S.J., Kano, M., Farmer, A.D., et al.: Neuroticism influences brain activity during the experience of visceral pain. Gastroenterology. **141**(3), 909–917 (2011)

Inclusion

Understanding the Educational Landscape of Children with Autism in Bangladesh

Anurata Prabha Hridi[1]([✉]), Shameem Ahmed[2], Ifti Azad Abeer[3],
Anik Saha[3], Anik Sinha[3], Mohammad Sorowar Hossain[4],
Nova Ahmed[3,4], and Moushumi Sharmin[2]

[1] Clemson University, Clemson, USA
ahridi@g.clemson.edu
[2] Western Washington University, Bellingham, USA
{ahmeds,sharmim}@wwu.edu
[3] North South University, Dhaka, Bangladesh
{ifti.azad,aniksaha,anik.sinha,
nova.ahmed}@northsouth.edu
[4] Biomedical Research Foundation, Dhaka, Bangladesh
sorowar.hossain@brfbd.org

Abstract. Early childhood education and teachers providing them play an imperative role in the development of children with autism, which motivated us to examine the current educational practices, teachers' experiences, needs, and expectations in Bangladesh. Findings from our qualitative study with teachers (N = 20) from four schools specializing in autism reveal that despite not having the required training for these kids they join the profession and even after getting a meager salary they continue to teach them. We also found that their relationship with the parents is complex, resulting from lack of effective communication about student progress. We propose a set of guidelines to design ICT tools which are a first step in addressing how to improve the educational experience of the teachers and their students by leveraging existing ICT tools. We believe our findings will open avenues for future researchers and guide them in envisioning robust technology to aid the existing educational process.

Keywords: Autism · Special education · Autism in Bangladesh · ICT

1 Introduction

Autism Spectrum Disorder (ASD) has become a global issue recently and Bangladesh is no exception. In 2012 it was estimated that globally 17 out of 10,000 children had ASD with an additional 62 out of 10,000 experiencing pervasive developmental disorder [13]. In Bangladesh, the prevalence of ASD is unknown; however, a pilot study conducted in 2013 estimated the prevalence rate as 0.15% [16].

Bangladesh is a developing country with a population of over 160 million. Being a less privileged country in terms of facilities - be it healthcare or technological, it has

---

A. P. Hridi and S. Ahmed—Contributed equally to this work.

© Springer Nature Switzerland AG 2020
A. Sundqvist et al. (Eds.): iConference 2020, LNCS 12051, pp. 441–455, 2020.
https://doi.org/10.1007/978-3-030-43687-2_35

undergone multiple phases of evolutions over the years. Until recently, ASD has not been considered as a problem, let alone an area requiring resource allocation. To reduce the negativity and stigmatization and to better support the needs of children with neurodevelopmental disorders including ASD, the government of Bangladesh has taken some initiatives which include but are not limited to raising awareness, establishing child development centers, facilities for neurodevelopment and ASD care, and introducing information on these challenges in academic materials. Consequently, the number of special schools focused on educating children with autism has increased, particularly in the urban areas [17].

Previously, two studies were conducted to understand the educational scenario at autism schools in Bangladesh [6, 7]. These studies highlighted the necessity of special schools for children with autism. Recently, Faisal et al. examined the perceptions of teachers of both special and mainstream schools regarding the inclusion of children with autism in the mainstream educational programs [8]. These prior studies offered important insights about autism schools in Bangladesh and the scope of integration of children with autism into mainstream schools. However, the current process of educating children with autism and challenges in improving the educational process is still unexplored.

Our primary objective is to understand the current context of ASD in educational settings in Bangladesh through the lenses of the special school teachers. We conducted in-depth face-to-face interviews with 20 teachers from four autism schools to understand the challenges and needs of special school teachers in helping children with autism in Bangladesh. There could be many ways to address these challenges and needs; however, as researchers of ICT (Information and Communication Technology), we chose to examine how the use of ICT can support these teachers in their role as educators. Our secondary objective is to explore what types of ICT tools will be the most effective for assisting them.

Therefore, this paper makes the following contributions:

(a) We report findings from our interviews with special education teachers in Bangladesh, which provide a deeper understanding of current practices, challenges faced and the needs of educators in helping children with autism.
(b) We propose ICT-based design guidelines (e.g., building a digital daily routine for each kid, creating an app to track developments of the kids so that parents can see as well) to address existing problems experienced by the educators.

2 Related Work

Prior research primarily focused on how technology can benefit children with autism in addressing many challenges faced during their everyday lives. For instance, in 2018, researchers analyzed 149 peer-reviewed research articles that discussed the use of smart technology for children with autism [12]. Here, we focus on research relevant in the context of educational settings of children with autism in Bangladesh.

2.1   Prevalence of Autism in Bangladesh

Bangladesh is relatively new in the realm of research on ASD. Rahman reported the number of individuals with autism in the USA is 1 in 150 and extrapolated it to be 1.5 million out of 165 million people in Bangladesh [1]. Hossain et al. conducted a systematic review of epidemiological studies of ASD in eight South Asian countries (Bangladesh, India, Pakistan, Nepal, Sri Lanka, Bhutan, Maldives, and Afghanistan) to identify gaps in existing knowledge about case definition, screening devices, and criteria [2]. In this corpus, six articles focused on identifying the prevalence of ASD in Bangladesh, India, and Sri Lanka, which reported a prevalence of 3%, 0.90% and 1.07% in Bangladesh (only Dhaka), India, and Sri Lanka respectively. The authors aimed to offer an understanding of the scale of the prevalence of ASD in Bangladesh and tried to identify the causes for such prevalence.

2.2   Autism-Related Technology in the Context of Bangladesh

The scarcity of information regarding ASD in Bangladesh makes it difficult to detect and diagnose ASD in toddlers and children properly. Bardhan et al. proposed an automated ASD screening device for developing countries like Bangladesh, where advanced treatment options were unavailable [3]. They proposed a smartphone-based app, Autism Barta, which represents M-CHAT (Modified Checklist for Autism in Toddlers) questions in a pictorial format to determine if a toddler is on the spectrum [5]. Mamun et al. proposed a cloud-based screening framework to automate the diagnosis of ASD where an application consisting of screening questionnaires with relevant pictorial representation (e.g., pictures, animation, and video) was utilized [4]. Muslima et al. focused on validating a Rapid Neurodevelopmental Assessment (RNDA) tool to determine neurodevelopmental impairments (NDIs) in children in Bangladesh [18–20]. Khan et al. conducted a similar experiment with toddlers and reported that RNDA could be used effectively in a clinical setting [20]. Ahmed et al. proposed a strategy for primary screening of autism by utilizing the well-established vaccination platform to avoid infrastructure and deployment cost where parents and caregivers would answer the autism-screening questionnaire during the vaccination schedule [11]. If a positive screening is found, parents can seek further help from specialized personnel. This process may reduce the burden on the limited number of experts and parents and caregivers to conduct and participate in the initial screening respectively.

This thread of research focused on designing tools and techniques for early diagnosis of autism in developing countries where professional expertise is sparse. In contrast, we focus on identifying challenges in the educational setting in Bangladesh and how to design technological solutions to address these challenges. Ehsan et al. stated infrastructural and cultural challenges (e.g., Bangladeshi people are still new to mobile technology and their overall poor socioeconomic condition denotes their attitude towards children with autism) for designing mobile assistive technologies for ASD in Bangladesh [27] which partially resonate with our thoughts as we investigate the challenges faced by the teachers for now, not the caregivers at home.

2.3   Autism in Educational Settings in Bangladesh

Majumdar conducted an in-depth study to identify the needs of children with ASD after they were enrolled in autism schools [6]. By collecting data from teachers, parents, and the school environment, the authors identified parameters that hindered the educational advancement of children with ASD and suggested to prioritize personal needs while developing an educational plan for children with autism.

Akanda identified factors that made teaching at special schools difficult and challenging in Bangladesh while reiterating the necessity of special schooling for children with autism [7]. A notable difference with our research and [7] is that we aim to identify factors that would make the educational process effective for the teachers and the students instead of focusing on improving the experience of schools and teachers. Through a cross-sectional quantitative study, Faisal et al. reported that teachers of children with autism are more optimistic than teachers at mainstream schools about the idea of inclusive programs at mainstream schools [8]. They reported that teachers in special schools considered that children with mild autism who are verbal and non-aggressive could be taught in mainstream schools. Teacher groups from autism schools and mainstream schools agreed that limiting the environmental noise and distraction will facilitate a smooth transition of children with autism into the mainstream. Our findings are well-aligned with findings reported in [8], which contradicts Akanda's suggestion that mainstream schools were mostly unsuitable for children with autism. Our work also extends this thread of research by uncovering challenges in the educational setting that could be addressed by utilizing ICT-based solutions.

3   Research Methodology

3.1   User Recruitment

After receiving permission from the ethical board of WWU, the study-initiating institution, we recruited study participants using convenience sampling. First, we contacted the corresponding authorities of multiple autism schools in Bangladesh to grant us access to their teaching staff. Upon receiving written permission from four schools, we recruited 20 participants (m = 3, f = 17) who are working as teachers in one of these four schools. This gender disparity is reflective of the male and female educator ratio in autism schools in Bangladesh, which is also reported by other researchers [6]. The distribution of the participants is as follows: first school (N = 6), second school (N = 3), third school (N = 5), and fourth school (N = 6). All these four schools are in Dhaka. We opted not to disclose the names of the schools and participants' affiliation to limit any consequences on our participants who shared sensitive information about the educational practices and processes utilized in their schools.

3.2   User Profile

The minimum, maximum, and average ages of our participants are 20, 50, and 32.7 years respectively. Before starting their job at the corresponding schools, only three participants changed their jobs. In terms of the highest educational degree earned, all participants had at least a high school (12th grade) degree. The distribution of advanced degrees is: Master's degree (N = 10), Bachelor's degree (N = 7), Diploma (N = 1), High school degree (N = 1), and did not disclose (N = 1). The minimum, maximum, and average number of years of job experience were 0.25, 14, and 6.1 years respectively.

3.3   Semi-structured Interviews

We conducted semi-structured interviews to understand current educational practices, challenges faced by educators and their needs in autism schools in Bangladesh. During the study, we used a questionnaire to guide our discussion. All interviews were conducted in Bengali, the official language of Bangladesh, and the native language of both the participants and the interviewers. The study dates and times were scheduled via telephone and the study was conducted at the schools of the participants where they were employed. Interviews were audio-recorded and lasted up to 66 min.

Our interviews were designed and conducted based on contextual inquiry methodology [15], which helped us to observe the teachers in their own environment and the resources they have access to. During the study, we asked our participants a series of questions, which focused on (1) participant's demographic information, (2) training and previous knowledge about autism, (3) process of adaptation in autism schools, (4) experience with ICT in the education process, and (5) suggestions to design ICT solutions to address their challenges. The questionnaire consisted of 29 questions. We allowed tangents from participants to get a clear picture of their overall experience. Each participant had the right to skip a question and/or stop participating in the study at any time. Participant 4 skipped a question when she was asked about her age and participant 7 did not disclose her highest educational degree.

3.4   Post-fieldwork Analysis

After transcribing the interview audio recordings, we imported these transcriptions into Atlas.ti software [14]. We then carefully read the transcripts and identified 35 initial codes (e.g., motivation, professional experience, teaching method, challenges, current responsibility, training, private tuition, and electronic devices). After refining these codes in an iterative fashion and reviewing those with team members, we agreed on 51 codes. We then grouped the similar codes together to identify high-level themes.

4   Findings

We report findings emerging from the high-level themes we discussed in the research methodology section. Although some of these are commonly known in autism-related studies globally (e.g., kids' non-responsiveness for quite a long time at a stretch when social interaction is initiated [24], their adherence to regime hence strict obedience to plans, etc.), we report these and also novel findings to provide a holistic view of the current educational practices, teachers' experiences, needs, and expectations in the context of Bangladesh. All quotes are translated from Bengali to English and include information about the participants' gender and years of experience, which may influence their opinion about teaching, challenges faced, and needs.

4.1 Structure of a Typical Autism School in Bangladesh

A Typical Day: Structure is Key. Children with autism prefer to follow a routine and teachers in most of the schools try to maintain the same routine whenever possible. Majumdar stated about the preference to structure [6] which resembles our observation that educators consider this structured activity an integral part of their teaching process:

> *Typically, the day starts with an assembly followed by 'My Choice' class where the kids select a toy of their choice. Since they hardly know how to play with such objects meaningfully, we teach them how to do so. For example, we show them a toy car and how it works. (P9, f, 3 months)*
> *We have a daily lesson plan which we follow every day. I think this is a very effective process. Having a fixed plan makes it easier for us to teach them that they can understand easily too. (P20, f, 6 years)*

Segregation Between Special and Mainstream Schools. Three out of four schools we visited offered no opportunity to children with autism to interact with neurotypical children, which reflects the existing segregation of special schools and mainstream schools in Bangladesh:

> *Mainstream schools do not want to take them [as students]. (P6, m, 4 months)*

Educators have varying opinions regarding enrollment of children with autism in mainstream schools:

> *Let them [autistic and neurotypical children] mingle and play together. They should interact no matter what. (P3, f, 4 years)*
> *The [autistic] child must hold a minimum IQ, so that effort can be put to bring them into the mainstream. (P12, m, 12+ years)*

IEP-Based Teaching: To Modify or Not to Modify. All four schools use the IEP (Individualized Education Program)-based teaching method [10], where a small set of targets is set for the students based on their deficiencies in different cognitive and behavioral areas. The fourth school follows JSS Behavioral Services [9] along with IEP. When a child gets enrolled, teachers build an IEP based on a thorough assessment of the child and try to help the student reach his/her target:

> *We have a health educator who prepares a report which diagnoses whether the child has autism or not. A customized plan is formed in the presence of teachers, physicians, and coordinators. (P1, f, 8 years)*
> *While working with IEP, we try to teach them step-by-step. We focus on the things they lack. (P13, f, 10 years)*

When asked about deviation from the designed IEP, most teachers (N = 13) commented that such adjustment is beneficial for children with autism:

> *We [teachers] have full rights to bend the procedures stated in the IEP so that learning becomes more fruitful and meaningful for the child. (P11, f, 11 years)*

Few participants (N = 4) advocated for the non-modified version of the IEP while rest was agnostic in terms of deviation. Strong belief on the effectiveness of IEP was mentioned as a rationale behind it:

(IEP is based on) Research to find out the exact way to drive the children towards better communication, social and cognitive skills. (P10, f, 14 years)

4.2   Teaching Journey: Not a Straight Path

Most teachers associated with special schools at some point in their career faced a dilemma regarding continuing their profession due to the demanding physical and mental workload and lack of enough monetary benefits.

Professional Commitment: A Mixed Review. Educators participating in our study lacked special education training or professional experience related to autism when they started their jobs whereas in the US it is mandatory to have a bachelor's in special education to get into this profession [26]. Out of 20, only four participants were aware of autism before joining the schools. Remaining 16 participants had little to no prior knowledge about autism:

Earlier I had no idea about autism. After joining here, I came to know about that. (P11, f, 11 years)

Lack of related background caused difficulty for most educators early in their careers. It is a common phenomenon among them since most of the people in Bangladesh are unfamiliar with autism. After getting more aware of autism and working with children with autism, they became more empathetic towards them:

I was emotionally devastated when I first joined here. I found that I must be very patient, hardworking, affectionate, and dedicated. I wanted to leave immediately. However, I completed seven years so far and over the years have learned a lot about these kids. I hope to learn more. It makes me happy. (P4, f, 6+ years)

When asked about motivations behind embracing this profession despite their lack of training and knowledge, attachment to children and having extended family members in the spectrum were provided as reasons (N = 3 in both cases), while others simply chose this profession as they needed a job.

From Zero Experience to Full-Fledged Training. After getting involved in the profession, our participants received formal training on autism to better prepare themselves for teaching roles from several Bangladeshi organizations including Bangladesh Protibondhi Foundation, Centre for the Rehabilitation of the Paralyzed (CRP) and Society for the Welfare of Children with autism, etc. Some teachers (N = 3) received training from multiple organizations. School authorities arranged their enrolment in training sessions and these included specific intervention techniques (e.g., ABA: Applied Behavior Analysis and PECS: Picture Exchange Communication System), life-skill training (e.g., self-help training, toilet training, challenging behavioral training, and cognitive skill development training):

We were assigned under an experienced special teacher and we had to follow him/her to get a hold of everything that we needed to learn about the children. (P6, m, 4 months)

The training contents were straightforward, combined theoretical and hands-on experience, and were considered useful by the teachers:

We were taught about the structured and disciplined routine we had to follow for each child. From assembly to academics, physical exercise to other therapies - we were given all sorts of exposure. (P8, f, 11 months)
Those training sessions were very helpful and effective for us. (P16, f, 7 years)

Although teachers valued these training sessions and spoke highly of them, they could not apply theoretical knowledge all the time and needed improvisation to handle new or different situations:

Theoretical knowledge does not always help. (P1, f, 8 years)
Training materials vary from school to school. Hence, we need to improvise [the training materials]. (P3, f, 4 years)

Insufficient Fund Affects Teachers' Financial Satisfaction and Overall Educational Experience. The percentage of male teachers in autism schools in Bangladesh is significantly low, which resulted in a similar disparity (17f:3m) among our participants. However, there is a high demand for male teachers as female teachers lack the physical strength to manage relatively older, restless kids:

For little children, any mother figure is the best caregiver. However, as they grow up, it is not possible for a female teacher to handle all the activities of a hyperactive child. (P12, m, 12+ years)

Despite this demand, since this job alone does not provide enough money to cover even the basic needs of a small family in Bangladesh, males are not showing interest in these positions:

When the school wants to hire male teachers, salary should be thought over because it's a challenging job! It requires a lot of patience and a fellow feeling. (P12, m, 12+ years)

Financial inadequacy also impacts the experience of the students:

We can neither ensure any separate rooms to calm down those who get extremely restless nor afford to take the children out by a car for some time as the school has no transportation facilities. (P12, m, 12+ years)
They [children with autism] should be given a field to play. Unfortunately, we do not have that yet. (P4, f, 6 years)

Teachers' Role Outside of the Classroom. Some teachers (N = 4) have paid positions (through the parents) as 'in-home private tutors' for the children with autism to teach them the same materials they covered at school. Teachers feel that these additional appointments create a stronger bond with the kids and improve their relationship with the parents:

Sometimes parents make a request to give time to their children if they are busy. What we do is teach them the same things at home. As a result, there is a synchronization between home and school and no time is wasted [to acclimatize with the child] since the same teacher is dealing with the child. (P1, f, 8 years)
Yes, I go for tuition. I feel more connected to the child and his/her family in this way. The parents also recognize us as an integral part of their child's life. (P12, m, 12+ years)

4.3   Relationship Between Teachers and Parents: It's Complicated

Teachers considered educating a child with autism as a joint responsibility where parents and teachers should play equally important roles:

> *Neither teachers nor parents can handle them [children with autism] alone. (P20, f, 6 years)*
> *It [development of children with autism] demands teamwork from the teachers and the parents. (P11, f, 11 years)*

Our findings suggest that the relationship between teachers and parents/caregivers is a complex one. After working with children with autism, teachers became more empathetic towards parents:

> *They [parents] share their pain with us. (P13, f, 10 years)*
> *I do feel for them. I face only a part of the hassle. I cannot even imagine what they go through. (P9, f, 3 months)*

However, many educators (N = 6) believe that parents are not committed to the success of their children with autism and do not spend enough time and energy on them compared to their other neurotypical children. Many teachers (N = 12) showed skepticism towards parents' contribution and blamed the parents for lack of patience and lack of dedication towards their children with autism:

> *Parents do not provide as much effort as we do. Otherwise, there could be some good outcomes. Perhaps they have another neurotypical child. The effort behind that [neurotypical] child affects their concentration about the autistic child. (P1, f, 8 years)*

Some teachers (N = 6) considered parents responsible for the slow or lack of progress of children with autism:

> *We prepare a routine for the [autistic] children which they should follow both in school and at home. The parents do not understand that. As a result, even if we are moving the development process forward, the process is going backward because of them. (P4, f, 6 years)*
> *Parents do not follow the structure or the IEP designed for their children at home. They do not put an effort to help the children complete the homework. This hinders the overall progress. (P11, f, 11 years)*

Schools often organize training sessions for parents aiming to expose the techniques that would enable them to take better and structured care of their children. Such sessions also help parents to recognize teachers' efforts towards educating their children. However, according to teachers, many parents are reluctant to join these sessions or discontinue after attending a couple of sessions due to additional time requirements, other responsibilities, etc. This lack of effort to manage time for the children with autism led the teachers to believe that parents are not committed to the betterment of their children with autism.

5 Discussions

Financial need is one of the major reasons why teachers took up this job. The nature of this job (teaching is socially considered as a respected profession for women in Bangladesh) and the urge to become economically solvent inspired many women to engage in this profession. However, in contrast to the workload, the salary is not enough to run even a small family in Bangladesh. In the patriarchal society of Bangladesh, this job alone is insufficient for males to maintain their families. This also contributed to the uneven ratio of female and male teachers in this area.

Before starting their career in autism schools, most of the teachers lacked educational and professional training in special education, and most of the teachers had no awareness or experience with children with autism. This lack of awareness led to suboptimal experience for the educators and may have influenced the quality of education and care received by the students. Currently, there is a scarcity of training resources for educators and many schools address this inadequacy by creating their own training programs. However, teaching children with autism introduces unique challenges that require special training, empathy, and skills that may be difficult to acquire from these makeshift training programs.

Teachers empathized with parents' 'difficult' situations but also held them responsible for 'not caring enough' or 'not being there' for their children. In developed countries, educators and parents communicate regularly at IEP meetings regarding students' progress and concerns. However, in Bangladesh, these meetings are not the norm. There is a communication gap between teachers and parents about their respective roles in a student's development. Among the papers we reviewed, none of them mentioned a systematic progress report of the students. Many teachers also work as home-tutors for their students, which is uncommon in other countries. Since home-tuition for the conventional education system is vastly popular in Bangladesh, this practice is also accepted without much controversy. However, as there is no systematic monitoring system, it is unclear whether this tutoring makes a positive impact on the children's lives.

Mainstream schools in Bangladesh do not have educational or training programs for children with autism. Research signifies the benefit of an inclusive classroom environment, which is reflected by programs such as AIM (Access and Inclusion Model) utilized in the US among other developed countries [25]. Educators in Bangladesh also commented on the potential benefit of such inclusive programs where children with autism will have access to the same opportunities as neurotypical students and have an opportunity to learn firsthand from their peers. This segregation may contribute to the limited awareness of autism in Bangladesh.

Exposing children with autism to real-life situations (going to grocery stores, using public transportation, playing in a park) is challenging in Bangladesh due to lack of funds available for field trips, lack of manpower in maintaining the security and safety of the children outside the classroom environment, and lack of social awareness from the general population, which may lead to unwanted situations. Creating awareness about autism may bring a positive social change where people may become more accepting of children with autism.

6 Design Implications

The total number of mobile phone users and Internet subscribers in Bangladesh are 152.5 million and 88.7 million respectively [22]. When teachers were asked about their perception and interest in using ICT tools (e.g., mobile phones, Internet, digital games, etc.) in an academic setting, they showed a keen interest in using ICT-based tools to enhance the feasibility of their teaching methods. According to them, students' inter-action with ICT tools seem natural and effortless (e.g., listening to songs on YouTube, playing games using tablets):

> They can operate everything on their own! Perhaps I myself won't be able to do that. (P12, m, 12+ years)

Our participants highlighted possibilities of independence for kids with autism through a technology-based career. They reported that these children are interested in technology and can learn skills that can prepare themselves for the job market:

> Autistic children can be independent by learning technology-based works – how to operate photocopy machines, perform computer-related jobs, and design websites. (P9, f, 3 months)

While our participants mostly considered the inclusion of ICT as teaching tools as positive, a few of them were a bit cautious and wanted to restrict the use of ICT tools. Participant P15 was concerned about kids' natural attraction towards these tools, which might result in attention deficit and distract them from socialization or meaningful learning activities.

Considering the pervasive nature of ICT among mass people in Bangladesh and our participants' keen interest in using ICT as teaching tools, we suggest some ICT-based solutions to support teachers in their role inside and outside the classroom. Our rec-ommendations stem from our observations of the schools we visited, analysis of the interviews we conducted, and our prior experience working in the domain of autism and technology.

6.1 Technology-Aided Synergistic Platform for Learning: Bridging Communication-Gap Between Teachers and Parents/Caregivers

Student learning can be enhanced through a synergistic approach by educators and parents where they follow the same processes in a synchronized manner using the same resource. Educators expressed a need for such platforms that will enable children to learn the same things in different contexts (school vs. home), which will support repeated exposure, thus enhancing cognitive abilities:

> There could be some visual materials that can be used at home too in the absence of us [teachers]. (P6, m, 4 months)

This will also ensure that children are following the same process for a specific task - limiting confusion and reducing the performance gap at school and at home, a common concern expressed by teachers. With technological support, concepts and materials introduced at schools can be shared seamlessly without worrying about limitation of access and portability with parents, who can use them to reinforce the learning process outside school. Moreover, communicating 'processes utilized' in school without technological aid (video) may be difficult as written or verbal narration may fail to capture the nuances of such processes. Technology can also be used to capture the activities students are doing at school with their teachers and at home with their parents/caregivers. For example, in the US, many elementary schools are currently using Seesaw [23], a free web and mobile-based platform for teachers, students and parents to actively engage in the education process. Such a shared platform will help to bridge the gap between educators and parents, as they would have access to the activities performed and the resulting outcome.

6.2   Creation of Visually Enhanced Educational Materials and Daily Routine

Children with autism learn better when information is presented visually. Besides, many children with autism are non-verbal and/or experience challenges in expressing themselves. Educators commented on the advantage of using mobile applications where audio along with visuals can help children to imitate the 'correct behavior' (e.g., the correct pronunciation of words) and images can offer a solution where children can touch or point to materials, activities, or even emotions to indicate their needs or feelings:

> There can be something where children can touch – it can be a picture or a scene to express what they are asking for. (P6, m, 4 months)

While such applications are widely available in the Google Play and Apple app store, they do not provide culturally relevant or accessible content, which limits their applicability as a teaching tool in Bangladesh. For example, most available apps for children with autism include images of LEGO, strawberry, and hamsters which unlike the developed countries are unfamiliar in Bangladesh due to their unavailability. Besides, such applications use English as the primary language - a barrier for Bengali-speaking children. Members of this research team have created the first mobile application in Bengali to make it accessible and culturally relevant [21], which received positive feedback from parents of children with autism. Figure 1 shows four interfaces of the prototype of the app.

We also found that teachers create a structured plan for the students that they must follow and keep track of their success and/or failure in these tasks which is critical for the kids' progress. The current approach of creating it lacks efficiency and cannot be reused as educators create and update it manually for each student as they follow the steps. Simplifying the process of creating a daily planner and updating them as students go through their day were considered a huge help. As the set of activities is limited and has well-defined structures, creating an application that would enable selection of a specific activity, visualize associated steps, and let educators select the appropriate status of a student's performance, should not present many technological challenges. Such applications can also facilitate adding new activities and removal of unwanted ones. From a technological point of view, this idea is not novel, however, such a tool has the potential to alleviate a lot of burden from the busy day of an educator.

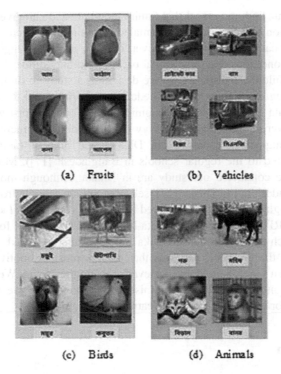

        (a) Fruits   (b) Vehicles

        (c) Birds   (d) Animals

Fig. 1. Culturally relevant information presented in an interactive mobile application as a teaching tool [21].

6.3 Digitalization to Create Accessible, Context-Aware Educational Contents

While showing children the physical objects used in schools may help recognition, it does not teach them how to utilize this knowledge in real life. Exposing children to real-life scenarios where such concepts are used can be very beneficial but also very expensive in terms of resources needed. Technology can offer a viable solution where real-life scenarios are captured and shared with the students to help them understand what they can do with this new knowledge. For example, showing a note of taka (the Bangladeshi currency) does not convey the concept of money and how it can be used to purchase things. Augmenting 'role-play' scenarios with interactive digital content to show students how 'taka' can be used in different situations, may offer a better understanding.

7 Limitations and Future Work

Our research goal was to gain a deeper understanding of the current educational process of children with autism in Bangladesh. As a first step, we conducted contextual inquiry inspired qualitative study with special education teachers. While we focused on educators only, our findings reveal that family members and caregivers play a critical part in the education process and it is essential to learn their perspective to get a holistic picture of the educational process. Moreover, existing research suggests that parents' socio-economic conditions and educational background may influence the educational facility of their children. Currently, we are designing a study to understand their role and experiences regarding their children's education. Although for the current study we did not collect data about the socio-economic strata of the parents, we can speculate that the parents were moderately tech-savvy (since mobile and internet penetration is very high in Bangladesh, especially in Dhaka) and affluent (autism schools are expensive compared to the regular schools in Bangladesh [17]). Moreover, the four schools where we conducted our study are in Dhaka. Although most of the autism schools in Bangladesh are in Dhaka [17], selecting autism schools from other cities or rural areas of Bangladesh may have resulted in different insights. In fact, many training institutes (e.g., CRP, IPNA) are still Dhaka-based and it is difficult for the teachers to have access to such resources outside Dhaka and get properly trained. Besides, another observation from the teachers' part was that parents must be motivated so that the feasibility of such a synergistic tool is achieved at the highest level. We look forward to this in our next ongoing study. By promising to address this, we hope to bring a positive change for these kids and their learning process here.

8 Conclusion

Like many other countries worldwide Bangladesh is experiencing an increase in the number of children diagnosed with autism. Early intervention through specialized education and training is imperative for the proper development of children with autism. Recognizing the immense importance of early childhood education and teachers' role in shaping the lives of children with autism, we focused on understanding current educational practices and teachers' experiences, needs, and expectations. Our findings being the novelty of this study reveal that ICT tools can be used to address many of the issues. Among others, technology to create accessible and contextual educational materials, a shared communication platform for parents and teachers, and applications to create interactive activity planners and progress tracker may aid the education process.

References

1. Rahman, M.M.: Autism spectrum disorders. J. Bangladesh Coll. Phys. Surg. **28**(3), 143–144 (2010)
2. Hossain, M.D., et al.: Autism spectrum disorders (ASD) in South Asia: a systematic review. BMC Psychiatry **17**(1), 281 (2017)
3. Bardhan, S., et al.: Autism Barta—a smart device based automated autism screening tool for Bangladesh. In: 5th International Conference on Informatics, Electronics and Vision (ICIEV), pp. 602–607. IEEE (2016)

4. Al Mamun, K.A., et al.: Smart autism—a mobile, interactive and integrated framework for screening and confirmation of autism. In: 38th Annual International Conference of the IEEE Engineering in Medicine and Biology Society (EMBC), pp. 5989–5992. IEEE (2016)
5. M-CHAT. http://mchatscreen.com/. Accessed 16 Sept 2019
6. Majumdar, A.: Exploring the state of educational and care giving services for autistic children in Dhaka city: a case study of two schools. Diss. BRAC University (2011)
7. Akanda, M.D.: Writing a thesis on teaching challenges at autism schools-teachers perception. Diss. BRAC University (2010)
8. Faisal, R.A., Hossain, S.: Teachers' perspectives on the mainstreaming of autistic students in Bangladesh. Teacher's World **42**, 25–36 (2015). ISSN 0040-0521
9. JSS Behavioral Services. http://newsite.jssbehavioral.com/. Accessed 16 Sept 2019
10. Individualized Education Plan (IEP). https://www.understood.org/en/school-learning/special-services/ieps/understanding-individualized-education-programs. Accessed 16 Sept 2019
11. Ahmed, N., et al.: Managing autism spectrum disorder in developing countries by utilizing existing resources: a perspective from Bangladesh. Autism **23**(3), 801–803 (2019)
12. Sharmin, M., et al.: From research to practice: informing the design of autism support smart technology. In: Proceedings of the 2018 CHI Conference on Human Factors in Computing Systems (2018)
13. Elsabbagh, M., et al.: Global prevalence of autism and other pervasive developmental disorders. Autism Res. **5**(3), 160–179 (2012)
14. ATLAS.ti: The Qualitative Data Analysis & Research Software. https://atlasti.com/. Accessed 16 Sept 2019
15. Holtzblatt, K., Jones, S.: Contextual inquiry: a participatory technique for system design. In: Schuler, D., Namioka, A. (eds.) Participatory Design: Principles and Practices, pp. 177–210. Lawrence Erlbaum Associates (2017)
16. Global Autism Movement and Bangladesh. http://cri.org.bd/2014/09/03/global-autism-movement-and-bangladesh/. Accessed 16 Sept 2019
17. Autism School and Resource Center in Bangladesh. https://www.autismwing.com/autism-school-and-resource-center-in-bangladesh/. Accessed 16 Sept 2019
18. Muslima, H., et al.: Validation of a rapid neurodevelopmental assessment tool for 10-to 16-year-old young adolescents in Bangladesh. Child Care Health Dev. **42**(5), 658–665 (2016)
19. Khan, N.Z., et al.: Validation of rapid neurodevelopmental assessment for 2-to 5-year-old children in Bangladesh. Pediatrics **131**(2), e486–e494 (2013)
20. Khan, N.Z., et al.: Validation of rapid neurodevelopmental assessment instrument for under-two-year-old children in Bangladesh. Pediatrics **125**(4), e755–e762 (2010)
21. Abeer, I.A., et al.: Reinforcement based learning through communicative Android app for autism personnel. In: Proceedings of the 20th International Conference on Human-Computer Interaction with Mobile Devices and Services Adjunct, pp. 132–138 (2018)
22. Bangladesh Telecommunication and Regulatory Commission Data Statistics. http://www.btrc.gov.bd/data-statistics. Accessed 16 Sept 2019
23. Seesaw. https://web.seesaw.me/. Accessed 16 Sept 2019
24. McConnell, S.R.: Interventions to facilitate social interaction for young children with autism: review of available research and recommendations for educational intervention and future research. J. Autism Dev. Disord. **32**(5), 351–372 (2002)
25. AIM program. http://aim.gov.ie. Accessed 16 Sept 2019
26. Requirements of special education teacher. https://www.alleducationschools.com/teaching-careers/special-education-teacher/. Accessed 16 Sept 2019
27. Ehsan, U., et al.: Confronting autism in urban Bangladesh: unpacking infrastructural and cultural challenges. EAI Endorsed Trans. Pervasive Health Technol. **4**(14), e5 (2018)

Digital Comics Reading Program for Reducing the Digital Exclusion of People with Hearing Impairments

Zinaida Manžuch[(⊠)] [iD] and Elena Macevičiūtė

Faculty of Communication, Vilnius University,
Saulėtekio Ave. 9, 10222 Vilnius, Lithuania
zinaida.manzuch@mb.vu.lt, elena.maceviciute@gmail.com

Abstract. The paper explores experiences of people with hearing impairments that facilitate their digital inclusion. It is based on the case study of the educational program in digital reading and creating of comics in the Šiauliai municipal public library in Lithuania. Eleven deaf and partially hearing respondents and two trainers participated in the research. The data were collected by means of graphic questionnaire survey, a focus group with the deaf and hard-of-hearing respondents and the semi-structured interviews of the trainers. The findings showed that the digital reading program reinforced personally significant behavior to deaf and hard-of-hearing persons. It resulted in high motivation and engagement with the course content. The training helped the respondents to get oriented in the rapidly changing digital technologies and to acquire useful ICT skills and knowledge to make more informed choices of digital tools in future. They also learned about digital means for visual communication to support their personal interaction in future. The research revealed that deaf and hard-of-hearing people were active users of the digital technologies and they did not experience physical barriers in accessing the basic ICT equipment. Obstacles in ICT use were related to gaps in general literacy skills.

Keywords: Digital exclusion · Digital reading · Deaf and hard-of-hearing people · Digital inequalities · Lithuania

1 Introduction

In digital societies, information and communication technology (ICT) adoption is high on the political agendas because it expands or limits the possibilities to access and use the society's resources and services, participate in societal processes and effectively solve daily life problems [8]. According to Goggin [7], current studies about digital exclusion of people with disabilities are much fewer in comparison to the research on other social groups and excessively focus on access barriers. Disability is often treated as a single factor shaping digital exclusion, although it is tightly woven in a thread of various social contexts and inequalities that also play their role in ICT adoption [3, 7].

Studies show that digital technologies and online platforms brought both opportunities and limitations to people with hearing impairments (e.g., see [3, 7]). Often limitations and opportunities are not straightforwardly influenced by the accessibility of

A. Sundqvist et al. (Eds.): iConference 2020, LNCS 12051, pp. 456–469, 2020.
https://doi.org/10.1007/978-3-030-43687-2_36

digital tools, but rather shaped by social contexts and factors. For instance, Kožuh, Hintermair, Debevc [9] found that a strong identification of a person with hearing impairment with either community of the deaf or hearing online had a positive effect on the frequency of communicating in written language on social networking sites and community building activities. It means that much more subtle factors than just accessibility of the device of digital service contribute to digital inclusion of person with hearing impairments.

In this paper we would like to contribute to the existent knowledge of the factors that stimulate digital inclusion of persons with hearing impairments. The paper explores experiences of people with hearing impairments (including behavior, perceptions and attitudes, contextual factors) that facilitate their digital inclusion. The paper is based on the case study of digital reading and creating of comics in the Šiauliai municipal public library in Lithuania.

Using Van Dijk's [14] theoretical framework, we treat digital exclusion as inequalities that emerge due to differences in motivation, access, skills, usage of information and communication technologies (ICT) and lead to limitations in solving life problems and participation in society's processes. To study the experiences of deaf and hard-of-hearing people we also employ social cognitive theory (SCT) by Bandura [1] that explains how individuals learn and adopt new patterns of behaviors. By combining Van Dijk [14] and Bandura [1] theoretical frameworks we seek to answer the following research questions:

- What personal attitudes and perceptions that emerged during the digital reading program could help to reduce the digital exclusion of people with hearing impairment?
- What behavior of people with hearing impairments that emerged during the program could help to reduce their digital exclusion?
- Which elements of the digital reading program contribute to reducing the digital exclusion of people with hearing impairment?

This case study presents a part of the findings of the project "Digital reading as a means of reducing the digital divide" (2017–2018) funded by the Lithuanian Research Council. The project analyzed the effect of digital reading interventions on socially disadvantaged groups. The project team conducted a natural social experiment that studied the experiences and changes in behavior of respondents from three disadvantaged groups in educational program of digital reading and creating of comics. In this paper we use the findings from the graphical questionnaires, the focus group with deaf and partially-hearing respondents as well as in-depth interviews with digital reading trainers.

This study provides a micro-level approach to understanding the mechanisms of digital exclusion and factors that lead to reducing this gap and gives an insight to subtle human perceptions and behavior that may lead to digital inclusion. The study has a practical value to practitioners involved in designing educational programs to increase ICT adoption among persons with hearing impairments.

2 Literature Review

When studying the digital exclusion of people with hearing impairments it is important to realize that hearing disability is accompanied and reinforced by other factors. In his concept of digital divide Van Dijk [14] highlighted the reciprocal relations between social and digital inequalities. Additionally, Goggin [7] noted that disability experience is dynamic and may be caused or influenced by various conditions (e.g., aging) and situations (e.g., violence, traumatic experiences). Current studies on the disabilities and digital divide confirm these observations. Dobransky and Hargittai [3] in the large-scale study of the American adults with different disabilities argued that a lower socioeconomic status, older age and education were common to the disabled respondents. In this study after controlling demographic and socioeconomic parameters there were no significant differences in terms of engagement in online activities between people with and without disabilities; however, gaps in ICT access persisted except for deaf and partially hearing persons [3].

To understand perceptions, attitudes, behavior and contextual factors that may influence the digital exclusion of deaf and partially hearing persons, one may consult large-scale national ICT access and use studies (e.g., [3, 11]), thematic surveys (e.g., elearning – [10]; the use of social networking sites – [9]); small-scale experiments or interventions – [4, 5]). The studies often analyze the level of ICT acceptance, in some cases – digital inequalities, others focus on learning and accessible ICT design.

Although as shown by Dobransky and Hargittai [3] the basic access gap experienced by people with hearing impairments is not such severe as in case of other disabilities; ICT accessibility is an important factor. Inaccessible devices that reproduce dominating auditory communication practices can reinforce the feeling of being excluded [2]. In other context, for instance, e-learning, accessibility is a crucial condition that may affect the decision to enroll [10].

In terms of digital skills, the studies observe general literacy gaps. They are preconditioned by differences in spoken and sign languages and multiple constraints in acquisition of literacy skills. The outcome is that deaf and partially hearing people experience constraints in searching or surfing the web when written text comprehension skills are required [4], and in getting oriented in long unstructured texts [12]. However, some research prompts the importance of personal attitudes in practicing the use of written text online that, presumably, can lead to improvements. For instance, Kožuh, Hintermair and Debevc [9] found that deaf and hard-of-hearing persons who identify themselves with hearing communities online demonstrated better written language skills and used them more frequently on social networking sites. According to Carberoglio, Dickson, Cawthon and Bond [6], there is a link between intensive online communication and better reading comprehension skills.

Text comprehension and literacy development is also in the focus of digital educational initiatives for deaf and hard-of-hearing children. Experiments with using digital technologies and blending digital reading tasks with storytelling involving a lot of visual materials and creative tasks can lead to increasing student motivation to learn [5] and in some cases – better learning outcomes [15].

Large-scale quantitative research of the U.S. adults reports active engagement of deaf and hard-of-hearing people in online activities such as playing games, creating and sharing their own content, watching videos [3, 11]. Dobransky and Hargittai [3] associate these activities with the purposes of socialization, self-expression and community building, in other words, developing the deaf culture. Kožuh, Hintermair and Debevc [9] also observed that frequent written communication on social networking sites was intended to build online communities. Interestingly, Dobransky and Hargittai [3] observe that the deaf culture is also a subject of inequalities between more and less educated, high and low income, and other segregation features within the group of people with hearing impairments.

Although the studies discussed here provide interesting insights to experiences of deaf and hard-of-hearing people, most of them are small-scale researches or quantitative analyses relevant to one country. This paper adds Lithuanian experience to this body of research.

3 Research Design

3.1 Theoretical Framework and Methods

To study the experiences of deaf and partially hearing persons we used SCT [1] that explains various factors underpinning human learning and is widely applied in information science and ICT adoption research [13]. SCT frames learning experiences within a system of three components – environment, person and behavior. Environment embraces the factors emerging in a person's social setting, which could be observed, used for learning and become the source of inspiration or pressure. Person element indicates personal thoughts, opinions, attitudes and feelings that, in turn, shape decisions to learn, learning processes and outcomes. Behavior can be treated as an outcome of environmental and personal factors, but also mastering certain behavior impacts on personal attitudes and feelings and may encourage a new learning cycle. It means, that all three SCT components should be studied in interaction as their reciprocal influence allows researchers to construct a rich picture of learning experiences [1, 13].

To understand the links between learning experiences and reducing the digital exclusion we applied the model by Van Dijk [14] that provides a guidance on different nature and levels of digital divide that shape specific environment conditions, personal attitudes and provoke specific behavior. Van Dijk's model allowed us to avoid simplification of the digital divide phenomenon. There are four levels of digital divide in the model: a foundational motivation level that shapes individual decisions to engage or avoid ICT, access level that covers physical and intellectual barriers that prevent access and use of certain digital tools and internet, skills level that indicates the presence/absence of abilities to master digital tools and content, and finally, digital usage level that shows if (how much) an individual is able to make use of digital technology in different setting to reach his/her goals [14].

The research was carried out as a part of the educational digital comics reading program we designed and implemented in collaboration with Šiauliai municipal public library. Comics were chosen as a reading medium due to the success of the library

Table 1. The content of research instruments according to SCT elements [1]

Research instrument/collected data	Environment	Person	Behavior
Graphic questionnaire	–	I liked:…	I did:… I learned:… I remembered:…
Focus group	What helped/hindered learning the most important things in this program? What did you like the most in learning about comics and Tablet PC?	What was the value of this program for you, if any?	What are three most important things you have learned in this programme? Are you going to: use Tablet PCs/read comics in future?
Semi-structured interview	What were the most successful organizational and training solutions in this program? What contributed/hindered the respondents' learning success?	Did you noticed any changes in the respondents' perceptions of and attitudes toward Tablet PCs, internet and comics during the program? If yes, what were the changes? What were the most/least exciting and the easiest/most difficult elements of the program for the respondents?	What skills did the respondents acquire by participating in this program?

educational programs delivered at its Comics Center to the general public. However, at the time of the project, the Comics Center did not offer any programs to deaf and hard of hearing people. Previous library experiences showed that the users were very engaged with this medium. Additionally, due to a combination of images and text comics were versatile for training various skills (e.g. seeking, analyzing and assessing, creating, editing and sharing both textual and visual information online, etc.).

The program focused on developing competencies in digital comics reading and using a Tablet PC and consisted of 8 thematic lessons (according to the wishes of respondents, 2 lessons were studied at one meeting, so the program was accomplished in 4 meetings) over the period of two months. We designed three research instruments to get different perspectives on the research questions:

- a graphic questionnaire that was offered to the participants after each meeting to collect the data on the respondents' immediate attitudes and behaviors. The graphic questionnaire was a learning self-report template that contained brief open-ended statements and honeycomb-shaped spaces for the respondents to fill in. Being short and easily comprehended, it reduced the burden of reading and writing that is common to traditional questionnaires;

- a focus group with the respondents was conducted at the end of the program to collect the data on their overall experiences;
- a semi-structured interview with the trainers was conducted after completing the program to get another perspective on the participants attitudes, the influence of lesson settings and interpersonal dynamics.

The research instruments were focused on the factors underlying the respondents' experiences as outlined in SCT [1]: environment, person and behavior (see Table 1). Additionally, different levels of digital divide by Van Dijk [14] were considered in research instrument design.

Table 2. Factors affecting various levels of digital exclusion of the respondents

Levels of the digital divide	Environment	Person	Behavior
Motivation	Creative practical tasks (GQ, FG, INT) Level of awareness about ICT in the group (INT, GQ)	Interest in the novel subject of comics (GQ, FG, INT)	Practical use of visual communication (FG, INT)
Access	Sign language translation services (INT) Ability to access otherwise unavailable tool (FG)	Importance of digital tools for communication in everyday life (FG)	Increased use of library services (INT) Active use of digital tools in everyday life (FG)
Skills	Social support and friendly environment (FG, INT)	Independent learning (FG, INT)	General communication and literacy skills (INT) Tablet PC usage skills (GQ, FG, INT) Information seeking skills (GQ)
Usage	The wide selection of tasks (FG)	The need to get oriented in rapidly changing digital tools (FG)	Informed choices of digital technology (FG, INT) Finding new ways to enrich their personal communication with visuals (INT)

NOTE: abbreviations used in Table 2 indicate what research instruments enabled to get specific findings: GQ – graphic questionnaire, FG – focus group, and INT – interview

3.2 Selecting Participants, Data Collection and Interpretation

The data were collected in April-May 2018 during and after the implementation of the educational program in Šiauliai municipal public library. Šiauliai was selected for the data collection due to a concentration of deaf and partially hearing persons in this city and an active local community of disabled people. Šiauliai public municipal library was an experienced partner in serving persons with hearing impairments. It also founded a Comics Centre several years ago and delivered educational comics programs to the users. Two librarians – one experienced comics educator and another – specializing in educating the deaf and hard of hearing population, were recruited as trainers.

We aimed to select the respondents that experienced digital exclusion on different levels. The selection of participants was conducted through a questionnaire surveying their condition in the use of digital technologies. Despite some changes in the group we have data from twelve participants, five men and seven women. Seven participants attended 2–4 meetings, while 5 respondents – dropped out after one meeting.

With the library assistance, the program and research instruments were adapted to - the special needs of respondents. Sign language translators mediated all interactions with the respondents during training and the research data collection sessions. Focus group with 9 participants of the program and in-depth interviews with 2 trainers were recorded and transcribed. We performed thematic analysis on the graphic question-naire, interviews and the focus group data.

3.3   Limitations of the Study

The nature of the study – research interventions in the course and after the end of the program, while interacting with the respondents in their natural learning environment caused several limitations of this study. Participation in the digital comics reading program was voluntary and in order to avoid any bias we didn't reward or elsewhere encouraged the respondents to participate. The respondents were informed about the research interventions and their right to stop whenever they felt appropriate.

One of the limitations was the lack of continuous participation of the respondents in the learning and, accordingly, research sessions. Therefore, this research does not study the continuous and evolving experiences of the learners, but rather focuses on immediate ones. Additionally, two months period and a small number of training meetings could be too short for revealing certain changes in the respondents' perceptions, behavior and environment. We realize that some of these factors can be observed over a longer period and are outside the temporal scope of this study.

All persons invited to participate in the program were deaf or partially hearing people, but their ICT knowledge, skills, usage habits significantly differed. So, these persons usually experienced digital exclusion effects to a different extent and in a different way. Due to this reason we considered this study an explorative inquiry in the learning experiences of people with hearing impairments.

3.4   Findings

Eleven deaf and hard-of-hearing respondents participated in the educational program that consisted of four meetings and was guided by two trainers. We collected the following data: 22 graphic questionnaires (7 participants filled in 2–4 questionnaires, while each of the rest 5 participants – returned one questionnaire), one transcript of the focus group and two transcripts of interviews with the trainers.

Basing on the theoretical framework, we aimed at identifying subtle factors in the learning setting, personal attitudes and behavior (according to SCT model) that could contribute to changes on each level of digital exclusion (according to Van Dijk model). For instance, we started our analysis by seeking contextual factors, attitudes and behaviors that affected the motivation to engage with Tablet PCs. Then, in a similar manner, we studied other levels of digital exclusion. The factors that contribute to reducing (or increasing) the digital exclusion of persons with hearing impairments were discovered in the data (see the summary in Table 2).

We observed a number of factors (see Table 2) that could influence the motivation to engage in the digital reading program and, consequently, actively engage in adopting and using digital tools in the future. The analysis revealed that the course design could contribute to increasing the motivation of the participants. It was obvious that engagement in practical tasks of creating their own comics was an exciting and motivating experience for the respondents because it allowed them to imagine the story, search for appropriate visual solutions and to explore how the Tablet PC and comics software can make their story live. Both excitement and engagement in creative tasks were obvious in all three datasets:

- in the graphic questionnaire the respondents mentioned that they liked to design their own comics (e.g., "I liked to create my own comics");
- the focus group participants also described the exciting experience of their own comics project. For instance: "the most interesting was to create my own comics", "I liked to create my own comics, to tell the story", "I thought what my story could be like, how to make it in pictures, what text bubbles to put; it was a very interesting task".
- Both interviewed trainers also observed the participants engagement with creative tasks: "when the participants started to design their own comics, it was the most interesting part", "some participants were so engaged that they designed comics not only during the lessons, but also at home", "[the most interesting was] the opportunity to tell their own story, idea by using digital technology".

However, we identified one aspect that could reduce the motivation to engage in learning about digital technology – a different level of awareness about ICT among the group members. In the graphic questionnaire some participants noted that they "didn't learn anything new about computers and the internet" in contrast to others. One of the trainers also indicated that diversity in level of skills, usage practices and knowledge about ICT negatively affected the engagement in the program: "Those participants that were not so skilled in ICT were interested, while others who were younger and used those things we explained every day, told us that they didn't learn anything new and stopped attending the classes".

Comics was a novel subject to most respondents, and it stimulated their positive attitude and curiosity. All research interventions indicated the attractiveness of the new subject. For instance, in the graphic questionnaire the respondents mentioned that they liked to "get new knowledge about comics", "imagine comics story". The focus group participants indicated that "it was very interesting to learn how comics emerged, it was great to find out more about their history, I learned a lot of new things", "I have seen some movies about superheroes, but a closer look at comics was very interesting".

Consequently, the trainers also observed the excitement about the new subject (e.g., "one of the reason for success was that they hadn't heard about comics media before", "introduction to comics was an interesting experience for them", "[the most interesting] was the discovery of comics, their genres and the opportunity to tell the story").

Naturally, the stimulating effect of comics was deeply related to the importance and practical use of visual communication in the everyday life of the respondents. Images played an important part in the respondents' socialization and were significant expressive mean; therefore, the respondents were excited to enrich their knowledge and skills in understanding and creating visual stories. This motivating effect was noted by various respondents in the focus group:

- "When I was in school, teachers tried to show us things in pictures. It was very difficult for them to teach us because we could hardly understand. They tried to teach us by drawing and showing pictures. Maybe this is the reason that I have been engaged with images since childhood and I got very interested during the program".
- "It [image] is very important for deaf people. By reading pictures you can understand a story".
- "When I was a little girl, I liked to read fairy tales and look at the pictures. I had friends who could hear, so while they were reading aloud, I was looking at the pictures. So, I liked the pictures here as well because I have this hobby since childhood".

One of the trainers also noted the importance of images in the social life of people with hearing impairments: "In general they take a lot of photos to compensate their hearing disability with their vision".

The research also revealed several important aspects related to the accessibility of ICT. The first accessibility condition was the participation of experienced sign language translators in all interactions between the learners and the trainers and the researchers. It ensured the accessibility of course materials that could otherwise become a significant barrier to learning. One of the trainers noted that the sign language translators played an important role in the program success: "Sign language translators contributed to the training success because they made the course materials understandable to deaf and partially hearing people".

The second accessibility condition – availability of otherwise inaccessible tool, was observed by the focus group participants (e.g., "I think it was useful to learn about Tablet PC; at home I use a computer and a mobile phone, I have never used Tablet PCs. And now I can make a choice in case more technologies will be available to me"). Important to note, these and other comments by the focus respondents indicated that they actively use digital technologies in everyday life (e.g., "I use computer at home; so it was a new experience to use Tablet PC here"; "computer and mobile phone are the best tools for me. I use them for a long time and got accustomed to them, they are very convenient"). However, constant availability of digital tools was perceived as an important condition for the respondents to connect to the surrounding world (e.g., "if you sleep and feel that the mobile phone vibrates, you wake up and look what happened. I can communicate with my deaf friends and foreign friends by using the camera, I can also arrange meetings that way").

And finally, one of the trainers observed that the digital reading program was a good chance for the participants to learn about the library services: "in general, those who had never visited us before, learned about the Šiauliai municipal public library and they can come and use all services". Knowledge about the providers of free digital services and resources can reduce deaf and partially hearing persons ICT access barriers as well.

The participants and the trainers reported about the wide spectrum of skills acquired in the course of the program and an important condition to facilitate the learning. The skills fall into three groups:

- Tablet PC usage skills included mastering hardware and software and was mentioned by the respondents in the graphic questionnaire (e.g., "I learned how to use Tablet PC", "I learned how to use the software", "I learned how to make photos"), the trainers' interviews (e.g., "their skills to use tablet PCs improved, indeed", "in the end of the classes they understood the advantages of tablet PCs", "in the beginning some of them could hardly switch the Tablet PC on, they confused buttons, but in the end they did well") and focus groups (e.g., "I learned about tablet PCs, how to use them").
- Information seeking skills mostly were observed in the graphic questionnaires (e.g., "I learned how to find the Lithuanian comics online", "I learned how to find comics online").
- General communication and literacy skills included the ability to create a consistent story and express ideas and were highlighted both by the participants in the graphic questionnaires (e.g., "I created a comics story", "I tried to create a comics story") and the focus group (e.g., "we made photos of the food and thought how to make a funny story with those photos"). One of the trainers revealed the general literacy difficulties usually experienced by deaf and partially hearing persons and the improvement of those skills during the program: "Creating their own comics story, making connections between photos and making it interesting, attractive and funny was a huge challenge to most participants. In general, deaf persons experience a lot of difficulties in writing down their thoughts; those who are older have difficulties in communicating in Lithuanian [...]. They acquired not only computer literacy skills, but also improved language skills and grammar. I had foreseen it, although it was not included in the program".

When needed the respondents were brave to seek for the assistance of their teachers, peers and friends, but mainly preferred independent learning and practical explorations of the subject on their own:

- "I just was taking photos of what I saw around and was trying to draw something, sometimes the trainers helped a little bit, when at home I asked my friends for help".
- "I tried to create [the comics] on my own, I used my own photos and tried to arrange them myself".
- "I did everything on my own and used my own ideas".

Self-sufficiency of the learners was also noted by the trainer: "They succeeded when working on their own".

Social support contributed to creating a safe, friendly and relaxing atmosphere during the lessons. One of the trainers reflected that "communication made the participants feel closer to each other [...]. During the lessons they felt confident in the library space, relaxed and felt good. I think it also contributed to the learning success". Although the participants were self-sufficient learners, they enjoyed the availability of help, support and meeting people. One focus group participant commented: "I think that this training was very useful. If I didn't understand something, people would help me and repeat it. It was the first time when I got so much information from people, not online".

The value of the program was also in the opportunity to enrich common interactions with digital tools with new ways to use technology for everyday needs. In the focus group discussion, the participants noted the variety of tasks and learning opportunities offered by the program. For instance, one respondent shared her greatest impression as following: "I have learned how to use Tablet PCs, how to create comics by using the software, how to arrange photos and how to make them; I made the photos of flowers, people and their faces by using various software, tried to put flowers on the photos of people, all of it was new to me". The variety of learning paths and opportunities enabled the participants to make choices about the most personally relevant things to learn (e.g., "perhaps, I won't use the Tablet PC at home, but creating my own comics was the most interesting occupation").

The participants of the focus group reported that the program was useful in raising awareness about rapidly changing digital technologies: "We will use those tablet PCs anyway. It was important to learn how to use them here. We don't know if we have an opportunity to use them in the future; but the most important thing is that we had an introduction to this equipment. Nowadays, technology changes very fast".

Consequently, the participants and the trainers indicated that the program could affect future behavior in terms of the practical application of digital tools to informed choices of digital technology:

- For instance, the respondent of the focus group asserted: "I think it was useful to learn about Tablet PC; at home I use a computer and a mobile phone, I have never used Tablet PCs. And now I can make a choice in case more technologies will be available to me".
- One of the trainers also mentioned that "although digital tools will not be available immediately, the majority will have an opportunity to apply different digital tools for consuming and creating content; so learning and testing the opportunities of digital technologies will encourage them to plan their activities, communicate, and use those tools for different purposes".

Due to the importance of visual communication to deaf and partially hearing participants they are likely to enrich their personal communication practices by using visual materials in various ways. One of their trainers argued: "I think they can apply Tablet PC for making and processing the photos [...]. Adults actively use Facebook and publish photos. They don't write texts as those who can hear, but upload photos and communicate that way".

4 Discussion and Conclusion

The social cognitive theory provides an important advantage for analyzing the findings of this research. It argues that all elements – behavior, perceptions and attitudes and environmental factors influence and shape one another [1]. By considering this statement, we can see several groups of factors and their interactions, which allow us to uncover how they all work together and could possibly contribute to reducing digital exclusion of the respondents. These are: common everyday life behavior and attitudes of the deaf and hard-of-hearing participants, features of the digital reading program, and behavior and attitudes that resulted from participation in the program.

In the findings, it was obvious that the digital reading program reinforced behavior and attitudes that were not only common but also personally significant to deaf and hard-of-hearing persons in their everyday lives. They cover the active use of visual communication and digital tools and a resulting attitude about the high relevance of digital tools for communication.

The course features activated the common and personally relevant behavior and attitudes and encouraged the participants' engagement in learning. Combined with digital hardware and software, comics enabled the participants to create and tell their own stories and find the means to express themselves. Additionally, the program offered a wide selection of tasks, including creative tasks that allowed a reasonable space for choice in excelling in visual communication and using digital tools for communication purposes. The training was fully accessible and created a welcoming and safe environment for learning. It stimulated an independent creative exploration of visuals and digital tools.

The participants responded to the course content, methods and organizational solutions by developing new values and attitudes as well as with new ICT related behavior. Personal relevancy of comics and digital tools in the lives of the respondents generated high motivation and engagement with the course content. It also encouraged the respondents to acknowledge that the training helped them to get oriented in the rapidly changing digital technologies. As a result, the participants acquired useful ICT skills and were equipped with the knowledge to make more informed choices of digital tools in the future. They also managed to get useful knowledge in digital means for visual communication to support their personal interaction in the future.

When analyzing the findings from the digital exclusion perspective by Van Dijk [14] we can summarize the following:

- The motivation of the participants was crucial to the overall success of engaging people with ICT. As shown by the research, the motivation to engage with ICT is deeply connected with the general life context of deaf and hard-of-hearing people. A deep understanding of how ICTs are woven into the lives of people enables the trainers to create content and tools that make people willing to respond to.
- Deaf and hard-of-hearing people are active users of digital technologies and they do not experience significant physical barriers in accessing the basic ICT equipment. This conclusion is in line with previous research [3, 11].

- In terms of skills, the obstacles to using ICT by deaf and hard-of-hearing people are often related to general literacy skills, such as written text comprehension and expressing thoughts and ideas in writing. This observation is also in line with previous research [4, 12].
- The digital educational program is an important tool to expand the ICT usage repertoire of the deaf and hard-of-hearing people and, especially, to facilitate the use of digital tools for personal communication, which is a personally significant objective in their lives as pointed by Kožuh, Hintermair and Debevc [9].

We believe that small-scale qualitative research of experiences of deaf and hard-of-hearing persons in digital interventions is an important addition to large-scale quantitative inquiries. Although in line with the major findings of the previous research, our analysis showed how different factors interacted and reinforced each other. The understanding of such interaction provides important insights not only to quantitative researchers to interpret their findings, but also to digital educators who design the training for deaf and hard-of-hearing people.

References

1. Bandura, A.: Social Foundations of Thought and Action: A Social Cognitive Theory. Prentica Hall, Englewood Cliffs (1986)
2. Bitman, N., John, N.A.: Deaf and hard of hearing smartphone users: intersectionality and the penetration of ableist communication norms. J. Comput.-Mediat. Commun. 24(2), 56–72 (2019)
3. Dobransky, K., Hargittai, E.: Unrealized potential: exploring the digital disability divide. Poetics 58, 18–28 (2016)
4. Fajardo, I., Abascal, J., Cañas, J.J.: Bridging the digital divide for deaf signer users. In: Proceedings of the 15th European Conference on Cognitive Ergonomics: the Ergonomics of Cool Interaction, p. 37. ACM, Madeira (2008)
5. Flórez-Aristizábal, L., Cano, S., Collazos, C.A., Benavides, F., Moreira, F., Fardoun, H.M.: Digital transformation to support literacy teaching to deaf children: from storytelling to digital interactive storytelling. Telemat. Inform. 38, 87–99 (2019)
6. Garberoglio, C.L., Dickson, D., Cawthon, S., Bond, M.: Bridging the communication divide: CMC and deaf individuals' literacy skills. Lang. Learn. Technol. 19(2), 118–133 (2015)
7. Goggin, G.: Disability and digital inequalities: rethinking digital divides with disability theory. In: Ragnedda, M., Muschert, G.W. (eds.) Theorizing digital divides. Routledge, New York (2018)
8. Helsper, E.J., van Deursen, A.J.A.M.: Digital skills in Europe: research and policy. In: Andreasson, K. (ed.) Digital Divides: The New Challenges and Opportunities for E-Inclusion. Taylor & Francis Group, Boca Raton (2015)
9. Kožuh, I., Hintermair, M., Debevc, M.: Community building among deaf and hard of hearing people by using written language on social networking sites. Comput. Hum. Behav. 65, 295–307 (2016)
10. Lago, E.F., Acedo, S.O.: Factors affecting the participation of the deaf and hard of hearing in e-learning and their satisfaction: a quantitative study. Int. Rev. Res. Open Distrib. Learn. 18(7), 267–291 (2017)

11. McKeown, C., McKeown, J.: Accessibility in online courses: understanding the deaf learner. TechTrends **63**, 506–513 (2019)
12. Maiorana-Basas, M., Pagliaro, C.M.: Technology use among adults who are deaf and hard of hearing: a national survey. J. Deaf Stud. Deaf Educ. **19**(3), 400–410 (2014)
13. Middleton, L., Hall, H., Raeside, R.: Applications and applicability of social cognitive theory in information science research. J. Libr. Inform. Sci. **4**(51), 927–937 (2018)
14. Van Dijk, J.: The Deepening Divide: Inequality in the Information Society. Sage Publications, Thousand Oaks (2005)
15. Wang, Y., Paul, P.V.: Integrating technology and reading instruction with children who are deaf or hard of hearing: the effectiveness of the cornerstones project. Am. Ann. Deaf **1**(156), 56–68 (2011)

Utilization of Assistive Technologies Among Visually Impaired Students in University Libraries in Uganda: Users' Experiences

Patience Agabirwe[✉] and George W. Kiyingi

East African School of Library and Information Science, College of Computing
and Information Sciences, Makerere University, Kampala, Uganda
pagabirwe@gmail.com, wkiyingi@gmail.com

Abstract. This paper presents visually impaired students' experiences on the utilization of assistive technologies to access digital information resources for academic work. It reports preliminary findings from an ongoing Doctoral study on Information Practices of Students with Visual Impairment using Digital Information Resources in Public University Libraries in Uganda. Using a qualitative approach; stratified purposeful, snowball and convenience sampling techniques were used. Data was obtained from twenty visually impaired students using face to face in-depth open ended interviews. Data was analyzed using software Atlas ti v.7.5.5 following the study themes. Findings revealed exclusion in the provision and utilization of assistive technologies in the libraries studied. Skills, competency and capacity constraints by both staff and visually impaired students on the use of assistive technologies, coupled with insufficient assistive technologies impacted on the gainful utilization of digital information resources for academic undertaking. Obsolescence, limited supervisory and technical support from the librarians, and inadequate information, communication and technology (ICT) facilities were major impediments to utilization of assistive technologies to access digital information resources among visually impaired students. Provision of assistive technologies does not guarantee their utilization therefore, the study recommends designing tailor-made courses in ICT for visually impaired students for library staff, equipping visually impaired students with requisite skills and competencies, purchasing or subscribing to up-to-date assistive technologies, acquiring more computers and designating library staff to manage the special needs section in libraries.

Keywords: Assistive technologies · Digital information resources · Visually impaired students · University library

1 Introduction

The advancement of information, communication and technology (ICT) has increased utilization of digital information resources for learning and research in university libraries. For visually impaired students, this advancement is vital in their academic pursuits. For instance, closed circuit television (CCTV), Braille embossers, Braille translation software, Braille writing equipment, Refreshable braille display, scanners, modified computer keyboards, audio web browsers, screen magnifiers and screen

© Springer Nature Switzerland AG 2020
A. Sundqvist et al. (Eds.): iConference 2020, LNCS 12051, pp. 470–479, 2020.
https://doi.org/10.1007/978-3-030-43687-2_37

readers, Adaptive Multimedia Information System are now available to ease access and use of digital information resources by the visually impaired [1–6].

Several authors [7–10] have noted that although, assistive technologies are available in university libraries, most library staff lack skills and competencies to support visually impaired students in their adoption, utilization, and incorporating it in the library user education programmes. Relatedly, [11, 12] mentioned that assistive technologies are expensive and require regular upgrades, which is a challenge to many university libraries especially in developing countries. Additionally, limited University budgetary provision constrains the acquisition and maintenance of such ICT facilities [11]. Visually impaired students, who are minority, tend to be excluded. The absence or inadequacy of assistive technologies means that access and use of digital information resources by visually impaired students is denied [2, 7]. Without assistive technologies, visually impaired students do minimal work to overcome access to and usage challenges of digital information resources for their academics [2, 4, 13].

In this paper, visually impaired students refer to students who have both low vision and are blind [14]. Assistive technologies are products used to maintain, increase or improve the functional capabilities of people with disabilities [15]. Digital information resources are all academic library materials that are produced in digital formats including library websites and other web-based resources. This paper sought to explore the utilization of assistive technologies among Visually Impaired Students in University Libraries in Uganda.

1.1   The Ugandan Context

Uganda's population stands at 34.6 million, of which 6.5% are visually impaired [16]. The recent study by the [17] puts visual impairment at 31% as the second largest category of people with disabilities (PWDs). While 5% of these are aware of assistive technologies, only 1% have access to and are utilizing them. This low uptake is largely due to high cost, low levels of ICT and disabilities literacy among policy makers, stakeholders and non-implementation of ICT policies for PWDs [18, 19]. Among these policies is the ICT policy which provides for implementation of special ICT training programs to equip PWDs in the education sector with ICT skills [20].

In support of inclusive education, the Universities and other Tertiary Institutions Act 2001 requires public universities to admit students with disabilities [21]. However, the current joint admission list on disability scheme indicates that, only Kyambogo and Makerere Universities out of the nine public universities, admit visually impaired students [22]. This translates approximately to twenty visually impaired students every academic year out of a total of 57,898 students admitted approximately 0.035% [23, 24]. Therefore, the study was conducted in these two universities that admit and cater for persons with disabilities in their ICT policies. Kyambogo University's ICT policy 2015 section 5.2 states that "the University shall provide ICT services and infrastructure that is responsive to the needs of persons with disabilities to enhance their ability to contribute to the attainment of the University's vision and mission" [25]. Similarly, Makerere University's ICT policy section 12.2, states that "the university shall implement provisions for ICT usage for special user groups within the teaching, learning and research units towards enabling equal access to information and knowledge". Section 12.4 further urges for "the provision of appropriate digital mechanisms within the library for special user groups" [26].

Having policy and legal frameworks in place however, is one thing, implementing them is another. Despite the installation of assistive technologies to enable visually impaired students to utilize digital information resources in the two universities [27, 28], no study has been conducted to investigate the experiences of visually impaired students on the utilization of assistive technologies to access digital information resources for learning and research. Earlier studies on library inclusiveness were of a general nature, visually impaired students and their utilization of assistive technologies on digital information resources formed a small part of those studies [27–31]. It is imperative, therefore, to explore the utilization of assistive technologies among students with visual impairment to access digital information resources in public university libraries in Uganda. Their experiences may inform better ways to serve visually impaired students by university libraries and formulate strategies that would ensure inclusiveness in their academics.

1.2 Research Questions

RQ1: What assistive technologies do visually impaired students use in the libraries of public universities in Uganda?

RQ2: What are the visually impaired students' experiences in utilizing the assistive technologies in their learning and research provided by Ugandan public university libraries?

2 Methodology

2.1 Research Approach and Design

The study was qualitative and explorative, involving descriptive and in-depth understanding of the experiences visually impaired students in utilizing assistive technologies to access digital information resources in public university libraries in Uganda [32]. Exploratory research design is used to gain vital insights about a phenomenon that is literary less known [33].

2.2 Population

The study focused on two public universities; Kyambogo and Makerere that admit students with visual impairment [22]. Their libraries have established library sections for students with disabilities; 60 undergraduate visually impaired students from the two public universities were involved in the study.

2.3 Sample Strategy and Size

Due to the nature of the study population, this study employed stratified purposeful, snow ball and convenience sampling techniques to select the study participants.

Stratified purposeful sampling describes samples within samples and uses small samples for generalization [34]. Snowball is where each person interviewed may be asked to suggest additional people for interviewing [35]. The researcher initially contacts a small group of people who are relevant to the research topic and then uses these to establish contact with others [36]. Convenience sampling is simply available to the researcher by virtue of its accessibility [36]. For this study, stratified purposeful sampling technique categorized students according to their academic year (freshmen and continuing students). Initially the researcher obtained the list of all visually impaired students from the university disability departments, which contained only visually impaired students admitted on disability scheme. Strata of the potential study participants according to the year of study and programmes were made, that is, first and continuing students, then selected the continuing students (year two and above). It was assumed that continuing students had been longer at the University and have used digital information resources or other library services more than first years, therefore could provide comprehensive information for the study. Due to inadequate contact information, at least six students were identified from the list. They consented to participate in the study. They later on referred the researcher to others. Through a referral system, more participants were accessed and they too consented to participate in the study. Some of the other potential study participants were accessed at the university without prior referral. Following the researcher's eligibility inquiries and explanation regarding the study, they too consented and participated. In total, 20 visually impaired students have participated in the study. The researcher expects to reach a point of saturation with the sample size of between 25 and 30 study participants.

2.4 Data Collection Procedure

Data was collected through face-to-face in-depth open ended interviews that ranged from 45–80 min. Interviews helped the researcher to probe the assistive technologies the visually impaired students used and their experiences regarding their utilization to access digital information resources in the two universities.

2.5 Data Analysis

Data from interviews was transcribed, coded, categorized thematically and analyzed using the software Atlas ti v.7.5.5.

3 Study Limitations

Inadequate documentation on students with visual impairment in the universities studied affected the determination of the target population. The list got from the disability offices only contained students admitted on disability scheme.

The study focused on visually impaired students from two public universities, the results may therefore not be generalizable in other universities.

4 Preliminary Findings

4.1 Study Participants

Four of the twenty participants were privately sponsored, twelve on disability scheme and two on national merit. Six had low-vision while fourteen were totally blind. Causes of their visual impairment included damaged retina, glaucoma, measles, child games, accident and medical failure during eye sight operation.

4.2 The Assistive Technologies that Visually Impaired Students Use in the Public University Libraries

The study revealed that most visually impaired students use assistive technologies to access digital information resources. The available assistive technologies that students use in the university libraries studied were the screen reader Job Access with Speech (JAWS) and an embosser (a printer for the blind). However, JAWS is obsolete and the embosser is dysfunctional.

> *"JAWS is there, but it is very old. In fact I tried to explain to the university librarian about its malfunctioning and he said that they bought that software long time ago."- (Participant1).*

In these circumstances, participants use plextalk (talking book player and recorder), free assistive mobile phone Apps with loud voice and magnification capabilities alongside proprietary unlicensed assistive technologies or trial versions. Mobile phone apps with loud voice helped participants to search for information required to accomplish assignments because they are conveniently portable. However, they are slow and often freeze with heavy documents. This hampers easy access and use of digital information resources.

Participants similarly revealed that unlicensed assistive technologies are ineffective, unreliable and restrict their operations. For instance, they sometimes crashed before completion of the tasks.

Participants with low vision indicated that due to lack of assistive technologies for them, they had no option but to use available screen readers in the libraries.

> *"I am partially blind but because the university does not provide me with screen magnifiers I use a screen reader even when I do't like it"-(participant14).*

4.3 Experiences of Visually Impaired Students in Utilizing Assistive Technologies to Access Digital Information Resources

Supervisory and Technical Support from the Library. The study revealed inadequate librarians' support to visually impaired students. Assistive technologies in the section for students with disabilities were often vandalized by other students with disabilities. One participant noted that generalized access to assistive technologies hampers their use, especially when one is uninterested in JAWS that it makes noise for them, quits it and no librarian is available to help-*(Participant1).*

Due to inadequate monitoring, supervisory and technical support, some participants resorted to taking computer maintenance decisions into their hands. For example one of the participants revealed that when the computers in their section were very slow they sought help from a sighted student to format all computers and reinstalled the operating system and trial version of JAWS.

Limited Knowledge and Capacity of Library Staff to Operate Assistive Technologies. The study established that when the visually impaired students needed assistance from the library due to technical problems with assistive technologies, librarians could not support them because they were unfamiliar with the dysfunctional machines.

To one participant,

"Some of them are willing to help but they don't know how those technologies work.... They are not exposed to assistive technologies that we use"-(participant6).

Librarians seemed less acquainted with assistive technologies. In this light, [10, 11] noted that library staff tend to lack specialised knowledge beyond that of general instructional technology support.

Limited Knowledge and Capacity of Visually Impaired Students to Utilise Assistive Technologies. It was revealed that, just like the library staff, some visually impaired students were not conversant with using assistive technologies. There seems to be no deliberate user library orientation initiatives for visually impaired students on assistive technologies upon admission. Therefore they find it hard to comprehend the assistive technologies. One participant noted that,

"Inductions are made but they are generalized on many other things while leaving out the sensitive issues that we need most."-(participant2).

In contrast, [28] reported that librarians in one of the universities understudy are trained in ICT and related library services for students with visual impairment and these in turn have ably equipped the students with the same skills. However, this study reveals a lack of such training from the users' perspective. Nevertheless, findings established that some students with visual impairment possessed knowledge and ICT skills that enabled them to utilise assistive technologies in academic work through prior ICT trainings and 'used these to access electronic reading materials'-(participant4). However, these trainings are incomprehensive to expose them to sophisticated assistive technologies hence their desire for the support of experienced library staff.

Inadequate ICT Facilities. Participants noted that computers with assistive technologies in the libraries do not commensurate with visually impaired students.

"...computers are very few...they are like five or six but those we can access as VIs are only two that have JAWS. Because if you give me a computer that doesn't have JAWS it's like a toy to me"-(participant5).

Others complained that while sighted students have access to computers in their college and faculty libraries, visually impaired students had to come to the library section for disability to access assistive technologies. They considered this discriminative and inconveniencing because they had to walk long distances from their residences and classrooms to the library despite unfriendly university walkways.

Despite the unpleasant experiences, participants revealed that they often turn to peers and social networks for help to learn assistive technologies and access digital information resources. This collaborate with [37–39]. Participants however, preferred peer assistance for they appeared well conversant with the assistive technologies. To them, a visually impaired person appreciates the challenge of disability, unlike one without the disability-*(participant8)*.

5 Discussion

Participants admitted that both university libraries provided JAWS and an embosser to enable utilisation of digital information resources. However, it was revealed that JAWS is obsolete and an embosser is dysfunctional. In the absence of adequate and up-to-date assistive technologies participants used plextalk, free assistive mobile phone Apps with loud voice and magnification capabilities, proprietary unlicensed assistive technologies or trial versions. Whereas Emong reported that, one of the university libraries under study has a CCTV reader, a Braille printer, a voice synthesizer, the participants never mentioned such assistive technologies [40]. Relatedly, [28] reported the availability of a screen magnifier and open book which none of the participants mentioned. From a policy perspective, this could be attributed to lack of explicit policies on orientation programs organized by library staff to acquaint visually impaired students with all the necessary information on available assistive technologies.

The experiences of the participants on the use of assistive technologies were unpleasant due to institutional and individual constraints imposed in the areas of supervision as well as capacity building. Participants also felt excluded from access to digital information resources due to inadequate supervisory and technical support, inadequate ICT facilities and training on the use of assistive technologies. Besides, the fact that visually impaired students were assisted to reinstall the operating system and trial version of JAWS without the knowledge or permission of library staff is a case in point. Furthermore, universities do not subscribe to or purchase the sophisticated assistive technologies due to financial constraints, as argued by [11].

6 Conclusion

The provision and utilization of assistive technologies by visually impaired students in the university libraries is constrained by institutional and individual factors which translate to exclusion from effective utilization of digital information resources for academic work. Existing provision are insufficient in enabling effective utilization of digital information resources due to obsolescence, limited supervisory and technical support from the librarians, limited knowledge and capacity of librarians to use and train in assistive technologies, limited knowledge and capacity of visually impaired students to use assistive technologies, and inadequate ICT facilities. Thus, the provision of assistive technologies alone may be insufficient to guarantee utilization of digital information resources by visually impaired students.

In light of these institutional and individual capacity constraints, University libraries need to design and implement capacity building and skills enhancement courses tailored to ICTs for library staff to effectively serve the visually impaired students, purchase or subscribe to up-to-date assistive technologies, acquire more computers and designate adequate library staff to support students with special needs. Short of this, there is the risk of excluding visually impaired students from utilizing the existing assistive technologies to access digital information resources. Finally, university libraries need to design and implement regular training programs for visually impaired students to equip them with the requisite skills and competencies to effectively use the assistive technologies.

References

1. Bhardwaj, R.K., Kumar, S.: A comprehensive digital environment for visually impaired students: users' perspectives. Libr. Hi Tech. **35**(4), 549–564 (2017). https://doi.org/10.1108/lht-01-2017-0016
2. Majinge, R.M., Stilwell, C.: ICT use in information delivery to people with visual impairment and on wheelchairs in tanzanian academic libraries. Afr. J. Libr. Arch. Inform. Sci. **24**(2), 151–159 (2014)
3. Butucea, D.: Personalized e-learning software systems: extending the solution to assist visually impaired users. Database Syst. J. **IV**(3), 41–49 (2013)
4. Lucky, A., Achebe, N.E.: Information service delivery to the visually impaired: a case study of hope for the blind foundation Wusasa, Zaria (Nigeria). Res. J. Inform. Technol. **5**(1), 18–23 (2013)
5. Kleynhans, S.A., Fourie, I.: Ensuring accessibility of electronic information resources for visually impaired people. The need to clarify concepts such as visually impaired. Libr. Hi Tech. **32**(2), 268–372 (2014)
6. Kumar, S., Sanaman, G.: Preference and use of electronic information and resources by blind/visually impaired in NCR libraries in India. J. Inform. Sci. Theory Pract. **1**(2), 69–83 (2013). https://doi.org/10.1633/jistap
7. Ekwelem, V.O.: Library services to disabled students in the digital era: challenges for outcome assessment. Libr. Philos. Pract. 1–28 (2013). https://digitalcommons.unl.edu/cgi/viewcontent.cgi?article=2352&context=libphilprac
8. Zaid, Y.A.: Information provision for students with visual impairments in nigerian universities: charting a course from project to service delivery. J. Appl. Inform. Sci. Technol. **10**(1), 1–10 (2017)
9. Majinge, R.M., Stilwell, C.: Library services provision for people with visual impairments and in wheelchairs in academic libraries in Tanzania. South Afr. J. Libr. Inform. Sci. **79**(2), 39–50 (2013). https://doi.org/10.7553/79-2
10. Foley, A.R., Masingila, J.O.: The use of mobile devices as assistive technology in resource-limited environments: access for learners with visual impairments in Kenya the use of mobile devices as assistive technology in resource-limited environments: access for learners with visual impairment in Kenya. Inform. Health Care (2014). https://doi.org/10.3109/17483107.2014.974220

11. Eligi, I., Mwantimwa, K.: ICT accessibility and usability to support learning of visually-impaired students in Tanzania. Int. J. Educ. Dev. Inform. Commun. Technol. **13**(1), 87–102 (2017)
12. Majinge, R.M.: Library services' provision for people with visual impairments and in wheel chars in academic libraries in Tanzania. Doctoral thesis, University of KwaZulu-Natal, Pietermaritzburg (2014)
13. Vigo, M., Harper, S.: Coping tactics employed by visually disabled users on the web. Int. J. Hum. Comput. Stud. **71**(11), 1013–1025 (2013). https://doi.org/10.1016/j.ijhcs.2013.08.002
14. World Health Organization: International Statistical Classification of Diseases and Related Health Problems 10th Revision (ICD-10)-WHO Version for 2016 (2016)
15. Koulikourdi, A.: Assistive technologies in Greek libraries. Libr. Hi Tech. **26**(3), 387–397 (2008). https://doi.org/10.1108/07378830810903319
16. Uganda Bureau of Statistics: National household survey, Kampala (2014)
17. Uganda Communications Commission: Access and Usage of Information and Communications Technologies (ICTs) by People With Disabilities (PWDs) in Uganda, Kampala (2018)
18. Kalemera, A.: Promoting Accessible ICT in Uganda. Promoting effective and inclusive ICT policy in Africa (2018). https://cipesa.org/2018/12/promoting-accessible-ict-in-uganda/
19. Busuulwa, A.: From disparity to parity: understandig the barriers to inclusion of persons with visual disabilities in the digital revolution of Uganda. A doctoal thesis, University of Twente, The Netherlands (2015). https://doi.org/10.3990/1.9789036538473
20. Ministry of Information and Communications Technology: The republic of Uganda ministry of information and communications technology: National Information and Communications Technology policy for Uganda (2014)
21. Republic of Uganda: The universities and other tertiary institutions Act (2001)
22. Public University Disability Scheme: Makerere University and other Public Universities Admissions for students with disability 2014–2018 (2018)
23. Kyambogo University: Kyambogo University: Fact Book 2018/2019, Kampala (2018)
24. Makerere University: Makerere University: Fact Book 2018–2019, Kampala (2019)
25. Kyambogo university: Kyambogo university Information Communication policy, Kampala (2014)
26. Makerere University: Makerere University Information & Communication Technology Policy, Kampala (2016)
27. Buwule, R.: The adoption of assistive technologies in academic libraries : a casestudy of library users with visual and hearing impairement at Kyambogo University in Uganda. In: 20th Standing Conference of Eastern, Central and Southern Africa Library and Information Associations, Nairobi (2012)
28. Musoke, M.: University library infrastructure for persons with special needs: the Makerere university library experience. In: 21st Standing Conference of Eastern, Central and Southern Africa Library and Information Associations Conference Proceedings on Information and Knoweldge Management as a Driving Force for Social-Economic Development in Africa, Malawi, pp. 189–196 (2014)
29. Naluwooza, M.: Inclusiveness: the provision of information services to persons with disabilities at Makerere university library. In: QQML Conference (2014)
30. Nelson, H.E., Kamusiime, N.: Promoting effective friendly information and service delivery to persons with disabilities in Uganda. In: 21st Standing Conference of Eastern, Central and Southern Africa Library and Information Associations Conference Proceedings on Information and Knoweldge Management as a Driving Force for Social-Economic Development in Africa, pp. 179–187 (2014)

31. Nabwaami, E.: Information seeking behaviour of students with disabilities at the faculty of special needs and rehabilitation library. A masters dissertation, Makerere University (2015)
32. Brantlinger, E., Jimenez, R., Klingner, J., Pugach, M., Richardson, V.: Qualitative studies in special education. Except. Child. **71**(2), 195–207 (2005)
33. Malterud, K., Siersma, V.D., Guassora, A.D.: Sample size in qualitative interview studies: guided by information power. Qual. Health Res. **26**(13), 1753–1760 (2016). https://doi.org/10.1177/1049732315617444
34. Patton, M.Q.: Qualitative Research & Evaluation Methods: Integrating Theory and Practice, 4th edn. Sage, Thousand Oaks (2015)
35. Babbie, E.: The Practice of Social Research, 12th edn. Wadsworth, Belmont (2007)
36. Bryman, A.: Social Research Methods, 5th edn. Oxford University Press, Oxford (2016)
37. Seyama, L.S., Morris, C.D., Stilwell, C.: Information seeking behaviour of blind and visually impaired students: a case study of the university of Kwazulu-Natal. Pietermaritzburg Campus. Unisa Press **32**(1), 1–22 (2014)
38. Awais, S., Ameen, K.: Information accessibility for students with disabilities: an exploratory study of Pakistan. Malays. J. Libr. Inform. Sci. **20**(2), 103–115 (2015)
39. Appiah, M., Deborah, K.: Information seeking behavior of visually challenge students in public universities: a study of university of Ghana, Legon and university of education, Winneba. Doctoral thesis, University of Ghana (2017)
40. Emong, P.: The realisation of human rights for disabled people in higher education in uganda: a critical analysis drawing on the UN convention on the rights of persons with disabilities. A doctoral thesis, University of Leeds (2014)

"It Could Have Been Us in a Different Moment. It Still Is Us in Many Ways": Community Identification and the Violence of Archival Representation of Disability

Gracen M. Brilmyer(✉)

University of California Los Angeles, Los Angeles, CA 90095, USA
gracenbrilmyer@gmail.com

Abstract. Using data collected through semi-structured interviews, this paper outlines two ways disabled people relate to their representation in archives. First, many participants reflected on the prevalence of disability stereotypes, tropes and limited perspectives within the records that document us. Witnessing these representations—or rather, misrepresentations—and their violent effects is emotionally difficult for many disabled people researching our histories. Second, many interviewees saw themselves in archival subjects and related to the threat of institutionalization they faced. Yet, as they see pieces of themselves in other times, disabilities and geographies, disabled researchers are also aware of the activation of present politics, vocabularies, and critical lenses that they apply when addressing the historical record. As part of a larger research project that investigates the impacts of archival representation, these findings lay the foundation for the multifaceted ways in which disabled communities are affected by witnessing themselves in history through digital and physical archives.

Keywords: Disability · Archives · Records · Representation · Qualitative research

1 Introduction

As part of a larger research project that investigates the complexity of archival representation, misrepresentation and underrepresentation of disability, this paper addresses the ways disabled communities are impacted by and relate to their representation in archives. Disabled people are often represented within archival material through records documenting their criminalization, institutionalization and spectacularization [1–6]. Although many of these records are used to tell parts of disability history, little scholarship has been produced about *how* this type of archival representation—in both digital and physical archives—impacts disabled people today.

This paper outlines two themes that emerged in data collected through semi-structured interviews with disabled people who use archives. First, this data illustrates the prevalence of disability stereotypes, tropes and limited perspectives within the records that document disabled people. In witnessing such representations, disabled people described how they are affectively impacted: witnessing the violence of the past

© Springer Nature Switzerland AG 2020
A. Sundqvist et al. (Eds.): iConference 2020, LNCS 12051, pp. 480–486, 2020.
https://doi.org/10.1007/978-3-030-43687-2_38

is emotionally difficult for many disabled people researching their histories. Second, these quotes show that many interviewees see themselves in archival subjects and relate to the threat of institutionalization they faced. At the same time, however, they also poignantly noted the temporal differences between experiences represented in records from the past and lived experiences today. Given the limits of historical representations of disabled people, this paper lays a foundation for future research into not only the impacts of archival representation on marginalized communities, but also the value of elevating the voices of and archival uses specific to disabled communities.

2 Literature Review

Archives and the materials they contain have the power to influence how we understand history, others, and ourselves. Many scholars in the field of Disability Studies have used records to illuminate pieces of disability history. Susan Schweik, for instance, uses archival records to examine late nineteenth and early twentieth century legislation called "the Ugly Laws" [3]. Under these laws, people found "unsightly" were often policed, arrested, and institutionalized, which created a plethora of arrest records, asylum, and medical documentation, as well as newspaper articles that reinforced the idea that disability is something to be feared, contained, and eliminated. Similarly, Rosemarie Garland-Thomson traces how performer Julia Pastrana ("The Bear Woman") "was managed by a man who married her after she became extremely profitable, perhaps to assure his control over her exhibition" [6]. Records, such as her marriage certificate that ensured her husband's profit, medical journals that documented and debated her physical differences, and advertisements for her shows, demonstrate the power others had over her life and the power that records had in documenting and controlling her narrative.

Much historical documentation of disability is produced by those in power, and the voices of those whose lives were affected by such representations are often missing from records. Susan Wendell tells us that "The lack of realistic cultural representation of experiences of disability not only contributes to the 'Otherness' of people with disabilities by encouraging the assumption that their lives are inconceivable to non-disabled people but also increases non-disabled people's fear of disability by suppressing knowledge of how people live with disabilities" [8]. Not only has disability had a fraught relationship with archives and records, but such records have the potential to maintain harmful rhetorics that continue to impact disabled people's lives today.

Recent literature in Archival Studies has revealed that some marginalized groups are affectively impacted by under- or mis-representation in mainstream archives (read: large institutions) [7]. Caswell, Cifor, and Ramirez, for example, investigate the impact of archival representation on communities marginalized by race, ethnicity, sexuality, and gender [9]. Using data collected through focus groups consisting of users of community-based archives, they describe how some marginalized groups feel erased in history due to their underrepresentation and misrepresentation in archival material. In contrast to the negative impacts of mainstream archives, Caswell et al. have also investigated how community-based archives—communities documenting themselves in their own archives—have drastic positive affective impacts: seeing oneself and one's community represented in history can positively inform a feeling of belonging [10].

Located alongside this work, this short paper begins to fill a gap in the literature: using empirical data from interviews with disabled archival users, this paper investigates how disabled people relate to and are impacted by their representation, misrepresentation and underrepresentation in archival material today.[1]

3 Methods

The data for this paper was collected through ten semi-structured interviews with disabled scholars, artists, activists, and community members living in North America. Research participants (a) self-identified as disabled; (b) had conducted research in an archive and found records about people with disabilities; (c) were 21 years of age or older. Participants were recruited through email and social media, primarily using personal and professional networks, listservs, and organizations who shared the call for participation. This snowball sample—participants and community members recommending other participants—is not representative, thus the data is not generalizable; however, this research is concerned with developing in-depth analysis and providing deep, rich narratives from qualitative research, rather than acquiring a large quantity of generalizable data.

The interviews were conducted via video, phone, and in person. This array of methods both centered the access needs and comfort of disabled participants as well as permitted long-distance communication. Interviews ranged from 60 to 100 min in length and were audio recorded with consent from interviewees. Participants had the option of being quoted anonymously, and nine of the ten interviewees gave consent to be cited by name. The recordings were then transcribed, coded, and analyzed in an iterative manner, using constant comparative analysis, to allow themes to emerge within and across interviews [11, 12].

This research is deeply influenced by my personal experiences as a Disabled person working in archives and in the field of Disability Studies. Therefore, this research is done in an interpretivist paradigm where I am part of the social situations and relationships being observed. Although I share some axes of identity with the interviewees, they also held a variety of racial, ethnic, age, size, gender, sexuality, illness and disability identities, many of which differ from my own. Although there are common themes and experiences across disabilities, disabled people are not a single unified group, but have vastly differing identities, experiences, opinions and politics, and this diversity surfaced in the interviews.

---

[1] The digital and physical archives interviewees worked with varied: some would be considered mainstream archives and special collections, while others identified disability-specific collections or framed themselves as a disability-centered archives.

4 Findings

4.1 Finding 1: Violence in Representation and Erasure

One theme that emerged from the interviews was the prominence of stereotypical representations of disability—as pitiable, as dangerous, as a medical 'problem' to be eliminated. Many interviewees talked about the prevalence of these forms of representation of disability and expecting them within their research. A disabled postdoctoral researcher, who requested to be anonymous, states, "I had become aware of certain tropes in the representation of blind musicians. So part of me was guarded as a researcher in studying these materials and remaining alert to the manifestation of these tropes". Cody Jackson, a disabled, gay graduate student researching 19th century conduct manuals, spoke about the frequency of representations that work towards the eradication of disability. He states, "honestly, I think it [the record] was about eradicating both [queerness and disability] because I think the conduct manuals are about maximizing productivity and maximizing normality because when we see conduct manuals, they're usually reproducing norms". Along these lines, Megan Suggitt, a disabled undergraduate student who researches a Canadian asylum for developmentally disabled people, expresses concern about how stereotypes are easily accessible within archival materials. She states, "There's the side that the records will perpetrate how disabled people are seen [in negative ways]... people could see Huronia Regional Centre as something that was very helpful in the sense that they, you know, they 'kept' people... versus like instilling them in the community". Such stereotypical representations of disability were described as pervasive—and anticipated—within many different archives in which interviewees worked.

Although many participants described being unsurprised by the stereotypical representations of disability in records, they professed that such representations were still emotionally difficult to witness. Disability activist and author Corbett OToole describes looking at institutional records from a Californian asylum in a newspaper digital archive:

> "When I looked at the archives, I mean, clearly they were all labeled as disabled, which is why they were easy to find because institutional[ized] people, right?... It was like every page was a new kind of horror. As I would look through the records... to see what was there about the people and that's when I realized how incredibly capricious it was that they were even institutionalized".

Michelle Ganz, a hard of hearing archivist, similarly spoke about her experience looking at pension records of injured soldiers. She states:

> "It was so dehumanizing, and I really felt for so many of these soldiers, because so many of them were incredibly young and then were permanently disabled.... And then couple that with their disability and the fact that there was no support whatsoever. It really caused some of these people to go into horrible depressions and all these other mental issues that come along with the isolation of disability. It's heartbreaking because, especially when you're looking at people who are already in an area that was already economically depressed before the war happened, and then after the war, they never recovered".

Jackson continues, "I think that a lot of the 'overcoming [disability]' narratives that we get kind of erase the people who have been left behind by these very toxic and very violent systems that place value on our bodies". Suggitt says that witnessing past violences in the archive can affect one's ability to conduct research: "It almost made me not want to go back after I looked at all the documents. I just couldn't physically do that to myself because I knew after talking to the survivors, I had actual real history and then going there and seeing such a huge lack of information, [I thought] 'I don't physically think I can do that again'". OToole echoes, "it's a particular kind of hard work spiritually to do: to witness institutional stuff, trauma and abuse".

These quotes illustrate how disability often gets misrepresented through stereotypes and limited tropes of disabled people. Yet, a familiarity with these dominant forms of representation doesn't necessarily protect disabled researchers from the emotional impact of encountering these tropes in archival material.

4.2 Finding 2: Temporal Relations and Distances to Archival Subjects

Another prominent theme emerged around interviewees' feelings of connection with archival subjects. Specifically, the historical and ongoing threat of institutionalization and eradication of disability drew many interviewees to relate to archival subjects. OToole articulates that connection as follows:

"I grew up with the threat of institutionalization. They told my parents to institutionalize me when I was a baby. So I always feel the specter of institutionalization is literally that hand that's almost on my shoulder.... Also, my degree is in special ed. I visited a number of the state locked facilities for people that had labels of developmental disabilities. So I had spent some time in those places as a student so I had a very real sense of what those places feel like and look like. And so I had a lot of feelings about it".

While institutionalization has directly impacted some interviewees' lives, others understand that in another time, they, too, could have been institutionalized. Nonbinary disabled scholar Jess Waggoner reflects, "I have a really strong affective response to thinking about institutions.... Especially as I find more of my community, the more I think about it, at a certain point or a certain period in time, myself or my friends could have been in this". As disabled poet and scholar Travis Chi Wing Lau expands, this understanding of what could have been is also connected to a realization that for some, discrimination and the threat of institutionalization is still present: "It could have been us in a different moment. It still is us in many ways. Right? It's haunting. And maybe it's a defense mechanism of mine, but I try to make sense of it in terms of theory and history, but it's a powerfully emotional experience, to encounter it". Likewise, blind historian Alida Boorn identified with the struggles of past blind and low vision academics. She states, "they had a heck of a time breaking into getting full time [and] becoming a professor at full time because they were told, 'Well, how can you teach if you're blind?' And I can totally relate to that because there have been occasions [when people have told me], 'Well, how can you do this if you can't see?'"

While many disabled people connected to disabled people in records, they also acknowledged the temporal distance between them and the archival subjects. Dr. Therí A. Pickens, a Professor of English, reflects:

"There are Black women's experiences or hospital experiences I see and recognize in the archives or looking at other people's scholarly work where they've addressed that in the archive, and I can see myself in the folks that they're talking about, or I can understand that 50 years ago I would have been one of the folks that they were talking about. That is the straightforward 'yes'. The part that's tricky about that is that when I've looked through archives as a scholar, I have often attempted to keep reminding myself that my personal experiences are not the ones that I'm reporting on. And, as a scholar, my responsibility is not to talk about myself singularly, but to think about the experiences I research in aggregate".

Along these lines, Jackson states, "It's also about situating oneself within and without the archive and trying to figure out what separates us and what binds us together". Another interviewee, who wished to remain unnamed, reflects on his experiences in contrast to the disabled people he studies: "We cannot always apply present-day standards to the past without maintaining a certain degree of nuance. As a researcher, I now want to go back to representations of disability and disabled bodies in the archive, and to ask how do I productively engage those difficult questions, not solely from the perspective of publics, or of researchers, but by situating these perspectives in dialogue with the experiences of the disabled people represented, and by centering the latter".

As they have deep and personal connections to institutionalization, discrimination and oppression, disabled people also understand the temporal distances—across different disabilities, other intersecting identities, and temporal specificities with contemporary lenses. This theme illustrates how disabled researchers often feel connected to the archival subjects they encounter, while also often feeling a desire to counter or complicate the violence of the stereotypical representations. Yet, at the same time, many interviewees expressed a wariness about that desire and an awareness around applying contemporary critical lenses to historical documents.

5   Conclusion

This short paper, by investigating disabled people's relationship with their representation in archives, has expanded upon the ways archival users relate to and are affectively impacted by records. It has shown that witnessing problematic, limited, and stereotypical representations of disability is an emotional experience for many disabled people. Witnessing historical violence against disabled people is often unsurprising, but because researchers may relate to past experiences of institutionalization—either because they've experienced it, understand how they could have been in similar situations in another time, or feel the threat of it under the current U.S. administration—witnessing the history of discrimination, oppression and violence against disabled people is often personal and political. While relating to experiences of the past that span different times, disabilities, and geographies, disabled people also hold a complexity in relating to their representation in archives: researchers are aware of the activation of present politics, vocabularies, and critical lenses that they apply when addressing the historical record.

This paper reveals just two facets of the relationship between disabled communities and archival material in both physical and digital archives. Understanding the complex impacts of archival representation on disabled communities is just the beginning of thinking through archival interventions. Future applications could ask: how might archivists describe or frame records around disability to cultivate deeper connections with living disabled communities? And how might digital projects and technological interventions potentially foster, sustain, or expand the temporal connections and disconnections between disabled communities and their historical representation?

References

1. Snorton, C.R.: Black on Both Sides: A Racial History of Trans Identity, 1st edn. University of Minnesota Press, Minneapolis (2017)
2. McMillan, U.: Embodied Avatars: Genealogies of Black Feminist Art and Performance. New York University Press, New York (2015)
3. Schweik, S.: The Ugly Laws: Disability in Public. New York University Press, New York (2010)
4. Imada, A.: Promiscuous Signification: leprosy Suspects in a Photographic Archive of Skin. Representations 138(1), 1–36 (2017)
5. White, S.: Crippling the archives: negotiating notions of disability in appraisal and arrangement and description. Am. Arch. 75(1), 109–124 (2012)
6. Garland-Thomson, R.: Extraordinary Bodies: Figuring Physical Disability in American Culture and Literature, 1st edn. Columbia University Press, New York (1996)
7. Cifor, M.: Affecting relations: introducing affect theory to archival discourse. Arch. Sci. 16(1), 7–31 (2016)
8. Wendell, S.: The Rejected Body: Feminist Philosophical Reflections on Disability, 1st edn. Routledge, New York and London (1996)
9. Caswell, M., Cifor, M., Ramirez, M.: "To suddenly discover yourself existing": uncovering the impact of community archives. Am. Arch. 79(1), 58 (2016)
10. Caswell, M., Migoni, A., Geraci, N., Cifor, M.: "To be able to imagine otherwise": community archives and the importance of representation. Arch. Rec. 38(1), 5–26 (2016)
11. Lofland, J., Snow, D., Anderson, L., Lofland, L.: Analyzing Social Settings: A Guide to Qualitative Observation and Analysis, 4th edn. Wadsworth Publishing, Belmont (2005)
12. Strauss, A., Corbin, J.: Basics of Qualitative Research: Grounded Theory Procedures and Techniques, 2nd edn. SAGE Publications, Inc., Newbury Park (1990)

Creating Inclusive Library Spaces for Students with Disabilities (SWDs): Perceptions and Experiences

Caroline Ilako[1(✉)], Elena Maceviciute[2],
and Joyce Bukirwa Muwanguzi[1]

[1] Makerere University, P.O. BOX 7062, Kampala, Uganda
carolineilako0@gmail.com
[2] University of Bora, Allegatan 1, 503 32 Boras, Sweden

Abstract. Students with disabilities are enrolled in different academic programs in institutions of higher education and universities have to provide the required standards to cater for the needs of these students. One important area of focus is the library building and spaces within them. Although there are laws governing the construction of public buildings, students with disabilities may face accessibility barriers to library spaces, implying that they are not benefiting from the services and facilities. Therefore, it is imperative for academic libraries to create architectural designs and spaces that invite more students with disabilities into their buildings so as to enjoy the right of access to facilities and services. This paper takes a normative stance to the accessibility of library spaces by students with disabilities. A qualitative ethnographic study was used to investigate the perceptions and experiences of students with disabilities in physical library spaces using participant observation and in-depth interviews. The data was analyzed using thematic approach.

Keywords: Inclusive spaces · Access and usage · Students with disabilities

1 Introduction

A library is a learning environment that combines both architectural expressions and flexible physical spaces in supporting the teaching, learning and research and providing places that are individually adopted by users without any barriers [1]. These barriers may be different and affect library users differently degree, especially students with Disabilities (SWDs). By law, library buildings should be designed with this special category of users in mind. The Persons with Disabilities Act of Uganda [2] defines disability as "a substantial functional limitation of daily life activities caused by physical, mental or sensory impairment and environmental barriers resulting in limited participation" (p. 4). Persons with disabilities are a varied group of people and may include those that are physically handicapped, visually impaired, partially impaired, albinos, deaf and dumb, dwarfs, and those with learning or cognitive disabilities etc. [3].

© Springer Nature Switzerland AG 2020
A. Sundqvist et al. (Eds.): iConference 2020, LNCS 12051, pp. 487–494, 2020.
https://doi.org/10.1007/978-3-030-43687-2_39

According to the World Bank report [4], 15% of the world's population experience some form of disability, with the highest occurrence in developing countries. In Uganda, where this study was conducted, 16% of the country's population includes persons with disabilities [2]. A number of laws and policies pertaining to persons with disabilities have been adopted including those that address their right to access public and private buildings and information. In institutions of higher education, persons with disabilities are enrolled in different programs. This means that these institutions should be in a position to meet different needs of persons with disabilities at each given point of service. One important area of focus is the library building and the inclusive spaces. The importance of access to physical library spaces cannot be neglected, especially in developing countries where students have different literacy levels and meet a variety of pedagogical approaches. Availability of digital resources, though alleviating some access problems, cannot reduce the need for physical spaces in libraries. So, the needs of students with disability should be taken into account, though libraries meet a number of challenges, not least the budget cuts that reduce their ability to introduce necessary measures.

There are several options offered in library space design that promote social, educational and cultural activities. Digitalization of higher education also brings special demands on library as a place where computer equipment has to be provided or brought in by users. A library becomes an ecosystem of digital and analogue media, equipment and users. As library physical space evolves, emphasis should be put on increasing learning spaces, which are responsive, flexible, convenient, adaptive, accommodating, welcoming and extensible "spaces that meet the needs of SWDs as well. These characteristics may be encompassed in the qualities of library spaces i.e. functional, adaptable, accessible, varied, interactive, conducive, environmentally suitable, safe and secure, efficient, suitable for information technology, these qualities are intended for any form of space" [5].

The designs of library spaces are dictated by the needs of the users, therefore libraries should provide a comfortable, accessible and desirable environment for users, including students with disabilities. Based on a study that dates back in the 1980s, students' with disabilities access to the library buildings is not limited by the individual inability but rather by the limited facilities such as walk paths and ramps that favor the disabled users [6]. This perspective corresponds well with the understanding of disability as the environmental limitation, rather than personal [7]. Therefore, it is imperative for academic libraries to provide architectural designs and spaces that are more inviting to all.

Although academic libraries have created spaces based on users' needs and requirements, an on-going concern is how these spaces interface with users with disabilities and how they enhance their perception of physical library space [8, 9]. In this context, we take a normative stance to the accessibility of library spaces by focusing on the following research Questions:

1. What are the perceptions of library users about the architectural designs of library buildings?
2. What are the experiences of students with disabilities within library spaces?

2   Literature Review

International Federation of Library Institutions and Associations (IFLA) developed Library Building guidelines for planning and designing libraries. Though not set standards, they offer insights that can be used by the implementing libraries [10]. Constructing, extending or restructuring a library building requires planning in order for it to be successful [11]. IFLA PWD checklist ensures that persons with disabilities are presented with equal opportunities to access the libraries without any hindrances, it focuses on three aspects: physical access (outside and inside the library building), access to materials, and access to services. [12]. This paper focuses on physical access.

[13] have noted that library space plays an important role in helping the library achieve its user-centric goal therefore space planning and designing should focus on user habits, requirements and preferences. The library as place consists of the physical space where users display their experiences and behavior while using the space that is meant to be convenient and offering a pleasant experience to all [14]. Library should offer adaptable spaces that accommodate different modes of learning as well as different learners. Inclusion of students with disabilities in all aspects of life pertaining to their education is imperative if they have to achieve their information aims. Academic libraries have reported designing services specifically for students with disabilities; however, there is a need to assess the accessibility of their buildings [12].

Academic libraries should put in place conducive surroundings, pictograms, and reachable shelves, aisles, ramps, elevators favorable for users in wheelchairs. This would facilitate access to library services and resources. In Iran, the absence of ramps and parking spaces was as an important factor hindering access into library buildings [15]. Similarly, a study [16] at the University of Limpopo in South Africa revealed that the library didn't have adequate shelves and that most students with disabilities were observed struggling to browse through them. [17] also emphasized that library buildings should provide suitable and user-friendly layouts with adequate elevators, rails, sizeable doors, washrooms specifically designed for students with disabilities.

Space designs have an effect on what users can do, how they move and communicate while using the space [18]. Spaces created with users in mind are aimed at eliminating access barriers by creating an environment where users easily participate equally, confidently and independently [3]. Meeting the participation and accessibility needs of students with disabilities is dependent on how the individual libraries creatively and innovatively design and create spaces. Re-echoing Goldman's statement, "Persons with disabilities must be able to enjoy the psychological aspects of a structure, not only the individual points or planes within it" (as cited in [3], p. 19]). Students with disabilities should be able to feel an emotional attachment to using a particular space as well as a sense of belonging. [19], suggested five principles for building an inclusive space:

1. "Inclusive designs place people at the heart of the design"- indicate the importance of consultations with space inhabitants. How then can they accommodate all one may ask?

2. Through creating "Inclusive designs that acknowledge diversity and difference"- appreciated spaces meet the needs of many people without limiting access to only a few.
3. Inclusive designs should offer choice to all users - Different users should be allowed to choose which spaces they want to use at a particular time without any limitation.
4. Everybody enjoys using spaces that are convenient and can support their activities at any given time, inclusive spaces should be as convenient as possible.
5. Flexibility should be considered while designing inclusive space: users should be given an opportunity to use the space for their changing needs and not force themselves to fit into the already built and available spaces.

2.1   Context of the Research

Library building policies for students with disabilities vary from country to country. In Uganda, the Constitution advocates for elimination of discrimination against people with disabilities. Persons with Disabilities Act, section 19 stipulates that all PWDs should have access to buildings and that every building owner shall be responsible for providing suitable features, particularly the act emphasizes easy to use entrance and exit, access to parking areas, accessible washrooms, supportive staircases and ramps, elevators, embossed signage etc. as a measure to eliminate access restrictions.

3   Methods

This study is part of a larger study on physical space utilization in academic libraries. It used qualitative data collection methods particularly participant observations and in-depth interviews with library users. This study was conducted in four University libraries in Uganda i.e. Makerere University (Maklib), Uganda Christian University (Hamlib), Kampala International University (IBML) and Ndejje University Libraries. Data collected using participant observations utilized the IFLA disability checklist with the aim of investigating the appropriateness of the library building and spaces for Students with Disabilities (SWDs). The period of observation was from 28th May 2019 to December 2019. During the observation period, participants were asked questions in relation to architectural designs. An in-depth interview was then scheduled with those who were purposively selected as frequent users. 23 In-depth interviews were conducted and out of those 6 users were SWDs (2 physical disabilities, 1 Albino, 2 Partial visual impaired, 1 deaf and dumb). Credibility in this study was ensured by prolonged engagement with students with disabilities while asking several questions regarding topics on library spaces and probing participants to support their answers. Methodological triangulation using observations, short and in-depth interviews was applied. Data was analyzed using Atlas-Ti software by thematic analysis method generating themes related to the research questions. The researchers obtained both the Makerere university Ethical and Uganda National Council of Science and Technology clearances.

4 Findings and Discussions

Results are presented in Sect. 4.1; provides a brief overview of participants. The main findings will then be described in Sects. 4.1 and 4.2. Access and usage, coping strategies emerged as themes. This section combines results from participant observation and In-depth interviews (Table 1).

Table 1. Participant categories

Category	Gender	Participants
Library users	F(4) M(13)	P1-17
Students with disabilities	F(1) M(5)	P1-IDIPWD-P6-IDIPWD

Note: That the study was voluntary and that only those who agreed to be included in the study were considered for participation.

As we observed the library building, different libraries had ramps, elevators, high shelves and signage, thus, it was possible for Students with disabilities (SWDs) to access the library premises at least to the ground floor. It was noted that some academic library had special spaces for SWDs with supportive facilities and equipment. In addition, printed signs were visible within the spaces but these were only favorable for users without form of visual impairment.

4.1 Access and Usage

This section outlines how participants talked about the library spaces as a facility that facilitates access to and usage of resources. Several sub-themes emerged as discussed below:

Universal Design Features. The notion of universality of spaces was repeatedly brought about by the participants. Participants indicated that the library limited access to spaces, and resources such as textbooks and digital resources; they indicated that the spaces were not ideal for SWDs because of the inaccessible design features:

"...if a PWD wanted to use the floor above, how do they get there? I don't see any ramps for them so they are not ideal...even for the blind I don't see any services...so I would recommend anybody else to use the library but not PWDs because they won't be supported given that their resources are not there..." (P2-IDI).

Here the library spaces and resources are seen as exclusive and limited to users with disabilities. Many students with disabilities indicated to be affected by the architectural designs which do not respond to their needs and physical challenges hence creating an access barrier [20].

"...students with disabilities, in wheelchairs do not have access to certain places within the library, the only level you will access in a wheelchair is the 3rd floor of the main library... and the lift is not working... That makes it so hard for a student in a wheelchair to access it" (P2-IDI PWD).

The data revealed that library users were comfortable using a particular space if access to the physical library materials was guaranteed. However, the SWDs accessed the spaces because they were designated for them regardless of whether their needs were met or not while within those spaces:

"... I am confined to this space basically because of the presumption and the mental setup that it is space which is good for "these people" [P2-IDPWD].

Although academic libraries have made effort to create and design spaces for students with disabilities, these spaces are perceived as limiting and that for SWDs to enjoy comfort within the library, convenience and access to all library spaces should be guaranteed as an assurance for full participation [16].

Besides, participants also revealed that, the tables and chairs were not properly aligned and therefore they experienced challenges while writing because the chairs could not elevate them to the table level:

"...I also want my writing position to be good, I don't want to sit on a lower level and stretch my hand to write on the table. The chairs in the law level don't get me to the level of comfort while writing so I have to go to that level for that reason" [P1-IDI].

Inept dimensions of furniture provide writing difficulty to the users' especially to students with physical disabilities. In such incidences, the users' would find spaces with the furniture that suit their requirements. It is so unfortunate for some Students with Disabilities (SWDs) whose engagements are limited to specific spaces and this can't warrant change of space as echoed by [3].

Signage. Some participants urge that creating appropriate signage is important for all users, in such a case, all the academic libraries had signs written in print and fonts that are not easily visible by all, and this doesn't cater for Students who are visually impaired as echoed by one of the participants:

"...such printed signs are not relevant to visually impaired users...I think they should find a way to make signs that suit even those who can't read" [P3-IDI PWD).

On the other hand, a participant with hearing impairment (deaf and dumb) indicates that he is not able to access any resources while in the library because the library staff do not know sign language:

"...I am deaf and dumb and therefore I have a communication barrier because the librarians don't know sign language therefore it is difficult for me to access any library resources or services" (P6-IDIPWD).

Thus, serving students with sign language is a communication avenue that librarians should take for equitable access to information among users with hearing impairment [21]. Space planning and designing should include an inclusive approach in order to remove all access and usage barriers. To the other participants, the choice of space is influenced by its accessibility, they indicated that their choice of space is not limited to the different space attributes but rather to the kind of disability one has. It is from experience that SWDs devised coping strategies as will be presented in the next section.

4.2 Coping Strategies for Students with Disabilities

Several challenges are experienced by SWDs within library spaces. Participants described a number of coping strategies that they have used. In-depth interviews indicated using alternative spaces such as ground floor, digital spaces and their residences. Some do not agree with these strategies and they indicate that there is need for inclusive spaces. However, they appreciate the fact that library management designated spaces for SWDs, this offers them a sense of belonging and acceptance hence satisfaction. Although another participant argues that for space to be satisfactory, it has to be accessible to all and not a particular group. His argument was based on the fact the designated space accommodates SWDs and therefore limits their engagement with other users who don't have permission to access the same space. The coping strategies employed by the students with disabilities are intended to reduce on access barriers within both the physical and virtual spaces. This underlying effort doesn't eliminate the unsatisfactory perception of students with disabilities about the limiting architectural designs.

5 Conclusion

Academic libraries play a major role in meeting the information as well as space needs of SWDs. Innovations are evident in the different spaces, but little effort has been put to ensure that students with disabilities are inclusively represented in these spaces. Although the general perception and views of the participants seemed to indicate that the library has done well towards developing library spaces created spaces for SWDs some architectural hindrances have excluded Students with disabilities from accessing and navigating different spaces. In short, for students with disabilities access and usage are mainly influenced by architectural designs, universal designs and signage creates a convenient, comfortable and sustainable library experience. The use of alternative spaces by SWDs is a way of creating sustainable spaces that support their needs and requirements.

References

1. Freeman, G.T.: The Library as Place: Rethinking Roles, Rethinking Spaces. Council on Library and Information Resources, Washington, D.C. (2005)
2. The Persons with Disabilities Act: Ministry of Gender. Labour and Social Development, Kampala, Uganda (2006)
3. Morena, M., Truppi, T.: Inclusive Design-Architecture for Everyone. https://www.politesi.polimi.it/bitstream/10589/19143/1/Inclusive%20design%20-%20Architecture%20for%20Everyone.pdf. Accessed 6 Sept 2019
4. World Bank. https://www.worldbank.org/en/topic/disability. Accessed 6 Sept 2019
5. McDonald, A.: The ten commandments revisted: the qualities of good library space. LIBER Q. 6(2) (2006). http://doi.org/10.18352/lq.7840
6. Finkelstein, V.: Attitudes and Disabled People: Issues for Discussion. World Rehabilitation Fund, New York (1980)
7. Visagie, S.: Factors related to environmental barriers experienced by persons with and without disabilities in diverse African settings. PLoS One 12(10), 1–14 (2017)
8. Simon, M.: US Projects and Trends: Better Library and Learning Space: Projects, Trends and Ideas. Facet, London (2013)

9. Watson, L., Howden, J.: UK Projects and Trends, Better Library and Learning Space: Projects, Trends, Ideas. Facet, London (2013)
10. Saur, K.G.M.: IFLA Library Building Guidelines: Developments & Reflections. Strauss GmbH, Biebergemünd (2007)
11. Bisbrouck, M.F.: Evaluation of university library buildings in France, the second survey (2000–2007). LIBER Q. **18**(2), 209–229 (2008)
12. Irvall, B., Nielsen, G.S.: Access to Libraries for Persons with Disabilities: A Checklist. International Federation of Library Associations, The Hague (2005)
13. Beard, J., Dale, P.: Library design, learning spaces and academic literacy. New Libr. World **111**(11/12), 480–492 (2010)
14. Cocciolo, A.: Alleviating physical space constraints using virtual space?: A study from an urban academic library. Library Hi Tech **28**(4), 523–535 (2010)
15. Forrest, M.: Towards an accessible academic library: using the IFLA checklist. IFLA J. **32** (13), 13–18 (2006)
16. Phukubje, J., Ngoepe, M.: Convenience and accessibility of library services to students with disabilities at the University of Limpopo in South Africa. J. Librarianship Inf. Sci. **49**(2), 180–190 (2016)
17. Uzohue, C.E., Yaya, J.A.: Provision of library and information services to the visually impaired pupils in Pacelli school for the Blind, Lagos, Nigeria. Biomed. Health Inform. **1**(1), 1–5 (2016)
18. Lefebvre, H.: The Production of Space. Blackwell, Oxford (1991)
19. Fletcher, H.: The principles of inclusive design (they include you). https://www.designcouncil.org.uk/sites/default/files/asset/document/the-principles-of-inclusive-design.pdf. Accessed 5 Sept 2019
20. Scheer, J., Kroll, T., Neri, M.T., Beatty, P.: Access barriers for persons with disabilities: the consumer's perspective. J. Disabil. Policy Stud. **13**(4), 221–230 (2003)
21. IFLA: Guidelines for Library Services to Deaf People, 2nd edn. International Federation of Library Associations and Institutions, The Hague (2000)

Education

Expanding the REU Model Within an iSchool Context: Exploring iConference's Potential Role in Addressing Underrepresentation

Kayla M. Booth[1,6]([✉]), Elizabeth V. Eikey[2,6], Joe Sanchez[3,6],
Josue Figueroa[4,6], and Aderinsola Falana[5,6]

[1] University of Pittsburgh, Pittsburgh, PA 15213, USA
kbooth@pitt.edu
[2] University of California, San Diego, CA 92093, USA
[3] Queens College, Flushing, NY 11367, USA
[4] University of Michigan, Ann Arbor, MI 48109, USA
[5] Highmark Inc., Pittsburgh, PA 15222, USA
[6] The iSchool Inclusion Institute (i3), Pittsburgh, PA 15213, USA

Abstract. This paper briefly explores the extant literature surrounding both the potential and critiques of undergraduate research initiatives built to address underrepresentation and develop pipelines for underrepresented students into graduate programs within the information (and related) fields. We then discuss one particular US-based iSchool program whose structure aims to address common criticisms and embeds presenting research at iConference into its curriculum. While not a formal study, this paper presents students' reflections that emerged during program evaluation, discusses potential implications and next steps to systematically examine the role iConference, and perhaps other conferences, may play in addressing underrepresentation.

Keywords: Undergraduate research · Diversity · Inclusion · Recruitment and retention · iSchool education

1 Introduction

Within the United States (US), the computer, information, and library sciences are widely regarded as suffering from severe underrepresentation in terms of the undergraduate students, graduate students, and faculty who are successfully recruited and retained within these disciplines [1–4]. Underrepresentation refers to the misalignment between the who lives in the US and who is represented in these fields and professions. The US population is comprised of approximately 50% women and 38% underrepresented racial and ethnic populations (e.g., Hispanic, Black, American Indian/Alaskan Native, Native Hawaiian/Pacific Islander, Multiracial), yet the faculty and student populations across these fields are largely homogenous in terms of race/ethnicity and gender [5]. Computer and information science are largely comprised of white men. As of 2017, over 80% of PhDs awarded in computing and information fields were awarded to men, and American Indian/Alaskan Native, Black, and Hispanic students earned less than 4% of all PhDs in those fields [6]. Master's degree programs mirror these

© Springer Nature Switzerland AG 2020
A. Sundqvist et al. (Eds.): iConference 2020, LNCS 12051, pp. 497–510, 2020.
https://doi.org/10.1007/978-3-030-43687-2_40

demographics [6]. Similarly, library science is dominated by white women who make up 73% of university credentialed librarians, while only 11% of university credentialed librarians identify as Latino, African American, Asian, Pacific Islander, or Native American [4].

Homogeneity and underrepresentation in these fields has dire consequences, including but not limited to: the development of products and technical solutions that neglect the needs of those not represented, the embedding of cultural bias in technology, stifled innovation, failure to fill jobs in an expanding market, an inability to understand the very communities librarians are meant to serve, and exacerbating social inequality [3–5, 7, 8]. As a result of these consequences, many scholars, corporations, and government entities have developed and implemented a multitude of interventions aimed at addressing underrepresentation and broadening participation across these fields. This paper is particularly focused on academic and university-led initiatives.

iSchools and other computer, information, and library science entities have developed and implemented a myriad of interventions to address underrepresentation within their domains. Many of these interventions are designed to address recruitment (who is being recruited into academic programs and faculty application pools) and/or retention (who remains and matriculates to graduation or promotion). Some initiatives are implemented at the administrative level and are designed to address systemic barriers and policies (e.g., auditing curriculum to embed equity and inclusivity, developing diversity and pedagogical training for faculty, assessing salary equity, evaluating student admissions and faculty search processes) [7, 9]; other initiatives work directly with students in order to recruit them into undergraduate and graduate programs and/or retain them through graduation. This paper focuses on the latter, specifically student-facing initiatives aimed at recruiting and retaining undergraduate students from underrepresented populations, as this is often the earliest stage of higher education and students' engagement with a university.

One of the most common academic initiatives to address underrepresentation in these fields is the development of undergraduate research opportunities, such as Research Experiences for Undergraduates (REUs). Participation in and engagement with research is suggested to increase undergraduate students' retention within their major, understanding of their discipline, and grade point averages (GPAs), while also building direct pipelines into graduate programs through exposure and experience [10–12]. These experiences may be particularly helpful in reducing some of the barriers underrepresented students often experience within information and computing fields, such as less access to faculty role-models and mentors [3, 12].

This paper briefly explores the extant literature surrounding both the potential and critiques of undergraduate research initiatives. Within these initiatives, this paper focuses on those built to address underrepresentation and develop pipelines for underrepresented students into graduate programs within the information (and related) fields. Following this overview, we then discuss one particular US-based iSchool program whose structure aims to address common criticisms and embeds presenting research at iConference into its curriculum. While not a formal study, this paper presents students' reflections that emerged during program evaluation, discusses potential implications and next steps to systematically examine the role iConference, and perhaps other conferences, may play in addressing underrepresentation.

2 Background

2.1 Research Experiences for Undergraduates (REUs)

REU Overview. As previously discussed, engaging in research may increase rates of undergraduate retention, build recruitment pipelines into graduate programs, develop students' problem-solving and collaboration skills, and increase students' comprehension of the research process, graduate school/career opportunities, and their field of study [1–3, 11, 12]. As a result, many academic schools and departments within the information sciences and related disciplines have implemented opportunities for undergraduates to formally participate in research. Similarly, federal agencies have developed funding opportunities to support these initiatives. For example, in the United States, the National Science Foundation (NSF) currently funds almost 100 Research Experiences for Undergraduates (REUs) sites at various colleges and universities across the country, specifically within computing-related fields. While these programs are often open to all students, NSF specifically states that, "REU projects offer an opportunity to tap the nation's diverse student talent pool and broaden participation in science and engineering," and that they are "…particularly interested in increasing the numbers of women, underrepresented minorities, and persons with disabilities in research. REU projects are strongly encouraged to involve students who are members of these groups. (Underrepresented minorities are African Americans, Hispanics, American Indians, Alaska Natives, and Native Hawaiians or Other Pacific Islanders.) …" [13].

REU Program Structure. While the exact structure of each REU varies, these federally funded initiatives typically have several core elements built into their models based on NSF requirements and guidelines. The majority of REUs:

- Recruit students nationally across colleges and universities
- Employ a cohort-based model in which students begin, experience, and conclude their REU participation together
- Provide funding for student travel, housing, and stipends
- Take place during the summer (although some take place during the academic year)
- Are structured around students participating in ongoing research projects or projects specifically designed for the REU experience
- Formally connect participating students with role models and mentors to guide their learning and research experiences
- Embed an element where students present their work to an audience

Critiques of Undergraduate Research Initiatives. There are a myriad of studies examining the successes that individual undergraduate research initiatives and their participants experience. However, several scholars point out that these initiatives, along with other interventions with similar goals, have ultimately failed to move the needle when it comes to addressing underrepresentation across computer, information, and library sciences [4, 7, 14]. Some scholars point out that while these cohort-based initiatives have tremendous impact on individuals, they are challenging to fund long-term and difficult to scale in ways that would create a statistical shift [X]. Both cohort-based research and scholarship programs show promising results in terms of recruitment and retention on an individual level, but there are administrative and financial barriers to scaling. For example, NSF typically funds REU sites on average between three to five years and cohort-based programs are limited in the number in the number of students they can accept each year.

In addition to funding and scalability limitations, cohort-based research programs typically only have one point of contact in which cohorts are together collaborating (often during a summer institute). These initiatives operate separately across undergraduate, graduate, and professional contexts and provide little continuity across students' education and careers. Programs that are built on a singular point of interaction (e.g. a ten-week summer institute) are sometimes considered to be "one and done" initiatives without long-term infrastructure of support. Some scholars point out that this approach speaks to a larger issue of the tendency for institutions and organizations to treat diversity and inclusion initiatives as "bolted-on" rather than "built-in." That is to say, diversity initiatives are often added as afterthoughts separate from an organization's main activities, rather than "built-in" from the beginning as institution's core value that is deeply embedded into all business processes [3]. This often leads to disjointed efforts that successfully recruit underrepresented students into graduate programs, who may experience feeling abandoned and forgotten once they begin their graduate careers [4, 7, 14]. This withdrawal of support can be particularly jarring given the hostility, isolation, and othering many Professionals of Color experience at work and within the field. Gaps in support and feelings of isolation are major barriers to retention [6, 7, 9], and successfully recruiting underrepresented individuals into the field profession means little if programs fail to retain them [8, 9].

2.2   The iSchool Inclusion Institute (i3)

The previous section outlined the successes, structures, and critiques surrounding undergraduate research initiatives. This section, however, focuses on a single undergraduate research program designed to combat underrepresentation specifically within an iSchool context. Uniquely aligned with this year's conference theme, Sustainable Digital Communities, this program expands the traditional REU model by leveraging both digital communication tools and multiple points of contact (including iConference) to develop and *sustain* a sense of community and belonging amongst its participants and alumni. This extended model seeks to foster long-term community and relationships to combat the isolation underrepresented students often experience within the information, computer, and library sciences.

Program Overview. Now in its tenth year, The iSchool Inclusion Institute (i3) is an undergraduate research and leadership development program designed to prepare students from underrepresented populations for graduate study and careers in the information sciences (IS). Each year, 25 undergraduate students from a myriad of colleges and universities across the country are selected in a nationwide search to become i3 Scholars. Each year, cohorts are comprised of students enrolled in majors across social science, humanities, and STEM majors. To date, 210 students have participated in i3.

Program Structure. While i3 is not federally funded or considered a traditional REU, its structure shares several foundational features with their model. Students are recruited as part of a national search to participate in a cohort-based research experience, funding is provided for student travel, housing, meals, and stipends, and students are actively connected to role models and mentors throughout the program.

Despite these similarities, there are some intentional differences in i3's structure that aim to address the aforementioned critiques of single points of contact or "one and done" approaches. Rather than taking place over a single summer or semester, the undergraduate research experience takes place over the course of 20 months. Students first attend a summer-long institute introducing them to the information sciences, research design, computational thinking and tools, and professional development. Upon returning to their home institutions, they work in distributed teams on a guided, yearlong research project with a mentor and return to i3 the following summer to "put the pieces together" and present their work. While at their home institutions, students' communication, collaboration, and relationship building is supported via digital platforms. These include Slack and Basecamp for project management, Skype and Google Hangouts for their weekly team meetings with their research mentors, and private i3-specific Snapchat and Facebook groups used by not only their cohort, but alumni from previous cohorts to promote cross-generational community building.

The i3 model is also unique in its multiple points of contact built into the 20-month program structure, which is meant to foster community and relationship building amongst the cohorts and mentors over an extended period of time. In addition to the two summer institutes, students submit their preliminary work to iConference after Summer 1 and their final projects after Summer 2. With the opportunity for each i3 Scholar to attend and present in back-to-back years, iConference plays a pivotal role in i3's mission to address underrepresentation in the information sciences. Rather than presenting in a space designed for the program or highlighting specifically undergraduate research, students interact with and present their work in the same spaces as graduate students and faculty in the IS field. While operating within similar budgetary constraints, i3 expands the "one and done" model by leveraging digital platforms and iConference to build a twenty-month long infrastructure that centers community building and support.

Program Evaluation. i3's success is annually evaluated based on a series of metrics including retention across the program's 20-month structure, acceptance, enrollment and completion rates in iSchool graduate programs, students' peer-reviewed publications, and a series of student and alumni surveys.

While iConference has always been an important touch-point for i3 Scholars to reunite and present their work, more and more i3 Scholars are submitting their work and attending year after year. A total of 50 i3 projects have been presented at the conference.

Based on this evolution, program administrators expanded program evaluation to include a survey post-iConference 2019 in order to: (1) Understand i3 Scholars' experiences and strategies surrounding their participation in iConference, and (2) assess how and to what extent students attending and presenting at iConference supports the program's ultimate goal of increasing the recruitment and retention of underrepresented students in information science graduate programs and faculty careers. It is important to note that this paper is not presenting a formal research study, but rather discussing preliminary program evaluation data as they relate to combating underrepresentation within the iSchools and information field. This paper outlines potential implications, limitations, and areas for future work to more systematically explore these preliminary insights.

3   Evaluation Methods

As previously discussed, i3 is evaluated via a myriad of metrics and tools. This paper specifically focuses on the preliminary program evaluation data collected and analyzed to understand students' experiences at and strategies for navigating iConference, as well as to what extent their participation supports the program's ultimate goal.

3.1   Survey Instrument

A survey designed in Qualtrics was sent to all i3 Scholars who participated in iConference 2019 via email. This survey was divided into two parts.

Part one of the survey contained a series of open-ended questions developed to encourage participants to reflect on their experiences and strategies surrounding their participation in iConference. Questions were developed to understand their feelings and preparation strategies leading up to the conference, their experiences and navigation strategies during the conference, and their perceptions of how their iConference experience impacted their future plans.

Part two of the survey was designed to assess the extent to which students' participation in and experiences at iConference aligned with and support the program goal of addressing underrepresentation in the information sciences. The program aims to increase students' confidence and skills surrounding research, interest in applying to graduate school, and understanding of the information sciences, all of which informed the survey questions. Using a 5-point Likert scale (1-Strongly Disagree to 5-Strongly Agree), participants were asked to first reflect on how they felt before they attended iConference and then asked to reflect on how they feel now that they have attended iConference (e.g., "Before attending iConference, I felt confident in my ability to…") on eight dimensions (i.e., presenting a paper, presenting a poster, networking with faculty, networking with students, ask speakers questions, conduct research, be part of the information science community, and attend graduate school). Likert scales were chosen to provide a quantitative assessment that we could compare across cohorts as part of our program evaluation data. To provide space for reflection and explanation, participants were also asked open-ended questions about how their iConference experience affected how their feelings about graduate school, their careers, research, and the information sciences.

The survey was sent to students after iConference 2019 concluded on April 2, 2019 and all responses were completed between April 5–10, 2019. As part of program evaluation, participants were given the options to skip questions and to remain anonymous.

The full survey instrument (including the open-ended questions and scales) were developed as standard data collection procedures for our program evaluation. The program evaluation survey discussed in this paper has two goals. The first is to assess the alignment between our students' needs/strategies and the guidance our program provides. For example, as part of the preparation for iConference, we provided students with a two-part webinar series about how to secure travel funding and how to navigate academic conferences. During the conference, we also provided support in the form of group meetings as well as practice paper and poster presentations. Therefore, we asked questions to understand what was most effective from students' perspectives in preparing them for this conference. Our second program evaluation goal is to assess how and the extent to which students' iConference experiences supports the program's ultimate goal of recruiting and retaining i3 Scholars into graduate study and careers within the field. We leveraged ten years of data from our scholars to develop other questions, including the aforementioned eight dimensions. These areas have been standardized as part of reporting and aim to assess self-efficacy around important conference aspects (presenting and networking) and general sense of belonging, which are all key to retaining individuals from underrepresented backgrounds in the information sciences.

3.2 Analysis

Survey data were organized and analyzed in Excel. Open-ended responses were analyzed via inductive, thematic coding. For each open-ended question, two of the authors identified recurring themes across responses. The authors iteratively discussed and organized each response by which theme it aligned with, iteratively refining the themes throughout the analysis. Because our quantitative data are descriptive, we computed and report frequencies.

4 Findings

Sixteen out of the 23 students who attended iConference 2019 as part of i3 participated in the survey (approximately 70% response rate). All student respondents presented either a poster or a paper at iConference, with some of them also participating in the Undergraduate Symposium. Of the 13 who specified their type of participation, six presented a poster, seven presented a paper, and six participated in the Undergraduate Symposium. For the majority of students who filled out the question (n = 9/13), this was their first iConference experience, followed by four who had attended one other iConference before this one as part of the i3 program.

4.1 Experiences and Preparation Strategies Prior to iConference

To aid in the continuous improvement of program infrastructure surrounding iConference, participants were asked about their experiences and preparation strategies leading up to iConference after their acceptance notification, but prior to their arrival. Specifically, participants were asked to reflect on their excitement, fears, and expectations, as well as the preparation strategies they employed.

In response to an open-ended question asking students to describe what they were most excited about prior to attending iConference, all 16 participants indicated that they had been looking forward to one or more of the following: (1) reconnecting with their i3 cohort (n = 11/16), (2) presenting their research (n = 6/16), (3) networking (n = 4/16), learning more about the iSchools and information science (n = 3/16), and experiencing a new location (n = 2/16). The most common source of excitement across responses was reuniting with their cohort and colleagues. Many participants had not seen their i3 colleagues in-person since the previous summer (eight months prior to the conference). While students meet via video call each week with their teammates and communicate with the rest of their cohort and program alumni throughout the year via formal and informal digital channels (e.g., Slack, SnapChat, Basecamp, etc.), several responses emphasized feeling excitement about seeing everyone together face-to-face. For example, one respondent exclaimed, *"Seeing my team in person!"* was the aspect of iConference they were most excited for.

In addition to reuniting with their i3 colleagues, six participants indicated that they were excited to present their research. Several participants specifically mentioned that they were excited to receive quality feedback. One participant explained that they thought this experience would be markedly different than the feedback they receive at their home institution, stating, *"...If I gave a presentation in school, the questions/feedback I got after that presentation was very high-level and not particularly useful in terms of taking it into consideration and using the guidance for future endeavors. I knew iConference would be different. The feedback I would receive on our team poster would be thoughtful, critical, and aimed towards making adaptations and coming from a place of reason."* Similarly, participants were excited to network with researchers in the field (n = 4) and learn more about the iSchools and information science (n = 3). One participant reflected, *"I was excited to network with people who are directly related to my future plans. What an amazing opportunity to speak DIRECTLY to the dean of an iSchool (this happened with Michigan and Drexel) who would be reading my application 8 months from then. It's barely even hyperbole to say there literally is no opportunity better than that."* Students were excited to have the opportunity to present to, receive individualized feedback from, and interact with scholars in the field and at the iSchools they intend to apply for graduate school.

In addition to their sources of excitement, participants were also asked to reflect on what (if anything) they were nervous about prior to attending iConference. All 16 participants responded. Almost every participant (n = 15/16) reported feeling nervous about one or more of the following themes: (1) presenting (8/16), (2) networking (n = 5/16), (3) finances (n = 2/16), and navigating the conference and time-management (n = 2/16). Participants reported presenting and networking as two of the top three things they were both excited *and* nervous about prior to attending the conference. An emergent theme across responses was that their nervousness stemmed from uncertainty about what language and research terminology to use when talking to faculty and graduate students. For example, one participant explained, *"I was primarily concerned with using the correct terminology when people asked me questions about my poster. An example of this could be if someone who was more knowledgeable than myself was asking about our methods, I wanted to make sure I could accurately reproduce exactly what we did in a way that was appropriate for the audience. I know that I knew my stuff, but I wanted to make sure I was explaining it in a way that['s] 'normal' in the research world. (inductive vs deductive, sentiment analysis, thematic analysis..stuff this like this)."* Many participants were excited to present and felt that they understood their research, but were nervous about communicating appropriately to their "more seasoned" and experienced audience.

When asked how they prepared for iConference, all sixteen participants indicated that one or more of the following helped them prepare: (1) i3 webinars (n = 9), (2) working with i3 mentors (n = 7), (3) developing materials (n = 4), (4) practicing presentations (n = 4), (5) seeking feedback or advice from i3 Scholars (n = 2), and (6) feeling confident about their research (n = 1). More than half of participants directly mentioned the two webinars i3 hosted prior to the conference. The first was hosted after acceptance decisions were announced and covered how to navigate funding, budgeting, and travel logistics. The second webinar was hosted one month prior to iConference and covered the format and schedule of the conference, presentation tips and guidelines, and items to pack and prepare. Several participants specifically indicated that the content surrounding the format of the conference and what was required of them was particularly helpful, with one participant stating, *"The webinar [helped me prepare] because it helped me understand what was expected of me and what to expect at the conference."* In addition to expectations, several participants reported that the act of preparing the specific materials outlined during the webinars together was particularly helpful. Participants specifically mentioned how useful it was to prepare business cards, their elevator pitches, and a list of people they want to meet based on their research interests and prospective graduate programs.

Participants also turned to their i3 network, including the program directors and research advisors (n = 7), as well as fellow i3 Scholars (n = 2). One participant responded that the program mentors *"gave us the ability to ask questions regardless of how strange or oddly specific they might seem."* Prior to their presentations and poster sessions, each team practiced their presentation with at least one i3 mentor. An emergent theme across responses was the role of the feedback during these sessions. One participant explained that their research advisor *"was able to tell us what to expect, test us on our knowledge, and then give honest feedback on the areas that needed improvement."*

4.2 Experiences During iConference

In order to understand students' experiences at iConference and assess whether this element of the program structure aligns with the program's goals, participants were asked to reflect on their experiences and navigation strategies at the conference. Participants were encouraged to consider what they liked and disliked, whether the conference was what they expected, what was interesting or surprising, what they found challenging, and the strategies they employed to overcome the challenges they faced. Thirteen out of 16 participants responded to these open-ended questions.

Participants also turned In terms of elements that surprised participants, two themes emerged across responses: (1) the breadth of research topics presented, and (2) the welcoming environment. The first and most common was the breadth of topics covered at iConference. For example, one participant reported, *"I did not expect to encounter so many different people from so many different parts of the world and hear about the various research that is being conducted in the field."* Participants were also surprised at how "friendly" faculty and graduate students were, with one individual stating that the conference was *"more diverse and welcoming than I expected it to be."* Several participants also noted that they were surprised at how interested graduate students and faculty were in their research.

In terms of challenges, once again, participants reported mixed emotions about networking. Six participants indicated that it was particularly challenging to network with strangers, while four indicated that they specifically enjoyed the networking aspect of the conference. When asked how they overcame any challenges they faced at iConference, eight participants indicated that talking with and being surrounded by i3 colleagues was the biggest source of support. While some responses indicated that their peers' general presence helped them feel more comfortable (*"nothing specific it was just being in the present of my i3 family"*), others explained that they worked with their colleagues to overcome the elements of the conference they found most challenging. In addition to practicing their presentations and soliciting feedback from their peers, some participants shared that they would network in small groups. For example, one participant said *"...sticking with other i3 people, I brought them with me to talk with professors."* While several participants indicated presenting and networking were difficult, being surrounded and supported by their i3 peers and navigating challenges together was an essential part of overcoming challenges.

Similarly, the majority of participants indicated that having their i3 colleagues with them enhanced their iConference experience. For example, one participant explained that *"iConference was an enjoyable experience on its own, but my i3 colleagues definitely made it better,"* while another expressed similar sentiments, stating *"It was a lot friendlier than I expected, but I am not sure how much that was due to the fact that I was surrounded and supported by my cohort and i3 throughout the event."*

4.3   iConference's Impact and Future Plans

When asked to reflect on how attending iConference influenced their confidence in their abilities on a Likert scale from 1 to 5, some striking trends emerged, as shown in Fig. 1 (below). We saw increases in reported confidence on all items (i.e., presenting, networking, asking speakers questions, conducting research, belonging, and attending graduate school) as students reflected on their perceptions before and after attending iConference. In terms of presenting at academic venues, only six of ten at least somewhat agreed that they were confident in their ability to present papers and only five of 11 in their ability to present posters before attending iConference. Whereas after iConference, these numbers increased to eight of ten and 11 of 11. We also saw increases in students' perceptions of their ability to network, with eight at least somewhat agreeing they were confident in networking with faculty and nine with students before attending iConference, jumping to 12 and 13, respectively after attending. Similarly, the number of students who felt confidence in asking speakers questions after presentations improved from eight to ten.

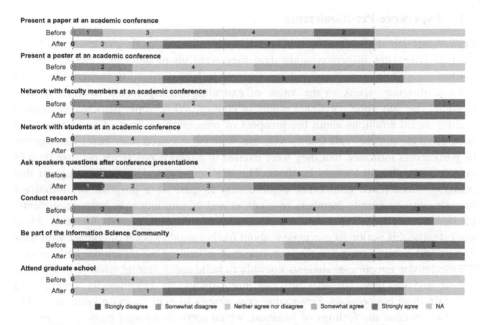

Fig. 1. Participants' perceptions of their abilities before and after iConference

We also saw increases in perceptions of ability to conduct research and attend graduate school from seven participants at least somewhat agreeing in their abilities prior to iConference and 11 (conduct research) and nine (attend graduate school) after having gone to the conference. Notably, we found a 53.85% change in perception of belonging. Before iConference, only six students at least somewhat agreed that they were confident in their ability to be part of the information science community, compared to all 13 (100%) after attending. Importantly, while before iConference some reported disagreeing about their confidence in their abilities to present papers and posters, network with faculty, conduct research, and be part of the information science community, we found that after iConference, no (0%) participants disagreed on any of those dimensions.

5 Discussion

i3 is an undergraduate research and leadership development program designed to combat underrepresentation and build inclusion within iSchools and the information sciences. This program extends the traditional REU model by leveraging digital communication and multiple points of contact (including iConference) in order to develop and maintain participants' sense of community and belonging that is critical to both recruitment and retention. Preliminary analysis of program evaluation data suggests that iConference may play an important role in cohort-based programs. These implications are discussed below.

5.1 Experience Pre-iConference

Prior to arriving at iConference, more participants reported that they were excited to see their i3 colleagues in-person again than they were about any other element of the conference. While it isn't unusual for students to look forward to reconnecting with friends, this may speak to the value of extending undergraduate research models beyond "one and done" or single points of contact. While some participants recalled feeling mixed emotions about the prospect of presenting in front of and networking with graduate students and faculty who are more experienced than them, the majority of participants indicated that they were excited to attend iConference because their i3 cohort and colleagues would be there. This preliminary evaluation data suggest that utilizing iConference (and other conferences) as part of a program or initiative's infrastructure to reunite members of a cohort and community may increase students' excitement about and participation in academic research and conferences. More importantly, this notion of excitement about having another point of contact with their cohort and mentors speaks to the importance of extending the traditional REU model. This extension encourages students not only to build and foster relationships with their cohort and mentors, but also provides infrastructure to intentionally support and maintain these connections. Leveraging conferences to help maintain systems of support may combat the feelings of isolation, which serve as a major barrier to retention within IS.

In addition to feeling excitement at the opportunity to reunite with their cohort and mentors, participants expressed mixed feelings towards presenting and networking. Participants who were excited to present and network at iConference specifically referenced looking forward to receiving meaningful feedback from faculty and engaging with faculty and leadership from graduate programs they are looking to apply to. It is possible that attending iConference and interacting with these individuals may help students feel like stronger applicants and gain a more nuanced sense of potential programs. Several students indicated that attending and presenting at iConference is a unique opportunity to pursue their academic goals, which suggests that iConference may play a role in increasing underrepresented students' sense of belonging.

For those who were nervous to network or present, several participants indicated that the program webinars helped them prepare for the conference and increase their confidence. This has two implications. The first is that leveraging digital communication tools may be a successful strategy in extending REU models and maintaining the mentorship and support underrepresented students are less likely to receive. The second is that simply adding conference attendance to undergraduate research initiatives is not enough - participation in conferences needs to be embedded within a larger infrastructure of support, preparation, and communication. This infrastructure also encourages long-term interactions between students and program mentors/research advisors, which may strengthen feelings of support and the ability to build trust.

5.2   Experience During iConference Experience

Participants were surprised at both the breadth of the research topics covered at iConference, as well as the friendliness of faculty, graduate students, and volunteers. iConference and other similarly interdisciplinary venues with broad ranges of topics may be opportunities for recruitment and retention. This myriad of topics at iConference may help students draw more personal connections to the field. Similarly, students were surprised that so many faculty and graduate students were interested in talking with them about their research. i3 Scholars were in a unique position in that they were not presenting their work at an undergraduate venue or in a special session dedicated to undergraduate researchers. Their work was submitted, evaluated, and accepted in the same way any experienced researchers' work is assessed and with the same criteria, which may foster an environment in which students can see themselves pursuing higher education and professional careers within the field.

i3 Scholars enjoyed spending time with their cohort and mentors, but also relied on those existing connections to develop strategies to help them overcome challenges they faced at the conference. Participants emphasized the importance of having their cohort members and mentors to practice their presentations with and to approach speakers in order to make connections. Underrepresented students often experience conferences as spaces in which they are the only person who looks like them, but i3 Scholars didn't experience that at their first and second conference experiences. Having a built-in systems of support at conferences can enhance feelings of belonging, which is essential in combating the isolation that underrepresented scholars often experience.

5.3   Impact and Future Plans

Participants reported perceived increases in confidence across research skills, interest in graduate school, and belonging in IS, all of which are the ultimate goals of the program. Participants indicated that being exposed to the vast array of topics within the information sciences and surrounded by scholars who were interested in their work increased their desire to apply to graduate school and their sense that they can belong within this academic community. iConference has the unique opportunity to serve as a space in which undergraduate researchers are introduced to and embedded within the larger scholarly community. As we talk about initiatives that are "built-in" to iSchools and universities rather than "bolted-on," iConference may play a pivotal role in "building" these initiatives into the larger information landscape.

6   Limitations and Future Work

As previously mentioned, this paper presents preliminary program evaluation data, rather than a completed research study. The survey was designed to evaluate a single program, rather than generalize to theory or a larger population. The survey was not administered before and after students attended iConference, thus the data points are not only limited in number, but only speak to participants' perceptions of the impact of their iConference experience. Future work will include a systematic examination of students' experiences incorporating a mixed methods approach to measure student's perceptions of their belonging and acceptance at the iSchool's conference and to understand the deeper experiences reported in the open-ended questions such as the significance of reconnecting with members of their cohorts. Open-ended interviews and formal field observations will be conducted to better define "belonging" and to further identify and classify the multiple layers of support students feel when they reconnect face to face.

Acknowledgements. The iSchool Inclusion Institute (i3) is funded by the Andrew W. Mellon Foundation. We would like to thank each of our participants and all i3 Scholars who have participated in the i3 program and iConference.

References

1. Cuny, J., Aspray, W.: Recruitment and retention of women graduate students in computer science and engineering: results of a workshop organized by the computing research association. SIGCSE Bull. **34**, 168–174 (2002)
2. Aspray, W., Bernat, A.: Recruitment and retention of underrepresented minority graduate students in computer science. In: Report on a Workshop by the Coalition to Diversity Computing (2000)
3. Redacted
4. Cooke, N.A.: Information Services to Diverse Populations: Developing Culturally Competent Library Professionals. ABC-CLIO, Santa Barbara (2016)
5. Women, Minorities, and Persons with Disabilities in Science and Engineering. National Science Foundation (2017). www.nsf.gov/statistics/wmpd/
6. Zweben, S., Bizot, B.: 2016 Taulbee survey: generation CS continues to produce record undergrad enrollment; graduate degree production rises at both master's and doctoral levels. Comput. Res. News **29** (2017). cra.org/crn
7. Jaeger, P.T., Cooke, N.A., Feltis, C., Hamiel, M., Jardine, F., Shilton, K.: The virtuous circle revisited: injecting diversity, inclusion, rights, justice, and equity into LIS from education to advocacy. Libr. Q. **85**(2), 150–171 (2015)
8. Townsend, G., Stewart, K.: Computing opportunities for students of color. In: Proceedings of the 2019 ACM Conference on Innovation and Technology in Computer Science Education, p. 324. ACM (2019)
9. Mason, S., Bailey, M., Wadia-Fascetti, S., Sorcinelli, M.D.: Advancing diversity and inclusivity in STEM education. In: Proceedings of the 17th Annual Conference on Information Technology Education, pp. 83–84. ACM (2016)
10. Peckham, J., Stephenson, P., Hervé, J.Y., Hutt, R., Encarnação, M.: Increasing student retention in computer science through research programs for undergraduates. ACM SIGCSE Bull. **39**(1), 124–128 (2007)
11. Dahlberg, T., Barnes, T., Rorrer, A., Powell, E., Cairco, L.: Improving retention and graduate recruitment through immersive research experiences for undergraduates. ACM SIGCSE Bull. **40**(1), 466–470 (2008)
12. Russell, H., Dye, H.: Promoting REU participation from students in underrepresented groups. Involve J. Math. **7**(3), 403–411 (2014)
13. NSF
14. IMLS

An Experience Report for Running an REU Program in an iSchool

Junhua Ding[✉], Jiangping Chen, Alexis Palmer, and Daniella Smith

University of North Texas, Denton, TX 76203, USA
{junhua.ding,jiangping.chen,alexis.palmer,daniella.smith}@unt.edu

Abstract. In this article, we report on our experiences and lessons learned from training undergraduate students in data science research in an iSchool, comparing this program to the experience of running a similar program in a computer science department. The undergraduate research training programs described were supported by the National Science Foundation (United States) through the Research Experiences for Undergraduates (REU) program. Through investigating the research tasks, reading materials, lectures, tutorials, research reports, publications, and project evaluation results, we summarize the differences in research focus of the same program running in an iSchool and in a Computer Science department. We develop a group of research activities that can be adopted for effectively training undergraduate researchers in an iSchool. Furthermore, we propose an enhancement of the undergraduate data science curriculum based on the experiences and lessons we learned from running the REU programs.

Keywords: Research Experiences for Undergraduates · Data analytics · Information retrieval · Computer science · Data science

1 Introduction

In this paper, we report our experience and lessons learned from training undergraduate students in research through the Research Experiences for Undergraduates (REU) program supported by the National Science Foundation (NSF) in the United States. Our particular REU site, at the University of North Texas, focuses on *Data Analytics and Information Retrieval* (DAIR) and is led by faculty with expertise in Information Science, Data Science, and Computational Linguistics. NSF's REU program as a whole supports undergraduate students to gain research experience in science and engineering disciplines by conducting guided research with research mentors in universities [3]. NSF's current REU program was established in 1987. A similar program called Undergraduate Research Participation Program ran from 1958 until it was abolished in 1982. There are two types of REU programs: REU site and REU supplementary. REU site program awards are independent awards that support a cohort of undergraduate

Supported by NSF award #1852249.

students to conduct research in a host university for 8 to 10 weeks. REU supplementary awards normally support individual undergraduate students to contribute to an ongoing research project through a supplement to a regular NSF award. This paper discusses only REU site programs.

REU site programs are supported by different directorates in NSF, including Engineering, Geosciences, Mathematical and Physical Sciences, and Computer and Information Science and Engineering (CISE). REU programs in computer science, information science, and data science are normally sponsored by the CISE directorate; this includes the REU programs discussed in this paper. Student participants in REU programs must be citizens, nationals, or permanent residents of the United States [3], as well as being a registered undergraduate student at a college or university. High school graduates who have been admitted by a university are also eligible to participate in the program. Most REU site programs run in summer semesters, with a few taking place in regular semesters. REU students are well paid for participating in the program. For example, each student participant receives a stipend of approximately $500 per week (figure from summer 2019; the stipend will be increased to $600 starting in 2020), in addition to lodging and meal allowances and travel support. The details of the REU program can be found at NSF website at: https://www.nsf.gov/funding/pgm_summ.jsp?pims_id=5517. Research results have shown that REU programs have great positive impacts on student participants choosing science and engineering as their graduate study fields or their future careers [16,17].

Admission to the program is quite competitive, with an average admission rate of about 10% for the REU site programs we ran during past 7 years.[1] According to the NSF website,[2] as of August 2019, the CISE directorate has supported a total of 98 REU site programs. These REU sites are hosted in different departments and at many different universities. Of the 98 CISE REU sites, 81 are hosted in computer science related departments such as departments of computer science, computer engineering, software engineering, and high performance computing centers; 6 are hosted in information science related departments or research centers. Among the 6 information science related departments, 4 are departments that include both computer science and information science, and 1 in a department of Informatics. None of these are designated iSchools. As of August 2019, the REU site on *Data Analytics and Information Retrieval* (DAIR host) at the University of North Texas (UNT) is the only CISE REU site that is hosted in an iSchool. The authors of this paper are also the co-principal investigators, each serving as either a faculty mentor or project evaluator for DAIR. The DAIR REU will run for three years, starting March 2019 and ending March 2022. Each summer, 10 undergraduate students selected from universities nationwide will conduct research for 10 weeks on the UNT campus, guided by the faculty mentors. Our first cohort of students came in summer 2019 and successfully completed several research projects.[3] In this paper, we share our

---

[1] The first author has been involved in multiple REU site programs, described below.
[2] https://www.nsf.gov/crssprgm/reu/list_result.jsp?unitid=5049.
[3] More information at the project website: https://reu.ci.unt.edu.

experience and lessons learned from running the REU program. One of the co-authors of this article was the principal investigator of two previous CISE REU site programs hosted in the department of Computer Science at East Carolina University (ECU) from March 2013 to March 2019. In this paper, we will compare how the research focuses and tasks, training objectives, and approaches differ between the REU programs hosted in a department of Computer Science, and that hosted in an iSchool. Based on the results of this comparison, as well as our related experiences, we propose a research training plan for running an REU in an iSchool. The plan also can be used for enhancing the current curriculum of undergraduate data science programs.

The rest of the paper is organized as follows: Sect. 2 describes the overarching objectives of CISE REU programs. Section 3 discusses the nature of student activities in REU programs. Section 4 compares the performance of an REU program hosted in an iSchool to that of an REU program hosted in a Computer Science department. We propose an enhancement of the undergraduate Data Science curriculum in Sect. 5, and summarize the paper in Sect. 6.

2 Objectives of REU Programs

In this section, we first introduce the objectives of CISE REU programs. After discussing the different research focuses of computer science and information science, we describe the sample objectives of our iSchool-hosted DAIR REU program.

2.1 Information Science *vs.* Computer Science

An REU program supported by CISE can be hosted in a department of Computer Science or in an iSchool, as long as its research themes are within the research scope of the CISE directorate. For example, the *REU on Software Analytics and Testing* co-author Ding led at ECU was hosted in the department of Computer Science. The *REU on Data Analytics and Information Retrieval* we are running at UNT is hosted in the department of Information Science, an iSchool. Both REU programs focus on Data Science, but each program has its own unique research focuses that are decided by the respective research focuses of information science and computer science.

"Information Science brings together and uses the theories, principles, techniques and technologies of a variety of disciplines toward the solution of information problems." [1]. A widely accepted definition of computer science is defined by the Computing Sciences Accreditation Board (CSAB) as "a discipline that involves the understanding and design of computers and computational processes." [2]. From these two definitions, it is not difficult to understand the difference between information science and computer science. Information science develops information solutions to serve human society, and computer science designs computers and algorithms for computers to solve real-world problems. The focus of information science research is human society, and the focus of computer science research is computers. Figure 1 illustrates the research focuses of information science and computer science. The differences in research focus should inform the research training offered by the respective departments.

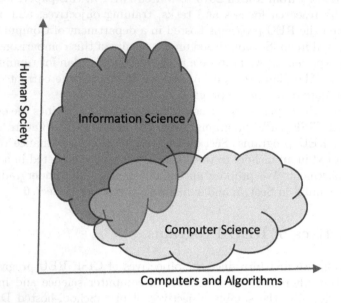

Fig. 1. An illustration of the different focus areas of information science and computer science.

2.2 Project Objectives

REU programs provide an opportunity for undergraduate students to build valuable research experiences through working on well-designed research projects. It is a great mechanism for attracting and retaining students in science and engineering disciplines and preparing them for careers in these fields [3]. NSF requires each REU site to have a common research focus that reflects the research expertise of the faculty mentors and the capabilities of the host department. These requirements must be considered when developing the project objectives for an REU site. Using the DAIR REU as an example, we might define the project objectives as follows [4]:

1. To provide a high-quality research and mentoring environment for REU students to conduct research and build research experience in data analytics and information retrieval.
2. To train REU students in broadly applicable research skills including problem solving, critical thinking, and research presentation.
3. To develop REU students in research collaboration and communication skills.
4. To guide REU students to explore their interest in graduate studies and professional careers in science and engineering.

These objectives, though, are quite general and, with only slight modifications, can be relevant for any REU program. They reflect neither the research focus nor the expertise of the faculty mentors of the REU program. The objectives can be improved by emphasizing the research focuses of information science and the research expertise of the faculty mentors. For a revised set of objectives, we keep Objectives 3 and 4 as they are and refine Objectives 1 and 2:

1. To provide a high-quality research and mentoring environment for REU students to conduct research and build research experience in data analytics and information retrieval. At the end of the summer training, students will be able to apply interdisciplinary knowledge including computing, computational linguistics, and information science to develop and evaluate data-intensive solutions for information problems.
2. To train REU students in broadly applicable research skills including problem solving, critical thinking, and research presentation. In particular, REU students will be able to understand information security and privacy issues related to solutions for information problems and to evaluate proposed solutions with respect to information security and privacy. REU students will also be able to understand and evaluate issues of ethics, fairness, and bias related to solutions for information problems.

In the revised and expanded objectives, we emphasize the skills to be developed for building solutions for information problems, especially emphasizing the *service to human society* of any solution. Therefore, the important information science concerns of information security and privacy, ethics, and fairness of an information solution should be addressed in the research training. The research and training activities for the DAIR REU program were designed with these refined objectives in mind.

3 Nature of Student Activities

Student activities are the core of any REU program, and they are designed to achieve the project objectives (as described in the previous section). The general activities include research preparation, tutorials and lectures, research seminars, group meetings, group research discussions, literature review, conducting research, research results presentation and reporting, etc. Table 1 lists the major activities of the DAIR REU [4]. In this section, however, our focus is on the specific research projects we developed for the REU students. Using the DAIR REU as an example, these projects were carefully designed to develop student's research skills in building solutions for information problems to serve human society. Similar projects were also used in the REU on *Software Analytics and Testing* led by co-author Ding at ECU before. We will discuss how the different project objectives were implemented by the same projects in different REU programs.

Table 1. The general schedule of the DAIR REU summer program

Activities	Topics
Research preparation	1. Reading, Lectures and Tutorials: Data analytics, information retrieval, and computational linguistics
	2. Sample research projects on data analytics, information retrieval, and computational linguistics
Orientation	1. Overview of the program and other useful information
Seminars	1. Preparation, writing and presentation of a research proposal and results
	2. The state-of-the-art of data analytics research, information retrieval research, and computational linguistics research
	3. Graduate study: application and scholarship
	4. Ethics issues in research
Tutorials	1. Basic concepts and preliminaries of data analytics, information retrieval, and computational linguistics
	2. Algorithms, models, and tools for data analytics, information retrieval, and computational linguistics
	3. Applications of data analytics, information retrieval, and computational linguistics
	4. Neural networks and deep learning
Social events	1. Research labs at UNT
	2. High-tech companies in the greater Dallas-Fort Worth area
	3. 2 to 3 local social events
Meeting and reporting	1. One-hour group discussion and oral presentation of research results every week
	2. Each student gives a 20-min presentation of his or her research results in the 6th week, and a 30-min presentation at the end of the 10th week
	3. Each student submits a midterm research report of his or her research results in the 6th week, and a final research report at the end of the 10th week
	4. Each student gives a poster presentation of his or her research results on the last day of the summer program

Although activities such as research preparation, research seminars, tutorials, and lectures cover the most important information science research questions in building solutions for human society, research training on information security and privacy, as well as research ethics and fairness, is mainly implemented by conducting the research projects. Here we share the sample research projects we developed for the DAIR REU program and map the research activities to the training objectives.

1. *Data Analytics of Large Volume of Biomedical Images.* This project includes two closely-related research components: auto-labeling and image classification of cytopathology images including pap smear images collected by one faculty mentor. The auto-labeling project studies how to automatically label the type of each image using clustering and classification methods based on semi-supervising learning. The classification is to study the deep learning-based classification of the images and the approach for improving the classification accuracy. In this project, students learn feature engineering, supervised learning, unsupervised learning, and semi-supervised learning; machine learning algorithms including Convolutional Neural Network (CNN), clustering algorithms including Gaussian Mixture Model (GMM) and K-means, and Support Vector Machine (SVM); understand the processes for building a machine learning application. Students also program machine learning models in Python, conduct experimental study, validate models, present and report results [4].

   The project is a typical computer science project for building computing solutions without considering the concerns of information science research such as how the project result would positively or negatively impact human society. For example, suppose the classification software has higher classification accuracy than a human pathologist on some datasets. Which result should be considered to be more reliable, if a pathologist and the classification software produce different classification results for a particular case? Is it possible a pathologist won't make an independent decision due to the different result produced by the classification software? How reliable are the datasets that were used for training the classification software? For example, Rajpurkar et al. introduced a deep learning system called ChexNet for diagnosing pneumonia diseases based on chest X-ray images in 2017. They claimed *"We find that CheXNet exceeds average radiologist performance on pneumonia detection on both sensitivity and specificity"* [6]. However, Oakden-Raynera, a radiology student and machine learning researcher, questioned the dataset used by ChexNet. He suspected the dataset was not fit for training medical machine learning systems to do diagnostic work due to its problems with image labelling [7]. Therefore, the quality of the datasets is critical to the usefulness of the information solution that is built on the datasets. It is important to evaluate the quality of datasets before the system is released. We will add new components into the research projects to train students on evaluation of data quality and fairness in machine learning systems, to emphasize the research focus of information science.

2. *Information Retrieval of Large-Scale Text Collections.* This project also includes two sub-projects: one is on re-ranking with machine learning approaches for precision medicine information retrieval, and the other is on cross-language information retrieval for low-resource languages. Precision medicine provides evidence-based treatment and prevention of diseases that are customized to individual patients according to data analysis results. Precision Medicine Information Retrieval (PMIR) specifically retrieves relevant cancer treatment literature to find treatment evidences using a patient's

genomics and demographic information. The challenge is how to put the most relevant information into the top list of the returned retrieved results. We explore and compare a supervised learning algorithm based on regression analysis, an unsupervised learning algorithm based on language models such as Doc2Vec [8] or BERT [9], and traditional information relevance feedback approaches. In addition, we explore the modeling of human precision medicine knowledge as a re-ranking process. In this project, students learn fundamentals of information retrieval, existing information retrieval models and tools, document modeling including sentence-level language modeling and word-level modeling, word embeddings, and evaluation of information retrieval tools. The project also trains students to understand the usability of information systems and makes them familiar with cognitive models for improving the usability [4]. The research focus of information science has been well addressed in this project.

The goal of Cross Language Information Retrieval (CLIR) is to find relevant information that is written in a language that is different from that of the user's queries. CLIR is expected to remove language barriers to information and knowledge sharing. This project aims to investigate effective and efficient methods for locating text and speech content in "documents" in low-resource languages using English queries. We explore the use of machine learning and data analytics to understand new languages, to perform machine translation of the queries, and to re-rank retrieval results. Students learn CLIR and machine translation principles, algorithms, tools and system implementation in text analysis and mining. It is also important to teach students about the necessity of providing information solutions for low-resource languages and the subsequent impact to human society by expanding access to information [4].

3. *Social Media Information Retrieval for Disaster Research.* In this project, we study the retrieval, processing, and analysis of crisis-related Twitter data. It also includes two sub-projects: one is retrieval and processing of crisis-related Twitter data, and the other is content-based filtering and analysis of crisis Twitter data. The first sub-project gives students training in data management, data pre-processing, and natural language processing (NLP) tools for Twitter data. They also learn system implementation, verification, and validation. In the second project, students learn deep learning methods such as word embeddings and CNNs; training of domain-specific word embeddings; feature engineering and feature extraction for both supervised classification and neural network approaches; and neural network methods for sentiment analysis. They perform comparative evaluation of the different filtering approaches. Both projects also train students in ethical considerations around data collection and re-use, especially in the social media context [10]. Students additionally learn about preparation of data for scholarship and analysis in the humanities and social sciences [4].

From above discussion, it is likely clear that projects 2 and 3 were specifically designed for the DAIR REU program. Both include significant research tasks related to building solutions for human society, and both consider ethical issues as an integrated research component. Project 1, on the other hand, was adapted from the previous REU program and, as such, didn't specifically address the research focus of information science. The REU programs led by Ding at ECU were also in the realm of data science, but they offered different research projects from DAIR, as it was hosted in the department of Computer Science and the faculty mentors involved had different research expertise and interests. Some sample research projects offered by the previous REU programs hosted at ECU are:

1. *Software Testing and Data Analysis of Scientific Software.* Students learn the basic principles of software testing, as well as new techniques of test generation, test oracle development, and automated evaluation of test adequacy in the scope of testing scientific software [5].
2. *Software Testing and Data Analysis of Web Security.* Students learn fundamentals of web security and the skills for testing security of web applications using state-of-the-art testing techniques [5].
3. *Fault Detection Effectiveness and MC/DC Coverage of Combinatorial Test Cases.* Students learn fundamentals of combinatorial testing, test adequacy criteria, and use combinatorial testing tools for creating adequate MC/DC test cases as well as for the evaluation of the test effectiveness.
4. *Program Analysis for Mobile DSL Construction.* Students learn the principles and tools of program analysis, analyzing patterns in software repositories, and skills for applying the techniques for analyzing usage patterns in a mobile domain specific language.

The research focus of all of these projects is on building computing solutions for analyzing or testing software or software repositories. These projects in their current form reflect the research interests of computer science, but they could be extended by an REU program hosted in an iSchool. For example, for a mobile application that may collect private information from its users, possible extensions of the research questions to be addressed could include: *(a) what are the minimal security and privacy requirements for the application, and (b) how can we check and ensure the satisfaction of security and privacy requirements.* These are still open questions, and they fit directly within the research scope of information science.

4   Project Evaluation

Every REU program is required to build regular and thorough project evaluation into the activities of the program. Project evaluation ensures that an REU program running effectively, as well as providing feedback for improving the program's effectiveness. In this section, we discuss the project evaluation process and evaluation results of the DAIR REU program for summer 2019. Project evaluator Smith, one of the co-authors of this paper, led the project evaluation. The evaluation plan for the DAIR REU program is described as follows, precisely as it appears in the project proposal [4]. For each project objective, several assessment activities were developed.

Objective 1:

1. Evaluation of research results from each student.
2. Pre-program and exit interview from each student.
3. Evaluation of research publications and presentations from each student after the summer program.

Objective 2:

1. Evaluation of the research proposal, oral presentations and project reports from each student.
2. Pre-program and exit interview from each student.

Objective 3:

1. Evaluation of research group plans, meeting minutes, weekly presentations and group research results.
2. Evaluation of activities in social network accounts.
3. Pre-program and exit interview from each student.

Objective 4:

1. Pre-program and exit interview from each student.
2. Each student's education and career path after the summer program.

The project evaluation process is conducted continually throughout and beyond the project period, with periodic formative evaluations and yearly summative evaluation reports. The project evaluator developed an interview questionnaire to measure the students' pre-program attitudes toward the project, self-evaluation of their competencies, and then administer it again after the program to measure desirable changes in the students. A total of 29 survey questions were asked for student participants for summer 2019. On a scale of 1–7, with 1 being the lowest level and 7 being the highest level, a student participant rates her or his ability or understanding of the tasks (rating before summer camp, and rating after summer camp) such as: ability to develop a research proposal; understanding of the basic processes and activities of data analytics and information retrieval. More tasks can be found in Table 2.

For the comparative assessments, the project evaluator performs statistical analysis to evaluate any significant improvement. Basic descriptive statistics are performed on the data collected from assessment activities. In addition, the program uses the CISE REU evaluation toolkit offered by Dr. Audrey Rorrer from University of North Carolina (UNC) Charlotte to evaluate the program.

The survey results of DAIR REU 2019 summer program show the program was successful, with a change from the average rating before the summer camp of less than 4 to the average rating after the summer camp of between 5 and 6. Partials results are shown in Table 2, where we list only those survey tasks that are related to research training. The evaluation results provided by Dr. Rorrer from UNC Charlotte showed similar performance improvement, although the

Table 2. Survey result of 2019 REU summer program

Tasks	Before	After
Ability to develop a research proposal	3.67	5.11
Understanding of the basic processes and activities of data analytics and information retrieval	4.11	6.11
Understanding the background, basic concepts, and current challenges to data analytics and information retrieval	4.56	6.00
Familiarity with the data analytics tools used in modern research	3.56	5.22
Familiarity with the information retrieval tools used in modern research	3.56	4.89
Familiarity with several case studies related to data analytics and information retrieval	3.44	5.67
Gathering and recording the data necessary to address the questions being researched	4.33	5.67
Analyzing those data to help answer those questions	4.00	5.78
Being able to prepare a written report in which research results are presented and interpreted	4.11	5.22
Being able to plan additional research to address questions suggested by the results of just completed research	4.22	5.33
Figuring out the next step in a research project	4.11	5.22
Formulating a research question that could be answered with data	3.67	5.33
Identifying the limitations of research methods and designs	3.89	5.56

evaluation included different questions. The project evaluator also conducted interviews with student participants. The interview results also showed the attitude of the student participants toward 2019 DAIR REU summer program was positive. Sample responses include:

"I feel like I improved my social skills and reading comprehension. Trying to do research to find data sets and papers helped my comprehension. All of this was out of my comfort zone. I grew a lot."

"My previous experience with research was different. I was approached by an older student to do research. I felt like an assistant. This is more of my own research. I found my own data and developed my own questions. I am more by myself collecting and organizing data for a goal that I am working towards. I have good ideas to take back with me. The ideas go hand in hand with my major. This will help me with my projects in the future."

"The REU opened my mind for considering machine learning. I never looked into this fascinating subject before. I see the connection with my undergraduate area. I learned new algorithms, what cybersecurity is and how computers work.

It is cool seeing an algorithm that computer science developed implemented in data science."

The project evaluation results are comparable to the project evaluation results of the REU programs that were led by Ding at ECU. Considering the DAIR REU summer program was the first REU program that was ever hosted at the College of Information at UNT, and also the first time this team worked together, we consider the program a success so far. We believe the experience and lessons learned from running the 2019 REU summer program will be helpful for improving the program in the future. We also hope it might be useful for other researchers running similar undergraduate research programs at their universities.

The DAIR REU summer program received 42 qualified applicants nationwide for the 2019 summer program, which is significantly lower than the number of the applicants of the REU programs led by Ding before, which had around 100 applicants each year. The major reason was due to the late confirmation of the REU award from NSF, limiting the amount of time available to develop program materials and spread news of the program. We selected 10 students from 6 different universities, including 2 students from UNT in summer 2019. Among the 10 students, 3 were female and 2 were Hispanic. This is notable because both women and Hispanic students are traditionally underrepresented in technical fields. In addition, 6 of the students were from universities that offer limited research opportunities for undergraduate research. Therefore, the 2019 DAIR REU summer program met the requirements for student participants according to the program solicitation. However, seven of the 10 students were majoring in Computer Science, two students in Linguistics, and one in Economics. In the future, we will increase our efforts to promote the DAIR REU program among iSchools and increase the number of students from information science programs.

5   A Recommendation for Data Science Curriculum

Based on our experiences running an REU program in data science, we would like to recommend a specific enhancement to the curricula of programs currently offering a bachelor of science in data science (BSDS). Many universities, such as UNT [15], University of Texas at Dallas [11], University of Houston Downtown [12], Purdue University [13], Tufts University [14], offer or have offered the BSDS as an interdisciplinary program. The specific courses of these programs differ from university to university, but the curricula all include six categories of courses:

1. foundation and pre-major courses,
2. courses on statistics and probability,
3. courses on statistical analysis and data mining,
4. computing courses,
5. machine learning courses, and
6. courses on applications of data science.

All of these programs tend to consider the data science degree an extension of computer science, with more data analytics courses. We, however, believe a data science program should include information science courses that target the development of solutions for information problems in order to better serve human society. Therefore, components addressing important societal issues should be integrated into the content of most data science courses. For example, the curriculum should include courses related to information and data quality, information security and privacy, information behaviors, usability, and ethics and fairness of data science applications. We will develop research components that are related to these topics in our 2020 summer REU program, and will share the experience with the data science education and research community.

6   Summary

In this paper, we reported our experience and lessons learned from running an REU summer program in data science in the department of Information Science at UNT, an iSchool. The REU program is the only NSF CISE REU site program hosted in an iSchool in 2019. Through investigating the nature of student activities and project evaluation results, particularly in comparison to a previous REU program hosted in a Computer Science department, we summarized the unique research focus of an REU program in an iSchool. Based on the discussion, we also propose an enhancement of the curriculum of BSDS with more information science components. The materials and experience shared in this paper would be useful to other researchers for effectively running an undergraduate research program.

References

1. Williams, M.E.: Defining information science and the role of ASIS. Bull. Am. Soc. Inf. Sci. **14**(2), 17–19 (1987/1988)
2. McGuffee, J.W.: Defining computer science. SIGCSE Bull. **32**(2), 74–76 (2000)
3. NSF, Research Experiences for Undergraduates (REU) Sites and Supplements, Program Solicitation, NSF 19-582 (2019). https://www.nsf.gov/pubs/2019/nsf19582/nsf19582.htm. Accessed 10 Aug 2019
4. Ding, J., Chen, J., Palmer, A., Smith, D.: REU Site: Data Analytics and Information Retrieval, NSF REU Proposal (2018)
5. Ding, J., Tabrizi, N., Ding, Q., Hill, M., Vilkomir, S.: REU Site: Software Analytics and Testing, NSF REU Proposal (2015)
6. Rajpurkar, P., et al.: CheXNet: Radiologist-Level Pneumonia Detection on Chest X-Rays with Deep Learning. CoRRabs/1711.05225 (2017)
7. Oakden-Rayner, L.: Exploring the ChestXray14 dataset: problems (2017). https://lukeoakdenrayner.wordpress.com/2017/12/18/the-chestxray14-dataset-problems. Accessed 19 June 2019 (2017)
8. Le, Q.V., Mikolov, T.: Distributed Representations of Sentences and Documents. CoRR, abs/1405.4053 (2014)

9. Devlin, J., Chang, M.-W., Lee, K., Toutanova, K.: BERT: Pre-training of Deep Bidirectional Transformers for Language Understanding. CoRR, abs/1810.04805 (2018)
10. Jules, B., Summers, E., Mitchell Jr., D. V.: Ethical considerations for archiving social media content generated by contemporary social movements: challenges, opportunities, and recommendations, Documenting the Now, Technical report, April 2018 (2018)
11. UTD, BS in data science program in the University of Texas at Dallas (2019). https://catalog.utdallas.edu/2018/undergraduate/programs/data-science. Accessed 09 June 2019
12. UHD, BS in data science program in University of Houston Downtown (2019). https://www.uhd.edu/academics/sciences/mathematics-statistics/Pages/MS-BS-DataScience.aspx. Accessed 09 June 2019
13. Purdue, BS in data science program in Purdue University (2019). https://www.cs.purdue.edu/undergraduate/curriculum/datascience.html. Accessed 09 June 2019
14. Tufts, BS in data science program in Tufts University (2019). https://engineering.tufts.edu/cs/bachelor-science-data-science. Accessed 09 June 2019
15. UNT, BS in data science program in the University of North Texas (2019). https://informationscience.unt.edu/bs-data-science-program-requirements. Accessed 09 June 2019
16. Connolly, F., Gallian, J.A.: What students say about their REU experience. In: Proceedings of the Conference on Promoting Undergraduate Research in Mathematics, pp. 233–236 (2007)
17. Garcia, R., Wyels, C.: REU design: broadening participation and promoting success. Involve: J. Math. **7**(3), 315–326 (2014)

The Cost of Entry: Internships in Galleries, Libraries, Archives, and Museums Education

Marika Cifor[1](✉) ⓘ and Brian M. Watson[2] ⓘ

[1] University of Washington, Seattle, WA 98195, USA
mcifor@uw.edu
[2] Indiana University Bloomington, Bloomington, IN 47405, USA

Abstract. Internships are widespread in GLAM and have become the cost of entry to the field for many students and early career professionals. This paper reports on preliminary findings from a content analysis of internship related information on the websites' of 178 graduate-level GLAM education programs in the U.S. and Canada. We contextualize the study in relation to the available literature on internships, and recent professional discussions. We discuss the implications our findings that: (A) there is a high prevalence of internships in the field; (B) there are significant differences in internship practices by GLAM discipline and by specialization, focus, certificate, or other master's degree enhancement; (C) the wide variances in internship practices by geographic region, setting, and institution type; and (D) the diversity of internship requirements and structures within these professional education programs. We address the implications of internships for diversity and inclusion throughout our analysis.

Keywords: Internship · Education · Diversity

1 Introduction

In July 2019, the Society of American Archivists (SAA) began prohibiting listings for unpaid internships on their job boards [1]. A month earlier, the Association of Art Museum Directors called for an end to unpaid internships [2]. These are not solitary events: significant conference, listserv, and social media discussion around internships, particularly those that are unpaid, is taking place within the Galleries, Libraries, Archives, and Museums (GLAM) community. For aspiring and early career professionals, the cost of entry into the field has become an inclination and ability to complete often un- or under-compensated internships [19].

Internships, which have in some instances replaced training programs and entry-level jobs [3] are employment experiences of finite duration, assumed to include a learning component, completed during and/or closely following graduate-level education. Competition for permanent GLAM positions means that entry-level applicants are now required to be highly-qualified and to demonstrate a commitment to the sector beyond educational qualifications—this is often accomplished through internships. In response to market shifts and calls to increase graduates' employability, professional

© Springer Nature Switzerland AG 2020
A. Sundqvist et al. (Eds.): iConference 2020, LNCS 12051, pp. 525–535, 2020.
https://doi.org/10.1007/978-3-030-43687-2_42

graduate-level education programs now routinely require or strongly encourage internships within core or specialization curricula.

It is widely accepted that internships are an important aspect of professional training, and that they correlate positively with securing future job prospects and enhanced earnings. Yet, the empirical data as to the prevalence and structure of GLAM internships is insufficient to assess their implications on students' abilities to complete their education and to compete and succeed in the marketplace. The real benefits or costs of internships for key stakeholders–students and early career professionals, employers, faculty, and granting agencies–remain unknown. The purpose of this paper is to investigate what curriculum requirements and recommendations currently constitute internship programs in GLAM. By discovering and characterizing the internships offered and required in relevant degree programs, this study extends the literature on GLAM curriculum composition and provides insights for students, faculty and administrators, and employers who offer or engage in internships or are considering the establishment of a new or revision of an existing internship program in their curricula.

This paper reports findings from our preliminary content analysis of internship related information on the publically available websites' of 178 graduate-level education programs in the U.S. and Canada. This research is the pilot for a larger study. First, we contextualize the study in relation to literature on internships, and recent professional discussions. Second, we detail and discuss the implications our findings on: (A) the prevalence of internships; (B) differences in internship practices by discipline and program specialization/concentration; (C) differences in internship practices by geographic region, setting, and institution type; and (D) wide variances in internship requirements and structures. This data on internships will enable faculty, administrators, and staff to ensure that internships within our programs are high quality experiences that abide by the core values and ethics of our professions, that they align with related programs and practices, and that they are being structured as to benefit diverse students and employers.

2 Literature Review

Internships emerged from within the medical profession in the nineteenth century, and were subsequently taken up in national, state, and local public administration beginning in the 1930s [35]. By the 1960s, service and socially-oriented fields such as teaching, social work, psychology, and journalism began to establish and formalize internships [35]. The spread of internships to publishing, finance, and technology was in full swing by the 1980s. It is now abundantly clear that internships have also become widespread in GLAM, including within graduate-level education [19]. As Hunt and Scott summarize in their review of literature on graduate-level internships most research concurs that students undertake internships in order to gain access to "particular industries or careers and improve their employability through the provision of 'real world' experience and opportunities to develop social networks and industry-specific knowledge and skills" [14]. In this section, we contextualize our study within literature on internship practices and curricula within GLAM education and in guidelines and best practices aimed at this sector. Finally, we briefly outline recent discussions about internships, especially unpaid internships, in relation professional to ethics and diversity, equity, and inclusion in GLAM.

There are no formal professional standards specific to GLAM internships and guidelines from professional organizations are often limited or outdated. The American Library Association (ALA), for example, does not publish a guide on best practices—the most cited guide is Multnomah County's 2012 *Effective Library Internships: A Toolkit for Success* [20]. In 2008, SAA created a broad-brush guide recommending internship agreements, onsite and faculty supervisors, evaluation, and compensation. Despite their explicit recommendation that "graduate internships without any form of compensation should be rare to avoid devaluing the professional nature of archival work," unpaid internships are still common and were promoted by SAA until 2019 [1].

There are a few studies of internships in the GLAM sector, however the small literature on graduate-level education and internships is primarily in the form of practical guides or brief case studies experiences implementing and running internship programs authored by professionals [15, 19]. Practical guides for educators, such as Bastian and Webber's 2008 *Archival Internships* [23], are an important resource for faculty, administrators, employers, and students, as are more qualitative studies such as Schwartz's 2012 M.A. thesis [38]. However, such guides are limited in focus or have rapidly become outdated. There are a number of case studies by professionals leading internship programs in their institutions that point to the scale, significance, and current best practices for such experiences. These include Kopp's recent article on the potential of special collections internships for experiential learning and that posits their potential positive impacts not only on student's professional life, but for their academic success and personal growth using the case of the L. Tom Perry Special Collections at Brigham Young University's Harold B. Lee Library [36]. Additionally, there are some discussions of individual programs that tangentially mention compensation, such as the Jazz Archives Fellowship or the Wolf Trap Foundation for the Performing Arts internship [21, 22].

Assumptions regarding the positive benefits and outcomes of internships, paid and unpaid, are commonplace across workplace sectors, despite a lack of empirical findings to support such claims [3]. Recent discussions about internships in GLAM have focused largely on unpaid internships and their implications for the profession's core values, professional ethics, and the continued racial and class homogeneity of the field. This study includes data (where available) on internship characteristics, including compensation. Some data, including from allied fields, shows that unpaid internships have different outcomes. Broad surveys of college graduates found consistent results over a five-year period that unpaid interns are less likely to get a full-time job offer after the internship ends than paid interns (44% vs. 72%) and are more likely to be paid less in future positions [17, 18]. Similarly, an annual census of graduates in the United Kingdom, reveals that unpaid internships appear to be "more likely to lead to underemployment and less favorable career development outcomes" [14–16].

There is agreement that the lack of diversity in the GLAM workforce is widespread, problematic, and will only become increasingly so if significant measures are not undertaken. A major response has been to focus on diversifying incoming students, based on the premise that a more diverse student body will encourage future diversity at all levels. A small, but powerful literature by professionals identifies unpaid internships as being the most harmful aspect of GLAM education, for less economically privileged and/or minoritized students, especially students of color. The ubiquity of unpaid internships, they argue, results in a majority middle-class and overwhelmingly-white workforce in libraries (86% [23]), archives (87% [28]), and galleries and museums (87% [23–27]). However, as Wildenhaus notes, "no comprehensive studies have yet been published quantifying the extent of unpaid internships within archives and libraries" [19].

It is clear that there is some important GLAM literature on how to improve internship outcomes for employers and students. However, there is a lack of comprehensive empirical research that faculty, administrators, granting-agencies, and employers can use as a guide. Data is required to effectively plan and implement both required and recommended internships in core and specialization courses and to make informed choices about the extension or restructuring of existing internships. Ours is the first graduate-and-discipline-specific study on internship practices. As conference and literature discussion around internships has become commonplace, and discourse about unpaid internships have become increasingly contentious [4, 6, 21, 29–31], and professional organizations have called for an end to some internship practices [1, 2, 32], this study is urgently needed

3 Methods

We conducted quantitative and qualitative content analyses of internship programs and courses in GLAM graduate-level education programs in the U.S. and Canada. The data collection process was twofold. The initial step in data collection was to identify relevant programs and institutions. Second, we collected information regarding the use of internships within those degree programs. The goal was to understand the current landscape of internship practices and to identify patterns in internship requirements and structures across the field. We developed the list of programs analyzed using directories of accredited, recommended, or otherwise listed education programs by the leading professional organizations in each respective GLAM area: ALA, SAA, and American Alliance of Museums (AAM).

Next, we compiled a list of all education programs fitting our criteria: graduate-level degree in a GLAM area with a publically accessible website by sampling from online directories in June-July 2019. ALA provides a comprehensive list of 60 accredited master's programs at colleges and universities [39]. We then sampled from the SAA Directory of Archival Education, identifying 26 programs beyond those listed by ALA [40]. Finally, we sampled AAM's Directory of Museum Studies and Related Programs identifying 102 programs [41]. After removing defunct, discontinued, minor or certificate-only programs we were left with 52 ALA accredited institutions, 27 SAA programs, and 102 AAM programs, most focusing on Museum Science/Studies (42 programs) or Arts Administration (23 programs). When programs appeared in more than one directory, we included only one entry per degree program in our data. Some institutions offered more than one relevant program, we included entries for each relevant program.

Using a spreadsheet, we charted the name of the program, website, degrees offered, and internship courses offered for the 178 programs identified into their respective fields. Then, we analyzed any internship-related information available indicating in additional fields with yes, no, or uncertain whether an internship was required to complete the degree in that program's core/foundational courses, or to complete in program specialization/concentration. Using the same criteria, we indicated whether a credit-granting internship course was offered, whether paid internships could be used to fulfill degree requirements, and the duration of internships by hours, in cases where the website only mentioned credits, we used the Carnegie Credit Hour formula [37] to generate estimated hours. We also included an open data field for any additional internship-related information that could be obtained.

We compiled data on the frequency of activities in each category and then aggregated the data to describe the percentage of institutions that incorporated no, few, moderate or high uses of internships within their program(s). Finally, we mapped relevant data from 96 data points the Carnegie Classification of Institutions of Higher Education (CCIHE) onto our sample [33]. As our focus was on graduate programs, we retained 46 Carnegie data fields on which to base our analysis. After independent initial data analysis by each researcher, we met and iteratively reviewed examples of the themes detailed below.

4 Findings and Discussion

Our analysis of the data collected is ongoing, yet our preliminary analysis has significant findings on: (Sect. 4.1) the prevalence of internships in GLAM graduate-education; (Sect. 4.2) the differences in internship practices by GLAM discipline and associated program specialization; (Sect. 4.3) differences in internship practices by geographic region, setting, and institution type; and (Sect. 4.4) wide variances in internship requirements and structures.

4.1 Prevalence of Internships

Our findings reveal that internships are widely required within GLAM education. In our sample of 178 GLAM degree programs, we found that 147 (83%) required completion of an internship or internships as a component of their graduate level program. This number includes 83 schools that required an internship to complete degree requirements, and 116 programs that required internship/s to complete a specialization, focus, certificate, or other master's degree enhancement. The latter means that some, but not all students are required to complete an internship.

4.2 Internships by GLAM Discipline

We found that whether an internship is required for degree completion, whether in a core or foundational course, or as an independent internship course completed for credit, varied significantly by GLAM field. Internships were most common in archives and museum focused education. Of 60 ALA-accredited programs 13 (25%) required an internship. Of 26 SAA-recommended programs 6 (24%) require an internship for degree completion. Of the 27 ALA and SAA combined programs that focus on archives, 10 (35%) include a required internship for degree completion. In contrast, out of 102 AAM programs 64 (63%) mandated an internship to fulfill graduation requirements. These numbers indicate a wide variance by GLAM discipline and professional area, with museum and archives programs being far more likely, than library programs to require internships in order to obtain a master's degree.

Our findings reveal that whether students are required to an internship or internships in order to complete a specialization, focus, certificate, or other master's degree enhancement also varied significantly by GLAM field. We found that of 60 ALA-accredited programs, 28 (54%) required an internship for one or more degree specializations. Of 27 programs focused on archives from the ALA and SAA lists 23 (88%) required an internship for specialization completion. In comparison, of 102 AAM programs 64 (63%) required an internship to fulfill specialization requirements. These numbers indicate a wide variance in internship requirements by GLAM area specialization, with archives focused enhancements including more often than all other programs an internship requirement.

4.3 Internships by Environment

Using CCIHE data, we found notable differences in internship by environment and region of U.S (Table 1). Programs that required graduate students to complete internships to obtain degrees are significantly more likely to be located in the Mideast (29 programs), Great Lakes (28 programs) and Southeastern regions (33 programs). There may be historical reasons for this regional specificity that areas of yet are unknown.

Table 1. Number of programs by CCIHE-defined area

CCIHE-defined area	Number of programs
Mideast	58
Southeast	33
Great Lakes	28
Far West	18
Southwest	13
New England	13
Plains	8
Mountain	5

Drilling down further by region, we found a wide variance in internship requirements by state (Table 2). New York places top for both the number of schools (17 programs) and most required internships for degree completion (13 programs) and specialization (20°) within those programs. While, California has 10 relevant programs, the second highest number, only 3 programs there require internships to obtain a degree. Indeed, the Northeast has both the most GLAM programs and most required internship programs, despite California having nearly 70% of the population of all Northeast states combined. Another noteworthy regional trend was that the schools that prohibited paid internships for pay are, with the exception of one Northeast school, in the Southeast.

Table 2. Top 10 states that require internships for degree or specialization:

State	CCIHE-defined area	Number of programs
New York	13	20
Illinois	6	6
Michigan	6	7
Texas	6	5
Washington D.C.	5	4
Maryland	4	4
Pennsylvania	4	6
Virginia	4	6
California	3	6

We also examined the setting of GLAM programs by level of urbanization as established by CCIHE. In addition, we analyzed internship practices in line with institution type as established by Carnegie Classification, and found that require specialization internships are more likely to be in heavily urbanized areas and belong to the Coalition of Urban and Metropolitan Universities or the Coalition of Urban Serving Universities (39 schools). Although there is not enough data to make substantive statements, of the 6 programs that explicitly do not allow paid internships to be considered for degree completion, it is potentially significant that 4 are at religious-based institutions.

Our findings reveal potentially important variances that hold implications for diversity and inclusion within the student body of GLAM programs, and for the future of the field. Schools that require an internship for specialization completion are generally urbanized, are more likely to be in the CUMU or CUSU and 33% more likely to be serving minority students—28 of the 39 schools in this category are either historically Black colleges and universities, women's colleges, minority-serving, or Hispanic majority institutions.

Overall, the variances we found by setting mean that GLAM graduate-programs that require internships to obtain a degree are generally urbanized, R1 universities that offer more STEM degrees and serve more diverse students. They are more likely in the Great Lakes or the Southwest regions of the country.

4.4   Internship Requirements and Structures

Our data reveals that not only do the prevalence of internships vary greatly by program, specialization, focus, certificate, or other master's degree enhancement within that program. Additionally, required internships are structured in meaningfully different ways within GLAM programs, including intern hours spent on site, compensation or lack thereof, and eligibility for academic credit. There is a significant lack of uniformity, even among similar programs, in current internship practices.

We found that the number of hours required within an internship or by a series of internships to complete a degree or specialization varied tremendously, with the least number of hours being 60 and the greatest being 400. Museum programs were mostly likely to include the highest number of hours on site for student interns. On average, ALA programs that required an internship obligated students to complete an average of 140 h (mean), with a range of 60 to 360 h. SAA programs required an average of 220 h, with a range of 120–400 h. Combined archival programs from ALA and SAA require 170 h, with a range of 60–400 h. In AAM programs, requirements were much higher, with an average of 250 h and range from 120 to 480 h. The variance of the number of required hours is greater than mere differences in credit hours completed.

Most of the sampled programs, 148 out of 178 (83%) that included an internship component whether for degree or specialization within a degree program permitted the internship to count for course credit. There was little available information on whether paid work could be utilized for program's internship requirements. Of those same 178 of programs approximately half, 96 (53%), do not publicly disclose whether paid internships are eligible for credit. It is clear given the state of discourse about compensation and internships in the GLAM community, that greater transparency about these practices is required.

5 Conclusion

This article describes an early attempt to understand the prevalence and implications of internships in the GLAM education. There are significant limitations to our findings.. We only sampled from public information on GLAM graduate-education program websites in the U.S. and Canada, therefore our perspective is limited by the quality and completeness of the website offerings. There were a few program websites where our analysis may be particularly limited due to limited language skills requisite to analyzing French and Spanish-language programs. Out analysis does not allow us to gain insight into the nuances of internship structures and courses or the experiences of students, faculty, and employers with internships. Greater knowledge of timing of internships within a graduate curriculum, of potential distinctions between online or in-person instructions, of specific academic assignments required, and details about opportunities for learning and mentorship in the internships might shift our conclusions.

The data collected and analyzed in this preliminary study does not permit a definitive conclusion as to the ways that required internships in GLAM education may have significant implications for diversity, equity and inclusion. The lack of racial and socio-economic diversity in GLAM professions is widely acknowledged [4–7]. A focus on diversifying students enrolled in graduate programs has been a major response [6–13]. There is evidence from other sectors that internships perpetuate structural inequities [3, 14–18]. Emphasizing internships in and beyond graduate education may therefore be contributing to GLAM workers' homogeneity and associated failures to serve diverse communities. Further research is needed to understand these vital implications of our internship practices.

In revealing the high frequency of internships and lack of uniformity and best practices across our field, this research raises a host of issues for future exploration. How prevalent are internships without remuneration versus paid opportunities? How does compensation or lack thereof shape the expectations, training, and experiences of interns and of employers? How can faculty effectively evaluate and structure internship resources and requirements to ensure they support diverse students and employing institutions? Does the capacity building of internships positively correlate to long-term employability advantages? How do internships impact the lives and professions of workers, particularly workers from minority populations? We hope to explore these issues in future research.

Further research on internships is urgently needed if we are, as an academic field and a profession, to truly understand the nature, function, and impact of internships. Our initial findings point to the urgency of examining internships and their characteristics. This work is timely, given recent changes to rules and regulations around internships by the U.S. Department of Labor, who has made it significantly easier for businesses to offer unpaid internships [34]. Now, more than ever, it is important that GLAM educators and professionals consider the implications of internship requirements.

References

1. Society of American Archivists.: Only Paid Internships to Be Posted to the SAA Career Center (2019). https://www2.archivists.org/news/2019/only-paid-internships-to-be-posted-to-the-saa-career-center
2. Greenberger, A.: Association of Art Museum Directors Calls for End of Unpaid Internships (2019). http://www.artnews.com/2019/06/20/aamd-resolution-paid-internships/
3. Hora, M., Wolfgram, M., Thompson, S.: What Do We Know About the Impact of Internships on Student Outcomes? Center for Research on College to Workforce Transitions, Wisconsin Center for Education Research, University of Wisconsin-Madison. Madison (2017). http://ccwt.wceruw.org/documents/CCWT-report-Designing-Internship-Programs.pdf
4. Dooley, J.: Feeding Our Young 2013 Society of American Archivists Presidential Address (2013). https://www2.archivists.org/history/leaders/jackie-m-dooley/2013-saa-presidential-address-by-jackie-dooley
5. Taylor, C.: Getting our house in order: moving from diversity to inclusion. Am. Arch. **80**, 19–29 (2017). https://doi.org/10.17723/0360-9081.80.1.19
6. Poole, A.H.: Pinkett's charges: recruiting, retaining, and mentoring archivists of color in the twenty-first century. Am. Arch. **80**, 103–134 (2017). https://doi.org/10.17723/0360-9081.80.1.103
7. Greene, M.A.: One archivist's struggles with diversity, community, collaboration, and their implications for our profession. In: Caldera, M., Neal, K.M. (eds.) Through the Archival Looking Glass: A Reader on Diversity and Inclusion, pp. 23–59. Society of American Archivists, Chicago (2014)

8. Blaser, B., Ladner, R.E., Burgstahler, S.: Including disability in diversity. In: 2018 Research on Equity and Sustained Participation in Engineering, Computing, and Technology (RESPECT), pp. 1–4. IEEE, Baltimore (2018). https://doi.org/10.1109/RESPECT.2018. 8491717

9. Gilliland, A.J.: Pluralizing archival education. In: Caldera, M., Neal, N., Kathryn, M. (eds.) Through the Archival Looking Glass: A Reader on Diversity and Inclusion, pp. 235–271. Society of American Archivists, Chicago (2014)

10. Neely, T.Y.: Diversity initiatives and programs: the national approach. J. Libr. Adm. **27**, 123–144 (1999). https://doi.org/10.1300/J111v27n01_09

11. Black, K.: Recruiting under-represented groups to librarianship. In: Multicultural Learning and Teaching, vol. 13 (2018). https://doi.org/10.1515/mlt-2017-0004

12. Jeffries, C.: Diversity, Inclusion, Access, & Equity: An Analysis of Otherness in Cultural Organizations. (1960). https://commons.emich.edu/honors/593

13. Lewis, J.: Diversity, Equity, and Inclusion: Impacting Leadership Roles in Art Museums. Drexel University, Philadelphia, PA (2018). https://idea.library.drexel.edu/islandora/object/ idea%3A8225

14. Hunt, W., Scott, P.: Paid and unpaid graduate internships: prevalence, quality and motivations at six months after graduation. Stud. High. Educ. **45**(2), 1–13 (2018). https://doi. org/10.1080/03075079.2018.1541450

15. Holmes, K.: Experiential Learning or exploitation? Volunteering for work experience in the UK Museums sector. Mus. Manag. Curatorsh. **21**, 240–253 (2006). https://doi.org/10.1016/j. musmancur.2006.06.001

16. Smith, S., Smith, C., Caddell, M.: Can pay, should pay? Exploring employer and student perceptions of paid and unpaid placements. Active Learn. High. Educ. **16**, 149–164 (2015). https://doi.org/10.1177/1469787415574049

17. Held, D.K.: The Internship Gap: The Relationship Between Internship Salary and the Probability of Receiving a Job Offer (2016). https://repository.library.georgetown.edu/ handle/10822/1040792

18. National Association of Colleges and Employers: The class of 2014 student survey report (2014)

19. Wildenhaus, K.: Wages for intern work: denormalizing unpaid positions in archives and libraries. J. Crit. Libr. Inf. Stud. **2**, 1–26 (2018). https://doi.org/10.24242/jclis.v2i1.88

20. Multnomah County: Effective Library Internships: A Toolkit for Success. Multnomah County Library, Multnomah County, Oregon (2012). http://interns.multcolib.org/ EffectiveLibraryInternshipsFULL.pdf

21. Surles, E., Cuervo, A.P.: The Jazz archives fellowship: professional development and diversity at the Institute of Jazz Studies. J. Arch. Organ. **12**, 230–241 (2015)

22. Cuyler, A.C.: Diversity internships in arts management, do they work? Am. J. Arts Manag. **13**, 1–13 (2015). http://fsu.digital.flvc.org/islandora/object/fsu%3A330447

23. Bastian, J.A., Webber, D.: Archival Internships: A Guide for Faculty, Supervisors, and Students. Society of American Archivists, Chicago (2008)

24. Farkas, M.: Barriers to diversity: problems of LIS internships and practica. Am. Libr. **50**, 48 (2019)

25. Galvan, A.: Soliciting Performance, Hiding Bias: Whiteness and Librarianship (2015). http:// www.inthelibrarywiththeleadpipe.org/2015/soliciting-performance-hiding-bias-whiteness- and-librarianship/

26. Farrell, B., Medvedeva, M.: Cultural Policy Center: Demographic Transformation and the Future of Museums. AAM Press, Washington, DC (2010)

27. Westermann, M., Sweeney, L., Schonfeld, R.: Art Museum Staff Demographic Survey 2018. Ithaka S+R (2019). https://doi.org/10.18665/sr.310935

28. United States Office of Personnel Management: 2012 Federal Employee Viewpoint Survey Results: National Archives and Records Administration Agency. United States Office of Personnel Management, Washington, DC (2012)
29. Pena, K., Hinsen, K., Wilbur, M.: Why diversity programs fail and how to fix them. SMPTE Motion Imaging J. **127**, 56–69 (2018). https://doi.org/10.5594/JMI.2018.2860499
30. Goldman, R.: Sea change: a community approach to archives internships. In: Conference presentations, p. 71. La Salle University, Philadelphia (2016)
31. Tai, J., Jimenez, K., Larmon, O.H.: Building Frameworks for Ethical Paid Internships in Archives. Society of American Archivists, Students and New Archives Professionals Section Meeting (2019)
32. Fisher, M.M.: Culture Workers, Just Say No to All Unpaid Internships. ARTNews (2019). https://www.artnews.com/art-news/news/unpaid-interhips-art-museums-transparency-oped-12974/
33. Carnegie Classification of Institutions of Higher Education: Carnegie Classifications (2018). http://carnegieclassifications.iu.edu/downloads.php
34. Mason-Draffen, C.: New rules could lead to more unpaid internships. Newsday. https://www.newsday.com/business/unpaid-internships-federal-regulations-1.17225681
35. Perlin, R.: Intern Nation: How to Earn Nothing and Learn Little in the Brave New Economy, pp. 31–35. Verso Books, Brooklyn (2011)
36. Kopp, M.G.: Internships in special collections: experiential pedagogy, intentional design, and high-impact practice. RBM J. Rare Books Manuscr. Cult. Herit. **20**, 12 (2019)
37. Carnegie Unit Foundation: What is the Carnegie Unit? (2014). https://www.carnegiefoundation.org/faqs/carnegie-unit/
38. Schwartz, P.S.: Making it Count: Professional Standards and Best Practices in Building Museum Internship Programs. Seton Hall University, South Orange, New Jersey (2012). https://sustainingplaces.files.wordpress.com/2013/05/museum-internship-programs.pdf
39. American Library Association: Directory of ALA-Accredited and Candidate Programs in Library and Information Studies (2019). http://www.ala.org/educationcareers/accreditedprograms/directory
40. Society of American Archivists. Directory of Archival Education (2019). https://www2.archivists.org/dae
41. American Alliance of Museums: Accreditation & Excellence Programs (2019). https://www.aam-us.org/programs/accreditation-excellence-programs/accreditation/

Temporality in Data Science Education: Early Results from a Grounded Theory Study of an NSF-Funded CyberTraining Workshop

Elliott Hauser[1]([✉])[iD] and Will Sutherland[2][iD]

[1] The University of North Carolina at Chapel Hill, Chapel Hill, NC, USA
eah13@email.unc.edu
[2] University of Washington, Seattle, WA, USA
willsk88@uw.edu

Abstract. Interest in data science, especially within the context of graduate education, is exploding. In this study we present initial results from an ongoing qualitative study of an interdisciplinary cyberinfrastructure-focused NSF-funded graduate data science education workshop hosted at an iSchool in the US. The complexity of the workshop curriculum, the participants' and instructors' disparate disciplinary backgrounds, and the technical tools employed are particularly suited to qualitative methods which can synthesize all of these aspects from rich observational, ethnographic, and trace data collected as part of the authors' role on the grant's qualitative evaluation team. The success of the workshop in equipping participants to do reproducible computational science was in part due to the successful acculturation process, whereby participants comprehended, altered, and enacted new norms amongst themselves. At the same time, we observed potential challenges for data science instruction resulting from the rhetorical framing of the technologies as inescapably new. This language, which mirrors that of a successful grant proposal, tends to obscure the deeply embedded and contingent history of the command-line technologies required to preform computational science, many of which are decades old. We conclude by describing our ongoing work, future theoretical sampling plans from this and future data, and the contributions that our findings can provide to graduate data science curriculum development and pedagogy.

Keywords: Data science education · Temporality · Grounded theory

1 Introduction

Data science education is a pressing concern for funding agencies, universities around the world, and members of the iSchools caucus. Recent work has explored

This work was partially supported by National Science Foundation grant 1730390.

A. Sundqvist et al. (Eds.): iConference 2020, LNCS 12051, pp. 536–544, 2020.
https://doi.org/10.1007/978-3-030-43687-2_43

the role that iSchools might play in data science education, both as a mechanism for modernizing the iSchool curriculum and a form of university service [9]. Data science is commonly presented as a 'cross-cutting' field which can be applied to any 'domain' [13]. In this way it is similar to many of the fields that proceeded it, such as statistics or, most pertinently, the so-called 'metadiscipline' of information science [3]. As such, the iSchools and the broad fields of information studies have much to bring to the initiatives, funded research, and curriculum updates.

The iSchools are particularly well-suited to contribute a socially informed and yet technically rigorous perspective to data science education. While some recent work has sought to clarify the role that iSchools might play in data science education [9], more work is clearly needed. Other disciplines are bringing their disciplinary norms and perspectives to bear upon this problem [6], and it is critical that the information fields do so as well so that we remain full partners in the transformations under way. While some of these contributions should come from applications of existing literature or lessons learned from analogous transitions in the field's past, there is still much that is unique to the field of data science that we don't fully understand.

The present study is intended as a contribution in the latter vein. Our broader study applies disciplinary perspectives from information studies to a qualitative analysis of an NSF-funded data science workshop focused on cyberinfrastructure skills at a US-based iSchool. Here we present some initial results of our ongoing work, based on a grounded theory analysis of interview, survey, observational, and digital trace data sources. We consider data science education a sociotechnical phenomenon, where neither social or technical methods alone can adequately explain what is observed [14]. iSchools initiatives such as the Data Science Education Committee seek to help define the iSchools' role in higher education's data-scientific future. Studies which apply the insights of information studies to rich data collected at the sites of ongoing efforts at transformation will be well-positioned to help the iSchools not only find their way in this future but do so in a manner that is consistent with the long history of holistic sociotechnical innovation and research in the field.

2   Theoretical Methods

Given the nascence of data science methods in the sciences, we avoid applying a ready-made frame, and instead rely on a grounded theory approach to sensitize ourselves to the critical points of engagement emerging between data science and scientific practice. Grounded theory has a range of different traditions, idioms, and disciplinary adaptations [2]. For this work, the authors primarily rely on Charmaz [4]. Grounded theory has a history of application in information studies [15], and has been widely used to study both software development [1,10,11] and educational issues in technical and scientific education [7,8]. Though qualitative work commonly relies upon ethnographic observation as a primary data source, Charmaz emphasizes that "All is Data" in grounded theory. This study takes advantage of grounded theory's data agnosticism to combine traditional qualitative data sources such as ethnographic observation, participatory interaction, semi-structured interviews, and surveys with trace ethnography of the extensive digital artifacts generated at the study site by both participants and instructors [5]. While trace ethnography has traditionally applied to the large scale data such as server logs, our application of it here applies it to small scale but rich digital artifacts created by the participants, described in detail in Sect. 3. Treating these as material artifacts with specific situated histories [12], they became essential supplementary pieces of our constant comparative analysis of our data.

3   Study Setting and Data Collection Methods

The site of the study was a workshop aimed at instructing scientists and engineers from a wide variety domains in using computational and data management tools in their work. The workshop was held at an information school at a large US public university, and hosted doctoral and postdoctoral participants from a large number of institutions across the US. Instructors were professors in the fields of information or computer science, research scientists, and research staff from NSF-funded cyberinfrastructure projects. A summary of the participants and some descriptive information is provided in Table 1.

The workshop was designed as a two-week, intensive introduction to reproducible computational science. The workshop's class sessions lasted most of the day each day, and breakfast and lunch were provided on-site. The first week of the workshop consisted of class sessions, including lecture as well as significant hands-on work. In the second week, the participants worked on a variety of group projects, which involved applying computational methods, such as machine learning, or reproducing scientific processing pipelines (in some cases the participants' own).

Table 1. Instructors (n = 17) and participant (n = 21) career stages. All staff, including those who did not formally teach sessions, are listed as instructors.

	PhD students	Postdocs	Asst. prof.	Assoc. prof.	Full prof.	Staff	Industry
Instructors	3	–	–	2	2	8	2
Participants	13	8	–	–	–	–	–

3.1   Data Collection, Analysis, and Theoretical Sampling

The study utilizes a variety of data sources and formats. Surveys, conducted after the first and second week of the workshop, provided more broadly comparable textual responses to the course content. Participants provided anonymous feedback by filling out sticky note responses identifying what went well and what did not go well about each session, which were collected and transcribed. Direct observation was carried out as the authors participated in the workshop as mentors, helping participants with technical breakdowns and project work throughout the workshop and over the intervening weekend. Informal interactions during meals and breaks supplemented formal observation and helped develop rapport. One of the authors taught two sessions on project collaboration tools Git and GitHub during the workshop, by request of the organizers. In addition to the above, the authors had access to and reviewed a large amount of digital artifacts generated by instructors and/or participants. These include:

- Group Slack chats
- Collaborative notetaking via HackMD
- GitHub code repositories and documentation created by participants
- Instructor presentations
- Participant final presentations

Interviews were conducted in the second half of the second week of the workshop, lasting from 20–60 min each. Interviews contained a structured common core of questions and were supplemented by a changing list of topics which had emerged from the current state of our constant comparative analysis and theoretical sampling process. For participants, these included:

- The nature of technical difficulties encountered by the participants.
- Problems participants had conceptualizing the tools and procedures being taught.
- The participants' experience and history with computational tools.
- The relevance of the workshop content to problems they were facing in their work.
- The relevance of the workshop content to their careers as researchers.

Finally, the authors completed many of the workshop activities themselves, producing field notes from this process. Constant comparative analysis has continued with digital traces and field notes after the event, and theoretical sampling has guided the researchers' engagement with the voluminous amount of digital trace data.

4   Initial Results

The initial results presented here all deal with the construction of temporality in the workshop: where the present is situated in relation to the past, and what value the past might have to understanding the present. These topics were chosen for their theoretical saturation, coherence with each other, and as examples of the insights we are seeking to generate with our work.

4.1   "Five Years Ago": The Temporal Framing of Computational Tools

Multiple instructors framed the importance of their subjects by emphasizing the differences between the present and "five years ago." A variety of tool names, usually proper nouns, were cited as evidence for this, tools that either had changed scientific practice during that time or, sometimes, were invented during this time. Rhetorically, this places the learner at the cusp of a new and exciting technological world, one which the instructor is familiar with. The names of particular tools stood in for acquired or desired skillsets ("machine learning with Keras", "reproducibility with Docker", "workflows with Snakemake", etc.), and, on a larger scale, the broad application or literacy with these tools established a temporal framing in which a participant, or even a scientific field might be "behind" or "ahead" others in adopting computational methods.

An implication of this construction is that the currently used technologies will themselves be obsolete five years hence, an implication conspiratorially acknowledged by Instructor 10: "of course, no one wants to think about that the technologies we're learning today will be obsolete in five years' time, but that's another story." This implication is held up as justification for the need for constant training, and perhaps to make learners glad that they are getting caught up now. Participant 3 described his motivation for attending the workshop as, "I think I fell back a bit so I need to keep up and learn these new technologies". This sea of constant change is presented as an easy-to-deny but ultimately undeniable fact, and one that will allow learners to separate themselves from their peers and maintain their professional relevance.[1]

4.2   The Obscured Past

When the workshop participants sat down to learn these cutting edge computational methods, they immediately stumbled upon an array of older, prerequisite technologies. In order to learn cloud systems participants had to struggle with accessing remote machines using SSH, and editing files with command line editors like nano or vim. Furthermore, where participants were able to quickly understand the tools being presented, it was often because they had encountered older technologies that were analogous in some way. Some participants reported picking up the concept of containers more easily, for instance, because of their prior experience with virtual machines.

These encounters with invisible old technologies highlighted a disconnect in the narrative of 5-year technological churn. That narrative obscured the fact that many, if not most, of the technologies, operating systems, platforms, and protocols used during the workshop were comparatively ancient. Command line utilities like ssh, vi, and bash have existed for decades and have a deep history. Version control and social collaboration site GitHub, cited by many participants as one of the most revolutionary tools encountered during the workshop, was founded in 2007 as an easier way to host git repositories. Open source version control software git, first developed in 2005 by Linux inventor Linus Torvalds,

---

[1] Professional relevance in this context is not limited to academic science. A major theme we will address in future work is the role and involvement of industry in scientific training. Genomics researchers we talked to, for instance, noted that many of their peers completed their doctorate and went to work for, for instance, social media or finance companies.

uses the Vim command-line text editor by default. Vim was first released in 1991.[2] Git and GitHub both make use of SSH (the binary program and the file transfer protocol), first released in 1995. The historical contingencies and mutual dependencies of these technologies extend in all directions. We cannot give a complete account of them here but rather seek to place the notion of "five years ago" into the context that it helps obscure. Five years hence, it is very likely that GitHub, git, Vim, and SSH will all still be in use. The technologies developed in this span will most likely be as deeply imbricated with current-day technologies as each of these is with the then-current technologies at the time of its initial development.

4.3   "Freezing" the Past: Versions, Tags, and Names

The complex relationship with the past informs the nexus of innovation and preservation constituted by practices of unambiguous naming in software development. Software is deeply embedded within a complex network of historically contingent binaries, programming languages, protocols, interfaces, and idioms. And yet there is immense pressure to collapse this complexity into comprehensible concepts, like "deep learning," "cloud," "container," or "workflow". This pressure is in one respect cognitive, making 'hooks' for understanding. In another respect it is a commodification, an implied equivalence that allows this cloud platform to be substituted for that one, this container to be equivalent from that one (provided they were built from the same image), and this workflow to generate the same results. Technological labels such as Python, Docker, or Ubuntu encapsulate a range of potential versions of their type: Python 3.7, Ubuntu 14.04 LTS, etc. They allow someone to say "I can code Python" or "I know Docker" even as the precise referent of these statements changes over time, sometimes markedly.[3] The version name, the commit, and the tag play dual roles in this process, marking innovation and enabling preservation. Version control technology marks a potential boundary between cultures which seek to innovate, those that seek to preserve, and those that are negotiating the relative value of each.

4.4   Honoring Legacy Code: Resisting Invisibility

The constructions of temporality we observed were not univocal, or even necessarily consistent. Participants and instructors also utilized constructions of

---

[2] Vim was a clone of and improvement on vi, first released in 1976 as a visual mode improvement on the ex line editor program for UNIX systems. Vim itself was based upon the 1988 C code of an Amiga port of STEVIE (ST Editor for vi Enthusiasts), a 1987 vi clone for the Atari ST. Development of Vim has been near-constant since the 1990s, and new versions are released every few months.

[3] An example of this is the discontinuities between Python 2 and 3, which played a role in the workshop as a Participant 7 updated his old processing pipeline from Python 2 to Python 3 as part of the workshop's project phase.

temporality that placed their work in dialog with technologies and computational artifacts from the past. In many cases these constructions emphasized the scientific relevance of work completed in the past. Instructor 3 framed her lecture around a story that many participants could relate to: when she started her PhD, she inherited code from an outgoing student and then spent almost a year trying to get it working, before being able to get started on any "real" science. The point of her framing was to help stoke participants' interest in the principles of reproducibility, and it was successful in doing so. During this lecture we learned that, in addition to the instructor, two other participants had used code written in FORTRAN 77 that was critical to their research. FORTRAN 77 was finalized in 1978 and was heavily used in scientific research for decades, but obscure and rarely used today.[4] This instructor defined "legacy code" as old software that does its job well but is hard to run on modern computers. This is a non-idiomatic usage of a term originally from software engineering. Legacy code in the software industry is any old software that is difficult to work with, prone to breakage, and expensive to maintain. It remains merely because it is too expensive or impractical to replace it with something better. For Instructor 3, legacy code represented something deserving of respect: a valuable, 'validated' computational artifact, a literal legacy left to the field by prior researchers. The history it represents is a connection with disciplinary expertise and scientific values.

5   Discussion

The construction of temporality in the workshop we observed placed the participants at the culmination of the past five years of development, and situated the course content as the cusp of innovation in scientific methodology. While this may be an appealing rhetorical framing for funding agencies, deans, and other units of the university, when applied too forcefully it can obscure the deeply historical and embedded nature of the command-line tools used in data science.

We observed participants encounter and successfully utilize many kinds of software tools for the first time. Some, like Singularity, were recently developed, while others, like Git, vi, SSH, or bash, were decades old. All of the software used existing protocols, libraries, conventions, and data formats in ways that were not novel and many activities would have been technically feasible five years ago. What this suggests to us is that computational tools do not travel alone. They embody a history of technological accretion, contain an array of literal and figurative dependencies, and embed practices which give them scientific meaning and value. This has strong implications for how researchers learn data science and scientific software development, but also for the changes that might emerge in various disciplines as computational methods are adopted. The negotiated temporality we observed in our workshop, simultaneously emphasizing

---

[4] FORTRAN stands for Formula Translator and was intended for easily translating mathematical formulas, which many scientists were familiar with, into compiled machine code, which they were not.

novelty and mobilizing the past to inform the present, is perhaps a microcosm of larger processes that are playing out in all disciplines which must contend with the adoption and integration of computational methods into their practices and norms.

Our findings show this dynamic at work for participants and instructors alike. On the one hand they were committed to the new cutting edge methods of data science which are redefining their work. On the other hand they were committed to the meticulous preservation activities of reproducibility, through which they work to construct continuity with the past. These combined as a motivation to use tools for computational reproducibility, as a way of making their present work valuable to a hypothetical future.

6 Future Work

The authors continue to study data science workshops as site to further develop this work. More broadly, though, the authors would like to expand out methods to include other data science education formats. Many data science curriculum initiatives are underway, including semester-length NSF CyberTraining programs at several institutions in the US. The authors hope to select one or more of these longer format classes as a future site. The less intensive data collection schedule should allow for a more thorough constant comparative analysis than the opportunistic short-term access utilized in this study can provide.

As data science becomes integrated more completely into curricula at iSchools and beyond, shaping what happens in the classroom and its effects upon subsequent research will become all the more important. The authors hope to employ insights from what is working at their study sites to the semester-length graduate data science curriculum at an iSchool. The resulting work will to contribute to the ongoing conversation about the role the iSchools can plan in the future of data science education.

References

1. Adolph, S., Hall, W., Kruchten, P.: Using grounded theory to study the experience of software development. Empir. Softw. Eng. **16**(4), 487–513 (2011)
2. Apramian, T., Cristancho, S., Watling, C., Lingard, L.: (Re)Grounding grounded theory: a close reading of theory in four schools. Qual. Res. (QR) **17**(4), 359–376 (2016)
3. Bates, M.J.: The invisible substrate of information science. J. Am. Soc. Inf. Sci. **50**(12), 1043–1050 (1999)
4. Charmaz, K.: Constructing Grounded Theory: A Practical Guide Trough Qualitative Analysis. Sage Publications, London (2006)
5. Geiger, R.S., Ribes, D.: Trace ethnography: following coordination through documentary practices. In: 2011 44th Hawaii International Conference on System Sciences, pp. 1–10, January 2011
6. Hicks, S.C., Irizarry, R.A.: A guide to teaching data science. Am. Stat. **72**(4), 382–391 (2018)

7. Kampov-Polevoi, J., Hemminger, B.M.: A curricula-based comparison of biomedical and health informatics programs in the USA. J. Am. Med. Inform. Assoc. (JAMIA) **18**(2), 195–202 (2011)
8. Kinnunen, P., Simon, B.: My program is ok - am I? Computing freshmen's experiences of doing programming assignments. Comput. Sci. Educ. **22**(1), 1–28 (2012)
9. Ortiz-Repiso, V., Greenberg, J., Calzada-Prado, J.: A cross-institutional analysis of data-related curricula in information science programmes: a focused look at the ischools. J. Inf. Sci. Eng. **44**(6), 768–784 (2018)
10. Pang, A., Anslow, C., Noble, J.: What programming languages do developers use? A theory of static vs dynamic language choice. In: 2018 IEEE Symposium on Visual Languages and Human-Centric Computing (VL/HCC), pp. 239–247, October 2018
11. Prechelt, L., Schmeisky, H., Zieris, F.: Quality experience: a grounded theory of successful agile projects without dedicated testers. In: 2016 IEEE/ACM 38th International Conference on Software Engineering (ICSE), pp. 1017–1027, May 2016
12. Ribes, D.: Materiality methodology, and some tricks of the trade in the study of data and specimens. In: Vertesi, J., Ribes, D. (eds.) digitalSTS, pp. 43–60. Princeton University Press, Princeton (2019)
13. Ribes, D., Hoffman, A.S., Slota, S.C., Bowker, G.C.: The logic of domains. Soc. Stud. Sci. **49**(3), 281–309 (2019)
14. Sawyer, S., Jarrahi, M.: Sociotechnical approaches to the study of information systems. In: Topi, H., Tucker, A. (eds.) Computing Handbook, vol. 19, 3rd edn, pp. 5-1–5-27. Chapman and Hall/CRC, London (2014)
15. Star, S.L.: Living grounded theory: cognitive and emotional forms of pragmatism. In: Bowker, G.C., Timmermans, S., Clarke, A.E., Balka, E. (eds.) Boundary Objects and Beyond: Working with Leigh Star, pp. 121–142. MIT Press, Cambridge (2015)

Physical Computing in Library and Information Science Master's Program Curriculum: A Pilot Course Offering and Future Possibilities

Monica G. Maceli[✉]

School of Information, Pratt Institute,
144 W. 14th Street, 6th Floor, New York, NY 10011, USA
mmaceli@pratt.edu

Abstract. Informal library practitioner publications have detailed the use of low-cost physical computing devices (such as micro-controllers and single-board computers) and sensors in broad library applications, such as: running digital signage, hosting OPAC stations, assessing space crowdedness, or automating reference statistics collection. Though physical computing topics have an increasing presence in makerspace-related curriculum within ALA-accredited library and information science Master's programs, there is a lack of general-purpose coverage suitable to tackling novel problems in the information professions, outside of the makerspace context. This paper presents the development of a Masters-level course in physical computing and rapid prototyping, considers its suitability to wider iSchool curriculum, and details future work in this area.

Keywords: Technology education · Physical computing · Rapid prototyping · iSchool curriculum

1 Introduction

Libraries have traditionally offered the public's first exposure to novel technological innovations, such as providing patrons with access to the burgeoning Internet in the 1990s. In the present, many of these novel technologies have found a home within library makerspaces, which are spaces dedicated to creative activities and educational programming, and may include anything from crafts, to do-it-yourself (DIY) electronics platforms, 3D printers, or audio-video recording technologies. Further in line with the maker ethos, library practitioner publications have detailed the use of such low-cost physical computing devices and sensors in broader library applications and *outside* of the makerspace, such as in running digital signage, hosting OPAC stations, assessing space crowdedness, or automating reference statistics collection.

Though maker-technologies are becoming increasingly common, and desirable to learn by librarians (e.g. as in the survey results presented in [1]), these technologies have largely been constrained to use within the boundaries of the makerspace or making-related events and patron programming. Existing early adopter publications

© Springer Nature Switzerland AG 2020
A. Sundqvist et al. (Eds.): iConference 2020, LNCS 12051, pp. 545–552, 2020.
https://doi.org/10.1007/978-3-030-43687-2_44

have indicated that broader application of maker-technologies within libraries and information organizations can yield additional services and features to the physical and digital library offerings, as well as leverage growing information professionals' skillsets in this realm.

A pilot course, offered at Pratt Institute School of Information in Spring 2019 and currently offered in a revised format in Spring 2020, explored rapid prototyping using such devices, with an emphasis on understanding both the technical possibilities and theory behind the maker movement. This short paper describes the design of the pilot course, specific to physical computing projects broadly within the information professions, but potentially outside of the bounds of the makerspace. Prior research suggests that such projects are increasingly common within libraries and information organizations, but poorly supported through Library and Information Science (LIS) curriculum and lacking in published resources. This paper reports on the developed course materials, findings, and generalizability of such curriculum to other iSchools.

2 Background

Though physical computing devices, such as sensors, microcontrollers, and low-cost single board computers, have found a natural home within the library makerspace, further opportunities exist to employ these technologies in aiding the broader work done by information professionals. A growing collection of published tutorials, blog posts, and case studies have detailed use of maker-technologies in broader library applications such as: increasing automation of reference statistics collection [2, 3], hosting information kiosks and signs [4, 5], or serving as OPAC terminals [5–7]. These projects largely employed the Raspberry Pi™, a low-cost single-board computer originally developed for educational purposes by the Raspberry Pi Foundation, which has become immensely popular in a wide range of do-it-yourself (DIY) projects. Also well-represented were: Arduino microcontrollers, a variety of sensors, and user interface components (such as push buttons and screens). These technologies are likely in use in other LIS circumstances that have yet to be formally documented.

The construction of such systems requires technological skills and knowledge typically associated with makerspace projects in the library and information science realm. Prior research work has investigated librarians' related knowledge and competencies, as well as how they acquire such skills. Koh and Abbas' [9] survey of library makerspace practitioners found the top required competency reported by all groups of participants was technology skills, but that the top competency which participants felt unprepared for was "new technology and making tools", with 48% of participants citing this need. Participants specifically related that they had *not* learned skills in new technologies, making tools, and makerspaces within their higher education.

Moorefield-Lang [10] conducted interviews with librarians who had makerspace locations in their libraries and noted significant struggles in librarian training, with reliance on peers, online resources, and trial-and-error; the author states "Makerspace training is evolving slowly... adult training is still lacking" (p. 110). This lack of existing makerspace training was echoed in Bowler's [11] experiences in introducing an experimental course in this area at the University of Pittsburgh. Closer to the present, Williams and Folkman [12] reiterated this finding, noting that very little in MLS graduate programs was being taught on the makerspace subject. In 2019, Maceli [8] identified a total of 8 courses from 7 ALA-accredited MLS programs relating to makerspace and making topics. A series of past and current makerspace-related continuing education opportunities were noted, with a variety of durations and structures, all offered in online format. As compared to prior research, these findings describe a notable increase in training and curriculum relating to library makerspaces. However, education in this realm for librarians and library staff appears to still be in its nascence and focuses more on the use of these technologies within makerspaces for patron programming and educational efforts [8] then broader applications of physical computing devices.

Thus, there is clear evidence that librarians and library staff currently feel unprepared to leverage maker-technologies in broader library context (or even within the makerspace itself), though many potential use cases exist. A handful of librarians and library staff are beginning to explore the possibilities. This gap provided the motivation to design and develop a course in rapid prototyping and physical computing, available as an elective to all graduate students in the School of Information at Pratt Institute. The initial pilot version of the course, offered in the spring of 2019, explored prototyping using such physical computing devices, with an emphasis on understanding both the technical possibilities and theory behind the maker movement.

3   Course Design

A review of related literature, as briefly summarized above, first indicated the lack of makerspace and making-related curriculum within MLS programs that could support information professionals in applying such physical computing tools to solve problems outside the makerspace. In response to this need, in Spring 2019 the author designed and taught a special topics course focused on using physical computing tools within design activities, as well as employing them in hardware-focused projects. Within design activities, physical computing devices can be used to craft interactive prototypes, experiment with different design solutions, and facilitate end-user collaboration and input. The course exposed students to a broad array of maker-technologies and tools, without bounding these ideas in the library makerspace context as has commonly been the case in prior MLS curriculum. The developed course description is as follows:

This course covers rapid prototyping using physical computing devices, with an emphasis on understanding both the technical possibilities and theory behind the maker movement. The course introduces programming, electronics, sensors, and other interaction technologies. Students will prototype with electronics, microcontrollers and engage in computer programming. The obtained knowledge will culminate in an applied final hardware project on a topic of the student's choosing.

The course goals and objectives (Table 1, below) emphasized understanding and exploring the role of making in creative processes, as well as endowed students with practical implementation skills.

Table 1. Course goals and learning objectives for the graduate-level "Rapid Prototyping and Physical Computing" course

Course goals	Course learning objectives
- Gain a broad understanding of the maker movement and related theory - Build knowledge of programming and electronics - Provide practical hands-on experience with prototyping using physical computing devices and electronics	- Understand the theory behind the maker movement, maker space designs, and implementations - Understand and critically analyze the possibilities of new physical computing technologies - Build skills in designing, creating, and evaluating physical computing systems - Create small interactive projects using microcontrollers, microcomputers, basic electronics, sensors, and related programming languages

The technologies explored, and used in student projects, included: Arduino microcontrollers, a variety of sensors (such as light sensors, RFID reader boards, load cells to determine weight, and sound sensors), motors, 3D printing, screens and LEDs, the Raspberry Pi single board computer, and others. On the theoretical side, the course explored the origins of the maker movement, as well as maker-focused pedagogical theory. Topics included critical making [e.g. 13], in which critical thinking and making activities are entwined within a reflective design process, as well as exploring the growing connection between making and library and information organizations [e.g. 14].

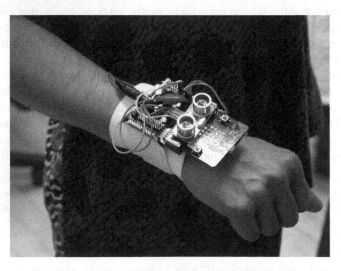

Fig. 1. Wearable accessibility system to alter blind users with a vibration when approaching walls (project of Kexin Cha)

Typical class sessions included a mix of discussions of design-related reading, hands-on learning of programming concepts, and exploratory exercises with relevant sensors and physical computing technologies. The early weeks of the course emphasized learning physical computing concepts using the inexpensive and education-focused BBC Micro:Bit device (visible in Fig. 1, above). In the semester-long final project, students were encouraged to identify and create a personal or professionally meaningful information system, based on the physical computing devices covered (and any additional technologies they chose to explore further). The project required students to include some form of user interface, in any modality, and the use of at least one microcontroller and one sensor, though all students went well beyond these base requirements.

Fig. 2. Museum-in-a-box system, consisting of a collection of RFID-scannable 3D artifact models (in box to the left) and a base station (to the right) to scan artifacts and play educational audio files (project of John Decker)

Fig. 3. Collection of RFID-scannable 3D artifact models for the Museum-in-a-box system (project of John Decker)

Final student projects included: a wearable accessibility system that could sense distance and alert blind users via vibration when approaching obstacles (Fig. 1, above), a "museum in a box" which played educational audio files after a 3D printed replica of a historical artifact was scanned (Figs. 2 and 3, above), a data visualization sculpture that moved in tandem with sea level variations as a result of climate change, and an interactive LED art installation driven by the user's heart rate.

Students presented their final projects to the School's community during a show-case held in finals week, as well as at an end-of-the-year event that highlighted student work. The course was taught in partnership with the Interactive Services department of the Information Technology unit, which collaborates with faculty on custom technology solutions to support research and teaching activities. The implications of this collaboration will be discussed in the following section. The course was well received by students, with 100% stating they strongly or moderately agree with the statement "I would recommend this course to another student". Student comments highlighted that the "course gives every student space to develop ideas" and that students enjoyed the opportunities to work with novel technologies, collaboratively problem-solve, and learn by experimentation.

4 Discussion

ALA-accredited Masters programs in library and information science are beginning to include courses relating to maker-technologies and makerspaces [8], with many of these courses positioned within iSchools. However, no courses support information professionals directly in employing similar technologies outside of the makerspace in other useful contexts within libraries and cultural heritage organizations. Given the extensive nature of the skills and knowledge required to complete physical computing projects, it is difficult to cover these technical needs and those of patrons in library makerspace programming within one class. To separate these use cases, the course designed and presented in this work emphasized the general capabilities of physical computing devices and how they might be integrated into design processes to any end. These devices could then be employed in any aspect of information professionals' work.

As detailed earlier, in the novel Rapid Prototyping and Physical Computing course, School of Information students created a range of personally meaningful maker projects that motivated them to go beyond course materials in solving their particular challenges. The technology skills covered introduce students to the broad range of possibilities with potential to drive novel technical ideas in the information professions, particularly around Internet-of-Things and sensing systems. These efforts lower the barriers for other institutions interested in offering similar courses and/or topics in the future as well as begin to raise awareness around existing projects of relevance. This is of particular importance to the LIS field currently, as recent research indicates that there is a small but growing number of maker-related courses offered within MLS programs and other programs will likely follow suit [8]. The initial pilot course syllabus is provided publicly in the School's syllabus repository.

4.1   Collaborative Technological Approach

A key success of the first offering of the Rapid Prototyping and Physical Computing course was the new relationships fostered with other schools, and the identification of departments within Pratt Institute that had intersecting interests in physical computing. In its initial offering, the course was conceived as a partnership between the School of Information and the Interactive Services department, with the two entities sharing cost of supplies and hosting of class activities. This model helped to connect School of Information stakeholders (faculty and students) directly with the Interactive Services staff, and thus created a shared understanding of the needs and possibilities around growth in the physical computing realm. This partnership model also helped overcome budget, staff, and space limitations that would become limiting if the course was hosted by the School of Information alone. Raising awareness of the physical computing needs across the campus as a whole, has facilitated an ongoing discussion around creating a shared space for making activities, which is currently under consideration by the administration.

5   Conclusion and Future Work

The initial goal of this work was to design and develop a general-purpose physical computing course that would endow future information professionals with the skills and knowledge to use such technologies to solve problems within their libraries and information organizations. The ongoing work in this area also seeks to improve knowledge sharing around the possibilities of maker-technologies outside of the makerspace within libraries and information organizations, as well as raise the profile of innovative library practitioners in this realm and increase visibility of their projects.

Longer-term goals for this project include sharing the code and instructions for successful projects developed to a wider library audience and allow for the collaborative growth of such code over time. In the context of library and information science curriculum, this research seeks to give library and information science students the opportunity to increase their skills and knowledge in the area of maker-technologies, and provide the wider LIS education and continuing education communities with course materials to facilitate their own educational offerings in the potential applications of maker-technologies outside makerspaces.

Future work will include using the related literature as a starting point for identifying active projects within libraries employing maker-technologies outside of the makerspace. Project developers will be approached for semi-structured interviews addressing the current or past uses of maker-technologies within the library, the successes and challenges encountered, the required librarian skills and knowledge, and the potential for sharing across the wider library community. The interview findings will be used to inform a follow-up physical computing course design, which will emphasize the design and construction of specific physical computing projects with application to broader library and information organization context. The course materials may also be used, in part or in whole, within continuing education efforts, such as conference workshops that illustrate the construction of such projects.

The maker ethos has clearly resonated with the LIS community and offers benefits to both our patrons and ourselves, as librarians, information professionals, educators, and researchers. Using maker-technologies to solve problems within libraries and information organizations allows the design and construction of systems tailored exactly to our needs and gives complete control over the software's functionality and data collection procedures. This may be a useful path for libraries and information organizations that want to leverage novel Internet-of-Things services within their spaces, but seek to avoid the privacy and other issues that emerge with the use of "black box" proprietary software systems.

References

1. Burke, J.J.: Survey says…: how library staff members are using technologies. In: Burke, J. J. (ed.) The Neal-Schuman Library Technology Companion. A Basic Guide for Library Staff, 5th edn, pp. 30–40. American Library Association, Chicago (2016)
2. Ribaric, T.: Redux: tabulating transactions with Raspberry Pi and visualizing results. Code4lib J. **40** (2018)
3. Younker, J., Ribaric, T.: Beyond open source software: solving common library problems using the open source hardware Arduino platform. Partnersh. Can. J. Libr. Inf. Pract. Res. **8** (1), 1–15 (2013)
4. Terlaga, A.: Take a look at the Raspberry Pi – library technology buzz. http://publiclibrariesonline.org/2013/08/take-a-look-at-the-raspberry-pi-library-technology-buzz/. Accessed 4 Apr 2019
5. Schiller, N.: Adventures with Raspberry Pi: a librarian's introduction. https://acrl.ala.org/techconnect/post/adventures-with-raspberry-pi-a-librarians-introduction/. Accessed 25 July 2019
6. Cooper, J., Knight, J.: Evaluating possible uses of a Raspberry Pi in an academic library environment. D-Lib Mag. **20**(5/6), 1–11 (2014)
7. Phillips, J.: Building small, cheap, dedicated catalog stations: do-it-yourself Raspberry Pi OPACS. http://publiclibrariesonline.org/2015/05/building-small-cheap-dedicated-catalog-stations-do-it-yourself-rasberry-pi-opacs/. Accessed 24 Apr 2019
8. Maceli, M.: Making the future makers: makerspace curriculum in library and information science graduate programs and continuing education. Library Hi Tech (2019)
9. Koh, K., Abbas, J.: Competencies needed to provide teen library services of the future: a survey of professionals in learning labs and makerspaces. J. Res. Libr. Young Adults 7(2), 1–22 (2016)
10. Moorefield-Lang, H.: Change in the making: makerspaces and the ever-changing landscape of libraries. TechTrends **59**(3), 107–112 (2015)
11. Bowler, L.: Creativity through 'maker' experiences and design thinking in the education of librarians. Knowl. Quest **42**(5), 58–61 (2014)
12. Williams, B.F., Folkman, M.: Librarians as makers. J. Libr. Adm. **57**(1), 17–35 (2017)
13. Ratto, M.: Critical making: conceptual and material studies in technology and social life. Inf. Soc. **27**(4), 252–260 (2011)
14. Britton, L.: Making space for creation, not just consumption: libraries around the United States offer tools for patrons to learn by doing. Libr. J. **137**(16), 20–23 (2012)

Public Libraries

Spatial Accessibility and Equity of Public Libraries in Urban Settings

Lingzi Hong[1](✉), Jiahui Wu[2], and Zhenpeng Zou[3]

[1] College of Information, University of North Texas, Denton, TX 76207, USA
lingzi.hong@unt.edu
[2] College of Information Studies, University of Maryland,
College Park, MD 20742, USA
jeffwu@umd.edu
[3] Urban and Regional Planning and Design, University of Maryland,
College Park, MD 20742, USA
zhenpeng@umd.edu

Abstract. Spatial accessibility of libraries affects their usage. It is, therefore, crucial to consider spatial accessibility's impacts on equity and inclusiveness of public libraries, which are part of public spheres for information services and community activities. We proposed a method to evaluate spatial accessibility and equity of public libraries in urban settings and conducted a preliminary study for public libraries in Washington D.C. Spatial accessibility is evaluated from two perspectives: the minimum distance to the nearest library of a community and the total number of libraries within certain distances. Spatial equity is evaluated as the correlation between the spatial distribution of libraries and community characteristics, which indicate the priority in need for library resources. We find that the spatial distribution of public libraries in D.C. can satisfy residents' basic need for library resources, as most communities can access at least one public library within an average distance of 2,500 m. However, the minority population, children and youth have inequitably less diverse library resources on average than the other subpopulations.

Keywords: Public libraries · Spatial accessibility · Equity · Urban setting

1 Introduction

Accessibility has always been a vital research question studied in library and information science. Equal accessibility to library resources and services is a civil right at heart and is a key tenet held by the American Library Association according to the Library Bill of Rights [1]. Accessibility has a multitude of meanings. Previous literature mainly focused on the accessibility of library services to patrons. For example, researchers studied how to make digital resources equally accessible to users of different physical or cognitive abilities [3]; how to ensure accessibility to infrastructures and services for patrons who are physically challenged or differently-able [9]. However, few paid attentions to the spatial allocation of libraries and the spatial accessibility to libraries. Spatial accessibility, interchangeable to "accessibility" in geographic

© Springer Nature Switzerland AG 2020
A. Sundqvist et al. (Eds.): iConference 2020, LNCS 12051, pp. 555–563, 2020.
https://doi.org/10.1007/978-3-030-43687-2_45

science refers to the cost or effort one takes to travel between places [10]. Spatial accessibility to certain amenity is positively correlated with how frequently the amenity is utilized [7]. The geographic location of a library determines the frequency of its usage, thereby affecting its equity and inclusiveness to local residents.

People may argue that physical distance to a library building is no longer a critical issue, since library information and resources can be easily accessed online these days. People with this opinion may ignore that public libraries often play a bigger role than simply managing publications and providing information. Public libraries are gradually seen as a type of facility that supports a sustainable community [2], which provide common space for residents to engage in community activities [12]. Public libraries are knowledge centers that provide varieties of learning programs for children, K-12 students, and adults [4, 24]. Public libraries also serve as a common space for people to build connections and develop social capital [25]. Such public services require physical access to public libraries and cannot be substituted by digital services. Meanwhile, they are of crucial importance for personal development and even community development. A previous study showed that having a library in the neighborhood is negatively correlated with the crime rate and the high school dropout rate [12]. Accessibility to libraries ensures the freedom for patrons to attend activities and access public resources. Especially for socioeconomically disadvantaged subpopulations, such as immigrants [24], free public resources provide opportunities for their upward social mobility.

Public resources are discretely distributed, which inevitably generates the differences in spatial accessibility of individuals. It is almost impossible to ensure that everyone has the same level of spatial access to public resources. However, it is possible to choose such locations that enable people of different demographic backgrounds and socioeconomic statuses to have equitable spatial access to these resources. Equity not only means equal distribution of resources to everyone, but that the disadvantaged have the resources in accordance to their need. For example, people with a low socioeconomic status may have a higher demand for the access to a library, since they cannot afford private Internet access or expensive books. While the criteria of equity may differ under different circumstances, there is no doubt that we need to make favorable decisions towards people who are either in a disadvantageous socioeconomic status or a subpopulation with a special need in certain public resources. This brings up the concept of spatial equity, in which the spatial variations in resource allocation is evaluated by a consideration of the equity impacts on residents in need [22].

In this paper, we will discuss about the evaluation of spatial accessibility and equity in the case of public libraries in urban settings. The urban setting is quite different from the suburban and rural setting in that car ownership is lower due to limited parking spaces and high parking cost. In addition, residents can adopt a multimodality lifestyle with convenient public transit, waking, and cycling [8]. While spatial accessibility is usually assessed based on travel distance, travel costs significantly differ between the urban and rural setting even with the same travel distance and mode (e.g. Fuel cost is usually higher in a city than in the suburbs). Therefore, distance-based spatial accessibility should be evaluated separately for urban, suburban and rural areas. Many U.S. cities today are faced with the challenge of spatial disparity in neighborhood demographics, such as a concentration of the urban poor [15], which makes the examination of spatial equity more critical than it has ever been.

We measure spatial accessibility to libraries in two ways: (1) the distance-based accessibility to at least one public library and (2) the number of libraries one can reach in certain distance. The first measurement focuses on the accessibility to meet the minimum need for a public library; The second measurement evaluates how many diverse library resources one can access within certain travel distance. We compute spatial accessibility to public libraries in different communities in Washington D.C. (DC for short), where distinct demographic and socioeconomic characteristics are spatially located due to historical redlining [14]. By examining the relationship between the spatial accessibility to public libraries and the characteristics of communities, we can make an inference about whether there exists a spatial disparity in accessibility to public libraries that may negatively impact the disadvantaged communities.

Specifically, we first measured the spatial accessibility to public libraries for all communities in DC. Then, we combined the accessibility level with the socioeconomic and demographic characteristics of these communities and examined their correlations. Our findings suggest that the spatial accessibility to public libraries in DC is mostly equitable in terms of satisfying the basic needs to access library resources by different subpopulations. However, for communities with a higher percentage of minority population or a higher percentage of children and youth, the number of libraries one can access within a certain distance is usually fewer than the communities with a concentration of white and single working professionals. This implies that spatial equity is yet to be fully achieved in terms of allocating more library resources to communities with more people in need. The rest of the paper is organized as follows: In Sect. 2, we concisely review related work about spatial accessibility and equity in public resources including public libraries. We describe the methodology and present the results in Sects. 3 and 4, and briefly discuss the implications and future work in Sect. 5.

2 Related Work

Spatial accessibility is often measured at two levels. One is at the household level, where the spatial accessibility for users of libraries or other public facilities is computed as the road-network based distance from the household location to the nearest public library [19, 21, 23]. However, this method requires detailed household location information of library users, which is usually not available. The second is at the community level, where the spatial accessibility is calculated as the Euclidean distance between the geographic centroid of a given community and the nearest public resources to the centroid [6]. Certainly, this measurement does not provide fine-grained information and averages the accessibility of all households in a community. Nevertheless, it is reasonable to assume that residents are uniformly located within a community in the urban setting with a high population density [21]. In this study, we conduct the analysis at the community level. Additionally, we evaluate the equity of spatial accessibility in this study.

Spatial equity is an important issue in public services, including parks [23], schools [18], playgrounds [21], primary healthcare facilities [13] and libraries [6]. The perspectives to analyze spatial equity may differ for different kinds of facilities. For example, considering people tend to go to the nearest playgrounds, the minimum-distance is a good metric to evaluate spatial equity. But this is not the case for public libraries that people may choose slightly further libraries for activities of interest.

Spatial equity to library resources has been studied from different perspectives. Donnelly compared the spatial accessibility to public libraries at the regional level in the United States [6]. The study compared the average distance to the nearest library at census tracts in different regions. The results show significant regional variances. While regional studies provide an overview of the spatial distribution of library resources, they are unable to identify local level issues. Sin evaluated funding and service level for public libraries nationwide [20]. Results show disparities in distribution of digital materials while no difference in public Internet terminals. Park analyzed the average travel distance for library users of different demographic characteristics and found that Caucasians, households with children, and well-educated individuals tended to travel further distance to access public libraries [19]. Spatial equity, in the context of allocating resources in accordance to people in need, was seldom studied.

3 Method

We measure spatial accessibility at the census tract level. In addition to the average travel distance for a community to reach the nearest public library, we also consider the number of public libraries can be reached within a certain radius. The spatial equity to public libraries is evaluated by comparing the spatial accessibility among communities of different socioeconomic and demographic characteristics.

DC is chosen as the study area mainly for two reasons. First, DC has the typical urban setting with a multimodal transportation network and good accessibility to public resources in general. In addition, the 179 census tracts in DC differ significantly in socioeconomic and demographic characteristics. Figure 1 shows the distribution of percentage of minority population, median household income in 2015, and proportion of population under 18 years old for these census tracts. The percentage of minority population ranges from 13.10% to 99.75%. The median household income for a few census tracts is greater than $100,000 a year, while about 40% of the census tracts have a median household income of up to $40,000 a year. The proportion of population under 18 years old, different from the other two indicators, tends to be normally distributed with an average of 17.41%.

The list of public libraries (1 central library and 25 branch libraries) in DC was obtained from the database of Institute of Museum and Library Services (IMLS) [17]. The locations of these libraries were geolocated in Google Places API, as shown in Fig. 2. The census tract data were obtained from the DC government dataset [5].

For this preliminary study, we simplified the measurement of spatial accessibility by considering walking as the primary travel mode to access public libraries, since parking spots are usually limited near the libraries. According to the 2017 National Household Travel Survey (NHTS) trip data, only 42.7% of trips are car trips. For a

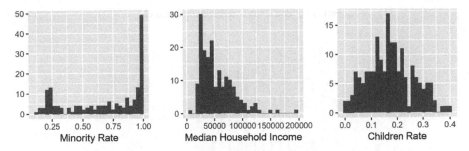

Fig. 1. Histogram of minority population rate, median household income and rate of residents under 18 of census tracts in DC

given census tract, we found its geographic centroid and calculated the Euclidean distance from the centroid to the nearest public library. The Euclidean distance is appropriate in this analysis because we consider spatial equity at the community level instead of the individual level. It enables us to compare the relative equity, although it is not as an accurate measurement as the transportation network distance. For each census tract, we also counted the number of libraries within a distance buffer of 1000 m, 1500 m, and 2000 m, approximately corresponding to 10, 15, and 20 min of walk.

Finally, the spatial equity of library accessibility is evaluated by correlating the spatial accessibility indicators and the socioeconomic and demographic indicators at the census tract level. The strength of correlations will imply whether certain sub-population have better spatial accessibility to public libraries than the others.

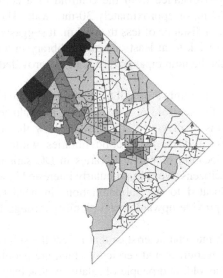

Fig. 2. Locations of public libraries in DC. (Public libraries indicated as triangle. One is closed and not shown. The Census Tracts are colored by median household income, darker blue represents higher median household income) (Color figure online)

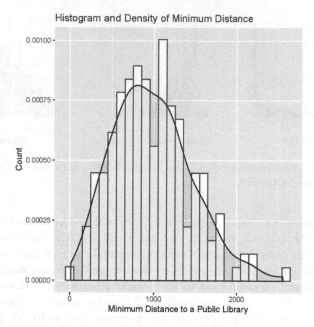

Fig. 3. Distribution of the minimum distance from census tracts to public libraries.

4   Results

Figure 3 shows the distribution of the distance to the nearest library for 179 census tracts in DC. The longest distance from the centroid of a community to its nearest public library is 2562.69 m, or approximately 30-min walk. Half of the communities have an average minimum distance of less than 1 km. It suggests that residents in most communities of DC can walk to at least one public library in a reasonable amount of time, which indicates that the municipal government has provided basic public resource equitably to all citizens.

Besides, we count the number of public libraries within the radius of 1000 m, 1500 m and 2000 m to the centroid of a community to evaluate the spatial equity of library resources in terms of diversity. The results show that more than half of the communities can access at least two public libraries within 2000 m on average. Although the spatial allocation of public libraries in DC satisfies the basic need for library resources for all citizens, we are particularly interested in understanding whether more resources are allocated to the subpopulations in need (e.g. the low income, minority, the youth) to provide upward social mobility through favorable public good provision.

We specifically look into characteristics that reflect the subpopulations in need for favorable public library resources and services, which are people of racial minorities, population under 18 years old, and people of relatively low income. As we are unable to find information about poverty, we use the median household income to signal the average socioeconomic status of a community. A previous study shows that poverty is highly correlated with the median household income [11].

Table 1 shows the correlation results between the spatial accessibility indicators and the socioeconomic and demographic characteristics of communities. The minimum distance from community centroid to a nearby library is only significantly related to the population density. When the population density is high, the distance to a nearby library is shorter. The minimum distance to public libraries is not biased toward any groups.

However, if we consider the diverse resources communities can access, there are significant disparities. As Table 1 shows, the percentage of minority population has negative correlation between number of libraries in 1000 m ($cor = -0.1476$, $p = 0.0493$), 1500 m ($cor = -0.1645$, $p = 0.0283$) and 2000 m ($cor = -0.2734$, $p = 0.0002$) radius. It means that for communities with more minorities, there are usually fewer libraries within the distance of 1000 m, 1500 m and 2000 m. The correlation between percentage of population under 18 is also significantly negative. Although there is not much difference in satisfying the basic need (spatial accessibility to the nearest library), communities with people who are potentially in higher need of public libraries are disadvantaged in the diversity of resources or the spatial accessibility to multiple libraries.

Meanwhile, we see that the median household income of communities is not correlated with any of the spatial accessibility indicators, which means public libraries present relatively equal spatial accessibility to communities with different socioeconomic levels.

Table 1. Correlations between spatial accessibility indicators and socioeconomic/demographic of communities

Spatial accessibility	Need indicators						
	Population	Minority population	Population under 18	Population density	Minority rate	% Under 18 population range	Median income
1. Min distance	0.0126	0.0135	0.0488	−0.2749***	0.0273	0.0250	0.0500
2. #Lib in 1000 m	0.0685	−0.1009	−0.0512	0.1631*	−0.1476*	−0.1044	0.0612
3. #Lib in 1500 m	−0.0703	−0.1349	−0.1349	0.2875***	−0.1645*	−0.1178*	0.1175
4. #Lib in 2000 m	−0.1326	−0.2512***	−0.3176***	0.4033***	−0.2734***	−0.2922***	0.1206

Significance levels: 0 '***'; 0.001 '**'; 0.01 '*'; 0.05 '.'; 0.1 ' '

5   Conclusion and Future Directions

Spatial accessibility measures the convenience for physical access to amenities and activities. The location choices of public libraries inevitably generate variances in spatial accessibility for individuals and communities. We argue that spatial equity of libraries doesn't mean everyone has the same level of accessibility, but that spatial accessibility should match the needs of different groups of people. We analyzed spatial accessibility and equity of public libraries at the community level in Washington D.C., where communities are highly heterogeneous in socioeconomic and demographic characteristics. Our results show that most of the communities in DC have good spatial accessibility to at least one public library within walking distance. The distance to the nearest library has no correlation with the socioeconomic or demographic characteristics of communities. The local level analysis shows a different pattern that the distribution of public libraries is not biased towards communities with high socioeconomic levels. However, we find that spatial equity may be improved as communities with more minority population or more children and youth have lower access to multiple libraries than the other communities. Considering that minorities and the youth and children could be in higher need for diverse learning resources and more engagement in community activities, there appears to exist a spatial inequity in public libraries against these subpopulations in need.

The initial study also has limitations that can be potentially addressed in future work. First, we simplified the evaluation of spatial accessibility by only considering walking distance. It is not the best indicator considering that DC also has a convenient public transportation system, which is supposed to enhance spatial accessibility. Whether public transportation can improve or worsen spatial equity remains to be studied. In addition to distance, travel time by modes of transportation could also be an indicator for accessibility [16]. Second, we use the number of libraries as a measurement of diversity of library resources. It would be interesting to also take into account funding and other heterogeneous characteristics that can differentiate each public library in the evaluation of spatial equity. Lastly, library is only one of the important public resources. We can also explore how the integrated urban public space featuring libraries, community centers, and other resources can jointly impact spatial accessibility and equity. By considering the joint effect of public resource allocation, we can not only help stakeholders equitably distribute public library resources, but also inform the decision-making process in urban planning and design.

References

1. American Library Association: Interpretations of the library bill of rights. http://www.ala.org/advocacy/intfreedom/librarybill/interpretations. Accessed 22 Aug 2019
2. Audunson, R., et al.: Public libraries as an infrastructure for a sustainable public sphere: a comprehensive review of research. J. Doc. **75**, 773–790 (2019)
3. Carlo Bertot, J., Snead, J.T., Jaeger, P.T., McClure, C.R.: Functionality, usability, and accessibility: iterative user-centered evaluation strategies for digital libraries. Perform. Meas. Metrics **7**(1), 17–28 (2006)
4. Celano, D., Neuman, S.B.: The role of public libraries in children's literacy development an evaluation report. Pennsylvania Library Association (2001)
5. District of Columbia Government: Census tracts in 2010. 30 November 2017. https://opendata.dc.gov/datasets/6969dd63c5cb4d6aa32f15effb8311f3_8. Accessed 02 July 2019
6. Donnelly, F.P.: Regional variations in average distance to public libraries in the United States. Libr. Inf. Sci. Res. **37**(4), 280–289 (2015)
7. Glander, M., Dam, T., Chute, A.: Households' use of public and other types of libraries. https://nces.ed.gov/pubs2007/2007327.pdf. Accessed 27 Aug 2019

8. Hamre, A., Buchler, R.: Commuter mode choice and free car parking, public transportation benefits, showers/lockers, and bike parking at work: evidence from the Washington, DC region. J. Public Transp. **17**(2), 4 (2014)
9. Hill, H.: Disability and accessibility in the library and information science literature: a content analysis. Libr. Inf. Sci. Res. **35**(2), 137–142 (2013)
10. Janelle, D.G.: Spatial reorganization: a model and concept. Ann. Assoc. Am. Geogr. **59**(2), 348–364 (1969)
11. Jesuit, D., Smeeding, T.: Poverty and income distribution. Technical report, LIS Working Paper Series (2002)
12. Johnson, C.A.: Do public libraries contribute to social capital? A preliminary investigation into the relationship. Libr. Inf. Sci. Res. **32**(2), 147–155 (2010)
13. Knox, P.L.: The intraurban ecology of primary medical care: patterns of accessibility and their policy implications. Environ. Plan. A **10**(4), 415–435 (1978)
14. Lloyd, J.M.: Fighting redlining and gentrification in Washington, D.C.: the Adams-Morgan organization and tenant right to purchase. J. Urban Hist. **42**(6), 1091–1109 (2016)
15. Lynch, J.W., et al.: Income inequality and mortality in metropolitan areas of the United States. Am. J. Public Health **88**(7), 1074–1080 (1998)
16. Miller, H.J.: A measurement theory for time geography. Geogr. Anal. **37**(1), 17–45 (2005)
17. Institute of Museum and Library Services: Library search & compare. https://www.imls.gov/labs/search-compare/details?fscs_id=DC0001. Accessed 18 June 2019
18. Pacione, M.: Access to urban services the case of secondary schools in Glasgow. Scott. Geogr. Mag. **105**(1), 12–18 (1989)
19. Park, S.J.: Measuring public library accessibility: a case study using GIS. Libr. Inf. Sci. Res. **34**(1), 13–21 (2012)
20. Sin, S.C.J.: Neighborhood disparities in access to information resources: measuring and mapping U.S. public libraries funding and service landscapes. Libr. Inf. Sci. Res. **33**(1), 41–53 (2011)
21. Smoyer-Tomic, K.E., Hewko, J.N., Hodgson, M.J.: Spatial accessibility and equity of playgrounds in Edmonton, Canada. Can. Geogr./Le Géographe canadien **48**(3), 287–302 (2004)
22. Talen, E., Anselin, L.: Assessing spatial equity: an evaluation of measures of accessibility to public playgrounds. Environ. Plan. A **30**(4), 595–613 (1998)
23. Tsou, K.W., Hung, Y.T., Chang, Y.L.: An accessibility-based integrated measure of relative spatial equity in urban public facilities. Cities **22**(6), 424–435 (2005)
24. Vårheim, A.: Gracious space: library programming strategies towards immigrants as tools in the creation of social capital. Libr. Inf. Sci. Res. **33**(1), 12–18 (2011)
25. Vårheim, A.: Public libraries, community resilience, and social capital. Inf. Res. **22**(1) (2017)

Theorizing Public Libraries as Public Spheres in Library and Information Science

Håkon Larsen[✉]

Oslo Metropolitan University, P.O. Box 4 St. Olavs Plass, 0130 Oslo, Norway
hakon.larsen@oslomet.no

Abstract. During the 21st century, library and information scholars have set out to theorize the role of public libraries as public spheres. Most of this research is engaging with Habermas' early work on the structural transformation of the public sphere. Even though Habermas has continued to develop his theories on the public sphere and deliberative democracy throughout his carrier, library and information scholars have to a limited degree engaged with his more recent work. Simply relying on Habermas's early work when theorizing public libraries as public spheres is limiting, but in addition to getting up to speed on Habermas' theoretical development, library and information scholars should also familiarize themselves with a broader set of public sphere theories. In this paper, I will give a short presentation of Habermas' work of relevance for public libraries, I will give a short presentation of some additional theories of public spheres, and I will present key concepts in studies of public libraries as public spheres within library and information science. I will conclude with some thought on how to move forward when theorizing public libraries as public spheres within library and information science.

Keywords: Public sphere · Public libraries · Habermas · Democracy · Social theory

1 Introduction

During the 21st century, scholars of library and information science have set out to theorize the role of public libraries as public spheres [1–4]. Most of this research is engaging with the work of Jürgen Habermas, and in particularly his early work on the structural transformation of the public sphere in Europe [5, 6]. This classic study has had a strong impact on several disciplines in the human sciences, and Habermas has remained an influential scholar and thinker throughout his career. Most disciplines have kept up with his intellectual development and particularly the work of relevance to one's own discipline. As pointed out by Michael Widdersheim, this has not been the case with library and information science where scholars to a limited degree have engaged with Habermas' more recent work [7]. This is remarkable, considering that Habermas has continued to develop his theories on the public sphere [8, 9] and deliberative democracy [10] throughout his career. These are works that should be of great interest to scholars seeking to understand and theorize the role of public libraries as public spheres, especially when concerned with libraries role as meeting places.

© Springer Nature Switzerland AG 2020
A. Sundqvist et al. (Eds.): iConference 2020, LNCS 12051, pp. 564–570, 2020.
https://doi.org/10.1007/978-3-030-43687-2_46

I fully agree with Widdersheim [7], in that simply relying on Habermas's early work when theorizing public libraries as public spheres is limiting. But I think we need to take it one step further: Getting up to speed on Habermas' theoretical development is not enough for amply theorizing public libraries as public spheres; library and information science scholars must also familiarize themselves with a broader set of public sphere theories. As digitalization frees up space in the physical libraries and digital culture seems to enhance the need for physical meeting places, the societal mission of public libraries has to an increasing degree been related to their role as public spheres [11, 12].

In this paper, I will give a short presentation of Habermas' work of relevance for public libraries, I will give a short presentation of some additional theories of public spheres, and I will present key concepts in studies of public libraries as public spheres within library and information science. I will conclude with some thoughts on how to move forward when theorizing public libraries as public spheres within library and information science.

2 Habermas' Public Sphere Theory and Public Libraries

Habermas describes in his 1962 book how the public sphere in Germany, Great Britain, and France in the seventeenth and eighteenth centuries went through a transformation from being a sphere where the rulers were displaying their power, to becoming a bourgeois public sphere inhabited by property-owning and literate men discussing central social and cultural issues (it later evolved to also include other social groups). In these public discussions, arguments were to transcend the individuals' social status, no topic should be foreign for critical discussion, and the audience should in principle be totally open [6]. For Habermas, this sphere where "private people come together as a public" [6] represented an ideal liberal public sphere. But Habermas' theory ended on a negative note: He believed it to be deeply problematic that the new mass media of the time (such as tabloid newspapers, radio and popular cinema) transformed the public to be consumers of culture, rather than critically discussing citizens. According to Habermas, this led to the dissolving of the bourgeois public sphere; due to the mass media, citizens were no longer capable of performing arguments in public.

Habermas later changed his perception of the role of mass media for democracy: 30 years after the publication of his dissertation, he launched a theoretical model for liberal democracies [10]. According to this model, any political decision must be supported by a majority of the population in order to be considered legitimate. A public sphere that strives to live up to the ideals of the bourgeois public sphere plays a key role in this model, as a majority will be attained through public deliberations. Habermas is no longer a pessimist. He now considers the mass media to play a key role in the communicative structure of the public sphere, where different groups from civil society can communicate their interests to a broader public. Depending on the kind of support they manage to achieve, these interests can be channeled to the political system and potentially end up in political decisions, and at best changes in law. Within such a democratic power circuit, public libraries can play a role as an open and inclusive space where citizens can get together and discuss cultural and political matters, in addition to be a free and open space for citizen education.

Public libraries have increasingly emphasized their role as public meeting places and hosts of cultural and political events, especially in the Nordic countries [11, 12]. Scholars of library and information science has also emphasized this aspect of public libraries in recent years, deeming public libraries an important element in the infrastructure of a sustainable public sphere [1]. Habermas' theory has proven helpful when conceptualizing this aspect of the mission of public libraries. When we take other dimensions of the mission into account, dimensions that also point to public libraries being public spheres, simply relying on a habermasian approach will come short. In order to theorize the complex role that public libraries play as public spheres, we need a broader set of theories.

3 Theories of Public Spheres

Since Habermas published his influential book, the thesis of the book has been discussed and criticized by several influential scholars [13], in turn leading Habermas [8] to revise his initial thesis. Habermas' thesis has also had considerable impact on theorization of the public sphere, as his influence has led scholars to develop perspectives on the public sphere that position themselves as an explicit alternative to a habermasian perspective, with the work of Negt and Kluge [14] and Mouffe and Laclau [15–17] as prominent examples (the public sphere has also been theorized by scholars prior to Habermas' work [18]). Where Negt and Kluge argued that Habermas in his theory of the bourgeois public sphere missed out on counter public spheres, especially proletarian ones, Mouffe does not consider consensus as a goal. Instead, she looks at conflict and emotional involvement as a value in itself and believes that this serves democracy better than an unattainable ideal of consensus and communicative rationality, which is a central tenet in Habermas' oeuvre.

Another influential theory on the public sphere and democracy has been developed by Alexander [19]. With his theory of *The Civil Sphere*, he has developed a theory of democracy and the public sphere, emanating from a cultural sociological perspective, with its strong focus on the role of meaning in social life [20]. Alexander [19] adheres to Habermas' [6] definition of the public sphere as "the sphere of private people coming together as a public", but criticizes Habermas for assuming that the idealizing principles of deliberation and rational discussion "actually grow out of speaking, deliberating, or being active in the public sphere" [19]. Where the public sphere for Habermas is an arena for rational discussions, it is for Alexander an arena for social performances, since "the ideal of rational dialogue and dispassionate deliberation is only one of several performative modes available to cultural actors in the public sphere" [21]. Habermas' [22] theory is based on an idea that there exists a specific form of rationality in the lifeworld that sets it apart from the instrumental rationality of the systems of market and state. Through communicative rationality, Habermas [23] argues that we meet each other as equals and let the power of the best argument decide the winners of every discussion. For Alexander, on the other hand, solidarity rather than rationality is the guiding principle of the public sphere. For Alexander [19], such a civil public sphere "relies on solidarity, on feelings for others whom we do not know but whom we respect out of principle." The civil sphere is "a world of values and institutions that generates the capacity for social criticism and democratic integration at the same time" [19]. For Alexander, the discourse of the civil sphere has at its core a set of binary cultural codes separating the civil from the anti-civil. This discourse is in turn sustained by specific communicative institutions (public opinion, mass media, polls, associations) and regulative institutions (voting, parties, office, law). This leaves no room for public libraries as an explicit part of his theory. Nevertheless, as public libraries are tied to the civil side of the binary code of civil sphere discourse, basing its legitimacy on such civil values as inclusion and openness, public libraries can be viewed as civil organizations. At the same time, it is important to remember that the public library can fail to live up to its ideals. In the US, for example, the public library has throughout its history gradually dissolved its tendencies for exclusion and anti-civil actions [24].

As public libraries have a strong mandate to serve the whole community through various inclusive practices [25], Alexander's civil sphere theory, with its heavy focus on solidarity, can be helpful when theorizing the democratic and inclusive mission of public libraries. Lacking in Alexander's theory is a focus on the public sphere as a place, as a physical location, an aspect that is captured by Habermas' theory, as well as other theories of public spheres, particularly those developed by Sennett [26, 27]. My argument is therefore that simply relating to one theory of the public sphere is not sufficient to amply theorize public libraries as public spheres. Instead, we need to develop a sophisticated theory of public libraries as public spheres by critically engaging with several theories of public spheres and seek to develop them as fitted to public libraries.

4 Public Libraries as Public Spheres

In recent years, library policies have been developed to emphasize the public sphere function of the public library. This is especially true in the Nordic countries, where several national laws on public libraries have been reformulated to encompass the libraries roles as public spheres [11, 12]. Most of these are explicitly or implicitly inspired by the work of Habermas. In Norway, Habermas' work has had a profound impact on the social sciences and humanities, and through that also the formation of cultural policies [28] and laws on freedom of speech [29, 30]. This is due to a tradition for involving scholars as experts when developing policies [11, 30]. Even though policies emphasize public libraries as public spheres in a habermasian sense, there is nevertheless a leap to argue that the public library is merely a public sphere institution in a habermasian sense, in that rational discussions of cultural and political matters are but one aspect of the democratic mission of public libraries. As free and open public spaces, public libraries are just as much about social solidarity as about democratic deliberation. In order to capture the totality of the democratic mission of the public library, it makes more sense to combine insights from Alexander and Habermas, rather than simply relying on one of the theories. From Habermas, we can get a precise definition of what constitutes a public sphere. "Private people coming together as a public" [6], serves as a description of certain aspects of the life at a public library. Nevertheless, Habermas' theory is too focused on democratic deliberation. If we instead turn to Alexander's theory of the civil sphere, we get to include democratic aspects of public libraries that goes beyond deliberative events taking place within the libraries, as his theory is not build on rational deliberation as the basis for a civil public sphere. Public libraries can most certainly be considered an institution of the civil sphere, as it "generates the capacity for social criticism and democratic integration at the same time" [19]. In public libraries patrons can attain knowledge deemed important for participation in public sphere discourse, and potentially also feel as part of a community simply by being present in the library and engaging with its various offerings. The *public* in public libraries relates both to the library as a physical "meeting place" for various activities involving some form of deliberation (be they debates, book club meetings or language cafés) and it being an open and inclusive space (at least in principle, although not true throughout the history of the institution [24]).

Social scientists have developed many concepts that can capture the *public* in public libraries. In library and information science public libraries have been conceptualized as low intensive meeting places [31], as meeting spaces [32], as public spheres [2, 4], as third places [12, 33] and as palaces for the people [34]. Library and information scholars activate sociological theories when developing models and concepts for public libraries, irrespective of whether the original theory emphasizes public libraries as a part of the theory. Oldenburg hardly mentions libraries in his book [33], while library and information scholars talk about libraries as third places [12]. Similarly, libraries make up a minor part of Habermas' theory, yet library and information scholar rely heavily on his theory when conceptualizing libraries as public spheres [1–4]. Alexander does not mention libraries, yet his theory has been activated when theorizing the role of libraries in society [35]. Klinenberg is an exemption as he is a sociologist writing explicitly about public libraries (New York Public Library) when developing his argument on the importance of social infrastructures for creating a more just and united society. Combined, these different perspectives provide us with a rich conceptual language for understanding public libraries. Yet, there exists no fully developed theory of public libraries as public spheres.

Scholars of library and information science have relied heavily on Habermas' early work when conceptualizing public libraries as public spheres [7]. In going forward with this theorizing in library and information science, scholars should engage with Habermas' more recent work as well as with alternative theories of public spheres. Only then will we be able to develop a theory capturing the many aspects of public libraries as public spheres.

References

1. Audunson, R., et al.: Public libraries as an infrastructure for a sustainable public sphere: a comprehensive review of research. J. Doc. **75**(4), 773–790 (2019)
2. Buschman, J.: The public sphere without democracy: some recent work in LIS. J. Doc. https://doi.org/10.1108/JD-06-2019-0115

3. Vårheim, A., Skare, R., Lenstra, N.: Examining libraries as public sphere institutions: mapping questions, methods, theories, findings, and research gaps. Libr. Inf. Sci. Res. **41**(2), 93–101 (2019)
4. Widdersheim, M.M., Koizumi, M.: Conceptual modelling of the public sphere in public libraries. J. Doc. **72**(3), 591–610 (2016)
5. Habermas, J.: Strukturwandel der Öffentlichkeit: Untersuchungen zu einer Kategorie der bürgerlichen Gesellschaft. Luchterhand, Darmstadt (1962)
6. Habermas, J.: The Structural Transformation of the Public Sphere: An Inquiry into a Category of Bourgeois Society. MIT Press, Cambridge (1989[1962])
7. Widdersheim, M.M.: Late, lost or renewed? A search for the public sphere in public libraries. Inf. Res. **22**(1), CoLIS paper 1664 (2018)
8. Habermas, J.: Further reflections on the public sphere. In: Calhoun, C. (ed.) Habermas and the Public Sphere, pp. 421–461. MIT Press, Cambridge (1992)
9. Habermas, J.: Political communication in media society: does democracy still enjoy an epistemic dimension? The impact of normative theory on empirical research. Commun. Theory **16**, 411–426 (2006)
10. Habermas, J.: Between Facts and Norms. Contributions to a Discourse Theory of Law and Democracy. MIT Press, Cambridge (1996)
11. Koizumi, M., Larsen, H.: Public libraries and democracy in the Nordic model. In: Gašo, G., Ranogajec, M.G., Žilić, J., Lundman, M. (eds.) Information and Technology Transforming Lives: Connection, Interaction, Innovation. Proceedings of the XXVII Bobcatsss Symposium, Osijek, Croatia, BOBCATSSS, pp. 452–457 (2019)
12. Audunson, R., et al.: Physical places and virtual spaces. Libraries, archives and museums in a digital age. In: Audunson, R., et al. (eds.) Libraries, Archives and Museums as Democratic Spaces in a Digital Age. De Gruyter Saur, Munich (2020)
13. Calhoun, C. (ed.): Habermas and the Public Sphere. MIT Press, Cambridge (1992)
14. Negt, O., Kluge, A.: Öffentlichkeit und Erfahrung: Zur Organisationsanalyse von bürgerlicher und proletarischer Öffentlichkeit. Suhrkamp Verlag, Frankfurt (1972)
15. Laclau, E., Mouffe, C.: Hegemony and Socialist Strategy: Towards a Radical Democratic Politics. Verso, London (1985)
16. Mouffe, C.: The Return of the Political. Verso, London (1993)
17. Mouffe, C.: On the Political. Routledge, London (2005)
18. Gripsrud, J., Moe, H., Molander, A., Murdock, G. (eds.): The Ideal of the Public Sphere. A Reader. Lexington Books, Lanham (2010)
19. Alexander, J.C.: The Civil Sphere. Oxford University Press, Oxford (2006)
20. Alexander, J.C.: The Meanings of Social Life: A Cultural Sociology. Oxford University Press, New York (2003)
21. Townsley, E.: Media, intellectuals, the public sphere, and the story of Barack Obama in 2008. In: Alexander, J.C., Jacobs, R.N., Smith, P. (eds.) The Oxford Handbook of Cultural Sociology, pp. 284–317. Oxford University Press, Oxford (2012)
22. Habermas, J.: The Theory of Communicative Action. The Critique of Functionalist Reason, vol. 2. Beacon Press, Boston (1987)
23. Habermas, J.: The Theory of Communicative Action. Reason and the Rationalization of Society, vol. 1. Beacon Press, Boston (1984)
24. Wiegand, W.: Part of our Lives. A People's History of the American Public Library. Oxford University Press, Oxford (2015)
25. Johnston, J.: The use of conversation-based programming in public libraries to support integration in increasingly multiethnic societies. J. Librariansh. Inf. Sci. **50**(2), 130–140 (2018)
26. Sennett, R.: The Fall of Public Man. Norton, New York (1992[1977])

27. Sennett, R.: Quant. The Public Realm. https://www.richardsennett.com/site/senn/templates/general2.aspx?pageid=16&cc=gb. Accessed 02 Dec 2019
28. Ministry of Culture: Meld. St. 8 (2018–2019) Kulturens kraft: Kulturpolitikk for framtida. Ministry of Culture, Oslo (2018)
29. Ministry of Justice and the Police: NOU 1999:27 "Ytringsfrihet bør finde Sted" Forslag til ny Grunnlov §100. Ministry of Justice and the Police, Oslo (1999)
30. Kalleberg, R.: Ytringsfrihet, demokratiteori og demokratiet som uferdig prosjekt. Sosiologi i dag **45**(4), 11–37 (2015)
31. Audunson, R.: The public library as a meeting-place in a multicultural and digital context: the necessity of low-intensive meeting-places. J. Doc. **61**(3), 429–441 (2005)
32. Jochumsen, H., Rasmussen, C.H., Skot-Hansen, D.: The four spaces – a new model for the public library. New Libr. World **113**(11/12), 586–597 (2012)
33. Oldenburg, R.: The Great Good Place: Cafés, Coffee Shops, Bookstores, Bars, Hair Salons, and Other Hangouts at the Heart of a Community. Paragon House, New York (1989)
34. Klinenberg, E.: Palaces for the People. How to Build a More Equal and United Society. The Bodley Head, London (2018)
35. Larsen, H.: Archives, libraries and museums in the Nordic model of the public sphere. J. Doc. **74**(1), 187–194 (2018)

Creating a Library Privacy Policy by Focusing on Patron Interactions

Shandra Morehouse(✉), Jessica Vitak, Mega Subramaniam,
and Yuting Liao

University of Maryland, College Park, MD 20742, USA
{shandra,jvitak,mmsubram,yliao598}@umd.edu

Abstract. As sensitive transactions continue to move online, public libraries are becoming a critical resource to patrons without access to the internet. This paper shares insights on how library staff negotiate privacy risks when working with patrons handling sensitive and private information. Based on findings from an analysis of library policies on technology use, as well as focus groups and participatory design sessions with library staff from around the United States, we categorize primary risks patrons face when using library computers to complete information tasks requiring submission of sensitive information, as well as how library staff navigate the tensions between their professional values and privacy concerns. We conclude the paper with a discussion of how these findings are informing our development of a framework that library staff can use to navigate privacy risks patrons face.

Keywords: Libraries · Information needs · Privacy · Security · Information policy

1 Introduction

For low-income neighborhoods in the United States, one of the most important resources public libraries offer is access to computers and the internet. Data suggests that low-income Americans are much less likely to have internet access at home and many only access the internet through their smartphone [1]. At the same time, forms and services (e.g., job applications, banking, healthcare) increasingly require online transactions. Therefore, public library staff who assist patrons using public computers play an important role in helping patrons get access to a variety of services to satisfy their information needs and provide useful guidance when it comes to protecting patron's privacy. In this paper, we conceptualize privacy in terms of the control one has (or does not have) over the disclosure of their personal information. Control has historically been a popular way of framing the concept in the social sciences and is heavily influenced by the work of Westin [2] and Altman [3], who defined privacy as "selective control of access to the self" (p. 24).

To understand how library staff are assisting patrons navigate privacy risks, we evaluated the local, state, and national policies that provide guidance to library staff on how they should assist patrons conducting online transactions, especially when it involves personally identifiable information (PII). By identifying the gaps in these

© Springer Nature Switzerland AG 2020
A. Sundqvist et al. (Eds.): iConference 2020, LNCS 12051, pp. 571–578, 2020.
https://doi.org/10.1007/978-3-030-43687-2_47

policies for staff/patron interactions, we make policy recommendations to ensure library staff provide the needed services without running into liability risks [4]. We also analyze data collected by our team through focus groups and participatory design sessions with library staff to get their insights on the privacy issues patrons face when using public computers, the existing procedures that work (or don't work) as staff assist these patrons; and the policies they'd like to guide patron interactions. Our research is guided by two primary research questions:

> **RQ1:** What privacy issues do patrons face when they use public library computers?
> **RQ2:** How do library staff navigate tensions between professional core values and patron privacy?

Based on our analysis of these data sources, we conclude this paper by presenting considerations for the development of a patron-focused privacy policy framework for public libraries. The resulting framework will provide guidelines for front-line library staff who respond to time-sensitive requests for assistance from patrons that may deal with patrons' PII.

2   Related Work

2.1   Privacy Policies in Public Libraries

A major resource for library administrators creating or revising their library's privacy policy is the American Library Association's (ALA) Privacy Toolkit [5]. This toolkit outlines how to build a privacy policy, including how to conduct a privacy audit[1] at a library and how to implement the policy once it has been created or updated. In addition to the toolkit, ALA's privacy materials include guidelines and checklists on privacy concerns like third party vendors, public access computers, and library websites [6, 7].

ALA's privacy resources provide detailed guidance on the precautions libraries as an institution should take to protect patrons' data. Similarly, much of the research on privacy in libraries focuses on library administration. For example, Pekala [8] considers privacy issues arising when third parties collect patron information, while Houghton [9] considers how to provide patrons the services they expect and still protect their privacy. Klinefelter [10] argues that circulation, reference, and interlibrary loan services are additional weak points of privacy within libraries. Building on prior work, this paper examines how libraries and library staff can assist patrons with privacy issues they face when using public computers.

---

[1] A privacy audit is often the first step in creating or revising a privacy policy. It evaluates current policies and practices in the library and can reveal strengths and weaknesses of existing policies and library culture.

2.2 Core Values of Librarianship

As a profession, librarians are led by a set of 12 core values that form their foundation of practice [11]. Most relevant to this paper are the values of Access, Intellectual Freedom, Service, and Privacy/Confidentiality. Access means that all information resources are equally available to all patrons. Intellectual Freedom refers to the profession's commitment "to resist all efforts of censoring library resources" [11]. Service reflects the commitment of library staff to provide the "highest level of service to all library users" [11]. While Privacy/Confidentiality states that "protecting user privacy and confidentiality is necessary for intellectual freedom and fundamental to the ethics and practice of librarianship" [11].

3 Methods

3.1 Virtual and In-person Focus Groups with Library Staff

Throughout 2017, we conducted 11 focus groups with 36 library staff at local and national library conferences and via Webex video conferences. Staff were recruited through ALA's communication channels and social media posts. Each focus group lasted approximately 90 min. Sessions included discussions on the challenges staff faced as they work with patrons, how they handle information requests involving sensitive information, and the types of resources and training they wanted to enhance their and their library's ability to resolve patrons' information needs. For a detailed discussion of data collection and analysis, see [4].

3.2 Evaluation of Local, State, and ALA Policy Guidelines

To better understand privacy issues being discussed in libraries, we conducted a review of existing policies from ALA, state libraries, and various library systems around the US. State and library system policies included in this review were gathered using snowball sampling from the ALA toolkit [5], as well as reviewing major metropolitan library systems. These policies were gathered and analyzed to develop thematic categories of privacy policies in libraries. Policies were collected until saturation was reached. In total, 16 state and public library policies were reviewed.

From these policies, we developed an initial list of eight categories for library privacy policies, including: Unlawful Use of Library Computers, Privacy at Public Terminals, Confidentiality of Patron's Search Data, Filtering, Internet Privacy and Security Practices, Rules Governing the Use of Library Computers, Guidelines for Minors, and What Staff Can and Cannot Do. These categories were then used in the participatory design sessions described below to get feedback from library staff who had experience interacting with patrons to determine what did and did not work, and what was missing in these policies.

3.3   Participatory Design Sessions with Library Staff

In the first half of 2019, we conducted four in-person participatory design (PD) sessions (see Bonsignore et al. [12] for details on PD techniques) with 24 public library staff. Two sessions were held at an ALA conference, one at a state library association conference, and one at a public library. Staff were recruited through ALA and state library channels, as well as social media. Each session lasted 90–120 min. In the first part of each session, library staff were given copies of different types of library policies (described in Sect. 3.2 above). After a large group discussion, staff were divided into smaller groups, each focusing on a different category of privacy policies. Members in each group collectively created draft policies or topics of interest that were missing in their category and added them to sticky notes. Afterward, they regrouped and discussed why these policies are needed and how these policies may vary based on communities that they serve. See Fig. 1 for an example of this process.

Fig. 1. An example of policy ideas generated during PD sessions.

Research team members took detailed notes during each session. PD activities were audio recorded and pictures were taken. The research team transcribed the audio and created a summary document for each session that weaved the audio, observation notes, pictures, and the resulting ideas that came out of each session.

4 Findings

4.1 Privacy Issues Faced by Patrons When Using Public Library Computers

Through our focus groups and PD sessions, it became clear that library staff want to help patrons protect their data, but the rapid change in technology and new data threats make it difficult. Below, we identify three contexts emerging from our data where a patron's privacy was at risk.

Privacy Knowledge and Skills: Everyday Basics. Many patrons do not fully understand privacy risks or care about their privacy, which adds to the challenge library staff face when helping those on public computers. For example, a librarian from urban New York said, *"...many customers are not savvy at all. One man, I was questioning him about his information, and he said, 'Oh, don't worry, I'm not worth anything.' He was joking, but at the same time, that's their attitude. It's like, 'What's to steal?'"* In addition, library staff said many patrons are unaware of the digital traces they leave behind when using public computers, like not logging out of an account or storing credit card information on a retail site. Another New York-based librarian noted, *"They know there are certain things that need to be kept secure, but when they're done with their session, they're done, and they don't think about closing things out."* This issue is exacerbated for libraries that don't have safety protocols in place to delete personal information after each use. From our conversations with library staff, policies and technology for clearing user history varied significantly across library systems.

Library staff spend a lot of time helping patrons with passwords. A tech services coordinator in rural Tennessee, estimated they help patrons reset a password at least three or four times a week. Some patrons expect staff to remember their passwords for them; a librarian from suburban New York said, *"I've definitely had...patrons who are like, 'Why can't you remember it?' And it's like, we see hundreds of you guys every week. We can't remember all of your email addresses...We don't want to know your passwords."*

Privacy While Obtaining Critical Government Assistance. As described in Thompson et al. [13]—and as shared by library staff we spoke with—government and social service agencies often send patrons to libraries to get help with online assistance programs. These forms require transmission of PII, which makes it challenging to assist patrons in completing the forms. A librarian from urban New York noted, *"I've had folks come in and say, 'Oh, I'm just going to give you all my tax information. I need you to fill this out for me.' I can't sit down and do that for them as a librarian... I can help point you in the right direction, but I'm not allowed to put in any information for you."*

Privacy When Accessing Library-Contracted Third-Party Vendor Sites. An emerging concern that library staff have is the amount PII collected by third-party vendors who have contracts with library systems. Oftentimes, patrons have no idea when they move from a library site to a third-party site while using the public computers. Like Houghton [9], several library staff expressed concerns regarding the amount of data third parties collect and how to inform patrons regarding third-party data sharing policies. A branch manager from urban North Carolina expressed their concern over third parties, saying, *"[I was] talking to [a] vendor about novels and whatnot...and he was like, 'Have you heard about linked service, using GPS to see how* *close you are to the library...' Makes me nervous...to see what's close by and whether a book is on the shelf."*

4.2   Staff Tensions Between Their Core Values and a Patron's Privacy

Below, we discuss how library staff navigate the tensions between some of their professional values (like Intellectual Freedom, Access, and Service) and the core value of Privacy and Confidentiality.

Providing Access to Information vs. Preventing Risky Privacy Practices. Staff we spoke to had an expectation of neutrality when it came to digital privacy and security, in line with core values of Intellectual Freedom and Access. They discussed challenges they faced when trying to balance helping their patrons and preventing them from making risky decisions. As a librarian from Washington D.C. noted, the goal is to *"communicate the risks without dictating what they can and cannot do."* Similarly, another librarian from Maryland described the expectation that library staff remain neutral: *"I think that's what can get tricky helping serve customers because sometimes they're doing something that probably isn't the best privacy practice...and trying to remain that neutral party or give them verified resources to assist them."*

In practice, however, risk assessment by library staff seems largely idiosyncratic, rather than based on specific policies. Other library staff we spoke with described situations where they explicitly warned patrons about risky situations. A tech services coordinator from rural Tennessee said, *"If [you] see something on there that they really shouldn't have on [their] device, you're like, 'Hey, this is spyware, you need to get rid of this.' ...You cross a very fine line of wanting to help your patrons while trying to stay neutral."*

Library staff also recognize that libraries are trusted institutions [14] and that this trust goes hand in hand with neutrality. A librarian from urban California explained, *"I think a lot of it, is patrons trust the library. We're the neutral place where it's okay. No one's going to come after them. Whatever they share stays with us... So they're always willing to share information. And sometimes, I feel like they share a little bit too much."*

Providing the Highest Level of Service vs. Protecting Patron's Privacy. Many library staff we spoke to struggled to find a balance between providing high-quality service to patrons while still protecting their privacy. A librarian from urban California explained, *"I think a lot of patrons are so desperate to get assistance...[that] I don't think they realize they are handing us sensitive or private information."* A librarian from urban North Carolina had similar experiences: *"We get people who are in a hurry and just wanna get something done really, really fast. So they'll want us to do things that are beyond that policy. And that's when we have to say, 'This is your task and we will show you how to do it, but you need to do it yourself.'"*

Some patrons prefer library staff complete their computer tasks because of physical disabilities or a lack of digital literacy. This creates an additional strain on library staff between following stated policies and recognizing many situations fall into gray spaces. A librarian from urban Maryland explained how they handle these situations: *"...if it becomes overwhelming, like, 'okay, I really need you to bring someone with you to help you,' that's some of the ways that I've dealt with working with customers and their sensitive information. "*

5   Discussion

This analysis is part of a larger research project, with a goal of developing a patron-focused privacy framework to guide US library staff in assisting patrons with their information needs and encourage patrons to develop privacy skills and keep their information secure in public spaces. The themes presented in this paper form the basis of this patron-focused framework that will be created to be used as a companion to the existing ALA privacy toolkit [5]. ALA's privacy framework focuses on how libraries can protect patron's data but does not fully address how library staff can help patrons protect their own information on public computers.

We asked library staff to talk about the utility of policies or other resources they could use when helping patrons navigate privacy risks and the tensions described above. The overwhelming response was that while it was an appealing idea, the process of building a privacy policy focused on staff/patron interactions is easier said than done. As staff responses have highlighted, patrons' privacy skills, interest, and knowledge vary significantly, and their expectation and trust with library staff assumes that staff are comfortable handling their PII. This variation creates challenges for designing a framework that can be applied to many different library contexts.

To make this framework applicable to all libraries and library staff, the completed framework should be flexible enough to allow for variations in situations/contexts while still providing enough guidance for library staff on where to draw the line. To be inclusive and scalable, the framework should be written in a straightforward language —not full of technical jargon. In addition, any privacy framework needs to be general enough to allow for changing technology and any new privacy risks that will arise.

When discussing what types of content are most important for a policy resource, most staff stressed that discussions of privacy should be connected to patrons' everyday technology use rather than covering high-level topics like encryption. The framework should also address the three contexts we discussed above – basic privacy knowledge, privacy when completing government forms, and privacy when using third party sites. Additionally, the framework should address the tensions between librarians' core values and privacy concerns by providing suggested solutions that work best for their own library system and population.

6   Conclusion

This study provides an important step in developing a privacy framework that allows library staff and administrators to personalize policy based on their branches' privacy configurations and patron population. Next, we will be co-creating this patron privacy framework through PD sessions with library staff and sharing examples with the larger library community across the US. We will work with technology policy and privacy scholars to ensure policy language alleviates the tensions library staff have indicated in this study, as well as allowing patrons to safely utilize public computers in the libraries to complete everyday transactions.

References

1. Mobile Technology and Home Broadband 2019. https://www.pewinternet.org/2019/06/13/mobile-technology-and-home-broadband-2019/. Accessed 16 Sept 2019
2. Altman, I.: The Environment and Social Behavior: Privacy Personal Space Territory and Crowding. Brooks/Cole Publishing Co., Monterey (1975)
3. Westin, A.F.: Privacy and Freedom. Atheneum, New York (1967)
4. Vitak, J., Liao, Y., Kumar, P., Subramaniam, M.: Librarians as information intermediaries: navigating tensions between being helpful and being liable. In: Chowdhury, G., McLeod, J., Gillet, V., Willett, P. (eds.) iConference 2018. LNCS, vol. 10766, pp. 693–702. Springer, Cham (2018). https://doi.org/10.1007/978-3-319-78105-1_80
5. Privacy Tool Kit. http://www.ala.org/advocacy/privacy/toolkit. Accessed 15 Sept 2019
6. Library Privacy Guidelines. http://www.ala.org/advocacy/privacy/guidelines. Accessed 07 Sept 2019
7. Library Privacy Checklists. http://www.ala.org/advocacy/privacy/checklists. Accessed 07 Sept 2019
8. Pekala, S.: Privacy and user experience in 21st century library discovery. Inf. Technol. Libr. **36**(2), 48–58 (2017). https://doi.org/10.6017/ital.v36i2.9817
9. Houghton, S.: The challenge of balancing customer service with privacy. J. Intell. Freedom Privacy **4**(1), 8–9 (2019)
10. Klinefelter, A.: Privacy and library public services: or, I know what you read last summer. Legal Ref. Serv. Q. **26**(1–2), 253–279 (2007). https://doi.org/10.1300/J113v26n01_13
11. Core Values of Librarianship. http://www.ala.org/advocacy/intfreedom/corevalues. Accessed 07 Sept 2019
12. Bonsignore, E., et al.: Embedding participatory design into designs for learning: an untapped interdisciplinary resource. In: CSCL 2013 (2013)
13. Thompson, K.M., Jaeger, P.T., Taylor, N.G., Subramaniam, M., Bertot, J.C.: Digital Literacy and Digital Inclusion: Information Policy and the Public Library. Rowman & Littlefield, Lanham (2014)
14. Gomez, R., Gould, E.: The "cool factor" of public access to ICT: Users' perceptions of trust in libraries, telecentres and cybercafés in developing countries. Inf. Technol. People **23**, 247–264 (2010)

Evaluating Public Library Community Engagement and Impact for Sustainable Information Services

M. Asim Qayyum[(✉)] , Waseem Afzal , and Linda Mahony

Charles Sturt University, Wagga Wagga, Australia
aqayyum@csu.edu.au

Abstract. Public libraries have always had a pivotal function within the community. However, libraries are undergoing rapid changes, as are many industries in a globalised world. Therefore they need to re-evaluate their operations and services to provide for the changing needs of their users. In this paper, we describe a pilot study underway that measures the engagement and impact of two library programs/services for young children and their families – *Giggle and Wiggle*, and *Story Time* – that are offered by the Australian Capital Territory (ACT) Libraries in Canberra, Australia. Exploring the impact of these services will help in understanding the factors that ensure the sustainability of public libraries and their engagement with the communities they serve. These factors will focus on four key domains as have been identified from the literature: the educational, social, cultural, and economic impact these programs have on their communities. The findings of this study are expected to generate some practical strategies that public libraries can adopt to maximise community impact and engagement.

Keywords: Public libraries · Community engagement · Early childhood education · Library impact

1 Introduction

People from diverse backgrounds engage with public libraries as libraries perform a number of vital functions within the community. For example, public libraries provide spaces for work, leisure and relaxation; and the digital divide is reduced through equitable access to information, activities and resources [1, 2]. Public libraries also offer a place where people can become part of the community, and connect with local services. However, in an era of changing technology and ever-increasing user expectations, public libraries need to remain agile to meet the evolving needs of the communities they serve.

The aim of the current pilot project is to measure and evaluate the engagement and impact of two library programs/services for young children and their families, *Giggle and Wiggle* and *Story Time,* offered by Libraries ACT - Australian Capital Territory (ACT) - in Canberra, Australia. Outcomes and impact of these two programs will be studied across four domains: educational, social, cultural, and economic. These

A. Sundqvist et al. (Eds.): iConference 2020, LNCS 12051, pp. 579–587, 2020.
https://doi.org/10.1007/978-3-030-43687-2_48

domains have been proposed in many library impact studies to be of great value in determining impact (e.g. [5]).

Exploring the impact of these services is critical for ensuring the sustainability of public libraries and communities to ensure development meets the needs of the present community without compromising the needs of future generations. This pilot study will also identify practical strategies that public libraries can adopt to evaluate and maximise the impact and engagement with their communities. Therefore, the study's significance is that the findings will enable public library sector administrators to have a comprehensive view of the social, cultural, educational, and economic contributions made by services such as the ones studied in this project. The administrators will also be able to demonstrate the value of their library services in tangible terms to their funding bodies across a wide range of impact domains.

2   Review of the Literature

The conceptual framework of the current study is informed by many landmark studies in library services assessment (e.g. [3, 4]) and underpinned by the standards and guidelines proposed by peak professional associations and/or government bodies including Australian Library and Information Science Association (ALIA), the Australian Department of Education and Training, and the National Early Literacy Panel (NELP)-USA.

The conceptual framework is focused across four domains: educational, social, cultural, and economic. These domains, in one or another form, have been identified as being of great value in library impact studies. Examples include, a study by Huysmans and Oomes [5], a study by Detez et al. [6], and a study commissioned by State Library of New South Wales [4]. Our assessment will look at the gains in knowledge and skills of children as linked to the six variables identified by NELP being strong predictors of later literacy development. These variables include (a) alphabet knowledge, (b) phonological awareness, (c) rapid automatic naming, (d) rapid automatic naming of objects or colours, (e) writing or writing name, and (f) phonological memory. The perceptions of participants in these programs (both parents/care givers and librarians) will be explored around the four domains identified above.

The review of the literature indicates that remaining agile and engaged with community might simply encompass provision of free internet services and training in technology use [7]. But if public libraries are to maintain an image of being trusted places [8, 9] then greater agility and new forms of service diversity may be required to remain relevant to the needs of the communities they serve. For example, the ALIA 2014 futures report [7] recognises the need for more social and work spaces where people can connect, or disconnect from the stress of being perpetually connected. Such spaces may serve as an access point from which individuals can be encouraged to connect with each other and to community programs [10].

2.1   Value of Public Libraries

Public libraries form an essential part of any community. An indicator of this perceived value is the willingness of community members to pay for library services. For example, Oliphant [11] in their study of 1201 individuals, comprising both library users and non-users, found respondents were willing to pay a median of $20 per year for library membership. In another study, Barron, Williams [12] found that the key perceived benefits of public libraries are that they: (1) nurture a love of reading, (2) help people obtain a new job, (3) assist people in being more productive with their current job, and (4) support them with life-long learning.

Other studies have examined the impact and engagement of public libraries with their communities to assess their value. These research efforts have adopted various methodologies including surveys of users and non-users perceptions of public libraries, as well as the analysis of usage statistics collected by public libraries. For example, Barron et al. [12] large online study of 3,689 public library users conducted at the University of South Carolina found that public libraries had an impressive array of positive impact on the community, not the least of which was the improvement in quality of life reported by 92% of the sample. In another large study [11] 88% of survey respondents reported that they, or someone in their household, had used a public library in the previous 12 months. Participants in that study indicated having access to their local library was important or very important, thus indicating the high value they placed on public libraries.

Value of public libraries in terms of their social and economic impact on the community is varied and well documented. For example, social impact includes promotion of social cohesion and opportunities to work collectively to help build a sense of local community [13]. Economic impact can include benefits to financial well-being through the provision of access to financial information, job and career resources, computer technology and services, and business resources [14]. Other impacts of public libraries are cultural and educational [15]. For example, some cultural benefits to communities include supporting and promoting learning and development, while libraries can promote education and learning and are increasingly providing both adult and child literacy skills development programs.

2.2   Impact of Public Libraries on Children

Public libraries play a major role in promoting children's literacy learning. These institutions expose children to print books as well as other literacy learning experiences such as arts and crafts, songs, drama, storytelling, and puppet shows. Research shows that the early years are crucial to develop literacy skills [16]. Children from environments lacking in rich language experiences have shown declines in tests of preschool educational development [17]. These children often fail to catch up, thus falling further behind in school achievement. As Burchinal et al. [17] elaborate, exposing young children to quality language and initial literacy learning experiences begins in early childhood.

Public libraries also have the potential for promoting emergent literacy skills and pre-reading skills of young children (e.g. [18]). Many public libraries in Australia focus their early years' programs to incorporate emergent literacy techniques. Emergent literacy skills refer to interest and enjoyment with books, phonological awareness, letter knowledge, and vocabulary. It is an interactive and holistic approach to reading development which emphasises the natural literacy behaviours of young children. Many public libraries focus their early years' programs to incorporate emergent literacy techniques as it helps narrow the gap in academic achievements in later years for students (e.g. [19]). For example, the Better Beginnings Project is a program linking Western Australian libraries with primary schools to promote reading for enjoyment and improve literacy skills among children [16]. Thus, library programs do more than simply encourage a love of reading [20]; they also offer opportunities for children to develop language and literacy skills which provides the foundations for success in literacy.

2.3   Children's Library Programs in Libraries ACT: 'Giggle and Wiggle' and Story Time

Two popular children's programs hosted by Libraries ACT include *Giggle and Wiggle (G&W)* and *Story Time* where the former is hosted for 0–2 year old children. During G&W sessions, children and their parents/carers share songs and rhymes to support language development. Songs and rhymes are important in the development of phonological awareness. For very young children, songs and rhymes provide rich linguistic, cognitive, and social stimulation for a young child's developing brain [21]. Babies are quick to learn to discriminate between phonemes, which are the sounds in words. Children need to acquire phonological awareness at the word level, that is, be aware that speech is composed of a series of separate words. This awareness can be promoted by rocking, clapping, or counting words in a spoken phrase or sentence [22].

The other program, *Story Time*, at Libraries ACT is an interactive session of stories, rhymes and songs suitable for 3–5 year old children and their parents/carers. The aim of Story Time is to encourage a love of books and to promote pre-reading skills, listening and language skills. It has been shown that reading aloud to children improves their pronunciation, comprehension skills and increases their vocabulary [16]. Rich language experiences in the prior-to-school years plays an important role in developing children's literacy and vocabulary skills and are related to later literacy success [23]. Children's books contain almost twice as many infrequently used words as adult conversations therefore reading children books that have rich vocabulary are useful to promote their vocabulary. Large vocabularies have been known to be linked to later reading success [9, 24]. Stories stimulate children's emotions and imaginations; introducing them to conflict and problem-solving skills, adventure through real or imaginary worlds, and supporting the development of empathy for others.

2.4   Research into Children's Library Programs

Children's programs have long been an important part of library services and due to their long-standing traditions, many research studies have examined the impact of these programs. For example, studies by McKechnie [25], Campana et al. [26], and Mills et al. [27] represent that scholarly tradition. Campana et al. examined early literacy outcomes in library story-telling sessions, whereas Cahill [28] analysed use of language in stories. Yet, in another study McKechnie explored the ways in which story-telling can help to understand what transpires during these sessions and the contributions made by these sessions to the participants.

However, the focus of these studies has been primarily on understanding the impact these programs have on early literacy, or broadly speaking on educational development of children. This line of enquiry is highly valuable but there is a need to examine the impact of these programs not only on children but also on all of the participants, including parents/carers and librarians. Furthermore, it is also important to understand the impact these programs have across a broad range of domains including educational, social, cultural, and economic aspects.

3   Project Methodology

The methodology to be used in this study will be dictated by the research aim listed above, as has been recommended by others [29–31]). As such, a qualitative approach utilising semi-structured interviews will be used to collect data from library program participants, as well as the librarians who administer these programs. Both open-ended and closed-ended (survey type) questions will be used. Open-ended questions will gather participant and librarian's perceptions about educational, social, and cultural value of these programs, while closed-ended questions will help in gathering information about their general usage and economic value. This methodology is consistent with a majority of literature examining the impact of public libraries, and indeed it has been argued that the qualitative methodology is best suited to examining the different types of impact of public libraries [8, 32].

3.1   Participants

Two groups of participants will be recruited to share their stories in semi-structured interviews:

1. 20–30 library program participants (expected to be parents/carers of a child) who attend the two programs will be interviewed for their perspectives about the programs they have attended at the library with their young children. Interviewing library program participants will allow the researchers to best explore the intimate knowledge they hold of their experiences with these programs.
2. Around 10 librarians responsible for these programs will be interviewed to identify and document their perceptions of the effectiveness of the programs they offer.

3.2   Data Collection

Research data for this study will be collected in December 2019 at those ACT library sites where the two identified programs are being held. Ethics approval has been obtained from the university's Human Research Ethics Committee.

A challenges foreseen during data collection is that fewer than expected participants agree to take part in the study that can necessitate a longer data collection time period. Another challenge will be that question wording can be challenging for participants from different cultural backgrounds, and may necessitate use of appropriate prompts/clarifications by the researchers.

3.2.1   Semi-structured Open-Ended Interview Questions

Semi-structured interviews have a predetermined set of questions. However, the interviewer is not bound by open-ended questions as they only provide a focus for the interview, while allowing the flexibility [33, 34] to follow leads from participants, and probe for further information that might arise during the interview. Through interviewing library program participants (parents/carers) and librarians in this study, the effectiveness of the library services and the barriers and enablers to maximise engagement with the community can be explored and described.

At the beginning of the interview, basic demographic data will be gathered from all participants. Following that, a grand tour question will introduce the topic to begin conversation. For example, library program participants will be asked: 'Tell me about your experiences of coming to Giggle and Wiggle and/or Story Time', and librarians will be asked 'Tell me about your experiences managing Giggle and Wiggle and/or Story Time sessions.'

Guiding questions will follow the grand tour questions as they assist to clarify what was requested and guide the conversation [33, 35]. The following are examples of guiding questions for library program participants:

- How long have you been coming to the library?
- What would you like/what could be improved?
- What other programs do you, or have you attended? Why/why not?

Guiding questions for the librarians will include:

- How do you decide what program to run?
- What is your perception of the success of the program?
- How long have you been involved in the program?

Finally, probing questions will provide back up and clarification to the grand tour and guiding questions for both participant groups, and will add depth to the interview data by asking the participant to be more specific [29, 33–36]. Probing questions will evolve from the interview as it takes place and will include [33, 36]:

- Tell me more.
- Can you give me an example?

3.2.2   Closed-Ended, Structured Interview Questions

Structured closed-ended question will allow the researchers to measure the economic value and the economic activity generated by these two programs as quantitative data. All library program participants and librarians affiliated with the Giggle and Wiggle, and Story time programs will be asked these structured interview questions to:

The economic impact will be assessed using 'Contingent valuation method'. This method is considered to be a very useful and valid measure of public libraries' economic value (e.g. [37]), and is one of the best-known methods for assessing the economic value of library programs. The method was originally developed for identifying the financial value of non-profit organisations and services [37] and is expected to work well for this study's purposes. By engaging this method, users will be asked a hypothetical question 'if this service is not funded by the government anymore how much would you be willing to pay to maintain community's access to this service'. A cross check is that the economic activity generated involves assessing the real financial activity in the form of exchange of goods and services, and that can be calculated using 'industry multipliers' available from the Australian Bureau of Statistics [38].

3.3   Data Analysis

All interviews will be digitally audio recorded with permission from participants, and later transcribed verbatim. The gathered interview data will be analysed qualitatively through thematic analysis, while the data from the closed ended survey type questions will be analysed using descriptive statistical analysis.

4   Conclusion

Public libraries in the 21st Century are undergoing rapid change. Engagement and use of public libraries is continually under scrutiny to determine the viability of this community resource. Current programs and services need to be evaluated to ascertain their ongoing service to communities. In this paper we described a current pilot study to measure engagement and impact of early childhood programs for the communities which they service. Outcomes of this study will enable us to better understand the educational, social, cultural and economic impact of public libraries on the communities they serve. Preliminary findings will be reported at the conference.

Acknowledgements. The authors acknowledge with thanks the financial support provided by the Faculty of Arts and Education, Charles Sturt University. They are particularly grateful to the Australian Capital Libraries (ACT) management and staff for their assistance with this research.

References

1. Svanhild, A., Ragnar, A., Andreas, V.: How do public libraries function as meeting places? Libr. Inf. Sci. Res. **32**, 16–26 (2010)
2. Australian Library and Information Association, Statement on public library services. https://www.alia.org.au/about-alia/policies-standards-and-guidelines/statement-public-library-services. Accessed 12 Nov 2019
3. SGS Economics and Planning, Dollars, Sense and Public Libraries: The landmark study of the socio-economic value of Victorian public libraries (2011)

4. Library Council of New South Wales, Enriching communities: The value of public libraries in NSW (2008)
5. Huysmans, F., Oomes, M.: Measuring the public library's societal value: a methodological research program. IFLA J. **39**(2), 168–177 (2013)
6. Detez, J., et al.: Performance metrics towards 2030: Investigating the news to measure and report on our activities (2014)
7. Australian Library and Information Association, Future of the Library and Information Science profession. https://www.alia.org.au/futureoftheprofession. Accessed 10 Nov 2019
8. Aabø, S.: The role and value of public libraries in the age of digital technologies. J. Libr. Inf. Sci. **37**(4), 205–211 (2005)
9. Anderson, K., et al.: Better beginnings: public libraries making literacy links with the adult community. Libri **63**(4), 272–281 (2013)
10. Scott, R.: The role of public libraries in community building. Public Libr. Q. **30**(3), 191–227 (2011)
11. Oliphant, T.: "I'm a library hugger!": public libraries as valued community assets. Public Libr. Q. **33**(4), 348–361 (2014)
12. Barron, D.D., et al.: The economic impact of public libraries on South Carolina. University of South Carolina (2005)
13. Kerslake, E., Kinnell, M.: Public libraries, public interest and the information society: theoretical issues in the social impact of public libraries. J. Libr. Inf. Sci. **30**(3), 159–167 (1998)
14. McClure, C.R., et al.: Economic benefits and impacts from public libraries in the State of Florida, Final Report (2000)
15. Abram, S.: Communicating value and impact through advocacy: dealing with the scalability issue in the province of ontario. Public Libr. Q. **36**(2), 96–122 (2017)
16. Ewing, R., Callow, J., Rushton, K.: Language & Literacy Development in Early Childhood. Cambridge University Press, Cambridge (2016)
17. Burchinal, M., Lee, M., Ramey, C.: Type of day-care and preschool intellectual development in disadvantaged children. Child Dev. **60**(1), 128–137 (1989)
18. Kupetz, B.N.: A shared responsibility: nurturing literacy in the very young. Sch. Libr. J. **39**(7), 28–31 (1993)
19. Baydar, N., Brooks-Gunn, J., Furstenberg, F.F.: Early warning signs of functional illiteracy: predictors in childhood and adolescence. Child Dev. **64**(3), 815–829 (1993)
20. Celano, D., Neuman, S.: The role of public libraries in children's literacy development: An evaluation report (2001)
21. Fellowes, J., Oakley, G.: Language, Literacy and Early Childhood Education, 3rd edn. Oxford University Press, Oxford (2019)
22. Gleason, J.: The Development of Language. Pearson, Boston MA (2005)
23. Snow, C.E., Dickinson, D.K.: Skills that aren't basic in a new conception of literacy. In: Jennings, E.M., Purves, A.C. (eds.) Literate Systems and Individual Lives: Perspectives on Literacy and Schooling, pp. 179–191. State University of New York, Albany (1991)
24. Lehr, F., Osborn, J., Hiebert, E.H.: Research-based practices in early reading series: A focus on vocabulary (2004)
25. McKechnie, L.: Observations of babies and toddlers in library settings. Libr. Trends **55**(1), 190–201 (2006)
26. Campana, K., et al.: Early literacy in library storytimes: a study of measures of effectiveness. Libr. Q. **86**(4), 369–388 (2016)
27. Mills, J.E., et al.: Early literacy in library storytimes, part 2: a quasi-experimental study and intervention with children's storytime providers. Libr. Q. **88**(2), 160–176 (2018)

28. Cahill, M., Joo, S., Campana, K.: Analysis of language use in public library storytimes. J. Libr. Inf. Sci. (2018). https://doi.org/10.1177/0961000618818886
29. Berg, B.L.: Qualitative Research Methods for the Social Sciences, 5th edn. Pearson Education, Boston (2004)
30. Crotty, M.: The Foundations of Social Research: Meaning and Perspective in the Research Process. Allen & Unwin, St Leonards (1998)
31. Denzin, N.K., Lincoln, Y.S.: The Sage handbook of qualitative research. Sage, Thousand Oaks (2011)
32. Miller, P.A., Crabtree, B.: Depth interviewing. In: Hesse-Biber, S.N., Leavy, P. (eds.) Approaches to Qualitative Research: a Reader on Theory and Practice, pp. 185–202. Oxford University Press, New York (2004)
33. Hatch, J.A.: Doing Qualitative Research in Education Settings. State University of New York, Albany (2002)
34. Warren, C.A.B.: Qualitative interviewing. In: Gubrium, J.F., Hostein, J.A. (eds.) Handbook of Interview Research: Context and Method, pp. 83–102. Sage, Thousand Oaks (2002)
35. Corbin, J.M., Strauss, A.L.: Basics of Qualitative Research, 3rd edn. Sage, Thousand Oaks (2008)
36. Bogdan, R., Knopp-Biklen, S.K.: Qualitative Research for Education: An Introduction to Theories and Methods, 5th edn. Pearson, Boston (2007)
37. Poll, R.: Can we quantify the library's influence? creating an ISO standard for impact assessment. Perform. Meas. Metrics **13**(2), 121–130 (2012)
38. Information paper: Australian national accounts: Introduction to input-output multipliers, Australian Bureau of Statistics [Canberra] (1995)

Cultural Policies, Social Missions, Algorithms and Discretion: What Should Public Service Institutions Recommend?

Kim Tallerås[✉], Terje Colbjørnsen, Knut Oterholm,
and Håkon Larsen

Oslo Metropolitan University, P.O. Box 4 St. Olavs Plass, 0130 Oslo, Norway
kim.talleras@oslomet.no

Abstract. Digital media services, and streaming services in particular, filter and recommend content to their users by the use of algorithms. In this paper, we ask what happens when institutions like public service broadcasters, public libraries, as well as other media institutions who base their operations on public funding and social mission statements, implement similar algorithms. Can we think of alternate algorithmic principles? What should public service algorithms recommend, who would decide, and based on what criteria? In order to address questions such as these, we argue for a broad approach based on not only technological considerations, but also complementing perspectives touching upon how such institutions are situated in the media industries, relevant cultural policy frameworks and practices for handling quality assessments. Using examples from Scandinavian public service and media institutions, we indicate how the coding of algorithms have profound social and cultural implications. This short paper thus initiates a project with the aim of examining various algorithmic perspectives that could - and perhaps should - be taken into account when approaching issues of cultural policies, social missions and discretion in publicly funded culture institutions.

Keywords: Social missions · Public service · Recommender systems

1 Introduction

Can you code a social mission?

In a study of the availability of media content in streaming services, Tallerås, Colbjørnsen and Øfsti [1] found that Netflix tend to recommend their own "originals". In a newspaper article [2] following up on the study, a representative from Netflix commented the findings by stating that their recommendation system simply was favorizing movies and TV series matching previous preferences of their users; if they watch Netflix originals, they will be exposed to more of those. This is a legitimate way of targeting an audience in the commercial streaming market, but what happens when institutions like public service broadcasters and public libraries, based upon public funding and operating principles, implement similar algorithms? What should they recommend, who would decide, and based on what criteria?

© Springer Nature Switzerland AG 2020
A. Sundqvist et al. (Eds.): iConference 2020, LNCS 12051, pp. 588–595, 2020.
https://doi.org/10.1007/978-3-030-43687-2_49

These are grand questions forming a complex problem area. In order to approach them, we need an appropriate technological perspective, but also complementing perspectives touching upon how such institutions are situated in the media industry, relevant cultural policy frameworks and not least practices for handling quality assessments. There exist a variety of previous research relating to this problem area, including papers that thoroughly outline and describe the area as an important one to research [3]. Most related studies, however, are focused on limited perspectives, for example on certain branches of public service institutions or on how the technology in itself can be designed and developed to provide better recommendations. Such studies provide important contributions, but in order to respond satisfactorily to the questions outlined above, it is imperative to bring together a series of perspectives, including political, social and cultural aspects.

This short paper initiates a project which aims at doing that. The objective at this stage is not to answer the grand questions directly, but to examine various perspectives that could – and perhaps should – be taken into account when approaching issues of cultural policies, social missions and discretion in publicly funded culture institutions.

In the remainder of the paper, we present perspectives from the fields of information science, media studies and cultural sociology. The presentations exemplify the problem area by drawing on practical cases from a broad conception of what we may term Scandinavian public service institutions. These include public service broadcasters, public libraries, but also commercial media organizations in the book industry. Our discussions reference streaming services as specifically interesting sites of algorithmic considerations. At the end, we provide some concluding remarks.

2 Streaming, Recommender Systems and Public Service

In Norway, as in other Scandinavian countries, streaming services have become increasingly popular over the last few years. Like most digital media services, streaming services rely on algorithms for search, recommendation, personalization and presentation. Indeed, streaming services with databases containing hundreds of thousands or even millions of titles can be said to rely even more heavily on algorithmic filtering. Spotify, Netflix and YouTube are the most common examples of such algorithm-driven streaming services. Other examples include streaming services for ebooks and audio books, such as Storytel and Kindle Unlimited. Besides these international companies, national and regional actors, some commercial, some funded by taxpayers' money, also run streaming services. Some form of algorithmic filtering is typically part of these as well. Even public libraries apply the streaming model, one example being US public libraries that subscribe to the Kanopy service for providing access for patrons to films.

The government-owned Norwegian broadcasting corporation (NRK), has increasingly made their media content freely available online and in the recent years, offered access through a streaming platform. In 2017, the "sandbox" department for tech-testing at NRK, NRKbeta, published two blog post [4, 5] presenting a recommender system that had been implemented on this platform. The postings addressed a challenge of skewed consumption: A few titles from their considerable collection of available media content, account for most of the usage. To meet the challenge, NRK set out to bring forward titles from the long tail of content and that would match the relevant context of the user [4]. The technique described by NRKbeta combines and utilizes two similarity measures; similarities that can be found between media objects, e.g. based on metadata describing genres and responsibilities, and similarities that can be identified between users based on their behavior and feedback patterns. These techniques resemble the most common way of classifying recommender systems as so-called content filtering, collaborative filtering, or through the combination of these in hybrid systems. Recommender systems, and the tweaking of such techniques are part of a long tradition of research in information and computer science [6], where the overall research problem is to design systems that provide useful and effective suggestions, e.g. in order to sell more products or to increase user satisfaction in streaming systems.

Although the NRKbeta postings do not mention or relate directly to a concrete mission statement providing a premise for their developments, the identification and formulation of their problems suggest that their main ambition is to increase the diversity of usage, or at least to provide an alternative method for dissemination that does not reinforce the popularity of already popular objects. The diversity problem represents a vital branch of research on recommender systems, often referring to diversity of sales, or a strategic problem of balancing diversity with the need to provide accurate recommendation. More recently, "exposure diversity" has been discussed as a design principle in its own right, e.g. based upon a general concern for a "decrease in the diversity of information to which users are exposed" [7]. Others have questioned the use of recommender systems for discretion in public service institutions as such, given the challenge to implement the systems without risking mimicking "data-driven approaches [that] operate within commercial frameworks" [8].

With a mission to serve the public, rather than commercial interests or the state, public service broadcasters differ from commercial services like those found in the book industry (which is discussed in the next section). Public service broadcasters have a long history of balancing broad and narrow content in their programming, and it is in line with their historical mission that they seek to remain a common cultural arena in a society that is moving towards individualized culture consumption.

In Norway, NRK has since it faced competition from commercial actors in the national TV-market in the 1990s, based a significant part of its legitimacy on being the largest actor in the Norwegian TV market. Being popular among the citizens, measured in viewing numbers as well as trust surveys, has served as the basis for the organization's legitimacy. That is, as the most popular and most trusted actor in the market, they were not in need of active legitimation work on the part of the broadcasting organization [9].

As a public service broadcaster, the NRK is obliged to work towards fulfilling some cultural policy goals set by the Ministry of Culture. Operating at arm's length from the Ministry, NRK nevertheless exert editorial freedom and autonomy in its content programming. However, the Ministry and citizens will not be content simply with being provided with popular content. Basing its legitimacy on being popular, must go hand in hand with the provision to the citizens of programs that are considered important due to their artistic quality or their importance for society. When algorithms decide which content to recommend to the individual consumer, this leave the data programmers with a significant amount of power in managing the public service mission. Are they aware of this, and how does it manifest itself in their work?

Public service broadcasters have throughout their history been an important arena were citizens can take part in a common (national) culture, and acquire a shared set of cultural references etc. In today's individualized digital culture, these arenas are dismantling. How are the public service broadcasters relating to this part of their history, in developing streaming services? Is it at all possible to maintain a common arena based on algorithmic logics?

3 Streaming Services for Digital Books and Their Social Contracts

While public service broadcasters are clearly bound to some form of social mission, it is arguably less evident that commercial streaming services need to take other considerations than related to their core business. Nonetheless, book industry actors in countries with strong cultural policy measures (such as the Scandinavian countries) often proclaim that they adhere to a social or cultural mandate, a public service remit that separates them from purely commercial actors. Conversely, cultural policy makers expect more than merely monetary considerations from such actors. This implicit social contract may, we argue, have consequences for how algorithmic filtering is done.

Algorithms make certain types of content more easily available than other types. The question, which applies to commercial as well as public organizations, remains: What types? Since companies like Storytel (International), Fabel (Norwegian), Mofibo (Denmark), Bookbeat (Sweden) and Nextory (Sweden) are commercial entities, independent from government control, we may expect them to apply algorithmic filters in any way they see fit. That could mean promoting only bestsellers or titles associated with the company (all the services are in some way affiliated with a publisher). On the other hand, these companies (some more than others) enjoy public support, directly through subsidies or indirectly through policy measures that promote the production and dissemination of culture. In Norway, such measures include tax exemption, fixed prices, artist support, public libraries and government-funded purchasing programmes for libraries.

We ask what kinds of algorithmic filtering can be expected from commercial services with significant public support, departing from the Norwegian situation and with specific reference to streaming services Storytel and Fabel. Norwegian cultural policy provides support for book industry actors, and specific measures on pricing and inventory applies to booksellers. As booksellers, Storytel and Fabel are required to provide all available titles upon request, as per a 2017 addendum to the Norwegian Book Agreement. Nonetheless, the selection of titles in both services is contingent on ownership by publishers Cappelen Damm (Storytel) and Lydbokforlaget (Fabel) [1]. Thus, the algorithms are already incapable of promoting "anything, anywhere, anytime", as the streaming hyperbole claims.

Then, as the algorithms of Storytel and Fabel are put to work, the programmed actions that they take may further limit cultural choice and thwart practices that go beyond the mainstream and the predictable. The fear of filter bubbles is a well-known concern [10]. A different variation of the algorithmic unease stems from the impression that taste patterns can grow increasingly narrow, as recommendation algorithms seek to avoid deviations from the preferences already indicated [11]. Finally, it is important to note that the user interfaces ("shop fronts") of streaming services are very restricted in terms of how many items can be shown simultaneously. It follows that concentration on the few items displayed can be a concern, even considering the personalization efforts made. In a recent study, we looked at recommendations in Storytel, based on the "Personal book recommendations" category. We found that the 15 most frequently recommended titles were part of 45 per cent of all recommendations in this category. Only three of these 15 titles, were published by other publishers than Cappelen Damm, Storytel's parent company [1].

In digital platforms, curation and recommendation, traditionally the task of culture industry gatekeepers, is delegated to algorithms whose work is typically hidden or made difficult to monitor. While it is far from politically uncontroversial, it can be argued that even private and commercial organizations need to code social missions into the algorithms they operate.

4   Recommendations, Discretion and Questions of Cultural Quality

The basic assumption of this paper is that recommendation services, both digital and analogue, address the questions of quality, discretion and values. The most obvious is perhaps, that by recommending, displaying, or highlighting some media objects others are made less visible, less valued and less used. From this follows that changes in the infrastructure of recommendation practices have an impact on cultural values, qualities, how discretion is performed etc.

For Norwegian public libraries, key concepts guiding their dissemination practice, directly expressed in the Public Library Act of Norway, are actuality, quality and versatility [12]. According to Tygstrup [13] the logic behind the algorithms, now used in recommender systems, is not a simple trial-and-error structures, but based on a type of feedback: "the intuitive handling of a book, a film, or a playlist is recorded as feedback, which can be included in the production of improved versions" [13, p. 94]. One question is thus, to which extent do recommender technology based on user behavior, interaction and other types of feedback displace the balance between these concepts and their related, but different values.

When NRKbeta motivates their implementation of recommender systems [4], they highlight the importance of a broader use of their collections, but also express that the core of their concept of quality is relevance. The new systems have a capacity that the staff do not have, to make the media objects more used. More use becomes a symptom of relevance: "The numbers speak for themselves. Those who are exposed to the recommendations are clicking more. [...] Our interpretation of this result is that the systems enable us to present more exciting content. The programs that we recommend are more relevant." [4, our translation]. The success criteria, relevance, slides in their interpretation towards personal aesthetic preference: *exciting content.*

The data NRKbeta puts forward also shows that the time user spent watching the recommended program also increased. This also fit the narrative of success: "clicks are not enough. We want people to watch the TV shows they click on" [4]. If we accept that discretion and valuation is a complex interaction between context, work (œuvres) and users, it is reasonable to question the consequences of only focusing on user preference as a recommendation criterion. This narrative is, of course, more complex. If a motivation for implementing a recommender system "was to display and expose users to a greater diversity of the catalogue", another one following from this is expressed as that "people would discover content they didn't know they wanted to see" [4]. Taken at face value this statement is interesting. Firstly, because the phrasing is very similar to what we find in another public institution with a clear mandate to recommend or disseminate cultural items. In e.g. a public library context, it has been worded like this: "The libraries must be a place where people not only get what they want, but also get opportunities to discover what they didn't know about beforehand" [14, p. 55]. In this context, one connotation of facilitating the opportunities of discovery is Bildung; i.e. the reader or film watcher's possibility for growth and development in interaction with their environments [15, 16]. In this argument, growth and development are concepts relying upon an open future, that the logic of feedback technology doesn't necessarily provide [13]. Secondly, following the first: The question that lurks under this twofold strategy are how to balance serendipity (to value the unplanned) with more direct patterns of user preference? Do they stimulate our social habits of discovering or do they stimulate repetitive habits or behavior? This is an even more interesting question, since the values/qualities, we often ascribe to art and culture is exactly to stimulate the possibility to discover, to be challenged and even to be transformed.

5   Concluding Remarks

Associated with public institutions with long historical roots is often the impression that they are not keeping up with technological development [14, 15]. In NRK's own strategies, it is stated directly that "NRK must be present, and develop services on, all major media platforms [...]." The ambition may imply that NRK continuously obtain and implement technology developed under other conditions than public service, for example for commercial purposes. As we have touched upon, mimicking the algorithm design of Netflix and Amazon is an example of such isomorphism between public and private actors. Public funded organizations are guided by their commitments to society as a whole and their individual members with their needs and preferences [16]. The use of new and emergent technology is not a problem, if the technology fit NRK's social mission to address the public as citizens and not consumers. Here, we have mostly been concerned with raising this issue. Future work will have to address the specific questions of how to fit algorithms and social missions of PSB.

As our paper has pointed out, PSB`s are not the only institutions where these concerns are raised. Public libraries are bound by similar commitments. Even commercial book industry actors and others who benefit from public support and funding may have their algorithms scrutinized by concerned citizens, scholars and policy makers.

Developing algorithms for recommendation, presentation, personalization etc. is not typically the work of traditional curators, although the function that algorithms perform is (partly) curatorial. There is a concern that the principles of algorithmic design (similarity, relevance) are not necessarily in harmony with cultural values (diversity, quality, Bildung). Thus, it takes a conscious interdisciplinary effort to develop public service algorithms.

According to Nielsen and Langsted [16, 17], in the domain of cultural policies, this implies that quality should not equal individual taste or preference. The question one should ask, is "whether the given cultural/artistic activity is experienced as appealing, inspiring and challenging by the contemporary public and to what degree it contributes to the development of cultural life and the cultural public debate" [18, p. 242].

References

1. Tallerås, K., Colbjørnsen, T., Øfsti, M.: Relativ tilgjengelighet. Norsk medietidsskrift **26**(1), 1–20 (2019). https://doi.org/10.18261/ISSN.0805-9535-2019-01-02
2. Pedersen, B.E.: Anbefalte ingen norske filmer (2019). https://www.dagsavisen.no/kultur/anbefalte-ingen-norske-filmer-1.1458750
3. Fields, B., Jones, R., Cowlishaw, T.: The case for public service recommender algorithms. In: FATREC Workshop (2018)
4. Holmstad, Ø.: Slik skal NRK TV bruke algoritmer for å anbefale deg nytt innhold (2017). https://nrkbeta.no/2017/01/09/slik-bruker-nrk-tv-algoritmer-for-a-anbefale-deg-nytt-innhold/
5. Holmstad, Ø.: Hvor godt virker algoritme-drevne anbefalinger i NRK TV? (2017). https://nrkbeta.no/2017/05/18/hvor-godt-virker-algoritme-drevne-anbefalinger-i-nrk-tv/
6. Ricci, F., Rokach, L., Shapira, B.: Recommender systems: introduction and challenges. In: Ricci, F., Rokach, L., Shapira, B. (eds.) Recommender Systems Handbook, pp. 1–34. Springer, Boston, MA (2015). https://doi.org/10.1007/978-1-4899-7637-6_1
7. Helberger, N., Karppinen, K., D'Acunto, L.: Exposure diversity as a design principle for recommender systems. Inf. Commun. Soc. **21**(2), 191–207 (2018). https://doi.org/10.1080/1369118X.2016.1271900
8. van Es, K.F.: An impending crisis of imagination: data-driven personalization in public service broadcasters. Media@LSE Working Paper Series (43) (2017)
9. Larsen, H.: Legitimation strategies of public service broadcasters: the divergent rhetoric in Norway and Sweden. Media Cult. Soc. **32**(2), 267–283 (2010). https://doi.org/10.1177/0163443709355610
10. Pariser, E.: The Filter Bubble: What the Internet Is Hiding from You, Kindle edn. Penguin, London (2011)
11. Uricchio, W.C.: Recommended for you: prediction, creation and the cultural work of algorithms. Berlin J. **28**, 6–9 (2015)
12. Folkebibliotekloven [Public Library Act of Norway]. Lov om folkebibliotek (folkebibliotekloven) (2014)
13. Tygstrup, F.: Culture quality, and human time. Contested Qualities: Negotiating values in arts and Culture. Fagbokforlaget, Bergen (2018)
14. Colbjørnsen, T.: Continuity in Change: Case Studies of Digitalization and Innovation in the Norwegian Book Industry 2008–2012. Doctoral thesis, University of Oslo (2012)
15. Larsen, H.: Legitimering av allmennkringkasting i Norge og Sverige. Doctoral thesis, University of Oslo (2011)

16. Nielsen, H.K.: Smagskulturer, kvalitet og dannelse. In: Smagskulturer Og Formidlingsform, pp. 14–31. Klim, Århus (2006)
17. Langsted, J.: Kvalitet i kulturpolitik: kvalitet i kunst. Nordisk Kulturpolitisk Tidskrift **2000** (2), 6–34 (2000)
18. Nielsen, H.K.: Cultural policy and evaluation of Quality. Int. J. Cult. Policy **9**(3), 237–245 (2003). https://doi.org/10.1080/1028663032000161678. NCS Homepage http://www.springer.com/lncs. Accessed 21 Nov 2016

Archives and Records

Records-Making During Crisis Management – Rule Based or Discretion Driven?

Erik A. M. Borglund[✉]

Mid Sweden University, 85170 Sundsvall, Sweden
erik.borglund@miun.se

Abstract. During large crises, e.g. forest fires, flooding, terrorist attacks, or aircraft crashes, temporal organizations are set up to manage the crisis and minimize negative impacts on society. These temporal organizations are often called situation rooms. The purpose of this paper is to study what regulates the record-making practice in a police situation room. Qualitative research methods were used. Data was sourced from five different case studies in the Swedish police service. The tension between discretion and rule-based regulation has been used as the theoretical lens in this paper. Through the application of this theoretical lens of regulation, whereby the two extremes found were discretionary creation on the one hand and rule-based creation on the other, one can identify a real challenge in record-making practice. Much of the record-making was regulated discretionary, i.e. each regulated and motivated by a police officer's own judgment. This kind of record-making is difficult to predict and consequently the created records may also be difficult to capture, simply because no-one knows that they exist. In non-temporal organizations' recordkeeping practice, entire work processes can be identified, the records created in the processes can be identified in advance and the process can be supported by various information systems. But in the temporal organization, proactivity is more difficult to achieve and thus records created based upon discretion will probably not be proactively identified as being part of an activity in a process.

Keywords: Crisis management · Discretion · Police · Records-making · Situation room

1 Introduction

The White House has since long had a situation room that allows the American leadership unprecedented access to situational awareness regarding a range of critical geo-political events [1]. This type of setting seems no longer to be exclusive to global political leaders, but is also a reality for a range of organizations involved in crisis response and civil security. During a crisis, the governmental authorities responsible will often activate temporal organizations for crisis management and response, which are often led from a situation room. Situation rooms, control rooms and operation rooms are synonyms, and share common characteristics due to their common focus on a continuous need to achieve overview, support the management, and respond to the crisis. Research has been conducted regarding what happens in situation rooms during

© Springer Nature Switzerland AG 2020
A. Sundqvist et al. (Eds.): iConference 2020, LNCS 12051, pp. 599–615, 2020.
https://doi.org/10.1007/978-3-030-43687-2_50

large crises, but work practices are less studied. Large crises are often analyzed afterwards, and quite often the lack of relevant documentation is presented as a large problem [2, 3], although research strongly emphasizes the importance of documenting during a crisis [4].

This paper focuses on *Record-making*, that is, records creation for a particular use in a particular situation, in this case the contextual setting of the situation room that is activated during large police operations. It also contributes to the field of research about records use see e.g. [5–7]. The situation room is a less stable organization compared to organizations where records are normally created. Records are an important source of information in police work, and can play an important role in operational as well as strategic police work [see e.g. 5, 6, 8, 9]. The primary reason for police use of records has mostly been for their informational value [10]. However, only limited interest in record-making can be found in the literature. Foscarini and Gillian Oliver have identified the need to further scrutinize how records are used by individuals and in organizations. For example, they have applied the concept of genre in order to discuss and present the different flavors that exist related to records use [11–13].

The purpose of this paper is study what regulates the record-making practice in a police situation room. The situation room is a both a temporal and a time-critical place for work, and the findings from this research are transferable to other time-critical and temporal work places and work situations, e.g. project organizations or temporal team work. Although records are evidence of activities, Swedish archival practice implies that records are born in organizations and in activities that can be identified in advance [14, see e.g. in 15]. From a records continuum perspective a proactive approach is almost a requirement for the possibility to capture, organize and ultimately pluralize archival records [16, 17]. Therefore, it is argued that studying record-making in a time critical environment, where the work cannot always be identified in advance is of theoretical interest.

In this article we make two very basic assumptions. The first is that to be able to develop records management systems or systems that manage records, unknown use of records is an obstacle to successful system design and development [supported by e.g. 18–20]. The second assumption is that extensive understanding of how records are created and used is important for developing recordkeeping theories applicable in an era of digital transformation.

2   Research Approach

The situation rooms in focus in this paper differ from similar studies found in e.g. the field of Computer Supported Collaborative Work (CSCW), which have focused on more traditional control rooms, or dispatch centrals as, for example, the Swedish national emergency centre [21], control rooms in the London Underground [22], urban traffic control [23], and command and control rooms [24]. The interest in this article is, as stated above, the situation room that is set up and initiated when some larger crisis or event happens. When a situation occurs that cannot be managed with the ordinary available police recourses, other predefined organizations are used. These intermittent organizations are called *staff*. The central task for the staff is to provide the commander in chief with relevant information to support strategic and tactical decisions. Therefore, the staff work must focus on creating and continuously developing a Common Operational Picture (COP), which can be defined as: 'A single identical display of relevant information shared by more than one command. A common operational picture facilitates collaborative planning and assists all echelons to achieve situational awareness.' [25]. FEMA defines a COP as follows:

"a common operational picture is established and maintained by the gathering, collating, synthesizing, and disseminating of incident information to all appropriate parties involved in an incident. Achieving a common operating picture allows on-scene and off-scene personnel to have the same information about the incident, including the availability and location of resources, personnel, and the status of requests for assistance" [26].

A common awareness of what is going on is needed for the successful management of a large crisis [27, 28]. The COP has been described by the Swedish Civil Contingencies Agency (MSB) as a selection of available information at a certain time aggregated to present an overview of what is going on [29]. Beside the work with the COP there is another central task for the staff and that is information sharing. Information sharing takes place within the police service, between different police units, or between the police and other authorities involved in handling the crisis [30, 31].

Since records today are mostly digital, created and managed within various IT-systems, it is natural to study the creation, capturing and organizing of records in its natural element, i.e. what best can be described as workplace studies, a term often found in Computer Supported Collaborative Work (CSCW) literature [32–34]. In CSCW the workplace studies are often design-oriented, where new or improved IT-artefacts are the goal. In this research the aim is not yet design of new technology; it is to understand and gain new knowledge, which is necessary for later design of IT-support for records creation, records capturing, and records organizing. Ethnography, a classic research method applied in CSCW research has been applied in this study [35–37].

The paper rests upon an extensive ethnographical research effort [35], where five primary studies have been used as data sources, hereafter named A, B, C, D, and E. **Study A** was a case study conducted during the EU Energy and Environment Ministers meeting held in Åre, Sweden, in 2009, between July 23 and 25. Planning and preparing the police operation, which aimed to guarantee safety during the whole meeting of Ministers, started many months ahead of the meeting. The operation itself started July 20th and ended July 25th, when the Ministers left Åre. The research was therefore conducted between July 20th and July 25th. **Study B** was a case study of a large regional disaster training exercise that took place in April 2010 in the Swedish County of Jämtland. The scenario of the exercise was an airplane incident where a Boeing 737 from Arlanda Airport crashed during landing at Åre-Östersund Airport. The exercise involved almost 1,000 participants, and aimed to test the region's capacity to manage a large crisis. The exercise also aimed to stimulate cooperation between different actors involved in crisis management in the region. Data collected during this training exercise was confined to the police authority, and also included two preparation days arranged by the police. **Study C** was a longitudinal case study in a three-year long research project, *Gaining security symbiosis* (GSS), where the project's main focus was to run three training exercises for the Norwegian and Swedish police, fire departments, municipalities, county administrative boards, and medical services. **Study D** was based on active participation in two week-long courses in operation center management and operation center organization, at the Swedish National Police Academy in Stockholm during 2014. **Study E** consisted of active participation in two educational courses at the National Swedish Police Academy, each one week long. The two courses were "Introduction to staff work", and "Chief of staff". The researcher participated as a student in the first course and as one of the teachers of the second course. All participants in the course were informed of the researcher's presence and that the researcher was there to collect data. The data was gathered during all of the minor exercises that constituted part of the courses. When the researcher was a student the data was collected from a participant's point of view, and during the second course it was collected as an observer rather than participant.

Although the time period of the data collection stretches over five years, the work practices found in the situation rooms are based upon the same internal police regulations. Before 2009 a large education effort was made to prepare Swedish police to ensure security during several EU meetings. If there are important nuances in the data this is highlighted in the following sections. The primary data collection is from exercise and training events, which is natural when situations where a situation room is established is hard to foresee and therefore also difficult to access as a researcher during an ongoing crisis.

Table 1 presents a summary of the studies, their duration and methods of data collection used.

Table 1. Summary of the primary research studies

Study	Research context	Extent	Data collection
A	Police work during an EU Energy and Environment Ministers meeting	6 days	Observation Interviews
B	Police work during a large regional disaster training exercises	1 day exercise 2 days' preparation	Observation Interviews
C	Collaborative cross-national project focusing on training and development exercises	Total 12 days	Observation Interviews Network analysis Radio communication
D	Local police authority education and training	1 day	Observation Interviews
E	2 Courses "Introduction to staff work" and "Chief of staff"	10 days	Observation Interviews

The data collection methods were primarily various forms of field studies with participatory observations. Short notes were taken in a notebook during the observations. At the end of each day the collected notes were summarized [38]. In order to revisit areas of interest as well as gathering experiences from events not covered by the aforementioned observations, informal interviews were done [39]. During each study an on-going analysis was done with the aim to make sense of the activities observed and studied. The ethnographic approach has a strong research tradition within CSCW [40, 41] and is very helpful in identifying design implications [42, 43]. The main focus of this paper and the data collection was record-making. This automatically included the study of the artefacts involved in record-making, such as computers, white boards, flip charts, maps etc.

The analysis of the data has been iterative, where the notes from the research have been manually revised and patterns and structure in the data identified. The empirical data from studies 1–5 were re-analyzed by overlaying the theoretical lens applied, which is described below. The findings have also been discussed with two police superintendents who have been in charge of many large police operations.

2.1 Analytical Lens

It is hard to find any mention or analysis in the literature of what the underlying forces might be that drive people to record or not record activities. Since our aim is to further elaborate what record-making practice looks like, it is also important to understand what might be regulating that practice. In this article the concept of 'discretion' is used. Merriam-Webster[1] describes 'discretion' as "a: individual choice or judgement" or "power of free decision or latitude of choice within certain legal bounds". Implicitly this means that during a large emergency situation, the police officers involved can take non-standard approaches to recording activities. The concept of 'rules' and/or 'rule-based' is also used, often contrasted with 'discretion'. Here, 'rules' means requirements for how an officer must act, setting out very specific procedures. 'Discretion' has been used in police research to describe and put into words the freedom to act within stated legal boundaries [As e.g. is presented by 44]. Police discretion is important to enable police officers to carry out their job in the most efficient way, whereas a more rule-based approach could hinder police work. In the police environment, 'rules' should be interpreted as laws and other regulations.

In this article 'rules' and 'discretion' are not used as strict concepts in our analysis. We are more interested in using 'rules' and 'discretion' as the two extremes on a scale. Fukuyama [45] uses 'discretion' on a scale where 'subordination' is at one end of the scale and 'autonomy' is on the other. Full autonomy is characterized by "excessive discretion", and subordination by "too many rules". This article aim can therefore be extended to show what record-making practice during extraordinary events looks like: is the record-making practice driven by an autonomous ideal or by subordination?

2.2 Use of the Records Continuum Model

The Records Continuum Model [17, 46] (Fig. 1) is an archival theoretical contribution that is applied in this paper as a way to frame the record-making. The Records continuum model consists of four dimensions: Create, Capture, Organize and Pluralize. The dimensions can be interpreted at a very simple level as follows: first a document is

---

[1] https://www.merriam-webster.com/dictionary/discretion.

created and when it is **captured** it becomes a record. When records are **organized** in e.g. an archive it can then become useful for many in the **pluralize** dimension. In this article record-making is located in the 1st and 2nd dimension. The axes in the model are, in very simple terms, about who (**identity**) did what (**transactionality**), what traces of evidence can be found about that (**evidentiality**), and where and how can that be retrieved from document, records, and archives? (**recordkeeping containers**). Primarily the Records Continuum Model is used in this paper to clearly show that record-making is an active process.

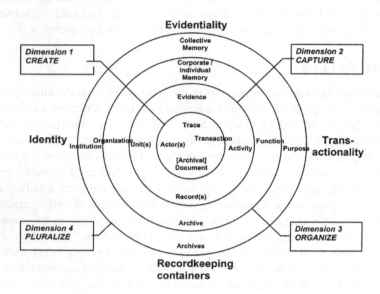

Fig. 1. The records continuum model [17, 46]

3   How Police Are Organized in a Situation Room

In police work, the name used for the team in the situation room during a large crisis or extraordinary event is *staff* [47], structured similarly to the regulations that existed during the period of empirical data collection for this article [27]. The staff were organized by function according to the national standard for how large police operations should be arranged [47], and had the following competences and units:

Chief of Staff
P1 – Human resource manager: Responsible for making sure there are enough police officers, that they get to rest when required etc.
P2 – Intelligence: Responsible for intelligence work during the extraordinary event.
P3 – Operational management: Responsible for coordinating the operational police work.
P4 – Logistics and equipment
P5 – Planning and co-operation: Supporting planning and establishing co-operation with other authorities

P6 – Operational analysis

P7 – Information: Responsible for information sharing with press and information gathering from the press.

P8 – Various tasks: Dependent upon the event, this position can have various aims.

P9 – Documentation: Responsible for capturing important decisions made by the staff, and document them according to internal instructions.

The staff is normally located either in a specially designed room with lots of technology or in a room more like a conference room. It is not uncommon for the room where the staff meets and works to look like Fig. 2 below: i.e. a room with whiteboards and video projectors.

4 Record-Making Practice

The findings are very descriptive, following the ethnographic research tradition [see e.g. 35].

In the results a records continuum [17, 46] perspective is used to present the results. That means that first something (a transaction) takes place and it is documented. When the document is captured in some activity, it becomes a record. In the following the term document is used, and by that is also meant the first phase in a record-making process. That is, creation of a record for a particular use in a particular situation. From a records continuum perspective, the use of 'document' in the text means that the document not yet is captured as a record: documentation is the art of documenting. In this article documents that do not need to be captured as a record into a recordkeeping system are not discussed. However, there were very few such documents within the empirical data.

On a daily basis, 4–6 ordinary staff meetings were held (including meetings where staff teams take over from each other). During these meetings, the Chief of Staff and the P1–P8 were gathered in the staff room and each of the staff members presented for the others what new information had been received since the last meeting. The staff meeting was always documented in a word processor document that was accessible to all through the police intranet. Normally the staff meetings are where a more official COP is formed. Each P-function is represented and an aggregation of available and relevant information is made, to form the COP upon which all participants can agree. One can say that the COP developed during the staff meeting is a time stamped, shared, and documented understanding of what is going on.

Between the staff meetings each P-function reported to the Chief of Staff all events judged to be important. It was then up to the Chief of Staff to decide if the entire staff should be gathered. This was communicated face to face, by telephone or by mail, even if the last was very rare. If the P-functions needed to document their work they used the ordinary police IT-systems available for this purpose. The P3-unit was the unit that had the main responsibility for managing and updating the common operational picture, as it had operational responsibility for all police units on duty. The P-3 unit was divided into 3 subunits, *P-3T* responsible for the traffic, *P-3O* responsible for all other police units, and *P-3C* responsible for criminal investigations. The P-3 units had at least 2 dispatch operators that managed the radio traffic among the police units. The dispatch operator also recorded all on-going events in the command and control system. The P-3 unit plotted all upcoming events on whiteboards. For example, in study A, they had the preliminary schedule of when they expected each minister to arrive at Östersund Airport. Every change was added in a different colour on the whiteboard.

Collaboration is embedded in the structure of the roles expected of staff. For example, Operational Management (P3) are reliant upon correct information from Intelligence (P2), and Logistics and Planning (P4) need to collaborate with the Human Resource Manager (P1).

Fig. 2. The situation room, with all P-functions gathered around the table

Between the staff meetings each P-function either works in the room set aside for the staff or they return to their own offices. If the situation is time-critical and the stress level is high, a higher tendency to stay in the staff room has been observed in the five studies. When the staff room was a well-equipped situations room (as in studies A, B & D) the members of the staff tended to stay in the room throughout the entire operation. There are also some events that require the staff to work in the same room for security reasons. This requires functioning staff logistics supporting the staff with drinks, food and other necessary equipment.

4.1   Computers and the Documentation Systems

In the situation rooms studied, two computer-based systems were used for documenting and sharing of the on-going activities. **1.** The command and control system (STORM), was used to document all operational activities involving police units. For example, if 2 groups of police officers were sent to an address, this was recorded in STORM, together with the reason for the job. **2.** The more tactical and strategic decisions were documented using Microsoft Office Word™, and were stored in common folders on the police intranet. All minutes were written and documented in Microsoft Office Word™. In addition to the minutes each P-function could write a "diary" of on-going activities, but not all P-functions did. When the whole staff was gathered, there were discussions about what situations should be documented and if all agreed to document a situation, this was what was done. STORM could be running on a computer in the staff, and also be projected on a wall with a video projector and in that way enable sharing the content of the system. From a records continuum perspective [17, 46] the documents described become records as they are captured and labelled with some metadata.

Microsoft Office Word™ was used as more of a hidden repository, as very few police officers read what others had written. Only in the two command posts during the police operation in Åre, were Microsoft Office Word™ documents read and used by someone other than the author. Although each document was accessible from a computer connected to the police intranet, and each document was named with a time stamp, they were rarely used. To be fully updated, all sub-folders, in which the minutes, diaries, etc., had been stored, had to be opened. The complete list of documents needed to be manually read one by one. However, the Word documents were often found to information rich. Typical Word documents were intelligence analyses, various reports, etc. That is, the Word documents are all, per definition, evidence of activities and they should all be treated as documents that ought to be captured as a record.

4.2   Whiteboards and Flipcharts

Whiteboards are important in large police operations, which was very apparent in the three case studies. Every situation room and the command posts had whiteboards, which were used as operational plotting tools.

In the situation rooms where the staff worked, one whiteboard was always used to plot all planned events in chronological order. The plotting of planned events helped the staff to be prepared for the future and increase their knowledge of what was to come. If there was a change in e.g. the schedule for the minister meeting in Åre, the information was updated and also marked as "updated". It is common to find that a whiteboard was allocated for plotting all important decisions given either by the police operational commander or the strategic commander. Sometimes the overall decisions taken were found in the common folders on the police intranet. During these three case studies (A, B and D), all three staffs that were studied used a third whiteboard which they used to plot the important events that took place, i.e. a timeline of the activities that affected the police operation. An example of this timeline can be seen in Fig. 3.

On one additional whiteboard found at the two command posts, they had plotted descriptions of individuals that the police intelligence unit had analysed and identified as a potential threat to the police operation. Pictures of these persons were also attached to the whiteboards with magnets.

When a whiteboard was filled with content as can be seen in Fig. 3, they either prioritized documentation of the content in a Microsoft Office Word™ document, or they brought in another whiteboard upon which they continued to write, so the traceability was of high quality. Snap shots with a camera were sometimes used to document the content.

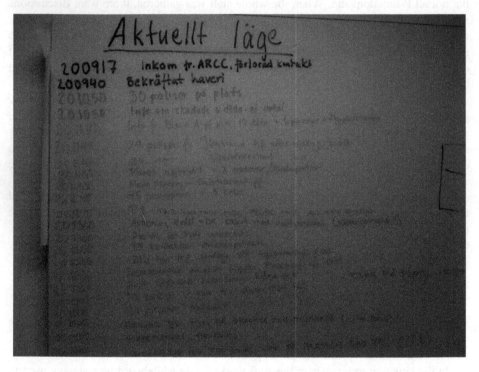

Fig. 3. One whiteboard was used to plot all events in chronological order

During stressed and more chaotic situations the whiteboards played an important role in documenting on-going activities and decisions taken. The person writing on the whiteboard could write on the whiteboard at the same time as he/she was giving information through the mobile, and everyone in the room could immediately see what was written. In case A, B, & D in this research, the situation rooms' whiteboards were used as presented above. If something extra needed to be documented in the same way, the flip charts were used. The flip charts were used when there was a temporary need for urgent and easy documentation.

For example, during the training exercise they started to plot how many uninjured, injured, severely injured, dead, and missing people there were from the simulated plane crash site. In this situation this was plotted on flipchart papers instead of trying to find room on a whiteboard. Another example of when the flipchart was used was when it was important to map out the location of all available police units.

Flipcharts were mostly used to document needs of a more temporal character. During the police operation in Åre, telephone numbers, call signs on the radio and flight numbers were the most frequent information written on the flipcharts. Some of this information was either transcribed into Microsoft Office Word™, or the page of the flipchart was torn off and put on a free space on a wall with adhesive tape. In Fig. 2, some charts can be seen taped to the wall in the picture's upper right corner. When the information on the flipchart (or the charts on the wall) was no longer important for the management of the police operation, the chart was torn off. This is an example of a (potential) record that was meaningful for a very short time. But if it wasn't captured into a recordkeeping system, is it really a record? According to McKemmish use of the Record continuum model will lead to "accessibility of meaningful records for as long as there are of value to people, organizations, and societies – whether that is for a nanosecond or millennia." [48].

4.3 Maps

Maps are traditional artefacts that police are used to using. Every time a police unit intervenes in the surrounding society, a geographical location is connected to the actual police unit's work, which is documented in the command and control system STORM.

In this research the police used maps amongst many things to plot where the available units were allocated, where the plane crash had happened, to plan alternative escape routes for the motorcade, landing sites for the police helicopter and other spatial plotting needs. Permanent plotting was done on an electronic map and projected on one wall. But when the map was used as basis for decisions the staff sometimes used a printed map instead, and the persons involved put the map on a table and stood around the map, discussing, pointing, but not drawing on the map. In Fig. 2, both a map with plotting and a picture of the same area taken from a helicopter can be seen. In the three exercises within the GSS project, maps were used all the time. When incidents are taking place in areas unfamiliar to the police, the maps play a very important role. For example, the GSS project incident took place in the border region between Sweden and Norway. In the situation room the map was used to plot resources, find alternative routes for rescue vehicles, and to identify the roads that must be closed. Sometimes the map was projected on to a white board and police officers in the situation room could draw with whiteboard markers on the map. These hybrid constructs were an alternative when the available systems for managing the map did not support drawing, and were never saved as a whole.

4.4 Categories of Documentation

The way activities are documented can be categorized in three different document types presented below.

IT-Based Documentation. IT-based documentation is the documentation taking place with the help from various forms of Information Technology, or in this context primarily by computer-based information systems. IT has been used in the police domain for more than 50 years [49]. In this research we divide the IT-based documentation taking place in either formal IT-use or non-formal IT-use. Formal IT-use is the use of various specially designed police information systems. It can be the command and control system, or the police report system. These systems where the police normally document activities during everyday work are also used during a crisis. In the three case studies in this research the command and control system, STORM was the primary and most frequently used IT-system. The system is used to document every activity of the various police units. Non-formal IT-use is characterized in this study by use of software provided in the police workstations for various documentation purposes, mostly MS Word™ and MS Excel™. In the Word documents and in the Excel spread sheets a wide range of activities that could not be added into the more formalized IT-systems were documented. examples included minutes of staff meeting, lists of telephone numbers, lists of cars, etc.

It is not what was documented that is problematic, it is rather the effect of the more non-formal IT-use. A CSCW researcher (Computer Supported Cooperative Work) would probably define the Microsoft Office suite as a common artifact [50, 51] an artifact that is available and that can be used for common business activities. By using for example Microsoft Office Word™ without any further system support for managing the created documents, there is a large risk that these documents will be stuck in the folders in which they were originally stored. What would ultimately happen to them was very unclear. If there was a plan to capture these documents, it was never seen during these five studies.

Non-IT-Based Documentation. As presented in the results section, much of the documentation happens without any IT-support. The whiteboards, flipcharts, sticky notes are all examples of common artifacts that serve as an important component of cooperation taking place in the situation room context. They can be defined as common artefacts, because they are common in most modern organizations. As seen in both Figs. 2 and 3, the "plotting" that is easily done on a whiteboard can be seen as more formal, where the information is written into a structure. These more formal kinds of use are important in the work that takes place in the situation room. But we also find that the whiteboard, flipchart and sticky notes are used for very temporal needs for documentation that arise suddenly. The police in the situation room write their own notes on these artefacts because they are present and available.

The challenge and problems related to the rather large and less easy to move artefacts are that they are not IT-based. Although it is easy to write on sticky notes and post them on a wall, and easy to write on the whiteboard and the flipchart, these kinds of documentation are not easy to capture in a digital format. The police officers normally took pictures of the whiteboard, but how the picture is further treated is very ad hoc. Sometimes the picture was sent by email to police officers involved, sometimes the picture was just kept in the camera or phone.

Hybrid Documentation. The last kind of documentation category that has been found in this research is the Hybrid. Hybrid documentation is when digital information is projected upon a wall on which more analogue information is added. For example, maps are projected upon a whiteboard and the police in the situation room write on the whiteboard. Even if the map software most commonly used by the police can add text and symbols upon a map, it seems to be easier to write with a pen upon the whiteboard. Although this hybrid form of documentation may not be very common, it has been observed during the three case studies in this research.

The most obvious problem about these hybrids is capturing what has been documented. Because the digital projection is linked with the analogue information they must be kept together as a whole.

5   Rule Based Record-Making vs. Discretion Driven Record-Making

The "tales from the field" above [35] present what characterizes the documentation practice in the police during crisis management in an police situation room, managed by the police staff during an extraordinary event. There are several examples of documentation that have their roots in various regulations that police officers must follow. For example, documentation of the decisions made during staff-meetings is regulated by various staff instructions. Accountability is very dependent upon the documentation that represents and covers the decisions taken in the course of their work. The existing regulations are either internal police regulations concerning documentation that not always are followed, even if they are mandatory. However, as the police is one of few authorities that have the right to intervene against citizens and organizations, this means that they also affect individuals' freedom. These situations occur when police units have used their legally supported right to use various means of compulsion. Such interventions require documentation and are regulated by law.

In the rich description of the documentation practice above it has been very obvious that the majority of the documentation is not ruled based, it is rather regulated by discretion amongst the police officers. Each function within the police staff acts with autonomy within a legal boundary. Discretion is probably necessary for the majority of documentation. It is impossible to know in advance what will happen during a crisis, or what will not happen. It is therefore necessary to document based upon one's own judgement. What is going to happen next cannot be stated in advance by the police staff in the situation room. What probably will happen can eventually be identified. When it comes to more situational dependent activities it is difficult to know what will happen and even if one would know what will happen, and in what chronological order it will happen. Therefore, it is natural that the documentation is more likely to be regulated and guided by discretion. The situations that can be identified in advance are the staff meetings, and certain decisions that are normally taken during a crisis. Those activities also regulate how and what is meant to be documented.

From a record-making perspective, it is very difficult to proactively work with identifying what kind of documents will be created, in what kind of work process they occur, and so on. Discretion gives police officers freedom to decide when and what to document, but the downside is that there is a huge risk that the documents will seldom be captured, and even more rarely be organized.

6 Concluding Remarks

This research has focused upon record-making practice. Record-making is a rarely studied phenomenon and the article with its rich empirical material contributes knowledge about the record-making and what it can look like in practice. Application of the theoretical lens of regulation, wherein the two extremes were discretion and rule-based, allowed identification of a real challenge in the observed record-making practices.

As stated above, the rule-based record-making could be referred to decisions, and similar activities within the police domain that by law or other regulation require written documentation. On the other hand, much of the record-making that was identified in this research was regulated by discretion, i.e. each regulated and motivated by police officers' own judgment. This type of record-making is difficult to predict, and a proactive approach for records capture is difficult, when their existence or potential existence cannot be known. In recordkeeping practice in non-temporal organizations, entire work processes can be identified and the records created in those processes can be identified in advance, hence the process can be supported by various information systems. But in the temporal organization proactivity is more difficult to achieve and that means that records created based upon discretion probably will not be proactively identified as being a part of an activity in a process. It does not follow that discretion should be avoided in regulating records creation. It rather means that there is a challenge to design support for records capture when the record-making is not known.

Analysis of reports that highlight lack of documentation as a problem during large crises [see e.g. 2, 3], reveals that the documents that are lacking are those that help us to understand why they did what they did in certain way and what were the reasons for certain decisions: documents that contribute to what can best be described as tacit knowledge.

In this research we have not studied the role played by the records that are created based upon a police officer's judgement (i.e. regulated by discretion) in the work taken place the situation room. Are those records more important for the outcome of the crisis or do they play another role? This question is a potential area for continuing research. Designing technology for easier records capture is also a relevant design-oriented research possibility.

References

1. Bohn, M.K.: Nerve Center: Inside the White House Situation Room. Brassey's, Washington, D.C. (2003)
2. Myndigheten för samhällsskydd och beredskap: Ansvar, samverkan, handling: åtgärder för stärkt krisberedskap utifrån erfarenheterna från skogsbranden i Västmanland 2014. Myndigheten för samhällsskydd och beredskap, Stockholm (2016)
3. Skogsbrandsutredningen: Rapport från Skogsbrandsutredningen. In: Regeringskansliet (ed.). Regeringen (2015)
4. Landgren, J.: "Glöm inte dokumentera!" Hantering av dokumentation vid krishantering. vol. MSB 315. MSB (2011)

5. Borglund, E.A.M., Öberg, L.-M.: How are records used by organizations? Inf. Res. **13** (2008). Paper 341 (2008)
6. Borglund, E.A.M.: Electronic records use changes through temporal rhythms. Arch. Soc. Stud.: J. Interdisc. Res. **2**, 103–134 (2008)
7. Sundqvist, A.: The use of records – a literature review. Arch. Soc. Stud.: J. Interdisc. Res. **1**, 623–653 (2007)
8. Valtonen, M.R.: Documentation in pre-trial investigation: a study of using the records continuum model as a record management tool. Rec. Manag. J. **17**, 179–185 (2007)
9. Kostiainen, E., Valtonen, M.R., Vakkari, P.: Information seeking in pre-trial investigation with particular reference to records management. Arch. Sci. **3**, 157–176 (2003). https://doi.org/10.1007/BF02435656
10. Schellenberg, T.R.: Modern Archives: Principles and Techniques. SAA (Original work published 1956), Chicago (1956/1998)
11. Foscarini, F.: Organizational records as genres: an analysis of the "Documentary Reality" of organizations from the perspectives of diplomatics, records management, and rhetorical genre studies. In: Theory in Information Studies, pp. 115–132 (2015)
12. Foscarini, F.: Diplomatics and genre theory as complementary approaches. Arch. Sci. **12**, 389–409 (2012). https://doi.org/10.1007/s10502-012-9173-6
13. Foscarini, F.: Understanding the context of records creation and use: 'Hard' versus 'soft' approaches to records management. Arch. Sci. **10**, 389–407 (2010). https://doi.org/10.1007/s10502-010-9132-z
14. Sahlén, T.: Informationsförvaltning i offentlig och privat sektor. Näringslivets arkivråd, Stockholm (2016)
15. Sahlén, T.: Kaos eller struktur - om modern dokumenthantering. In: Sundqvist, A. (ed.) Dokumentstyrning i processorienterade organisationer, pp. 7–56. Folkrörelsernas arkivförbund & Näringslivets arkivråd, Stockholm (2005)
16. Upward, F.: The records continuum. In: McKemmish, S., Piggott, M., Barbara, R., Upward, F. (eds.) Archives: Recordkeeping in Society, pp. 197–222. Charles Sturt University, Centre for Information Studies, Wagga Wagga (2005)
17. Upward, F.: Modeling the continuum as paradigm shift in recordkeeping and archiving processes, and beyond - a personal reflection. Rec. Manag. J. **10**, 115–139 (2000)
18. Borglund, E.A.M.: Design for recordkeeping: areas of improvement. Department of Information Technology and Media, Mid Sweden University, Sundsvall (2008)
19. Borglund, E.: A first step towards general quality requirements for e-records. In: Nilsson, A. G., Gustas, R., Wojtkowski, W.G., Wojtkowski, W., Wrycza, S., Zupancic, J. (eds.) Advances in Information Systems Development: Bridging the Gap Between Academia & Industry, pp. 745–756. Springer, New York (2006). https://doi.org/10.1007/978-0-387-36402-5_64
20. Borglund, E.: Operational use of electronic records in police work. Inf. Res. **10** (2005). Paper 236
21. Pettersson, M., Randall, D., Helgeson, B.: Ambiguities, awareness and economy: a study of emergency service work. Comput. Supp. Coop. Work **13**, 125–154 (2004). https://doi.org/10.1023/B:COSU.0000045707.37815.d1
22. Heath, C., Luff, P.: Collaboration and control: crisis management and multimedia technology in London underground line control rooms. Comput. Supp. Coop. Work **1**, 69–94 (1992). https://doi.org/10.1007/BF00752451

23. Filippi, G., Theureau, J.: Analyzing cooperative work in an urban traffic control room for the design of a coordination support system. In: de Michelis, G., Simone, C., Schmidt, K. (eds.) Proceedings of the Third European Conference on Computer-Supported Cooperative Work 13–17 September 1993, Milan, Italy ECSCW 1993, pp. 171–186. Springer, Dordrecht (1993). https://doi.org/10.1007/978-94-011-2094-4_12

24. Luff, P., Heath, C.: The collaborative production of computer commands in command and control. Int. J. Hum.-Comput Stud. 52, 669–699 (2000)

25. Department of Defense: Department of Defense Dictionary of Military and Associated Terms. In: Department of Defense (ed.) Department of Defense (2010)

26. FEMA - Emergency Management Institute: National Incident Management System (NIMS) Student Manual IS-700.A. Communication and Information Management. In: Institute, F.-E. M. (ed.), vol. IS-700.A National Incident Management System, An Introduction, I-700.A (2009)

27. Nylén, L.: Operativ ledning: bedömande och beslutsfattande: lednings- och fältstaber vid särskild händelse: en handledning. Rikspolisstyrelsen. CRISMART, Försvarshögskolan, Stockholm (2006)

28. Svensson, S.: Staber och stabsarbete vid kriser, risker och olyckor. Studentlitteratur, Lund (2007)

29. Borglund, E., Landgren, J., Lintzen, M.: Lägesbilder: Att skapa och analysera lägesbilder vid samhällsstörning. Myndigheten för samhällsskydd och beredskap, Stockholm (2014)

30. Myndigheten för samhällsskydd och beredskap: Gemensamma grunder för samverkan och ledning vid samhällsstörningar. Myndigheten för samhällsskydd och beredskap (MSB) (2014)

31. Myndigheten för samhällsskydd och beredskap: Aktörsgemensamma former för inriktning och samordning vid samhällsstörningar: Vägledning för aktörer på lokal och regional nivå med utgångspunkt i geografiskt områdesansvar. In: Enheten för samverkan och ledning (ed.) Myndigheten för samhällsskydd och beredskap (2017)

32. Schmidt, K.: Cooperative Work and Coordinative Practices: Contributions to the Conceptual Foundations of Computer-Supported Cooperative Work (CSCW). Springer, London (2011). https://doi.org/10.1007/978-1-84800-068-1

33. Schmidt, K., Simonee, C.: Coordination mechanisms: towards a conceptual foundation of CSCW systems design. Comput. Supp. Coop. Work (CSCW) 5, 155–200 (1996). https://doi.org/10.1007/BF00133655

34. Schmidt, K., Bannon, L.: Taking CSCW Seriously. Comput. Supp. Coop. Work 1, 7–40 (1992). https://doi.org/10.1007/BF00752449

35. Van Maanen, J.: Tales of the Field: On Writing Ethnography. University of Chicago Press, Chicago (1988)

36. Puddephatt, A.J., Shaffir, W., Kleinknecht, S.W.: Ethnographies Revisited: Constructing Theory in the Field. Routledge, London; New York (2009)

37. Button, G., Harper, R.: The relevance of 'work-practice' for design Comput. Supp. Coop. Work (CSCW) 4, 263–280 (1996)

38. Taylor, S.J., Bogdan, R.: Introduction to Qualitative Research Methods: A Guidebook and Resource. Wiley, New York (1998)

39. Kvale, S.: Den kvalitativa forskningsintervjun. Studentlitteratur, Lund (1997)

40. Blomberg, J., Karasti, H.: Reflections on 25 years of ethnography in CSCW. Comput. Supp. Coop. Work (CSCW) 22, 373–423 (2013). https://doi.org/10.1007/s10606-012-9183-1

41. Schmidt, K., Bannon, L.: Constructing CSCW: the first quarter century. Supp. Coop. Work (CSCW) 22, 345–372 (2013). https://doi.org/10.1007/s10606-013-9193-7

42. Dourish, P.: Responsibilities and implications: further thoughts on ethnography and design. In: Proceedings of the 2007 Conference on Designing for User eXperiences, pp. 2–16. ACM, Chicago (2007)
43. Dourish, P.: Implications for design. In: Proceedings of the SIGCHI Conference on Human Factors in Computing Systems, pp. 541–550. ACM, Montreal (2006)
44. Carrington, P.J., Schulenberg, J.L.: Structuring police discretion: the effect on referrals to youth court. Crim. Justice Policy Rev. **19**, 349–367 (2008)
45. Fukuyama, F.: What is governance? Governance **26**, 347–368 (2013)
46. Upward, F.: The records continuum and the concept of an end product. Arch. Manuscr. **32**, 40–62 (2004)
47. Polismyndigheten: Polismyndighetens riktlinjer för operativ ledning vid särskilda händelser. In: Polisen (ed.) (2016)
48. McKemmish, S.: Placing records continuum theory and practice. Arch. Sci. **1**, 333–359 (2001)
49. Benson, D.: The police and information technology. In: Button, G. (ed.) Technology in Working Order: Studies of Work, Interaction and Technology, pp. 81–97. Routledge, London (1993)
50. Pekkola, S.: Designed for unanticipated use: common artefacts as design principle for CSCW applications. In: GROUP 2003: Proceedings of the 2003 International ACM SIGGROUP Conference on Supporting Group Work, Sanibel Island, Florida, USA (2003)
51. Berlage, T., Sohlenkamp, M.: Visualizing common artefacts to support awareness in computer-mediated cooperation. Comput. Supp. Coop. Work **8**, 207–238 (1999). https://doi.org/10.1023/A:1008608425504

On the Breakdown of the Controlled Environment Paradigm in Norwegian Archival Repositories

Herbjørn Andresen[(✉)][iD]

OsloMet – Oslo Metropolitan University, Oslo, Norway
Herbjorn.andresen@oslomet.no

Abstract. The rules and arrangements that govern transfer of digital records to the archive repositories in Norway, rely on a controlled environment paradigm. This paradigm is the basis for assuming the authenticity and evidential values of the archives. The concept of a paradigm is borrowed from the theory of science, but it can also be relevant to fields of practice. In the theory of science, it denotes distinct concepts, methods and thought patterns that guide what contributions are perceived as valid within a field. If or when a paradigm ceases to provide adequate guidance in a field, it may break down, possibly leaving the field in need of a new paradigm. The discussion in this paper apply a theory of different responses to paradigm breakdowns in order to explore stakes and opportunities at a point of crisis for the current paradigm on transfer of born-digital records to archive repositories.

Keywords: Digital repositories · Archives life cycles · Theory of science

1 Introduction

The incitement for this short paper is a recent Norwegian proposition for new legislation on records and archives [1]. The proposition report contains bold changes in many areas, most of them left out from this paper. One of the areas that is discussed, albeit very briefly, is a possible need to change the ways transfer of born-digital records to the repositories is arranged and controlled. The current rules require the semantics of an electronic archive to be interpreted, tested and determined at transfer time. Later use of the archives must, and do, rely on the transformations that have been carried out earlier. The discussion, contained in a brief paragraph on the concept of data lakes, suggests transformations, and with them interpretations and verifications, might better be postponed to the time of use. This would have an impact on the entire basis for assuming authenticity and evidential value of records in the archive repositories. That is probably a good thing.

© Springer Nature Switzerland AG 2020
A. Sundqvist et al. (Eds.): iConference 2020, LNCS 12051, pp. 616–621, 2020.
https://doi.org/10.1007/978-3-030-43687-2_51

2 Theoretical Perspective, Responses to Paradigm Breakdowns

The rudimentary discussion in this paper labels the existing rules and assumptions on transfer to repositories in Norway a "controlled environment paradigm". An account of its main ingredients is given below in Sect. 3. The discussion itself draws on the concept of paradigms, known from the theory of science. In Kuhn's famous book on the structure of scientific revolutions, paradigms are defined as "universally recognized scientific achievements that for a time provide model problems and solutions to a community of practitioners" [2]. Following such an achievement, further contributions are made as "puzzle-solving" within the confines of the paradigm that was established. A working paradigm is a mechanism for building cumulative knowledge effectively. The paradigm provides concepts, methods and thought patterns that guide what is seen as legitimate contributions to the knowledge base, and what is not. However, the paradigms do not last forever. The clause element "for a time" is a crucial part of Kuhn's definition. When new results or knowledge do not fit well into the paradigm, they are perceived as anomalies, often not valued on their own merits, but instead judged as incompatible with the paradigm. If anomalies are persistent, and throw important assumptions of a paradigm into doubt, the paradigm may break down. Crises are a necessary precondition for the emergence of novel theories, or paradigm shifts, in Kuhn's terminology.

Kuhn includes in his writing some reflections on responses to crises, intertwined in historical examples. For the purpose of this paper, responses to paradigm breakdowns are instead taken from another paper, by Alexander, that develops a more stringent typology of different responses to paradigm breakdowns [3].

Alexander labels the first type of response 'ritual response'. This is a pattern of responding in denial of the breakdown. Even though the evidence of an untenable paradigm emerges, the ritualist will ignore the crisis and cling to the existing paradigm.

A second type is the 'avoidance response'. Avoiding is not denial. The evidence of a crisis in the current paradigm is acknowledged, by accepting that it is happening. An avoidance response will often even emphasize the anomalies, but keep perceiving them as anomalies viewed from within the paradigm. Though the breakdown as such is recognized, the practical implications are ignored.

A third type is the 'abandonment response'. The breakdown is recognized, and current models are abandoned as they appear unnecessary and dysfunctional. An abandonment response could for example be framed as a determination to "adopt the intuitive wisdom of the practitioner" and stay away from grand theories. By rejecting the need for model problems and solutions, the mechanism for judging new contributions will also be lacking.

The fourth type of response is the 'search response'. The starting point for this response is to recognize the breakdown for what it is, and at the same time acknowledge the need for new model problems and solutions. Even though, as according to Kuhn's definition, one is aware that new paradigms are also only for a time.

3   The Controlled Environment Paradigm in Norway

Rules on how government agencies should create and organize their records have been around in Norway since early 18th century. At the heart of these rules was the *registraturprinzip*, a system of creating current registries organized by cases, and archiving according to the original order. This principle has remained prevalent for most of the public records practices.

From an early start in the mid-20th century, the National Archives has also, increasingly, given guidance and exercised powers of control and auditing over the records practices in government agencies. Therefore, a regime where the different government agencies adhered to rules and conventions imposed by the National Archives had already been established when the first version of a national standard for electronic records management systems was issued in 1984 [4]. This implied an expectation that electronic archival materials ending up in their repositories would be based on structures and functionalities that safeguarded reliable content, of known provenance and internal structure, and with a high perceived evidential value. 1984 appears to be really early for a standard on electronic records systems, but the first versions only covered registry information. The actual documents were still transferred on paper, until the 1999 version of the standard allowed for transferring electronic documents, either as scanned picture files or as output files from word processing systems or similar.

Also, in 1999, to maintain the control over records creation in electronic systems, the National Archives introduced a scheme for approving electronic records management systems to be used by government agencies. Each agency can buy a system from some vendor in the market, or develop the records systems themselves, but they will have to keep paper files unless the system they use have been approved.

Even before the OAIS reference model [5], the National Archives had decided the transfer of electronic records to the repository should only be a transfer of the data content and context information, and not a transfer of systems hardware or executable program needed to display or render the records. The government agencies, when they are prompted to transfer records, produce an extract from the system conforming to extraction requirements in the national standard [4]. In the vocabulary of OAIS [5], they produce a SIP, a submission information package.

After the SIP has been transferred, the National Archives performs a testing procedure, to verify if the submitted package conforms to the prescribed structure and metadata requirements. After passing these test procedures, the National Archives approves the transferred archival unit, and accept a conferred responsibility for the further maintenance and adherence to access rights and limitations and whatever else an archival institution assumes responsibility for.

The controlled environment paradigm builds in part on the Jenkinsonian notion of an unbroken chain of custody as a warrant for the evidential value of the archives [6]. The requirements pertaining to born-digital materials transferred to the National Archives repository are modelled on a similar assumed need for an end-to-end control throughout a linear life cycle of the records. Jenkinson did not, however, support the view that archival institutions should intervene in the records management activities before transfer. Other theorists have spoken in favour of such practices, for instance

Terry Cook, "...no reliable record will even survive to be available to the archivist to preserve in the traditional way unless the archivist intervenes in the active life of the record, sometimes before it is even created" [7].

4   Anomalies in the Controlled Environment Paradigm

The controlled environment paradigm, as ordained in Norway, puts a huge demand for quality and compliance in a long series of complex processes. The first severe signs of anomalies showed up in the middle of the chain, as errors in the run of the test procedures to verify the submitted transfers. There were more often than not a high number of errors, such as missing metadata, inconsistent data, structural flaws and so on. Quite often the errors were not imposed by wrong implementations of the records management systems or extraction procedures, but in the recordkeeping practices.

One example of perceived errors in the records, that were often discovered at the time of testing transfers, was case files "left open" in the records management system. A demand imposed by the ancient *registraturprinzip* is that case files must be closed. This is a step that users of the system might not even be aware of. The immediate interpretation of such errors was that the systems, even though they adhered to the national standard, were used in a wrong way. When it turned out such errors were frequent and pervasive, it was no longer tenable to view them as mere user errors. In some cases, it might even be counter-intuitive to close case files. The interpretation of such errors encountered in the testing of transfers shifted gradually, from perceiving them as non-conformance to perceiving them as possible anomalies to the controlled environment assumption.

The disheartening test results caused time-consuming, and therefore expensive, iterations of sending new corrected versions of the extracted transfer files back and forth. A very strict adherence to the commitment to an unimpeded controlled environment made it virtually impossible to get archives through to a conferred status. A possible side effect of the slow transfer and acceptance process may have been to slow down the deployment of more innovative digital preservation technologies, therefore what might be viewed as an avoidance response may in fact be influenced by the available tools. A part of the National Archives' solution to the acknowledged anomalies was to relax the testing procedures, in two aspects. First, the requirements for consistency and accuracy in the records metadata could be a bit more flexible than the requirements laid down in the standard [4]. Second, and slightly more heretical to the controlled environment paradigm, minor and obvious errors in the extractions could easily be corrected by the National Archives testing unit themselves, instead of requiring the record creating agency to submit a revised version of the extract. The limit to what corrections may be made by the testers without impeding the warrant of authenticity is hard to define in a principled way. Instead, there has been some practice-based rules of thumb to draw this line.

The problems of achieving an acceptable test result revealed further problems to the asserted controlled environment from records creation to continuous custody. When extracts were sent back and forth to make it pass the tests, the necessary corrections would have to be made either to the actual records, or to the records management system, or to the extraction procedure generating the extracted files to be transferred. Making changes to the actual records, for instance closing case files that the records manager had left open, would solve the problem of consistency, but at the cost of no longer reflecting the actual case-handling practices in an accurate way. If the problems were either in the records management system or in the extraction program, it would be the same vendor who interpreted the error reports from the repository, and who tried to come up with solutions. The actions of the programmer are not necessarily transparent, even if the records management system as such has been approved at an earlier stage. It might be hard to tell whether any tweaking of the extraction procedure in order to make the transfer pass the test blurs the strict requirements on how the extract to be transferred should correspond to the actual records.

The anomalies as a fundamental problem proliferated mainly from the middle of the chain, verification of transfers, to the antecedents in the records management and extraction processes. However, there are also some concerns on the other side of the transfer process, to the usability of the transferred archives. Even though a number of extracted, born-digital archives by now have been received and verified, they appear to be hard to put into use beyond retrieving specific records residing in a known archival information package. The semantics of the records management systems have been evolving, even with a common standard for records management systems, different archives are not easily linked or compared. Semantic structures and metadata schemes that are interpreted, fixated and closed at transfer time do not provide much leeway for exploring possibly interesting combinations of data from different parts of the archives. The limits on usability have not been explored to the same extent as the anomalies of records management, extraction and transfer.

5   Perceiving and Responding to the Anomalies

The first perceptions of problems with the value chain for electronic archives were in the low efficiency of testing and verifying transfers. At first, this was handled within the paradigm, as a slow process, taking as long as it had to, in order to keep in line with the controlled environment paradigm. It was thought to be a learning process, soon ready for speeding up. The anomalies were perceived as such when decisions were made to relax the tests in order to speed up the transfer process. The profoundness of the problems was discovered and understood gradually. The anomalies were persistent and amounted to a crisis for the paradigm.

Responses to the crisis have been varying and have included all the four types listed in Sect. 2 above. The ritualist response was seen when the problems were mainly dealt with at a department level, as a need for improvement, and taking the necessity of the controlled environment paradigm for granted. A choice between the three other different responses require an acknowledgement of the crisis, severe difficulties in maintaining the controlled environment from records creation to continuous custody for born-digital materials as a warrant for the evidential value. At the organization level, a project was established to present and compare different model concepts for the transfer and maintenance of archives [8]. The project looked into different ways to improve the transfer process, including relaxing requirements and accepting more diversified submissions. Still, none of the proposed model concepts were clear and outspoken departures from the notion of a controlled environment, where the evidential value depends on adherence to the tenets of this paradigm.

The model concept that was eventually chosen, was named the "zero plus"-alternative. Essentially, this alternative implies keeping the same processes going, the "plus"-part signifying a need for systematic work on improvement. The outcome of this evaluation process, viewed as a response to a paradigm breakdown, is the avoidance option.

6   Conclusion

The project for modernizing receipt and ingestion of born-digital materials was never in denial of the anomalies vexing the current paradigm. It was, in a way, a search response, ending in avoidance. This is understandable, and not really deserving of too much criticism. The archival community would need a very strong stomach to abandon a controlled environment paradigm, as it would put the justification of the whole endeavor in jeopardy. The only viable alternative to avoidance therefore seems to be the search response.

The proposed new legislation on archives in Norway, that was briefly mentioned in the introduction, is promising. Not because it necessarily provides clear solutions to how the breakdown of the controlled environment paradigm should be handled, but because it indicates that the search for a new and viable paradigm can still be an option.

References

1. Official Norwegian Report. NOU 2019:9 Fra kalveskinn til datasjø. Ny lov om samfunns-dokumentasjon og arkiver. ["From Vellum to Data Lakes". Proposal for enactment of new legislation on societal documentation and archives] (2019)
2. Kuhn, T.S.: The Structure of Scientific Revolutions, 2nd edn. University of Chicago Press, Chicago (1970)
3. Alexander, E.R.: After rationality, what? A review of responses to paradigm breakdown. J. Am. Plan. Assoc. 50(1), 62–69 (1984)
4. National Archives Norway. NOARK Norsk arkivstandard [Norwegian national standard for public sector electronic records and archives]. (First edition 1984, 5th generation from 2008, current version is version 5.5)
5. ISO 14721:2012 Space data and information transfer systems – Open archival information system (OAIS) – Reference model. International Organization for Standardization, Geneva (2012)
6. Jenkinson, H.: A Manual of Archive Administration Including the Problems of War Archives and Archive Making. Clarendon Press, Oxford (1922)
7. Cook, T.: What is past is prologue: a history of archival ideas since 1898, and the future paradigm shift. Archivaria 43, 17–63 (1997)
8. National Archives Norway. Konseptutredning om modernisering av arkivvedlikehold og overføring til arkivdepot (MAVOD) [Report on evaluation of concepts for modernizing archives maintenance and transfer to archival repositories] (2018)

Identifying Challenges for Information Organization in Language Archives: Preliminary Findings

Mary Burke[✉] and Oksana L. Zavalina

University of North Texas, Denton, TX 76201, USA
{mary.burke, oksana.zavalina}@unt.edu

Abstract. Language archives are repositories of linguistic data about a selected set of languages, typically including recordings, transcripts, translations, and linguistic annotations. Digital accessibility of primary language data, particularly that of endangered languages, has long been recognized as necessary for research reproducibility, production of pedagogical materials, and typological discovery, though their potential currently lies dormant because these resources are rarely accessed by linguists or language communities. Reasons for the under-utilization of language archives include the lack of data standardization and decreased focus on metadata quality. The present work seeks to elucidate the issues facing language archive managers and users through two steps: content analysis of information organization in language archives, and semi-structured interviews with language archive managers and users. Primary challenges identified include lacking institutional support and a range of factors which impact authority control in language archives.

Keywords: Language archives · Information organization · Metadata · Digital repositories

1 Introduction

Language archives are repositories of linguistic data about a selected set of languages, typically including recordings, transcripts, translations, and linguistic annotations, essential for facilitating language preservation and revitalization and providing access to data on severely endangered languages (Henke and Berez-Kroeker 2016). Digital accessibility of primary language data, particularly that of endangered languages, has long been recognized as necessary for research reproducibility, production of pedagogical materials, and typological discovery, though their potential currently lies dormant because these resources are rarely accessed by linguists or language

This research has been funded by the US Institute for Museum and Library Services through a planning grant IMLS LG-87-18-0197. We also thank our project team members, Dr. Shobhana Chelliah and Mark Phillips, in addition to the members of our advisory board, Myung-Ja Khan, Drs. Christina Wasson, Gary Holton, Susan Smythe Kung, for help in identifying language archives for analysis and interpreting results.

© Springer Nature Switzerland AG 2020
A. Sundqvist et al. (Eds.): iConference 2020, LNCS 12051, pp. 622–629, 2020.
https://doi.org/10.1007/978-3-030-43687-2_52

communities. Reasons for the under-utilization of language archives include the lack of data standardization and decreased focus on metadata quality. To address this, the Open Language Archives Community (OLAC) was formed in the early 2000's to develop protocols for language archiving and creating interoperable repositories for storing language data. Between OLAC and the Digital Endangered Languages and Musics Archive (DELAMAN), awareness of metadata has significantly increased in the linguistics community. Still, linguists are unsure if the widely used metadata schemes are appropriate for representation of language datasets and if these will ensure the use of their data. They often do not expect non-linguists (who normally make metadata-related decisions and create metadata in data repositories) to adequately represent language data for information retrieval. Need for detailed and accurate metadata to facilitate resource discovery, as well as ease of search in language archives is documented by user studies (Al Smadi et al. 2016; Wasson et al. 2016), informed by a user-centered design approach. Wasson et al. (2016) identified five stakeholder groups central to language archives, acknowledging that individuals may belong to multiple groups: language communities, linguists, archivists, user-centered design practitioners, and representatives of funding agencies (p. 659). Representatives of each group gathered at a workshop and shared their perspectives, which were recorded, transcribed and coded using qualitative analysis software Dedoose. While Wasson et al. (2016) report significant insights of these user groups, still, the current knowledge of users' tasks and needs are insufficient to determine whether the present state of information organization is facilitating user tasks, whether additional metadata elements for representing language data, or methods of searching are required to increase the usability of language archives.

To understand more thoroughly the issues facing language archive managers and users, we have undertaken a project funded by the Institute of Museum and Library Services with two phases: Phase 1 included a content analysis of the websites of 20 digital language archives; Phase 2 involves semi-structured interviews with archive users and managers. Findings from Phase 1 are reported in Sect. 2, and the preliminary results from Phase 2 in Sect. 3. Section 4 concludes. The goal of the exploratory study presented in this paper was to identify:

- information organization tools and practices currently employed by language archives across the United States, and
- the needs of depositors and end-users (linguistics researchers, instructors, and students) for information organization functionalities in language archives.

The following information organization tools and practices were considered:

- What item-level and (if applicable) collection-level metadata scheme(s) are used?
- To what extent metadata records are displayed to end users?
- Does the archive allow self-depositing and, if so, are metadata creation guidelines and/or documentation of a metadata application profile used in language archives available?
- How is authority control implemented? What data value standards are used?

- What options for advanced search against indexed metadata fields are available?
- Are metadata records available for harvesting/download?
- What Semantic Web applications are available? For example, is metadata available as Linked Data?

1.1 Scoping Definitions

For the purpose of this project, we define language data as any audio, video or textual material representative of authentic language use. A list of words, a speaker explaining how to cook a particular variety of rice, or a traditional song are just a few examples of the various forms language data can take. Language data should be accompanied by metadata describing its relevance and context (minimally, how and where it was collected, name of speaker, and a simple description of the content).

We define a language archive as containing at least one collection (two or more items) of language data. Crucially, language archives do not need to identify as such to be considered in this analysis. For example, many university repositories contain collections of language data (e.g., University of North Texas Digital Library's Lamkang Language Resource, Indiana University at Bloomington's Ethnomusicology Multimedia Materials Collection), but identify more broadly as digital libraries or university repositories. Language archives have materials available for public access with the intent of long-term preservation. For example, Kaipuleohone, housed at the University of Hawai'i at Mānoa (http://ling.hawaii.edu/kaipuleohone-language-archive/), exemplifies a language archive because it contains individual items, makes items available for public access, has structured metadata, and accept deposits of material (or has accepted in the past).

Resources not considered in this analysis, though in no way dismissed, are corpora and resource aggregators. The Language Data Consortium (LDC), a collection of corpora, does not organize corpora into collections, have structured metadata, nor provide public access to its content. Resource aggregators, such as the Karuk Archives (http://karuk.org/) are also excluded from this definition. Such websites provide links to resources available on other websites and archives, but do not house language data itself, nor do they provide structured metadata. So, while these platforms may store language data, they are not considered a language archive for the purpose of this investigation.

2   Phase 1: Content Analysis

In the first phase of our research project, we conducted an exploratory content analysis of websites of language archives to identify the information organization practices currently employed by language archives in the United States.

To answer these questions, we examined a total of 20 language archives, including 16 within the United States and 4 outside the United States for comparison (2 in Europe, 1 in Australia, 1 in Canada). Of the 16 US archives, 6 are collections housed in university libraries, 4 are standalone archives not affiliated with a university, and 6 are archives associated with universities. Burke and Zavalina (2019) provide a full report of Phase 1 findings. Phase 2, discussed below, focused on the decision-making process for these information organization decisions and on the gaps between user needs and the way information is organized in language archives. This preliminary report partially addresses the overall findings of the study.

2.1 Phase 1 Findings

The findings of Phase 1 displayed a variety of information organization strategies in language archives.

Metadata Schemes Used. Though language archives make some information available on an item landing page, it is often unclear which metadata schemes the elements belong to. It seems that many language archives are using locally developed schemes to suit their needs. Often, local metadata application profiles based on Dublin Core are constructed for use in data repository. One such example, Kaipuleohone, makes two versions of each record available, a simple and full record. 'Simple item records' can be expanded by selecting 'Show full item record.' The full record displays the namespace 'dc' along with qualifiers that clearly indicate the use of the Qualified Dublin Core metadata scheme. Records from other archives typically contain many of the same elements (e.g., Identifier, Title, Contributor/ Depositor/ Creator, Language, Date, Description, Format, Notes) but do not include any explicit indications of the metadata scheme being used. Only 2 of the 20 archives, both collections within a university digital libraries, have metadata records available for download in RDF (i.e., University of North Texas Digital Library and University of British Columbia Open Collections).

Controlled Vocabularies. Use of controlled vocabularies is not consistent across language archives. ISO 639-2 Language Codes, DCMI Type Vocabulary, and Traditional Knowledge Labels are frequently used. Collections within digital libraries include Library of Congress Subject Headings, while other archives designed for language data do not include a Subject element. Dates are typically encoded using W3CDTF. Because most language archives make records available only on the object's landing page, it is unknown whether additional metadata, including more extensive use of controlled vocabularies, exists on the back end.

Advanced Search Capabilities. 18 of the 20 archives have advanced search capabilities, though not all fields are indexed for advanced search. 10 archives have only a subset of fields available for advanced search; minimally, Title, Author, and Language fields.

Metadata Creation Guidelines. Self-depositing is not available in most cases; only ELAR, AILLA, the Tromsø Repository of Language and Linguistics (TROLLing), and Language Commons allow users to upload data without an intermediary. Few of the university repositories analyzed have information on making deposits. In these cases, it is unclear whether they are not open to deposits, or whether a potential depositor would have to contact the university library directly to discuss depositing. Similar to the use of controlled vocabularies, the availability and level of detail of metadata creation guidelines vary widely. While some language archives (e.g., PARADESIC, AILLA,

Kaipuleohone) provide detailed guidelines including examples and tutorials, others require only a title and a description of the deposit.

2.2 Phase 1 Conclusions

Through content analysis alone, many of our research questions remain unanswered, or only partially answered. For example, we were able to identify that there are no records available for download in RDF on most archive's websites; however, this does not preclude the possibility that such RDF records exist, but are inaccessible to users. Similarly, because full metadata records are not always exposed, there may be controlled vocabularies in place that are not shown in the user interface. Further, content analysis did not indicate whether the archive manager(s) plan to implement any such features, and what factors might impact those choices. To gain a more detailed view of the information organization strategies employed in language archives and user needs, we interviewed these groups in Phase 2.

3 Phase 2: Semi-structured Interviews

3.1 Methodology

In Phase 2, we assess the needs of depositors and various stakeholders for information organization functionalities in these archives via semi-structured interviews. Stakeholders include:

- Linguistics researchers depositing their datasets in language archives and using or planning to use language archives in their research
- Language and linguistics educators using or planning to use language archives for teaching (K12-higher education)
- Students who would benefit from using language archives in their studies (linguistics students and information science students)
- Language community members interested in heritage language materials
- Language archiving practitioners and managers.

The semi-structured interviews were conducted with the purpose of language archive analysis and user needs assessment, as well as to collect information on how these requirements are met by information organization in language archives based on the previous experiences of respondents in using language archives. In addition to the users of archives, we interviewed archivists to learn about the use of metadata schemes and controlled vocabularies in these archives. Participants who already use language archives were also observed depositing data and/or searching and browsing language archives and interacting with metadata in the process. Observations represent the evaluation of information organization techniques in a selection of the language archives examined in Phase 1.

Participants were recruited from major language archives and from language documentation scholarly communication networks (e.g., the Linguistics Society of America's Committee on Endangered Languages and their Preservation (CELP) blog, the LinguistList). To date, we have interviewed and observed 7 archivists and 9 users of language archives. Of the 9 users, 4 had deposited data to a language archive. The present work reports our preliminary findings from the data collection and early data analysis stage of the project.

Interviews and observations were conducted over the Zoom video-conferencing tool. Zoom provides an automated transcription which was then manually corrected. Transcripts were coded according to the recurrent themes in the data using NVivo 12 Plus. The code list was developed based on the interview guide, and was later refined according to topics which emerged from the transcripts and consultation with project team members. Because the data analysis is ongoing, the code list may be further modified as necessary.[1]

3.2   Preliminary Findings

With data analysis still ongoing, the final results from the content analysis of interview transcripts is not yet prepared; rather, we share the compelling themes emerging from interviews.

Lacking Resources. Many archive managers identified a lack of funding as a primary barrier they face to maintaining their archive or implementing any new functionalities. With budget cuts to universities throughout the United States, institutions must rely on funding from federal grants to stay afloat. Full-time staff members are vital to the maintenance of the archive, but there is insufficient funding to support them, as short-term funding is not guaranteed renewal. One archive manager remarked "an archive is an institution, and it should be funded at the hundred-year level, not at the one-year level" (arch_5, 2019).

In 2011, the National Science Foundation (NSF) mandated the inclusion of a Data Management Plan (DMP) for all projects to increase transparency of research; this affects language archives directly because one of the most common ways language documentation projects are funded is through NSF's Documenting Endangered Languages (DEL) program. Specifications for the DMP in DEL projects require a Letter of Collaboration from the institution where the data will be archived, confirming their agreement and ability to ingest the material resulting from the project (National Science Foundation 2018). Another major source of funding for language documentation projects, the Endangered Languages Documentation Program (ELDP) requires that the resulting data be archives in the Endangered Languages Archive (ELAR). This has increased substantially the amount of materials language archives receive each year, creating additional strain on these under-funded institutions.

This issue is reflected on the user end during the depositing process—in some cases, researchers utilize student assistants in order to manage the often cumbersome and tedious work of archiving their primary language data. While the DMP has caused a prioritization of archiving, there has not been a corresponding increase in funding to

---

[1] Data collection instruments and the current code list can be found at https://docs.google.com/document/d/1EGn_34QyQlpV1EcIj1wuevbvsorbe4UAA9uqw1vLfco/edit?usp=sharing.

support this additional task not previously emphasized in language documentation projects, and both depositors and archivists alike are striving to meet the shifting demands.

Under-Utilization of Authority Control. Interviews reveal that language archives do not implement authority control to the extent typical in traditional library settings. This is especially true for proper names of people. In some cases, archives maintain local name authority files for the depositors in their archive, but do not link this to a higher authority (e.g., the Library of Congress Name Authority File). The use of authority control is connected to the lack of funding; for example, one archive management team explained that they do have a locally developed name authority file, but have not applied it to names in every record because staff must address basic access issues before they can devote time to standardizing data values across thousands of records.

Subject headings are not typically assigned to language data; rather, the language of the data (typically referred to as 'subject language') seems to be of primary importance to users. The long-standing struggle with languages having multiple names has popularized the use of the ISO codes for language names. Still, the ISO 639-3 does not have a value for all existing languages, further complicating the issue of authority control in language archives.

Though this study focuses on language archives based in the United States, there are global factors affecting information organization, namely the General Data Protection Regulation (GDPR) in place throughout the EU. The GDPR is tightening restrictions on personal data use, even if that data is archived outside of the EU, so language archives in the United States must develop solutions to these restrictions. One archive manager noted the effect GDPR is having on their decision to include the names and years of birth of individuals featured in archived recordings, despite the potential value that information, particularly the year of birth, would add for researchers using the archive. It is expected that, in coming years, GDPR and similar legislation will affect information organization in language archives, most notably name authority control.

User Preference for Social Media. Finally, linguists depositing to language archives may feel their archival deposit is not being utilized by other researchers, and especially not by the language communities they work with. Though researchers understand and appreciate the purpose of archiving for long-term preservation of the materials, many express frustration with the inadequate access to materials archives provide. Depositors interviewed compared the depositing process with major language archives to the ease of uploading a video to YouTube or Instagram: [on social media,] "the transaction costs for, let's say, the depositor are extremely low, and yet, the findability and the accessibility is extremely high. So somehow we're at the opposite end in linguistics where, like the burden on the depositor is extremely high, and yet, the findability and accessibility is extremely low" (user_4, 2019). Indigenous language communities, another primary user group of language archives, often rely on mobile devices, making streaming significantly more feasible than downloading large files, which creates a preference for a social media-type user interface over the archival access point.

4 Conclusions

This project is the first step in a series of research and demonstration projects aimed at improving the information organization in language archives throughout the United States. Initial analysis of the interviews reveal several elements of the language archiving process which are problematic for users, depositors, and archivists, including lacking institutional support and a range of factors impacting authority control. These preliminary results are promising; we are confident that this project will yield fruitful data for developing strategies to improve the usability of language archives, and help bridge the gap between what users need and what archivists are able to provide.

References

Henke, R., Berez-Kroeker, A.: A brief history of archiving in language documentation, with an annotated bibliography. Lang. Doc. Conserv. **10**, 411–457 (2016)

Al Smadi, D., et al.: Exploratory user research for CoRSAL: report prepared for S. Chelliah, Director of the Computational Resource for South Asian Languages. University of North Texas. Department of Anthropology (2016)

Wasson, C., Holton, G., Roth, H.: Bringing user-centered design to the field of language archives. Lang. Doc. Conserv. **10**, 641–671 (2016)

Burke, M., Zavalina, O.L.: Exploration of information organization in language archives. Proc. Assoc. Inf. Sci. Technol. **56**, 364–367 (2019)

National Science Foundation Documenting Endangered Languages (DEL) program solicitation. https://www.nsf.gov/pubs/2018/nsf18580/nsf18580.htm. Accessed 13 Sept 2019

Challenges in Organizing and Accessing Video Game Development Artifacts

Jin Ha Lee[✉], Marc Schmalz, Stephen Keating, and Jeewon Ha

University of Washington, Seattle, WA 98195, USA
jinhalee@uw.edu

Abstract. Artifacts created during the game development process are vital for understanding and appreciating the history and context of video games. However, few have explored how to organize and preserve the digital ephemera created during game development, critically endangering these media artifacts. Through interviews of various stakeholders interested in these types of artifacts, we explore the game development process. Participants discussed various challenges in organizing and finding game development artifacts for their work due to multiple factors: organization culture, the technical work environment, and a lack of standard vocabulary and practices. They also discussed the disconnect between game library, archive, and special collections lacking ways to note relationships among relevant materials. Based on these findings, we discuss two main implications from an organizational point of view.

Keywords: Video games · Game development artifacts · Video game preservation

1 Introduction

Today, digital games are deeply embedded within our social, cultural, and economic activities. The Entertainment Software Association reports that more than 164 million Americans play video games and that 75% of US households have at least one game player [5]. Numerous colleges and universities offer degrees or coursework to prepare game industry professionals, and games are used in education, science, and engineering as learning and literacy tools.

Like print publishing, film, and music, digital games are cultural products, which produce and distribute social symbolism [6]. To properly understand their history, we need to know the context and details of their creation. Draft manuscripts, research notebooks, and other related artifacts are key to garnering a deeper understanding regarding the processes of creators and their intentions.

Unfortunately, unlike many of its counterparts in the cultural industries, digital games have received relatively little attention and support from academia, museums, libraries, and other institutions concerned with the study and preservation of culture and cultural objects [4]. Only recently have we seen academia and memory institutions accelerate their acceptance of digital games as cultural objects. Radio, television, and film were also subject to this form of neglect in their infancy, and media historians and

© Springer Nature Switzerland AG 2020
A. Sundqvist et al. (Eds.): iConference 2020, LNCS 12051, pp. 630–637, 2020.
https://doi.org/10.1007/978-3-030-43687-2_53

archivists have lost access to significant cultural works due to society's slow realization of their cultural impact [1].

Fortunately, an increasing number of institutions are now collecting and providing access to digital games as part of our cultural heritage, working to catalog, classify, archive, and preserve digital games. A growing number of university libraries also circulate video games for the purposes of academic inquiry. However, this new effort is often limited in scope and largely uncoordinated with other organizations involved in cultural preservation or digital game production [12].

Most digital games created during the industry's relatively short history are no longer easily accessible for study and play [12]. Even when we preserve games, finished products are only part of the story. Researchers and memory institutions have given far less attention to artifacts associated with game development, such as game design documents (GDDs), technical design documents (TDDs), art bibles, style guides, musical scores, test builds, voice-over auditions, and marketing material. Many of these artifacts are born-digital themselves, making their preservation even more challenging [16]. While few are currently aware of the challenges, all involved recognize the loss, from curious fans to students and historians of the industry, media, and culture, as well as librarians, museum professionals, and archivists at the memory institutions who serve those individuals. It is imperative that we begin to address the challenges in organizing and preserving these endangered artifacts.

This research aims to advance our understanding of how to organize and represent artifacts related to the development of video games. As the first step in this larger research effort, this paper focuses on the following research question: *What issues and challenges do stakeholders in game development artifacts (including game developers, librarians, museum curators, game researchers) currently face in organizing and accessing these materials?*

2 Related Work

To date, there have been few projects that have focused on video game development processes, organization, and preservation. The Preserving Virtual Worlds project was a joint effort by Rochester Institute of Technology, Stanford University, the University of Maryland, and the University of Illinois at Urbana-Champaign, and was supported by the Library of Congress. This project focused on preserving older video games and software and began establishing best practices and strategies for game preservation. The second phase of the project, funded by the Institute of Museum and Library Services, focused on determining significant properties for educational games [8]. While this project laid preliminary groundwork for basic metadata standards, the final report specifically calls for future work in establishing relationships and entities, and states that the project barely scraped the surface for standardized ontologies in this domain [14].

Responding to this call, a conceptual model for video games and interactive media —the Video Game Metadata Schema (VGMS)—and seven related controlled vocabularies (CVs) were created by the University of Washington Game Research (GAMER) Group and Seattle Interactive Media Museum in 2012 [10, 11]. GAMECIP, led by the

University of California, Santa Cruz Library, UCSC Computer Science, and Stanford University Library, also investigated metadata needs and citation practices surrounding computer games in institutional collections, producing a schema and best practices for cataloging and classifying computer games [3, 15]. However, both projects mainly focused on the product: finished representations rather than materials created during development.

One exception is Winget's work [18, 19], confirming the game development process does "produce significant and important documentation as traditionally conceived by collecting institutions (p. 29)" but also finding that standard practices fail to adequately collect and preserve the full range of artifacts created. Our work complements prior research by addressing the organization and preservation of game-related materials that have been excluded by previous projects, analyzing the needs of creators and users of these artifacts.

3   Method

We adopted a user-centered approach, focused on identifying the needs of our target users, exploring their practices regarding game development artifacts, and mapping their conceptualization of the domain. This approach helps to ensure results will be relevant to stakeholders. We conducted in-depth, semi-structured interviews with a total of 29 users recruited via email after being identified through snowball sampling which started with recommendations from the project's advisory board. The participants included 12 game industry professionals (producers and developers), 6 game historians, and 11 participants from memory institutions including museums, libraries, and archives. We asked how these different user groups perceive and express their needs for organizing and accessing game development artifacts, and how they expect to find materials they need. We also asked about current practices and challenges when dealing with these materials. Interviews were transcribed and inductively coded for analysis as prescribed by Corbin and Strauss [2]. We followed a consensus model [7] where two coders independently coded the data, discussed discrepancies, and utilized a third researcher as tie-breaker when consensus could not be reached.

4   Preliminary Findings and Discussion

This work is part of a larger ongoing two-year project, working towards a practical solution for organizing game development artifacts. Here, we discuss several key points learned from our interview data during the first phase of the project.

4.1   Challenges in Organizing and Finding Game Development Artifacts

Participants unanimously shared that they currently have challenges in organizing and finding game development artifacts for their work. They described several factors—including organization culture, technical work environments, and a lack of standard vocabulary and practices—as the main reasons for these challenges.

Our industry participants included game developers as well as game platform developers. Platform creators—those creating technical resources that must be shared with developers using their platform—were more focused on creating and organizing development artifacts since materials needed to be shared with clients. Developers working on games were less concerned about maintaining development artifacts. Organization size is also often a factor in the quality and availability of documentation. Smaller companies often adopt *ad hoc* solutions while larger organizations have firmer policies. Little concern was expressed by game development professionals about facilitating hand-offs to memory institutions as they were primarily concerned about product development. Memory institution workers were concerned with all aspects of preserving these materials and making them available to others.

Organization Culture. Perceptions of organizational culture were mentioned as an influence on creating, storing, sharing, and organizing development artifacts. Several participants described a video game industry that does not currently encourage or incentivize documentation processes despite recognizing the value of well documented and organized game development assets and materials. The lack of documentation caused difficulties when people were searching for relevant artifacts.

> *"If you're in a company that's been making content for 20 years and you go try to find an art asset, it's like a needle in a stack of needles."* (P11)

However, many developers also do not see documentation as part of their main job, as using time to document is not perceived as productive or rewarding as actually working towards building a game.

> *"Culture is also another one. If your company doesn't have a culture around—If the developers are used to just working or running off and doing a task– Here's another thing, documentation is not fun. That's not why a game designer came to work, to write shit down so that other people on some other team could understand what you're doing."* (P11)

P1 also stated that companies might be unwilling to share some of the game development artifacts:

> *"I've already noted there are some significant disadvantages for them releasing design documents, potentially, if someone put like a feature they really liked which was cut from the development of that game."* (P1)

The same participant also pointed out that people may be more likely to share certain game development artifacts than others. For instance, some companies might be more unwilling to share organization-related information than game assets. While digital objects created during the development process evoke a desire for sharing, information related to process and budgeting are often closely guarded.

Technical Work Environment. Technical environments were also seen to influence creation, storage, sharing, and organization development artifacts. Overwhelmingly, game studios have embraced agile development principles, a fact that is presented by our developer participants. According to the Agile Manifesto, agile developers value "Working software over comprehensive documentation" [13]. Participant 11 reported that it can be unclear what to document, especially at the beginning of game projects, since specifics change frequently and dramatically. Most industry participants disclosed that employees of their company often do not maintain early design and technical documentation as living documents. Some create official systems for supplemental work but others simply do not track these changes in a central location.

The constant need to make new products also creates gaps in the process, meaning retrospectives are few and far between.

"If your team is telling you they have the information to build what needs to get built, it can be very hard to find the justification then the additional time documenting it." (P13)

Some companies deliberately chose less documentation because they felt it suited their design process,

"For better or worse we are kind of allergic to design documents. We tend to evolve the design and show, rather than describe." (P17)

Participants also mentioned that documenting becomes more difficult as "living games" become more common, with updates and patches releasing frequently. In addition, P12 and P15 mentioned that open office layouts impact the documentation process.

"Yes, we're trying to keep things efficient and quick. That is the main benefit of a close open office like this is, you can just go, 'Hey, where's the thing?' And, 'Yes, it's here.' Boom and you're done." (P15)

P12 believed this increased efficiency resulted in decreased need for describing and documenting artifacts in the short-term but admitted that personnel changes and increasing complexity diminish these perceived benefits.

Lack of Standard Vocabulary and Practices. Our participants report that there are several tools used to document various game development artifacts. These tools include specific platform tools, enterprise software (e.g., Confluence), cloud-based services (e.g., Dropbox, Google Drive), and wikis. Each of these allows developers to name and organize assets and structure documentation. However, participants mentioned a lack of standard terminology and naming conventions for these processes and artifacts. Numerous environments, both for creating and preserving these artifacts, has led to a lack of consistency in the industry and even among concerned memory institutions. Participants were often left to their own devices without clear standards to follow.

"We have an industry of terrible at this naming conventions. Every person who writes some-thing or comes up with something, names it themselves which makes it very difficult then to search anything because I might call something a one-page or because I think it's a one sheet document. Another person might call it a game design document. Then the naming of the features also can change multiple times over the course." (P13)

This problem becomes compounded as the number of development artifacts increases. Participants reported that tools allowed for easy storage of assets but were less helpful for finding and retrieving them later. Standardization problems are exac-erbated when the work is international in nature, as when dealing with assets created in foreign studios.

Participants from memory institutions also complained about the lack of standard vocabulary to describe games and related artifacts, resorting to homegrown CVs. Participants detailed the challenges caused by the lack of such standards.

"We've been using Argus for a while and that comes with an entire lexicon-controlled vocabulary. Most of which is not incredibly useful for my particular collection. Over time I definitely have had to add to that on a local level that basically is just in our servers." (P25)

"I don't have a controlled vocabulary for that. It's just based on experience. Then there are times that I don't know what something is and I check with some of the IT folks. Recently, we got a collection and that is from [a corporate donor]. They did some early electromechanical games and shuffleboard and stuff like that. I was like, 'I have no idea what I'm looking at.'" (P27)

Memory institutions that had created their own CVs had not shared them with other memory institutions, resulting in a highly fractured, siloed language for game development artifacts.

4.2   Disconnect Between Libraries, Archives, and Special Collections

Participants from memory institutions described a disconnect among their libraries, archives, and special collections. They explained that different systems exist for each collection type (e.g., Argus or PastPerfect for museum collections, and WorldCat for library collections). Connections between relevant objects scattered around these collections—a video game in the special collections, a related publication in the library collection, and related development artifacts in the archive—are not explicitly related in the organizational system. This is an obstacle for users seeking all materials relevant to a game even within one memory institution. Other challenges seemed to involve institution culture.

"It would be theoretically possible if one hand knew what the other hand was doing, but in practical terms, probably not. We wouldn't be in communication enough to know that one of us had a related item." (P6)

5   Conclusion and Future Work

By interviewing stakeholders interested in video game development artifacts, we were able to uncover several challenges regarding their organization and access. Some challenges are more difficult to address, such as the low value the game industry gives the documentation process and the pressures of fast game development cycles. However, we also observed two phenomena that could be addressed from an organizational perspective:

(1)   There is a need for standard vocabulary and naming conventions to better organize and represent video game development artifacts in the game industry and memory institutions. Standardized and thorough descriptions of these materials afford improved access to museum curators, archivists, and librarians who acquire, catalog, and provide reference services; users of these collections; and commercial organizations trying to organize and preserve their own development assets. We are currently in the process of developing a taxonomy of video game development artifacts which will enable information professionals to describe game related materials more accurately and thoroughly, improving the quality of metadata

shared with users and organizations alike. This taxonomy will be published as a complement to and extension of prior work with the VGMS [17], the conceptual model for video games and interactive media [9], and research from GAMECIP research team [3] as well as extending and complementing archival standards.

(2) It would be fruitful to explore ways to better connect relevant items in multiple collections of varying nature. We plan to more closely examine the different systems and metadata standards that are currently used in libraries and archives, aiming to generate a best practice document on how to better represent the entities and relationships in the domain of video game and interactive media development.

While we focus on video game development in our work, many other forms of electronic, born-digital, and interactive media (e.g., e-books, computer software, digital images, and smartphone applications) can benefit from research on non-book metadata. Inquiry into the differences in organizational needs for physical and digital artifacts speaks to larger questions about the transition from physical to digital materials and the implications of that transition for libraries, archives, and museums. Our work may also be applicable to other segments of the cultural industries, such as film and animation, which are also created from a complex development process where many intermediate development artifacts are produced and are also in the throes of transition to digital materials.

The challenges for video game media and their accompanying digital artifacts are numerous. Further inquiry into how best to preserve them is necessary to provide robust documentation for the game development process, while wider acceptance and distribution of standards will greatly aid in a shared understanding of the artifacts. While this research firmly targets informing the latter, without better practices and an industry-wide drive towards documentation, much of preserving the process, history, and context of video games remains threatened.

Acknowledgement. This project was made possible in part by the Institute of Museum and Library Services LG-86-18-0060-18.

References

1. Bamberger, R., Brylawski, S. (eds.): The state of recorded sound preservation in the United States: A national legacy at risk in the digital age. Council on Library and Information Resources & Library of Congress, Washington, D.C. (2010)
2. Corbin, J., Strauss, A.: Basics of Qualitative Research, 4th edn. SAGE Publications, Thousand Oaks (2015)
3. Core Metadata Schema for Cataloging Video Games. Version 1. Game Metadata and Citation Project (GAMECIP) Tech Report 1. https://gamecip.soe.ucsc.edu/sites/default/files/GAMECIP-Tech-Report-1_0.pdf. Accessed 14 Sept 2019
4. Digital Preservation Coalition. Critically Endangered. http://www.dpconline.org/our-work/bit-list/critically-endangered. Accessed 14 Sept 2019
5. Entertainment Software Association. 2019 Essential Facts About the Computer and Video Game Industry. https://www.theesa.com/esa-research/2019-essential-facts-about-the-computer-and-video-game-industry/. Accessed 12 Sept 2019

6. Hesmondhalgh, D.: The Cultural Industries, 3rd edn. SAGE Publications, London (2012)
7. Hill, C., Thompson, B., Williams, E.: A guide to conducting consensual qualitative research. Couns. Psychol. **25**(4), 517–572 (1997)
8. Institute of Museum and Library Services. LG-06-10-0160-10. https://www.imls.gov/grants/awarded/lg-06-10-0160-10. Accessed 09 Sept 2019
9. Jett, J., Sacchi, S., Lee, J.H., Clarke, R.I.: A conceptual model for video games and interactive media. J. Assoc. Inf. Sci. Technol. **67**(3), 505–517 (2016)
10. Lee, J.H., Cho, H., Fox, V., Perti, A.: User-centered approach in creating a metadata schema for video games and interactive media. In: Proceedings of the 13th ACM/IEEE-CS Joint Conference on Digital Libraries, pp. 229–238 (2013)
11. Lee, J.H., Tennis, J.T., Clarke, R.I., Carpenter, M.: Developing a video game metadata schema for the Seattle Interactive Media Museum. Int. J. Digit. Libr. **13**(2), 105–117 (2013)
12. Lowood, H., Monnens, D., Vowell, Z., Ruggill, J., McAllister, K., Armstrong, A.: Before it's too late: a digital game preservation white paper. Am. J. Play **2**(2), 139–166 (2009)
13. Manifesto for Agile Software Development. https://agilemanifesto.org/. Accessed 15 Sept 2019
14. McDonough, J., et al.: Preserving virtual worlds final report, Champaign, IL (2010). http://hdl.handle.net/2142/17097
15. Online Audiovisual Catalogers, Inc. Best Practices for Cataloging Video Games Using RDA and MARC21. Version 1.0, June 2015. http://olacinc.org/sites/capc_files/GameBestPractices.pdf. Accessed 14 Sept 2019
16. Ries, T., Palkó, G.: Born-digital archives. Int. J. Digit. Hum. **1**(1), 1–11 (2019). https://doi.org/10.1007/s42803-019-00011-x
17. Video Game Metadata Schema. http://metadataregistry.org/schema/show/id/132.html. Accessed 14 Sept 2019
18. Winget, M., Murray, C.: Collecting and preserving videogames and their related materials: a review of current practice, game-related archives and research projects. In: Proceedings of the 71st ASIS&T Annual Meeting, pp. 1–9 (2008)
19. Winget, M., Sampson, W.: Game development documentation and institutional collection development policy. In: Proceedings of the 11th Annual International ACM/IEEE Joint Conference on Digital Libraries, pp. 29–38 (2011)

An Exploration of Contributor-Created Description Field in Participatory Archives

Ana Roeschley(✉) ⓘ, Jeonghyun Kimⓘ, and Oksana L. Zavalinaⓘ

University of North Texas, Denton, TX 76207, USA
ana.roeschley@unt.edu

Abstract. Participatory archive initiatives are an emerging phenomenon in the archives field. These initiatives are defined by the participation of the individuals that archival materials are created by or about. This often includes the description of materials by their creators. However, participatory archival description brings forth several questions: What knowledge and insights can be gained about items in a digital collection when they are described by their record creators and contributors? And what risks are there when the data values for are not created in a standardized format? To answer these questions, this paper examined the outcome of participatory archival description – i.e., free-text description metadata field created by participatory archives' contributors. Using the Boston Harbor Islands Mass. Memories Collection Dublin Core-based description metadata records, contributor-created Description field length and attributes were analyzed through a combination of quantitative and qualitative content analysis methods. Study results show that data value of contributor-created description metadata was dominated by utterances that provide contextual information regarding archival objects, particularly about the individuals and physical environment that contributors associate with the items, while item content itself can be under-described.

Keywords: Metadata · Contributor-created metadata · Free-text description metadata field · Participatory archives

1 Introduction

"Participation" and "participatory culture" are growing topics of interest in the field of archives. Various methods and levels of participation in archival work have been discussed [1–3] by exploring concepts such as participatory archives, where "people other than archives professional contribute knowledge or resources, resulting in increased understanding about archival materials" [4]. Participatory archive initiatives have arisen as part of this participatory movement, including The Mass. Memories Road Show,[1] Europeana Migration Collection Days,[2] and Inspiring Ireland,[3] and Harvey Memories.[4]

---

[1] https://openarchives.umb.edu/digital/collection/p15774coll6.

[2] https://www.europeana.eu/portal/el/collections/migration/collection-days.html.

[3] https://www.dri.ie/documenting-1916-rising-through-public-memorabilia-collection-days.

[4] https://harveymemories.org/news.

© Springer Nature Switzerland AG 2020
A. Sundqvist et al. (Eds.): iConference 2020, LNCS 12051, pp. 638–648, 2020.
https://doi.org/10.1007/978-3-030-43687-2_54

Such initiatives involve the active participation of the individuals who the archival records are created by or are about. The contributions to participatory archives can include an individual's involvement with archival tasks, such as appraisal, description, and restrictions and access to archival materials. Shilton and Srinivasan [2] argue that this new archival practice allows "the creator [to] own the choices they have made, ensuring that they speak with their own voices, and empowering their representation into the future." For participatory archival description in particular, Caswell and Mallick [5] asserted that the practice of allowing community members to describe the content acknowledges the importance of community knowledge and works toward integrating that knowledge into the archival record.

However, questions remain about participatory archival description: What knowledge and insights can be gained about items in a digital collection when they are described by their record creators and contributors? And what risks are there when the data values for are not created in a standardized format? To answer these questions, this paper examined the outcome of participatory archival description – i.e., free-text description metadata field created by participatory archives' contributors.

2 Literature Review

The literature on participatory archives includes works that provide both theoretical and practical frameworks for understanding participatory archives [1, 2, 6, 7]. These include information on archive formations, collection policies, and their potential to connect archives with social justice movements [8, 9]. Because these archives are an emerging phenomenon, many aspects of participatory archives continue to be unexplored. Particularly, little to no attention has been paid to how contributor-created metadata is affects our understandings of participatory archive collections.

Nevertheless, there is a breadth of literature on the processes of participatory and crowdsourced metadata creation [10–12]. Liew [13] explains that there is potential for cultural institutions to use crowdsourced metadata as a window into collective memory. In the realm of archives, Benoit [14] discusses the role of social tagging in supplementing under-described digital archives.

Metadata is created to ensure that repository users can find the data which they need. Through standardization, metadata records are comparable within and across digital collections. Describing Archives: A Content Standard (DACS) is the current standard for the description of archival collections, personal papers, and manuscript collections [15][5]. Gracy and Lambert [16] found that in using DACS, "most archival institutions employ people who have knowledge and experience in preparing descriptions of archival materials." DACS currently does not include a free-text Description element.

---

[5] https://www2.archivists.org/standards/DACS.

There are a number of metadata standards that have been created for both domain-specific and for generic collections. A widely used generic metadata scheme, Dublin Core is often applied by participatory archives. The simple version of Dublin Core (Dublin Core Metadata Element Set 1.1)[6] consists of 15 broadly-defined elements (e.g., Date, Format, Relation, etc.) embodied in databases as metadata fields. The more extended version of Dublin Core item-level metadata standard – Dublin Core Metadata initiative (DCMI) Metadata Terms[7] consists of both DCMES 1.1 elements and a number of more specific elements (e.g., DateSubmitted, Extent, HasPart, etc.). Unlike several other Dublin Core metadata elements that commonly rely on controlled-vocabulary data values (e.g., Subject, Coverage, Type, Format, etc.), the Description element is intended to provide a free-text account of the resource being described. The definition of Dublin Core Description element is broad and can include an abstract, a table of contents, a graphical representation, or a free-text account of the resource.

Best practice recommendations have been developed regarding data values for the free-text metadata elements in different metadata schemes (including Dublin Core Description element and semantically similar elements in other metadata standards) for metadata records that describe individual information objects or items in the collections: Cataloging Cultural Objects (CCO) [17], Categories for the Description of Works of Art (CDWA) [18], etc. CCO and CDWA suggest recording information about subject, significance, and function in free-text description element.

Guidelines also exist for Description fields and its semantic equivalents in metadata records describing physical collections of manuscripts [19] and collections of archival materials [20, 21]. For example, National Union Catalog of Manuscript Collections [20] suggests that collection-level metadata creators for manuscript collections provide in the Description element: information about types of materials included in the collection; topics and geographical areas with which the materials in the collection deal; associated dates, events, and historical periods; names, dates, and biographical identification of persons and names of corporate bodies significant to the collection; and specific phases of career/activity of the major person or corporate body responsible. Summary Notes for Catalog Records [21] recommends inclusion of information about specific types and forms of materials present; significant people, topics, places, and events covered; span of dates covered by the collection; history of the work; unique characteristics of the collection; reason and function of the collection; audience; and user interaction. The Encoded Archival Description [21] recommends inclusion in the data values of Description field information about form and arrangement of materials; significant subjects represented; places and events represented; significant organizations and individuals represented; collection strengths; functions and activities that generated the materials being described, and gaps in the materials to help the user evaluate the potential relevance of these materials.

---

[6] https://www.dublincore.org/specifications/dublin-core/dces/.

[7] https://www.dublincore.org/specifications/dublin-core/dcmi-terms/.

Archival materials are usually described at the level of collections, rather than items. Collection-level metadata can provide abundant information regarding the provenance and context of archival and other cultural collections [22–24]. However, because participatory archive collections are created by many contributors rather than one or several members of a collective unit, a number of these projects, including the Mass. Memories Road Show, the North Texas History Harvest, Our Marathon etc., focus on creating item-level metadata. The metadata records for these participatory archive projects are created in a number of ways, from contributor-created, as in the case of Mass. Memories, to professionally created as in the case of Our Marathon [26].

While there is a strong body of literature on metadata and on the emerging phenomenon of participatory archives, there is no evidence of literature on participatory archive contributor-created metadata. This exploratory study attempts to close this gap in the literature by examining data values in the participatory archive contributor-created Description metadata fields in order to ascertain what knowledge can be gained about archival objects when they are described by their contributors.

3 Method

We examined the Boston Harbor Islands Mass. Memories Road Show (BHI-MMRS) collection, a participatory archive that is housed by the University of Massachusetts Boston's Digital Collections. This collection includes 154 digitized archival objects, mostly photographs, which were contributed by community participants. This project relies on contributors to create the free-text Description metadata through filling out the Photo Form for each contributed object (Fig. 1). As can be seen in Fig. 1, contributors are given concise but broad written instructions for the creation of their item descriptions, giving them leeway in creating the free-text metadata [26].

To serve as the main dataset, we downloaded a copy of BHI-MMRS collection metadata. These metadata records utilized a modified version of Dublin Core, and though a number of metadata elements were present, only Description field was analyzed as part of this study.

The data value length of the Description field was analyzed using descriptive statistics, using mean, standard deviation, and variation. The data value attribute of the Description field was analyzed using a combination of qualitative and quantitative content analysis through Dedoose, a web-based qualitative analysis tool. To identify attributes, we used an inductive open coding approach of grounded theory. Through the iterative construction of analytic codes, we analyzed the data according to the constant comparative method introduced by Glaser and Strauss [27]. As a result, we developed two categories and 11 codes which reflect the processes of description and contextualization that are present in the BHI-MMRS description metadata fields. The content category relates to the substance of the contributed archival object itself with free-text metadata describing the content of archival object. Conversely, the context category

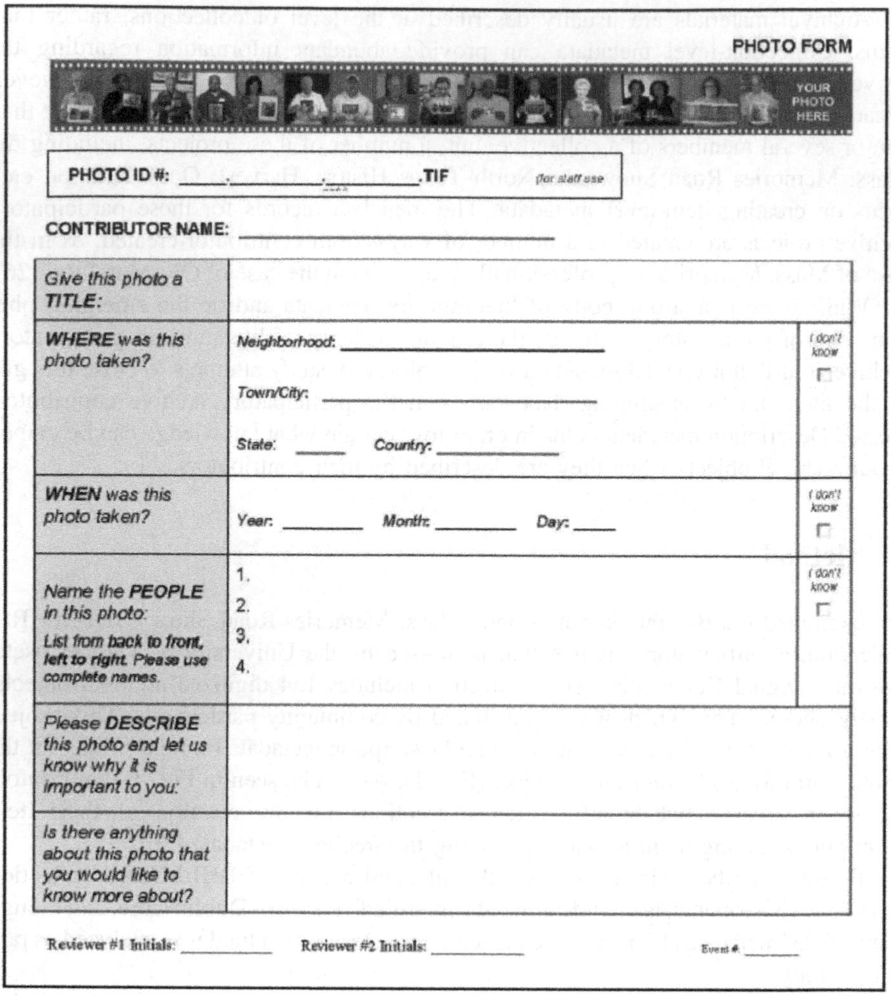
PHOTO FORM

YOUR PHOTO HERE

PHOTO ID #: ______ .TIF (for staff use)

CONTRIBUTOR NAME: ______

Give this photo a *TITLE:*		
WHERE was this photo taken?	Neighborhood: ______ Town/City: ______ State: ______ Country: ______	I don't know ☐
WHEN was this photo taken?	Year: ______ Month: ______ Day: ______	I don't know ☐
Name the *PEOPLE* in this photo: List from back to front, left to right. Please use complete names.	1. 2. 3. 4.	I don't know ☐
Please *DESCRIBE* this photo and let us know why it is important to you:		
Is there anything about this photo that you would like to know more about?		

Reviewer #1 Initials: ______ Reviewer #2 Initials: ______ Event # ______

Fig. 1. Photo Form includes the instructions on metadata creation for contributors to the BHI-MMRS participatory archive. The Mass. Memories Road Show [26].

relates to the contextual information provided by the contributor, which is information that helps users understand the context of archival object. The coding scheme is presented in Table 1.

To test the inter-coder reliability, the primary researcher coded all 154 records, and subsequently the second coder coded every fifth record in the dataset. Cohen's Kappa coefficient was found to be 0.84, indicating high agreements between the two coders.

Table 1. Data value attribute of Description field

Category	Code	Definition	Example
Content	Archival Object Type	Statement of archival object type	"This *photograph* gives a moving account of…"
	Physical Environment	Physical environment (including buildings, rooms, landmarks, etc.) represented in archival the object	"*Location: Thompson Pond*"
	People	Individual(s) featured in archival object	"Pictured: *Giuseppe Cioffi* (top middle with hat and cigarette)"
Context	Provenance	Information about the context of contributed archival object	"This photo is *among many from my husband's collection of local informal scenes of Boston Harbor*"
	Event	Information about a specific event associated with archival object	"On *June 12, 1949, we married…*"
	Action	Information about actions and activities individuals engage in	"While Patrick *was painting the portrait* of the Director of Long Island Hospital,…"
	Information about Physical Environment	Provisional information about physical environment	"*The park was developed by the MWRA to provide a sanctuary for those who walk, run, bike-ride, and watch the sunrise and sunset. It is also a place to fish*"
	Information about People	Detailed information about individuals related with archival object	"They are being shuttled on the 'Irene' by *Richie, who was a small private boat-owner and part of our island family for years*"
	Party of Associates	Information about groups and organizations associated with archival object	"I became a member of the *famous 'First Boys' Band in the United States..*"
	Experiential Narrative	Re-telling of a personal or shared memory	"*We would take the boat out on nights and weekends in the river and the harbor…*"
	Evidence of Affect	Use of language that alludes to or embodies affect	"It was a beautiful day. *It was delightful…*"

4   Results

The data value length of Description field metadata in our dataset varies with the shortest entry at five words and the longest at 229 words. The average length is 59.78 words, with a standard deviation of 38.27, and a variance of 1,465.16. When compared with the previous work on the length of Description field metadata value in DPLA, which was generated by professionals [28], this average length of contributor-created Description field is short. But it should be noted that BHI-MMRS collection contains mostly photographs whereas the DPLA includes a variety of object types, including photographs, manuscripts, books, sounds, and moving images.

Table 2. Summary of data value attribute of Description field

	Number of records	Percentage
Content		
Archival object type	34	22%
Physical environment	49	32%
People	96	62%
Context		
Provenance	39	25%
Event	75	49%
Action	118	77%
Information about physical environment	142	92%
Information about people	136	88%
Party of associates	57	37%
Experiential narrative	53	34%
Evidence of affect	61	40%

In terms of data value attributes, we found that context was found in all 154 records, while content was found in 153 records. As presented in Table 2, data value of contributor-created metadata was dominated by utterances that provide contextual information of archival objects; this is reflected by the fact that context category includes eight codes that are applied to the data set in 681 instances. It is also noted that 92% of records include circumstantial depiction of physical environment, like town, neighborhood, landmarks, and buildings. Similarly, detailed sketch of individuals constitutes 82% of the records. Figure 2 illustrates how context can be more prevalent in contributor-created free-text description.

As can be seen in the contributor-created free-text description in Fig. 2, the account of the item is rather limited, and the majority of the lengthy utterance is about the contributor's stories behind the item she contributed to the archive. The contributor explores several topics in her description, which is written in a conversational style. This data value is in direct contrast to most metadata input guidelines, which not only indicate that the description should be predominately about the item, they also include a rule for brevity: "Enter information clearly and concisely" [17].

While the contributor-created free-text description in Fig. 2 does not comply with guidelines, the data value does provide rich contextual information. These contextual details reveal substantial information regarding life for visitors to the historic Boston Harbor Islands which have experienced significant changes over the past several decades. These rich details and the use of conversational language provide evidence of affect as in the case of the contributor who describes her "*numerous happy memories*" and how she "*loved walking around the island* (Fig. 2)."

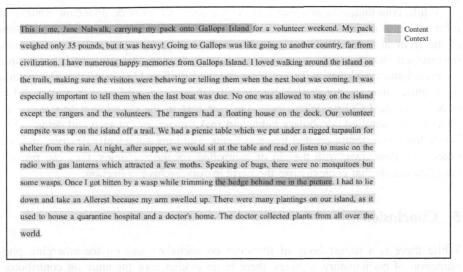

This is me, Jane Nalwalk, carrying my pack onto Gallops Island for a volunteer weekend. My pack weighed only 35 pounds, but it was heavy! Going to Gallops was like going to another country, far from civilization. I have numerous happy memories from Gallops Island. I loved walking around the island on the trails, making sure the visitors were behaving or telling them when the next boat was coming. It was especially important to tell them when the last boat was due. No one was allowed to stay on the island except the rangers and the volunteers. The rangers had a floating house on the dock. Our volunteer campsite was up on the island off a trail. We had a picnic table which we put under a rigged tarpaulin for shelter from the rain. At night, after supper, we would sit at the table and read or listen to music on the radio with gas lanterns which attracted a few moths. Speaking of bugs, there were no mosquitoes but some wasps. Once I got bitten by a wasp while trimming the hedge behind me in the picture. I had to lie down and take an Allerest because my arm swelled up. There were many plantings on our island, as it used to house a quarantine hospital and a doctor's home. The doctor collected plants from all over the world.

Content
Context

Fig. 2. Example of a contributor-created Description field that shows content and context categories.

Affect exists at the intersection of feeling, being, and knowing as it ties historical records to memory [29]. While affect is often evoked by personal archival materials, its presence is unexpected in standardized metadata in institutional repositories. However, through our iterative coding, we found that affect is openly added in the BHI-MMRS Description fields by the contributors and is present in 40% of the records as contributors describe personal connections and emotional ties to their items. For example, one excerpt was tagged for "Evidence of Affect" code because it speaks to how the item represents family relationships: "This photo is *important because it shows how close our family was* during our summers on Peddock's." Rather than describing the photograph, the contributor describes the photograph's importance as an embodiment of the contributor's family ties.

The conversational language and the use of first-person narration present in the BHI-MMRS metadata also allow for personal and collective memories to shine through. These instances, coded as "Experiential Narrative," lack any objective tone. Rather, they invite archive users to view the past through the eyes of the contributors. The "Experiential Narrative" code is present in 34% of the records and is often cross-coded with "Event" which is present in 49%.

The personalized first-person narrations reveal how the contributors view archival objects and the memories that are tied to these objects. For example, in describing a photograph of a singing group, a contributor writes, "*Many, many fond memories* of rehearsals at our home." In pointing to the fond memories of the rehearsals, the contributor explains what it is about this particular item that makes it worthy of inclusion in the archive.

While contributor-created free-text descriptions can provide abundant contextual information, some also provide confusing or limited information regarding the content of the archival items. While the generally understood purpose of metadata is to relay information about the items or collections it is describing, this situation is not unique for participatory archives as Tarver, Zavalina, and Phillips [28] found that Description field entries that are not contributor-created can also be confusing or vague. Additionally, as the CCO guidelines note, the free text in the description acts as a supplement to controlled-vocabulary fields and make room for "nuance and detail" [17]. While these contributor-created free-text fields could not sufficiently describe archival objects on their own, with the aid of controlled-vocabulary fields, they can provide complex details that contextualize the participatory archive collection.

5 Conclusion

While there is a robust body of literature on metadata and on the emerging phenomenon of participatory archives, there is no evidence of literature on contributor-created metadata in participatory archives. This exploratory study attempts to close this gap in the literature by examining a participatory archive's contributor-created free-text description metadata in order to ascertain what knowledge can be gained about archival objects when they are described by their contributors. This study's findings suggest that contributor-created description can provide nuanced contextual information on archival objects. This supports Caswell and Mallick's [5] assertion that participant description enriches our understandings of archival collections by contextualizing the archival objects with archive contributors' personal and community knowledge. Including such description in contributor-created Description metadata fields is one way in which such contextual information can be easily accessed in digital participatory archives.

While this study explored metadata in a collection with a small number of contributed items, our future research would be replicated on a much larger scale, as a comparative study incorporating multiple collections to develop the understanding of the role of metadata in participatory archives. In particular, further research is needed on the role of free-text descriptive metadata, its correlation with controlled-vocabulary metadata within the same metadata records, and best practices of such metadata creation in participatory archives.

References

1. Huvila, I.: The unbearable lightness of participating? Revisiting the discourses of "participation" in archival literature. J. Doc. **71**(2), 358–386 (2015)
2. Shilton, K., Srinivasan, R.: Participatory appraisal and arrangement for multicultural archival collections. Archivaria **63**, 87–101 (2007)
3. Yakel, E.: Balancing archival authority with encouraging authentic voices to engage with records. In: Theimer, K. (ed.) A Different Kind of Web: New Connections Between Archives and Our Users, pp. 75–101. Society of American Archivists, Chicago (2011)

4. Theimer, K.: Exploring the participatory archives. Presentation at the 2011 Society of American Archivists Annual Meeting (2011). http://www.slideshare.net/ktheimer/theimer-participatory-archives-saa2011

5. Caswell, M., Mallick, S.: Collecting the easily missed stories: digital participatory microhistory and the South Asian American Digital Archive. Arch. Manuscripts **42**(1), 73–86 (2014)

6. Eveleigh, A.: Welcoming the world: an exploration of participatory archives. In: International Council on Archives (ICA) Conference (ICA 2012), August 2012

7. Roeschley, A., Kim, J.: "Something that feels like a community": the role of personal stories in building community-based participatory archives. Arch. Sci. **19**(1), 27–49 (2019). https://doi.org/10.1007/s10502-019-09302-2

8. Rolan, G.: Agency in the archive: a model for participatory recordkeeping. Arch. Sci. **17**(3), 195–225 (2017). https://doi.org/10.1007/s10502-016-9267-7

9. Wick, A.: We're all vegans here: the twenty-first century archival ecosystem. J. Arch. Organ. (2018). https://doi.org/10.1080/15332748.2018

10. Barber, S.T.: The ZOONIVERSE is expanding: crowdsourced solutions to the hidden collections problem and the rise of the revolutionary cataloging interface. J. Libr. Metadata **18**(2), 85–111 (2018). https://doi.org/10.1080/19386389.2018.1489449

11. Chen, A.T., Carriere, R.M., Kaplan, S.J.: The user knows what to call it: incorporating patient voice through user-contributed tags on a participatory platform about health management. J. Med. Internet Res. **19**(9), e292–e292 (2017). https://doi.org/10.2196/jmir.7673

12. Varin, J.: iTunes metadata and classical music: issues and solutions for crowdsourced metadata in iTunes. Ser. Libr. **69**(1), 70–76 (2015). https://doi.org/10.1080/0361526X.2015.1036196

13. Liew, C.L.: Social metadata and public-contributed contents in memory institutions: "crowd voice" versus "authenticated heritage"? Preserv. Digit. Technol. Cult. **45**(3), 122 (2016). https://doi.org/10.1515/pdtc-2016-0017

14. Benoit, E.: MPLP part 2: replacing item-level metadata with user-generated social tags. Am. Archivist **81**(1), 38–64 (2018). https://doi.org/10.17723/0360-9081-81.1.38

15. Surles, E.: Sharing notes: a qualitative analysis of description of archival music materials. Music Ref. Serv. Q. **22**(3), 111–130 (2019). https://doi.org/10.1080/10588167.2019.1570739

16. Gracy, K.F., Lambert, F.: Who's ready to surf the next wave? A study of perceived challenges to implementing new and revised standards for archival description. Am. Archivist **77**(1), 96–132 (2014). https://doi.org/10.17723/aarc.77.1.b241071w5r252612

17. Baca, M., et al.: Cataloging Cultural Objects: A Guide to Describing Cultural Works and Their Images. American Library Association, Chicago (2006)

18. Baca, M., Harpring, P. (eds.): Categories for the Description of Works of Art (CDWA). Getty Research Institute, Santa Monica (2009)

19. National Union Catalog of Manuscript Collections: Online data sheet for participating institutions (2011). http://www.loc.gov/coll/nucmc/lcforms.html

20. OLAC Cataloging Policy Committee, Summary/Abstracts Task Force: Summary notes for catalog records (2002). http://www.olacinc.org/drupal/?q=node/21

21. Encoded Archival Description: EAD3 (2015). http://www2.archivists.org/sites/all/files/TagLibrary-VersionEAD3.pdf

22. Bearman, D.A.: Documenting documentation. Archivaria J. Assoc. Can. Archivists **34** (Summer), 33–49 (1992)

23. Miller, P.: Collected wisdom: some cross-domain issues of collection level description. D-Lib Mag. **6**(9) (2000)

24. Zavalina, O.L., Palmer, C.L., Jackson, A.S., Han, M.J.: Evaluating descriptive richness in collection-level metadata. J. Libr. Metadata **8**(4), 263–292 (2009)
25. Northeastern University Libraries: Our Marathon (n.d.). https://marathon.library.northeastern.edu/
26. The Mass. Memories Road Show. The Mass. Memories Road Show project handbook: A planning guide for local communities. University of Massachusetts Boston, Joseph P. Healey Library, Boston (2016)
27. Glaser, B., Strauss, A.: Grounded theory: the discovery of grounded theory. Sociol. J. Br. Sociol. Assoc. **12**(1), 27–49 (1967)
28. Tarver, H., Zavalina, O.L., Phillips, M.: An exploratory study of a Description field in the Digital Public Library of America. In: Proceedings of the International Conference and Workshop on Dublin Core and Metadata Applications, Copenhagen, Denmark, 13–16 October 2016 (2016)
29. Stewart, K.: Ordinary Affects. Duke University Press, Durham (2007)

Future of Work

AI Models and Their Worlds: Investigating Data-Driven, AI/ML Ecosystems Through a Work Practices Lens

Christine T. Wolf[✉]

IBM Research – Almaden, San Jose, CA, USA
ctwolf@us.ibm.com

Abstract. When we invoke the "future of work," to whose work do we refer? This paper considers everyday work practices through which contemporary artificial intelligence (AI) and machine learning (ML) ecosystems are made possible. The "future of work" is often talked about in relation to the anticipated domain settings where AI/ML systems might be implemented and the labor conditions such implementations might re-configure (foreseeing or noting changes in medical/health, legal, or manufacturing work, for example). This paper turns our attention to the various forms of labor that must be undertaken to conceive of, train/test, deploy, and ongoingly maintain AI/ML systems in practice. In particular, this paper draws on an ongoing ethnographic endeavor in a large, global technology and consulting corporation and leverages a work practices lens to examine three themes: *curating datasets* (everyday work practices of data pre-processing); *tending models* (everyday work practices of training, deploying, and maintaining predictive models); and *configuring compute* (everyday work practices of back-end infrastructuring, commonly called "DevOps"). This paper considers the value of a work practices lens in studying contemporary sociotechnical labor ecosystems. By locating the work practices through which AI/ML systems emerge, this paper shows that these technologies indeed require considerable human labor, at the same time they are often talked about as drivers of automation and displacers of work. This extends discourses around the "future of work," giving light to the various standpoints and experiences of labor such imaginaries implicate and ongoingly re-configure.

Keywords: Artificial intelligence · Machine learning · Future of work · Data science · AI worlds · Work practices · Invisible labor · Ethnography

1 Introduction

This paper considers the "future of work" from the vantage of the labor that must be undertaken to conceive of, train/test, deploy, and ongoingly maintain AI/ML systems in practice. Concerns over the future of work (rapid changes to the nature and experience and everyday work brought on by advances in computational technologies) are not new. The computerization and personal computer (PC) movements of the 1970s and 1980s also portended an imagined future where the everyday experiences of labor would be improved through increased efficiency and the reduction of tedious and

© Springer Nature Switzerland AG 2020
A. Sundqvist et al. (Eds.): iConference 2020, LNCS 12051, pp. 651–664, 2020.
https://doi.org/10.1007/978-3-030-43687-2_55

boring dimensions of everyday work tasks [21]. The future of work narratives of recent years have been precipitated by the "Big Data" boom, an explosive growth in the volume, velocity, and variety of data in the past decade [20]. This growth in data, alongside increased computational processing capabilities (often in the form of graphical processing units or GPUs) which are available in distributed configurations (i.e., via cloud computing) have rekindled widespread fascinations and hopes of researchers, entrepreneurs, and developers that the possibilities of artificial, machine intelligence, often referred to as artificial intelligence (AI) and machine learning (ML), might transform human experience and provoke social change.

The "future of work" is often talked about in relation to the anticipated domain settings where AI/ML systems might be implemented and the labor conditions such implementations might re-configure – i.e., in transforming heavily structured domains like the health/medical domain [28, 29] or creating entirely new domains, like casual/gig and app-based work (which is often organized via AI/ML sorting algorithms) [27]. Other approaches examine AI/ML implementations in work contexts more generally, looking at, for example, the impact of smart office software on everyday workplace tasks like email and calendaring [33], organizational decision-making processes [17] or the experiences of knowledge workers [10, 30].

This paper considers the "future of work" from the vantage of the technical, software engineering and design work practices that render contemporary AI/ML systems possible. All AI is "work" for someone – that is, it is someone's job to conceive of, train/test, deploy, and ongoingly maintain AI/ML systems in practice. We consider this point of view, which is often rendered invisible in much of the "future of work" discourses today. Drawing on ethnographic fieldwork and participatory design projects at a large, global technology and consulting corporation, we consider three dimensions of the everyday work practices of AI/ML: *curating datasets* (everyday work practices of data pre-processing); *tending models* (everyday work practices of training, deploying, and maintaining predictive models); and *configuring compute* (everyday work practices of back-end infrastructuring, commonly called "DevOps").

From recent work, we gain a rich understanding of the everyday data work practices of a number of uniquely situated domain settings, for example research scientists [24] or hospital administrative staff [25]. But, as others have noted, we understand little about the work of everyday data science "on the ground" [5, 31, 34]. Recent work by Wolf [32] has investigated the information behavior practices of ML developers, noting their role in shaping professional identity and social belonging. That work suggests that the everyday work practices of data-intensive developers is a rich site for inquiry into the experiences of contemporary information professionals. A situated, qualitative examination of everyday technical work practices follows a tradition of ethnographic studies of such practices, for example, the foundational work of Julian Orr in studying the practices of photo-copier repair technicians at Xerox [23]. Organizational studies scholars such as Bechky [1] have called for a renewed attention to technical work practices, particularly in providing thick descriptions of these activities. Bechky [1] argues such inquiries provide empirical insight into occupational communities and the ways in which knowledges flow across networks of practices. In turning our attention to the everyday work practices that make contemporary AI/ML systems possible, we set out to develop a rich, thick understanding of these technical work practices and their everyday acts of ingenuity and social knowledge production.

In doing so, we extend scholarly conversations around the "future of work" by locating the work practices through which AI/ML systems emerge. To borrow language from feminist theorist Donna Haraway, no AI model is "without it's world" (as quoted in [2]). This statement relates to the notion of feminist standpoint epistemology, which holds that all knowledge claims (epistemes) are socially situated within particular subject-positions [13, 14]. Such a view asks us to consider knowledges (plural) rather than knowledge (singular) and provokes an interrogation of how knowledge claims and ways of knowing are situated, contingent, and differently positioned.

In providing thick descriptions of AI models and their worlds, we complicate dominant narratives of the "future of work" by showing that these technologies indeed require human labor, at the same time they are often talked about as drivers of automation and displacers of work. Whose point of view do we invoke when we say the "future of work"? This paper prompts reflection on the work practices that make AI/ML systems (the catalyzing technologies behind the "future of work") possible and makes two primary contributions – one empirical and another conceptual. Grounded in ethnographic fieldwork, this paper answers the call of others [5, 31] in providing rich descriptions of everyday data science work. Conceptually, this paper drives forward conversations around the sociotechnical nature of contemporary AI/ML systems. By interrogating the production of such systems through a work practices lens, the situated and sociotechnical nature of such systems is rendered visible. Giving light to the everyday labor that goes into creating AI/ML systems highlights how they are, at their core, human endeavors – at the same time they are powerful, era-shaping, and for many life-changing, these systems emerge from the day-to-day doings of real people, in their daily work, which they experience to be ordinary. Deep understandings of these work practices – and the points-of-view they encode, embody, and make (im)possible – provides a necessary cleave in which the seeds of critical interpolations may be planted.

2   Field Setting and Methods

This paper draws on ethnographic fieldwork at a large, global technology and consulting corporation headquartered in North America (referred to as "TechCorp" or "the company"). This ethnographic endeavor began in Fall 2017 and includes several sources of qualitative data, including semi-structured interviews (both formal and informal), participant observations, and artifact analysis. This paper draws on analyses of four projects from this broader investigation: two long term (>12 months) projects; and two shorter term (<6 months) projects. The two long-term projects focused on building a software/system service, while the short-term projects were exploratory in nature. Details are provided in Table 1 below, all proper names (including the names of informants and projects) are pseudonyms. Data were analyzed inductively, following techniques similar to those in constructivist grounded theory [6].

Table 1. Describes the four projects from the larger ethnographic study.

Project pseudonym and description	Time period	Sources of data
Alpha – software development project building an intelligent decision-support system to support the design work of IT architects, who design IT infrastructures	Dec. 2017 – Aug. 2019	Semi-structured interviews and usability testing (with members of the user community of IT architects) and participant observation of technical development work on this project; also design and execution of a user feedback program to facilitate exchange between user community and technical team (72 informants)
Beta – exploratory interview study of ML developers' experiences and work practices	June 2018 – Aug. 2018	Semi-structured interviews and participatory design of an interface for a novel, open-source AI/ML toolkit (13 informants)
Gamma – software development project building a system to support the model improvement practices of data scientists	Oct. 2018 – Sept. 2019	Semi-structured interviews and participant observations of model improvement practices; participatory design of a system to support those practices (8 informants)
Delta – exploratory interview study of those who work on natural language processing (NLP) projects	July 2019 – Sept. 2019	Semi-structured interviews (30 informants)

3   A Model and Its World: Everyday, AI/ML Work Practices

We organize our findings into three thematic sections. First is *curating datasets*, which examines the everyday work practices of data pre-processing. Second is *tending models*, which examines the everyday work practices of training, deploying, and maintaining predictive models. Third is *configuring compute*, which examines everyday work practices of back-end infrastructuring, commonly called "DevOps."

3.1   Curating Datasets

First, we begin by examining the work of *curating datasets*. There is considerable labor involved even before algorithms may process training data and convert them into models. These efforts are often referred to as "data pre-processing" or "data engineering." *"Dealing with your data, that's everything, I think it's like the most important part in my opinion, of the whole process,"* explained Bernadette, an ML developer in an interview. *"Dealing with your data and making the data consumable and making it full, complete, you know dealing with problems, with entity resolution problems and stuff like that.*" (Bernadette, ML developer, Beta interview). In many accounts, informants reflected on the amount of "prep" work needed to pre-process data. Phillip, an ML developer, similarly emphasized: "*I feel like I spend so much time working on really data-dependent problems, fixing my datasets to be just right,*" he said, "*of course I didn't realize that when I started (laughs) that's like the whole thing, data is pretty much the thing (emphasizes) that you do in machine learning.*" (Phillip, ML developer, Beta interview).

Pre-processing involves gaining an intimate understanding of one's dataset. This can be seen clearly in Aisha's recounting of a recent project. She was working on developing an image processing model; even though she was using a "standardized" dataset (meaning it was a publicly-available dataset used throughout the AI/ML community to train, test, and benchmark different algorithms [32]), she still had to do considerable work to get the images in appropriate order for her task:

> So the most annoying part was pre-processing the data because I had to align all the images into one line, make sure the [objects in the images] were all aligned and square inside the frame... that was the most time consuming task. Then I also had to adjust the brightness levels, Or I mean, yes, the brightness levels are very important because it was affecting on the pixel colors. But I had to - they had to all have a similar brightness level.

She went on to continue: "*After pre-processing the data, running the actual algorithms was pretty straightforward.*" Reflecting, Aisha noted: "*That's a big challenge for different data because you can't just throw all of the data through your algorithm and expect that it can work well. I mean adjusting all of the brightness level.*" (Aisha, ML developer, Beta interview). In these accounts we are able to see how data – the requisite precursor to AI/ML model development – are seen as the complex and messy part of the development pipeline.

It is not only that developers must cultivate an intimate knowledge of the dataset as a meticulous collection, but they must also work to carefully tie that data to the domain question or problem. We can see this interplay – between dataset and domain question – in D'von's reflection:: "*When you have your data, you have to ask yourself, is this a good candidate dataset? Will it highlight the thing I'm trying to talk about or not? It can take a long time.*" (D'von, ML developer, Beta interview). Developers often must develop a lot of domain knowledge, gaining a deep understanding of both the underlying phenomena of interest and the ways in which it is and can be manifested in the data. For example, one case study in the Gamma project, Sage, centered around text analytics for the legal domain. The case focused on developing predictive models capable of assigning labels to segments or strings of natural language found in legal documents, such as contracts or purchase orders. This is typically referred to as a *classification task* (the model's job is to classify data segments into classes or labels) in the broader natural language processing (NLP) domain. Several of the data scientists on the Sage project reflected on having to get "up to speed" on the legal domain. While nearly all of the seven data scientists on the team had prior experience in NLP (which typically involves an understanding of linguistics/semantics), none had worked with legal language before. "*I didn't know anything, really, about the legal domain before this project,*" reflected Layla, a data scientist on the project. "*It took me a while to get up to speed,*" she continued, "*to get comfortable and understand the language because things are written in peculiar ways.*" (Layla, data scientist, Gamma interview). Similarly, Chandra described the process of becoming adept in the domain, which involved working closely with a subject-matter expert (SME), in this case a paralegal. "*I worked closely with an SME, well a couple of SMEs on the project,*" Chandra said. "*It involved working through examples, I would take some starter documents to read and try and label myself and then discussing specific examples with the SMEs where I wasn't sure or didn't understand.*" (Chandra, data scientist, Gamma interview). Beyond the Sage project, many informants talked proudly of the domain knowledge they built up over the course of their projects. Marianne's broader research interest was in privacy, for example, and because health/medical is an industry where regulatory compliance with privacy laws was a key business concern, she found herself working on many health/medical-related projects. "*I learned so much from those projects,*" Marianne recalled, speaking of the first several projects she worked on in grad school. "*Just a lot about how hospitals actually function, things administration finds important and their 'known issues,' like things they know are weird about their data,*" she said, "*it's so, so messy. Any real-world dataset is gonna be messy.*" (Marianne, data scientist, Delta interview).

Reflecting on how his understanding of the domain has grown over time, Alexei noted:

> *I think at this point I'm fairly confident. I might have started out with less than 10% just some understanding of law from my general knowledge. And I think that now I would put myself at about 90, 95%. And I say that because legal is like quite broad and I'm sure there's a few other things that we have not covered yet that may come up.* (Alexei, data scientist, Gamma interview)

In Alexei's account we can see how one's confidence grows substantially through the experiential learning that comes from working on AI/ML projects. But Alexei also leaves room for ongoing learning, "*...things that we have not covered yet may come up.*" Such perspectives recognize the amount of work undertaken to learn a domain, yet also acknowledges that such work is never complete.

In addition to developing domain fluency, curating datasets can also involve orchestrating the hand-labelling of training data by people. In a *supervised learning* approach, AI/ML algorithms learn patterns from labeled data[1] – the data instance itself in the input (e.g., an image) and the label is the desired output (e.g., class label "dog"). The resulting model devises optimized approaches to map input/output based on the training examples. Achieving standard, systematic labeled data, though, can be difficult. Often, hand-labelling of training data is accomplished via crowdsourcing platforms, such as Amazon Mechanical Turk or Figure Eight [12, 16]. As we've discussed above, many industrial applications of AI/ML require domain expertise. This means that often data labelling must be done by SMEs, or members of the development team who have appropriate expertise/knowledge of the topic. Often the amount of labelled data needed far exceeds what can feasibly be done by one or even a handful of labelers.

---

[1] In an unsupervised approach, by contrast, the algorithmic modelling techniques take only input and devise their own outputs; unsupervised approaches are often used in exploratory data analysis.

The distributed nature of this effort requires oversight and can mean establishing protocols and procedures to ensure labelling done by groups of SMEs is consistent and robust. *"We actually ended up developing a little tool, an interface to help systematize the labelling process,"* Andy, a researcher, said of his experiences working on a recent project (Andy, researcher, Delta interview). He recounted how it took many iterations for the team to agree on the label definitions and develop a codebook, which could then be embedded inside the interface they created. Ongoing iteration and calibration around labelling also came up in the Sage project. *"We had to go back and forth with the SMEs several times,"* Nadia, a data scientist on the project, explained. *"Sometimes they were confused or we realized we needed to add in an additional parameter to the class-label definition."* (Nadia, data scientist, Gamma interview). For any qualitative researcher experienced in team research, such concerns will sound familiar. In pointing to these efforts, we further illuminate the wide sets of work practices that can comprise the curating of datasets.

3.2 Tending Models

Next, we examine the theme of *tending models*, which involves the work of ongoingly maintaining AI/ML models which are implemented into environments of end-use. The day-to-day micro-practices of contemporary software engineering work are typically organized using Agile methods [7]. Agile is an iterative[2] approach, where feedback from users shapes the direction of the development team in a process of "continuous improvement." In the context of applications where AI/ML models are deployed, end-users typically provide feedback on the model's performance (e.g., noting incorrect classifications) in a process that is often referred to as "human in the loop" or "interactive machine learning" [15]. This feedback must then be analyzed (to identify root causes of the issues raised) and then prioritized and woven into ongoing development and maintenance work of the technical team (cycles which, in Agile, are called "sprints").

Before feedback may be analyzed, though, there must be coordination amongst different "squads," what functionality-focused teams are called in Agile projects. For example, in the Sage project, there was one squad focused on developing and maintaining the text classification model and another focused "upstream" on a text extraction model (text documents must be extracted and parsed into text strings or spans, which are then classified, this can be done in a single model but in the Sage project it was split into two models). And another Sage squad focused on designing the user experience (UX) and interface where end-users interact with that model.

Similarly, the Alpha project had several squads. Alpha was developing an intelligent decision-support system for IT architects, who design IT infrastructures. The system included two key AI/ML functionalities, one being the extraction and classification of

---

[2] Agile stands in contrast to more traditional methods of organizing software engineering work, such as the Waterfall Method, where user requirements are gathered and analyzed at the beginning of a project (top of the Waterfall) before development efforts proceed. Once the project progress to the subsequent phase (i.e., moving from requirements analysis to development work) it does not revert back to prior phases (i.e., water falls in one direction).

unstructured text (in this case, the IT infrastructure requirements found in RFP documents) and two being an optimization model that matched those classified requirements to a set of offerings in an IT services catalog. Here the extraction/classification was done in a single model, and thus owned by a single squad (rather than two, as in the Sage project). But the system's optimization model was owned by a different squad. In addition, there were two other squads on the Alpha project who owned other non-AI/ML functions in the tool.

The classification squad on Sage had to work closely with the interface squad to design an application programming interface (API) that they could query and collect feedback instances which the platform collected and stored in the Cloud. This was iterative and involved some back-and-forth to get the API to store the feedback in a standard format (e.g., JSON) they could then further analyze.

Establishing a feedback protocol on the Alpha project was more challenging, as the system was complex and involved multiple models. In addition to collect *in situ* feedback from users in the interface (i.e., feedback on individual classified text instances) there was a recognition that further usability testing mechanisms would be needed. This involved designing not only the individual usability sessions with users (working out specific user flows to test) but also what the team called the "closed loop feedback process" where qualitative data learned in the usability sessions was aggregated and reported across the projects numerous squads. As we know, distributed collaboration is challenging [11] and the global and distributed nature of the Alpha development team made feedback reporting effortful, not only in noting different feedback from users in different geographies, but also the practical concern of time zone conflicts and limited windows of shared working hours between continents.

Then once a protocol had been established to routinize the collection of user feedback, the squads must still analyze that feedback. In the case of model errors, this can involve a root cause analysis (RCA) to understand why the model mis-classified a data instance (precision error) or did not classify a data instance (recall error). But feedback can also involve bugs or other code defects or new feature/function requests. In the case of bugs/defects, such feedback is typically investigated via RCA also. New feature/function requests, though, can require further analysis to design and "size" them (understanding the amount of effort that would be needed to implement the feature and the dependencies it would raise for other portions of the system). In some cases, the design and sizing process involved further follow-up with users who offered the feedback to develop a deeper understanding of the feedback and also its business value (i.e., how crucial it was to complete the work tasks and business processes the system is meant to support).

Deciding if and how feedback is incorporated into subsequent development sprints depends on several factors. Of course, resources are a concern and the capacity of a squad to accomplish priority development tasks. In the Agile approach, members of the user community are active stakeholders in shaping the future of the application. Thus, any decisions made over whether and how to incorporate feedback into squads' actual development work need to be communicated back to the users. This can be difficult to convey, as these decisions are complex and multi-faceted. *"Just because users give feedback, it doesn't mean it will be taken up right away,"* Dafna, a designer explained. *"There are resource considerations and also the strategic direction of the system.*

Additionally, if the feedback is on model errors, we need to feel confident it truly was an error by triangulating across users." (Dafna, designer, Delta interview). Furthermore, there can be inherent mismatches between AI/ML capabilities and user expectations [19]. It can be difficult to explain the mechanics of AI/ML models (which, by their inferential constitution, are inherently incapable of 100% confidence) to users, who often have mental models shaped by science-fiction and marketing narratives around machine intelligence as a corollary to human sentience and reasoning. In the Alpha project, for example, this was an ongoing issue that caused friction between the development team and the user community. As the extraction/classification squad consistently showed gains in technical measures of performance and accuracy (e.g., single-digit increases in key metrics like precision/recall rate and F1 score), members of the user community continued to comment on what they perceived to be very low accuracy. Ultimately, this points-of-view were clearly distinguished in progress reports to strategic leadership, noting a difference between technical accuracy and what the team called "*user reality.*" In calling out the difference, a compromise was made possible where both the squad and the users' point-of-view over the model's accuracy could be honored, allowing them to work forward on how to address the user reality in relation to the overarching business process the system supported (i.e., how do we adjust the overall process so IT architects are comfortable with what they perceive to be low accuracy). As these examples show, tending models involves caring for complex sociotechnical relations which are configured around the models themselves – and the various points-of-view, priorities, ambitions, and ambivalences such configurations encompass.

3.3 Configuring Compute

Next we examine the theme *configuring compute*, which investigates the everyday work practices commonly called "DevOps." DevOps is a portmanteau of *development* and *operations* and refers to the back-end infrastructuring work upon which contemporary cloud computing systems are built [9]. Our use of the word *infrastructuring* is inspired by the concept as developed in Karasti et al. [18], which gerunds infrastructure to emphasize the processual quality of infrastructures and the vast and often distributed collective efforts to accomplish what is experienced as "infrastructure."

Cloud computing is a key infrastructural component of the contemporary AI/ML boom. Cloud computing is a model of computational architecture "enabling ubiquitous, convenient, on-demand network access to a shared pool of configurable computing resources (e.g., networks, servers, storage, applications, and services) that can be rapidly provisioned" [22]. In cloud environments, individual programs are often packaged inside "containers" (like Docker or Kubernetes) which are virtual objects that can house code and its requisite dependencies, allowing for greater modularity at lower levels of computation processing (e.g., at the virtual machine (VM) or operating system (OS) levels) [3].

Cloud computing co-constitutes the recent AI/ML explosion in a number of ways. Most notably, cloud computing fuels AI/ML because of the vast amounts of data stored and accessible in distributed cloud servers. The ability to leverage large-scale, distributed networks of processing power via cloud computing as also an important ingredient in engineering AI/ML systems, which require enormous amounts of "compute" (the term-of-art within the computer science field to refer issues of speed, performance, and resource demands of running computer programs).

A key hardware leveraged by contemporary AI/ML systems is the "GPU" which stands for *graphics processing unit*. At their core, AI/ML algorithms perform complex statistical operations to render a model which represents the training dataset's underlying relations in high dimensionality. These statistical operations can be optimized and run with great speed in parallel via GPUs. Spending any length of time around AI/ML engineers, and you will soon hear talk of GPUs, particularly the cost of GPUs, both monetarily (to rent the processing time) and temporally (the length of time it takes to run functions) being a factor in training and testing AI/ML models. For veteran technologists, such concerns echo long-forgotten laments of scheduling "mainframe time" in the early days of digital computing [26]. For contemporary technicians working in AI/ML, GPUs represent a key resource that makes the intense computational power needed to train such complex models possible.

Configuring compute means dealing with constraints, which we can see arose during the Beta project. One part of the Beta project was leveraging participatory design (PD) methods in designing an interface for a novel, open-source AI/ML toolkit. ML developers were invited to imagine using the toolkit in a particular task (which, in this case, involved inspecting a dataset for tampering or the presence of "poisoned" data). They interactively engaged with initial designs for the toolkit's interface, offering their feedback which improved further design iterations. In planning the PD study, the research/design team initially planned to run a "live" case for the developers to work though, training an artificial neural network (ANN) from scratch (as they would in their typical, day-to-day ML work practices) and then utilize the toolkit to inspect for poison. This would mimic an *in situ* run of the toolkit and offer the most true-to-life experience, save for actual "in the wild" implementation. Discussions amongst the research/design team, though, revealed several issues around gaining access to GPUs to train multiple ANNs, as well as concerns over the time it would require to train and then re-train a model (after identifying and removing the poisoned data). After some brainstorming, the final resolution reached was to create a mock experience for the ML developers to offer feedback on, simulating the training/re-training components via Wizard of Oz techniques [8] and instead focus the PD sessions on the interface designs.

Informants also discussed experiences where GPU access were constraints for projects to proceed, with stakeholders being reluctant to invest in such a costly resource, particularly for experimental or exploratory projects. "*The hardware requirements can also be an issue,*" Delaney, a data scientist, explained, "*so in addition to the cost or time involved in labelling, paying for GPU time can sometimes be an issue.*" She went on to explain how she takes great care to explain such constraints to clients early on in projects, when they are working together to set goals and reasonable expectations for the project. "*I've learned it's important to take time upfront, really discuss what they are trying to do and what data they have, what's feasible and what it would take to achieve what they are trying to do,*" she explained. "*Then I try to work with them, if the expectations are just way too high, to set some more reasonable goals that still work on addressing their business problem but fit more with the scope of the engagement.*" (Delaney, data scientist, Delta interview). In her account, we are able to see the care practices involved in defining possibilities together with clients.

The back-end infrastructuring work practices involved in configuring compute also include other concerns as well. The overall speed and performance of an AI/ML model at inference/prediction time (i.e., when a user enters an input, which the model processes and produces an output). Any changes or improvements to the models or overall ML architecture must be evaluated for impacts to speed/performance before they may be implemented. "*Even adding seconds, you know, even half seconds to run time can cause problems,*" Jiro, an ML developer said, "*so we are always testing those impacts before we implement any changes.*" (Jiro, ML developer, Delta interview). In addition to aligning AI/ML models with hardware/compute capabilities, another type of infrastructuring work raised by many informants was aligning versions between opensource ML frameworks and libraries like TensorFlow or Keras. Software libraries are collections of coding programs that are pre-packaged and shared for ready re-use by others [4]. Kwame shared a story during his interview about joining an ongoing project and picking up his teammates code. He kept getting errors returned when he tried to execute the code, which was stumping him and the teammate (who originally wrote the code). They were both using Keras, so what gives? Kwame described searching online forums but couldn't find anything particularly useful. "*Keras is known for not having the best documentation,*" he explained, noting he is almost always able to find out answers to coding problems in online forums (or at least an adjacent answer that can give some ideas to springboard off). Disappointed, Kwame felt stuck and shared his frustration with others who shared his workspace. "*That's when I was just talking about it in our room, asking if anybody else had this problem when they started,*" Kwame said, continuing: "*It was kinda funny,*" he said with a playful laugh, "*after all those issues and trying everything I could think of, trying for several days, [Edgar] was like 'Oh yeah, what version of Keras are you using? The most recent release caused a lot of portability issues.' And just like that, we figured it out.*" (Kwame, ML developer, Beta interview).

4 Discussion and Conclusions

What do we gain from recognizing that AI/ML is work? In taking seriously a work practices perspective, we are tasked with considering deeply the ongoing and emergent human labor – the improvisational and careful struggling through which things get done – that undergird contemporary sociotechnical ecosystems. Our built world is full of modern marvels – everyday human experiences are shaped by vast, entangled sociotechnical systems which are made possible through the highly-skilled, meticulous, and ongoing ingenuity of trades and professions. Consider the electricity powering the building we are sitting in, the roadway or transit systems we recently traversed, or the educational and scholarly enterprises we apprenticed in and aim to contribute to. The computational devices, too, which our fingertips touch come about through the ongoing technical labor of many. AI/ML models are a particular type of computational configuration which, too, require extensive efforts to be brought about. Work is hard, it is an ongoing practice where we strive to artfully apply skills to emergent problems, while we engage in thoughtful, experimental knowledge practices along the way.

In the words of feminist theorist Donna Haraway: "nothing comes without its world" (as quoted in [2]). In threading together feminist standpoint epistemology [13, 14] with our ethnographic inquiry, we are provoked to consider the pluralities that are implicated in contemporary discourses of the "future of work." The experiences of contemporary data-driven ecosystems – of the AI/Ml models and the outputs they present to us – are situated and contingent in specific standpoints and particular sociotechnical encounters. The cutting-edge, data-driven AI/ML systems that are increasingly incorporated into a number of everyday technologies, too, are not "without their world." A central, *sine qua non* dimension of those worlds are the vast, entangled sociotechnical networks of highly-skilled, technical work practices that makes such systems possible.

Wolf [32] recently examined the information behavior practices of AI/ML developers. There, Wolf was making the point that highlighting information practices (as ongoing improvisational crafty practices, rather than sets of pure techniques or skills that are rotely applied) could work to decrease barriers to entry in that profession. Such a claim is political in that it attempts to extend the professional image and identity of "ML developer," trying to diminish gatekeeping and instead enable broader and more inclusive imaginaries around that kind of work. This paper makes a related though distinct argument. In drawing attention to the technical work practices that undergird AI/ML systems, this paper complicates discourses around the "future of work" by dismantling the "black box" of AI/ML worlds. In investigating the work of technicians in AI/ML ecosystems, as we have done here, we are forced to recognize the effortful, caring practices these forms of work involve. Often, the human effort behind AI/ML systems is rendered invisible or blackboxed in discussions of such systems. AI/ML is not magic, nor is it near a science-fiction "singularity," as many might colloquially refer to it. AI/ML is work, and as we have shown, it is often complex, difficult work. To recognize the humanity and dignity of the work is to say there are points of mutuality and caring across data-driven ecosystems of contemporary labor experiences. Those who work in the tech industry, those who are building, testing, deploying, and maintaining models, are connected to those who experience the "end use" effects of workplace transformation made possible by AI/ML. Recognizing this helps us see the ways in which individual lives, careers, and professions – our deeply personal cares and concerns – are imbricated in societal-level labor transformations. Tracking the day-to-day hum-drum aspects, the work practices, of AI/ML development as we have done in this paper offers insights into the various standpoints that are involved in the future of work – and the ways in which hyped and blackboxed technologies can be experienced as "business as usual" for some, at the same time they are experienced as magical, esoteric, and even frightening by others. What remains to be figured is how best to leverage these tracings to incite interventions and collective actions – if people are behind systems capable of creating great social change, how do we work together to ensure such changes are healthy, sustainable, and mutually beneficial for all, and not just some? How do we alter the portrait of labor to render a sketch more full, one where spaces exist for many points-of-view to not only be made visible, but also be equitably valued, honored, and fortified?

Acknowledgements. Thank you to informants and collaborators for sharing their time, insights, and points-of-view. All opinions are my own and do not reflect any institutional endorsement.

References

1. Bechky, B.A.: Talking about machines, thick description, and knowledge work. Organ. Stud. **27**(12), 1757–1768 (2006)
2. de la Bellacasa, M.P.: Matters of care in technoscience: assembling neglected things. Soc. Stud. Sci. **41**(1), 85–106 (2011)
3. Bernstein, D.: Containers and cloud: from LXC to Docker to Kubernetes. IEEE Cloud Comput. **1**(3), 81–84 (2014)
4. Burton, B.A., et al.: The reusable software library. IEEE Softw. **4**(4), 25–33 (1987)
5. Carter, D., Sholler, D.: Data science on the ground: hype, criticism, and everyday work. J. Assoc. Inf. Sci. Technol. **67**(10), 2309–2319 (2016)
6. Charmaz, K.: Constructing Grounded Theory: A Practical Guide Through Qualitative Analysis. SAGE, London (2006)
7. Cohen, D.: Agile Software Development. Super Star Press, California (2010)
8. Dahlbäck, N., et al.: Wizard of Oz studies: why and how. Knowl.-Based Syst. **6**(4), 258–266 (1993)
9. Erich, F.M.A., et al.: A qualitative study of DevOps usage in practice. J. Softw. Evol. Process **29**(6), 1885 (2017)
10. Faraj, S., et al.: Working and organizing in the age of the learning algorithm. Inf. Organ. **28**(1), 62–70 (2018)
11. Goggins, S.P.: Collaboration in isolation: bridging social and geographical boundaries in two rural technology firms. In: IDEALS: iConference 2013 Proceedings (2013)
12. Gray, M.L., Suri, S.: Ghost Work: How to Stop Silicon Valley from Building a New Global Underclass. Houghton Mifflin Harcourt, Massachusetts (2019)
13. Harding, S.: Rethinking standpoint epistemology: what is "strong objectivitiy?". Centen. Rev. **36**(3), 437–470 (1992)
14. Harding, S.: Whose Science? Whose Knowledge?: Thinking from Women's Lives. Cornell University Press, New York (1991)
15. Holzinger, A.: Interactive machine learning for health informatics: when do we need the human-in-the-loop? Brain Inform. **3**(2), 119–131 (2016)
16. Irani, L.C., Silberman, M.S.: Turkopticon: interrupting worker invisibility in Amazon mechanical turk. In: Proceedings of the SIGCHI Conference on Human Factors in Computing Systems, pp. 611–620. ACM, New York (2013)
17. Jarrahi, M.H.: Artificial intelligence and the future of work: human-AI symbiosis in organizational decision making. Bus. Horiz. **61**(4), 577–586 (2018)
18. Karasti, H., Baker, K.S.: Infrastructuring for the long-term: ecological information management. In: Proceedings of the 37th Annual Hawaii International Conference on System Sciences, January 2004, pp. 1–10. IEEE, Honolulu, Hawaii (2004)
19. Kay, M., et al.: How good is 85%? A survey tool to connect classifier evaluation to acceptability of accuracy. In: Proceedings of the 33rd Annual ACM Conference on Human Factors in Computing Systems, pp. 347–356. ACM, New York (2015)
20. Kitchin, R., McArdle, G.: What makes big data, big data? Exploring the ontological characteristics of 26 datasets. Big Data Soc. **3**(1) (2016)
21. Kling, R., Iacono, S.: The mobilization of support for computerization: the role of computerization movements. Soc. Probl. **35**(3), 226–243 (1988)

22. Mell, P., Grance, T.: The NIST definition of cloud computing. Technical report #NIST Special Publication (SP) 800-145, National Institute of Standards and Technology (2011)

23. Orr, J.E.: Talking About Machines: an Ethnography of a Modern Job. Cornell University Press, New York (1996)

24. Paine, D., et al.: Examining data processing work as part of the scientific data lifecycle: comparing practices across four scientific research groups. In: IDEALS: iConference 2015 Proceedings (2015)

25. Pine, K.H., Wolf, C.T., Mazmanian, M.: The work of reuse: birth certificate data and healthcare accountability measurements. In: IDEALS: iConference 2016 Proceedings (2016)

26. Rankin, J.L.: A People's History of Computing in the United States. Harvard University Press, Massachusetts (2018)

27. Sutherland, W., Jarrahi, M.H.: The sharing economy and digital platforms: a review and research agenda. Int. J. Inf. Manag. **43**, 328–341 (2018)

28. Willis, M., Jarrahi, M.H.: Automating documentation: a critical perspective into the role of artificial intelligence in clinical documentation. In: Taylor, N.G., Christian-Lamb, C., Martin, Michelle H., Nardi, B. (eds.) iConference 2019. LNCS, vol. 11420, pp. 200–209. Springer, Cham (2019). https://doi.org/10.1007/978-3-030-15742-5_19

29. Willis, M., Meyer, E.T.: Work that enables care: understanding tasks, automation, and the national health service. In: Chowdhury, G., McLeod, J., Gillet, V., Willett, P. (eds.) iConference 2018. LNCS, vol. 10766, pp. 544–549. Springer, Cham (2018). https://doi.org/10.1007/978-3-319-78105-1_60

30. Wolf, C.T., Blomberg, J.L.: Evaluating the promise of human-algorithm collaborations in everyday work practices. In: Proceedings of ACM Computer-Supported Cooperative Work, pp. 143:1–143:23. ACM, New York (2019)

31. Wolf, C.T.: Conceptualizing care in the everyday work practices of machine learning developers. In: Companion Publication of the 2019 ACM Conference on Designing Interactive Systems Conference, pp. 331–335. ACM, New York (2019)

32. Wolf, C.T.: Professional identity and information use: on becoming a machine learning developer. In: Taylor, N.G., Christian-Lamb, C., Martin, M.H., Nardi, B. (eds.) iConference 2019. LNCS, vol. 11420, pp. 625–636. Springer, Cham (2019). https://doi.org/10.1007/978-3-030-15742-5_59

33. Wolf, C.T.: Seeing work: constructing visions of work in and through data. In: Proceedings of the 19th ACM International Conference on Supporting Group Work, pp. 509–512. ACM, New York (2016)

34. Wolf, C.T.: The work of AI: sociotechnical contours of accessibility in contemporary software engineering. In: Proceedings of Applied Human Factors and Ergonomics (AHFE) 2020 Conference. Springer, Heidelberg (2020, to appear)

Diversifying the Next Generation of Project Managers: Skills Project Managers Must Have in the Digital Age

Abidemi Atolagbe$^{(\boxtimes)}$ ⓘD and Schenita Floyd ⓘD

University of North Texas, Denton, TX 76203, USA
{abidemiatolagbe-olaoye, schenitafloyd}@my.unt.edu

Abstract. In the digital age, many jobs are susceptible to reduction or elimination. This study examines how project managers can improve their skill set to avoid elimination and lead successful projects to help build a sustainable future. This study addresses three research questions using open data to assess project management essential skills, trending job titles, and skills for a sustainable future. The results of the study indicate project managers should retain their traditional project management skills and develop their digital technical, quantitative, and marketing skills. Digital, agile, data, quantitative, cybersecurity, cloud, and technical project managers are a few of the new job title trends. Finally, in the digital age, it is vital for project managers to stay abreast of societal needs, trends, and technological advances that can promote a sustainable future.

Keywords: Project management · Sustainability · Job skills · Digital age · Artificial intelligence

1 Introduction

In the digital age, will bots replace project managers? As technology advances, many jobs are susceptible to elimination; however, having foresight and acquiring the skills needed for the digital age is essential to avoiding elimination and securing a position in the new job market. Each industrial revolution eliminates jobs, but creates new jobs and careers beyond the original jobs in existence. As we enter the fourth industrial revolution, it is imperative that project managers hone in on their skills and acquire new skills to meet the demands of communities striving for a sustainable future.

The purpose of this study is to assess job skills vital to project managers by addressing the following research questions:

- What traditional skills are essential to the project management profession?
- What are the developing job title trends within the project management profession?
- What skills should project managers acquire to facilitate a sustainable future in the digital age?

A. Sundqvist et al. (Eds.): iConference 2020, LNCS 12051, pp. 665–676, 2020.
https://doi.org/10.1007/978-3-030-43687-2_56

To address these questions, we examine data from the Project Management Body of Knowledge (PMBOK), Association for Project Management Body of Knowledge, Occupational Information Network Database, and job postings.

2 Related Work

A review of the literature reveals similar studies on essential project management skills and trending job titles. The studies are under the themes project management competencies, critical success factors for the future, skills for project success, other professions' usage of project management skills, and project management skills in the digital age. Each theme surmises from keyword searches of peer-reviewed articles found on the EBSCO database and Google Scholar within the last ten years, 2009–2019.

2.1 Core Project Management Competencies

The project management community develops core project management competencies and standards through project management organizations such as the International Project Management Association (IPMA), Project Management Institute (PMI), and the Association for Project Management (APM) [1]. IPMA's project management competencies align along three areas: technical, behavioral, and contextual [2]. PMI outlines its project management competencies in the Project Management Body of Knowledge. APM, a European based project management organization, core competencies are in its APM Body of Knowledge [3].

Core project management competencies are important for a project manager's career and project success, but should project management students and young professionals focus on the core competencies? Engel, Susan, and Laura Simpson Reeves [4] argue for more focus on core competencies as many schools promote practical skills and reduce the instruction of core competencies. Practical skills are important, and they will help young professionals to some extent. Conversely, another study notes hiring managers look for core competencies in their candidates to promote success in the current open position and for future job opportunities in the organization [5]. Both viewpoints are valid, but we believe a balance and the ability to exercise all skills are essential. An unbalanced skill set could make the project manager too rigid or too flexible. Rigidness can cause friction on the team, whereas too flexible could increase scope creep; therefore, a balance of practical skills and core competencies are critical success factors for young professionals.

2.2 Critical Success Factors and Skills for the Next Generation

Critical success factors for project managers are discussed throughout the literature pinpointing skills and frameworks for the next generation of project managers to be competent and successful. According to Bredillet, Tywoniak, and Dwivedula [6], a competent project manager is someone who has the qualities to fulfill his or her role and demonstrates a particular level of performance. Alias, Zawawi, Yusof, and Aris [7] developed a conceptual framework for project success. However, their model did not include a CSF component. They propose project managers should define CSFs from their perspective. Chang and Torkzadeh [8] classify information systems project management skills into four categories, namely: communication and relationship management, resource management, change management, and administrative skills. Liikamaa's [9] study identifies achievement drive, leadership, conflict management, and initiative skills as the most important for project managers.

Keil, Lee, and Deng [10] argue that "leadership, organization skills, relationship building, and multitasking skills" are the most important Information Technology (IT) project management skills. Similarly, Kerzner [11] identifies leadership, team building, conflict resolution, technical expertise, planning, organization, entrepreneurship, administrative, management support, and allocation of resources as the skills required to manage complex programs and projects. PMI states that project managers need technical project management skills, leadership skills, and strategic and business management skills in order to deliver successful projects [12]. These skills are also known as the PMI talent triangle.

Although many studies have been conducted on project management competencies, some presented consistent findings while others did not, especially in the order of importance. The PMI talent triangle sums up all the various project management skills into three major skills – technical project management skills, leadership skills, and strategic and business management skills. However, there is a need to examine the important skills to equip project managers in the era of evolving digital transformation. Kerzner [11] argues that knowledge of the business, risk management, and integration management are the three main skills for effective project management in the twenty-first century; however, the skills are consistent with what existing studies presented even before the twenty-first century. Others suggest elimination of skills, with business process automation and the capabilities of artificial intelligence; Gartner's report suggests that 80% of traditional project management tasks will be replaced by artificial intelligence [13]. However, there is a need to assess the trend and current situation regarding the skills that project managers need for relevance and effectiveness in the digital age.

2.3   Skills for Project Success

We have discussed core project management competencies and critical success factors as they relate to project success, but what other skills are required for project success? One recent study listed client performance or involvement affects project success [14]. A project manager's relationship building, engagement, and facilitating skills can improve the client's performance, thereby ensuring project success. Brown and Albright express that leadership, teamwork, and communication played a major role in their projects' success [15]. Analytical, decision-making ability, and a high level of project management skills are essential for construction projects success [16]. Transferable skills such as communication, critical thinking, and the ability to work in a collaborative environment can be overlooked in some technical fields [17]. Despite being overlooked, these skills are essential to technical and non-technical project success. In the IT industry, project managers are expected to have some of the technical knowledge and transferable skills. For IT project managers, the ability to communicate at multiple levels and a diversified range of competencies are needed for project success [2]. Whether it is a construction or an IT project, each of these skills can benefit all project managers' successful implementation of their projects.

2.4   Other Professions

Project managers function across all major industries, and they have the ability to crossover from one industry to another by understanding the basic concepts of the business. In the literature, project management is listed as an important skill set for chemists [18], librarians [15, 19–21], engineers [22, 23], research professionals [5, 24], IT professionals [17, 25], and engineers [16]. For example, Watson observed a decrease in job opportunities for chemists due to limited government funding and changes in agricultural needs. He recommends young chemists master the fundamentals of their profession and dedicate time to other essential skills, such as project management. He emphasizes resource management and stakeholder analysis as two critical project management skills that will affect different aspects of chemists' lives [18]. Gallagher, Kaiser, Simon, Beath, and Goles [23] echoed the importance of project management skills, but they discuss project management skills in the IT industry. They state, "the skills most critical to retain in-house and most sought in new mid-level employees are non-technical skills such as project management, business domain knowledge, and relationship skills". Librarians believe in the importance of project management skills, and they do not think of it as a soft skill, but an essential professional skill all librarians should possess [20]. Librarians, scientists, and technical professionals are examples of how other professions utilize project management skills, but there are many other examples inspired by innovation.

2.5   Digital Revolution and Innovation in Project Management

Digital transformations are "changes in ways of working, roles, and business offerings caused by the adoption of digital technologies in an organization" [26]. The authors propose that changes could also occur at various levels such as process, organization, business domain, and society. Innovation is "the process by which organizations use their resources and competences to develop new and improved products" [27]. However, embarking on an innovative endeavor comes with a high level of risks as "only 12% to 20% of research and development projects" successfully advance to market [27]. The goal of project management is to create business value [12]. Value creation activities require the use of innovative approaches that would increase the number of successful projects, and in turn, improve the number of products to market. Since businesses exist to make profits, it is imperative to examine the factors that could enhance competitive advantage, one of which is project management skills in the age of the digital revolution.

3 Methodology

This study was conducted to determine which traditional skills are essential to the project management profession, which project management job titles are trending, and what skills should project managers acquire to facilitate a sustainable future. We obtained open data from the Project Management Institute, Association of Project Managers, the O*NET Resource Center, and job posting websites to identify skills and job title trends in the project management profession. In addition, data were analyzed from these sources to determine how to facilitate a sustainable future. Table 1 contains detailed information about the data set used for this study.

Table 1. Project management skills data sets.

Source	File name/search criteria	Date updated by source
PMI	6th edition Project Management Body of Knowledge	September 6, 2017
APM	APM Body of Knowledge	September 5, 2019
LinkedIn	Project Management Job Postings	September 7, 2019
O*NET	Skills Data File	September 7, 2019
Indeed	Project Management Job Postings	September 10, 2019
Dice	Project Management Job Postings	September 10, 2019

Data sets were obtained from each website and relevant fields were extracted, cleaned, and organized for data analysis.

4 Results and Discussion

4.1 Project Management Book of Knowledge – 6th Edition

The Project Management Institute (PMI) is one of the largest project management organizations that maintain the standards for the project management profession. PMI produces and updates periodically the Project Management Book of Knowledge that includes its project management competencies and skills. Project managers from across the world study the PMBOK to pass a comprehensive exam to become a certified Project Management Professional. The PMBOK contains forty-nine unique skills project managers should have to ensure successful projects as shown in Figs. 1, 2 and Table 2 [12].

Fig. 1. A word cloud output of the raw data before removing duplicates and cleaning the data.

Table 2. PMBOK 6th edition skills.

Skills				
Team	Integration	Project Resource Mgmt	Insightful	Interactive comm
Communication	Presentation	Motivation	Project Mgmt Knowledge	Tech Knowledge
Influence	Decision Making	Coaching	Verbal Comm	Soft Skills
Planning	Interpersonal	Coordination	Written Comm	Manage People
Relationship Mgmt	Strategic	Knowledge Mgmt	Business Mgmt	Action-Orient
Expert	Leadership	Conflict Mgmt	Emotional Intelligence	Business Intelligence
Technical	Political Awareness	Observant	Personnel Admin	Visionary
Data Analytics	Problem Solver	Active Listening	Technical PM	Facilitating
Collaboration	Competent	Networking	Meeting Mgmt	
Project management	Negotiation	Cultural Awareness	Nonverbal Comm	

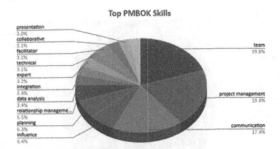

Fig. 2. The top skills with a word count over 100x in the PMBOK 6th edition. Team, project management, communication, influence and technical are in the top skills shown.

4.2 Association of Project Managers Body of Knowledge

Association of Project Managers (APM) is a European based organization, and their book of standards is called the APM Body of Knowledge. APM core competencies are under one of its five professional dimensions. The five dimensions are breadth, depth, achievement, commitment, and accountability [3]. For data analysis, we examine the entire APM Body of Knowledge 6th edition to identify traditional project management skills. The APM Body of Knowledge contains thirty-two unique skills project managers should have to ensure successful projects as shown in Figs. 3 and 4 [28].

Fig. 3. A word cloud output of the raw data

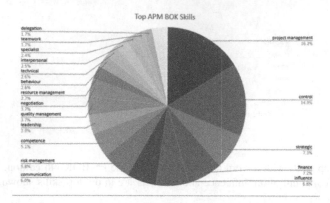

Fig. 4. The top skills with a word count over 10x in the APM BOK 6th edition. Project management, teamwork, technical, influence, and communication are the top-ranking skills.

4.3 O*NET Project Management Skills

O*NET Resource Center provides open data on the United States occupational data. O*NET is a joint venture with the Department of Labor and corporations to help standardize job titles and skills. Since O*NET data is organized and structured we use the skills data file to create 35 unique skills for project managers as shown in Fig. 5 [29].

Fig. 5. A word cloud output of the raw data.

4.4 Association of Project Managers Job Postings

The APM website has job postings for opportunities in the United Kingdom. Most of the job titles are generic project manager openings; however, a few titles are surprisingly different. Table 3 displays trending job titles on the APM website job postings, excluding the generic project manager titles [3].

Table 3. APM trending job titles.

Trending job titles
Collaborative Lead/Facilitator
Project Delivery Manager
Digital Project Manager
Integrated Senior Project Manager
Agile Project Manager - Digital Marketing
Transformation Project Manager
Quant Project Manager

4.5   LinkedIn Job Postings

LinkedIn has a webpage dedicated to project and program manager jobs. The website provides insights, main types of project management jobs, popular job titles, other trending job titles, and job functions. Table 4 displays the top job title trends extracted from LinkedIn website for program and project managers, excluding the generic project and program manager titles [30].

Table 4. LinkedIn trending job titles.

Trending job titles
Digital Project Manager
Agile Transformation Program Manager
Compliance Project Manager
Technical Program Manager
Global Lead
Scientific Project Manager
Deputy Program Manager
Clinical Project Manager
Implementation Manager

4.6   Indeed Job Postings

Table 5 displays job title trends extracted from Indeed job website for program and project managers, excluding the generic project and program manager titles [31].

Table 5. Indeed trending job titles.

Trending job titles
Agile Project Manager/Scrum Master
Analytics Project Manager
Change/Transformation Program Manager
Cyber Security Project Manager
Data Center Project Manager
Digital Project Manager
Engineering Project Manager
ERP Project Manager
Healthcare Project Manager
Supply Chain Project Manager

4.7 Dice Job Postings

Table 6 displays job title trends and skills extracted from Dice job website for program and project managers, excluding the generic project and program manager titles [32].

Table 6. Dice trending job titles.

Trending job titles
Agile Project Manager/Scrum Master
Analytics Project Manager
Change Management Team Lead
Cloud Project Manager
Cyber Security Program Manager
Data Center Project Manager
Digital Project Manager
ERP Project Manager
Facilities Project Manager
Healthcare Project Manager

5   Conclusion

The purpose of this study was to assess job skills vital to project managers by addressing three research questions on traditional project management skills, job title trends, and the skills project managers should acquire to facilitate a sustainable future in the digital age. This study was meant to benefit current and future project managers who desire a sustainable future in the digital age. It is also expected to combat fears of traditional project management tasks will be replaced by artificial intelligence. Artificial intelligence will not only impact project managers but all jobs, including jobs driving artificial intelligence. However, project managers possess many transferable skills, and the digital age should not be a time to fear job loss, but an opportunity to embrace the superjobs of the future and promote sustainability throughout all industries to meet societal needs.

The results of this study found that project managers should retain their traditional project management skills and develop digital technical skills, quantitative skills, marketing skills, and having a sense of humor is a plus. Digital, agile, data, quantitative, cybersecurity, cloud, and technical project managers are a few of the new job title trends among project management job postings. Despite the success in addressing the research questions, there are some limitations in this study. The limitations were biases towards the United States and European countries as the data came from the United States and the United Kingdom. A technical bias was another limitation as many of the jobs are technical, especially Dice job postings. Future research should focus on other countries and on project management tasks difficult to automate in the digital age.

References

1. Chipulu, M., Neoh, J., Ojiako, U., Williams, T.: A multidimensional analysis of project manager competencies. IEEE Trans. Eng. Manage. **60**(3), 506–517 (2012)
2. Silva de Araújo, C., Pedron, C.: IT project manager competencies and IT project success: a qualitative study. Organ. Proj. Manage. **2**(1), 53–75 (2015)
3. APM Homepage. https://www.apm.org.uk. Accessed 5 Sept 2019
4. Engel, S., Reeve, L.: What do they need to know? Core skills for postgraduate development studies students. Asia Pac. Viewpoint **59**(2), 212–225 (2018)
5. Henderson, L.: Catch (& keep) a rising star. Appl. Clin. Trials **27**(3), 12–14 (2018)
6. Bredillet, C., Tywoniak, S., Dwivedula, R.: What is a good project manager? An aristotelian perspective. Int. J. Project Manage. **33**(2), 254–266 (2015)
7. Alias, Z., Zawawi, E., Yusof, K., Aris, N.: Determining critical success factors of project management practice: a conceptual framework. Proc.-Soc. Behav. Sci. **153**, 61–69 (2014)
8. Chang, J., Torkzadeh, G.: Perceived required skills and abilities in information systems project management. Int. J. Inform. Technol. Proj. Manage. **4**(1), 1–121 (2013)
9. Liikamaa, K.: Developing a project manager's competencies: a collective view of the most important competencies. Proc. Manuf. **3**, 681–687 (2015)
10. Keil, M., Lee, H., Deng, T.: Understanding the most critical skills for managing IT projects: a Delphi study of IT project managers. Inf. Manage. **50**(7), 398–414 (2013)
11. Kerzner, H.: Project Management: A Systems Approach to Planning, Scheduling, and Controlling, 11th edn. Wiley, Hoboken (2013)
12. PMBOK Guide: A Guide to the Project Management Body of Knowledge. Sixth Edition Project Management Institute, Inc. (2017)
13. Gartner Press Room webpage. https://www.gartner.com/en/newsroom/press-releases/2019-03-20-gartner-says-80-percent-of-today-s-project-management. Accessed 07 Sept 2019
14. Hatmoko, J., Khasania, R.: Comparing performance of government and private clients in construction projects: contractors' perspective. Civ. Eng. Dimension **18**(2), 85–92 (2016)
15. Brown, R., Albright, K.: The Google online marketing challenge and distributed learning. J. Educ. Libr. Inform. Sci. 22–36 (2013)

16. Hegazy, T., Abdel-Monem, M., Saad, D., Rashedi, R.: Hands-on exercise for enhancing students' construction management skills. J. Constr. Eng. Manage. **139**(9), 1135–1143 (2013)
17. Wikle, T., Fagin, T.: Hard and soft skills in preparing GIS professionals: comparing perceptions of employers and educators. Trans. GIS **19**(5), 641–652 (2015)
18. Watson, K.: The changing landscape of careers in the chemical industry. Nat. Chem. **3**(9), 685 (2011)
19. Burns, J.: Role of the information professional in the development and promotion of digital humanities content for research, teaching, and learning in the modern academic library: an Irish case study. New Rev. Acad. Libr. **22**(2–3), 238–248 (2016)
20. Currier, B., Mirza, R., Downing, J.: They think all of this is new: leveraging librarians' project management skills for the digital humanities. Coll. Undergr. Libr. **24**(2–4), 270–289 (2017)
21. Walther, J.: Developing personal course plans (PCPs) as an example of self-directed learning in library management and project management education. J. Libr. Adm. **58**(1), 91–100 (2018)
22. Dubikovsky, S., Kestin, J.: Project management as an active component of the aeronautical Engineering technology program. J. Aviat. Technol. Eng. **1**(2), 3 (2012)
23. Snider, C., Gopsill, J., Jones, S., Emanuel, L., Hicks, B.: Engineering project health management: a computational approach for project management support through analytics of digital engineering activity. IEEE Trans. Eng. Manage. **66**(3), 325–336 (2018)
24. Wilson, G., Bryan, J., Cranston, K., Kitzes, J., Nederbragt, L., Teal, T.: Good enough practices in scientific computing. PLoS Comput. Biol. **13**(6), 1–20 (2017)
25. Gallagher, K., Kaiser, K., Simon, J., Beath, C., Goles, T.: The requisite variety of skills for IT professionals. Commun. ACM **53**(6), 144–148 (2010)
26. Parviainen, P., Tihinen, M., Kääriäinen, J., Teppola, S.: Tackling the digitalization challenge: how to benefit from digitalization in practice. Int. J. Inform. Syst. Proj. Manage. **5**(1), 63–77 (2017)
27. Jones, G.: Organizational Theory, Design, and Change. Pearson, Upper Saddle River (2013)
28. Association for Project Management: APM body of Knowledge. 6th edn. Association for Project Management, Buckinghamshire (2012)
29. O*NET Homepage webpage. https://www.onetcenter.org. Accessed 07 Sept 2019
30. LinkedIn Project Manager webpage. https://www.linkedin.com/jobs/browse/program-and-project-management. Accessed 07 Sept 2019
31. Indeed website. https://www.indeed.com/jobs?q=Project%20manager&l=Anywhere. Accessed 10 Sept 2019
32. Dice project management jobs page. https://www.dice.com/jobs?q=Project+management. Accessed 10 Sept 2019

Information Sources, Early-Career Worker Activities, and Workplace Learning in Large Technology Organizations: Developing a New Framework for the Future of Work

SeoYoon Sung[✉️]

Rutgers University, New Brunswick, NJ 08901, USA
seoyoon.sung@rutgers.edu

Abstract. This paper introduces an initial stage of theory-building on information sources and how people navigate the evolving workplace. The purpose of this research is two-fold. First, this work aims to build a useful theoretical framework needed to better understand how workers navigate in an environment where new sets of information sources and materials produce new kinds of worker activities. Second, information behavior has been understood in isolation from its workplace landscape, and relevant theories have contributed very little to the growing research domain around the future of work. By empirically testing a designed framework, this study aims to provide a useful theory. The author uses Lloyd's [1] conceptualization of information sources in the workplace, and Marsick's [2] workplace learning theory to construct a combined framework. This framework is being tested through an initial set of data gathered from interviews with eight young, early-career workers from marketing sectors in media and technology companies. By analyzing how early-career professionals navigate their information landscape, this initial study seeks to understand how the increasingly nuanced variations of information sources may interact with workplace activities. This paper shares initial preliminary findings and presents a plan to move forward with its research agenda.

Keywords: Human information behavior · Future of work · Information sources · Workplace learning · Informal learning · Information practice

1 Introduction

With the proliferation of modern technologies, scholars have begun to explore complex issues related to the changing work landscape. Numerous global-scale reports commonly highlight the need to reskill or upskill workers alongside increasingly capable machines [3–5]. For example, the Organization for Economic Cooperation and Development (OECD) issued a report on future of work and skills which suggests that young people need to be prepared for jobs in the future and "successfully navigate through an ever-changing, technology-rich work environment, and give all workers the opportunity to continuously maintain their skills...." [5, p. 2]. However, little attention has been paid to depicting what this "navigation" looks like, and how understanding

© Springer Nature Switzerland AG 2020
A. Sundqvist et al. (Eds.): iConference 2020, LNCS 12051, pp. 677–684, 2020.
https://doi.org/10.1007/978-3-030-43687-2_57

this can help support young people to be prepared for the changing workplace environments by providing continuous learning to succeed in such a dynamic workplace environment.

To better assist young people to successfully adapt to the changing workplace demands, it is important to first understand how young people currently navigate the evolving workplace environments. Thus, the following research questions guide the overall direction and objective of this research study:

RQ1: How do young early-career employees in fast-pace, technology-heavy workplace environments engage with various information sources to resolve daily learning challenges as well as gain knowledge or expertise needed for work?
RQ2: In what ways do they perceive these sources to be helpful for their knowledge work?
RQ3: How is technology used and perceived by the young early-career for their daily work practice?

This study first removes the assumption that young people at work are currently lacking opportunities to engage in their practice of knowing – as "knowing-in-practice" is achieved through engagement in practice [6], and they are in fact navigating through the challenging workplace environment where social configurations, environmental features, and technologies are laid out as information sources for them to navigate through. By removing the assumption, this study seeks to explore how they learn to make choices between available information sources and produce sustained work activities, thereby achieving workplace information literacy.

This paper is part of an overall research aim build theory needed to explore the interaction between young people's work practice and new forms of organizational and material resources. As an initial phase, a theoretical framework is first designed and is being tested through empirical data gathered. This paper briefly discusses a theoretical model that combines Lloyd's [1] conceptualization of information sources in the workplace and Marsick's [2] workplace learning theory. The combined framework has been devised to first understand what variations of work activities are produced as a result of people's navigating activity in the workplace.

The research aims to offer a solid theoretical model that helps to explore the evolving nature of a workplace exhibiting key elements of social, organizational and material resources, as well as young people's information behaviors with respect to how they navigate in ever-evolving and technology-rich work environments. The results of this study may provide a better depiction of how organizational or educational programs could construct appropriate opportunities for young people to prepare themselves for future work.

2   Theoretical Framework

Lloyd's research can address how early-career workers might navigate the evolving landscape of work in a fast-changing, technology-driven work environment. Table 1 summarizes Lloyd's conceptualization of information sources. Information is represented through text, talk, embodied action, as well as physical and material resources.

Individuals pick up various cues by using their senses, thought, and body [7]. Hence, information practice in the workplace is as much about understanding the tacit know-how as it is simply about interacting with information artifacts that are typically associated with textual information [8]. From this point of view, information practice is achieving "knowing-in-practice" [6] where people play with and navigate their information landscapes using various information sources such as textual, social, and physical/sensory sources [9, 10]. Information landscapes are what affords a range of opportunities for people to engage with these information sources [10]. In a workplace landscape, a range of activities, symbols, practices, and artefacts afford people who work in that space to facilitate their learning and knowing. Through this "navigation process" one comes to know "know-how".

Table 1. Lloyd's conceptualization of information sources

Information sources	Description
Textual	Outlines the formal requirements documents (i.e., policy and procedures, rules and regulations) of work. Learning to find, access and use this information engenders an institutional understanding of the workplace practice
Social	Facilitates the formation of a shared view of practice. Connects newcomers to information valued by the collective. Difficult to represent textually but makes a significant contribution to the transition of novice to expert
Physical/sensory	Facilitates embodied learning and observed through practice and the bodies of other practitioners. They act as a collector of sensory information, a site of knowledge and as a disseminator of physical experience

This framework offers a systematic understanding of the interaction between workers and their workplace environments. It also illuminates social and physical aspects of information that have largely been overlooked in information studies. For example, information about work practice and culture is "inscribed on the body through the social actions", [11, p. 90] and a distinct organizational culture that is typically tied to high tech organizations can play an important role in shaping individual and organizational practices. Furthermore, such cultural aspects, which are linked both with social and sensory sources, need to be examined when understanding information behavior within the confines of particular organizational boundaries. Broader social and environmental representations of information play a critical role in shaping workers' practices of work, hence, attention needs to be paid to these overlooked areas.

This framework can be examined in parallel with a workplace learning theory to better explain how people's social, physical, and textual relationships with information interact closely with a range of human's learning activities within a work environment. The following Table 2 introduces a workplace learning framework suggested in Watkins and Marsick [12] and Marsick [2]:

Table 2. Marsick's conceptualization of workplace learning

Workplace learning	Description
Formal	Discrete planned events organized for learning
Informal	Learning from experience that takes place outside formally structured activities. Can be planned or unplanned. Involves some degree of conscious awareness that learning is taking place
Incidental	Learning from experience that takes place outside formally structured activities. An unintended by-product of some other activity. Highly unintentional, unexamined and embedded in people's closely held belief systems

Informal learning is best situated in the context where individuals can have a control over what and how they learn. It involves not only cognitive activities of individuals, but also learning from others (e.g., networking, coaching, mentoring) and from non-interpersonal sources. In addition to informal learning, learning can also happen incidentally as a byproduct of other activity, such as task accomplishment, trial-and-error experimentation, and sensing the organizational culture [12].

As Lloyd acknowledges the close interconnection between one's ways of knowing and learning and the practices of navigating the sources, it is evident that how one comes to *know* can be represented in his or her workplace activities which interact closely with how they choose to use surrounding information sources in the landscape. Learning, in this case, constitutes people's navigating activity in an information environment where they learn to make choices between available sources. Thus, it can be said that in a workplace landscape, how one comes to know (or Lloyds would also explain as gaining information literacy) is a socio-cultural practice [9]. Information behavior is a learning behavior where "knowing-in-practice" is achieved through engaging in the evolving configurations of information sources. Thus, a combined framework has been constructed (Table 3) in the attempt to systematically exhibit nine dimensions that display examples of work activities that workers might engage in at work. It also offers a productive framework to describe early-career workers' experience in technology-heavy, and fast-changing environments, where workers pick up environmental cues from sources of the information landscape and achieve their know-how.

It is important to note that the boundaries of these dimensions are blurry and penetrable in a real-life context. It is also possible that one could be categorized as multiple elements as it has been demonstrated during the initial analysis. For example, while textual information (e.g., company manuals, policy documents) could be experienced through formal learning, it is also possible that one can experience informal learning if he or she searches for and engages with such information in a self-directed way to fulfill one's learning needs. There were a few categories that fell within more than one type of information sources and learning types during the coding process. Overall, this conceptual framework has guided the overall process of data analysis needed to refine the framework and test its usefulness to progress the study.

Table 3. Combined framework for workplace activities

Information sources/learning types	Textual	Social	Physical/sensory
Formal	Learning Management Systems (LMS) used by organization	Regular team/unit/department meetings, orientations	On-the-job training, workshops, simulations, demo sessions
Informal	Navigating through company documents, Using databases and archives, online tutorials, Internet search	Networking, informal/ad-hoc meetings, talking to colleagues, asking questions, social media, mentoring/coaching	Observations, working with others on the job, joining a project
Incidental	Discovering what is not in textual documentations, reading between the lines	Observing organizational culture, picking up messages from role modeling, cultural climate	Trial-and-error experimentation, task accomplishment

3 Methods

This study takes a qualitative methodological approach with the use of semi-structured interviewing methods [13]. Eight participants were recruited for this study through purposive and snowball sampling based on the following criteria:

- Full-time employees at large-size technology companies in the U.S.
- Working in digital marketing or advertisement
- Early 20s to mid-30s in age
- Early-career professionals whose total years of full-time work experience is five years or less
- Non-managerial position or have limited experience managing others

Eight professionals (5 female; 3 male) from seven technology companies in digital marketing and media sector were interviewed. Six participants reported working for a large-size company (1000 to 25,000 employees or more), and two reported working at a medium-size (100 to 1000 employees) company. The average age of the participants was 26.5 years (range = 23–30 years). Participants' work involved developing products or services related to media, social media, or technology (i.e., 5 advertising/marketing; 2 business development related to marketing; 1 product operations).

All interviews were voice recorded and transcribed. The interviews were 50 min in average. Two coding methods (i.e., open coding, process coding) were used for the initial analysis, following Saldaña [14] and Miles and Huberman [15]'s work. Analytic memo writing has been incorporated also as part of open coding, which was appropriate at this stage to make a coherent sense of the data and tie together pieces of data into a cluster based on a concept [15]. Process coding has then been conducted to exclusively reveal action in the data by using gerunds ("-ing" words), as it was deemed appropriate to best identify participants' work activities that could be understood in relation to the nine dimensions proposed.

4 Preliminary Findings

The analysis resulted in few initial visual frameworks where workers' activities can be understood to align with workplace resources. As expected, activities related to social sources of information and informal learning stood out as the most visible workplace activities. Following previous information studies of workplace context, participants relied most on other people for their information [16, 17]. When they encountered a challenge with their daily tasks, they sought others who may have answers to their problems ("Going back to the people who actually developed the thing"). Their co-workers and team members were regarded as "experts" who hold unique knowledge or expertise ("I feel like everybody on my team, in some way, is a master of something"). The challenge, however, was that they needed to first learn who the experts, or the knowledge providers are. This, in and of itself, was the knowledge that needed to be gained by the participants (i.e., who knows whom and who knows what).

While people seek others for information, other sources of information became intricately intertwined. In other words, people can seek a source to directly get to the information they need (e.g., talk to a colleague), but they can also find other sources that would lead to another source with information needed (e.g., accessing a database to find a person who has the information). Hertzum and Pejtersen [16] support this finding and discuss that over time individuals learn to make choices between different sources depending on varied work situations. Lloyd [10] also points out that people gain their ability to navigate diverse and complex information sources through the holistic process that is influenced by social, physical and textual relationships.

As expected, participants engaged in textual information both formally and informally, as they tried to navigate through available company documents using various tools and databases. Participants not only referred to documentations to align their own practices to others in the organization (e.g., matching procedures), but they also created documentations on their own for future records for themselves and others at work. Types of databases and space for such textual creation, sharing and distribution differed across organizational contexts.

Another major theme noticed was that when it comes to how workers use workplace technologies or tools to engage with textual information, there seem to be more room for incidental learning gained through combination of textual and physical/sensory sources. Participants interacted frequently with textual information (e.g., types of user or market data) using internal tools, and due to the uncertain nature of what these data can do to help their performance at the time of retrieving such data, participants experimented with what data or content might work best for specific situations and clients. Such activities seemed to represent incidental learning through engagement with both textual and physical sources in the information landscape. It was sensory engagement in that they were being immersed in the experience of a particular task using a specific tool and types of data ("knowing where data lives"). It was incidental in that these types of activities were in the form of a "trial-by-fire". Participants favored the learning-by-doing approach, as they expressed that "putting yourself out there" and gaining the embodied learning experience is the best way to gain knowledge for their work.

5 Discussion and Future Direction

The primary findings suggest that in a high-technology workplace context, the boundaries of information sources are much broader than what tends to have been viewed as information source. These boundaries are also blurry and permeable: one's engagement in one kind of information source could lead to another or involve two or more kinds simultaneously. Being information literate means being able to navigate diverse information within a particular landscape that characterizes the ecologies of information [10]. The information landscapes and being familiar with the affordances of information sources can facilitate how one comes to know in the workplace. Then the sources and learning can be understood together to examine how they produce different types of work activities.

Refinement of the framework and further analyses are needed to better frame how workers may navigate their workplace landscape and understand nuanced characteristics of different (or combinations of) sources of information available in today's workplace context. Along with further analyses and model refinements, the next stage of research will focus on investigating organizational and material resources that are available in marketing domains of technology organizations and how they play a role in shaping workers' navigating activities.

One limitation learned from this phase was that the interview method makes it difficult to investigate the intricacy of social configurations and environmental features that are available for the workers. For example, this investigation focused on individuals, although it is apparent that young workers often are assigned to teams, which means that they expected to acquire and use information in a collective way. Also, the combined theoretical framework guiding this study could benefit from other perspectives offering explanations, such as how tech companies function that are unique compared to other organizational contexts. It would be useful to identify key features of the organizational and material structures associated with organizational environments of media and technology industry. Articulating this might be a helpful next step to acquiring a better understanding of worker activities in a chosen environment to examine in depth how workplace activities and available social and physical configurations in contemporary technology organizations interact. A large technology company has been chosen to text this and work is now underway to further explore this area.

References

1. Lloyd, A.: Working (in) formation: conceptualizing information literacy in the workplace. In: Proceedings of the 3rd International lifelong learning conference, Yeppon, Queensland, Australia, pp. 218–224 (2004)
2. Marsick, V.J.: Toward a unifying framework to support informal learning theory, research and practice. J. Workplace Learn. **21**(4), 265–275 (2009)
3. McKinsey&Company.   https://www.mckinsey.com/ ~ /media/mckinsey/featured%20insights/future%20of%20organizations/what%20the%20future%20of%20work%20will%20mean%20for%20jobs%20skills%20and%20wages/mgi-jobs-lost-jobs-gained-report-december-6-2017.ashx
4. World Bank Group: World development report 2019 (in press). http://pubdocs.worldbank.org/en/816281518818814423/2019-WDR-Draft-Report.pdf
5. OECD: Future of work and skills. In: the 2nd Meeting of the G20 Employment Working Group, Hamburg, Germany, pp. 1–24 (2017)
6. Orlikowski, W.J.: Knowing in practice: enacting a collective capability in distributed organizing. Organ. Sci. **13**(3), 249–273 (2002)
7. Lloyd, A.: Information literacy as a socially enacted practice: sensitising themes for an emerging perspective of people-in-practice. J. Doc. **68**(6), 772–783 (2012)
8. Jarrahi, M.H., Thompson, L.: The interplay between information practices and information context: the case of mobile knowledge workers. J. Am. Soc. Inform. Sci. Technol. **68**(5), 1073–1089 (2017)
9. Lloyd, A.: Information literacy: different contexts, different concepts, different truths? J. Libr. Inform. Sci. **37**(2), 82–88 (2005)
10. Lloyd, A.: Information literacy landscapes: an emerging picture. J. Doc. **62**(5), 570–583 (2006)
11. Cheville, J.: Confronting the problem of embodiment. Int. J. Qual. Stud. Educ. **18**(1), 85–107 (2005)
12. Watkins, K.E., Marsick, V.J.: Towards a theory of informal and incidental learning in organizations. Int. J. Lifelong Educ. **4**(11), 287–300 (1992)
13. Creswell, J.W.: Qualitative Inquiry and Research Design: Choosing Among Five Approaches, 3rd edn. Sage, Thousand Oaks (2013)
14. Saldaña, J.: The Coding Manual for Qualitative Researchers, 3rd edn. Sage, Thousand Oaks (2016)
15. Miles, M.B., Huberman, A.M.: Qualitative Data Analysis: An Expanded Sourcebook, 3rd edn. Sage, Thousand Oaks (2014)
16. Hertzum, M., Pejtersen, A.M.: Information-seeking practices of engineers: searching for documents as well as for people. Inf. Process. Manage. **36**(5), 761–778 (2000)
17. Cross, R., Sproull, L.: More than an answer: information relationships for actionable knowledge. Organ. Sci. **15**(4), 446–462 (2004)

Open Data

The *What* of Data: Defining Which Scientific Research Is Appropriate to Share

Bernadette M. Boscoe(✉) iD

University of Washington, Seattle, WA 98195, USA
boscoe@uw.edu

Abstract. Increasingly, scientists are releasing research data to the public for potential (re)use. Yet, the *what* of data–what gets shared (or kept private), by whom, and why–is difficult for data curators and stewards to determine. Scientific field-specific norms play an important role in decision-making processes to define what data are deemed acceptable to release. I explore the framework of *contextual integrity* (CI), which operationalizes appropriate flows of information that reflect context-dependent norms. CI is essentially a theoretical framework for privacy *in* data; however, in this work, appropriate data sharing *surrounds* the data. In this paper, CI methods are applied to a case study in astronomy and show how CI can guide an understanding of which data can be shared by tracing how people move information within contexts. The aim is to provide both researchers and repository maintainers an approach to make data available in an appropriate way that does not violate rapidly evolving sharing norms.

Keywords: Data · Sharing · Infrastructures

1 Introduction

In compute-intensive science, the availability of data has skyrocketed in recent years, paired with an interest in making these data available for potential (re)use. Much scholarly work has sought to understand the complex landscape of incentives, restrictions, and policies within open science that both support and limit data sharing [16]. Shifts in data access and control are occurring in scientific research fields as data are increasingly seen as being valuable and, therefore, worthy of greater attention. In this paper, I limit my inquiry to a narrow aspect: Assuming researchers are willing to make their research data available, what are "the data" that can be appropriately shared so as to best reflect community norms? In scientific research processes, "the data" are impossible to define: data enjoy numerous evidentiary and statistical iterations throughout the research

Supported by the Alfred P. Sloan Foundation, grant numbers 201811217 and 201514001. Special thanks to Nic Weber.

© Springer Nature Switzerland AG 2020
A. Sundqvist et al. (Eds.): iConference 2020, LNCS 12051, pp. 687–694, 2020.
https://doi.org/10.1007/978-3-030-43687-2_58

process and are contingent upon their eventual purpose [5]. Previous work has explained the circulation of data as a commodity governed by both property rights and contextual social norms [17]. In what follows, I focus on the latter, norms-based governance, through the framework of contextual integrity (CI), a descriptive and diagnostic framework that makes it possible to judge appropriate flows of information given context dependent norms. Many applications of CI have focused on normative violations that involve data content of a sensitive nature (e.g. personally identifiable information (PII)), however the strength of CI is that it provides a comprehensive means of analyzing not just the content of data, but the broader sociotechnical environment in which data are shared. Here, I apply CI to a case study in astronomy. This work aims to surface relationships between norms and data to best inform the design of relevant infrastructures for making research data available for potential reuse within spaces where data sharing is contested.

2   Data to Share

More than ever, digital infrastructures such as data repositories offer researchers opportunities to make their data publicly available. Researchers' motivations and disincentives to share and reuse research data have been explored by a number of scholars in information science fields [3,13,14]. Reproducibility rises to the fore as a motivation to share for purposes of scientific rigor, but the laborious nature of its implementation can be a challenge for scholars [7,15]. At the same time, individual researchers can receive greater visibility for their work by relying on open-science tools and linkages, perhaps leading to more citations and thus justifying efforts to make data more available to the public [6]. Motivations aside, should researchers decide to make their data available, the question of *what* to make available involves choosing and organizing data, metadata, and code, drawing from–in essence–a flowing stream of information that can be placed into a data repository. Sharing proves more challenging for small research groups who lack enterprise-scale support structures and staff to assist in data sharing practices.

3   Contextual Integrity *Around* Data

CI is a framework developed by Nissenbaum et al. [10,12] that defines *privacy* as appropriate information flows based on norms specific to contexts. CI was developed for use with data containing information about individuals and has been adopted by researchers studying the Internet of Things and social media, to name a few examples [2]. Five parameters characterize information flow: subject, sender, recipient, information type, and transmission principles. Senders and recipients are actors that can be individuals or groups of people. Information type is a description of the form information takes, for example, an email. Transmission principles are defined as constraints imposed upon the information flows. Privacy is breached when an information flow fails to map onto expected values. Importantly, to ascertain privacy norms when evaluating a scenario, all five parameters must be specified. Some transmissions can be a violation in one sphere yet not in others. Additionally, transmission principles that change over time can result in violations from previously acceptable flows.

The main purpose of CI is to examine information flows that contain data about individual privacy; however, researchers can also violate data sharing norms by behaving in ways deemed unacceptable to others in their field (or other fields). In the research world, information is a highly coveted commodity–and the published results are often rewarded for being novel and first. Nissenbaum's [11] new work employs the metaphor of a *data food chain*, a hierarchical construct where "data of a higher order are a function of data of a lower order" (p. 236) thus stratifying data into layers that can be mapped to effects on privacy. Nissenbaum [11] notes that *data primitives*, which are event imprints such as electrical signals or activated pixels or GPS coordinates, are challenging to map onto norms; it is the higher levels of semantic data that can be more easily evaluated. For example, a mouse "click" is a meaningless trace until it is put into the context of higher-level data-processing layers. Thus, CI cannot be applied at the click level. In acknowledging the complexities of the data layers and related actors and norms, I turn this problem on its head and consider researchers, with their layers of data and multiple normative spheres through which to navigate, as a way of evaluating that information which is acceptable to share.

4   Data Sharing in Astronomy

Astronomy (including astrophysics, cosmology, and related fields) is a digital data-rich field with a multitude of data sources from observational and theoretical domains, often one serving to verify one another. Observational instruments collecting data take many forms, from ground and space telescopes to weather balloons and radio dish arrays. Compared with other science fields, astronomy has a well-established history of sharing data with the public [8]. However, a more granular inspection of data sharing practices reveals differences between countries, sub-fields, locations, projects, and instruments, as well as between PIs and among their teams. Microsoft's database guru, the late Jim Gray, famously said that his interest in astronomy data stemmed from the fact that it had no commercial value [9]. The ones and zeros that make up digital explorations into the night sky may not possess a market value, but the scores of scientists, data wranglers, archivists, instrument operators, and others working within the realm certainly are involved in the ethical entanglements that are part and parcel in doing science.

4.1   A Brief History of Norms of Astronomy Data Sharing

In the 1970s, acquiring astronomy data was a physical act and a heavy one at that: Astronomers had to lug reels of tapes from mountaintop observatories and drag heavy suitcases of data into cars and onto planes to return home and begin analyzing their data. By the 1990s, the digitization of astronomy was nearly complete, the Internet might not have been capable of transmitting astronomically large amounts of data, but media in the form of hard drives or discs made it easier for astronomers to share. In the United States, a plethora of telescopes were in the process of being built on Earth or launched into space, such as Hubble (1990), Chandra (1999), Spitzer (2003), and Keck (1992). At this time, U.S. space missions were generally funded by NASA and ground-based telescopes tended to be funded by private organizations. As a result, data sharing norms differed widely between the privately and publicly funded operations and between national and international entities [18]. Hubble Space Telescope is a canonical example of NASA data sharing practices. From the initial planning stages, Hubble data were to be put in an archive made available to the public. Levels of data reductions were categorized, with Level 0 data being "raw" data from the telescope, and subsequent numbers indicating that more processing had been done to the data. To collect Hubble data, astronomers submit proposals to observe various phenomena in the night sky, which are then processed by Hubble staff and given to the observer team. The observer is typically given a grace period of 12–18 months, offering them the opportunity to develop and publish results; after this time, the data are made available to the public.

It is important to stress that data released in large, mission-based public archives differs from research data created in the act of doing science as a result of analysis to be used for publications. The latter form of data may be shared by being placed on team or individual repositories, on university servers, or within platforms such as Zenodo or GitHub. Often, the research datasets that are made available with publications are voluntarily determined by the PI of the project, making them especially nebulous and unpredictable across cases.

4.2   Methods

To show examples of CI frameworks demonstrating data sharing practices, I draw from findings from a three-year qualitative case study of astronomy [4]. I conducted ethnography and participant observation at six locations, including observatories and universities with astronomy research groups, interviewing 40 astronomers and other related staff, such as programmers, and data repository stewards. The findings also stem from a corpus of interviews of astronomers done by information scientists within the Center for Knowledge Infrastructures at UCLA, led by Dr. Christine Borgman. I also spent two years embedded in an astronomy research group studying their data and code practices. A detailed understanding of data sharing practices grew from this in-depth and up-close scrutiny. Three vignettes follow from discussions with astronomers in the case study.

4.3   Scenario 1: "Horse Trading" as a Sharing Mechanism Between Teams

{*Subject*: Observational data. *Sender*: Japanese research team. *Receiver*: U.S. research team. *Information type*: Analyzed, reduced data from the Japanese telescope. *Transmission principle*: Data to be shared in between the two teams only; not explicitly stated but intended for the single use of producing one collaborative research paper}.

In 2018, members of a Japanese astronomy research group were working on a project about stars in the Milky Way Galaxy similar to that of a U.S.-based research team. The Japanese team sent a long formal email letter to the U.S. team requesting to share data and code with each other. In return for the U.S. team's data, the Japanese team would give the U.S. team their data plus authorship on a related publication. After some consideration as to whether it was beneficial to do so, the U.S. team agreed to the exchange. Recall, transmission principles are constraints imposed upon the information flow; so in this case the data shared was to remain private between the two groups. Therefore, if the U.S-team were to share this data with a third party or place it into a public repository without the Japanese group's permission, this would be considered a norm violation.

This type of *horse trading* (a term used by astronomers) predates newer scenarios to make research data available with an associated publication. I recommend that a data steward, such as an archivist or repository manager, be made aware of the provenance of various datasets, as well as any associated understandings and agreements, especially because assumptions might not have been explicitly stated. Some research groups in astronomy choose to share all data and code associated with their research, but others are forbidden from doing so by their PIs. To borrow from mathematical set theory, these datasets might be thought of as *clopen*–both open and closed and thus requiring more care in terms of curation. Repository designers' implementations might evolve as a result of surfacing norms via CI approaches. So, too, can CI be used to formalize design requirements in a way that can be translated into technical solutions [1].

In follow-up interviews, the U.S. team said they did end up sharing with the Japanese team, and the results were published in a journal that required the data to be made available to the public. However, it was unclear whether it would be acceptable to use the Japanese data for further projects, even though the data are public. Questions of ownership and appropriate use remain. One collaborator with the U.S. team said, when asked what an infrastructure could look like to improve sharing, "If data is shared for a one-time use, you could put a key on it so that it expires". He continued to explain his own relationship with the U.S. team data and said, "I must respect the data. I can access it but cannot use it unless the [U.S.] PI says yes". Another team member of the U.S. team opined that "We need a real data release policy beyond the PI informally deciding what gets shared. We want things to be clearer".

4.4   Scenario 2: Changing Transmission Principles

{*Subject*: Exoplanets. *Sender*: PI of research group. *Receiver*: Astronomy journal. *Information type*: DOI and links to repository. *Transmission principle*: Must include DOI and links in a particular way}.

CI can reveal changing transmission principles by comparing parameters over time and by examining norms. The following example demonstrates this. In September 2019, an astronomer in a small research group discussed reviews of her article recently accepted by an astronomy journal. She explained, "This is the first time I have ever seen explicit instructions for how to share the data associated with this paper. I share my data in GitHub, and the reviewer told me to get a DOI from Zenodo and link to my GitHub repository and use the DOI in my citations".

This is an interesting constraint imposed upon the researchers: As a condition to publish, they must share data in a way specified by the journal. Whether this is a norm violation is contingent upon the person or group evaluating this case; for all intents and purposes, the introduction of new contingencies placed on sharing practices is of importance to the repository designer and maintainer; knowing that researchers must share in a specific way allows for codification of a set of rules with which the repository can align. This case study also demonstrates potentially clashing norms of research groups, publishers, repositories, and even prior field norms that have dictated previous sharing practices.

4.5   Scenario 3: Violating the "Gentleperson's Agreement"

{*Subject*: Data in an archive. *Sender*: A rival research team. *Recipient*: A journal. *Information type*: A paper and associated data for publication. *Transmission principle*: Paper submitted to this journal and not elsewhere}.

I asked astronomers to give an example of a norm violation that might be construed as egregious across the board. An astronomer explained the following case: "Let's say a team took a series of observations and were working on a paper. The embargo period passes, and the raw data is released into the public archive but the team isn't finished with the paper yet. Another group uses the data from the archive to publish the same result first, scooping the other team". Other astronomers agreed that was "not cool" and that it is a problematic practice. I asked what would happen in this case, and astronomers replied that nothing would really be done, but that the offending team might get a bad reputation for doing this. "It is just something that should not be done" opined another astronomer, and added, "We call them archive vultures".

5   Conclusion

As fields such as astronomy have amassed increasing amounts of data and are fostering larger than ever collaborations among research groups, informal forms of sharing break down. Research repositories are but one way to make rules of reusing data more explicit, especially within public frameworks. A better understanding of what data gets shared can result in improved infrastructures to promote appropriate reuse. I have shown that by using the framework of CI, potential norm violations in the transmitting of information can occur in many situations of data sharing. Instead of looking at a dataset as an entity that can or cannot be shared, I instead evaluate its transmission within the various contexts in which it might be shared. A deeper understanding of these nuances can better inform the design and maintenance of repositories tasked with sharing data with different rules attached. As data sharing in science increases, creating more sophisticated ways to share data on different levels will help address the problem of what data can be shared and with whom. In particular, understanding who makes these decisions within a science field has a pronounced effect on what data get shared. As field norms shift over time, repository designers can enable functionality to determine what data to share.

References

1. Barth, A., Datta, A., Mitchell, J.C., Nissenbaum, H.: Privacy and contextual integrity: framework and applications. In: 2006 IEEE Symposium on Security and Privacy (S P 2006). 15pp.–198, May 2006. https://doi.org/10.1109/SP.2006.322
2. Benthall, S., Gürses, S., Nissenbaum, H.: Contextual integrity through the lens of computer science. Found. Trends Priv. Secur. **2**(1), 1–69 (2017). https://doi.org/10.1561/3300000016
3. Borgman, C.L.: Big Data, Little Data, No Data: Scholarship in the Networked World. MIT Press, Cambridge (2015). http://mitpress.mit.edu/big-data
4. Boscoe, B.M.: From blurry space to a sharper sky: keeping twenty-three years of astronomical data alive. Ph.D. thesis, UCLA (2019). https://escholarship.org/uc/item/2jv941sb5
5. Collins, H.M.: The meaning of data: open and closed evidential cultures in the search for gravitational waves. Am. J. Sociol. **104**(2), 293–338 (1998). https://doi.org/10.1086/2100406
6. Curty, R.G., Crowston, K., Specht, A., Grant, B.W., Dalton, E.D.: Attitudes and norms affecting scientists' data reuse. PLoS One **12**(12), e0189288 (2017). https://doi.org/10.1371/journal.pone.01892887
7. Darch, P.T., Borgman, C.L.: ShipSpace to database: motivations to manage research data for the deep subseafloor biosphere. In: Proceedings of the 77th Annual Meeting of the Association for Information Science and Technology, Seattle, WA, November 2014. http://www.asis.org/asist2014/proceedings/submissions/papers/156paper.pdf,000008
8. Genova, F.: Data as a research infrastructure CDS, the Virtual Observatory, astronomy, and beyond. In: EPJ Web of Conferences, vol. 186, p. 01001 (2018). https://doi.org/10.1051/epjconf/201818601001
9. Hey, T.: The big idea: the next scientific revolution. Harv. Bus. Rev. (2010). https://hbr.org/2010/11/the-big-idea-the-next-scientific-revolution10
10. Nissenbaum, H.: Privacy as contextual integrity. Wash. Law Rev. **79**, 39 (2004)
11. Nissenbaum, H.: Contextual integrity up and down the data food chain. Theor. Inq. Law **20**(1), 221–256 (2019). https://www7.tau.ac.il/ojs/index.php/til/article/view/161412

12. Nissenbaum, H.F.: Privacy in Context: Technology, Policy, and the Integrity of Social Life. Stanford Law Books, Stanford (2010)
13. Palmer, C.L., Weber, N.M., Cragin, M.H.: The analytic potential of scientific data: understanding re-use value. Proc. Am. Soc. Inform. Sci. Technol. **48**(1), 1–10 (2011). http://onlinelibrary.wiley.com/doi/10.1002/meet.2011.14504801174/full14
14. Pasquetto, I.V., Randles, B.M., Borgman, C.L.: On the reuse of scientific data. Data Sci. J. **16** (2017). https://doi.org/10.5334/dsj-2017-008. http://datascience.codata.org/articles/10.5334/dsj-2017-008/,0000015
15. Stodden, V., et al.: Enhancing reproducibility for computational methods. Science **354**(6317), 1240–1241 (2016). https://doi.org/10.1126/science.aah6168
16. Tenopir, C., et al.: Data sharing by scientists: practices and perceptions. PLoS One **6**(6), e21101 (2011). https://doi.org/10.1371/journal.pone.0021101
17. Vertesi, J., Dourish, P.: The value of data: considering the context of production in data economies. In: Proceedings of the ACM 2011 Conference on Computer Supported Cooperative Work, CSCW 2011, pp. 533–542. ACM, New York (2011). https://doi.org/10.1145/1958824.1958906
18. Williams,T.: The philanthropy of stargazing: we're in a new golden age of mega telescope projects (2014). http://www.insidephilanthropy.com/home/2014/12/18/the-philanthropy-of-stargazing-were-in-a-new-golden-age-of-m.html

Of Seamlessness and Frictions: Transborder Data Flows of European and US Social Science Data

Kristin R. Eschenfelder[1]([⊠]) [iD] and Kalpana Shankar[2]

[1] University of Wisconsin-Madison, Madison, WI 53706, USA
eschenfelder@wisc.edu
[2] University College Dublin, Belfield, Dublin 4, Ireland

Abstract. Open science initiatives are predicated upon managing research data to overcome "data frictions," or the points of resistance in the movement of data time [12]. This paper explores organizational creation of data frictions to manage the flow of data from one data organization to another. We describe the creation and modification of data frictions between European data organizations and between data organizations in Europe and the USA. We analyze historical documentary data from CESSDA, an umbrella organization representing European data organizations that has served as a platform for development of international data sharing arrangements from the 1960s through today.

Keywords: Data sharing · Data archives · Data management · Transborder data flows

1 Introduction

Sharing of data promotes verification of research results, makes publicly funded research accessible, enables new questions and methods, and generally advances the state of research and innovation [5]. Today's open science initiatives encourage the idea that access to and reuse of data be seamless. However, as data move across boundaries – from one spreadsheet to another, from one researcher to another, or across organizations or national borders, data meet resistances or "data frictions" [12]. In this paper, we explore intentionally created data frictions in the context of research data sharing between formal social science data organizations (DO) and across international borders. Our research goal is to increase understanding how and why social science DO structure the movement of data between themselves and across national boundaries. This paper is part of a larger project about the history of social science DO as organizations from the 1960s to today [11]. But the insights are applicable to contemporary infrastructural projects that imagine seamless data sharing such as the European Open Science Cloud.

This paper focuses on the Consortium of European Social Science Data Archives (CESSDA) as a focal point to examine movement of data between European and American DOs. CESSDA is an umbrella organization of European DO, and a European Research Infrastructure Consortium (ERIC) based in Norway. CESSDA has existed

© Springer Nature Switzerland AG 2020
A. Sundqvist et al. (Eds.): iConference 2020, LNCS 12051, pp. 695–702, 2020.
https://doi.org/10.1007/978-3-030-43687-2_59

informally since the 1960s but formalized in 1992. Part of the CESSDA mission is to support cross border data sharing, providing "integrated and sustainable data services" for researchers in partnership with national social science DO [6]. CESSDA is a federation of national DO: Data and core service functions remain within national DO.

2 Methods

We focus on social science data organizations (DO) because they provide a longitudinal analysis lens for examining transborder data sharing agreements. Social science DO predate both computers and the Internet, they have operated in many nations facilitated data sharing since the 1960s, allowing longitudinal analysis of transborder data agreements. Their collections are primarily quantitative, resulting from survey research or polling including regularly repeated data collection events, government agency data, and data from individual PIs. Some data is restricted due to sensitivity, national privacy laws, PI request, or DO business model.

The sources for paper include organizational documents from 1968 to the early 2000s obtained from the CESSDA Archive and two related large social science DO (the UK Data Archives (UKDA) and the Inter-university Consortium for Political and Social Research (ICPSR)), contemporary (2002-present) documents obtained from the CESSDA website, and secondary literature written by current and former CESSDA members or others. Our collection of CESSDA documents included over 800 digitized documents. We paid special attention to reports, position statements, meeting agendas and notes. Emails threads debating controversies were also very insightful. Many documents, including numerous logistics emails, were put aside after initial review.

We employed inductive thematic analysis on the relevant documents. The first author first read all the documents and developed summary memos for each year documenting participants, major projects and funders, the emergence of debates and the positions of CESSDA members, and the resolution of the debates (or not). She then summarized major motivators and concerns in decade memos. In many cases she supplemented this with secondary information about particular CESSDA projects. From this preliminary analysis, both authors decided on foci based on prominent themes and areas of most interest to the scholarly community. They then developed theme specific memos that pulled together data from across time and across sources related to the chosen themes. This paper includes data focused on the theme of tensions surrounding sharing of data across national boundaries.

3 Data Sharing and Interoperability

This paper describes results from a study that focus on CESSDA, a field level cooperative data organization that exist in a web of interlinked governmental and research stakeholders and international DO partners. But the actions of CESSDA are driven by a larger data sharing and reuse context. This includes changing data sharing practices between individual scholars or labs [18], the cultural and economic factors impacting deposit or reuse of data in science fields [15, 16, 18], the challenges faced by member

DO in light of shifting expectations and resources [4], and challenges of coordinating field-level initiatives and shared services [17].

One goal of the CESSDA has been to promote data exchange or the flow of data across border to promote comparative research. Bates, Lin and Goodale [2] complain that the metaphor of "data flow" implies a smoothness that does not exist. As Borgman argues, "data do not flow…" but data movement occurs with stops [3, 4]. Where a DO, or its components, are geographically located matters because location influences mission, host relations and funding, regulations, and national political loyalties. Instead of thinking about data frictions solely as impediments to flows of data between DO, we look at data frictions as a means of structuring relationships and activities. Looking at points of disagreement, and the creation of processes between DO, illuminates how different nations or different science cultures organize work around data sharing to make data move across boundaries [1].

4 Fishing Zones, Request Routing and Other Data Sharing Arrangements Within Europe

The development of European social science DO in the late 50s and 60s sought to promote cross-national data analysis and sharing. But at the same time, in order to justify their budgets, DO needed to show the impact of their activities. Further, professional values required that DO steward data and ensure their proper use. These parallel motivations encouraged DO to create protocols to track and (to some extent) control who used data. The tension between promoting data flows and the need to track and control were complicated by the emergence of the new technologies of FTP that researchers could use to self-distribute data.

Early discussions about how to manage the movement of data between national DO started in the 1960s through the UNESCO sponsored International Social Sciences Council (ISSC) Standing Committee on Social Science Data Archives. This group of prominent quantitative social scientists contained many of the founding members of CESSDA, as well as representatives from ICPSR and Roper in the USA. European participants at the ISSC, who later formed CESSDA, by 1964 had developed a norm known as the "Fishing Zone Agreement" which outlined expectations that national DO had rights and responsibilities for data produced in their country [13]. One underlying stewardship assumption that national DO should be gatekeepers for their nation's data and manage their access and use. European DO saw themselves as national service providers with an obligation to provide data services for free, or low cost, to research centers and scholars in their national territory. These ties between data and the geographical/political location in which they were produced were strong enough that at least one CESSDA member used the term "data raiding" to refer to outside others (e.g., US DO) acquiring data out from under from their rightful European stewards. While DO have a legal obligation to protect certain data (e.g., data with personal identifiers, sensitive data), our data indicate that the fishing zone expectations extended further to non-sensitive data collections held by national DO.

The Fishing Zone expectations of national control were bolstered by the need for DO to get credit for their curation work and justify their budgets. First, they needed to show funders that DO work was impactful and they did so by creating data use and control procedures that generated usage data. These protocols typically tracked which researchers from which nations had requested data and for what purpose. For example, in formal data transfer procedure described by 1979, all data requests had to be routed through national DO on both the sending and receiving end to ensure that all use was counted and that the request was legitimate and appropriate. Second, DO clearly labelled the materials they shared to ensure that they received credit for their curation work. Materials identified the originating archive as the home archive to ensure that reusers knew who had done the labor to make the data set sharable [13].

The introduction of procedures, or frictions, to track use, and ensure stewardship and credit, slowed down the flow of data across borders. Increasing demands for faster transfers led CESSDA to modify these arrangements. Social science scholars increasingly wanted to do cross-national data analysis [7]. CESSDA members reported complaints about wait times for cross border requests. CESSDA members therefore soon modified their protocol to allow a European DO to directly fulfill a European cross-border request without routing the request back to the home country archive of the requester in order to speed fulfillment. The new arrangement still required documentation and counting, and the DO fulfilling the request was supposed to inform the researcher's national DO about the request after the fact, and no national DO should give another DO's data to a third party country like a US DO [8].

Technological change also put pressure on the original arrangements created to manage transborder data flows, ensure stewardship, use counting and credit. After 1981 it became possible to FTP files through via various European computer networks, and by 1983, one could send data across the Atlantic via EARN/BITNET. Personal computers and FTP gave researchers more options about where to deposit their data as they could avoid expensive tape drive shipping fees. Researchers could now set up their own FTP sites and distribute data themselves, giving researchers more options for data distribution.

Researchers also began to demand more control over reuse and distribution that conflicted with existing CESSDA data sharing norms. Previously CESSDA members agreed to always provide peer copies of deposited data to each other at cost. But in 1984, the German DO reported (rather apologetically) that a group of investigators would only deposit their data if the German DO agreed not provide copies to other DO (in violation of the previous peer data sharing norms). The PIs wanted a higher level of control over reuse. These changing researcher expectations pushed CESSDA members to again change their Data Sharing Agreement to account for depositor requested limitations on data sets [9].

5   Creation of EU-US Transborder Data Flow Agreements

Relationships between CESSDA members and American DO like ICPSR and Roper that have gone through periods of lower trust and tension, requiring the creation of new transborder sharing agreements. Tensions stemmed in part from differences in how these DO generate revenue to pay for their staff, operations, and infrastructure. Many (but not all) European DO receive funding as part of national governmental budgets.

In contrast, in the US, large DO like ICPSR and Roper relied on membership fees (and later contracts). European DO tended portray themselves as national service providers for all scholars in their national territory. In contrast, in the US, there has never been a national social science DO; rather, large DO like ICPSR and Roper positioned themselves as membership organizations serving their dues paying members.

Strains began as US DO sought to expand their membership bases into European university campuses and acquire European data for their collections. The direct solicitation to European universities to become paying members conflicted with European DO norms about proving data at no (or low) cost to other DO. Further, the US DO move to acquire European data for their collections conflicted with the Fishing Zone norm. As one DO head described, US acquisition of European data would "interfere with operational needs" of European DO because of the expectation that national governments funded European DO to be the gatekeepers and stewards for all their nation's social science data.

ICPSR adapted to European conditions and developed national-level membership for European DO that better fit with the model of European DO being national service providers. But this arrangement still conflicted with the CESSDA norm that DO provide data to one another at cost. In a series of "balance of trade" debates that played out on email lists, some voiced the opinion that it was unfair that European DO had to pay ICPSR membership fees to distribute American data, while there was no similar arrangement for European DO to get revenue from distribution of European data in the US.

A quid-pro-quo or fee-based Europe-US data exchange norm developed in the late 1970s as the outcome from a heated exchange between CESSDA members and ICPSR. Many CESSDA members were deeply frustrated both by ICPSR's (and Roper's) European data acquisition activities and their need to pay a membership fee to provide their users access to ICPSR data. ICPSR countered that during the 1970s, the amount of data transferred from the US to Europe was much higher than the amount transferred from Europe to the US, which justified national fees. A counterargument was that while the volume of European data moving to the US might be smaller, reuse of the European data in the US was higher value and this merited reduced ICPSR fees for CESSDA members.

CESSDA members debated these issues and then developed a white paper [10]. The white paper suggested that ICPSR accept the European peer DO data exchange traditions including exchange on a cost-only or quid-pro-quo data swapping basis. In instances of data sharing, it sought to guarantee exchange of usage data, and ensure that originating archives got provenance credit for any shared materials. Further, the white paper reasserted the Fishing Zone expectation that European DO ought to have primary responsibility for European data. In its response, ICPSR refused to acknowledge the CESSDA fishing zone tradition or any nationality based "right of first refusal" to data produced in country. It argued that ICPSR had to remain free to serve its global audience by collecting data globally. ICPSR claimed that if they just all communicated better about planned activities, there would be no need for assertion of rights, or that "full exchange of information should usually eliminate the need to refer to an archive's right" [14 p. 85] But in instances where data exchange was sought, ICPSR agreed the exchange could be quid pro quo, or involve a fee or other compensation. ICPSR and

European DO have subsequently exchanged data on a DO to DO bilateral basis based on a variety of compensation or trade arrangements. This example illustrates that the working out of transborder data sharing agreements is part of the development of trust leading to increased data flows.

6 Conclusions

In this paper, we analyzed historical documents from CESSDA, a field-level organization representing data organizations (DOs) in Europe from the 1960 to the 1990s to understand how and why DO create and modify data sharing agreements to manage the exchange of data between DO. CESSDA members shared a goal of data sharing and meeting increasing researcher demands for convenient international data.

But DO also had expectations, manifested in the Fishing Zone Agreement, about national rights and responsibilities for data produced in a home nation. DO also had goals of ensuring data stewardship, impact tracking and ensuring they received credit for curation work. We described how they managed these related, and sometimes conflicting goals, through creation and modification of international data sharing norms and processes.

Our first story told of the fishing zone norm in Europe and changes to early international data agreements. DO had expectations, manifested in the Fishing Zone Agreement, about national rights and responsibilities for data produced in a home nation. DO also had goals of ensuring data stewardship, impact tracking and ensuring they received credit for curation work. We described how CESSDA members created DO to DO data flow procedures to try to balance the goals of increased access and sharing with the need to steward the data, and ensure usage counts and credit to the home archive of the data. This story also shows how CESSDA DO had to adjust their procedures in light of changing technology and research expectations.

Our second story told of development of European-US data flow arrangements in the 1970s and illustrated how data sharing agreements were necessary to overcome lack of trust between US and European archives. It illustrates how US DO demands blocked extension of European DO to DO data sharing norms and required more bespoke arrangements that might involve fees, trades of labor or any other agreed upon exchange of value.

From a practical perspective, our stories illustrate limits on the dream of seamless data flows. These limitations are important because the motivators that have shaped DO to DO data sharing in the past, will shape data sharing in the future through new federated data organizations such as the European Open Science Cloud. The question of where data produced by one nation ought to sit is still contentious even in the age of clouds. DO still need to show evidence of impact, they need to ensure stewardship of data, and ensuring rewards for and funding of curation work is still problematic. The challenge is to design systems in ways that leads to higher "flow" performance from and end user perspective but also accomplish DO goals.

This paper contributes to the larger literature on data curation by examining data sharing between DO, and by highlighting the role of field-level DO organizations like CESSDA as a social platform through which DO make and modify practices. Our focus on DO to DO data sharing agreements provide different insights into questions about data sharing and trust that complements studies of data sharing between researchers or labs and also studies of depositor relationships with DO. Our long term analysis frame also provides new insights about changes in DO practices over time.

Theoretically, our stories illustrate how looking at points of disagreement, and the creation of data regulatory processes between DO, provides a lens for understanding how different nations or different science cultures organize work around data sharing. Frictions bring actors together to explore differences in understandings and work out alignments as they work out ways to make data move across boundaries [1]. Instead of thinking about data frictions solely as impediments to inter-organizational data collaboration, new questions arise if we look at data frictions as a means of structuring relationships and activities.

References

1. Bates, J.: The politics of data friction. J. Doc. **74**(2), 412–429 (2018)
2. Bates, J., Lin, Y.W., Goodale, P.: Data journeys: capturing the socio-material constitution of data objects and flows. Big Data Soc. **3**(2), 1–12 (2016)
3. Borgman, C.L.: Big Data, Little Data, No Data: Scholarship in the Networked World. The MIT Press, Cambridge (2015)
4. Borgman, C.L., Scharnhorst, A., Golshan, M.S.: Digital data archives as knowledge infrastructure: mediators of data Sharing and reuse. J. Assoc. Inf. Sci. Technol. 1–17 (2019)
5. Borgman, C.: The conundrum of sharing research data. J. Am. Soc. Inf. Sci. Technol. **63**(6), 1059–1078 (2012)
6. CESSDA: http://www.springer.com/lncs. Accessed 14 Sept 2019
7. Committee of European Social Science Data Archives: Meeting Minutes, Brussels, 20 April 1979
8. Committee of European Social Science Data Archives: CESSDA Agreement Re: Transborder Data Transfer, Cologne, 4 August 1982
9. Committee of European Social Science Data Archives: Meeting Minutes, Salzburg, 11 May 1984
10. Committee of European Social Science Data Archives: Position Paper on Relationships Between ICPSR and CESSDA, Louvain-la-Nouve, 21 May 1977
11. Downey, G., Eschenfelder, K.R., Shankar, K.: Talking about metadata labor: social science data archives, professional data librarians, and the founding of IASSIST. In: Aspray, W. (ed.) Historical Studies in Computing, Information, and Society. HC, pp. 83–113. Springer, Cham (2019). https://doi.org/10.1007/978-3-030-18955-6_5
12. Edwards, P.N., Mayernik, M.S., Batcheller, A.L., Bowker, G.C., Borgman, C.L.: Science friction: data, metadata, and collaboration. Soc. Stud. Sci. **41**(5), 667–690 (2011)
13. International Social Sciences Council (ISSC) Standing Committee on Social Science Data Archives: Principles of a federation of European social science data archives. In: Second ISSCIICSSD Conference on Data Archives, Paris, September, pp. 28–30 (1964)
14. Inter-university Consortium for Social and Political Research: ICPSR Response to Louvaine-la-Neuve Discussions, Ann Arbor, MI, p. 85, 14 July 1977
15. Pasquetto, I., Randles, B., Borgman, C.: On the reuse of scientific data. Data Sci. J. **16**(8), 1–9 (2017)

16. Piwowar, H.A.: Who shares? Who doesn't? Factors associated with openly archiving raw research data. PLoS One **6**(7) (2011)
17. Ribes, D.: Notes on the concept of data interoperability: cases from an ecology of AIDS research infrastructures. In: Proceedings of the 2017 ACM Conference on Computer Supported Cooperative Work and Social Computing, pp. 1514–1526. ACM (2017)
18. Tenopir, C., Allard, S., Douglass, K., Aydinoglu, A.U., Wu, L., Read, E., et al.: Data sharing by scientists: practices and perceptions. PLoS One **6**(6), e21101 (2011)

Exploring Open Data Initiatives in Higher Education

Yang Julia Zhu and Luanne Freund$^{(\boxtimes)}$ ⓘ

University of British Columbia, Vancouver, BC V6T1Z1, Canada
yang.j.zhu@gmail.com, luanne.freund@ubc.ca

Abstract. Open data is the name given to datasets that are online, machine-readable, open-licensed, available for bulk download and redistribution, and free of charge. Although open data in universities is still a relatively new concept, several universities have begun to participate in making their data public. This paper offers an initial investigation to open data in post-secondary education systems, to identify opportunities and challenges, and to offer case studies on select open data movements in higher education.

Keywords: Open data initiative · Open education · Higher education

1 Introduction

The availability of open data has grown considerably, as public organizations respond to external pressure and internal motivation to release administrative data in formats and under conditions that enable reuse. Open data is an international phenomenon that is strongly associated with the open government movement and motivated by the desire for increased transparency and social and economic benefits made possible by data reuse [1]. In the government realm, open data initiatives include the growing 2003 Public Sector Information (PSI) Directive in Europe, the Open Government Partnership established in 2011, and the expanding G8 Open Data Charter developed in 2013 [1]. In March 2011, the government of Canada launched its first-generation Open Data Portal and Canada is now a leader in the open data movement, currently chairing an international Open Data Working Group through its involvement in the Open Government Partnerships [2]. Given this context, we became interested in the impact of the open data movement on other, non-governmental public institutions, and specifically in higher education, where open data could be thought to bring the same or similar benefits. Further, a working group at our university began to investigate the feasibility of establishing an open data initiative, and wished to know if this was a widespread practice. Therefore, we set out to determine: do university-based open data initiatives exist, what forms do they take, and what challenges do they face? We conducted an environmental scan of open data initiatives and data sharing practices within major Canadian and international universities and present the results in this short paper.

© Springer Nature Switzerland AG 2020
A. Sundqvist et al. (Eds.): iConference 2020, LNCS 12051, pp. 703–710, 2020.
https://doi.org/10.1007/978-3-030-43687-2_60

2 Background

The key feature of open data have been identified and codified over time, from the seminal 8 Principles of open government data established at the Sebastopol meeting in 2007[1] to the more comprehensive Open Definition, which has its roots in the open source movement[2]. Generally, to be considered "open", the data must be available online, in machine readable format, licensed as open without restrictions, complete, available for bulk download and redistribution, and free of charge [3]. Governments, businesses, and individuals can use open data to bring about social and economic benefits and to hold organizations accountable for their actions. Open data can be of many types, including data that governments have traditionally shared, such as census and other statistical data and geographical data; and administrative data produced in the process of carrying out organizational activities, which in the past may have been subject to Freedom of Information requests, but are not open by default. In the higher education context, research data is a category of open data that has seen a recent and dramatic surge of interest. However, in this project, we have focused on open administrative data in higher education, referred to by Borgman as "grey data" [5].

2.1 Motivations and Barriers

One of the primary motivations for open government data initiatives is corruption, an international problem that threatens economic growth and undermines peoples' faith in the government [8]. It is believed that because of open data, open data initiatives could be a promising step towards minimizing corruption. According to a systematic review of open government data initiatives, there are three main reasons for open government data [1]:

- *Transparency* – a complete disclosure of information, rules, plans, processes and actions of companies, organizations and government;
- *Releasing social and commercial value* – data about the city, province, or nation have both social and commercial value which could be used for policy development or new service implementation; and
- *Participatory Governance* – as government data is made public, citizens can feel more involved with government processes such as decision- and policy-making as opposed to passively voting in elections.

Although open data initiatives have been successful, with widespread adoption at all levels of government, the movement faces a number of barriers that prevent it from reaching its full potential. Atenas and Havemann [7] summarize the following challenges: the heterogeneity of data formats and tools to work with data; low consumer data literacy; poor metadata leading to data discoverability issues; inadequate budgets for open data projects; and concerns over liability due to inaccuracies or exposure of

---

[1] The original Sebastopol principles and additional open data principles are outlined at opengovdata. org.

[2] See the full Open Definition here: http://opendefinition.org/od/2.1/en/.

sensitive data. Given these challenges, it is important to acknowledge that many open data initiatives, fail to thrive and are abandoned [9].

2.2   Open Data in Higher Education

In comparison to a very substantial body of research on open data in government, relatively little has been written on open data in higher education. As noted above, data produced by educational institutions can be categorized into research data or "grey data" [5]. Grey data is an umbrella term that includes the large array of data that universities produce, apart from that produced by research activities [5]. Typically, grey data refers to reference data, such as the location of academic institutions; internal data, such as staff names, personnel data, or identity data; curriculum data such as learning objects or course data; or user-generated data such as learning analytics, performance data, or job placements [6]. Arguably, one of the most valuable types of grey data that universities collect is student data. By collecting grey data about students, some universities are able to create unique learning paths or develop profiles of students according to their choice of majors, financial aid status, scholarships, and other matters [5]. Such profiles can be used internally for recruitment, student support, and service improvements; however, as with all personally identifiable information, data privacy concerns are paramount.

With all this information produced and collected, universities are stewards of immense amounts of data that can provide countless opportunities for local and global partnerships in teaching, research, and strategic planning [5]. Indeed, according to Krumova [6], public universities have an obligation to commit to openness, including open data and open access to scholarly information, in keeping with their mission and to maintain public trust and confidence [6]. Some universities do share grey data as linked open data (LOD), and a number of such initiatives have been supported by the Joint Information Systems Council in the UK [10]. Another motivation for universities to adopt open data initiatives is the "campus as a living lab" concept, in which universities aim to achieve sustainable operations through ongoing experimentation and evaluation, which requires the acquisition and sharing of campus data [11].

As with government data, there are many challenges in adopting an open data stance within universities. Borgman points out that data originate from various sources within the university and take various forms, such that exact data ownership may be ambiguous. Therefore, it is difficult to allocate responsibility for these types of information [5]. Grey data stewards include libraries, instructional development units, food services and campus retail businesses, to list a few [5]. Furthermore, the methods and financial resources required for effective data stewardship in universities are still currently poorly understood, as few universities have data governance plans in place [5]. In contrast, governments are more likely to have resources and staff with data expertise available, for example through regional or national statistical agencies. Compared to government entities, which work for the benefit of the general public, universities primarily serve their students, faculty and staff, who expect the institution to achieve a balance between openness, including academic and intellectual freedom, and confidentiality, security, and responsibility towards their data [5].

3 Methods of Data Collection

We carried out a semi-structured environmental scan seeking information on university data sharing practices and open data initiatives. We initially focused on major Canadian and English language international universities, targeting the 15 major research universities in Canada (U15)[3] and major universities in the United States, the UK and Australia, based on their ranking in the 2018 QS rankings[4]. The 36 institutions included in the scan are listed in the appendix. Using this systematic approach, we found only a few examples of open data initiatives. We then broadened our scope by searching the Web for any mentions of university-based open data initiatives. After looking at a large number of universities, we found a limited number of open data initiatives. In total we report on six cases that we examined in detail.

In conducting the scan, we relied upon a combination of Google keyword searches and browsing to explore each university website. We looked for any references to "open data" (specific queries such as "open data initiatives in post-secondary education" or "open datasets in universities") and sought out the units responsible for information and data management within the university. When we identified an open data initiative, we documented: the administrative unit responsible, the stated motivation or goals, the types of data and number of datasets available, and the platform used to share the data, and any policies or licenses regarding data use.

4 Results

The primary findings are that the open data movement has not yet had a substantial impact in the higher education domain. The scan identified six cases of open data initiatives in major universities. These cases are presented briefly below. While open data commitments are rare, all the universities included in the scan do share select administrative data in some form on their websites, typically through institutional planning or information technology units. The most common format for the sharing of data by North American universities is in a "fact book," – an annual snapshot of data on a number of set topics, such as degrees offered and completed, admissions and student demographics. In most cases, fact books are shared in non-machine readable formats, such as Portable Document Format (pdf). However, in a small number of cases, this data is available in open formats, such as csv and/or via interactive platforms such as Tableau. Some US universities participate in the Common Data Set initiative[5] in which they share a standard set of data with publishers in order to support consistent reporting and student information. However, these Common Data Set files do not meet open data standards. In many cases, information on accessing and using open data is provided by the institution's library through subject guides, but, generally, these are not focused on access to administrative data from the home institution.

---

[3] U15.ca/.

[4] www.topuniversities.com/university-rankings/world-university-rankings/2018.

[5] http://www.commondataset.org/.

4.1 Open Data Cases

The first stage of the environmental scan identified open data initiatives in the following major universities: Waterloo (Canada); Harvard (USA), Cornell (USA) and Oxford (UK). Further dedicated searching identified two more: Concordia (Canada) and Southampton (UK). As this environmental scan was not exhaustive, these serve primarily as examples of the types of approaches taken to open data. A summary of these six open data initiatives is presented in Table 1.

The University of Waterloo's Open Data Initiative (http://uwaterloo.ca/open-data/) is managed by the Information Systems and Technology unit and offers access via API to approximately 80 datasets from more than 20 sources within the university. Data is shared via GitHub and available to registered users through the university's Open Data License 1.0. This seems to be an active and well-managed initiative that is clearly documented and which contains a substantial number and range of datasets, including courses, scholarships, news, job opportunities, and buildings.

Concordia University's Open Data initiative (http://www.concordia.ca/web/open-data.html) is managed by a cross-functional team led by Concordia Library, which collects datasets from across the university. These are available via API to registered users through GitHub and as CSV downloads subject to the Creative Commons Attribute 4.0 license. Sixteen datasets are available, including library catalogue data, facilities, and unit and course data. The site appears to be up to date and is well-documented.

Harvard University shares institutional data through a Dataverse instance (data.harvard.edu/). The portal offers 23 datasets in a mix of formats, most of which are licensed through a Creative Commons 0 "no rights reserved" license. Datasets are wide-ranging, including library catalogue data, financial and scholarship data, and look up directories for faculty. The portal is maintained by the Harvard IT unit. In addition to this centralized initiative, there is a Harvard College student and faculty led open data project (hodp.org), which shares about 40 datasets in a simple portal and also publishes analyses of the data.

The Cornell Open Data Initiative (codi.engineering.cornell.edu/) is a student run project that shares institutional data via its website and GitHub. While there are only a small number of datasets currently available, including map, calendar, transit and event data, this initiative seems to be transitioning to allow for API access to increase the number of datasets. In comparison with the other cases, which have institutional support, there is less available documentation about the initiative and the datasets, and licensing information is unavailable.

The University of Southampton's Open Data Service (data.southampton.ac.uk/) is an early and award winning initiative that shares data in static and linked open formats and creates apps and services based on the data. It is managed by the university's IT services and offers a large number of datasets that are collected on an ongoing basis, aggregated and converted to RDF format. These include data on events, facilities, food, parking, course offerings, and more. Most of the data is available through the UK Open Government License.

The University of Oxford shares institutional data through its linked open data store (data.ox.ac.uk). The Open Data program is managed by IT services and offers only 4

Table 1. Summary of cases of university open data initiatives.

Institution	Platform	Number and formats of datasets	Unit responsible	License
Waterloo, Canada	GitHub	80+; API, multiple	Info Systems & Technology	Open Data License 1.0
Concordia, Canada	GitHub	16; API and CSV	Library+ institutional partners	CC Attrib. 4.0
Harvard, USA	Dataverse	23; CSV, PDF, API +	IT Department	CC0
Cornell, USA	GitHub	16; CSV, JSON, +	Engineering student volunteers	Unknown
Oxford, UK	Local database	4; RDF + multiple	IT Services	CC-by-SA-2.0
Southampton, UK	In-house systems	47 RDF + multiple	IT Services	UK Open Government License

datasets, including data on open positions, on course offerings and a geospatial dataset. The data are available through the Creative Commons BY-SA 2.0 license. This data store has been offered as a beta service since 2012, and given the limited number of datasets, it seems to be more of a proof of concept than a fully functional open data initiative.

5 Discussion and Conclusions

Based on the six case studies presented above, the overarching goal of open data initiatives in higher education seems to focus on making data more easily accessible to members of the campus community and to improve planning and decision making. At the same time, while some universities have chosen to shape their open data initiatives towards a more economic direction (targeted to app developers), other universities are more focused on data transparency.

With respect to limitations, there appears to be little order or consistency in the data offered. Some portals have data and services; some contain only the data. What is rather surprising is that most appear almost random in terms of the datasets included – this speaks to the challenge of pulling together data from many masters. Some datasets are shared, but not actually "open" in the sense that they are in PDF, which is not machine-readable.

Open data is increasingly provided by governments, but is a relatively new concept in higher education. Overall, open data initiatives in post-secondary institutions seem to be at an experimental stage, in which little systematic work has been done. Potential reasons for this could include difficulties gathering data from diverse sources and units, the lack of uniform requirements or guiding frameworks for open data in higher education, and lack of expertise and resources to handle the sharing of private or insensitive information.

Appendix

List of universities included in the environmental scan

Canada	USA	UK
Carlton University	Columbia University	Cambridge University
Concordia University	Cornell University	Edinburgh University
Dalhousie University	Duke University	Imperial College
McGill University	Harvard University	Manchester University
McMaster University	Princeton University	Oxford University
Queen's University	Rice University	University College London
University of Alberta	Stanford University	University of Southampton
University of British Columbia	University of Chicago	
University of Calgary	University of Pennsylvania	**Australia**
University of Manitoba	Yale University	University of Sydney
University of Ottawa		University of Melbourne
University of Saskatchewan		Australian National
University of Toronto		University
University of Waterloo		

References

1. Attard, J., Orlandi, F., Scerri, S., Auer, S.: A systematic review of open government data initiatives. Gov. Inf. Q. **32**, 399–418 (2015)
2. Open Data 101, December 2017. https://open.canada.ca/en/open-data-principles. Accessed 2 July 2019
3. Open Data Movement Reaches Turning Point, May 2016. https://gijn.org/2016/05/13/open-data-movement-reaches-turning-point/. Accessed 2 July 2019
4. 'Open data': Why it's making waves across Canada, May 2016. http://www.cbc.ca/news/technology/open-data-movement-canada-1.3557562. Accessed 2 July 2019
5. Borgman, C.: Open data, grey data, and stewardship: universities at the privacy frontier. Berkeley Technol. Law J. **33**(2), 365–412 (2018). https://doi.org/10.15779/Z38B56D489
6. Krumova, M.: Higher education 2.0 and open data: a framework for university openness and co-creation performance. In: ICEGOV, pp. 562–563 (2017)
7. Atenas, J., Havemann, L. (eds.): Open Data as Open Educational Resources: Case Studies of Emerging Practice. Open Knowledge, Open Education Working Group, London (2015). http://dx.doi.org/10.6084/m9.figshare.1590031
8. Ubaldi, B.: OGD: toward empirical analysis of OGD initiatives. OECD Working Papers on Public Governance, 22 (2013). https://doi.org/10.1787/5k46bj4f03s7-en

9. Sieber, R., Johnson, P.: Civic open data at a crossroads: dominant models and current challenges. Gov. Inf. Q. **32**(3), 308–315 (2015). https://doi.org/10.1016/j.giq.2015.05.003

10. Keßler, C., Kauppinen, T.: Linked open data university of Münster – infrastructure and applications. In: Simperl, E., et al. (eds.) ESWC 2012. LNCS, vol. 7540, pp. 447–451. Springer, Heidelberg (2015). https://doi.org/10.1007/978-3-662-46641-4_43

11. Verhoef, L.A., et al.: Towards a learning system for university campuses as living labs for sustainability. In: Leal Filho, W., et al. (eds.) Universities as Living Labs for Sustainable Development. WSS, pp. 135–149. Springer, Cham (2020). https://doi.org/10.1007/978-3-030-15604-6_9

Scientometrics

A Comparative Study on the Classification Performance of Machine Learning Models for Academic Full Texts

Haotian Hu[1] , Sanhong Deng[1] , Haoxiang Lu[2] ,
and Dongbo Wang[2,3]

[1] Nanjing University, Nanjing 210023, People's Republic of China
[2] Nanjing Agricultural University, Nanjing 210095, People's Republic of China
db.wang@njau.edu.cn
[3] KU Leuven, Leuven, Belgium

Abstract. [Objectives] The study aims to compare the classification performance of various machine learning models, explore the classification effects of traditional machine learning models and deep learning models, solve the problem of missing category information of chapter structure in academic literature, promote the retrieval of the content of the specified chapter structure in the academic literature, and automatically extract and customize the formation of specific text services. [Methodology] 31,888 academic articles in the journal "PLOS ONE" were selected. After data cleaning and segmentation, a text classification corpus containing 313,952 chapter structure category information was constructed. Based on traditional machine learning models NB, SVM, CRF, and the deep learning model RNN model group, Bi-LSTM model group, IDCNN model group, BERT model group, a total of 17 machine learning models were used to carry out chapter structure division experiment. [Results] Among the classification tasks, the BERT-Bi-LSTM-CRF model has the best classification performance, with an average F value of 71.18%, which is 0.51% and 3.31% higher than the second CRF and the third Bi-LSTM-CRF, respectively. For deep learning models, the use of BERT for text representation is better than word2vec. Adding the Attention mechanism and replacing the Softmax layer with the CRF layer can achieve better classification results. In addition, the online version of the Chapter Structure Recognition Presentation and Application Platform has been developed, which can visually display the overall situation of the research and the model training process, and can realize machine learning and deep learning models such as NB, SVM, CRF, Bi-LSTM, IDCNN. The models can perform online recognition application of chapter structure.

Keywords: Machine learning · Deep learning · BERT · Chapter structure · Classification

© Springer Nature Switzerland AG 2020
A. Sundqvist et al. (Eds.): iConference 2020, LNCS 12051, pp. 713–737, 2020.
https://doi.org/10.1007/978-3-030-43687-2_61

1 Introduction

The chapter structure of academic texts is a generalization of the structure and chapter functions of academic literature. English academic texts usually include five types of constituent elements, namely "Introduction", "Method", "Result", "Discussion" and "Conclusion".

At present, in the process of carrying out academic research, researchers often face the following three problems:

1. In the process of academic literature retrieval, almost all electronic journal databases only provide the retrieval approach for the whole article; that is to say, it is not possible to conduct a separate search for chapter structures such as "purpose", "method", etc. in the paper.
2. When conducting relevant research verification and analysis, most researchers adopt the traditional method of manually consulting papers to select literatures, that is, to obtain the required information by downloading the whole paper. If there is only the need to obtain the information of a specific structure function in the literature, the required functional structure needs to be extracted from the whole article manually; the structure function of the literature cannot be broken up automatically and customized push of specific chapter structure cannot be achieved.
3. For some older literatures, paragraph structure information may be lost in the process of digital extraction of paper literatures. In some cases, due to limitations, either incomplete text sections can be obtained, or chapter headings are lost. It is difficult for researchers to identify manually the category of chapter structure, which hinders subsequent research.

Therefore, this paper selects the PLOS ONE corpus to carry out the automatic classification of the chapter structure of academic papers. It sets to classify chapter and paragraph of academic literature by machine learning classification algorithm, hoping to solve the above problems. It also aims to realize the automatic recognition of the chapter structure type of academic literature, and promote the retrieval of specific chapter structure, and customized push services of chapter structures.

Common traditional Machine Learning classification methods include Naïve Bayes, Support Vector Machine, k Nearest Neighbor, and so on. At present, deep learning technology has been widely used in the field of text classification. The following are some major researches. Cao et al. [1] proposed a topical attention-based Bi-LSTM model (LAB-Bi-LSTM), by combining LDA, Attention mechanism and Bi-LSTM, it improved the F1-score of Web services classification. Ding et al. [2] proposed a Densely Connected Bidirectional LSTM (DC-Bi-LSTM) model, compared with Bi-LSTM, it can get better performance with fewer parameters. Kim [3] used convolutional neural network (CNN) for semantic analysis and topic classification tasks, and achieved good results in evaluating models on different classification data sets. Kalchbrenner et al. [4] introduced a dynamic convolutional neural network method that could be used for English sentence modeling. By means of k-max pooling operation, feature vectors of the whole text could be obtained to get rid of the dependence of decision tree method. A good text classification effect has been achieved in the evaluation of problem classification in the English language. Xian-yan et al. [5] proposed a multilingual text categorization model T-BLSTM-CNN, which use LDA and Bi-LSTM-CNN to gain both semantic and local features, thus obtaining a significant improvement on Chinese, English and Korean parallel datasets. Lai et al. [6] proposed the text classification model of circular convolutional neural network, which classified the text sets of 20 Newsgroups and Fudan database, and found that the text classification model of circular convolutional neural network could better obtain context information and achieve better effects than other models.

In this paper, large-scale experiments were carried out from the perspective of automatic classification of machine learning to compare the performance of traditional machine learning models with that of deep learning models in chapter structure classification in PLOS ONE corpus, so as to find the optimal model for effect and build a platform for chapter structure recognition, presentation and application. Therefore, this paper compared traditional machine learning algorithms, i.e. NB (Naive Bayes), SVM (Support Vector Machine) and CRF (Conditional Random Field), with deep learning models, i.e. RNN (Recurrent Neural Network), Bi-LSTM (Bidirectional Long Short-Term Memory), IDCNN (Iterated Dilated Convolutional Neural Network) and BERT (Bidirectional Encoder Representation from Transformers), in terms of their performance in chapter structure classification in the PLOS ONE corpus.

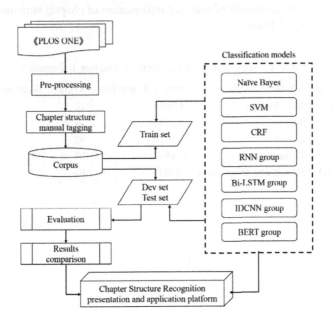

Fig. 1. The overall flow chart of this paper

The overall process of this paper is shown in Fig. 1, and the subsequent sections are arranged as follows: Sect. 2 introduces the data source and corpus preprocessing process. Section 3 briefly introduces the basic principles of machine learning and deep learning models used in experiments. In Sect. 4, the classification experiments of each machine learning model are carried out in PLOS ONE corpus, and the performances of different classification models are compared. The Sect. 5 introduces the web chapter structure recognition and application platform from the aspects of function introduction and application method. Finally, Sect. 6 summarizes this paper and points out further research direction.

2   Data Source and Corpus Preprocessing

The data source used in this paper is the full text data of 31,888 journal papers published in Public Library of Science One (PLOS ONE) from 2006 to 2013. The Bibliometric Analysis of this corpus was conducted by Python programming. Finally, 5 chapter structures such as "Introduction", "Method", "Result", "Discussion" and "Result and Discussion" were selected for classification experiments. In order to obtain a more accurate experimental result on the real PLOS ONE data, the "Result and Discussion" category is kept. Finally, we build a corpus containing 313,952 texts to be classified. The statistical results of relevant information of chapter structures are shown in Table 1 and Fig. 2 below:

Table 1. Statistical results of chapter structure information

No.	Tags	Chapter structures	Paragraph numbers	Average Word numbers
1	I	Introduction	67298	28
2	M	Method	88844	26
3	R	Result	33916	30
4	D	Discussion	113889	30
5	RD	Result and Discussion	10005	30

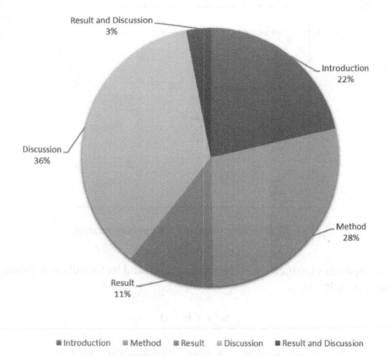

Fig. 2. Proportion of each chapter structure

3 Machine Learning and Deep Learning Model

3.1 Traditional Machine Learning Model

NB. Set the text set to be classified as $X = \{x_1, x_2, \ldots, x_i, \ldots, x_n\}$, set the text set $C = \{c_1, c_2, \ldots, c_i, \ldots, c_n\}$ as the category set of the text to be classified, and then Naïve Bayes classifier can be calculated by the following formulae:

$$P(c_i|x_k) = \frac{P(x_k|c_i)P(c_i)}{\sum_{j=1}^{m} P(x_k|c_j)P(c_j)} \tag{1}$$

$$F(x_k) = \arg\max P(c_i|x_k) \tag{2}$$

$$P(x_k|c_i) = \prod_{i=1}^{n} P(\omega_{kj}|c_i) \tag{3}$$

SVM. Support Vector Machine [7] can well solve nonlinear and high-dimensional data classification problems. The schematic diagram of SVM classification is shown in Fig. 3 below.

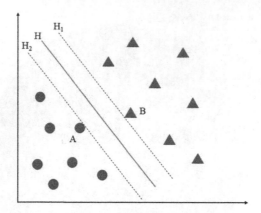

Fig. 3. Schematic diagram of SVM classification

H is the optimal classification Hyperplane sought, and its formula is expressed as the following Formula (4).

$$w^T x + b = 0 \tag{4}$$

CRF. Conditional Random Field is a kind of probabilistic undirected graph model used to solve the Sequence Tagging problem. The basic structure of the CRF model is shown in Fig. 4.

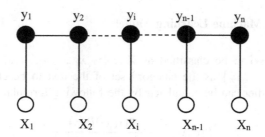

Fig. 4. Basic structure of CRF model

Let $x = \{x_1, x_2, \ldots, x_i, \ldots, x_n\}$ represent the observed input sequence and $y = \{y_1, y_2, \ldots, y_i, \ldots, y_n\}$ represent the output marker sequence. The conditional probability of the output labeled sequence y is calculated by Formulas (5) and (6):

$$p(y|x, \lambda) = \frac{1}{Z_x} \exp\left(\sum_{i=1}^n \sum_j \lambda_j f_j(y_{i-1}, y_i, x, i)\right) \tag{5}$$

$$Z_x = \sum_y \exp\left(\sum_{i=1}^n \sum_j \lambda_j f_j(y_{i-1}, y_i, x, i)\right) \tag{6}$$

3.2 Deep Learning Model

RNN. Recurrent neural network [8] is a neural network which is used to solve Sequence Tagging problems. At time t, the calculation formula of RNN hidden layer and output layer is:

$$h_t = f(Ux_t + Wh_{t-1}) \tag{7}$$

$$y_t = g(Vh_t) \tag{8}$$

Attention-Based Model. For input sequences, RNN treats each term equally. The addition of Attention [9, 10] allows the model to give greater weight to words that contribute more. For the output vector sequence of the previous hidden layer $\{v_1, v_2, \ldots, v_i, \ldots, v_n\}$, a_i^t is the Attention weight of the vector i at time t, then the input vector sequence c^t of the next hidden layer can be calculated by Formula (9):

$$c^t = \sum_{i=1}^{n} a_i^t v_i \tag{9}$$

RNN with Attention mechanism is called RNN-Attention model, which can pay more attention to words containing category information in the process of feature learning, so as to improve classification performance.

RNN-CRF. Replacing the Softmax layer with a linear CRF layer can make the original independent tag output be converted into the best tag sequence output, thus obtaining the RNN-CRF neural network model. The formula of calculating sequence label is as follows:

$$s(X, y) = \sum_{i=0}^{n} A_{y_i, y_{i+1}} + \sum_{i=1}^{n} P_{i, y_i} \tag{10}$$

In addition, by combining the Attention mechanism and the CRF layer, the RNN-CRF-Attention model can be obtained. Theoretically speaking, it has the advantages of both the RNN-Attention model and the RNN-CRF model.

Bi-LSTM. By introducing LSTM cell and three kinds of gate controllers, Long Short-Term Memory network (LSTM) solves the problem that RNN is liable to cause the phenomena of vanishing gradients and exploding gradients. The calculation formula of LSTM cell is as follows:

$$i_t = \sigma(W_i h_{t-1} + U_i x_t + b_i) \tag{11}$$

$$f_t = \sigma(W_f h_{t-1} + U_f x_t + b_f) \tag{12}$$

$$o_t = \sigma(W_o h_{t-1} + U_o x_t + b_o) \tag{13}$$

$$c_t = f_t \odot c_{t-1} + i_t \odot \tanh(W_c h_{t-1} + U_c x_t + b_c) \tag{14}$$

$$h_t = o_t \odot \tanh(c_t) \tag{15}$$

Bi-LSTM model is a bidirectional LSTM neural network with two parallel LSTM layers in opposite directions. At last, the probability of category label is predicted by Softmax classifier. Figure 5 is the structure diagram of Bi-LSTM model used for corpus classification in PLOS ONE.

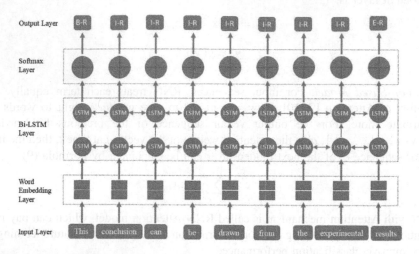

Fig. 5. The main architecture of the Bi-LSTM model

Bi-LSTM-CRF. The Bi-LSTM-CRF [11, 12] model uses the CRF linear layer instead of the Softmax layer to predict the label, so that it can not only consider the context information at the same time, but also calculate the joint conditional probability distribution of the entire state tag.

By the same token, the Bi-LSTM-Attention model [13] can be obtained by introducing the Attention mechanism. The Bi-LSTM-CRF-Attention model can be obtained by combining the CRF layer with the above model.

IDCNN. Iterated Dilated CNN (IDCNN) was proposed by Strubell et al. [14]. Compared with CNN, overfitting is prevented by sharing parameters and repeatedly iterating a series of dilated convolution layers. The following formulae express IDCNN model structure:

$$i_t = D_1^{(0)} x_t \tag{16}$$

$$c_t^{(j)} = r\left(D_{2^{L_c-1}}^{(j-1)} c_t^{(j-1)}\right) \tag{17}$$

$$c_t^{(L_c+1)} = r\left(D_1^{(L_c)} c_t^{(L_c)}\right) \tag{18}$$

$$b_t^{(k)} = B\left(b_t^{(k-1)}\right) \tag{19}$$

$$h_t^{(L_b)} = W_o b_t^{(L_b)} \tag{20}$$

Figure 6 is the IDCNN model structure used for the division of chapter structure in PLOS ONE. Embedded vector sequences are input into IDCNN layers for dilated convolution computing. Subsequently, the Softmax layer predicts the category label with the highest probability.

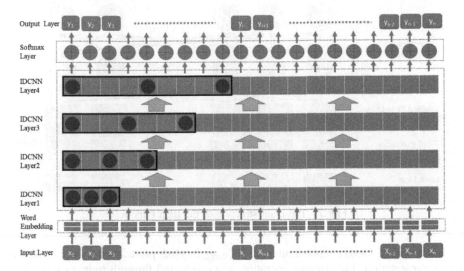

Fig. 6. The main structure of the IDCNN model

IDCNN-CRF. Replace the Softmax layer of IDCNN model with the CRF layer to get the IDCNN-CRF model. Compared with IDCNN model, its advantage is that when predicting output labels, the CRF layer can consider the transition probability of the current state and the previous state at the same time, thus obtaining better tagging accuracy for data with strong context dependency.

BERT. BERT [15] (Bidirectional Encoder Representation from Transformers) is proposed by Google in 2018 for language representation. Through the MLM (Masked Language Model) method, a bidirectional language representation model with bidirectional semantic information is finally obtained. The BERT model structure used in this study is shown in Fig. 7 below:

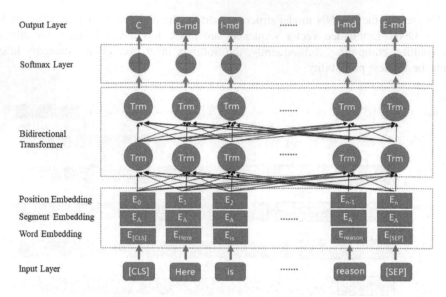

Fig. 7. The main structure of the BERT model

In this paper, Google open source BERT$_{BASE}$ English pre-trained model is used for text representation. Fine-tuning operation was conducted through training to continuously optimize and adjust initial parameters, and finally to output category labels through Softmax.

BERT-Bi-LSTM-CRF. The Softmax layer in BERT is on top of the transformer structure, by replacing it with Bi-LSTM-CRF [11, 12] neural network, the training text embedded with deep text representation can be further extracted and learned with Bi-LSTM-CRF neural network, so that BERT can also consider the contextual association when outputting, and output the class tag by calculating the joint probability.

4 Classification Experiment Based on Machine Learning Model

Based on 31,888 academic articles in PLOS ONE corpus, this paper constructs a corpus containing 313,952 texts to be classified. According to the ratio of 9:1, the data set is divided into train set and dev set, and dev set is taken as a test set to test the performance of the model. Each model uses a five-fold cross-validation approach.

4.1 Classification Performance Evaluation Indicators

In this paper, the evaluation of the performance of the automatic partition model of the chapter structure function of PLOS ONE is measured by three factors: Precision, Recall and F-value. The overall performance of the models is judged by Micro-P, Micro-R and Micro-F. The specific calculation formulae are as follows:

$$P = \frac{TP}{TP + FP} * 100\% \qquad (21)$$

$$R = \frac{TP}{TP + FN} * 100\% \qquad (22)$$

$$F = \frac{2 * P * R}{P + R} * 100\% \qquad (23)$$

$$Micro\_P = \frac{\sum_{c \subset C} TP_c}{\sum_{c \subset C} TP_c + \sum_{c \subset C} FP_c} \qquad (24)$$

$$Micro\_R = \frac{\sum_{c \subset C} TP_c}{\sum_{c \subset C} TP_c + \sum_{c \subset C} FN_c} \qquad (25)$$

$$Micro\_F = \frac{2 * Micro\_P * Micro\_R}{Micro\_P + Micro\_R} \qquad (26)$$

For each category, TP indicates the number of chapter structures correctly classified, FP indicates the number of chapter structures belonging to the category that are incorrectly classified, and FN indicates the number of chapter structures belonging to the category that are misclassified into other categories. When calculating the overall classification performance of Micro-P, Micro-R, and Micro-F, C indicates all categories. The above six evaluation indicators are calculated using the open source evaluation tool conlleval.py.

4.2 Model Parameter and Hyperparameter Settings

Through exploratory experiments, the best parameters of each model are identified. Parameters of traditional machine learning model are set as follows: for both NB model and SVM model, vector space model (VSM) is used to represent the text as the document-word matrix of n * 500, where n is the total text number and 500 is the vector dimension. TF-IDF algorithm was used to extract the feature word set of various types, and the term frequency (TF) and TF-IDF values were used to construct the feature vector respectively.

The hyperparameters of the deep learning model are set as follows: For RNN group and Bi-LSTM group, the number of hidden units of each hidden layer is set to 100, the batch size is 64, the dropout rate of hidden units is 0.5, the learning rate is 0.001, the epochs is 100, and the clip is 5. Word embedding is done through word2vec, and the vector dimension is 100 dimensions. For IDCNN group, the number of convolution layers is 100, and the setting of other hyperparameters is the same as that of RNN group and Bi-LSTM group. For BERT group, the Max seq length is set to 128, the batch sizes for training, verification and testing are 32; the learning rate is 5e–5; warmup proportion is 0.1; and epochs is 50. For the BERT-Bi-LSTM-CRF model, clip is 5, hidden unit is 2048, and epochs is 50.

4.3   Chapter Structure Division Experiment

The computer configuration used in this experiment is as follows: CPU: Intel(R) Xeon(R) CPU E5-2650 v4 @ 2.20 GHz; Memory: 256 GB; GPU: NVIDIA® Tesla® P40 Memory: 24 GB; Operating System: CentOS 3.10. 0.

NB. The NB-based chapter structure partitioning experiment was performed using the naive_bayes tool encapsulated by the scikit-learn toolkit. After the previous experiments, this paper selects the BernoulliNB method which has the best classification effect. The classification results of constructing feature vectors by word frequency (TF) and term frequency-inverse document frequency (TF-IDF) are compared, as shown in Table 2 and Fig. 8.

Table 2. Comparison of NB classification results of constructing feature vectors with TF and TF-IDF

No.	Naïve Bayes (TF)			Naïve Bayes (TF-IDF)		
	Precision	Recall	F-value	Precision	Recall	F-value
1	64.53%	64.53%	64.53%	64.16%	64.16%	64.16%
2	64.57%	64.57%	64.57%	64.35%	64.35%	64.35%
3	64.01%	64.01%	64.01%	64.27%	64.27%	64.27%
4	64.69%	64.69%	64.69%	64.04%	64.04%	64.04%
5	63.98%	63.98%	63.98%	64.39%	64.39%	64.39%
Average	64.36%	64.36%	64.36%	64.24%	64.24%	64.24%

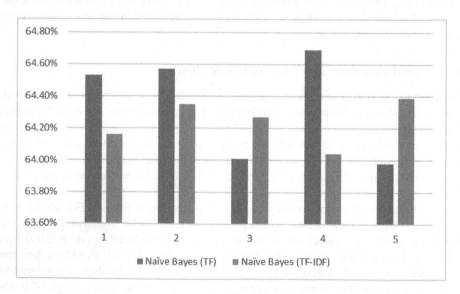

Fig. 8. NB classification five-fold cross-validation F-value comparison

The maximum and minimum F-values of NB classification model using TF as the feature vector differ by 0.59%, and the average F-value is 64.36%. The NB classification model with TF-IDF as the feature vector has an average F-value of 64.24%, and the difference between the highest and lowest F-value is 0.65%. The classification performance of Naïve Bayes (TF) model was slightly better than that of Naïve Bayes (TF-IDF) model, and the fluctuation range of F-value in each experiment was also relatively small, suggesting that NB model constructed with TF had a better classification effect and higher robustness.

SVM. This section uses the svm.LinearSVC tool provided by the scikit-learn toolkit to perform SVM chapter structure partitioning experiments. Similarly, the influences of constructing vector space with TF and TF-IDF on SVM classification performance are compared. The classification results are shown in Table 3 and Fig. 9.

Table 3. Comparison of SVM classification results of constructing feature vectors with TF and TF-IDF

No.	SVM (TF)			SVM (TF-IDF)		
	Precision	Recall	F-value	Precision	Recall	F-value
1	62.53%	62.53%	62.53%	63.42%	63.42%	63.42%
2	63.38%	63.38%	63.38%	63.56%	63.56%	63.56%
3	62.56%	62.56%	62.56%	63.12%	63.12%	63.12%
4	62.91%	62.91%	62.91%	63.48%	63.48%	63.48%
5	62.69%	62.69%	62.69%	63.05%	63.05%	63.05%
Average	62.81%	62.81%	62.81%	63.33%	63.33%	63.33%

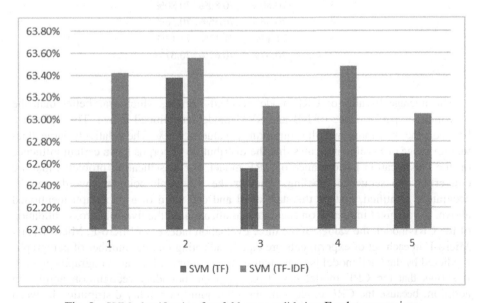

Fig. 9. SVM classification five-fold cross-validation F-value comparison

The average F-value of SVM (TF) is 0.52% lower than that of SVM (TF-IDF), indicating that for SVM models, better classification results can be obtained by using TF-IDF values to construct feature vector spaces. In addition, we noticed that in the overall classification performance evaluation index based on the NB model and SVM model, the Precision, Recall and F-values are numerically equal. It is found by further calculation that the value is equal to the Accuracy of the model. This is because when the Micro Average is calculated, the categories are not distinguished, and the number of labels with the correct classification and the wrong classification is directly counted as a whole. Considering that the overall performance of each model is evaluated according to this standard, and that the micro-average result is not easily affected by individual categories, it is more suitable to be used as the evaluation index of the overall performance of the model.

CRF. For the CRF model, this paper transforms the nonlinear classification problem into a linear sequence labeling problem, and converts the smallest units from paragraphs to words. For the original five categories, five sets of a total of fifteen tag sets {I-B, I-I, I-E, M-B, M-I, M-E, R-B, R-I, R-E, D-B, D-I, D-E, RD-B, RD-I, RD-E} are defined. The following RNN group, Bi-LSTM group, IDCNN group, and BERT group are also trained in a similar way. Table 4 shows the classification result of the chapter structure of the CRF model.

Table 4. CRF classification results

No.	Precision	Recall	F-value
1	69.60%	69.60%	69.60%
2	71.20%	71.20%	71.20%
3	70.80%	70.80%	70.80%
4	70.56%	70.56%	70.56%
5	71.17%	71.17%	71.17%
Average	70.67%	70.67%	70.67%

The average F-value of CRF model reached 70.67%, which was better than the classification performance of NB and SVM models mentioned above. The difference between the maximum and the minimum F-value is 1.6%. The relatively large fluctuation range of F-value indicates that the distribution of corpus has a certain influence on the classification performance of CRF model. For classification problems that are converted into sequence labeling, whether the paragraph boundary words can be accurately identified, that is, the start word and end word of a paragraph mentioned above, have a great influence on accurate classification. In the five-fold cross-validation of the CRF model, the values of the three evaluation indexes of Micro-P, Micro-R, and Micro-F in each set of experiments are equal, indicating that the number of paragraphs predicted by the CRF model is consistent with the number of actual paragraphs present. It shows that the CRF model has strong segment boundary recognition ability. In addition, because the CRF model calculates the joint probability distribution between the current state and the previous state when predicting tags, this ensures that the category tags of words in the same paragraph must be consistent when tagging them. It also ensures that the number of predicted paragraphs is equal to the actual situation.

RNN. Table 5 and Fig. 10 show the experimental results of chapter structure division based on RNN, RNN-CRF, RNN-Attention and RNN-CRF-Attention.

From the average F-values of the four neural network models, it can be concluded that their chapter structure classification performance from high to low is: RNN-CRF-Attention > RNN-CRF > RNN-Attention > RNN. Compared with the RNN model, the addition of the Attention mechanism increases the F-value by 6.98%. This indicates that the Attention mechanism does make the RNN model pay more attention to the words that can reflect the category information during the training process, and targeted to enhance the feature learning of texts containing category information, thereby improving the accuracy of the classification. The recall of the RNN-CRF model is 62.37%, which is the highest value of the four models. The recall is 10.86% higher than that of the RNN model and 4.10% higher than the that of the RNN-Attention model, indicating the effect of using the CRF layer in category prediction is better than that of using the Softmax layer in label probability prediction. To the RNN-CRF-Attention model are simultaneously added both the Attention mechanism and the CRF layer. It is not only the best classification model among the four models, but also compared with the RNN model, its accuracy, recall and F-values are increased by 11.31%, 10.06% and 10.45% respectively. This fully demonstrates the superiority of the Attention mechanism and CRF layer in probability calculation.

Table 5. Comparison of RNN group classification results

Models	No.	Precision	Recall	F-value
RNN	1	44.69%	56.12%	49.76%
	2	50.06%	47.67%	48.84%
	3	51.89%	51.47%	51.68%
	4	45.97%	50.70%	48.22%
	5	52.67%	51.59%	52.13%
	Average	49.06%	51.51%	**50.13%**
RNN-CRF	1	51.78%	64.09%	57.28%
	2	53.65%	62.26%	57.64%
	3	53.59%	64.66%	58.61%
	4	57.44%	58.36%	57.90%
	5	53.38%	62.50%	57.58%
	Average	53.97%	62.37%	57.80%
RNN-Attention	1	56.98%	57.68%	57.33%
	2	55.84%	62.04%	58.78%
	3	57.01%	59.50%	58.23%
	4	54.45%	53.46%	53.95%
	5	55.97%	58.65%	57.28%
	Average	56.05%	58.27%	57.11%

(continued)

Table 5. (*continued*)

Models	No.	Precision	Recall	F-value
RNN-CRF-Attention	1	61.21%	59.71%	60.45%
	2	61.74%	59.16%	60.42%
	3	63.78%	52.43%	57.55%
	4	59.90%	63.13%	61.47%
	5	55.21%	73.41%	63.02%
	Average	60.37%	61.57%	**60.58%**

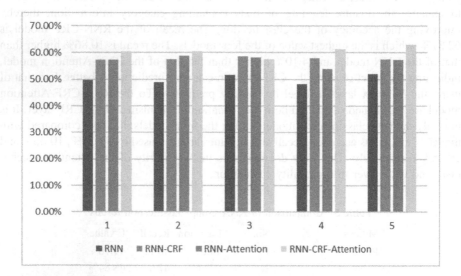

Fig. 10. Comparison of RNN group classification five-fold cross-validation F-values

Bi-LSTM. Table 6 and Fig. 11 summarize the classification performance of the four models in the Bi-LSTM group in the experiment of chapter structure division.

Table 6. Comparison of Bi-LSTM group classification effects

Models	No.	Precision	Recall	F-value
Bi-LSTM	1	20.88%	46.87%	28.89%
	2	30.96%	60.32%	40.92%
	3	47.54%	63.72%	54.46%
	4	38.30%	60.15%	46.80%
	5	20.76%	47.87%	28.96%
	Average	31.69%	55.79%	**40.01%**

(*continued*)

Table 6. (*continued*)

Models	No.	Precision	Recall	F-value
Bi-LSTM-CRF	1	68.98%	68.98%	68.98%
	2	67.98%	68.01%	67.99%
	3	67.85%	67.88%	67.87%
	4	67.00%	67.00%	67.00%
	5	67.51%	67.51%	67.51%
Bi-LSTM-Attention	1	57.86%	59.18%	58.52%
	2	55.38%	68.44%	61.22%
	3	59.87%	59.82%	59.84%
	4	59.04%	65.94%	62.30%
	5	64.54%	51.83%	57.49%
	Average	59.34%	61.04%	59.87%
Bi-LSTM-CRF-Attention	1	68.37%	55.02%	60.97%
	2	58.99%	69.32%	63.74%
	3	65.51%	62.30%	63.86%
	4	60.14%	68.06%	63.86%
	5	63.71%	62.89%	63.30%
	Average	63.34%	63.52%	63.15%

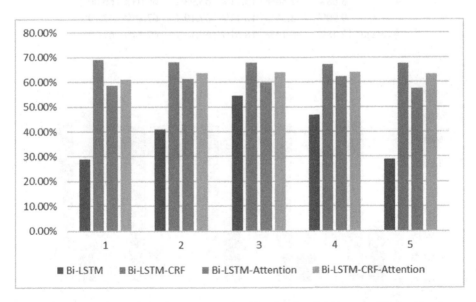

Fig. 11. Comparison of Bi-LSTM group classification five-fold cross-validation F-values

It can be seen from Table 6 that the order of the F-value from high to low in chapter structure division is as follows: Bi-LSTM-CRF > Bi-LSTM-CRF-Attention > Bi-LSTM-Attention > Bi-LSTM. The precision, recall, and F-value of the Bi-LSTM-CRF model are 36.17%, 12.09%, and 27.86% higher than those of the Bi-LSTM model, respectively, which again shows that using the CRF layer instead of the Softmax layer for the probabilistic prediction of classification labels can yield more accurate results. Different from the RNN model group, the classification performance of the Bi-LSTM-CRF-Attention model is higher than that of the Bi-LSTM model, but lower than that of the Bi-LSTM-CRF model. This indicates that the Attention mechanism for the Bi-LSTM model can improve the model's feature learning of related vocabulary, but the learned features are not conducive to the final CRF layer for category prediction, which affects the CRF layer's judgment on the category output to some extent.

IDCNN. The five-fold cross-validation results of the chapter structure division based on the IDNN model and the IDCNN-CRF model are shown in Table 7 and Fig. 12 below.

Table 7. Comparison of IDCNN group classification results

No.	IDCNN			IDCNN-CRF		
	Precision	Recall	F-value	Precision	Recall	F-value
1	16.79%	39.55%	23.57%	68.32%	68.32%	68.32%
2	7.14%	30.06%	11.53%	66.96%	66.97%	66.97%
3	19.89%	45.06%	27.59%	67.19%	67.19%	67.19%
4	8.68%	32.54%	13.71%	65.98%	66.03%	66.00%
5	9.90%	43.56%	16.14%	67.19%	67.19%	67.19%
Average	12.48%	38.15%	18.51%	67.13%	67.14%	67.13%

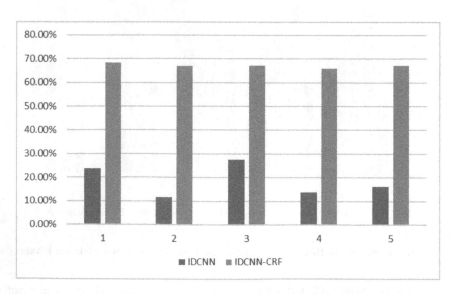

Fig. 12. Comparison of IDCNN group classification five-fold cross-validation F-values

From Table 7, it can be held that the IDCNN model is almost impossible to carry out the task of dividing the chapter structure. However, the accuracy, recall and F-value of the IDCNN-CRF model have reached more than 60%, and the F-value is even 48.62% higher than that of IDCNN. This shows that for the IDCNN model, when performing text categorization tasks with strong contextual relevance, its ability to extract contextual and implicit semantic features is insufficient. It is necessary for the model to use the CRF layer to jointly consider the context feature to obtain a better classification performance.

BERT. Table 8 and Fig. 13 show the experimental results of the BERT and BERT-Bi-LSTM-CRF models in the chapter structure division task.

Table 8. Comparison of BERT group classification results

No.	BERT			BERT-Bi-LSTM-CRF		
	Precision	Recall	F-value	Precision	Recall	F-value
1	61.49%	63.82%	62.63%	70.83%	71.91%	71.37%
2	61.52%	62.77%	62.14%	70.85%	71.43%	71.14%
3	59.99%	62.13%	61.05%	70.64%	70.73%	70.69%
4	63.80%	65.16%	64.47%	71.49%	72.10%	71.79%
5	60.70%	63.48%	62.06%	70.91%	71.27%	71.09%
Average	61.50%	63.47%	62.47%	70.97%	71.38%	71.18%

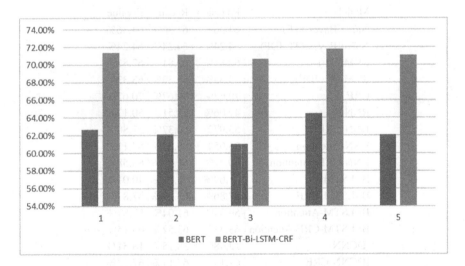

Fig. 13. Comparison of BERT group classification five fold cross-validation F-values

The average F-value of the BERT with Softmax predictive labels is 62.47%, which is higher than the average F-value of RNN group. On the one hand, this indicates that the classification performance of the Transformer architecture is better than that of the

RNN architecture. On the other hand, BERT can embed more context information than word2vec. The average F-value of the BERT-Bi-LSTM-CRF model is 71.18%, which is 3.31% higher than that of the Bi-LSTM-CRF model. This shows that using BERT for text representation can learn more deep semantic features than word2vec, which demonstrates the powerful feature learning capabilities of the two-way Transformer. The average F-value of the BERT-Bi-LSTM-CRF model is 8.71% higher than that of the BERT, indicating that the deep text representation by BERT pre-training model is not enough to complete the chapter structure division task for PLOS ONE. It is necessary to further learn the inter-word relationship, context information and category features of the corpus by means of neural networks such as Bi-LSTM-CRF.

Comparison of Classification Performances of Machine Learning Models. Table 9 and Fig. 14 show the classification performances of the 17 traditional machine learning models and deep learning models in chapter structure division tasks in this paper.

For the traditional machine learning models, the CRF model has the best classification performance, and the SVM (TF) model has the worst classification performance. As regards the deep learning models, BERT-Bi-LSTM-CRF has the best classification effect, and IDCNN has the worst effect. After comprehensive comparison, the 17 classification models are ranked according to their classification performances from high to low. The top three are: BERT-Bi-LSTM-CRF > CRF > Bi-LSTM-CRF, and the bottom three are RNN > Bi-LSTM > IDCNN.

Table 9. Comparison of classification performances of machine learning models

Models	Precision	Recall	F-value
Naïve Bayes (TF)	64.36%	64.36%	64.36%
Naïve Bayes (TF-IDF)	64.24%	64.24%	64.24%
SVM (TF)	62.81%	62.81%	62.81%
SVM (TF-IDF)	63.33%	63.33%	63.33%
CRF	70.67%	70.67%	70.67%
RNN	49.06%	51.51%	50.13%
RNN-CRF	53.97%	62.37%	57.80%
RNN-Attention	56.05%	58.27%	57.11%
RNN-CRF-Attention	60.37%	61.57%	60.58%
Bi-LSTM	31.69%	55.79%	40.01%
Bi-LSTM-CRF	67.86%	67.88%	67.87%
Bi-LSTM-Attention	59.34%	61.04%	59.87%
Bi-LSTM-CRF-Attention	63.34%	63.52%	63.15%
IDCNN	12.48%	38.15%	**18.51%**
IDCNN-CRF	67.13%	67.14%	67.13%
BERT	61.50%	63.47%	62.47%
BERT-Bi-LSTM-CRF	70.97%	71.38%	**71.18%**

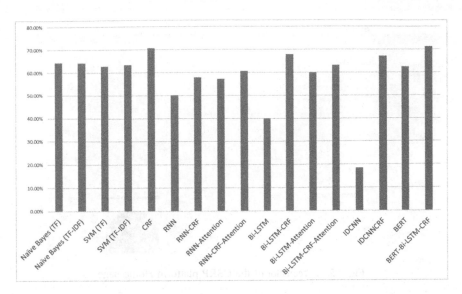

Fig. 14. Comparison of the classification F-values of the machine learning models

5 Chapter Structure Recognition Presentation of Online Version of Academic Literature and Application Platform

In order to display the research content and results more easily and visually, and meanwhile realize the automatic recognition function of the text structure function of academic literature, we developed the chapter structure recognition presentation and application platform, hereinafter referred to as CSRP. The front-end development of the CSRP platform uses HTML, CSS, JavaScript, Bootstrap, Echarts and other web programming languages and tools. The back-end is developed using Python3.5.2, built on Django1.11.5, and Tensorflow1.3.0 is used as the deep learning backend. Figure 15 is a screenshot of the Home page of the CSRP platform.

The CSRP platform includes four pages: Home, Train, Application, and About us. Their functions are as follows: sketch of the overall content of the research (including research purposes, introduction to data, introduction to method and model, model application), online display of model training process, applications of machine learning and deep learning models in automatic identification of online chapter structures, as well as introduction to our research group.

Fig. 15. Screenshot of the CSRP platform Home page

Figure 16 is a screenshot of the Train page of the CSRP platform. This page dynamically demonstrates the training process of the machine learning model through ajax technology. Click the "Start" button, the text box will dynamically load the model training process information, including the setting of the model hyperparameter, the step and loss value of each iteration, the accuracy, precision, recall and the F-value of the model training.

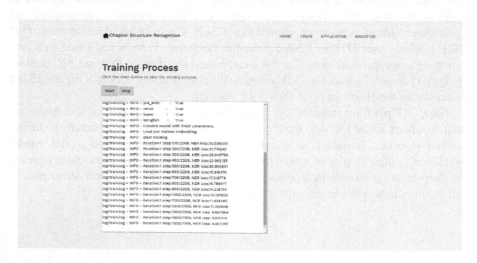

Fig. 16. Screenshot of the TRAIN page of the CSRP platform

Figure 17 is the screenshot of the Application initial page of the CSRP platform. User inputs the text of the academic document paragraph to be recognized in the text box. In the drop-down box of "Choose model", CSRP platform provides three machine learning models such as NB, SVM and CRF, and four deep learning models such as Bi-LSTM, Bi-LSTM-CRF, IDCNN and IDCNN-CRF for users.

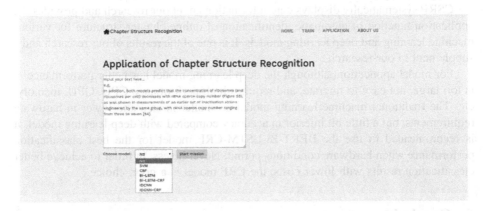

Fig. 17. Screenshot of CSRP platform APPLICATION initial page

After entering the text and selecting the model, click on the "Start mission" button to get the content of Fig. 18 below.

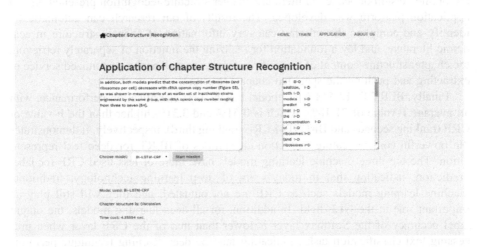

Fig. 18. Screenshot of CSRP platform APPLICATION page calling Bi-LSTM-CRF model for chapter structure online recognition

Figure 18 is a screenshot of the online recognition result of the Application page of the CSRP platform, which is shown here using the Bi-LSTM-CRF model as an example. Compared with the initial interface of Fig. 17, three lines of information appear below the text input box, indicating the model used for chapter structure recognition, the chapter structure category of this text, the time taken for online recognition, respectively. In addition, on the right side of the text input box, a text output box appears, showing the result of the Bi-LSTM-CRF model automatically labeling the chapter structure label on the text at the word level.

CSRP systematically displays core information about our research and provides the application function of automatic identification of online chapter structure for various machine learning and deep learning models. It is one of the results of our research and a supplement to our research.

For model application, although the deep learning model has better performance, it is too large, not easy to migrate, and requires high-performance CPU, GPU, memory, etc. The traditional machine learning model is smaller in size and lower in hardware requirements, but a little bit inferior in accuracy compared with deep learning model. It is recommended to use the BERT-Bi-LSTM-CRF model for the best classification performance when hardware conditions permit. Nevertheless, in order to achieve better classification results with lower costs, the CRF model is a good choice.

6   Conclusion

In this paper, large-scale chapter structure classification experiments of machine learning models were carried out on the corpus of PLOS ONE. The classification performance of 17 types of machine learning models were explored respectively, and the online version of academic literature chapter structure recognition presentation and application platform was developed. The results of our research can automatically identify and complete the missing category information of chapter structure in academic literature, and lay a foundation for realizing the function of separately retrieving the chapter structure content of a specific category, as well as the customized service of extracting and pushing the specified chapter structure.

Finally, BERT-Bi-LSTM-CRF model has the best classification performance, with an average F-value of 71.18%, which is 0.51% and 3.31% higher than the F-value of CRF (ranking second) and Bi-LSTM-CRF (ranking third), respectively. It demonstrates the powerful context feature extraction capabilities of BERT for deep text representation. The top three machine learning models have more or less used CRF for label prediction, indicating that in today's era of deep learning technology, traditional machine learning models such as CRF are not outdated, and they will still play an important role in the NLP field. In addition, for all deep learning models, the output label accuracy of the Softmax layer is lower than that of the CRF layer when processing text classification tasks, indicating that the deep learning technique performs well in deep semantic feature extraction. There is, however, still much space for improvement in the output of predictive labels. In the future, we will explore more classification performance of machine learning models and conduct large-scale classification performance comparison studies on various corpora. What's more, we will select the optimal model, and construct academic literature chapter structure retrieval system and chapter structure customization extraction and pushing system.

References

1. Cao, Y., Liu, J., Cao, B., Shi, M., Wen, Y., Peng, Z.: Web Services classification with topical attention based Bi-LSTM. In: Wang, X., Gao, H., Iqbal, M., Min, G. (eds.) CollaborateCom 2019. LNICST, vol. 292, pp. 394–407. Springer, Cham (2019). https://doi.org/10.1007/978-3-030-30146-0_27

2. Ding, Z., Xia, R., Yu, J., Li, X., Yang, J.: Densely connected bidirectional LSTM with applications to sentence classification. In: Zhang, M., Ng, V., Zhao, D., Li, S., Zan, H. (eds.) NLPCC 2018. LNCS (LNAI), vol. 11109, pp. 278–287. Springer, Cham (2018). https://doi.org/10.1007/978-3-319-99501-4_24

3. Kim, Y.: Convolutional neural networks for sentence classification. arXiv preprint arXiv: 1408.5882 (2014)

4. Kalchbrenner, N., Grefenstette, E., Blunsom, P.: A convolutional neural network for modelling sentences. arXiv preprint arXiv:1404.2188 (2014)

5. Xian-yan, M., Rong-yi, C., Ya-hui, Z., Zhenguo, Z.: Multilingual short text classification based on LDA and BiLSTM-CNN neural network. In: Ni, W., Wang, X., Song, W., Li, Y. (eds.) WISA 2019. LNCS, vol. 11817, pp. 319–323. Springer, Cham (2019). https://doi.org/10.1007/978-3-030-30952-7_32

6. Lai, S., Xu, L., Liu, K., Zhao, J.: Recurrent convolutional neural networks for text classification. In: Proceedings of the Twenty-Ninth AAAI Conference on Artificial Intelligence. AAAI 2015, pp. 2267–2273. AAAI Press (2015)

7. Cortes, C., Vapnik, V.: Support-vector networks. Mach. Learn. **20**(3), 273–297 (1995). https://doi.org/10.1007/BF00994018

8. Pham, T.-H., Le-Hong, P.: End-to-End recurrent neural network models for vietnamese named entity recognition: word-level vs. character-level. In: Hasida, K., Pa, W.P. (eds.) PACLING 2017. CCIS, vol. 781, pp. 219–232. Springer, Singapore (2018). https://doi.org/10.1007/978-981-10-8438-6_18

9. Bahdanau, D., Cho, K., Bengio, Y.: Neural machine translation by jointly learning to align and translate. arXiv preprint arXiv:1409.0473 (2014)

10. Vaswani, A., et al.: Attention is all you need. In: Guyon, I., et al. (eds.) NIPS, pp. 6000–6010 (2017)

11. Lample, G., Ballesteros, M., Subramanian, S., Kawakami, K., Dyer, C.: Neural architectures for named entity recognition. arXiv preprint arXiv:1603.01360 (2016)

12. Huang, Z., Xu, W., Yu, K.: Bidirectional LSTM-CRF models for sequence tagging. arXiv preprint arXiv:1508.01991 (2015)

13. Zhang, K., Ren, W., Zhang, Y.: Attention-based Bi-LSTM for Chinese named entity recognition. In: Hong, J.-F., Su, Q., Wu, J.-S. (eds.) CLSW 2018. LNCS (LNAI), vol. 11173, pp. 643–652. Springer, Cham (2018). https://doi.org/10.1007/978-3-030-04015-4_56

14. Strubell, E., Verga, P., Belanger, D., McCallum, A.: Fast and accurate entity recognition with iterated dilated convolutions. arXiv preprint arXiv:1702.02098 (2017)

15. Devlin, J., Chang, M.W., Lee, K., Toutanova, K.: BERT: pre-training of deep bidirectional transformers for language understanding. arXiv preprint arXiv:1810.04805 (2018)

Ranking-Based Cited Text Identification with Highway Networks

Shiyan Ou[✉] and Hyonil Kim

School of Information Management, Nanjing University, Nanjing, China
oushiyan@nju.edu.cn, univcol001@163.com

Abstract. In recent years, content-based citation analysis (CCA) has attracted great attention, which focuses on citation texts within full-text scientific articles to analyze the meaning of each citation. However, citation texts often lack the appropriate evidence and context from cited papers and are sometimes even inaccurate. Thus it is necessary to identify the corresponding cited text from a cited paper and examine which part of the content of the paper was cited in a citation. In this study, we proposed a novel ranking-based method to identify cited texts. This method contains two stages: similarity-based unsupervised ranking and deep learning-based supervised ranking. A novel listwise ranking model was developed with the use of 36 similarity features and 11 section position features. Firstly, top-5 sentences were selected for each citation text according to a modified Jaccard similarity metric. Then the selected sentences were ranked using the trained listwise ranking model, and top-2 sentences were selected as cited sentences. The experiments showed that the proposed method outperformed other classification-based and voting-based identification methods on the test set of the CL-SciSumm 2017.

Keywords: Content-based citation analysis · Cited text identification · Listwise ranking · Text similarity · Deep learning

1 Introduction

Citations are very important signals to indicate the impact and relations of scientific articles. A citation is often accompanied with a short textual description (named as *citation text*) to explain the author's citation motivation and attitude or mention the related content of a cited work. With the increasing availability of full-text scientific databases and the development of natural language processing techniques, content-based citation analysis (CCA) has obtained great attention in recent years. It focuses on citation texts within full-text scientific articles to analyze why and how a work was cited in a citing paper [1]. However, it is not enough to examine the meaning of a citation only from the side of a citing paper. The citation texts in a citing paper often lack the appropriate evidence and context from cited papers (i.e. reference papers) to justify or complement the citation information, and are sometimes even inaccurate due to the citing authors' misunderstanding or misquoting [2]. Thus, it is necessary to identify the corresponding text (named as *cited text*) that originally describes the

© Springer Nature Switzerland AG 2020
A. Sundqvist et al. (Eds.): iConference 2020, LNCS 12051, pp. 738–750, 2020.
https://doi.org/10.1007/978-3-030-43687-2_62

content mentioned in a citation text from the cited paper and examine which part of the content of the paper was cited in a citation.

As a result, the identification of cited texts has attracted the attention of some scholars in computer science and information science in recent years. Most of previous studies regarded this issue as a binary sentence categorization task, i.e. for a citation text in a citing paper, categorize all the sentences in its reference paper into cited sentences or non-cited sentences. Since 2014, a related competition series, the CL-SciSumm Shared Task, was launched and held once a year to promote relevant research. It focuses on extracting cited texts in terms of the citation sentences in citing papers to comprise a summary for a reference paper, and provides the training and test corpus for the task in each year's competition [3]. In this paper, we proposed a ranking-based method to identify cited texts with the use of a deep learning algorithm— highway network. A listwise ranking model was developed for this task. On the one hand, this method can avoid the data imbalance problem in text categorization; on the other hand, it has more flexibility than categorization-based methods.

2   Related Work

Most of previous studies performed the identification of cited texts at the sentence level and regarded it as a classification problem, i.e. categorizing whether a sentence in a cited paper is the corresponding cited sentence of a citation sentence or not, and thus used some machine learning algorithms like SVM, Random Forest, CNN to train text classifiers. To build the classifiers, various features were explored by researchers. Ma et al. chose Jaccard similarity, cosine similarity and some position information as features, and trained four classifiers including a Decision Tree-based, a Logistic Regression-based and two SVM-based [4]. Finally, they used a weighted voting method to combine the categorization results of the four classifiers and achieved the best performance in the CL-SciSumm 2017 competition. Yeh et al. considered some lexical features, knowledge-based features, corpus-based features, syntactic features, surface features to represent the feature vector of a text and adopted a majority voting method to combine the results of the six classifiers like KNN, Decision Tree, Logistic Regression, Naive Bayes, SVM and Random Forest [5]. They got the F-value of 14.9% by running their system on the corpus of the CL-SciSumm 2016 competition.

There are two main issues in the categorization-based methods: no ranking and class-imbalanced data. On the one hand, it is difficult to clearly divide the sentences in a cited paper into cited sentences and non-cited sentences. In a cited paper there may be quite a few sentences that are related to the citation sentence(s) more or less, and we only intended to identify those that contain more similar content with the citation sentence(s). Thus the cited text identification problem should be regarded as a ranking problem rather than a classification one. On the other hand, since there are only few real cited sentences (usually not more than five) in a target cited paper, the proportion of the negative and positive sample in a corpus is not balanced. Ma et al. used Nearest Neighbor (NN) rule to reduce data imbalance and increased the F_1-score from 11.8% to 12.5% [4].

With respect to the ranking-based cited text identification, a few studies have been done. Pramanick et al. ranked the sentences in a target paper according to the cosine similarity between each of them and the citation sentences and then selected the top five sentences as the cited sentences [6]. However, this unsupervised method did not obtain reasonable performance. Therefore, we proposed a listwise ranking method for identifying cited sentences, which is a supervised method trained by a deep learning mechanism.

3   Methodology

In this study, we deemed that a cited text should contain more similar content with its corresponding citation text, and thus regarded cited text identification as a ranking problem. A ranking-based method was proposed to identify sentence-level cited text (named as *cited sentences*) based on deep learning. This method includes two stages of ranking: a similarity-based unsupervised ranking and a supervised listwise ranking as shown in Fig. 1. In the first stage, we ranked all the sentences in a cited paper (named as *cited-paper sentences*) according to each sentence's similarity with a citation text, and then choose top K sentences as candidate sentences for the second-stage ranking. In the second stage, we trained a listwise ranking model to rank the K candidate sentences, and finally choose top N sentences ($N < K$) as cited sentences.

We used the training data in the CL-SciSumm 2017 corpus to train the listwise ranking model as well as determine the parameter K (i.e. the number of the selected candidate sentences) and N (i.e. the number of the selected cited sentences). The CL-SciSumm 2017 corpus was created by randomly sampling 40 target papers from the ACL Anthology corpus and then selecting some of their citing papers [7]. 30 target papers were used as training data and 10 target papers as test data. Each target paper (i.e. cited paper) is associated with 10 of its citing paper. In a citing paper, each citation text that refers to a target paper was first identified by human coders, which may include one or multiple continuous sentences (named as *citation sentences*). For a citation text in a citing paper, each sentence in the target paper was marked as a cited sentence or not by human coders. In order to simplify word vector space and ensure the robustness of our proposed method, we performed a simple preprocessing for the citation texts in the citing papers and the full texts of the target papers by removing the stopwords with the NLTK library[1].

3.1   Unsupervised Similarity-Based Ranking

In this section, we explored different similarity metrics between two texts to rank all the sentences in a cited paper (i.e. cited-paper sentences) for a given citation text in one of its citing paper, whereas a citation text may contain one or more sentences. Five kinds of similarity metrics were considered as follows.

---

[1] https://www.nltk.org.

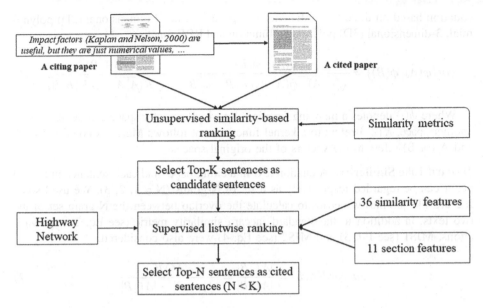

Fig. 1. Two-stage ranking for the identification of cited text.

Cosine Similarity Based on TFIDF Weighted Vector Space Model. In this kind of similarity metrics, N-grams were extracted from a text as its features, and the text was represented as a TFIDF weighted feature vector based on Vector Space Model (VSM). Then the cosine similarity between the feature vectors of the two texts (i.e. citation text and cited text) were calculated. We tested two TFIDF-based cosine similarity metrics: when N = 1 and when N = 2 respectively for N-grams.

Cosine Similarity Based on Word Embedding. In this kind of similarity metrics, a text was represented as a document vector based on word embedding. First, the vector of each word in a text was trained with Word2vec. Then three kinds of document vectors were calculated based on the word vectors using three different weighting mechanisms: TF-weighted average of the word vectors (TF-AWV), TFIDF-weighted average (TFIDF-AWV), and T-statistics-weighted average (Tstat-AWV). Here, TF-AWV and TFIDF-AWV were proposed for citation sentences identification in our previous study [8]; Tstat-AWV is the average value of all the word vectors weighted by each word's T-statistics in a text, whereas the T-statistics of a word refers to the T-test statistics of the hypothesis that whether the word appears in a text or not is independent of whether or not the text is a cited text.

Cosine Similarity Based on SVM Kernel Functions. As we know, a linearly insep-arable sample can become linearly separable by projecting a low-dimensional space to a high-dimensional one. Thus, we considered to transform the TFIDF-weighted average word vector (TFIDF-AWV) to a higher-dimensional space by using three SVM kernel functions, so as to make a text more distinguishable from others. Thus three kinds of kernel function-based cosine similarity metrics were calculated with the following equation based on three kernel functions respectively, i.e. 2-dimensional (2D) polynomial, 3-dimensional (3D) polynomial function and RBF function.

$$cos(\phi(A), \phi(B)) = \frac{\phi(A) \cdot \phi(B)}{\sqrt{\phi(A) \cdot \phi(A)} \cdot \sqrt{\phi(B) \cdot \phi(B)}} = \frac{K(A,B)}{\sqrt{K(A,A)} \cdot \sqrt{K(B,B)}} \quad (1)$$

Where $\phi(\cdot)$ denotes a mapping function, by which a vector space can be mapped to another space, $K(\cdot, \cdot)$ refers to a kernel function that follows Mercer's condition [10], and A (or B) refers to the vectors of the original space.

Jaccard-Like Similarity. A citation text in a citing paper and each sentence in a cited paper can be regarded respectively as a set of N-grams (N = 1, 2, 3). We used some Jaccard-like similarity metrics to calculate the overlap between the N-gram set of the two texts. In addition to the standard Jaccard similarity metric (see Eq. 2), two variations, MJS1 (see Eq. 3) and MJS2 (see Eq. 4) were also considered.

$$Jaccard(A, B) = \frac{|A \cap B|}{|A \cup B|} = \frac{|A \cap B|}{|A| + |B| - |A \cap B|} \quad (2)$$

$$MJS1(A, B) = \frac{|A \cap B|}{|A|} \quad (3)$$

$$MJS2(A, B) = \frac{|A \cap B|}{|B|} \quad (4)$$

Additionally, the two weighting mechanisms, IDF-weighted and T-statistics-weighted, can also be applied to the above N-gram set respectively to improve the Jaccard-like similarity metrics.

BM25 Measure. The identification of cited text can also be regarded as an information retrieval task, where a citation text corresponds to a query and the sentences in a cited paper correspond to documents to be retrieved. BM25 measure is a well-known relevance metric in classical information retrieval and may also serve as a similarity metric in our work.

In total, there are 36 similarity metrics (as shown in Table 1), each of which can be used for ranking. We will test the performance of each similarity metric in the following step to discover the best metric for the first-stage unsupervised ranking.

3.2   Top-K Sentence Selection Based on Similarity Ranking

To select the sentences that are the most similar with the citation sentences, we ranked all the sentences in the cited paper according to each of the 36 similarity metrics and evaluated which metric can obtain the best result. The number K of the selected top sentences can be set as 1, 2, 3, 4, 5, 6, 7 and 8. The evaluation indicators include Precision, Recall and $F_{1.5}$ (β = 1.5) as shown in Eqs. 5, 6 and 7. Here, $F_{1.5}$ was used instead of the most popular F_1 because there is only few corresponding cited sentences in a cited paper for a citation text, and thus Recall is more important than Precision in order to select as many candidate sentences as possible.

$$P@K = \frac{the\ number\ of\ the\ real\ cited\ sentences\ among\ the\ top-K\ sentences}{the\ number\ of\ the\ top-K\ sentences} \quad (5)$$

$$R@K = \frac{the\ number\ of\ the\ real\ cited\ sentences\ among\ the\ top-K\ sentences}{the\ total\ number\ of\ the\ real\ cited\ sentences\ among\ the\ training\ data} \quad (6)$$

$$F_\beta@K = \frac{(\beta^2 + 1)PR}{\beta^2 P + R} \quad (7)$$

Table 1. The similarity metrics used in the similarity-based ranking.

Similarity metrics	Model	Weighting mechanism/transforming function	Number of features
Cosine similarity metrics	Unigram Vector Space Model Bigram Vector Space Model	TFIDF	2
	Word2vec model	TF TFIDF T-statistics	3
	SVM Kernel transforming model	2D polynomial function 3D polynomial function RBF function	3
Jaccard similarity metrics	Unigram Jaccard Unigram Jaccard variation 1 (MJS1) Unigram Jaccard variation 2 (MJS2)	Non-weighted IDF T-statistics	9
	Bigram Jaccard Bigram Jaccard variation 1 (MJS1) Bigram Jaccard variation 2 (MJS2)	Non-weighted IDF T-statistics	9
	Trigram Jaccard Trigram Jaccard variation 1 (MJS1) Trigram Jaccard variation 2 (MJS2)	Non-weighted IDF T-statistics	9
BM25			1
Total			36

We used the training data of the CL-SciSumm 2017 corpus to evaluate the performance of each similarity metric. Figure 2 shows the $F_{1.5}$ value of the top-K (K = 1 ∼ 8) sentence selection based on various similarity metrics respectively. As shown in Fig. 2, the 33th metric, i.e. T-statistics weighted trigram Jakarta variation (MJS1), obtained the best result for most of the K values. Thus, we used this similarity metric to rank all the cited-paper sentences and selected top-K sentences as candidate sentences. Table 2 shows the $F_{1.5}$ value of the top-K sentence selection for different K values (K = 1, 2, 3, 4, 5, 6, 7, 8) based on the MJS1 similarity metric. According to the results shown in Table 2, the best $F_{1.5}$ value of the top-K sentence selection was obtained when K equals to 5 or 6. Thus we determined to set the parameter K = 5, i.e. only select top-5 sentences, in the first-stage ranking.

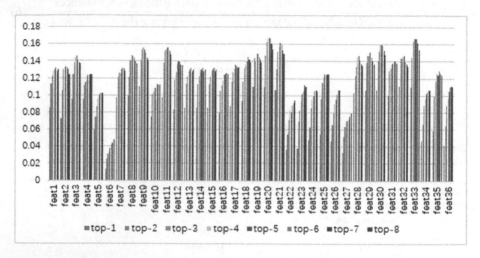

Fig. 2. $F_{1.5}$ values of the top-K sentence selection based on each of the 36 similarity metrics on the training data.

Table 2. The performance of different top-K sentence selections based on the T-statistics weighted trigram Jaccard variation similarity on the training data

K values	Recall	Precision	$F_{1.5}$
1	9.96	14.35	10.99
2	16.17	11.65	14.45
3	21.79	10.46	16.35
4	25.74	9.27	16.64
5	**29.39**	**8.47**	**16.69**
6	32.94	7.91	16.69
7	35.40	7.28	16.18
8	36.98	6.66	15.40

3.3 Supervised Listwise Ranking Based on Deep Learning

In the second-stage, we intended to use a supervised ranking, *Learning to Rank*, to combine various similarity metrics, in order to rank the candidate sentences and precisely identify cited sentences from them.

For learning to rank, there are three kinds of methods: pointwise, pairwise and listwise. Pointwise ranking does not consider the relative order of the candidate sentences. Pairwise ranking can be regarded as a binary classification problem to determine the relative order of each pair of the candidate sentences, but does not consider the position of each candidate sentence in the whole ranking list. Thus these two kinds of ranking methods are not suitable for our task. Listwise ranking can directly output the overall rank of all the candidate sentences and was selected as the ranking method in our study. However, this method requires a training corpus in which the corresponding cited sentences of a citation text need to be not only identified but also ranked. In fact, it is very difficult, even almost impossible, to annotate such a ranked training corpus for our study. Therefore, the classical listwise ranking algorithm, such as ListNet [9], cannot be applied to our cited text identification task directly. We thus proposed a novel deep learning-based listwise ranking model based on ListNet.

In the training set of the CL-SciSumm 2017 corpus, each cited-paper sentence was annotated as a real cited sentence or not, but there was no ranking order among the real cited sentences. We applied the first-stage unsupervised ranking to the training data and selected top-K sentences from the cited paper for each citation text. The candidate sentences selected from the training data formed a subset of the training set, which were then used for training the proposed listwise ranking model. It is possible that few real cited sentences may be eliminated after the first-stage ranking and not included in the candidate sentences. However, since lots of noisy sentences can be filtered out at the same time from the subset of the training set, the performance of the trained listwise ranking model should be improved.

In the subset of the training data, for each citation text $c^{(i)}$, a list of K candidate sentences $\left(r_1^{(i)}, r_2^{(i)}, \ldots, r_j^{(i)}, \ldots, r_K^{(i)} \right)$ was annotated with a corresponding list of labels $(l_1^{(i)}, l_2^{(i)}, \ldots, l_j^{(i)}, \ldots, l_K^{(i)})$. If $r_j^{(i)}$ is a cited sentence, $l_j^{(i)} = 1$, otherwise $l_j^{(i)} = 0$.

We first denoted a scoring function $F(\cdot)$ based on a neural network model, which can assign a relevance score $s_j^{(i)}$ between a citation text $c^{(i)}$ and the j-th candidate sentence $r_j^{(i)}$, i.e. $s_j^{(i)} = F\left(c^{(i)}, r_j^{(i)} \right)$. In the second-stage ranking, the candidate sentences will be ranked again, according to their relevance score.

In this study, we implemented the scoring function by using highway network [10], which is a deep learning algorithm that can overcome the learning difficulty of a large number of layers in deep learning. In order to train the scoring function, we used the probability that a cited sentence is ranked first as the measure to evaluate the scoring function. This means, if a candidate sentence is assigned a greater score, it has higher probability to be ranked first. This probability can be obtained from the scoring function with the use of a transformation function Softmax shown as Eq. 8.

$$p_j^{(i)} = \frac{\exp\left(s_j^{(i)} \right)}{\sum_{j=1}^{K} \exp\left(s_j^{(i)} \right)} \tag{8}$$

For a list of candidate sentences, the evaluation measure of the scoring function can be formulated as Eq. 9.

$$P\left(s_1^{(i)}, \ldots, s_j^{(i)}, \ldots s_K^{(i)}\right) = \sum_{j=1}^{K} l_j^{(i)} \cdot p_j^{(i)} \tag{9}$$

The training of the proposed ranking model is to maximize the probability $P\left(s_1^{(i)}, \ldots, s_j^{(i)}, \ldots s_K^{(i)}\right)$ for each citation text $c^{(i)}$ in the training corpus (the total number of the citation texts is denoted as M). The optimization task can be defined in Eq. 10.

$$maximize \sum_{i=1}^{M} P\left(s_1^{(i)}, \ldots, s_j^{(i)}, \ldots, s_K^{(i)}\right) \tag{10}$$

The whole process of the listwise ranking is shown in Fig. 3. The input is the feature vector of each candidate sentence for a citation text. With the scoring function based on a highway network, each candidate sentence is assigned a relevance score. The output is a list of ranked candidate sentences according to the scores. Finally top-N sentences (N < K) were selected as cited sentences.

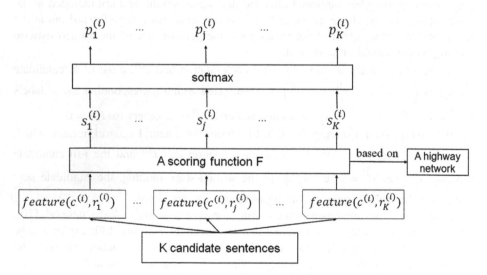

Fig. 3. The listwise ranking model for cited text identification.

To create the feature vectors of the candidate sentences, we used all the 36 similarity metrics described in Sect. 3.1 as features. In addition, we also involved the location information of a candidate sentence in the cited paper as additional features. There are 11 location features in total, which represent whether a candidate sentence occurs in a kind of section or not. The location information is determined based on a rule-based method, which only considers rough string matching in section headings. For example, if a section heading contains the keyword "Method", the section is considered to be a METHOD section.

In order to obtain the best listwise ranking model during the training process, we need determine the appropriate values of two parameters: one is the number of training iterations and the other is the number of the selected cited sentences (i.e. N). Thus we tested the F_1 values[2] of the top-N (N = 1, 2, 3 and 4) listwise ranking model while the model was being trained on the training data with different numbers of training iterations (see Fig. 4). As shown in Fig. 4, all the F_1 curves of the top-N ranking converges gradually with the increase of the number of training iterations, and become stable after 40000 training iterations. The top-2 listwise ranking obtained the best performance whereas the performance of the top-4 ranking is the worst.

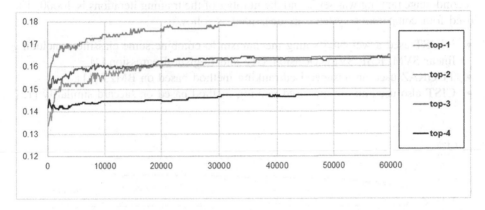

Fig. 4. The F_1 curves of the top-N listwise ranking on all the training data. The horizontal axis refers to the number of the training iterations and the vertical axis refers to the F_1 values.

4   Experiments and Results

Once the listwise ranking model was trained, we needed to evaluate its performance on the test data. The test data was also from the CL-SciSumm 2017 corpus, which contains 10 reference papers and 100 citing papers (10 citing papers for each reference paper). To validate the parameters determined during the training process, we tested four values of N (N = 1, 2, 3 and 4) and different numbers of training iterations on the test data again. To detect whether a trained model is overfitted or not, we also applied the top-1 and top-2 ranking model respectively to the training set and calculated their F_1 values as contrast. Figure 5 shows the F_1 values of the top-N listwise ranking with different number of training iterations. The results show that the F_1 curves of the top-2 listwise ranking on the training set and on the test set both have the same increasing trend. It means that there is no overfitting on the model for the top-2 ranking. On the other hand, the F_1 curve of the top-1 ranking on the training set goes up with the

---

[2] In the fist-stage ranking, we wanted to identify more candidate sentences and thus used $F_{1.5}$ as the evaluation measure which gives more weight to recall than to precision. In the second-stage ranking, we wanted to identify cited sentences exactly and thus used F_1 as the evaluation measure which gives equal weight to recall and precision.

increase of the number of the training iterations whereas the F_1 curve on the test set goes down. It means the model for the top-1 ranking is overfitted.

In the final evaluation, we evaluated our ranking-based cited text identification method on the test set by comparing it against the top-3 systems reported in CL-SciSumm 2017. To test the effectiveness of the second-stage listwise ranking, we reported the results of our ranking-based method in two stages respectively: ① only using the first-stage unsupervised ranking, and ② using both the first-stage unsupervised ranking and the second-stage unsupervised listwise ranking. The three parameters in our method had been predefined: the number K of the selected candidate sentences in the first-stage ranking was set 5, the number N of the selected cited sentences in the second-stage ranking was set 2, and the number of the training iterations is 40000. The used four comparative systems are described as follows:

- NJUST used a weighted voting mechanism to combine some classifiers including linear SVM, RBF SVM, Decision Tree and Logistic Regression [4].
- TUGRAZ used an unsupervised ranking method based on BM25 [11].
- CIST also used an unsupervised ranking method based on Jaccard similarity [12].

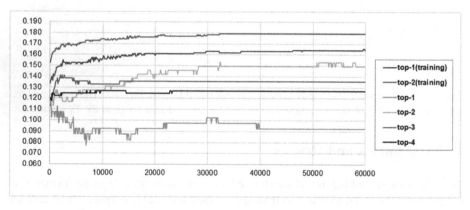

Fig. 5. The F_1 curves of the top-N listwise ranking on the test data against on the training set. The horizontal axis refers to the number of training iterations and the vertical axis refers to F_1 values.

To evaluate the performance of these systems, two kinds of metrics were used: sentence overlaps and ROUGE-N scores [13]. Sentence overlap focused on the number of overlapping sentences between the system's output and the human-annotated gold standard. ROUGE-N, a widely used evaluation metric in automatic summarization, focused on the number of overlapping N-grams (here set N = 2). Based on the two kinds of metrics respectively, the micro-average and macro-average of the F_1 values were calculated and shown in Table 3. The results of the comparative systems are from Jaidka's reports on the CL-SciSumm 2017 [7]. As shown in Table 3, our unsupervised similarity-based ranking method used in the first stage obtains slightly worse results than the other four comparative systems. After applying the supervised listwise ranking in the second stage, the performance of our ranking-based method can increase greatly and obtain the best results among all the tested systems.

Table 3. The F_1 values of our system and the top-3 systems on the test data of the CL-SciSumm 2017

System	Sentence ID overlaps		ROUGE
	Micro-Avg	Macro-Avg	Micro-Avg
Our system (unsupervised ranking + listwise ranking)	**15.3**	**18.3**	**14.3**
NJUST	12.3	14.6	11.4
TUGRAZ	11.0	13.5	10.8
CIST-BUPT	10.7	11.3	4.7
Our baseline (unsupervised ranking)	11.7	12.9	4.9

5 Conclusion and Discussion

In this paper, we focused on the issue of cited text identification and proposed a ranking-based identification method involving an unsupervised similarity-based ranking and a supervised listwise ranking. A novel listwise ranking model was developed with the use of the Highway Network deep learning algorithm based on the classical listwise ranking algorithm ListNet.

The contributions of this study lie in two main aspects: several novel similarity features and a novel listwise ranking model. Firstly, we proposed new similarity features for ranking to roughly identify the candidate sentences that are probably cited sentences, such as word embedding–based cosine similarity, SVM kernel function-transformed cosine similarity, and modified N-gram Jaccard similarity. Different weighting mechanisms were also explored in these similarity features, including TF-weighting, TFIDF-weighting, and T-statistics weighting. The experiment results showed that the T-statistics weighted Jaccard variation similarity metric based on the trigram language model was the most useful feature for unsupervised ranking. A simple unsupervised ranking only depending on this similarity feature can obtain reasonable identification results. Secondly, we proposed a novel listwise ranking model with the use of the Highway Networks deep learning algorithm. Unlike the classical ListNet ranking model that was usually used in information retrieval, our model did not require ranked training data and was thus more suitable for the cited text identification task. The experiment results showed that this novel ranking-based method outperformed other classification-based and voting-based approaches.

In this study, we identified the cited text of a citation text at sentence level, i.e. identifying individual cited sentences. In this case, the identified cited sentences are sometimes not continuous to comprise a cited text. In the future work, we will also identify cited texts at paragraph level, i.e. identifying a set of continuous cited sentences. In addition, we will perform fine-grained citation content analysis based on the identified cited text.

Acknowledgement. This paper is one of the research outputs of the project supported by the State Key Program of National Social Science Foundation of China (Grant No. 17ATQ001).

References

1. Ding, Y., Zhang, G., Chambers, T., Song, M., Wang, X., Zhai, C.: Content-based citation analysis: the next generation of citation analysis. J. Assoc. Inf. Sci. Technol. **65**(9), 1820–1833 (2014)
2. Cohan, A., Goharian, N.: Scientific document summarization via citation contextualization and scientific discourse. Int. J. Digit. Libr. **19**(2-3), 287–303 (2017). https://doi.org/10.1007/s00799-017-0216-8
3. Jaidka, K., Chandrasekaran, M.K., Rustagi, S., Kan, M.-Y.: Insights from CL-SciSumm 2016: the faceted scientific document summarization Shared Task. Int. J. Digit. Libr. **19**(2), 163–171 (2017). https://doi.org/10.1007/s00799-017-0221-y
4. Ma, S., Xu, J., Zhang, C.: Automatic identification of cited text spans: a multi-classifier approach over imbalanced dataset. Scientometrics **116**(2), 1303–1330 (2018). https://doi.org/10.1007/s11192-018-2754-2
5. Yeh, J.Y., Hsu, T.Y., Tsai, C.J., et al.: On identifying cited texts for citances and classifying their discourse facets by classification techniques. J. Inf. Sci. Eng. **35**(1), 61–86 (2016)
6. Pramanick, A., Mandi, S., Dey, M., Das, D.: Employing word vectors for identifying, classifying and summarizing scientific documents. In: Proceedings of the 3rd Computational Linguistics Scientific Summarization on Shared Task (CL-SciSumm 2017), pp. 94–98. CEUR-WS.org (2017)
7. Jaidka, K., Chandrasekaran, K.M., Jain, D., Kan, M-Y.: The CL-SciSumm shared task 2017: results and key insights. In: Proceedings of the 3rd Computational Linguistics Scientific Summarization on Shared Task (CL-SciSumm 2017), pp. 1–15. CEUR-WS.org (2017)
8. Ou, S.Y., Kim, H.I.: Unsupervised citation sentence identification based on similarity measurement. In: Chowdhury, G., McLeod, J., Gillet, V., Willett, P. (eds.) iConference 2018. LNCS, vol. 10766, pp. 384–394. Springer, Cham (2018). https://doi.org/10.1007/978-3-319-78105-1_42
9. Cao, Z., Qin, T., Liu, T.Y., Tsai, M.F., Li, H.: Learning to rank: from pairwise approach to listwise approach. In: Proceedings of the 24th International Conference on Machine learning, pp. 129–136. ACM, New York (2007)
10. Srivastava, R.K., Greff, K., Schmidhuber, J.: Training very deep networks. In: Proceedings of the 29th Annual Conference on Neural Information Processing Systems 2015 (NIPS 2015), pp. 2377–2385. Neural Information Processing Systems Foundation, Inc. (NIPS), California (2015)
11. Felber, T., Kern, R.: Query generation strategies for CL-SciSumm 2017 shared task. In: Proceedings of the 3rd Computational Linguistics Scientific Summarization on Shared Task (CL-SciSumm 2017), pp. 67–72. CEUR-WS.org (2017)
12. Li, L., Zhang, Y., Mao, L., Chi, J., Chen, M., Huang, Z.: CIST@CLSciSumm-17: multiple features based citation linkage, classification and summarization. In: Proceedings of the 3rd Computational Linguistics Scientific Summarization on Shared Task (CL-SciSumm 2017), pp. 43–54. CEUR-WS.org (2017)
13. Lin, C.Y.: ROUGE: a package for automatic evaluation of summaries. In: Proceedings of the Workshop on Text Summarization Branches Out (Post-Conference Workshop of ACL 2004), pp. 74–81. Association for Computational Linguistics (2004)

A Method for Measuring Journal Discriminative Capacity and Its Application in WOS

Hao Wang[1,2], Baolong Zhang[1,2(✉)] [iD], Sanhong Deng[1,2], and Xinning Su[1,2]

[1] School of Information Management, Nanjing University, Nanjing 210023, China
zbl@smail.nju.edu.cn
[2] Jiangsu Key Laboratory of Data Engineering and Knowledge Service, Nanjing 210023, China

Abstract. Journal discriminative capacity refers to the degree of difference between the journals in research subjects, and is of great significance for detecting the level of journal differentiation. Current research on journal discrepancies is predominantly focused on the quantitative analysis of journal content, and rarely measures the degree of journal difference. To address this lapse in research, a method from the perspective of difference is proposed in this paper to quantitatively measure and analyze the discriminative capacity of journals. Using the bibliographic of Science Citation Index (SCI), Social Science Citation Index (SSCI), and Arts & Humanities Citation Index (A&HCI) journals from 2015–2017 as the data source, the contents differences of 23 Library and Information Science (LIS) journals are analyzed through hierarchical clustering and journal discriminative capacity (JDC) measurement. The discriminative capacity of disciplines is then calculated and combined with multidimensional scaling analysis to detect the difference characteristics of journals in ten disciplines, and the mean JDC is used to explore the overall differences of disciplines. Results show that the discriminative capacity of LIS journals is obviously stratified, the journals of library science are the most discriminating, and the journals of evaluation and review are the weakest. In addition, the journals of different disciplines have distinct disciplinary characteristics, with the discriminative capacity of SCI journals as the most notable, followed by SSCI journals, and with A&HCI journals displaying the weakest discriminative capacity.

Keywords: Journal discriminative capacity · Journal difference · MDS dimension reduction · Disciplinary difference

1 Introduction

The analysis and evaluation of academic journals is an important research topic in library and information science, and plays an important role in guiding the responsible development of academic journals [1]. However, in the era of the knowledge explosion,

A. Sundqvist et al. (Eds.): iConference 2020, LNCS 12051, pp. 751–767, 2020.
https://doi.org/10.1007/978-3-030-43687-2_63

research hotspots continue to emerge in the innovation of ideas, technologies, and methods. Some journals have gradually lost their own research characteristics in order to pursue popular topics, displaying a homogenizing trend. This gradual weakening of differences between journals is harmful to the individualized development of journals and academic innovation. Therefore, accurately measuring and evaluating the differences of journal research content is a highly important research topic, which plays an important role in keeping the characteristics of journals and improving the innovative development of journals.

Most current research into the difference in journal research content utilizes the clustering method to analyze the differences between journals. Few studies use algorithms to quantitatively measure the degree of difference in journal content. And it seems like a historical qualitative approach to differences according to their intellectual evolution could also be a useful way to discriminate between disciplines. But such studies are subjective and local to a certain extent. So the existing methods are difficult to measure the differentiation in the research content of academic objects. Therefore, a novel indictor, Journal Discriminative Capacity (JDC), is proposed in this study to measure the differentiation in research content of the academic journal. This indicator is mainly used to describe the degree of discriminative capacity among journals in a specific group. The greater the degree of discriminative capacity, the more unique the research content is, and the more significant the differences are. This indicator can measure and detect the difference of journals scientifically and effectively, providing a theoretical basis for the differential analysis of journals.

From the perspective of difference, this study uses the JDC to quantitatively analyze the difference in research content among journals. Taking titles and abstracts in the bibliographic data as experimental data, the difference characteristics of Library and Information Science (LIS) journals are first analyzed through the calculation of JDC, and the journals with unique or "homogeneity" characteristics are located, so as to determine the differentiated level of LIS journals. The distinct features of the journals in different disciplines are then comparatively analyzed by JDC calculation and analysis, as well as the overall level of discriminative capacity of different disciplines. This study may not only facilitate the exploration of differentiation characteristics of journals but provide managers a basis for guiding for journals' diversity development and adjusting the research focus of academic journals.

The present research is guided by the following questions:

RQ1. To what extent are journals within library and information science different from one another? And what are the discriminative features?
RQ2. To what extent are journals in a multi-disciplines group different from one another? And what are discriminative features of journals in different disciplines in individual and in overall?

2 Related Research

Research into the difference of journals aims to explore the degree of difference of academic journals by analyzing the contents of published papers. Current study can be generally divided into two categories. The first predominantly uses various external data such as impact factors and downloads [2] to study the relationship between journals from the perspectives of quality [3, 4], influence [5–7], development level [8], and citation efficiency [9]. These studies mainly explore the external characteristic diversity of academic journals, and rarely involve the analysis of differences in research content. The second category mainly examines the internal title data (such as title, keywords, and abstracts) and citations to analyze the contents of journal papers. Such methods tend to adopt hierarchical clustering [10, 11], multi-dimensional scaling, visualization of similarities (VOS) [12, 13], and other methods to detect the degree of aggregation of journals in different dimensions, so as to analyze the similarity or difference of different categories of journals. These studies explore the differences in journal research content based on the aggregation of journals and qualitative analysis, but can only analyze the differences between journal groups, failing to quantify differences between journals of the same group and different groups. Meanwhile, very few studies have been able to accurately quantify the differences in journal content. Additionally, some studies use similarity to quantitatively analyze the research content of journals to detect their differences [14, 15], but this method can only measure the similarity between two objects and cannot detect the degree of difference between different journals in different groups.

In view of the research on differences in research content, some studies have analyzed papers, topics, scholars, and other academic objects. With regard to academic papers, González-Albo [16], Liu [17], and Lamba [18], discussed the differences in research hotspots, topics, and quality of different academic papers through quantitative analysis. Boyack [19] analyzed the differences of document objects in groups by using Jensen-Shannon divergence method [20]. For research topic analysis, Weismayer [21], Song [22], and Fang [23] used hierarchical clustering, co-occurrence network, and latent Dirichlet allocation (LDA) topic mining to conduct quantitative research on the differences of research topics. With regard to scholars, Yang [24], Ding [25], and Zhang [26] explored the differences of scholars in research fields and topics by using methods including citation network, similarity, and multi-layer clustering. Some researchers have also discussed the differences between institutions [27], disciplines [28–30], and other large-grained academic objects. Most of these studies use clustering, multidimensional scale, co-occurrence network, topic mining, and other methods to explore the differences between different objects, and rarely measure the degree of differences in research content. A small amount of studies have also explored the quantitative measurement methods of academic object differences. The term discrimination model proposed by Salton [31, 32] can be used to calculate the differences of terms in information retrieval. While this method has some limitations, such as high algorithm complexity and a large amount of computational cost, and can only measure term difference indirectly by using document content, its core concept can be used to measure the difference of journals.

In summary, current research on the differences between academic objects consists of the following problems. (i) Existing research on the differences of journals is focused on exploring external features such as quality and influence, while research using the journal's inner data to more thoroughly explore research content differences is relatively rare. (ii) Content difference research for journals and other academic objects mainly uses clustering, multi-dimensional scaling analysis, and various network models to explore the differences of individual target groups, but the differences of individual subjects cannot be quantitatively analyzed. (iii) The existing term discrimination model has high time complexity and is only applicable to measure the differences of the term. It is also difficult to process large-scale data and measure the differences of academic journals directly using the current model. Therefore, this paper takes the difference as a research perspective and proposes a measurement method for the difference of journal content, providing a new method and concept for the evaluation of academic journals.

3 Data and Methods

3.1 Data Preprocessing

To explore the differences of journals and provide a comparison among disciplines, this study selects ten disciplines from Science Citation Index (SCI), Social Science Citation Index (SSCI), and Arts & Humanities Citation Index (A&HCI) journals (as shown in Table 1), using journals included in Q1 and Q2 of the Journal Citation Report from 2015 to 2017 as candidates. Candidate journals of History and Philosophy are collected from A&HCI by random sampling. It is generally believed that titles and abstracts can reveal the research content of journals to a large extent, and can be successfully utilized to explore differences in the research content of journals. Therefore, the bibliographic data of the candidate journals of ten disciplines from 2015 to 2017 are obtained from Web of Science database, and the titles and abstracts in the bibliographic data are used as experimental data.

Table 1. List of disciplines

Disciplines	Abbr.
Optics	OP
Mathematics	MH
Materials Science, Multidisciplinary	MS
Engineering, Mechanical	EM
Computer Science, Artificial Intelligence	CR
Information Science & Library Science	LIS
Business	BS
Sociology	SS
History	HS
Philosophy	PH

The preprocessing of data mainly includes two aspects. The first is data cleaning and journal screening, in which data that is missing from the abstract field is treated as invalid data to be eliminated. Journals with less than 30 valid bibliographic data points every year are excluded, and the top 20 journals in each discipline are selected as the research object according to impact factor (IF) ranking from the remaining journals. The second aspect of data preprocessing is data sampling and text processing. Stratified random sampling is used to extract 30 records from each journal every year as experimental samples. The titles and abstracts are then extracted, and word segmentation, de-stopping, and stemming are performed using the bibliographic information analysis software SATI [33]. The obtained information is then regarded as a term and converted into a triple of <Journal number, term, term weight> after computing the term weight.

3.2   Calculation of Journal Discriminative Capacity

A journal discriminative capacity method based on the term discriminative model is proposed in this paper. The technique is divided into three parts: journal space construction, journal space density computation, and JDC calculation. The specific process is described as follows.

(1) Construction of journal space: The triple must first be converted into a journal-term matrix (JTM) with dimensions m * n, consisting of columns of journals and rows of terms. Subscript m is the number of journals, n is the number of terms included in m journals, and the matrix element is the term weight value, calculated by using Eq. (1):

$$TFIDF = TF \times IDF = tf_t \times lg(m/m_t + \varepsilon) \tag{1}$$

where tf_t is the frequency of term t appearing in journal i, m_t $(m_t \neq 0)$ is the frequency of term t appearing in the term vector, and ε is the adjusting factor. In this study, let $\varepsilon = 1/m_t$ to ensure that the inverse document frequency (IDF) is not zero when $m = m_t$.

Next, JTM is transformed into a journal-journal matrix (JJM) by cosine similarity. The JJM is a symmetric similarity matrix which is defined as journal space according to Eq. (2):

$$JJM = \begin{pmatrix} S_1 \\ S_i \\ \vdots \\ S_m \end{pmatrix} = \begin{pmatrix} s_{11} & \cdots & & s_{1m} \\ & \cdots & s_{ij} & \cdots \\ & \cdots & & \\ s_{m1} & \cdots & & s_{mm} \end{pmatrix} \tag{2}$$

where $S_i = \{s_{ij} \mid i, j \in m\}$ is the journal vector and s_{ij} represents the cosine similarity of journals i and j.

(2) Computation of journal space density: Journal space density (JSD) is calculated by using the average similarity of the all journal vector S_i and journal space centroid, as expressed in Eq. (3):

$$JSD = \left(\frac{1}{m}\sum_{i=1}^{m}DS(S_i)\right) \tag{3}$$

where DS is the similarity of S_i and $Centroid$ that can be calculated by distance-based similarity [34], as shown in Eq. (4):

$$DS(S_i) = \frac{1}{c^{Dist(S_i,Centroid)}}, \quad c = 1.3 \tag{4}$$

The distance in Eq. (4) is measured by the cosine distance between S_i and $Centroid$. The calculation method is shown in the following Eq. (5):

$$Dist(S_i, Centroid) = \left(\sum_{i=1}^{m}\left(s_{ij} - \frac{1}{m}\sum_{j=1}^{m}s_{ij}\right)^2\right)^{1/2} \tag{5}$$

where $Centroid$ is calculated using Eq. (6):

$$Centroid = \left(\frac{1}{m}\sum_{j=1}^{m}s_{1j}, \frac{1}{m}\sum_{j=1}^{m}s_{2j}, \ldots\ldots, \frac{1}{m}\sum_{j=1}^{m}s_{mj}\right) \tag{6}$$

(3) Calculation of journal discriminative capacity: The JDC is calculated by the average change in the JSD after the certain journal is removed, as shown in Eq. (7):

$$JDC_{S_k} = \frac{JSD_{S_k} - JSD}{AVG\_JSD} \tag{7}$$

where JSD_{Sk} is the journal space density after journal S_k is removed and AVG_JSD is the average density difference of the journal space. The calculation method is shown in Eq. (8):

$$AVG\_JSD = \frac{1}{m}\sum_{k=1}^{m}|JSD_{S_k} - JSD| \tag{8}$$

where the absolute value of the difference is used to avoid the positive values counteracting the negative values.

4 Results and Analysis

4.1 Calculation and Analysis of Journal Discriminative Capacity in Library Science and Information Science

Result of Data Preprocessing in LIS Journals. Through cleaning the bibliographic data of LIS candidate journals from 2015 to 2017, 23 journals are selected. The titles and abstracts are then extracted from the valid bibliographic data obtained by random sampling. A total of 10,936 terms and 43,607 triples are obtained after text processing and term weight computing, and the data preprocessing results are provided in Table 2.

Table 2. Data preprocessing results of LIS journals

No.	Journals	Abbr.	Valid data	Sample size	Number of terms
1	College & Research Libraries	CRL	141	90	1462
2	European Journal of Information Systems	EJIS	99	90	1922
3	Government Information Quarterly	GIQ	170	90	1848
4	International Journal of Geographical Information Science	IJGIS	344	90	2220
5	International Journal of Information Management	IJIM	273	90	1841
6	Information & Management	IM	233	90	1448
7	Information Processing & Management	IPM	211	90	1929
8	Information Systems Research	ISR	141	90	2105
9	Information Technology & People	ITP	116	90	2149
10	Journal of Academic Librarianship	JAL	207	90	1701
11	Journal of The American Medical Informatics Association	JAMIA	502	90	2254
12	Journal of the Association for Information Science and Technology	JASIST	610	90	1929
13	Journal of Health Communication	JHC	455	90	2062
14	Journal of Knowledge Management	JKM	222	90	1989
15	Journal of Management Information Systems	JMIS	127	90	1984
16	Journal of Informetrics	JOI	247	90	1676
17	MIS Quarterly	MISQ	153	90	2110
18	Online Information Review	OIR	177	90	2005
19	Portal-Libraries And The Academy	PLA	116	90	1429
20	Telematics And Informatics	TI	372	90	1964
21	Research Evaluation	RE	109	90	1848
22	Social Science Computer Review	SSCR	135	90	1895
23	Scientometrics	STM	1087	90	1837
Total			6247	2070	43607

Cluster Analysis of LIS Journals. Journals can be divided into different groups by hierarchical clustering to initially explore the differences among individual groups. Therefore, the triples obtained by data preprocessing are transformed into JTM (dimension is 23 * 10936), and clustered by hierarchical clustering. The result is shown in Fig. 1.

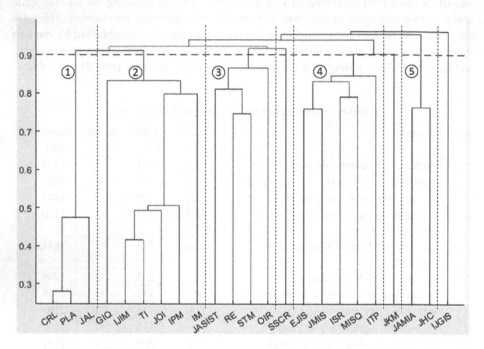

Fig. 1. Clustering results of 23 journals in LIS discipline

As illustrated in Fig. 1, the 23 journals are clustered into five major categories and three individuals. (1) ① is predominantly made up of library science journals, ② is mainly information management journals, ③ is mainly evaluation and review journals, ④ is mainly information system journals, and ⑤ is medical information journals. (2) According to the results, the clustering is reasonable and different categories of journals can be clearly distinguished. It can be seen from the categories that the research field of LIS journals is more extensive, and there are obvious differences among the five categories of journals. Among the three individual journals, IJGIS mainly presents geographic information, which is notably different from other LIS journals, so it is reasonable to separate this journal. Alternatively, JKM and SSCR are close to ③ and ④, respectively, indicating that there is a certain degree of difference between the two journals and two categories, but it is limited. (3) From the inter-group distance (vertical axis), the smaller the distance between groups, the greater the similarity between the journals in the group, and the smaller the similarity of journals in different groups. Therefore, the journals in ① and ② are obviously different from the journals in other groups, while the difference of journals in ③, ④, ⑤, and the other three separated journals may not be significant. In general, the clustering results are reasonable, and there are obvious differences among journals, indicating that the differential measurement and analysis of these journals is scientifically feasible.

Analysis of Journal Discriminative Capacity in LIS. Cluster analysis can only observe the difference between various periodical groups, but cannot measure the degree of difference accurately. Therefore, the degree of difference of LIS journals is calculated by JDC method, and the results are compiled into a scatter diagram as shown in Fig. 2. Multi-dimension scaling analysis (MDSA) is then adopted to conduct a two-dimensional visualization of JJM (as shown in Fig. 3), so as to assist in the analysis of the differences of journals in combination with the spatial distribution of journals.

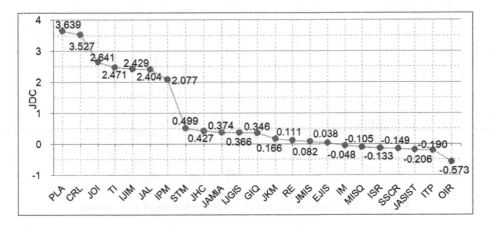

Fig. 2. JDC results of LIS journals

It can be seen from Fig. 2 that most JDC values of the LIS journals are positive, indicating that the research content of these journals has certain uniqueness and is well differentiated among the groups. There are seven journals with negative JDC values, indicating that the research content of these journals may have the characteristics of "homogeneity". (i) The range distribution of JDC presents a gradient, and most JDC values are concentrated in the $(-1, 1)$ interval. The first and second levels of JDC are mainly library science journals (such as *PLA*, *CAL*, *JAL*) and information management journals (such as *JOI*, *TI*, *IJIM*, and *IPM*). These two kinds of journals are distributed in the outer space (within the real coil in Fig. 3), which indicates that the academic research of these journals is unique, among which library science journals are the most distinctive. The JDC gap between the third level and fourth level (negative value) is very small, which illustrates that the research content of these journals is not distinctively prominent, and there may be different degrees of assimilation. This result can be verified by the spatial distribution of journals, that is, journals with negative JDC are distributed centrally in the box area in Fig. 3, which can be seen amplified in the dotted ellipse area to right of the figure. (ii) The journals with negative JDC values are mainly information system journals and evaluation & review journals, which present the comprehensive characteristics of these two kinds of journals. These journals have a wide range of research content, such as *MISQ* and *JASIST*, which play an important role in the LIS discipline, and the research content is of mutual interest of LIS disciplines. Among them, the comprehensive characteristics of evaluation & review journals such as *OIR* are more outstanding. Although *JAMIA*, *JHC*, and *IJGIS* are separated in hierarchical clustering, their JDCs are at a low level, indicating that the research features of these three journals in medicine and geography are not prominent and there may be a tendency of "homogenization".

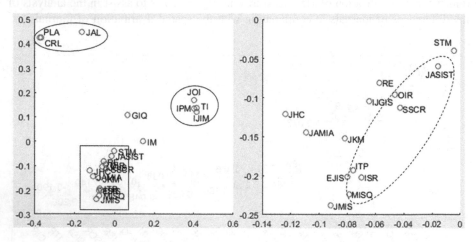

Fig. 3. Spatial distribution and partial amplification of LIS journals

4.2 Comparative Analysis of Journal Discriminative Capacity Among Disciplines

A total of 200 journals are selected by cleaning the bibliographic data of candidate journals of ten disciplines from 2015 to 2017. The 60,928 terms and 396,362 triples are formed after stratified random sampling and text processing. The JDCs of 200 journals are then calculated and analyzed using this data.

Analysis of the Differences Among Top and Bottom Ten Journals. To analyze the difference characteristics of individual journals of ten disciplines, the top ten and bottom ten ranked by JDC are selected as representative journals for analysis, as shown in Table 3.

It can be seen from the JDC results that the journals in the top and the bottom ten have obvious inclination among disciplines. Seven of the top ten journals in JDC are from Optics, which indicates that Optics journals have unique academic research features among ten disciplines. Two of the other three journals are Materials Science journals and the other is Mathematics journals, which shows that these three journals demonstrate high discriminative capacity and their research content has distinct disciplinary characteristics. The journals in the bottom ten are all negative values and from different disciplines, indicating that their research contents may be interdisciplinary to some extent. Among them, *IJGIS*, which has the smallest JDC, is a typical journal of cross-geography and information science, showing strong cross-disciplinary characteristics. The JDCs with three Engineering & Mechanical journals are also small, illustrating that these three journals may have overlapping fields with other science and engineering journals. Generally speaking, the JDC may have great differences in disciplines, that is, the journals in the humanities and social sciences field may have a smaller discriminative capacity than those in the science and engineering field, and are more likely to interdisciplinary.

Table 3. JDC results of the top ten and bottom ten journals in ten disciplines

The top ten JDC			The bottom ten JDC		
Disciplines	Journals	JDC	Disciplines	Journals	JDC
OP	Light-Science & Applications	3.078	BS	Supply Chain Management-an International Journal	−0.475
OP	Laser & Photonics Reviews	3.054	EM	Tribology Letters	−0.484
OP	Optica	3.026	EM	Drying Technology	−0.517
OP	Nanophotonics	2.854	EM	IEEE-ASME Transactions on Mechatronics	−0.537
OP	ACS Photonics	2.773	HS	International Journal of the History of Sport	−0.541
MS	ACS Nano	2.635	CR	International Journal of Neural Systems	−0.551
MH	Nonlinear Analysis-Theory Methods & Applications	2.538	BS	Journal of Intellectual Capital	−0.554
OP	IEEE Journal of Selected Topics in Quantum Electronics	2.523	LIS	Journal of The American Medical Informatics Association	−0.566
OP	Nature Photonics	2.523	SS	Agriculture and Human Values	−0.609
MS	NANO Letters	2.502	LIS	International Journal of Geographical Information Science	−0.841

Analysis of Numerical Distribution of JDC Among Disciplines. To analyze the JDC characteristics of different disciplines intuitively and comprehensively, all JDC values of ten disciplines are drawn into a scatter diagram, as shown in Fig. 4. The horizontal axis is the journal number, and the vertical axis is the JDC value.

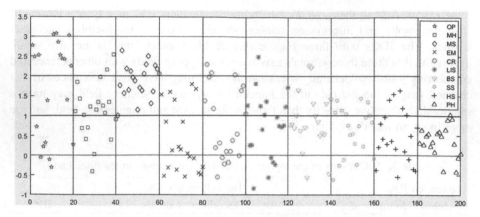

Fig. 4. JDC numerical distribution in ten disciplines

Statistics show that 162 journals in ten disciplines have positive JDC values, among which 88 journals have JDC values greater than 1, indicating that most journals in the journal group have obvious differences. Moreover, the distribution of JDC values of ten disciplines is obviously different in both science and engineering and humanities and social sciences journals. (i) The JDC of science and engineering journals is generally large, while that of humanities and social science journals is relatively small, indicating that science and engineering journals have distinct disciplinary characteristics and their research content is more unique than that of humanities and social science journals. (ii) There are obvious differences between science and engineering journals. The JDC range of Optics journals is the largest, indicating that some journals in Optics have outstanding research features, while others possess interdisciplinary features. The JDC range of the Materials Science discipline is the smallest and at a high level, indicating that the research field of this discipline is relatively concentrated and its research content is highly unique. The JDCs of Engineering & Mechanical journals show polarization and more negative values, indicating that journals of this discipline may have more cross-fields and the interdisciplinary feature of the journals is obvious. (iii) Compared with science and engineering journals, the JDC distribution of humanities and social sciences journals is relatively dense and at a low level, indicating that there may be overlapping fields in the research of these disciplines. Among them, the Business journals are the most prominent, distribution of JDC is more scattered, and some journals show a greater degree of differentiation, while the JDC of Philosophy journals are at a lower level, indicating that the journals of this discipline show strong comprehensive characteristics.

According to the above analysis, journals of different disciplines may display certain associations. In order to detect the difference characteristics of journals, MDSA is adopted to reduce dimensions of JJM (as shown in Fig. 5), and two-dimensional distribution is used for visual analysis, so as to prove the difference and relevance of journals of different disciplines.

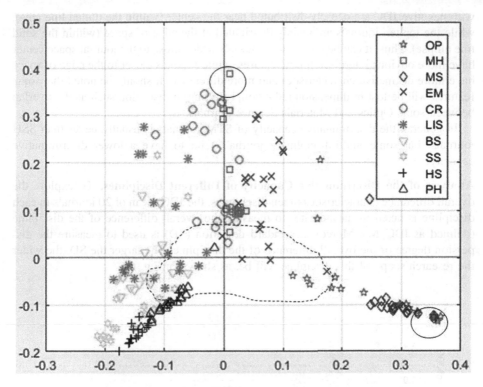

Fig. 5. Visualization of the spatial distribution of journals in ten disciplines

As illustrated in Fig. 5, science and engineering journals and humanities and social sciences journals are divided into two parts by $Y = 0$, which accurately reflects the significant differences in research contents between them. (i) Science and engineering journals are distributed discretely in the first and fourth quadrants, and are relatively far from the center of space. Consequently, the JDCs of these journals are at a high level. However, humanities and social science journals are concentrated in the third quadrant, showing a strong correlation, which makes the JDCs of these journals at a low level. (ii) The Computer Science journals are distributed discreetly around the Y axis and have a certain cross-correlation with Mathematics, Engineering & Mechanical, and LIS disciplines, which fully reflects their cross-disciplinary characteristics. The LIS discipline is distributed in the second and third quadrants, which is closely related to Business and Sociology, while Engineering & Mechanical and Materials Science journals are isolated in the outer space, showing great uniqueness. The distribution of Engineering & Mechanical journals is relatively discrete, and these JDCs display an obvious polarization. However, the distribution of History and Philosophy journals is almost mixed together, illustrating the close relationship between the two disciplines, so the JDCs of these journals are generally small. From the spatial distribution, the overlap in social science and humanities (SSH) journals is reasonable, because the disciplinary culture (both epistemic and social) is totally different in science, technology, and material (STM) and SSH fields. The result is expected. (iii) Most journals with negative JDC are densely distributed near the center (within the dotted line area), while the top ten journals are mainly distributed at the edge of space (within the solid line ellipse). Thus, it can be proven that journals which close to the journal space center have more obvious interdisciplinary features, while journals closer to the edge of space have more distinctive characteristics and more difference. It should be noted that some features will be lost in dimension reduction, resulting in distortion such as the overlap between some Optics and Materials Science journals.

In general, the discriminative capacity of STM journals is usually better than SSH journals, but some multi-disciplinary journals tend to have a lower discriminative capacity.

Analysis of the Discriminative Capacity of Different Disciplines. To explore the overall difference characteristics of ten disciplines, the JDC mean of 20 journals in each discipline is taken as an indicator to measure the overall difference of the discipline (defined as JDC_M). Moreover, standard deviation (SD) is used to measure the dispersion degree of the overall difference of the discipline. The larger the SD, the wider the research scope of this discipline will be, as shown in Fig. 6.

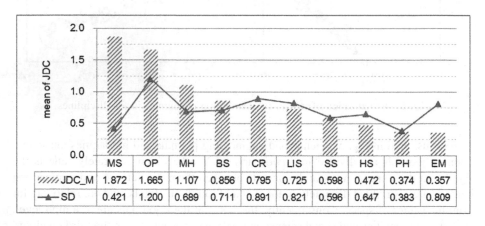

	MS	OP	MH	BS	CR	LIS	SS	HS	PH	EM
▨ JDC_M	1.872	1.665	1.107	0.856	0.795	0.725	0.598	0.472	0.374	0.357
▲ SD	0.421	1.200	0.689	0.711	0.891	0.821	0.596	0.647	0.383	0.809

Fig. 6. Results of JDC_M and SD of ten disciplines

As illustrated in Fig. 6, the JDC_M of the ten disciplines is obviously different, and the JDC_M of science and engineering disciplines is generally higher than that of humanities and social sciences. (i) The JDC_M of Materials Science and Engineering & Mechanical are the largest and smallest, respectively, while their standard deviation performance is opposite. This significant difference indicates that Materials Science journals have more concentrated research fields and outstanding academic research uniqueness, while Engineering & Mechanical journals contain a wide range of research, displaying interdisciplinary characteristics. (ii) The JDC_M of Optics and Mathematics is relatively large, but the standard deviation of Optics is the largest, indicating that the overall difference between the two disciplines is significant, and the interdisciplinary nature of some Optics journals sees them display a relatively large dispersion. (iii) The overall JDC_M of social sciences & humanities is at a low level, among which the JDC_M of Business, LIS, and Sociology is higher than History and Philosophy, indicating that the research of social sciences is more unique, while the research of humanities is more comprehensive.

5   Conclusion

This study measured and analyzed the discriminative capacity of LIS journals from the perspective of difference, presenting a comparative analysis of individual and overall difference characteristics of ten discipline journals. The results show that: (i) In LIS journals, the research contents of library journals have distinct uniqueness and their discriminative capacities are at the first level. Information management journals are at the second level, and the third and fourth level journals are mostly information system journals and evaluation journals, which show signs of "homogeneity". This is particularly so for the fourth level journals represented by *OIR*, which have obvious comprehensive characteristics. (ii) Among WOS journals, the discriminative capacity of SCI journals is largest, followed by SSCI journals and A&HCI journals. The differences of journals display distinct disciplinary features in which Materials Science journals have the most distinctive disciplinary features and the largest overall discriminative capacity, the discriminative capacity of Optics and Engineering & Mechanical discipline journals is polarized, and some journals are obviously interdisciplinary. The research fields of History and Philosophy discipline journals are relatively concentrated and the overall differentiation degree is relatively small.

This study verifies the wide applicability of JDC through the difference measurement of journals and the comparative analysis of disciplines, and is of significance to enrich and improve the current academic evaluation system. However, some issues in the research process require further exploration. Notably, only part of the journals is selected as a research object to explore the differences of LIS journals which may make the research results one-sided. Subsequently, the sample will be expanded to explore the differences of journals at a larger and more comprehensive scale.

Acknowledgments. This study was supported by the Natural Science Foundation of China (No. 71503121). We would also like to express our special thanks to the editor and three reviewers for their very constructive comments and suggestions.

References

1. Zhang, F.: Evaluating journal impact based on weighted citations. Scientometrics **113**(2), 1155–1169 (2017). https://doi.org/10.1007/s11192-017-2510-z
2. Vaughan, L., Tang, J., Yang, R.: Investigating disciplinary differences in the relationships between citations and downloads. Scientometrics **111**(3), 1533–1545 (2017). https://doi.org/10.1007/s11192-017-2308-z
3. Beets, S.D., Lewis, B.R., Brower, H.H.: The quality of business ethics journals: an assessment based on application. Bus. Soc. **55**(2), 188–213 (2016). https://doi.org/10.1177/0007650313478974

4. Beets, S.D., Kelton, A.S., Lewis, B.R.: An assessment of accounting journal quality based on departmental lists. Scientometrics **102**(1), 315–332 (2015). https://doi.org/10.1007/s11192-014-1353-0

5. Da Silva, J.A.T., Memon, A.R.: CiteScore: a cite for sore eyes, or a valuable, transparent metric? Scientometrics **111**(1), 553–556 (2017). https://doi.org/10.1007/s11192-017-2250-0

6. Zhang, C., Liu, X., Xu, Y., Wang, Y.: Quality-structure index: a new metric to measure scientific journal influence. J. Am. Soc. Inf. Sci. Technol. **62**(4), 643–653 (2011). https://doi.org/10.1002/asi.21487

7. Saha, S., Jangid, N., Mathur, A., Narsimhamurthy, A.M.: DSRS: estimation and forecasting of journal influence in the science and technology domain via a lightweight quantitative approach. Collnet J. Scientometr. Inf. Manag. **10**(1), 41–70 (2016). https://doi.org/10.1080/09737766.2016.1177939

8. Gazni, A., Ghaseminik, Z.: Internationalization of scientific publishing over time: analysing publishers and fields differences. Learn. Publ. **29**(2), 103–111 (2016). https://doi.org/10.1002/leap.1018

9. Lee, H., Shin, J.: Measuring journal performance for multidisciplinary research: an efficiency perspective. J. Informetr. **8**(1), 77–88 (2014). https://doi.org/10.1016/j.joi.2013.10.004

10. Leydesdorff, L., Bornmann, L., Wagner, C.S.: Generating clustered journal maps: an automated system for hierarchical classification. Scientometrics **110**(3), 1601–1614 (2017). https://doi.org/10.1007/s11192-016-2226-5

11. Tseng, Y.H., Tsay, M.Y.: Journal clustering of library and information science for subfield delineation using the bibliometric analysis toolkit: CATAR. Scientometrics **95**(2), 503–528 (2013). https://doi.org/10.1007/s11192-013-0964-1

12. Gómez-Núñez, A.J., Vargas-Quesada, B., Chinchilla-Rodríguez, Z., Batagelj, V., Moya-Anegon, F.: Visualization and analysis of SCImago Journal & Country Rank structure via journal clustering. Aslib J. Inf. Manag. **68**(5), 607–627 (2016). https://doi.org/10.1108/AJIM-12-2015-0205

13. Gómez-Núñez, A.J., Vargas-Quesada, B., de Moya-Anegón, F.: Updating the SCImago journal and country rank classification: a new approach using Ward's clustering and alternative combination of citation measures. J. Am. Soc. Inf. Sci. Technol. **67**(1), 178–190 (2016). https://doi.org/10.1002/asi.23370

14. Wolfram, D., Zhao, Y.: A comparison of journal similarity across six disciplines using citing discipline analysis. J. Informetr. **8**(4), 840–853 (2014). https://doi.org/10.1016/j.joi.2014.08.003

15. Wang, F., Wolfram, D.: Assessment of journal similarity based on citing discipline analysis. J. Am. Soc. Inf. Sci. Technol. **66**(6), 1189–1198 (2015). https://doi.org/10.1002/asi.23241

16. González-Albo, B., Bordons, M.: Articles vs. proceedings papers: do they differ in research relevance and impact? A case study in the Library and Information Science field. J. Informetr. **5**(3), 369–381 (2011). https://doi.org/10.1016/j.joi.2011.01.011

17. Liu, G., Yang, L.: Popular research topics in the recent journal publications of library and information science. J. Acad. Librariansh. **45**(3), 278–287 (2019). https://doi.org/10.1016/j.acalib.2019.04.001

18. Lamba, M., Madhusudhan, M.: Mapping of topics in DESIDOC Journal of Library and Information Technology, India: a study. Scientometrics **120**(2), 477–505 (2019). https://doi.org/10.1007/s11192-019-03137-5

19. Boyack, K.W., Newman, D., Duhon, R.J., et al.: Clustering more than two million biomedical publications: comparing the accuracies of nine text-based similarity approaches. PLoS One **6**(3), e18029 (2011). https://doi.org/10.1371/journal.pone.0018029

20. Lin, J.: Divergence measures based on the Shannon entropy. IEEE Trans. Inf. Theory **37**(1), 145–151 (1991). https://doi.org/10.1109/18.61115

21. Weismayer, C., Pezenka, I.: Identifying emerging research fields: a longitudinal latent semantic keyword analysis. Scientometrics 113(3), 1757–1785 (2017). https://doi.org/10.1007/s11192-017-2555-z

22. Song, M., Heo, G.E., Lee, D.: Identifying the landscape of Alzheimer's disease research with network and content analysis. Scientometrics 102(1), 905–927 (2015). https://doi.org/10.1007/s11192-014-1372-x

23. Fang, D., Yang, H., Gao, B., Li, X.: Discovering research topics from library electronic references using latent Dirichlet allocation. Libr. Hi Tech 36(3), 400–410 (2018). https://doi.org/10.1108/LHT-06-2017-0132

24. Yang, S., Wang, F.: Visualizing information science: author direct citation analysis in China and around the world. J. Informetr. 9(1), 208–225 (2015). https://doi.org/10.1016/j.joi.2015.01.001

25. Ding, Y.: Scientific collaboration and endorsement: network analysis of coauthorship and citation networks. J. Informetr. 5(1), 187–203 (2011). https://doi.org/10.1016/j.joi.2010.10.008

26. Zhang, L., Liu, X., Janssens, F., Liang, L., Glänzel, W.: Subject clustering analysis based on ISI category classification. J. Informetr. 4(2), 185–193 (2010). https://doi.org/10.1016/j.joi.2009.11.005

27. An, L., Yu, C., Li, G.: Visual topical analysis of Chinese and American Library and Information Science research institutions. J. Informetr. 8(1), 217–233 (2014). https://doi.org/10.1016/j.joi.2013.12.002

28. Zhang, L., Janssens, F., Liang, L., Glänzel, W.: Journal cross-citation analysis for validation and improvement of journal-based subject classification in bibliometric research. Scientometrics 82(3), 687–706 (2010). https://doi.org/10.1007/s11192-010-0180-1

29. Leydesdorff, L.: Visualization of the citation impact environments of scientific journals: an online mapping exercise. J. Am. Soc. Inf. Sci. Technol. 58(1), 25–38 (2007). https://doi.org/10.1002/asi.20406

30. Htoo, T.H.H., Na, J.C.: Disciplinary differences in altmetrics for social sciences. Online Inf. Rev. 41(2), 235–251 (2017). https://doi.org/10.1108/OIR-12-2015-0386

31. Salton, G., Yang, C.S.: On the specification of term values in automatic indexing. J. Doc. 29(4), 351–372 (1973). https://doi.org/10.1108/eb026562

32. Salton, G., Yang, C.S., Yu, C.T.: A theory of term importance in automatic text analysis. J. Am. Soc. Inf. Sci. 26(1), 33–44 (1975). https://doi.org/10.1002/asi.4630260106

33. Liu, Q., Ye, Y.: A study on mining bibliographic records by designed software SATI: case study on library and information science. J. Inf. Resour. Manag. 2(1), 50–58 (2012). (in Chinese)

34. Zhang, J., Korfhage, R.R.: A distance and angle similarity measure method. J. Am. Soc. Inf. Sci. 50(9), 772–778 (1999). https://doi.org/10.1002/(SICI)1097-4571(1999)50:9%3c772:AID-ASI5%3e3.0.CO;2-E

How Does Media Reflect the OA and Non-OA Scientific Literature? A Case Study of Environment Sustainability

Tahereh Dehdarirad(✉) ⓘ, Jonathan Freer,
and Alexander Mladenovic

Department of Communication and Learning in Science,
Chalmers University of Technology, Göteborg, Sweden
tahereh.dehdarirad@chalmers.se

Abstract. News outlets and popular science magazines have played an important role in increasing the public's knowledge, engagement with and understanding of global environmental issues in recent years. Increased access to scholarly outputs might foster a culture of greater scientific education, which in turn could have a direct impact on public policy. This paper aimed to study: (i) Which topics in the area of environmental sustainability have been communicated to the members of the public via News and Popular Science articles. (ii) If these topics were also found in OA and Non-OA scientific articles. Three data sets comprising documents published between 2014 and 2018 were obtained from ProQuest and Scopus databases. Our findings showed four topics have been communicated to the general public via News and Popular Science articles. *'Environmental protection'* and *'Socio-economic aspects of environmental sustainability'* were the common topics amongst OA, Non-OA and News and Popular Science articles. Although the three sets had two topics in common, they placed different levels of importance on different topics. In the OA set *'Biodiversity management & wildlife conservation'* and *'Sustainable agriculture'* were regarded as motor topics. In the News and Popular Science set, *'Environmental policy'* appeared as a well-developed and motor topic.

Keywords: Environmental sustainability · Science journalism · Open Access · General public · News · Popular Science articles · Strategic diagram · Clustering · Visualization

1 Introduction

News outlets and popular science magazines have played an important role in increasing the public's knowledge, engagement with and understanding of global environmental issues in recent years. They have become influential communicators of climate change, linking science and policy with the public [4]. Newspapers have been one of the media sources used most by students and the lay public to find information about environmental issues [11, 14]. Climate concerns have also been widely reflected upon and addressed by popular culture as shown, for example, by the computer-animated Hollywood film *Ice Age 2: The Meltdown* [17].

© Springer Nature Switzerland AG 2020
A. Sundqvist et al. (Eds.): iConference 2020, LNCS 12051, pp. 768–781, 2020.
https://doi.org/10.1007/978-3-030-43687-2_64

Good science journalism can make complex topics accessible to the general public, whilst still being scientifically accurate. However, science journalism can also over-simplify and present subject material in a misleading manner [5]. Thus, science communication by journalists might be impeded by different factors such as scientists' lack of control over the communication process, journalist's misunderstanding of scientists' language, and the fact that scientists and journalist are driven by different agendas [19].

Removing paywalls from scholarly literature and providing universal access to all readers, including members of the public is a global goal of the Open Access movement [18, 21]. In 2002, the Budapest Open Access Initiative provided the Open Access (OA) movement with a tangible goal and strategies to make this happen [7]. The goal of making research output freely available in this manner has been widely accepted as a desirable phenomenon. It has become a reality in many academic spheres [16].

Since 2006, the European Commission has been developing policies for Open Access [22]. In September 2018, 11 top national research funders and the European Research Council created *cOAlition S* and launched *Plan S*, an initiative that focuses on broad accessibility. It is driven by the view that "free access to all scientific publications from publicly funded research is a moral right of citizens" [9]. Increased access to scholarly outputs might foster a culture of greater scientific education, which in turn could have a direct impact on public policy [24], particularly in domains such as climate change and global health. This could also increase public engagement in scientific research [20, 21]. Nevertheless, problems such as fragmented institutional spending on publication costs and a lack of transparency regarding publication fees have been raised regarding open access publishing [12, 13]. Thus, it would be interesting to compare the performance of OA articles and Non-OA articles in terms of the topics being communicated to the public via News and Popular Science articles.

Therefore, this paper has two aims:

(i) to investigate which topics in the area of environmental sustainability have been communicated to the members of the public via News and Popular Science magazines

(ii) to study if these topics were also found in OA and Non-OA articles

To achieve the aims of this study, the three following objectives were pursued:

• to identify the topics studied in OA, Non-OA and News and Popular Science articles

• to study which topics of OA and Non-OA articles were also found in News and Popular Science articles

• to compare the importance placed on different topics by OA, Non-OA and News and Popular Science articles.

2 Methodology

2.1 Data Collection and Processing

The chosen field for this paper was environmental sustainability. Three data sets comprising documents published between 2014 and 2018 were obtained:

(i)   Open Access (OA) set: 11,387 Open Access articles and reviews obtained from ProQuest and Scopus databases
(ii) Non-Open Access (Non-OA) set: 32,626 Non-Open Access articles and reviews obtained from ProQuest and Scopus databases
(iii) News and Popular Science magazines set (News and Popular Science set): 117,292 news articles and popular science magazine articles obtained from the ProQuest *News & Newspapers* database.

In order to obtain the data, the following three queries were performed in the ProQuest *Science & Technology, Business, Health & Medicine, Art & Social Sciences* and *News & Newspapers* databases:

- *MAINSUBJECT.EXACT("Sustainable development") OR SU ("Environment* sustainab*")*
- *SU (sustainab*) AND SU (environment*)*
- *MAINSUBJECT.EXACT("Sustainability   reporting")   OR*
  MAINSUBJECT.EXACT("Environmental   management")   OR
  MAINSUBJECT.EXACT("Environmental   protection")   OR
  MAINSUBJECT.EXACT("Economic   policy")   OR
  MAINSUBJECT.EXACT("Sustainability   management")   OR
  MAINSUBJECT.EXACT("Industrial   policy")   OR
  MAINSUBJECT.EXACT("Environmental   policy")   OR
  MAINSUBJECT.EXACT("Natural   resource   management")   OR
  MAINSUBJECT.EXACT("Sustainable   design")   OR
  MAINSUBJECT.EXACT("Sustainable   agriculture")   OR
  MAINSUBJECT.EXACT("Environmental   economics")   OR
  MAINSUBJECT.EXACT("Sustainable   materials")   OR
  MAINSUBJECT.EXACT("Environmental stewardship")

This resulted in a total of 33,866 unique documents for the first and second sets and 117,292 news articles for the third set.

To ensure that the largest possible number of documents relevant to the first and second sets were included in our analysis, we also conducted a search in Scopus using SciVal Topic Prominence section. To do this, we defined a new research area called *environmental sustainability*, based on the following topics: environmental sustainability, environmental management and sustainable development. This resulted in a total of 10,147 OA and Non-OA documents. As a result of using the two search methods, our total data set comprised 44,013 documents. Of these, 11,387 were defined as Open Access and 32,626 Non-Open Access. The Open Access status of the documents was obtained from *Unpaywall.org*. The papers obtained from Scopus were tagged using the subject terms provided by the ProQuest database. This was done by converting all author, index, title keywords and topics of the Scopus documents to ProQuest subject terms using the ProQuest thesaurus.

The reasons for choosing for Scopus were twofold. Firstly, using Scopus, we were able to use the SciVal Topic Prominence section and define a new research area called environmental sustainability. Secondly, each paper in Scopus is clustered into 97,000 Topics, based upon direct citation analysis. Each of the 97,000 Topics have been matched with one of the 1,500 Topic Clusters, using the same direct citation algorithm that creates the Topics. Using these Topic Clusters, we were able to convert the topics assigned to each paper to subject terms provided by the ProQuest database.

There were two reasons for using the ProQuest database. First, this database provides standard subject terms for all indexed items in the database using the ProQuest thesaurus. Using these standard subject terms, we were able to compare the topics obtained from three sets. Second, by using the News & Newspapers database, we were able to query and retrieve news articles from more than 3,000 of the world's news media sources.

2.2 Data Analysis and Procedures

The analysis and visualisation in this paper have been done using the udpipe, igraph R packages, Gephi and VOSviewer.

To identify the clusters in each data set, we applied Blondel et al. [3]'s Louvain method, a popular greedy optimization method. This iterative heuristic method works well for large-scale networks. It performs better and produces higher quality community partitions than several other algorithms [3, 15, 23]. Furthermore, in our study, this method provided a better modularity than other clustering methods such as the fast-greedy method and hierarchical clustering. It should be considered that the cluster analysis for the three sets was done after data cleaning was performed, in relation to stop words, punctuations and the removal of subject terms with a low frequency. In this paper, the analysis was based on subject terms that had a minimum frequency of 5. This frequency was chosen, as it provided us with a list of more relevant subject terms for our analysis. Furthermore, in all data sets, these terms accounted for more than 80% of the data.

In order to decide regarding the number of clusters in each set, we used Gephi and ran the Louvain cluster analysis at different resolution values (for example 1, 0.5, etc.). We compared the obtained modularity values, the number of corresponding clusters and their visualizations. We checked to see if the clustering made sense to a scholar with knowledge in the area of Environmental sustainability, and where required, we repeated the task with different resolution values.

To provide a visualized overview of the most co-occurrent subject terms in each cluster, VOSviewer heatmaps were used. The size of subject terms in each heatmap in the results section is equal to the co-occurrence frequency of each subject term. It should be considered that each term can appear only in one cluster.

In order to identify and visualize the position and importance of clusters obtained from using the Louvain method, strategic diagrams were built for each set. A strategic diagram is a two-dimensional space, built by plotting themes according to their centrality and density, where the abscissa axis represents the centrality, the ordinate axis represents the density, and the origin is denoted by the median or mean value of the two, centrality and density [6, 8, 10].

In this paper the origin was calculated using the mean value of centrality and the mean value of density. The density, or the internal cohesion index, indicates the strength of the linkage that each word has with other words within the same cluster (or theme). The centrality, or the external cohesion index, indicates the strength of the linkage that each keyword has with other keywords in other clusters [10].

A strategic diagram divides the space into four quadrants, such that there are four types of themes according to their location [6, 8].

- *Motor topics (upper-right quadrant)*: The topics that are most developed and are important for the structure of a research field.
- *Specialized topics (upper-left quadrant)*: These topics are considered to have marginal importance to the field, are very specialized and peripheral in nature.
- *Emerging or disappearing topics (lower-left quadrant):* These are the topics that have received temporary importance in a field. Thus, they could be either emerging or disappearing.
- *General, basic and transversal topics (lower-right quadrant):* These are the topics that are important for a research field in the development stage.

3   Results

3.1   Clusters Identified in the News and Popular Science Set

The results of Louvain cluster analysis on 117,292 News and Popular Science documents showed 4 clusters (see Fig. 1). For this data set, there were 5,541 unique subject

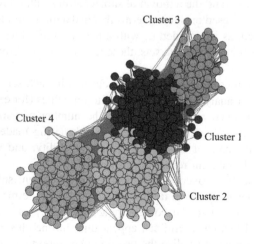

Fig. 1. Clusters identified in the field of environmental sustainability (2014–2018) for the News and Popular Science set

terms with the minimum frequency of five. The origin of the strategic diagram for the News and Popular Science set was based on the centrality value of (0.74) and density value (0.06).

Table 1 and Fig. 2 show the number of terms, the name and the heat map of each cluster which is named as a topic.

Table 1. Clusters identified in the field of environmental sustainability (2014–2018) for the News and Popular science set

Cluster number	Number of terms	Topic name	Centrality	Density	Topic type
1	2,051	Socio-economic aspects of environmental sustainability	0,67	0,04	Emerging/disappearing
2	2,079	Environment Protection (Water & Air Quality)	0,95	0,05	Basic
3	571	Environmental policy	0,82	0,11	Motor
4	840	Environmental stewardship and education	0,54	0,04	Emerging/disappearing

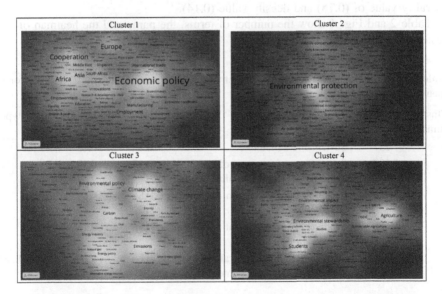

Fig. 2. Heatmaps of the clusters identified in the field of environmental sustainability (2014–2018) for the News and Popular Science set

3.2 Clusters Identified in the OA Set

By applying Louvain cluster analysis on 11,387 open access documents, we identified 5 clusters (see Fig. 3).

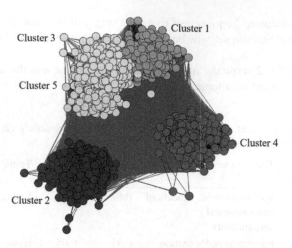

Fig. 3. Clusters identified in the field of environmental sustainability (2014–2018) for the Open Access set

For this data set, there were 5,306 unique subject terms with the minimum frequency of five. The origin of the strategic diagram for the OA set was based on the centrality value of (0.75) and density value (0.14).

Table 2 and Fig. 4 show the number of terms, the name and the heatmap of each cluster which is named as a topic.

Table 2. Clusters identified in the field of environmental sustainability (2014–2018) for the Open Access set

Cluster number	Number of terms	Topic name	Centrality	Density	Topic type
1	757	Sustainable agriculture	0.78	0.15	Motor
2	1,459	Socio-economic aspects of environmental sustainability	0.77	0.10	Basic
3	1,433	Environmental protection (Water & Air quality)	0.86	0.09	Basic
4	1,111	Biodiversity management & wildlife conservation	0.76	0.15	Motor
5	276	Computer & mathematical models for water resources management	0.60	0.20	Specialized

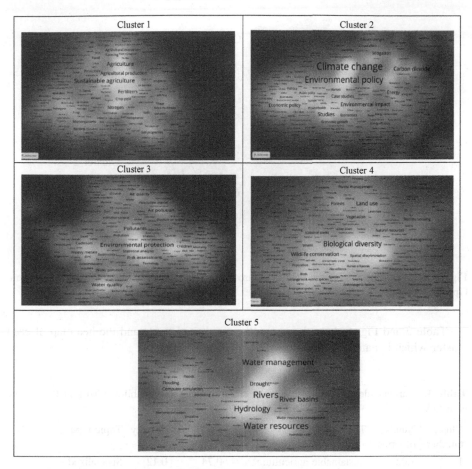

Fig. 4. Heatmaps of the clusters identified in the field of environmental sustainability (2014–2018) for the Open Access set

3.3   Clusters Identified in the Non-OA Set

By applying Louvain cluster analysis on 32,626 Non-OA documents, 6 clusters were identified (see Fig. 5).

For this data set, there were 8,360 unique subject terms with the minimum frequency of five. The origin of the strategic diagram for the Non-OA set was based on the centrality value of (0.76) and density value (0.11).

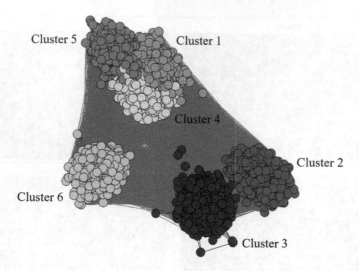

Fig. 5. Clusters identified in the field of environmental sustainability (2014–2018) for the Non-Open Access set

Table 3 and Fig. 6 show the name, the number of terms and the heatmap of each cluster which is named as a topic.

Table 3. Clusters identified in the field of environmental sustainability (2014–2018) for the Non-OA set

Cluster number	Number of terms	Topic name	Centrality	Density	Topic type
1	1,021	Sustainable agriculture	0,74	0,12	Specialized
2	1,126	Biodiversity management & wildlife conservation	0,75	0,11	Both specialized and emerging/disappearing
3	3,119	Socio-economic aspects of environmental sustainability	0,78	0,07	Basic
4	790	Computer & mathematical models for water resources management	0,69	0,16	Specialized
5	1,074	Sustainable energy and environmental impact	0,79	0,10	Basic
6	1,230	Environmental Protection (Water & Air Quality)	0,83	0,10	Basic

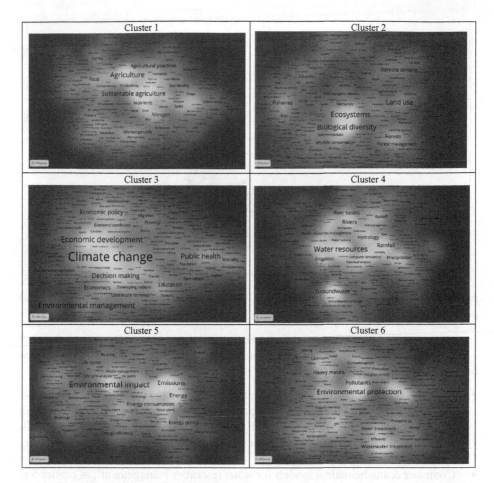

Fig. 6. Heatmaps of the clusters identified in the field of environmental sustainability (2014–2018) for the Non-Open Access set

3.4 The Comparison of Clusters Among the Three Data Sets

To make the comparison between the three networks easier, the same topics were shown with similar colours throughout the entire paper.

Comparing the networks of three data sets, it can be seen that all networks have two clusters in common (see Fig. 7). These clusters, shown in yellow and blue, are 'Environmental protection' and 'Socio-economic aspects of environmental sustainability', respectively. Additionally, when comparing the networks of OA and Non-OA sets, it is interesting to see that all clusters are the same, except for cluster 5, 'Sustainable energy and environmental impact', only found in the Non-OA set. Therefore, similar topics have been studied in the field environmental sustainability between 2014 and 2018 for both the OA and Non-OA data sets.

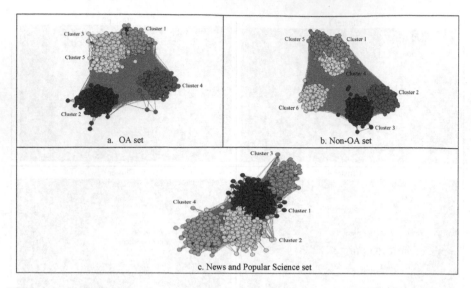

Fig. 7. Comparison of the three networks in terms of the clusters identified in the field of environmental sustainability (2014–2018)

When comparing clusters in the three sets using strategic diagrams (see Fig. 8), the following results were obtained:

- In the OA set 'Biodiversity management & wildlife conservation' and 'Sustainable agriculture', shown as 4 and 1, were regarded as well-developed topics, whereas, in the News and Popular Science set, 'Environmental policy' appeared as a well-developed and motor topic. This cluster is shown in grey. No motor topics were found in the Non-OA set.

- 'Computer & mathematical models for water resources management', as cluster 5 in the OA set and as cluster 4 in the Non-OA set was the smallest topic and appeared as a specialized topic in the both sets.

- The biggest cluster in both OA and Non-OA sets was 'Socio-economic aspects of environmental sustainability' (shown in blue), whereas for the News and Popular Science set, this was 'Environmental protection' (shown in yellow). In all three sets, these two big topics appeared as basic topics. This means that these topics are important for the field and are in the development stage. The second biggest cluster for the News and Popular Science set was 'Socio-economic aspects of environmental sustainability' (shown in blue), which had a marginal size difference when compared with the first biggest cluster in the same set.

- While there were no emerging/disappearing topics for the OA set, 'Environmental stewardship and education' and 'Socio-economic aspects of sustainable development', shown as clusters 4 and 1, were the emerging topics in the News and Popular Science set. This means that these topics are both weakly developed and are marginal.

- In the Non-OA set there was only 'Biodiversity management & wildlife conservation', shown as cluster 2, which appeared as both a specialized and an emerging/disappearing topic. This means that this topic is emerging and is very specialized and peripheral in nature.

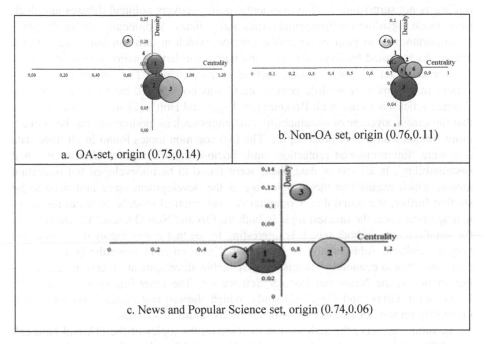

a. OA-set, origin (0.75,0.14)

b. Non-OA set, origin (0.76,0.11)

c. News and Popular Science set, origin (0.74,0.06)

Fig. 8. Comparison of the three networks in terms of importance of topics identified in the field of environmental sustainability (2014–2018)

4   Conclusion and Discussion

This paper aimed to study which topics related to 'Environmental sustainability' have been communicated to the public via News and Popular Science articles and to also ascertain if these topics were found in OA and Non-OA scientific articles. Our findings showed that four topics were communicated to members of the public via News and Popular Science between 2014 and 2018. These topics were 'Socio-economic aspects of environmental sustainability', 'Environment Protection', 'Environmental policy' and 'Environmental stewardship and education'. Two topics were found in common between Open Access, Non-Open Access, and the News and Popular Science articles. These were 'Environmental protection' and 'Socio-economic aspects of environmental sustainability'. When comparing OA and Non-OA topics, it was interesting to see that both OA and Non-OA articles addressed the same topics, with the exception of 'Sustainable energy and environmental impact', which was found only in the Non-OA set. Therefore, we conclude that both OA and Non-OA data sets have focused on similar topics in the field of 'Environmental sustainability' between 2014 and 2018.

Our findings also showed that although the three data sets had two topics in common, they placed different levels of importance on different topics. For example, 'Biodiversity management & wildlife conservation' and 'Sustainable agriculture' were found to be motor topics in the OA set, whilst in the News and Popular Science set, 'Environmental policy' appeared as a well-developed and motor topic. The latter finding is not surprising, as 'Environmental policy' covers political debates and decisions made regarding environmental issues and policies. Additionally, the media plays an important role in influencing public opinion, which in turn can influence political actors. As indicated by Lyytimäki [17] the media can have a major influence on how the agenda is set for policy issues, such as climate change. The finding that 'Biodiversity management & wildlife conservation' was not covered by News and Popular Science articles is in line with Barkemeyer, Figge and Holt's [1] study, which showed that the media coverage of sustainability challenges such as biodiversity has been much more limited than that of other topics. The two common topics found in all three data sets were 'Environmental protection' and 'Socio-economic aspects of environmental sustainability'. In all sets of data, these were found to be undeveloped but important topics, which means that these topics are at the development stage and need to be studied further. We found that 'Computer & mathematical models for water resources management', was the smallest topic in both the OA and Non-OA sets. Although this is the smallest topic in both sets, it is interesting to see that it was highly developed and very specialized. Additionally, the topics of 'Environmental stewardship and education' and 'Socio-economic aspects of sustainable development' received temporary importance in the News and Popular Science set. The latter finding is in line with Barkemeyer, Givry, and Figge' [2] study, which showed that media coverage of sustainability related socioeconomic issues showed seasonal patterns.

In future research, the authors aim to compare the topics of the OA and Non-OA scientific articles which have been cited in News and Popular science articles.

References

1. Barkemeyer, R., Figge, F., Holt, D.: Sustainability-related media coverage and socioeconomic development: a regional and north-south perspective. Environ. Plann. C: Govern. Policy **31**, 716–740 (2013)
2. Barkemeyer, R., Givry, P., Figge, F.: Trends and patterns in sustainability-related media coverage: a classification of issue-level attention. Environ. Plann. C: Polit. Space **36**, 937–962 (2017)
3. Blondel, V.D., Guillaume, J.-L., Lambiotte, R., Lefebvre, E.: Fast unfolding of communities in large networks. J. Stat. Mech: Theory Exp. **2008**, P10008 (2008)
4. Boykoff, M., Luedecke, G.: Elite News Coverage of Climate Change. Oxford University Press, Oxford (2016)
5. Brownell, S.E., Price, J.V., Steinman, L.: Science communication to the general public: why we need to teach undergraduate and graduate students this skill as part of their formal scientific training. J. Undergrad. Neurosci. Educ. **12**, E6–E10 (2013)
6. Callon, M., Courtial, J.P., Laville, F.: Co-word analysis as a tool for describing the network of interactions between basic and technological research: the case of polymer chemsitry. Scientometrics **22**, 155–205 (1991)

7. Chan, L., et al.: Budapest open access initiative (2002)
8. Cobo, M.J., López-Herrera, A.G., Herrera-Viedma, E., Herrera, F.: An approach for detecting, quantifying, and visualizing the evolution of a research field: a practical application to the fuzzy sets theory field. J. Inform. **5**, 146–166 (2011)
9. European Commission: 'Plan S' and 'cOAlition S' – Accelerating the transition to full and immediate Open Access to scientific publications (2018)
10. Dehdarirad, T., Villarroya, A., Barrios, M.: Research trends in gender differences in higher education and science: a co-word analysis. Scientometrics **101**, 273–290 (2014)
11. Detjen, J.: The media's role in science education. Bioscience **45**, S58–S63 (1995)
12. Green, T.: Is open access affordable? Why current models do not work and why we need internet-era transformation of scholarly communications. Learn. Publish. **32**, 13–25 (2019)
13. Jahn, N., Tullney, M.: A study of institutional spending on open access publication fees in Germany. PeerJ **4**, e2323–e2323 (2016)
14. Keinonen, T., Yli-Panula, Y.-P., Svens, M., Vilkonis, R., Persson, C., Palmberg, I.: Environmental issues in the media – studentsí perceptions in the three nordic-baltic countries. J. Teach. Educ. Sustain. **16**, 32 (2014)
15. Kirianovskii, I., Granichin, O., Proskurnikov, A.: A new randomized algorithm for community detection in large networks**the results of the paper have been obtained at IPME RAS under support of Russian Foundation for Basic Research (RFBR) grant 16-07-00890. IFAC-PapersOnLine **49**, 31–35 (2016)
16. Kriegeskorte, N., Walther, A., Deca, D.: An emerging consensus for open evaluation: 18 visions for the future of scientific publishing. Front. Comput. Neurosci. **6**, 94 (2012)
17. Lyytimäki, J.: Mainstreaming climate policy: the role of media coverage in Finland. Mitig. Adapt. Strat. Glob. Change **16**, 649–661 (2011)
18. Matthias, L., Jahn, N., Laakso, M.: The two-way street of open access journal publishing: flip it and reverse it. Publications **7**, 23 (2019)
19. Peters, H.P.: Gap between science and media revisited: scientists as public communicators. Proc. Natl. Acad. Sci. **110**, 14102 (2013)
20. Stodden, V.: Open science: policy implications for the evolving phenomenon of user-led scientific innovation. J. Sci. Commun. **9**, A05 (2010)
21. Tennant, J.P., Waldner, F., Jacques, D.C., Masuzzo, P., Collister, L.B., Hartgerink, C.H.: The academic, economic and societal impacts of open access: an evidence-based review. F1000Research **5**, 632 (2016)
22. Togia, S., Koseoglou, E., Zapounidou, S., Nikolaos, T.: Open access infrastructure in Greece: current status, challenges and perspectives. In: ELPUB 2018, Toronto, Canada (2018)
23. Wakita, K., Tsurumi, T.: Finding community structure in mega-scale social networks: [extended abstract]. In: 16th International Conference on World Wide Web, Banff, Alberta, Canada (2007)
24. Zuccala, A.: Open access and civic scientific information literacy. Inform. Res.: Int. Electron. J. **15**(1) (2010)

Using Link Prediction Methods to Examine Networks of Co-occurring MeSH Terms in Zika and CRISPR Research

Meng-Hao Li[✉]

George Mason University, Arlington, VA 22201, USA
mlill@gmu.edu

Abstract. This research applied the Literature-based Discovery approach and supervised link prediction methods to predict previously unknown research links between medical subject headings (MeSH) terms in Zika and CRISPR research. Both Zika and CRISPR research was extracted from the PubMed dataset and analyzed respectively. For Zika research, the timeframe for the data extraction was between 1952 and 2017, containing 1,939 research articles and 2,546 distinct MeSH terms. For CRISPR research, the data were collected from 2002 to 2016, including 4,572 research articles and 4,203 distinct MeSH terms. The link prediction measures, Common Neighbor, Jaccard's Coefficient, Adamic/Adr, Preferential Attachment, and Resource Allocation Index, were generated as input variables to predict whether a non-linkage between two MeSH terms is formed in the future. This research applied the Logistic Regression, Naïve Bayes, Decision Tree, and Random Forests algorithms to build classification models. Because the outcome variables are highly unbalanced, the stratified sampling and under/over-sampling methods were used to generate representative training and testing sets. The results indicate that the Logistic Regression has better performance for predicting a MeSH link in Zika research. In contrast, the Naïve Bayes has better performance for predicting a MeSH link in CRISPR research. Thus, the methods proposed by this research can be used to discover possible research areas of MeSH terms and new research directions. For biomedical policymakers, the results can be considered as an evidence-based source for the decisions of public fund allocation.

Keywords: Link predictions · Literature-based Discovery · Text mining

1 Research Purpose

The purpose of this research is to apply the Literature-based Discovery approach and supervised link prediction methods to predict unknown connections between biomedical concepts. The Literature-based Discovery is a text mining methodology that is used to discover hidden or unknown relationships from existing knowledge (publication). The Literature-based Discovery has been applied to several fields including discovering disease candidate genes, finding drug-drug interaction or predicting interactions between diseases and proteins. The Swanson's seminal hypothesis is an example of using this approach to discover a potential research link between fish oil

© Springer Nature Switzerland AG 2020
A. Sundqvist et al. (Eds.): iConference 2020, LNCS 12051, pp. 782–789, 2020.
https://doi.org/10.1007/978-3-030-43687-2_65

and Raynaud's disease [1]. Previously, Raynaud's disease did not have effective treatments, so Swanson analyzed 489 Raynaud's disease related research articles and found that there is a research link between fish oil and blood thinners, and another research link between blood thinners and Raynaud's disease. Swanson then suspected that there is likely a research connection between fish oil and Raynaud's disease and hypothesized that fish oil may be a possible treatment for Raynaud's disease (Fig. 1).

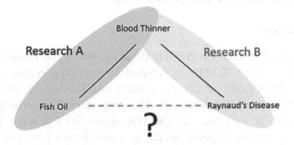

Fig. 1. Swanson's hypothesis (1989)

Kastrin, Rindflesch, and Hristovski applied the similar approach to seek potential research linkages between medical subject headings (MeSH) in biomedical research [2]. Their research collected PubMed database's entire articles (21,850,751) between 1951 and 2010 and constructed co-occurring MeSH-MeSH networks. However, the research used previous research articles as a training set and current research articles as a testing set. This approach tends to overlook the time varying covariates and over-estimate the models (Fig. 2). Because the previous existing co-occurring MeSH-MeSH linkages are highly possible to be continually researched by scholars, the classification models are likely to fail to learn potential new MeSH-MeSH linkages in current research articles. That is, the models may be good to predict a research linkage in a network without time varying covariates but poorly predict for a linkage formation with time varying covariates. Thus, this research built classification models using both T1 and T2 data points for training and testing sets (Fig. 3) and examined how a non-linkage of MeSH terms becomes a linkage of MeSH terms. This research selected Zika and CRISPR as examples to demonstrate how link prediction and machine learning methods can be used to explore potential research areas.

Training models [input, output]	Testing models [input, output]
T1	T2

Fig. 2. Kastrin, Rindflesh & Hristovski [2]

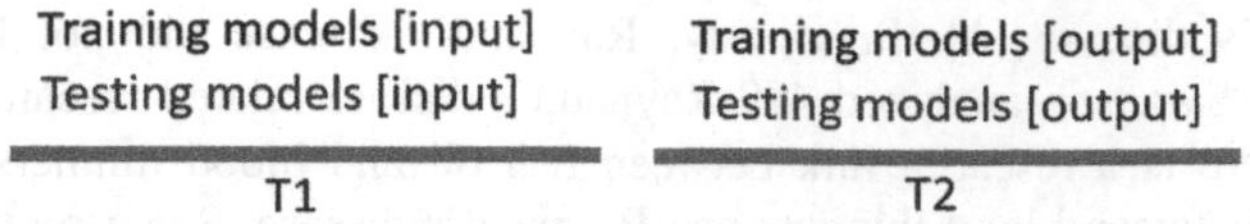

Training models [input]   Training models [output]
Testing models [input]   Testing models [output]

T1   T2

Fig. 3. Present research

2 Data Collection and Pre-processing

2.1 Data Collection

The data were collected from the PubMed database, the largest biomedical database in the world [3]. Zika and CRISPR are selected as examples in this research because (1) according to the Center for Disease Control and Prevention, there is no specific medicine or vaccine for Zika virus [4]. It is important for researchers to find out effective treatments or vaccines. (2) CRISPR stands for Clustered Regularly Interspaced Short Palindromic Repeats, which is a simple yet powerful technology for editing genomes. The American Association for the Advancement of Science's awarded it as breakthrough of the year in 2015 [5]. All the papers published in PubMed have MEDLINE format [6], containing journal citations, abstracts, date of publication et al. for biomedical literature. MEDLINE also contains MeSH terms that used to describe article content, for example, DNA microarray analysis, Receptor Activity-Modifying Protein 2, Transcription Factors, Molecular Sequence Data, Diagnostic Errors or Travel Medicine. MeSHs are standardized terms which are assigned to articles by NIH experts. This research extracted MeSH terms from Zika and CRISPR's MEDLINE to construct MeSH-MeSH networks.

The following search rule was used to search Zika research articles published between 1952 and November 27, 2017. The total number of Zika articles is 1,939 and most of them were published in 2016 and 2017.

"zika virus" [MeSH Terms] OR ("zika" [All Fields] AND "virus" [All Fields]) OR "zika virus" [All Fields] OR "zika" [All Fields] OR "zika virus infection" [MeSH Terms] OR ("zika" [All Fields] AND "virus" [All Fields] AND "infection" [All Fields]) OR "zika virus infection" [All Fields]

The following search rule was used to search CRISPR research articles published between 2002 and 2016. The total number of CRISPR articles between 2002 and 2016 is 4,572.

"clustered regularly interspaced short palindromic repeats" [MeSH Terms] OR ("clustered" [All Fields] AND "regularly" [All Fields] AND "interspaced" [All Fields] AND "short" [All Fields] AND "palindromic" [All Fields] AND "repeats" [All Fields]) OR "clustered regularly interspaced short palindromic repeats" [All Fields] OR "crispr" [All Fields]

2.2 Data Pre-processing

All the data were downloaded from PubMed database and pre-process in MS SQL server. The MeSH terms were projected from article-MeSH relationships to MeSH-MeSH relationships. For example, two MeSH terms belonging to an article were assumed to have a linkage (association) between both (Fig. 4). Hence, if an article only includes one MeSH term, it is not possible to make any MeSH linkage of this article. This article then would be removed from analysis.

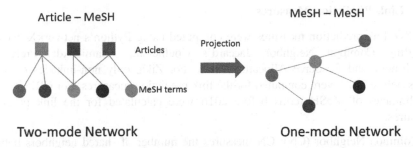

Fig. 4. Network projection

The data were organized as a node list, an edge list, and an outcome list for Zika and CRISPR research respectively. For Zika, the node list for Zika includes 2,546 nodes (distinct MeSH terms) in the network. The nodes were recoded as a sequence of numbers. The edge list is non-linkages (3,203,609) of MeSH terms before 2017 (1952–2016), which was built by removing linkages (36,167) of MeSH terms before 2017 from all possible linkages (3,239,785) of MeSH terms. The outcome list is whether non-linkage pairs of MeSH terms before 2017 have a linkage in 2017. The number of linkages of MeSH terms in 2017 is 14,445. The number of non-linkages of MeSH terms in 2017 is 3,189,164 (Table 1). Similar to the Zika data preparation process, the node list for CRISPR includes 4,203 nodes (distinct MeSH terms) in the network. The nodes were recoded as a sequence of numbers. The edge list is non-linkages (8,755,745) of MeSH before 2016 (2002–2015), which was built by removing linkages (74,758) of MeSH terms before 2016 from all possible linkages (8,830,503) of MeSH terms. The outcome list is whether non-linkage pairs of MeSH terms before 2016 have a linkage in 2016. The number of linkages of MeSH terms in 2016 is 47,333. The number of non-linkages of MeSH terms in 2017 is 8,708,412 (Table 1).

Table 1. The distributions of MeSHs

		N
Zika	Distinct MeSH terms	2,546
	All possible linkages of MeSH terms	3,239,785
	Linkages of MeSH terms before 2017	36,176
	Input: Non-linkages of MeSH terms before 2017	3,203,609
	Output: Linkages/Non-Linkages in 2017	14,445/3,189,164
CRISPR	Distinct MeSH terms	4,203
	All possible linkages of MeSH terms	8,830,503
	Linkages of MeSH terms before 2016	74,758
	Input: Non-linkages of MeSH terms before 2016	8,755,745
	Output: Linkages/Non-Linkages in 2016	47,333/8,708,412

Those data sets were imported to Python for computing link prediction measures (networkX package [7]) and building supervised machine learning models (sklearn package [8]).

2.3   Link Prediction Measures

The five link prediction measures were computed using Python's networkX package, including Common Neighbor, Jaccard's Coefficient, Adamic/Adr, Preferential Attachment, and Resource Allocation Index. For Zika, only non-linkages of MeSH terms before 2017 were computed for the link prediction measures. For CRISPR, only non-linkages of MeSH terms before 2016 were calculated for the link prediction measures.

- Common Neighbor (CN): CN measures the number of shared neighbors between two nodes.

$$s_{CN}(u,v) = |\Gamma(u) \cap \Gamma(v)|$$

- Jaccard's Coefficient (JC): JC is a normalized score of CN. It computes the ratio of common neighbors out of all neighbors.

$$s_{JC}(u,v) = \frac{|\Gamma(u) \cap \Gamma(v)|}{|\Gamma(u) \cup \Gamma(v)|}$$

- Adamic/Adar (AA). AA refines the counting of common neighbors by assigning the lower-connected neighbors with higher weights, which means that those neighbors are more unique to the nodes.

$$s_{AA}(u,v) = \sum_{z \in \Gamma(u) \cap \Gamma(v)} \frac{1}{\log|\Gamma(z)|}$$

- Preferential Attachment (PA). PA is the product of the degrees of two nodes.

$$s_{PA}(u,v) = |\Gamma(u)| \times |\Gamma(v)|$$

- Resource Allocation Index (RA): RA is fraction of a "resource" that a node can send to another through their common neighbors.

$$\sum_{w \in \Gamma(u) \cap \Gamma(v)} \frac{1}{|\Gamma(w)|}$$

3 Data Description

Table 2 show the distributions of each link predication measure. For Zika, most input variables (i.e. CN, JC, RA, AA, and PA) have about 50% zeros. The output variable (year 2017) has a highly skew distribution toward left. The mean of the output variable is about 0.45%. As for CRISPR, most input variables have about 75% zeros. The output variable (year 2016) has a highly skew distribution toward left. The mean of the output variable is 0.54%.

Table 2. Data description

		CN	JC	RA	AA	PA	Output
Zika	Count	3,203,609	3,203,609	3,203,609	3,203,609	3,203,609	3,203,609
	Mean	2.14	0.04	0.01	0.33	593.22	0.0045
	Std	3.48	0.05	0.02	0.60	1852.83	0.07
	Min	0	0	0	0	0	0
	25%	0	0	0	0	0	0
	50%	1	0.02	0	0.13	147	0
	75%	3	0.07	0	0.43	492	0
CRISPR	Count	8,755,745	8,755,745	8,755,745	8,755,745	8,755,745	8,755,745
	Mean	1.92	0.02	0	0.30	929.12	0.0054
	Std	4.71	0.03	0.02	0.80	3773.73	0.07
	Min	0	0	0	0	0	0
	25%	0	0	0	0	0	0
	50%	0	0	0	0	0	0
	75%	2	0.04	0	0.29	520	0

4 Modeling and Randomization Strategies

The Logistic Regression, Naïve Bayes, Decision Tree, and Random Forests algorithms were used to build classification models. The data were split 80% sample for the training set and 20% sample for the testing set. Because the outcome variables are highly unbalanced, the stratified sampling method was used to make representative training and testing sets. Additional over-sampling and under-sampling methods for Logistic Regression and Naïve Bayes were employed. The goal of over-sampling minority with replacement is to make minority to have a same number as majority.

For Zika, the minority group has 14,445. The minority group was sampled with replacement to make the number to 3,189,164 as the number of majority. For CRISPR, the minority group has 47,333. The minority group was sampled with replacement to make the number to 8,708,412 as the number of majority. Then, new samples were split into 80% for the training sets and 20% for the testing sets. The goal of under-sampling without replacement is to make majority to have a same number as minority. For Zika, the majority group has 3,189,164. The majority group was sampled without replacement to make the number to 14,445 as the number of minority. For CRISPR, the majority group has 8,708,412. The majority group was sampled without replacement to make the number to 47,333 as the number of minority. Next, new samples were split into 80% for the training sets and 20% for the testing tests.

5 Model Evaluation

All the models were built using Python's sklearn package with default settings. Table 3 show the model evaluation results for both training and testing sets. For Zika, the results show that Logistic Regression (LR), Naïve Bayes with over-sampling (NB-Over), and Naïve Bayes with under-sampling (NB-Under) have better AUC performance than others. Logistic Regression with over-sampling (LR-Over), Logistic Regression with under-sampling (LR-Under) and Decision Trees (DT) are not appropriate algorithms for predicting links in Zika research. For CRISPR, Naïve Bayes (NB), Naïve Bayes with over-sampling (NB-Over), and Naïve Bayes with under-sampling (NB-Under) have better AUC performance than others. Decision Trees performs worst for predicting links in CRISPR research.

Table 3. Model evaluation

			LR	LR-Over	LR-Under	NB	NB-Over	NB-Under	DT	RF
Zika	Training	Accuracy	0.9313	0.6473	0.6425	0.9737	0.6369	0.6350	0.9970	0.9969
		AUC	0.7685	0.5633	0.5594	0.7282	0.7359	0.7348	0.8953	0.8953
	Testing	Accuracy	0.9313	0.647	0.6457	0.9738	0.6368	0.6310	0.9939	0.9951
		AUC	0.7698	0.5627	0.5607	0.7289	0.7361	0.7400	0.5811	0.6658
CRISPR	Training	Accuracy	0.9156	0.6024	0.6044	0.9756	0.6486	0.6488	0.9969	0.9967
		AUC	0.7039	0.6363	0.6359	0.7169	0.7306	0.7300	0.8719	0.8719
	Testing	Accuracy	0.9151	0.7627	0.6063	0.9753	0.6485	0.6484	0.9924	0.9943
		AUC	0.7030	0.6362	0.6361	0.7180	0.7302	0.7305	0.4980	0.6256

6 Conclusion

The aim of this research is to use link prediction methods for predicting previously unknow research links between MeSH terms. Common Neighbor, Jaccard's Coefficient, Adamic/Adr, Preferential Attachment, and Resource Allocation Index were used as input variables to predict whether is a MeSH linkage between two MeSH terms. The results indicate that Logistic Regression has better performance for predicting a MeSH link in Zika research, and Naïve Bayes has better performance for predicting a MeSH link in CRISPR research. However, some limitations for this research are worthy to address. First, the classification of MeSH terms changes over time. New terms are growing up and would not reassign to previous articles. This might underestimate the models. Second, new research findings may be named or assigned to new MeSH terms after a couple of years. There is a delay between new findings and new MeSH terms, which may result in model under-estimation. Third, all the calculation in this research is based on unweighted networks. For the future research, scholars may consider using weighted networks to reassess the models.

References

1. Cameron, D., Bodenreider, O., Yalamanchili, H., et al.: A graph-based recovery and decomposition of swanson's hypothesis using semantic predications. J. Biomed. Inform. **46**(2), 238–251 (2013). https://doi.org/10.1016/j.jbi.2012.09.004
2. Kastrin, A., Rindflesch, T.C., Hristovski, D.: Link prediction on a network of co-occurring MeSH terms: towards literature-based discovery. Methods Inform. Med. **55**(4), 340–346 (2016). https://doi.org/10.3414/ME15-01-0108
3. PubMed Homepage. https://www.ncbi.nlm.nih.gov/pubmed/. Accessed 11 Sept 2018
4. Centers for Disease Control and Prevention homepage. https://www.cdc.gov/zika/symptoms/treatment.html. Accessed 11 Sept 2018
5. Science Homepage. http://www.sciencemag.org/news/2015/12/and-science-s-2015-break-through-year. Accessed 11 Sept 2018
6. MEDLINE®/PubMed® Resources Guide Homepage. https://www.nlm.nih.gov/bsd/pmresources.html. Accessed 11 Sept 2018
7. NetworkX Homepage. https://networkx.github.io. Accessed 11 Sept 2018
8. Scikit-learn Homepage. http://scikit-learn.org/stable. Accessed 11 Sept 2018

Extracting Methodological Sentences from Unstructured Abstracts of Academic Articles

Ruping Wang, Chengzhi Zhang$^{(\boxtimes)}$, Yingyi Zhang, and Jinzhu Zhang

Department of Information Management,
Nanjing University of Science and Technology, Nanjing 210094, China
{wangrp, zhangcz, zhangjinzhu}@njust.edu.cn,
zyyzjzs@163.com

Abstract. Methodological sentence is the smallest unit that depicts how the research method is used in one paper. Researchers can understand a method by reading these sentences. So, extracting methodological sentences automatically is meaningful for them to evaluate and select appropriate methods in their research process. However, previous studies rely too much on manually annotated corpus, in which the quantity is limited. Furthermore, some studies do not perform well when generalized to testing sets. In this paper, we use structured abstracts as training data to alleviate the burden of manually annotation. The label for each sentence is determined by its corresponding title in the abstract. Moreover, in order to extract methodological sentences more precisely, a rule-based method is applied for pruning the prediction result. In experimental results, the P, R, and F_1 value after pruning are 65.14%, 57.00% and 60.80% respectively, which are all higher than those are not pruned.

Keywords: Methodological sentences extraction · Information extraction · Text classification · Text mining

1 Introduction

The number of scientific articles published all over the world has reached a million level, and continues to increase at a rate of about three percent each year [1]. These articles outpace human being's reading and understanding capacities. It is time consuming for researchers to find an appropriate method for solving a problem from a large number of papers.

Methodological sentences are the content that describe the research methods used in an academic article. Figure 1 is an example of methodological sentences. This example shows "survey" and "structural equation modeling" are methods for implementing the task of "path analysis". The research method is the key to solve the research problems in the article. Extracting methodological sentences from scientific articles can help summarize and organize the methods distributed in the scientific articles, and help researchers to learn methods of their research field and thereby assist them to solve problems more efficiently. In this paper, we try to extract methodological sentences from unstructured abstracts. We treat the task of methodological sentences extraction as a sentence classification task here.

A. Sundqvist et al. (Eds.): iConference 2020, LNCS 12051, pp. 790–798, 2020.
https://doi.org/10.1007/978-3-030-43687-2_66

This study targeted community members who had purchased a specific cosmetic brand's products and had been members of an official brand fan page for at least one year. Using a survey of 488 valid samples and structural equation modeling was used to conduct path analyses.

Fig. 1. An example of methodological sentences.

Although few studies address the problem of methodological sentences extraction, there are some studies about general sentences extraction. Basing on annotated corpus, Noriega-Atala et al. extracted inter-sentence relation in biological research papers; they regarded the task as a classification task and employed Support Vector Machine, Logistic Regression and so on for predicting [2]. Wang et al. extracted evidence sentences that can explain/support answer predictions for multiple-choice MRC tasks. They used rule-based way to generate standard corpus and applied a Kernel-based Bayesian Network classification model [3]. To design a method for extracting clinically useful sentences that contain most clinically information, Morid et al. built a Kernel-based Bayesian Network classification model based on a gold standard corpus [4]. In summary, there is a problem in existing studies: many studies depend on the corpora annotated manually, which is time consuming and only can generate very few annotated corpora.

In this paper, we propose a new training set constructing strategy, through which we select structured abstracts of academic articles as our training set. This avoids manual annotation and facilitates the research process. Then, we apply deep learning method (BiLSTM and CON1D) to train our classifiers. Also, we use rule-based method for pruning the prediction result. Experimental results show that our strategy has a significant improvement in the task of methodological sentences extraction.

2   Methodology

2.1   Dataset

Structured Abstracts. We select five journals in Information Science (IS) as training data source. These five journals all have structured abstracts. We collect 3,282 articles of the five journals from their websites. Statistical information is shown in Table 1. After statistical analysis, we found that approximately 93.39% of the abstracts contain four common components: Purpose, Design/methodology/approach and Findings. So, we regard other types of components as "Other".

We use tokenization tool from NLTK[1] to tokenize sentences and obtain 30,542 sentences totally. According to our task, we focused on extracting methodological sentences. So, we divide sentences into 2 classes, i.e., methodological sentences and

---

[1] http://www.nltk.org/.

non-methodological sentences. The methodological sentences are obtained from the Design/methodology/approach component, and the non-methodological sentences are from other types of components. Finally, we get 23,480 non-methodological sentences and 7,062 methodological sentences.

Table 1. The research articles' information we obtain from five journals.

Journal	#articles	#sentences	#MS	#Non-MS
aslib Journal of Information Management	216	1,973	441	1,532
Journal of Documentation	733	6,735	1,512	5,223
Library Hi Tech	682	6,064	1,362	4,702
Online Information Review	785	7,006	1,618	5,388
The Electronic Library	866	8,764	2,129	6,635
Total	3,282	30,542	7,062	23,480

Note: MS and Non-MS denote methodological sentence and non-methodological sentence, respectively.

Unstructured Abstracts. We choose the journal **JASIST**[2] as our testing data resource. We collect 820 research articles of JASIST from 2003 to 2008. Since review articles contain many references, and rarely involve descriptions of research methods, we remove review articles from our corpus. To evaluate testing performance, we randomly choose 100 articles and annotate the sentences from their unstructured abstracts into MS class or Non-MS class.

2.2   Research Methodological Sentences Extraction Model

Neural Network Model. We apply CNN [5] and BiLSTM [6] for our sentence classification task. The optimal classifier will be selected according to the values of Precision, Recall and F_1. Then we will use the optimal classifier to extract research methodological sentences from unstructured abstracts.

Convolutional Neural Network (CNN). Convolutional networks (ConvNets) are a special type of neural network that are especially well adapted to computer vision applications [7]. It is one of the most popular algorithms for deep learning, a type of machine learning in which a model learns to perform classification tasks directly from images, video, or sound. Some studies have used Convolutional Neural Network for text classification task [8]. We use pre-trained word embedding (100 dim) as its input. The pre-trained word embedding is trained based upon the full-texts downloaded from the five journals.

---

[2] https://onlinelibrary.wiley.com/loi/23301643.

Bi-Directional Long Short-Term Memory (BiLSTM). BiLSTM is a combination of forward LSTM and backward LSTM, which is also utilized for text classification [9]. Same as CNN, we also use the 100-dimensional pre-trained word embedding for training BiLSTM.

Baseline Model. We use three traditional machine learning models as our baseline models.

Support Vector Machine (SVM). SVM is a binary-classification model [10]. For training this classifier, we apply Bag of Words (BOW) model to build vector space. We tokenize our training data into word set and select 100 feature words according to Chi-square. Then the vector space model (VSM) is constructed by computing the tfidf of these words. Ten-fold cross validation is applied for effect validation.

Naive Bayes (NB). NB is a classification method based on Bayes' Theorem and characteristic condition independent hypothesis [11]. This hypothesis is often not established in practical applications, which may influence the correctness of the classification. We use the BOW model as its input to train the classifier.

K-Nearest Neighbors (KNN). KNN means each sample can be represented by its nearest k neighbors. The major drawbacks of KNN is its low efficiency, which is because it needs to calculate the distance of each pair of points [12]. Here, we also use the BOW model to train KNN.

2.3 Extraction Results Pruning of MS from Unstructured Abstracts

Through our preliminary trials, we found that some sentences that are obviously not methodological sentences were predicted to be methodological sentences. So we further process the prediction result to obtain more correct classification results.

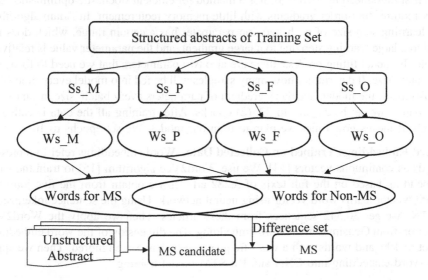

Fig. 2. The processing of further pruning the result predicted by BiLSTM.

Processing of pruning is shown in Fig. 2. As mentioned in 2.1, the structured abstracts consist of four types of components: Purpose (P), Design/methodology/approach (M), Findings (F) and Other (O). According to the function title of every part in the structured abstracts, we can easily obtain four types of sentence sets belonging to the four types of components respectively, denoted as Ss_P, Ss_M, Ss_F and Ss_O. Next, we acquire four types of word sets from the four sentence sets. We denote the four types of word sets as Ws_P, Ws_M, Ws_F and Ws_O. For every type of component, we calculate document frequency (DF) of every word in the sentence sets from which it comes. Then the words are sorted in reverse order according to the document frequency. We choose top N words from Ws_M as words for MS (Methodological Sentence); and we choose top M words from other three types of words sets respectively for words for Non-MS (Non-Methodological Sentence). These words are utilized to filter out sentences that may not be methodological sentences. Our experimental results show that this strategy has higher performance in extracting methodological sentences.

3   Experiments and Results Analysis

3.1   Experimental Setup

Parameters for Deep Learning. In order to get a good training performance, we tune some important parameters for CNN and BiLSTM. When compiling our model, we should set two main parameters. (1) loss function. Minimizing the loss function, a classifier can get the best model configuration. Here, we select binary_crossentropy as our loss function, which is applied to binary classification and calculates the distance between true value and predicted value. (2) optimizer. A classifier also needs optimizer to reduce the value of loss function. Adam algorithm is selected as the optimizer. Adam was first introduced in 2015 [13]. It is a method for efficient stochastic optimization that only requires first-order gradients with little memory requirement. In Adam algorithm, the learning step size of each iteration parameter has a certain range, which does not lead to a large learning step due to a large gradient, and the parameter value is relatively stable. In model fitting process, there are also two parameters that we need to focus on. (1) batch_size. It determines how many samples will be fed into model every time. That is also to say the model calculates gradient of parameters every batch_size instances. In this paper, we set batch_size to 32. (2) epochs. After training all the data is called an epoch. It means how times we plan to train our model. We set epochs to 10.

Word Embeddings Trained on Collected Data. Word embeddings refer to represent words as continuous vectors [14]. We use Word2Vec algorithm [15] to train the word embedding based on the full texts of 3,282 articles we obtain from the five journals. Word2vector learns word vector using neural network. Using the sentence tokenizer in NLTK, we get 30,542 sentences from these articles. Then we apply the Word2Vec function from Gensim to train word embedding. The dimension of the word embedding is set to 100, and words with a word frequency less than 5 are ignored. Then we apply this word embedding into CNN and BiLSTM model training.

3.2   Classification Model Selection of Methodological Sentences

In this section, we analyse the performance of classifiers on structured abstracts. Table 2 shows the results of methodological sentences classification.

From Table 2, we can find that deep learning methods perform better than traditional machine learning classifiers. CNN and BiLSTM have higher overall performance with F_1 value at 74.18% and 75.54% respectively. The best baseline model KNN only has F_1 value at 66.40%.

BiLSTM has an optimal performance overall. It gets the highest F_1 value at 75.54%. It is approximately 9 percentage points more than KNN, which is the best baseline model. Due to the low F_1 value, the baseline models are excluded from extracting methodological sentences from unstructured abstracts.

BiLSTM extracts methodological sentences more precisely. By comparing P value between CNN and BiLSTM, we can find that P value of BiLSTM is slightly higher than that of CNN by 1.72%.

BiLSTM also performs best in extracting method comprehensively. Its recall is 76.43%, also the best recall, which means that it is also superior to the other classifiers in extracting more methodological sentences.

Table 2. Performance of five classifiers on training set (%).

Model	Metrics		
	P	R	F_1
KNN	74.39	60.00	66.40
NB	74.61	56.29	64.15
SVM	**83.07**	45.21	58.53
CNN	72.96	75.44	74.18
BiLSTM	74.68	**76.43**	**75.54**

In summary, BiLSTM has the best classification effect, and will be selected for extracting methodological sentences from the unstructured abstracts.

3.3   Extracting Result of Methodological Sentences from Unstructured Abstracts

By evaluating classifiers' performance, we select BiLSTM as the final model to extract methodological sentences from unstructured abstracts.

Firstly, we randomly choose 100 articles from the selected 795 JASIST articles. 741 sentences in total are acquired from their unstructured abstracts. the average counts of sentence per abstract is about 7.35. Then we annotate these sentences into class 0 and class 1, which denote non-methodological sentence and methodological sentence respectively. Specifically, we carry out the process of annotation task as follows:

(1)   A coding schema is set by one researcher.
(2)   Two annotators from information science major together studied and discussed the coding schema.

(3) Pre-annotation is started: sentences from the same 25 abstracts are annotated independently by the two annotators.
(4) After the stage of pre-annotation, a meeting is held to revise the coding schema.
(5) Finally, the remaining 75 abstracts are annotated and the Kappa [16] is then calculated.

Landis and Koch [17] suggest that values of kappa above 0.60 denote excellent agreement; values between 0.41 and 0.60 show medium-level agreement and values of 0.40 or less show fair to poor agreement. The Kappa value in this research is about 0.46, which is medium-level agreement.

Then we use the optimal classifier BiLSTM to extract methodological sentences from sentences of the unstructured abstracts and get the final prediction result after pruning it using our proposed strategy. The results comparison is shown in Table 3.

Our proposed pruning strategy is significant in extracting more correct methodological sentences from unstructured abstracts. Pruning strategy can just achieve P, and F_1 value at 30.82%, and 44.63%. But its R is at a high value that is 81.00%. The reason may be that the feature words in rule-based method are very limited, which may lead to large number of sentences misjudged as methodological sentences. Before pruning the prediction result, BiLSTM just has very low P, R, and F_1 value at 38.82%, 30.10% and 33.91% respectively. After the result pruning, the model achieves better effect. It has a higher P value at 65.14%, indicating that it can make a precise prediction. And its R value is also higher at 57.00%. In general, BiLSTM after pruning has an overall good performance with F_1 value at 60.80%.

Table 3. Extraction results of pruning before and after (%).

Strategy	Metrics		
	P	R	F_1
Pruning	30.80	81.00	44.63
BiLstm	38.82	30.10	33.91
BiLstm+ pruning	**65.14**	**57.00**	**60.80**

In this section, we evaluate the training results of every classifier from aspects of P, R and F_1 to select the classifier which performs the best. Then we use the best classifier BiLSTM to test on the unstructured abstracts. However, when we analyse the prediction result, we find that some obviously not methodological sentences are predicted to be methodological sentence class, so we choose a strategy for pruning our prediction result. Finally, we get a good extraction effect.

4 Conclusion and Future Work

This paper aims to extract methodological sentences from unstructured abstracts of research articles. We apply structured abstracts to alleviate the burden of annotating corpus manually. Then we train classifiers for getting an optimal one to test on unstructured abstracts.

In our training results, the BiLSTM classifier has the best performance. So, we use it to extract methodological sentences from unstructured abstracts. Although abstract components of articles from the same field are similar, structured abstracts are more standardized than unstructured abstracts, and there are some differences between them. In order to compensate for the loss caused by these differences, we adopt the rule-based way to prune the results predicted by BiLSTM. The results indicate that our proposed pruning strategy is proved effective.

Here, we just extract methodological sentences from unstructured abstracts. However, more details about research methodology exist in the main body of an academic article. Moreover, the trained model works for the field of LIS, which may be not a good model for other fields. In the future, we will try to extract methodological sentences from full texts; we will explore the characteristics of research methodological sentences in different chapters; Furthermore, we will compare methodological sentences under different research methodologies. It will be significant for researchers especially for new researchers to evaluate and select appropriate research methods in their research process.

Acknowledgment. This work is supported by Major Projects of National Social Science Fund (No. 17ZDA291) and Postgraduate Research & Practice Innovation Program of Jiangsu Province (No. KYCX19_0246).

References

1. Bornmann, L., Mutz, R.: Growth rates of modern science: a bibliometric analysis based on the number of publications and cited references. J. Assoc. Inform. Sci. Technol. **66**(11), 2215–2222 (2015)
2. Noriega-Atala, E., Hein, P.D., Thumsi, S.S., Wong, Z., Wang, X., Morrison, C.T.: Inter-sentence relation extraction for associating biological context with events in biomedical texts. In: 2018 IEEE International Conference on Data Mining Workshops (ICDMW), Singapore, pp. 722–731 (2018)
3. Wang, H., et al.: Evidence sentence extraction for machine reading comprehension. arXiv preprint arXiv:1902.08852 (2019)
4. Morid, M.A., Fiszman, M., Raja, K., Jonnalagadda, S.R., Del Fiol, G.: Classification of clinically useful sentences in clinical evidence resources. J. Biomed. Inform. **60**, 14–22 (2016)
5. Venkatesan, R., Li, B.: Convolutional Neural Networks in Visual Computing: A Concise Guide. CRC Press, Florida (2017)
6. Wakuya, H., Zurada, J.M.: Bi-directional computing architecture for time series prediction. Neural Netw. **14**(9), 1307–1321 (2001)

7. Hadji, I., Wildes, R.P.: What do we understand about convolutional networks? arXiv preprint arXiv:1803.08834 (2018)
8. Rezaeinia, S.M., Ghodsi, A., Rahmani, R.: Text classification based on multiple block convolutional highways. arXiv preprint arXiv:1807.09602 (2018)
9. Chengliang, G., Hua, X.U., Kai, G.: Attention-based BiLSTM network with part-of-speech features for chinese text classification. J. Hebei Univ. Sci. Technol. (2018)
10. Cristianint, N.: An Introduction to Support Vector Machines and Other Kernel-Based Learning Methods. Printed in the United Kingdom at the University Press (2000)
11. Palous, J.: Machine Learning and Data Mining. Horwood Publishing, Chichester (2007)
12. Guo, G., Wang, H., Bell, D., Bi, Y., Greer, K.: KNN model-based approach in classification. In: Meersman, R., Tari, Z., Schmidt, D.C. (eds.) On The Move to Meaningful Internet Systems 2003: CoopIS, DOA, and ODBASE. OTM 2003. LNCS, vol. 2888, pp. 986–996. Springer, Heidelberg (2003). https://doi.org/10.1007/978-3-540-39964-3_62
13. Kingma, D., Ba, J.: Adam: a method for stochastic optimization. Comput. Sci. (2014)
14. Levy, O., Goldberg, Y.: Dependency-based word embeddings. In: Proceedings of the 52nd Annual Meeting of the Association for Computational Linguistics (Volume 2: Short Papers) (2014)
15. Mikolov, T., et al.: Efficient estimation of word representations in vector space. arXiv preprint arXiv:1301.3781 (2013)
16. Cohen, J.: A coefficient of agreement for nominal scales. Educ. Psychol. Meas. $20(1)$, 37–46 (1960)
17. Landis, J.R., Koch, G.G.: The measurement of interrater agreement for categorical data. Biometrics 33, 159–174 (1977)

AI and Machine Learning

Identifying Historical Travelogues in Large Text Corpora Using Machine Learning

Jan Rörden[1]([⊠]) [iD], Doris Gruber[2] [iD], Martin Krickl[3] [iD],
and Bernhard Haslhofer[1] [iD]

[1] AIT Austrian Institute of Technology, Vienna, Austria
jan.roerden@protonmail.com
[2] Austrian Academy of Sciences, Vienna, Austria
[3] Austrian National Library, Vienna, Austria

Abstract. Travelogues represent an important and intensively studied source for scholars in the humanities, as they provide insights into people, cultures, and places of the past. However, existing studies rarely utilize more than a dozen primary sources, since the human capacities of working with a large number of historical sources are naturally limited. In this paper, we define the notion of *travelogue* and report upon an interdisciplinary method that, using machine learning as well as domain knowledge, can effectively identify German travelogues in the digitized inventory of the Austrian National Library with F1 scores between 0.94 and 1.00. We applied our method on a corpus of 161,522 German volumes and identified 345 travelogues that could not be identified using traditional search methods, resulting in the most extensive collection of early modern German travelogues ever created. To our knowledge, this is the first time such a method was implemented for the bibliographic indexing of a text corpus on this scale, improving and extending the traditional methods in the humanities. Overall, we consider our technique to be an important first step in a broader effort of developing a novel mixed-method approach for the large-scale serial analysis of travelogues.

Keywords: Travelogues · Machine learning · Digital humanities

1 Introduction

Travelogues offer a wide range of information on topics closely connected to current challenges, including mass tourism, transnational migration, interculturality and globalization. By definition, documents considered to be travelogues contain perceptions of *Otherness* related to foreign regions, cultures, or religions. At the same time, travelogues are strongly shaped by the socio-cultural background of the people involved in their production. Comparative analysis allows us, in turn, to scrutinize how (specific) cultures handled *Otherness*, as well as to examine the evolution of stereotypes and prejudices. This high degree of topicality fosters the continuous growth of studies on travels and travelogues, as can be observed by the sheer flood of publications appearing every year (c.f. [23]). While heuristic approaches proved to be fruitful [2,

© Springer Nature Switzerland AG 2020
A. Sundqvist et al. (Eds.): iConference 2020, LNCS 12051, pp. 801–815, 2020.
https://doi.org/10.1007/978-3-030-43687-2_67

29], many fundamental questions connected to travelogues remain unanswered, among other reasons, because previous analysis of travelogues rarely exceeded a dozen primary sources.

In response, we seek to leverage the possibilities offered by large-scale digitization efforts, as well as novel automated text-mining and machine learning techniques, for the first time, on travelogues. This allows us to significantly increase the quantity of text we can analyze. The overall goal of our work is to develop a novel mixed qualitative and quantitative method for the serial analysis of large-scale text corpora and apply that method to a comprehensive corpus of German language travelogues from the period 1500–1876 (ca. 3,000–3,500 books) drawn from the Austrian Books Online project (ca. 600,000 books) of the Austrian National Library (ONB).

As a first step, and this is the focus of this paper, we seek to provide automated support for scholars in identifying travelogues in large collections of historical documents, which have been scanned and undergone an optical character recognition (OCR) process by Google. A major challenge clearly lies in finding an effective method that can be scaled for large collections, is robust enough to support documents with varying OCR quality and can deal with the evolution of the German language over almost four centuries. Previous studies have already demonstrated the potential of quantitative methods for investigating cultural trends [15] or types of discourses in the past [22], and the effectiveness of automated machine learning techniques for subject indexing [14]. However, to the best of our knowledge, no method has previously been tailored to the specific characteristics and unique challenges of identifying travelogues.

To this end, our contributions can be summarized as follows:

- We reviewed the characteristics and commonalities of travelogues and combine our findings into a generic definition of a *travelogue*.
- We provided a manually annotated dataset of documents that match our working definition of a travelogue in the range of the 16th to the 19th century.[1]
- We employed that dataset as a ground-truth for evaluating a variety of document classification methods and found that a multilayer perceptron (MLP) model trained with standard bag-of-words (BOW) and bag of n-grams (range 1, 2) feature set can effectively identify travelogues with an F1 ratio of 1 (16th c.), 0.94 (17th c.), 0.94 (18th c.) and 0.97 (19th c.).[2]
- We found that approximately 30 manually annotated documents are needed for training an effective classifier.

Our results show that standard machine learning approaches can effectively identify travelogues in large text corpora. When we applied our most effective model on the ONB's entire German language corpus, we unearthed 345 travelogues that could not be identified using a traditional keyword search. Thus, we were able to create the most extensive collection of early modern German travelogues to date. This will provide us a solid baseline for determining subsequent steps to develop a serial text-analysis

---

[1] We will share the corpus here: https://github.com/Travelogues/travelogues-corpus.

[2] The code (as Jupyter notebook) that we used for the classification is available here: https://github. com/Travelogues/identifying-travelogues.

method, which will focus on the specific phenomena of intertextuality and analysis of semantic expressions referring to *Otherness*.

We will present our definition of travelogue and closely related work in the next section. Afterward, in Sect. 3, we outline our methodology before presenting our results in Sect. 4. Finally, we discuss the implications and limitations in Sect. 5 and conclude our paper in Sect. 6.

2   Background

2.1   Characteristics of Travelogues

For identifying travelogues we needed, first of all, a precise definition of the notion of a *travelogue*. In previous research, very broad and general definitions were suggested that, unfortunately, did not resolve all of our questions connected to the classification [20, 33]. There was, for instance, no conclusive answer whether or not missives, letters of consuls, or texts only partly including descriptions of actual travel are to be considered travelogues. Consequently, we had to generate our own definition, which aims to apply to all historical eras, geographical regions and media types. Our considerations, however, which are based on an analysis of printed (early) modern travelogues in German, have been formed accordingly and can be characterized as follows:

A travelogue is a specific type of media [7] that reports on a journey which, if detectable, actually took place. Consequently, a travelogue is formed by two relations: the first is content-based (description of a journey) and the second biographical (factuality of the journey).

Our definition builds upon and refines the careful reflections of Höfert [9], who provides a narrower characterization: Fictional narratives are excluded, but there is no binary distinction between fictionality and factuality, since a certain amount of fictionality is part of every travelogue [17, 24], apparent factuality was often generated artificially, and fictional narratives influenced reports at times [27].

A journey is a movement in space and time that begins at a starting point and then moves through a variable set of further points outside of the well-known cultural environment of the traveler. In contrast to Treue [28] we include (forced) emigrations and relics of people who died while traveling, but exclude movements on a permanent level (e.g., nomads, vagabonds).

Travelogues can be handed down in various forms, whether through oral speech, non-verbal communication, text, an image or video. Travelogues obtained from the (early) modern period and available for research consist of text and/or images. The available text is predominantly in prose and can be attributed to several text genres, such as reports, diaries, letters or missives. Notwithstanding that there are many mixed forms and transition zones here, especially since certain guidelines for the creation of travelogues (the so-called *Ars Apodemica*) only emerged and were, if at all, partially applied by the authors during the course of the study period [12, 26].

The only decisive element of a text to be classified as travelogue is the mention of the fact that it reflects the experiences of an actual journey that was undertaken, with all of the imaginable variations of spellings and semantic forms. A frequent, but not always included, feature is an itinerary listing different stations along the journey and the connected experiences associated with the stops. Images in travelogues are usually mimetic, predominantly including portraits, landscapes, and depictions of plants, animals or architecture, but may also incorporate abstract representations. The decisive element here is the inclusion of any pictorial form that is a reflection about experiences that occurred during a journey. Thus, a series of pictures, which originated from an actual journey and contain no text, are also understood to be travelogues, but are not collected within the current project that is focusing specifically on text.

Most of the travelogues from the (early) modern period were written by the traveling persons themselves, are therefore known as *ego documents* [21], and, predominantly, in a narrower sense considered to be *self-testimonies* (Selbstzeugnisse) [11, 13]. Consequently, the personal experiences and cultural background of the authors, as well as other persons involved in the production of the final document, strongly shape the content of the resulting texts.

However, (early) modern travelogues should not be considered detached from each other, since they depend on each other and/or other (types of) media intertextually [19], interpictorially [8], intermaterially or intermodally [3]. For the definition itself it is considered irrelevant whether, in the case of a publication, a travelogue was published by the traveling person or by someone else (e.g., posthumous publications, later editions, written/edited by a related person), whether they are independent publications, appear in the context of a travel collection, as part of a larger publication (e.g., autobiography, historiography) or in the form of an excerpt.

2.2 Known Document Identification Methods

Generally, linear classifiers have demonstrated solid performance for text classification tasks. This includes support vector machines (SVM) and logistic regression, as shown in [10] and [6]. We build on these findings and evaluate both methods in our experiments.

A recent study in the digital library field, by Mai et al. [14], compared the effectiveness of classification models trained on titles only versus models trained on fulltexts and found that the former outperform the latter. They used multilayer perceptron (MLP), convolutional neural network (CNN) and long short-term memory (LSTM) architectures, and found that MLP outperformed the other methods in most cases. Although their models were trained on large-scale datasets from other domains (PubMed, EconBiz) and therefore not directly applicable, we consider MLPs for building a travelogue identification model.

Dai et al. [5] use an unsupervised method based on word embeddings to cluster social media tweets as related or unrelated to a topic, in their case influenza. Although they use much shorter texts (Twitter posts, or tweets, were limited to 140 characters until 2018), their task is similar to the one we present here in that both are binary classification tasks. The authors report an F1 score as high as 0.847, using pre-trained word embeddings from the Google News dataset. Additionally, the authors compared their approach to other methods such as keyword or related-word analysis but found their solution to perform better. In this paper, we will show that similar scores can be achieved without using pre-trained word embeddings.

In [31], Yang et al. use hierarchical attention networks for document classification, in their case sentiment estimation and topic classification (multi-class). Their model outperforms previous methods, depending on the dataset, reaching F1 scores between 0.494 and 0.758. Additionally, they are able to visualize the informative components of a given document. This might be a suitable method for identifying possible subject indexing terms (classes) in an entire corpus and a subsequent document classification task. However, since the identification of travelogues is a binary classification problem, we refrain from these methods at the moment.

Zhang et al. [32] use character-level convolutional networks for text classification, comparing them against methods such as BOW, n-grams and other neural network architectures. They test on several large-scale datasets (e.g., news, reviews, question/answers, DBPedia), showing that their methodology outperforms most of the other approaches, having up to 40% fewer errors. While the authors do not report F1 scores, they illustrate that treating text as just a sequence of characters, without syntactic or semantic information or even knowing the words, can work well for classification tasks. While we do not apply their findings directly, we take inspiration from their work and use BOW and bag-of-n-grams features.

3 Methods

3.1 Overview

Our overall goal is to develop a novel mixed qualitative and quantitative method for the serial analysis of large-scale text corpora. Since serial analysis typically focuses on a specific topic or type of document, in this case travelogues, we first need to define a systematic method that supports scholars with diverse backgrounds (historical science, library and information science, data science) in iteratively training a machine learning model that ultimately supports them in locating travelogues within a huge collection of digitized documents.

Figure 1 summarizes the overall workflow and involved participants from a high-level perspective: in the first step, domain experts use the keyword search feature of the Austrian National Library's catalog to search the overall corpus for documents meeting our definition of a travelogue. They manually inspect each result and annotate those matching our definition as being a travelogue. In parallel, the data scientist automatically selects a randomized sample of documents from the overall corpus, which are

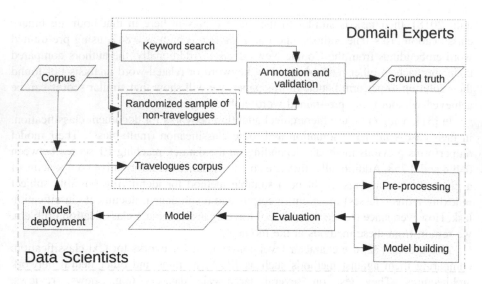

Fig. 1. High-level overview of our interdisciplinary approach. Creation of the ground truth is primarily the responsibility of domain experts (with data scientists contributing to identify non-travelogues). Model creation is completed by data scientists, with the results of the model deployment on the whole corpus being evaluated by the domain experts again.

then manually inspected and verified by the domain experts as being non-travelogues. This process, which is described in more detail in Sect. 3.2, yields a balanced ground truth corpus consisting of travelogues and non-travelogues documents, which can then be used for subsequent machine learning tasks.

Before building machine learning models, documents in the ground truth corpus need to be pre-processed, which includes cleansing, normalization and feature engineering steps. Section 3.3 explains in more detail the steps we applied to our documents. Next, we use the pre-processed documents for *model building*, which includes training various machine learning models, such as SVMs and MLPs. This process is described in Sect. 3.4. Following this, we evaluate the effectiveness of the trained models (see Sect. 3.5).

The top-performing model was then deployed and used to classify the remaining documents in our corpus, in an attempt to identify additional, potentially previously unknown travelogue documents. As a result, our iterative method yields a growing *travelogue corpus*, which can be used for refining the effectiveness of machine learning tasks and for other quantitative and qualitative analytics tasks. In the following sections we describe each step in more detail.

3.2   Dataset and Ground Truth Creation

In our work, we are focusing on prints published between 1500 and 1876, which are part of the historical holdings of the ONB. Since 2011, more than 600,000 books (volumes) from that period have been digitized and OCR-processed in a public-private partnership with Google (Austrian Books Online, ABO[3]). Therefore, nearly all of the library's historical books are currently accessible in a digital form. Within this corpus, we are specifically searching for travelogues.

As a first step, we identified German volumes in the overall ABO corpus, and then split the corpus by century. Then we initiated a ground truth by querying over titles and subject headings. We searched for different keywords in German, namely truncated spellings of 'Reise' (travel) and 'Fahrt' (journey) along with their known variants and with wildcard affixes and suffixes (in alphabetical order: *faart*, *fahrt*, *fart*, *rais*, *raiß*, *raisz*, *rays*, *rayß*, *raysz*, *reis*, *reiß*, *reisz*, *reys*, *reyß*, *reysz*, *rys*, *ryß*) as well as common subject-headings in the library's catalog including 'Forschungsreise' (expedition), 'Reise' (travel) and 'Reisebericht' (travelogue).

As these queries still generated many false positives, we cleaned up the dataset manually. Results were double-checked intellectually by two annotators fluent in German and experienced with early modern German, a historian and a librarian, who read parts of the texts and utilized external bibliographies, biographies and catalogs,[4] to confirm whether a document meets our definition of travelogue or belongs to another genre. Uncertainties were resolved unanimously and there were no disagreements on the final annotations. The result of this step is a manually annotated and verified sample of travelogues, which took approximately three months of full-time work for both annotators.

Since training and validation of machine learning models also requires counterexamples, in this case, non-travelogues, we implemented an automated procedure for randomly selecting an equally sized sample of documents from the subset of German volumes. Via a manual investigation process conducted by the same annotators, we ensured that those documents were not travelogues. This provides a manually verified sample of non-travelogues.

In total, our travelogues ground truth dataset contains a balanced sample of 6,048 volumes, representing 3.67% of 167,570 German language volumes from the complete ONB corpus. Table 1 provides an overview of our ground truth and its distribution over centuries. One can easily observe that the number of volumes, as well as the size of each publication increases with time. To provide insight into how likely it is to find a travelogue randomly, we also included the number of travelogues that were found while reviewing the randomized sample we used as counterexamples. This approach was replicated for the 16th, 17th, 18th and 19th centuries. Volumes that were not

---

[3] https://www.onb.ac.at/en/digital-library-catalogues/austrian-books-online-abo.

[4] E.g.: https://www.deutsche-biographie.de/, https://lb-eutin.kreis-oh.de/, https://kvk.bibliothek.kit.edu/, https://www.oclc.org/de/worldcat.html, http://www.vd16.de/, http://www.vd17.de/, http://www.vd18.de/, https://viaf.org/, Wikipedia.

evaluated remain in the *candidates* pool, upon which we applied our classifier after identifying the best-performing model.

Table 1. Dataset overview. Our corpus consists of the total number of digitized German-language books available to us. The ground truth contains an equal amount of travelogues and randomly selected counter examples; in brackets, we provide the number of travelogues we found by chance. Books not evaluated remain in the *candidates* pool. A token contains at least two alphanumerical characters, punctuation etc. is not counted.

Corpus				
Century	No. candidate volumes	No. ground truth volumes	Total tokens	Average tokens
16th	8,526	67/67	362,244,353	41,829
17th	8,763	161/161	651,957,983	71,762
18th	55,971	873/873	5,041,741,840	82,274
19th	88,262	1,897/1,897	11,464,645,150	124,539
$\sum$	161,522	5,996	17,520,589,326	104,589

3.3   Pre-processing

The preprocessing phase involves several steps. First, the texts were tokenized at the word level, using blanks and interpunctuation as separators. The German language uses upper- and lowercase spelling, depending on the word type and their position in the sentence, but to compensate for OCR and orthographic errors we transformed all tokens to lowercase. Furthermore, we removed all tokens that do not contain at least two alphanumeric characters, as this removes OCR artifacts, which are often special characters. For the same reason, each token needs to appear at least twice in the whole corpus.

3.4   Model Building

As shown in Table 1 the documents that we seek to classify are rather large, as they contain on average 41,000–124,000 tokens. We decided to use a combination of BOW and bag-of-n-grams, as shown by Wang and Manning [30]. With this approach, we can both handle intricate problems with our data, while having a computationally effective method that still provides competitive results.

Experiments were performed on the above-mentioned ground truth. We tested different classification algorithms:

- Multinominal Naive Bayes (MNB)
- Support Vector Machine (SVM)
- Logistic regression (Log)
- Multilayer perceptron (MLP)

For the MNB, SVM and Log algorithms we used the sklearn [18] implementation. We use the Tensorflow [1] and Keras [4] implementation for the MLP. The data for all algorithms was vectorized and hashed with the sklearn HashingVectorizer.

3.5   Evaluation Procedure

As a baseline, we applied a random classification. In all the experiments, we treat every book as a single document.

First, we split the ground truth into both a training (75%) set and a validation (25%) set, for every time period. We evaluated all classifiers presented here first through a five-fold cross evaluation along the training split. This essentially means that the training set was split into five equally sized subsets, and for each fold one subset serves as a test, and the other four become the training data. When the results across the cross-evaluation are comparable, good scores are less likely to occur by chance. Subsequently, we applied the classifiers on the held-out validation data. The classification results are discussed in Sect. 4.

The evaluation of our work follows a two-step approach. First, we gauge the effectiveness of a given method by precision, recall and F1 metrics on our training set. Precision is the number of correct results, divided by the number of all returned results. Recall shows how many of the documents that should have been found are actually found, dividing the number of correctly classified documents by the number of documents that actually belong to that class. F1 is the harmonic mean of precision and recall (with a range between 0 and 1, with 1 representing the perfect result).

For the second step of our evaluation, we apply the model that performs best on our training data to the remaining documents of our corpus. This results in a list of all those documents, with probability scores indicating how likely they belong to our travelogues class. Starting with the highest probability, those documents are then manually evaluated by domain experts (see Sect. 4), to judge how well this model identifies travelogues in a set of unseen documents.

3.6   Minimal Ground Truth Requirements

Additionally, we wanted to understand how many ground truth documents are needed to train an effective classifier. We approached this by testing the top classification approach against different amounts of ground truth documents and evaluated the results. The same setup as described above is used, but we varied the number of ground truth documents, as well as randomizing their selection.

For each time frame, we evaluated 5, 10, 15, 20, 25, 30 and 50 examples each for the positive class (travelogue) and the negative class (anything else); for the 18th and 19th centuries, we extended to 100 examples each. The model created with those documents was then tested on the remaining ground truth documents. For each sample size, we repeated this a total of five times with a different randomized sample each time.

4 Results

4.1 Classification Results

Table 2 shows the evaluation of our classification algorithms.

Table 2. Classification results. We provide precision, recall and F1 scores for multinominal naive Bayes (MNB), support vector machine (SVM), logistic regression (Log) and a multi-layer perceptron neural network (MLP).

Century	MNB			SVM			Log			MLP		
	P	R	F1	P	R	F1	P	R	F1	P	R	F1
16th	0.73	**1.00**	0.85	0.96	**1.00**	0.98	0.95	0.95	0.95	**1.00**	**1.00**	**1.00**
17th	0.75	0.97	0.84	0.82	0.92	0.87	0.82	0.92	0.87	**0.95**	**0.93**	**0.94**
18th	0.79	**0.94**	0.86	0.88	0.90	0.89	0.84	0.88	0.86	**0.96**	0.93	**0.94**
19th	0.86	0.92	0.89	0.91	0.90	0.91	0.88	0.91	0.90	**0.97**	**0.96**	**0.96**

Our results show that it is possible to achieve good classification scores with our dataset, even without extensive feature engineering or pre-trained word embeddings. We assume that this is based in the comparably[5] large size of our data points, as can be seen in Table 1. Additionally, through the randomness involved in the selection of non-travelogues, those volumes are expected to have a high variance in genres, which matches the whole corpus as well. Comparing numerous examples of one genre against an equal number of volumes covering many more genres certainly benefits the classification, especially when taking into account the length of the documents.

Taking the results from this evaluation, we were confident in approaching our main task, which was the identification of travelogues from a much larger dataset: the other digitized books in our corpus not yet evaluated by us.

Following the training of models suitable for classification, one specifically designed for each century, we applied it to our pool of candidates. We used this process to create a list of books that are potentially travelogues, ranked from highest to lowest, and evaluated the first 200 items. The results of this are shown in Table 3 and have been subject to the same scrutiny as our initial ground truth.

We can show that our methodology proves a clear improvement over a less guided evaluation: within our evaluated findings, true positives made up 12.5% (16th c.), 30% (17th c.), 41.5% (18th c.) and 89.5% (19th c.) respectively. Due to time constraints, our evaluation was discontinued after the first 200 items, but this already means that we discovered 345 books of the travelogue genre that were not found by traditional search queries on meta data, as we explained in Sect. 3.2. Discovery by chance only resulted in 3% (16th c.) and 0.8% (18th c.) positives, or none at all (17th c., 19th c.).

---

[5] Many works focus on datasets that have more, but shorter documents, c.f. [31] for comparisons of multiple classification methods and datasets.

It also has to be noted that the increase in the percentage of true positives in a diachronic perspective is connected to the equally increasing number of travelogues. There simply are many more travelogues that were printed in the 19th century than in the previous time periods.

Table 3. Applying the classifier on the candidates pool. *By chance* shows how many travelogues were found when randomly selecting examples for the ground truth.

Century	No. candidates	Confirmed (top 200)	By chance
16th	8,526	25	2 (from 67)
17th	8,763	60	0 (from 161)
18th	55,971	83	7 (from 873)
19th	88,262	177	0 (from 1,897)

4.2 Error Analysis

During this evaluation, it became apparent that the majority of potential findings with a high probability belong to the group we attribute as historiography. Due to their nature, they have strong a overlap with travelogues but lack the required criteria of describing a journey actually experienced by the author. This crucial information can in many cases only be gathered from external sources.[6] From a purely technical perspective, there is no difference with the content of the books between travelogues and historiographies. This means that while, for the purposes of this project, they are very different, right now we cannot further differentiate between them. Additionally, in the 18th century, many false positives include publications on geography; a possible explanation here is that they often describe locations, which naturally overlap with travelogues as well.

4.3 Ground Truth Requirements

The result of our efficiency evaluation is depicted in Fig. 2. We provide the average F1 score for each time frame, as well as the variance between the samples.

For every time frame, our general observation is that the performance of the MLP classification fluctuates heavily when only a small dataset is available. With at least 20 documents, but it is better with 30 examples, each for the positive and negative class a stable performance of above a 0.8 F1 score can be reached. After that it slowly increases up to a 0.9 F1 score at 50 examples each, with only very minor changes for 100 examples each.

This experiment shows that it is possible to create a working classification methodology, which reaches acceptable results with a modest time investment[7] upfront, as shown in Table 2.

---

[6] C.f. Sect. 2.1.

[7] Depending on the sources, and if additional definitions etc. are needed, between several hours and up to a few weeks of full-time work.

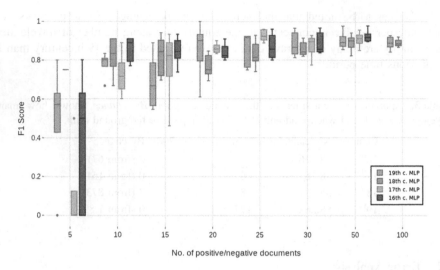

Fig. 2. Classifier efficiency evaluation for MLP. Every step has a balanced number of travelogues and non-travelogues (5/5, 10/10, 15/15, 20/20, 25/25, 30/30, 50/50 and 100/100). The experiment was repeated five times for each step.

5   Discussion

Our results show that standard machine learning techniques combined with relatively easily computable features (BOW and bag-of-n-grams) can effectively support scholars in identifying travelogues in a large-scale document corpus. Using the same features for an MLP neural network generates even superior results. This is an important first step in the development of a broader mixed-method approach for the large-scale serial analysis of travelogues.

Specifically, we discovered a total of 345 travelogues in the evaluated time periods using the top 200 findings with the highest confidence scores each (800 in total). We previously were not able to find any of these files through search queries based on meta data or manual search in our catalog, hence this directly translates into a re-discovery of sources for scholars in the humanities.

Additionally, a large fraction of false positives is, at the level of words and their semantics, extremely similar to the true positives. However, going by the definition provided earlier we are required to use external information that could not be included as a feature, as it is dependant on domain knowledge. This severely limits the efficacy of unsupervised machine learning and deep learning approaches.

A clear limitation of our effort lies in the time and effort required to create a high-quality ground truth. While this effort could possibly be reduced by applying unsupervised clustering techniques beforehand, annotations provided by domain experts will always be key for effective learning techniques. Applying active learning techniques (c.f. [25]) for iteratively developing ground truths could be a possible strategy for reducing this manual annotation effort. Another limitation of our approach lies in the focus on entire volumes, which currently neglects the fact that volumes may include travelogues and non-travelogues. Using a wider spectrum of semantically richer features (c.f. [16]) such as named entities could support classification at the paragraph or page level.

Nonetheless, our experiments on the efficiency of the classification method presented here show that it is possible to achieve robust results above an F1 score of 0.8 with a relatively small ground truth size. Knowing this, future research in different domains should require substantially less time investments to get started.

A remaining challenge lies in the distinction between highly similar genres, in our case historiographies or geographic books and travelogues. We hope that this can be tackled by further refining the ground truth to fit the given genres, taking into account a wide range of external sources, to include domain knowledge in a structured way.

6   Conclusions

In this paper, we have described a methodology to identify historical travelogues in a large dataset. Our approach combines the knowledge of both domain experts (historical science, library and information science) and data scientists to create a ground truth and subsequently build an MLP model, successfully identifying 345 previously unknown travelogues. Furthermore, we have shown that a ground truth for this kind of data can be as small as 30 examples each for the positive and negative class and still perform well.

In the upcoming weeks and months, we will begin looking at the discovered travelogues in more detail. In a first step, we will identify intertextual relations in our corpus to find out in what way the travelogues depended on each other, why and how (certain) stereotypes and prejudices were handed down, evolved or disappeared over the centuries.

Ultimately, we want to know how foreign cultures, places and people were perceived, and if the perceptions differed depending on the socio-cultural background of the involved people. This will allow us to come to an understanding how and why something was perceived as Other, if and how this changed across the centuries. For this, we have done the groundwork here, as it is crucial to rely on as much data as possible; concrete next steps in this direction include creating a formal description of intertextuality and *Otherness*, and translating it into a set of machine-readable text features.

Acknowledgments. The work in the Travelogues project (http://www.travelogues-project.info) is funded through an international project grant by the Austrian Science Fund (FWF, Austria: I 3795) and the German Research Foundation (DFG, Germany: 398697847).

References

1. Abadi, M., et al.: TensorFlow: large-scale machine learning on heterogeneous systems (2015). https://www.tensorflow.org/
2. Agai, B., Conermann, S. (eds.): "Wenn einer eine Reise tut, hat er was zu erzählen". Präfiguration – Konfiguration – Refiguration in muslimischen Reiseberichten. ebv, Berlin (2013)

3. Bellingradt, D., Salman, J.: Books and book history in motion: materiality, sociality and spatiality. In: Bellingradt, D., Nelles, P., Salman, J. (eds.) Books in Motion in Early Modern Europe. NDBH, pp. 1–11. Springer, Cham (2017). https://doi.org/10.1007/978-3-319-53366-7_1

4. Chollet, F., et al.: Keras (2015). https://keras.io

5. Dai, X., Bikdash, M., Meyer, B.: From social media to public health surveillance: word embedding based clustering method for twitter classification. In: SoutheastCon 2017, pp. 1–7. IEEE (2017)

6. Fan, R.E., Chang, K.W., Hsieh, C.J., Wang, X.R., Lin, C.J.: LIBLINEAR: a library for large linear classification. J. Mach. Learn. Res. 9(Aug), 1871–1874 (2008)

7. Genz, J., Gévaudan, P.: Medialität, Materialität, Kodierung: Grundzüge einer allgemeinen Theorie der Medien, pp. 201–209. Transcript, Bielefeld (2016)

8. Greve, A.: Die Konstruktion Amerikas: Bilderpolitik in den "Grands Voyages" aus der Werkstatt de Bry, Europäische Kulturstudien, vol. 14. Böhlau, Köln, Weimar und Wien (2004)

9. Höfert, A.: Den Feind beschreiben. >>Türkengefahr<< und europäisches Wissen über das Osmanische Reich 1450–1600, pp. 120–122. Ferdinand Schöningh, Paderborn (2014)

10. Joachims, T.: Text categorization with Support Vector Machines: learning with many relevant features. In: Nédellec, C., Rouveirol, C. (eds.) ECML 1998. LNCS, vol. 1398, pp. 137–142. Springer, Heidelberg (1998). https://doi.org/10.1007/BFb0026683

11. von Krusenstjern, B.: Was sind Selbstzeugnisse? Begriffskritische und quellenkundliche Überlegungen anhand von Beispielen aus dem 17. Jahrhundert. Forum Historische Anthropol. 2, 462–471 (1994)

12. Kürbis, H.: Hispania descripta: Von der Reise zum Bericht. Deutschsprachige Reiseberichte des 16. und 17. Jahrhunderts über Spanien. Ein Beitrag zur Struktur und Funktion der frühneuzeitlichen Reiseliteratur, pp. 345–356. Peter Lang, Frankfurt am Main (2004)

13. Lüdtke, A., et al. (eds.): Selbstzeugnisse der Neuzeit. Böhlau, Weimar (1993)

14. Mai, F., Galke, L., Scherp, A.: Using deep learning for title-based semantic subject indexing to reach competitive performance to full-text. In: Proceedings of the 18th ACM/IEEE on Joint Conference on Digital Libraries, pp. 169–178. ACM (2018)

15. Michel, J.B., et al.: Quantitative analysis of culture using millions of digitized books. Science 331(6014), 176–182 (2011)

16. Momeni, E., Tao, K., Haslhofer, B., Houben, G.J.: Identification of useful user comments in social media: a case study on flickr commons. In: Proceedings of the 13th ACM/IEEE-CS Joint Conference on Digital Libraries, pp. 1–10. ACM (2013)

17. Nünning, A.: Zur mehrfachen Präfiguration/Prämediation der Wirklichkeitsdarstellung im Reisebericht: Grundzüge einer narratologischen Theorie, Typologie und Poetik der Reiseliteratur. In: Gymnich, M., et al. (eds.) Points of Arrival: Travels in Time, Space, and Self/Zielpunkte: Unterwegs in Zeit, Raum und Selbst, pp. 11–32. Francke, Tübingen (2008)

18. Pedregosa, F., et al.: Scikit-learn: machine learning in Python. J. Mach. Learn. Res. 12, 2825–2830 (2011)

19. Pfister, M.: Intertextuelles Reisen, oder: Der Reisebericht als Intertext. In: Wetzel, H.H. (ed.) Reisen in den Mittelmeerraum, pp. 55–101. Passavia Universitätsverlag, Passau (1993)

20. Piera, M.: Travel as episteme–an introductory journey. In: Piera, M. (ed.) Remapping Travel Narratives (1000–1700), pp. 1–22. Arc Humanities Press, Leeds (2018)

21. Presser, J.: Memoires als geschiedbron. In: Presser, J. (ed.) Uit het werk van Jacob Presser, pp. 277–282. Athenaeum-Polak & Van Gennep, Amsterdam (1969)

22. Purschwitz, A.: Netzwerke des Wissens – Thematische und personelle Relationen innerhalb der halleschen Zeitungen und Zeitschriften der Aufklärungsepoche (1688–1818). J. Hist. Netw. Res. **2**(1), 109–142 (2018)

23. Salzani, C., Tötösy de Zepetnek, S.: Bibliography for work in travel studies. CLCWeb Library p. travelstudiesbibliography (2010). https://docs.lib.purdue.edu/clcweblibrary/travelstudiesbibliography

24. Sandrock, K.: Truth and Lying in early modern travel narratives: coryat's crudities, lithgow's total discourse and generic change. Eur. J. English Stud. **19**(2), 189–203 (2015)

25. Settles, B.: Active learning. Synth. Lect. Artif. Intell. Mach. Learn. **6**(1), 1–114 (2012)

26. Stagl, J.: Apodemiken. Eine räsonnierte Bibliographie der reisetheoretischen Literatur des 16., 17. und 18. Jahrhunderts, Quellen und Abhandlungen zur Geschichte der Staatsbeschreibung und Statistik (QASS), vol. 2. Ferdinand Schöningh, Paderborn et al. (1983)

27. Stagl, J.: Eine Geschichte der Neugier. Die Kunst des Reisens 1550–1800, pp. 77–122. Böhlau, Köln, Weimar und Wien (2002)

28. Treue, W.: Abenteuer und Anerkennung. Reisende und Gereiste in Spätmittelalter und Frühneuzeit (1400–1700), p. 8. Ferdinand Schöningh, Paderborn (2014)

29. Van Groesen, M.: The Representations of the Overseas World in the De Bry Collection of Voyages (1590–1634). Brill, Boston and Leiden (2008)

30. Wang, S., Manning, C.D.: Baselines and bigrams: simple, good sentiment and topic classification. In: Proceedings of the 50th Annual Meeting of the Association for Computational Linguistics: Short Papers, vol. 2, pp. 90–94. Association for Computational Linguistics (2012)

31. Yang, Z., Yang, D., Dyer, C., He, X., Smola, A., Hovy, E.: Hierarchical attention networks for document classification. In: Proceedings of the 2016 Conference of the North American Chapter of the Association for Computational Linguistics: Human Language Technologies, pp. 1480–1489 (2016)

32. Zhang, X., Zhao, J., LeCun, Y.: Character-level convolutional networks for text classification. In: Advances in Neural Information Processing Systems, pp. 649–657 (2015)

33. von Zimmermann, C.: Texttypologische Überlegungen zum frühneuzeitlichen Reisebericht: Annäherung an eine Gattung. Archiv für das Studium der neueren Sprachen und Literaturen **154**, 1–20 (2002)

Detecting Machine-Obfuscated Plagiarism

Tomáš Foltýnek[1,2](✉)(iD), Terry Ruas[1,4](iD), Philipp Scharpf[3](iD),
Norman Meuschke[1,3](iD), Moritz Schubotz[1](iD), William Grosky[4](iD),
and Bela Gipp[1](iD)

[1] University of Wuppertal, Rainer-Gruenter-Str. 21, 42119 Wuppertal, Germany
`{foltynek,ruas,meuschke,schubotz,gipp}@uni-wuppertal.de`
[2] Mendel University in Brno, Zemědělská 1, 613 00 Brno, Czechia
`tomas.foltynek@mendelu.cz`
[3] University of Konstanz, Universitätsstraße 10, 78464 Konstanz, Germany
`{philipp.scharpf,norman.meuschke}@uni-konstanz.de`
[4] University of Michigan-Dearborn, 4901 Evergreen Rd, Dearborn 48128, USA
`{truas,wgrosky}@umich.edu`

Abstract. Research on academic integrity has identified online paraphrasing tools as a severe threat to the effectiveness of plagiarism detection systems. To enable the automated identification of machine-paraphrased text, we make three contributions. First, we evaluate the effectiveness of six prominent word embedding models in combination with five classifiers for distinguishing human-written from machine-paraphrased text. The best performing classification approach achieves an accuracy of 99.0% for documents and 83.4% for paragraphs. Second, we show that the best approach outperforms human experts and established plagiarism detection systems for these classification tasks. Third, we provide a Web application that uses the best performing classification approach to indicate whether a text underwent machine-paraphrasing. The data and code of our study are openly available.

Keywords: Paraphrase detection · Plagiarism detection · Document classification · Word embeddings

1 Introduction

Plagiarism is a severe form of academic misconduct and a pressing problem for educational and research institutions, publishers, and funding agencies. Students who submit plagiarized works can receive credits without achieving their educational objectives. Researchers who plagiarize can inflate their publication and citation counts, secure research funding for the ideas of others, and advance to job positions for which they are not qualified [13,42].

To counteract academic plagiarism, many institutions employ *plagiarism detection systems (PDS)*. These tools reliably identify duplicated text yet are significantly less effective in detecting paraphrases, translations, and other concealed forms of plagiarism [19,24,43].

© Springer Nature Switzerland AG 2020
A. Sundqvist et al. (Eds.): iConference 2020, LNCS 12051, pp. 816–827, 2020.
https://doi.org/10.1007/978-3-030-43687-2_68

Recent studies [37,39] show that an alarming proportion of students nowadays employ *online paraphrasing tools (OPT)* (also known as text rewriting or text spinning tools) to obfuscate text taken from other sources. According to Rogerson and McCarthy [39]: *"[...] spinning tools are equally available to academics who may be enticed with the notion of re-purposing already published content as a way of increasing research output"*.

OPT typically employ artificial intelligence approaches to paraphrase a text, e.g., by replacing words with their synonyms [45]. The tools were initially designed for Search Engine Optimization [22] by inflating a website's PageRank. The idea is to re-use the content of the promoted website to create numerous bogus websites that link to the advertised website. OPT serve to alter the content so that Web search engines do not recognize the fraudulent websites as duplicates and thus include them for calculating the PageRank of the promoted site. If successful, the approach negatively affects the users of Web search engines since the inflated PageRanks do not reflect the impact of the websites but rather the effort invested into producing fraudulent websites.

In academia, OPT help to obfuscate plagiarism, facilitate collusion, and support ghostwriters in producing work that appears original. The tools severely threaten the effectiveness of plagiarism detection systems, which are crucial for ensuring academic integrity. Rogerson and McCarthy [39] call for technical solutions to identify machine-paraphrased text and their integration with educational and policy actions to counteract the use of OPT. The International Journal for Educational Integrity even devoted a special issue[1] to this topic.

This paper answers the call of the academic integrity community by devising an automated approach that reliably distinguishes human-written from machine-paraphrased text and providing the solution as a free and open-source Web application. We structure the presentation of our contributions as follows. Section 2 briefly reviews related work on paraphrase identification and the application of dense vector models for natural language processing (NLP). Section 3 describes the training and selection of dense vector models and machine learning classifiers for our task. Section 4 presents the evaluation of the automated classification approach using the judgments of experts and the capabilities of the leading plagiarism detection system Turnitin as baselines. Section 5 summarizes our contributions and presents future work.

2   Related Work

The research on plagiarism detection has yielded many approaches that employ lexical [4,18], syntactical [33,44], semantic [27,41], or cross-lingual text analysis [12,14]. These approaches reliably detect copied or moderately altered plagiarism. Some approaches can also identify paraphrased and translated text.

Most research on paraphrase identification focuses on quantifying to which degree the meanings of two sentences are identical. Approaches for this task

---

[1] https://edintegrity.biomedcentral.com/mbp.

employ lexical and syntactic analysis, semantic similarity measures that are either knowledge-based (i.e., derived from dictionaries, thesauri, or other lexical resources) or corpus-based (e.g., LSA [9], ESA [15], or word embeddings), as well as shallow and deep machine learning [2].

Approaches analyzing nontextual content features, such as academic citations [16,28], images [11,25], and mathematical content [26,29], complement the text analysis approaches to improve the detection of concealed plagiarism.

The problem we address, i.e., distinguishing human-written and machine-paraphrased text at the level of documents and passages is still in its early stages. The work of Zhang et al. [45] is most related to our contributions. The authors provided a tool that determines if two articles are derived from each other and clusters these related articles. However, Zhang et al. did not investigate the task of distinguishing original and machine-fabricated text. Dey et al. [10] applied an SVM classifier to identify semantically similar tweets and other short texts.

Regarding techniques to accomplish the task at hand, the use of dense vectors to represent words in documents has attracted much research in recent years. Word embedding techniques, such as word2vec [31], have alleviated common problems in bag-of-words (BOW) approaches, e.g., scalability issues, and the curse of dimensionality. In addition to word embeddings, representing entire documents [21] and characters [7,36] in a single fixed-length dense vector is another successful approach. The two techniques can capture latent semantic meaning from textual data using efficient neural network language models. The superiority of token-based embedding models over count-based models has been observed for several NLP problems, such as word similarity, document classification, and sentiment analysis [35]. However, the use of neural language models comes at the cost of requiring large amounts of data to derive the models. Moreover, the embedding process does not observe word order, and its quality strongly depends on the selection of hyperparameters [3,17,30,38].

3   Methodology

To devise an approach for classifying texts as either human-written or machine-paraphrased, we analyzed the performance of pre-trained word embedding models that convert texts into fixed-length vectors. We investigated both classifying entire documents and paragraphs. Classifying paragraphs represents the more realistic detection task since plagiarists more often copy and obfuscate passages rather than whole texts [39,43]. After training the models, we used features thereof in machine learning classifiers, as we describe hereafter.

3.1   Datasets for Training and Testing

To create training sets, we used all 4,012 *featured articles* from the English Wikipedia because they objectively cover a wide range of topics in great breadth and depth[2]. Senior Wikipedia editors select articles of superior quality as featured articles (approx. 0.1% of all articles). Featured articles typically have

---

[2] https://en.wikipedia.org/wiki/Wikipedia:Content_assessment.

numerous authors and undergo many revisions. Thus, they are written in high-quality English and unlikely to exhibit a bias towards the writing style of specific persons. Lastly, the articles are publicly available, which increases the reproducibility of our research.

To obtain a *training set for documents*, we machine-paraphrased (*spun*) all articles using the SpinBot[3] API. The service is the technical backbone of several widely-used OPT, e.g., Paraphrasing Tool[4] [39] and Free Article Spinner[5]. Thus, the training set comprises of 8,024 articles (4,012 original, 4,012 spun).

To create a *test set for documents*, we selected 1,990 Wikipedia articles labeled as *good articles* at random. To receive this label, articles must be well-written, verifiable, neutral, broad in coverage, stable, and illustrated by media (see footnote 2). We paraphrased all articles using the SpinBot API to obtain the test set of 3,980 articles (1,990 original, 1,990 spun).

To obtain the *training and test sets for paragraphs*, we split the original and spun articles from the document training set (8,024) and the document test set (3,980) into paragraphs. We discarded paragraphs with fewer than three sentences, as these typically represented titles or subtitles. The resulting training set consists of 200,767 paragraphs (98,282 original, 102,485 spun); the test set consists of 79,970 paragraphs (39,241 original, 40,729 spun).

3.2 Word Embedding Models

We evaluated the following pre-trained word embedding models for the classification task: GloVe[6] [34], word2vec[7] [31], fastText[8] [5], and USE[9] [7]. GloVe and fastText use a corpus of Wikipedia articles to derive their vector representations. Word2vec uses Google News articles; USE employs a mixed collection including Wikipedia articles, Web news, question-answer Web pages, discussion fora, and the Stanford Natural Language Inference (SNLI) corpus [7].

Additionally, we trained a paragraph-vector (PV) model [21] from scratch. This model uses a Wikipedia Dump [40] as the training corpus, a distributed bag-of-words training model (DBOW), a window size of 15 words, a minimum count of 5 words, trained word-vectors in skip-gram fashion, averaged word vectors, and 30 epochs. We chose the distributed bag-of-words training model for paragraph vectors (PV-DBOW) over a distributed memory model for paragraph vectors (PV-DM) because of its superiority for semantic similarity tasks [20]. Parameters we do not describe, correspond to the default values in the *gensim*[10] API. All the word embedding models have 300 dimensions, except for USE, which has 512 dimensions. Table 1 summarizes the word embedding models we analyzed.

---

[3] https://spinbot.com/API.
[4] https://paraphrasing-tool.com/.
[5] https://free-article-spinner.com/.
[6] https://nlp.stanford.edu/projects/glove/.
[7] https://code.google.com/archive/p/word2vec/.
[8] https://fasttext.cc/docs/en/english-vectors.html.
[9] https://tfhub.dev/google/universal-sentence-encoder/2.
[10] https://radimrehurek.com/gensim/models/doc2vec.html.

Table 1. Word embedding models in our experiments.

Algorithm	Main characteristics	Training corpus	Dimensions
GloVe	Word-word co-occurrence matrix	Wikipedia dump 2014 + Gigaword 5	300
word2vec	Continuous Bag-of-Words (CBOW)	Google News	300
Paragraph vectors	Distributed Bag-of-Words (PV-DBOW)	Wikipedia Dump 2010	300
fastText-rw	Skip-gram without sub-words	Wikipedia Dump 2017 + UMBC	300
fastText-sw	Skip-gram with sub-words	Wikipedia Dump 2017 + UMBC	300
USE	Deep Average Network	Wikipedia + Various sources	512

Each text is represented as the average of its constituent word vectors according to the word embedding models in Table 1. We accessed the pre-trained model and retrieved the vectors for the words occurring in each of the texts. If none of the words in a document existed in the pre-trained model, the document would have been discarded. However, this case did not occur.

All the models in Table 1, except for PV-DBOW, yield a vector representation for each word. In PV-DBOW, the embedded tokens represent entire texts. Thus, a match of an unseen text, i.e., a text not part of the external training corpus, and the pre-trained PV-DBOW model is unlikely. Inferring the vector representations for unseen texts requires an additional training step. Both training steps, i.e., building the document embeddings model (similar to the model used in word2vec) and inferring the vector representations, require parameter tuning. For all texts in our training and test sets, we performed this extra training step using the following hyperparameters for the *gensim* API: alpha = 10^{-4}, min alpha = 10^{-6}, and 300 epochs. The resulting PV-DBOW document embedding model requires at least 7 GB of RAM to be loaded and used. All word-based embedding models require between 1 GB to 3 GB of RAM. The higher memory consumption of PV-DBOW can make it unsuitable for some use cases.

3.3   Machine Learning Classifiers

After applying the pre-trained models to our training and test sets, we passed on the results to five machine learning classifiers: k Nearest Neighbors (kNN) [1], Random Forests (RF) [6], Logistic Regression (LR) [23], Support Vector Machines (SVM) [8], and Naïve Bayes (NB) [32]. We used multiple classifiers to explore the stability of the word embedding models concerning each classifier's characteristics. We adjusted the parameters for each classifier using a grid-search approach for the parameter values shown in Table 2.

Table 2. Grid-search configuration.

Classifier	Parameter	Range
kNN	Neighbors	1, 5, 15, 25 ... 95
Logistic Regression	Solver	newton-cg, lbfgs, sag, saga
	Maximum iteration	500, 1000, 1500
	Multi-class	ovr, multinomial
	Tolerance	0.01, 0.001, 0.0001, 0.00001
Support Vector Machine	Kernel	Linear, radial bases function, polynomial
	Gamma	0.01, 0.001, 0.0001, 0.0001
	Polynomial degree	1, 2, 3, 4, 5, 6, 7, 8, 9
	C	1, 10, 100
Random Forest	Number of estimators	100, 325, 550, 775, 1000
	Maximum features	auto, sqrt
	Maximum depth	10, 32, 77, 100, None
	Minimum samples split	2, 5, 10
	Minimum samples leaf	1, 2, 4

4 Evaluation

Section 4.1 presents the results of applying the combinations of word embedding models and machine learning classifiers to the test sets. Sections 4.2 and 4.3 establish two baselines for the results of the automated classification approach by indicating how accurately human experts (Sect. 4.2) and respectively, a leading PDS (Sect. 4.3), identify machine-paraphrased articles.

4.1 Automated Classification

Tables 3 and 4 show the accuracy of the classification approaches at the document level and the paragraph level, respectively. Due to resource limitations, we did not employ kNN and RF for the paragraph classification task but will investigate these classifiers in the future.

At the document level, PV-DBOW outperformed the other techniques for four of the five classifiers, followed by word2vec, and fastText-rw. However, at the paragraph level, PV-DBOW consistently yielded the worst results for all tested classifiers. This finding is in line with results by [20], who reported a performance drop when using PV-DBOW for short documents.

For paragraph classification, the fastText-rw embedding model, in combination with an SVM classifier, achieved the best result followed by word2vec in combination with SVM. For fastText, we evaluated two training models, one using complete words (-rw) and the other using sub-words (-sw). The sub-words model uses the sum of the character n-grams of its constituent vectors. For example, using n = 3, the word $java$ is represented as $\{ja, jav, ava, va\}$ and the word $java$ itself. Thus, the sub-model can embed words that are not in the training corpus. In theory, this approach can capture more semantic information from the corpus. However, as Tables 3 and 4 show, on average, the whole word model (-rw) outperformed the sub-word one (-sw).

Table 3. Classification accuracy for documents.

Classifier	GloVe	word2vec	PV-DBOW	fastText-rw	fastText-sw	USE
kNN	0.8874	**0.9085**	0.8867	0.8920	0.7696	0.8525
RF	0.9085	0.9397	**0.9606**	0.9246	0.8791	0.8533
LR	0.9457	0.9563	**0.9829**	0.9191	0.6950	0.7734
SVM	<u>0.9716</u>	<u>0.9744</u>	**0.9900**	<u>0.9789</u>	<u>0.9518</u>	<u>0.9437</u>
NB	0.7427	0.7437	**0.8829**	0.7492	0.6920	0.7455

Boldface indicates the best value of a row.
<u>Underlining</u> indicates the best value of a column.

Table 4. Classification accuracy for paragraphs.

Classifier	GloVe	word2vec	PV-DBOW	fastText-rw	fastText-sw	USE
LR	0.7758	**0.8050**	<u>0.5806</u>	0.7757	0.6068	0.6615
SVM	<u>0.7908</u>	<u>0.8225</u>	0.5244	**0.8336**	<u>0.7896</u>	<u>0.7815</u>
NB	0.5390	0.5163	0.5094	0.5229	0.5297	**0.5519**

Boldface indicates the best value of a row.
<u>Underlining</u> indicates the best value of a column.

We conclude from the experiments that OPT often introduce rare and out-of-context words that allows the spun text to be identified. Prentice et al. [37] also reported unusual words as a means to manually identify spun essays.

4.2   Human Baseline

To gauge how well humans can distinguish original from machine-paraphrased text, we conducted a quiz. We randomly selected ten featured Wikipedia articles with various topics. For each article, we extracted the first one or two paragraphs to obtain a text of approximately 100 words. We paraphrased six of the excerpts via the SpinBot API and used the other four extracts unaltered. Using Quiz-Maker[11], we prepared a Web-based quiz that showed the ten excerpts one at a time. Participants could vote (by clicking one of two buttons) whether the text had been machine-paraphrased and optionally submit a freely worded comment after completing the quiz. We shared the quiz via e-mail and a Facebook group with researchers from the academic integrity community.

During three weeks, 73 subjects completed the quiz. The completion times ranged between 2 min 12 s and 36 min 51 s with an average of 9 min and 18 s. The accuracy of the participants ranged between 40% and 100%, with an average of 78.4%. One subject, who classified all cases correctly, commented: *"I paid special attention to any oddness in the text. I never read student works so carefully"*.

The experiment showed that experienced educators who read carefully and expect to encounter machine-paraphrased text could achieve an accuracy between 90% and 100%. However, even in this setting, the average accuracy was

---

[11] https://www.quiz-maker.com/.

below 80%. We expect that the efficiency will be lower in a realistic scenario, in which readers do not pay special attention to spotting machine paraphrases.

4.3   Plagiarism Detection System Baseline

To quantify the benefit that our approach (word2vec + SVM) provides over-current PDS, we compared it to the leading PDS Turnitin. Using the PDS, we checked ten machine-paraphrased articles selected at random from the document test set. In all cases, Turnitin found the correct source. The reported text similarity ranged between 49% and 67%, with an average of 55.2%. In other words, if the entire document was spun, Turnitin reliably identified the text overlap.

In a second experiment, we tested Turnitin's detection effectiveness for documents that mix original and machine-paraphrased text. We created nine documents (each approx. 3,000 words long) that contained between 10% and 90% machine-paraphrased text with the remainder being random text generated by a free online generator[12]. In a document that contained only one machine-paraphrased paragraph (298 words), Turnitin failed to identify the spun text. For the other documents, Turnitin correctly marks parts of the spun text as plagiarized but in 2 cases, fails to identify Wikipedia as the source.

These results are in line with the findings of Rogerson & McCarthy [39], who used two OPT (one of them based on the SpinBot API) to paraphrase a paragraph from a prior publication. When the unchanged paragraph was used as the input to Turnitin, the system found a 100% match with the source. However, for the two machine-paraphrased versions of the paragraph, Turnitin computed a similarity score of zero for the source.

We conclude from these experiments that if a plagiarist employs OPT to paraphrase a few paragraphs, the resulting similarity is often below Turnitin's threshold, thus causing the plagiarism to remain undetected.

5   Conclusion and Future Work

A combination of the word2vec embedding model and an SVM classifier achieved the best trade-off between accuracy, computation time, and memory consumption for classifying entire documents and paragraphs as original or machine-paraphrased (cf. Sect. 4.1). Consequently, we chose this approach for realizing the demonstration system available at

https://purl.org/spindetector.

The presented approach outperformed human experts in distinguishing original and machine-paraphrased text (cf. Sect. 4.2). Compared to existing PDS, the method achieved a better detection performance for cases in which a few paragraphs have been machine-paraphrased (cf. Sect. 4.3). If plagiarists spin entire documents, PDS can typically identify the source. However, PDS often fail to

---

[12] http://www.randomtextgenerator.com/.

identify cases in which individual paragraphs have been taken over from a source and been obfuscated using OPT.

The presented classification approach demonstrates the feasibility of devising effective and efficient technical measures to counteract the use of OPT for disguising academic plagiarism. Including the presented methods in plagiarism detection systems can mitigate the weaknesses of current systems and assist educators in more reliably identifying disguised instances of plagiarism.

We are aware that the selection of high-quality Wikipedia articles and the inclusion of a single OPT limits the ability to generalize our findings. Distinguishing well-written Wikipedia articles from their machine-paraphrased counterparts does not entirely reflect the task that educators face in their everyday work. Students for whom English is a second language often use rare or out-of-context words due to their insufficient command of English.

Our future work will address the limitations of the current study by including articles from more repositories (e.g. ArXiv[13] and Reuters[14]) and additional OPT (e.g. Seo Tools Centre[15], EZ Rewriter[16], or Spinner Chief[17]). Moreover, we plan to collect original texts produced by non-native speakers of English and a dataset of texts paraphrased via cyclic machine translation. Plagiarists often employ cyclic machine translation to obfuscate duplicated text. These additions will increase the diversity of the texts used for training and testing and hence, the complexity of the classification task. To increase the classification effectiveness, we will investigate the performance of deep neural network approaches.

We are confident that the good results of the presented approach can be replicated and improved in future work. To ensure the reproducibility of our experiments and to facilitate future research on this task, the data and code for our study, as well as for the Web-based demonstration system, are available at

https://doi.org/10.7302/bewj-qx93

References

1. Aha, D.W., Kibler, D., Albert, M.K.: Instance-based learning algorithms. Mach. Learn. **6**(1), 37–66 (1991). https://doi.org/10.1007/BF00153759
2. Altheneyan, A., Menai, M.E.B.: Evaluation of state-of-the-art paraphrase identification and its application to automatic plagiarism detection. Int. J. Pattern Recogn. Artif Intell. (2019). https://doi.org/10.1142/S0218001420530043
3. Altszyler, E., Sigman, M., Fernandez Slezak, D.: Corpus specificity in LSA and word2vec: the role of out-of-domain documents. In: Proceedings 3rd Workshop on Representation Learning for NLP, pp. 1–10 (2018). https://doi.org/10.18653/v1/W18-3001

---

[13] https://arxiv.org/.
[14] http://qwone.com/~jason/20Newsgroups/.
[15] https://seotoolscentre.com/article-rewriter-tool.
[16] http://www.ezrewrite.com/.
[17] http://www.spinnerchief.com/.

4. Alvi, F., Stevenson, M., Clough, P.: Plagiarism detection in texts obfuscated with homoglyphs. In: Jose, J.M., et al. (eds.) ECIR 2017. LNCS, vol. 10193, pp. 669–675. Springer, Cham (2017). https://doi.org/10.1007/978-3-319-56608-5_64
5. Bojanowski, P., Grave, E., Joulin, A., Mikolov, T.: Enriching wordvectors with subword information. Trans. Assoc. Comput. Linguist. **5**, 135–146 (2017). https://doi.org/10.1162/tacl_a_00051
6. Breiman, L.: Random forests. Mach. Learn. **45**(1), 5–32 (2001). https://doi.org/10.1023/A:1010933404324
7. Cer, D., et al.: Universal sentence encoder for English. In: Proceedings Conference on Empirical Methods in Natural Language Processing: System Demonstrations, pp. 169–174 (2018). https://doi.org/10.18653/v1/D18-2029
8. Cortes, C., Vapnik, V.: Support-vector networks. Mach. Learn. **20**(3), 273–297 (1995). https://doi.org/10.1023/A:1022627411411
9. Deerwester, S., Dumais, S.T., Furnas, G.W., Landauer, T.K., Harshman, R.: Indexing by latent semantic analysis. J. Am. Soc. Inform. Sci. **41**(6), 391–407 (1990). https://doi.org/10.1002/(SICI)1097-4571(199009)
10. Dey, K., Shrivastava, R., Kaushik, S.: A paraphrase and semantic similarity detection system for user generated short-text content on microblogs. In: Proceedings International Conference on Computational Linguistics (Coling), vol. 42, pp. 2880–2890 (2016)
11. Eisa, T., Salim, N., Alzahrani, S.: Figure plagiarism detection using content-based features. In: Patnaik, S., Popentiu-Vladicescu, F. (eds.) Recent Developments in Intelligent Computing, Communication and Devices. AISC, vol. 555, pp. 17–20. Springer, Singapore (2017). https://doi.org/10.1007/978-981-10-3779-5_3
12. Ferrero, J., Agnes, F., Besacier, L., Schwab, D.: Using word embedding for cross-language plagiarism detection. In: Proceedings Conference of the European Chapter of the Association for Computational Linguistics (EACL), vol. 2, pp. 415–421 (2017)
13. Foltýnek, T., Meuschke, N., Gipp, B.: Academic plagiarism detection: a systematic literature review. ACM Comput. Surv. **52**(6), 112:1–112:42 (2019). https://doi.org/10.1145/3345317
14. Franco-Salvador, M., Gupta, P., Rosso, P., Banchs, R.E.: Cross-language plagiarism detection over continuous-space- and knowledge graph-based representations of language. Knowl.-Based Syst. **111**, 87–99 (2016). https://doi.org/10.1016/j.knosys.2016.08.004
15. Gabrilovich, E., Markovitch, S.: Computing semantic relatedness using wikipedia-based explicit semantic analysis. In: Proceedings International Joint Conference on Artificial Intelligence (IJCAI), pp. 1606–1611 (2007)
16. Gipp, B., Meuschke, N., Breitinger, C., Pitman, J., Nürnberger, A.: Web-based demonstration of semantic similarity detection using citation pattern visualization for a cross language plagiarism case. In: Proceedings International Conference on Enterprise Information Systems (ICEIS), vol. 2, pp. 677–683 (2014). https://doi.org/10.5220/0004985406770683
17. Goldberg, Y., Hirst, G.: Neural Network Methods in Natural Language Processing. Morgan & Claypool Publishers, San Rafael (2017). https://doi.org/10.2200/S00762ED1V01Y201703HLT037
18. Kanjirangat, V., Gupta, D.: Investigating the impact of combined similarity metrics and POS tagging in extrinsic text plagiarism detection system. In: Proceedings International Conference on Advances in Computing, Communications and Informatics (ICACCI), pp. 1578–1584 (2015). https://doi.org/10.1109/ICACCI.2015.7275838

19. Kanjirangat, V., Gupta, D.: Study on extrinsic text plagiarism detection techniques and tools. J. Eng. Sci. Technol. Rev. **9**(5), 9–23 (2016). https://doi.org/10.1109/ICACCI.2015.7275838

20. Lau, J.H., Baldwin, T.: An empirical evaluation of doc2vec with practical insights into document embedding generation. In: Proceedings Workshop on Representation Learning for NLP (2016). https://doi.org/10.18653/v1/w16-1609

21. Le, Q., Mikolov, T.: Distributed representations of sentences and documents. In: Proceedings 31st International Confernce on Machine Learning, vol. 32, pp. 1188–1196 (2014)

22. Madera, Q., García-Valdez, M., Mancilla, A.: Ad text optimization using interactive evolutionary computation techniques. In: Castillo, O., Melin, P., Pedrycz, W., Kacprzyk, J. (eds.) Recent Advances on Hybrid Approaches for Designing Intelligent Systems. SCI, vol. 547, pp. 671–680. Springer, Cham (2014). https://doi.org/10.1007/978-3-319-05170-3_47

23. McCullagh, P., Nelder, J.: Generalized Linear Models, 2nd edn. Chapman & Hall, Boca Raton (1989)

24. Meuschke, N., Gipp, B.: State of the art in detecting academic plagiarism. Int. J. Educ. Integr. **9**(1), 50–71 (2013). https://doi.org/10.5281/zenodo.3482941

25. Meuschke, N., Gondek, C., Seebacher, D., Breitinger, C., Keim, D., Gipp, B.: An adaptive image-based plagiarism detection approach. In: Proceedings 18th ACM/IEEE Joint Conference on Digital Libraries (JCDL), pp. 131–140 (2018). https://doi.org/10.1145/3197026.3197042

26. Meuschke, N., Schubotz, M., Hamborg, F., Skopal, T., Gipp, B.: Analyzing mathematical content to detect academic plagiarism. In: Proceedings ACM Conference on Information and Knowledge Management (CIKM), pp. 2211–2214 (2017). https://doi.org/10.1145/3132847.3133144

27. Meuschke, N., Siebeck, N., Schubotz, M., Gipp, B.: Analyzing semantic concept patterns to detect academic plagiarism. In: Proceedings International Workshop on Mining Scientific Publications (WOSP) at the 17th ACM/IEEE Joint Conference on Digital Libraries (JCDL), pp. 46–53 (2017). https://doi.org/10.1145/3127526.3127535

28. Meuschke, N., Stange, V., Schubotz, M., Gipp, B.: HyPlag: a hybrid approach to academic plagiarism detection. In: Proceedings 41st International ACM SIGIR Conference on Research and Development in Information Retrieval, pp. 1321–1324 (2018). https://doi.org/10.1145/3209978.3210177

29. Meuschke, N., Stange, V., Schubotz, M., Kramer, M., Gipp, B.: Improving academic plagiarism detection for stem documents by analyzing mathematical content and citations. In: Proceedings ACM/IEEE Joint Conference on Digital Libraries (JCDL), pp. 120–129 (2019). https://doi.org/10.1109/JCDL.2019.00026

30. Mikolov, T., Chen, K., Corrado, G., Dean, J.: Efficient estimation of word representations in vector space. In: Proceedings Workshop Track 1st International Conference on Learning Representations (ICLR) (2013)

31. Mikolov, T., Sutskever, I., Chen, K., Corrado, G.S., Dean, J.: Distributed representations of words and phrases and their compositionality. In: Proceedings 27th Conference on Neural Information Processing Systems (NIPS), pp. 3111–3119 (2013)

32. Mitchell, T.M.: Machine learning. International Edition. McGraw-Hill, New York (1997)

33. Mohebbi, M., Talebpour, A.: Texts semantic similarity detection based graph approach. Int. Arab. J. Inf. Technol. **13**(2), 246–251 (2016)

34. Pennington, J., Socher, R., Manning, C.D.: GloVe: global vectors for word representation. In: Proceedings Conference on Empirical Methods in Natural Language Processing (EMNLP), vol. 14, pp. 1532–1543 (2014). https://doi.org/10.3115/v1/D14-1162

35. Perone, C.S., Silveira, R., Paula, T.S.: Evaluation of sentence embeddings in downstream and linguistic probing tasks. arXiv abs/1806.06259 (2018)

36. Peters, M., et al.: Deep contextualized word representations. In: Proceedings Conference of the North American Chapter of the Association for Computational Linguistics (2018). https://doi.org/10.18653/v1/n18-1202

37. Prentice, F.M., Kinden, C.E.: Paraphrasing tools, language translation tools and plagiarism: an exploratory study. Int. J. Educ. Integr. **14**(1), 11 (2018). https://doi.org/10.1007/s40979-018-0036-7

38. Roberts, K.: Assessing the corpus size vs. similarity trade-off for word embeddings in clinical NLP. In: Proceedings Workshop on Clinical NLP, pp. 54–63 (2016)

39. Rogerson, A.M., McCarthy, G.: Using Internet based paraphrasing tools: original work, patchwriting or facilitated plagiarism? Int. J. Educ. Integr. **13**(1), 2 (2017). https://doi.org/10.1007/s40979-016-0013-y

40. Shaoul, C., Westbury, C.: The Westbury Lab Wikipedia Corpus (2010). http://www.psych.ualberta.ca/~westburylab/downloads/westburylab.wikicorp.download.html

41. Velásquez, J.D., Covacevich, Y., Molina, F., Marrese-Taylor, E., Rodríguez, C., Bravo-Marquez, F.: DOCODE 3.0 (DOcument COpy DEtector): a system for plagiarism detection by applying an information fusion process from multiple documental data sources. Inform. Fusion **27**, 64–75 (2016). https://doi.org/10.1016/j.inffus.2015.05.006

42. Weber-Wulff, D.: False Feathers. Springer, Berlin Heidelberg (2014). https://doi.org/10.1007/978-3-642-39961-9

43. Weber-Wulff, D.: Plagiarism detectors are a crutch, and a problem. Nature **567**, 435 (2019). https://doi.org/10.1038/d41586-019-00893-5

44. Yokoi, T.: Sentence-based plagiarism detection for Japanese document based on common nouns and part-of-speech structure. In: Fujita, H., Selamat, A. (eds.) SoMeT 2014. CCIS, vol. 513, pp. 297–308. Springer, Cham (2015). https://doi.org/10.1007/978-3-319-17530-0_21

45. Zhang, Q., Wang, D.Y., Voelker, G.M.: DSpin: detecting automatically spun content on the web. In: Proceedings Network and Distributed System Security (NDSS) Symposium, pp. 23–26 (2014). https://doi.org/10.14722/ndss.2014.23004

Comparing Intelligent Personal Assistants on Humor Function

Irene Lopatovska[1(✉)], Pavel Braslavski[2,3], Alice Griffin[1],
Katherine Curran[1], Armando Garcia[1], Mary Mann[1], Alexandra Srp[1],
Sydney Stewart[1], Alanood Al Thani[1], Shannon Mish[1], Wanyi Wang[1],
and Monica G. Maceli[1]

[1] Pratt Institute, New York, NY 10011, USA
ilopatov@pratt.edu
[2] Ural Federal University, Yekaterinburg 620002, Russia
[3] Higher School of Economics, Saint Petersburg 190068, Russia

Abstract. Intelligent personal assistants (IPA) use humor to engage and entertain users as well as mitigate performance limitations. In order to understand the types of users' humorous interactions with IPA, we developed a classification of humorous utterances that included categories of questions about IPA personality, requests for jokes, rhetorical statement, and others. In order to illustrate the usefulness of classification for analyzing IPA interactions, we used it for comparing the four major IPAs on their responses to humorous utterances. A representative sample of 96 humorous utterances in each humor category and IPA type was developed and tested by 14 participants. The study found that IPA responses to specific requests for jokes received the highest humor ratings from users. The study also found that, overall, Alexa was rated as the most humorous IPA, followed by Google Assistant and Cortana. Interpretation of the findings in light of humor theories and IPA features are provided.

Keywords: Intelligent personal assistants · Digital conversational agents · Voice user interfaces · Humor

1 Introduction

Humor serves an important communicative function: it helps humans develop an image of self and others, build relationships and correct unwanted behaviors. The use of humor in machines aims to make them appear more personable. Evidence suggests that intelligent personal assistants (IPAs including Amazon Alexa, Google Assistant, Apple Siri, Microsoft Cortana and others, also known as digital/voice assistants) use humor to develop attachment and mitigate situations when IPAs are unable to respond appropriately [3, 11].

As part of a larger study of IPA usage, we examined humorous interactions with IPAs and developed classifications of humorous user utterances and system responses. This paper presents the classification of humorous user utterances and discusses its application for comparing four dominant IPA systems: Alexa, Google Assistant, Siri and Cortana.

© Springer Nature Switzerland AG 2020
A. Sundqvist et al. (Eds.): iConference 2020, LNCS 12051, pp. 828–834, 2020.
https://doi.org/10.1007/978-3-030-43687-2_69

2 Literature Review

Many disciplines study humor and its definitions often depend on the purpose for which it is used [24]. Most researchers agree that humor is a cognitive state of joy, which can be manifested through facial and vocal expressions (e.g., smiles, laughter) [1].

A good summary of humor theories and functions can be found in Meyer [16]. The author summarizes the three main theories of humor, including:

- relief theory, which emphasizes the use of humor to reduce the sense of stress and tension;
- incongruity resolution theory, which focuses on the humor derived from unusual/illogical pairings, and
- superiority theory, which describes situations when humor arises when people feel superior to others.

Meyer [16] also outlines the four functions of humor for social bonding, improving interaction memorability, rule enforcement and support of personal identities.

Martin et al. [14] emphasizes that the use of humor depends not only on social and communicatory needs, but the personality type of the person generating humor. For example, individuals with an aggressive humor style use humor to advance themselves at the expense of others.

Studies also point to the cultural influences on humor production and perception. Yue et al. [27] found that Chinese students were more likely to regard humor as an undesirable and unimportant quality than Canadian students.

Within human computer interaction (HCI) literature, humor is discussed as a feature that can improve engagement, usability and personification of technology. Two main areas of research include humor generation and recognition.

Humor generation research usually focuses on identifying humor and algorithmically replicating it for users [24]. Most humor generation studies focus on puns due to their relatively simple structure [4, 7, 25].

Computational humor recognition algorithms aim to recognize human-generated humor. Some studies focus on detecting humor in simple-structure texts, such one-liners [17, 26]. Other studies aim at understanding irony and sarcasm, more complex manifestations of humor which are hard to detect even by humans [22]. Recent studies of complex humor algorithms were tested with social media content [21, 28].

Within the context of IPAs, humor is discussed as a feature that helps IPAs to appear more likable and personable [11, 12]. Not much is known on how companies develop humorous responses for IPAs, but reports suggest that some are hiring professional writers for creating comedic responses [10]. Humor generated by IPAs is usually perceived as "corny" [2], old-fashioned and simplistic [11]. While there are many anecdotal reports of IPA humor, we focus on a more systematic approach of classifying humorous IPA interactions and report some of the preliminary findings here. We also illustrate the usefulness of such classification by applying it to compare several IPAs on humor function.

3 Methods

In order to capture elements of humorous interactions with IPAs, we collected data via online diaries and printed questionnaires. Twenty-eight participants recorded a total of 162 interactions, including the utterance directed toward the IPA, the IPA's response, and the user's rating of that response on a 5-point scale of how funny they thought it was. The collected data were content analyzed to identify the main types of user utterances and system responses.

The study produced a classification of the types of user humorous utterances directed towards IPAs (reported by Lopatovska [13] and summarized in Table 1 below). To validate the classification, we tested it on publicly available online sets of funny prompts, phrases, and questions for IPAs published between August 2015 and January 2019 [5, 6, 8, 9, 18–20, 23]. We were unable to find very recent articles for Cortana, as most of them were published between August 2015 and December 2016. We focused on English-language sources from U.S. websites because our initial classification was developed in the same linguistic and cultural context. While we found that Amazon Alexa had the highest number of published jokes, we crafted a balanced list of about 110 prompts per IPA. Each prompt was classified according to the initial classification: two hundred and thirty joke prompts were coded as personality test questions, 110 as rhetorical, 26 as funny prompts, 19 as joke requests, 14 as action requests, and 6 as funny sounds. During the classification, we refined our initial schema by adding sub-themes under the theme of rhetorical questions, including philosophical questions and self-expressions directed at the self and at the IPA system. Informational requests and action requests based on the IPA's functionality were removed from the schema because they did not match up against the humorous utterances suggested by published sources. These themes emerged from the initial study where users logged their own humorous utterances which may have been accidental and/or more context would be required to understand why users rated informational and action requests as humorous.

We then randomly selected utterances in each humor category, with the total of 21–29[1] utterances for each of the four most popular IPAs (Amazon Alexa, Apple Siri, Microsoft Cortana and Google Assistant), resulting in the list of 96 total jokes across 4 IPAs.

In order to compare the performance of the four IPAs in each humor category, fourteen participants tested a randomized list of utterances over multiple sessions and four different IPAs, and rated their "funny-ness" on the 5-point scale mentioned previously. The data were collected over three days, and participants could enter their ratings at the time and place of their convenience. The fourteen participants were all native English speakers and U.S. residents, representing age groups in the teens, 20s, 30s and 40s. The averages of their ratings provided an initial comparison of the four IPA responses to humor.

---

[1] Amazon Alexa list was the longest and included 29 utterances due to wide availability of publicly published humor for this IPA. Google Assistant had the lowest number of publicly available humor, resulting in a shorter list of 21 test utterances.

4 Findings and Discussion

Overall, the classification of humor utterances derived from our initial ethnographic study matched the categories of humor in the dataset composed from publicly published sources of IPA humor. The categories of humor utterances generated by users towards IPAs, such as questions about IPA personalities, joke requests and rhetorical statements, generally fell under relief and superiority theories of humor. Since humorous utterances in our study were intentional, we were unable to fully capture incongruity of humor that emerges from unexpected interactions (for example, instances when the system response does not match user expectation, resulting in an accidentally funny interaction).

None of the tested utterances were rated with the perfect score, 5. Some IPA responses were rated as high as 4 by individual raters but the averages across the raters never reached 4. The averages across the categories were below 3 (in the not-funny range). The "funniest" responses were delivered in the joke request category, with the most consistent scores across the 4 IPAs. This finding confirms the IPA strength in the "canned" (pre-programmed) humor category [10, 11].

Questions about the IPA's personality were among the most frequent in our initial study and also the most frequent in the public datasets. High frequency of such questions might be explained under superiority theory which describes situations when humor is used to emphasize superiority of one agent over the other, in this case human over IPA. However, it was one of the least humorous categories across all the tested IPAs, with the average rating of 1.81. While IPAs usually have answers to personality questions or statements, these answers are frequently vague and deflective, and never show that the IPA is a robot-like entity. This illustrates that companies want to maintain an illusion of IPAs as a human-like entity, but also that users do not find such responses humorous.

The funniest responses were delivered by Alexa when users requested funny sounds.

Each humor category ratings reveal gaps in IPAs' abilities to produce humor, but also reveal elements of their general functionality. For example, Google Assistant has a lower rating in responding to rhetorical utterances because it often responds with search results, instead of a humorous response or admission that it does not understand the utterance. Active search functionality for Google Assistant makes sense for an IPA powered by Google Search, but it does not support intentionally humorous interactions well. We noticed that different devices enabled with Google Assistant (i.e. phone or Google Home Mini) sometimes gave our participants different responses to the same utterance, and not only for jokes where you would expect a range of responses, like "knock knock" jokes.

Despite not being able to find recent prompts for Cortana, it was often rated comparably to the other IPAs. Perhaps we were not able to find more recent data for Cortana because it is not as well-known for its connection to smart speakers, other smart home devices or mobile phones.

While our sample was small enough for any statistical tests, we observed that the ratings were dependent on participants' age. In general, younger raters found IPA responses funnier, a finding that is in line with humor theories linking age to changing perceptions of humor [15]. Understanding cultural references also affected ratings. Some younger participants did not have the background to appreciate responses based on older pop culture references.

5   Conclusion

Through analysis of user interactions with IPAs, we developed classification of user-generated humor and validated it on publicly available datasets of IPA humor. The classification has methodological and practical significance and can be used for making improvements to existing IPA functionality. To illustrate the usefulness of IPA humor classification for understanding user interactions with this technology, we used the classification to compare performance of the four major IPAs' on humor function. The development of a classification is an early step in creating a strong body of research around IPAs, technology and humor. Future researchers may use this classification to help develop their own projects in these areas. Future plans include validating classification on a larger sample and testing IPA performance on different types of humor. This paper aims to start the discussion and solicit ideas for future research.

Acknowledgments. The study was partially supported by the Pratt Institute Seed Grant. Special thanks to our participants and Pratt iSchool administration for their help with the study.

Appendix

Table 1. IPA responses to humorous utterances.

User-generated humor category *Example of jokes*	Amazon Alexa	Google Assistant	Apple Siri	Microsoft Cortana
	(Number of jokes in the category from large dataset/number of jokes tested) Average reaction rating (1–5)			
Personality test questions (20 total tested/avg rating 1.81) *Are you a robot?*	36/4 – 1.69	65/4 – 1.81	58/5 – 1.78	71/7 – 1.97
Joke request (11 total tested/avg rating 2.3) *Make me laugh*	2/2 – 2.48	4/3 – 2.48	4/3 – 2.02	9/3 – 2.25
Rhetorical (27 total tested/avg rating 1.8) *Why are we here?*	36/7 – 2.14	23/3 – 1.53	34/10 – 2	17/7 – 1.53
Funny prompts (17 total tested/avg rating 2.01) *Where do babies come from?*	8/5 – 2.16	6/6 – 2.12	8/3 – 2.15	6/3 – 1.61
Action request (13 total tested/avg rating 1.73) *Do a barrel roll*	10/6 – 2.08	4/4 – 1.85	3/2 – 1.11	2/1 – 1.9
Funny sound (8 total tested/avg rating 2.05) *Can you sneeze?*	5/5 – 3.55	1/1 – 2.58	1/1 – 1.35	2/1 – 0.7

References

1. Apte, M.L.: Humor and Laughter: An Anthropological Approach. Cornell University Press, Ithaca (1994)
2. Attkisson, A.: Siri vs. Alexa: why Amazon won our 300-question showdown. https://www.tomsguide.com/us/siri-vs-alexa,review-3681.html. Accessed 17 May 2018
3. Binsted, K.: Using humour to make natural language interfaces more friendly. Paper Presented at the International Joint Conference on Artificial Intelligence Workshop on AI and Entertainment, Montreal, Quebec (1995)
4. Binsted, K., Pain, H., Ritchie, G.: Children's evaluation of computer-generated punning riddles. Pragmat. Cogn. **5**(2), 305–354 (1997)
5. Bolluyt, J.: 90 questions Cortana has funny and interesting answers for. https://www.cheatsheet.com/gear-style/funny-questions-ask-cortana.html/. Accessed 26 Apr 2018
6. Chacos, B.: Ask Cortana anything: snarky answers to 59 burning questions. https://www.pcworld.com/article/2148940/windows-phone-os/ask-cortana-anything-sassy-answers-to-58-burning-questions.html. Accessed 19 May 2018
7. He, H., Peng, N., Liang, P.: Pun generation with surprise. In: Proceedings of the 2019 Conference of the North American Chapter of the Association for Computational Linguistics: Human Language Technologies, Volume 1 (Long and Short Papers), pp. 1734–1744. Association for Computational Linguistics, Minneapolis (2019)
8. Hesse, B.: Bothering the bots: funny questions and commands to pose to Google assistant. https://www.digitaltrends.com/mobile/funny-things-to-ask-google-assistant/. Accessed 22 Mar 2018
9. Hill, S.: The funniest questions to ask Siri. https://www.digitaltrends.com/mobile/funny-questions-to-ask-siri/. Accessed 14 May 2018
10. Kelly, A.: Siri, tell me a joke. No, not that one. Could machine learning help the voice-activated assistant find its comedic chops? Signal **71**(7), 11–12 (2017)
11. Knight, W.: Siri may not be the smartest AI in the world, but it's the most socially adept. MIT Technol. Rev. **115**(3), 80–82 (2012)
12. Lee, N.: Siri and Alexa walk into a bar: how AI assistants found their funny bone. https://www.engadget.com/2018/06/26/siri-alexa-cortana-google-jokes/. Accessed 28 Apr 2018
13. Lopatovska, I.: Classification of humorous interactions with intelligent personal assistants. J. Libr. Inform. Sci. (Accepted for publication)
14. Martin, R.A., Puhlik-Doris, P., Larsen, G., Gray, J., Weir, K.: Individual differences in uses of humor and their relation to psychological well-being: development of the humor styles questionnaire. J. Res. Pers. **37**(1), 48–75 (2003)
15. Martin, R.A.: The Psychology of Humor: An Integrative Approach. Elsevier Academic Press, Burlington (2007)
16. Meyer, J.C.: Humor as a double-edged sword: four functions of humor in communication. Commun. Theory **10**(3), 310–311 (2000)
17. Mihalcea, R., Strapparava, C.: Learning to laugh (automatically): computational models for humor recognition. Comput. Intell. **22**(20), 126–142 (2006)
18. Moon, S.: Funny things to ask Alexa (2018). https://thoughtcatalog.com/sari-moon/2018/03/funny-things-to-ask-alexa/. Accessed 13 May 2018
19. Owens, S.J.: More than 60 funny and silly things to say to Siri (2018a). https://www.lifewire.com/funny-things-to-say-to-siri-4171645. Accessed 09 May 2018
20. Owens, S.J.: 99 funny questions to ask Google Home (2018b). https://www.lifewire.com/funny-questions-to-ask-google-home-4161209. Accessed 09 May 2018

21. Rajadesingan, A., Zafarani, R., Liu, H.: Sarcasm detection on Twitter: a behavioral modeling approach. In: Proceedings of the Eighth ACM International Conference on Web Search and Data Mining (WSDM 2015), pp. 97–106. ACM, New York (2015)
22. Reyes, A., Rosso, P., Veale, T.: A multidimensional approach for detecting irony in Twitter. Lang. Resour. Eval. **47**(1), 239–268 (2013)
23. Stables, J.: 115 brilliant Alexa Easter eggs: Funny things to ask your Amazon Echo. https://www.the-ambient.com/guides/best-alexa-easter-eggs-167. Accessed 11 Apr 2018
24. Taylor, J.M., Mazlack, L.J.: Computationally recognizing wordplay in jokes. In: Forbus, K., Gentner, D., Regier, T. (eds.) Proceedings of the Twenty-Sixth Annual Conference of the Cognitive Science Society, pp. 1315–1320. Cognitive Science Society, Mahwah (2004)
25. Valitutti, A., Toivonen, H., Doucet, A., Toivanen, J.M.: "Let everything turn well in your wife": generation of adult humor using lexical constraints. In: Proceedings of the 51st Annual Meeting of the Association for Computational Linguistics, pp. 243–248. Association for Computational Linguistics, Stroudsburg (2013)
26. Yang, D., Lavie, A., Dyer, Ch., Hovy, E.: Humor recognition and humor anchor extraction. In: Proceedings of the 2015 Conference on Empirical Methods in Natural Language Processing, pp. 2367–2376. Association for Computational Linguistics, Lisbon (2015)
27. Yue, X., Jiang, F., Lu, S., Hiranandani, N.: To be or not to be humorous? Cross cultural perspectives on humor. Front. Psychol. **7**, 1495 (2016)
28. Zhang, R., Liu, N.: Recognizing humor on Twitter. In: Proceedings of the 23rd ACM International Conference on Information and Knowledge Management (CIKM 2014), pp. 889–898. ACM, New York (2014)

Identifying FinTech Innovations with Patent Data: A Combination of Textual Analysis and Machine-Learning Techniques

Lu Xu, Xiaobin Lu[✉], Guancan Yang, and Bingfan Shi

Renmin University, Beijing 100872, China
luxb@ruc.edu.cn

Abstract. Financial technology, or FinTech, has recently attracted considerable attention both in the financial industry and academia. It covers a large range of technologies, including big data, cloud computing, and cryptocurrency, and is widely used in the finance industry. Despite the broad application of FinTech, little academic research has explored the development of this new wave of technological innovations. Our study aims to identify, classify, and track the development of FinTech innovations using patent data. A difficulty is that there are no accurate International Patent Classification (IPC) codes that we can refer to as FinTech innovations. Hence, in this paper we provide a comprehensive method for identifying FinTech patents. We first use a text-based filtering technique to locate potential FinTech patents and get a data set comprising 37,156 records. We then construct a training sample of FinTech patents by reading those patent files manually. Next, textual analysis and machine-learning techniques are applied to identify all FinTech patents in the whole data set, based on the initial sample. We classify FinTech patents into seven categories according to the key underlying technologies and track the development of each category. Thus a whole picture of FinTech innovations is formed.

Keywords: FinTech innovation · Textual analysis · Machine-learning technique

1 Introduction

Financial Technology, often abbreviated to FinTech, was first proposed in 2011 and refers to the transformation of the traditional financial industry using block chain, big data, cloud computing, and other emerging technologies. As an innovative financial approach that combines finance and technology, FinTech has the potential to radically change, and to some extent already has changed, traditional finance sectors, including banking, payments, asset management, and insurance. FinTech has grown rapidly, attracting a huge amount of attention and investment in recent years. Figure 1 shows investment in the field of FinTech from 2012 to 2018. It shows that the total investment

Financial support is gratefully acknowledged from the Chinese National Natural Science Foundation (No. 71903189), the China Postdoctoral Science Foundation (No. 2019M660052).

A. Sundqvist et al. (Eds.): iConference 2020, LNCS 12051, pp. 835–843, 2020.
https://doi.org/10.1007/978-3-030-43687-2_70

is gradually increasing despite some small fluctuations. In the first half of 2018, financial technology companies in the Americas, Europe, and Asia received a total investment of 57.8 billion US dollars, an increase of 51.7% over the whole year of 2017. Accordingly, FinTech has been considered one of the most valuable investments for financial firms [1].

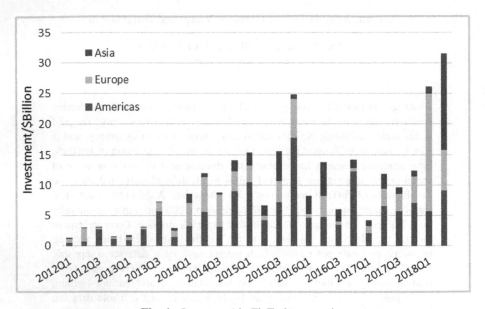

Fig. 1. Investment in FinTech companies

Despite the wide interest and huge investment in FinTech, little is currently known about how to identify, classify, and track these new technological innovations. Previously, researchers have studied specific technological breakthroughs that promote the development of FinTech. They have modeled the new social network propagation dynamics of worms [2] and used aggregating correlated naïve Bayes predictions to study internet traffic classifications [3]. These studies are closely related to mobile networks. Data analysis is another area of intense research, with researchers discussing how to use big data to preserve privacy on the cloud [4]. Other researchers have tried to ascertain the whole FinTech framework using a bibliometric method [5, 6]. In contrast to previous research, we use patent data to study FinTech innovations.

However, a challenge in identifying FinTech patents is that there is no standard definition of FinTech. FinTech is a combination of finance and technology, so there are no exact IPC codes we can refer to as FinTech patents. Thus, in this paper, we combine textual analysis, manual reading, and machine-learning techniques to provide a comprehensive method to identify FinTech patents and classify them into several categories. Our research questions include: Which patents can be defined as FinTech innovations? How do we classify FinTech innovations into different categories? What are the key underlying technologies of each category? We try to answer these questions in the following paper.

2 Data and Category

In this section, we describe how we acquired our data set and the seven categories of FinTech innovations.

2.1 Data

All our patent data is from the recently launched Lens database, which is jointly developed by Cambia and the Queensland University of Technology. The database covers nearly all patent documents worldwide, containing the latest statistics of coverage, date range, and other various accessible metadata. Currently, the update takes three to four weeks. The patent data absorbed and integrated in Lens mainly includes: (1) European Patent Office DocDB bibliographic data from 1907 to the present, comprising 81 million documents from nearly 100 jurisdictions; (2) U.S. patent and trademark office applications since 2001, with full text and pictures; (3) grants from the European Patent Office (EP) since 1980, with full text and images.

We selected a time range from January 1, 2014 to December 31, 2018 within the legal jurisdiction of the United States. To gain an initial understanding of FinTech patents, we search terms related to the key underlying technology of FinTech, such as "big data", "cloud computing", "AI" and so on. The results show that patent areas almost all concentrate in broad IPC codes G (phsics) and H (electricity). Thus, we narrowed our data set to all granted patents in Classes G and H. This allows the data set to cover digital computing technologies that are necessary elements of FinTech.

Next, we applied a text-based filtering method to further narrow the data set. We used a list of filtering terms explicitly associated with financial services. To compile the filtering terms, we referred to a lexicon of terms associated with financial services [7]. For example, the lexicon contains single-word terms (e.g. "banking", "bid", or "cashier") and bi- or trigram terms (e.g. "asset management" and "cash transaction"). Also, new words recently identified as FinTech terms were added, such as "digital currency" and "smart contract". In total, there were 478 unique terms closely related to financial service on the final list[1]. Using these filtering terms, we further excluded patents that did not contain any of these terms in their patent file title, abstract, or claim. The final data set comprised 37,156 patent records including title, abstract and claim. Table 1 below shows the process of constructing the final data set.

Table 1. Construction of FinTech patent dataset

Construction step	Remaining patents
All granted patents from January 1, 2014 to December 31, 2018 within the legal jurisdiction of the United States	1528774
Remove patents not belonging to IPC Classes G or H	200151
Remove patents not related to finance using the list of filtering terms	37156

---

[1] The final list of filtering terms is available on request.

2.2   Category

In 2017, the Financial Stability Board (FSB) issued a report titled "Financial Stability Implications from FinTech", in which it defined FinTech as a technological innovation in financial service that could result in new business models, applications, processes, or products [8]. The report classifies FinTech activities into five categories according to their economic functions: insurance; market support; investment management; payments, clearing, and settlement; and deposits, lending, and capital raising. The report also shows that different technology may have very different applications. For example, cloud computing is mainly used for market support, while big data has a wide range of economic functions, including payments, insurance, investment, and market support.

Referring to but differing from FSB's FinTech classification system, we classify FinTech patents based on both their underlying technologies and applications. To proceed with our analysis, we begin from the premise that FinTech is made up of a group of recently developed technologies that have been applied or will likely be applied to financial services in the future. We classify FinTech innovations into seven categories below.

Encryption & Security. Hardware or software technologies used to protect the system from damaged, changed, or leaking data due to accidental or malicious reasons and to ensure that the service is not interrupted.

Mobile Payment. Hardware or software designed to facilitate payments by consumers via mobile wireless devices.

Big Data Analytics. Technologies used to enhance the analysis of financial big data, such as cloud storage, cloud computing, machine learning, and artificial intelligence.

Blockchain. Distributed ledger technology (DLT) applications and other blockchain technology with a primary application to financial services.

Online Lending. Technologies used in online consumer-to-consumer financial transactions, such as crowd-funding, group payments, and marketplace lending.

Expert Advisor. Software or machines that capable of intelligent behavior, such as robo-advising which provide automated financial advisory services to help customers achieve the purpose of diversifying risks and long-term profitability.

Internet of Things (IoT). Hardware or software that interrelate computing devices, mechanical and digital machines, objects, animals, or people without requiring human-to-computer interaction.

3   Method and Procedure for Identifying and Classifying FinTech Innovations

We used a two-step procedure to identify and classify FinTech patents based on the data set and seven categories we outlined in Sect. 2. First, we constructed an initial sample by reading manually. Then, using the initial sample, we applied machine-learning technique to the whole data set described in Sect. 2.1. We will explicitly describe these two steps and the methods in this section.

3.1   Constructing an Initial Training Sample by Manual Reading

We randomly selected patents from the data set described in Sect. 2.1. Reading through the title, abstract, and claim, we manually classified the patents into nine different categories. Categories 1 to 7 are the different FinTech categories we defined in Sect. 2.2. Category 8 is finance-related patents that do not qualify as FinTech innovation. Category 0 includes the residual patents that are unrelated to financial service. 1800 patents were selected from the final data set. We manually read through the titles, abstracts, as well as claims, and classified them into the nine categories in Sect. 2.2. Thus, in total we have 1800 classified FinTech patents as the initial sample.

3.2   Identifying and Classifying FinTech Patents

First, we preprocessed the text of the patent documents to prepare them to be applied to the machine-learning algorithm. We used the Stanford NLP English Word Tokenizer to conduct tokenization of the patent documents. The documents are processed to remove punctuation marks (i.e. ","), numbers (i.e. "35"), and stop words (i.e. "a"). Then, we used a "bag of words" model to convert the document into numeric vectors. We mapped them onto term-frequency-inverse-document-frequency (tf-idf) vectors. Tf-itf combines both the frequency counts of words and the inverse document frequency so that it can normalize the word frequency and eliminate the influence of the document's length.

Next, we used a supervised machine-learning algorithm the random forest method to identify and classify the FinTech patents. Random forest is an ensemble learning model based on a decision tree as a basic classifier. It contains multiple decision trees trained by ensemble learning techniques. When a sample to be classified is input, the final classification result is the output of a single decision tree. It is widely used in practical fields such as business management, language modeling, text classification, economics and finance, etc. Using the random forest method, we provided a classification of all the patents in final data set described in Sect. 2.1. In total, 3,620 patents were classified into FinTech category 1–7. In the next section we will report detailed accuracy and results.

4   Results and Conclusion

Our work provides a comprehensive method for identifying FinTech innovations, combining textual analysis, manual reading, and machine-learning techniques. It is useful for identifying new technology in fields that, like FinTech, do not have a clear definition and cannot be identified by IPC codes. In this section, we will first test the accuracy of our method and then outline our main results.

4.1   Accuracy

We select 80% of the initial labeled sample as the training set, and 20% as the validation set. Then, we calculated the confusion matrix (also known as the error matrix), as shown in Table 2. The row represents our manual classification, and the column represents the machine prediction classification. The values on the diagonal represent the number of patents that the machine-learning algorithm has correctly classified in each category. The average accuracy of our method for the identification and classification of FinTech patents is 71.67%.

Table 2. Confusion matrix of FinTech classification

Category	0	1	2	3	4	5	6	7	8
0	193	2	0	3	0	0	2	0	4
1	10	9	1	1	0	0	0	0	3
2	1	2	11	0	0	0	0	0	7
3	8	1	0	4	0	1	1	0	2
4	4	0	0	0	1	0	0	0	2
5	1	0	3	0	0	2	0	0	0
6	1	0	0	0	0	0	9	0	1
7	4	0	1	0	0	0	0	4	0
8	27	1	7	0	0	0	1	0	25
Correctly classified: 258					Wrongly classified: 102				
Accuracy: 71.67%					Cohen's kappa (k): 0.51				

4.2 Keywords Extraction

Next, in order to further identify the characteristics of FinTech innovations and to make an intuitive judgment, we extracted the keywords of all patent documents in categories 1–7. We applied the n-gram keyword extraction method, which considers both words (e.g. bank) and phrases (include bigram and trigram, e.g. block chain, payment authorization request). We extracted 15 keywords according to the tf*idf value in each category. The results are shown in Table 3.

Table 3. Keywords in each FinTech category

Category	Keywords
1 Encryption & Security	Card payment; identity theft; fraud prevention; payment card; configuration; computer system; payment account; cyber; user device; card information; fraud score; transaction datum; transaction card; policy; datum
2 Mobile payment	Payment transaction; payment card; payment system; field communication; information payment; payment method; method system; device payment; system method; address; settlement; transaction payment; message payment; payment amount; phone payment

(continued)

Table 3. (*continued*)

Category	Keywords
3 Big data analytics	Datum center; bank; cloud storage; storage service; datum record; cloud computing; datum stream; method cloud; web; datum source; datum store; datum request; storage device; message; source datum
4 Blockchain	Block chain; transaction record; game; transaction request; payment account; currency account; cryptocurrency; encryption; payment service; event; rule; node; currency user; fraud; bill
5 Online lending	Merchant device; payment entity; payor; offer; payment application; lendee; payment server; payment processing; payment authorization; payment processing system; phone; payment authorization request; purchase amount; transaction datum; payment request
6 Expert advisor	Insurance; game; information asset; node; asset class; portfolio manager; module; asset allocation; file; memory; sleeve; engine; image; loan; index
7 Internet of Things (IoT)	Client device; sensor datum; vehicle; computing device; iot device; activity; hub; packet; card; network device; communication device; signature; iot; device; management device

From Table 3, we see these keywords match their categories well. For example, keywords in category 1, "Encryption & Security", are closely related to payment, fraud, and datum, and representative keywords include "card payment", "identify theft", "fraud prevention", and so on. This alignment also indicates that our identification and classification results are relatively accurate. Also, the keywords in Table 3 can help us recognize key technologies and the potential applications in each category. For example, in category 3, "Big data analysis", top keywords include "bank", "cloud storage", and "cloud computing". Thus we can infer FinTech innovations of big data analysis are widely applied in banking industry and their key underlying technologies must contain cloud computing.

4.3   Track the Trends of FinTech

Finally, we tracked the development trend of FinTech innovations. We calculated the percentage of each category of FinTech innovations in the total number of FinTech innovations every year from 2014 to 2018. The results are shown in Fig. 2 below.

From Fig. 2, we see the percentage of different FinTech category is constantly changing. Among all seven categories, online lending accounts for the smallest percentage, while big data analytics accounts for the largest percentage. The percentages of encryption & security and blockchain are relatively stable. The category of IoT has a burst around 2015 and 2016 but then decreases. Expert advisor diminishes over these years, while mobile payment has been gradually increasing since 2016.

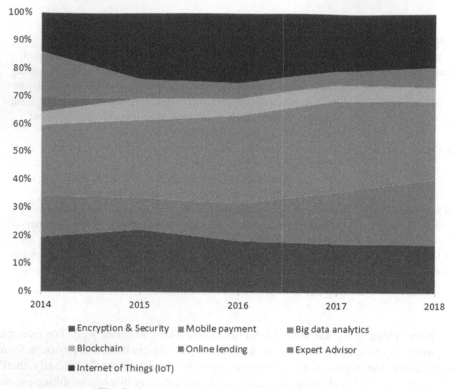

Fig. 2. Development of FinTech from 2014 to 2018

5 Future Work

Our work provides a basic way to identify, classify, and track FinTech innovations using patent data. In the future, we will work to improve our accuracy, as well as track the development and even make some predictions about important new technologies. First, we plan to refine our training sample based on our current work. Second, we will also improve the construction of the word vector, considering n-gram phrases, word order, and grammar. Third, rather than simply relying on one machine-learning algorithm, we will use several different machine-learning techniques. For example, the Support Vector Machine (SVM) is an important kind of supervised machine-learning algorithm in document analytics, and the Deep Neural Networks (DNN) plays a leading role in many complex tasks involving large data sets. Other popular classification methods include Naive Bayes (NB) method, and k-nearest neighbors (kNN) method. By using and comparing these techniques, we expect to further improve the accuracy of our identification and classification.

References

1. Wigglesworth, R.: Fintech: search for a super-algo. https://www.ft.com/content/5eb91614-bee5-11e5-846f-79b0e3d20eaf. Accessed 20 Jan 2016
2. Wen, S., Zhou, W., Zhang, J., Xiang, Y., Zhou, W., Jia, W.: Modeling propagation dynamics of social network worms. IEEE Trans. Parallel Distrib. Syst. **24**(8), 1633–1643 (2013)
3. Zhang, J., Chen, C., Xiang, Y., Zhou, W., Xiang, Y.: Internet traffic classification by aggregating correlated naive Bayes predictions. IEEE Trans. Inform. Forensics Secur. **8**(1), 5–15 (2013)
4. Zhang, Q., Yang, L., Chen, Z.: Privacy preserving deep computation model on cloud for big data feature learning. IEEE Trans. Comput. **65**(5), 1351–1362 (2016)
5. Gai, K., Qiu, M., Sun, X.: A survey on FinTech. J. Netw. Comput. Appl. **103**, 262–273 (2018)
6. Milian, E.Z., Spinola, M.D.M., de Carvalho, M.M.: Fintechs: a literature review and research agenda. Electron. Commer. Res. Appl. **34**, 100833 (2019)
7. Chen, M.A., Wu, Q., Yang, B.: How valuable is fintech innovation? Rev. Financ. Stud. **32**(5), 2062–2106 (2019)
8. Board, F.S.: Financial stability implications from FinTech: supervisory and regulatory issues that merit authorities' attention, Basel, June 2017

Methodological Innovation

Continuities and Discontinuities: Using Historical Information Culture for Insight into the Sustainability of Innovations

Fiorella Foscarini[1] , Charles Jeurgens[2] , Zhiying Lian[3] ,
and Gillian Oliver[4(✉)]

[1] University of Toronto, Toronto, ON M5S 3G6, Canada
fiorella.foscarini@utoronto.ca
[2] University of Amsterdam, 1090 GN Amsterdam, The Netherlands
[3] Shanghai University, Shanghai, China
[4] Monash University, Caulfield East, VIC 3145, Australia
gillian.oliver@monash.edu

Abstract. The analysis of information cultures of the past can provide insight into the likelihood of sustainability of innovative information practices, and can help design sustainable information strategies for the future. This article focuses on three instances of innovation in three different parts of the world – namely, Italy, China, and the Netherlands – in the 1930s, a time period that was characterized by political unrest and significant societal changes in all three locations. Genres, workarounds, and infrastructure are used as diagnostic indicators to demonstrate the utility of an information culture model which distinguishes cultural factors according to their susceptibility to change. The three case studies discussed in this article not only shed light on continuities and discontinuities in information practices over time; they also show the complexities of successfully changing specific existing information attitudes. The ultimate goal of this article is to illustrate the benefits of conducting comparative and longitudinal research on historical information cultures.

Keywords: Information cultures · Genres · Workarounds · Infrastructure

1 Introduction

The emphasis in current research into information culture has been on understanding contemporary workplaces, from the perspective that identifying the values and attitudes that influence information practices will enable the development of culturally appropriate information management strategies. However, knowledge and understanding of the historical antecedents of these cultural influences is patchy and difficult to synthesise because of geographical specificity. Insight into information cultures of the past will enhance our understanding of the present, and contribute to the development of sustainable innovations in information practice.

The purpose of this paper is to raise awareness of insight that can be gained from research into historical information cultures and the socio-political contexts that shaped, and were shaped by, such cultures. This paper builds on previous research carried out by

© Springer Nature Switzerland AG 2020
A. Sundqvist et al. (Eds.): iConference 2020, LNCS 12051, pp. 847–859, 2020.
https://doi.org/10.1007/978-3-030-43687-2_71

Oliver and Foscarini [1]. Our aim is to contribute to the discussion on the reasons for the continuity and discontinuity of information practices and the implications for the sustainability of innovations.

The next section briefly outlines our approach to information culture. The following section details particular innovations which were characteristic of the information cultures in the 1930s' governments in three non-Anglophone settings – Italy, China, and the Netherlands. The discussion section reflects on some of the reasons for the continuity or discontinuity of innovative information practices, and the implications for the sustainability of innovations. The conclusion provides recommendations for further research.

2 The Information Culture Model

Values accorded to information, and attitudes towards it are indicators of an information culture. Information culture can be viewed as a multi-layered model comprising several factors, some of which can be changed or modified relatively easily, while others cannot.

2.1 Diagnostic Indicators

A series of case studies conducted in the course of research aiming to develop a toolkit for the application of the information culture model [1] resulted in the identification of the following diagnostic indicators: genres, workarounds, and infrastructure. These three indicators may overlap and not be mutually exclusive; but where they occur they do provide insight into information culture and can be associated with a particular layer in the information culture model.

Genres – Identification of this diagnostic indicator requires the application of a Rhetorical Genre Studies lens [2], which interprets genre as "typified social action" [3] that people invoke when the situations they participate in appear to be recurrent. This will include any written, oral or acted "texts" which are characteristic of a particular setting, ranging from the repeated use of specific documentary forms for communication to the enactment of a recurrent type of meetings for decision making.

Workarounds – These are the unofficial systems and tools that people develop and use in order to achieve their work objectives. Motivation for workarounds is often the problems experienced with official systems and tools which can be perceived as hampering the completion of primary objectives (e.g., organizational requirements to use a specific repository to store digital documents and emails which entail a number of processing steps to be undertaken by users). Workarounds may be explicitly prohibited by organizational policies, in which case their use is particularly striking.

Infrastructure – This refers to the formal systems, tools and resources that exist to support and facilitate the management of information. This could range from information technology systems to the people with information management responsibilities and everything in-between, such as physical space and storage equipment.

3 Historical Information Cultures

Snapshots of information cultures in the 1930s provide examples of innovations that were introduced into three different environments. The 1930s were selected as the time period for this study not only because the social and political changes underway provide many examples of new and innovative information practices, but also because of emerging similarities with today's turbulent environment. The cases are reported chronologically here, beginning with the insurgence of Fascism in Italy, followed by the reform of records and archives management in China, and concluding with changing parliamentary procedures in the Netherlands. Each case identifies one or more diagnostic indicators.

3.1 The "Machine Bureaucracy" in Fascist Italy

As a consequence of the so-called "March on Rome" in October 1922, Benito Mussolini was appointed Prime Minister, and the National Fascist Party he had founded a few years earlier started to get growing influence within the government and in the everyday life of Italians. Italy was going through a period of economic recession, and Mussolini was seen as the *homo novus* the country needed to recover from World War I and to become a "great nation again" – with reference to the Roman Empire, a central theme of the fascist rhetoric. Without pursuing a traditional political career and by relying on both legal and illegal means, Mussolini became Head of State in 1925, and between 1925 and 1927, progressively dismantled all constitutional and conventional restraints on his power in order to build a police state [4]. But was Fascism a complete revolution? Did Mussolini and his dictatorship – which reached its peak in the mid 1930s in terms of public support, and ended in 1943, after bringing Italy into a second, disastrous World War – manage to "fascistize" everything and everyone? By examining the bureaucratic machine established by the fascist regime – a machine that Mussolini envisioned as the core of his idea of a "strong state" – and focusing on some of the genres invented or reimagined by "the leader" (in Italian, *il duce*), we will attempt to answer these questions, which speak to the sustainability of innovative information practices.

Mussolini, "Italy's First Clerk". It is impossible in these few pages to provide a full account of the complex socio-cultural, political, and economic background in which Mussolini developed his own character, his particular notion of a state, and his vision for the future of Italy [5, 6]. Besides his personal charisma and exuberant personality, historians recognize the strong influence on his ideas and attitudes of the artistic and social movement of Futurism, which originated in Italy in the early 20th century [7]. The emphasis on youth, speed, power, and technology, which characterized Futurism in the arts, became the essence of "modernity" for the generation that was young during World War I and was still thirsty for change when the war ended. In this cultural climate, Mussolini forged his "radically alternative governing style" [8] which was in marked contrast to that of the old liberal world and centred on administration as a key factor for a healthy and well-functioning state.

Mussolini loved to describe himself as "Italy's first clerk" [8, p 74]. A few features of his work habits will illustrate what he meant. Mussolini used to spend approximately 12–15 h in his office every day. He considered it "a point of honour to be in the office before anyone else" [9, pp 348–349]. Intensity was another characteristic of his work behaviour. He would browse through around 350 newspapers (both Italian and foreign) daily, scribble notes on them with a red-and-blue pencil, and cut out articles of interest, that he would then send to his collaborators or to the archives. In his work breaks, he was keen on engaging in various sports activities, including reckless car drives – thus epitomizing the vitalism professed by the Futurists.

Mussolini's idea of the bureaucratic state was that of a highly centralized and overall simple mechanism steered by means of easy-to-use devices which had to be in the capable hands of a strong man. In his words, "Bureaucracy is (…) like a gigantic engine that runs regularly and fervidly, but can also be subject to sudden arrests. (…) Then, I intervene: I press a lever and the machine restarts with its regular rhythm" (cited in [8, p 12]). The language of Futurism and the fascist image of the "demiurge" (a supreme being responsible for the creation of the universe) are both present in this quote from an interview Mussolini gave to the *Giornale d'Italia* in December 1923. During the time of Fascism, the strong bureaucratic machinery wanted by Mussolini actually became increasingly more complex and inefficient, due to the very fact that "he did not trust anyone, and therefore needed to see and control everything" [5, p 472].

The cultural artefacts, or genres, that every society produces in order to allow collaborative action among its members embed and form the values and attitudes of the people using them [10]. Thus, looking at specific information products (not only written records, but also oral ones, information systems, writing technologies, gestures, etc.) can provide insights into the cultural characteristics of a community. Although Rhetorical Genre Studies insists that genres shape and are shaped by groups rather than single individuals, it also warns us that we should not discount the importance of "charisma" in certain environments [11]. In the case of Italy under Fascism, "the leader" certainly played the role of genre innovator, by imposing a new language and oratory style, and creating new rhetorical devices.

One of the most interesting genres reinvented and heavily used by Mussolini was the "note to the Head of Government" ("*Appunto per Sua Eccellenza il Capo del Governo*" [8, p 75]). The "note" was a very brief summary (one or maximum two pages of typewritten text) of a complete case or procedure, involving more administrative units, where the content of complex matters was schematically encapsulated often by means of numbered bulleted lists. All laws and regulations pertaining to the note's subject had to be meticulously referenced, and the exposition of facts had to be "neutral". All possible options and their consequences had to be described, so that Mussolini could quickly make up his mind. He would usually write down his decisions on the note itself with his notorious red-and-blue pencil (another genre he introduced in the Italian administrative practice). His annotations were rapid and resolute (e.g., "sounds good", "move ahead", "yes", "no", "to the archives"), and he would rarely ask for additional documentation or further investigation.

The Central Political Police Records Office (*Casellario Politico Centrale*) was established in 1894 for purposes of political surveillance; however, its activity exploded during Fascism with approximately 12,000 new cases opened every year between 1929 and 1933 [8, p 372]. A genre that was typical for this office was a yellow kangaroo pocket folder containing all the information collected by the police on each "suspect" since the individual started to be kept under surveillance. All essential data (including physical descriptions and a summary of political activities) were recorded on the cover page of the folder. The *Casellario* was not only interested in criminals or people potentially dangerous to the regime. Any citizens who might have had some suspect behavior in the course of their public or private activities could have their life minutely recorded in one of these folders, where all personal relations and "bad habits" were noted down. In this case, one may notice some continuity with the past; but never before in Italy state surveillance had been so pervasive and "scientific" as it was during the fascist era.

One of the first new offices established by Mussolini when he came into power was the Leader's Personal Secretariat (*Segreteria Particolare del Duce*). This office would soon start overseeing all kinds of affairs, not only those that were legitimately considered confidential, due to Mussolini's fear that something might escape him [6]. Personnel matters, public policy and security issues, but also new rules about ceremonies, uniforms, rankings, attendance at public events, language to be used in written and oral communications at home and on the street, every subject could be treated as "confidential correspondence" (*carteggio riservato* [8, pp 77–78]). The term "confidential" was the new, threatening word of the fascist administrative jargon. The goal of Mussolini and his entourage was to standardize, centralize, and bureaucratize all aspects of life.

However, the fascist regime was overall an "imperfect machine", as historian Melis entitled one of his latest books on the Italian administration of that period [8]. This expression emblematically encapsulates the contradiction between the image of the fascist state, which aimed to be a "perfect machine", and its reality.

3.2 Reform of Records and Archives Management in the Nanjing Nationalist Government

In the 1930s, the situation for the Nanjing Nationalist Government (1927–1948) was very complicated: on the one hand, the government needed to fight against the Japanese invasion; on the other hand, they needed to suppress the Communist Party. Handling all of these issues required modern administration and high administrative efficiency. However, being affected by the old administrative system of the late Qing Dynasty (1840–1912), the administrative structure was unreasonably complex and administrative efficiency was very low. Gan, deputy minister of Interior and a central figure of the reform of records and archives management, compared the government of that time to a new automobile which still relied on an ox to pull it [12, p 34]. At the proposal of some officials and intellectuals, including Gan, who were influenced by the movement of administrative efficiency in America, the Nanjing Nationalist Government decided to initiate an administrative efficiency movement.

The reform of records and archives management of the 1930s is the prologue and heart of this administrative efficiency movement. Records and archives were regarded as important tools of administration by the reformers, but their management was separated and messy, thus hampering administrative efficiency.

However, many government staff regarded records as a tool to shirk responsibility. For example, the subordinates tended to ask their superiors for instructions on nearly all kinds of work, including trivia, using written records. This created a huge number of records, and the procedures for records processing were cumbersome and time-consuming: "there are 196 procedures for processing a record" [13, p 194]. A record was registered and numbered many times according to different methods. Archives managers were just in charge of keeping archives and had a very low rank in the government. Archiving the valuable records or not depended on the government staff; archives managers had no power to require them to transfer archival records to the archives depository in a timely fashion, so many archival records were kept by the staff in their offices for convenient use; if archives were borrowed by staff loans were not recorded, and archives managers had no power to ask the staff to return the archives [13, pp 197–198]. This resulted in the loss and destruction of many archives.

Records and archives management in the 1930s still followed the tradition of the late Qing Dynasty. It was based on the experiences kept in the minds of record mangers and archives managers, and these managers did not share their experiences and knowledge on records and archives with others for fear that they might be replaced, if others knew about it. Therefore, there were no unified methods on records and archives management; methods varied in different agencies and even in different units within an agency. To find archives was time-consuming and usually depended on the archives managers' memory of the location of the needed archives, which gave some archives managers opportunities to use archives for illegitimate interests. Zhou commented: "The young archives managers cannot get training on archives management, so they lack knowledge and experience. The senior archives managers are conservative and complacent, and they control the archives as their tools for making a living" [14, pp 578–579].

Meanwhile, the reform of records and archives management was regarded as a safe starting point for the administrative reform. According to Gan, "to conduct administrative reform in China is not easy. It should be based on theoretical study and the actual needs; it also needs feasible plans, but the most important for the reform is to avoid political unrest" [12, p 25]. In order to avoid political unrest, Gan asserted that the reform should begin with issues on "things", not with issues on "people". He believed that records and archives management was concerned with the "things", and to reform the "things" would not lead to political unrest. This is the possible reason why he just focused on the reform of records and archives management method *per se*, and neglected the reform of records and archives managers. But "things" cannot be separated from "people".

The chain method of records and archives management was the core of the reform of records and archives management. It was proposed by Naiguang Gan in 1933. Gan [15] believed that records and archives could not be separated since archives were filed records and records were unfiled archives. Therefore, he proposed that records and archives management should be integrated and that the mailroom, which was previously only in charge of receiving and dispatching records, should comprehensively classify, register and number all incoming and outgoing records according to a classification scheme which was drafted by the leaders of all of the units in the agency and then dispatched to the relevant units. After the records were handled, the units would file and transfer them to the archives depository of the agency where they would be kept according to the classification assigned to them by the mailroom. By doing this it would be also convenient to find archives related to the incoming or outgoing records, so the related archives could be attached to the incoming or outgoing records and be sent together to the relevant units, which was helpful for the administration [16, p 96].

The chain method is an innovation in the infrastructure of government information management in the 1930s. It is based on the recognition of the relationship between records and archives. It reflects the idea that the process from the creation, current use, filing and keeping of records is a continuous one, as well as the idea of front-end control of recordkeeping. The chain method was initially trialed in the Ministry of Interior in 1934, and it worked well. Gan and his followers wrote about the method in journals such as *Administrative Efficiency* and *Administration Research*. The method was later adopted by the Ministry of Education and such provinces as Jiangxi and Guangxi. However, after Gan was transferred to Wuchang in 1935, the method was no longer sustained in the central government. Gan promoted the method in Wuchang and Sichuan in 1935, but the method was not adopted widely by other local governments.

3.3   The Dead Bodies Archive in the Netherlands

Since the middle of the 19th century, openness, publicity and transparency in parliament were shaped by publishing verbatim proceedings, having a public and a reporters' gallery in parliament. However, these infrastructural tools by which openness and transparency were shaped do not explain the level of openness and transparency. Although Dutch politicians like to show off the advanced state of openness and transparency of Dutch parliamentary tradition [17], there are at the same time many signals that reveal at least an ambivalent attitude towards openness and transparency. Historian Aerts argued that compared to other countries, the Dutch parliamentary tradition is more focused on negotiating partners than being open to the citizens. In that tradition, it is typical "to conceal and to make furtive arrangements" to achieve results [18, p 466]. This raises the question of how solid and sustainable the glorified and vital values of openness, publicity and transparency are in parliamentary information culture. Is it possible to reveal some deeply rooted characteristics of parliamentary culture of openness in the Netherlands?

To investigate parliamentary information culture, the rules of procedure are a good starting point. The rules of procedure provide the norms and guidelines for parliamentary behavior. The history of the genesis of the rules of procedure mirrors a laborious process in which the parliamentary rules of the game continuously changed and gradually became stricter and more detailed. The first rules of procedure in 1815 counted only 20 rules; in the 1930s, the number of articles had risen to more than 160.

In the 1910s, 1920s and 1930s, parliament was confronted with fundamental societal changes. With the introduction of general male suffrage in 1917, followed by female suffrage in 1919 and the introduction of the system of proportional representation the political set-up changed fundamentally and marked the end of the hegemony of liberal bourgeoisie and the beginning of a more diverse composition of parliament. Before the elections of 1918, seven political parties were represented in parliament; after the elections as much as 17, and among these were three radical left-wing parties, followed by fascist parties in later years. These parties had in common that they did not want to abide by the parliamentary habits. Adaptations of the rules of procedure in 1919 and 1934 were aimed at curbing the radical parties in parliament and gave the speaker of parliament more disciplinary power to regulate the meetings.

Since the mid 19th century, the rules of procedure stipulated that if a member of parliament used offensive language, he would be corrected by the speaker. Dozens of examples are known, recorded and publicized in the proceedings [19, p 282]. After a new modification of the rules of procedure in February 1934, the speaker of parliament received the authority not only to correct a member of parliament but also to refuse to accept inappropriate language. In order to implement this rule, the speaker received the extensive power to delete these words and sentences from the official proceedings. Despite fierce opposition from the radical parties in parliament who considered this expansion of authority of the speaker as a far-reaching measure to silence the revolutionary voices in parliament and to protect bourgeois interests [20, p 1217] and despite some fundamental objections expressed by several members from the traditional parties against deleting parts from the proceedings which made them "no longer a historically correct and accurate representation of the deliberations" (cited in [21, p 27]), an overwhelming majority in parliament agreed. Since then, the speaker of parliament autonomously decided what was regarded as inappropriate. What were the implications of this new authority of the speaker of parliament on recordkeeping, on the praised values of openness and transparency and on the style of debating in parliament?

Producing verbatim proceedings was not easy. With the introduction of stenography in 1849 it was emphasized that "full, immediate publicity is the essence of our constitutional form of government. Every word spoken in the meeting room of Dutch Parliament must be recorded immediately (…) and every citizen must have the opportunity to read in a short time what has been discussed" (cited in [22, p 212]). To put this in practice, on-duty stenographers in parliamentary sessions alternated with each other every ten minutes. This procedure was designed in such a way that the parliamentary debates could be revealed without delay. The substituted stenographer immediately transcribed his shorthand notes before taking over again. The draft proceedings could be sent to all speakers of the day right after the end of the debate to give them an opportunity to make some style corrections. The aim was to have the proceedings printed within 24 h after the meeting was closed. The shorthand notes and the manuscripts which were sent to the printing office were kept at the registry, and since everything was recorded and published in the verbatim proceedings the notes and manuscripts were destroyed two weeks after closing the parliamentary year [23, pp 457–460]. Seen in this light, the proceedings were the infrastructural pillars to support the values of full publicity and transparency.

However, producing proceedings was always balancing between what was said in parliament and how to represent what was said in written language in such a way that it could be read fluently, without being confronted with disturbing stuttering, stopgaps and other noise without meaning. Producing verbatim proceedings created some sort of polished reality. Furthermore, not everything was recorded. For instance, disapproving or supporting remarks made by members of parliament who did not participate in the debate were usually not noted [21, pp 37–40]. The new authority of the speaker to delete parts of what was said from the proceedings was however a much more radical and intrusive polishing of reality. This concealing effect was even enlarged since the proceedings published between 1934 and 1940 almost never reveal that the speaker made such interventions. Bootsma and Hoetink calculated that between February 1934 and the outbreak of the war in May 1940, the speaker of parliament used his new authority 298 times. Members of the left-wing Marxist parties were the prime victims of the new order [21, pp 46–47]. The stenographers recorded what was said, but they would take out from the transcribed shorthand notes the sentences that the speaker of parliament considered inappropriate, thus preventing that these would come in the public domain.

Dutch historian Woltjer has argued that although values such as openness and freedom of press were anchored in the constitution of 1848, this did not mean that "the printed or spoken word (…) could be contrary to public order and good morals" [24, p 17]. It is likely that protecting public decency and civil order according to bourgeois values and standards were also at the basis of the measures taken in parliament to ban inappropriate language from the proceedings. According to the authors of the new rule of procedure, dignity of parliament should be protected and the government should be prevented from becoming responsible for the dissemination of inflammatory and offensive texts, financed by the state and published in official proceedings [20, pp 1228–1229]. The deleted parts, which were called "dead bodies", would be stored in separate files, arranged per case. To prevent that the "dead bodies" could still be used as unwelcome and indecent means of communication, the content of the files remained secret and could (and still can) only be accessed after explicit permission from the speaker of parliament. The new rule aroused much dissatisfaction among those who fell victim to the new authority. Already in 1934, left-wing radical Sneevliet complained that "it cannot be the purpose that we, in this country and in this parliament, want to store such expressions in the historical archive and keep it secret" [21, p 89]. Nevertheless, many radical members experimented and occasionally succeeded in finding workarounds. For instance, they sometimes managed to avoid a ban by citing disputable phrases taken from (preferably authoritative) people such as journalists, politicians and famous writers in order to be able to say what they wanted to say without being accused of using inappropriate language themselves [21].

It may seem paradoxical that the vast majority in parliament emphasized and defended the importance of full and immediate transparency by publishing verbatim proceedings, and at the same time considered it legitimate not to publish a complete account of what happened in case a member was accused by the speaker of using inappropriate language. The key to this paradox is located in understanding the tacit bourgeois values such as public decency and civil order which were embraced by the majority of the members of parliament. Protection of public decency was a widely accepted rule of conduct in society and its solid foundation may also explain why, for instance, the press was not against the authority of the speaker to delete inappropriate language from the proceedings. There were no attempts made to muzzle the press. On the contrary, it was admitted that the press had its own responsibility. Most newsagencies in the 1930s were however very cautious in reporting on cases when the speaker made use of his authority. Usually they did not publish the banned sentences journalists could witness from the reporters' gallery. It shows how self-evident these tacit values were. In the eyes of contemporaries there was no contradiction, which was best expressed by the newspaper *De Tijd*, by claiming that "no majesty is more inviolable than the word, if it does indeed behave in a royal way" [25].

4   Discussion

The cases discussed above – particularly the new genres created during Italian Fascism, the infrastructural reforms impacting records and archives management in China in the 1930s, and the workarounds enacted to game the official system of rules governing parliamentary debates in the Netherlands around the same time period – provide examples of innovative information practices having different levels of sustainability.

The central figure of the Italian case, Mussolini, had a simplistic vision of the state. He believed in "governing through bureaucracy", an idea that was based on two assumptions: (1) that administering essentially means to execute orders – thus, Mussolini strived to build rigid hierarchical structures in all government branches and to impose quasi military obedience on his subordinates; and (2) that he, "the leader", was absolutely capable of seeing what needed to be done and directing people accordingly [8, p 74]. By focusing on the bureaucratic machine and its cogs (i.e., the new genres he invented and imposed) and on himself as its unstoppable pilot, Mussolini discounted the fact that deeply rooted values, unconscious preferences and pre-existing infrastructures are very hard if not impossible to change. Thus, he did not manage to "fascistize" the Italian institutions and population as thoroughly as he had wished. The persistence and resistance of a pre-fascist generation of high-level officials and bureaucrats who had been educated to liberal values was one of the elements that made it relatively easy for post-war, democratic politicians and administrators to re-establish the authority of traditional mechanisms as soon as Fascism collapsed. "Pre-existing institutions 'metabolized' the fascist order not through open opposition, but rather through assimilation of the new norms into the old system" [8, p 341].

This brings us to another point of interest, that is, the "conservative nature" of genres [26]. The mix of innovation and tradition characterizing Italy during the twenty years of the fascist regime may be read as a result of the resilience that belongs to any genres – especially the official, bureaucratic ones. Mussolini's focus on bureaucracy to change Italy did not take into consideration the "immobilism" inherent in the apparatus that should have, in his mind, spurred the revolution.

The war against Japan (1931–1945) and the subsequent civil war in China (1945–1949) certainly had a negative influence on the promotion of the reform of records and archives management. From the perspective of information culture, however, the reason that the chain method was not sustainable in the central government and was not widely adopted in local governments also lies in the fact that this innovation was contrary to the values accorded to records and archives by the staff and archives managers of the time and preexisting infrastructures. The new method involved managing records and archives collaboratively and transparently, so that archives could be accessed and found quickly and conveniently. However, most officials did not realize the value of records and archives for the administration, and did not attach importance to records and archives management. For the staff who regarded records as tools to shirk responsibility and the archives managers who regarded aichlves as tools to pursuing their illegitimate interests, this innovation represented an impediment. He commented: "there are a lot of difficulties in the work (i.e. the reform of records and archives management). Most difficulties are not in the techniques, but in the human factors" [27, p 115]. Another cultural reason to be highlighted is the inadequacy of the professional skills of records and archives managers. The reform was mainly dependent on a central figure – Naiguang Gan – and very few records and archives managers had sufficient professional expertise to be able to apply the new model. As He put it, "because the government does not attach importance to archives management, they do not know the importance of competent archives managers, and some incompetent people occupy the positions of archives managers" [27, p 115]. Yin also commented: "it has been over ten years since the creation of the chain method, but it has not been widely adopted. It is a pity that such a good method is seldom applied. (…) This is mainly because there are few professionals, and the current managers cannot understand the essentials of the chain method" [28, p 789].

One should also consider that the few information channels that were available in the 1930s (e.g., newspapers, magazines, telephones, telegrams) did not help the transmission of the innovation. Though the method was effective, a lot of agencies, especially many local governments, simply had no possibility to learn about it. While this is an objective factor, Gan's focus on the "things" as if they could be separated from the "people" was a result of his shortsightedness and a sign of that time. In another part of the world, Mussolini too thought that his goal was to build a "strong machine" (a thing), and the "people" would just obey and run.

Our close look at the actors and the processes involved in the making of the "verbatim" proceedings of the Dutch parliament around the same time has provided us with a nuanced and situated understanding of the meaning of openness and transparency, which defeats any easy generalization. One of the lessons learned from this case study is that digging deep into an historical information culture allows identifying the origins of ambivalent behaviours or misplaced perceptions that may continue until the present day. What we saw at play in the Dutch parliament of the 1930s as a specific context of genre production was a clash of values within the same culture: on the one hand, government transparency, civil rights and freedom of press were praised and, in some way, implemented, and on the other, principles of "good morals", public decency and civil order – the bourgeois values – pervaded and shaped the political and public discourse. To fight censorship, some more radical members of parliament turned to the "words of others", thus creating unexpected solutions that would circumvent the rules (workarounds).

5   Conclusion

Studying historical information cultures, that is, exploring the values, motives, and attitudes underpinning the information practices of the past through an interrogation of the practices themselves, is essential to understanding why certain approaches to information had been more or less successful, and how we can design sustainable information strategies for the future.

The cases examined in this article not only provide insight in continuities and discontinuities and in more and less successful innovations in information practices over time, but also generate new information culture-oriented research questions. All the cases show the complexities of successfully changing specific existing information practices and information habits. Mussolini did not succeed in fascistizing all preexisting information structures. Comparative research into information practices in times of regime change may provide more clarity about which factors may be more conducive to successful transformations. The innovative chain model in China was not firmly adopted due to resistance of practitioners who feared to lose their jobs. Comparative research may shed more light on the question of what influences professionals' willingness to adopt new methods. The Dutch case shows clashes of values concerning transparency and secrecy within the same culture. Comparative research between such identified clashes in different contexts may help identify regularities and irregularities in state and civil servant centered information practices. The ultimate aim of historical information culture research is to find explanations for successful and unsuccessful transitions. Comparative and longitudinal research on genres, workarounds, and infrastructures, and the cultural, social, and political implications of continuities and discontinuities can help us get a better understanding of our apparently new world.

Note: All translations from non-English sources have been carried out by the article authors.

References

1. Oliver, G., Foscarini, F.: Records Management and Information Culture: Tackling the People Problem. Facet Publishing, London (2014)
2. Foscarini, F.: Record as social action: understanding organizational records through the lens of genre theory. Inf. Res. **18**(3) (2013). paperC08. http://InformationR.net/ir/18-3/colis/paperC08.html. Accessed 01 Sept 2019
3. Miller, C.R.: Genre as social action. Q. J. Speech **70**(2), 151–167 (1984)
4. Lyttelton, A.: The Seizure of Power: Fascism in Italy, 1919–1929. Routledge, New York (2009)
5. De Felice, R.: Mussolini il fascista. Volume 1, La conquista del potere: 1921–1925. Einaudi, Turin (1966)
6. De Felice, R.: Mussolini il duce. Volume 1, Gli anni del consenso: 1929–1936. Einaudi, Turin (1974)
7. Gentile, E.: The Struggle for Modernity: Nationalism, Futurism, and Fascism. Foreword by Payne S.G. (Italian and Italian American Studies). Praeger, West-port (2003)
8. Melis, G.: La macchina imperfetta. Immagine e realtà dello Stato fascista. Il Mulino, Bologna (2018)
9. Milza, P.: Mussolini. Carocci, Roma (2000)
10. Russell, D.R.: Rethinking genre in school and society. An activity theory analysis. Writ. Commun. **14**(4), 504–554 (1997)
11. Bazerman, C.: The Languages of Edison's Light. MIT Press, Cambridge (1999)
12. Gan, N.G.: New Theory on Chinese Administration. The Commercial Press, Chongqing (1943)

13. Chen, G.C.: The Simplification and Management of Records. World Publishing Corporation, Shanghai (1945)
14. Zhou, L.K.: The Method of Archives Management. World Publishing Corporation, Shanghai (1942)
15. Gan, N.G.: Trial on the chain method of records and archives management—the report on the initial trial in the Interior Ministry. Adm. Effic. 1(10), 423–429 (1934)
16. Gan, N.G.: Retrospect and Prospect on the Reform of Records and Archives Management. World Publishing Corporation, Shanghai (1937)
17. De Volkskrant, Imagoprobleem van het Europees Parlement (newspaper), 21 May 2019. https://www.volkskrant.nl/nieuws-achtergrond/zo-veel-invloed-zo-weinig-bekend-bij-burgers-het-imagoprobleem-van-het-europees-parlement ~ bed39fa9/
18. Aerts, R.: Iemand moet het doen. Tweehonderd jaar beeld en zelfbeeld van de Tweede Kamer. In: Aerts, R., Van Baalen, C., Oddens, J., Smit, D., Te Velde, H. (eds.) Twee Eeuwen Tweede Kamer, pp. 439–467. Boom, Amsterdam (2015)
19. Pippel, J.G.: Het Reglement van Orde van de Tweede Kamer der Staten-Generaal. Zijne Geschiedenis en Toepassing. Algemeene Landsdrukkerij's, Gravenhage (1925)
20. Handelingen der Staten-Generaal, 14 February 1934. https://repository.overheid.nl/frbr/sgd/19331934/0000053610/1/pdf/SGD_19331934_0000340.pdf
21. Bootsma, P., Hoetink, C.: Over Lijken. Ontoelaatbaar taalgebruik in de Tweede Kamer. Boom, Amsterdam (2006)
22. Baalen, C., Tanja, E.: In dienst van de Kamer. De ambtelijke ondersteuning van de volksvertegenwoordigers. In: Aerts, R., Van Baalen, C., Oddens, J., Smit, D., Te Velde, H. (eds.) In dit Huis. Twee Eeuwen Tweede Kamer, pp. 193–221. Boom, Amsterdam (2015)
23. Bonenkamp, B.J.: Zwijgend medewerker en aandachtig luisteraar. 150 jaar Stenografische Dienst der Staten-Generaal. SDU, Den Haag (1999)
24. Woltjer, J.J.: Recent Verleden. De Geschiedenis van Nederland in de Twintigste Eeuw. Uitgeverij Balans, Amsterdam (1992)
25. De Tijd, Victor de Stuers en de kunst van het debat, (newspaper), 23 February 1934. https://www.delpher.nl
26. Bazerman, C.: Systems of genres and the enactment of social intentions. In: Freedman, A., Medway, P. (eds.) Genre and the New Rhetoric. Taylor & Francis, London (1994)
27. He, L.C.: Archives Arrangement and Management. World Publishing Corporation, Shanghai (1937)
28. Yin, Z.Q.: New Theory on Chinese Archives Management. World Publishing Corporation, Shanghai (1949)

Bridging DH and Humanistic HCI

John S. Seberger(⊠) Ⓘ

University of California, Irvine, Irvine, CA 92697, USA
jseberge@uci.edu

Abstract. Bowker's Age of Potential Memory describes a new era characterized by a culture of knowledge production that fosters and stifles certain forms
of statements depending on the logics that subtend them. Through processes of
ubiquitous data collection, analysis, and feedback, individuals are increasingly
reduced to users; users are re-created as data doubles or data doppelgangers,
post hoc, through the aggregation and analysis of their data traces. This discursive transformation of the human that will arise in relation to living alongside
and through these doubles or doppelgangers is difficult to understand within the
framework of extant disciplinary silos. And yet methods that connect disciplines
are emerging. To realize these connections, translational work is required. This
paper explores the complementarity of digital humanities (DH) and humanistic
human-computer interaction (hHCI) through the lens of distant reading. I focus
on distant reading—topic modelling in particular—because of its methodological popularity and relation to discourse. I argue that distant reading comprises a
useful connection between these two young domains: a pivot that allows for the
inter- or transdisciplinary study of the future human through the analysis of its
potential sociotechnical, discursive compositions.

Keywords: Digital humanities · Humanistic HCI · Discourse · Distant
reading · Sociotechnical

1 Introduction

I write this essay as a practitioner of humanistic HCI [1]: *from* an interdisciplinary
position and *to* an intended audience of scholars who are frustrated by, or wary of, the
increasingly common rebranding of disciplines and methodologies as 'digital.' By
these I mean, digital humanities (DH), digital sociology [2], digital ethnography [3],
and perhaps most recently, digital STS [4]. It is not my intention to downplay the
importance of these endeavors or the validity of the work they represent, but rather to
take on the unpopular task of addressing the extent to which the epistemic colonization
of digital phenomena according to the old allegiances of disciplinary silos risks
obfuscating and frustrating emergent opportunities for transdisciplinarity and further
risks defining digital phenomena in terms of outmoded domain logics [5]. These
practices are subtended by a potent form of radical presentism: one that primes us to
overlook the possibility that one day, 'the digital' will disappear as a modifier as in the
promise of infrastructure and technological success [6, 7], as though the world of
phenomena will remain oriented towards the digital turn as it manifests currently.
Whereas presentism usually refers to the inappropriate smuggling of the present tense

© Springer Nature Switzerland AG 2020
A. Sundqvist et al. (Eds.): iConference 2020, LNCS 12051, pp. 860–873, 2020.
https://doi.org/10.1007/978-3-030-43687-2_72

into historical research, here it refers to the assumed discursive stability *of* that present tense: that the Archive [8] of the future will be built upon the discursive structures of today's (unstable) transformations.

The world is changing in ways that reach beyond historical boundaries of culture, society, and geography, and it is changing in no small part because of 'the digital.' But within this digitality emerge questions of appropriateness: the appropriateness of maintaining the homeostasis of disciplinary rigidity versus encouraging the homeorhetic process of interdisciplinary paradigmatic shifts. We *can* divide the digital era and its phenomena along the historical lines of disciplinarity. The question is, '*Should* we?'[1]

Empiricism—the apparent Zeus relative to the Olympian pantheon of episte-mologies—produces knowledge, but it also produces absences in knowledge: any mode of perception is also a mode of imperception. It is to find a signal within the noise, thus defining that which is unperceived *as noise*: irrelevant. But as Michel Serres argued [10], we walk alongside the noise. It cannot be overlooked or assumed to be irrelevant. The noise created by the durability of disciplinary siloes might, indeed, be the anthem of our futures. I write this paper to address two very difficult questions: (1) 'What potential signals are we reducing to the status of noise by forcing them into the extant domain logics of historical disciplines, despite the emendation of the term 'digital'?' and (2) 'How might we leverage methodological complementarity within emerging domains to render these noises as signals?' In other words, 'How might we foster emerging sites of interdisciplinary collaboration in order to study the potential futures of the human, rather than (unintentionally) limiting those futures by fitting them to known disciplines, or 'knowledge reservoirs'?' [9].

In the digital age—what Bowker [11] refers to as the Age of Potential Memory and more recently what Zuboff [12] has called the Age of Surveillance Capitalism—the human is a matter of concern [13]. This matter of concern is framed not only by the human drive to classify [14], but also to dichotomize [15]. In the lingering structure of Snow's two cultures [16]—a broad dichotomization of a more nuanced classification system—both sides race towards the middle to claim it. That middle is 'the digital,' and it becomes a pivot point between the two cultures. In the humanities camp, the emergence of DH allows indirect commune with the sciences because of its quantitative tendencies; in the scientific camp, humanistic human-computer interaction (hHCI) (among others) allows indirect commune with the humanities because of its theoretical foundations.

And yet both DH and hHCI are apparently separate from one another. Bardzell et al. [17] have highlighted the synergistic relationship between the humanities and HCI, while Bardzell and Bardzell [1] have also explicitly drawn a line between DH and hHCI: DH uses digital tools to study humanistic phenomena; hHCI uses humanistic epistemologies to study the digital. While this line in the sand was likely drawn in order to aid in defining an emergent sub-domain of HCI, I argue that it has served its purpose. Surely the relationship is more productive than mutual differentiation. In identifying the nature of its potential productivity, I seek to understand how DH and hHCI can

---

[1] I am not a sociologist and am therefore ill-equipped to engage in a mechanistic analysis of how one might alter modes of scholarly communication and validation in such a way as to foster an easier transdisciplinarity. For those interested in pursuing this issue, I recommend the work of Becher and Trowler [9] as a starting point.

complement each other to provide scholarly access to the archive [8] of the future human: the future world of discourse in which the human will reside.

This paper explores the complementarity of DH and hHCI through the lens of distant reading [18, 19]. In particular, I focus on Latent Dirichlet Allocation topic modeling (LDA) [20] and its relationship to discourse: LDA topic modeling as a discourse; and LDA as a means of exploring the contemporary Archive through textual discourse. LDA's relationship to discourse is essential and justifies my focus on it: where discursive systems constitute the greater archive [8], and LDA provides access to the discourses that subtend a corpus of texts (see Sect. 4.1), LDA can be used to identify current discursive systems [21], but also to abduce [22] their potential transformations. I argue that LDA provides unique access to The Archive—the set of all possible discursive statements relative to a given historical era [8, 23]—in the present tense. Such access identifies LDA as not only a mechanism of discursive transformation, but also a suitable tool for analyzing the potential future discursive construction of the human.[2]

In the relationship between DH and hHCI as seen through the lens of topic modeling, DH takes on the quantitative role of the probabilistic computer sciences, and hHCI takes on the qualitative role of the humanities. That subdomains within both of Snow's two cultures evidence epistemic tendencies generally associated with their opposite camp indicates a site for interdisciplinarity.

2   Across the Great Divide

The interplay of humanistic and computational epistemologies will come to define the human experience *of being human* through digitally mediated experience: of being thrown [25] into an era defined by the set of possible statements that subtend it. The tug-of-war between human phenomenology and the phenomenology of the Computational Other, which pre-processes the world prior to human perception, bounds the imaginary of the future. It therefore bounds the possible experience of being human *in* the future. So, not only are we sociotechnical, but we are future-sociotechnical; not only are we embodied in a present tense and interpolated by digital versions of ourselves derived from trace data and algorithmic knowledge production, but we are both of these things in the complex temporality of the imaginary. In these toddling years of the Age of Potential Memory, the human—as much as any individual user—resides as a set of potentials, each of which is predicated on the path dependencies of contemporary knowledge production, which is itself broadly predicated on the adoption of either humanistic or computational epistemologies. Do we computerize the human, or do we humanize the computer? Do we envision the human through the lens of the computer, or do we envision the computer through the lens of the human?

---

[2] Further, discussion of the epistemic roots of LDA and its relation to archive theory allows us to sidestep the (important) issue of data visualization, which can be seen as an obfuscating, but primary motivating factor for the use of digital methods [24].

Unfortunately, It's just not as simple as those binary formulations. The ontology of subject and object is changing: we are entering an new ontological madness [26], new mode of relationality between the members of the triple—Aristotelian, Heraclitean, and Parmenidean—ontology. The sociotechnical is simultaneously both social and technical; the physical conditions of humans and computers create different *umwelts* [27] that occupy the same space, both exerting onto-epistemological influence over the other. The human-computer dialectic dissolves into a unity, a new mode of hybrid contextuality. The gathering of the thing [28] extends beyond the physicality and affordances [29] of discrete subjects and objects into the philosophical realm of subjectivity and objectivity: not only do discrete subjects and objects gather to form things, but so, too, to the ontological categories to which they belong. The subjectival and objectival comprise the gathering *through* the predicative, and as scholars we must be open to the idea that this gathering cannot be studied adequately within the extent structures of academia. To study change within a fixed framework is to predefine the limits of how that change might be studied. Where the digital offers potentially myriad new constellations of discourse, we risk rendering these discourses as noise rather than signal by classifying them in terms of historical disciplines.

To further complicate the matter, while the phenomenological domains of the human and the computer do, in fact, overlap and exert mutual influence over each other, they are apparently separate and separable. Their apparent separability emerges from the broader paradigm of 'domain logic' [5] within academia. The object of study is in-part created by the scholarly domain that studies it [30–32]. We are what we are through any one of the kaleidoscopic facets of scholarship, where each one is valid under certain epistemological conditions: I am governed [33]; I am a patient in the clinical gaze [34]; I am my digital traces [35]. I am both a user and more than a user. And yet tremendous tension exists between humanistic and (computer) scientific approaches. This tension gives rise, in part, to a bifurcated human subject: a schizoid actant embedded in culture and history yet *made* schizoid by the processes of reductionist domain logics that operationalize them as 'user.'

In the context of ostensibly flattening ontologies [36] and our deepening sociotechnicality, it is germane to examine the points at which humanistic and scientific domain logics—descendants of Snow's famous 'two cultures' [16]—are no longer functionally separate: points at which the schizoid is avoidable, treatable. If new epistemologies are required to understand the future of the human—for example, the human as they will exist in a realized imaginary of the Internet of Things (IoT), or any other manifestation of Bowker's Age of Potential Memory [11]—so, too, are new and hopefully permanent modes of transdisciplinarity.

3 Humanistic HCI and DH in a Nutshell

While DH and hHCI are at the very least related through their use of the terms 'humanities' and 'humanistic,' the nature of their relationship is somewhat vaguer. In this section, I provide an overview of what they are: their epistemic assumptions, common practices, and potential points of productive overlap.[3]

3.1 Humanistic HCI

In the past twenty years or so, HCI has taken a phenomenological turn (e.g., [37]). For practitioners of third paradigm HCI [38], context is everything (e.g., [39]). But for even the most phenomenologically minded HCI scholars, it can be difficult to think beyond the discourse of context as it emerges through such problems as the framing problem [40, 41] and the cognitive-scientific foundations of second paradigm HCI [38]. Techno-centric approaches to context confound human-centered approaches: human experience, and therefore humanistic definitions of context, is/are envisioned through the lens of computation. Our designed devices—even those designed in a values sensitive [42], reflective [43], or participatory [44] framework—ultimately reconstruct us, reconfigure us [45].[4]

The move towards humanistic HCI within third paradigm HCI shifts focus from understanding digital phenomena through the epistemologies of computation to understanding them through humanistic epistemologies [1]. Thusly, humanistic HCI emerges as proximal, but not identical, to DH. But the question remains as to whether or not there is productive overlap between the two nascent traditions, and what this potential overlap might contribute to the greater discourse of context.

3.2 Digital Humanities

Broadly, DH uses digital tools and methods to interpret and analyze humanistic phenomena. Almost as frequently as DH scholars employ digital methods to study texts, DH scholars debate what DH is (e.g., [46–56]). These contributions to the literature, focus on appropriately bounding the use of digital tools in DH. That is, they perform a gatekeeping function intended to delineate between a humanities that is digital and the rest of academia, which is also faced with (no less problematic) transitions to digital modes of knowledge production. But the logic here is unfortunately exclusionary. We struggle to define disciplines that have existed for many generations in light of emergent methodologies; we embrace the radical presentism of the 'digital' disciplines in order to maintain purchase on a changing sociotechnical and philosophical landscape.

But these methodologies are inherently transdisciplinary: digital methods emerge as means of understanding digital phenomena; digital phenomena are not relegated to either the humanities or the sciences. Rather, digital phenomena are transdisciplinary in

---

[3] The treatments of DH and hHCI presented here are purposefully broad. While they will likely not satisfy specialists in either DH or hHCI, to seek a middle ground is always to fail in satisfying disciplinary purists.

[4] That design implies reconstruction is a primary impetus for the design practices referenced.

that they constitute their own domain of study that transcends extant disciplinary silos and domain logics.

I argue that hHCI and DH are not mutually exclusive, but rather complementary and synergistic. In their synergy, one finds the potential for a newly concretized domain: a human sciences that accepts the digital as a set of phenomena, but does not eschew broader historical, critical, and cultural narratives for the presentism and attraction of 'digital this,' or 'digital that.' One method of digital humanities knowledge production —LDA Topic Modeling [57–60]—is particularly useful in highlighting their synergistic relationship and points to a method, suitably framed, for accessing and describing the discursive structure of the contemporary historical archive: the archive into which the human-as-user is thrown; the archive that emerges from the contemporary imaginary of future computing. We will become digital, and when we have become digital the 'the digital' will be naturalized, and we will become human already again.

4 Distant Reading and the Contemporary Archive

Distant reading [18] has come to be a public standard for DH. Perhaps because of its widespread adoption in DH, it has not readily been adopted as an object of humanistic HCI study. Through its execution, it combines the terms 'digital' and 'humanities' in an approachable way: digital methods (and tools) for textual data. This combination— perhaps juxtaposition is a better term—however, betrays what might be seen as a primary shortcoming of DH: a focus on tool-building [55]. By tool-building, I mean a DH paradigm wherein digital tools are (built and) used to analyze textual materials that would otherwise be analyzed using the more traditional toolkit of the human reader, thus unintentionally calling into question the validity of (pre-digital) humanistic methods, while fostering the theory-agnostic tendencies of big data [61, 62]. Where the human reader is involved in the process of distant reading—setting the algorithm's parameters, reading its output—their work is ultimately in service to a computationally derived 'text as process' [63]. Only in the broadest sense of functionalism—a car is the same as a horse because they both get you somewhere!—are the roles of the human reader in traditional interpretation and distant reading the same.

In this particular framing of DH—which is by no means the only framing—non-practitioners are primed to think of DH as a means by which outdated or obsolete humanists catch up with the digital era.[5] Such an approach does no one—least of all Digital Humanists—any good. Given the tremendous inertia of epistemic cultures or paradigms [64, 65], such a rhetorical implication is woefully counterproductive to the survival of humanistic knowledge production in an increasingly data-driven world. Indeed, it overshadows the very style of knowledge production (and its resultant contributions) for which the humanities have historically been valued. The expert subject, if augmented by computerized empiricism, may appear as an expert reader, but their expertise is predicated, in part, on the prosthetic of the computer: an actant

---

[5] I do not hold the position that humanistic analysis is out of date or outmoded, but rather make this statement as it appears to be the elephant in the room whenever DH comes up at non-DH conferences.

fundamentally external to the condition of embodiment that give rise to subjectivity (whether expert or not).

4.1 Topics as Discourses

In work that predates the emergence of distant reading and the concretization of DH, Olsen [66] presaged the role of computers in approaching the discourses that subtend a text. In so doing, Olsen implied the ever-present status of (Foucauldian) discourse: that is, discourse is not only a purely historical concept—observed *post hoc*—but one that must always already exist in any given present tense, even as it slips into the future as in the case of writing upon a page. As Olsen [66, p. 313] writes:

> [...] systematic analysis of sign or language use across large blocks of text is amenable to both qualitative and quantitative analysis. The image of the Fortunate Islands (later the Canaries) or 'women's anger' can be examined systematically in a large database without resorting to quantification at all, simply by reading and comparing descriptions across many texts of many years. By contrast, one can examine the changing meaning of words that constitute the discourse of gender over long periods of time using quantitative methods that are well known and understood.

While Olsen's situating of discourse in a 'long period of time' most clearly hints at the relationship between his concept of 'discourse' and that analyzed by Foucault in his grand historical project, it also hints at the continued existence of such discourse across temporalities: if it exists in one, and if we are to assume the experiential validity of the continuity of time, then it must exist at all possible scales of time that can be experienced or theorized. Thusly, the form of analysis Olsen describes becomes a tool for analyzing discourse in the present tense: it renders the archive accessible.

If discourses are present in an historical text or corpus so as to be analyzable at a temporal remove (as is the basic case in historical study), then they must also be present in a text at the moment of writing and the moment of reading.[6] Discourse is inscribed into a text at the jussive moment of the text's inscription: it is always there, latent or overt, within the linguistic weave of the inscription—a linguistic weave that stretches like gossamer into cultural histories, geological histories, the history of materiality and embodiment expressed through signifiers. Discourse abounds and envelopes, and by it we, as historical animals, abide. We have only to develop and implement the means to access it in the present tense, lest it be approached solely *post hoc*.

Olsen [66, pp. 313–314] continues with a consideration of the relationship between the author and the symbolic constellations of discourses to which they have access:

> Authors function within symbolic universes of which they can only be partially conscious. If I am correct in assuming that computer analysis of large bodies of material for relatively simple constructions reveals elements of discourse that are beyond the control or awareness of an author, then studies of individual authors and texts will be rendered more intelligible by highlighting the ways in which an author uses, modifies, or rejects contemporary symbols.

---

[6] That discourses are present or materialized in texts at the moment of writing does not imply their stability. The text, therefore, constitutes a heterotopia combining both the historical *a priori* condition in which it was written and the analogous condition in which it is read. It is doubly temporal; doubly historical.

Indeed, selection of interesting or important rhetorical shifts or manipulations would seem to presuppose careful identification of general patterns of discourse. Knowing what language is available to an author—the symbolic universe in which he/she operates—is a vital part of interpreting the intentions and limitations of the text.

The symbolic universe of the author has expanded—rather, the potential for its visibility has increased. Text now extends in the form of metatextuality and hyper-textuality into the realm of the digital: all texts potentially reside in a quantum-like state of primary textuality and metatextuality. The mode of materialization by which a text becomes inscribed is therefore necessarily a universal discourse subtending the discourse of textuality. It is therefore not enough to use digital methods to analyze the discursive content of a given text. Any project that hopes towards completeness must also concern the materiality of the text, which—given the logic of Olsen's statement above—must extend to those materialities employed in the analysis of the text. The digital-scientific must interpret the textual; the humanistic must interpret the digital-scientific. The complementary and synergistic relationship between DH and hHCI comes into view.

The need to concern ourselves with the materiality that produces topics and therefore effects an onto-epistemological shift in the text it analyzes is evident in interpretations made by leading DH scholars. Underwood [67], for example, argues that the topics derived from LDA topic modeling "probably always have the character of 'discourses,' despite the fact that the size of the corpus analyzed is likely to have an effect on the granularity of topics generated." That is, the term 'topic' is ambiguous in its usage and application across differently sized corpuses. (As Underwood notes, Blei was pointedly 'agnostic' as to the theoretical value of the term 'topic,' preferring to reduce the notion of 'topic' to that of a 'latent variable.') If the discourses identified as relevant to a given corpus are predicated, to a certain extent, on the size of that corpus, then the machinery used to compile and 'read' that corpus effects a sort of infrastructural inversion [68]: that which was invisible, but ostensibly always already present in the form of latent discourse, becomes visible. The 'text' emerges as a part of the 'Text,' where the latter is a discourse unto itself, as in the 'oeuvre' for Foucault [8]. Through the assembly of the corpus and its preparation for digital-distant analysis, the text (i.e., that which is printed on the page) is thrown into the heady space of discourse (i.e., the forces that allow for printing on a page, up to and including the technology of the page [and the digital reader] itself). The text as a function of the Text becomes visible through the eye of the machine. Where the eye of the machine and the embodied eye of the human are different, such a difference must be accounted for. In the need to account for that difference, we see the first hint that traditional humanistic analysis— that which was perfected prior to the digital era—must still play a fundamental role in any distant reading endeavor, but not only in reading a topic model's output: in reading the mechanics of the topic modeling algorithm (and its material manifestations) as well. As such, DH aligns with humanistic HCI: both are predicated on the validity of humanistic epistemology.

Underwood [67] compares his own LDA work on 'volumes of 18th and 19th century works' to Lisa Rhody's work that focuses on much smaller documents: poems. Rhody's work [59] highlights the value of LDA analysis in identifying and partially explicating the:

> types of questions we are looking for as humanists. What this small discovery shows is that topic modeling as a methodology, particularly in the case of highly-figurative language texts like poetry, can help us to get to new questions and discoveries—not because topic modeling works perfectly, but because poetry causes it to fail in ways that are potentially productive for literary scholars [59].

Underwood [67] reaches a similar conclusion in describing his own use of LDA: certain topics are particularly difficult to parse, 'but for a literary scholar, that's a plus.' He further writes that he wants 'this method to point [him] towards something [he] doesn't understand' yet, noting further that he 'almost never finds that the results are too ambiguous to be useful.' That ambiguity is useful further implies the role of the machine in the construction of Text: the machine and its logics constitute part of the text that is analyzed in terms of the Text. That words are ripped from the page n-gram by n-gram in order to be assembled into the larger puzzle of discourse connotes a textual function of the machine no smaller than the function played by the page, the chapter, or the binding itself. The text is deconstructed to be reconstituted as the Text, which is a state change rather than a vantage from which to view the traditional state of the text. While effecting such a state change possibly allows for the generation of theories and findings relative to the time or tradition in which a work was written, it also certainly necessitates reflexive analysis: distant reading effects an epistemological change on the humanities. The expert subject merges with the probabilistic objectivity of the computer.

Here, we see a reciprocity between DH and hHCI: the former moves towards the sciences; the latter towards the humanities. DH becomes poised to approach the archive as it emerges through the 'text as process', while hHCI is poised to approach the process by which that archive is created as 'text as process.' Put differently, DH approaches a new condition of textuality and its relationship to discourse and discursive transformation; hHCI approaches the means by which this new condition of textuality emerges *as discourse*. They meet in the middle in the emerging epistemology of the digital human, the human sciences. This change deserves as much scrutiny as the texts that it reassembles.

Topic modeling uses the form of the book as a metaphor allowing the model's interpreter to assign to the corpus a transient textuality that ultimately allows for the creative destruction of such textuality: one imagines a text so as to index it [*cf* 69]; one indexes it in the form of a topic model so as to erase the imagined image, to move beyond the metaphor of the book. In a longer historical view, we invented the book to destroy it through the seeking of some deeper and yet more abstracted knowledge; we built a doorway to the realm of discourse and Texts only to destroy the known library from which it leads.

But the nature of the access granted is paradoxical: just as a book is read in different eras, and those eras shape and color the meaning a reader derives from that text, so, too, does discourse change depending on the means of access to that discourse [70].

To grant digital access to works from the 18th century is not to access the 18th century or its history: it is to access that century through a critical wormhole of the present tense, pregnant with its own discursive contents. As such, the historiographical epistemology of topic modeling is summed up nicely by Pascal and Pierre Nora: "*Pascal peut-etre avait raison: «Toute histoire qui n'est past contemporaine est suspecte.»*" [71], and again by Benedetto Croce: 'All history is a history of the present tense' [72].

5 Conclusion: The Human Between DH and hHCI

It is productive to view topic modeling as a boundary object [73] between any number of fields increasingly enrolled into the epistemic culture of big data. For example, the LDA algorithm exists as a boundary object between DH and Information Sciences. Both, to one extent or another, are predicated on the assumptions of Bayesian probability, but interact with the logics contained therein differently. As the human continues its evolution in the shadow of Bayesian logics—as in the imaginary of IoT and future computing (FC), machine learning (ML), and the latest-greatest approach to artificial intelligence (AIx)—topic modelling presents itself as uniquely suited for reflexive research. Not only does it allow for access to the discourses that subtend the imaginary of the future human, but it is also a discourse unto itself: an algorithmic statement that limns the structure of The (Digital) Archive, the archive in-motion [74]. This kernel statement of this future Archive—in human-readable format—reads something like the following: "We have the data, so now can know and be known." Topic modelling is both a mode of knowledge production and an archive of potential statements that evolves from previous statements. The statements it might generate are, themselves, bound by the greater archival superset of statements that comprise computerized empiricism and the long slouch towards an epistemic culture of big data. LDA presents not only as a means of accessing discourse, but as a mode of discursive transformation. It is both a method of studying discourse and an agent of discursive transformation; it is as simultaneously humanistic and scientific as any of its users.

A complete usage of the LDA algorithm requires a convergence of community members from both/all sides of the boundary object [73], and therefore the effacement of the boundary object's boundary qualities: the practice of distant reading effectively forms a bridge between the 'two cultures' [16]. It presents as a means of digital analysis relative to textual phenomena; it presents as a site of humanistic analysis of the digital wherein we might understand the modes by which we produce knowledge and the impacts they will have on the experience of being human. It is the meeting point of DH and hHCI. This meeting point deserves to be structured as a big tent (to borrow a phrase from DH): within it linger the answers to fundamental questions about the future discourse of the human: what it might means to say, 'I am human,' in future predicated on the infrastructuralization of IoT, FC, and ML. Designing a lasting structure for that bridge should now be a core focal point within the DH and HCI writ large. The emergence of digital culture portends a flattened ontology [36, 75]. Why should disciplines be exempt from this flattening?

We are moving into a future that is characterized by rampant and ubiquitous data collection. Such ubiquity will only further concretize the importance of big data: we will continue to know (and naturalize) our worlds through the lens of big data, as problematic as that is [30, 76]. The ontological and epistemological colonial force of big data will have lasting impacts not only the experience of being an individual human in the temporality of the day-to-day, but it will also have confounding effects on the disciplinary structure of scholarship. Rather than focusing on the extent to which one field or another, one tradition or another, can differentiate themselves, or make themselves more relevant through the use of digital technologies, it is high time to return to a framework of unification. The topics and societal problems with which we now have to grapple are inherently transdisciplinary: they not only require interdisciplinary and multi-disciplinary teams of scholars, but they also often necessitate the emergence of new fields entirely. As new fields emerge, it will be of the utmost importance to ensure that (Digital) Humanists have a place at the table alongside HCI scholars—not as an after-thought, but as indication of the central place of humanities scholarship in the production of worlds in which humans *want* to live *as humans*. Similarly, it is of equal importance to ensure the continuation of humanistic HCI research.

At a point in time when the Digital Humanities has begun to concretize around the practice of distant reading, it becomes necessary to consider the future-oriented ramifications of this media format—the materiality of the algorithm, as well as its modes of interactivity (e.g., MALLET) [77]. What are the knowledge producing characteristics of a disciplinary infrastructure such as that which emerges through the widespread use of distant reading? What contributions can DH make to the ongoing paradigmatic shift towards a ubiquitous epistemic culture of big data?

With regard to the latter question, the answer appears clear: DH has, like a colonial collaborator, allowed computerized empiricism into its territory. At first glance, this is worrying. Another look, however, primes us to consider that perhaps this is simply a symptom of paradigmatic shift: the emergence of a new transdisciplinarity. While calls for the end of theory [61] have not yet been echoed in humanistic circles (to my knowledge), they are likely not far behind. Similarly, with a focus on tool-building, DH aligns itself with the problematic aspects of tech culture [55, 56]. When such an alignment occurs relative to a set of disciplines from which postcolonial theory, deconstruction, critical theory, and the like emerged, doubts as to the future validity of these approaches come directly into view. As I demonstrated above, however, distant reading practices—when combined with methodologies historically grounded in the pre-digital humanities, as in hHCI—can be leveraged to reflect on themselves. Where text—the traditional and rightful domain of humanistic inquiry—expands into the realm of the digital, let that serve as the corpus. No translation necessary.

I suggest that DH and hHCI scholars take a cue from the field of science studies: first, to leverage the tools of distant reading in order to analyze the practice of humanities and humanistic scholarship as it occurs across the two cultures and in the emergent, interstitial spaces between; second, to apply the lessons learned from the DH experiment to the broader and transdisciplinary space of digital life. No one is better equipped to see the trends of culture and the trajectories of history than humanistic scholars. These trends present as raw data in the form of digital texts—texts that converge across scrolling feeds of Tweets, newsfeeds, images, and memes. As humanists living with, alongside, and through the digital—DHers, hHCIers, and the rest—we have been so caught up with validating our (already valid) methodologies in the context of the digital era, that we have forgotten or overlooked the value we can contribute to the analysis of this digital era through the simple act of reflexive study.

References

1. Bardzell, J., Bardzell, S.: Humanistic HCI. Morgan & Claypool Publishers, San Rafael (2015)
2. Lupton, D.: Digital Sociology. Routledge, Abingdon (2014)
3. Boellstorff, T., Nardi, B., Pearce, C., Taylor, T.L.: Ethnography and Virtual Worlds: A Handbook of Method. Princeton University Press, Princeton (2012)
4. Vertesi, J., Ribes, D.: digitalSTS: A Field Guide for Science & Technology Studies. Princeton University Press, Princeton (2019)
5. Ribes, D., Hoffman, A.S., Slota, S.C., Bowker, G.C.: The logic of domains. Soc. Stud. Sci. **49**, 281–309 (2019). https://doi.org/10.1177/0306312719849709
6. Star, S.L., Ruhleder, K.: Steps toward and ecology of infrastructure: design and access for large information spaces. Inf. Syst. Res. **7**, 111–134 (1996)
7. Weiser, M.: The computer for the 21st century. Sci. Am. **265**, 94–104 (1991). https://doi.org/10.1038/scientificamerican0991-94
8. Foucault, M.: The Archaeology of Knowledge. Pantheon Books, New York (1972)
9. Becher, T., Trowler, P.: Academic Tribes and Territories: Intellectual Enquiry and the Cultures of Discipline. Open University Press, Philadelphia (2001)
10. Serres, M.: The Parasite. University of Minnesota Press, Minneapolis (2013)
11. Bowker, G.C.: Memory Practices in the Sciences. MIT Press, Cambridge (2005)
12. Zuboff, S.: The Age of Surveillance Capitalism: The Fight for a Human Future at the New Frontier of Power. PublicAffairs, New York (2019)
13. Latour, B.: Why has critique run out of steam? From matters of fact to matters of concern | bruno-latour.fr. In: Brown, B. (ed.) Things. University of Chicago Press, Chicago (2004)
14. Bowker, G.C., Star, S.L.: Sorting Things Out: Classification and Its Consequences. The MIT Press, Cambridge (2000)
15. Dawkins, R.: Gaps in the Mind. In: The Great Ape Project, pp. 80–87 (1993)
16. Snow, C.P.: The Two Cultures. Cambridge University Press, Cambridge (2012)
17. Bardzell, J., Bardzell, S., DiSalvo, C., Gaver, W., Sengers, P.: The humanities and/in HCI. In: CHI'12 Extended Abstracts on Human Factors in Computing Systems, pp. 1135–1138. ACM, New York (2012)
18. Moretti, F.: Distant Reading. Verso, London (2013)
19. Moretti, F.: Graphs, Maps, Trees: Abstract Models for Literary History. Verso, London (2007)
20. Blei, D.M., Ng, A.Y., Jordan, M.I.: Latent dirichlet allocation. J. Mach. Learn. Res. **3**, 993–1022 (2003)
21. Seberger, J.S.: Becoming Objects: IoT, The Archive, and the Future of the Human (2019)
22. Tavory, I., Timmermans, S.: Abductive Analysis: Theorizing Qualitative Research. University of Chicago Press, Chicago (2014)
23. Derrida, J.: Archive Fever: A Freudian Impression. University of Chicago Press, Chicago (1998)
24. Venturini, T.: Building on faults: how to represent controversies with digital methods. Public Underst. Sci. **21**, 796–812 (2012). https://doi.org/10.1177/0963662510387558

25. Heidegger, M.: Being and Time. Harper, New York (1962)
26. Flusser, V.: On Doubt. University of Minnesota Press, Minneapolis (2015)
27. Von Uexküll, J.: A stroll through the worlds of animals and men: a picture book of invisible worlds. Semiotica **89**, 319–391 (2009). https://doi.org/10.1515/semi.1992.89.4.319
28. Heidegger, M.: What is a thing? H. Regnery Co., Chicago (1968)
29. Gibson, J.J.: The theory of affordances. In: Shaw, R., Bransford, J. (eds.) Perceiving, Acting, and Knowing, pp. 67–82. Lawrence Erlbaum Associates, New York (1977)
30. Gitelman, L. (ed.): "Raw Data" Is an Oxymoron. The MIT Press, Cambridge; London (2013)
31. Gitelman, L.: Paper Knowledge: Toward a Media History of Documents. Duke University Press, Durham (2014)
32. Drucker, J.: Graphesis: Visual Forms of Knowledge Production. Harvard University Press, Cambridge (2014)
33. Foucault, M.: Governmentality. In: Burchell, G., Gordon, C., Miller, P. (eds.) The Foucault Effect: Studies in Governmentality, pp. 87–104. University of Chicago Press, Chicago (1991)
34. Foucault, M.: The Birth of the Clinic. Routledge, London (2012)
35. Boullier, D.: The social science and the traces of big data: society, opinion, or vibrations? Revue francaise de science politique (Engl. Ed.) **65**, 71–93 (2015)
36. Harman, G.: Object-Oriented Ontology: A New Theory of Everything. Penguin, London (2018)
37. Dourish, P.: Where the Action Is: The Foundations of Embodied Interaction. MIT Press, Cambridge (2004)
38. Harrison, S., Tatar, D., Sengers, P.: The three paradigms of HCI. In: Alt. Chi. Session at the SIGCHI Conference on Human Factors in Computing Systems, San Jose, California, USA, pp. 1–18 (2007)
39. Harrison, S., Dourish, P.: Re-place-ing space: the roles of place and space in collaborative systems. In: Proceedings of the 1996 ACM Conference on Computer Supported Cooperative Work, pp. 67–76. ACM, New York (1996)
40. Dennett, D.C.: Brainstorms: Philosophical Essays on Mind and Psychology. MIT Press, Cambridge (2017)
41. Bermudez, J.L.: Philosophy of Psychology: Contemporary Readings. Routledge, Abingdon (2007)
42. Friedman, B., Kahn, P.H., Jr.: Value Sensitive Design: Theory and Methods (2002)
43. Sengers, P., Boehner, K., David, S., Kaye, J.J.: Reflective design. In: Proceedings of the 4th Decennial Conference on Critical Computing: Between Sense and Sensibility, pp. 49–58. ACM, New York (2005)
44. Binder, T., Michelis, G.D., Ehn, P., Jacucci, G., Linde, P., Wagner, I.: Design Things. MIT Press, Cambridge (2011)
45. Woolgar, S.: Configuring the user: the case of usability trials. Sociol. Rev. **38**, 58–99 (1990). https://doi.org/10.1111/j.1467-954X.1990.tb03349.x
46. Burdick, A., Drucker, J., Lunenfeld, P., Presner, T., Schnapp, J.: Digital Humanities. The MIT Press, Cambridge (2012)
47. Gold, M.K.: Debates in the Digital Humanities. University of Minnesota Press, Minneapolis (2012)
48. Jones, S.E.: The Emergence of the Digital Humanities. Routledge, New York (2013)
49. Kirschenbaum, M.: Digital humanities as/is a tactical term. In: Debates in the Digital Humanities, pp. 415–428. University of Minnesota Press, Minneapolis (2012)
50. Kirschenbaum, M.: What is "digital humanities", and why are they saying such terrible things about it? Differences **25**, 46–63 (2014). https://doi.org/10.1215/10407391-2419997
51. Liu, A.: Digital humanities and academic change. Engl. Lang. Notes **47**, 17–35 (2009)

52. Pannapacker, W.: "Big Tent Digital Humanities," a View From the Edge, Part 1 (2011). http://chronicle.com/article/Big-Tent-Digital-Humanities/128434/
53. Porsdam, H.: Digital humanities: on finding the proper balance between qualitative and quantitative ways of doing research in the humanities. Digit. Humanit. Q. **7** (2013). http://www.digitalhumanities.org/dhq/vol/7/3/000167/000167.html
54. Raley, R.: Digital humanities for the next five minutes. Differences **25**, 26–45 (2014). https://doi.org/10.1215/10407391-2419991
55. Ramsay, S.: On building. In: Terras, M., Nyhan, J., Vanhoutte, E. (eds.) Defining Digital Humanities: A Reader. Routledge, Abingdon (2011)
56. Seberger, J.S.: How long is now? The "digital" in DH. Presented at the DH 2015, Paramatta, NSW (2015)
57. Blei, D.M.: Topic Modeling and Digital Humanities. http://journalofdigitalhumanities.org/2-1/topic-modeling-and-digital-humanities-by-david-m-blei/
58. Meeks, E., Weingart, S.: The Digital Humanities Contribution to Topic Modeling. http://journalofdigitalhumanities.org/2-1/dh-contribution-to-topic-modeling/
59. Rhody, L.M.: Topic Modeling and Figurative Language. http://journalofdigitalhumanities.org/2-1/topic-modeling-and-figurative-language-by-lisa-m-rhody/
60. Weingart, S.: Topic Modeling for Humanists: A Guided Tour. http://www.scottbot.net/HIAL/?p=19113
61. Anderson, C.: The End of Theory: The Data Deluge Makes the Scientific Method Obsolete (2008). https://www.wired.com/2008/06/pb-theory/
62. Bowker, G.C.: The theory/data thing. Int. J. Commun. **8**, 1795–1799 (2014)
63. Fitzpatrick, K.: Planned Obsolescence. NYU Press, New York (2011)
64. Cetina, K.K.: Epistemic Cultures: How the Sciences Make Knowledge. Harvard University Press, Cambridge (1999)
65. Kuhn, T.S.: The Structure of Scientific Revolutions, 3rd edn. The University of Chicago Press, Chicago (1996)
66. Olsen, M.: Signs, symbols and discourses: a new direction for computer-aided literature studies. Comput. Humanit. **27**, 309–314 (1993)
67. Underwood, T.: What kinds of "topics" does topic modeling actually produce? (2012). https://tedunderwood.com/2012/04/01/what-kinds-of-topics-does-topic-modeling-actually-produce/
68. Bowker, G.C.: Science on the Run: Information Management and Industrial Geophysics at Schlumberger, 1920–1940. MIT Press, Cambridge (1994)
69. Day, R.E.: Indexing It All: The Subject in the Age of Documentation, Information, and Data. MIT Press, Cambridge (2014)
70. Rogers, R.: Digital Methods. MIT Press, Cambridge (2013)
71. Nora, P.: L'événement monstre. Communications **18**, 162–172 (1972). https://doi.org/10.3406/comm.1972.1272
72. Croce, B.: History. Its Theory and Practice. Harcourt, Brace (1921)
73. Star, S.L.: This is not a boundary object: reflections on the origin of a concept. Sci. Technol. Hum. Values **35**, 601–617 (2010). https://doi.org/10.1177/0162243910377624
74. Røssaak, E.: The Archive in Motion: New Conceptions of the Archive in Contemporary Thought and New Media Practices. Novus Press, Oslo (2010)
75. Shaviro, S.: The Universe of Things: On Speculative Realism (Posthumanities). Lulu Press Inc, Morrisville (2016)
76. Boyd, D., Crawford, K.: Critical questions for big data. Inf. Commun. Soc. **15**, 662–679 (2012). https://doi.org/10.1080/1369118X.2012.678878
77. McCallum, A.K.: MALLET: A Machine Learning for Language Toolkit (2002)

A Phenomenographic Approach to the Effect of Emotions on the Information Behaviour of Doctoral Students: A Narrative Inquiry

Amira Ahmed(✉) [iD], Frances Johnson, Geoff Walton,
and Sumayah Bayounis

Department of Languages, Information and Communication, Manchester
Metropolitan iSchool, Manchester Metropolitan University, Manchester, UK
amira.ahmed@stu.mmu.ac.uk

Abstract. This article is to examine how emotions affect the doctoral student's journey by analyzing diverse aspects of the information behaviour that emerged from their narratives through a phenomenographic perspective. Narratives are a rational way of communication that focuses on how people perceive different phenomena regarding themselves, their inner thoughts, their states of mind, and how it affects their lifeworld's. This phenomenographic study employs interview data from 36 doctoral students. The data collected from the narratives were studied drawing from the variation theory and iterative data analysis resulted in categories of doctoral student experiences and their emotional journey. The holistic phase of the thematic analysis revealed a relatively balanced interplay of positive and negative emotions. The rich data obtained in the phenomenographic approach exposed significant links between participants' heightened emotions in five common themes during looking for information, their interactions with key individuals (supervisors and peer) and situations in their doctoral lives. Whilst this paper focuses on the approach taken to explore the narratives, recommendations are made based on the findings and to further explore the information-seeking behaviour patterns of doctoral students.

Keywords: Doctoral students · Phenomenography · Emotions · Information behavior

1 Introduction

This research explores the lived emotional information-seeking experiences of doctoral students. In so doing, it will provide a clearer understanding of how these doctoral students' past histories and current commitments may impact the affective, cognitive, and physical elements of their experience of doctoral research. The doctoral study involves numerous challenges. These range from the everyday pressures associated with living on a reduced income to the demanding task of constructing a scholarly identity in the research world. Consequently, many doctoral students experience what has been described as a 'rollercoaster of confidence and emotions' [1, 2]. There is evidence that doctoral students conceal their emotions [3, 4] and perhaps there is fear that discussing students feelings might morph into concern for therapeutic rather than

A. Sundqvist et al. (Eds.): iConference 2020, LNCS 12051, pp. 874–883, 2020.
https://doi.org/10.1007/978-3-030-43687-2_73

pedagogic [5] yet 'the emotional aspects of research practice and the management of emotions are deeply embedded in being a successful doctoral student' [6]. Information scholars such as [6–8] argue that the stress and negative emotions sparked by learning a new and occasionally counter-intuitive skill may be an inevitable aspect of the information-seeking process. However, some, [9], sees students' experiences of emotional barriers during the information search process as a sign that a student is genuinely transcending his or her comfort zone of knowledge, and gaining a deeper understanding of a topic. Despite the shreds of evidence and various Information Seeking Process (ISP) models, few works have been carried out to investigate this aspect of emotional behaviour in doctoral student's study to gain insight into the emotions they faced during their research career and how various sources of information influence it.

This paper explores the emotion-infused experiences of thirty-six international and local doctoral candidates studying in the United Kingdom. The data is collected in the form of interviews conducted over a one-year period. Based on phenomenographic study, a very 'open' view of this phenomenon has been the starting point of this research, and the overall thrust is that of a process of discovery rather than a search for predetermined categories. The results revealed through the participants' narratives indicate a relatively balanced interplay of positive and negative emotions. The rich data obtained in the phenomenographic approach uncovered significant relations between participants' heightened emotions and their interactions with key individuals such as supervisors and research peers and circumstances in their doctoral lives. The paper first analyses relevant investigations into the previous studies of information-seeking behaviour and emotions before outlining the study's theoretical framework, then it describes the study's research design and methodology—next, the participants' accounts of the emotion's episodes. The final section considers the discussion and conclusion. The focus of the paper is to describe the phenomenographic approach taken and the insights obtained from the participants' narratives of their emotional incidents experienced during their doctoral study.

2   Emotions, Information Behavior and Doctoral Students

Emotions are fundamentally implicated in all human behaviour. They shape perceptions, influence thinking, affect the ability to share knowledge and motivate action [10]. Emotions provide doctoral students with motivational energy to persist until graduation [11]. However, they can also inhibit thinking. For example, anxiety has been shown to interfere with doctoral candidates' ability to write [12]. Emotions can also help in achieving desired outcomes, as demonstrated in [13] account of doctoral students' experiences dealing with stress. Furthermore, studies have been investigated to evaluate the effect of emotions, specifically on users' information-seeking behaviour. According to [14], emotional factors affect search strategies and performance, search results, motivation, and satisfaction. In [15], they investigated the cognitive and affective aspects of information-seeking behaviour among novice users. The study found that need for confirmation, hesitation, surprise, and fear affected the strategies that the users applied in the search process. [16] describes different information behaviour according to anxiety or relaxation, and need for control, and under/oversupply of information among other factors. According to [17], factors such as course, age, level, native language, and religion have a substantial effect on the information-seeking behaviour of college students.

Finally, different researchers have focused on diverse elements of information-seeking behaviour among university students. Previous studies have delved the differences in the information-seeking behaviour of local and international students (e.g. [18–21]. [22] compared the information-seeking behaviour of local and international students at the University of Illinois. While focusing on professionals, [23] offer insights regarding the information-seeking behaviour expected of academics. This study draws on the above studies that information seeking has an affective dimension, and that doctoral student will seek information to support their study from various sources, such as from the literature, other researchers, their peers and supervisors.

3 Methodology

This paper acknowledges an important aspect on how doctoral students perceive emotion and poses the following research question:

- What is the effect of emotions on the information behaviour of doctoral students' research journey?

To answer this, a phenomenographic approach was chosen based on the variation theory [24, 25].

3.1 Study Design and Approach

The objective of phenomenography is to describe qualitatively the various ways in which individuals conceive phenomena in their unique worlds [26]. The investigators aim to classify conceptions of a phenomenon of interest as accurately as possible and refrain from interjecting their preconceived concepts. Analysis within the phenomenographic approach is discussed in the literature [27–29]; however, there is, as yet, no clear one 'best' method of phenomenographic analysis. The objective, however, is largely to describe the data in the form of qualitative categories, often referred to as the 'outcome space', looking to find similarities or differences. Usually, the categories of description are related to one another in some manner, often in a hierarchical manner. In addition, our decision to use a person-centred approach as opposed to a segment-centered approach was because our research question was aimed at investigating specifically the variation in how doctoral students lived experiences influenced by emotions.

3.2 Setting, Participants and Their Recruitment

One of the essential elements when designing a phenomenographic study is the selection of the participants. Since the purpose of phenomenography is to uncover the qualitatively different ways that a specific phenomenon is understood, the participants should be selected to obtain the maximum possible diversity. This implies the use of a purposeful sampling method [30]. To obtain the maximum possible variations, participants selection was based on the demographic attributes of gender, age, race, nationality (domestic/international), intended doctoral major, family orientation and overall personalities. The students come from a diversity of majors but were screened to ensure that they had a recent researching experience to be included in the study. The participants were recruited with all the approachable mediums and were introduced to the study individually, followed by filling consent forms. The demographic variations of participant samples are shown in (Table 1).

Table 1. Demographic variation in participant sample

Categories	Groups	Counts
Gender	Female	21
	Male	15
Age	18–28	8
	29–38	15
	39–48	10
	58+	3
Nationality	Domestic	11
	International	25
Enrolled Course (PhD)	Arts and Humanities	13
	Computer Science	10
	Science & Technology	4
	Health & Social Care	3
	Business & Economics	2
	Other	1
Family Status	Married	6
	Married with kids	15
	Single	6
	Single with kids	3
	Separated	2
	Engaged	1
	Other	0

3.3 Data Gathering

This article draws on the transcripts of 36 h-long interviews conducted between a year-long period and a small number of email exchanges aimed at clarifying issues identified during the transcription process. The researcher conducted interviews with each participant on their campus. The fact that the researcher was also a doctoral student who helped establish rapport with the participants, despite differences in age and background.

3.4   Explication of the Findings

In a phenomenographic approach, data are explained rather than analyzed. The six steps include **bracketing**; **defining** emotional aspects; **clustering** lived experiences of interviews lifeworld and defining a **relation** for each emotion episodes; **summarizing** each interview/discussion and validating it and, where necessary, modifying it (results); and **extracting** general and unique themes (discussion) [31]. Bracketing refers to containing the researchers' views and preconceptions, so they do not influence the interview/discussion of the findings. The investigator repeatedly listened to the audio recordings to familiarize with the contributors' words and develop a holistic sense. The tapes were transcribed and read and reread multiple times to develop a holistic sense harmoniously. Significant statements related to the study goal were marked. The emotional aspects of the phenomenon of doctoral students during their study were identified.

4   Emotion Incidents in Doctoral Narratives

This section reports emotion incidents that emerged in the participants' (subjects') narratives while conducting open-ended interviews regarding their information-seeking behaviour. The findings reveal seven categories, which directly affected the emotional state of doctoral students lived experiences while researching for information Some individual's variance themes were also identified which are depended on individual's demographics (Table 2).

Table 2. Common themes and emotional episodes

DIMENSIONS OF VARIANCE	COMMON THEMES				
	Language Barriers	Personal Problems	Self Motivation / Passion	Profes-sional Communities	Supervisor Relationship
Family Status *Health Issues* *Finance* *Gender* *Nationality* *Past Experiences*	EMOTIONAL EPISODES				

4.1   Language Barrier

Almost all of the doctoral students indicated one common theme, writing and given the salience of review in writing activities; this is hardly surprising. The trials associated with writing in English generated mainly strong emotions:

> sometimes… I know what I'm doing, but it's hard for me to express in a different language … and sometimes I get irritated with myself ah yeah you know. You know what you want to say, but it's not actually there. (P13, 747–753)

In addition to triggering anger, anxiety and frustration, participants (P28, P24, P12) whined that writing was time-consuming and took time away from other activities. Given these challenges, participants expressed joy and pride when their scripts were accepted for publication. All international students did mention that looking for the right keyword to research for information is troublesome for them and results in high anxiety and frustration.

> I feel reluctant to use new keywords… during research, I found new keywords…, which I never used before, so it worries me, and felt…uhm… I am incapable of using library services… Sometimes I do feel I did not know how to research umm…. I cannot continue my PhD (P4, 117–120).

4.2   Personal Problems

Doctoral studies have numerous challenges and the most common theme which generated strong emotions are a personal problem. Every individual has their own circumstances which directly affect their doctoral journey, especially not meeting deadlines, and participants indicated finance, health and family commitments. P19 reported that she and her husband had started discussing job prospects:

> P: We started discussing about that [the future]. Yeah, for him I think, I don't concern about him at all. And ah for myself, I am sceptical.
> R: Why?
> P: Ah, ah about what kind of job I can find and ah I have to get a good publication to get a good… academic career. (P19, 1556–1562)

Her anxiety about finding an academic post was exacerbated by knowing that her student visa would expire shortly after she submitted her thesis. If she was to remain in the UK, she needs to find a job offer.

4.3   Self Motivation/Passion

Self Motivation or Passion emerged as a critical theme that affected doctoral students in very different ways. Although P17, P16 and P27 spent large parts of interview eagerly sharing what they had learned about her two different methodologies, P9 and P22 could barely remember either of her data collection techniques and didn't talk much about one. P27 repeatedly stated that she was 'passionate 'about learning new things and sharing them with her professors, friends and future clients. However, P22 overriding passion seemed to be directed toward completing assessments (which she described as 'obstacles 'and 'blocks') that required information-seeking through brute force.

While neither motivation is better than the other, their different passions may have led to different approaches to information seeking.

4.4   Professional Communities

Almost three-quarter of international candidates referred to feelings concerning interactions with members of their different communities which caused the information searching. Their experiences within their departments were consistently negative, while their interactions in their respective communities were (in all but one case) extremely positive.

P7 complained about her department's unfriendly culture and felt 'very, very troubled' (741) at what she perceived as a lack of welcome and orientation when she first arrived. P18, P24, P30 also regretted the absence of peers with whom to discuss ideas. This lack of departmental community sent a powerful (unintended?) message that scholarly research is a solitary affair. In contrast, participants' interactions with their disciplinary communities at conferences and in the publication process were highly positive. P18's account of attending a 'very prestigious' international conference in Europe conveys his pleasure and pride:

> that was really interesting because. . . it gave me really good feedback. . . during the break, people were coming to me. . . and they were telling me they are impressed about what I am doing. . . (P18, 271–280).

By participating in this conference, P18 experienced the satisfaction of being recognized as a researcher by others in his disciplinary community. P24 contacted two international experts in his field about a paper he was writing and was delighted to receive positive feedback on the work he was doing. In both cases, this emotional boost was converted into enhanced confidence and motivation.

4.5   Supervisor Relationships

The last aspect of the participants' experiences which has so many emotions involved was their interactions with their supervisors. Most of the participants' comments about their supervisors were positive, with individuals acknowledging their efficiency, support, feedback and friendly manner. P34 explained that his supervisors' trust in his ability had given him the confidence to begin writing:

> P: when. . . you are a person from an environment that does not really value publication as it is here, and then you come to this place –
> R: – to compete on an even footing –
> P: Yes. . . I was thrilled that my supervisors yeah they trust me, tried to motivate me – 'Yes you can, you have experienced' and. . . when we discuss content-based knowledge,... (P34)

On the other hand, P18 considered the role his supervisor assigned him is unsuitable and face-threatening. However, conscious of the power dynamics at work, he chose not to counterattack. Instead, he lowered his sights and chose to focus on 'just finishing' the PhD:

I guess there was a lot of drive, but. . . you just reach a point where you don't really care anymore what occurs, all you want to do is just. . . try to see if you can have the results and try to finish. (P18, 902–913)

When asked to explain, the interesting way P18 paraphrased his supervisor's appraisal of his work revealed his suppressed anger:

P: at the beginning well I could write stuff and. . . he doesn't understand it so 'it's bullshit... it's rubbish'. Well, I would like –
R: Would he actually use that word with you?
P: Of course, he would say it doesn't make sense to him. (P18, 918–923)

5 Discussion and Conclusion

Emotions play an intricate role in doctoral experiences. This paper focuses on the phenomenographic approach taken to explore the participants' narratives and to identify the categories (or themes) that describe their emotive incidents, and that was chosen based on variation theory seeking similarities and differences across the participants' experience within each incident.

Language barriers, personal problems, self-motivation/passion, professional communities and supervisor relationship all play a part in doctoral narratives. Writing English for those whose first language is not English experienced particularly strong emotions. Personal problems also generated concern, especially with respect to future job prospects. Self-motivation/passion was a core driver and talking about professional communities was emotive and which appeared to influence action. Perceived lack of time affected the students emotionally as did supervisor relationships, especially concerning the influence the supervisor can have.

Hence, it can be seen that emotions underlie all of these themes and it is anticipated that the approach taken will allow us to further explore how the emotions within these incidents have influenced thinking and motivated action in the doctoral student journey from start to finish. The depth of insight afforded results in a model of the emotional journey and one which acknowledges how emotion may be influenced (especially by information resources and services encountered) and managed to inspire, guide and enhance the doctoral student and their research trajectory. In doing so, the doctoral journey will not only become more effective but also more enjoyable for both supervisors and students alike.

References

1. Ezzy, D.: Theorizing narrative identity: symbolic interactionism and hermeneutics. Sociol. Q. 39(2), 239–252 (1998)
2. Schutz, P.A., Hong, J.Y., Cross, D.I., Osbon, J.N.: Reflections on investigating emotion in educational activity settings. Educ. Psychol. Rev. 18(4), 343–360 (2006)
3. Herman, C.: Emotions and being a doctoral student. In: Thomson, P., Walker, M. (eds.) Routledge Doctoral Student's Companion: Getting to Grips with Research in Education and the Social Sciences, pp. 283–294. Routledge, London and New York (2010)

4. Manathunga, C.: Early warning signs in postgraduate research education: a different approach to ensuring timely completions. Teach. High. Educ. **10**(2), 219–233 (2005)
5. Beard, C., Smith, K., Clegg, S.: Acknowledging the affective in higher education. Br. Educ. Res. J. **33**(2), 235–252 (2007)
6. Thomson, P., Walker, M. (eds.): Routledge Doctoral Student's Companion: Getting to Grips with Research in Education and the Social Sciences. Routledge, London and New York (2010)
7. Kuhlthau, C.C.: Seeking Meaning: A Process Approach to Library and Information Services, 2nd edn. CTLibraries Unlimited, Westport (2004)
8. Nahl, D., Bilal, D.: Information and Emotion: The Emergent Affective Paradigm in Information Behaviour Research and Theory. Information Today, Medford (2007)
9. Julien, H., Genuis, S.K.: Emotional labour in librarians' instructional work. J. Doc. **65**(6), 926–937 (2009). https://doi.org/10.1108/00220410910998924
10. Lupton, D.: The Emotional Self: A Sociocultural Exploration. Sage, Thousand Oaks (1998)
11. McCormack, C.: Postgraduate research students' experience: it's all about balancing living. In: Tight, M., Mok, K.H., Huisman, J., Morphew, C.C. (eds.) The Routledge International Handbook of Higher Education, pp. 181–193. Routledge, New York and London (2009)
12. Castello, M., Inesta, A., Monereo, C.: Towards self-regulated academic writing: an exploratory study with graduate students in a situated learning environment. Electron. J. Res. Educ. Psychol. **7**(3), 1107–1130 (2009)
13. Hopwood, N., Stocks, C.: Teaching development for doctoral students: what can we learn from activity theory? Int. J. Acad. Dev. **13**(3), 175–186 (2008)
14. Lopatovska, I.: Emotional aspects of the online information retrieval process. Ph.D. Rutgers University-Graduate School-New Brunswick (2009)
15. Nahl, D., Tenopir, C.: Affective and cognitive searching behaviour of novice end-users of a full-text database. J. Am. Soc. Inf. Sci. **47**(4), 276–286 (1996)
16. Heinstrom, J.: Fast surfing, broad scanning and deep diving: the influence of personality and study approach on students' information-seeking behaviour. J. Doc. **61**(2), 228–247 (2005)
17. Devi, S.T., Dlamini, N.N.: Information needs and seeking behaviour of Agricultural students at the University of Swaziland: a case study. Int. J. Digit. Libr. Serv. **4**(2), 1–15 (2013)
18. Abdoulay, K.: Information seeking behaviour of African students in Malaysia: a research study. Inf. Dev. **18**(3), 191–195 (2002)
19. Dalglish, C.L., Chan, A.O.: Expectations and reality–international student reflections on studying in Australia. In: Australian International Education Conference (2005)
20. Deumert, A., Marginson, S., Nyland, C., Ramia, G., Sawir, E.: The social and economic security of international students in Australia: study of 202 student cases (Summary report). Monash University, Melbourne (2005)
21. Liu, M., Redfern, B.: Information seeking behaviour of Multicultural students: a case study at San Jose State University. Coll. Res. Libr. **58**(4), 348–354 (1997)
22. Song, Y.S.: A comparative study on information-seeking behaviours of domestic and international business students. Res. Strat. **20**(1/2), 23–34 (2005)
23. Shafique, F., Mahmood, K.: Variable affecting the information needs and seeking behaviour of educational administrators: a review. Pak. J. Libr. Inf. Sci. **14**, 26–32 (2013)
24. Marton, F.: Phenomenography—describing conceptions of the world around us. Instr. Sci. **10**(2), 177–200 (1981)
25. Yates, C., Partridge, H.L., Bruce, C.S.: Exploring information experiences through phenomenography. Libr. Inf. Res. **36**(112), 96–119 (2012)
26. Reed, B.: Phenomenography As a Way to Research the Understanding by Students of Technical Concepts, Nucleo de Pesquisa em Tecnologia da Arquitetura eUrbanismo (NUTAU): Technological Innovation and Sustainability, São Paulo, Brazil (2006)

27. Svensson, L.: Theoretical foundations of phenomenography. High. Educ. Res. Dev. **16**(2), 159–171 (1997)
28. Ashworth, P., Lucas, U.: What is the 'World' of phenomenography? Scand. J. Educ. Res. **42**(4), 415–431 (1998)
29. Larsson, J., Holmstrom, I.: Phenomenographic or phenomenological analysis: does it matter? Examples from a study on anaesthesiologists' work. Int. J. Qual. Stud. Health Well-Being **2**(1), 55–64 (2007)
30. Bowden, J.A., Green, P. (eds.): Doing Developmental Phenomenography. RMIT University Press (2005)
31. Åkerlind, G., Bowden, J.A., Green, P.: Learning to do phenomenography: a reflective discussion. In: Bowden, J., Green, P. (eds.) Doing Developmental Phenomenography, pp. 74–100. RMIT University Press, Melbourne (2005)

Social Network Analysis: Making Public Library Communities Visible

Deborah Hicks[1]([⊠]), Mary M. Cavanagh[2], and Amy VanScoy[3]

[1] School of Information, San Jose State University, San Jose, CA 95192, USA
deborah.hicks@sjsu.edu
[2] School of Information Studies, University of Ottawa, Ottawa, Canada
[3] Department of Information Science, University at Buffalo, Buffalo, USA

Abstract. This paper argues for applying social network analysis (SNA) theoretically and methodologically to study information organizations, specifically the contemporary public library and its network relations with its communities. A brief review of SNA's origins, theoretical underpinnings, and key concepts is followed by a discussion of why and how public library research could benefit from taking this perspective, and the multiple options available for defining the library-user relational tie as the unit of analysis. Constraints affecting data collection and analysis are also noted.

Keywords: Social network analysis · Information organizations · Community

1 Introduction

By design, public libraries have always been networked organizations. Long before the digital era, they functioned as mediated informational, cultural, and interactional spaces within their physical communities. Their primary purpose, historically, and persisting still today, is to connect their public spaces, staff, collections, and information networks with individuals, groups, and whatever formal or informal associations of people assemble [6]. In relational and uniquely human terms, public libraries create ties, enable ties, extend ties, and gather ties together into clusters, nodes, and network neighborhoods. The impact of the "Triple Revolution" [23], framed as the combined impact of the social, mobile, and internet revolutions on individuals, has been well established and documented by Wellman and network researchers over many years. However, as actors in those individual or community networks and social ecosystems, public libraries have been overlooked, or rendered so institutional as to be often invisible or ignored by social science researchers. Social network analysis (SNA) offers library and information science (LIS) researchers an approach to better envision the relationships public libraries have with their communities both in-person and online by exploring the kinds of ties they have, how these ties lead to relationships, and how these relationships can be characterized.

© Springer Nature Switzerland AG 2020
A. Sundqvist et al. (Eds.): iConference 2020, LNCS 12051, pp. 884–891, 2020.
https://doi.org/10.1007/978-3-030-43687-2_74

2 Social Network Analysis

Social network analysis is a common methodological approach in the broad field of LIS for examining the patterns and relationships among individuals, groups, or organizations. With its roots in sociology, and pioneered in LIS research by sociologist Barry Wellman [12, 28, 29], social network analysis has been used to study a broad range of topics in information science, such as information exchange [13], how people use Twitter to form and maintain social connections [11], and the co-authorship networks of researchers [1, 2]. But as Sheble, Brennan, and Wildemuth state: "Though there has been considerable use of social network analysis in ILS [Information and Library Science], we have yet to realize its full potential" (p. 339 [25]). We argue that one area where the potential of SNA as research methodology has yet to be exploited is in the study of information organizations. To date, there has been limited use of SNA to examine the relationships and communities that information organizations build and uphold with their clients and each other.

In describing SNA, Mische said: "Relational thinking is a way to overcome stale antinomies between structure and agency through a focus on the dynamics of social interactions in different kinds of social settings" (p. 80 [18]). Relationships are ties between social actors. A social actor, also known as an agent, node, social entity, or vertex, can be an individual, organization, or other group. Ties, also known as links or edges, that connect social actors represent an exchange of information or other resources, such as social support or influence, between actors [13]. Ties can be both material and/or immaterial and online, these ties are often symbolic [14]. For instance, adding someone as a "friend" on Facebook does not necessarily suggest there is a real-life friendship between two people, only that there is a desire for some form of social connection.

Relationships can be both directed and undirected. In a directed relationship, the tie flows from one actor to another, meaning the information or resources flow in one direction. For example, on Twitter, it is possible to follow someone without them following you back. Their tweets, therefore, will flow to a follower without any reciprocation. An undirected relationship is a mutual relationship in which the direction of the information flow is irrelevant. A friendship is an example of an undirected relationship. Relationships between people can be complex and multifaceted; however, the focus of SNA is not on the complexity of the interactions, but on the structure of the relationships [22]. In the case of public libraries, for instance, a client may have many different ties to the library. A client may borrow a popular book, attend a program, and volunteer all in one week. However, for the purposes of SNA, only one of these ties would be the focus of the analysis.

Two types of networks are the foci of SNA studies: egocentric networks and whole networks. Egocentric networks focus on the connections an individual actor has with others (known as alters). A whole network, or socio-centered network, examines the ties that exist among a specific target population or social group. These networks can be one-mode or two-mode networks, meaning the ties can be between similar social actors, as would be the case in a friendship network, or the ties can be mediated in some way, such as downloading the same reading app from the library, resulting in no direct connections. An example of a two-mode network is co-membership in an organization where the only connection between the actors is the organization [25].

The data sources and collection methods for SNA include questionnaires, surveys, interviews, observations, research diaries, and even historical research [22, 25]. Digital data is also a common data source for SNA-based studies. This data can be gathered from bibliographic databases, knowledge networks (e.g., scholarly communication), or web sources such as Twitter or Facebook, and can be collected using application programming interfaces (APIs) or downloaded from bibliographic databases.

Data analysis for SNA consists of identifying patterns in how actors interact with each other [22]. This can be done descriptively or statistically. Typically, results are presented visually to "provide insight into overall network structure, subcomponents, and specific nodes and their relationships" (p. 344 [25]). Specialized SNA software, such as UCINET [3], NodeXL, [26], and Netlytic [10], are commonly used to analyze the data and create network visualizations. Certain kinds of analysis are appropriate for each network type. Whole networks can be analyzed for concentration of power, the flow of information or other resources, and the emergence of hierarchical social structures [4, 7]. Ego-centered networks can be analyzed for their size, structure, and composition, which enable researchers to examine questions such as: How many people is the actor connected to? Does the actor connect nodes that would otherwise be unconnected? And, are the nodes to whom the actor is directly connected (i.e., alters) similar to each other [16]?

When analyzing social networks, a few core principles guide the analysis: cohesion, reciprocity, and centrality. These principles can be measured at the node-level or network-level of analysis. At the node-level, they measure the influence of particular actors in a network. At the network-level, they measure the whole and not an aggregate of individual actors [14].

At the node-level of analysis, centrality and reciprocity are two core analytical measures. Centrality measures a particular actor's position in a network. Two degrees of centrality exist: in-degree and out-degree. In-degree centrality measures the relationships that others have initiated with an actor (e.g., a Twitter follower), while out-degree centrality measures the relationships that the actor has initiated (e.g., someone an actor is following on Twitter). These measures are particularly important when using SNA to examine social media networks as they help researchers identify network hubs, or network stars. A hub is an actor in the network who has more connections than other actors in the same network, which places them in a position to influence the flow of information and other resources in a network [13]. Reciprocity measures whether or not the ties between two actors are mutual. It allows researchers to measure the homophily, or the similarities and differences, among connected actors of the network [25].

A core network-level measure is cohesion. Cohesion measures the relationships within a network. The cohesiveness of a network is usually described through its density and centralization. Density measures interconnectedness by comparing the number of possible connections, or links, with the number of actual connections. The more dense a network, the more likely it is for information to flow between network members. Centralization measures whether or not actors are connected through a central node. In highly centralized networks, information flows through the central node, which places that node in a gatekeeper role [14].

Figure 1 offers an example of a network visualization for the Vancouver Public Library's tweets from September 10–23, 2017, using Netlytic [10]. What can be observed in the visualization is that the library's network is small, with low density and reciprocation. Information largely flows from the library's Twitter account to its followers with little or no two-way communication. The library is a central node and the focus of the network's most prominent cluster. Distinct communities, or clusters, in the network can be observed (in this example, the different colors of the ties indicate different network clusters).

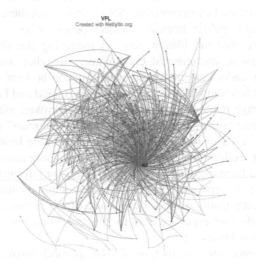

Fig. 1. Network Analysis of the Vancouver Public Library's Tweets from September 10–23, 2017, using Netlytic.org [10]

3   Social Network Analysis and Public Libraries

Practically and philosophically, community is the *sine qua non* of a public library. Buschman and Warner asserted that the central idea of community is at the core of contemporary public library goals. They suggested that the public library's institutional standing in the community makes a unique contribution, constituting "co-operative coping" among citizens as they negotiate their day-to-day lives (p. 15 [5]). Extending these ideas into sociological and network terms, the public library's community consists of clusters of individuals and groups that use, endorse, include, and imagine their libraries into agency. It is individuals who come together and constitute public libraries into action and ongoing interaction.

This defining concept of relationship that continually connects a library with its community, individually and collectively, poses an ongoing challenge for LIS researchers [11]. Past LIS research that has focused on forms of public library interaction concentrated around information behavior and library user theories and models. Some studies looked specifically at public library-community relationships at the macro-level. For instance, the work of Durrance and Fisher and others examined these relational connections, but relied on in-depth qualitative methods which enable different types of analyses [8, 20, 21]. Importantly, these studies do not address core questions that SNA could enable researchers to explore: What does a public library relationship in a relational context or social network look like? Are public libraries the network stars they envision themselves to be? SNA allows LIS researchers to better understand and possibly even expand our notions of public library communities, relationships, and ties. For example, an ego-centered examination of a public library's network would illuminate how many different communities the library is a part of. This could highlight previously unknown and under-explored community ties. But, perhaps most importantly from an LIS perspective, SNA offers researchers the opportunity to better understand how public libraries connect people who would otherwise be unconnected and the role the library plays in mediating the flow of information between these otherwise unconnected communities. In other words, SNA enables researchers to better understand the different information brokerage roles that public libraries play in the communities they are connected to. Gould and Fernandez identified five types of brokerage relations: coordinator, itinerant broker, gatekeeper, representative, or liaison. These brokerage roles are "concrete social *roles*" (p. 93, emphasis in original) that actors in a social network can occupy [9]. These brokerage roles can be within-group or can facilitate interactions with outside communities. Public libraries have long considered themselves to be community hubs for information exchange, and research into public perceptions of public libraries supports this self-image [15]; however, such research tends to focus on the role of the physical library as a community hub. SNA offers an expanded way for researchers to think about the different social roles that public libraries play.

A significant consideration in any type of SNA approach involving a public library is identifying and gaining access to either existing secondary data sources or creating new researcher-defined data. A major constraint on data access relates to the public library's long-standing commitment to user data privacy. As a general practice, public libraries neither collect nor store their member-generated transactional logs in any form. In the case of the online catalog and other third-party application interfaces, the vendor supplying the front-end social interface (e.g., Bibliocommons™) may collect and store that data, doing so under a terms of use agreement made directly with the library user, and respecting only their proprietary data. These reasons may explain in part why SNA studies have rarely been conducted using existing public library user interaction data. The data dashboard of the Toronto Public Library is one illustration of how these interactional data are already aggregated and reported; though it still lacks any formal network analysis [27].

Traditional data collection techniques, such as surveys, interviews, and even observations, do offer LIS researchers a straightforward way of collecting data for SNA studies. Other potential data sources include, for example, digital library-user interactions or a public library's programming calendar. Digital library-user interactions, such as those scraped from social media sites or transactional logs, may be accessible as secondary data sources while simultaneously meeting ethical research standards, although there may be limitations with this data associated with current public library privacy policies. The programming calendar offers the opportunity to track library-community relationships through library events, speakers, topics, dates, and times.

Coding such a program catalog over a period of time could begin to map the library-community relationships of expertise as they relate to library programming. Such a mapping could then be compared to the same or other library Twitter feeds to look for patterns in topics, speakers, and to track the momentum of current knowledge topics in a particular community.

Analyzing public library networks follows the same principles as analyzing other social networks. Examinations of public libraries' network size would provide insights into how nodes in their networks access social support, resources, and information. Looking at the composition of the networks would shed light onto the probability of exposure to the resources the library has to offer. Examining the homophily or heterogeneity of the libraries' networks would help researchers understand the kind of people who dominate library's networks, which would shed light on their influence over the library itself. In addition, SNA offers researchers the opportunity to identify structural holes in libraries' networks. Where do they lack community ties? And how do those ties influence the libraries' ability to meet their stated missions?

SNA can also be combined with ethnographic methods. At the start of a project, ethnography can help researchers to write survey and interview questions to be used in the SNA data collection and at the end of the project ethnographic data can be used to help interpret results [7]. In other words, by adding an ethnographic component to an SNA study, researchers can explore not just the characteristics of a public library's social network, but also the meanings and understandings that members attach to the network. Such insights would help researchers understand how different communities make sense of their relationship with the public library, see the effect of powerful community groups on not just the shape, but also the function of the network, and identify the needs of communities that are missing from the library's existing network.

4 Conclusion

Recently, the ways in which public libraries engage and interact with their communities has moved radically to the foreground in the forms of maker cultures, library spaces as community living rooms, and a vastly expanded array of both library-led and community-led programming connecting spaces, collections, and expertise. Community librarianship [24] and community-led librarianship [19] are service orientations where libraries look on their horizons to all forms of communities and interactions to collaboratively develop and deliver 21st-century library services [17]. Fundamental to this orientation is connection, relationship, and interaction. For example, in 2015, one of the world's largest public library systems, Toronto Public Library, logged more than 100 million user interactions in the form of visits, circulation, program attendance, technology logins, reference interactions, and more. Virtual visits accounted for 31% of those interactions. What could be uncovered and then learned by mapping these ties, over time, into library-community network diagrams along a variety of dimensions? The quantitative orientation of an SNA approach combined with its methods of data analysis in the forms of networks and hubs could give libraries the "hard" data they so often need to demonstrate their value to their political leaders, and could uncover new directions in library use and library relationships.

References

1. Abbasi, A., Altmann, J., Hossain, L.: Identifying the effect of co-authorship networks on the performance of scholars: a correlation and regression analysis of performance measures and social network analysis measures. J. Inform. **5**, 594–607 (2011)
2. Andrews, J.: An author co-citation analysis of medical informatics. J. Med. Libr. Assoc. **91**, 47–56 (2003)
3. Borgatti, S.P., Everett, M.G., Freeman, L.C.: UCINET for Windows: Software for Social Network Analysis. Analytic Technologies, Harvard (2002)
4. Borgatti, S.P., Everett, M.G., Johnson, J.C.: Analyzing Social Networks. Sage, Los Angeles (2018)
5. Buschman, J., Warner, D.A.: On community, justice, and libraries. Libr. Q. Inf. Commun. Policy **86**(1), 10–24 (2016)
6. Cavanagh, M.F.: Structuring an action net of public library membership. Libr. Q. **85**, 404–426 (2015)
7. DeJordy, R., Halgin, D.: Introduction to ego network analysis. http://www.analytictech.com/e-net/pdwhandout.pdf. Accessed 9 Sept 2019
8. Durrance, J.C., Fisher, K.E.: Determining how libraries and librarians help. Libr. Trends **51**, 541–570 (2003)
9. Gould, R.V., Fernandez, R.M.: Structures of mediation: a formal approach to brokerage in transaction networks. Sociol. Methodol. **19**, 89–216 (1989)
10. Gruzd, A.: Netlytic: software for automated text and social network analysis. http://Netlytic.org. Accessed 9 Sept 2019
11. Gruzd, A., Wellman, B., Takhteyev, Y.: Imagining Twitter as an imagined community. Am. Behav. Sci. **55**, 1294–1318 (2011)
12. Hampton, K., Wellman, B.: Long distance community in the network society: contact and support beyond Netville. Am. Behav. Sci. **45**, 476–495 (2001)
13. Haythornthwaite, C.: Social network analysis: an approach and technique for the study of information exchange. Libr. Inf. Sci. Res. **18**, 323–342 (1996)
14. Himelboim, I.: Social network analysis (social media). In: Matthes, J. (ed.) The International Encyclopedia of Communication Research Methods. Wiley, Hoboken (2017)
15. Horrigan, J.B.: Libraries (2016). https://www.pewinternet.org/2016/09/09/libraries-2016/. Accessed 9 Sept 2019
16. Jordan, K.: Seperating and merging professional and personal selves online: the structure and processes that shape academics' ego-networks on academic social networking sites and Twitter. J. Assoc. Inf. Sci. Technol. **70**, 830–842 (2019)
17. Lankes, R.D.: The New Librarianship Field Guide. The MIT Press, Cambridge (2016)
18. Mische, A.: Relational sociology, culture, and agency. In: Scott, J., Carrington, S. (eds.) The SAGE Handbook of Social Network Analysis. SAGE, Thousand Oaks (2011)
19. Pateman, J., Williment, K.: Developing Community-Led Public Libraries: Evidence from the UK and Canada. Ashgate Publishing Limited, Farnham (2013)
20. Pettigrew, K.E., Durrance, J.C., Unruh, K.T.: Facilitating community information seeking using the Internet: findings from three public library–community network systems. J. Am. Soc. Inform. Sci. Technol. **53**, 894–903 (2002)
21. Pettigrew, K., Durrance, J., Vakkari, P.: Approaches to studying public library networked community information initiatives: a review of the literature and overview of a current study. Libr. Inf. Sci. Res. **21**, 327–360 (1999)

22. Quan-Haase, A., McCay-Peet, L.: Social network analysis. In: Jensen, K.B., Craig, R.T., Pooley, J., Rothenbuhler, E.W. (eds.) The International Encyclopedia of Communication Theory and Philosophy. Wiley, Hoboken (2016)
23. Rainie, L., Wellman, B.: Networked: The New Social Operating System. The MIT Press, Cambridge (2012)
24. Scott, R.: The role of public libraries in community building. Public Libr. Q. **30**, 191–227 (2011)
25. Sheble, L., Brennan, K., Wildemuth, B.M.: Social network analysis. In: Wildemuth, B.M. (ed.) Applications of Social Research Methods to Questions in Information and Library Science, pp. 339–350. Libraries Unlimited, Santa Barbara (2016)
26. Smith, M., et al.: NodeXL: a free and open network overview, discovery and exploration add-in for Excel 2007/2010/2013/2016. https://www.smrfoundation.org. Accessed 9 Sept 2019
27. Toronto Public Library: Key performance indicators. https://www.torontopubliclibrary.ca/content/about-the-library/pdfs/board/meetings/2016/apr25/15-2015-annual-performance-measures-and-benchmarking-att-1.pdf. Accessed 9 Sept 2019
28. Wellman, B., Tindall, D.: Canada as social structure: social network analysis and Canadian sociology. Canad. J. Sociol. **26**, 265–308 (2001)
29. Wellman, B., Wortley, S.: Different strokes from different folks: community ties and social support. Am. J. Sociol. **96**, 558–588 (1990)

The Evolution of Bonded Design: From Elementary School to Higher Education

Valerie Nesset[1(✉)], J. Brice Bible[1], and Nicholas Vanderschantz[2]

[1] University at Buffalo (SUNY), Buffalo, NY, USA
{vmnesset, bible}@buffalo.edu
[2] University of Waikato, Hamilton, New Zealand
vtwoz@waikato.ac.nz

Abstract. This paper introduces an alternative model of the participatory design (PD) methodology, Bonded Design (BD). Bonded Design originated from research investigating the use of participatory design methods to foster collaboration between two potentially disparate groups, adult researchers/designers and elementary school children. Previous work has shown that by using design techniques selected from various existing PD models, executed in a particular order, the Bonded Design methodology can successfully empower two distinct groups of participants to conceive ideas for innovative technologies they could not have produced alone. For these reasons the BD methodology was chosen as the framework for a university-wide initiative of a Research 1 university to foster meaningful communication and interaction between faculty and IT professional staff with the intent to create innovative technology solutions. Findings from this study indicated that while several Bonded Design features were useful in achieving the end goal, modifications needed to be made to the methodology as a whole to accommodate not only the increased sophistication and knowledge base of the adult participants, but also the design of a tangible final deliverable that could be directly implemented.

Keywords: Participatory cultures · Participatory design · Bonded Design · BD · Technology solutions

1 Introduction

In spring 2017, under the purview of the Office of the Vice President-Chief Information Officer of a large Research 1 university in New York State, a university-wide survey of faculty members' IT needs and uses was conducted [1]. It was anticipated that the survey would identify where there were needs for upgrades to hardware and software as well as gaps in IT support services. While these goals were achieved, an unexpected, but important finding was revealed in the open-ended comments where faculty were asked for suggestions to improve IT services. These comments identified a disconnect between faculty and IT professional staff. It appeared that while IT professionals had a good understanding of *how* particular technologies were designed to work, they were not necessarily aware of how faculty were actually using them. Indeed, although they worked for the same institution, neither group seemed to know much about the other.

A. Sundqvist et al. (Eds.): iConference 2020, LNCS 12051, pp. 892–900, 2020.
https://doi.org/10.1007/978-3-030-43687-2_75

This was not an unusual finding as IT professionals' interactions with faculty are most often limited to troubleshooting problems. Yet, it was clear that to make IT services more responsive to faculty needs, more meaningful communication and interaction needed to be fostered between these two disparate groups. The big question, then, was *how?* A complex problem, it would not be solved through the administration of another survey. More in-depth research methods were required. Enter the Faculty IT Liaison (FITL) Program.

The FITL Program was developed primarily as a means to facilitate the generation of recommendations for modifications to existing technologies and IT programs and services to make them more faculty-friendly. It was reasoned that this could be best accomplished by bridging the communication and interaction gap between faculty and IT professionals to encourage meaningful collaboration. Participatory design methods have been shown to enable such collaboration [2–4], particularly the participatory design methodology of Bonded Design. Bonded Design [5–7] emerged from research investigating the collaboration between two distinct and disparate groups, adult researchers and children. While the Bonded Design methodology had been used only with intergenerational teams, it was considered a good fit for the FITL Program because it is predicated on the notion that each group possesses unique expertise, and that within the shared experience of the design team, these two groups are able to come together to create something that could not have been created alone or with their peers. Yet, as this would be the first time the methodology would be used with two distinct groups of adults, it was anticipated that some modifications would need to be made.

This paper presents and discusses the modifications to the Bonded Design framework to enable it to be an effective tool to promote better communication and interaction between university faculty and IT personnel to enable development of an innovative and implementable final deliverable.

2 Bonded Design in the Context of Participatory Design

The decision to use a participatory design process bringing together faculty members and IT professionals, draws from the literature on user-centered and participatory design [8] and from the researchers' previous experience in developing new approaches to designing technology alongside elementary school students [5–7]. Unlike some user-centered design (UCD) approaches that may only include end-users in certain stages of development such as system testing, [9] participatory design promotes a design process that is not just human-centered, but rather, human-involved. Marti and Bannon [10] describe this as, "users are not simply viewed as objects of study but as active agents within the design process itself...so those who will be affected by change have an influence on the kind of changes that will be made" (p. 8). In participatory design, users move from extrinsic roles (e.g., observer) to intrinsic roles (e.g., peer co-designer) [9–11]. Participatory design has flourished in recent decades and has evolved into many different approaches with different methods of engaging end-user communities in the design process. For example, participatory design techniques have been used to design more user-friendly systems with and for children [8, 12–14], in planning library spaces [15], and in business [16]. What unites these approaches is the over-arching concept of active participant involvement leading to better outcomes. What differentiates these approaches is the level and duration of the participants' involvement [9]. As Bowler et al. [17] assert, "participatory design recognizes that users are the experts in how *they* will use technology in the real world and that they should, therefore, be part of the design process. The single-most important characteristic of participatory design and one that distinguishes it from other methods which incorporate a face-to-face inter-action with users, is that users are "in essence co-designers" throughout an iterative, circular process of design" (p. 734). Thus, PD takes on aspects of action research, promoting through a reflective process the collaborative solving of real-world problems directly affecting its participants [18–20].

Bonded Design (BD) emerged from research investigating how children design web portals [21]. BD integrates elements of participatory design and user-centered design approaches, especially those of Cooperative Inquiry [12] and Learner-Centered Design [22, 23], bringing two disparate groups together in the shared experience of the design team. Its team approach, where participants are considered equal but different, each sharing their own expertise with their teammates throughout the design process was considered ideal for bringing together faculty members and IT professionals. Another reason it seemed the best fit as a framework for the FITL Program was its flexible methodology consisting of six different design techniques: needs assessment, or determining what the user community wants in terms of design deliverable; eval-uation through team discussion of exemplars of similar technology designs; discussion of design issues; brainstorming design ideas (where all ideas, no matter how whimsical, are given equal value); prototyping low-tech models of potential designs; and con-sensus building related to the final design of the low-tech prototype.

3   The Evolution of Bonded Design

This section will describe and explain the Bonded Design model/methodology in the context of the original intergenerational team studies and its recent use in the Faculty IT Liaison Program, outlining the changes made to accommodate the latter, and why they were made.

3.1   Purpose of the Studies

The purpose of the original study was to determine if intergenerational teams could work together to develop a low-tech prototype of a technology, specifically, a web portal as the researchers had expertise in web portal design. The Bonded Design methodology/model [5–7] emerged from the data collected during the design sessions. In the university study, however, it was the Bonded Design methodology itself that was under investigation – how efficacious it was in fostering meaningful communication and collaboration to produce a tangible final deliverable in an organization-wide environment where instead of intergenerational disparity, there was now employee hierarchy disparity. Differing from the original BD use case that explored web portal design, the final deliverable in this case were recommendations to make three everyday technologies—email, course management software, and data storage—more faculty-friendly to use.

3.2   The Origins of the Bonded Design Methodology

As it was the results of the original studies [5–7] that informed the Bonded Design methodology, it is necessary to briefly revisit how they were formed. To structure the intergenerational team design sessions, several design techniques were selected from different participatory design models including Co-operative Inquiry [12], Informant Design [24], Contextual Design [25] and Learner-Centered Design [22, 23]. Bonded Design is comprised of those techniques that were found to be the most effective in encouraging the two groups to communicate and collaborate.

As shown in Fig. 1, the original Bonded Design methodology/framework consists of two groups, designers and users, that collaborate in the shared experience of the design team. The design sessions are structured using the six design techniques which are accomplished individually or in teams, depending on the activities associated with a particular technique. The design techniques are applied in a specific order, leading to the creation of a team low-tech prototype.

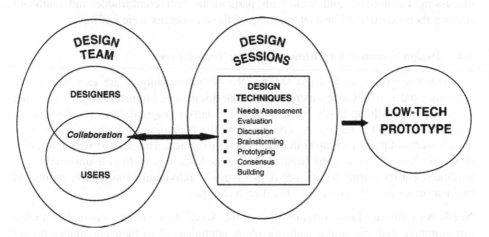

Fig. 1. Original Bonded Design Model [5–7]

3.3   Design Team Recruitment, Makeup and Authority Issues

In terms of recruitment, in the original studies, volunteer student names were picked randomly from a hat. As this was not a feasible nor desirable method for the much larger university population, potential faculty volunteers filled out an application form. The purpose of the form was threefold: (1) to control numbers of participants, (2) to ensure the greatest diversity among academic units, and, perhaps most importantly, (3) to ensure the greatest disparity between the two groups comprising each team.

As mentioned in Sect. 3.2, planning for the original studies was informed by the participatory design model, Cooperative Inquiry (CI) [12] which also involved inter-generational teams where the children team members were treated as complete equals with the adults. However, the CI model was predicated on the study of intergenerational teams that ran for long periods of time with the same members within a laboratory specially equipped for this purpose. Since the Bonded Design studies were to be conducted in an operational environment (a classroom over the lunch hour) the researchers had concerns regarding potential authority issues, specifically, how to maintain equality so that the students would feel comfortable; while still maintaining some control. To accomplish this, all team members called each other by their first names, and each group's expertise (the researchers in web portal design, the students in their unique worldviews and perspectives) respected.

In terms of the Faculty IT Liaison Program, while the university design teams were comprised of adults and there were therefore no authority concerns over age disparity, there were other power dynamics that needed to be considered, namely that IT professionals are considered support staff. At the outset of the project, it was not clear if or how this would make a difference to collaboration between these two very different groups within the design team sessions. Prior to the outset of the FITL the researchers held concerns such as; whether the faculty would "take charge" and condescend to the IT participants, would the two groups be able to share a common terminology when discussing technology, and would all participants feel comfortable and confident sharing their expertise? Fortunately, none of these concerns were realized.

3.4 Design Sessions: Execution of Design Techniques

As shown in Fig. 1, in Bonded Design, the design techniques are executed in the following order: needs assessment, evaluation, discussion, brainstorming, prototyping and consensus building [5–7]. In the Faculty IT Liaison Program, however, because all team members had extensive experience using the technologies, many of these techniques were omitted, rearranged in order, and/or modified. This section will discuss in-depth the developments of the Bonded Design methodology within the university with particular enhancements to the needs assessment, individual prototyping, individual brainstorming, and the consensus building techniques.

Needs Assessment. In the original studies, the Needs Assessment consisted of a short questionnaire that the young team members administered to their classmates during recess. Included as a design technique, it was mainly a team-building activity, although it did provide some insight into the students' design preferences for web portals. In the university, however, a survey sent out to all faculty members to identify and assess their technology needs and uses served as the needs assessment. Indeed, the results of this survey were the catalyst for the creation of the FITL Program, thus making the needs assessment a crucial part of the process instead of just an add-on activity.

Individual Prototyping. Although not designated as a design technique in the inter-generational studies (it was included within the design technique of brainstorming) individual prototyping took place in the form of drawing one's own mental model of the ideal web portal. In the FITL Program, since technology evaluation and discussion were omitted for the reasons listed in the previous section, the sessions devoted to each technology started with this activity. As such, it was considered a separate design technique [26, 27]. As might be expected, in the original studies the young students quite enjoyed the freedom of this activity, yet for some faculty members this task was not an enjoyable one. Unlike the children (and surprisingly, the IT staff participants who appeared happy to be able to think out of the box and dream), some faculty members were limited by their concerns that their ideas were not implementable, or that their drawing skills were poor.

Individual Brainstorming. In the intergenerational teams, this design technique consisted of drawing and presenting orally each team member's mental model of the ideal technology. The young students, although they enjoyed drawing very much, found brainstorming a more difficult exercise because they tended to interpret things at a very literal level [5, 6]. Thus, features of each drawing were recorded and from these, the researchers developed a team prototype for the students to critique. In the FITL Program this technique was more complex. It started in the same way with individual oral presentations of each team member's drawing. It should be noted that often during these drawing presentations the level of enthusiasm of the discussions increased to the point where everyone was animatedly talking at once. This was likely stimulated by the fact that the researcher/facilitator, who is a terrible artist presented her drawing first. A further enhancement to the BD method for its use in the FITL Program was that each team member was asked to write down on sticky notes the three features (one per note) of their ideal system they felt were the most important. This differed from the intergenerational teams where the individual brainstorming phase ended with the presentations of drawings.

Consensus Building. In the intergenerational teams this technique consisted of discussing the low-tech prototype developed by the researchers. It was difficult for the students to reach consensus as they were loath to let go of their own ideas for the low-tech prototype however impractical or unpopular with the team as a whole they might have been. To achieve final consensus, the researchers had to include at least one feature of each child's drawing in the final design.

In the FITL Program, because of the sophisticated nature of the final deliverable – recommendations for technology modifications – and the advanced educational levels of the FITL team members, consensus building was more complex. To begin, as a team, four to five categories relating to the workings of the technology (e.g., interface design, content organization) were identified. Each team member then categorized their ideas by affixing the sticky note under a category heading they believed to be the most appropriate. Consensus was achieved via team discussion where all of the ideas on the sticky notes were further fleshed out and depending on the team's decision, left alone, moved to another category, superseded by other similar ideas, or discarded. Consensus was fairly easily achieved, perhaps because many of the individual ideas were shared by other team members and because the deliverable, a list of recommendations and not one team design as in the intergenerational studies, allowed for expression of the majority of them.

Final Deliverable. As discussed earlier, the main purpose of the original studies was to establish whether participatory design methods could empower children and adults to work together in intergenerational teams to develop a low-tech prototype of a web portal for children. It was not important that the prototypes be useful, although they did inform the interface for a working web portal on Canadian History, *History Trek*. [21] Therefore, the results of the studies not only indicated that children and adults could effectively work together within a participatory design framework, but also that the process encouraged generation of creative and innovative ideas that each group would not have produced alone. These findings served as the catalyst for the creation of the Bonded Design methodology. In the university, however, the investigation concentrated on whether or not the Bonded Design methodology was an appropriate framework to enable efficient and effective development of an innovative, tangible deliverable that could be implemented.

4 Bonded Design: The Evolution Realized

Taking into consideration all of the issues raised in Sect. 3, a new model was developed to better reflect the Bonded Design methodology as realized in the Faculty IT Liaison Program. Figure 2 presents this new process flow where the needs assessment and the development of the final deliverable, rather than simply vehicles to encourage collaboration, comprise crucial elements of the methodology.

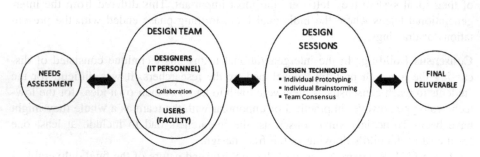

Fig. 2. Bonded Design Methodology – Faculty IT Liaison Program ©

5 Conclusion

The participatory design method, Bonded Design, developed from the findings of two studies of children and adults working together in intergenerational teams, was used as a framework for the Faculty IT Liaison Program, a university initiative. The FITL Program was established to encourage meaningful communication, interaction, and collaboration between faculty and IT professional staff. Unlike in the original studies [6, 7], the participants in the FITL Program were all adults but from two very different groups, faculty and IT professional staff. The FITL Program was a demonstrated success as within the shared experience of the design team, these two disparate groups were able to come together to create recommendations for improving existing technologies that could not have been created alone or without the combination of teams with mixed areas of expertise. It has been reported by the University IT Department that many of these recommendations have been or will be incorporated into the technologies under consideration. Furthermore, the depth of collaboration enabled by the methods of Bonded Design was the catalyst in building upon the Bonded Design methodology to be used with disparate groups of adults. Indeed, future research funded by the US Institute of Museum and Library Services (IMLS) will investigate the efficacy of this new BD methodology in the public library context to enable librarians and older adults to work together to develop targeted and meaningful programming and services.

References

1. 2017 Faculty IT Survey. http://www.buffalo.edu/content/dam/www/ubit/docs/reports/2017FacultyITSurvey-Final.pdf. Accessed 20 Jan 2020
2. Schuler, D., Namioka, A.: Participatory Design: Principles and Practices. L. Erlbaum Associates, Hillsdale (1993)
3. Carmel, E., Whitaker, R.D., George, J.F.: PD and joint application design: a transatlantic comparison. Commun. ACM **36**(4), 40–48 (1993)
4. Muller, M., Kuhn, S.: Participatory design. Commun. ACM **36**(6), 24–28 (1993)
5. Large, A., Nesset, V.: Bonded Design. In: Khosrow, M. (ed.) Encyclopedia of Information Science and Technology, 2nd edn. Information Science Reference, Hershey, PA, pp. 383–388 (2009)
6. Large, A., Nesset, V., Beheshti, J., Bowler, L.: "Bonded Design": a novel approach to intergenerational information technology design. Libr. Inf. Sci. Res. **28**, 64–82 (2006)
7. Large, A., Nesset, V., Beheshti, J., Bowler, L.: Bonded Design: a methodology for designing with children. In: Zaphiris, P., Kurniawan, S. (eds.) Advances in Universal Web Design and Evaluation: Research, Trends and Opportunities, pp. 73–96. Idea Group, Hershey (2007)
8. Torraco, J.: Theory development research methods. In: Swanson, R.A., Holden, E.F. (eds.) Research in Organizations: Foundations and Methods of Inquiry, pp. 351–374. Berrett Koehler Publishers, San Francisco (2005)
9. Robertson, T., Simonsen, J.: Challenges and opportunities in contemporary participatory design. Des. Issues **28**(3), 3–9 (2012)
10. Marti, P., Bannon, L.J.: Exploring user-centered design in practice: some caveats. Knowl. Technol. Policy **22**, 7–15 (2009)
11. Bowler, L., Large, A.: Design-based research for LIS. Libr. Inf. Sci. Res. **30**, 39–46 (2009)
12. Druin, A.: Cooperative inquiry: developing new technologies for children with children. In: Williams, M., Altom (Chairpersons), M. (eds.) Proceedings of the SIGCHI Conference on Human Factors in Computing Systems, pp. 592–599. ACM Press, New York (1999)
13. Nesset, V., Large, A.: Children in the information technology design process: a review of theories and their applications. Libr. Inf. Sci. Res. **26**(2), 140–161 (2004)
14. Yip, J.C., et al.: The Evolution of engagements and social bonds during child-parent co-design. In: Proceedings of the 2016 CHI Conference on Human Factors in Computing Systems, pp. 3607–3619. ACM Press, New York (2016)
15. McLaughlin, J.E.: Focus on user experience: moving from a library-centric point of view. Internet Ref. Serv. Q. **20**(1/2), 33–60 (2015)
16. Nielsen Norman Group: How to collaborate with stakeholders in UX research. https://www.nngroup.com/articles/collaborating-stakeholders/. Accessed 20 Jan 2020
17. Bowler, L., et al.: Issues in user-centered design in LIS. Libr. Trends **59**(4), 721–752 (2011)
18. Atkins, L., Wallace, S.: Qualitative Research in Education. Sage Publications, London (2012)
19. Rapoport, R.N.: Three dilemmas in action research. Hum. Relat. **23**, 499–514 (1970)

20. Wilson, V.: Research methods: action research. Evid. Based Libr. Inf. Pract. **8**(4), 160–162 (2013)

21. Large, A., Beheshti, J., Nesset, V., Bowler, L.: Designing web portals in intergenerational teams: two prototype portals for elementary school students. J. Am. Soc. Inform. Sci. Technol. **55**(13), 1140–1154 (2004)

22. Soloway, E., Guzdial, M., Hay, K.: Learner-centered design: the challenge for HCI in the 21st century. Interactions **1**(2), 36–48 (1994)

23. Guzdial, M.: Learner-Centered Design of Computing Education: Research on Computing for Everyone. Morgan & Claypool Publishers, San Rafael (2016)

24. Scaife, M., Rogers, Y., Aldrich, F., Davies, M.: Designing for or designing with? Informant design for interactive learning environments. In: Pemberton, S. (ed.) Proceedings of the SIGCHI Conference on Human Factors in Computing Systems, pp. 343–350. ACM Press, New York (1997)

25. Beyer, H., Holtzblatt, K.: Contextual design. ACM Interact. **6**, 32–42 (1999)

26. Nesset, V., Bible, J.B.: Building understanding between users and designers through participatory design: the Bonded Design approach. In: Chowdhury, G., McLeod, J., Gillet, V., Willett, P. (eds.) iConference 2018. LNCS, vol. 10766, pp. 515–520. Springer, Cham (2018). https://doi.org/10.1007/978-3-319-78105-1_56

27. Nesset, V., Bible, J.B.: The faculty IT liaison program: using participatory design to build possibilities with technology. In: Proceedings of ICKM 2018: A Profession and Discipline of Action. University of North Texas, Denton (2018)

Author Index

Printed in the United States
By Bookmasters